The Penguin Archaeology Guide

The Penguin Archaeology Guide

Edited by Paul Bahn

PENGUIN BOOKS

PENGUIN BOOKS

Published by the Penguin Group
Penguin Books Ltd, 80 Strand, London WC2R ORL, England
Penguin Putnam Inc., 375 Hudson Street, New York, New York 10014, USA
Penguin Books Australia Ltd, Ringwood, Victoria, Australia
Penguin Books Canada Ltd, 10 Alcorn Avenue, Toronto, Ontario, Canada M4V 3B2
Penguin Books India (P) Ltd, 11, Community Centre, Panchsheel Park, New Delhi – 110 017, India
Penguin Books (NZ) Ltd, Private Bag 102902, NSMC, Auckland, New Zealand
Penguin Books (South Africa) (Pty) Ltd, 24 Sturdee Avenue, Rosebank 2196, South Africa

Penguin Books Ltd, Registered Offices: 80 Strand, London WC2R ORL, England

Collins Dictionary of Archaeology first published by HarperCollins Publishers 1992
This completely revised, expanded and updated edition first published 2001
1

Set in TheAntiqua and TheSans
Typeset by Rowland Phototypesetting Ltd, Bury St Edmunds, Suffolk
Printed by WSOY, Finland

ISBN 0–140–29308–6
ISBN (US) 0–140–51448–1

Contents

List of Illustrations

Photographic acknowledgements are given in parentheses: Every effort has been made to trace all copyright holders. The publishers will be happy to make good any missing or erroneous acknowledgement in future reprints.

List of maps

Contributors

Dr Paul Bahn, Hull, England
(editor; western Europe, early periods; prehistoric art)

Professor Gina Barnes, Dept of East Asian Studies, University of Durham, England
(Far East)

Dr Caroline Bird, Greenmount, WA, Australia
(Australasia)

Dr Peter Bogucki, School of Engineering and Applied Science, Princeton University, Princeton, New Jersey, USA
(Central and eastern Europe and ex-USSR, later periods)

Dr Philip Duke, Dept of Anthropology, Fort Lewis College, Durango, Colorado, USA
(North America; theory)

Dr Christopher Edens, American Institute for Yemeni Studies, Sana'a, Yemen
(Near East; Central Asia)

Dr David Gill, Dept of Classics and Ancient History, University College of Swansea, Wales
(classical archaeology)

Dr Ian Glover, Ditton Priors, Shropshire, England
(Southeast Asia)

Dr Edwin Hajic, Santa Fe, USA
(methods and techniques)

Dr John Hoffecker, Institute of Arctic and Alpine Research, University of Colorado at Boulder, Colorado, USA
(Central and eastern Europe and ex-USSR, early periods)

Dr Geoffrey G. McCafferty, Dept of Archaeology, University of Calgary, Alberta, Canada
(Mesoamerica)

Dr Christopher Mee, School of Archaeology, Classics and Oriental Studies, University of Liverpool, England
(Aegean)

Elena Miklashevich, Dept of Archaeology, Kemerovo State University, Kemerovo, Russia
(Siberia, Central Asia)

Dr Christopher Scarre, McDonald Institute for Archaeological Research, University of Cambridge, England
(western Europe, later periods)

Dr Katharina Schreiber, Dept of Anthropology, University of California, Santa Barbara, USA
(South America)

Dr Steven Snape, School of Archaeology, Classics and Oriental Studies, University of Liverpool, England
(Egypt and the Levant)

Dr Anne Thackeray, Dept of Archaeology, University of Witwatersrand, South Africa
(Africa)

Dr Joyce Tyldesley, Bolton, Lancs, England
(western Europe, early periods)

There are many kinds of archaeological reference books – dictionaries, gazetteers, atlases, encyclopedias, anthologies and so forth. The subject is now so vast and all-encompassing that no single book can hope to do it justice. This new *Penguin Archaeology Guide* is no exception, but nevertheless we hope that it will prove an invaluable tool for professionals, students and amateur enthusiasts alike. We have called it a guide because that is precisely what it is intended to be – a guide to definitions and dates, to locations and achievements, to sites and cultures, to peoples and empires, and to the theories and methods of archaeology. This is more than a dictionary, since the detailed maps provide locations, and more than an atlas, since the maps and cross-references can lead the reader to a whole range of entries that are relevant to a region, period or culture.

This book's core is derived from the *Collins Dictionary of Archaeology*, published in 1992. Almost all of that original team was reunited to produce this revised and updated text, but at the same time new specialists were brought in to expand on or add areas which merited inclusion or better coverage, such as parts of the New World, Southeast Asia, Africa and the later periods of Siberia and Central Asia. We feel the result has a far better global balance, and even less Eurocentrism, a charge we had already sought to avoid in 1992. In these times of world archaeology, with every part of the globe producing important new data, there is no excuse for inherent bias.

Despite our best efforts, however, the coverage is still inevitably imperfect, given the constraints on number of words and pages available to us. As before, we have accorded relatively little space to the more recent periods in Europe and elsewhere (Viking and later) and virtually none to industrial archaeology. However, this seemed preferable to the course chosen in one recently published dictionary of archaeology which omitted virtually the whole of the classical world, a most bizarre decision, given that area's crucial role in the history and development of our subject.

As always, tough compromises constantly had to be made between the number of entries and their length.

Since this is a guide rather than an encyclopedia, we have tended to choose concise entries rather than long essays, because the book is above all meant to be for quick reference – to remind oneself of a meaning or a date or a location. There are plenty of encyclopedias or specialized dictionaries available where in-depth information on a more limited sphere – such as Egyptology or Prehistoric Europe – can be found. We wanted ours to be compact, light and within the means of the average student. We believe it is the most comprehensive and up-to-date work of its kind, since it covers not only artifacts, materials, features, sites and cultures, but also deceased archaeologists of world importance, and also the methods, theoretical approaches and jargon of recent decades.

A few ground-rules should be underlined here. The entries are in strict alphabetical order: places beginning with 'Tell' or 'Tepe' are under the name which follows, while those beginning with 'Le/La/Les' or 'El' are under those letters. We have used bc, ad or bp (the latter meaning before the radiocarbon method's present, i.e. before 1950) where the dates are uncalibrated absolute ages; but we have used BC, AD or BP where the dates are calibrated or (far more often) where they are general estimated ages.

In closing, the editor and contributors would like to thank the following friends and colleagues for advice and information of various kinds: Bernadette Arnaud, Bettina Arnold, Ofer Bar Yosef, Nick Barton, Peter Bellwood, Carmen Cacho, Jane Callander, Ron Clarke, Angela Close, Glen Doran, Lyubov Ermolenko, Francesco d'Errico, Lidia Clara García, Naama Goren-Inbar, Martha Graham, Roberte Hamayon, Ludmila Iakovleva, Alice Kehoe, Kathy Kuman, Mary Leslie, Adrian Lister, Marcel Otte, Estelle Potgieter, Margarete Pruech, Sergio Ripoll, Peter Robertshaw, Avraham Ronen, Andrew B. Smith, Andrea Stone, Eitan Tchernov, Francis Thackeray, Phillip Tobias, Jan Wisseman Christie and João Zilhão; and our warmest gratitude also goes to Nigel Wilcockson, Jenny Rayner, Molly Mackey and David Watson of Penguin for their patience and fortitude in transforming our work into such a handsome and user-friendly product.

abacus the top part of the CAPITAL which is in contact with the bottom part of the ENTABLATURE of a CLASSICAL building. It is thicker on capitals of the DORIC ORDER than on those of the IONIC ORDER.

Abada, Tell a 2–3 ha (5–7.5 acre) 'UBAID period (c.5000–3800 BC) site in the Hamrin district of eastern-central Iraq, where S. Jasim's excavations during the 1970s provided the first wide exposure of 'Ubaid residential architecture. The site contains three phases of occupation: the lowest corresponds to the CHOGA MAMI Transitional and 'Ubaid 1 of neighbouring regions, and also contains a little SAMARRAN pottery; the upper two levels belong to the 'Ubaid 2–3 in which a little Late HALAF POLYCHROME painted pottery appears. The domestic buildings of the village consist of rooms that are (largely) symmetrically grouped on both sides of a long and often 'T'-shaped central hall; each building may have contained an extended family household. This tripartite floor plan is found in other 'Ubaid settlements (e.g. KHEIT QASIM), and also appears in religious architecture of the 'Ubaid and URUK periods.

Abaj Takalik a middle and late PRECLASSIC site on the Pacific slope of Guatemala. Famous for monumental sculpture in OLMEC style, and with later iconography relating to the IZAPA style and early MAYA.

Abbevillian an outdated term denoting the early ACHEULIAN industries of western Europe, named after the type-site of Abbeville in the Somme Valley, France (see BOUCHER DE PERTHES). The Abbevillian was formerly called the CHELLEAN.

Abdul Hosein, Tepe an ACERAMIC NEOLITHIC site in the uplands of the Zagros Mountains (western Iran), excavated by Judith Pullar in the 1970s. Its sequence of architecture indicates a transition from ephemeral occupation marked by pits and scattered debris to one of rectilinear mud-brick structures with green- or red-painted plaster floors. The material culture includes chipped and ground stone equipment, and figurines and geometrics (see TOKENS); the botanical evidence indicates cultivation of two-rowed hulled barley and of emmer.

Abejas phase a phase in the TEHUACÁN VALLEY, Mexico, beginning about 3500 to 1500 BC. The phase comes after the initial introduction of maize in the valley, when agricultural production begins to make up a significant part of the diet. See also AJUEREADO PHASE.

Abel see BAHR EL GHAZAL.

Abercromby, John, Lord (1841–1924) a Scottish antiquary, author of the seminal *Bronze Age Pottery of Great Britain and Ireland* (1912), which opened a new phase in the study of the British Bronze Age. In 1904 Abercromby introduced the term 'beaker' for decorated handleless drinking vessels characteristic of the late Neolithic/Early Bronze Age, subdividing them into three types, A, B and C, a classification which remained the basis of British Beaker typology until the 1960s.

Abeurador, Balma a cave-site in Hérault, France, on the southern edge of the Massif Central, with ten distinct layers of human occupation from EPIPALAEOLITHIC to late Neolithic, c.9000 to 2500 bc. Carbonized remains of lentils, peas and chick peas, morphologically indistinguishable from early cultivated forms of Southwest Asia, were found in AZILIAN levels dated to c.8000 bc, and have suggested incipient cultivation of these species in a formally pre-Neolithic context.

Abingdon a Neolithic CAUSEWAYED CAMP, dating from c.3200 BC in Berkshire, England, with remains of two widely spaced concentric ditches with several entrance-gaps. Located on Thames Valley river gravels, this was the first causewayed camp to be found in a low-lying location.

Abraq, Tell a small mounded site in Ras al Khayma (United Arab Emirates), with a unique Bronze and Iron Age sequence of occupation excavated by D. Potts in the early 1990s. The occupation focused on an UMM AN-NAR period mud-brick tower which continued in use through the 2nd millennium BC; an Iron Age platform constructed upon the tower helped to preserve it. Among the finds are evidence for interaction with the Indus, Dilmun,

MESOPOTAMIA, and the Iranian plateau (see PERSIAN GULF TRADE).

abri see ROCKSHELTER.

abri Dufaure see DURUTHY.

Abri Pataud an Upper Palaeolithic rockshelter in LES EYZIES, Dordogne, southwestern France, which has yielded a detailed stratigraphy with radiocarbon dates from 34,250 to c.19,000 bc. The abundant artifacts have been classed as AURIGNACIAN, Upper PERIGORDIAN (or GRAVETTIAN) and Proto-MAGDALENIAN. The shelter, excavated by MOVIUS in 1958–64, was primarily a winter site, its faunal remains heavily dominated by reindeer. A number of human remains were discovered, including a sixteen-year-old girl of the Proto-Magdalenian. Fallen fragments in all levels indicate that the shelter's wall was always painted, engraved and sculptured.

Abri Zumoffen see ADLUN.

Absolon, Karel (1887–1960) a Czech archaeologist who excavated a number of major Palaeolithic sites, including DOLNÍ VĚSTONICE, ONDRATICE, PEKÁRNA and BÝČÍSKÁLA.

absolute dating the process of utilizing dating methods that allow ages to be reported in years either as years before present (bp), uncorrected for carbon flux in the atmosphere, or as calendar years (AD/BC/BP), corrected for carbon flux. A margin of uncertainty as compared with standards, usually expressed in years, is reported as well. Compare RELATIVE DATING. See also CHRONOMETRIC DATING.

absolute pollen counting the process of counting pollen grains for each species per sample unit volume or unit weight. Because SEDIMENTATION rates may vary among sampled intervals, pollen counts are reported as a pollen influx rate for each species per sample. The pollen influx rate is the number of pollen grains of a species accumulating on a unit sediment surface area per unit time. Sedimentation rates are required to perform the calculation, and these are obtained with multiple radiocarbon ages through the sampled column. Using pollen influx rates circumvents the problem that relative pollen counting of species percentages is co-dependent on percentages of other species being counted, and therefore does not necessarily reflect changes in vegetation composition. See also PALYNOLOGY.

Abu Ballas a series of mud pans in the Western Desert of Egypt, occupied between 10,000 and 5,000 years ago. The ceramics indicate a cultural relationship with the KHARTOUM NEOLITHIC.

Abu Duwari, Tell an OLD BABYLONIAN city, the ancient Mashkan Shapir in northern Babylonia, investigated by an American project during the late 1980s. Essentially a single-period settlement, the site makes available as surface observations important details about Mesopotamian urban fabric, including location of canals, major monuments, special-function (religious, administrative, mortuary) walled quarters, and craft production.

Abu Ghurab the site of the SUN TEMPLE of King Niuserre of the 5th Dynasty of Egypt, excavated by Borchardt and SCHÄFER in 1898–1901.

Abu Hureyra, Tell an EPIPALAEOLITHIC (late NATUFIAN) to early ceramic Neolithic site on the middle Euphrates. A. M. T. Moore's excavation in the 1970s provides considerable detail on the beginnings of food production in this part of Syria. The Epipalaeolithic levels contained an abundance of wild einkorn, and of other wild cereals, legumes, nuts and seeds; the excavator suggests that the einkorn at least was cultivated. The ACERAMIC (PRE-POTTERY) NEOLITHIC (PPNB) levels contain rectilinear mud-brick structures with plastered and painted walls and floors, and a material culture that included stone vessels, bone tools, a variety of personal ornaments, clay figurines and a wide variety of exotic materials in addition to the chipped stone. In the 7th millennium BC, exploitation switched abruptly from gazelles to sheep and goats.

Abu Roash a site northwest of GIZA, Egypt; the unfinished pyramid of King Radjedef, the immediate successor of KHUFU, is the northernmost of those associated with the capital MEMPHIS.

Abu Salabikh, Tell set in southern MESOPOTAMIA on an extinct watercourse just northwest of NIPPUR, Abu Salabikh was first excavated by V. Crawford in the 1960s. This work exposed part of a large building complex of EARLY DYNASTIC III date, in which were found over 500 texts including the earliest-known literary works of SUMERIAN literature (the 'Instructions of Shuruppak' and the 'Kesh Temple Hymn'). They also define a scribal tradition different from that previously known in Sumerian Mesopotamia (at Fara), remarkable for the Semitic names of many of its scribes and resemblance to the documents from KISH as well as from EBLA in Syria. I. J. Gelb has proposed the name 'Kish civilization' to identify the cultural patterns of northern BABYLONIA during the mid 3rd millennium. Nicholas Postgate and his collaborators excavated at Abu Salabikh during the 1970s and 1980s. The site is composed of eight separate mounds, six of which fall within a 100 ha (250 acre) area. The latter collectively date to URUK-Early Dynastic III times, with some later 3rd millennium occupation also occurring. Not all the mounds were inhabited simultaneously, and the settlement focus shifted through time. Major contributions of the project include: application of extensive surface scraping to reveal urban architectural layout during several periods; analysis of production and use of pottery and chipped stone during the middle Uruk period; identification of walled house compounds of Early Dynastic I date, probably a material reflection of extended families; documentation of the layout of a major Early Dynastic III settlement; and detailed analysis of Early Dynastic pottery that entails a correction to the ceramic chronology based on the older Diyala evidence (at KHAFADJE, Tell ASMAR), and identification of regional variations in the Early Dynastic pottery of southern Mesopotamia that may reflect Gelb's 'Kish civilization'.

Abu Shahrain see ERIDU.

Abu Sifian see HAYONIM CAVE.

Abu Simbel the site, in LOWER NUBIA, of two ROCK-TEMPLES constructed under RAMESSES II. The Great Temple has a façade of two pairs of colossal seated figures (approximately 22 m [72 ft] tall) of the king, flanking the entrance. The Small Temple has a more modest, but nonetheless impressive, frontage of standing figures of Ramesses and his principal queen, Nefertari. Both temples were dismantled and reconstructed on higher ground during the NUBIAN RESCUE CAMPAIGN.

Abusir the site of the pyramids of the 5th Dynasty Egyptian Kings Sahure, Niuserre, Neferirkare and (probably) Raneferef, excavated by Borchardt in 1902–8. Between these pyramids and ABU GHURAB lies the SUN TEMPLE of King Userkaf, also of the 5th Dynasty, excavated by Ricke and Haeny in 1954–7.

Abydos a much-excavated site in UPPER EGYPT containing a series of important structures, including royal tombs of the ARCHAIC PERIOD and the temples of the early 19th Dynasty. Abydos was considered to be the burial-place of OSIRIS, and as such became an important 'national' cemetery and place of pilgrimage, giving rise to the construction of a large number of tombs, and of monuments (including royal examples) commemorating individuals buried elsewhere, especially from the MIDDLE KINGDOM onwards.

The pyramid of King Sahure at ABUSIR, Egypt. The ruined condition of the pyramid illustrates the poorer construction methods of the late Old Kingdom.

Acacus or **Tadrart Acacus** broken country in the Sahara Desert of southwestern Libya with many rock paintings. Exfoliated pieces of paintings incorporated into a cave deposit enabled depictions of domestic cattle to be radiocarbon-dated to c.4800 BP. Faunal remains from the TI-N-TORHA and UAN MUHUGGIAG rockshelters provide the most complete sequence of Holocene subsistence behaviour in the central Sahara.

accelerator mass spectrometry (AMS) a RADIOCARBON DATING method that utilizes an accelerator mass spectrometer to determine the actual numbers of ^{14}C atoms present in a sample, rather than the relatively small numbers of ^{14}C atoms that decay radioactively during the measurement time of the conventional β-counting method. Both methods have about the same dating age limit of about 50,000 bp. The greatest advantage of the AMS method is the sample size requirement of only 1 mg (0.035 oz) of carbon, and in some cases, as little as 100 μg (0.0035 oz) of carbon. A second advantage is that actual measurement time takes about an hour, whereas conventional β-counting can take days. The cost of AMS analysis is a drawback and, if enough sample is available, the finest conventional counters can achieve a slightly greater precision. In addition to dating standard materials such as charcoal, bones and other organic residues of occupation, the AMS method allows dating of individual seeds, textiles and artifacts without totally destroying the sample.

Aceramic Neolithic 1 another term for the PRE-POTTERY NEOLITHIC. The word Neolithic was originally technological, referring to peoples using ground stone and pottery, whatever their subsistence practices. It is now exclusively used to refer to communities with food production as the central basis of subsistence. The differentiation between technology and economy became apparent with the discovery of food-producing communities in western Asia that did not use pottery; the reverse situation – i.e. foragers who use pottery – also occurs but is not given a special name.

2 a transitional phase identified on a number of sites in Greece, Crete and Cyprus such as ARGISSA, SESKLO, KNOSSOS, KALAVASOS and KHIROKITIA, in which agriculture is the basis of the economy but pottery is not yet in use.

Achaeans one of the terms used by Homer for the Greeks at TROY which may have been current in the Bronze Age, if HITTITE Ahhijawa is correctly identified as a MYCENAEAN state, but which is not attested in LINEAR B.

Achaemenids a branch of the Persian tribes that moved into western Iran early in the 1st millennium BC (if not earlier) and settled in Fars. From there, the ruling house (who claimed descent from Achaemenes, eponymous founder of the royal line in the early 7th century BC) expanded during the 6th century BC to create a world empire that stretched from Central Asia and northern India to THRACE and Egypt. Notable Achaemenid rulers include CYRUS II (559–530 BC), Darius I (522–486 BC) and Xerxes I (485–465 BC). The Macedonian Alexander the Great conquered the Achaemenid empire in 330 BC.

Achenheim a prehistoric French site situated 10 km (6 miles) to the west of Strasbourg and investigated by a number of workers since 1835. The loess layers have produced abundant faunal remains, including mammoth, rather poor Lower Palaeolithic artifacts, MOUSTERIAN-like tools dating to the RISS GLACIATION and some Upper Palaeolithic material.

Acheulian or **Acheulean 1** (*European*) the main Lower Palaeolithic tradition of biface makers which lasted from over one million years ago until the early part of the last GLACIATION *c*.100,000 BP. Acheulian industries have been identified over much of Africa, across western and Central Europe and as far east as India. Their tool-kits are characterized by the presence of bifaces, waste flakes and flake tools, with considerable local and regional variation within the same Acheulian tradition. The Acheulian takes its name from the type-site of Saint-Acheul, Amiens, in the Somme Valley, France.

2 (*African*) an EARLIER STONE AGE industrial complex. A very early Acheulian is known at 1.65 million years ago west of LAKE TURKANA in Kenya, and between 1.5 and 1.4 million years ago at KONSO-GARDULA in Ethiopia, the KARARI escarpment east of Lake Turkana and in northern Tanzania at OLDUVAI GORGE and PENINJ. The African Acheulian was replaced by the MIDDLE STONE AGE between 250,000 and 200,000 years ago. It is characterized by the production of bifaces, especially hand axes and cleavers, manufactured by an early HOMO species, known variously as early African *H. erectus* or *H. ergaster*, and later by early *H. sapiens*.

acinaces (*Gk* akinakes) a short (40–60 cm [16–24 inch]) dagger-like sword, a thrusting weapon used in hand-to-hand fighting by the SCYTHIANS and the Persians in the middle and 2nd half of the 1st millennium BC. Early acinaces were made of bronze, and then were replaced by iron specimens. They were carried in a wooden or leather scabbard. Acinaces had a heart-shaped guard and a plain pommel, which were both sometimes decorated with zoomorphic images depicted in the SCYTHIAN-SIBERIAN ANIMAL STYLE.

Acropole of Susa structures at SUSA in lowland Khuzistan, southwestern Iran. Among the many excavations there, perhaps the most important are those named

ACINACES.

'Acropole 2' and 'Acropole 1', dug in the 1970s by P. Canal and A. Le Brun respectively. Acropole 2 addresses the context of the large cemetery and large platform that de Morgan had exposed in Susa's initial occupation levels. Dated to the end of the 5th millennium BC, these structures and their contents imply a degree of social complexity at this time in lowland Khuzistan. Acropole I provides a sequence of twenty-seven levels running from the initial settlement of the place to AKKADIAN times. In this sequence may be observed the replacement of painted pottery in the local style (levels 27–23) by an URUK ceramic inventory (22–17), followed by an abrupt change in pottery (16–14); the transition between these two phases, of uncertain duration, seems to be absent from the sequence. The latter two ceramic phases correspond to important developments in writing: levels 18–17 contain tablets marked only with numbers, and TOKENS in BULLAE (which themselves are often marked with numbers), while levels 16–15 contain tablets bearing PROTO-ELAMITE script. This developmental sequence of writing parallels that found at WARKA, but here represents a different language.

acropolis see AKROPOLIS.

acroterium see AKROTERION.

activity area an area of a site in which a specific activity, such as stone tool or pottery manufacture, was practised.

actualistic study an investigation of the actual processes through which the archaeological record, or artifacts common in the archaeological record, comes about. Under the NEW ARCHAEOLOGY, actualistic studies were an important way to develop BRIDGING ARGUMENTS and WARRANTING ARGUMENTS. Studies of ETHNO-ARCHAEOLOGY and TAPHONOMY, as well as replication experiments, are actualistic studies.

AD an abbreviation for Anno Domini, Latin for 'in the year of the Lord', in a calendrical system first used by a 6th-century AD abbot, Dionysius Exiguus (or 'Little Dennis'), who calculated dates from his estimate of the birth of Jesus Christ, designated AD 1, to replace the Roman calendar, which was based on the reigns of Roman emperors. Dates before AD 1 were labelled BC ('before Christ'). There was no year 0, because the concept of zero was unknown in western Europe at the time. The BC/AD system was not widely used in Europe until the 10th century AD. Some now prefer a calendrical system without reference to Christian religion and use the abbreviations CE ('the Common Era') instead of AD, and BCE ('before the Common Era') instead of BC. Where these letters appear in lower case (ad, bc) they generally denote uncalibrated estimates of dates obtained by the RADIO-CARBON method; where they appear in upper case, they generally denote calendar years, rough dates or calibrated radiocarbon estimates (see CALIBRATION).

Addaura a cave in the Monte Pellegrino group at Palermo, Sicily, with parietal engravings, discovered in 1952, which are usually attributed to the final Upper Palaeolithic (ROMANELLI period). They comprise horses, bovids and deer, but especially a series of humans, some possibly masked and apparently dancing, while two in the centre seem to be bound and lying down.

Adena a complex located in the central Ohio Valley, USA, between approximately 500 and 100 BC, which shows great internal cultural variation. Adena is characterized by pottery, the construction of earthen enclosures and earthen mounds built over burials. Grave-goods are made from a variety of materials found in various parts of the American Midwest and Southeast. Habitation structures vary in size, from single-family dwellings to communal houses. See also GRAVE CREEK MOUND.

Adlun or **Abri Zumoffen** a Palaeolithic site on the Lebanese coast between SIDON and TYRE which was investigated by GARROD. Excavations have revealed an AMUDIAN industry followed by JABRUDian occupation.

adobe dried mud (mixed with plant fibre), often called *jacal*, used in the wattle-and-daub method of building construction. See also MUD-BRICK.

Adrar Bous a volcanic ring complex in northern Niger with archaeological material dating from ACHEULIAN times until about 4,500 years ago. The sites offer important information on the beginnings of cattle domestication in the Sahara.

adyton or **adytum** an enclosed room which formed the innermost sanctuary of a CLASSICAL temple. It was normally entered via the OPISTHODOMOS and was located to the rear of the CELLA.

adze 1 a stone tool made of flakes or pebbles, with steep flaking or battering along one or both sides, hafted and used for woodworking. Adzes approximately 25–40 mm (1–2 inches) long are found in small numbers in most southern African LATER STONE AGE sites, particularly those dating to the last few thousand years. In Australia several types have been recognized, but only the TULA is clearly defined. Australian archaeologists often use the term loosely to describe flake scrapers with heavily retouched step-flaked edges. Repeated resharpening and reversal in the haft results in the production of a heavily flaked 'slug'.
2 a tool made of ground stone found throughout the Pacific. There is a wide variety of forms, which are important cultural and chronological markers. The most widely used classification was devised by DUFF. Shell adzes are also found in MICRONESIA and POLYNESIA. See also POLISHED STONE ADZE.

Adzhi-Koba a Palaeolithic cave-site in the Crimea, Ukraine. The lower occupation horizon contains an assemblage of Middle Palaeolithic artifacts, including sidescrapers. The upper horizon contains an Upper Palaeolithic occupation, rare in the Crimea, with artifacts apparently similar to those from SYUREN' I. Adzhi-Koba was excavated by Bonch-Osmolovskij in 1932–3.

aedicula a small Roman shrine usually projecting from a wall inside a building. Two columns supported a miniature ARCHITRAVE and above that a PEDIMENT. A small statue of a deity may have been placed inside. Wall-paintings, in particular those at POMPEII, often include aediculae in an attempt to give depth to the room.

Aegina an island in the Saronic Gulf between PIRAEUS and the Peloponnese. An Early Bronze Age site has been excavated at Kolonna adjoining the modern town. Over this settlement was constructed a temple of the DORIC ORDER. Elsewhere on the island was the temple of Aphaia, rebuilt in the early years of the 5th century BC. The PEDIMENTS of the new building showed the two sacks of TROY.

Aeneolithic see ENEOLITHIC.

aeolian or **eolian** *adj.* of the wind. The term is applied to deposits caused by, material carried by, or processes related to the wind. Aeolian deposits can easily bury archaeological deposits intact or with little disturbance, whereas aeolian erosion can cause collapse of the archaeological record and displacement of debris. Aeolian particle movement may modify archaeological debris through abrasion and create a PATINA.

Aeolic order an architectural order defined by an ornate type of CAPITAL that seems to have been widely used in the northwestern part of Turkey (the ancient Aeolis) as well as the island of Lesbos. The capital was formed by two VOLUTEs which are separated by a spreading PALMETTE. The ECHINUS rests below the bottom of the volutes and tends to be formed by water-lily leaves. See also IONIC ORDER.

aerial photography a survey tool used to locate sites, detail site structures, and map GEOMORPHOLOGY and soils in site vicinity. It is based on contrasting tonal patterns due to differences in soil texture, soil moisture content, organic matter content and vegetation type and vigour. Photography is usually from an aircraft utilizing a range of film type depending on needs, and can be oblique or vertical, the latter taken with overlap to allow stereoscopic examination.

aerobic *adj.* denoting an environmental state where free molecular oxygen is available. An aerobic environment is not conducive to preservation of plant, animal and human remains, or of artifacts made from them, because the presence of oxygen facilitates the chemical or biochemical decay of organic structures. Compare ANAEROBIC.

Afanasievo culture an ENEOLITHIC culture of southern Siberia (MINUSINSK BASIN, ALTAI MOUNTAINS, Tuva) and northwestern Mongolia. It was first distinguished by S. A. TEPLOUKHOV in the 1920s from materials unearthed in his excavation of the Afanasieva Gora cemetery in the Minusinsk Basin. The Afanasievo culture is known primarily from graves, in which multiple inhumations were interred in a central pit with grave-goods, above which was a low mound surrounded by a low circular wall up to 12 m (13 yds) in diameter. Most of these burials occur in groups of up to twenty, such as at the sites of Afanasieva Gora and Karasuk III. The people of the Afanasievo culture were of Europeoid type, and were the first stock-breeders and first metallurgists in Siberia. The most typical Afanasievo ceramics are egg-shaped vessels and incense cups, which find their closest analogies in the YAMNAYA CULTURE, far to the west.

Afontova culture an Upper Palaeolithic culture of southern-central Siberia, dating to c.20,000–10,000 BP. Diagnostic artifacts include wedge-shaped microcores, microblades and scrapers. Retouched blades, which are common in sites of the roughly contemporaneous KOKO-REVO CULTURE, are rare. The Afontova culture was defined by Abramova in 1979.

Afontova Gora a group of four Upper Palaeolithic open-air sites on the Yenisei River in Krasnoyarsk, southern-central Siberia. At each locality, artifacts and faunal remains are buried in slope deposits overlying ALLUVIUM of the second terrace. Most of the occupation layers date to the late GLACIAL. Among the fauna, reindeer is generally the most abundant species, although woolly mammoth and arctic fox are also common. The artifact assemblages contain wedge-shaped microcores, microblades and scrapers. Afontova Gora I was discovered and excavated by Savenkov in 1884–93; subsequent investigations by Auerbakh, Gromov and others occurred in 1912–14 and 1923–30.

Afrasiab an ancient fort, formerly Marakanda, located on the outskirts of Samarkand in ancient SOGDIANA (Uzbekistan) where excavations carried out since 1874 have uncovered HELLENISTIC period (late 1st millennium BC) buildings, pottery and small finds similar to materials at AI KHANUM. The fort existed from the 6th century BC until it was destroyed by Mongols in AD 1220. It consists of a citadel, inner town and a suburb. Excavations have unearthed residential and handicraft areas, a mosque and the remains of a palace from the 7th to the 8th centuries AD in which multi-coloured murals were discovered in 1965, in a style that strongly parallels those found in Xinjiang at sites like Tun-huang and Turfan, differing mainly in the degree of SASSANIAN influence in Sogdiana.

Africa Evidence from eastern and southern Africa indicates that the human archaeological record began on the African continent. Although early traces of this record are usually rare and fragmentary, and invariably offer only tantalizing and debatable glimpses of the details of the human past, the broad outlines are well established.

Modern humans are the only surviving species of the HOMINID family, which probably branched off from the great ape line in the period between 9 and 7 million years ago in Africa, the only continent on which fossils of the first hominids have been found. Some researchers claim that 6-million-year-old fossils of ORRORIN *tugenensis* from Kenya may represent the earliest known hominid and ancestor of HOMO. Others have suggested that a small ape-like ardipithecine (see ARDIPITHECUS) hominid that lived in Ethiopia some 4.4 million years ago could represent an early stage in the lineage from which humans later evolved. In the period between 4.2 and 1 million years ago, several species of ape-like bipedal australopithecines (see AUSTRALOPITHECUS) lived in regions stretching from Chad in northeastern Africa through eastern Africa to northern South Africa. Some lightly built species of these creatures are widely considered to have been distant human ancestors. A recent suggestion that they could rather represent a side branch on the human family tree is the subject of current debate. They probably made tools from organic materials, just like modern wild chimpanzees have been observed doing. The oldest-known stone tools, dating to some 2.5 million years ago from GONA in Ethiopia, could have been made by australopithecines. A 3.5-million-year-old flat-faced hominid from Kenya, KENYANTHROPUS *platyops*, which probably had a diet different from that of australopithecines, indicates that australopithecines were not the only hominids present at that time, and that the details of the relationships between early hominids are unclear.

Creatures belonging to the human genus *Homo* first appeared in Africa when australopithecines still existed. The criteria for distinguishing hominid fossils as *Homo* are currently under debate. Some suggest 2.3-million-year-old remains from HADAR are the oldest known *Homo* fossils, while others prefer to attribute this claim to *H. ergaster* or African *H. erectus* fossils from eastern Africa dating to about 1.9 million years ago. At about this time, early humans appear to have spread to Asia for the first time, according to the 'OUT OF AFRICA 1' hypothesis.

The period between about 2.5 million and 250,000 years ago saw the use of EARLIER or EARLY STONE AGE technology, in North Africa also termed Lower Palaeolithic, in which simple tools were made from stone as well as organic materials like bone and wood. This stage of stone tool technology is divided into two main technological traditions or complexes. Between about 2.5 and 1.5 million years ago, tools of the Earlier Stone Age OLDOWAN COMPLEX, named after OLDUVAI GORGE, were made by early *Homo* and possibly also by australopithecines. Between about 1.5 million and 250,000 years ago, at first early *Homo* and later, after some 800,000 years ago, archaic *H. sapiens* made tools of the Earlier Stone Age ACHEULIAN tradition. There is no unequivocal evidence for the controlled use of fire, construction of shelters or existence of art or burial of the dead during this period, and it is thought that the hominids were omnivores who were more successful at foraging and scavenging than hunting big game.

From some 250,000 or later years ago until as recently as about 30,000 or later years ago, the MIDDLE STONE AGE, in North Africa the Middle Palaeolithic, saw the production of more deliberately shaped stone tools, some of which appear to have been hafted on to handles, widespread occurrence of colouring materials like ochre, and frequent examples of deliberately constructed hearths. Possible examples of burials and, in the latest Middle Stone Age, of rock art, have also been recorded. Middle Stone Age tools are particularly abundant after about 130,000 years ago, when the earliest-known fossils of anatomically modern *H. sapiens* have been found at sites like KLASIES RIVER MOUTH. These fossils, together with genetic studies, are the basis for the 'Out of Africa 2' hypothesis that modern humans, like the first of their kind, originally evolved in Africa and then spread to the rest of the world.

After some 40,000 years ago, the LATE or LATER STONE AGE, or in North Africa the Upper Palaeolithic, saw the widespread use of microlithic stone tools, bone tools, specialized fishing, hunting and gathering equipment, and an explosion of evidence for art and decoration as well as deliberate burial of the dead.

In North Africa, increasingly sedentary lifestyles and intensive use of local resources around water sources after about 18,000 years ago paved the way for the adoption of agriculture and appearance of Neolithic communities with pottery probably from shortly before 7,000 years ago. Exotic domesticated plants and animals spread throughout Africa, and indigenous African plants like millet and sorghum became cultivated. The agricultural wealth of the Nile Valley contributed to the development of centres which, by 3100 BC or slightly before, became a unified kingdom in which the ancient Egyptian civilization flourished for the following 3,000 years (see EGYPT). PASTORAL NEOLITHIC societies appeared in eastern Africa after about 5,000 years ago, while Stone Age pastoralists with pottery, the ancestors of the KHOE-KHOEN, were present in the western parts of southern Africa by 2,000 years ago.

Apart from Egypt and some regions of North Africa, most of the continent did not experience a Bronze Age but moved directly from the Stone to the Iron Age. Knowledge of iron smelting from western Asia reached North Africa in about the 8th century BC. Iron metallurgy spread through Africa from this source or possibly developed independently in several regions. There is evidence of iron working or Iron Age pottery in West Africa from about the 7th century BC, in eastern Africa from at least the late 1st millennium BC, if not earlier, and in southeastern Africa by AD 400. The spread of iron through most of Central, eastern and southern Africa is usually linked to migrations of BANTU-speaking peoples originally from the Nigeria-Cameroon border, but it has been suggested that these migrations could have begun before the Iron Age. Iron Age people were farmers who lived in permanent villages and who brought domesticated animals and cultivated plants as well as pottery and metallurgy to much of sub-Saharan Africa. The development of local and long-distance trade networks during the 1st millennium AD led to the growth of indigenous towns such as JENNE-JENO, social stratification such as exemplified at IGBO-UKWU and MAPUNGUBWE, and culminated in the emergence of pre-colonial states in many areas of sub-Saharan Africa, including GHANA, MALI, SONGHAY, KANEM and BENIN in West Africa, and GREAT ZIMBABWE in southern Africa.

African Red Slip ware a type of red-glossed pottery (see SLIP) produced in North Africa, particularly from the 3rd to the 6th centuries AD. A range of shapes was produced. The stamped decoration included simple motifs such as PALMETTES as well as figured scenes, some of which were drawn from biblical passages. The fabric has a wide distribution, being found as far north as Britain. Its export may be linked to the demand for African olive oil.

Afunfun early copper-working sites in the Agadez region of Niger, of the 2nd and 1st millennia BC (a furnace dated to 4140 bp provides the earliest date), containing a series of furnaces, quantities of slag and copper objects. The Agadez region of Niger is one of two areas in West Africa with evidence of pre-Iron Age metallurgy (see AKJOUJT).

Agade the city founded by SARGON of Akkad as the capital of his empire; its location is unknown, but is probably in the neighbourhood of KISH.

Agadez see AFUNFUN, AZELIK.

Agate Basin 1 a PALAEOINDIAN site located in eastern Wyoming, USA, probably used as a bison KILL-SITE. It shows evidence of both the killing and butchering of animals.

2 a late Palaeoindian point form recognized at its type-site.

3 an archaeological complex centred in the northwestern Plains of North America. It is dated at the HELL GAP site to 10,500–10,000 BP. Besides the distinctive point form, the complex is characterized by its scrapers and eyed bone needles. The Agate Basin occupation at Hell Gap had evidence of POSTHOLES, possibly representing small circular structures.

agger 1 the raised causeway which served as the foundations for the construction of Roman roads.

2 a rampart forming part of a series of fortifications.

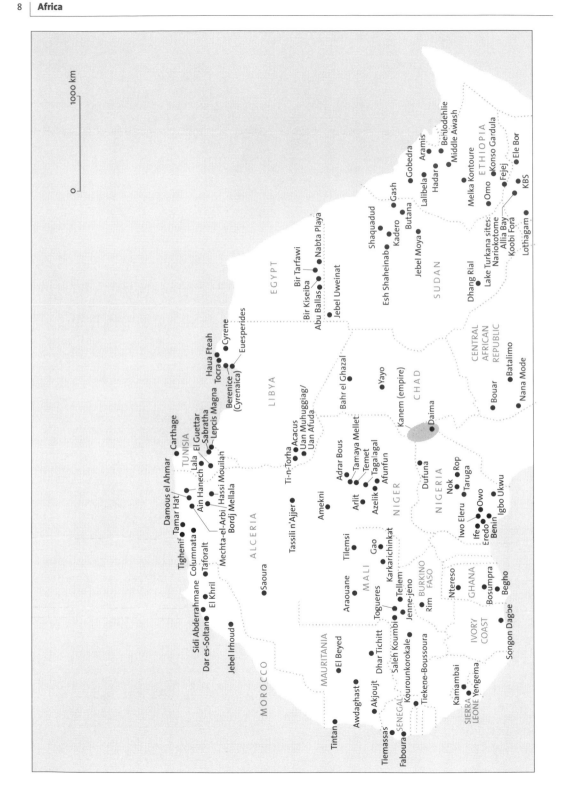

1000 km

0

Behodehlie
Middle Awash
Aramis
Hadar
Gobedra
Lalibela
Gash
Butana
Melka Kontoure
ETHIOPIA
Konso Gardula
Omo
Fejej
Ele Bor
KBS
Shaquadud
Kadero
Jebel Moya
Esh Shaheinab
SUDAN
Lake Turkana sites:
Nariokotome
Allia Bay
Koobi Fora
Lothagam
Dhang Rial

Bir Tarfawi
Nabta Playa
Bir Kiseiba
Abu Ballas
Jebel Uweinat
EGYPT

CENTRAL
AFRICAN
REPUBLIC
Batalimo
Bouar
Nana Mode

Cyrene
Euesperides
Haua Fteah
Tocra
Berenice
(Cyrenaica)
Lepcis Magna
Sabratha
El Guettar
Carthage
Lala
TUNISIA
Damous el Ahmar
Tamar Hat
Ain Hanech
Hassi Mouilah
Mechta-el-Arbi
Bordj Mellala
Tighenif
Columnata
Taforalt
Sidi Abderrahmane
El Khril
Dar es-Soltan
Jebel Irhoud

LIBYA

Bahr el Ghazal
Yayo
Kanem (empire)
CHAD
Daima

Ti-n-Torha
Acacus
Uan Muhuggiag/
Uan Afuda
Adrar Bous
Tamaya Mellet
Temet
Tagalagal
Afunfun
Amekni
Arlit
Azelik
NIGER
Dufuna
Nok
Rop
Taruga
NIGERIA
Iwo Eleru
Ife
Owo
Eredo
Benin
Igbo Ukwu

Tassili n'Ajjer
ALGERIA
Saoura

Tilemsi
Gao
Karkarichinkat
MALI
Araouane
Togueres
Jenne-jeno
Tellem
BURKINO
FASO
Rim
Ntereso
GHANA
Bosumpra
Begho
IVORY
COAST
Songon Dagoe

MAURITANIA
El Beyed
Akjoujt
Dhar Tichitt
Saleh Koumbi
Kourounkorokale
Tiekene-Boussoura
MOROCCO

Tintan
Awdaghast
Tiemassas
SENEGAL
Faboura
SIERRA
LEONE
Kamambai
Yengema

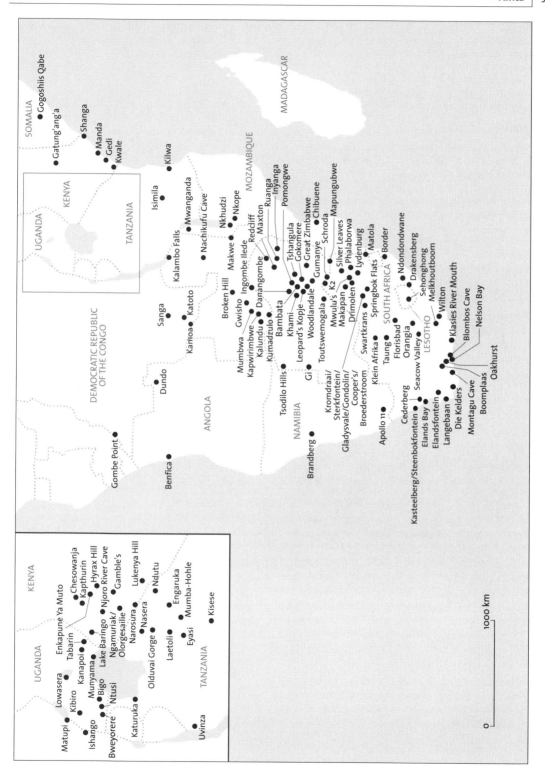

Aggsbach an Upper Palaeolithic open-air site located on the River Danube in northeastern Austria. Artifacts and faunal remains (e.g. woolly mammoth, reindeer, giant deer) are buried in deposits of loess yielding radiocarbon dates of 25,700–22,450 bp. The assemblages contain end-scrapers, backed blades and retouched blades; they are assigned to the EASTERN GRAVETTIAN.

Aggtelek see DOMICA.

agora a focal point for civic life in the Greek city. The area tended to be surrounded by buildings linked to the government of the state (see BOULEUTERION, PRY-TANEION) and the law-courts. It could also include markets as well as spaces for athletic events and festivals. The perimeter of the agora could be marked by boundary stones. From the HELLENISTIC period agoras throughout the Greek world could be lined by STOAS. As the civic centre the agora attracted the erection of honorific statues. One of the best understood agoras is that at ATHENS excavated by an American team. Compare FORUM.

Agrigento (*Gk* Akragas, *Lat.* Agrigentum) a Greek colony in southern Sicily traditionally founded by GELA c.580 BC. It became a prosperous city, probably flourishing on the rearing of horses, vineyards and olives. Its wealth is reflected in the large number of temples of the DORIC ORDER which continue to dominate the ridge forming the southern edge of the city. In the late 2nd century BC there was substantial rebuilding, with the streets laid out in a grid pattern (see HIPPODAMIAN PLANNING).

Agrileza see LAURION.

Agris helmet an Iron Age helmet discovered in the Grotte des Perrats, Agris, Charente, France, by cavers in 1981. One of the finest works of LA TÈNE art to be discovered in recent years, it was of iron, overlaid by bronze bands with decoration in raised relief covered by thin gold sheet. Further decoration of coral was fixed to the helmet with silver rivets. PALMETTES are prominent among the decorative motifs, and the helmet is attributed on stylistic grounds to the 4th century BC.

A-Group a culture which emerged in LOWER NUBIA during the late 4th millennium BC and disappeared by c.3000 BC; it was influenced by the GERZEAN of UPPER EGYPT. The economy was based on the herding of cattle, sheep and goats, and there is a concern for burial ritual hitherto unknown among populations in Nubia.

Aguadulce Shelter a rockshelter on the Pacific coastal plain of central Panama where PRECERAMIC horizons have yielded starch grains of manioc, yams and arrowroot on plant milling stones dating to between 7,000 and 5,000 years ago, which, together with phytoliths and pollen from the site, constitute the earliest direct evidence for root crop cultivation in the New World.

Ahar a prehistoric site in southern Rajasthan, just south of the Aravalli Hills in western India. The settlement of Ahar falls into two distinct periods: CHALCOLITHIC (Ahar IA–C) and Iron Age (Ahar IIA–C). Radiocarbon dates for Ahar I indicate occupation between 2500 and 1500 BC. The community lived in fairly large structures of stone and mud-brick, and by the end of the period grew rice, sorghum (?and millet) as well as other crops, herded cattle and kept other animals, and smelted a great deal of copper. The latter feature, most clearly evident in Ahar IB, reflects the settlement's proximity to the copper sources in the Aravalli Hills. The pottery displays changes through time. A white-painted BLACK-AND-RED WARE and black-on-cream-slipped ware are present in Ahar IA; Lustrous Red ware appears in Ahar IC. The Iron Age settlement begins with levels containing NORTHERN BLACK POLISHED ware (Ahar IIA), followed by early historic period levels (Ahar IIB–C).

Aharoni, Yohanan (1919–76) an Israeli archaeologist, an active excavator whose sites include ARAD, LACHISH and BEERSHEBA.

Ahmose the first king of the Egyptian 18th Dynasty and therefore of the NEW KINGDOM. During the reign of Ahmose (c.1550–1525 BC) the HYKSOS were expelled from Egypt, and territorial gains were made in NUBIA and Palestine.

Ahrensburgian *adj.* relating to an EPIPALAEOLITHIC culture found in northern Germany and Holland, in many ways similar to the HAMBURGIAN of the same area, but much later in date (c.8500 BC). The northern German site of Stellmoor has yielded both Hamburgian and Ahrensburgian levels; the Ahrensburgian phase, dated to the last cold phase of the final GLACIATION, appears to be a temporary reindeer-hunting camp. The tool-kit includes flint scrapers, burins, tanged points which were probably used as arrowheads, wooden arrow shafts, and clubs which were used to kill reindeer. See also BROMMIAN.

ahu a rectangular ceremonial platform on EASTER ISLAND and the Society Islands, related to the POLYNESIAN MARAE, and usually built of stone slabs encasing a rubble core. On Easter Island, where ahu sometimes supported human statues (MOAI), the earliest appear c.AD 600 and the latest date to c.AD 1500. In most of eastern Polynesia, the term referred only to a raised platform at the end of a rectangular court, but in the northern Marquesas and Easter Island it denotes the whole ceremonial centre.

Ahualulco a ceremonial complex in western Mexico, best known as part of the SHAFT TOMB complex, which is found in association with a distinctive architectural style. This style is characterized by habitation zones dominated by a large multiple-circle complex with BALL

COURTS and elite residential architecture. Ahualulco was made up of six circles and one ball court, enclosing about 42,510 sq. m (50,840 sq. yds). This architectural style was characteristic from about 200 BC until AD 900/1000.

ahuapua'a a basic unit of land division in the Hawaiian Islands, cross-cutting all major environmental zones from the uplands to the coast, and under the control of a chief. Several have been studied intensively by archaeologists, including HALAWA VALLEY, KAWELA, LAPAKAHI and MAKAHA VALLEY.

Ai a site in Palestine, excavated by GARSTANG in 1928, by Marquet-Krause in 1933–5 and by Callaway in 1964–72. Ai was occupied during the EARLY BRONZE AGE when its AKROPOLIS included a palace/temple and a rectangular stone tower, part of the fortifications of the 'citadel'; some of this building work may have involved Egyptian craftsmen of the ARCHAIC PERIOD. Ai was destroyed and abandoned at the end of the Early Bronze Age, but was occupied as an unfortified town in the Iron Age.

Aibunar a late Neolithic copper mine in Bulgaria, located near KARANOVO and AZMAK, and dated by pottery found in the workings to the Karanovo VI period. Eleven galleries have been identified, totalling approximately 500 m (550 yds). The longest gallery was 110 m (120 yds) long at a depth of 20 m (66 ft). Antler axes and picks were found in the galleries.

Aichbühl a late Neolithic settlement on the Federsee in southwestern Germany, dated to c.4200 BC. Small rectangular houses, often with two rooms, were arrayed in rows along the lake shore. The excavation of Aichbühl and similar sites in the early 20th century led to a reappraisal of the LAKE DWELLINGS of Central Europe and the realization that they had been built on lake shores rather than out over water.

Ai Khanum a Greek city founded late in the 4th century BC at the confluence of the Kokcha and Oxus Rivers in Bactria (northern Afghanistan). The city included a citadel and ACROPOLIS as well as a walled lower town. French excavations in the lower town documented a large administrative complex, religious buildings, a gymnasium and theatre. Architectural design and artistic products reveal a progressive combination of Greek, Mesopotamian, Iranian and local Bactrian elements during the two centuries of the city's existence.

'Ain Ghazal an extremely large settlement on the east bank of the River Jordan occupied from late PRE-POTTERY NEOLITHIC into ceramic Neolithic times, that was excavated during the 1980s by Gary Rollefson. The excavation revealed a Pre-Pottery Neolithic B (PPNB, c.7600–6000 BC) settlement which grew steadily through time, from 4 ha (10 acres) at c.7250 BC to 9 ha (22 acres) at c.6500 BC and ultimately reaching 12 ha (30 acres) in 6000 BC, making it one of the largest known PPNB sites. The Aceramic levels are remarkable for the three caches of plaster human statues, perhaps reflecting an ancestor cult connected with the famous PPNB PLASTERED SKULLS. The lithic changes seen in the terminal Aceramic period, designated PPNC, are dated to 6000–5700 BC. This lithic distinction may also capture deeper economic shifts: the PPNB community kept goats, while PPNC herders also tended cattle, pigs and perhaps sheep, and are thought to have begun long-distance movements to seasonal pasture. The subsequent ceramic Neolithic settlement (the YARMOUKIAN) represents seasonal occupations, perhaps by pastoralists connected to farmers in the western Levant.

Ain Hanech an early Pleistocene site in northern Algeria, yielding pebble tools, particularly spheroids and battered stones, associated with extinct riverine and lacustrine fauna. ARAMBOURG carried out palaeontological work here in 1931–66. Recent excavations by Sahnouni have shown that the main stratified cultural horizon is OLDOWAN in technology, and Lower Pleistocene in age. The low density of artifacts includes cores and flakes of local FLINT, as well as limestone river cobbles. Handaxes and cleavers are absent. Microwear analysis shows that some flakes were used on meat.

Ain Mallaha see EYNAN.

Ainu former hunter-gatherer-farmers occupying Hokkaido and Sakhalin Islands (Japan and Russia). In Hokkaido, they are now settled as farmers with heavy intermarriage with the Japanese. They are morphologically related to the prehistoric JOMON population, which in northern Japan was culturally transformed to the northern YAYOI and then EMISHI. The Ainu were first documented in the 14th–16th centuries AD. The Ainu language has no known relatives. See also AMURIAN.

Ajanta the location of Buddhist cave temples in central India, renowned for their wall paintings that illustrate events from the Buddha's previous lives. The earliest murals date to the 1st century AD (or slightly earlier), but the majority belong to the GUPTA period (4th–5th century AD).

Ajuereado phase the earliest phase in the TEHUACÁN VALLEY, Mexico. Ranging from 10,000 to 7000 BC, the subsistence activities during the Ajuereado phase include hunting small animals and gathering wild plants.

Ajvide Neolithic coastal settlement and cemetery of the PITTED-WARE CULTURE on the island of Gotland, Sweden, occupied primarily between 3100 and 2700 BC. Over fifty graves have been excavated. Many of the graves contain pig jaws, possibly those of wild animals brought to the island. Other grave-goods include hedgehog quills and ornaments of shell and bone. Fishing and seal hunting were important in the diet of the Ajvide community.

Akapana see TIAHUANACO.

Akashi the site of fossil HOMO finds near Kobe City, Japan, discovered by Naora Nobuo in 1931. Only the cast of the innominate bone survived the Second World War. Because of their fossilization, the remains were first thought to be Pleistocene in date, but now they are assessed as Holocene. See also NISHIYAGI.

Akhenaten a king of the 18th Dynasty who reigned c.1353–1337 BC, remarkable among ancient Egyptian monarchs for rejecting the traditional pantheon of gods (especially the cult of AMEN) in favour of a monotheistic worship of the ATEN. Akhenaten, accompanied by his chief wife NEFERTITI, moved the capital of Egypt from THEBES to EL-AMARNA. His memory, together with that of his immediate successors who were associated with the 'Aten heresy', including TUTANKHAMEN, was reviled by later kings.

akinakes see ACINACES.

Akjoujt a region of Mauretania, Africa, containing a series of copper mines dating back to the 1st millennium BC. This is one of two areas in West Africa with evidence of pre-Iron Age metallurgy (see also AFUNFUN, AZELIK). Copper mining was established here between the 8th and 3rd centuries BC. Hundreds of copper objects, especially arrowheads, have been found with little or no archaeological context but linked to the mines through chemical composition.

Akkadian(s) a linguistic term denoting a group of Semitic languages in MESOPOTAMIA, first reflected in CUNEIFORM texts of the mid 3rd millennium BC in the northern part of the Mesopotamian ALLUVIUM, the ancient Akkad. The later languages BABYLONIAN and ASSYRIAN belong to this language group. The term 'Akkadians' is often used to denote people speaking this language during the 3rd millennium BC, as distinct from SUMERIANS, and ethnic differences are often ascribed to this distinction (see ABU SALABIKH, KISH). In the political history of Mesopotamia, the term is applied to the rule of SARGON's dynasty (c.2330–2150 BC), with its capital at AGADE in Akkad; by extension the term also describes the material culture (especially CYLINDER SEALs, artistic production and ceramics) of this period.

Ak-Kaya a group of fourteen Middle Palaeolithic sites in the Crimea, Ukraine, which includes Ak-Kaya I–V and ZASKAL'NAYA I–IX. Artifact assemblages from these sites have been assigned to the AK-KAYA CULTURE.

Ak-Kaya culture a Middle Palaeolithic culture defined on the basis of artifact assemblages from the AK-KAYA sites in the Crimea, Ukraine. It is characterized by a high percentage of bifacial foliates, including PRONDNIK knives and BOCKSTEIN knives.

akropolis or **acropolis** literally 'the high point of a (Greek) city'. It could form a refuge as well as a location for the cults of the city (see TEMENOS). One of the best known is at ATHENS where several highly decorated temples (see PARTHENON, ERECHTHEION) were built. It also attracted dedications (see KOUROS, KORE) from private individuals from all over its territory of Attica.

akroterion a decorative element found on the roof of a CLASSICAL building, above the apex or the corners of the PEDIMENT. Various forms were used, including PALMETTES, victories and SPHINXes.

Akrotiri on the CYCLADIC island of THERA or SANTORINI in the Aegean archipelago, the site of a Bronze Age town buried by volcanic ash in the 16th century BC. The excavations by MARINATOS and Doumas have revealed houses two or even three storeys high, with brilliant polychrome frescoes still *in situ* on the walls. It is evident from the finds that the inhabitants of Akrotiri maintained close links with MINOAN CRETE.

Aksum see AXUM.

alabaster see GYPSUM.

alabastron a Greek unguent container which should strictly be made of alabaster but can be of clay.

Alaca Höyük a 7 ha (17 acre) prehistoric settlement some 160 km (100 miles) east of Ankara, not far from BOĞAZKÖY in Turkey. The excavations of H. Kosay starting in the 1930s revealed a succession of CHALCOLITHIC, Bronze Age and Iron Age and later (Roman to medieval) settlements. Belonging to the late 2nd millennium BC is a HITTITE occupation consisting of a walled town with several temples, residential areas and a formal gateway (the 'Sphinx gate'); the excavation revealed an iron foundry within the town. Much of this town, including its monumental aspects, belongs to the Old Hittite period (mid 2nd millennium BC), and is often identified with the Hittite cultic centre Arinna. Of the earlier settlements, the Early Bronze contains the famous 'royal graves', dated to the Early Bronze II (the early-to-mid 3rd millennium BC). These thirteen tombs are rectilinear stone- or wood-lined pits, each with one to two inhumations and extremely rich grave-goods, including a series of 'standards' (animal figures in bronze inlaid and plated with precious metals), weapons (many of bronze, but also including iron daggers, an early appearance of this metal), vessels in precious metals, bronze human figurines, and much metal and stone jewellery. The cultural origins of this Early Bronze complex are not easily discerned, since many elite goods had an extremely wide currency in western Asia of the time; the animal figure 'standards' are often cited in suggesting a Pontic origin (somewhere around the Black Sea).

Alalakh see ATCHANA, TELL.

Alambra-Mouttes in eastern CYPRUS, the site of an early Middle Cypriot settlement of rectangular stone-built houses excavated by Coleman in 1976–82.

Alamgirpur a small site in Uttar Pradesh, northeast of Delhi in northern India, excavated in the late 1950s by Y. D. Sharma, which was inhabited at four separate times. The earliest period is characterized by a ceramic assemblage having extremely strong resemblances to the Mature HARAPPAN, in a village of brick and wattle-and-daub architecture. The work at Alamgirpur presented the first evidence of the Harappan ceramic tradition in the Ganges Yamuna doab (alluvial plain). The presence at Alamgirpur of typically Mature Harappan elements (ceramic forms, terracotta cakes), within a cultural assemblage that as a whole is still distinguishable from the Mature Harappan of the Sind (Pakistan), has been interpreted either as a regional variant of the Mature Harappan or as a representative of a Late Harappan tradition that perhaps overlapped in time with the Mature Harappan. The first alternative seems preferable. The later occupations at Alamgirpur, separated from the earlier by a weathering surface, belong to the PAINTED GREY WARE tradition, and then to the 3rd–2nd centuries BC and medieval times.

Alashiya mentioned in Near Eastern texts of the 2nd millennium BC, evidently a source of copper and therefore presumed to be CYPRUS. If this is correct, it would appear that Cyprus was an ally of the Egyptian PHARAOH in the 14th century BC but may subsequently have been incorporated in the HITTITE empire. The texts also record the devastation inflicted by the SEA PEOPLES in c.1200 BC.

Alaska Refugium a large area comprising interior Alaska that was never GLACIATED during the latter part of the Pleistocene. The refugium was connected to BERINGIA and eastern Siberia, both of which also remained free of glaciers. This huge region allowed unimpeded access for early peoples between Asia and North America.

Albany a LATER STONE AGE industry (sometimes called the OAKHURST industry), a regional variation of the Oakhurst complex, known from the Western Cape and Eastern Cape Provinces of South Africa, and dated to between 12,000 and 8000 BP. It is characterized by few formally patterned stone artifacts other than scrapers more than 20 mm (0.8 inch) long, but some assemblages have a range of sophisticated bone tools. See also LOCKSHOEK.

Albright, William Foxwell (1891–1971) an American orientalist and linguist whose archaeological work in Palestine included the excavations at BEIT MERSIM.

Alcalà a cemetery in the Algarve, Portugal, of thirteen

CHAMBERED TOMBS of 'THOLOS' type, with a long passage leading to a circular CORBEL-VAULTED chamber, sometimes with additional side-chambers. The richest, tomb 3, had CALLAIS beads, amber pendants and copper flat axes, daggers and awls. Four of the daggers had raised mid-ribs on both sides, once considered evidence for the early use of a two-piece mould, but now thought to have been hammered-up. The tombs were probably built in the 4th millennium BC, but grave-goods indicate their continued use in the 3rd millennium.

Aleria (*Gk* Alalia) a 6th-century BC colony in eastern Corsica founded from Phocaea in Turkey. The tombs show close similarities with those in ETRURIA, and contained a considerable amount of Etruscan material. This has been seen by some as evidence for an Etruscan presence on the island.

Alésia an Iron Age OPPIDUM in Côte d'Or, France, site of the last stand by the CELTIC chieftain Vercingetorix against Roman invasion forces of Julius Caesar in 52 BC. The oppidum occupies a steep-sided plateau 97 ha (240 acres) in area, with short stretches of walling, including some of the MURUS GALLICUS type described by Caesar. Excavations undertaken for Napoleon III in 1861–5 to the west of the oppidum uncovered remains of Caesar's siege works. A bronze statue of Vercingetorix was erected at the site in 1865.

Aleutian tradition a tradition found in western Alaska and the adjacent Aleutian Islands, which originated in approximately 5000 BP and continued with some modification virtually to the historic period. It is characterized by specific stone projectile points and carved harpoon heads.

Alexandria a coastal city in Egypt founded by Alexander the Great in 331 BC. Little of the city has been excavated, although the cemeteries lying to the east and west of the settlement have been explored (see HADRA WARE). Important buildings included the tomb of Alexander, the Museum, the Serapeum (the temple of Serapis), the library and the Pharos (lighthouse), one of the SEVEN WONDERS. The cult site of Caesar (the Caesareum), and later of Augustus (the Sebasteum or Augusteum), was marked by two obelisks (one of which is Cleopatra's Needle in London).

Alföld see SZAKALHÁT-LEBO GROUP.

Alfred the Great the ruler of the ANGLO-SAXON kingdom of Wessex (AD 871–99), he successfully opposed the assault by the 'Great Army' of the Danes who since 865 had overrun the northern Anglo-Saxon kingdoms of Northumbria, Mercia and East Anglia. In a series of battles with mixed outcomes, Alfred gained the upper hand over the Danes and laid the foundations of the Anglo-Saxon reconquest of the northern territories in the early 10th century. The '*Alfred Jewel*', found in Somerset in 1693, bears the inscription 'AELFRED MEC HEHT GEVVYRCAN' ('Alfred had me made') and may have been a gift from Alfred himself.

Algar do Bom Santo a cave in central Portugal, discovered in 1993, which contains a major Neolithic cemetery, with at least 121 skeletons laid out on the cave floor, both young and adult, dated by radiocarbon to between 4860 and 4430 bp. Some are accompanied by polished axes and pottery, while a few still wear armlets and bracelets of shell.

al Hiba first tested by KOLDEWEY in 1887, and systematically investigated by Donald Hanson since 1968, al Hiba is the city of Lagash, one of the centres of the ancient MESOPOTAMIAn city-state Lagash. The site, on a former branch of the Euphrates, covers nearly 700 ha (2.7 sq. miles) in a series of low mounds. It has a sequence of EARLY DYNASTIC levels capped by an ED III temple oval (as found at KHAFADJE and 'UBAID). Occupation at the site continued into OLD BABYLONIAN times, though after its absorption into the UR III state, Lagash declined in importance.

alidade a surveying instrument used in conjunction with a PLANE TABLE to map a site topographically or locate features in the field. Although somewhat overtaken by electronic measuring instruments and PHOTOGRAMMETRY, this is still the only instrument that enables maps to be created in the field as work progresses. It consists of a focusing telescope for long sightings mounted on a flat metal base with a straight edge that rests on, but is not attached to, the plane table. The alidade is also equipped with a striding-level to level the scope; a bull's-eye level to level the plane table on which it rests; a vernier scale for measuring vertical angles; stadia and cross hairs for determining distances with measurements taken from a stadia rod; and a compass for determining magnetic bearings.

alignment a setting of standing stones or wooden posts characteristic of the British Isles and northwestern France during the late Neolithic and Bronze Age. Alignments sometimes consist of several parallel lines containing hundreds of stones; the most famous are those of CARNAC in Brittany. Such alignments are normally considered to have had a ritual or religious significance, and some were clearly oriented towards solar or lunar phenomena.

Ali Kosh see DEH LURAN.

Alışar Höyük a 12 ha (30 acre) site to the southeast of BOĞAZKÖY in northern Cappadocia, central Anatolia, which was occupied from at least the beginning of the EARLY BRONZE AGE (perhaps even into the late CHALCOLITHIC) up to medieval times. The excavation standards of H. van der Osten's work here in the 1920s and 1930s were fairly low, and the STRATIGRAPHIC associations of his vertical sequences are difficult to reconstruct, leaving this early work at Alışar somewhat compromised. The best-known aspect of the site is the early 2nd millennium BC settlement, characterized by a material culture that has strong similarities with those of contemporary Cappadocian sites such as KÜLTEPE; like these contemporary towns it also contains an Old ASSYRIAN KĀRUM, represented by a small archive and scattered texts.

Allahdino a small village site near the Indus delta in the lower Sind in Pakistan that provides a rare glimpse into a small agricultural community of the Mature HARAPPAN CIVILIZATION. Walter Fairservis's work at the site revealed that most of the artifacts found in urban settings also occur in this rural settlement.

allée couverte sometimes translated as 'gallery grave', one of the two classic types of French megalithic tomb, the other being the PASSAGE GRAVE. *Allées couvertes* are long rectangular monuments, sometimes with the remains of a covering mound, and are distinguished by the absence of a division between passage and chamber, though some have a small antechamber. Dating from the 3rd millennium BC, they are especially characteristic of Brittany and the Paris basin, those of the latter region often holding the remains of several hundred individuals.

Allens Cave a limestone doline on the Nullarbor Plain, South Australia, near KOONALDA CAVE. Two excavations have produced evidence of human occupation below a hearth dated by radiocarbon to about 20,000 bp. THERMOLUMINESCENCE dates of 40,000 years are claimed for the earliest occupation. If confirmed, this would be the oldest evidence of settlement in Australia's arid zone.

Allerød Interstadial a warm period occurring during the final stages of the last (WEICHSEL) GLACIATION in Europe and starting at c.11,800 bp.

Allia Bay a bay on the eastern shore of LAKE TURKANA, northern Kenya, where twelve early HOMINID fossils, comprising dental and arm remains, ascribed to the early bipedal species AUSTRALOPITHECUS *anamensis*, were found in or below the 3.9 million-year-old Moiti TUFF in the KOOBI FORA Formation between 1982 and 1995.

alluvial fan a depositional landform, usually located along valley margins and mountain fronts where tributary streams enter larger valleys or broad lowlands. It is created by the accumulation of ALLUVIUM sedimented as channelized flow becomes unconfined, velocity and depth of flow decrease as waters spread laterally and channels shift position. Fans were, and still are today, prime locations for settlement because they provide a well-drained landscape position in otherwise relatively poorly drained valleys, and they are situated so that upland and floodplain resources are both easily accessible. Archaeological remains tend to be buried more or less intact in alluvial fans as their sediments are deposited.

alluvium a general term for sediment deposited by rivers, including material at the river bed, margins, and as over-bank deposits, which is the primary sediment constituent in floodplain, ALLUVIAL FAN and estuarine depositional environments. The material tends to be organic-rich, producing fertile soils suitable for farming.

Almagro Basch, Martín (1911–84) a Spanish archaeologist, best known for his work on megaliths, and on the dating and interpretation of Spanish prehistoric cave art, and for his excavation and publication of the northeastern Spanish site of AMPURIAS (Emporion).

Almeria a dry region of southeastern Spain with an important sequence of later prehistoric remains, including the middle Neolithic Almerian culture, represented by villages such as EL GARCEL, the rich CHALCOLITHIC settlements and tombs such as LOS MILLARES, Gates and ALMIZARAQUE, and the fortified villages of the Argaric Early Bronze Age (see EL ARGAR).

Al Mina a harbour settlement at the mouth of the River Orontes in Turkey, excavated by WOOLLEY in the 1930s. Exploration confined itself to the town and the associated warehouses. Ten levels (I–X) were identified, dating back to c.700 BC. The earliest (X–VII) contained a significant quantity of imported Greek pottery, especially from Euboea (see LEFKANDI). As a result the site has been interpreted by some as a Euboean settlement and has come to be regarded as one of the key sites for the channelling of eastern ideas and art to the Greek world (see ORIENTALIZING). Others maintain that the earliest levels are part of a PHOENICIAN settlement, and that the presence of Greek pottery merely reflects trading contacts with the Greek world. The next key period (VI–V) covers the 7th century BC. In the 5th century BC, the settlement was replanned with new warehouses. Some contained batches of Greek pottery, transport AMPHORAE and other items of trade. The site seems to have fallen out of use towards the end of the 4th century BC. See also ATCHANA.

Almizaraque a CHALCOLITHIC settlement and nearby CHAMBERED TOMB in Almeria, Spain. The settlement had a defensive wall and ditch enclosing a number of oval houses with storage pits. Finds included an ivory 'sandal', alabaster idols, decorated pottery and over 100 copper objects together with copper-working slag. The nearby PASSAGE GRAVE contained remains of some fifty skeletons, together with CALLAIS beads, V-perforated buttons, copper tools and POTSHERDS with incised double 'eye' motifs.

Alpera a group of rockshelters near Albacete, southeastern Spain, containing LEVANTINE ART – small paintings of numerous humans, sometimes grouped in scenes, including archers, and women with garments and adornments. Animals are also represented, such as ibex and bulls.

Altai Mountains a mountain range in southwestern Siberia, on the border with Mongolia, important as a source of raw materials for early metallurgy in Central Asia including both tin and copper. The territory was inhabited from very ancient times. There are sites here related to the Palaeolithic, such as ULALINKA and UST'-KAN CAVE. Later archaeological cultures in the region are represented by the AFANASIEVO culture (ENEOLITHIC), the KARAKOL culture of the Bronze Age, the PAZYRYK culture of the Early Iron Age, especially known for its frozen tombs at Pazyryk and UKOK, and a series of cultures of the early Middle Ages. The Altai formed part of the Turkish KAGHANATE and of the Mongol empire of Genghis Khan. The Altai Mountains are also full of rock art sites of different periods.

Altaic a language family within the subdivision of Ural-Altaic including Turkic, Mongolian, Manchu (see MANCHURIA), Tungusic (see TUNGUS), and probably Korean and Japanese. The distribution of these languages in an arc across northern Eurasia argues for considerable continuity of population movement in the past, though the details of these phenomena are currently unknown.

Altamira a cave in Santander Province, northern Spain, where SANZ DE SAUTUOLA discovered Palaeolithic art on the walls in 1879, though his claims for its antiquity were rejected by the archaeological establishment for twenty years. Best known for its ceiling of polychrome bison figures, Altamira contains a wealth of other paintings and engravings, including 'masks' and quadrilateral signs like those of EL CASTILLO. Multiple-line engravings, both on the walls and on PORTABLE ART, have been dated to 13,550 bc. The cave's art probably spans a period from the late SOLUTREAN until its blockage in the mid-MAGDALENIAN. Black figures in different parts of the cave have produced direct dates from 16,480 to 14,650 bp. Charcoal in some of the ceiling's bison has yielded radiocarbon dates from 14,820 to 13,130 bp which, if valid, suggest that the ceiling may not be a single homogeneous composition after all.

Altamura Man in 1993, speleologists found the complete fossilized skeleton of an archaic human, encased in stalagmite, in the depths of the Lamalunga Cave at Altamura near Bari in southeastern Italy; so far it has been left in situ. It has been ascribed to the Middle Pleistocene, between 400,000 and 100,000 years old, and is probably pre-NEANDERTHAL in morphology.

Altar de Sacrificios a MAYA site in Guatemala on the western border of the Southern Lowlands. Data indicate the site was invaded during the 9th century AD by a non-CLASSIC Maya group from the Gulf Coast Lowlands.

Gordon Willey and Ledyard Smith of Harvard University excavated there from the late 1950s to the late 1960s. Evidence for conquest comes from analysis of FINE ORANGE POTTERY found at Altar de Sacrificios, SEIBAL and other sites. The designs on this pottery are distinct from those of the Classic Maya, but local clays, from the Usumacinta River drainage, were used in their manufacture. Such evidence of invasion helped undermine the traditional view of the Classic Maya as a peaceful, non-combative civilization.

Altithermal a climatic episode, dated approximately 7500–5500 BP, which created drier and warmer conditions throughout the world. In North America, it is thought by some archaeologists to have forced humans to abandon areas such as the Plains for higher regions.

altitude the distance an object, land surface or water surface lies above a DATUM plane, usually taken as sea level. Altitude is one of the three dimensions that define the spatial location of artifacts.

Altmühlian a Middle Palaeolithic industry of Central Europe characterized by BLATTSPITZEN, sidescrapers and retouched blades. The Altmühlian dates to the late Middle Palaeolithic, probably the middle of the last GLACIAL.

Alto Salaverry a Late PRECERAMIC site in the Moche Valley of the north coast of Peru, at which both domestic and ceremonial architecture were excavated by Shelia and Thomas Pozorski. It marks the first appearance of a sunken circular structure, a form that became widely distributed in ceremonial sites of the INITIAL PERIOD.

Altyn-depe a major site on the Kopet Dagh piedmont in southern Turkmenistan, Altyn contains deposits beginning with NAMAZGA I materials (later 6th millennium BC) and continuing to Namazga V times (late 3rd millennium). Initially a small settlement, the site was enclosed in a wall by the Namazga III period (late 4th millennium), and grew to a size of 25–30 ha (62–74 acres) during the 3rd millennium (Namazga IV and V periods). V. M. Masson's strategy of extensive horizontal exposure in Namazga V levels has allowed examination of an urban layout: city walls, ceremonial centre, elite quarters and other residential areas, cemeteries and intra-mural vaulted collective burials, and areas of craft production (potting and possible metallurgy). A massive multi-staged platform has been compared with the MESOPOTAMIAN ziggurat, and a number of artifacts with HARAPPAN materials. Altyn-depe represents the clearest example of Bronze Age urbanism in Central Asia.

Al-'Ubaid see 'UBAID, TELL-AL.

Amapa a site in Nayarit, Mexico, well known for its metal artifacts. From AD 250 to 700, Amapa was only a large village. After a period of abandonment, it was reoccupied from AD 900 to 1200. Metal was introduced to the site in about AD 900. Artifacts at the site suggest western Mexico was more integrated into the MESOAMERICAN culture at this time than previously.

Amarna Letters three hundred and seventy-nine clay tablets (plus fragments) found in the so-called 'Record Office' at EL-AMARNA in Egypt during the 1880s. The tablets, written in CUNEIFORM script, form part of the diplomatic correspondence between the Egyptian Kings AMENHOTE III, AKHENATEN and TUTANKHAMEN, and their vassals and rival powers in the Levant.

Amarna period part of the 18th Dynasty of Egypt during which AKHENATEN and his immediate successors ruled from EL-AMARNA and practised the worship of the god ATEN.

amber the translucent golden-yellow fossilized resin of a conifer which may occasionally reveal a trapped prehistoric animal or plant. Amber was regarded as a prestige item during the Upper Palaeolithic period. From the Neolithic onwards Baltic amber became an increasingly important trade item, and amber artifacts have been found in many of the megalithic monuments of northern Europe. Amber was used to make buttons, beads, figurines and other decorative items and, as some CLASSICAL authors suggest, was prized for its strong medicinal or magical powers. Its varying acid content makes it possible to source the fifty or so varieties of amber with some degree of accuracy.

Ambrona see TORRALBA.

Amekni a site linked to riverine resources then existing in the Hoggar or Ahaggar mountainous area of the Algerian Sahara, dated to about 9000 BP and later, with early decorated ceramics but no domestic animals. Several human skeletons are described as Negroid. See also 'AQUALITHIC'.

Amen a local god of the town of THEBES in UPPER EGYPT, becoming pre-eminent among the pantheon of Egyptian deities in the NEW KINGDOM as Amen-RE, patron god of the Egyptian empire.

Amenemhat see SENWOSRET.

Amenhotep or **Amenophis** the name of four of the monarchs of Egypt's 18th Dynasty (early NEW KINGDOM). The reign of Amenhotep III (c.1391–1353 BC) is regarded by many scholars as a 'golden age' of ancient Egypt. Amenhotep IV was later known as AKHENATEN.

Amenophis see AMENHOTEP.

America, North Archaeologists believe that the first humans to occupy the continent were immigrants from Northeast Asia who moved in sometime during the terminal years of the Pleistocene (c.15,000 years ago). During the Pleistocene, two huge glacial systems dominated the

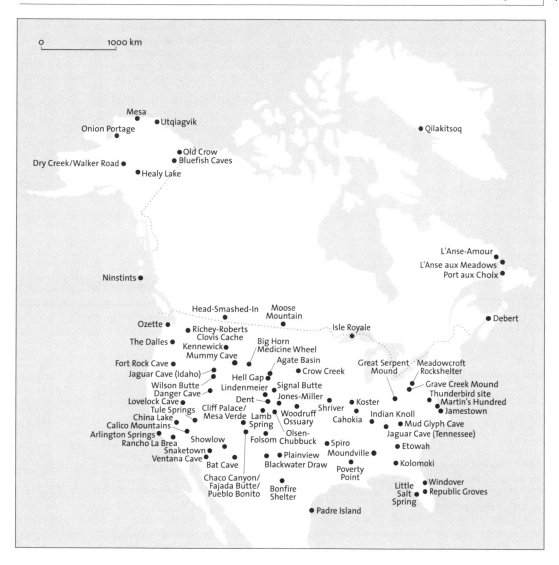

Mesa
Onion Portage
• Utqiagvik
• Qilakitsoq
Old Crow
• Bluefish Caves
Dry Creek/Walker Road •
• Healy Lake

Ninstints •

L'Anse-Amour
L'Anse aux Meadows
Port aux Choix

Head-Smashed-In   Moose
Mountain
Ozette •   Isle Royale   • Debert
• Richey-Roberts
The Dalles •   Clovis Cache
Kennewick•   Big Horn
Mummy Cave   Medicine Wheel
Fort Rock Cave •   Agate Basin
Jaguar Cave (Idaho)•   • Crow Creek   Great Serpent   Meadowcroft
Wilson Butte   Hell Gap   Mound   Rockshelter
Danger Cave   Lindenmeier   Signal Butte   Grave Creek Mound
Lovelock Cave •   Dent   Jones-Miller   Thunderbird site
Tule Springs   Cliff Palace/   Shriver   • Koster   • Martin's Hundred
China Lake   Mesa Verde   Lamb   Woodruff   • Jamestown
Calico Mountains   Spring   Ossuary   Cahokia   Indian Knoll
Arlington Springs •   Olsen-   Mud Glyph Cave
Rancho La Brea   Showlow   Folsom   Chubbuck   Jaguar Cave (Tennessee)
Snaketown   • Spiro   • Etowah
Ventana Cave   • Plainview   Moundville •
Bat Cave   Blackwater Draw   • Kolomoki
Chaco Canyon/   Poverty
Fajada Butte/   Bonfire   Point   Little   • Windover
Pueblo Bonito   Shelter   Salt   • Republic Groves
Spring
• Padre Island

continent, one originating in the Rocky Mountains and the other centred in northern Quebec. The lowered sea-levels, caused by the creation of these huge glaciers, opened up the Bering Straits and allowed pedestrian hunters and gatherers reliant on large megafauna like mammoth, mastodon, horse and now-extinct forms of bison to cross over into the New World. As the exact boundaries of these glaciers moved during the Pleistocene, so periodically did an 'ice-free corridor' between the two open up. This corridor, which roughly paralleled the eastern flanks of the Rockies, would have allowed human populations to move into the interior of the continent even when its northern half was ice-bound. An alternative route for the first entry is down the Pacific coastline.

Unfortunately this route is now mostly submerged by the Pacific and so there is little evidence to support this hypothesis. Regardless of their entry routes, these first Americans rapidly occupied the whole of the continent, perhaps hastening the extinction of the megafauna. Archaeological evidence for the earliest immigrants is scant, but sites like BLUEFISH CAVES in the Yukon and MEADOWCROFT ROCKSHELTER in Pennsylvania provide evidence for this earliest occupation.

The first well-defined period of human occupation on the continent is called the PALAEOINDIAN and is broken into three traditions, the CLOVIS (or LLANO), the FOLSOM and the PLANO. Most of our evidence for this period is biased to hunting activities, but includes habitation sites, kill-sites (where animals were dispatched), as well as burials. The distinctive points of this period are some of the most beautifully crafted anywhere in the world. Clovis peoples hunted Pleistocene fauna and there is evidence of them throughout most parts of the continent. The succeeding Folsom period is recognized only in the western United States. After the Folsom period, myriad projectile point forms developed, perhaps indicative of an increasing human population and greater territoriality. Western sites like BLACKWATER DRAW, Folsom and LINDENMEIER were among the first to be scientifically excavated. However, Palaeoindian sites from the eastern half of the continent are increasingly adding to the richness of our knowledge of this period.

By about 8,000 years ago, the continent's climate and environment was taking on its present-day characteristics. In some parts of the continent, most notably the Great Plains, a concentration on the hunting of large animals, specifically the American bison, continued. Indeed, this way of life continued until white settlers swept across the plains in the nineteenth century. Sites such as HEAD-SMASHED-IN show a long-term commitment to the communal hunting of bison.

However, elsewhere, there is evidence for the development of a subsistence economy that was based much more on a wide-spectrum pattern of exploitation, whereby dozens of plants were gathered and many animals, large and small, were hunted. This so-called ARCHAIC period (an unfortunate term) is recognized archaeologically by the widespread adoption of grinding stones and the appearance of a new form of projectile, the ATLATL, whereby the projectile is propelled by means of a throwing stick. Points tend to be both corner- and side-notched. In some parts of the continent, the end of the Archaic period saw a trend to increasing sedentism and an emphasis on particular plants, perhaps the precursor to domestication. There is also a suggestion of non-egalitarian societies forming in some parts of the continent, for example, in the ADENA and HOPEWELL cultures of the American Midwest.

Hunting and gathering is one of the great ways of life of the North American continent. The FORMATIVE constitutes the second and it begins to appear around 2,000 years ago. Formative-level traditions are recognized archaeologically by a dependence on agriculture, the appearance of village life, the development of specific crafts, especially pottery, and the adoption of the bow and arrow. The most highly developed (from a Western viewpoint) Formative traditions appeared in two areas.

In the deserts of the Southwest, agriculture, diffusing northwards from Mexico, began to have a major impact on lifestyles certainly by 2,000 years ago. Intensive farming of corn, beans, squash and cotton (often with extensive irrigation systems) allowed the development of three traditions: ANASAZI, HOHOKAM and MOGOLLON. These are exemplified by magnificent sites like MESA VERDE, CHACO CANYON and SNAKETOWN. In the Southwest there developed one the finest ceramic traditions of the New World. In the more humid climates of the Southeast, centred along the Mississippi, even larger communities developed. Again, dependent on farming, some of these communities may be termed cities. The largest of these is Cahokia, dominated by the huge earthen mound called Monk's Mound, but other sites like ETOWAH in Georgia and MOUNDVILLE in Alabama are equally impressive. There is very good evidence for continental trade patterns and a rich ceremonial life, as exhibited in the so-called SOUTHERN CULT.

The independence of the Native American tribes came crashing to an end in the 16th century when the European powers began to move on to the continent permanently. Francisco Vasquez de Coronado and others led Spanish expeditions into the American Southwest in quest of fabled cities of gold. In the Southeast, the conquistador, Hernan de Soto, invaded Florida and adjacent states and devastated the tribes of the area. The eastern seaboard was initially colonized by English merchant venturers looking for untapped resources of land and timber. Archaeological sites like MARTIN'S HUNDRED belong to this period. Ultimately, tribes in the northeastern part of the continent became caught up in the wider geopolitical struggles between England and France. Besides the military devastation caused by these invasions, European diseases caused the most severe impact on native populations. Some historians estimate that perhaps as many as 90 per cent (90 million) of the continent's population had been wiped out by AD 1600.

America, South The earliest human presence in South America has been documented at MONTE VERDE, in Chile, some 13,000 years ago, although controversial evidence from Brazil is said to support occupations up to 35,000 years old. Certainly by 10,000–8,000 years ago there were substantial Palaeoindian occupations throughout the continent, perhaps best represented by a series of sites in Patagonia (e.g. CUEVA FELL, CUEVA DE LAS MANOS). Gradually, with the warming of the climate, subsistence came to be based on the hunting and gathering of a broad spectrum of wild species, a way of life that persisted until European contact in parts of Patagonia and the Amazon and Orinoco Basins.

Settled villages became the norm in parts of Amazonia and the Andes by about 2500 BC. Ceramics first appeared in northern South America at this time, and the technology gradually spread southwards. Occupation of the Amazon Basin remained relatively sparse, given the relatively low productivity of the rain forest environment, but villages of substantial size did appear in some areas. The Andean region was the locus of the development of more complex societies. The INITIAL PERIOD (1800–800 BC) saw the emergence of complex societies on the central and north coast of Peru, which organized the

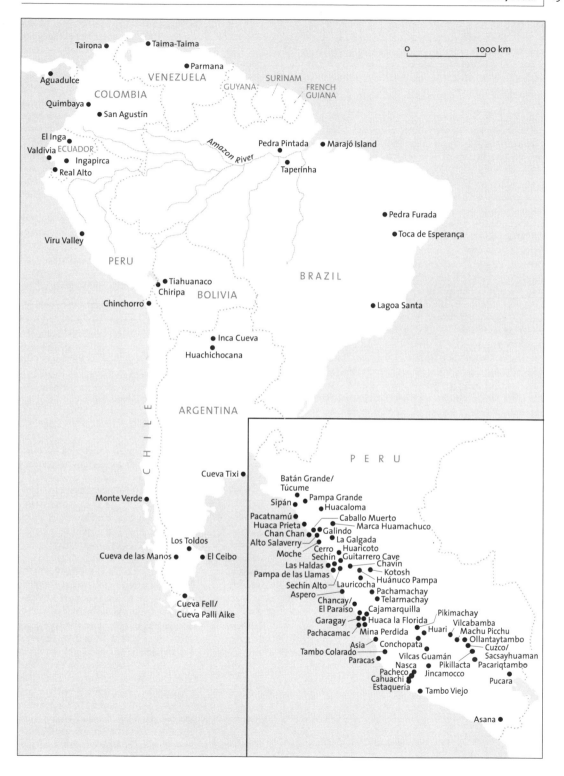

Tairona ● ● Taima-Taima

● Parmana

VENEZUELA

Aguadulce ●   GUYANA   SURINAM

COLOMBIA   FRENCH GUIANA

Quimbaya ●

● San Agustín

El Inga ●

Valdivia ● ECUADOR

● Ingapirca

● Real Alto

Amazon River

Pedra Pintada ●   ● Marajó Island

Taperinha ●

● Pedra Furada

● Toca de Esperança

Viru Valley ●

PERU

BRAZIL

● Tiahuanaco
Chiripa   BOLIVIA

Chinchorro ●

● Lagoa Santa

● Inca Cueva

Huachichocana

CHILE

ARGENTINA

0   1000 km

Cueva Tixi ●

Monte Verde ●

Los Toldos ●

Cueva de las Manos ●   ● El Ceibo

Cueva Fell/
Cueva Palli Aike

PERU

Batán Grande/
Túcume
● Pampa Grande
Sipán ●   ● Huacaloma
Pacatnamú ●   ● Caballo Muerto
Huaca Prieta ●   ● Marca Huamachuco
Chan Chan ● Galindo
Alto Salaverry ●   ● La Galgada
Cerro   ● Huaricoto
Moche   Sechín ● Guitarrero Cave
Las Haldas ●   ● Chavín
Pampa de las Llamas ●   ● Kotosh
Sechín Alto   Lauricocha   ● Huánuco Pampa
Aspero   ● Pachamachay
Chancay   ● Telarmachay
El Paraíso ●   ● Cajamarquilla
Garagay ●   ● Huaca la Florida   ● Pikimachay
Pachacamac ●   Mina Perdida   ● Huari   ● Vilcabamba
● Huari   ● Machu Picchu
Asia   ● Conchopata   ● Ollantaytambo
Tambo Colarado ●   ● Cuzco/
Paracas ●   Vilcas Guamán   Sacsayhuaman
Nasca ●   ● Pikillacta   ● Pacariqtambo
Pacheco ●   ● Jincamocco   ● Pucara
Cahuachi ●
Estaquería ●   ● Tambo Viejo

● Asana

building of massive platform mounds and pyramids, as well as their regular renewal and rebuilding. Religious traditions of the northern highlands stressed ritual interment and renewal of temples. The Titicaca Basin saw the emergence of a religious tradition based on pilgrimage.

The EARLY HORIZON (800 BC–AD 100) was characterized by the presence of complex chiefdoms on the coast and the northern highlands, and the emergence of an important pilgrimage centre at CHAVÍN de Huantar. Ceramics found in its subterranean galleries indicate that people travelled great distances to the temple to leave their offerings, and iconography associated with Chavín is found throughout northern Peru. Carved in great stone monuments at Chavín, the images depict what may have been a shamanic cult, with emphasis on animals of the jungle regions below and to the east. Advances in metallurgy at this time, especially gold working, led to further elaboration of metal technology in ensuing periods. South American metallurgical technology and artifacts would appear suddenly in western Mexico in about the 8th century AD.

Chavín influence ceased around 200 BC, at which time several regional cultures began to emerge. These and other developments would coalesce into a number of well-defined regional cultures in the EARLY INTERMEDIATE PERIOD (EIP) (AD 100–750), including Cajamarca and Recuay in the northern highlands, LIMA on the central coast, and PUCARA in the Titicaca Basin. Best known, however, is MOCHE on the north coast, probably the earliest Andean state. Moche controlled the entire north coast – some nine or ten river valleys, stretching a distance of 350 km (220 miles) from north to south by AD 750.

The south coast NASCA culture produced some of the most spectacular ceramic and textile art of the ancient world, and its ceramic style and technology strongly influenced subsequent cultures. The people of Nasca also constructed a vast complex of lines and figures on the desert plain.

In the MIDDLE HORIZON (AD 750–1000), two highland cultures came to dominate the Andes. The HUARI empire of Peru controlled most of the highlands and coast of Peru. In the Titicaca Basin, TIAHUANACO probably emerged as a regional culture in the earlier EIP, and in the Middle Horizon established long-distance economic relations with surrounding regions.

Following the collapse of Huari and Tiahuanaco regional cultures emerged once more in the LATE INTERMEDIATE PERIOD (AD 1000–1476), the largest and most powerful of which was the CHIMÚ state of the north coast. The Chincha of the south maintained a far-flung economic network based on seafaring trade. Small polities occupied discrete portions of the highlands. In the mid 15th century, one of those polities began a series of conquests that would culminate in the largest empire known in the New World: TAWANTINSUYU, the INCA

empire. During the LATE HORIZON (AD 1476–1533) the Incas controlled the coast and highlands of what today are Ecuador, Peru, Bolivia, northern Chile and northwestern Argentina. They ruled the empire from their capital at CUZCO, and a series of major administrative centres built throughout the empire. The empire was held together by an impressive system of royal roads, a feat of engineering that could hardly be exceeded with modern technology. Messages were carried throughout the empire by runners, who passed them verbally from one to another.

The Inca empire came to an end with the arrival of the Spanish in 1532, led by Francisco Pizarro, who captured and later killed the Inca emperor, bringing an end to indigenous control.

American Palaeo-Arctic tradition a broad tradition that includes several complexes or cultures of the North American Arctic and sub-Arctic dating to *c.*11,000–6500 bp. These complexes (e.g. DENALI COMPLEX) are characterized by the common occurrence of microblades, bifaces and burins. This tradition was defined by Anderson in 1968.

Amfreville helmet an Iron Age helmet discovered in 1841 in an old stream bed of the River Seine, Eure, France. A fine example of CELTIC workmanship, the helmet is of bronze decorated with gold leaf and enamel. Dated on stylistic grounds to the 3rd century BC, it is related to Italian models but was probably made by a local northern French craftsman.

amino acid racemization a biological dating method that utilizes postmortem changes in indigenous proteins in carbonate shells of molluscs and bones to estimate the time since death. Protein traces in carbonate fossils consist of amino acids that exist in one of two configurations, referred to as L-isomers and D-isomers. In living organisms, amino acids are molecularly structured in the L-isomer configuration. Upon death, amino acids begin to convert to the D-isomer configuration, a conversion process referred to as racemization. From the zero point at death, D/L ratios begin to increase with time and can be used as relative age indices to construct a CHRONOSTRATIGRAPHY. However, ages are only locally applicable because racemization rates are influenced by the thermal history of the site from which they are collected. Site temperature also causes the effective time range of the dating method to vary with latitude. In tropical areas, where reaction rates are relatively rapid, equilibrium is achieved after about 150,000–3 million years; in mid-latitudes after about 2 million years; in arctic sites, rates are unmeasurable within the Holocene and equilibrium is not achieved even in 10 million years. Problems with the method include converting D/L ratios to absolute ages because of the difficulties in reconstructing site thermal history, modelling of the racemization reaction, and differing racemization rates among different species.

With D/L ratios less than 0.3 and independent age control, the analysis is reliable to about ±15 per cent to 20 per cent. Certainty decreases with ratios greater than 0.3.

Amino acid racemization is also used to reconstruct palaeotemperatures. If the age of a site is known by other independent methods, the palaeotemperature can be calculated, utilizing similar equations used to determine age, with an uncertainty of about ± 1 °C.

Amorites peoples west of MESOPOTAMIA who are generally believed to have been nomadic. The AKKADIAN designation *amurru*, equivalent to the SUMERIAN term *mar.tu*, specified a lifestyle contrasting with that of urban Mesopotamia. Pressure from Amorite groups was a factor in the collapse of the UR III kingdom at the end of the 3rd millennium BC, and Amorite dynasties ruled many of the small kingdoms during the subsequent OLD BABY-LONIAN PERIOD (*c.*2000–1600 BC), including that of HAMMURABI at BABYLON. Later, the term Amorite referred to a small kingdom in northwestern Syria, as well as to a language in that area.

amphitheatre a construction formed by two roughly semicircular bands of seating facing inwards towards a central arena. These arenas were used mainly for wild-animal shows and gladiatorial combats throughout the Roman empire. See COLOSSEUM.

amphora a large jar, typically two-handled, used to store oil, wine or other such liquids.

Ampurias (*Gk* Emporion) a Greek trading port in north-eastern Spain founded from MARSEILLES in the 6th century BC. The initial settlement was located on an offshore islet. The cemeteries have yielded much imported Greek pottery. See ALMAGRO.

Amratian a phase of the PREDYNASTIC sequence of UPPER EGYPT, also known as NAQADA I, and dated to *c.*4500–4000 BC. The Amratian culture, which seems to have more affinities with the preceding BADARIAN than the following GERZEAN, displayed skill in stone-working, especially in flint, and in the production of painted pottery.

Amri a prehistoric site in the southern Sind in Pakistan, first explored by Majumdar in the 1920s and then excavated by J.-M. Casal in the 1950s, and containing Early HARAPPAN as well as Harappan and post-Harappan levels. The Early Harappan materials provide the definition of the Amri culture of the later 4th millennium BC, whose painted ceramics are similar to materials in the Indo-Iranian borderlands to the north. The overlying levels contain increasing amounts of Mature Harappan pottery until the site was clearly contained within the Harappan tradition, followed by Late Harappan materials similar to those at JHUKAR. The main significance of Amri is its contribution to understanding the formation of the Harappan civilization.

AMS see ACCELERATOR MASS SPECTROMETRY.

Amsadong a village site of the Korean CHULMUN culture near Seoul, first excavated in 1968 and again in the mid 1970s by a joint university team. Several of the twelve excavated pithouses are now reconstructed as a historical park. Net weights and sinkers indicate river fishing subsistence; QUERNS show plant utilization, but there was no evidence for agriculture despite the site's Neolithic status. It is the type-site of Classic Chulmun pottery and dates to 4490–1510 BC.

Amud Cave a Middle Palaeolithic site in the Wadi Amud, Israel, first surveyed (with Emireh and ZUTTIYEH caves) by TURVILLE-PETRE in 1923. Excavation by a Japanese team during the 1960s discovered an almost complete adult male NEANDERTHAL burial (Amud I) associated with a MOUSTERIAN industry. Subsequent excavations by an Israeli team (1991–4) recovered fragmentary remains of seventeen more individuals, mostly infants and children. Estimated dates for this presumed Neanderthal occupation are *c.*60–50,000 BP.

Amudian a brief Palaeolithic blade-producing industry dating to the last INTERGLACIAL and found at sites close to the Mediterranean coast such as TABUN, JABRUD, ADLUN and the HAUA FTEAH cave. The Amudian, previously termed the pre-AURIGNACIAN, was named by GARROD after the Wadi Amud in Israel, and occurs between the ACHEULIAN and the Middle Palaeolithic.

Amun see AMEN.

Amuq a plain through which flows the Orontes River in southern Turkey, where soundings were made on multiple sites (Tell Judeideh, Tell Kurdu, ÇATAL HÖYÜK, Tell Tayinat and several others) by a University of Chicago team. The combined results of these soundings produce a CULTURE HISTORY divided into twenty-two phases (Amuq A–V) that covers the 8,000 years between the beginning of the ceramic Neolithic and the late medieval period. The sequence is a standard for the relative chronology of northwestern Syria and southeastern Anatolia, and reflects some significant interregional ceramic relationships in western Asian prehistory (e.g. HALAF painted pottery in Amuq C–D, 'UBAID painted pottery in Amuq D–E, late URUK/JEMDET NASR in Amuq F–G, KURA-ARAXES/Khirbet Kerak burnished pottery in Amuq H–I).

Amurian a variant of HOMO *sapiens* who inhabited Northeast Asia at the end of the Pleistocene, and who may be the ancestors of the contemporary NATIVE AMERICAN. The present-day AINU of Japan are a remnant Asiatic population of this stock.

Amvrosievka an Upper Palaeolithic open-air site in southern Ukraine, comprising a massive bed of steppe bison bones (at least 983 individuals) and nearby artifact clusters. The artifacts include microblades, laterally-grooved bone points and simple ornaments. Recent studies, building on the earlier excavations of Pidoplichko and BORISKOVSKIJ in 1948–50, have produced radiocarbon dates of 18,220 to 18,700 bp. Amvrosievka, along with several other sites in the south Russian Plain such as BOL'SHAYA AKKARZHA and Zolotovka I (Lower Don River), may reflect a regional Upper Palaeolithic practice of killing bison herds, like Holocene tribes of the North American Plains.

amygdaloid *adj.* almond-shaped. A morphological term used by BORDES to refer to an elongated OVATE or cordiform biface.

An the supreme SUMERIAN god, the provider of life and fertility, and the source of authority; the AKKADIAN equivalent was Anu. An literally meant 'sky'. In the hierarchical divine world, An was replaced by other figures (ENLIL, MARDUK), but always remained behind the scenes as the ultimate source of authority. An has a close identification with the city of WARKA.

'Anaeho'omalu a site on the main island of Hawaii, initially in about the 10th century AD an intermittent fishing camp, but by late prehistoric times the site of a permanent fishing settlement centred on a large fishpond. The area also has several lava-tube caves used for burial, and one of the largest PETROGLYPH fields in the Hawaiian Islands, with over 9,000 figures.

anaerobic *adj.* of an environmental state in which free molecular oxygen is not available owing to depletion by soil bacteria. This condition is attained in waterlogged or relatively deeply buried situations, leading to the preservation of plant, animal and human remains, and of artifacts fashioned from these materials. Compare AEROBIC.

Anak a KOGURYO tomb cluster located near P'yongyang City, North Korea. It consists of mounded tombs with stone chambers, many painted as MURAL TOMBS. Tomb 3 is most famous, being the burial of a 4th-century AD Chinese governor whose portrait is painted on the tomb wall together with his wife and courtly entourage.

analogy the argument that if two objects or phenomena are similar in some attributes, they should be similar in others.

Ananino culture an Iron Age culture of the mid 1st millennium BC in the middle Volga basin, Russia. The Ananino culture had close connections with the SCYTHIANS, who occupied the territory to the south.

Anapchi a 7th-century AD garden pond in the palace site of the United SILLA Kingdom in Kyongju City, Korea. Excavations in 1975 recovered over 15,000 items including dug-out boats, Buddhist images, pottery and metal vessels, inscribed wooden tablets (see MOKKAN), wooden architectural components and roof and floor tiles

buried in the pond mud. Four palace pavilions have been reconstructed around the relandscaped pond to form a historical park.

Anasazi a Navajo word meaning 'Enemy Ancestors' that was applied by A. V. KIDDER in 1936 to the major prehistoric tradition of the northern part of the American Southwest. The Anasazi are believed to be the ancestors of some contemporary PUEBLO Indians. The tradition is broken into eight sequential stages. Basketmaker I is a hypothetical, late ARCHAIC pre-agricultural stage; Basketmaker II (AD 1–450) is defined by the appearance of agriculture; and Basketmaker III (AD 450–750) by the appearance of pottery, PITHOUSES and the bow-and-arrow. The Pueblo I–V stages are characterized by an increasingly complex subsistence technology based on the intensive farming of maize, beans and squash, the development of large, multi-room dwellings and sophisticated and regionally diverse pottery techniques and styles. The specific dates are: Pueblo I – AD 750–900; Pueblo II – AD 900–1150; Pueblo III – AD 1150–1300; Pueblo IV – AD 1300–1600; Pueblo V – AD 1600–present. The Anasazi tradition is also broken into regional variants: Chacoan, MESA VERDE and KAYENTA. See also CHACO CANYON, PUEBLO BONITO.

anathyrosis a Greek architectural technique, perhaps originating in Egypt, used to match two adjoining blocks or column-drums. Instead of the two touching along a complete face, the centre was hollowed out, thus leaving a point of contact only along the edges.

Anau a TELL site in Turkmenistan, 12 km (7.5 miles) east of Ashkabat, first excavated by an American expedition led by R. Pumpelly in 1904. Pumpelly's excavations established the first cultural chronology for Central Asia, from the late Neolithic throughout historical periods. The Anau reports emphasized the interaction of humans with their environment and included systematic analysis of faunal remains, bringing an interdisciplinary approach to archaeological investigation (importance of changing climate, interest in development of food production in arid environments, analysis of metals and of fauna) that was not repeated in western Asia until after the Second World War. The cultural sequence has since largely been superseded by later work; the painted pottery of Anau IA (early 6th millennium BC) fills the gap between the DJEITUN culture and the NAMAZGA sequence (now best seen at sites like Chakmaklik-depe in the Tedjen drainage to the east along the Kopet Dagh mountain range). A joint American–Turkmeni project reopened investigation of the site during the 1990s.

Anbangbang a large sandstone rockshelter in western ARNHEM LAND, North Australia. The earliest levels are undated but are probably Pleistocene. From about 6000 bp the intensity of occupation increased. The uppermost unit, spanning the last 1,000 years, is extraordinarily rich in well-preserved organic material.

Andernach see GÖNNERSDORF.

Andersson, Johan Gunnar (1874–1960) a Swedish geologist who was affiliated with the Geological Survey of China as a mining adviser in 1914–25. He is credited with the first discoveries of Neolithic painted pottery sites and of Palaeolithic HOMO *erectus* finds at ZHOUKOUDIAN.

andesite line a line dividing the Pacific region along the point of contact between the Asiatic and Pacific plates through western POLYNESIA. West of the line are varied continental rocks, including andesitic basalts. East of it are coral atolls and volcanic islands of olivine basalts and other basic rocks.

Andrae, Walter (1875–1956) a Near Eastern archaeologist who trained as an architect in his native Germany, and joined KOLDEWEY's Babylonian excavations in 1898. He went to ASSUR in 1903 to excavate independently, where he worked with great success until 1914. Andrae also worked at FARA and Hatra (a PARTHIAN city in northern MESOPOTAMIA) before the First World War began. After the war he worked in museums and universities in Germany.

Andronikos, Manolis (1919–92) a Greek archaeologist, excavator at Vergina-Aigai during the 1950s and 1960s. He is best remembered for his excavation of the Great Mound at VERGINA in 1977. This was found to contain rich tomb offerings of gold, silver and ivory. Studies of the cremated bones have led to the theory that this was the tomb of Philip II of Macedon.

Andronovo culture a Bronze Age culture of western Siberia, Russia, and adjacent parts of Kazakhstan, of considerable duration from before 1500 BC to about 800 BC. Both settlement and burial sites are known, with extensive traces of metallurgy using the rich mineral resources of this region. A variety of regional groups of the Andronovo culture have been distinguished. Andronovo settlements consist of up to ten semi-subterranean houses of log-cabin construction, ranging in size from 20 by 30 m (22 by 33 yds) to 30 by 60 m (33 by 66 yds). The Andronovo culture is succeeded by the KARASUK culture.

Aneityum a high volcanic island in Vanuatu, Melanesia, investigated by Matthew Spriggs. More than 800 sites document the development of intensive root-crop (*taro*) agriculture from dry land plots 1,000 years ago to the construction of large-scale irrigation systems during the last 400 years.

Anghelu Ruju a cemetery in Sardinia of thirty-five rock-cut CHAMBERED TOMBS of the 3rd millennium BC, first investigated by Taramelli in 1903. They consist of a passage or shaft leading to a chamber which can be round, oval, rectangular or irregular; subsidiary chambers lead off the main chamber. The chamber walls are decorated with carvings of animal horns and BUCRANIA. Gravegoods include marble and alabaster bracelets, copper tools and weapons, and small female figurines of local stone.

Angkor the area of the capital of the KHMER state of KAMBUJA, said to have been formed early in the 9th century AD from a group of small neighbouring states. The term is used frequently to refer to the phase of the state's history before the 14th century, when it dominated Cambodia, most of Thailand, southern Laos and south Vietnam. The best known of the hundreds of temples and structures surviving from this period are: Preah Ko and Bakheng (9th–early 10th century), Koh Ker, Pre Rup, BANTEAY SREI, Khleang and Phimeanakas (10th century), Ta Keo, Baphuon and Phimai (11th century), Wat Phu, Angkor Wat, Banteay Samre and Preah Khan (late 11th–12th century), Ta Prohm, Angkor Thom and BAYON (13th century); many of these are famous for their elaborate structure and fine reliefs.

Angles-sur-l'Anglin a MAGDALENIAN rockshelter known as the 'Roc aux Sorciers', in the Vienne region of France, where excavations by D. GARROD and S. de Saint-Mathurin led to the discovery in 1952 that the backwall and collapsed ceiling had been sculptured and painted. The bas-reliefs include bison, horses, ibex and four life-size human females from stomach to knee. The occupation layers, containing pigments, grinders, stone picks and PORTABLE ART objects, have been dated by radiocarbon to 14,160 bp.

Anglian see ELSTERIAN.

Anglo-Saxons the dominant inhabitants of Britain before the Norman conquest, the Angles and Saxons were Germanic peoples of northern Europe who crossed the North Sea to settle in eastern Britain after the decline of Roman rule in the 5th century AD. The scale of the

Some of the towers, each bearing four carved, smiling faces, at the Bayon, in ANGKOR Thom, Cambodia.

immigration may have been relatively small, but resulted in the adoption of the English language and in the establishment, by the 6th century, of a series of kingdoms dominated by Germanic elites. These kingdoms, including Northumbria (see YEAVERING), Mercia and Wessex, later unified into 'England', with its capital at Winchester, in Wessex.

During the course of the 7th century, the early Saxon period, a combination of Irish missionaries from the west and missionaries dispatched by the papacy at Rome began the conversion of the Anglo-Saxon kingdoms to Christianity. The story is recounted by the monastic historian Bede (673–735), who also tells of the early political history of the Anglo-Saxon kingdoms.

The international links of the early kingdoms were illustrated by the discovery in 1939 of the early 7th-century Anglo-Saxon ship burial at SUTTON HOO, which contained Merovingian coins and Byzantine metalwork. The rivalry between the Anglo-Saxon kingdoms and the development of international trading ports such as Ipswich and Hamwic (Southampton) was halted in the 8th century by the arrival of VIKING raiders from Scandinavia, who sacked the wealthy monastic centres and settled areas of northern (see YORK) and central England (as well as parts of Scotland and Ireland). In the ensuing struggle the Anglo-Saxon ruler ALFRED THE GREAT, King of Wessex 871–99, defeated the Viking army and laid the foundations for a unified kingdom of England which was brought to fruition by his successors Edward the Elder (899–924) and Athelstan (924–39). The Anglo-Saxon kingdom of England enjoyed prosperity during the 10th century marked by monastic revival, urban development and overseas trade. Renewed Scandinavian onslaughts in the early 11th century did little to interrupt the process and it was a prosperous state which the Norman invaders (themselves descendants of Viking settlers in northern France) conquered at the Battle of Hastings in 1066.

ankh an Egyptian HIEROGLYPHIC sign, appearing as a 'T' with a loop whose ends join the cross-bar close to the top of the upright stroke. The Egyptian word 'ankh' broadly speaking means 'life', and the sign often appears in Egyptian art with that symbolic connotation.

annealing a process used in metallurgy to reduce the brittleness caused by hammering and other working of metals, especially in the case of copper, silver and gold. It involves heating and slowly cooling the metal to increase its ductility. In Andean South America the technique was used especially in the case of copper-silver alloys by the MOCHE culture.

Anshan see ELAM, MALYAN.

anta 1 a short stub-wall found at the end of, and at right angles to, the long walls of a CLASSICAL temple CELLA.

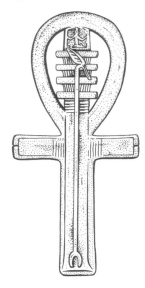

ANKH

Columns placed between these stub-walls are described as being *in antis*.

2 a Portuguese term for CHAMBERED TOMB. The earliest, in the Alto Alemtejo region of inland central Portugal, have mid 5th-millennium BC THERMOLUMINESCENCE dates: Anta 1 at Poço da Gateira 4510 BC; Anta 2 at Gorginos 4440 BC.

antefix a CLASSICAL decorative element concealing the outermost end of a tile. They can be made of marble or clay, and show a range of subjects such as a simple PALMETTE, a GORGONEION or a lion's head. They may be placed above the SIMA.

Antequera an important group of CHAMBERED TOMBS, in Málaga, Spain, each set in a natural hill. Most famous are: a) Cueva de Romeral: a long passage leads to two interconnected CORBEL-VAULTED chambers, one behind the other, in a mound 90 m (98 yds) across. The corbelled vaults are closed at the top by a single megalithic slab. The main chamber has plastered walls and floor, and measures 5 m (16 ft) in diameter by almost 4 m (13 ft) high; b) Cueva de la Menga: a bottle-shaped chamber with five huge cap-stones (the largest weighs about 180 tonnes), reached by a short entrance passage. The tombs probably date to the 4th millennium BC, but no grave-goods are known.

anthracology the study of human interactions with the plant environment through microscopic identification and statistical treatment of wood charcoal from archaeological sites.

anthropogenic soil a soil that physically, morphologically or chemically has been influenced by human activity. This may include the concentration of phosphorus, organic matter, debris and artifacts, and the physical mixing of differing soil and sediment components through human activities such as cultivation, deforestation or construction activities.

anthropomorph **1** an object or picture resembling a human form.

2 in prehistoric art, a figure providing visual information recognized by contemporary humans as resembling the human form (*Gk anthropos* man, *morphos* shape, form).

anthropomorphic *adj.* **1** treating a deity as having a human form or character.

2 attributing human motivation, characteristics or behaviour to animals, inanimate objects or natural phenomena.

3 in rock art, attributing human form to the depiction of a deity.

anthropomorphism the attribution of human form or character to a deity, or to non-human objects.

anthropomorphous *adj.* **1** having or suggesting human form and appearance.

2 in prehistoric art, providing visual information recognized by contemporary humans as resembling human form.

anthropophagy see CANNIBALISM.

Antilles the group of islands, stretching from the north coast of Venezuela to that of southern Florida, which experienced the first contact with Christopher Columbus and his successors (Columbus first landed on the Bahaman island of Guanahaní on 12 October 1492). The Antilles were first occupied around 5000 BC by groups of hunter-gatherers from South and Central America, and around 500 BC by the first farmers of Arawak origin. Archaeology has revealed several cultures here before the arrival of Columbus, including the BARREROIDS and BANWAROIDS (both non-farming); and the OSTIONOIDS and MEILLACOIDS (farmers) who developed local cultures. The most important group in 1492 were the TAINOS, who had developed a high degree of ceremonialism, but there were also the CARIBS, and residual groups of hunter-gatherers such as the CIBONEYES.

antler the branched horn of a deer used in the preparation of a variety of artifacts from the Palaeolithic onwards. Its resilience made antler particularly suitable for use as a soft hammer or punch during flint knapping, and as a sleeve used to hold a stone axe in a wooden haft. Antler artifacts, like those of bone and wood, are prone to decay and so appear under-represented in the archaeological record.

Antonine Wall the most northerly of the permanent Roman frontiers in Britain, which served to secure the Scottish lowlands. It was established during the reign of the emperor Antoninus Pius probably after AD 143. The line of the wall ran from the Firth of Forth in the east to the Clyde in the west and seems to have been constructed by legionaries. The wall was made of turf on a cobbled foundation, and it was protected to the north by a ditch. There were nineteen forts along its length in addition to three fortlets. It was probably abandoned in the 150s, and briefly reoccupied *c*.163.

Anubis an Egyptian deity depicted as a jackal or jackal-headed man. Anubis was the god associated with cemeteries and MUMMIFICATION.

Anundshög a large Iron Age, VIKING and early medieval complex of monuments in central Sweden, centred on a mound 60 m (197 ft) in diameter and 10 m (33 ft) high, next to which are two large SHIP SETTINGS, one of which is 54 m (177 ft) long. Near by are about twenty more burial mounds and three more ship settings. A large RUNE stone and a long row of standing stones that mark a prehistoric and medieval road complete the complex.

Anyang [An-yang] a late SHANG site near Anyang City, China, dating to the 13th century bc. Excavated between 1928 and 1937 by LI CHI, the site consists of an oval unwalled area, *c*.3.75 by 9.75 km (*c*.2.33 by 6 miles), encompassing: a royal cemetery at XIBEIGANG consisting of eleven SHAFT TOMBS; nearly 2,000 small graves and the FU HAO tomb; a temple complex at XIAOTUN of several worship halls and residential buildings; clusters of aristocratic houses; workshops for bronze casting; stone, jade, bone and shell workshops; and servants' quarters. Some interpret these remains as the late Shang capital, others as a mortuary complex. The Anyang bronze style with prominent TAOTIE designs suggests preoccupations with death and transformation in ancestor worship rituals, and its ORACLE BONES provide information on the social organization of the Shang state.

Anza an early Neolithic site in Macedonia (sometimes referred to in the literature as Anzabegovo). The earliest levels at Anza belong to the STARČEVO culture (*c*.6500–5800 BC), while the uppermost are of the VINČA culture (*c*.5500–4000 BC). Anza lies in a basin called 'Ovče Polje' ('sheep basin') and sheep/goat are the main component of the large faunal assemblage. Early houses resemble those of Bulgarian and Greek sites like KARANOVO and NEA NIKOMEDEIA, rectangular structures with mud-plastered post walls, while later structures have wattle-and-daub construction.

Apennine culture a Bronze Age culture of peninsular Italy, originally defined by its dark-burnished pottery with carefully incised designs. Puglisi argued in 1959 for an economy based on pastoralism from the high location of many of the sites and the discovery of perforated pottery 'milk boilers', but excavations at the Apennine village of Luni, with long houses cut into the soft rock, have demonstrated mixed farming. Pottery studies support a subdivision into three phases: Apennine, Subapennine and Protovillanovan (see VILLANOVAN), beginning around 1500 BC. West of the Alps the Apennine culture is preceded by a Protoapennine phase (2000–1500 BC), best represented at the site of Tufariello.

Aphaia temple see AEGINA.

Aphrodisias a 500 ha (2 sq. mile) CLASSICAL city on a tributary of the Meander River, southwestern Turkey, excavated by ERIM. Most of the extant remains belong to the Roman period and include the AGORA, the ODEUM, the temple of Aphrodite and baths. Many of these public buildings were highly decorated with free-standing statuary which has survived in sufficient quantities to allow study of the Aphrodisian 'school'. The settlement also has a long pre-classical history: soundings in two of the mounds within the city (the 'AKROPOLIS' and 'Pekmez' mounds) revealed traces of a late Neolithic occupation (with ceramic parallels to HACILAR VII) and then a sequence of late CHALCOLITHIC to Late Bronze Age materials that is strongly similar to that at BEYCE-SULTAN.

Apis an Egyptian god worshipped at MEMPHIS in the form of a living bull, chosen after the death of its predecessor by virtue of a number of identifying marks. Apis-bulls were interred in the SERAPEUM.

Apis Rock see NASERA.

apodyterium the changing-room of a Roman bath-house. Smaller examples may be equipped with niches for storing clothes. See also THERMAE.

Apollo 11 a cave in the Huns Mountains of southern Namibia, with MIDDLE and LATER STONE AGE remains, excavated by W. E. Wendt and named after the 1969 moon landing. Of particular interest are several small rock slabs painted with animal figures and lines, which are the oldest dated rock art in Africa, radiocarbon dates indicate that the layers in which the slabs were found accumulated between about 28,000 and 19,000 BP.

apsidal adj. (of a structure) having one end rounded.

Apulia (mod. Puglia) an area of southeastern Italy. Although containing no Greek colonies, it was strongly influenced by neighbouring Greek cities. In the 5th and 4th centuries BC it produced figure-decorated pottery (see APULIAN POTTERY, GNATHIAN WARE, SOUTH ITALIAN POTTERY).

Apulian pottery an important type of SOUTH ITALIAN POTTERY, mostly decorated in the RED-FIGURED technique. Production seems to have started in the late 5th century BC and may have been influenced by ATHENIAN POTTERY. One of the early centres seems to have been at

TARENTUM. In the middle of the 4th century the scenes became more ornate with additional figures inserted in the field and an increased use of added colours. Plain wares were also produced alongside (see GNATHIAN WARE).

Aqab, Tell a small prehistoric site in the Khabur region of Syria, just upstream from CHAGAR BAZAR, that provides an unbroken sequence from the Early HALAF into the 'UBAID periods. In addition to defining the presence of Early Halaf occupation, similar to that of ARPACHIYAH to the east, the excavations of T. Davidson and T. Watkins also identified a gradual transition from Halaf to 'Ubaid ceramic styles, where 'Ubaid elements are added to a modified Halaf pottery assemblage until it is fully 'Ubaid in character. Similar to the pottery in the basal levels at Tepe GAWRA, such transitional assemblages can now be identified elsewhere in western Syria and southeastern Turkey. The transitional phase shows that interpretations of the northern 'Ubaid as population movements and replacements cannot be upheld.

Aqar Quf the site of the KASSITE city of Dur-Kurigalzu in northern BABYLONIA (near Baghdad, central Iraq). T. Baqir's excavations in the 1940s provided the widest exposure of Kassite period architecture (in this case, dated roughly 1400–1150 BC) yet available. The Iraqi excavation concentrated on the ziggurat and a palace complex, about a kilometre (half a mile) apart. Aqar Quf's ziggurat is one of the best known. The palace complex, built and rebuilt four times, contained wall paintings (preserved only in its last phase), and also provided examples of Kassite period art (e.g. a famous lion head in clay), a small archive, and an ox-hide INGOT of copper belonging to the Aegean world, among other objects. Dur-Kurigalzu is poorly known, apart from these two excavated areas, but seems to have been a substantial settlement, approaching 200 ha (495 acres) in size.

Aquae Sulis see BATH.

'Aqualithic' an informal term denoting an early ceramic cultural complex adapted to riverine and lacustrine environments during the North African wet phase between about 10,000 and 8000 BP. The cultural material includes bone harpoons, which have a wide distribution from the confluence of the Blue and White Niles to the central Sahara and northern Kenya (see ARAOUANE, TA-GALAGAL, TAMAYA MELLET, AMEKNI, TI-N-TORHA).

aqueduct a channel for carrying water, often over considerable distances. Aqueducts became an important feature of Roman urban life, providing water for THERMAE and fountains. One of the most impressive surviving examples is the PONT DU GARD. ROME itself was served by numerous aqueducts, the earliest being the Aquae Appia constructed in 312 BC.

Arad a Palestinian site excavated 1962–83 by AHARONI

and by Amiran. The 'lower city' of the EARLY BRONZE AGE is a substantial settlement of 9 ha (22 acres), with well-planned fortifications. The excavations at Arad have produced an important corpus of Early Bronze Age pottery, including imports, which has helped to develop chronological links between CANAANITE ceramics and those of ARCHAIC Egypt. The 'upper city' (TELL Arad proper), on a natural hill, is the site of six successive ISRAELITE citadels and includes a sanctuary of the 9th century BC containing a MASSEBAH.

Arago see TAUTAVEL.

Aramaean **1** a linguistic designation for a western Semitic language.

2 a series of small Iron Age (i.e. after 1200 BC) POLITIES in Syria up to the ASSYRIAN border, which were eventually absorbed into the Assyrian empire. More nomadic and tribally organized Aramaean groups pushed through Assyria and BABYLONIA at the end of the 2nd and beginning of the 1st millennium BC to settle between the Tigris and the Zagros Mountains. The Aramaic language used an alphabetic script, and was increasingly adopted for administrative purposes by the Assyrian, Babylonian and ACHAEMENID empires during the 1st millennium BC. This process introduced the script to peripheral zones of empire, where it was applied to local languages (seen, for example, in the modern Armenian and Georgian alphabets).

Arambourg, Camille (1885–1969) a French geologist with wide-ranging interests in North African palaeontology and archaeology whose excavations include the important sites of AIN HANECH and TAMAR HAT in Algeria. See also TIGHENIF.

Aramis a locality in the Middle Awash area of the Afar Depression, Ethiopia, which in 1992–3 yielded seventeen HOMINID fossils comprising dental, cranial and postcranial specimens, and in 1994–5 a partial postcranial skeleton, dated to about 4.4 million years ago. The fossils were initially ascribed to AUSTRALOPITHECUS *ramidus*, but are currently placed within ARDIPITHECUS *ramidus*.

Araouane a basin of former lakes in western Mali, known particularly for information on lacustrine adaptations in the central Sahara between 9,000 and 8,000 years ago. Cattle remains thought to date to about 7000 BP have also been found.

Ara Pacis a monumental altar by the Tiber in the Campus Martius at ROME dedicated by the Senate on 30 January 9 BC. The altar was contained within a walled precinct which was decorated with a continuous frieze, part of which showed the procession to the altar. Many scholars have sought to identify the emperor Augustus and members of his family among those present. The earliest remains were found in 1568, but the most extensive exploration of the site leading to a reconstruction of the monument was conducted under Mussolini in 1937–8.

Arapi the site of a Neolithic-Early Bronze Age settlement mound in Thessaly, Greece, excavated by Milojcic in 1955. The site was first occupied in the ACERAMIC NEOLITHIC and defines the late Neolithic Arapi culture which is characterized by polychrome decorated pottery.

Aratta a placename in one of the SUMERIAN epics concerning Enmerkar, an EARLY DYNASTIC ruler of WARKA (Uruk), which deals with an episode of contact with the lord of Aratta, a place to the east, perhaps in eastern Iran. Enmerkar wished to build a temple, for which he required raw materials unavailable in southern MESOPOTAMIA. The epic is frequently cited in connection with long-distance trade in Mesopotamia during the 3rd millennium BC.

Arawak a number of pottery-using, farming groups (e.g. TAINO) who occupied an area from the northeast of South America over most of the Caribbean. They seem to have been linguistically associated, and probably originated, to the south, but influence from MESOAMERICA can be seen in the presence of BALL COURTS and ZEMI worship. The Arawak were displaced from many areas by aggressive CARIB migrants, but they were still extremely numerous at the time of Columbus's arrival in AD 1492.

Araya the type-site in Niigata Prefecture, Japan, for a Palaeolithic burin technology. The site, dating to 13,200 bp, yielded wedge-shaped cores, microblades and burin spalls, suggesting the manufacture of composite tools on site. Araya-type burins are known from Mongolia through northern Japan to Alaska.

archaeoastronomy a sub-discipline of archaeology and of astronomy which studies the extensive and accurate astronomical knowledge which, it is increasingly recognized, was possessed by ancient cultures, from large-scale civilizations to small-scale hunter-gatherer groups. Archaeoastronomers try to identify the material remains of this knowledge through an examination of such evidence as pottery designs and the spatial location of features and buildings, and place this knowledge within the context of the overall ancient culture (e.g. for what was the astronomical knowledge used).

archaeoethnobotany see PALAEOETHNOBOTANY.

archaeological geology the application of geological techniques and methods to the solution of archaeological problems. It differs from GEOARCHAEOLOGY in that the latter is essentially a subfield of archaeology whose explicit focus is the physical context of archaeological deposits.

archaeology the study of the past through the systematic recovery and analysis of MATERIAL CULTURE. The primary aims of the discipline are to recover, describe and classify this material, to describe the form and behaviour of past societies, and finally to understand the reasons for this behaviour. In the Old World the term tends to refer to the body of techniques and theories used in achieving these goals, whereas in the New World archaeology refers also to the subject matter. Archaeology is truly an interdisciplinary subject, and has borrowed many of its major theoretical and methodological concepts and approaches from history and anthropology.

archaeomagnetic dating a dating method based on the PALAEOMAGNETISM of archaeological materials, such as hearths and stationary kilns. Heating above the Curie point, about 650 °C for haematite, destroys any previous alignment of magnetic particles and as the material cools they realign in accordance with the Earth's magnetic field at that time. Local and regional chronologies are built up by taking series of measurements and can be independently dated.

archaeometry the use of techniques derived from the hard sciences in the interpretation and analysis of archaeological data.

archaeozoology or **zooarchaeology** a branch of archaeology involving the analysis of archaeologically recovered animal remains (mostly bones and teeth) for information such as physiology, ecology, etc.; for the interpretation of these remains in their association with artifacts and people; human use of and impact on ancient animal populations; and for data on subsistence, dietary and butchering patterns, animal domestication and PALAEOENVIRONMENT. See also CATASTROPHIC AGE PROFILE, TAPHONOMY.

Archaic (*North American archaeology*) cultures that have a wide-spectrum hunting and gathering base, ground stone tools and increasing sedentism. In many parts of the continent it is used erroneously to refer to the chronological period that follows the PALAEOINDIAN period, from approximately 7000 BP to the time of Christ.

archaic *adj.* **1** relating to an early phase of art or a culture.
2 in Egyptian art, relating to the first two dynasties, *c.*3000–2700 BC.
3 in Greek art, relating to the period of the emerging city-states from the mid 8th century BC. The traditional end of the period is the Persian attack on Greece in 480 BC, although there is a possibility that the archaic style continued for some time after this event. In sculpture the 'archaic smile' refers to the characteristic frozen smile (see KORE and KOUROS).

Archaic period an era of Egyptian history comprising the 1st and 2nd Dynasties (*c.*3000–2700 BC) and Egypt's earliest period as a unified state. The Archaic period (with the addition of the 3rd Dynasty) is sometimes referred to as the EARLY DYNASTIC PERIOD.

Archaim see ARKAIM.

archaistic *adj.* **1** (of an artistic style) attempting to evoke an earlier period.
2 in Greek art (of a phase of HELLENISTIC art, in particular sculpture) seeming to recall ARCHAIC art of the late 6th century BC.

Archanes or **Arkhanes** a major MINOAN centre on the island of CRETE. At Turkogeitonia there is a 16th-century BC structure which is palatial in character if not in scale. Phourni is an extensive cemetery complex which was in use throughout the Minoan period. Splendid offerings of gold, ivory and marble have been discovered. Finally, at Anemospilia, Sakellarakis has excavated a shrine which was destroyed, apparently by an earthquake, *c.*1700 BC. A youth, whose skeleton was found in the shrine, is thought to have been a propitiatory sacrifice.

Archéodrome de Beaune a museum of reconstructed buildings and EXPERIMENTAL ARCHAEOLOGY designed for the general public. It was founded in 1978 at a service station on the A6 motorway at Beaune, Côte d'Or, France. Reconstructions include a Palaeolithic encampment based on PINCEVENT, a Neolithic house from Charmoy, and the Roman siege works constructed by Caesar at ALÉSIA.

architrave a horizontal load-bearing block which spans the space between two columns on a CLASSICAL colonnade. See also ENTABLATURE.

Arctic Small-Tool tradition a prehistoric tradition (4200–2100 BP) that stretched through the high Arctic, from the Bering Strait in the west to Greenland in the east. It may have originated in the preceding AMERICAN PALAEO-ARCTIC tradition. Tool assemblages are dominated by uniformly shaped scrapers and blade tools, with some harpoon heads found in sites in the eastern part of the tradition's distribution. Its economy was based on hunting and fishing.

Arcy-sur-Cure a complex of nine caves near Avalon, northern France, excavated primarily by LEROI-GOURHAN. The best-known site, the Grotte du Renne, has yielded fourteen Middle and Upper Palaeolithic levels, including a series of industries apparently transitional between Middle (MOUSTERIAN) and Upper (CHÂTELPERRONIAN) Palaeolithic technology. Numerous ornaments were found in a Châtelperronian layer (*c.*36,000 bp) containing a NEANDERTHAL temporal bone; and it has recently been shown that these ornaments – including wolf and fox canines made into pendants, and other perforated objects – are not only attributable to Neanderthal craftsmanship, but display manufacturing techniques owing nothing to AURIGNACIAN populations.

There is PARIETAL ART in the Grotte du Cheval (engravings) and Grande Grotte (paintings), both dominated by mammoths. In the Grande Grotte, charcoal associated with burnt bone and traces of ochre has yielded radiocarbon dates from 30,160 to 24,660 bp, providing a likely time range for its parietal art.

The Arcy INTERSTADIAL is the name given to a mild climatic phase during the final GLACIATION of Europe (c.31,000 BP), though its existence is still somewhat hypothetical.

ard a simple form of plough used to cut a furrow through the soil without turning it over. As a result, it was usually necessary to plough at right angles to the initial direction of ploughing to stir the soil adequately. The earliest ards are known from Near Eastern representations of the 5th millennium BC and from preserved finds in Europe from the 4th millennium BC. Parallel furrows in subsoil identified as ard marks have been noted at several Neolithic and Bronze Age sites in Europe, including Snave in Denmark and GWITHIAN in Britain.

Ardipithecus a genus claimed to represent the earliest known HOMINID (but see ORRORIN), which may have used a form of bipedal locomotion, known from 4.4 million-year-old fossils of the species *Ardipithecus ramidus*, from ARAMIS, Ethiopia. *'Ardi'* means 'ground' or 'floor' and *'ramid'* means 'root' in the Afar language spoken in the Aramis area. Dental remains place the genus between chimpanzees and australopithecines (see AUSTRALOPITHECUS).

Arene Candide a large limestone cave on the coast of Liguria, Italy. Deep soundings revealed a rich GRAVETTIAN ochre burial with flint knife, BÂTONS PERCÉS and a cap decorated with hundreds of seashells. Further ochre burials were found in EPIPALAEOLITHIC levels dated c.11,000–10,000 BC. The cave is also famous for its important stratified sequence of later deposits which provided the key to the Neolithic sequence of northern Italy, from early Neolithic IMPRESSED WARE to middle Neolithic BOCCA QUADRATA and late Neolithic LAGOZZA.

Argissa the site of a prehistoric settlement mound in Thessaly, Greece, which was excavated by Milojcic in 1956–8. First occupied in the Palaeolithic period and then more or less continuously throughout the Neolithic and Bronze Age, Argissa has been a key site in defining the Thessalian cultural sequence.

argon-argon dating an isotopic dating method in which the isotopic composition of argon, thermally released from irradiated sample material, is measured by high sensitivity mass spectrometry. Material can be dated in the age range of 10,000 to greater than 1 million years, with varying degrees of precision. Datable material includes a range of common silicate minerals, including hornblende, orthoclase, plagioclase, muscovite and bio-

tite; basalt; slate; K-evaporites and metals. The method is used to date the timing of mineralization, evaporite formation and volcanic activity, as well as QUATERNARY GEOCHRONOLOGY and establishing stratigraphic relationships. Used in conjunction with other geochronologic techniques, the method can determine the age of formation and post-formation thermal history of various minerals, within a range of about 100–550 °C. See also MOJOKERTO, SANGIRAN.

Argos a site in the Argolid, Greece. The prehistoric settlement was on the Aspis hill and appears to have been extensive in the Middle HELLADIC period but this was not a major MYCENAEAN site. Rich GEOMETRIC graves testify to the rise of Argos as the most powerful city in the Argolid, but in the Peloponnese as a whole Argos was ultimately overshadowed by SPARTA and CORINTH. The most impressive archaeological remains are the HELLENISTIC theatre and the Roman baths. The city's principal sanctuary was the Heraion, northeast of Argos, which is also the site of the Mycenaean settlement and cemetery of Prosymna.

Arikamedu a port town of the first centuries AD, just south of Pondicherry on the Coromandel Coast in northeastern Tamil Nadu, southern India, which displays evidence of trade with the Roman world. The site, much of which has been eroded away, has been excavated by a number of different archaeologists, including M. WHEELER and J.-M. Casal in the 1940s. This work indicated the existence of a late 1st millennium BC settlement containing pottery similar to that of the megalithic grave complex of south India (see MEGALITHIC CULTURE). Over these levels are large brick buildings and other installations, among which occur sherds of ARRETINE WARE, AMPHORAS, Roman glass and other Mediterranean products; this occupation belongs to the final centuries BC and the first few centuries AD. Although no Roman coins were found in these excavations, hoards of 1st–2nd-century AD coins are relatively common in southern India. Arikamedu directly illustrates passages in CLASSICAL literature that speak of Roman trade with India.

Ariuşd or **Erosd** a painted pottery variant in Transylvania of the CUCUTENI-TRIPOLYE culture. Red or orange pottery is painted with elaborate rectilinear and curvilinear patterns in black and white. The site of Ariuşd, a TELL in Transylvania, with seven occupation levels, provided evidence of craft activity, specifically a workshop for pottery manufacture.

Arka an Upper Palaeolithic cave-site located along the Hernád River in northeastern Hungary. Artifacts and occasional faunal remains (reindeer, horse and bison) are buried in deposits of loam dated to 18,600–17,050 bp. The artifacts include endscrapers, burins and retouched blades, and are assigned to the GRAVETTIAN. Arka was excavated by VÉRTES in 1960–61.

Arkaim a site complex of the Middle Bronze Age (18th–16th centuries BC) in the southern Urals (Russia). It consists of a fortified settlement with adjacent economic areas, burial mounds and some unfortified settlements. The fortified settlement is round in shape and has a radial-concentric structure, i.e. a double ring of fortification walls and a round central area with houses situated between the walls and the centre radially, like spokes in a wheel. The diameter of the outer wall is 145 m (159 yds), and the area of the settlement is 20,000 sq. m (23,920 sq. yds). Arkaim was discovered in 1987 and is being excavated by G. B. Zdanovich. This complex, together with that of SINTASHTA, belongs to the so-called 'Land of Cities', which was discovered in the steppes of the southern Urals thanks to the analysis of satellite and AERIAL PHOTOGRAPHY. More than twenty fortified centres and related mortuary complexes are known, as well as hundreds of smaller unfortified settlements. These sites are presumably connected with the ancient Indo-Iranians (Aryans). Arkaim is the best preserved and most investigated complex among the sites of the 'Land of Cities'.

Arkhanes see ARCHANES.

Arkin the location in LOWER NUBIA of a number of Palaeolithic sites. Arkin 8 is a late ACHEULIAN campsite with traces of dwellings, while Arkin 5 produced clusters of MOUSTERIAN artifacts.

Arku Cave a cave-site in the CAGAYAN VALLEY, northern Luzon, Philippines, with a burial assemblage dated from 1500 BC, including red-slipped pottery.

Arlington Springs Woman the skeletal remains of an adult female, found in 1959 on Rosa Island off the California coast, USA. They were not scientifically studied until the late 1990s when new radiocarbon techniques were able to date the remains to approximately 13,000 years ago. Such an early date and the skeleton's location on an island lend support to the hypothesis that the initial peopling of the New World took place along the Pacific coast rather than in the interior of the continent.

Arlit several sites on the west side of the Air Mountains in Niger, with stone artifacts similar to those of the TENEREAN at ADRAR BOUS. Radiocarbon dates bracket the period 5400–2700 BP, but domesticated cattle and sheep/goats (ovicaprines) do not appear until about 5000 BP.

Arnhem Land a region of the Northern Territory of Australia with a remarkably complete regional sequence which may extend back more than 50,000 years at MALAKUNANJA 2. The region is rich in rock art and it is likely that this too extends back into the Pleisto-cene. Earlier paintings, in a dynamic style, depict land animals, including some extinct species, and MIMI FIGURES, often with artifacts that were not part of the local tool-kit at European contact. Later X-RAY paintings include depictions of estuarine species. See also ANBANGBANG, LINDNER SITE, NAUWALABILA I, MALANGANGERR.

Arpachiyah a tiny site near the Tigris in the area of NINEVEH in Iraq. Max MALLOWAN's excavation here in the 1930s revealed a ten-phase architectural sequence of 'UBAID levels (TT 1–4) over HALAF levels (TT 6–10), with an intermediate transitional phase. The architecture of the Halaf settlements focused on the typical Halafian THOLOS, the first examples of this form to be reported. Mallowan also found pre-TT 10 materials outside his principal sounding, and I. Hijara's investigation in 1976 revealed another six levels containing rectilinear architecture. Mallowan's results provided the basis for dividing Halaf pottery into the three phases still commonly applied to Halaf chronological development (Early: pre-TT 10; Middle: TT 10–7; and Late: TT 6).

Arras an Iron Age barrow cemetery, type-site of the Arras culture which is restricted to eastern Yorkshire, England, and is known almost exclusively from its burials. The rectangular barrows have a central burial pit with inhumation, often accompanied by weapons. A few contain cart burials, notably three at Arras itself, and others discovered in the 1980s at Wetwang, Garton Station and Kirkburn. The cart burials and barrow form can be paralleled in the Champagne area of northeastern France, for example at SOMME-BIONNE, and some have argued that the Arras culture represents immigration or invasion by warriors from that region. The earliest Arras culture graves may belong to the 4th century BC, but the cemeteries appear to have continued in use until the 1st century BC.

Arretine ware a popular type of Roman red-glossed pottery initially produced at Arezzo in Italy especially in the 1st century BC and the 1st century AD. It had a wide distribution in these centuries but it was replaced by other regional red-glossed fabrics. A study of stamps has provided information about the number of workshops. See also TERRA SIGILLATA.

arrow straightener see BÂTON PERCÉ.

Arslantepe a site on the Malatya plain in the upper Euphrates drainage (eastern Anatolia) which was occupied from CHALCOLITHIC to late Roman times. The best-known monuments of the site belong to the Syro-Hittite world (beginning of the 1st millennium BC) and include a fortification wall entered through a 'Lion gate' in the tradition of HITTITE and MYCENAEAN architecture; just as important, however, are the far earlier settlements that were interacting with MESOPOTAMIA during the

Late URUK period (mid 4th millennium BC). Excavations began here with L. Delaporte's work in the 1930s and continued with that of C. Schaeffer in the 1940s, focused on the Bronze Age and Iron Age occupations. Since the early 1960s an Italian team has conducted more methodical work on the earlier levels. Apart from the Syro-Hittite remains, the site's most important contribution lies in the Early Bronze Age period VIA (c.3300–2900 BC). These levels contain a large complex of public buildings identified as temples with wall paintings, and in which were stored many clay sealings as an administrative record of transactions; a rich, perhaps royal, burial belongs to the end of this period. Some items of material culture reveal contact with Uruk Mesopotamia, but elaborate architecture in earlier levels at Arslantepe indicates that social complexity emerged here before this connection with the Mesopotamian world.

Artamonov, Mikhail Illarionovich (1898–1972) a Soviet archaeologist best known for his fundamental work on three main problems: the history and culture of the SCYTHIANS, the history of medieval nomads, and the origin of the Slavs. He is also known as an organizer of Soviet archaeology: in 1938–45 he was a director of the Institute of History of Material Culture in Leningrad (the leading Soviet archaeological institution); in 1951–64 he was a director of the State Hermitage; and he initiated the publication of a number of very important Soviet archaeological series.

Artenac a cave-site near Angoulême, Charente, France, destroyed by quarrying in the 1960s, and type-site of the CHALCOLITHIC Artenacien culture, which includes copper beads, finely flaked flint daggers, and fine pottery decorated with bands of wavy lines, triangles or dot-filled lozenges, and *anses nasiformes* or beaked handles. Artenacien material is found on defended promontory settlements, in simple megalithic tombs and in burial caves over an area stretching from Aquitaine to the western edge of the Paris basin, and is dated to between 3000 and 2000 BC.

Arthur a shadowy figure of medieval legend which some have traced back to a real historical ruler of the 5th or 6th century AD. From the 9th century AD Arthur appears in history and literature as a warrior-hero leading the Britons to victory over the ANGLO-SAXONS. Tradition associates him with Tintagel in Cornwall, a sea-girt promontory fortress where excavation has revealed links with the Mediterranean world during the 5th to 7th centuries AD. Other interpretations associate Arthur with sites in northern England, and with the HILLFORT of South Cadbury in Somerset, which since the 16th century has been identified in local tradition as the site of Camelot, and which is known to have been refortified in c.AD 500.

articulation the joint between rigid parts of the body.

Studies of faunal remains from archaeological contexts frequently include attempts to rearticulate, or join, skeletal parts. These studies provide information on TAPHONOMIC processes at work at the site, indicative of the integrity of the site. These studies also provide insights for SITE STRUCTURAL analysis at the site. Methods of butchering, size and composition of herds and estimates of the number of individuals represented at the site are other types of information gained from articulating skeletal remains.

artifact any movable object that has been used, modified or manufactured by humans. See also MATERIAL CULTURE, TOOL.

Artsikhovski, Artemy Vladimirovich (1902–78) a Soviet specialist in Slavic-Russian archaeology. He became famous for his grandiose excavations (from 1932) of NOVGOROD, an early Russian urban centre, where the famous BIRCH-BARK MANUSCRIPTS were discovered. He also led RESCUE excavations of ancient Moscow when the construction of the Moscow Underground began. He was the founder-editor of the journal *Soviet Archaeology*, and was the first person to introduce a general Archaeology course into USSR universities.

aryballos a round container which seems to have been used by the Greeks for perfumed oil. It has a narrow neck with two small handles. In art they are often shown attached to the wrists of athletes by means of a thong. Many examples of the shape were made at CORINTH (see CORINTHIAN POTTERY) and some have been found in the GIGLIO ISLAND shipwreck.

Arzhan a KURGAN of the 8th–7th centuries BC, located in the valley of the Uyuk River in Tuva, southern Siberia. It was excavated by M. P. GRYAZNOV in 1971–4. The preserved mound was 120 m (131 yds) in diameter and 2.5 m (8 ft) high. Under the cairn he discovered a complicated wooden construction consisting of one main central timber with seventy other timbers arranged radially around it. In the central tomb were burials of the 'king' and 'queen'. They were surrounded by the remains of eight people and six horses. In total, the kurgan contained the burials of fifteen people, accompanying the 'king' and 'queen', and more than 160 horses. The human burials had already been looted. The principal finds were the horse equipment (bits, PSALIA, decorations of bridle belts, etc.). Bronze weaponry was also found: daggers, arrows and a CHEKAN, and objects made in the tradition of the SCYTHIAN-SIBERIAN ANIMAL STYLE, such as a famous bronze plaque depicting a curled-up panther. Radiocarbon dates span the period from 850–800 bc. Arzhan is a very important site for the problem of the origin of the SCYTHIAN TYPE CULTURES.

as a small Roman bronze coin, four of which made a SESTERTIUS and sixteen a DENARIUS.

Asana a seasonally occupied, open-air PRECERAMIC site located at an altitude of 3,430 m (11,253 ft) in the western slopes of the Andes in southern Peru. Excavations by Mark Aldenderfer have revealed domestic structures, circular to ovoid in plan, with prepared white-clay floors, set between large boulders. Dating to as early as 7870 bc, these may represent the earliest domestic structures in the Andean region. In addition, a ceremonial complex dating to 2660 bc has been identified at the site. The complex includes a prepared clay floor, clay-lined fire basins, surface hearths and two possible altars.

ash 1 unconsolidated detrital volcanic material less than 4 mm (0.16 inch) in diameter deposited as a result of volcanic eruption. Ash falls can quickly bury and preserve archaeological sites, create STRATIGRAPHIC separation of occupation surfaces, and in some instances in effect create archaeological sites by falling on occupied areas, causing death or evacuation, and effectively 'freezing' intact and undisturbed evidence of activities and structures. See TEPHRA.
2 soft and solid residual remains of burned organic material, including human or animal cremation.

Ashdod a Palestinian site. A CANAANITE city of the LATE BRONZE AGE which seems to have been destroyed by the SEA PEOPLES, it became one of the cities of the PHILISTINE Pentapolis.

Asherah see ASTARTE.

Ashkelon a Palestinian site, sporadically excavated since 1815, especially by GARSTANG in 1920–21, and again since 1985 by L. Stager. The LATE BRONZE AGE levels produced objects of Egyptian and Cypriot origin, while the Iron Age is represented by the PHILISTINE city. Much archaeological material of the Roman period has also been found at Ashkelon, including a probable brothel, with evidence of male infanticide.

ashlar masonry consisting of rectangular cut blocks of stone laid horizontally in regular courses.

ash mound a distinctive site type of the central Deccan in southern India, the remains of Neolithic cattle pens, dated to the 3rd millennium BC. Excavations of these sites in Karnataka show that they consisted of a double palisade of palm trunks, of which the inner enclosed the cattle, and the outer the herders' dwellings. The accumulation of dung inside the inner palisade fuelled the fires that seem to have been a regular (and perhaps intentional) event at these sites, thereby producing the salient characteristic of this site type.

Ashur see ASSUR.

Asia a Late PRECERAMIC site on the south-central coast of Peru. It covers some 30 ha (74 acres), and comprises a series of mounds that may have served as residential structures. Burials from the site indicate social distinc-

tions based on equal access to resources, especially cloth; some individuals showed evidence of TREPHINATION.

Asiab an early 7th millennium BC site in the Kermanshah district of the Zagros Mountains in western Iran; excavations here reveal a small community living in circular semi-subterranean structures, and relying heavily on goats. Although not morphologically domesticated, the age structure of the goats suggests herding.

Asia, Southeast Archaeological research in the various countries of Southeast Asia started in the late 19th century through the personal interests of colonial officials – mainly geologists – in Malaya, Burma, the territories of the former French Indochina and the Netherlands Indies. Colonial government organizations such as the Archaeological Department (Burma), the Oudheidkundige Dienst (Netherlands Indies) and the École Française d'Extrême-Orient (Indochina) extended these private investigations and up to the 1930s put much effort and resources into studying and conserving the great Hindu-Buddhist monuments of the medieval period at PAGAN, BOROBUDUR, PRAMBANAN, ANGKOR and many other locations while paying rather little attention to prehistory, except in Java, where the early finds of HOMO *erectus* (JAVA and SOLO MAN) by DUBOIS, van Oppenorth and von KOENIGSWALD attracted continuing research. The Pacific War and subsequent revolutions and civil turmoil leading to the establishment of the eight nation states of the region today (Burma/Myanmar, Laos, Thailand, Cambodia, Vietnam, the Philippines, Malaysia and Indonesia) led to a virtual cessation of research for some twenty years. Starting in the 1960s archaeological activity revived, often by local scholars working in co-operation with European and American professionals, and by the 1990s the research agendas and much of the fieldwork had been undertaken by local archaeologists.

Prehistoric times
The earliest evidence for human presence in the region dates to the late Middle or early Upper Pleistocene, with the discoveries by Dubois of PITHECANTHROPUS *erectus* (*H. erectus*) in central Java. Isolated teeth of pre-modern hominids have also been found in northern Vietnam, but clear evidence for human cultural activities in the form of flaked stone tools is ambiguous until about 30,000 years ago, when they are found in many limestone caves throughout Southeast Asia. With the resumption of warmer conditions some 10,000 years ago sea-levels rose, separating the islands of western Indonesia from the mainland about 6000 BC, though much earlier evidence of watercraft is provided by the first settlement of the islands of eastern Indonesia, Melanesia and ultimately Australia by at least 40,000 years ago.
The early to mid Holocene period was characterized by the extension of lowland tropical forests inhabited by small bands of hunters and gatherers, probably of

Melanesoid type, usually referred to as the HOABINHIAN cultures on the mainland of Southeast Asia and the Flake-Blade cultures in the islands. The transition to a more settled way of life on the mainland based on rice cultivation and the raising of pigs and cattle occurred around 2500 BC, and was brought, in all probability, by the southward expansion of southern Mongoloid populations speaking early forms of Austroasiatic languages.

The Metal Ages

In northern Vietnam, northeastern and central Thailand bronze metallurgy appeared about 1500 BC but whether this was a purely local development or was introduced from China is still debated. However, metal working did not spread widely through Southeast Asia until about 500 BC, with the introduction of iron, probably from India to most of the region, and from China into northern Vietnam. At this time both intra- and interregional exchange increased in volume and extent, bringing familiarity with Indian and Chinese technologies (iron working, glass making, brick making) and Hindu-Buddhist cultural values, which were adopted rapidly and with enthusiasm by aspiring local elites.

The historic period

From about the 3rd to the 5th centuries of the Christian era Sanskrit inscriptions on stone appear in central Vietnam, western Java and eastern Kalimantan, making it clear that local rulers had adopted many aspects of Indian religious ideology and taken on Indian names; and soon afterwards brick religious buildings and stone and bronze images of Hindu deities, Buddhas and various Avalokitesvaras are widely found. The 6th to c.15th centuries mark the mature period of Indianized civilization in Southeast Asia, with the construction of enormous temple complexes at Pegu, Halin and Pagan in Burma, at Angkor Borei and the Angkor Wat region in Cambodia, the Cham temple towers along the central Vietnamese coast and, of course, in central and eastern Java on the Dieng Plateau, at Borobudur, Prambanan and Kediri.

From the early centuries of the Christian era northern Vietnam came under the HAN and subsequent Chinese Dynasties, incorporating the indigenous DONG SON culture until the local Ly Dynasty gained independence from China in the 10th century and the subsequent Sino-Viet rulers expanded to the south from the 15th century, conquering in turn the various Cham principalities and taking most of the fertile Mekong River delta from the local Cham and Khmer populations.

Burma (Myanmar)

Prehistoric research has been far less developed in Burma than in Thailand and Vietnam – more comparable to Laos and Cambodia. But the potential for significant new discoveries in this country is very great. Myanmar is rich in metal ores and other natural resources and we can expect to find a rich series of bronze- and iron-using cultures through the 2nd and 1st millennia BC, as in Thailand and Vietnam. Setting aside the discoveries by T. O. Morris and H. Movius of various Palaeolithic industries of still unknown age along the terraces of the Irrawaddy River, and the finds from the Padah Lin Caves, probably of late Pleistocene to mid Holocene age, the first reliable information on metal age finds comes from the recent excavations at Nyaunggan northwest of Mandalay, where a number of burials were uncovered in the mid 1990s, some furnished with copper-alloy tools and weapons.

Laos

As in Burma, the study of prehistory in Laos is in its infancy, but similarly some new research shows promise, although with its lower population density and large areas covered by steep forested mountains it is unlikely that Laos will ever be a major archaeological research field. Early in the 20th century French scholars catalogued some archaeological finds from the country but it is from the research of the redoubtable Madelaine Colani on the stone jars and other megaliths of the Plain of Jars in Xieng Khouang Province that Lao prehistory is best known. More recently the work in this region has been taken up by Thongsa Sayavongkhamdy, excavating at three of the forty known stone jar sites: Phon Savan, Ban Xieng Dee and Pu Salato. In addition, a quarry site where the stone jars were made was located with unfinished jars lying in situ. A UNESCO team is using advanced GIS methods to study the distribution and association of the jars with landscape features.

Cambodia

As in Burma and Laos there were a few early reports on prehistoric sites in Cambodia, especially on the huge freshwater SHELL MIDDEN at SAMRONG SEN on a branch of the Mekong, where finds of bronze axes and finely decorated pottery attracted the attention of CARTAILHAC, the famous French archaeologist. But the demands of the monumental sites of the historic Khmer civilization at Angkor and elsewhere attracted most of the research funds and personnel. Only in the 1960s did some archaeologists start to look again at the rich prehistoric background to Khmer civilization. Mourer excavated in the LAANG SPEAN caves in Battambang Province, while Bernard-Philippe Groslier diverted his attention from Angkor to make preliminary excavations at some of the enigmatic circular earthwork sites in Mimot District (now Memot) near the Vietnamese border. Research on these sites has recently been taken up by a joint German-Cambodian team and their preliminary results (mainly from the Krek 62/52 site) were set out in a workshop/conference held in Phnom Penh in November 1999.

A US-led team from the University of Hawaii has initiated the 'Lower Mekong Archaeological Project' on the prehistoric background to the Khmer civilization. Until recently, the only archaeological data on the archaeology

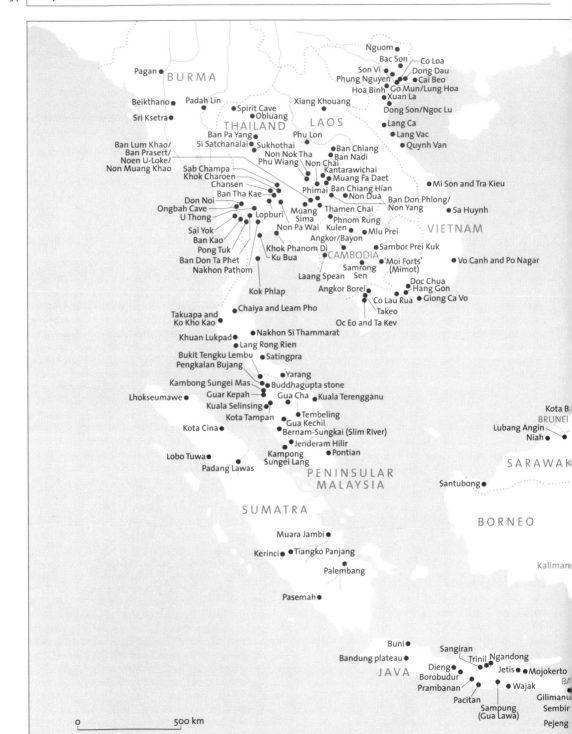

Nguom
Bac Son
Son Vi • • Co Loa
Pagan • BURMA Phung Nguyen • • Dong Dau
Hoa Binh • • Cai Beo
Go Mun/Lung Hoa
Xuan La
Beikthano • Padah Lin Xiang Khouang • Dong Son/Ngoc Lu
Sri Ksetra • Spirit Cave • Lang Ca
Obluang • Lang Vac
THAILAND LAOS
Ban Pa Yang Phu Lon • Quynh Van
Si Satchanalai • Sukhothai Ban Chiang
Ban Lum Khao/ Non Nok Tha • • Ban Nadi
Ban Prasert/ Phu Wiang \ Non Chai
Noen U-Loke/ Kantarawichai
Non Muang Khao Sab Champa • Muang Fa Daet • Mi Son and Tra Kieu
Khok Charoen • • Ban Chiang Hian
Chansen Phimai • • Non Dua
Ban Tha Kae • • Non Yang Ban Don Phlong/
Don Noi • Muang Thamen Chai • Sa Huynh
Ongbah Cave • Sima Non Yang
U Thong • Lopburi Phnom Rung • VIETNAM
Sai Yok Non Pa Wai Kulen • Mlu Prei
Ban Kao Angkor/Bayon Sambor Prei Kuk
Pong Tuk Khok Phanom Di 'Moi Forts' • Vo Canh and Po Nagar
Ban Don Ta Phet • Ku Bua CAMBODIA (Mimot)
Nakhon Pathom Samrong Doc Chua
Laang Spean Sen Hang Gon
Kok Phlap Angkor Borei • Giong Ca Vo
Co Lau Rua
Chaiya and Leam Pho Takeo
Takuapa and Oc Eo and Ta Kev
Ko Kho Kao
Khuan Lukpad • Nakhon Si Thammarat
• Lang Rong Rien
Bukit Tengku Lembu • Satingpra
Pengkalan Bujang
• Yarang
Kambong Sungei Mas • Buddhagupta stone
Lhokseumawe • Guar Kepah • Gua Cha • Kuala Terengganu
Kuala Selinsing
Kota Tampan • Tembeling
Kota Cina • Gua Kechil
Bernam-Sungkai (Slim River)
• Jenderam Hilir
Lobo Tuwa • Kampong • Pontian
Sungei Lang
Padang Lawas PENINSULAR
MALAYSIA
Kota B
BRUNEI
Lubang Angin
Niah •
SARAWAK
SUMATRA
Santubong •
BORNEO
Muara Jambi •
Kaliman
Kerinci • Tiangko Panjang
Palembang
Pasemah •
Buni •
Sangiran
Bandung plateau • Trinil Ngandong
Dieng • • Jetis • Mojokerto
JAVA Borobudur BA
Prambanan • Wajak
Pacitan Gilimanu
Sampung Sembir
0 500 km (Gua Lawa)
Pejeng

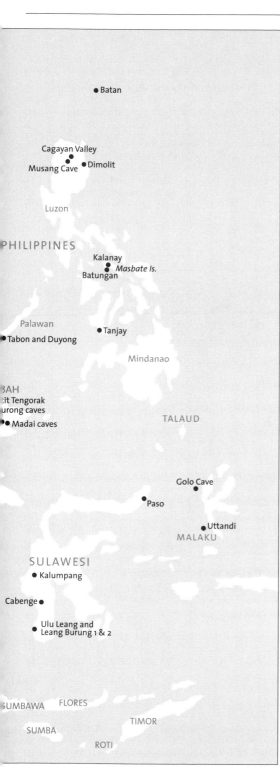

of the Mekong delta were from the surveys and excavations by Malleret in the 1940s at and around OC ÈO in Vietnam. Since 1996, the LOMAP project has undertaken research in and around the ancient site of Angkor Borei, Takeo Province, in southern Cambodia, long recognized as an important early settlement of the FUNAN period. Angkor Borei has produced the earliest Khmer inscription in Cambodia, dated to AD 611, as well as brick architecture, statuary and assorted valuables including precious metals and gems.

Thailand

Thirty years ago, Thailand had no known prehistory; investigation commenced with the work of the Thai-Danish group at Sai Yok and BAN KAO in Kanchanaburi Province in the early 1960s, which provided the first reliable and systematic descriptions of prehistoric material and sites. Since then surveys and excavations by many Thai and foreign researchers have proliferated, and a 1998 volume by Higham and Thosarat provides an authoritative survey of much of the archaeology undertaken in the kingdom up to the late 1990s.

One of the most interesting outcomes of the surveys and excavations of the past few years is the recognition of regional variability; that is to say that the emerging cultural sequence we know from the northeast does not make much sense in central, western or southern Thailand. In the northeast, for instance, there is abundant evidence for the casting of bronze tools and ornaments at many sites in the early 2nd millennium BC. Sites such as PHU LON and in the Wong Prachan Valley, northeast of Lopburi, show that the mining and smelting of local sources of carbonate and sulphide copper ores were being practised on a considerable scale by the middle of the 2nd millennium BC. It seems that these were specialized mining and refining sites exporting copper metal, which was mostly alloyed and cast into tools elsewhere, and the products of this industry are widespread and well known in eastern-central Thailand and on the KHORAT Plateau. Nevertheless, contemporary with these metal-making and metal-using complexes of eastern-central and northeastern Thailand we have the purely stone-using communities of Ban Kao and KHOK PHANOM DI, which were themselves involved in trading networks for exotic hard stone and pottery to the east and south.

Evidence for a preceding, purely stone-using phase of settled village agriculture without the use of bronze tools in northeastern Thailand is still weak and rests on a few burials without metal at NON NOK THA, BAN CHIANG, BAN PHAK TOP, Non Kao Noi and a few other sites, and it is not well identified nor closely dated. Despite the rather poor evidence, it looks as if agricultural communities were moving into this area through the northern valleys from about 2300 BC. These may have been Austroasiatic speakers bringing rice agriculture into

Southeast Asia from the centres of origin in the Yangzi Valley of China.

Secure dates for the appearance of iron in Thailand, let alone the whole region, are hard to come by, but on the basis of discoveries in the late 1980s there seems to be good evidence for burials dated to at least the 7th century BC, with iron and bi-metallic ornaments at the copper-smelting site of Nil Kham Haeng, northeast of Lopburi. When metal does appear in quantity in sites in western Thailand, it is iron, and the best documentation for this comes from BAN DON TA PHET, between Kanchanaburi and U THONG, where about 1,000 iron tools and weapons (including fragments) were recovered from three excavation seasons. No bronze tools or weapons were present, although bronze was in plentiful use for figurines, containers, bracelets, bells and rings. The site can now be dated to a rather short period in the 4th century BC – more exactly to 390–360 (calibrated). The transition in Thailand from small, dispersed, unstratified communities of basically bronze- and stone-using farmers to ranked, iron-using communities was rapid, starting about 700 BC; by 400 BC iron had replaced stone as a production tool in most places, and the region was becoming increasingly locked into a much broader system of interregional exchange which spread from the classical societies of the Mediterranean Basin, through India and Southeast Asia to China. Looking further afield, we can see that sea-communications also played a significant role in the growth of more complex societies in western Thailand and the incorporation of this region into the broader regional economy.

Aşıklı Höyük an ACERAMIC NEOLITHIC village of the 8th millennium BC near Aksaray in central Turkey. Excavations since 1989 by U. Esin have recorded ten building levels within the 14 m (46 ft) height of the 4 ha (10 acre) mound. The village houses abut one another to form a solid mass of architecture, a wide street creating two distinct neighbourhoods. Typical houses, constructed of mud-brick, are rectilinear affairs of one or two rooms, with access probably through the roof and burials beneath the floors. Several larger buildings with stone foundations and painted floors may be temples or other public buildings. The subsistence economy involved some domesticated cereals but also abundant wild plant foods; the animals are all wild.

askos a spouted vessel, used to pour oil or other liquids. The name comes from the Greek for a wineskin, which the askos sometimes resembles.

Asmar, Tell the ancient city of Eshnunna, excavated as part of FRANKFORT's Diyala project in the 1920s and 1930s, Tell Asmar (on the lower Diyala River in eastern-central Iraq) was inhabited from URUK to early OLD BABYLONIAN times. The excavations revealed an EARLY DYNASTIC I to AKKADIAN (2900–2150 BC) sequence at the Abu Temple, exposed an extensive residential district of later Early Dynastic and Akkadian date, and found a major industrial installation (in the 'Northern Palace', probably textile production) of the same date; the work also recovered monumental architecture of the early Old Babylonian period. A large cache of statuary from the Early Dynastic II Abu Temple, human figures in poses of supplication and awe, are some of the best-known examples of this genre. Together with the work at KHAFADJE and elsewhere in the lower Diyala, the excavations at Tell Asmar permitted the initial archaeological definition of the Early Dynastic and Akkadian periods. During the early 2nd millennium, just prior to the regional ascendancy of HAMMURABI, Tell Asmar was the centre of the regionally important kingdom of Eshnunna.

Asokan (or **Mauryan**) **pillars** polished sandstone columns, standing 12–14 m (40–46 ft) high and graced by capitals decorated with carved plants and animals; these are free-standing commemorative monuments erected by the MAURYAN king Asoka. Some fifteen pillars, of which ten bear inscriptions, are known across northern India as far west as TAXILA.

Asparn see LINEAR POTTERY CULTURE.

aspect see MIDWESTERN TAXONOMIC SYSTEM.

Aspero a Late PRECERAMIC site (4360–3950 bp) on the north-central coast of Peru. Covering some 12 ha (30 acres), it is one of the largest Preceramic settlements known in Andean South America, and represents the emergence of complex social organization. At least six PLATFORM MOUNDS and other structures were built along a natural hillslope through successive filling of small rooms. The largest mound, Huaca de los Idolos, measures 30 by 50 m (33 by 55 yds) and is 10 m (33 ft) high. Built in stages, each level comprises a series of rooms which were filled in with quarried rock held in mesh bags, and the next level superimposed. Dedicatory caches were buried as well, including small wooden artifacts, textiles, plant material, clay figurines and feathers. Subsistence was based primarily on maritime resources, with some cultigens playing a minor role; agriculture was devoted mostly to the production of industrial resources, such as cotton and gourds.

Asprochaliko a Palaeolithic rockshelter located on the Louros River in northwestern Greece. Artifacts are buried in a deep sequence of cave deposits; faunal remains (mostly deer and caprines) are rare. The lowermost cultural layers contain a MOUSTERIAN industry that includes sidescrapers and retouched flakes, and has been dated by THERMOLUMINESCENCE to 98,500 BP. Assemblages with similar tools occur in overlying levels. The upper cultural layers contain an Upper Palaeolithic industry with backed blades dated by radiocarbon to 26,100 bp.

assemblage a collection of artifacts that can be considered a single analytical unit. The size of an individual assemblage varies considerably. For example, an assemblage may represent artifacts used in a particular activity or the remains of a particular culture found at a site.

Assur **1** an ASSYRIAN god. Originally the principal deity of the city of ASSUR, eventually holding a place comparable to that of MARDUK at BABYLON, Assur became the more 'national' god of the NEO-ASSYRIAN empire. Here the god Assur provided the symbolic focus of a universalizing elite ideology that transcended the various boundaries within the empire; the adjective 'Assyrian' came to denote 'holy', and wars undertaken in Assur's name had ideological as well as more concrete value.

2 the ancient centre of ASSYRIA, set on a promontory overlooking the Tigris River in northeastern Iraq, where the excavations by W. ANDRAE exposed a wealth of 2nd and 1st millennium BC public and residential architecture. Much of the public architecture was built or largely reconstructed by SHAMSHI-ADAD I (1813–1781 BC), including the ziggurat of ENLIL, the temple of ASSUR (see **1** above), and the inner city walls. Later MIDDLE and NEO-ASSYRIAN kings persistently renovated these buildings and added further substantial construction, providing the city with three ziggurats and at least thirty-eight temples within the 140 ha (346 acres) contained by the city walls. Besides this religious architecture, the city contained at least two palaces. The 'old palace' was built in the early 2nd millennium and used through the Middle Assyrian period, but was subsequently adapted as a mausoleum of the 9th century (SARCOPHAGI of the kings AŠŠURNAṢIRPAL II and Shamshi-Adad V occur here). The 'new palace' was constructed by Tukulti-Ninurta I (1243–1207 BC), who also built KAR-TUKULTI-NINURTA just outside Assur. In the temple of ISHTAR, a deep sounding documented a sequence of temples on this site that begins (on virgin soil) in the mid 3rd millennium BC. The terminology Assur H to Assur A refers to this sequence; the architecture of Assur G, belonging to the AKKADIAN period, is the earliest with an adequately known floor plan. The latest substantial occupation of the site occurred in PARTHIAN times. The German work also recovered large numbers of Middle Assyrian tablets that provide important information about this time.

Aššurnaṣirpal II (883–859 BC) one of the great NEO-ASSYRIAN kings, who greatly extended ASSYRIAN domination westwards towards the Mediterranean, warring with such Syrian kingdoms as Bit-Adini, and taking tribute from the PHOENICIANS. He founded the new capital at KALHU, which was built and populated by people deported from conquered lands to the west and north; to inaugurate the city, he held a feast for some 52,000 guests from regions of the Assyrian empire and from neighbouring states, in addition to the 17,500

people from Kalhu itself. His son and successor, Shalmaneser III (858–824 BC), further expanded the empire in all directions.

Assyria the eastern section of northern MESOPOTAMIA in historic times, and named after the city of ASSUR, in the area of the Tigris River and its major tributaries, the Lesser and Greater Zab. This region participated in the broad development of northern Mesopotamia in prehistoric and early historic times (see ARPACHIYAH, ASSUR, GAWRA, HASSUNA, NEMRIK, NINEVEH, NINEVITE 5, OLD ASSYRIAN TRADE, SHAMSHI-ADAD). After a brief interlude under the domination of MITANNI, the kings of Assur created the MIDDLE ASSYRIAN empire (13th–12th centuries BC; see also KAR-TUKULTI-NINURTA). Following a period of weakness, the NEO-ASSYRIAN kings further extended the empire to encompass all the FERTILE CRESCENT (9th–7th centuries BC); NIMRUD, KHORSABAD and Nineveh served as the Assyrian capitals during the latter period (see also BALAWAT).

Astarte the goddess of love and war, a ubiquitous female deity of the ancient Near East. She was worshipped by the CANAANITES and PHOENICIANS; her cult was adopted by the PHILISTINES and by the ASSYRIANS and BABYLONIANS who knew her as ISHTAR.

Asturian a macrolithic industry of the Mesolithic period of northern Spain. Discovered in 1914 by the Conde de la Vega del Sella, it is known almost exclusively from *concheros* (SHELL MOUNDS) at cave mouths in the coastal area (see LA RIERA). The Asturian follows the AZILIAN, though it is not clear how the two are connected. Poor in cultural materials, it is characterized by a long, pointed unifacial QUARTZITE pick. Dates span the 9th and 8th millennia bp.

Asuka a region of Nara Prefecture, Japan, which was the focus of early Buddhist culture in the 6th–7th centuries AD. It is the location of the earliest temple built in Japan, the Asuka-dera of 588 (which is still extant but not architecturally continuous), the Kawahara-dera (which has been excavated and reconstructed in plan) and several contemporaneous palace sites, including FUJIWARA. Asuka was the seat of the RITSURYO government of Japan until the capital was removed to HEIJO. The region is now protected as a Historical District.

Aswan a modern town at the southern boundary of UPPER EGYPT. Archaeological remains in this region include granite quarries, rock-cut tombs of the OLD and MIDDLE KINGDOM, ELEPHANTINE, PHILAE and, since its re-erection during the NUBIAN RESCUE CAMPAIGN, the temple of KALABSHA.

Aszód a Neolithic settlement and cemetery of the LENGYEL CULTURE in northern Hungary, dating to the 5th millennium BC. Distributed among the settlement features are numerous clusters of graves, each with about thirty burials containing pots, boar jaws and SPONDYLUS ornaments.

Ataki I an Upper Palaeolithic open-air site on the Dnestr River in western Ukraine. Four occupation horizons are buried in slope deposits overlying ALLUVIUM of the second terrace; the second and third horizons have yielded radiocarbon dates of 15,375–16,600 bp. The principal excavations were undertaken by Chernysh in 1965.

Atapuerca a series of Lower Palaeolithic sites located in the Sierra de Atapuerca, 14 km (9 miles) east of Burgos, northern Spain, under investigation by a Spanish team headed by J. L. Arsuaga, J. M. Bermúdez de Castro and E. Carbonell. At the back of the Great Cave is the Sima de los Huesos (Pit of the Bones), a 12 m (40 ft) shaft; excavations at its base since 1983 have unearthed over 2,500 bones from at least thirty-two individuals of archaic HOMO *sapiens*, dating to more than 200,000 years ago. The presence of all parts of the body, and the lack of occupation material or carnivore marks, suggest strongly that this was a mortuary ritual, a purposeful disposal of the dead, the oldest known anywhere.

At another site, the Gran Dolina, simple stone tools have been recovered since the mid 1990s, together with teeth and bone fragments from at least six early humans which have been christened *H. antecessor*, and which date to about 800,000 years ago. *H. antecessor* has been claimed to be the last common ancestor of modern humans and NEANDERTHALS. Cutmarks on some of these bones are a possible indication of CANNIBALISM at this time.

Atchana, Tell the ancient *Alalakh*; WOOLLEY's excavations in the 1930s and 1940s at this site on the northern bend of the Orontes River in the Amuq plain (southern Turkey) defined seventeen phases of Middle and Late Bronze Age occupation. The lasting significance of his work here rests not so much on the exposure of residential, palatial and cultic architecture and the accompanying material culture, as on his recovery of two archives dated respectively to the 18th/17th (Alalakh VII) and the 15th (Alalakh IV) centuries BC. These archives throw considerable light on the political affairs of their times (the important Syrian kingdom of Yamkhad and a MITANNI client-state respectively), and on the progressive HURRIAN influence on Syrian societies. Woolley also explored AL MINA (literally 'the port') at the mouth of the Orontes, where he exposed ten levels dated between the 8th and 3rd centuries BC, which contained warehouses filled with Greek materials. Several kilometres upstream, he examined a settlement (Sabouni) with Bronze Age and 1st millennium habitation, where again strong interregional connections (MYCENAEAN and CYPRIOT painted pottery, as well as later Greek materials) are evident.

atelier a French word used to designate a primary stone, bone or metal working site.

Atelier de Commont an ACHEULIAN working site lying in the Somme River terrace, France, which has yielded elegantly worked bifaces of various shapes and flakes with secondary retouch.

Aten an Egyptian deity represented by the sun's disc. During the reign of AKHENATEN the Aten was elevated as the sole god of the monotheistic state religion promulgated by that king.

Aterian a Middle Palaeolithic stone industry with bifacial foliate points and/or tanged tools, and much use of the LEVALLOIS TECHNIQUE, found in North Africa from the Atlantic coast to the Nile from before 100,000 to about 50,000 years ago.

Athabascans NATIVE AMERICANS who speak languages belonging to the Athabascan or Dene language family. The Northern Athabascans comprise a variety of individual contemporary tribes who live mostly in Alaska and the Yukon. The Southern Athabascans, comprising Apache and Navajo, now live in the American Southwest, and are thought to have diverged from the northern group sometime around AD 500.

Athenian pottery pottery that was produced at ATHENS over a long period. In the late GEOMETRIC period monumental KRATERS and AMPHORAS, with scenes of mourning (see EKPHORA, PROTHESIS) and heroic events, were used to mark the tombs of members of the social elites. Athens is best known for its figure-decorated pottery (see BLACK-FIGURED, RED-FIGURED, SIX'S TECHNIQUE, WHITE-GROUND) produced during the ARCHAIC and CLASSICAL periods. Its products were widely exported and have been found throughout the regions bordering the Mediterranean and the Black Sea. Many examples have been found in tombs in CAMPANIA, ETRURIA (see CERVETERI, TARQUINIA, VULCI) and at SPINA. Alongside these decorated wares were produced the plain wares (see BLACK-GLOSSED). In the HELLENISTIC period Athens continued to export pottery (see MEGARIAN BOWLS, WEST SLOPE WARE).

Athens a Greek city which, as a result of being perceived as a centre of democracy, has received considerable archaeological attention. The main monuments include the local sanctuary on the AKROPOLIS, where there were several different cults. The main one was that of Athena (see PARTHENON). The political and commercial centre, the AGORA, has been excavated by the American School. The German excavations have revealed some of the cemeteries in the KERAMEIKOS. Although many of the monuments relate to the 5th century BC city, there are numerous Roman traces. The emperor Hadrian helped to finish the massive Olympieion (the temple of Olympian Zeus) and had an arch erected to mark the boundary between the City of Theseus and the City of Hadrian. See also ATHENIAN POTTERY.

Athribis (*Arabic* Tell Atrib) an Egyptian site in the central-southern Nile DELTA. Little now remains, or has been recovered archaeologically, of this important ancient Egyptian city. The excavations by Rowe in 1938 and the current work of the Polish Mission have uncovered a good deal of the Graeco-Roman city, but earlier periods at Athribis are only attested archaeologically by objects discovered by SEBBAKH-diggers.

Atkinson, Richard (1920–94) British prehistorian renowned for his excavations at major Neolithic sites in southern England from the 1940s to the 1960s, notably at Dorchester-on-Thames, WAYLAND'S SMITHY, SILBURY HILL and STONEHENGE. He also worked with Stuart PIGGOTT at the WEST KENNET long barrow. Atkinson's most famous excavations were at Stonehenge, where he reported the discovery in 1953 of axe and dagger carvings on some of the SARSENS; he also conducted experiments into the transport of the BLUESTONES to Stonehenge from South Wales.

Atlanthropus a genus used by ARAMBOURG in the 1950s for HOMINID fossils associated with handaxes and flaked pebbles as well as early Middle Pleistocene fauna from TERNIFINE (now Tighenif), and considered to have similarities with East Asian HOMO *erectus*.

Atlantic Bronze Age a regional tradition of the Late Bronze Age represented in western Iberia, western France and the British Isles, best known for its metalwork, including the distinctive CARP'S TONGUE SWORD.

Atlantic climatic period a POSTGLACIAL climatic and vegetational period of temperate Europe between c.7500 and 5000 bp, defined on the basis of POLLEN ANALYSIS by Blytt and Sernander. The Atlantic period is traditionally characterized by warmth and dampness in northern Europe, with mean annual temperatures approximately 2°C warmer than today, the result of polar air circulation having been displaced northwards (compare SUB-BOREAL CLIMATIC PERIOD).

atlatl a particular form of projectile technology, consisting of a throwing stick used as an extension of the arm to propel the pointed dart shaft through the air. The atlatl was introduced to the North American continent at the end of the PALAEOINDIAN period. It is associated with ARCHAIC stage cultures, although EXPERIMENTAL ARCHAEOLOGY has shown the feasibility of firing earlier Palaeoindian points with the atlatl technology. It was superseded by the bow-and-arrow. See also PROJECTILE POINT, SPEARPOINT, SPEARTHROWER.

Atlit drowned sites prehistoric settlements off the MOUNT CARMEL (Israel) coast, now submerged by rising Holocene sea-levels. Underwater excavations at several sites indicate that one, Atlit-Yam, is late PRE-POTTERY NEOLITHIC (PPNC; early 6th millennium BC) and others like Kfar Samir are late ceramic Neolithic (5th millennium) in date. The ANAEROBIC conditions produce excellent preservation of organics. Kfar Samir and other ceramic Neolithic sites contain concentrations of olive pulp and crushed olive stones, alongside the equipment used for processing this fruit, the oldest evidence yet found for olive oil production.

Atlitian an Upper Palaeolithic industry, including blades, scrapers and burins, which has only been found at a few sites in the Levant region. The best-known Atlitian site is EL-WAD.

Atlit-Yam see ATLIT DROWNED SITES.

atomic absorption spectrometry a technique used to determine quantitatively the chemical composition of artifactual metals, minerals and rocks to identify raw material sources, relate artifacts made of the same material, or trace material trade. A dissolved sample of material is atomized in a flame. A cathode lamp made from the element to be analysed is shown through the flame where atoms of the element in the atomized sample absorb light of the same wavelength produced by the lamp in proportion to the concentration of the element in the sample. After passing through the flame, the light intensity is measured with a photomultiplier and compared to the light intensity before passing through the sample to determine the amount of absorption.

atrium an open central court in a Roman or Etruscan house. An IMPLUVIUM may be placed in the centre for rain water.

Attic-Kephala the term proposed by Renfrew for the FINAL NEOLITHIC phase on sites such as ATHENS and THORIKOS in Attica and KEPHALA on Kea.

attribute **1** a characteristic element of a particular culture or group.
2 a specific element of an individual artifact, such as a pottery rim, or projectile point base.

attritional age profile see CATASTROPHIC AGE PROFILE.

Atwater, Caleb (1778–1867) an American antiquary whose essay in 1820 on the mounds of the American Midwest established him as one of the most important pioneers of American archaeology. Atwater meticulously described and measured many mounds around his Ohio home. He argued that they had been made by Hindus who had emigrated to Mexico from India. See also DAVIS, HAVEN, SQUIER, THOMAS.

Aubrey, John (1626–97) a Wiltshire antiquary sometimes called the first English archaeologist, who made the first detailed surveys of surviving field monuments including

STONEHENGE and AVEBURY, which he correctly recognized as places of prehistoric ritual but erroneously attributed to the Druids. In the 1660s Aubrey produced plans and descriptions of Avebury and Stonehenge for Charles II, in the course of his researches discovering the circle of holes within the ditch of Stonehenge now known as the Aubrey Holes.

auger a tool used to collect sediment and soil samples below the ground surface without hand excavation. The operation of an auger is based on rotation of a shaft with a spiral cutting surface. There are different types of augers ranging from economical hand-operated ones to large truck-mounted rigs. The twisting motion of the auger as it penetrates tends to mix samples, making them of limited use for analytical investigations. See also CORE.

aula the entrance hall in a Roman house.

Au Lac the pre-Chinese conquest Vietnamese state in the Red River Valley of the 3rd century BC, once thought to be legendary, but now linked to the DONG SON period in the region. The capital is thought to have been at the site of CO LOA.

Aulnat an Iron Age settlement site in Puy-de-Dôme, France, established in the 3rd century BC, with evidence of industrial activities including the working of gold, silver, bronze, coral, glass, bone and textiles. Gold and silver coins were among the products. Imported Mediterranean luxury goods indicate that this became an important site, but it was abandoned in the 1st century BC soon after the Roman conquest.

Aunjetitz culture see ÚNETICE.

aureus a Roman gold coin. Under Augustus there were forty-two to the Roman pound (327.45 g [11.56 oz]). Compare DENARIUS.

Aurignacian an Upper Palaeolithic industry which developed in the Near East and spread westwards, arriving in Spain by 39,000 bp (see SERIÑA, EL CASTILLO) and by at least 34,000 bp in France (see ABRI PATAUD), where it succeeded the CHÂTELPERRONIAN and preceded the GRAVETTIAN. The tool-kit is characterized by the presence of many burins, and also contains long blades, carinated (steep-ended) scrapers and split-based bone points. The name is derived from the Aurignac rockshelter in the French Pyrenees, first excavated by E. LARTET.

aurochs (*Bos primigenius*) the wild ancestor of domestic cattle, found throughout prehistory in western Eurasia, generally inhabiting open woodland. It had a dark coat, stood up to 1.8 m (6 ft) at the shoulder, and weighed up to one tonne. It became extinct through hunting, and by interbreeding with domesticated cattle, the last individual dying in Poland in AD 1627.

Australia Australia was the only continent occupied solely by hunter-gatherers until the colonial era. Archaeology in Australia was slow to develop. The 1960s and 1970s however saw an explosion of field research and data which both transformed Australian archaeology and had much wider implications. Mulvaney first established Pleistocene occupation at KENNIFF CAVE. By the 1970s, sites such as LAKE MUNGO and DEVIL'S LAIR had pushed occupation back to at least 40,000 bp and beyond. Claims of even greater antiquity, based on LUMINESCENCE rather than RADIOCARBON DATING methods, from sites such as MALAKUNANJA and NAUWALABILA suggest that first colonization may be at least 60,000 bp. What is clear is that early occupation is very widespread from TASMANIA to New Guinea, and even the arid zone was settled about 30,000 years ago.

Australian archaeologists have paid relatively little attention to TYPOLOGY and culture history and rely mainly on RADIOMETRIC DATING methods. Two broad divisions are recognized – the AUSTRALIAN CORE TOOL AND SCRAPER TRADITION and the AUSTRALIAN SMALL TOOL TRADITION – but it is now increasingly clear that these terms mask considerable regional variability. In the 1960s and 1970s, Australian archaeology was strongly influenced by ecological approaches and there was great emphasis on human interaction with the environment. Perennial debates about the role of fire in shaping the Australian landscape (see FIRESTICK FARMING) and the relationship between Aborigines and MEGAFAUNA reflect these influences, as does research on the long history of land management in the NEW GUINEA HIGHLANDS. In the 1980s and 1990s, much debate has focused on 'intensification' and the role of social factors in creating the social and economic complexity observed in indigenous societies at the time of European colonization.

Australian archaeologists have always drawn heavily

The 'Walls of China', Lake Mungo, AUSTRALIA.

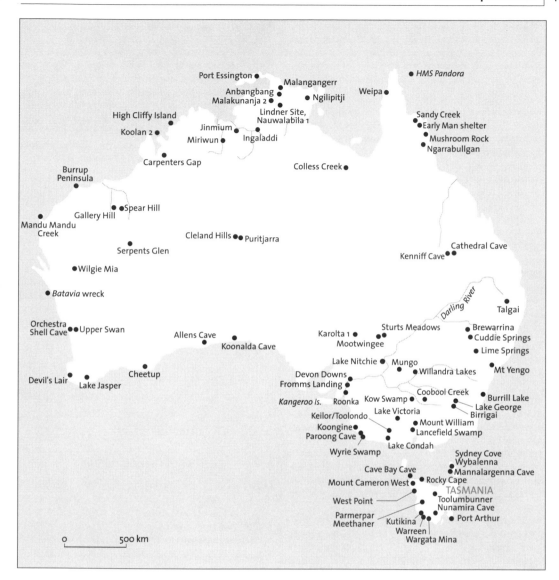

Port Essington ●
Malangangerr ●
Anbangbang ●
Malakunanja 2 ● ● Ngilipitji
Weipa ●
● HMS Pandora
Lindner Site, ●
Nauwalabila 1
High Cliffy Island ●
Jinmium ●
Koolan 2 ●
Miriwun ● ● Ingaladdi
Sandy Creek ●
● Early Man shelter
● Mushroom Rock
Ngarrabullgan ●
Carpenters Gap ●
Colless Creek ●
Burrup ●
Peninsula
Mandu Mandu ●
Creek
Gallery Hill ● ● Spear Hill
Cleland Hills ● ● Puritjarra
Cathedral Cave ●
Kenniff Cave ● ●
Serpents Glen ●
Wilgie Mia ●
Batavia wreck ●
Darling River
Talgai ●
Orchestra ● ● Upper Swan
Shell Cave
Allens Cave ●
Koonalda Cave ●
Karolta 1 ●
Mootwingee ●
Sturts Meadows ●
Brewarrina ●
Cuddie Springs ●
Lime Springs ●
Lake Nitchie ● ● Mungo
Devil's Lair ●
Lake Jasper ●
Cheetup ●
Devon Downs ●
Fromms Landing ●
Kangeroo Is.
Roonka ●
Kow Swamp ● ●
Lake Victoria ●
Keilor/Toolondo ●
Koongine ●
Paroong Cave ●
Lake Condah ●
Wyrie Swamp ●
Willandra Lakes ●
Mt Yengo ●
Coobool Creek ●
Burrill Lake ●
Lake George ●
Birrigai ●
Mount William ●
Lancefield Swamp ●
Sydney Cove ●
Wybalenna ●
Mannalargenna Cave ●
Cave Bay Cave ●
Mount Cameron West ●
● Rocky Cape
TASMANIA
Toolumbunner ●
Nunamira Cave ●
West Point ●
Parmerpar ●
Meethaner
Kutikina ●
Warreen ●
Wargata Mina ●
Port Arthur ●

0   500 km

on the rich ethnohistorical and ethnographic record. AUSTRALIAN ABORIGINES are now challenging the role archaeologists have played in the appropriation of their past. The development of Australian archaeology has occurred at the same time as Aborigines have become increasingly politically assertive. It is now usual for archaeologists to consult and involve indigenous communities in archaeological research and the Australian Archaeological Association has developed a code of ethics acknowledging Aboriginal ownership of their cultural heritage.

Australian Aborigines indigenous inhabitants of Australia. Many Indigenous Australians reject the term Abori-

gine and prefer to use tribal names or a regional name. Koori is an example of such a regional name; others include Murri, Nyungar and Nunga. Torres Strait Islanders also insist on their distinctive identity.

Australian Core Tool and Scraper tradition a Late Pleistocene and early Holocene stone artifact industry first defined at LAKE MUNGO by Rhys Jones and Harry Allen and characterized by chopping tools, horsehoof cores and steep-edged flake scrapers. All earlier attempts at classification of Pleistocene Australian assemblages were subsumed into the pan-continental Australian Core Tool and Scraper tradition, and terms such as Tartangan, GAMBIERAN and KARTAN largely fell out of use.

However, it is now increasingly clear that many Pleistocene assemblages do not fit the original characterization. The core tools are now usually considered cores. Large tools also occur in many recent sites. The concept is long overdue for revision, but no alternative scheme has been proposed.

Australian Small Tool tradition a term applied to mid-to-late Holocene stone artifact assemblages on the Australian mainland, but absent from TASMANIA. The Small Tool tradition dates from about 5,000 years ago and comprises a number of elements including a range of hafted tools such as BONDI POINTS, geometric MICRO-LITHS, TULAS, ELOUERAS, and unifacial and bifacial points, as well as blade technology. The distribution of these types varies in space and time. All except bondi points and geometric microliths were in use at the time of European contact. Like the AUSTRALIAN CORE TOOL AND SCRAPER TRADITION, the concept is overdue for revision. It certainly does not constitute a cohesive tradition: its elements do not appear together in the archaeological record, and their distributions are different. 'Australian Small Tool Phase' has recently been proposed as an alternative.

Australopithecus a genus of small-brained, bipedal, fossil HOMINID, known from sites in a belt stretching from East to southern Africa, as well as a single site in Chad (BAHR EL GHAZAL), of which some species are considered ancestral to humans (but see KENYANTHROPUS, OR-RORIN). Although hominid fragments from LOTHAGAM in northern Kenya dating between 6 and 5 million years ago may be australopithecine, the most ancient australopithecine currently identified is *A. anamensis*, known from 4.2–3.9 million-year-old deposits in East Africa. The best represented australopithecine is *A. afarensis* (see HADAR, LAETOLI, 'LUCY' – also sometimes assigned the generic name *Praeanthropus*), known from 4–3 million-year-old deposits in East Africa. *A. bahrelghazali*, from 3.5–3 million-year-old deposits in Chad, is considered to have similarities to *A. afarensis*, while *A. garhi*, represented by 2.5 million-year-old fossils from Ethiopia, is considered a descendant of *A. afarensis*. *A. africanus* (see DART, TAUNG) is best known from 3–2 million-year-old deposits at STERKFONTEIN and MAKAPANSGAT in South Africa. *A. afarensis* and *A. africanus* are sometimes called 'gracile' australopithecines because they were small and lightly built. Although details of the structure of the hominid family tree are widely debated among palaeoanthropologists, the gracile australopithecines are commonly regarded as direct ancestors of the human genus HOMO (but see *Kenyanthropus, Orrorin*).

More massive 'robust' australopithecines first appear later in time than the gracile species. They include 2.7–1.9 million-year-old *A. aethiopicus* and 2.3–1.4 million-year-old *A.* or *Paranthropus boisei* (see OLDUVAI, ZINJANTHROPUS) from East Africa as well as 1.9–1

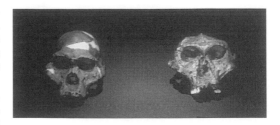

Australopithecine skulls – an AUSTRALOPITHECUS *africanus* from Sterkfontein (left) and an *A.* or *Paranthropus robustus* from Swartkrans (right).

million-year-old *A. robustus/Paranthropus* from South Africa (see KROMDRAAI, SWARTKRANS). These species overlap in time with early *Homo* and are generally not considered ancestral to later species of *Homo*.

Australopithecines were probably dark-skinned, hairy creatures. Males are estimated to have weighed 40–50 kg (88–110 lbs) and to have stood some 1.3–1.5 m (4 ft 3 inches–4 ft 11 inches) tall, while females are considered to have weighed only about 27–35 kg (60–77 lbs) and to have stood about 1 m (3 ft 4 inches) tall. Although australopithecine brain capacity was, on average, about 500 cc (30 cu. inches) or less (early *Homo* brains are larger than 600 cc [36 cu. inches]), there is speculation that australopithecines may have learnt to make stone tools: studies of australopithecine hand bones suggest they had the necessary co-ordination, while the earliest known stone tools (dated to between 2.6 and 2.5 million years ago at GONA in Ethiopia) pre-date the earliest known *Homo* fossils.

Austria see EUROPE, CENTRAL.

Austronesian the major language family spoken throughout island Southeast Asia, MELANESIA (except for most of Papua New Guinea), MICRONESIA and POLYNESIA. Austronesian speakers are commonly thought to have spread from Southeast Asia about 6,000 years ago, and LAPITA is regarded as the archaeological signature of their expansion into the Pacific.

Auvernier a lake dwelling on the northern edge of Lake Neuchâtel, Switzerland, with Neolithic and Late Bronze Age occupation. The Neolithic levels include early Neolithic CORTAILLOD, middle Neolithic HORGEN and late Neolithic CORDED WARE material. The rich Late Bronze Age material belongs to the HALLSTATT A2–B phase, c.1100–750 BC, and includes the remains of a metal workshop.

Avaris the capital of the HYKSOS in Egypt, possibly to be identified with the site of TELL ED-DABA.

Avars a nomadic people originally from the Caucasus who began to attack settlements along the Black Sea around AD 550 and subsequently moved further into

Central Europe, settling in the middle Danube region in the former Roman province of PANNONIA. Metal belt buckles decorated with animal motifs found in graves reflect the eastern origins of the Avars and are their most distinctive archaeological signature.

Avdeevo an Upper Palaeolithic open-air site on the Rogozna River (Sejm tributary) near Kursk in European Russia. The single occupation horizon is buried in ALLU-VIUM of the first terrace, and has yielded radiocarbon dates ranging between 11,950 and 22,700 bp. Woolly mammoth dominates the large faunal assemblage. A complex arrangement of pits and hearths appears to reflect the presence of several former structures. The artifacts, which include shouldered points and animal and 'VENUS' FIGURINES, are assigned to the KOSTENKI-WILLENDORF CULTURE or EASTERN GRAVETTIAN. Avdeevo was excavated in 1946–9 by Gvozdover, Voevodskij and ROGACHEV; investigations were resumed by Gvozdover in the 1970s.

Avebury a major Neolithic ritual complex in Wiltshire, England, comprising: a) the WEST KENNET long barrow c.3600 BC; b) the WINDMILL HILL CAUSEWAYED CAMP of approximately the same date; c) the Avebury HENGE monument, dated c.2900–2600 BC, over 400 m (440 yds) in diameter, surrounded by a deep ditch with outer bank and a setting of stones along its inner edge. Further stone settings stand within the monument, and an avenue of paired stones – the West Kennet Avenue – leads to the smaller circle known as the Sanctuary (a second western avenue – the Beckhampton Avenue – recorded in the 18th century has recently been rediscovered); d) SILBURY HILL, the largest prehistoric mound in western Europe, c.2600 BC. Recent investigations have revealed further earth and timber enclosures dating from the end of the Neolithic period (c.2300–2200 BC) at West Kennet Farm, and the Avebury area also has several Bronze Age barrow cemeteries, demonstrating its continued importance in the post-Neolithic period.

Avebury, John Lubbock, Lord (1834–1913) an English antiquary and author of *Prehistoric Times* (1865), which advanced archaeology as the 'link between geology and history' and helped bring it to the reading public. Avebury, in this book, was the first to use the terms Palaeolithic and Neolithic.

Aveline's Hole a cave-site in the Mendip Hills, Somerset, England, which has yielded a CRESWELLIAN EPIPALAEO-LITHIC industry and a MAGDALENIAN-style harpoon.

Aven des Iboussières a rich EPIPALEOLITHIC cave-site in the Drôme region of southeastern France, containing a multiple burial in a small chamber, with an AMS date of 10,210 BP. It has yielded 197 perforated and often decorated red deer canines, and thirty different types of grave-goods, including engraved bone and stone pendants,

notched hedgehog and rabbit mandibles, engraved scapulae, different species of marine shells including 1,112 *Dentalia*, and other faunal and lithic remains. These were associated with eight individuals (four adults, three juveniles and a new-born infant).

Awdaghast, Awdaghust or **Tegdaoust** a trading centre in Mali at the southern end of a trans-Saharan camel caravan route, with occupation from at least the 7th century AD, and later controlled by the ancient West African kingdom of GHANA.

awl a piercing implement made of bone, antler, wood, metal or stone, often found in prehistoric tool-kits.

axe factory site where outcrops of fine-grained rock were exploited, especially in the European Neolithic, as sources of stone for polished axes. PETROLOGICAL ANALYSIS of THIN SECTIONS can pinpoint the source, since each kind of rock has a distinctive crystalline structure, and studies of the distribution of different axe-types thus delineate the trading networks that were in operation.

axial-chambered tomb see SEVERN-COTSWOLD.

Axum the capital of an Ethiopian kingdom of the 1st to 7th centuries AD. Sporadically excavated since 1906, the most impressive monuments at the site are monolithic granite grave-markers, roughly dressed or elaborately carved, the largest being over 30 m (98 ft) tall.

Ayia Irini a site on the CYCLADIC island of Kea in the Aegean which was excavated by CASKEY in 1960–76. The site, on a promontory, appears to have been occupied more or less continuously throughout the Bronze Age. In the 2nd millennium BC Ayia Irini was a fortified town and maintained close links with MINOAN CRETE. Among the most remarkable finds were the large, in some cases almost life-size, female terracotta figures from the Temple.

Ayia Triadha the site of a MINOAN town on the island of CRETE, built around a magnificent Neopalatial villa. The sophisticated design and opulent decoration of the villa and the presence of an archive of LINEAR A tablets have led to the suggestion that Ayia Triadha may have superseded PHAISTOS as the administrative centre of southern Crete.

Ayios Epiktitos-Vrysi the site of a Neolithic II (later 5th millennium BC) settlement in northern CYPRUS, which was excavated by Peltenburg in 1969–73. A perimeter wall and ditch protected the settlement which consisted of semi-subterranean houses built of stone and PISÉ.

Aylesford an Iron Age cemetery in Kent, England, discovered by Sir Arthur EVANS in 1890 and associated with the BELGIC peoples of southern England encountered by the Romans. Together with the major cemetery of

Swarling (discovered in 1924), Aylesford became the type-site of the late Iron Age Aylesford-Swarling culture dated to between 75 BC and the Roman conquest of AD 43. The characteristic burial rite is cremation, sometimes in an elaborate bronze-bound bucket, within a flat grave, associated with wheel-turned pottery and, in richer examples, imported Roman wine AMPHORAS.

Aynan see EYNAN.

Ayub an urn-burial cave near Maitum, South Cotabato Province, Philippines, excavated 1991–5 and dated to the early centuries AD. Each of the anthropomorphous covers of the urns appears to represent a distinct individual; some are painted in red and black, and many had rows of small holes on the head to insert hair, now decayed.

Azelik a town in Niger, Africa, with evidence of copper smelting by the middle of the 1st millennium BC or perhaps earlier (see AFUNFUN). Like AKJOUJT, this provides evidence of a brief 'Copper Age' in this part of Africa before the adoption of iron. Azelik also has early evidence of iron technology dated to 2490 BP.

Azilian the final Palaeolithic/initial Mesolithic industry of southwestern Europe, first identified by PIETTE in 1887 at LE MAS D'AZIL where it filled the hiatus between the Palaeolithic and the Neolithic. It comprises microlithic tools, notably the Azilian point (a double-pointed backed blade), flat perforated and barbed harpoons of red deer antler, and small schist pebbles bearing red dots or stripes: the pebbles are known from France, northern Spain, Italy and Switzerland, but Le Mas d'Azil itself yielded over 1,000 harpoons and more than 75 per cent of the c.2,000 pebbles known. Dates for the Azilian fall primarily between 9000 and 8000 bc.

Azmak a Neolithic TELL site located near Stara Zagora in southern-central Bulgaria. The early Neolithic levels at Azmak are contemporaneous with those at KARANOVO I and have provided important evidence on subsistence and settlement layout. Later levels of the 8 m-high (26 ft) mound correspond to Karanovo V and VI and belong to the GUMELNIŢA culture. The Karanovo VI layer at Azmak contained two large multi-roomed structures.

Aztec *adj.* relating to the last great native MESOAMERICAn empire, defeated by CORTÉS in 1521. The Aztecs were originally a group of CHICHIMECS who moved east and south into the VALLEY OF MEXICO. They eventually settled at the site of TENOCHTITLÁN, having been given a sign by their tribal deity. The Aztecs are a fierce tribe who gained dominance in the area through their warring and political alliances (see also TRIPLE ALLIANCE), ultimately expanding their empire throughout much of Mesoamerica. The Aztecs had a complicated system of trade and redistribution that extended throughout Mesoamerica and beyond its frontiers (see POCHTECA). The city of Tenochtitlán and the Valley of Mexico were supported by this system of trade, tribute, and intensive agricultural production within the valley itself.

Azykh Cave a Palaeolithic site in Azerbajdzhan. The cave is situated at an elevation of 800 m (2,624 ft) in the Lesser Caucasus Mountains. The lower levels (X–VII) reportedly contain a pebble-tool industry without parallel in the region, associated with some isolated faunal remains; its age is unknown. Above these layers rest two levels (VI–V) containing assemblages with large bifaces and side-scrapers assigned to the ACHEULIAN and associated with Middle Pleistocene fauna (e.g. *Bison schoetensacki*). A level (III) containing a Middle Palaeolithic assemblage (dominated by sidescrapers) and remains of Merck's rhinoceros, cave bear and others overlies the Lower Palaeolithic industries; it is thought to date to the Late Pleistocene. Azykh Cave was discovered and investigated by Gusejnov during 1960–73.

B

Ba [Pa] see ZHOU, DIAN.

Baal the most important male deity of the CANAANITES, identified by the HYKSOS with the Egyptian deity SETH.

Baalbek (*Gk* Heliopolis) an important Roman religious centre in modern Lebanon. A major building was the monumental temple of Jupiter-Hadad.

Babadan A a Palaeolithic site in Miyagi Prefecture, Japan, with lithics, including choppers, dated between 50,000 and 70,000 bp. Unlike at SOZUDAI, the tools are of convincing human manufacture, giving support to the existence of an Early Palaeolithic in Japan.

Babylon the ancient capital of MESOPOTAMIA, and perhaps the most famous archaeological site in Iraq. Babylon was periodically the political centre of southern Mesopotamia, especially during OLD BABYLONIAN and NEO-BABYLONIAN times, when it was the seat of empires created by HAMMURABI and NEBUCHADNEZZAR respectively. At other times during the 2nd and 1st millennia, the city remained the focus of population and of traditional political feelings in southern Mesopotamia, and served as the regional capital of invading empires (NEO-ASSYRIAN, ACHAEMENID; Alexander the Great died in the city). The site was inhabited at least by the

EARLY DYNASTIC III and continued in use until medieval times. KOLDEWEY's work at the turn of the century, and that of others more recently, focused on the 1st millennium BC city, which covered some 850 ha (3 sq. miles) and contained such famous monuments as the ISHTAR Gate, the ziggurat Etemenanki (the 'tower of Babel'), and the palace of Nebuchadnezzar (which contains a structure Koldewey identified as the 'hanging gardens'). Earlier occupation has been uncovered only in the 'Merkes' section of the city, where excavation reached an Old Babylonian residential district beneath KASSITE period levels. See also SEVEN WONDERS.

Babylonia the region comprising the whole of the southern ALLUVIUM of MESOPOTAMIA from the ascendancy of HAMMURABI early in the 2nd millennium BC. It was roughly equivalent to the 3rd millennium designations SUMER and AKKAD combined. Although the name derives from the city of BABYLON, the region was not necessarily integrated and ruled from that centre, as this was a relatively infrequent circumstance (occurring notably under Hammurabi himself, and under the NEO-BABYLONIAN dynasty of NEBUCHADNEZZAR II).

Bacho Kiro a Palaeolithic cave-site located in the Balkan Mountains of central Bulgaria. Artifacts and faunal remains (e.g. horse, aurochs, cave bear) are buried in clay and rubble deposits. The two lowest layers contain Middle Palaeolithic tools (primarily sidescrapers), and are stratigraphically correlated with the end of the early GLACIAL and the early cold LAST GLACIAL MAXIMUM. Overlying layers contain early Upper Palaeolithic artifacts (e.g. endscrapers, retouched blades) dated to an early INTERSTADIAL of the last glacial (radiocarbon date of 43,000 bp), which represent the oldest Upper Palaeolithic industry ('Bachokirian') in Europe. AURIGNACIAN assemblages occur in the upper levels. Bacho Kiro was excavated by GARROD in the 1930s, and Kozlowski and others in the 1970s.

backed blade a blade with one long edge deliberately blunted by steep retouch. Some smaller backed blades and backed bladelets may have been used as arrow tips;

BABYLON: glazed frieze of a bull from the Ishtar Gate.

others were apparently used as knives. Backed blades are frequently encountered in GRAVETTIAN assemblages.

Bacsonian a term characterizing a stone industry, dating to *c*.8000–2500 BC, found in a series of cave-sites on the northern fringe of the Red River Valley in northern Vietnam, related to the HOABINHIAN, developing EDGE-GRINDING in later phases, when pottery was also in use. The type-site of the industry is Bac Son.

Bactrian Bronze Age a culture, initially identified from materials looted from graves in northwestern Afghanistan and sold on the antiquities market, that produced a range of materials (pottery, seals and other metal work, ornamented stone vessels, stone statuettes and other materials). Similar materials appear in the Murghab delta (ancient Margiana) of eastern Turkmenistan, giving rise to the name Bactrian-Margiana Archaeological complex (BMAC). Excavations at sites like DASHLY and SAPALLI-DEPE in Bactria and at GONUR-DEPE in Margiana date this culture to the end of the 3rd millennium and first third of the 2nd millennium BC. Bactrian-style artifacts are strongly represented in Baluchistan and the margins of the Indus (SIBRI), and also appear across the Iranian plateau as far west as SUSA.

Badarian the earliest phase of the PREDYNASTIC sequence of UPPER EGYPT, dating to *c*.5000–4500 BC. The Badarians probably practised a semisedentary economy; their most technologically accomplished product is a polished thin-walled pottery. A small number of copper objects, possibly imports, are found at Badarian sites.

Baden culture an ENEOLITHIC culture of eastern Central Europe, centred on Hungary and Slovakia but also reaching into the northern Balkans and southern Poland. The Baden culture is also frequently referred to as the Radial-Decorated Pottery culture, on the basis of the incised lines on its vessels which radiate upwards from the base. The chronology of the Baden culture is divided into three phases. The early phase (*c*.3400–2900 BC) is essentially equivalent to the Boleráz group of the Hungarian Plain, while the 'classic' and late phases (*c*.2900–2500 BC) saw the broader distribution of this culture. Baden settlements are generally dispersed sites with relatively thin deposits, which contrast with the stratified sites that characterize the preceding cultures of southeastern Europe. The appearance of evidence for wheeled vehicles, such as the wagon model from BUDAKALASZ, cups and vessels presumably associated with milk handling, large numbers of spindle whorls, and the shift to a dispersed settlement pattern are viewed as elements of the SECONDARY PRODUCTS REVOLUTION.

Bader, Otto Nikolaevich (1903–80) a Soviet archaeologist who investigated sites of many periods ranging from the Palaeolithic to the Iron Age in many regions of the USSR – in Crimea, the Urals, and the basins of the Volga and Oka Rivers. He created a first periodization of MOUSTERIAN sites for Crimea, and discovered a big group of Palaeolithic caves in the Urals. He is best known for his excavations at the Palaeolithic site of SUNGIR' and for the investigation of Palaeolithic parietal art in KAPOVA. He was also one of the pioneers of investigation of the Mesolithic in the USSR. Moreover, he discovered some cultures of the Bronze Age, studied the ancient metallurgy of copper and bronze, and made a specially important contribution to the problem of SEIMA-TURBINO BRONZES.

Bahrain tumulus fields dense fields of tumuli in Bahrain and at several places on the adjacent Saudi mainland that are constructed as single or multi-room chambers over which desert soils are heaped. The initial construction and use of these monuments belong to the Bronze Age BARBAR CULTURE, though many were reused at later times. Also associated with these tumulus fields are dense complexes of cist burials.

Bahr el Ghazal a region near Koro Toro in northern Chad where site KT 12 in 1993 yielded an australopithecine mandible similar in morphology to AUSTRALOPITHECUS *afarensis*, ascribed to *A. bahrelghazali* in 1996, associated with faunal remains estimated to date to between 3.5 and 3 million years ago. The mandible extends the known distribution of australopithecines outside eastern and southern Africa. The specimen has been nicknamed 'Abel'.

Băile Herculane a rockshelter site in southwestern Romania with early Mesolithic occupation levels which have provided information on the surrounding vegetation (Alpine forest-steppe, with juniper and willow predominant), subsistence (forest, steppe and riverine species) and the chipped stone industry (small blunted blades, denticulated blades and scrapers). In addition, there is a later occupation of the ENEOLITHIC SALCUŢA and COŢOFENI cultures.

Baite a group of sanctuaries (Baite I–III) on the desert plateau of Ustyurt in western Kazakhstan. The sanctuaries comprise KURGANs, ringed pavements, stone sacrificial places and the debris of over 100 broken stone statues (see also KAMENNAYA BABA). The statues depict a standing man with his right hand on his belly and his left hand at his side. On his belt, weapons are depicted: a sword, a dagger and a bow in a GORYTOS. The statues also display details such as a head-dress or hairstyle, bracelets or other adornments. The sanctuaries are attributable to SCYTHIAN or SARMATIAN tribes. Excavations are being carried out by the Russian archaeologists V. Olkhovsky and L. Galkin.

Baker's Hole, Northfleet an English Lower Palaeolithic working site in Kent which appears to have been a factory specializing in the production of large LEVALLOIS flakes.

Unfortunately the site was destroyed by quarrying before it could be properly excavated.

baktun a unit in the CLASSIC MAYA LONG COUNT, equalling 144,000 days, or about 400 years. See also TUN.

Bakun Tal-i a pair of prehistoric mounds (Bakun A and B) near PERSEPOLIS in Fars (southwestern Iran) that together span the 5th and the first half of the 4th millennium BC. Investigated by E. Herzfeld in 1928, an American group in the 1930s, and again by a Japanese team in 1956, the site presents dense village architecture and a sequence of painted pottery styles related to those of early SUSA. Several early 4th millennium BC buildings in Bakun A contained numerous sealings, including door lock sealings, indicating a concern for monitoring property.

Balakot a coastal site west of Karachi in Pakistan, where the excavations of George Dales revealed a settlement of the 4th millennium BC beneath Mature HARAPPAN levels. During the earlier period, the Balakotian ceramic connections are northwards into Baluchistan and have little connection with later developments at the site. The two periods of occupation contrast in subsistence patterns, with a Balakotian focus on cattle and a Harappan focus on sheep/goats and on maritime resources including a shell bangle workshop.

Balawat a 60 ha (148 acre) walled town with a 3 ha (7.4 acre) citadel near the Upper Zab River east of Mosul, northern Iraq, the ASSYRIAN town Imgur-Enlil, refounded by the king AŠŠURNAṢIRPAL II (883–859 BC) as a 'country retreat'. The work (by tunnelling) of H. Rassam in the 1880s recovered the objects for which the place is best known, the two Balawat bronze doors (actually bronze REPOUSSÉ strips covering wood), which narrate and illustrate campaigns of Aššurnaṣirpal II and of his successor Shalmaneser III (858–824 BC). MALLOWAN's brief work here in the 1950s focused on the Temple of Mamu, and recovered a third bronze door. Although certainly the best known and the most complete, the Balawat doors represent a common NEO-ASSYRIAN decorative practice, traces of which have been observed in most excavated Assyrian cities.

Ballana and Qustul two cemeteries on opposite sides of the Nile in LOWER NUBIA, excavated by EMERY and Kirwan 1931–4. The large tumuli contained the royal burials (including small numbers of sacrificed retainers) of the X-GROUP.

Ballana culture see X-GROUP.

Ballawinne see WARGATA MINA.

ball court see BALL GAME.

ball game a game played in MESOAMERICA with a rubber ball, possibly with a wooden core. While there is a certain amount of variation in the game throughout Mesoamerica, *ball courts* are a major functional class of formal architecture at Mesoamerican centres. There are historical accounts of the ball game from the time of the Spanish conquest, and the game appears to have originated during OLMEC times. The ball game served religious, political and recreational functions; for the MAYA it was a means of ritual communication between mortal and supernatural planes, and of enacting rituals of sacrifice and fertility. See also HOHOKAM.

Balma de Montbolo see MONTBOLO.

balneum a small Roman bath-house perhaps attached to a private house. Compare THERMAE.

Balof a limestone sinkhole on New Ireland in the BISMARCK ARCHIPELAGO, MELANESIA. Two shelters have been excavated, with basal dates of *c.*7000 bp at Balof 1 and *c.*14,000 bp at Balof 2. In the lower levels of both sites, obsidian from TALASEA occurs. Obsidian from LOU ISLAND appears about 3000 bp.

Bambandyanalo a rocky hill which forms the eastern boundary of the K2 site in the Northern Province, South Africa. It has given its name to a FACIES of Phase A of the southern branch of the LEOPARD'S KOPJE tradition of the southern African Iron Age, which dates to the 11th–12th centuries AD. The name is sometimes applied to the K2 site.

Bambata **1** a cave in the Matobo Hills of southwestern Zimbabwe, containing a long stratified sequence spanning the Upper Pleistocene and Holocene, as well as interesting rock paintings.

2 thin-walled, elaborately stamped pottery from the upper levels of cave and rockshelter sites in southwestern Zimbabwe, where it is sometimes referred to as Gwanda pottery; similar ware is also known from sites in Botswana, Namibia and South Africa, associated with dates from the 2nd century BC to the 9th century AD. Some researchers suggest that it is the consequence of Stone Age people imitating contemporary Iron Age pottery, while others consider that it is an Early Iron Age ware.

3 a MIDDLE STONE AGE industry of Zimbabwe and southern Zambia dating to at least 45,000–30,000 BP, characterized by unifacial points, scrapers and occasional bifacial points, as well as horizons containing small blades.

Bamiyan a highland valley in the Hindu Kush of Afghanistan, known for its long complex of Buddhist monasteries cut into a cliff face. Interior wall paintings of Buddhist themes combine Indian and Iranian stylistic elements. Outside, two images of the Buddha are carved into the cliff face, one standing over 50 m (164 ft) high. The complex dates to the first half of the 1st millennium BC.

Banawali a large prehistoric site in Haryana (northern

India), where excavations in the 1970s revealed three periods of occupation that span roughly the millennium between 2500 and 1500 BC. The earliest settlement contains pottery similar to that at KALIBANGAN during the Early HARAPPAN period. The second period is Mature Harappan in character, as shown by its typical urban form (two separately walled areas, with residential blocks on regular streets), pottery and small finds, though echoes of the Early Harappan pottery are still present. In the third period, the pottery is comparable to the Late Harappan wares of the eastern Punjab that are variously called Bara ware, Late Siswal ware or OCHRE COLOURED POTTERY.

Ban Chiang a World Heritage site, a prehistoric settlement in the Songkhram Valley, northern KHORAT, Thailand, occupied from the mid 3rd millennium BC to AD 300, a period spanning the transitions from the Neolithic to the use of bronze and then iron. Earlier claims for very early bronze manufacture c.3000 BC and iron about 1400 BC are now discounted. The site has been subjected to extensive looting and most 'Ban Chiang' objects in museums and collections around the world are of doubtful provenance. Nevertheless, many graves were richly furnished with bronze tools and ornaments and, towards the end of the settlement's history, with bi-metallic and iron weapons, glass ornaments and elaborately painted red-on-buff ware. Clay rollers found only in children's graves may have been used for printing textiles, many fragments of which (mainly hemp) are found embedded in metal corrosion.

Ban Chiang Hian a 38 ha (94 acre) moated mound (see MOATED SITES) in the middle Chi Valley, KHORAT, Thailand, occupied from the late 2nd millennium BC to the mid 1st millennium AD. As at BAN CHIANG, iron appears about 500 BC together with domesticated water buffalo, probably marking the beginning of intensive wet rice cultivation and increased inter-community conflicts.

band a type of social organization. It is most often associated with hunter-gatherers, and comprises small groups of people, with little or no social ranking, and a sexual division of labour. See also TRIBE, CHIEFDOM, STATE.

Bandkeramik see LINEAR POTTERY CULTURE.

Ban Don Phlong an Iron Age settlement in the eastern Mun Valley, northeastern Thailand, excavated in the 1990s, with seventeen smelting iron furnaces of the late 1st millennium BC overlying burials rich in bronze grave-goods.

Ban Don Ta Phet a late prehistoric burial site near U THONG, western-central Thailand, c.390–360 BC, which provides evidence for long-range trade linking sea and land routes. Grave furnishings included etched stone and other beads from India, a two-headed nephrite pendant from southern Vietnam, and a bronze SITULA probably from northern Vietnam (see DONG-SON). Local goods include iron tools distantly related to those of the Malay Peninsula, and high-tin cast bronze bowls with incised decorations. Similar bowls have been found in peninsular Malaysia and as far west as TAXILA in Pakistan.

Bandung microliths a mid Holocene obsidian industry of the Bandung Plateau, western Java, characterized by small backed flakes and other tools broadly similar to those of the TOALIAN in Sulawesi and the obsidians from TIANKO PANJANG and KERINCI in Sumatra.

Ban Kao a pair of sites (the Bang and Lue sites) in western-central Thailand on a tributary of the Khwae Noi, which served as occupation and burial sites, and which have yielded large numbers of polished stone adzes and a mass of pottery, including tripod pottery common to a number of sites in peninsular Thailand and Malaysia. No bronze was found, although corrected radiocarbon dates place the site in the middle of the 2nd millennium BC, when bronze was in regular use in parts of Thailand east of the Chao Phraya River. Caves at Ban Kao include Heap, Ment and Khao Thalu which together show a transition from HOABINHIAN hunting traditions to settled village agriculture.

Ban Koi Noi site of many stoneware kilns of the 10th–15th centuries AD near SI SATCHANALAI, on the Yom River, northern-central Thailand.

Red-on-buff ware pot from BAN CHIANG, Thailand.

Ban Lum Khao a large Bronze Age (*c*.1400–500 BC) mound, 5 km (3 miles) west of BAN PRASAT, with settlement debris and over 111 burials, excavated in 1995–6. The early settlement seems to mark the beginning of settled life in this part of the KHORAT Plateau. Fish, some of them enormous compared with modern specimens, together with shellfish were an important part of the diet. Pigs, dogs and cattle were raised, and water buffalo appear towards the end of the sequence.

Ban Nadi a small prehistoric settlement located about 30 km (19 miles) south of BAN CHIANG, in KHORAT, Thailand, occupied from *c*.1500 BC to *c*.AD 200–300. After 500 BC the settlement was the site of a local centre of tin-bronze production and trade, specializing in jewellery, axes and projectile points. From *c*.100 BC to AD 200 iron was also smelted and forged, to produce hoes, knives, spearheads and bangles. The site's bronze workshop (with clay furnaces) began to cast lead-bronze bells, bowls and bracelets at this time.

banner stone a ground and polished stone artifact that may have served either as an ATLATL weight or as a ceremonial object. The term is most often used in the American Midwest and East.

Ban Pa Yang site of many stoneware kilns of the 10th–15th centuries AD near SI SATCHANALAI, on the Yom River, northern-central Thailand.

Ban Phak Top a Neolithic site of the mid to late 3rd millennium BC near BAN CHIANG in the Sakon Nakhon basin, northeastern Thailand. It has been badly looted by villagers, and much of the fine black incised and carinated pottery in the world's museums said to come from Ban Chiang probably comes from this site.

Banpo [Pan-p'o] a Neolithic village site, dating to 3000–4000 BC, near Xian City, China. Excavated 1954–7 by the Institute of Archaeology, it became the type-site for the YANGSHAO phase of the early Neolithic in the central loess highlands. The site covers 5–6 ha (12–15 acres), including pit-houses and storage pits enclosed by a deep village ditch, examples of which are now openly exposed to view as a site museum. Kilns and cemetery remains occurred outside the ditched area, and remains of millet, pig and dog show it was part of the northern agricultural regime (see CISHAN).

Ban Prasat a late Bronze–Iron Age settlement and cemetery on the Prasat River, a tributary of the Mun, in northeastern Thailand. An exceptionally rich cemetery, dating from *c*.800 BC at about 5 m (16 ft) below the surface, was excavated in 1991. Highly burnished red pottery with a trumpet-shaped mouth is typical, and one interment contained fifty such pots. Iron appears late in the sequence.

Banshan [Pan-shan] one of five Neolithic cemeteries in the Banshan Hills of Gansu Province, China. ANDERSSON, the alleged discoverer of the Chinese Neolithic, obtained many splendid painted burial jars from here in the early 1920s and removed them to Sweden.

Ban Tamyae a settlement mound near PHIMAI on the upper Mun River of the KHORAT Plateau, northeastern Thailand, with a long occupation from *c*.1000 BC to AD 600.

Banteay Srei a small Sivite temple, 25 km (16 miles) northeast of ANGKOR, Cambodia, built in the late 10th century AD under Rajendravarman II, that is famed for its exquisite decorative carving in pink sandstone.

Ban Tha Kae a walled and moated mound (see MOATED SITES), northeast of LOPBURI in the Chao Phraya Valley, central Thailand, near the copper sources of Khao Wong Prachan and the copper-processing site of NON PA WAI. Occupation runs from the late Neolithic of the 2nd millennium BC to the early historic Buddhist DVARA-VATI civilization of the 1st millennium AD. The site has been extensively looted.

Bantu a group of languages within the Niger-Congo language family, traditionally spoken by black people in much of southern and Central Africa. The spread of the Iron Age through Central, eastern and southern Africa is generally linked to migrations of Bantu-speaking people, although some researchers suggest that the migrations may have begun before the Iron Age.

Ban Wang Hi an Iron Age settlement with burials in Uthai Thani Province, northern Thailand, furnished with carnelian and glass beads, some from India, bronze ornaments and iron tools. One burial had a large iron sword by the left hand, a find unique in Southeast Asia.

Banwaroids a prehistoric group of Indian hunter-gatherers who occupied the ANTILLES from *c*.3000 BC, originating on the coast of Venezuela, and named after the site of Banwari-Trace on the island of Trinidad. By 2500 BC they had reached Puerto Rico, Santo Domingo and Cuba. Their artifacts are characterized by polished stone.

Banyan Valley Cave see SPIRIT CAVE.

Baradostian see SHANIDAR.

Barakaevskaya Cave a small prehistoric cave in the northwestern Caucasus (Russia), containing several Middle Palaeolithic occupation levels buried in shallow deposits of loam and rubble. Associated mammal remains include steppe bison and sheep. Most of the occupations appear to date to a cold phase of the last GLACIAL. Among the large assemblage of tools, scrapers, notches, denticulates and points predominate. The jaw of a NEAN-DERTHAL child (estimated age 2–3 years) was recovered from the lowermost level. Barakaevskaya Cave was excavated by Liubin and Autlev during 1976–81.

bar and dot notation a MESOAMERICAN counting system in which a bar counts for five, a dot for one. The earliest example of the bar and dot system is on STELAS 12 and 13 at MONTE ALBÁN, dating to the late middle FORMATIVE PERIOD (c.500 BC). The system was in use throughout many parts of Mesoamerica, and is most closely associated with MAYA and ZAPOTEC writing systems.

Baraqish a walled city of South Arabia northwest of MARIB. During the 1990s Italian excavations in a temple reached levels datable to c.800 BC, and occupation continued into medieval times. The largely intact city walls incorporate numerous South Arabian inscriptions.

baray a Khmer term referring to the large rectangular water reservoirs associated with the ANGKOR period.

Barbar a site in northern Bahrain in the Persian Gulf consisting of a sequence of square temples built on an oval platform, dating from the late 3rd millennium to the mid 2nd millennium BC. The site gives its name to an archaeological culture, defined by pottery types, seals and other materials contained in the lower levels of the QAL'AT AL BAHRAIN, Barbar itself, the BAHRAIN TUMULUS FIELDS and other sites; this complex dates to the second half of the 3rd and earlier part of the 2nd millennia BC. Sites of this type are distributed along the southern coast of the Persian Gulf from Failaka (near the MESOPOTAMIAN delta) to Qatar, with materials appearing as trade goods in southeastern Arabia and on the Indus coast (see PERSIAN GULF TRADE).

barbotine a term used in ceramics to describe rough plastic relief on the surface of pottery.

Barca a Bronze Age fortified settlement of the OTOMANI culture in eastern Slovakia near Kosice. The most striking feature of the Barca settlement is its large houses. Twenty-three were found in the surviving portion of the enclosure, aligned in rows of four to seven and separated by intervals of 40 to 60 cm (16 to 24 inches). Between these rows of houses were 'streets' about 2.5 m (8 ft) wide. Most are three-room structures, many with hearths, although some have only one or two rooms.

bar hammer technique see SOFT HAMMER TECHNIQUE.

Barkaer two parallel rectangular Neolithic timber structures in Jutland, Denmark; approximately 8.5 m (28 ft) long, they are subdivided by twenty-one and twenty-eight wickerwork partitions respectively. Originally interpreted as houses (an early form of terrace!) they are now thought to be the timber frameworks of funerary long mounds built on the site of an earlier settlement c.4000 BC.

Barnenez one of the earliest Neolithic CHAMBERED TOMBS of western Europe, this sub-rectangular dry-stone cairn in Finistère, France, contains eleven chambers side by side reached by long, narrow, irregular passages. Excavations suggested the mound was built in two phases, an initial mound with five chambers (four dry-stone, one megalithic) being subsequently enlarged by an extension with six more (five dry-stone, one megalithic). The megalithic chamber of the first phase (chamber H) contained carved ORTHOSTATS including three axe motifs. Radiocarbon dates suggest that the initial mound was built c.4500 BC, with the extension following some 300 years later.

Barreroids a group of prehistoric Indian hunter-gatherers in the ANTILLES who originated in Central America, arriving around 4000 BC, and who used primarily flint for their tools. Their technology was very different from that of other gatherers such as the BANWAROIDS, since they made very little use of polished stone, and continued the use of flaked lithics. They are named after the site of Barrera-Mordán in southern Santo Domingo, and occupied parts of that island as well eastern Cuba.

barrow a burial mound, usually of earth in contrast to a stone-built cairn. Barrows cover burials, sometimes dug into the original ground surface, in other cases placed within the body of the mound itself. The term itself may be used of British burial mounds of any period, and covers monuments ranging widely in character and date. It was much used in the 18th and 19th centuries, when 'barrow-digging' became an amateur pastime among the educated or the simply curious. A broad distinction may be drawn between *long barrows* and *round barrows*. The former are usually Neolithic, and today are more properly referred to as 'long mounds'. The latter can date anywhere between the Neolithic and the early ANGLO-SAXON period.

A range of carefully differentiated barrow types characterize the Early Bronze Age of southern England, including *bell barrows* (small mounds surrounded by a BERM and ditch), *disc barrows* (where there is a wide berm between the round barrow and its encircling ditch), *saucer barrows* (with a broad low mound) and *pond barrows*, where there is no mound at all, but a circular concave depression in the ground, ringed by a bank. In the Later Bronze Age, cremation becomes common, and many barrows contain successive cremations deposited in cloth bags (now decayed) or funerary vessels. Iron Age burials in the ARRAS culture of southeastern Yorkshire differ from earlier types in being square and sometimes covering a chariot burial. Barrow burial continued to be practised by native aristocracies during the Roman period, as illustrated by the Bartlow Hills in Cambridgeshire. The latest British barrows date to the Anglo-Saxon period, before the conversion to Christianity, and include the famous barrow cemetery of SUTTON HOO. See also TUMULUS.

Barumini the site in Sardinia of a monument called Su Nuraxi, the most famous of the Bronze Age NURAGHI, consisting of a central round tower of massive basalt blocks and later outworks. The central tower was built c.1800 BC and was originally some 17 m (56 ft) high with three tall CORBEL-VAULTED chambers one above the other. The out-works – four round towers around the base of the central tower, and a perimeter wall with smaller towers enclosing a village – were built over a thousand years later, in the 8th century BC, possibly in response to the Carthaginian threat.

Base Ring Late Cypriot pottery which has a dark, lustrous SLIP and relief decoration. Base Ring juglets or *bilbils* resemble inverted poppy-heads and may have contained opium.

basilica a long, rectangular Roman building with an internal colonnade. They are often found in the vicinity of a FORUM and seem to have been used for judicial hearings and other civic functions. The term later came to be applied to church buildings which adopted this type of open-plan layout.

Basin of Mexico a closed basin surrounded by mountains, 2,400 m (8,000 ft) above sea-level. Cultural remains in the basin date as early as 19,000 BC at the site of Tlapacoya, which later became a large PRECLASSIC village. Tlatilco was also an important Preclassic site in the basin, well known for its spectacular burials. The Basin of Mexico contains the current capital of Mexico, Mexico City, as well as the remains of the AZTEC capital of TEN-

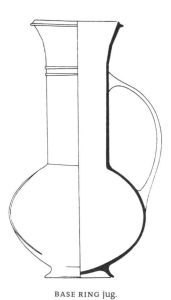

BASE RING jug.

OCHTITLÁN, and the cities of CUICUILCO and TEOTIHUACÁN. At the time of the Spanish conquest in 1521, the entire basin was intensively cultivated in order to support the resident population. In addition to dry farming SWIDDEN AGRICULTURE, irrigation techniques and CHINAMPAS were employed. The southern portion of the basin is better suited for agriculture, and was occupied earlier and more intensively than the northern part.

Archaeological research in the Basin of Mexico has focused primarily on the later stages of Teotihuacán and the Aztec period. Within the basin, there were two periods of florescence: the first from c.100 BC to AD 650 with the rise of Cuicuilco and then Teotihuacán; and the second from AD 1200 to 1520, with the appearance of the city-state of Azcapotzalco, and the subsequent rise to power of the Aztecs.

Basketmaker see ANASAZI.

Basse-Yutz a pair of bronze wine flagons with coral and enamel inlay discovered in 1927 in an uncertain context in Moselle, France, probably originally from a CELTIC chieftain's grave. The flagons combine a vessel shape copied from Italian models with Celtic-style decorative elements, including zoomorphic handles and lids. They are dated on stylistic grounds to c.400 BC.

Basta a large (8 ha [20 acre]) PRE-POTTERY NEOLITHIC (late PPNB, around 6400–6200 bc) settlement in Jordan, south of the Dead Sea. Joint German-Jordanian excavation uncovered three building phases, the lowest of which includes large multi-room houses erected on artificial terraces. Excellent preservation of architecture offers examples of details like windows, usually absent from other contemporary sites.

Bastam a large (21 ha [52 acre]) URARTIAN fortified settlement, just northwest of Lake Urmia in northwestern Iran, which represents one of the few thoroughly excavated Urartian sites. W. Kleiss's work exposed an administrative town set along a ridge, divided into upper and lower sections. The architecture of the citadel is dominated by monumental buildings ('palaces') with pillared halls; the administrative centre yielded several Urartian texts and a large number of sealed BULLAE (envelopes), reflecting monitored storage and flows of goods. The careful stratigraphic excavation permitted a detailed chronological ordering of Urartian and immediately post-Urartian pottery; this aspect of the German work is one of the most enduring contributions to Urartian studies in recent times.

Batalimo a site in the southern Central African Republic with large quantities of flakes, sidescrapers, flaked axes, and elaborately decorated dark brown or black pottery which has been included in the Batalimo-Maluba horizon dating to the first half of the 1st millennium AD. Pottery from Batalimo has a THERMOLUMINESCENCE date of

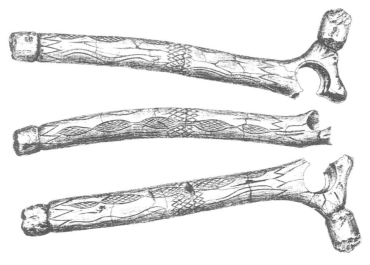

An engraved BÂTON PERCÉ or bâton de commandement from La Madeleine, France, broken at the perforation like many specimens.

AD 380, but there is no evidence for the use of iron at the site, which is usually labelled 'Neolithic'.

Batan an island in Batanes Province, northern Philippines, which lies midway between Luzon and Taiwan. As on nearby Sabtang island, there are numerous stone-lined, boat-shaped burials and hilltop, stone-built fortresses (*Ijang*) of undetermined age.

Batán Grande a large urban site located in the Lambayeque region of the far north coast of Peru, pertaining to the MIDDLE HORIZON and LATE INTERMEDIATE PERIOD, the centre of Sicán culture. Excavations by Izumi Shimada indicate that it was an important locus of metallurgy.

Batavia a Dutch East Indiaman, wrecked off Western Australia in AD 1629. Significant finds included military and navigation equipment and a complete sandstone portico intended for the fort at Batavia in the Dutch East Indies.

Bat Cave a series of adjacent stratified rockshelters, located in New Mexico, USA, which provided controversial evidence for early agriculture in the New World. The earliest evidence of humans in the cave is between 10,000 and 9000 BP. Up to 2800 BP, the site was used only occasionally by hunting groups. Between 2800 and 2200 bp large pits and hearths were constructed, and a more regular use of the site is indicated. The pits contained cultigens (maize and squash). The maize is primitive but similar to maize found in later PUEBLO sites. Beans were apparently not used at the site until later. Ceramic levels are dated between 1800 and 800 BP.

Bath (*Lat.* Aquae Sulis) a Roman spa town in England. The waters were sacred to the Celtic Sulis, who was identified with the CLASSICAL goddess Minerva. Excavations have revealed a temple built in the CORINTHIAN ORDER which lay in a precinct adjoining the extensive baths.

bâton de commandement see BÂTON PERCÉ.

bâton percé ('perforated baton') an Upper Palaeolithic artifact, occasionally encountered in AURIGNACIAN, GRAVETTIAN and SOLUTREAN assemblages but more typically found in MAGDALENIAN tool-kits. It consists of a decorated cylinder of antler with a hole through the thickest part. The baton may be decorated with intricate carving. Its function is unknown, although it is generally interpreted as a shaft-straightener, an interpretation which is supported by signs of use-wear in and around the hole.

Battersea Shield a bronze shield with glass inlays dredged from the River Thames, London, England, in 1857. The shield is sub-rectangular in shape with rounded ends and slight waisting in the centre. It would originally have been fixed to a wooden backing. The main face is decorated with three cast bronze discs with central bosses and tendril ornament. Stylistic criteria suggest a date in the early 1st century AD. The shield may have been deposited in the river as a votive offering.

Battle Axe culture a term, now somewhat archaic, applied to the CORDED WARE groups in southern Scandinavia and generally synonymous with the SINGLE GRAVE CULTURE of this region, dating to the 3rd millennium BC. Male graves, which occur singly under tumuli, often include a stone axe with a drilled shaft hole and a single, drooping blade, which has been fancifully termed a 'battle axe'.

battleship curve a graph, shaped like the profile of an early 20th-century battleship, that represents changes through time in the frequency of a particular attribute from increasing to decreasing popularity.

Batungan a Neolithic burial cave, on Masbate Island, central Philippines, yielding flaked stone tools and red-slipped, carinated, incised and dentate-stamped pottery that links it to the Yuan-Shan tradition of Taiwan.

Baturong Caves rockshelter sites, in Sabah, northern Borneo, including Hagop Bilo, yielding a stone industry characterized by long blade-like knives, dating to c.17,000–12,000 BP, succeeding the TINGKAYU industry and preceding that of the MADAI CAVES.

Bayon one of the greatest monuments of the ANGKOR complex, it probably started as a Hindu monument, and was then converted before completion between the late 12th and early 13th century to a Buddhist sanctuary under JAYAVARMAN VII. It is renowned for its fifty-four towers, each with four smiling faces of an Avalokitesvara (a future Buddha) **(see fig., p. 23)**, and the wonderful bas-reliefs with scenes of daily life in the 13th century.

BC/bc see AD.

BCE see AD.

be an administrative unit in the emerging YAMATO state organization of the 5th–6th centuries AD in Japan. Craftspeople and palace service personnel were assigned to *be* groupings and their products and labour collected for court use.

beaker a decorated, handleless drinking vessel, characteristic of the European late Neolithic–Early Bronze Age. See also BELL BEAKER.

bear see CAVE BEAR.

Beazley, Sir John Davidson (1885–1970) a British scholar who is best known for his work in identifying the 'hands' of the painters and potters of ATHENIAN POTTERY (see also BLACK-FIGURED, RED-FIGURED). These identifications supplemented the names of craftsmen which appear on the pottery. He named these anonymous people either after the museum in which one of the pieces was located (e.g. 'the painter of London E105'), a former owner (e.g. 'the Ready painter') or a mannerism of the style (e.g. 'Elbows Out').

bec a Palaeolithic flake tool retouched on one edge to form a point, used for boring.

bed the smallest formally recognized division of sediment or rock within a STRATIGRAPHIC series. It is greater than 1 cm (0.4 inch) thick and distinguished from overlying and underlying beds by well-defined divisional planes, or bedding planes. Excavations at archaeological sites and contextual interpretation are often conducted at the scale where recognition of individual beds, or even finer stratigraphic intervals, is significant.

Bede see ANGLO-SAXONS.

beehive tomb see THOLOS.

Beersheba a Palestinian site, the traditional southern boundary of the Land of Israel. It was substantially occupied only in the ISRAELITE period when massive fortifications surrounded a carefully planned city that included an impressive water-supply system, large storehouses and a building described as a 'Governor's Palace'.

beeswax figures figures in rock art made from the wax of native bees pressed on to rock surfaces to form abstract or figurative designs. They are found in northern Australia. Beeswax figures were made into the 20th century and have been radiocarbon dated to about 4000 bp.

Begho a central Ghanaian town-state dating between the 11th and 18th centuries AD. There are about 1,500 mounds representing the ruins of houses in a series of suburbs, and the site is estimated to have contained a population of some 10,000 at its peak in the 17th century. Evidence for a great variety of specialist subsistence, technological, commercial and political activities has been uncovered.

Begram ancient Kapisa in northeastern Afghanistan, a royal city of Indo-Greek and Kushana dynasties and an important caravan town. French excavation of the citadel-palace found two rooms packed with Indian carved ivories from India, Roman glass, bronzes and other objects and Chinese lacquers belonging to the 2nd century AD.

behavioural archaeology the study of the laws pertaining to the relationship between MATERIAL CULTURE and human behaviour, and the impact of human and natural agencies on material culture between its original use in the past and its subsequent discovery by archaeologists.

Behbet el-Hagar a site in the Nile DELTA, Egypt, the main cult centre of the goddess ISIS during the LATE PERIOD. Behbet el-Hagar now largely consists of a mass of fallen granite blocks from the temple, the construction of which was probably initiated by Nektanebo I (380–362 BC) and continued, in particular, by PTOLEMY II and Ptolemy III (285–221 BC).

Behistun see BISITUN.

Behlodehlie an Ethiopian site south of HADAR which in 1981 yielded a 3.9 million-year-old partial frontal bone ascribed to AUSTRALOPITHECUS *afarensis*.

Beidha a NATUFIAN and PRE-POTTERY NEOLITHIC

(PPNB) (11th–7th millennia BC) site in the highlands of southern Jordan, where Diana Kirkbride's excavations in 1958–67 produced a sequence of PPNB architecture that documents a shift from roughly circular (earlier) to agglomerated rectilinear (later) constructions. Subsistence at Beidha included probably domesticated goat as well as wild species; and barley and emmer, though not yet morphologically domesticates, seem to have been cultivated. The material culture includes small vessels and figurines of unfired clay and a wide range of exotic materials (including a little Anatolian obsidian) in addition to the chipped stone, ground stone and bone industries. Excavations also uncovered forty-three burials, including examples with detached skulls.

Beikthano a major early historic walled town and Buddhist religious site in central Burma, probably linked to the state centred on ŚRI KṢETRA of the early–mid 1st millennium AD. Bases of brick STUPAS recall those from eastern India, and elaborately moulded funerary urns reflect the transition from inhumation to cremation for the Southeast Asian elite.

Beit Mersim a Palestinian site excavated in 1924–32 by ALBRIGHT and Fisher. The TELL of Beit Mersim is important for its carefully excavated strata, especially of the MIDDLE BRONZE AGE, the pottery of which formed a basis for the ceramic chronology of Palestine.

Belarus see EUROPE, EASTERN.

Belgae the name given by Roman authors (notably Caesar) to the peoples of northeastern Gaul (modern northeastern France and Belgium) and southeastern Britain in the 1st century BC/AD. The continental Belgae were divided into twenty-seven different branches. Most of these were CELTIC, but the easternmost seem to have been purely Germanic. The Belgic confederation is thought to have come into being around 100 BC, and survived until conquered by Caesar in 57 BC. An important Belgic site excavated in recent years is the sanctuary at Gournay-sur-Aronde in Oise, France, dedicated to gods of war, death and fertility, with offerings of weapons and animal sacrifices. The Belgic peoples of Britain carried the same tribal names as their continental neighbours and may have been formed by an immigrant aristocracy. They are associated with the burials of the AYLESFORD-swarling culture.

Bel'kachi a stratified Neolithic site in the Lena basin of Siberia. The early Neolithic levels at Bel'kachi I have produced sand-tempered pottery with net or mat impressions, dated by radiocarbon to about 3000 BC. Overlying these deposits are layers of a 'developed' Neolithic which has been termed the 'Bel'kachinsk culture', whose pottery has distinctive cord-wrapped paddle impressions. The upper levels at Bel'kachi I have check-stamped pottery,

often tempered with animal hair. Bel'kachinsk stone tools and pottery are widespread in Siberia.

bell barrow see BARROW.

Bell Beaker a type of pottery vessel found throughout large areas of western and Central Europe in the FINAL NEOLITHIC or CHALCOLITHIC period c.2500–1800 BC. The name derives from the characteristic vessel form, which resembles an inverted bell, with globular body and flaring rim. Bell Beakers were objects of value and were highly decorated in a variety of regionally and chronologically specific styles, two of the most important early types being the Maritime Beaker of Iberia and the All-Over Ornamented Beaker of the Lower Rhineland. A range of special artifacts is often associated with Beakers in grave assemblages, including archer's WRISTGUARDS of polished stone, V-PERFORATED buttons and copper-tanged daggers.

BELL BEAKER.

Bellows Beach one of the earliest sites in Hawaii, on Oahu, dating to AD 600–1000. The assemblage of one-piece pearlshell fish-hooks, adzes and a shell grater, with bones of pig, dog and rat, is a typical early eastern Polynesian (see PACIFIC) one and resembles the material from the HALAWA dune site.

Belverde a Bronze Age ritual complex in Tuscany, Italy, consisting of ritual deposits among crevices and beneath overhangs among massive tumbled boulders. This unique site, nestling below a steep cliff, has yielded large numbers of bronze objects and items of pottery, including vessels containing carbonized foodstuffs. Basins and steps were carved on the tops of a few of the larger boulders. The plateau above the cliff is occupied by a fortified site, probably of the Late Bronze Age or Iron Age.

Belzoni, Giovanni Battista (1778–1823) an Italian theatrical strong-man who excavated for Egyptian antiquities, chiefly on behalf of Salt, the British Consul in Egypt. His best-known discovery is the tomb of Seti I, in the VALLEY OF THE KINGS.

bench **1** an erosional terrace landform consisting of an alluvial cut surface on bedrock confined to a valley.

2 an erosional landform consisting of a wave-cut surface, level to gently seaward-sloping, formed in coastal areas as a sea-cliff retreats from wave action. This type of bench is often referred to as a wave-cut platform.

Benfica a locality near Luanda on the Angolan coast with numerous SHELL MIDDENS, mostly associated with the 16th-century AD village of Benfica, but also comprising older stone artifact assemblages and Early Iron Age pottery dated to the 2nd century AD, and ascribed to the CHIFUMBAZE complex.

Beni Hassan a site in UPPER EGYPT, best known for its thirty-nine rock-cut tombs of the MIDDLE KINGDOM, some belonging to the NOMARCHS of the region. Painted scenes on the walls of some of these tombs provide much information on daily life and military activity during the period. Two km (1.2 miles) to the south is the ROCK-TEMPLE constructed by HATCHEPSUT called the Speos Artemidos.

Benin a southern Nigerian city which flourished from before the arrival of Europeans in the late 15th century AD, best known for its 4–7,000 CIRE PERDUE 'bronzes', most of which are brasses, in the form of near life-size human heads and plaques, a tradition which continued until the 19th century AD. Suggestions that the origins of the Benin brass-casting tradition may be traced to IFE are disputed.

Bennett, Wendell Clark (1905–53) an American archaeologist who undertook several major field projects in Andean South America, principally in Peru and Bolivia. In 1932 he worked in Bolivia, establishing a chronological sequence for the site of TIAHUANACO, and identifying the CHIRIPA culture. In 1936–8 he worked on the north coast and highlands of Peru, where he confirmed TELLO's assertion that CHAVÍN was the earliest complex civilization. He was one of the principal organizers of the Virú Valley survey of 1946–7. In 1950 he mapped and tested the site of HUARI, for the purpose of establishing a chronological sequence for the site.

Beowulf an epic ANGLO-SAXON poem, probably of the 8th century AD, about the conflict between good and evil, and the nature of heroism. Its importance to archaeology lies in the description of contemporary funerary customs like those displayed in the boat burials of SUTTON HOO. The poem opens with an account of a dead king being taken out to sea in a ship, with jewellery on his chest and armour and treasure placed around his body.

Berdyzh an Upper Palaeolithic open-air site on the Sozh

River (Dnepr tributary) in Belarus. The main horizon is buried in slope deposits overlying ALLUVIUM of the second terrace, and has yielded radiocarbon dates of 23,430 and 15,000 bp. The faunal remains are predominantly woolly mammoth, and as many as three former MAMMOTH-BONE HOUSES may be present.

Berekhat Ram an ACHEULIAN open-air site in the northern Golan Heights, Israel, which was discovered during agricultural work and excavated by N. Goren-Inbar in 1980–81. The site has yielded many waste flakes but comparatively few tools, including eight bifaces, LEVALLOIS flakes and sidescrapers. A tiny pebble was purposely modified, possibly to enhance its natural resemblance to a female figurine.

Berelekh the northernmost Palaeolithic site in the world, located at a latitude of 71 °N near the mouth of the Indigirka River in northeastern Siberia. The site contains a bed of over 8,000 mammal bones, primarily woolly mammoth, which apparently accumulated under natural conditions c.14,000–12,000 years ago, and an overlying Upper Palaeolithic horizon dating to 13,400–10,600 bp. The bone bed was studied by Vereshchagin, and the archaeological horizon by Mochanov, who assigned it to the DYUKTAI CULTURE.

Berenice the name of several HELLENISTIC foundations named after the various women of that name married to different PTOLEMYs. These cities include:

1 (mod. Benghazi) the harbour town on the coast of Cyrenaica, Libya, replacing the settlement at Euhesperides dug by the British.

2 a port on the Egyptian coast of the Red Sea founded by Ptolemy II. It was linked to Coptos on the Nile by a camel route. In the 1st and 2nd centuries AD it was an important port linking the Nile Valley, and ultimately the eastern Mediterranean, with Arabia, India and eastern Africa.

3 Pella in Jordan, said to have been called by this name.

beresty see BIRCH-BARK MANUSCRIPTS.

Beringia a land mass located in the present-day Bering and Chukchi Seas, formed by the drop in sea-levels as a result of the formation of continental glaciers at the end of the Pleistocene. This allowed humans to enter the New World, by a route called the Bering Land Bridge.

Bering Land Bridge see BERINGIA.

berm a flat area between a bank or barrow and its ditch.

Bernal García, Ignacio (1910–92) an eminent Mexican archaeologist, a pupil of Alfonso CASO, best known for his work at MONTE ALBÁN, DAINZÚ and other Oaxacan sites, and for excavations and restorations at TEOTIHUACÁN.

Bernam-Sungkai a district of peninsular Malaysia, including Slim River, known for its metal age (c.300 BC?) stone slab graves, perhaps contemporary with those of PASEMAH.

Bersu, Gerhard (1889–1964) a German archaeologist, Director of the Römisch-Germanischen Kommission at Frankfurt until removed by the Nazis in the 1930s. Bersu then emigrated to Britain, introducing continental methods of excavation including area excavation of settlement sites. These he put to good use in the now classic excavations at the Iron Age farmstead of LITTLE WOODBURY in 1938–9. During the Second World War, Bersu excavated Iron Age houses on the Isle of Man during his internment there as a German citizen.

Bessarabsky see BORODINO TREASURE.

beta ray backscattering a technique used to determine quantitatively the chemical composition of surface layers of materials such as the content of glass, glazes and slips. A sample is bombarded by a beam of electrons generated from a weak radioactive beta source producing backscattered electrons. The concentration of an element known to be present can be estimated based on the percentage of backscattering, which is dependent on the atomic number of the elements of the artifact surface layers.

Bethel a Palestinian site, excavated sporadically in the 1930s–1960s by ALBRIGHT and Kelso. Occupied non-continuously from the CHALCOLITHIC, the strongly fortified settlement of the MIDDLE BRONZE AGE included a fine stone sanctuary found to contain animal bones and ceramic cult-vessels, while ASTARTE-plaques were common. Following its conquest by the ISRAELITES Bethel became a comparative backwater, although it was a relatively large city in the Roman and BYZANTINE periods.

Beth-Shan a Palestinian site, the CLASSICAL Scythopolis, occupied virtually continuously from the CHALCO-LITHIC to the medieval period, and excavated sporadically by the University of Pennsylvania Museum from 1921 to 1933. Beth-Shan is best known for its successive strata of Late Bronze Age–Iron Age temples, which contained a large amount of NEW KINGDOM Egyptian material including STELAS and architectural elements. A monastery of the 6th century AD at Beth-Shan contains fine mosaic floors.

Beth-Shemesh a Palestinian site, excavated by Mac-kenzie in 1911–12 and by Grant in 1928–33. Probably founded in the MIDDLE BRONZE AGE, possibly as a HYKSOS fortified settlement, and later a significant LATE BRONZE AGE and PHILISTINE town.

Beth Yerah, Tell see KHIRBET KERAK.

Betovo a Middle Palaeolithic open-air site on the Desna River near Bryansk in European Russia. Artifacts and faunal remains are buried in a humic sand bed; although

their age is unclear, the predominance of arctic species among the fauna (e.g. snow lemming) indicates a cold interval (early last GLACIAL?). The artifacts include many denticulates. Betovo was dug by Tarasov in the 1970s and 1980s.

bevelled rim bowl a pottery form typical of the URUK culture in MESOPOTAMIA and surrounding regions. The bowls were mass-produced by pressing a coarse slab of clay into an open mould and then trimming the excess clay at the top of the mould to produce the characteristic rim. Found in huge numbers, often in temples or other 'public' buildings, the vessels are often regarded as instruments for apportioning rations to institutional personnel, but the evidence actually implies manifold uses.

Beycesultan a 15 ha (37 acre) prehistoric site on the upper Meander River in southwestern Anatolia excavated by S. LLOYD in the 1950s, which provides a key stratigraphic sequence of forty levels that run from the late CHALCO-LITHIC to the terminal Bronze Age. In addition to the pottery chronology (essentially equivalent to the Chalcolithic levels at HACILAR), Beycesultan provides early examples of MEGARON (porch and hall) architectures, possibly first in the late Chalcolithic level XXIV, and then certainly in EARLY BRONZE AGE III levels (X–VIII). The late Chalcolithic level XXXIV also contained a small hoard of copper tools, a particularly early concentration of metals. The MIDDLE BRONZE AGE walled town included the 'burnt palace', built of brick and timber walls and focused on pillared courtyards, which covered over half a hectare (1.25 acres). Other massive 'public' architecture was also present on the opposite side of the town. The Late Bronze Age occupation of the site was on a reduced scale, though still presenting large blocks of residential buildings (and still using the megaron form); the last occupation seems to have ended around 1000 BC.

Bhimbetka a rock ridge 45 km (28 miles) southeast of Bhopal in Madhya Pradesh, central India, which presents a large series of rockshelters that contain stratified

BHIMBETKA, India: late rock paintings showing a group of riders, together with animals.

Palaeolithic to historic period deposits and an extremely rich corpus of rock art. Excavations at several shelters (especially shelter IIIF-24) reveal a succession of ACHEULIAN (handaxes, cleavers, a high LEVALLOIS index), Middle Palaeolithic (disappearance of bifaces, increased blade frequency), Upper Palaeolithic (tendency towards bladelet production) and Mesolithic industries. The Mesolithic, the most frequently represented period at the rockshelters, is characterized by a bladelet industry and by grinding equipment; this lithic assemblage continues into levels in which occur copper tools and CHALCOLITHIC pottery. Radiocarbon determinations date the Mesolithic industry to 6000–1000 BC. The rock art belongs to the Mesolithic period and later into historic periods. The art, painted in a wide range of colours, presents a diverse array of human and animal figures which are either displayed individually or set in scenes of hunting, warfare or ceremony; some of the later art shows horse and elephant riders. As with most rock art, the chief means of dating are stylistic analysis and observation of superimposition (relative patination being not particularly pertinent here); V. S. WAKANKAR's proposed stylistic periodization for the entire Indian subcontinent is often cited in connection with the Bhimbetka corpus, but this system has uncertain validity. In 1990, PETROGLYPHS were found in one shelter.

bi a disc-shaped jade with a large central hole, used in early China to symbolize Heaven. It was worn suspended from the belt by court nobles in the HAN Dynasty.

Biblical Archaeology the study of the material remains of the Near East to the extent that it relates to the period of, and events referred to in, the Bible, especially the Old Testament. It is particularly concerned with exploring the sometimes ambiguous relationship between an ancient religious text and contemporary archaeological evidence.

Bibracte an Iron Age OPPIDUM mentioned by Caesar as the capital of the Aedui and now identified with Mont Beuvray, Nièvre, France. Excavations in the 19th and early 20th century by Bulliot and DÉCHELETTE found it to be the classic example of early urban development in France. The oppidum was divided into residential and industrial quarters by a regular system of streets, with houses based on Roman models. The site was replaced in the later 1st century BC by the new town of Augustodunum (Autun), 27 km (17 miles) away.

biface, handaxe or *coup-de-poing* a bifacially worked implement, usually a core tool, which forms the type-fossil for the ACHEULIAN but which is also found in certain MOUSTERIAN assemblages. Biface technology developed from African pebble-tool industries, spreading to Europe, India and Southwest Asia with clear variation in appearance and workmanship. Bifaces range in shape from triangular or pear-shaped to oval, and in length from approximately 8 to 20 cm (3 to 8 inches). They are

BIFACES or handaxes.

believed to be multi-purpose tools. See also BOUT COUPÉ, FICRON, OVATE, CORDATE.

bifacial foliate an artifact class comprising a variety of leaf-shaped stone tools characterized by complete or nearly complete flaking on both sides. See also BLATTSPITZEN, WILLOW-LEAF, LAUREL-LEAF.

Big Game Hunting tradition a North American cultural tradition, characterized by the hunting of MEGAFAUNA, such as mammoth and bison. This tradition was particularly widespread in the PALAEOINDIAN period, but was replaced in many areas of the continent by the ensuing ARCHAIC, except for areas like the Plains where it continued until European contact.

Big Horn Medicine Wheel a MEDICINE WHEEL located in the Big Horn Mountains of Wyoming, USA, that consists of a central D-shaped stone cairn, from which radiate twenty-eight spokes made of individual stones. The outer circumference of the 'wheel' is surrounded by six smaller cairns. It has been suggested that the site was astronomically aligned.

Bigo the capital site of a Central African interlacustrine state in western Uganda dating between the 13th and 16th centuries AD, containing extensive enclosures marked by earthworks running more than 10 km (6 miles) in total length. The remains of large circular houses with elaborate hearths resemble more recent royal residences of the region. See also BWEYORERE and NTUSI.

Bilzingsleben a Lower Palaeolithic open-air lakeshore site located near the confluence of the Wipper and Wirbelbach Rivers in eastern Germany. Artifacts are buried in spring deposits dated by the URANIUM/thorium method to c.230,000 bp; occupation extends back to c.350,000 bp; associated faunal remains include typical Middle Pleistocene forms (e.g. macaque). The artifacts include chopping tools, denticulates and scrapers and provide evidence of a Lower Palaeolithic industry without handaxes in Central Europe. Human skeletal remains, reflecting a mixture of HOMO *erectus* and *H. sapiens* traits, were also found, as well as some incised lines on bones which may be non-functional.

bipolar flaking the production of flakes by resting the core on an anvil and splitting or smashing it with a hammerstone. Bipolar flaking is widely distributed in time and space, but has often gone unrecognized because the products are difficult to identify. Discarded cores tend to be rectangular or wedge-shaped, with evidence of battering on both ends, and are often assumed to be tools. The flakes commonly lack the features of conchoidal fracture and can be difficult to recognize as artifacts. The bipolar technique is often associated with flaking quartz and is useful for reducing very small cores, such as small quartz pebbles.

birch-bark manuscripts or **beresty** early Russian letters and documents scratched on to thin pieces of birch-bark, dating to the 11th–15th centuries AD. They were first found in 1951 in NOVGOROD by A. ARTSIKHOVSKI, and form a very important source of information as no other documents earlier than the 13th century had survived because of the frequent fires in the wooden cities of Old Russia. The birch-bark manuscripts are quite well preserved because they were lost or thrown away by their addressees, and were found by archaeologists in layers that preserve organic materials. So far, 900 such letters have been found in Novgorod, together with sixty-seven in other Old Russian cities. More than 400 of them are related to the 11th–13th centuries.

Birch Creek the location of a series of stratified rockshelters in central Idaho, USA, with occupation ranging from approximately 8500 BP to the historic period. The sites are important for the construction of CULTURE HISTORY in this section of the Rocky Mountains and for understanding the prehistory of the Shoshonean, a widespread linguistic group of the American West.

Bird, Junius Bouton (1907–82) an American archaeologist who conducted field research primarily in South America. He excavated the site of CUEVA FELL in Tierra del Fuego, establishing the presence of a PALAEOINDIAN occupation in South America. He worked in the Atacama region of northern Chile, and also, as part of the Virú Valley survey, excavated the site of HUACA PRIETA on the north coast of Peru, establishing the existence of the PRECERAMIC period. He was especially interested in textile technology, and devoted much of his boundless energy to the study of textiles.

Birimi see KINTAMPO.

Birka Viking age trading centre on an island in Lake Mälaren, near Stockholm in Sweden, established in the early 9th century AD. Excavations over the last three centuries have revealed a large town with wattle-and-daub houses and workshops surrounded by earthen ramparts. Near by were several large cremation cemeteries. The thousands of objects found at Birka reveal far-reaching commercial contacts: east to Russia and even China, south to Byzantium, and southwest to the Rhineland and beyond.

Bir Kiseiba an area in the eastern Sahara of southern Egypt with early ceramics and bones arguably of domestic cattle dated to *c.*9500 BP (see NABTA PLAYA).

Birnirk a late prehistoric Arctic culture which is ancestral to the prehistoric Eskimo THULE culture, and dates to roughly AD 500–1200. Birnirk sites are found on the coast of Northeast Asia from the Kolyma River to the Bering Strait, and along the northwest coast of Alaska as far west as Barrow. Settlements were small and no more than a few houses (typically small with an entrance tunnel) were occupied at any one time. Material remains include toggle harpoon heads, sealing darts, bladder float nozzles, oil lamps, ground slate knives and skin-covered boats, and are similar to historic Eskimo artifacts. The economy was based primarily on marine mammal hunting (including some whale hunting) and fishing. The Birnirk culture is thought to be derived from OLD BERING SEA/Okvik culture in the Bering Strait region.

Birrigai a rockshelter in the southeastern highlands of the Australian Capital Territory, demonstrating occupation of this region at the LAST GLACIAL MAXIMUM. Intermittent occupation began *c.*21,000 bp, increasing in intensity from *c.*3000 bp.

Birsmatten an early Mesolithic rockshelter in northwestern Switzerland in which the complete skeleton of a woman dated to the BOREAL period, *c.*6200 BC, was found in 1944. Mesolithic habitation layers yielded bones of bear, bison, red deer, roe deer, wild pig and beaver, along with numerous triangular microliths.

Bir Tarfawi a small oasis in southwestern Egypt with ACHEULIAN and Middle Palaeolithic sites. The latter date between perhaps 175,000 and 90,000 BP and are associated with considerable evidence for meat- and plant-food processing and probably hunting.

birth-house see MAMMISI.

Bisitun a site located east of Kermanshah on the pass through the mountains towards Hamadan in western Iran, which is the setting for the famous trilingual CUNEIFORM inscription of the ACHAEMENID king Darius I, providing an account of his accession to the throne (by usurpation); the text accompanies a carved depiction of the king's triumph. The repetition of the text in the Old Persian, BABYLONIAN and ELAMITE languages allowed

RAWLINSON to initiate successful decipherment of cuneiform scripts. Monumental inscriptions and reliefs of other periods also appear at Bisitun, including a PARTHIAN relief which echoes that of Darius. Bisitun is also the location of a Palaeolithic cave-site excavated by Carleton Coon in the 1940s.

Biskupin a Late Bronze Age/Early Iron Age fortified site in northwestern Poland, excavated in 1933–9 by József KOSTRZEWSKI. Located on a peninsula, Biskupin is surrounded by a wooden-crib rampart which enclosed a settled area of 2 ha (5 acres). Streets paved with logs separated rows of houses. Excavations at Biskupin yielded many preserved artifacts of wood, cloth and bone. The main occupation at Biskupin is dated to the HALLSTATT D period, with the settlement being either abandoned or destroyed c.400 BC. The settlement at Biskupin has been reconstructed as an archaeological park open to the public.

Bismarck Archipelago islands off the HUON PENINSULA, Papua New Guinea, which were the subject of an intensive research programme, instigated by Jim Allen, to investigate the origins of the LAPITA cultural complex. The excavated sites include Pleistocene rockshelters and open-sites, and Lapita sites. The research has shown that occupation of the Bismarcks and exploitation of marine resources go back more than 30,000 years, and that obsidian from TALASEA was being transported 20,000 years ago. Evidence has also been presented for faunal introductions to the Bismarcks by humans: *phalanger* (possum) in the Late Pleistocene, and two species of rat and a wallaby in the mid Holocene. See also BALOF, ELOAUA ISLAND, LOU, MATENBEK, MATENKUPKUM, WATOM, YOMBON.

Black-and-Red ware a series of CHALCOLITHIC and Iron Age pottery wares in India. They are black on the interior surface and rim, and red on the exterior surface. Depending on the cultural contexts in which the ware appears, Black-and-Red pottery may bear painted decoration (e.g. at AHAR, KAYATHA, RANJPUR), while the specific characteristics of fabric, form and surface treatment of other Black-and-Red wares are highly variable through the Gangetic drainage (e.g. HASTINAPURA, KAUSAMBI, RAJGHAT, CHIRAND), the northern Deccan (e.g. INAMGAON, NEVASA) and further south (e.g. PIKLIHAL, MEGALITHIC GRAVES). This formal and temporal variability leaves the term with only a broad descriptive significance.

black-figured *adj.* (of pottery) characterized by figures or decorative elements that appear in black against the lighter clay background with the detail incised. The technique was also occasionally used on funerary plaques, and was first employed at CORINTH in the 7th century BC (see CORINTHIAN POTTERY), but it is often associated with ATHENS where it appeared in the late 7th century and was common well into the 5th century. However, it was not confined to these two centres (see CHALCIDIAN WARE, PONTIC WARE). Compare RED-FIGURED.

black-glazed see BLACK-GLOSSED.

black-glossed or **black-glazed** *adj.* (of pottery) characterized by a technique used to decorate plain wares giving them an appearance of a black sheen. Black-glossed wares were made alongside the figure-decorated wares (see BLACK-FIGURED, RED-FIGURED), but their popularity continued well into the HELLENISTIC period (see WEST SLOPE WARE). One of the most important centres of production was at ATHENS, from the 6th to the 2nd centuries BC (see ATHENIAN POTTERY), although it was also made at several centres throughout Italy and Sicily. From the middle of the 5th century BC, shapes were frequently ornamented with STAMPED DECORATION, and from the 4th century BC ROULETTING became common on open shapes.

Black Skull a striking robust australopithecine skull with a projecting face and large bony crests on the cranium, stained blue-black by manganese-rich minerals, dated to about 2.5 million years ago, found west of Lake Turkana in northern Kenya in 1985, also known by its catalogue number, KNM-WT 17000. It shows that robust australopithecines had evolved by at least 2.5 million years ago. The find is the subject of nomenclatural debate and ascribed to AUSTRALOPITHECUS *aethiopicus* or *A. boisei*.

Blackwater Draw an important site, actually a series of individual localities, in eastern New Mexico, USA, which is famous for the early investigations on CLOVIS and FOLSOM conducted there since the early 1930s. The surrounding area was once a series of glacial lakes and ponds, and the remains of camel, horse, bison and mammoth have been found, as well as extensive PALAEOINDIAN remains, which include not just Clovis and Folsom, but also AGATE BASIN, CODY and FREDERICK.

blade a long, flat and narrow flake with parallel sides struck from a prepared core, usually by indirect percussion involving the use of a punch placed between the hammer and the STRIKING PLATFORM. Traditionally, blades are defined as measuring at least twice as long as they are wide, with shorter narrower blades being classed as *bladelets*; however, different authorities use different length:breadth ratios. Blades were occasionally manufactured during the Middle Palaeolithic, but Upper Palaeolithic industries show a great increase in blade production and the development of specialized blade tools. See also BACKED BLADE, BURIN, SCRAPER.

bladelet see BLADE.

blank see CORE.

Blattspitzen a category of stone artifact, characterized by complete or nearly complete flaking of both sides and pointed at one or both ends. *Blattspitzen* are found in some late Middle and early Upper Palaeolithic industries of Central and eastern Europe.

Blegen, Carl William (1887–1971) an American archaeologist who excavated at KORAKOU, PROSYMNA and PYLOS in Greece, but who is perhaps best remembered for his extensive excavations at TROY.

Blombos a cave with a deep Stone Age sequence near STILL BAY on the southern coast of the Western Cape Province of South Africa. The upper layers contain LATER STONE AGE remains dating to the last 2,000 years, including large quantities of shellfish and fish bone, as well as pottery and bones of non-indigenous domesticated sheep directly dated to 1960 bp, one of the oldest known instances in the region. A layer of sterile dune sand separates these deposits from underlying MIDDLE STONE AGE material of the Still Bay industry, dated to at least 40,000 bp, and probably to one of the episodes of high sea-level that have been documented during the period between 100,000 and 50,000 bp. The artifacts comprise pressure-flaked bifacial points made on fine-grained silcrete raw material. Worked bone and fishbones in the Middle Stone Age layers could be the first standardized bone artifacts and evidence for fishing recovered from a reliable Middle Stone Age context older than 40,000 bp, with implications for the timing of the origins of modern human behaviour, but they await confirmation (see KATANDA).

bloodletting a MESOAMERICAN practice of piercing the tongue, ear, penis or other body part in order to draw blood. Blood-soaked paper was burned, with the smoke believed to communicate with deified ancestors.

blow-out an erosional landform consisting of a local trough, basin or hollow in sand-dominated material, caused by wind erosion as a local area is destabilized and becomes susceptible to deflation. The term often includes the resulting down-current accumulation of material that forms a blow-out dune. Blow-outs cause disturbance of original archaeological context, as coarser artifactual material settles in the hollow as a residual accumulation and finer material is winnowed out. Simultaneously, burial of artifactual material by the hollow fill may occur downwind.

blow sand see COVER SAND.

Bluefish Caves three small caves in the OLD CROW Basin of the northern Yukon, Canada, which may constitute the oldest archaeological site in North America. Discovered in 1975, they have been investigated by Cinq-Mars and Morlan since 1978. They contain excellently preserved deposits invaluable in reconstructing the environment during the late GLACIAL period. A small quantity of artifacts is buried in shallow loess and rubble deposits, associated with remains of woolly mammoth, Dall sheep, reindeer and other vertebrates. Sixteen radiocarbon dates on various bone fragments span 25,000–12,000 bp, but their relationship to the artifacts is problematic. There seems to be definite evidence for human occupation in deposits from at least 13,000–10,000 bp, including a wedge-shaped microcore, microblades and burins that are similar to tools manufactured in Siberia at the same time, and animal bones that may have been cut with a stone blade. In the lower levels (down to 20,000 bp) débitage flakes, cut and butchered animal bone, and the very large numbers of animal bones are also suggestive of human occupation.

bluestone a type of stone, bluish-grey in dry weather, used in the construction of the second phase of STONEHENGE. The main material is spotted dolerite, but the Stonehenge bluestones also include unspotted dolerite, rhyolite and volcanic. The source has been traced to the Preseli Hills of South Wales, 215 km (134 miles) away, from where the eighty or so bluestones, each weighing around 4 tonnes, are thought by some scholars to have been brought specially to Stonehenge, using river and sea transport as far as possible.

Bluff Cave see NUNAMIRA.

BMAC see BACTRIAN BRONZE AGE.

Boat Axe culture a subgroup of Scandinavia's SINGLE GRAVE/CORDED WARE cultures, characterized by a thin stone battleaxe whose shape resembles an upturned boat.

Boca Chica see CHICOID, TAINOS.

Bocca Quadrata or **Square Mouth** a middle Neolithic culture of northern Italy characterized by pottery vessels with a rounded body ending in a square mouth. Decoration consists mainly of incised geometric motifs. It is especially common in the Po plain and Liguria c.5400–3800 BC, and is present at the ARENE CANDIDE cave and the lake dwelling of Molino Casarotto.

Bockstein the collective name of a series of neighbouring open and cave-sites in the Lone Valley, Württemberg, Germany, which have yielded artifacts and faunal remains from the Middle and Upper Palaeolithic, and which have been excavated principally by Wetzel and Bosinski. The Bocksteinloch, a small cave, and the Bocksteinschmiede, the open area in front of the cave, are perhaps best-known sites, and have produced over 200 MICOQUIAN-style chert bifaces dated by STRATIGRAPHY to the end of the last INTERGLACIAL. The later material includes Bockstein knives.

Bodo a robust early archaic HOMO *sapiens* cranium, also described as *H. heidelbergensis*, found at Bodo d'Ar in Ethiopia in 1976 and thought to date to about 600,000 years ago. The specimen is considered to have the largest face in the human fossil record. Of particular interest near the eye sockets, on the cheekbone, and on the top and back of the head, are incisions which could only have been made by a stone artifact while the bone was fresh, either before or very shortly after death. This is one of the earliest documented cases of intentional defleshing, but it is not known whether CANNIBALISM was involved. The specimen is associated with ACHEULIAN stone artifacts and animal bones.

Bodrogkeresztúr an ENEOLITHIC culture of the Hungarian Plain which succeeds the TISZAPOLGÁR culture c.3800 BC and is followed in turn by the BADEN culture, contemporaneous with CUCUTENI-TRIPOLYE to its east. Bodrogkeresztúr grave-goods resemble those of Tiszapolgár, with undecorated globular pots on pedestals, massive copper shaft-hole 'axe-adzes', and virtually no figurines. Settlement pottery, however, is different, with the use of stab-and-drag (also known as 'Furchenstich') ornament in chequerboard and hatched patterns filled with white incrustation. Domestic cattle predominate in faunal samples.

bog a soft waterlogged area that supports a spongy vegetation community, including sedges, mosses, rushes and grasses, and is maintained by either relatively large amounts of rainfall, geomorphic setting, impedance to throughflow of groundwater, or a combination of these. Bog environments are usually ANAEROBIC and conducive to the preservation of organic remains; they are good sources of PALAEOENVIRONMENTAL information. Peat bogs are also a potential source of fuel. See also FEN.

Boğazköy the ancient Hattusha, the HITTITE capital in the Kizilirmak (Halys River) drainage of northern-central Anatolia, which has been the subject of long-term German research since the beginning of the 20th century. The Hittite city sprawls over a slope interrupted by several hills, the most important of which are Büyükkale and Büyükkaya; the walls of the city enclose about 180 ha (445 acres). The area was first occupied in CHALCOLITHIC times (at Yarıkkaya, about 3 km [2 miles] from the city), followed by EARLY BRONZE AGE occupation (at Büyükkaya). The settlement at the town itself began by the end of the EARLY and into the MIDDLE BRONZE AGE on and near Büyükkale; during the Middle Bronze Age the place was a KĀRUM involved in the Old ASSYRIAN CAPPADOCIAN TRADE. Although it was the royal seat of the Old Hittite period, relatively little of this occupation has been recovered (also on and near Büyükkale). By the time of the Hittite empire (third quarter of the 2nd millennium BC), the city consisted of a walled citadel (at Büyükkale) composed of large administrative buildings containing several extremely valuable archives, a separately walled inner town (about 80 ha [198 acres]) containing the massive Temple I along with residential areas to the northwest of Büyükkale, and a walled outer city (roughly 100 ha [247 acres]) upslope and south of Büyükkale with four excavated temples and several residential districts

also enclosed by a wall (covering about 100 ha). The walls of the latter part of town contain the famous 'Sphinx' and 'Lion' Gates which are often compared to the gate at MYCENAE. After the destruction of Hattusha and the collapse of the Hittite empire in c.1200 BC, the place was reoccupied by a far smaller settlement (at Büyükkale) down to the mid 1st millennium BC.

bog bodies human bodies, recovered from peat bogs all over northwestern Europe, and with their soft tissues well preserved by the humid, airless conditions. Hundreds have been found over the centuries. Men, women, youths and children have been found, and while they span periods from the Mesolithic to medieval times, most seem to belong to the Iron Age. Many met violent ends – cut throats, strangulation, blows – but it is unknown whether they were murder victims, executed criminals, or ritual sacrifices to water deities. Stomach contents sometimes point to a last meal of gruel, and the best preserved corpses also provide invaluable information on clothing and hairstyles. See TOLLUND, GRAUBALLE and LINDOW.

Bohai [Po-hai] 1 the bay at the northern end of the Yellow Sea separating the China mainland from the Korean peninsula. The coastal area of Bohai Bay includes the southern end of the DONGBEI region of China, containing the HONGSHAN, XINLE and XIAJIADIAN cultures.
2 a historic state succeeding KOGURYO in the Manchurian region, AD 698–926; it is spelled 'Parhae' in Korean.

Bohunice a Middle Palaeolithic open-air site located at the edge of Brno in Moravia, Czech Republic. Artifacts and occasional faunal remains are buried in loess deposits that date (on the basis of STRATIGRAPHIC correlation) to the early cold LAST GLACIAL MAXIMUM. The assemblage includes sidescrapers, denticulates, burins and laurel-leaf points, and has been used to define a distinct late Middle Palaeolithic industry (i.e. BOHUNICIAN).

Bohunician adj. of a Middle Palaeolithic industry of Moravia, Czech Republic, characterized by endscrapers and sidescrapers and some bifacial foliates. The industry occurs in the late Middle Palaeolithic (during the middle of the last GLACIAL), and may be transitional to the Upper Palaeolithic. The Bohunician was defined by Valoch in 1976, and seems to have emerged c.44–40,000 BP.

Boian culture a late Neolithic culture of the lower Danube basin (eastern Bulgaria and Romania), c.5000–4600 BC, generally discussed as part of a complex of cultures, including the MARITSA and VĀDASTRA, contemporaneous with layer V at KARANOVO. Boian fine pottery is characterized by narrow channelling, and in its later stages by graphite painted decoration which subsequently became the distinctive feature of the succeeding GUMELNIȚA culture. Notable sites of the Boian culture include Radovanu and the eponymous site of Boian A in southeastern Romania.

Boker Tachtit a stratified open-air Palaeolithic site in the central Negev, Israel, excavated in 1975–80 as part of Anthony Marks's Negev project. It has an industry transitional between the Middle and Upper Palaeolithic that differs from that found further north in the Levant. In the Boker Tachtit industry, dated to at least 43,000 BC, a LEVALLOIS technique produced both points and blades while opposed-platform blade cores are also present; typologically, the assemblages differ markedly from the local MOUSTERIAN industry.

Bökönyi, Sándor (1926–94) a Hungarian veterinarian and archaeozoologist, who was a curator in the archaeology department of the National Museum of Budapest, and from 1979 to 1993 headed the Archaeological Institute of the Hungarian Academy of Sciences. He studied the fauna of countless major archaeological sites, and did pioneering research on the origins and history of animal DOMESTICATION, especially that of the horse.

Boleráz see BADEN CULTURE.

Bølling Interstadial a warm period occurring during the final stages of the last (WEICHSEL) GLACIATION in Europe and starting at c.13,300 BP.

Bologna an important settlement in the Po Valley in northern Italy, where excavations have recovered remains of the VILLANOVAN cemetery. The town was to come under ETRUSCAN influence.

Bol'shaya Akkarzha an Upper Palaeolithic open-air site near the Black Sea coast outside Odessa in southwestern Ukraine. An assemblage of stone artifacts (age unknown) is associated with thousands of steppe bison bone fragments (see also AMVROSIEVKA). The site was excavated by BORSIKOWSKIJ in 1954 and 1961.

Bonampak a CLASSIC Lowland MAYA site in Chiapas, Mexico. The site is significant for its beautiful wall paintings, some of which depict a battle or raid. This graphic illustration of Maya warfare was important evidence suggesting that the traditional view of non-violent Maya civilization was inaccurate. These murals also provide detailed information about other aspects of Maya life, including dress, music and rituals.

Bondaian a regional variant of the AUSTRALIAN SMALL TOOL TRADITION in eastern New South Wales, characterized by BONDI POINTS and other microlithic implements.

bondi point an asymmetric backed blade, characteristic of the AUSTRALIAN SMALL TOOL TRADITION, distributed widely in southern parts of the continent, but absent from much of tropical northern Australia.

bone the substance from which bones are made. Bones are the components of the skeletal framework of vertebrates, formed of bone which consists of inorganic matter (calcium phosphate and calcium carbonate) and an organic matrix (largely collagen and fat). Animal bone was used from the Palaeolithic onwards in the manufacture of a variety of artifacts; it also provides a useful source of nutritious bone-marrow. As bone decays rapidly in acid soil, bone tools are almost certainly underrepresented in the archaeological record.

bone dating dating methods applied to collagen and mineral components of human and animal bones. Absolute ages with margins of uncertainty can be obtained by RADIOCARBON DATING, URANIUM SERIES DATING methods and, in some cases, AMINO ACID RACEMIZATION. RELATIVE AGES can be obtained by amino acid racemization, NITROGEN DATING and FLUORINE DATING methods. In *bone collagen dating*, protein collagen is extracted from bone and dated by radiocarbon. The collagen is selected for dating because it is less likely to be contaminated with modern carbon in the soil environment than the total organic carbon or apatite carbonate fraction.

Bonfire Shelter a bison KILL-SITE in Texas, USA, unusual because it has a long, albeit discontinuous, sequence of use (approximately 10,000 BC–AD 600) in an area that was not a primary bison habitat. The site is located in a rockshelter into which bison may have been driven from above, although new excavations of a portion of the site suggest that the earliest levels may have been associated with an animal trap, rather than a jump.

Book of the Dead modern designation of the ancient Egyptian 'Chapters of Coming Forth by Day', religious texts of the NEW KINGDOM whose purpose was to ensure a beneficial afterlife for the deceased, particularly with the god OSIRIS. The texts and illustrations of the Book of the Dead were placed in the tomb in the form of a papyrus roll, or painted on the walls of the tomb itself.

boomerang a curved throwing stick, one form of which can be made to return to the thrower. Returning and non-returning boomerangs are widely used by Australian Aborigines for hunting, fighting and as toys. The oldest Australian examples from WYRIE SWAMP are 10,000 years old. Although often thought of as uniquely Australian, they are known from other parts of the world. Archaeological examples have been found in Mesolithic Holland and Egypt, while a curved piece of mammoth tusk from OBLAZOWA, southern Poland, dating to 18,600 bp, is the oldest-known boomerang-like artifact. See also LITTLE SALT SPRING.

Boomplaas a cave in the Western Cape Province of South Africa, which contains a 5 m (16 ft) deep stratified deposit spanning the last 80,000 years, with successive MIDDLE and LATER STONE AGE industries excavated by H. J. Deacon in the 1970s. The excellent preservation and careful excavation of the large and small mammal remains, pollen, charcoal, sediments and artifacts have provided a unique record of environmental and cultural changes in the Western Cape.

Boqueirão see PEDRA FURADA.

bora ground or **bora ring** a group of Australian circular earthen structures, commonly linked by a pathway, used for ceremonies in northern-central New South Wales and southeastern Queensland. Similar features are also known from Victoria.

Border Cave a South African cave almost on the Kwa-Zulu-Natal Province/Swaziland border. Its stratified 2 m (6 ft) deep deposit contains MIDDLE STONE AGE assemblages dating from before 130,000 years ago, EARLY LATER STONE AGE assemblages dating to 45,000–33,000 BP, and, in the uppermost layers, recent Iron Age material. Although some human remains are of doubtful provenance, an adult mandible from deposits radiocarbon dated to more than 49,000 bp, as well as a partial cranium and an infant skeleton thought to be c.100,000 years old, may document the presence of anatomically modern HOMO *sapiens* in southern Africa during the early Upper Pleistocene. The infant skeleton is the only definite burial attributed to the Middle Stone Age in southern Africa.

Bordes, François (1919–81) a French prehistoric archaeologist best known for his pioneering study of the sediments of the River Seine, and for his classification of the MOUSTERIAN of southwestern France by means of the *système Bordes*, which involved the consideration of tool-type percentages plotted on CUMULATIVE GRAPHS and various technological and TYPOLOGICAL ratios. Bordes excavated at the Palaeolithic sites of COMBE-GRENAL and PECH DE L'AZÉ, and was an expert flint-knapper.

Bordj Mellala an Algerian early Neolithic site dating to c.7000 BP, associated with geometric microliths as well as numerous ostrich eggshell beads and decorated water containers. Refitting of the stone artifacts has led to the recognition of specialized activity areas within the site.

Boreal climatic period one of five POSTGLACIAL climatic and vegetation periods distinguished by Blytt and Sernander on the basis of POLLEN ANALYSIS, dated roughly to c.9600–7500 bp. The Boreal period in northern Europe represents the first real establishment of European woodlands, and sea-levels rose rapidly as the ice-sheets melted, separating Britain, Ireland and the Danish islands from the European continent.

boreal forest or **taiga** a group of related vegetation communities dominated by coniferous trees that exists in higher latitudes of the northern hemisphere but gener-

ally south of tundra. Climatic conditions that favour such communities are severe winters and short growing seasons; in some areas they are growing on PERMAFROST. During GLACIAL episodes of the QUATERNARY the location of the boreal forest shifted southwards. Boreal forests supported animals now extinct, such as the mastodon, that were potential food sources.

bored stone a roundish stone with a hole bored through its middle, found in a variety of sizes on sites throughout southern and Central Africa dating to the last 40,000 years. Some were impaled as weights on digging sticks used to uproot plant tubers, a practice which is depicted in rock paintings as well as recorded ethnographically in southern Africa and Ethiopia.

Borg early Viking chieftain's house on Vesvågøy, Lofoten islands, northern Norway, built in several stages between c.AD 600 and 900. The house at Borg is the largest Viking longhouse known, 83 m (272 ft) long and 9 m (30 ft) wide. It had four rooms including a large central room, storerooms and a stable at one end. Numerous artifacts, including pottery, glass and gold objects, reflect long-distance contact with England, Germany and France.

Boriskowskij, Pavel Iossifovitch (1911–91) an eminent Soviet Palaeolithic specialist, pupil of EFIMENKO, best known for his excavations at AMVROSIEVKA, BOL'SHAYA AKKARZHA, KOSTENKI and PUSHKARI. He was especially notable for addressing the social aspects of the Middle/Upper Palaeolithic transition, from a MARXIST perspective, in the early 1930s.

Bornu see KANEM.

Borobudur a great stone STUPA near Magelang in central Java, thought to be the largest in the world, and famous for its reliefs illustrating Buddhist literature, built in the late 8th–early 9th centuries AD by the rulers of MATARAM. The structure comprises six square terraces surmounted by three round terraces and a large bell-shaped stupa. The scenes in the reliefs fall into three zones: the lowest, on the hidden base, illustrate the 'world of desire' (*kamadhatu*); above this is the 'world of form' (*rupadhatu*); then comes the 'world of formlessness' (*arupadhatu*).

Borodino treasure (also known as **Bessarabsky**) a Bronze Age hoard found near the village of Borodino in Bessarabia (Odessa region, Ukraine) in 1912. The treasure consists of seventeen objects: silver spear-heads, a silver dagger and a big pin, stone finials of maces and polished jade pole-axes of a perfect form. The silver objects are decorated with fine ornaments such as gold inlay. The treasure has great importance from the chronological point of view, since it reflects different cultural influences: there are analogies from the SHAFT GRAVE in MYCENAE, from Caucasus bronzes, and especially among the so-called SEIMA-TURBINO BRONZES that were widespread on the territory of the EURASIAN STEPPES in the mid 2nd millennium BC. The objects had never been used, they were of undoubted value in ancient times, and they clearly constitute the extremely rare and spectacular ceremonial attire of a powerful chief or chieftain, who lived c.1550–1450 BC. The Borodino treasure is housed in the State Historical Museum in Moscow.

Bose a basin in the Guangxi Zhuang region of southern China where American and Chinese excavators have found thousands of Lower Palaeolithic tools at twenty-four sites, assigned by argon-argon dating to about 800,000 years ago, and buried in the molten debris of an ancient meteorite impact. They comprise implements flaked from cobbles of chert, sandstone and quartz, and somewhat resemble the handaxes of Africa, Europe and the Middle East in their sophistication and skill of manufacture.

Bosumpra a cave in central Ghana with evidence for occupation for some 3,500 years after the late 5th millennium BC, and a microlithic LATER STONE AGE industry with pottery and ground-stone tools, associated with charred oil-bearing seeds, which suggest a transition from the use of wild *Canarium* to the domestic oil palm, *Eleis*.

Bosutswe see TOUTSWE.

Botai an ENEOLITHIC settlement on the River Ishim in northern Kazakhstan, covering 15 ha (37 acres), and containing the remains of buildings, such as 153 round pithouses, workshops, structures for livestock, and burials, all suggesting at least four phases of occupation. The material culture comprises stone and bone tools, and half-egg shaped ceramics. Thousands of animal bones have been found, more than 99 per cent of them from horses. Wear on the teeth suggests that these horses had been tamed and were ridden, in addition to being a key food resource, and they are thus considered to be the oldest known domesticated specimens. The Botai settlement is currently being excavated by V. Zaibert. There are other similar sites concentrated between the Tobol and Irtysh Rivers, and together they form the Botai culture, of which Botai itself is the type-site.

bothros a pit in Greek archaeology, typically used for storage purposes or rubbish disposal.

Botta, Paul-Emile (1802–70) the first scholar to discover ASSYRIAN monuments when, as the French consul in Mosul, he excavated at NINEVEH and KHORSABAD in 1840–43. His collection of imperial Assyrian artwork now graces the Louvre.

Bouar a 130 by 30 km (81 by 19 miles) area in the Central African Republic with hundreds of megaliths, consisting of standing stones on oval tumuli, which may be burial grounds. Initial construction is thought to have taken place in the 6th–5th millennia BC, with later reutilization.

Boucher de Perthes, Jacques (1788–1868) a French customs official and amateur antiquary who first recognized the true antiquity of humankind in France by correctly identifying Lower Palaeolithic bifaces from the River Somme gravels as the tools of 'antediluvian (pre-flood) man' found in association with the bones of extinct animals. After gaining support from Joseph Prestwich and John EVANS in 1859, Boucher de Perthes' theories were slowly accepted by the French and British scientific establishments.

Bougon an important cemetery of megalithic tombs at Deux-Sèvres, France, comprising eight chambers in five mounds labelled A–F (D is a field boundary). Radiocarbon dates indicate that the oldest of the chambers (E1 and F0) date to the mid 5th millennium BC and hence are among the oldest CHAMBERED TOMBS in Europe. The cemetery was greatly aggrandized in later centuries with the construction of the large mounds A, C and F. Many of the mounds are multi-phase, but the scarcity of associated material has made it very difficult to establish the precise chronology of the sequence. Pottery ranges from possible early Neolithic sherds beneath one of the mounds, to material of the late Neolithic or Early Bronze Age.

boulder the size subdivision of gravel clasts larger than 256 mm (about 10.5 inches) in diameter, according to the Wentworth-Udden classification system. In the past, 'boulder' has carried the connotation of having been transported from a distance, and being somewhat rounded, although these inferences are not necessarily accurate.

bouleuterion a meeting place for the council (*boule*) in a Greek city normally adjacent to the AGORA. The buildings are usually square and contain a room which served as a debating chamber. Seats were normally placed around three sides, either in straight rows, or in curved tiers as found in theatres. At ATHENS, the bouleuterion contained seating for 500.

boundary the zone of vertical change from one soil horizon to another. Boundaries are described in terms of the vertical distance over which the change occurs, such as abrupt, clear or gradual, and the horizontal character of the boundary, such as whether it is smooth, wavy or irregular. Compare CONTACT.

Bouqras a multi-phase PRE-POTTERY NEOLITHIC (PPNB, c.7600–6000 BC) village of rectilinear mud-brick houses on the middle Euphrates River, opposite the confluence of the Khabur River in Syria. The interior walls of the houses sometimes bear painted decoration and human heads modelled in relief. Domesticated animals appear only at the end of the sequence, while the status of plants remains uncertain throughout.

Boussargues an enclosed village site in Hérault, France, with APSIDAL houses surrounded by a wall with projecting circular huts or towers, all built of dry-stone work. The circular huts had CORBEL-VAULTED roofs. Within the apsidal houses, pottery of the CHALCOLITHIC FONTBOUISSE culture (c.2500 BC) has been found. Finds of carbonized acorns and other nuts indicate that forest resources probably played an important part in the economy. The settlement is one of a number of enclosed Fontbouisse villages known in the area.

bout coupé *adj.* ('cut-end') a term used by some British archaeologists to describe a well-made cordiform or sub-triangular refined biface recovered from northwestern Europe, usually encountered as an isolated and undated find, but believed to be a diagnostic MOUSTERIAN tool.

bow-and-arrow an offensive weapon for firing small projectiles over great distances that is especially useful in the characterization of some North American cultures. The technology was introduced to North America as early as the PRE-DORSET in the Central Arctic, and quickly spread throughout many other regions as a distinct horizon. It is best recognized by small projectile points.

Boxgrove an ACHEULIAN site in West Sussex, England, excavated by Roberts, which has yielded a massive tibia of a man more than 1.8 m (6 ft) tall, and two teeth, dated to c.500,000 BP; and an extensive *in situ* biface manufacturing floor with lithic tools and débitage, bone tools and associated faunal material. The site has yielded clear evidence (spear-wounds, butchery marks) that its occupants were hunters rather than scavengers, killing and butchering rhinos, horses, deer and bison with great skill and organization.

Boyne Valley tombs a major cemetery of megalithic tombs in a bend of the River Boyne, Meath, Ireland, comprising three large tombs (Dowth, KNOWTH and NEWGRANGE) together with several smaller mounds. The tombs consist of circular mounds containing one or more PASSAGE GRAVES. Knowth and Newgrange are famous for the complex megalithic art which decorates the stones of their chambers and passages and of the kerbs which surround their covering mounds.

BP abbreviation for 'before present', by convention meaning before AD 1950; therefore, to convert a date from BP to BC (before Christ), it is necessary to subtract 1950 years. The use of lower case letters (*bp* or *bc*) indicates a radiocarbon date which has not been calibrated, and is therefore likely to appear younger than it should.

brachycephalic see CEPHALIC.

Bradshaw figures small red finely painted human figures in animated scenes common in the Kimberley region of Western Australia, and named after Joseph Bradshaw who 'discovered' them in the late 19th century. They are clearly of some antiquity because some artifacts depicted did not exist in recent Kimberley culture. Con-temporary Aboriginal people attribute them to spirits, and they often underlie polychrome WANDJINA paintings. They resemble the MIMI figures of ARNHEM LAND.

Brak, Tell a 40 ha (99 acre) site in the Khabur triangle of northeastern Syria known largely from the excavations by MALLOWAN in the 1930s, which revealed occupation at the site from 'UBAID to the mid 2nd millennium BC. Among Mallowan's more notable discoveries is a sequence of late URUK to JEMDET NASR temples (the 'Eye Temple', named after the recurrent eye motif within this building) beneath the palace of the AKKADIAN king NARAM-SIN and another of UR III construction; domestic architecture of the latter periods was also uncovered. In later levels, Mallowan found a MITANNI palace and temple. David and Joan Oates reopened investigation of Tell Brak during the late 1970s and 1980s, greatly refining the early 4th–mid 2nd millennium chronology of the site, and providing important new details about the 4th and the early 2nd millennium BC occupations. The evidence indicates the existence early in the 4th millennium of a complex society of indigenous character which in the middle centuries of the millennium became overwhelmingly southern MESOPOTAMIAn (middle Uruk) in character. The recent work has also revealed a massive Old ASSYRIAN building and traces of a city wall belonging to this time, perhaps a reflection of SHAMSHI-ADAD's empire building in the late 19th century BC.

Branč an Early Bronze Age inhumation cemetery in southwestern Slovakia, belonging to the so-called NITRA group (contemporaneous with the ÚNETICE culture further to the west). Susan Shennan's analysis of the approximately 300 burials produced clear evidence for social differentiation. A number of the female graves, including those of several children, were especially richly furnished, leading her to conclude that the females either achieved wealth by marriage or had it ascribed at birth. Several smaller cemeteries in this region suggest similar patterns.

Brandberg a mountain massif in the Namib desert of central Namibia with Stone Age and Iron Age material, particularly well known for its rock paintings, of which some 43,000 were documented by Harald Pager. One of the most celebrated of all rock paintings is the so-called 'White Lady of the Brandberg', made famous by the abbé BREUIL's romantic interpretation of it as a white woman with Mediterranean features. It seems, however, that Breuil was misled by natural marks on the rock and that the figure represents a male SAN or Herero.

Brassempouy a cave-site in the Landes, southwestern France, where excavations by PIETTE in the 1890s and by Delporte in the 1980s have revealed occupation from the MOUSTERIAN to the AZILIAN. The Grotte du Pape is best known for its series of ivory 'VENUS' FIGURINES and small ivory human head, generally attributed to the

GRAVETTIAN, but ascribed by BREUIL to an early AURIG-NACIAN or even CHÂTELPERRONIAN layer. The nearby Galerie des Hyènes contains Aurignacian material, together with a little MAGDALENIAN.

Brauron the TEMENOS of the goddess Artemis Brauronia in Attica, Greece, where young Athenian girls attended ceremonies dressed as bears. Excavations have revealed remains of a temple of the DORIC ORDER, as well as a STOA which included several dining-rooms (see SYMPOSIUM).

Brea, Luigi Bernabō (1910–99) Italian archaeologist best known for his extensive work in the Mediterranean, notably at ARENE CANDIDE, POLIOCHNI, and on Sicily and the Lipari islands.

breccia a rock consisting mostly of angular rock fragments larger than sand-size and cemented together. Uncemented counterparts, such as are found in some cave deposits or at the base of cliffs, are more accurately described as angular BOULDER or COBBLE GRAVELS, or DIAMICTON. Production of relatively large angular rock fragments is associated with cold climatic conditions where frost-related processes are intense. Caves that experienced human occupation may have archaeological deposits incorporated into or interstratified with deposits with abundant angular rock fragments.

Breitenbach an Upper Palaeolithic open-air site located on the Elster River in eastern Germany. Artifacts and faunal remains (e.g. woolly mammoth, reindeer) are contained in a buried soil probably dating to an INTERSTADIAL preceding the LAST GLACIAL MAXIMUM. The artifacts include endscrapers, burins and several bone points, and are assigned to the AURIGNACIAN.

Breuil, abbé Henri Edouard Prosper (1877–1961) a French priest and prehistorian, particularly noted for his typological classification of Palaeolithic artifacts and for his recording and 'sympathetic magic' interpretation of Palaeolithic art.

Brewarrina a freshwater fish trap system on the Darling River, northwestern New South Wales, Australia. It comprises a complex system of pens and weirs extending for 400 m (440 yds). The stone enclosures are built from cobbles and their different shapes, sizes and heights accommodate changes in river-levels. See also LAKE CONDAH, TOOLONDO.

Brézillon, Michel (1924–93) a French prehistorian who worked in Egypt, Nubia, Greece, Algeria and Japan, but whose principal work was conducted at the French sites of Mournouards (1960) and PINCEVENT (1964–70).

bridging argument an argument linking the materials in the archaeological record with interpretations about cultural systems (see also ACTUALISTIC STUDY, WARRANTING ARGUMENT). It allows the prediction of specific sets of phenomena based on prior generalizations (see also DEDUCTION).

bristlecone pine the most useful tree species (*Pinus aristata*) in DENDROCHRONOLOGY studies. It is found in the Sierra Nevada of California at higher elevations. With a life span of up to at least 4,600 years, the bristlecone pine provides continuous tree-ring records for dating purposes and PALAEOENVIRONMENTAL reconstruction.

Britain and Ireland The earliest evidence for human presence in Britain dates to the Lower Palaeolithic period around half a million years ago. From this period flint artifacts are found, notably handaxes, generally in the river terrace gravels but also at the undisturbed site of Boxgrove in Sussex, where they are associated with human remains generally attributed to HOMO *heidelbergensis*. During the height of each glacial episode most of Britain was uninhabited though at the same time lower sea-levels meant that it was connected to the Continent by dry land. Occupation of the Cheddar Gorge caves belongs to the latest cold period (in cultural terms the Upper Palaeolithic) (see GOUGH'S CAVE) and reveals bands of hunter-gatherers able to survive in the harsh conditions. The RED LADY OF PAVILAND (in fact a young male) documents forays as far north as South Wales and, covered in red ochre, is the earliest intentional burial in Britain.

With the resumption of warmer conditions some 10,000 years ago sea-levels rose, eventually separating Britain definitely from the Continent in c.6000 BC, though evidence of boats is given by the first settlement of Ireland c.7000 BC. The Mesolithic period from the end of the last GLACIAL to the beginnings of farming c.4000 BC was characterized by the spread of forest populated by small bands of hunters and gatherers exploiting the forest resources including deer and aurochs (wild cattle). The way of life is illustrated by the famous Mesolithic lake-side settlement of STAR CARR in Yorkshire.

The transition to the Neolithic period occurred around 4000 BC and marks the beginning of a tradition of monument building in Britain and Ireland which was to last over 2,500 years. Cereals were grown (adopted ultimately from the Near East via Continental neighbours) and domestic cattle, pig and sheep were raised, though several centuries of mobile lifestyles elapsed before settled farming became the norm. Rather than farming villages and field systems (which are absent from Britain until the Bronze Age), the British Neolithic is marked by CAUSEWAYED CAMPS, LONG MOUNDS, PASSAGE GRAVES, CURSUS monuments, HENGES and STONE CIRCLES. Polished stone axes from sources in the highlands of western and northern Britain circulated among these communities. The scale of communal endeavour is illustrated by STONEHENGE, AVEBURY and SILBURY HILL. In Ireland, the most impressive monuments are the passage graves with their wealth of 'mega-

0   200 km

Jarlshof

Maes Howe
Skara Brae
Quanterness
Isbister

Callanish

Oronsay

Antonine Wall

Newstead
Lindisfarne
Yeavering

Broighter
Mount Sandel
Tievebulliagh
Hadrian's Wall
Housesteads
Lyles Hill
Vindolanda
Heathery Burn

Carrowmore
Navan
Great Langdale
Stanwick
Cass ny Hawin
Star Carr
York
Knowth/Newgrange
Arras/Wharram Percy
Tara
Hanging Grimston

Dowris
Pontnewydd cave
Lindow
Graig Llwyd
Creswell

Lough Gur

Nene Valley
Wroxeter
Snettisham
Fengate/Flag Fen
High Lodge
Grimes Graves
Haddenham
Mildenhall
Hazleton
Wilburton
Hoxne
Crickley Hill
St Albans
Sutton Hoo
Stanton Drew
Bath
Wayland's Smithy
Colchester
Paviland Cave
Gough's Cave
Wolvercote
Clacton
Aveline's Hole
Abingdon
Yiewsley
Avebury/Silbury Hill/
London
Battersea
West Kennet/Windmill Hill
Danebury
Sweet Track/
Runnymede
Aylesford
Glastonbury
Baker's Hole
Oldbury
Little Woodbury
& Swanscombe
Hambledon Hill
New Forest
Boxgrove
Maiden Castle
Bush Barrow/
Rillaton
Hembury
Durrington Walls/
Hengistbury
Fishbourne
Stonehenge/Woodhenge
Gwithian
Head
Kent's Cavern &
Portchester
Windmill Cave
Mary Rose

lithic art', notably those of the Boyne Valley such as KNOWTH and NEWGRANGE (c.3000 BC). In contrast to Britain, Ireland has evidence of Neolithic houses as well as field systems (for example at CÉIDE in County Mayo), suggesting that the lifestyle may have been more settled here than in southern Britain.

In around 2500 BC, pottery vessels of the type known as BEAKERS become common throughout Britain, and shortly afterwards the first metal objects (of copper and gold) make their appearance. This marks the beginning of the Bronze Age (c.2200–700 BC). Around the middle of the 2nd millennium BC groups of small circular houses and systems of rectangular fields (the so-called CELTIC FIELDS) indicate growth in population and the spread of settled farming. First used mainly for ornaments, bronze becomes an increasingly utilitarian metal, and bronze slashing swords make their appearance in the Late Bronze Age (from c.1200 BC). This trend continues into the Iron Age (c.700 BC–AD 43), when HILLFORTS are constructed in many regions, including the famous MAIDEN CASTLE in Dorset. Defended by single or multiple lines of rampart and ditch, these were probably refuges rather than permanent settlements or townships, and politically the peoples of southern Britain retained the character of decentralized, small-scale farming societies. Only in the very late Iron Age, notably after the cross-Channel raids mounted by Julius Caesar in 55 and 54 BC and before the final Roman invasion of AD 43, does evidence suggest the emergence of native kingdoms such as that of the Catuvellauni centred on Colchester. Northern Britain and Ireland remained outside the range of these developments, however, with a dispersed settlement pattern of small fortified farmsteads including the BROCHS of northern and western Scotland and the DUNS and ringforts of Ireland. The kingdom of the PICTS in Scotland, and the traditional Irish kingdoms of Ulster, Munster, Leinster and Connaught, do not emerge as major political entities until the mid 1st millennium AD and coincide broadly with the adoption of Christianity in those areas.

Within thirty years of the Roman invasion under the emperor Claudius in AD 43 the conquest of England and Wales was complete. The northern frontier remained problematic and the emperor Hadrian in AD 122 ordered the construction of a wall, with associated forts, across the width of the island from the mouth of the River Tyne to the Solway estuary. Twenty years later the frontier was pushed north to the Forth-Clyde isthmus and a further wall (of turf and timber) was constructed, but the northernmost part of Britain was never conquered by the Romans and for most of the Roman period HADRIAN'S WALL formed the effective limit.

A network of roads and towns was built throughout lowland Britain, and the mineral resources and agricultural potential of the island were exploited. The provincial capital at LONDON was balanced by a northern centre at YORK, but municipal life was never well established

and the cities were in decline by the end of the 2nd century AD. Throughout the period, Britain remained a highly militarized province, and remains of legionary and auxiliary forts are among its most striking archaeological remains. During the 4th century Roman power weakened, and Britain was subject to raids and settlement by peoples from the low-lying countries on the eastern side of the North Sea (the ANGLO-SAXONS) and from Ireland. The end of Roman rule is conventionally placed at 410. The Anglo-Saxon settlement of eastern England gathered pace during the 5th and 6th centuries and a series of Germanic kingdoms was founded. The scale of the colonization is disputed but it is significant that in Britain alone of the western Roman provinces, Latin was replaced by the language (Old English) of the newcomers.

Christianity was reintroduced to the southeast in 597 but did not immediately replace Anglo-Saxon beliefs, as is illustrated by the richly furnished ship burial at SUTTON HOO in East Anglia, dated to the early 7th century AD. Other archaeological remains include cemeteries of flat graves, small villages of houses typically with sunken floored buildings, and 'royal' centres such as YEAVERING in Northumbria. Stone was largely reserved for religious buildings, including monasteries, though most churches were modest timber affairs. The west of Britain remained outside Anglo-Saxon rule, and retained its own 'Celtic' Christian tradition until Celtic and Roman traditions were reconciled in 664. Imported pottery at the clifftop centre of Tintagel in Cornwall illustrates how these western enclaves retained trade links with the mainland and continued to import wine in the 6th century. In the north, native kingdoms of Scots and Picts dominated Scotland, while the kingdoms of Ireland converted to Christianity in the 5th century and later sent missionaries to western and northern Britain. In Ireland, traces of religious and monastic buildings become prominent in the archaeological record, alongside the native duns and RATHS.

During the 9th century VIKING raids were followed by Scandinavian settlement in northern and eastern Britain, and also in Ireland. Many Irish towns including Dublin and Waterford were founded by the Vikings as trading settlements. In England, the Anglo-Saxon counteroffensive during the 9th century led to the creation of the first unified kingdom of England, but this lasted little more than a century until the conquest by William the Conqueror in 1066. A feudal kingdom developed in Scotland also during the 11th century, although the northern isles remained under Scandinavian control until the 15th century.

Broad Spectrum Revolution the concept of a subsistence shift in western Asia, from a relatively narrow to a wider array of foodstuffs, including small mammals, invertebrates, aquatic resources and a diversity of plants. In an attempt to explain the origins of food production,

The BROCH of Gurness, Orkney, Scotland.

several commentators (notably Kent Flannery) have suggested that late Pleistocene foraging communities in western Asia were able, through this shift, to live in larger and more sedentary communities, which could act as a buffer against environmental change. This 'broad spectrum revolution' (e.g. in the KEBARAN COMPLEX and the NATUFIAN in the Levantine sequence) would establish economic, demographic and social conditions conducive to experimentation with domesticated plants and animals, and so stands as a prelude to the 'Neolithic revolution'. Although the Broad Spectrum Revolution is still widely cited, more recent studies indicate that generalized foraging was a common pattern through much of the Upper Pleistocene in western Asia (and especially the Levant), and that the discontinuity in subsistence patterns implicit in the idea is overstated.

broch a circular dry-stone defensive tower found in coastal parts of northern and western Scotland and the islands. Up to 10 m (33 ft) tall with several stages of curving galleries within the thickness of the outer wall, brochs also had stone-built internal room divisions covered probably by a lean-to roof, leaving the central area open to the sky. Some, such as Gurness on Orkney, stood at the centre of a settlement of dry-stone houses within an outer defensive ditch. The origins of the broch lie in the mid 1st millennium BC, but most were probably built in the 2nd and 1st centuries BC/AD.

Broederstroom an extensive Early Iron Age site in the North-West Province, South Africa, consisting of a series of villages built between the 5th and 7th centuries AD. The excavation of Negroid human skeletal remains, collapsed circular huts, grain bins, iron-working debris, the bones of domestic sheep, goats and cattle as well as hunted animals, provides an unusually detailed picture of southern African Early Iron Age village life, and documents the existence of the CENTRAL CATTLE PATTERN in the 5th century AD.

Broighter a gold boat model, part of a hoard discovered in Co. Londonderry, Northern Ireland, by a ploughman in 1891, which also included a gold collar, twisted TORCS, necklaces and a hanging bowl. The boat, only 18.5 cm (7.3 inches) long, has oars, benches for the rowers and a mast. It may be LA TÈNE, late 1st century BC.

Broken Hill a mine near Kabwe in central Zambia, now quarried away, which has yielded remains including in 1921 a superbly preserved cranium with massive brow ridges, thought to be of the order of about 300,000 years old. The specimen shows indications of dental caries and abscesses, as well as of a healed wound near the left ear. Originally described as 'Rhodesian Man', HOMO *rhodesiensis*, an extinct species once thought to have been intermediate between *H. erectus* and *H. sapiens*, researchers now consider it difficult to identify links between the Broken Hill fossil and modern populations. Some group it together with a Middle Pleistocene cranium from Bodo in Ethiopia, and similar European specimens, in the species *H. heidelbergensis*.

Brommian a culture of Denmark, southern Sweden, northern Germany and Poland, dating to the ALLERØD and DRYAS III phases, and named after the Zealand lakeside reindeer-hunting camp of Bromme (c.10,000 bc). Of uncertain origin, and possibly derived from the MAGDALENIAN, it resembles the HAMBURGIAN, and may be the origin of the SWIDERIAN and AHRENSBURGIAN. It is characterized by the Lyngby point and Lyngby reindeer-antler 'axe' or club.

Bronocice a middle Neolithic hilltop site in southern Poland, with occupations of the FUNNEL BEAKER culture and a BADEN-like culture. The site at Bronocice, covering over 50 ha (124 acres), is extraordinarily large compared with contemporaneous sites in the same region. Notable among the Funnel Beaker finds is a pot with incised decoration believed to depict a wheeled vehicle.

bronze an alloy of copper, usually made by the addition of tin and sometimes including small amounts of other metals, used in the production of weapons, implements, art works and decorations. The Bronze Age cultural period takes its name from the proliferation during that time of items manufactured from bronze.

Bronze Age the period of antiquity in the Old World in which bronze became the primary material for tools and weapons. One of the elements of THOMSEN'S THREE AGE SYSTEM, the Bronze Age in Europe conventionally spans the period from 2200 to about 800 BC. The fact that tin and copper normally do not occur naturally in proximity resulted in a significant rise in trade, which was one of the factors in the progressive differentiation of access to status, power and wealth.

In *East Asia* the period of bronze use on the China mainland coincided with the stratification of society and state development in the SHANG and ZHOU periods of the 2nd–1st millennia BC (see CHINESE DYNASTIES). On the Korean peninsula, the Bronze Age commenced about 700 BC but was derived from a northern source (see TUNGUS). Iron was introduced from China c.400 BC, so that the Late Bronze Age and the Early Iron Age of Korea are contemporaneous (see KOREA). Both bronze and iron were transferred to the Japanese islands from the Korean peninsula c.300 BC at the same time as wet-rice agriculture. Thus the Neolithic, Bronze Age and Iron Age were all encompassed by the YAYOI culture in Japan (see JAPANESE PERIODIZATION).

See also EARLY, MIDDLE and LATE BRONZE AGE, with reference to the *Levant*.

bronze mirrors smooth-faced bronze discs with cast decoration on the back. Appearing in East Asia in the late 2nd millennium BC, they became a major toilette item of the HAN Dynasty elite in China; but in Korea and Japan, they fulfilled ritual or ceremonial functions, whether imported from China or manufactured locally. Korean mirrors of the Bronze Age are noted for their fine-lined geometric decoration, while some local Japanese mirrors of the KOFUN period bear CHOKKOMON designs. **(See fig., p. 94)**

Broom, Robert (1866–1951) a Scottish palaeontologist and physician who worked in Australia and South Africa, where he became renowned for his discoveries of mammal-like reptiles (therapsids) from the Karoo, and australopithecines from STERKFONTEIN (including the first australopithecine found at this locality in 1936, and in 1947 an australopithecine cranium nicknamed 'Mrs Ples'), KROMDRAAI (including in 1938 the first known robust australopithecines, which he named PARANTHROPUS *robustus*) and SWARTKRANS (which yielded early HOMO fossils, originally named *Telanthropus*, in 1948). He was one of few scientists who supported DART's interpretation of the 1924 TAUNG fossil as an early HOMINID before its widespread acceptance in the late 1940s.

Brørup see CHELFORD.

Bruchenbrücken see LINEAR POTTERY.

Brunn see LINEAR POTTERY.

Brynzeny I a cave-site in Moldova, located on a tributary of the Prut River, containing Palaeolithic, Mesolithic and younger artifacts. The lowest horizon is assigned to the early Upper Palaeolithic on typological grounds by the excavator, but no radiocarbon dates are available. A carved and decorated woolly mammoth tusk represents a rare Palaeolithic art object from this region. The site was discovered and excavated by Ketraru in 1963–5.

Brześć Kujawski a multi-period site in northern-central Poland first excavated by Konrad JAŻDŻEWSKI in 1933–9, with later excavations by Chmielewski in 1952 and by R. Grygiel and P. Bogucki in 1976–84. Over a dozen archaeological cultures are represented at Brześć Kujawski, with major settlements of the early Neolithic LINEAR POTTERY and LENGYEL cultures and later during the LA TÈNE period of the Iron Age. Brześć Kujawski is best known for the trapezoidal LONGHOUSES and rich burials of the Lengyel occupation, which have also been found recently at the nearby site of OSŁONKI.

Bubanj-Hum an ENEOLITHIC regional group in Serbia, centred on the sites of Bubanj and Hum near Niš in the Morava Valley. The Bubanj-Hum group succeeded the VINČA culture in this region and appears to have lasted through several long phases. Phase IA is the most distinctive, with graphite painted wares and burnished ware. Phase IB is contemporaneous with BADEN in northern Serbia and Hungary, while II is related to COŢOFENI and SALCUŢA in Bulgaria. The deposits at Bubanj itself have provided one of the more complete stratigraphic sequences for the central Balkans during this period.

Bubastis the CLASSICAL name for the Egyptian site of TELL Basta, situated in the southeastern Nile DELTA. Most of the construction of the major surviving monuments of the site, excavated by NAVILLE in 1887–9, was initiated by kings of the 22nd Dynasty (945–715 BC), who came from Bubastis.

bucchero a type of pottery produced in ETRURIA, especially in the ARCHAIC PERIOD. It was fired with a restricted supply of oxygen to give an even, black appearance through the fabric. It was burnished before firing, which resulted in a lustrous appearance. Decorative motifs, often consisting of semicircles or fans, were incised or impressed.

Buchau or **Wasserburg Buchau** a Late Bronze Age settlement in southern Germany excavated by Reinerth in the 1930s. It is located on an island in the moor surrounding the Federsee and has traces of two occupations. The first had thirty-eight rectangular post structures, thirty-seven of which were single-room buildings 4 by 5 m (13 by 16 ft) while one was a larger two-roomed building. The second settlement had nine complexes of large multi-roomed houses, along with assorted outbuildings. Both settlements were surrounded by a palisade. Buchau provides some of the rare settlement data for the URNFIELD period in Central Europe.

bucranium an ox-skull normally carved in relief and forming part of the decorative scheme of buildings in the Roman world. A second context for their use was funerary (see CINERARIUM, SARCOPHAGUS). They are often associated with garlands.

Buda industry a Lower Palaeolithic industry of Hungary characterized by the production of chopping tools on pebbles and flake tools. The industry was defined by

VÉRTES in 1965 and is best represented at the Middle Pleistocene site of VÉRTESSZÖLLÖS.

Budakalász a cemetery of the BADEN culture near Budapest in Hungary. It is known especially for the model of a four-wheeled wagon found in one of the graves, one of the first definite chronological markers of the use of a wheeled vehicle. Other finds at Budakalász include burials of paired cattle, which to S. PIGGOTT suggested the use of cattle for traction.

Buddhagupta stone one of several SANSKRIT language inscriptions of c.5th century AD found on the west coast of peninsular Malaysia, connected with a Buddhist traders' cult apparently unique to maritime Southeast Asia; related inscriptions have been found in western Kalimantan (Borneo) and Brunei.

Bug-Dniester culture a complex of sites in the valleys of the Bug and Dniester Rivers in Ukraine, in which pottery manufacture appears to have developed within a hunter-gatherer economic context about 6400–5500 BC. Short-lived sites like SOROCA were located on river terraces of the larger valleys. Bug-Dniester economy was based on red deer, wild pigs and cattle, roe deer, birds, shellfish and fish, with traces of plant gathering. CRIŞ and LINEAR POTTERY sherds suggest that the Bug-Dniester culture was in contact with neighbouring early agricultural groups, but evidence of farming is scanty.

Buhaya see KATURUKA, IRON AGE.

Buhen a site in LOWER NUBIA, excavated mainly by EMERY 1957–65. Buhen was occupied during the OLD KINGDOM, an early example of Egyptian expansion into Nubia, and was an important fortress during the MIDDLE and NEW KINGDOM.

Bukit Tengku Lembu a rockshelter site in peninsular Malaysia, with remains related to the BAN KAO Neolithic (see GUA KECHIL) and some later blackware pottery of uncertain origin, but which may be Indo-Roman ROULETTED ware like that found at SEMBIRAN and BUNI.

Bukit Tengorak a late Neolithic site in Sabah, eastern Malaysia, dated to c.1000 BC with red-slipped and incised pottery, shell beads and ornaments, adzes and obsidian blades imported from TALASEA in New Britain, Melanesia, 6,500 km (4,000 miles) to the east.

Bükk culture a regional late variant of the LINEAR POTTERY culture, centred on the Bükk Mountains of north-eastern Hungary, often in cave-sites. Bükk pottery is very finely made, with multiple parallel lines in spiral and curvilinear patterns. SHERDS of Bükk pottery sometimes appear at distant sites, such as OLSZANICA in southern Poland.

bulb of percussion a convex swelling found on the ventral or inside surface of a struck flake just below the point of impact. A small concave scar, the bulbar scar, is often found on the bulb of percussion.

Bulgaria see EUROPE, EASTERN.

bulla 1 a hollow ball of clay, characteristic of the writing systems of early MESOPOTAMIA, that contains TOKENS and bears a seal impression and/or numerical notations on its outer surface; such objects appear in late URUK contexts.

2 a clay sealing used to monitor flows of goods, to mark ownership and so forth. In the literature about western Asian civilizations these objects are commonly called *sealings*.

3 a round amulet worn on the chest. Etruscan examples are normally made of bronze and can be decorated in relief. In Roman society a gold bulla was worn by children of the social elite to signify free birth; it later came to be worn by the children of freedmen. When the child came of age, the bulla was placed in the household shrine or lararium. A fine example was found in the House of Menander at POMPEII.

Buni a port and burial site in western Java, of the first centuries AD, yielding crucibles and other remains of a bronze-working industry and Indo-Roman ROULETTED ware similar to that of SEMBIRAN on Bali; it was an important early Indonesian port on the spice trade route.

Buret' an Upper Palaeolithic open-air site on the Angara River in southern-central Siberia. The cultural layer is buried in slope deposits on a low terrace; it overlies a buried soil and is believed to date to c.20,000 bp. The features, which include traces of former structures, and the artifacts, which include human and animal figurines, are similar to the nearby site of MAL'TA. Buret' was discovered and excavated by OKLADNIKOV during 1936–40.

Burgäschisee-Süd a lakeside site of the CORTAILLOD CULTURE in western Switzerland, dated to the first half of the 4th millennium BC. Among the animal bones, a high proportion of red-deer bones attests to the continued importance of hunting for this farming community. Copper beads indicate contacts with copper-producing areas to the east.

burial the deliberate disposal of the dead. *Primary* burials are those in which the dead body has been laid down only once; *secondary* burials are those involving the deliberate movement and relocation of the body as part of the burial ritual; a *flexed* burial occurs when the body is coiled into a foetal position; an *extended* burial occurs when the body is stretched out, with the arms at its side. Archaeologists have traditionally assumed that the burial status of the dead reflected their social status while alive, but recent POSTPROCESSUAL critiques suggest that this assumption is no longer valid in all cases. See also PRIMARY/SECONDARY CREMATION, BURIAL.

Burial Mound period a term used in eastern North America for that period when cultures were characterized by the construction of BURIAL MOUNDS. See ADENA, HOPEWELL, TEMPLE MOUND PERIOD.

burial mounds earthen mounds deliberately constructed over burials. They are most often interpreted as marks of status or rank. Bodies were either interred on earthen platforms within log frames, or cremated and the remains placed in scooped-out basins. See also TUMULUS, TOUMBA, SOROS.

Burian, Zdeněk (1905–81) a Czech painter best known for his hundreds of outstanding and accurate pictures recreating extinct fauna, and the animals and people of prehistory, especially the last Ice Age, which have been reproduced in countless books.

buried soil soil covered by younger natural or ANTHROPOGENIC deposits with a vertical separation between the buried and modern soil or land surface; the buried soil is referred to as a PALAEOSOL. Buried soils represent former land surfaces with spatial, temporal and environmental significance, and form the basis for reconstructing former landscapes.

burin a characteristic Upper Palaeolithic blade tool with a sharp transverse chisel-like working-edge formed by the removal of a sliver of stone called a burin spall. Traditionally regarded as engraving tools used to work bone, ivory, antler, soft stone and wood, recent USEWEAR ANALYSIS suggests that burins may have been multi-purpose artifacts. By convention, the spall removal is indicated in drawings by a small arrow.

Burma see ASIA, SOUTHEAST.

burnish a polish applied to the surface of an object such as pottery or bronze to enhance its appearance or for decorative purposes. On a pot, burnishing is carried out, usually with a wooden or bone tool, between drying and firing, and makes the vessel more watertight.

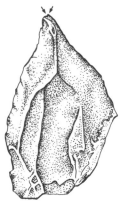

BURIN.

burren adze a term sometimes used by Australian archaeologists for flake scrapers, hafted for woodworking, which are not TULA adzes. They are also called non-tula adzes.

Burrill Lake a large sandstone rockshelter on the south coast of New South Wales, Australia, excavated in 1967–8 by Ron Lampert. First occupied about 20,000 years ago, the older levels are characterized by scrapers and flake tools of the AUSTRALIAN CORE TOOL AND SCRAPER TRADITION. From c.5000 years ago a range of small tools were added to the assemblage.

Burrup Peninsula an area of the northwestern coast of Western Australia rich in archaeological remains. Over 10,000 petroglyphs have been recorded on boulders, with very high concentrations at some sites. The subjects range from geometric figures to detailed representations of humans and animals, and include CLELAND HILLS faces. There are many open sites including quarries and artifact scatters, as well as SHELL MIDDENS ranging from 6700 bp to 200 bp. There are also many stone features including fish traps, standing stones and an enigmatic series of dry-stone walls and terraces.

Burzahom a site lying at 1,800 m (5,900 ft) in Kashmir. It was initially tested in 1939 by de Terra and Patterson, and then excavated in 1960–71 by T. Khazanchi, who defined four phases of occupation. In the earliest phase, the settlement is characterized by pit dwellings up to 4 m (13 ft) deep, wider at the top than the bottom, and surrounded by POSTHOLES to support a perishable superstructure, along with large storage pits; the material inventory includes a burnished handmade pottery with basal mat impressions, a rich bone industry, and a ground stone and chipped stone industry distinctive of this region of South Asia. The second occupation marks an architectural shift to above-ground mud-brick structures, though the basic material culture continues much as before. In the third phase a megalithic circle was constructed, while the pottery shifts to a coarse red ware; the last period is early historic. The chronology of the site is poorly known, but seems to cover the 3rd and early 2nd millennia BC.

Bush Barrow an Early Bronze Age burial mound in the Normanton Down cemetery (England), located approximately 1 km (half a mile) south of STONEHENGE. The barrow was opened by William Cunnington in 1808 and found to contain the remains of a single individual accompanied by rich grave-goods including a gold belt-fastener and lozenge-shaped breastplate, a stone mace-head with bone handle mounts, two bronze daggers and a low-flanged axe. The burial was probably that of a powerful Early Bronze Age chieftain buried around 2000 BC.

Bushmen see SAN.

Bus Mordeh see DEH LURAN.

Butana a Sudanese Neolithic group or industry within the KASSALA phase, dating to between 5500 and 4500 BP, which takes its name from a region east of the Nile in central Sudan. It is associated with large villages and cultural deposits 2 m (6 ft) deep containing ceramics as well as bones of wild and, in the upper layers, domestic animals. See also GASH, MOKRAM, SHAQADUD.

Butmir culture a late Neolithic culture of Bosnia, known from the type-site near Sarajevo and other settlements, including OBRE. Butmir ceramics are often elaborately decorated with incised geometrical and curvilinear patterns.

Buto a site in the Nile DELTA, today called Tell el-Fara'in (Mound of the Pharaohs). It seems to have been occupied continuously from the second half of the 4th millennium BC until the 6th century AD, but it is archaeologically important as one of the major sites in the north of Egypt which has evidence of a Neolithic tradition (sometimes called the MAADI culture), through the on-going excavations of the German Archaeological Institute and the University of Marburg.

Butser an experimental farm and open-air museum on the South Downs, Hampshire, England, the scene of scientific investigations into Iron Age plant cultivation and animal husbandry. Reconstructions of round-houses, granaries and storage pits of Iron Age type have also been made in order to test hypotheses about constructional details.

Butuan in northeastern Mindanao, Philippines, contains several waterlogged sites with the early evidence for trade in Asian glazed trade wares. Dated from between the early 10th to c.15th centuries, other finds include gold jewellery, coffin burials, and wooden boats of traditional Southeast Asian manufacture known locally as *balangay*.

Bweyorere a 2nd millennium AD capital of the inter-lacustrine Central African Ankole of southern Uganda, with extensive earthworks like those at BIGO. See also NTUSI.

Byblos a site in Lebanon, on a promontory overlooking the Mediterranean, excavated by MONTET in 1921–4 and by Dunand, chiefly in 1925–38. Occupied in the Neolithic and CHALCOLITHIC, it was a densely-packed, strongly fortified city, containing a series of religious structures including the 'obelisk temple', in the EARLY to MIDDLE BRONZE AGE. Byblos' importance stemmed from being a major trading centre, especially for the supply of raw materials to Egypt; it was ruled in the Middle Bronze Age by a line of princes whose 'court-style' in artistic taste was based on Egyptian models. Byblos' role as a trading centre later declined with the rise of TYRE and SIDON.

Býči Skála a prehistoric cave-site located northeast of Brno in the Moravian KARST zone, Czech Republic. Artifacts and faunal remains (e.g. cave bear, reindeer) are buried in loam deposits. The artifacts in the lowest cultural layer comprise a mixture of Middle and Upper Palaeolithic types (e.g. sidescrapers and burins), and their age and affiliation are unclear. Late Upper Palaeolithic and late prehistoric remains occur in the upper levels. Excavations in the late 19th century found about forty inhumation burials, as well as cremated bones, of the HALLSTATT period of the Early Iron Age. Three of the graves seem to be of particularly high-status individuals, with wagons with iron tyres. Numerous bronze objects, including buckets, kettles and bowls, a bull figurine with iron inlays, a helmet, and many pins, FIBULAE, and about 100 bracelets were found in the cave's deposits.

Bygholm a hoard from Jutland, Denmark, of four copper flat axes, a copper dagger and three copper spiral rings, found together with a TRB C vessel and dated to c.4000 BC. These are among the earliest metal objects to be found in Denmark.

Bylany a large settlement of the LINEAR POTTERY and STROKE-ORNAMENTED POTTERY cultures in Bohemia near Prague, excavated by B. Soudský. Bylany is an archetypal Linear Pottery site, situated on loess on the lower slope of a stream valley. Numerous rectangular LONGHOUSES were found, and detailed ceramic analysis has led to the identification of over twenty phases of settlement, each with five–six (rarely more than ten) houses. Soudský proposed a model of Linear Pottery cyclical shifting settlement, but recent work at other sites has led some to argue for occupations of longer duration.

Byzantium (*adj.* Byzantine) later Constantinopolis, a Greek colony founded in the 7th century BC on the European side of the Hellespont in Turkey. The city was destroyed after it stood against the emperor Septimius Severus in c.AD 195 and was refounded in AD 324 by the emperor Constantine; it was officially inaugurated in AD 330. One of the most magnificent buildings was the church of S. Sofia, later turned into a mosque. In the Hippodrome (see CIRCUS) the bronze serpent column from the Plataean monument at DELPHI may still be seen along with two obelisks.

Byzovaya an Upper Palaeolithic open-air site on the Pechora River in European Russia, and the northernmost Palaeolithic locality in Europe (65°N). Artifacts and faunal remains (predominantly woolly mammoth) are buried in fluvial deposits comprising the second/third terrace. The occupation probably antedates the LAST GLACIAL MAXIMUM (i.e. over 25,000 bp). Byzovaya was excavated in the 1960s by Kanivets.

C

C3, C4 and CAM plants see 13 CARBON/12 CARBON.

Caballo Muerto a complex of monumental constructions pertaining to the INITIAL PERIOD and EARLY HORIZON, located in the Moche Valley on the north coast of Peru. The site covers some 2 sq. km (0.75 sq. mile) and comprises seventeen mounds. The most complex construction at the site is the Huaca de los Reyes, a multi-level, U-shaped complex, roughly 240 m (260 yds) square, decorated with relief friezes painted yellow, white and red. An individual entering the complex from the east and moving towards the pyramid at the western end would pass through a series of structures, stairways, pillared halls and courtyard, rising to successively higher levels. This complex is considered to be an especially elaborate example of religious architecture pertaining to the late Initial period.

Cabalwanian industry a stone industry based largely upon flakes, recognized from surface collections made to the west of the CAGAYAN VALLEY in Luzon, northern Philippines. Once thought to be Lower Palaeolithic, it is now thought to date to the early Holocene and to represent a development parallel to the HOABINHIAN.

Cabengé an area in southwestern Sulawesi along the Wallanae River yielding a late PLIOCENE fauna, but the crude core and flake stone tools found in the river terrace with the bones are probably late Pleistocene in age, although earlier than the TOALIAN industry of the caves in the same region.

Cacaxtla a late CLASSIC (AD 650–900) site in central Mexico. Spectacular murals at the site portray warriors and merchants in MAYA costume, indicating highland-lowland interaction. The Battle Mural represents conflicting ethnic armies wearing bird and jaguar costumes, with the Jaguar warriors victorious. Leaders of the Maya Bird warriors are dressed in female costume, perhaps to indicate the capture of noble women who then become founding queens of a combined Bird/Jaguar dynasty.

Caere see CERVETERI.

Caeretan ware a type of ARCHAIC pottery found in ETRURIA and once thought to have been made at CERVETERI. It was decorated in a BLACK-FIGURED style and showed the influence of Greek craftsmen.

Caesarea a coastal site in Israel, the capital of the Roman province of Judaea. Sporadically excavated by many archaeologists, this substantial port is largely the result of an energetic building programme initiated in 22 BC by Herod the Great, although Caesarea also contains important remains of the BYZANTINE and medieval (Crusader) periods.

Cagayan Valley a region of northern Luzon, Philippines, yielding Early and Middle Pleistocene faunal remains. The stone tools once thought to have been in association with them are thought now to date to the early Holocene. See also CABALWANIAN INDUSTRY.

Cahokia a large site located a few miles east of St Louis, Missouri, USA, that was occupied from approximately AD 700 to 1500. Earliest occupation was associated with the WOODLAND stage, and this was followed by MISSISSIPPIAN stage groups in about AD 900. During this period, Cahokia developed into a large and complex regional economic and ceremonial centre of a once densely populated area now called the American Bottoms, and possibly even reached the state level of social organization. The most striking features of the Cahokia site, which at its peak occupation covered nearly 16 sq. km (6 sq. miles), are the numerous earthen mounds, possibly originally totalling more than 120. Mounds were either PLATFORM, BURIAL or ridge-top MOUNDS (shaped like an old-fashioned ridge tent). The largest of these is Monk's mound, a platform mound, which was built in the period AD 900–1200. It covers 6 ha (15 acres) and rises in four terraces to a height of over 35 m (115 ft). It was surmounted by a large building, probably a ceremonial centre and the home of the major ruler. Excavations at mound 72 unearthed nearly 300 burials, mostly of young women. These are thought to have been sacrificial burials, presumably related to the burial of a male ruler in the same mound. Nearby Woodhenge comprises the remains of a circle of upright logs, thought to have served as some form of calendar or as a celestial observatory. Cahokia derives its name from that of a local Indian group.

Cahuachi a large ceremonial site, the principal centre of the NASCA culture of Peru. The site comprises some forty adobe mounds and pyramids, and extensive cemeteries, but little habitation refuse. Excavations by Helaine Silverman suggest that the site was an empty ceremonial centre, occupied only during religious ceremonies. Excavation by an international team led by Giuseppe Orefici supports the ceremonial interpretation, but has also found evidence for perhaps several hundred permanent residents. The site was mostly built in Early Nasca times (phases 1–3), but probably continued to serve as a locus of ritual offerings through Late Nasca times (phases 4–7) and the MIDDLE HORIZON.

Cai Beo a 5th–4th millennium BC Neolithic settlement on Cat Ba island, Ha Long Bay, northern Vietnam. Discovered by Colani in 1938, the site was excavated in the 1970s and 1980s by Vietnamese archaeologists. The coarse sand-tempered pottery and flaked tools link the site to the HOABINHIAN traditions of the inland caves.

cairn a mound of stones. The most common examples are clearance cairns created when stones were cleared from a field in preparation for cultivation, and funerary cairns covering graves or burial chambers.

Cairo the modern capital of Egypt and major centre of Islamic civilization since its foundation by the Fatimid Dynasty in AD 969.

Cajamarquilla an urban site near Lima, on the central coast of Peru, a centre of the Lima culture of the EARLY INTERMEDIATE PERIOD. The nearby cemetery, Nievería, has produced many HUARI-related artifacts, suggesting intensive interaction with, if not control by, Huari.

Čaka a Late Bronze Age URNFIELD cemetery in Slovakia. One of the high-status burials at Čaka yielded a sheet-bronze breastplate, one of the oldest examples of body armour in Europe, dated to the 13th century BC.

Calakmul a very large MAYA site in Campeche, Mexico, which was occupied continuously from the middle PRE-CLASSIC until the terminal CLASSIC (c.500 BC–AD 850). Calakmul was located in a swampy region modified by an elaborate canal system used to drain the urban centre which was built around a low hill.

During the Preclassic period Calakmul developed as a contemporary of EL MIRADOR. During the Classic period it was a city of c.1,000 structures, with over 100 carved stone STELAS. It was allied with Caracol in war against PETÉN states such as TIKAL.

Calatagan a province in southwestern Luzon, Philippines, containing a large number of archaeological sites with abundant pottery that is poorly dated but mainly c.AD 1400–1600. One vessel has an Old Tagalog inscription around the neck.

caldarium the hottest room in a Roman bath-house. A plunge-bath was attached, which made it a very humid room. See also THERMAE.

calendar round a 52-year cycle used in MESOAMERICA. It is a combination of the 260-day almanac (TZOLKIN) and the 365-day, which run concurrently but reach a common starting point every fifty-two years. See also LONG COUNT.

calendric systems MAYA calendar systems, depending on astronomic calculations and the use of the LONG COUNT. The Maya believed in a cyclical history in which events (including disasters) literally repeated themselves. Calendric systems were used not only in timing agricultural activities, but also to calculate the occurrence of important events (such as solar and lunar eclipses) in order to prepare for them.

calibration the adjustment of data by means of some systematic change to exclude extraneous or error-producing information. For example, to achieve a result in calendar years in RADIOCARBON DATING, application of a correction factor is necessitated by the discovery, from ISOTOPIC and radiocarbon dating analysis in DEN-DROCHRONOLOGY of tree rings, that production rate of 14C in the atmosphere has not been constant through time, but rather variable. Radiocarbon ages are originally reported in uncalibrated radiocarbon years that assume no atmospheric 14C flux. Radiocarbon years are adjusted, or calibrated, to calendar years by taking this flux into account.

Calico Mountains an open-air site located on former Lake Manix in the Mojave Desert of southeastern California (USA). Lithic debris (fragments, flakes and blades) thought to represent artifacts is buried in fan deposits recently dated by the URANIUM-thorium method to c.200,000 BP. If accurately interpreted as a human site, Calico Mountains would constitute the earliest settlement in the New World (i.e. Lower Palaeolithic); however, the lithic debris is not widely accepted as of human manufacture. The site was investigated by Simpson, L. LEAKEY and others.

Calixtlahuaca a site in the Toluca Valley in the state of Mexico which has a ceramic sequence from TEOTIHU-ACÁN times to the AZTEC conquest period. There is also some evidence of occupation during the PRECLASSIC. It was occupied by the Matlatzincas, a NAHUA group, enemies of the Aztecs, from AD 1200 to 1472. The Matlatzincas were conquered by the Aztecs in the subsequent period (AD 1474–1510). The site is best known for the Temple of QUETZALCÓATL in his form as the wind god, Éhecatl. This temple is a circular structure, that went through three construction periods. The archaeologist

Jose García Payón directed most of the excavations carried out at the site in the 1930s.

callais an attractive greenish stone more properly known as either turquoise or variscite depending on the variety, used for the manufacture of beads and pendants found in Neolithic CHAMBERED TOMBS in Brittany and Iberia, in the SEPULCROS DE FOSA of eastern Spain, and in CHASSÉEN settlement sites of southern France. Neolithic variscite mines have been discovered at Gava near Barcelona; other sources are known in Brittany.

Callanish a Neolithic STONE CIRCLE on the island of Lewis, Outer Hebrides, Scotland, consisting of thirteen tall thin stones of local gneiss, the tallest 4.75 m (15 ft 7 inches) high. To one side within the circle is a round mound containing a small PASSAGE GRAVE. Rows of stones lead away from the circle to the west, north-northeast, east-northeast and south, the last of these double and forming an avenue. There are a number of other stone circles near by.

Całowanie an Upper Palaeolithic open-air site located on the Vistula River in eastern Poland. Artifacts are buried in stream and dune deposits. Two lower cultural layers are dated to c.11,500 BP and contain backed bladelets, while the overlying layers are dated to c.11,000–10,000 BP and contain tanged points.

Cambodia see ASIA, SOUTHEAST.

Camden, William (1551–1623) a Tudor antiquary and historian who travelled extensively in Britain looking at antiquities. He was the author of the first general account of British antiquities, the *Britannia* (1586), which was revised and reissued in several editions for over 200 years, and which helped awaken public interest in what he called 'the back-looking curiosity'.

cameo glass a Roman glass object made up of two or more layers of different coloured glass bonded together. Normally a lighter colour forms the top surface, through which the engraver cuts to reveal the darker base. The overall impression would be similar to the result of cutting cameos from onyx. An important example of this technique is the Portland Vase in the British Museum, although it was also used on decorative plaques in the House of Fabius Rufus at POMPEII as well as on finger-rings.

Campania an agriculturally rich area of Italy adjoining the Bay of Naples. It was the location of one of the earliest Greek colonies at CUMAE and it was also under the influence of the Etruscans (see ETRURIA). See also CAMPANIAN POTTERY, HERCULANEUM, OPLONTIS, POMPEII.

Campanian pottery a type of SOUTH ITALIAN POTTERY. Production seems to have started before the middle of the 4th century BC, perhaps under the influence of SICILIAN

CANAANITE AMPHORAS, bulk transport containers of the Late Bronze Age, excavated from the coastal site of Zawiyet Umm el-Rakham.

POTTERY. There seem to have been three main centres of production: two at Capua and one at CUMAE. Late in its production it seems to draw inspiration from APULIAN POTTERY.

Canaanean blade a type of extremely regular and large (2–5 cm [1–2 inches] wide and up to 25–30 cm [10–12 inches] long) flint blade produced by a specialized technique. The technology seems to have first appeared at the beginning of the 4th millennium BC in eastern Anatolia and adjoining areas, and was then introduced to the southern Levant ('Canaan') by 3500 BC; these blades were produced until 2000 BC.

Canaanite amphora common transport vessel of the LATE BRONZE AGE in the eastern Mediterranean. Canaanite AMPHORAS average c.75 cm (30 inches) in height and have a short, relatively narrow flaring mouth, a wide shoulder with two handles on it, and a tapering profile running down to a narrow pointed base. They were made in various centres in the eastern Mediterranean and were roughly contemporary with STIRRUP JARS.

Canaanites an ethnic group and land named in the Bible and in ancient cuneiform texts, archaeologically identified with the sophisticated urban culture of the Levant during the MIDDLE and LATE BRONZE AGE (2000–1200 BC). Canaanite towns (see HAZOR, JERICHO, LACHISH, BEIT MERSIM, MEGGIDO, DAN) typically were surrounded by massive earthworks entered through a formal arched gateway; elite urban architecture included well-appointed palaces and thick-walled temples of Syrian design. Foreign pottery points to regular contacts with Cyprus and the Aegean world after 1600 BC. Among other achievements, the Canaanites developed an early alphabet from which derived the PHOENICIAN and other scripts. The Egyptians controlled much of Canaan after 1500 BC, and town life declined under their rule. The

Canaanites were dislodged from much of their territory by the ISRAELITES and PHILISTINES, but much of their culture persisted among the Phoenicians.

candi a late 1st millennium–early 2nd millennium AD funerary temple of Java which combined imported Hindu or Buddhist religion with local ancestor veneration cults.

Can Hasan III an ACERAMIC NEOLITHIC site in southern-central Anatolia, where David French's excavations revealed a small settlement (somewhat less than a hectare [2.5 acres]) having a densely agglomerated complex of rooms and courtyards, with access seemingly through the roof in the Anatolian Neolithic manner (see ÇATAL HÖYÜK). French assigns this settlement to the middle of the 7th millennium bc. The significance of Can Hasan lies in its subsistence evidence: in addition to the wild animals (cattle and sheep/goat probably being herded), the site contains a wide variety of crop species (bread wheat, club wheat, emmer, einkorn, two-rowed hulled and possibly naked barley, lentils and vetch).

cannibalism or **anthropophagy** the consumption of human flesh by humans. Since the practice of eating one's own kind is known to exist among many species, including chimpanzees, our closest relatives, there is no reason to doubt its existence among early HOMINIDS (see ATAPUERCA, BODO). Claims are often made for the practice among later peoples, such as NEANDERTHALS (see KRAPINA, GROTTA GUATTARI), various Stone Age cultures (see KLASIES, FONTBREGOUA) and the ANASAZI; in the past, such claims were based on little more than wishful thinking. Today, thanks to careful bone analyses and TAPHONOMIC studies, some recent claims have become more plausible, but nevertheless the evidence remains ambiguous, and much of it could readily be explained by secondary funerary rituals, violence and warfare, etc.

canopic jars containers used by the Egyptians for the preservation of the internal organs removed during MUMMIFICATION. Canopic jars of the NEW KINGDOM often have lids in the form of the heads of the protective deities, the four sons of HORUS: Imset (human-headed, containing the liver), Hapy (baboon-headed, the lungs), Qebhsenuef (falcon-headed, the intestines), and Duamutef (jackal-headed, the stomach).

cantharus see KANTHAROS.

Cape Coastal ware a Stone Age pottery style, initially identified at coastal sites from southern Namibia to the Eastern Cape Province of South Africa, and more recently also at sites in the interior of western South Africa including the SEACOW River Valley, sometimes termed 'KHOEKHOE pottery'. It is characterized by thin-walled vessels with pointed bases, spouts and lugs, which were fired at relatively high temperatures, and which are associated with historically known Khoekhoe herding peoples. However, although thin-walled sherds fired at high temperatures occur in assemblages dating between about 2000–1600 BP, pointed bases and lugs are relatively rare until after about 1600 BP.

Cape du Couedic a rockshelter on KANGAROO ISLAND, Australia, with cultural deposits dating from 7550 to 5500 bp. The site demonstrates the early Holocene age of the KARTAN industry. Faunal remains suggest the exploitation of sea lion.

Cape Gelidonya see GELIDONYA.

Capeletti see DAMOUS EL AHMAR.

capital the top part of a CLASSICAL column comprising: in the DORIC ORDER, an ECHINUS and ABACUS; in the IONIC ORDER, VOLUTES, echinus and abacus; and in the CORINTHIAN ORDER, acanthus leaves.

Cappadocian trade the regular trade between a large number of ASSYRIAN family commercial firms of the 2nd millennium BC and areas to the west in Anatolia, particularly the regions of Cappadocia. The trade was organized as a series of foreign colonies (see KĀRUM, KANISH) attached to local towns but existing as largely self-regulating communities bound by treaty relations with the host government. The Cappadocian trade dealt largely with tin and textiles shipped via ASSUR from further east and south in exchange for Anatolian silver; the traders also peddled copper within Anatolia. The rich CUNEIFORM sources from Kanish, BOĞAZKÖY, ALIŞAR HÖYÜK and elsewhere make this the best documented trading system of ancient MESOPOTAMIA, but Assur of the early 2nd millennium may not be representative of other times and places in western Asian history.

Capsian the typical Capsian is an EPIPALAEOLITHIC stone industry found especially on SHELL MIDDENs in a restricted area of northern Algeria/Tunisia post-dating about 8500 BP and characterized by large burins and backed blades. At some sites after about 7500 BP it is overlain by the more widespread Upper Capsian, a microlithic stone industry also often associated with shell middens, and characterized by geometric-shaped backed microliths and notched or denticulated flakes as well as bone artifacts and engraved ostrich eggshells.

Capsian Neolithic or **Neolithic of Capsian tradition** a stone industry associated with pointed-base pottery, probably of several distinct traditions, from the Atlas Mountains of Algeria and the northern Sahara, dating from c.6200 to 5300 BP. It is characterized by notched pieces, scrapers and geometric microliths as well as ostrich eggshell, and is assumed to have affinities with the earlier CAPSIAN (see also DAMOUS EL AHMAR, HASSI MOUILAH).

capstone see also DOLMEN, CORBEL-VAULTED.

carbon 14 see RADIOCARBON.

Carchemish a city on the middle Euphrates, established no later than the mid 3rd millennium BC. It was an important political centre during the 2nd and first half of the 1st millennium BC, though often in clientage to stronger regional powers (HITTITES, NEO-ASSYRIANS), according to the fairly rich textual sources. The archaeological excavations there began in the 1870s and continued sporadically until 1920, when the newly drawn Turkish-Syrian border divided the site. Although these excavations produced EARLY BRONZE, LATE BRONZE and Early Iron Age materials, only the latter are published in any detail. During this period (the so-called Syro-Hittite), the city was separated into citadel, inner town and outer town, covering about 150 ha (370 acres) in all. The best-known archaeological aspects of the city are the Syro-Hittite sculptures and inscriptions. Some HALAF period round dwellings and pottery kilns were discovered at Yunus, on the outskirts of the city, and are frequently used to illustrate Halaf architecture.

Cardial ware the earliest Neolithic pottery type of the western Mediterranean and parts of Atlantic Europe. The vessels are often of fine quality and are sometimes decorated with the edge of a *Cardium* (cockle-) shell, from which the pottery takes its name, though other types of impressed decoration are also common (hence the alternative term IMPRESSED WARE). Cardial ware is dated to between *c*.6000 and 5300 BC, and is followed in some regions by an EPICARDIAL phase *c*.5300–4600 BC.

cardo the main street in a Roman town or camp usually laid out on a north-south axis. The FORUM was placed at the intersection with the DECUMANUS maximus. The rectangular blocks between the streets are described as INSULAE. The colonnaded cardo of the late antique city of JERUSALEM still dominates the street plan of the old city.

Carib a group of Indians who occupied the Lesser ANTILLES (from the Venezuelan coast to Guadeloupe) at the time of Columbus's arrival in AD 1492. Probably originating in northern South America, they migrated through the islands from the 13th century AD, and displaced the terrorized ARAWAK, from whom they differed through lack of ZEMI worship. Although pottery-using farmers like the Arawak, the Carib appear to have relied heavily on aggression and warfare, and, rightly or wrongly, gave their name to the phenomenon of ritual CANNIBALISM.

Caribbean see ANTILLES, ARAWAK, TAÍNOS.

carination a break in the profile of a pot which forms a keel or ridge, usually marking the junction of the body with the neck.

Carnac a complex of Neolithic ritual monuments around the Gulf of Morbihan, Brittany, France, including single standing stones (notably the Grand Menhir Brisé, now fallen and broken in four pieces), long mounds with several closed burial chambers (such as Er Grah and Le Manio), classic PASSAGE GRAVES with megalithic art (La Table des Marchand and Kercado), and massive ALIGNMENTS of standing stones. The most famous of these are the Le Menec alignments, consisting of eleven parallel lines of stones over 1 km (0.6 mile) long. Of the Carnac burial mounds the Tumulus de Saint-Michel is the most impressive, over 110 m (120 yds) long and 10 m (33 ft) high, with a chamber which contained a number of fine polished stone axes including several of jadeite. The Tumulus de Saint-Michel together with the Grand Menhir Brisé and the long mounds belong to the 5th or early

CARNAC, France: part of the Menec alignments.

4th millennium BC; the passage graves to the 4th or 3rd millennium, and the alignments to the mid 3rd millennium BC.

Carnarvon see CARTER.

Carnarvon Gorge an area in southern-central Queensland, Australia, outstanding for its stencilled rock art. Stencils include a range of artifacts and natural items and complex composite designs. Engravings and a few paintings also occur, while CATHEDRAL CAVE, one of the largest sites, also has occupation deposits.

Carpenters Gap 1 a rockshelter in the Kimberley region of Western Australia, recently excavated by Sue O'Connor. The base of the deposit is about 40,000 years old, and occupation continues through the LAST GLACIAL MAXIMUM. The site was then abandoned and only reoccupied in the late Holocene. Preservation of plant remains is excellent in the dry sediments.

carp's tongue sword a Late Bronze Age sword type, a characteristic product of the ATLANTIC BRONZE AGE, with a blade narrowing to an elongated, parallel-sided tip, in an attempt to combine the qualities of a slashing and a stabbing weapon.

Carrowmore a cemetery of megalithic tombs in Sligo, Ireland, consisting of circular boulder kerbs with central boulder-built chambers. Some consider this to be an early form of CHAMBERED TOMB, but despite the absence of pottery from some tombs, the associated radiocarbon date of *c.*4500 BC, which would make these the earliest chambered tombs of Ireland and among the oldest anywhere in western Europe, must be regarded with caution. A date in the late 5th or early 4th millennium BC is nonetheless likely.

carrying capacity the optimal population size that can be supported by a particular environment, a key concept in DEMOGRAPHY and PALAEOECONOMY. Stress between a population's size and the environment's ability to support it is cited in many studies as a fundamental cause of cultural change. However, some archaeologists consider the concept of carrying capacity to be essentially irrelevant for studies of human behaviour, because of the human ability to raise artificially the carrying capacity of a given area through changes in technology and subsistence practices.

Cartailhac, Émile (1845–1921) a French prehistorian who was a dominant figure in the development of the discipline, but who is best known for his initial vehement rejection of ALTAMIRA's authenticity, followed by a published *Mea Culpa*, after which he became a fervent champion of cave art.

Carter, Howard (1874–1939) an English artist and Egyptologist. His best-known archaeological work was financed by the Earl of Carnarvon, especially the discovery in 1922, and subsequent examination, of the tomb of TUTANKHAMEN.

Carthage a PHOENICIAN colony in modern Tunisia, traditionally founded in 814 BC. Excavations have revealed traces of the *tophet* (sanctuary) of the goddess Tanit which may date back to the 8th century BC. Recent excavations have uncovered traces of the circular harbour with ship-sheds. Despite the destruction of the city by ROME in 146 BC, a colony was established of which the AMPHITHEATRE and aqueduct remain.

cartonnage a material composed of layers of linen or papyrus cemented by plaster or glue and moulded to the required shape before drying and painting. Cartonnage was often used as a substitute for wood in the funerary equipment of LATE PERIOD Egypt.

cartouche an Egyptian HIEROGLYPHIC device consisting of a loop formed by a double thickness of rope with the end tied to form a straight line at the base of an elongated oval. Two of the names borne by the king, the throne-name and the birth-name, were each enclosed in a cartouche.

carved tree or **dendroglyph** a tree with designs, usually geometric, cut into the bark or heartwood. Such trees have a limited distribution in eastern and central New South Wales and southeastern Queensland, Australia, and were commonly associated with ceremonial activities such as burial or initiation. Carved trees also occur in the Chatham Islands. See also MORIORI. Compare SCARRED TREE.

caryatids columns in the form of standing women. Some of the earliest were used in treasuries at DELPHI in the 6th century BC. Six such figures formed a porch on the

The oval CARTOUCHES on this monument from Philae, Egypt, give two of the royal names of King Nectanebo I.

ERECHTHEION. Each seems to have held an OINOCHOE and a PHIALE, vessels used for pouring a LIBATION to the gods. Lord ELGIN removed one of them and it is now in the British Museum. Copies were made in the Roman period for Hadrian's villa at Tivoli.

Casamance see MEGALITHIC MONUMENT.

Casas Grandes a site located beyond the northern frontier of MESOAMERICA, about 160 km (100 miles) south of the United States border. Charles DiPeso, who excavated the site in the 1960s and 1970s, believed it was established by Mesoamerican merchant priests. Casas Grandes was built of adobe, and included workshops, ceremonial structures, integrated apartments and an underground drainage system. Although the interpretation is debated, at its height Casas Grandes is thought to have been a trading outpost between Mesoamerica and the American Southwest. The city was destroyed in AD 1340 by the indigenous population. The site is also called Paquimé.

Cascioărele an ENEOLITHIC settlement of the GUMEL-NIȚA culture in southern Romania, about 60 km (37 miles) south of Bucharest. The settlement is on an island in Lake Catalui about 100 m (110 yds) in diameter. Sixteen one-room posthouses occupy the interior of the settlement, widely spaced with varied orientations. Most houses contained a square hearth, evidence of weaving and food-processing equipment. Among the artifacts are a beam of red-deer antler interpreted as an ARD, one of the earliest in southeastern Europe, and an elaborate model of a house or shrine.

Caskey, John (1908–81) an American archaeologist who was Director of the American School of Classical Studies at Athens 1948–59, and who excavated at LERNA and AYIA IRINI on Kea.

Caso Andrade, Alfonso (1896–1970) a Mexican archaeologist who began his career in 1927, working first in the VALLEY OF OAXACA at MONTE ALBÁN. He also studied the Mesoamerican CALENDRIC SYSTEMS, and later worked on genealogies of the MIXTEC.

Cass ny Hawin a small Mesolithic settlement site on the Isle of Man, off the west coast of Britain, excavated by Woodman (1982–3). The site has yielded an unspecialized group of stone tools including microliths, but no faunal remains.

Castelluccio A 3rd-millennium BC cemetery of several hundred simple rock-cut tombs cut into limestone cliffs of the Cava della Signora, a narrow valley in eastern Sicily. Most consist only of a single chamber, circular or oval in plan, although some have a small ante-chamber. Two of the tombs had blocking stones with carved spirals. The burial rite was collective inhumation, accompanied by pottery, occasional copper objects, and curious bossed bone plaques, perhaps originally ornamental belt fasteners.

Castelnovian see CHÂTEAUNEUF-LES-MARTIGUES.

Castillo see EL CASTILLO.

Castor ware see NENE VALLEY WARE.

castro a fortified camp of the Portuguese Iron Age (see VILA NOVA DE SÃO PEDRO).

CAT see RADIOGRAPHY.

catacomb an underground set of galleries and rooms used as a cemetery. An extensive series have been explored outside ROME, although others are known. The Rome series have been an important source for early Christian art and iconography.

Catacomb Grave culture the second in the series of KURGAN (following YAMNAYA, preceding SRUBNAYA) cultures of the southern Russian and Ukrainian steppes between the Dniepr and the lower Volga, dated primarily to the early part of the Bronze Age between c.2200 and 1800 BC. The graves of this culture are not true CATACOMBS in the Roman sense, but rather are burials in which the skeleton and grave-goods were placed in a niche in the side wall of a shallow shaft. The filled-in shaft was then covered over by a barrow.

Çatal Höyük ('Fork Mound') the most celebrated Neolithic site of western Asia along with JERICHO. Located on the Konya Plain in southern-central Anatolia and excavated by J. Mellaart in the 1960s and now the object of renewed investigation by I. Hodder, at 13 ha (32 acres) it was one of the largest sites of its time. The architecture consists of tightly packed rooms, with access through the roof; the walls of many rooms are decorated with exuberant murals, and some (identified as shrines) also have BUCRANIA fixed to the wall or on benches. The dead were buried beneath the floors of houses, often in collective graves; some differentiation of wealth is evident. The community seems to have practised irrigation farming, and had access to a wide variety of exotic raw materials. Mellaart dated the fourteen building levels he explored to roughly 6500–5600 BC; the recent investigations suggest that these dates should be pushed back by half a millennium or more. In terms of wider developmental trends in western Asia, Çatal Höyük once appeared to be both precocious and without issue; the reasons for the existence of such a large town at this time and place excite considerable speculation, mostly concerning the control of the obsidian trade. However, excavations at other early large settlements like 'AIN GHAZAL, BASTA, HALULA and AŞIKLI HÖYÜK reveal contemporary or earlier developments of a similar character.

Catastrophe Theory a mathematical model that investigates how a small change in one variable can have major effects on other related variables. The model has applications in understanding the collapse of complex social systems as a result of apparently small factors.

catastrophic age profile some ancient cultures killed large groups of animals in single kill events. By analysing the skeletal remains of these herds, archaeologists obtain a snapshot profile of the age structure of the herd at the time of death. This gives clues to the health of the herd, and the existence of deliberate culling of only certain age groups by ancient hunters. This in turn helps archaeologists understand ancient hunting strategies. A catastrophic age profile is different from an attritional age profile, which represents the natural mortality rates of a population of animals over a period of time. See also ARCHAEOZOOLOGY.

catena a sequence of soils formed within the same parent material in a local area, under normal conditions of weathering and erosion, that have differing characteristics due to variation in landscape position. Systematic changes in soil characteristics with relief and drainage allow interpretation of former landscapes of which archaeological sites may be components.

Catfish Cave see SHAMARKIAN.

Cathedral Cave one of the richest art sites in CARNARVON GORGE, Australia, with sporadic evidence of occupation from about 3500 bp including stone and bone artifacts, together with well-preserved seeds from cycads. These are palm- or fern-like plants, which produce seeds high in food value but which must be processed to remove toxins. In some parts of Australia, cycad use is associated with ceremonial gatherings. The site was first occupied about 3500 bp and it has been suggested that large ceremonies and cycad processing are thus a recent phenomenon associated with the AUSTRALIAN SMALL TOOL TRADITION. Compare CHEETUP.

Catherwood, Frederick (1799–1854) an English architect, one of the first great explorers of MESOAMERICA, who, with his American companion, John Lloyd STEPHENS, explored the MAYA lowlands in 1841 and 1843. Catherwood's accurate and beautiful drawings of these expeditions provided insights into a relatively unknown culture, and are still useful for their details of Maya GLYPHS.

cation ratio dating a developing dating technique used to date GEOMORPHIC surfaces and artifacts, that is based on the premise that the ratio of calcium and potassium/titanium in rock varnish decreases exponentially with age. Whether it actually does so is controversial. Calibration to absolute ages for a region is accomplished by determining cation ratios associated with surfaces dated by independent means. See also DESERT VARNISH.

Caton-Thompson, Gertrude (1888–1985) a British archaeologist and student of Sir Flinders PETRIE, best known for her work in Egypt (see FAIYUM, EL-HAMMAMIYA, OASES) and for her 1929 excavation at GREAT ZIMBABWE which corrected myths by showing that it was of African construction. She also worked in the Northern Province of South Africa and the Arabian peninsula.

Caune de l'Arago see TAUTAVEL.

causewayed camp a Neolithic enclosure with one or more circuits of ditch interrupted by numerous causeways. An embankment or palisade stood within the ditch. The number of causeways and the location of the sites argue against a defensive purpose, and they have been interpreted as tribal meeting places or ritual centres; the latter explanation gains support from the presence of human remains in the ditches. Causewayed camps date mainly to the 4th millennium BC and are found throughout southern and eastern England: see WINDMILL HILL, CRICKLEY HILL, HAMBLEDON HILL, HEMBURY, MAIDEN CASTLE, ABINGDON.

cavea the tiered seating in a Roman theatre or AMPHITHEATRE.

cave art see PALAEOLITHIC ART.

Cave Bay Cave a rockshelter on Hunter Island off north-western TASMANIA, Australia. Excavations by Sandra Bowdler revealed three separate occupation episodes c.23,000 bp, 7000 bp and from 2500 bp. Faunal remains demonstrate a shift from a Pleistocene land-based economy, while the site was part of the mainland, to a marine economy in the early Holocene as the sea approached present levels. After abandonment in the mid Holocene, this and other sites on the island show seasonal specialized use over the last 2,000 years.

cave bear (*Ursus spelaeus*) an extinct species of bear which lived from about 300,000 to 10,000 years ago. It was restricted to central latitudes of Europe, from southern England to the northern Mediterranean, and eastwards to the Black Sea. Cave bears were up to 2.7 m (9 ft) long and weighed up to 300–400 kg (660–880 lbs), twice the weight of modern European brown bears (*Ursus arctos*). They had a relatively large head with a characteristic domed forehead, and relatively short, stocky legs. Studies of their tooth structure, as well as of the mineral content of their bones, indicate that their diet was almost exclusively vegetarian. Large numbers of cave bear fossils are found in certain caves, a result of animals occasionally dying during their winter hibernation.

Cave of Hearths see MAKAPAN.

Caverna da Pedra Pintada see PEDRA PINTADA.

Cayla de Mailhac, Le see MAILHAC.

Çayönü a 3 ha (7.4 acre) prehistoric site on the River Tigris drainage in the Diyarbakir district of Turkey excavated by H. Çambel and R. Braidwood. Its occupation dates to roughly 8200–6100 bc, with the main architectural phases falling after 7300 BC. The sequence of stone architecture at the site shows considerable sophistication, and includes at different times elaborate foundations and *terrazzo* floors (a decorative technique of coloured stones laid as patterns in cement and then polished). One late period building functioned communally in a mortuary cult, indicated by a collection of nearly 100 skulls, and an altar stone and flint knife that retained blood residues from wild cattle, sheep and humans. The material culture of the community encompassed various uses of unfired clay (figurines, geometrics [see TOKENS], basketry lining), hammered native copper, and rich lithic and bone industries. The community cultivated wheat and legumes, which increased in importance through time, and shifted from mostly hunted cattle, deer, sheep, goat and pigs to (probably) mostly herded sheep, goat and pig by the end of the occupation.

CE see AD.

Ceahlău-Cetăţica an Upper Palaeolithic open-air site located along a small tributary of the Siret River in eastern Romania. Artifacts and faunal remains (which include woolly mammoth and reindeer) are buried in loess deposits on a medium terrace. The lowermost levels contain small assemblages with bifacial foliates, sidescrapers and endscrapers and are assigned to the early Upper Palaeolithic (not clearly attributable to either the AURIGNACIAN or the SZELETIAN). The upper levels contain backed blades, and are assigned to the GRAVETTIAN.

Cebu City the site, in southern Visayas, Philippines, of the first Spanish settlement in the Orient. Excavated localities contained large quantities of glazed Asian trade wares, and a variety of impressed and incised earthenware pottery dating from c.10th century AD.

Cederberg a range of the Cape Fold Mountains north of Cape Town, South Africa, particularly known for its rock paintings, which date from the LATER STONE AGE to historical times. Depictions of humans, hand prints, animals (especially elephant and sheep), geometric designs and historical scenes are interpreted by a few scholars as related to the trance hallucinations of 'shamans'.

Céide Fields see Celtic fields

celadon a type of stoneware, with a revolutionary glaze containing calcium and feldspar, produced in quantity in China in the 9th–14th centuries AD (see CHINESE DYNASTIES). The glaze is most often dark greenish-blue from reduced firing, but some oxidized yellowish-brown glazes are also included. The northern Yaozhou and the southern Longquan kilns are best known. Celadon became the first trade ceramics to be exported from China in quantity (see SINAN) to many destinations in East and Southeast Asia, and the Koreans continued to develop the celadon tradition in the Koryo period (see also KOREA, WANDO; compare YUE ware).

cella the largest room in a CLASSICAL temple, which sometimes contained the cult-statue. To its rear was the ADYTON.

celt (from *Late Latin* 'celtis', chisel) an ancient chopping tool, a kind of a bronze socketed axe or adze, used for woodworking or for excavation. The main characteristic of a celt is a socket set perpendicular to the blade. The shaft was elbow-shaped. Celts were widespread in the 2nd–1st millennia BC almost everywhere in Europe and the EURASIAN STEPPES. See also SHOE-LAST ADZE.

Celtic fields regular systems of small rectangular enclosures found on the uplands of southern England, and generally dated to the pre-Roman Iron Age (1st millennium BC) though some go back to the 2nd millennium BC. Their edges are marked by small banks where processes of erosion (sometimes consequent on ploughing) have led to downslope slippage of soil. Similar field systems, of roughly the same date, are known from Denmark and the Netherlands, and excavations in lowland valleys of southern England and on the edge of the East Anglian Fens have revealed small fields marked out by rectilinear ditches. Some of these were livestock pens. Extensive field systems in upland regions such as Dartmoor, North Yorkshire and the Pennines have been traced back to the Bronze Age, but the earliest field system in northwestern Europe is that at Céide Fields in western Ireland, which dates to the 4th millennium BC.

Celts name frequently applied to the Iron Age peoples of Central and western Europe (including Britain and Ireland), and associated with the concepts of 'Celtic art' and 'Celtic languages'. The term 'Celt' was probably first used by the Greeks c.500 BC to refer to the people of southern France living north of the Greek colony of Massilia (MARSEILLES). It is cognate with the term 'Galatae' (the Galatians of the New Testament), a group or warband who invaded Asia Minor in the 3rd century BC, and with the 'Gauls' who attacked Rome in 390 BC and were themselves conquered by Julius Caesar in 58–52 BC. The term was never applied by any CLASSICAL writer to the peoples of Britain and Ireland and it was only in c.1700 that it came to be used to refer to the 'Celtic' languages of Brittany, Ireland, Cornwall, Wales and Scotland.

From the mid 19th century archaeologists began to define 'Celtic' cultures in Central Europe on the basis of new discoveries. This led to a two-phase scheme comprising a 'HALLSTATT' phase (c.1200–475 BC) followed by a LA TÈNE phase, which continued up to the Roman conquest. The La Tène art style, characterized by decorative use of interlacing plant motifs on mainly portable objects, became widespread in Central and western

Europe, and some see it continuing into the early medieval period in the Christian crosses and manuscripts of Britain and Ireland. Though loosely referred to as 'Celtic art', there is nothing to support the once-held view that all these objects are the work of a single Celtic people or tradition who spread from Central Europe to Britain and Ireland. See also DRUIDS.

Cenchreae the eastern harbour of the Roman colony of CORINTH giving access to the Saronic Gulf and the eastern Mediterranean. Although it was partially submerged due to the movement of the Peloponnese, American excavations have revealed remains of the temple of the Egyptian deity ISIS and a Christian basilica which contained coloured glass. The harbour itself was protected by artificial moles. A similarly complex harbour facility can be observed at Lechaeum on the Corinth Gulf, though this is now slightly above sea-level.

cenote a natural well or sinkhole created when bedrock has collapsed, exposing the water table. One of the most famous is the Sacred Cenote at CHICHÉN ITZÁ, 60 m (66 yds) in diameter with walls 26 m (85 ft) above the water-level. The MAYA offered rituals and sacrifices at the Sacred Cenote.

Central Cattle Pattern a southern African Iron Age homestead organization associated with most speakers of Eastern BANTU languages in the southern African Iron Age, who exchange cattle for wives. It is characterized by a central male area of stock byres, storage facilities controlled by a central political authority, high-status burials, and a men's court, which is surrounded by an outer arc of storage facilities and houses associated with women.

central place theory a model developed by geographers, which argues that sites are distributed evenly over a region, and that settlements are spatially organized in a hierarchy of importance, dependent on their control of resources.

centuriation a Roman technique for dividing up agricultural land into equal areas often of 200 *iugera* (approximately 50 ha [124 acres]). It was particularly common at colonies where each member of the foundation would be assigned an equal share. Centuriation may be noted by aerial photography where it shows as a grid pattern.

cephalic index a measure for the shape of the cranial vault, derived by Anders Retzius in 1842. The measure is the ratio of the maximum breadth divided by the maximum width of the skull. Retzius used the cephalic index to divide European populations into three types: *dolichocephalic* (long, narrow); *mesocephalic* (intermediate); and *brachycephalic* (short, broad).

ceque one of a series of imaginary lines radiating outwards from the INCA city of CUZCO. A total of forty-one ceques extended from the Temple of the Sun to the edges of the surrounding valley. Along each ceque were located a series of huacas (shrines) at which offerings were made on successive days. It has been argued that the sequence of huacas and ceques served to define the Inca solar-year calendar; and research by Anthony Aveni and Tom Zuidema suggests the possibility that some of the ceques may have had astronomical significance, although subsequent research has questioned these interpretations. A recent intensive study of the ceque system has found that the number and arrangement of huacas probably changed somewhat during the reign of each Inca emperor.

ceramic petrology the study of the composition, material sources and construction technology of pottery. Mineral constituents of ceramics that may help identify a material source are identified by one or more methods. Pottery can be broken down into particles with HEAVY MINERAL ANALYSIS conducted on the residue. More commonly, a PETROLOGICAL ANALYSIS is undertaken in which a THIN SECTION is made and mineral constituents are identified on the basis of their optical properties. Thin sections oriented perpendicular to vessel walls may reveal internal structures as well as mineral additives (temper), that provide clues to construction technology and techniques. If a clay source can be identified, the distribution of ceramics made from that source should hold clues to trade and economic systems.

ceramics baked clay or pottery, often used for containers. The plasticity and additive technology of ceramics make this medium one of the most culturally sensitive of all prehistoric artifacts that have been extensively used by archaeologists as time-markers, as well as for the information they can provide on social organization.

ceremonial centre a predominant form of urban centre in MESOAMERICA, especially among the OLMEC and MAYA cultures. Ceremonial centres are typically composed of monumental religious architecture, admin-

CERVETERI, Italy: Etruscan tombs.

istrative buildings, BALL COURTs and elite residential compounds. The non-elite lived in perishable structures around the centre.

Cerén, Joya de a MAYA 'POMPEII' in El Salvador, just west of San Salvador, discovered in 1976. Excavations by Payson Sheets have revealed that the village was buried under ash by a volcanic eruption in c.AD 600. The remarkable preservation has yielded wooden objects such as digging sticks and pestles inside houses, dishes of food left on hearths, and rows of maize in a cornfield.

Cernavodă a late Neolithic and ENEOLITHIC site complex in southeastern Romania. The best known is a cemetery of the HAMANGIA culture with over 300 inhumations. Many of the graves contained anthropomorphous figurines, including several with more facial and body detail than previous Balkan figurines. Near by is a later settlement with several metres of deposits, which is the type-site for the Cernavodă culture at the transition from the Eneolithic to the Early Bronze Age. Cernavodă shell-tempered, fluted pottery represents a break from that of the preceding GUMELNIŢA culture.

Cernica a late Neolithic cemetery near Bucharest, Romania, with 115 burials of the HAMANGIA culture. Among the grave-goods were copper beads made of malachite or a similar ore which had been cold-hammered but not heated. Other grave-goods included pottery, polished stone tools and bracelets of SPONDYLUS shell.

Cerny an early Neolithic culture of the Paris basin and middle Loire, France, characterized by round-based vessels with impressed decoration or applied cordons. Cerny (c.4400–4000 BC) follows the Villeneuve-St-Germain group in the Paris basin Neolithic sequence, and precedes the Chasseen (see CHASSEY).

Cerro Sechín a monumental site in the Casma Valley of the northern-central coast of Peru. A square central mound, measuring 53 m (58 yds) square and 4 m (13 ft) high, is faced with bas-relief stone carvings depicting warriors, captives, weapons and disarticulated human body parts. The dating of the site is unclear; some researchers consider it to date to the EARLY HORIZON, and suggest that it may commemorate the conquest of this region by a group from the highlands. Others argue for a date in the INITIAL PERIOD.

Cerveteri (*Lat.* Caere) – a walled city in southern ETRURIA. It is best known for its cemeteries, such as that at Banditaccia just to the north. A wide range of tombs have been found including some under tumuli and others cut into the TUFF. One of the more elaborate is the Tomb of the Reliefs, which is an underground room laid out like a TRICLINIUM with drinking vessels, armour and other items cut in relief. The tombs have been an important source for ATHENIAN POTTERY. Cerveteri was served by the port of Pyrgi, where three gold plaques have been found providing parallel texts in Etruscan and PHOENICIAN. See also CAERETAN WARE.

Čevdar see CHEVDAR.

C-group a population of LOWER NUBIA broadly contemporary, and sharing cultural traits, with the KERMA culture of UPPER NUBIA (c.2200–1500 BC). The C-group, like the PAN-GRAVE people, seem to have been primarily cattle-herders. Their most distinctive material product is hand-made black pottery with incised geometric designs. Links with the preceding A-group are uncertain. Elaborate buildings and the importation of luxury items from Egypt in late C-group times suggest that state formation was underway.

chacmool an anthropomorphous altar common at CHICHÉN ITZÁ and TULA but also found at other MESO-AMERICAN centres. The hands of reclining human figures, resting on the stomach, provided an altar on which offerings were placed. These sculptures are associated with temple entrances. Their name, meaning 'red paw' or 'great paw' in the Yucatec language, was first given to them by Augustus Le Plongeon in the 19th century.

CHACMOOL in the Temple of the Warriors, Chichén Itzá, Mexico.

CHACO CANYON, USA: walls and cliff at Pueblo Bonito.

ten HALAF levels, the lowest of which also contained SAMARRAN painted and AMUQ B-related sherds. NEUTRON ACTIVATION ANALYSIS of the later Halaf pottery at Chagar Bazar indicates that most of it was locally produced and distributed to smaller settlements to the north, an indication of economic specialization and possibly of socio-political complexity within the region. Elsewhere on the mound, Mallowan's work revealed five levels belonging to the 3rd and 2nd millennia BC. The uppermost of these levels contains a large building, possibly a palace, that contained a small archive dated to SHAMSHI-ADAD I. A recently initiated British project has documented additional 4th-millennium deposits.

chaîne opératoire a processing sequence, a form of lithic analysis which considers all stages of use from the initial collection of the raw material to the final discarding of the unwanted tool, combining traditional (TYPOLOGY, CONJOINING) and scientific (USE-WEAR ANALYSIS) approaches to lithic studies.

Chaironeia or **Chaeronea** a large Neolithic settlement mound in Boeotia, Greece, which is the source of distinctive red-on-cream middle Neolithic pottery. A stone lion in the village of Chaironeia guards the tomb of the Thebans who were killed in the battle of 338 BC.

Chaiya a city on the east coast of peninsular Thailand with two early historic sites: Wat Wiang, a moated settlement occupied in the late 1st–early 2nd millennium AD and source of inscriptions associating the town with Grahi, ŚRIVIJAYA and TAMBRALINGA; and Ban Phum Rieng, a site closer to the shore which has yielded finds linking it to the nearby port of LAEM PHO.

Chalandriani the site of a large Early CYCLADIC cemetery on the island of Syros in the Aegean, which was excavated by TSOUNTAS. The fortified settlement on the precipitous hill of Kastri is also Early Cycladic but appears to be later in date and to have been occupied by settlers from Anatolia.

Chalcatzingo a large PRECLASSIC community in Morelos, Mexico, known primarily for its carvings on boulders and other rock faces. The community was probably an important point on a trade route connecting the Mexican highlands with the OLMEC. The site was discovered by Eulalia Guzmán in 1934.

chalcedony a group of water-bearing silica minerals characterized by very fine grained (cryptocrystalline) quartz, colloidal silica, a small amount of water and submicroscopic pores. Chalcedony is transparent to opaque and is found in a wide range of colours. 'Chalcedony' is reserved for those specimens that are fairly uniform in colour, whereas *agate* is used for specimens characterized by colour bands or concentric rings. Some of the banded varieties are called *onyx*. In the archaeological record,

Chaco Canyon a wide canyon in northern-central New Mexico, USA. It is the location of some of the most visually impressive and important sites of the American Southwest. Chaco Canyon reached its zenith in the period approximately AD 1000–1150. The cluster of sites may have served as a ceremonial and/or trading centre for subsidiary sites, called Chacoan outliers, found throughout the northern Southwest. Many of these sites are connected to Chaco Canyon by roads up to 96 km (60 miles) long, some of which were merely depressions running along the surface while others were well constructed with stone edgings. See ANASAZI, FAJADA BUTTE, PUEBLO BONITO, WETHERILL.

Chadwick, John (1920–98) a British Classical scholar who helped VENTRIS to translate and interpret the LINEAR B documents.

Chaeronea see CHAIRONEIA.

Chagar Bazar a large (10 ha [25 acre]) prehistoric TELL site in the Khabur triangle in northeastern Syria. Max MALLOWAN's excavations during the 1930s occurred in separate parts of the mound. A deep sounding exposed chalcedony was used for beads, jewellery, seals, and was worked into stone tools by flaking and chipping.

Chalcidian ware a type of ARCHAIC BLACK-FIGURED pottery mostly found in ETRURIA and in the Chalcidian colony of Rhegium (*mod*. Reggio) situated on the 'toe' of Italy. The name is derived from the local style of lettering of the inscriptions which form part of the scheme of decoration. Recent clay analyses have been unable to identify the place of manufacture.

Chalcolithic a term for the Copper Age. See also ENEO-LITHIC.

Chaldeans a seminomadic ethnic group, associated with UR and Abraham in popular and biblical belief, which moved into southern MESOPOTAMIA early in the 1st millennium BC from the west; this movement, along with that of ARAMAEANS, contributed to the political and economic upheavals in ASSYRIA and BABYLONIA of that time. Unlike the Aramaeans, the Chaldeans became largely sedentary, though still organized as tribal descent groups, in southern Babylonia. These groups strongly resisted the Assyrian occupation of Babylonia in the 8th–7th centuries BC. Although the rulers of the NEO-BABYLONIAN empire are often referred to as the 'Chaldean dynasty', these kings (e.g. NEBUCHADNEZZAR II) are not known to be of Chaldean descent.

Cham an ethno-linguistic group belonging to the AUS-TRONESIAN family, once controlling the central coast of modern Vietnam, and forming the state of CHAMPA.

chamber(ed) tomb a tomb, either stone-built and covered by an earth mound or rock-cut, often used for multiple inhumations.

'Cham forts' see 'MOI FORTS'.

Champa a series of early Indianized kingdoms (see INDIANIZATION) formed by the Cham people on the central coast of modern Vietnam, comprising several distinct geographical foci: Amaravati, Vijaya, Kauthara and Pandurangga. Probably to be identified with Lin Yi, mentioned by the Chinese in the late 2nd century AD, it was one of the earliest Indianized states in Southeast Asia. It remained an important sea trading state until its progressive absorption by Vietnam after the 13th century. Major sites include: Vo Canh (earliest SANSKRIT inscription in Southeast Asia, from the 3rd century AD?); Po Nagar (centre of Kauthara); and, in Amaravati, Mi Son, Dong Duong and Tra Kieu (all major ceremonial centres).

Champ Durand a Neolithic enclosure in Vendée, France, consisting of three concentric rock-cut ditches with numerous entrance gaps. Rubble in the ditches probably came from a dry-stone rampart on their inner edge. Associated material is of late Neolithic type, and includes PEU-RICHARDIEN decorated pottery which allows the site to be dated to *c*.3300–3000 BC.

Champollion, Jean François (1790–1832) a French philologist instrumental in the decipherment of Egyptian HIEROGLYPHS, initially through his work on the RO-SETTA STONE.

Chancay a culture of the LATE INTERMEDIATE PERIOD on the northern-central coast of Peru. It is characterized by a distinctive ceramic style found in the Chancay and Chillón Valleys as well as to the north and south. A typical form is an elongated jar, with a face painted on a small neck; ceramics are not highly polished, and are typically painted in black geometric designs on an off-white SLIP. Numerous large cemeteries pertaining to this culture yield evidence of social stratification. One of several distinctive coastal cultures at this time, it was conquered by the INCA empire. See also CHIMÚ.

Chancelade or **Raymonden** two MAGDALENIAN rock-shelters in the Dordogne, France, which included hearths, harpoons, MOBILIARY ART and the tightly flexed ochre-covered burial of an adult male. The Chancelade man, found in 1888, was a HOMO *sapiens sapiens*, but skeletal analysis suggests that he would have been dissimilar in appearance to CRO-MAGNON man, being shorter and having a different facial shape.

Chan Chan an urban site covering over 6 sq. km (2.3 sq. miles), the capital of the CHIMÚ POLITY of the LATE INTERMEDIATE PERIOD, located in the Moche Valley on the north coast of Peru. Investigations by Michael E. Moseley, Carol Mackey, Kent Day and others indicate that the site comprises some nine large rectangular compounds each of which may have served as the administrative headquarters, ceremonial centre and subsequent mausoleum of each of the successive Chimú rulers. The presence of extensive secondary architecture suggests a resident population in excess of 10,000 persons. The lack of contemporaneous sites indicates that nearly the entire population of the Moche Valley may have lived at the site.

Chang'an [Ch'ang-an] the name of both the Early HAN and Tang capitals (see CHINESE DYNASTIES) of China. These two walled cities of the same name are located adjacent to each other in Shaanxi Province, the latter incorporating modern Xian City. The gridded street layout and gated walled enclosure of Tang period Chang'an, with the royal palace positioned for the first time in the north, became the model for urban development in the 7th century AD Korean states and Japan (see SILLA, HEIJO, PUYO, FUJIWARA).

Changjiang [Ch'ang-chiang] literally 'long river', the Chinese name for the Yangtze River, heartland of the wet-rice agricultural regime (see HEMUDU).

Chanhu-daro a group of three mounds covering nearly 20 ha (30 acres) (but originally larger) in the southern Sind (southern Pakistan). Chanhu-daro was excavated first by N. G. Majuindar and then by Ernest Mackay in the 1930s. Mackay's work revealed a Mature HARAPPAN city beneath ill-defined Late Harappan (JHUKAR) levels. Chanhu-daro's contribution to Harappan archaeology rests largely on the recovery of craftsmen's workshops (especially stone beads). Although it represents one of the few investigated Late Harappan sites in the Sind, Mackay's failure to excavate it by natural stratigraphic units leaves considerable confusion about the nature of the period.

Chania or **Khania** the site of ancient Kydonia, in the west of Crete, which was evidently a MINOAN administrative centre and should be the site of a palace, but the excavations at Kastelli in the old town have uncovered only a fraction of the Bronze Age settlement. Nevertheless LINEAR A and LINEAR B tablets have been discovered.

Chanka see INCA.

Chansen a moderate-sized protohistoric and early historic settlement north of LOPBURI in the Chao Phraya Valley, central Thailand. Evidence of trade with India dates to the first two centuries AD, and of trade with 'FUNAN' sites in the Mekong delta to the 5th and 6th centuries. Phase 5 of occupation (c.AD 600–800) is related to the state of DVARAVATI.

Charama or **Charaman** a post-ACHEULIAN and pre-BAMBATA early Upper Pleistocene Stone Age industry of Zambia and Zimbabwe, characterized by light-duty flake tools, especially scrapers, small picks and disc cores.

Charavines the LAKE DWELLING of Les Baigneurs, on the southern side of Lake Paladru, Isère, France, now under water. The well-preserved remains of timber houses and organic materials, excavated since 1972, have allowed a remarkably detailed picture of the settlement's history to be established through DENDROCHRONOLOGY of the structural timbers. The first village, of six or seven rectangular houses, was established in about 2740 BC. Repaired after nine years, these houses were then abandoned at the end of twenty years. Fifty-seven years later the village was rebuilt, and occupied for a further twenty years before final abandonment. Notable among the many organic remains recovered are finely flaked flint daggers with handles of coiled willow.

charcoal see ANTHRACOLOGY.

Charentian a major MOUSTERIAN variant rich in side-scrapers identified by BORDES in southwestern France. The Charentian tradition may be subdivided into the LA FERRASSIE type, which has few transverse scrapers but a frequent use of the LEVALLOISian technique, and the LA QUINA type, with many transverse scrapers but little Levallois material. See also LA QUINA, LA FERRASSIE.

chasing see REPOUSSÉ.

Chassey a promontory settlement, in Côte-d'Or, France, type-site of the middle Neolithic Chasséen culture found throughout much of eastern and southern France c.4500–3500 BC. The principal pottery forms are round-based bowls with sharp CARINATION, often of very fine fabric; and cubic or cylindrical objects with saucer-like tops and incised decoration of cross-hatched and dot-filled triangles known as VASE-SUPPORTS or 'incense-burners'. The latter term is probably nearer the true function of these enigmatic pieces. Chasséen material is found at promontory settlements in eastern and north-eastern France, at the large open sites of the Toulouse area including VILLENEUVE-TOLOSANE and ST MICHEL-DU-TOUCH, and in megalithic tombs of western France.

Châteauneuf-les-Martigues a rockshelter in the southern Rhône Valley, Bouches-du-Rhône, France, with Mesolithic and Neolithic occupation. The earliest layers (9 to 7) contain geometric microliths and other material of the late Mesolithic *Castelnovian* culture. This is followed c.5000 BC by early Neolithic layers with CARDIAL WARE pottery and bones of domestic sheep. Early radiocarbon dates from the site which suggested the appearance of Neolithic features before 6000 BC have now been discounted.

Châtelperronian the earliest Upper Palaeolithic French flake industry, named after the cave-site of Châtelperron, Allier, central France, and characterized by the presence of curved backed blades (Châtelperron points or knives), flakes, endscrapers and burins. It is generally accepted that the Châtelperronian represents a local development evolving c.40,000 bp from the final MOUSTERIAN of southwestern France. The Châtelperronian is occasionally termed the Lower PERIGORDIAN.

chattel art see MOBILIARY ART.

Chau Can a cemetery of the DONG SON culture in Ha Son Binh Province, 40 km (25 miles) south of Ha Noi, Vietnam, with eight log-coffin burials dated to between 530 and 200 BC and broadly contemporary with VIET KHE, but less richly furnished. Burial 3 contained a spear with fragments of a lacquered wooden haft, and a typical Dong Son asymmetrical axe with an intact haft, indicating that it was more likely to be a shoulder-pressure woodworking tool than an axe.

Chauvet see GROTTE CHAUVET.

Chavín a large town and temple complex located in the northern-central highlands of Peru, pertaining to the EARLY HORIZON. Investigations by Julio C. TELLO, Luis G. Lumbreras and Richard Burger indicate that the Old Temple complex (c.900–400 bc) was built originally to a U-shaped plan, arranged around a sunken circular courtyard. Deep inside the original structure is found a monolithic stone carving, the Lanzón, on which is depicted an anthropomorphous being with a fanged feline mouth and snakes for hair. It is one of the few large Chavín stone carvings still in its original location.

Later the complex was modifed, with the New Temple (c.400–200 bc) incorporating the old, and forming a new U-shaped layout surrounding a large sunken rectangular court. One of the stone carvings associated with the New Temple was the Raimondi STELA, on which was carved a human figure, with an elaborate head-dress, holding a staff in each hand. This may be one of the earliest representations of the Staff Deity, which is seen in the art of later civilizations, especially TIAHUANACO and HUARI.

Chavín probably functioned as a pilgrimage centre. (See also PACHACAMAC.) The art style of Chavín, together with new technological innovations in textile art and metallurgy, are found widely distributed through the northern highlands and the north, central and south coast of Peru. It is the spread of the Chavín style that originally gave definition to the Early Horizon, although at present its distribution is less extensive than originally thought. Work by Richard Burger indicates that many 'Chavinoid' sites actually pre-date the construction of Chavín. See also CUPISNIQUE, PARACAS.

Cheddar See GOUGH'S CAVE.

chedi a Thai term for STUPA.

Cheetup a granite rockshelter in southwestern Western Australia. The shallow deposits date to the Late Pleistocene. A pit containing well-preserved cycad seeds is dated to 13,200 bp. It resembles the pits described in 19th-century historical accounts that local Aborigines used to leach out the toxins from cycad seeds. Compare CATHEDRAL CAVE.

chekan a special kind of striking weapon for hand-to-hand combat. It was most widespread in southern Siberia and in Central Asia in the SCYTHIAN period. The chekan is a kind of a battle axe with a thin sharp point, made of bronze. It was fixed on to a long wooden shaft which had a bronze butt at its lower end, and was worn at the waist on a special belt. Chekans are quite often decorated with zoomorphic figures in the SCYTHIAN-SIBERIAN ANIMAL STYLE.

Chelford a Pleistocene site in Cheshire, England, which has given its name to the Chelford INTERSTADIAL, a warm phase during the early DEVENSIAN cold stage and dated to c.61,000 BP, which is accepted as the equivalent of the Continental BRØRUP Interstadial.

Chellean an outdated classificatory term used for the first primitive stage of biface manufacture believed to precede the ACHEULIAN, and named after the type-site of Chelles in the Somme Valley, France. It is now generally accepted that Chellean implements should correctly be classified as early Acheulian. The term Chelleo-Acheulian, which was once applied to African EARLIER STONE AGE

biface assemblages, has also been replaced by the term Acheulian. See also ABBEVILLIAN.

chemical analysis a general term for the quantitative or qualitative determination of the chemical composition of material utilizing a range of physical and chemical analytical techniques. Chemical analyses have been applied to nearly the full range of artifactual materials, soil and sediment recovered from archaeological contexts to solve problems of material characterization, correlation, material source identification, manufacturing technology and artifact composition.

Chenjiawo [Ch'en-chia-wo] see LANTIAN.

Chenla see ZHENLA.

Cheops see KHUFU.

Chephren see KHAFRE.

Chersonesos see SCYTHIANS.

chert 1 a member of the CHALCEDONY group of water-bearing silica minerals characterized by its opaqueness. 'Chert' is used to refer to such material where it occurs as strata or massive deposits, but it can also occur as NODULES. Flint is often distinguished from chert by its dark or black colour, although mineralogically they form a continuum, with chert having less water and being slightly coarser-grained. The hardness of chert, its interlocking fine grains, and ability to fracture concoidally producing razor-sharp edges made it a principal raw material used in tool manufacture.

2 a sedimentary silicious rock mostly consisting of chert, the mineral.

Chesowanja a central Kenyan site with faunal remains and OLDOWAN stone tools associated with small clay clasts, which some interpret as early evidence that HOMINIDs were using and controlling fire 1.42 million years ago. However, because it has been shown that erosion of naturally burnt clay areas can result in fragments like those at Chesowanja, some researchers consider the case for the controlled use of fire at Chesowanja unproven.

chevaux de frise term for a defensive system comprising rows of closely spaced stones or stakes, stuck in the ground, often found in front of vulnerable parts of HILLFORTS, CASTROS or other Iron Age defences from Britain to Iberia, and highly effective against cavalry charges or infantry.

Chevdar or **Čevdar** an early Neolithic TELL site located on the Topolnitsa River in Bulgaria. In one of the earliest uses of flotation in European archaeology, soil samples from floors and ovens at Chevdar yielded considerable information on plant use by the earliest Neolithic communities of the Balkans. The faunal sample consisted primarily of sheep and goat, with fewer cattle, pigs and some wild animals. The subsistence data from Chevdar, as at KAZANLUK, have been interpreted as reflecting both an arable component, based on a rotational system of cultivation, and a mobile pastoral component.

Chiapa de Corzo   a site in western-central Chiapas, Mexico, which not only has some of the earliest evidence of occupation in Chiapas, but has also been occupied almost continuously from the early PRECLASSIC (1500–1000 BC) through the Spanish conquest and into modern times. Its primary importance lies in its well-stratified deposits, the chronology that has been developed subsequently and the ability to tie this chronology to the remainder of MESOAMERICA. It has been excavated by a number of scholars working with the New World Archaeological Foundation.

Chibuene   a trading settlement on the Mozambique coast, occupied from at least the mid 1st millennium AD, which developed into an important link in the trade between the East African coast and interior sites such as MAPUNGUBWE and GREAT ZIMBABWE in the first half of the 2nd millennium AD.

Chichén Itzá   a MAYA CEREMONIAL CENTRE in central Yucatán, Mexico, one of the best-known sites in MESOAMERICA, whose ceramic evidence indicates occupation from the late PRECLASSIC to the late POSTCLASSIC. The features at this site include El Castillo, a square based, stepped pyramid, approximately 25 m (82 ft) high; the Sacred CENOTE, a natural well 60 m (66 yds) in diameter, with sides 26 m (85 ft) above the water surface, into which human and other sacrifices were thrown; El Caracol ('snail' in Spanish), a name referring to the building's spiral stairway: El Caracol was probably an observatory, and is the only round structure at Chichén Itzá. The centre also contains the Temple of the Warriors, which at one time was attributed to 'TOLTECS' during their occupation of the city. Many Mesoamericanists now reject the Toltec invasion theory, and see Chichén Itzá as having dual, complementary styles of architecture, with the 'Toltec' buildings perhaps built by the Putun or Chontal non-Classic Maya from southwestern Yucatán.

Chichimec   a general term applied specifically to peoples moving south into the Basin of Mexico from the north between AD 1175 and 1425. The term is used more generally to refer to 'barbarian' cultures on the northern frontier of MESOAMERICA. The Chichimec were typically portrayed as fierce, warring peoples, new to Mesoamerican civilization and culture. Perhaps the most famous descendants of the Chichimec were the AZTECS. Chichimec is also a linguistic group. See also GRAN CHICHIMECA.

Chicoid   a ceramic series that, like the MEILLACOID, developed from the OSTIONOID series in the ANTILLES around AD 1000 and lasted until the arrival of Europeans. The type-site is Boca Chica, in the Dominican Republic,

and the culture's influence extended over much of the eastern Antilles.

chiefdom   a type of social organization characterized by a degree of social ranking and larger population aggregates. They are led by individual chiefs who control access to resources and have specific political and economic powers.

Chifumbaze or **Mwitu tradition**   an Early Iron Age complex distributed over an enormous area of eastern and southeastern Africa, dating from about 2,500 years ago to at least the 11th century AD. Sites contain the first evidence in eastern and southeastern Africa for settled village life and metallurgy, and, in southeastern Africa, for the manufacture of pottery. The complex is generally divided into an Eastern Stream or UREWE tradition and a Western Stream or KALUNDU tradition (see CHONDWE, GOKOMERE, KAPWIRIMBWE, KWALE, MATOLA, NKOPE).

Childe, Vere Gordon (1892–1957)   one of the leading archaeologists of the 20th century. Born in Australia, he emigrated to Britain where he spent the whole of his professional life. Never a prolific excavator (SKARA BRAE being a rare exception), he is most famous for his massive syntheses of prehistory. Early work on European languages and ethnicity, published as *The Aryans* in 1926, broadened into a general survey of European prehistory in the Neolithic and Bronze Age, *The Dawn of European Civilization* (which, revised and corrected, ran through six editions between 1925 and 1957), and *The Danube in Prehistory*, published in 1929. For Childe, the succession of cultures at the VINČA TELL near Belgrade formed the key to the chronology of Southeast Europe. He subsequently widened his interests to include the early farming communities and civilizations of the Near East with *The Most Ancient East* (1928) and *Man Makes Himself* (1936). In 1927 he became the first Professor of Prehistoric Archaeology at the University of Edinburgh, moving in 1946 to be director of the newly established Institute of Archaeology in London. Widely respected for his knowledge of European languages and prehistory, he has also had a profound influence on later generations of archaeologists through his writings on the nature of archaeological concepts and entities, including the idea of the culture, still a major building block of European prehistory. The theoretical underpinnings to his work are strongly MARXIST.

Chimú   a large urban society located on the north coast of Peru during the LATE INTERMEDIATE PERIOD. The Chimú capital was at CHAN CHAN, in the MOCHE Valley, and Chimú control extended from the central coast of Peru nearly to Ecuador; it was the largest POLITY conquered by the INCA. The Chimú first began to expand in the 13th or 14th century AD, and controlled several valleys to the north and south. A second expansion, accomplished in the mid 15th century, brought the Chimú to their maximum extent; this later expansion may have been related to the fact that the Inca were also beginning to expand at this time. The Chimú built many impressive hydraulic constructions, and brought large tracts of land under cultivation. One canal may have served to connect the Chicama and Moche Valleys, but there is some dispute over whether or not the canal actually functioned, and over the reasons for its abandonment. The Chimú were conquered by the Inca empire after a bloody struggle, and the Chimú political apparatus was gradually dismantled.

China Between the late LAST GLACIAL MAXIMUM (18,000–15,000 BC) and the end of the former Han Dynasty in AD 9, the formation of China's coastlines had come to an end. China proper now extends approximately 1,000 miles from north to south and east to west, with mountain ranges and two great rivers, the Yellow River in the north and the Yangzi in the south. The regions drained by these rivers differ in soils, topography, temperature and rainfall, with a colder climate in the north and shorter growing seasons, while the warmer south allows rice cultivation.

Early human beings, like HOMO *erectus*, appeared in China over a million years ago, spreading from Africa and western Asia, as was proved by the discovery in 1920 of Peking Man at ZHOUKOUDIAN, close to today's capital Beijing. Simple chipped stone tools have survived from this period. In the later part of the Palaeolithic period (100,000–10,000 BC) hunters and gatherers (attributed to *H. sapiens*) appeared. By 5000 BC, a series of Neolithic cultures with agriculture, pottery and villages had emerged in many of the river valleys, with the main focus on rice growing in the south and millet in the north. Archaeological discoveries from these cultures have revealed remains of wooden houses on stilts, lacquered bowls and refined ceramic products (HEMUDU) and primitive burials with painted pottery (YANGSHAO). Spectacular finds of Neolithic jade are known from the HONGSHAN (*c*.3500 BC) and the LIANGZHU cultures (*c*.2500 BC), with small figurines in the shape of turtles, dragons or birds, suggesting a ritual significance.

Along with permanent settlements, new forms of social organization arose and, around 2000 BC, out of the diverse Neolithic cultures some more complex Bronze Age civilizations emerged in the area of the middle Yellow River. The earliest bronze vessels, such as cups, goblets and steamers, were found at ERLITOU, a region traditionally attributed to the earliest stage of this transition, the XIA Dynasty. However, no archaeological discovery attributed to Xia has yielded written documents so far, and it is still a matter of intense debate as to whether there was a fully fledged Xia Dynasty before the SHANG Dynasty (1600–1050 BC), with large-scale city-like cult centres such as ZHENGZHOU and ANYANG.

Domestication of the horse, bronze casting and the cultivation of grain and rice were the main achievements of the period. ORACLE BONES and bronze inscriptions constitute the first written records in Chinese history. They were placed in large burial sites, pit tombs with tomb passages and adjacent lateral pits. The following ZHOU Dynasty (1027–221 BC) inherited its cultural traditions from the Neolithic cultures and parts of the material culture of the Shang, whom they defeated in a battle in 1050 BC. The early Zhou is the first period from which written texts have come down to us. It is also the time when important changes emerged in ideas about death and the afterlife. Human sacrifices and divinations with oracle bones declined, and changes in bronzes and pottery took place. The concept of heaven supporting the rulers as mediators between heaven and earth was introduced.

The intellectual conceptions of China were established during the Eastern Zhou Dynasty (770–221 BC). Confucianism and Daoism were the main philosophical approaches at this time. Iron casting, coinage and infantry armies were introduced. It was also a period of decline in the Zhou royal house, accompanied by a fragmentation of political power. Rebellion by subordinate kings led to the annexation of smaller states and to the defeat of the Zhou. Finally, with the victory of the state of QIN, the first emperor, Qin Shihuangdi (221–207 BC) unified China. He standardized weights, the writing system, administration and currencies. His large tomb, with its TERRACOTTA ARMY, emphasizes his military power and his concern for the afterlife.

This was also the time when the GREAT WALL was built as a protection against the 'barbarians' in the north and south. The following Han Dynasty (206 BC–AD 220) asserted sovereignty over vast regions of today's China with a policy of continuous expansion. This period also saw the beginning of intensive trade with foreigners along the Silk Road. The hope for immortality found expression in large tombs with precious lacquer or silk grave-goods, found at MANCHENG and MAWANGDUI.

China was fragmented for more than three centuries after the fall of the Han. None of the smaller states in the south or north could gain control over the whole territory. Buddhism filtered into China from India, and was slowly adopted by the Chinese, as shown by cave temples at DUNHUANG/MOGAO. Cultural exchange and assimilation, facilitated by diplomacy and trade, opened China up to the outside world. China proper, finally united by the Tang rulers (618–907), extended from southern Vietnam to Inner Mongolia. The culture of the two major cities of CHANG'AN and Luoyang was enthusiastically cosmopolitan. Foreign merchants not only transported precious goods along the Silk Road but also brought religions, including Islam, Judaism and Nestorian Christianity to China. Buddhism finally became an integral part of Chinese life. This was the time when woodblock printing was used for calendars or sutratexts, and work in gold and silver reached its zenith.

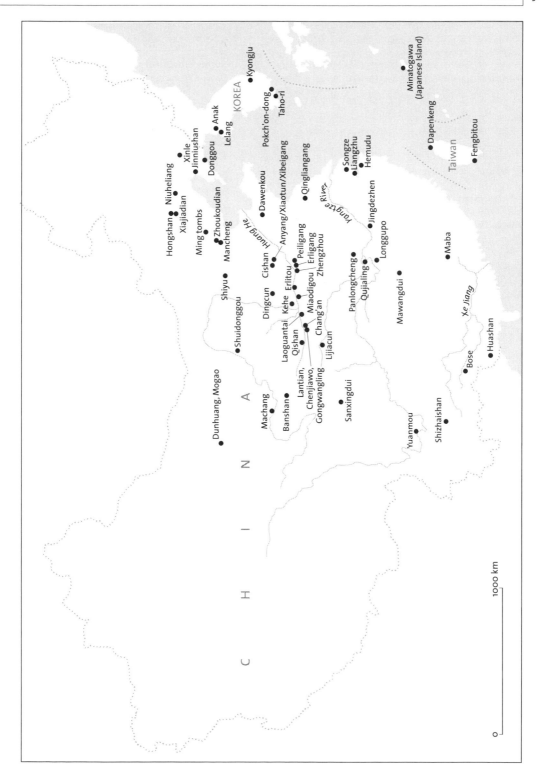

Kyongju

KOREA

Minatogawa
(Japanese Island)

Anak
Lelang
Donggou
Pokch'on-dong
Taho-ri

Dapenkeng

Xinle
Jinniushan
Niuheliang

Taiwan

Fengbitou

Hongshan
Xiajiadian
Ming tombs
Zhoukoudian
Mancheng

Dawenkou
Anyang/Xiaotun/Xibeigang
Qingliangang
Songze
Liangzhu
Hemudu

Jingdezhen

Maba

Shiyu
Dingcun
Cishan
Peiligang
Erligang
Zhengzhou
Erlitou
Miaodigou
Longgupo
Panlongcheng
Qujialing
Mawangdui

Shuidonggou

Laoguantai
Kehe
Qishan
Chang'an
Lijiacun

Xe Jiang

Huashan

Dunhuang, Mogao

Machang
Banshan
Lantian,
Chenjiawo,
Gongwangling
Sanxingdui
Yuanmou
Shizhaishan
Bose

Huang He

Yangtze River

C H I N A

1000 km

0

Decentralization and natural disasters led to the short-lived Five Dynasties (907–960) and the Northern Song Dynasty (960–1172) situated in North China. Finally, under the Southern Song (1172–1279) foreign trade, especially maritime trade, was encouraged by the government. Industries such as silk, lacquer or porcelain achieved their highest level of technical perfection. Rice became a central element in the Chinese diet. A refined examination system played a central role in creating a new elite for the civil service (bureaucracy).

Over the course of four centuries, large parts of China were under the control of tribal Asian people, culminating in 1276 with the siege of Kublai Khan, grandson of Ghengis Khan and founder of the Yuan Dynasty. During this time, China was attached to their Eurasian empire. Marco Polo is said to have visited the Mongolian court. Horses played an important role, as shown by famous silk paintings by various artists. A peasant revolt finally overthrew the alien rulers, and the Ming Dynasty rulers (1368–1644) gained power, strengthening the identification of China proper. Of the material artifacts of the Ming, none is appreciated more than the fine porcelains from JINDEZHENG, especially pieces in blue and white underglaze and polychrome enamels. The emperors built the Forbidden City, a palace only for royalty, and the Temple of Heaven in Beijing. In 1409 the first construction work on the royal graveyard began, and thirteen Ming emperors were buried there within a time span of 230 years (see MING TOMBS). See CHINESE DYNASTIES for chronology of Chinese dynasties.

China Lake an area containing a group of prehistoric open-air sites on the margins of the Mojave Desert in southern California, USA. At one locality, artifacts (two flakes) and mammoth remains were found on the surface of lake deposits, associated with an ancient soil. Although a URANIUM SERIES date of 42,350 bp was obtained on a mammoth tooth, the surface context precludes reliable dating of the artifacts, and the site is not widely accepted as evidence of settlement prior to 12,000 BP in North America.

chinampa an intensive agricultural technique used in the BASIN OF MEXICO, and often referred to as 'floating gardens'. Agricultural production takes advantage of the standing water, ALLUVIUM and mouldering vegetation in swampy or marshy areas.

To start a new chinampa, long rectangular mats of floating plants were grown in open, deeper ponds, and then dragged to a new location and secured with cypress stakes. A number of such mats were stacked on top of each other. The resulting chinampa was about 10 by 110 m (11 by 120 yds), and raised above the water-level. Canals were dug on three or four sides of the chinampa, which were laid out in a grid. The lake mud from constructing the canals was then piled on the vegetation. Seedlings started elsewhere were then transplanted to the chinampa. Special canoe-latrines carried human waste from TENOCHTITLÁN to the chinampas, providing a rich fertilizer.

The farmland created was extremely efficient because it existed where previously no agricultural produce could be grown. The chinampa grew staple root, vegetable, grain and fruit crops. A household would support itself using several chinampas, which were kept in production all year round. In 1519, 10,000 ha (39 sq. miles) of chinampa reportedly supported about 100,000 people.

Chinchorro a site on the coast of northern Chile, at which the earliest-known intentionally mummified humans have been found. Dating to c.7000 bp, the bodies were eviscerated, skinned, covered with clay and frequently painted in red pigments. Clay masks were placed on the faces.

Chindadn point a small teardrop-shaped bifacial type of point found in early prehistoric sites of central Alaska, dating to c.12,000–10,000 bp. First discovered by Cook at HEALY LAKE, they have also been found at WALKER ROAD and are diagnostic of the NENANA COMPLEX.

Chinese dynasties the traditional subdivisions of Chinese history based on dynasties, each comprising a series of emperors, usually blood relatives, who succeeded each other on the throne. A change in dynasty meant a change of family holding power. Chinese dynasties did not necessarily encompass the whole country, but often merely parts of it (e.g. in the THREE KINGDOMS). In chronological order, the dynasties are: XIA [Hsia] (17th century BC), though it is currently a matter of debate whether the Xia structure actually constituted a dynasty; SHANG (16th–11th centuries BC); ZHOU [Chou] (1027–221 BC); QIN [Ch'in] (221–207 BC); HAN (206 BC–AD 220); Three Kingdoms (Wei, Shu Han, Wu)/Six Dynasties (AD 220–280); Western Jin [Chin] (265–316); Eastern Jin [Chin] (317–420); Northern and Southern (420–581); Sui (581–618); Tang [T'ang] (618–907); Five Dynasties (907–960); Song [Sung] (960–1279); Liao (916–1125); Jin [Chin] (1115–1234); Yuan (1271–1368); Ming (1368–1644); Qing [Ch'ing] (1644–1911); Republic of China (1912–1949); People's Republic of China (1949–present). See also NEOLITHIC, BRONZE AGE, IRON AGE.

Chinhan see SAMHAN.

Chiot pottery pottery produced in the ARCHAIC period on the Greek island of Chios, although some have suggested that it was also made at NAUCRATIS. The pots, often chalices, were decorated with a cream SLIP and decorated on the exterior with figured scenes either in outline or in silhouette. In the glazed interior, floral patterns such as PALMETTES were often added in red.

chipping floor or **knapping floor** an archaeological site where stone tools have been knapped, characterized by the presence of rejected tools, discarded hammerstones and waste flakes or débitage.

Chirand a site on the ALLUVIAL plain of the lower Ganges River in Bihar in northeastern India, where excavations during the 1960s and 1970s revealed five periods of occupation. The last two of these are early 1st millennium AD and medieval respectively; the first three are Neolithic (Chirand I), CHALCOLITHIC (Chirand IIA–B) and NORTHERN BLACK POLISHED WARE (NBPW) (Chirand III). Chirand I, dating to the earlier 2nd millennium BC (and perhaps extending into the 3rd), is a village of plastered bamboo, with a blade lithic industry, hand-made red and grey burnished pottery, and a subsistence based on the cultivation of rice and other cereals, fishing and hunting. Chirand II, which is divided into two phases belonging to the later 2nd and earlier 1st millennium BC respectively, is largely a continuation of the Neolithic culture, though a BLACK-AND-RED WARE now occurs; copper artifacts first appear in Chirand IIA levels and iron in Chirand IIB. In Chirand III, beginning around 500 BC, NBPW replaces the black-and-red ware, and mud-brick architecture appears (baked brick by the end of the period); with this development, this part of the Gangetic drainage was culturally united with upstream regions in the second great episode of urbanization and state formation in northern India.

Chiripa a culture pertaining to the EARLY INTERMEDIATE PERIOD on the Bolivian altiplano. The site that gives its name to the culture was first occupied in the EARLY HORIZON; in the Early Intermediate period a large ceremonial component was built, including a series of sixteen structures symmetrically arranged around a rectangular sunken plaza. The Chiripa culture is roughly contemporaneous with the PUCARA culture of the Peruvian altiplano, and precedes the TIAHUANACO culture.

chocolate flint a variety of high-quality flint from the HOLY CROSS MOUNTAINS in central Poland, used by prehistoric peoples from the Mesolithic to the Early Bronze Age. It occurs in round flat nodules and in slabs no more than 10 cm (4 inches) thick. Chocolate flint is very homogeneous and has excellent flaking qualities. It was usually mined from shallow pits about 2.5 m (8 ft) deep. Four chocolate flint mines have been investigated, at Tomaszów, Wierzbica-Zele, Polany and Polany-Kolonie.

Choga Mami a 3 ha (7.4 acre) site near Mandali, to the east of the Tigris in central Iraq, where Joan Oates's excavations have revealed a SAMARRAN (c.5000–4500 BC) settlement with HALAF materials in certain contexts, under transitional levels (later occupations had been eroded away). In addition to exposures of architecture that complement those found at Tell es SAWWAN, Oates's work revealed a Samarran period irrigation canal, the first direct confirmation of water works in this culture. The 'Transitional' pottery shows both Samarran and 'UBAID I characteristics, and is similar to the newly defined 'Ubaid 0 pottery at 'OUELI (and especially the earliest levels at the latter site). The question remains open, however, whether this pottery at Choga Mami represents a chronological or geographical transitional style.

Choga Mish a 15 ha (37 acre) site in the Susiana plain (Khuzistan, southwestern Iran). American excavations during the 1960s and 1970s revealed settlement from the late 6th millennium BC into the 3rd millennium BC, with traces of later ACHAEMENID and PARTHIAN occupation. The town was an important centre in the Susiana plain, its settlement preceding that of SUSA itself, and then became a secondary centre during the 4th millennium.

Choga Zanbil a walled city of nearly 100 ha (247 acres), founded on the Karun River near SUSA in lowland Khuzistan, southwestern Iran, in the 13th century BC by a king of ELAM. R. Ghirshman's extensive excavations exposed a walled ziggurat compound, numerous other temples, and three large buildings, at least one of which was a funerary cult centre. Choga Zanbil provides a particularly clear example of a planned religious centre that is relatively unobscured by later occupation (down to the 6th century BC).

Choisy-au-Bac a lowland settlement site at the confluence of the Rivers Oise and Aisne, in France, occupied without break from Late Bronze Age to the late HALLSTATT. Three principal phases of occupation have been recognized, with rectangular houses, some 5 by 7 m (16 by 23 ft) in size. In the second phase, the settlement was defended by a ditch and rampart. Among the remains of the first and second phases was bronze-working debris, while iron-working furnaces were found in the third phase.

Chojnice-Pienki culture a late Mesolithic cultural group of the Vistula and Oder drainages in Poland, overlapping spatially and chronologically with the JANISŁAWICE culture during the late BOREAL and ATLANTIC CLIMATIC PERIODS (9600–5000 bp). The Chojnice-Pienki culture is viewed as having been derived from the preceding KOMORNICA culture, with the addition of trapeze-shaped projectile points.

chokkomon a design of shattered spirals engraved on a variety of artifacts of KOFUN period Japan. Its symbolism is unknown.

Chokurcha two Middle Palaeolithic cave-sites in the Crimea, Ukraine. At Chokurcha I, three occupation levels were identified in shallow loam and rubble deposits; associated faunal remains are predominantly of woolly mammoth, steppe bison and wild ass. The artifacts were lost during the Second World War, but apparently included both sidescrapers and bifacial foliates. At Chokurcha II, a single occupation horizon was found. The faunal remains are dominated by wild ass; the tools

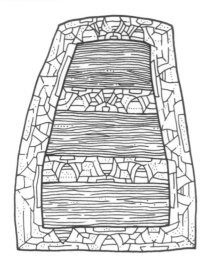

CHOKKOMON.

include many sidescrapers. Some specimens of figurative MOBILIARY ART, otherwise unknown in the Middle Palaeolithic, were reported. Chokurcha I was excavated by Ernst in 1928–40. Chokurcha II was discovered and investigated by Bader in 1974; recent excavation has been conducted by Stolbunov.

Cholula an urban MESOAMERICAN centre in Puebla, Mexico, founded in the middle PRECLASSIC and occupied without interruption up to the present, making it the oldest continuously occupied city in the Americas. Archaeological research has focused on the huge TEMPLE MOUND, known as Tlachihualtepetl ('man-made mountain'), which underwent four stages of sequential expansion, until it covered 16 ha (40 acres) and reached a height of 60 m (197 ft). It is the largest single Precolumbian structure in the New World.

After the fall of TEOTIHUACÁN, Cholula exerted authority over much of central Mexico, and interacted with EL TAJÍN on the Gulf Coast and the MAYA region. Its greatest period of expansion and influence was during the POSTCLASSIC period, when it was the centre of the cult of QUETZALCÓATL. Cholula POLYCHROME POTTERY is among the most beautiful in Mesoamerica, and was decorated in the MIXTECA-PUEBLA style with widely recognized religious iconography.

Chondwe an Early Iron Age group of the CHIFUMBAZE complex in central Zambia, dating to the middle of the 1st millennium AD.

Chontal see CHICHÉN ITZÁ, COZUMEL.

chopper/chopping tool a simple Lower Palaeolithic core tool with a sharp cutting edge formed either by the removal of flakes from one side of the implement (chopper) or by bifacial flake-removal to create a transverse edge

(chopping tool). Chopper and flake industries have been found in Africa (OLDOWAN), Europe (see e.g. CLACTONIAN) and the Near East, but are particularly associated with East and South Asia, where the earliest sites such as ZHOUKOUDIAN are regarded as forming an Asian Chopper/Chopping Tool tradition, considered by MOVIUS to be more primitive than the Handaxe tradition of Europe. They appear in assemblages labelled PACITANIAN and NGANDONG in Java, CABENGE in Sulawesi and CABALWANIAN in the Philippines. Recent work has thrown doubt on earlier assumptions, and it appears that some of the Southeast Asian assemblages of this type may be late Pleistocene or Holocene in date.

Choris see NORTON.

Chosen the Japanese name for pre-modern Korea; see also CHOSON.

Choson an early POLITY on the northwestern Korean peninsula mentioned in the HAN Dynasty chronicles of China. Extant from at least 197–108 BC, it was conquered by the Han and incorporated into the LELANG COMMANDERY.

Chou see ZHOU.

Choukoutien see ZHOUKOUDIAN.

chous 1 a Greek measure equal to 12 KOTYLAI. This varied from city to city, but at ATHENS it was the equivalent of 3.2 litres (5.6 pints).

2 a type of OINOCHOE made at Athens which may have served as a measure. The mouth normally had three

CHOPPER (Oldowan).

points to the spout ('trefoil'). A miniature version is often decorated with scenes of children playing.

Christy, Henry (1810–65) an English businessman and banker who was also an ethnologist (especially in Mexico) and was the partner of LARTET in his pioneering excavations in the Palaeolithic sites of southern France in the 1860s.

chromatography a qualitative method of chemical analysis used to separate and identify substances in a complex mixture; in archaeology it is used to identify and distinguish AMBER from different sources. Substances are separated by passing the solution through a selectively absorbing medium where they migrate at different rates. The result is a STRATIFICATION of constituent layers on the absorbing medium, or a chromatogram, with identification based on the location and colour of the resulting layers.

chronology the order or sequence of events with respect to time and determination of ages. Chronologies can be based on RELATIVE DATING, where events or materials are related to one another but not to absolute ages. Relative chronologies can be established based on STRATIGRAPHY and CORRELATION, ARTIFACT TYPOLOGIES or CROSSDATING; or chronologies can be based on ABSOLUTE DATING, where events or materials are assigned ages in years.

chronometric dating dating methods that report results as absolute ages. In chronometric studies, it is typical to report results with a measure of uncertainty, usually a standard deviation. DENDROCHRONOLOGY has the possibility of providing the most precise age estimates, although it is applicable only locally. Other chronometric dating techniques include RADIOCARBON DATING, POTASSIUM-ARGON DATING, URANIUM SERIES DATING, THERMOLUMINESCENCE DATING and, in some cases, AMINO-ACID RACEMIZATION.

chryselephantine *adj.* (of luxury Greek statues) combining ivory and gold. Two of the most famous in CLASSICAL antiquity were the cult-statues of Athena and Zeus in the PARTHENON and at OLYMPIA respectively, dating to the 5th century BC. Examples of chryselephantine statues have been found from ARCHAIC deposits at DELPHI. The workshop for the statue at Olympia, created by the sculptor Pheidias, has been discovered.

Chubu a modern district in central Honshu Island, Japan, often used in archaeological writings, comprising Niigata, Toyama, Ishikawa, Fukui, Gifu, Nagano, Yamanashi, Aichi and Shizuoka Prefectures. See also JOMON, IDOJIRI.

chullpa a tower, generally cylindrical in shape, which seems to have had a primarily funerary function, serving as a centre for ancestor cults. Built of adobe or stone, chullpas are found in the altiplano of southern Peru, close to Lake Titicaca, and date to the LATE INTERMEDIATE PERIOD and the INCA period.

Chulmun a type of Neolithic textured-surface pottery (the term Chulmun means 'comb-patterned') giving its name to the POSTGLACIAL horticultural/hunter-gatherer culture of the Korean peninsula. The Chulmun period, spanning the 7th–2nd millennia BC, probably saw the beginnings of millet cultivation at its end (see KOREA). Chulmun pottery was succeeded by MUMUN pottery and the introduction of rice *c.*1500 BC. Regional styles of Chulmun pottery include Classic Chulmun, typified by the AMSADONG site, which has incised herringbone patterns on conical pots, the decoration receding from base to rim through time. Other important Chulmun culture sites are TONGSAMDONG and OSAN-RI. (Compare JOMON, DAPENGENG, SHENGWEN, XINLE.) The PALAEOASIATIC peoples of the Chulmun period were probably succeeded by TUNGUS-speakers.

chultun an underground storage chamber. The term is most commonly used in the context of lowland MAYA settlements. Today, bell-shaped chultuns are dug and plastered and serve as water reservoirs during the dry season in the northern part of the Yucatán. A chultun at the prehistoric site of KABÁH has been renovated as a water reservoir, and chultuns are thought to have served this purpose during prehistoric times as well. They also provide excellent storage facilities for ramon nuts, a highly nutritious food still relied on by the modern Maya. The ability to store ramon nuts for extended periods of time would imply less dependence on maize production, since they are plentiful and are cultivated in trees located around the residence. A lower dependence on maize production in turn suggests a higher CARRYING CAPACITY, thus suggesting higher population estimates for the area than previously thought. Finally, cultivation and harvesting of ramon nuts could be carried out by women and children, thus freeing the men in households to build and maintain CEREMONIAL CENTRES.

Chwalim An Upper Palaeolithic and Mesolithic site along the Oder River in western Poland. In the latest occupation phase, dated to the SUBBOREAL climatic period during the 3rd millennium BC, pottery with a technical resemblance to GLOBULAR AMPHORA ware appears alongside Mesolithic flint tools and a faunal sample of wild species, suggesting that a small group of foragers persisted for many centuries alongside agricultural communities in nearby regions.

Ciboneyes a group of prehistoric hunter-gatherers on the island of Cuba, who used woodworking tools made from large shells and artifacts of polished volcanic rocks. They seem to have arrived *c.*3190 bc, and were still present when Columbus arrived.

Ciempozuelos a group of Beaker burials discovered in

1894, notable for their fine pottery and characteristic of the second Beaker phase on the central Meseta, in Spain. The graves were simple pit burials with twelve pottery vessels, a copper dagger and a copper awl. The pottery was heavily incrusted with white paste, and highly decorated bowls were prominent alongside the typical Bell Beakers.

Cimmerians a horse-riding group, with a probable origin in the steppes north of the Black Sea, who moved across the Caucasus Mountains and severely disrupted first the URARTIAN state and then the northwestern and western marches of the NEO-ASSYRIAN empire in the 8th century BC. The Cimmerians seem to have occupied the region of northern Anatolia near the Black Sea and exerted considerable pressure on Anatolian states, destroying PHRYGIA shortly after 700 BC and warring with the Lydians (see SARDIS), until the Assyrian king Aššurbanipal (668–627 BC) defeated them in Cilicia, southwestern Anatolia.

cinerarium a container for cremated remains, often placed in the niches of a COLUMBARIUM. At ROME they are frequently in the shape of a small box made of marble. A small panel may be inscribed with the name of the deceased. Cineraria may be decorated with simple patterns often consisting of garlands.

circus a long enclosure for chariot-racing in the Roman world. A central barrier divided the space into two tracks. Seating for the spectators was on banks, sometimes tiered, on the outside. The earliest example at ROME was the Circus Maximus, which measures some 600 m (656 yds) long, and 150 m (164 yds) wide. In the Greek world the circus is normally called a *hippodrome* (see BYZANTIUM). See also STADIUM.

cire perdue see LOST WAX.

Cishan [Tz'u-shan] a site in Hebei Province, China, belonging to the earliest Neolithic millet agricultural regime of the north. Pit-houses, storage pits and burials have been excavated. Artifacts include QUERNS with knobbed legs; serrated ground-stone sickles; tripod vessels, hailed as one of the earliest 'Chinese' cultural elements to appear (see DING); and bone and stone fishing and hunting implements. A case has been made here for the world's first domestication of the chicken, from the Common Jungle Fowl. Pig, dog and millet were also domesticated, in contrast to the southern agricultural regime known from HEMUDU. Cishan is dated to the early 6th millennium BC. See also PEILIGANG.

cist grave a grave, the sides of which are typically formed of stone slabs set on edge, but may be constructed of rubble or brick, and which is covered by stone slabs. From the Greek *kiste*, a box.

Clactonian a British Lower Palaeolithic flake tool industry named after the site of Clacton-on-Sea, Essex, and characterized by the presence of thick flakes, choppers and flake cores, the use of the hard hammer flaking technique and the absence of bifaces. A yew spear point, 36.7 cm (14.45 inches) long, recovered from Clacton represents the only surviving wooden artifact from Lower Palaeolithic Britain. The Clactonian is dated to the HOXNIAN INTERGLACIAL (c.3–200,000 BP), as is the early ACHEULIAN in Britain. Originally it was believed that these were two chronologically separate industries with the less developed Clactonian being succeeded by the more advanced biface-manufacturing Acheulian. It is now apparent that the two are contemporary, and that the presence or absence of bifaces in an assemblage can no longer be attributed to simple cultural tradition.

Clairvaux-les-lacs a series of Neolithic village sites which occupied the shores of Lake Clairvaux, Jura, France, from 3700 to 2400 BC. The earliest of these, La Motte-aux-Magnins, consisted of twelve buildings on a small island near the northern edge of the lake. Access would only have been possible by skin boat or dug-out canoe. Among the wealth of organic remains recovered were fishing floats of tree bark and pottery with remains of carbonized food. Some of the pottery, which belonged to the Burgundian middle Neolithic group, had been decorated with bands of tree bark cut into lozenge shapes.

Clark, Sir John Grahame Douglas (1907–95) a British prehistorian, for many years Disney Professor of Archaeology at Cambridge University. He pioneered the environmental approach to archaeology, in which the natural environment was seen as a major determinant to human behaviour. His work at the Mesolithic site of STAR CARR still stands as a model for archaeological site excavation and reporting.

Clarke, David Leonard (1937–76) a British archaeologist, noted for his outstanding contributions to theoretical archaeology. His work has much in common with NEW ARCHAEOLOGY, although his ideas developed essentially independently from that school of thought. In *Analytical Archaeology* in 1968, Clarke argued that archaeology must become a science by developing an explicitly archaeological theory based on GENERAL SYSTEMS THEORY.

classical *adj.***1** relating to the Greek and Roman civilizations, hence classical sculpture, art, period, etc.

2 relating to a period of Greek art dating to the 5th and 4th centuries BC. It traditionally starts after the Persian invasion of Greece in 480 BC (see ARCHAIC). The 4th-century phase is sometimes known as the Late Classical period.

Classic period a phase from AD 250 to 650–900 that represents the general period of large populations and elaborate social organization throughout MESOAMERICAN culture. The end of the period varies from region to region. The concept of the Classic period in Mesoamerica refers generally to the peak of artistic and religious endeavours in Precolumbian society. This term is partly an historical expression of archaeological reconstructions; recent research at many Mesoamerican sites negates some of the traditional assumptions associated with the term.

clast an individual grain that is a constituent of a sediment body. Archaeological debris, once culturally deposited, consists of clasts in an otherwise natural sediment body and is subject to the same processes and factors as the rest of the deposit.

clay 1 a size term for sediment or soil particles that are less than 0.004 or 0.002 mm in diameter depending upon the classification system used. As a particle size term, the definition of clay-size particles is independent of mineral composition or other properties other than size. Compare SAND.

2 an abbreviated term for clay minerals, the finely crystalline water-bearing alumino-silicate minerals belonging to the phyllosilicate mineral group. Clay-size particles consisting all or in part of clay minerals are a chief constituent in ceramics.

3 a texture term used in describing sediment and soils, defined, depending on the classification system used, as containing a certain percentage of clay-size particles relative to sand- and silt-size particle content.

4 a descriptive term for a sediment body (deposit) composed primarily of clay-size particles that is typically soft and plastic when moist. Material collected from this type of deposit is used in making pottery, tiles, bricks and cement.

Clazomenae see EAST GREEK POTTERY.

cleaver a bifacial stone artifact typically found in ACHEULIAN assemblages dating to the Lower and Middle Pleistocene. It is similar to a handaxe but has a broad axe-like cutting edge instead of a pointed end.

Cleland Hills a PETROGLYPH site in central Australia. Most of the heavily weathered pecked engravings are tracks or circles characteristic of PANARAMITEE ART. Sixteen small engravings seem to portray human faces and these are paralleled only in the Pilbara region of Western Australia, notably on the BURRUP PENINSULA.

Cleopatra's Needle see ALEXANDRIA.

Cliff Palace a major site in MESA VERDE, Colorado, USA, this ANASAZI PUEBLO is located in a large cliff overhang. The site is a multi-storey pueblo, with over 200 rooms and twenty-three KIVAS. The site was abandoned with the rest of Mesa Verde at the end of the 13th century AD and was discovered by WETHERILL in 1888.

clinker-built *adj.* (of a ship) built by a North European shipbuilding technique in which the hull is formed first

CLOVIS points.

of overlapping planks caulked together and the internal frame only added later. The Halsnoy boat c.350 BC is the earliest known clinker-built vessel; later examples include the SUTTON HOO ship of c.6th century AD and the famous Viking ships of Oseberg and Gokstad of the 8th–9th centuries AD. Clinker-construction remained in use in some parts of northern Europe into the 20th century.

cloisonné *adj.* relating to a technique used in the manufacture of jewellery whereby strips of metal are attached to an item so as to form cells, or *cloisons*, which are then enamelled or inlaid.

Clovis 1 the earliest fluted point type of the PALAEO-INDIAN period. The point is characterized by its symmetry, careful flaking and the removal of a small flute from its face. Until recently the date range for Clovis was approximately 11,500–11,000 BP. However, new calibrations of existing dates indicate that the tradition may have begun as early as 13,500 BP. The classic Clovis sites lie west of the Mississippi, USA, but increasing numbers of Clovis sites are being found in the eastern portion of the continent. Although this point type was first found at the DENT site in Colorado, it was not formally recognized as a new type until excavations were conducted at BLACKWATER DRAW locality 1.

2 a complex which forms part of the LLANO TRADITION, found mainly in the southern and central Plains of North America, although increasing numbers of Clovis-type points are now being recovered in the eastern half of the continent, forcing a reassessment of the complex and what it represents in terms of prehistoric social organization. The complex also comprises mammoth bones, and associated artifacts such as distinctive stone knives, smooth ivory and bone cylinders, bone points and bone foreshafts. The complex shows similarities in particular stone tool types, ivory artifacts and the use of red ochre to Upper Palaeolithic complexes in Asia and eastern Europe.

Cmielów a settlement of the FUNNEL BEAKER CULTURE located on the eastern slopes of the HOLY CROSS MOUNTAINS in central Poland. Cmielów appears to have served as a 'production settlement' at which 'banded' flint, extracted from nearby mines such as the ones at KRZEMIONKI, was reduced into cores and semi-finished axes. Excavations at Cmielów also produced evidence for copper metallurgy and a large sample of faunal and botanical remains.

Côa Valley a valley in northeastern Portugal, a tributary of the Douro, where rock art – hundreds of pecked and engraved figures of animals (primarily horses, aurochs, deer, ibex, fish) – was discovered in the mid 1990s, a discovery which led to an international, ultimately successful campaign to save them from being drowned by a major dam. The area is now a World Heritage site. Some figures are attributed to the Iron Age and historic periods, but the vast majority are clearly Palaeolithic in style, making this the foremost example of open-air PALAEO-LITHIC ART. A number of open-air Palaeolithic occupation sites have since been excavated in the vicinity, dated by THERMOLUMINESCENCE to the GRAVETTIAN and the MAGDALENIAN.

Coalescent tradition see PLAINS VILLAGE INDIAN.

cobble a size subdivision of gravel that ranges between 64 and 256 mm (2.5 and 10 inches) in diameter, according to the Wentworth-Udden classification system. Cobble gravel was commonly employed as building stone.

Cochise culture see PICOSA.

codex (*pl.* codices) a hand-drawn manuscript recording historic, tribute or religious information. In MESO-AMERICA the manuscripts were of bark or animal skin, lightly covered with plaster. HIEROGLYPHIC writing and pictures were then painted on the manuscript.

Cody see PLANO, BLACKWATER DRAW.

Coedès, George (1886–1969) a French epigrapher who was a leading authority in Southeast Asian studies, best known for discovering the Indonesian empire of ŚRIVI-JAYA in 1918, and for his books *The Indianized States of Southeast Asia* (1944) and *Les Inscriptions du Cambodge* (8 vols., 1942–66).

Cognitive Archaeology see STRUCTURAL ARCHAE-OLOGY.

coinage a standardized series of metal tokens, their specific weights representing particular values, and usually stamped with designs and inscriptions. They were used in many parts of the ancient world for everyday exchange.

Greek coinage first appears in the ARCHAIC foundation deposit of the Artemision at EPHESUS. Much early coinage was struck in silver, though the weight of the different coins changed from city to city (see OBOL, DRACHMA). Many of them bear the device of the city; for example, the owl of ATHENS, or the turtle of AEGINA. See also MINA, STATER, TALENT.

Roman coinage was struck at ROME and at various points throughout the empire. Different materials were used: gold (AUREUS), silver (DENARIUS) and bronze (AS, SESTERTIUS). Although Rome was the main mint, even quite minor cities could strike coins; these often show the head of the emperor and a relevant motif, such as a deity, for the city. See also RADIATE.

Colchester (*Lat.* Camulodunum) a Roman colony in England, established on the site of the Iron Age capital and mint. In AD 49 the emperor Claudius founded Colonia Claudia Victricensis, and tombstones of veterans have been found. One of the most impressive buildings was the temple (now forming the foundations of Colchester castle) which an inscription shows was dedicated to Claudius. The colony was extensively damaged during Boudicca's revolt in AD 60, but was rebuilt. The city was walled towards the end of the 2nd century, and remains may be seen of the main west gate (Balkerne Gate). To the west of the city over thirty kilns have been found, whose wares were widely distributed (see SAMIAN WARE). See also WHEELER.

collagen a protein which, together with fats, makes up the organic component of BONE. After death, while the fats rapidly disappear, the collagen lingers in the bone in diminishing amounts. The collagen content of bone can be measured by virtue of its constituent nitrogen, and so offers a useful analytical tool. Collagen is also found in other body parts including skin and teeth.

Collared urn the most important and widespread type of cinerary urn of the British Bronze Age. Developed probably from Neolithic vessels of the PETERBOROUGH WARE tradition, the first Collared urns appear around 2000 BC. They remained in use for some 600 years, commonly holding cremated remains beneath a burial mound. The Collared urn is characterized by a heavy overhanging rim or collar, usually bevelled internally; incised decoration is found on both collar and bevel. In addition to the Collared urn, several other varieties of Bronze Age cinerary urn are known, including the Cordoned urn, the Trevisker urn, the Bucket-shaped urn and the Wessex biconical urn.

collective tomb a tomb which is used for multiple, usually successive, interments.

Colless Creek a rockshelter with a rich artifact assemblage in northwestern Queensland, Australia. Occupation

CO LOA, Vietnam: the tympanum of the great bronze drum.

substantially pre-dates 17,350 bp and the site may have been used for at least 30,000 years.

colluvium an unlithified deposit resulting from mass wasting processes where gravity plays a significant role. Colluvium includes the relatively thin veneer of material in transport down HILLSLOPES, material behind barriers to downslope movement and potentially thick deposits found at the base of hillslopes and cliffs as fans and wedges. Major processes leading to accumulation of colluvial deposits are soil erosion, SOLIFLUXION, various debris flows and debris and rockslides and falls. Archaeological deposits may be buried in colluvium along valley margins, or mixed and displaced by colluvial processes. Human activities that lead to erosion are also likely to enhance some colluvial processes by destabilizing the landscape.

Co Loa a large settlement site on the Red River in northern Vietnam, belonging to the DONG SON period and thought to have been the capital of the early Vietnamese state of AU LAC. The site has two sets of moats and three sets of ramparts, the outermost enclosing an area of some 600 ha (2.3 sq. miles). The main find from the site is the 72 kg (40 lb) bronze drum containing over 100 bronze ploughshares.

Cologne (*Lat.* Colonia Claudia Ara Augusta Agrippinensium) a Roman colony in Germany founded in AD 50 in honour of Agrippina, wife of the emperor Claudius. It became the base for the Rhine fleet as well as an important commercial centre. Its cemeteries have yielded large quantities of glass, which was produced locally. Fine mosaics have been found including one of the god Dionysos and another of Greek philosophers.

Colosseum an especially ornate form of AMPHITHEATRE at ROME. The outside is decorated in the three main architectural orders: DORIC, IONIC and CORINTHIAN. Construction seems to have started under the emperor Vespasian (AD 69–79) and it was finally dedi-

cated under Titus in AD 80. It may have held around 50,000 spectators.

Colossi of Memnon a pair of massive seated statues of AMENHOTEP III, one of the few remnants still standing of that king's MORTUARY TEMPLE at THEBES (EGYPT)-WEST BANK.

columbarium **1** a dovecot in the Roman world.
 2 an underground burial chamber in the Roman world. Its walls were covered in small niches, hence the name, into which were placed CINERARIA. Inscriptions at ROME suggest that they were normally the place of burial for slaves and freedmen.

Columnata a major, if enigmatic, site in the Atlas Mountains of northern Algeria with good preservation including several human burials of Mechtoid type dated to 8300–7300 BP (see MECHTA AFALOU). The site also contains rare examples of hafted microliths.

Combe Capelle a rockshelter in Dordogne, France, which has yielded CHÂTELPERRONIAN, AURIGNACIAN, GRAVETTIAN and SOLUTREAN industries and, in 1909, an early burial of a short, robust male HOMO *sapiens sapiens* whose stratigraphic position remains uncertain.

Combe-Grenal a well-stratified southwestern French cave and rockshelter, excavated by BORDES in 1953–65 and best known for its fifty-five distinct MOUSTERIAN levels which have been dated to the early WÜRM GLACIATION. The site has played an important part in the interpretation of the Mousterian variants of southwestern France. Its nine ACHEULIAN levels are dominated by reindeer, while some Mousterian layers display a more temperate forest fauna.

comitium a building often sited near the FORUM in a Roman town and used for voting and for other political assemblies.

commandery a military establishment in HAN Dynasty China for governing 'barbarian' or newly conquered areas. It contrasts with 'principality', the established regional administrative unit governed through a local elite. See also LELANG.

compartmented seal the typical seal form of the Bronze Age in western Central Asia and northern Afghanistan (with a focus in the BACTRIAN BRONZE AGE), and usually made of metal. They are often round, but may also be square, cruciform, star-shaped or scalloped. The seals' motifs are comparably geometric (most often cruciform or radiating 'petals' or lines) but may be naturalistic (eagles, scorpions, goats, mythical animals, etc.). Many of the seals are open work, composed simply of the frame and the motif cast in metal, with the remaining space within the frame left hollow.

complex a collection of traits and artifacts that make up a separate class or taxon. The complex may or may not be equivalent to an ancient people. Very often the term is used to designate classes whose origins are unclear.

compluvium the central opening in the roof over the middle of the ATRIUM in a Roman house. The IMPLUVIUM was placed underneath it.

component a STRATIGRAPHIC layer within a site that belongs to a single culture, and is interpreted as the remains of a single people deposited in a relatively short time period. Similar components in a region are grouped into the same culture or PHASE.

composite soil a SOIL PROFILE that imposes its characteristics upon more than one parent material. Each parent material may have been affected by earlier PEDOGENESIS and have preserved features of older soil profiles. Recognition of composite soils, although not always straightforward, is important because of STRATIGRAPHIC, temporal and archaeological contextual implications. Synonymous with composite soil are 'welded soil', 'superimposed soil', and 'polypedomorphic soil'.

computed axial tomography see RADIOGRAPHY.

Conchopata a MIDDLE HORIZON site in the Ayacucho region of Peru, at which two major offering-deposits of HUARI ceramics have been found. The offerings comprise large quantities of smashed pottery, buried in unstructured pits. The first, excavated by Julio C. TELLO, is characterized by large open urns on which are painted an elaborate iconography similar to that of the Gateway of the Sun at TIAHUANACO. These depictions of the Staff Deity suggested to early researchers that Huari iconography was derived from the site of Tiahuanaco. The second offering-deposit includes a series of elaborately painted face-neck jars, which may represent Huari rulers.

concretion the rounded to irregular segregation of mineral matter in a soil that exhibits concentric internal fabric formed by periodic deposition of minerals from solution, usually around a central nucleus that may consist of archaeological debris. Because concretions form under certain conditions, mineralogical, ISOTOPIC and RADIOMETRIC characteristics of concretions are aids to environmental reconstruction and to determining the age of those conditions. Compare NODULE.

cone mosaic a typical decoration of building façades in the 'public' architecture of the URUK period of southern MESOPOTAMIA and surrounding regions. It was made of cones with painted ends which were pressed flat into plaster and brickwork to form mosaics of coloured geometric patterns. The best examples of this technique are found in several buildings within the EANNA precinct at WARKA.

conjoining or **refitting** the rejoining or fitting together of struck stone flakes to recreate the original core, or the refitting of waste flakes to finished or unfinished tools. The technique is used to study the dispersal of implements and débitage at ancient working sites, and to gain an understanding of the knapping process.

Con Moong a cave in Cuc Phuong National Park, 100 km (62 miles) southwest of Ha Noi, Vietnam, excavated in 1976. The 3.5 m (11 ft) deep deposits show a three-phase sequence from the late Pleistocene SON VI pebble industry, through the HOABINHIAN, to the BACSONIAN of the mid Recent period (c.5th–3rd millennia BC).

consistency a soil property defined by the forces of cohesion and adhesion, or by resistance to deformation or rupture. It is one of the properties routinely noted in describing and interpreting soils. Consistency can vary greatly with both soil-water and clay content.

Constantinopolis see BYZANTIUM.

contact the interface of surfaces between two vertically or laterally successive STRATIGRAPHIC units. Description and interpretation of contacts is significant in working out the geological history of an area, and in making inter- and intraregional correlations. Contacts may be conformable, where depositional conditions were not significantly altered or interrupted between adjacent units. An UNCONFORMITY occurs where a surface of non-deposition or erosion separates adjacent units. Both types are likely to be expressed in the field and can be described as abrupt, gradational or intercalated. Numerous sedimentary, palaeontological and structural criteria are used to distinguish the two contact types. Compare BOUNDARY.

contamination extraneous material that is not a part of the natural assemblage. Depending on the nature of the archaeological sample, contamination can be caused by post-depositional additions, intrusions or alterations. In dating methods, contamination is the inclusion of any extraneous substance that can cause an erroneous age determination.

context the situation or circumstances in which a particular item or group of items is found, or in which a particular event or group or series of events occurs. For example, the context of archaeological debris can refer to the physical or cultural associations of the debris, and their interrelationships; it can also refer to, and be defined by, what physically and culturally preceded and followed the use, manufacture, discard and transformations of the debris.

Coobool Creek part of the MURRAY BLACK COLLECTION of Australian Aboriginal skeletal remains, comprising over 100 individuals collected from the Wakool River, southern New South Wales. The collection resembles the KOW SWAMP material, and Brown's analysis suggests that artificial cranial deformation is a component of variation in Pleistocene Aboriginal crania.

Cook, James (1728–79) an English navigator who conducted three voyages of exploration in the Pacific between 1769 and 1779. The accounts of the peoples of Australia, POLYNESIA and MELANESIA in his journals are key sources of information about those societies at the time of European contact.

Cooper's a site between KROMDRAAI and STERK-FONTEIN in Gauteng Province, South Africa, with australopithecine and animal remains of the order of 2 million years old.

copal a MAYA term for an incense made of pine resin. The incense was used extensively during ceremonies throughout MESOAMERICA, and continues to be used today in religious contexts.

Copán a site in Honduras, thought to be one of the intellectual and artistic centres of MAYA culture. It was the largest Lowland Maya city during the late CLASSIC, and is well known for its sculpture and the dynastic sequence recorded in HIEROGLYPHIC writings at the site, featuring the ruler '18 Rabbit' and his son. The first archaeological expedition to Copán was made by Colonel Juan Galindo for the Guatemalan government in 1834. Many other archaeologists and institutions have subsequently carried out work at the site.

Coppa Nevigata a small mounded prehistoric settlement near a former lagoon at the northern edge of the Tavoliere plain, Puglie, Italy. At the base of the mound was an early Neolithic layer rich in cockle-shells associated with CARDIAL WARE pottery but no domestic animal remains or QUERNSTONES. The flint industry in this earliest layer, known as the Sipontian, is found only at this site and is probably a specialized tool-kit for the opening of cockle-shells. An early radiocarbon date suggesting an occupation before 6000 BC should be regarded with caution, but the site may well date from the 6th millennium BC.

copper a ductile, malleable metallic element, used in the manufacture of functional and decorative artifacts, that occurs as nodules of native copper or as a constituent in copper ores such as malachite. Copper was obtained from ores by smelting; it could be cold worked or cast, and was used to make bronze alloys.

Copper Age see ENEOLITHIC.

copper hoard a hoard of copper artifacts, many of which occur in the Ganges-Yamuna *doab* (alluvial plain) and in the area south of the lower Ganges, the former occasionally associated with OCHRE COLOURED POTTERY. The hoards, dated broadly to the 2nd millennium BC, include flat axes, anthropomorphous axes, barbed harpoons and sword blades. They have in the past been cited as evidence of the Vedic arrival (see SANSKRIT) but this correlation seems spurious. Other copper hoards, with different artifact typologies, also occur elsewhere in India and Pakistan.

coprolite preserved or fossilized faeces (excrement) of humans or animals. Preserved in arid or waterlogged environments, coprolites provide dietary and PALAEO-ENVIRONMENTAL information. Remains in human faeces are an indication of what was consumed by the individual. Remains in animal faeces not only indicate diet, but reflect to some degree what the surrounding regional environment was like. See also COPROLOGY.

coprology the study of preserved or fossilized faeces (excrement) of humans or animals. See also COPROLITE.

coral red a rare technique used on Attic pottery in late 6th- and early 5th-century Greece. On cups it was often used to give the bowls a bright red colour which would contrast with the shiny BLACK-GLOSSED lip.

corbelled vault a simple system of roofing whereby successive courses of masonry are laid, each overlapping the previous one, until they meet in the centre and the vault can be closed by a capstone, in some cases a megalithic slab. The technique was often used in the Neolithic CHAMBERED TOMBS of western Europe, especially those of dry-stone construction, and in MYCENAEAN THOLOS tombs **(see fig., p. 445)** and Sardinian NURAGHI.

corbel-vaulted *adj.* characterized by a CORBELLED VAULT.

cordate *adj.* a morphological term used to describe a refined heart-shaped (cordiform) biface with a flat profile, characteristic of the MOUSTERIAN of western Europe.

Corded Ware culture a late Neolithic culture of eastern and Central Europe, widely distributed in various related variants from European Russia to Holland during the 3rd millennium BC. The Corded Ware culture takes its name from the characteristic cord-marked decoration on its pottery, although it should be noted that cord marking occurs in other Central European Neolithic cultures such as FUNNEL BEAKER and GLOBULAR AMPHORA as well. Corded Ware burials, which constitute the primary source of information about this culture, are typically single graves under low tumuli. The Corded Ware culture was once argued, by archaeologists such as CHILDE and GIMBUTAS, to represent a wave or series of waves of migrants from the steppe region of southern Russia into Europe, possibly pastoralist INDO-EUROPEAN speakers. On the other hand, the Czech archaeologist Neustupny has argued that the economy of the Corded Ware culture was based on agriculture, suggesting that these were sedentary communities. In southern Scandinavia, the Corded Ware culture is known as the SINGLE GRAVE or BATTLE AXE culture, while local variants such as RZUCZEWO and

ZŁOTA reflect specific social and economic developments within the broader Corded Ware complex.

Cordilleran See LAURENTIDE.

core 1 *n*. intact solid cylinders of soil or sediment collected with a coring device and used to obtain undisturbed samples. Cores are used to evaluate the geological context of archaeological material and surrounding environments; to evaluate vertical and horizontal limits of cultural debris, MIDDEN and structures; to sample lake or bog sediments for pollen and macrobotanical remains for palaeoenvironmental reconstruction; and for STRATIGRAPHIC and correlation purposes (see DEEP-SEA CORES). Unlike an auger, the core is undisturbed; sediment contacts, soil boundaries and structures are intact and can be described accurately.

2 *n*. a sampling tool consisting of a hollow cylindrical barrel used to collect a core sample. Continuous cores can be obtained by returning repeatedly to the same hole and withdrawing increments the length of the core barrel. Coring devices range from hand-operated to truck-mounted rigs.

3 *n*. (also called **blank** or **nucleus**) the original piece of stone which is worked during knapping. The core either may be itself shaped by the removal of waste flakes to create a core tool such as a biface or chopper, or may simply be the raw material for the manufacture of flakes which are then further retouched to make flake tools. A prepared-core knapping technique involves the planned working of the core before removing a flake or blade. See DISCOIDAL NUCLEUS TECHNIQUE, LEVALLOIS TECHNIQUE.

4 *vb* to collect a core.

core-formed glass a form of glass created by twisting melted glass round a core. Different colours may be used to give a striped effect. It is a technique used in the eastern Mediterranean especially in the CLASSICAL and HELLENISTIC periods.

Coricancha the 'enclosure of gold' in CUZCO, Peru, this was the most sacred religious site of the INCA empire. The enclosure included temples dedicated to the worship of the sun, stars, rainbow, thunder and (possibly) the moon. Ritual offerings of maize beer were made into subterranean aqueducts under the enclosure. According to early Spanish reports, the walls were covered with sheets of gold; life-size models of llamas and maize plants of gold and silver were found here. The Coricancha was plundered at the time of the Spanish conquest and the gold artifacts melted down.

Corinth (*Gk* Korinthos, *Lat*. Colonia Laus Julia Corinthiensis) a city located where the Peloponnese meets the isthmus which links it to the Greek mainland. The site was important as it also controlled the short overland crossing from the Saronic Gulf to the Corinthian Gulf through the ports of Kenchreai and Lechaion respectively. The city was a major centre in the ARCHAIC period and CORINTHIAN POTTERY was widely exported. In 146 BC the city was destroyed by the Roman general Mummius, and the site seems to have been virtually vacated until the foundation of a Roman colony in 44 BC. Remains of this Roman city, the FORUM, surrounding administrative buildings, theatre and THERMAE, have been uncovered by recent excavations by the American School. See also PERACHORA.

Corinthian order a scheme of architecture closely related to the IONIC ORDER. It differs in the type of CAPITAL, which is formed by a mass of acanthus leaves out of which spring small VOLUTES. All four sides were similar, unlike Ionic capitals. The earliest-known Corinthian capital was used in the interior of the temple of Apollo at Bassae, along with the Ionic order; on the exterior the temple is of the DORIC ORDER. The order became more popular during the HELLENISTIC period and was widely used in the Roman empire.

Corinthian pottery a widely distributed fabric made at CORINTH and found throughout the Mediterranean. Production was mainly during the ARCHAIC period, although it continued into the CLASSICAL. A range of shapes were made, from small perfumed-oil containers (see ARYBALLOS, ALABASTRON) to AMPHORAS and KRATERS. PAYNE devised a chronological scheme which was divided into different phases: Protocorinthian, Transitional, Early, Middle and Late Corinthian.

cornice the uppermost part of the ENTABLATURE located above the TRIGLYPHs and METOPES in the DORIC ORDER, or above the frieze in the IONIC ORDER.

correlation the demonstration of equivalency of STRATIGRAPHIC units. Because there are multiple classes of stratigraphic units, equivalency can be expressed in lithological, palaeontological, cultural or chronological terms. In any case, the basis for equivalency should be clearly stated.

There are many methods of correlation and normally multiple methods are used together. Correlation of units defined by objective lithological criteria (lithostratigraphic units, see STRATIGRAPHY) can be done by tracing lateral continuity, lithological identity and position in a stratigraphic sequence, identifying structural relationships to UNCONFORMITIES, faults and folds, intrusions, and by other methods. Equivalency of biostratigraphic units (see STRATIGRAPHY) is demonstrated by identifying similar characteristics of fossil content and fossil assemblages. Correlation of chronostratigraphic units can be based on palaeontological criteria and correlation, ABSOLUTE DATING methods, RELATIVE DATING methods, CROSS-DATING methods, and position relative to the GLACIAL-INTERGLACIAL cycle as determined by physical and biological attributes.

corrugation a decorative technique on pottery, whereby the individual circular coils making up the walls of the vessel are left unsmoothed on the exterior, thus forming a distinctive overlapping surface. Corrugation also improves a vessel's conductivity of heat.

Cortaillod a Neolithic village site on the shore of Lake Neuchâtel, representing the second phase of Neolithic occupation of Switzerland, following the EGOLZWIL phase shortly before 4000 BC. Although the Cortaillod villages had domestic livestock and may have practised cereal cultivation, wild plant and animal resources continued to play an important part in the diet. In eastern Switzerland, the Cortaillod was replaced by the PFYN culture shortly after 4000 BC; in western Switzerland it was replaced by the HORGEN assemblage in around 3300 BC.

Cortés, Hernán or **Hernando Cortez** (*c.*1485–1547) the Spanish conqueror of the AZTEC empire and founder of the colony of New Spain. Cortés landed near Yucatán in April 1519. After capturing Tabasco and founding the city of Veracruz, he began a forced march to the interior of Mexico and TENOCHTITLÁN. Cortés gained the support of a number of enemies of the Aztec empire. This support, and the advice and aid of a MAYA princess (Doña Marina, or Malinche), allowed him to take Moctezuma, the Aztec ruler, hostage, and rule the city. In 1520 the Spanish were driven from Tenochtitlán, but it was finally conquered and destroyed in 1521 when Cortés defeated Moctezuma's successor, Cuauhtémoc. Subsequently, Cortés was appointed governor of Mexico, completing the conquest of the surrounding area, and building the colonial capital. He later led a number of other expeditions through Mexico, not always with success. His later years were spent primarily in Spain.

CORINTHIAN ORDER capital on a column at Jerash, Jordan.

Cortes de Navarra an URNFIELD settlement in the Ebro Valley, Navarre, Spain, consisting of stone-built rectangular houses grouped together in terraces. The occupation falls at the Late Bronze Age/Early Iron Age transition, 8th/7th century BC. The settlement was excavated primarily by MALUQUER DE MOTES.

cortex a tough, dull-white, powdery and porous covering or crust found over the outer surface of newly exposed flint NODULES and tabular flint. The cortex is usually discarded during the knapping process.

Cosquer see GROTTE COSQUER.

Coțofeni culture a late ENEOLITHIC culture of the eastern Balkans, centred on southern Romania. The Coțofeni culture succeeded the CERNAVODĂ culture and the KRIVODOL group in the lower Danube basin during the late 4th millennium BC. Its ceramics are reminiscent of the contemporaneous BADEN culture to the northwest with handled mugs and pitchers, and of the BUBANJ-HUM IB phase of Serbia. Coțofeni settlements are generally small and short-lived.

Cotte de St Brelade see LA COTTE.

Cotton Preceramic see PRECERAMIC PERIOD.

Cougnac a decorated Palaeolithic cave-site in the Quercy region of France, discovered in 1952. Best known for its paintings of MEGALOCEROS and ibex, its art was originally considered homogeneous and assigned on stylistic grounds to the SOLUTREAN period, *c.*18–16,000 years ago, but charcoal in dots on the wall has been dated to 14,290 and 13,810 bp, while dates for the megaloceros figures span a range from 25,120 to 19,500 years ago. If valid, these results point to several possible episodes of use.

coup-de-poing see BIFACE.

court cairn a type of Neolithic CHAMBERED TOMB common in Ireland, in which the burial mound encloses a courtyard in front of the passage leading to the burial chamber. The design may be considered a development from the horned cairn in which the horns have grown to completely enclose the space in front of the tomb.

Covalanas a cave near Ramales, northern Spain, containing Palaeolithic PARIETAL ART – outline paintings of a horse, a bovid or reindeer and eighteen hinds, all of them done with red dots, and all probably by a single artist; their style ascribes them to *c.*20,000 BP. Very similar figures are known in the nearby cave of La Haza, as well as in the more remote caves of Arenaza, El Pendo and La Pasiega (see EL CASTILLO).

cover sand or **blow sand** a sheet of sand deposited by the wind. Cover sand may be found on terraces within outwash plains of GLACIAL meltwater streams and the adjacent uplands where it may be interstratified with loess. Sand beaches can be the source for cover sand deposited in coastal areas. Deposition can effect rapid burial of archaeological deposits. If deposition is thick and rapid enough, artifact associations are likely to be preserved intact. See also DUNE.

Coveta del Or a cave-site on the Mediterranean coast of Valencia, Spain, with early Neolithic CARDIAL WARE pottery, bones of domestic animals and remains of cultivated wheat, with radiocarbon dates of c.4500 bc.

Coxcatlán phase the occupation phase from c.5000 to 3400 BC in Mexico's TEHUACÁN VALLEY, during which maize first appeared. Wild and semi-domesticated plants continued to make up a large part of the diet. In addition to collecting wild plants and producing some gardens, the society also hunted small game.

Cozumel an island off the east coast of the Yucatán peninsula, Mexico, that was both an important trade port and a place of pilgrimage to honour the cult of Ix Chel, MAYA goddess of women, childbirth and the moon. The island was first occupied by the Maya at about the time of Christ, but began its climb to prominence from AD 800 to 1000. During its peak (AD 1400), Putun, or Chontal, Maya traders (a Maya-speaking group of the Gulf Coast Lowlands, not part of the CLASSIC Maya culture) used it to store goods; long causeways from the coast led to large inland storage platforms.

crannog an artificial island in a lake or marsh forming the foundation for a small settlement. Crannogs are found in northern Britain and Ireland and date from the Late Bronze Age to early Christian period.

crater see KRATER.

Crawford, Osbert Guy Stanhope (1886–1957) British archaeologist who highlighted the geographical approach to the subject. He was Archaeological Officer of the Ordnance Survey, improving standards of mapping of British archaeological sites; he was a pioneer of aerial photography of archaeological sites, and in 1927 he founded the journal *Antiquity* and was its first editor until his death.

cremation see PRIMARY CREMATION, SECONDARY CREMATION.

crescent see SEGMENT.

Creswellian British late Upper Palaeolithic industry named after the sites of Creswell Crags in the Peak District of Derbyshire, and found at caves as far south as the Mendips in Somerset, the Gower Peninsula in Wales, and Devon. The assemblage includes a variety of backed blades including points and trapeze shapes. The industry is associated with cold fauna and dates to the end of the DEVENSIAN cold period.

Crete

Prehistoric period

The earliest occupation of Crete dates to the Neolithic period, from c.7000 BC, and is represented by a small settlement at KNOSSOS. By the 4th millennium BC Neolithic sites were established throughout the island. The Neolithic farmers cultivated cereals and legumes and reared sheep/goat, cattle and pig, all introduced to the island from Anatolia. Obsidian from Melos was used to make blades. The transition to the Bronze Age occurred c.3500 BC. This is subdivided into three phases: Early Minoan (EM), Middle Minoan (MM), Late Minoan (LM). Agricultural innovations in the 3rd millennium BC include the domestication of the olive and vine, plough agriculture and the use of pack animals. Alongside these changes there was an increase in population and from EM II (c.2900–2300 BC) the development of larger village communities, such as VASILIKI and MYRTOS-FOURNOU KORIFI. Contacts with Egypt are represented by imports of Old Kingdom stone vases. Burial practices indicate increasing social complexity, especially the communal tholos (circular) tombs of the MESARA, and the wealthy house-tombs at MOCHLOS.

Palatial period

The appearance of the palaces – notably Knossos, PHAISTOS, MALLIA and ZAKROS – in MM I, c.1900 BC, marks a major change in the social and political organization of Crete. There are two architectural/cultural phases: the earlier, Old Palace period (MM I–III, c.1900–1675 BC) and the New Palace period (MM III–LM I, c.1675–1500 BC). The palaces were the centre of Minoan economic, political and religious life. Economic transactions were recorded on clay tablets, first in Hieroglyphics and later in LINEAR A. The palaces were also centres of craft specialization: stone carving (vases and seal-stones), ivory carving, goldwork and wall paintings. The palatial period is characterized by urbanization, illustrated by GOURNIA and PALAIKASTRO. The Minoan landscape was densely inhabited and was dominated by luxurious country villas, including AMNISOS and VATHYPETRO. There is substantial evidence in LM IA (c.1675–1600 BC) for considerable Cretan influence throughout the Aegean islands, illustrated by the use of the Minoan metric system, Linear A, Minoan-style architecture and Minoanizing wall paintings, most notably at AKROTIRI on Thera. In the early 2nd millennium BC Minoan pottery is found at sites throughout Egypt and Syro-Palestine, evidence for flourishing trading contacts, and Egyptian Dynasty 18th tomb paintings depict people from Keftiu wearing Minoan-style costume. Minoanizing wall paintings have been found at TELL ED-DAB'A, in the Nile Delta, and on the coast of the southern Levant, at TEL KABRI. Following a period of apparent depopulation, the palaces, villas and towns were destroyed by fire in LM IB (16th century BC). Only the palace at Knossos was rebuilt and there was a

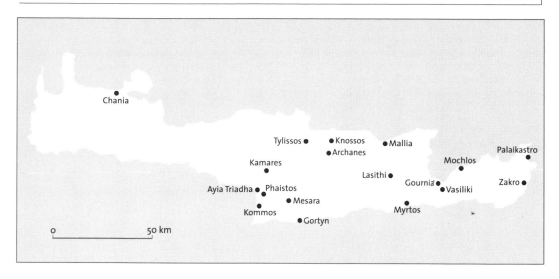

decline in the number of inhabited sites. Linear B inscriptions (written in Greek) have been found at Knossos and KHANIA. These and other changes, such as the appearance of warrior burials, suggest Mycenaean control of the island from LM II (*c*.1500–1440 BC).

Postpalatial period
Conditions were very unsettled at the end of the Late Bronze Age, between *c*.1190 and 970 BC (LM IIIC and Sub-Minoan periods), illustrated by a decline in population and a move away from coastal settlements to refuge sites in the mountains, such as KAVOUSI, KARPHI and VROKASTRO. In the Early Iron Age there was a new type of political organization, the polis or city-state, usually centred on defensive hill sites, like DREROS and GORTYN. The coastal site of KOMMOS shows signs of precocious contact with the Near East, especially its 9th-century Phoenician temple. There was little internal development during the CLASSICAL period (*c*.480–330 BC) but in the HELLENISTIC period (from *c*.330 BC) Crete played an important role in maritime trade and piracy. Between 68–66 BC Quintus Caecilius Metellus invaded the island, which was incorporated in a Roman province with CYRENE, North Africa, its capital at Gortyn. Roman Crete was densely inhabited and there was again settlement in the lowlands. In AD 330 Crete became part of the Eastern or Byzantine empire, until the Arab invasions of AD 824.

Crickley Hill a Neolithic CAUSEWAYED CAMP and Iron Age HILLFORT in Gloucestershire, England. The causewayed camp was replaced in the late Neolithic period by a defended enclosure with houses and streets within. This met its end in violence, as shown by the scatter of leaf-shaped flint arrowheads along the rampart, fanning out into the interior of the enclosure from the gates. A rectangular timber shrine was erected later in the Neolithic in the centre of the earlier causewayed camp, and was succeeded by a long mound and STONE CIRCLE. The site was reoccupied in the 7th century BC when an Iron Age promontory fort was constructed. This had two phases of construction, the first around 700 BC, with timber-laced rampart and rectangular long houses, the second, destroyed in the 5th century, with round houses and a massive curving hornwork to defend the entrance passage.

Criş culture an early Neolithic culture of Romania and Moldova, part of the vast complex of Balkan early Neolithic cultures that includes KARANOVO I, KREMIKOVCI, STARČEVO and KÖRÖS. As is the case with Starčevo and Körös sites, Criş settlements do not appear to be TELLS but rather flat open habitations. An important aspect of the Criş culture is the apparent contact that it had with forager populations of the BUG-DNIESTER culture to its east.

CRM see CULTURAL RESOURCE MANAGEMENT.

Cro-Magnon a French rockshelter in LES EYZIES, Dordogne, which in 1868 yielded AURIGNACIAN artifacts and associated HOMO *sapiens sapiens* burials, including four adults and various fragmented bones and infant remains. The bones indicate tall and muscular people with a long skull, high forehead and broad face. Compare CHANCELADE. The finds gave their name to the modern form of *Homo*.

cromlech 1 (*Brittany*) a STONE CIRCLE.
   2 (*Wales*) the general term for any megalithic tomb. The word is a traditional CELTIC term.

cross-beds a sedimentary structure in which fine strata or LAMINAE between bedding planes (e.g. within a BED) are inclined relative to the bounding bedding planes.

Cross-bedding forms in granular material as the result of migration of dunes and sandwaves within a current more or less at right angles to the prevailing current and are larger in scale than CROSS-LAMINAE. The type, size, constituents and orientation of cross-bedding are the result of prevailing hydrological or AEOLIAN conditions. Orientation of cross-bedding gives information on prevailing palaeocurrent direction, which can be used to reconstruct past depositional environments that may have related archaeological deposits.

cross-dating a correlation dating technique which can yield a relative or absolute age or chronology. Cross-dating is assignment of an age to an artifact at a location, based on the age of a TYPOLOGICALLY similar, or diagnostic, artifact, determined by some dating method or established chronology, at another location. If in the latter case the artifact is from a context dated by some CHRONOMETRIC DATING method, then an absolute age estimate can be applied to the artifact in the former case. Also, associated material found in the same context can be assigned the same age. The method is typically interregional and is necessarily based on assumptions of rates of typological evolution and diffusion. Ideal artifacts are those with a short but well-dated life-span with a wide geographic range. The method is always subject to some error because the assumption of diffusion implies a DIACHRONIC nature.

cross-laminae a sedimentary structure in which LAMINAE are deposited at an inclined angle to the main depositional surface (bedding plane). Cross-laminae form in granular material as the result of migration of ripples within the current more or less at right angles to the prevailing current, and are smaller in scale than CROSSBEDS. The type, size, constituents and orientation of cross-laminae are the result of prevailing hydrological or AEOLIAN conditions, and can be used to reconstruct prevailing palaeocurrent direction and past depositional environments.

Crow Creek a habitation site in South Dakota, USA, which belongs to the beginning of the Coalescent tradition of the PLAINS VILLAGE INDIANS. Recovered at the site were over 500 human skeletons, the remains of individuals who were massacred and later mutilated. The bodies were then buried *en masse* at the bottom of the settlement's fortification ditch. The conflict may have been over territory or access to scarce resources, since many of the skeletons showed signs of malnutrition. Burial sites of this magnitude are rare on the Plains, and thus Crow Creek gave archaeologists an invaluable opportunity to examine ancient DEMOGRAPHY and disease patterns.

Crvena Stijena a stratified prehistoric cave-site located near the Adriatic coast in Montenegro. Palaeolithic artifacts and faunal remains (including red deer, bison and marmot) are buried in loam and gravel deposits dating to the last GLACIAL. The lower layers contained a Middle Palaeolithic industry dominated by scrapers while overlying layers yielded Upper Palaeolithic assemblages often assigned to the AURIGNACIAN. Above several levels of Mesolithic occupation was a layer with IMPRESSED WARE pottery, from which the animal bones suggest that a hunting and gathering economy continued after the introduction of pottery. Later levels include one of the DANILO culture of the late Neolithic, and an uppermost layer with HALLSTATT A–B metalwork.

cryoturbation the disturbing or mixing of sediment or soil material by frost action, and the freezing of the active layer of PERMAFROST late in the melt-season. Advance of the freezing front leads to expansion and heave, and growth of ice lenses (thin layers of ice) disrupts the soil mass. Among the results of cryoturbation are complex INVOLUTIONS which signify former cold climatic conditions. Frost activity in caves tends to produce angular CLASTS that accumulate in greater concentrations during colder climatic episodes. In STRATIFIED cave deposits these rubble zones are often indicative of more severe climatic episodes.

cryptoportico an underground corridor, usually in the substructure of a large Roman building complex.

cubiculum 1 the bedchamber in a Roman house.
2 a chamber in a CATACOMB where groups of people perhaps gathered for rites linked to the dead.

Cucuteni-Tripolye one of the major ENEOLITHIC cultures of southeastern Europe, distributed throughout a broad region in southwestern Ukraine (where it is known as the *Tripolye* culture), Moldova and northeastern Romania (where it is known as the *Cucuteni* culture), named after the eponymous sites of Cucuteni in the Siret Valley of Romania and Tripolye near Kiev in Ukraine. The chronology of this culture is complicated by differing regional sequences, which have each been finely subdivided, spanning the late 5th and early 4th millennia BC. Romanian archaeologists recognize the existence of a 'pre-Cucuteni' culture whose antecedents appear to lie in the late Neolithic BOIAN culture of central Romania. Cucuteni-Tripolye settlements have benefited from the excavation of large contiguous areas, which have often revealed large village plans as at KOLOMIISHCHINA and VLADIMIROVKA. House sites are indicated by PLOSHCHADKI, fired clay and timber platforms. Cucuteni-Tripolye sites in Ukraine often occur on high promontories, as at POLIVANOV YAR, while many in Romania are surrounded by elaborate defensive ditch systems. Cucuteni-Tripolye trichrome (red-black-white) painted pottery reflects a high level of technological skill in its decoration and firing.

Cuddie Springs an open site in northwestern New South

Wales, Australia, where stone artifacts are reported in association with MEGAFAUNA bones dating back to about 30,000 bp. The artifacts include flakes with blood residues, suggesting use in butchering, and, surprisingly, fragments of grindstones.

Cuello a middle PRECLASSIC settlement in northern Belize with a long occupation sequence useful for defining the early development of MAYA civilization.

Cueva de la Sarsa a cave near Valencia, Spain, where excavations from 1928 to 1939 revealed a rich early Neolithic occupation with CARDIAL WARE, a wide variety of stone and bone tools and jewellery of shell, bone and stone. The economy was based on cattle, sheep and goats, and remains of carbonized wheat were also recovered.

Cueva de las Manos a PALAEOINDIAN site in southern Patagonia (Argentina) whose earliest occupation dates to c.9300 bp. The assemblage contains triangular points and a bola stone, in association with late Pleistocene fauna (guanaco, puma, fox and birds). The cave is best known for the PICTOGRAPHS of a later occupation, c.8000 bp; these comprise negative images of hundreds of human hands.

Cueva de los Murciélagos see MURCIÉLAGOS.

Cueva Fell an Early PRECERAMIC (PALAEOINDIAN) site (9050–8770 bc) in far southern Patagonia (Chile), at which fluted stemmed 'FISHTAIL' points were found by Junius B. BIRD in his excavations in the 1930s. The tools were found in a sealed deposit, associated with horse, mylodon (giant sloth) and camelid bones. The excavation of this site provided the first scientific evidence of very early human occupation near the southern extremity of South America in late Pleistocene/early Holocene times (see EL INGA).

Cueva Morin a northern Spanish Palaeolithic cave-site in Santander, best known for its seven MOUSTERIAN levels, some with fragments of living floors and associated tools including flake cleavers; a lower PERIGORDIAN layer dated to 36,350 bp; and its AURIGNACIAN levels including dwelling structures and burials. The site was most recently investigated by Freeman and González Echegaray in 1966–9, and was one of the first Spanish sites to be dug by the scientific method of controlled horizontal excavation.

Cueva Palli Aike a PALAEOINDIAN site in southern Patagonia (Chile) in which a late Pleistocene fauna (ground sloth, horse) was found in association with human bones and artifacts. The site is thought to represent very early human occupation of Patagonia, similar to CUEVA FELL, although it has come under recent scrutiny. The site was completely excavated by Junius B. BIRD in the 1930s, leaving no remaining archaeological context through which to evaluate his interpretations. A radiocarbon date

of 8600 bp has been obtained from bone fragments, but their association with the artifacts is unclear.

Cueva Tixi a site in the province of Buenos Aires, Argentina, with a history of at least four occupations spanning some 10,000 years. The earliest occupation (10,375–10,045 bp) is represented by hearths and lithic artifacts associated with extinct late Pleistocene fauna. Subsequent hunter-gatherer occupations extend the occupation of the cave up to 440 bp. The site provides a reliable long-term chronology for eastern-central Argentina.

Cuicuilco a ceremonial site containing the earliest monumental and ceremonial architecture found in the BASIN OF MEXICO. These monumental constructions date to 600–200 BC, when Cuicuilco was the major centre in the valley. Cuicuilco's supremacy ended in c.50 BC when the volcano Xitle erupted, covering much of the area in lava and forming the Pedregal, or volcanic desert. Ironically, the principal deity at Cuicuilco was a fire god, known in AZTEC times as Xiuhtecuhtli (Huehueteotl).

In 1922, Byron Cummings and Manuel GAMIO recognized that a 'hill' on the Pedregal was not a natural formation. Subsequent excavation uncovered a large TEMPLE MOUND. The site is famous for this massive circular pyramid, a truncated cone with stepped sides and ramps. It is over 100 m (110 yds) in diameter at the base and approximately 20 m (66 ft) high, and shows at least three phases of construction.

Cuiry-lès-Chaudardes an early Neolithic village site of the Paris Basin LINEAR POTTERY culture, Aisne, France, occupied c.4800 BC. The village consisted of a number of timber longhouses, between 10 and 39 m (33 and 128 ft) in length and 5 to 7 m (16 to 23 ft) broad, represented today only by POSTHOLES. The remains of the settlement cover 7 ha (17 acres) but the houses were rebuilt from time to time and only a few of them would have been in use at any given moment. Alongside the houses were pits from which clay had been dug to seal the house walls. These pits were later used for rubbish disposal and have yielded a variety of remains including bones of domestic animals (principally cattle), POTSHERDS decorated in the typical Bandkeramik style, grindstones for the preparation of flour and flint tools and waste flakes.

Cu Lao Rua a late Neolithic (shouldered polished stone adzes) to Bronze Age settlement in the Dong Nai River Valley, near Ho Chi Minh City in southern Vietnam, overlapping with HANG GON.

cult temple a term used to distinguish a temple erected to serve the cult of a particular deity (who was regarded as dwelling therein) from a MORTUARY TEMPLE.

cultural resource management the legally mandated protection of archaeological sites located on public lands in the USA that are threatened by destruction through development, energy exploration and other such activities. The most extensive laws have been enacted to protect sites on federal lands, but states and even some cities have enacted similar legislation.

culture 1 non-genetically determined human behaviour. **2** the constellation of beliefs, behaviours and customs peculiar to a specific people. **3** in archaeology, the constellation of specific elements of MATERIAL CULTURE, thought to represent a particular people. This term is most often used in the Old World.

culture areas major anthropological subdivisions of the North American continent, which are individually characterized by relatively uniform environments and relatively similar cultures. The culture area concept was devised at the end of the 19th century, as a means of organizing museum data. Although it was conceived for ETHNOGRAPHIC displays, the divisions have been used extensively by archaeologists also, on the assumption that the culture areas had a considerable time depth. Examples include the Southwest, the Plains and the northwest coast.

culture history the organization of the archaeological record into a basic sequence of events in time and space. Culture history is based on INDUCTION and the NORMATIVE view of culture. Explanations for changes in culture-historical sequences include DIFFUSION and migration, and have been criticized by PROCESSUAL ARCHAEOLOGISTS for not being explanations at all, but merely descriptions of behaviour. Culture history remains the primary goal of most archaeological work in many areas, despite the addition of processual studies to the discipline.

Cumae (*Gk* Kyme) a Greek colony in CAMPANIA dating to the mid 8th century BC. Tombs have yielded some of the earliest Greek pottery in Italy. On the AKROPOLIS, temples of Apollo and Jupiter were located. See also CAMPANIAN POTTERY.

cumulative graph a statistical method used by archaeologists to compare assemblages on the basis of ARTIFACT TYPOLOGY. BORDES used the method to subdivide the MOUSTERIAN industries of southwestern France, noting the presence, absence and percentage-value of well-defined tool types and plotting his results as a cumulative percentage frequency graph (or 'ogive').

cuneiform the characteristic wedge-shaped writing of western Asia, used for over 3,000 years, cuneiform was produced by impressing sharpened reeds into clay tablets. The writing system emerged during the 4th millennium BC in southern MESOPOTAMIA as a system of accountancy (see TOKENS) during the URUK period, and by the end of the 4th millennium BC (the JEMDET NASR period) was being used to record lexical lists (occupations, place names). Royal inscriptions appeared by the mid 3rd millennium, and recording of literary works

CUNEIFORM TABLET.

began soon after that (represented by texts from ABU SALABIKH in southern Mesopotamia and from EBLA in northern Syria). Cuneiform continued in use until the end of the 1st millennium BC, and was used to represent many different languages of ancient western Asia in addition to SUMERIAN and AKKADIAN (for example, EL-AMITE, HITTITE, URARTIAN, PERSIAN).

cup-and-ring mark a common motif in the rock art of Great Britain, consisting of a roughly circular central hollow surrounded by one or more concentric rings.

CUP-AND-RING MARKS at Carschenna, Switzerland.

These and other motifs are found on the backs of stones in the megalithic CHAMBERED TOMBS of the BOYNE VALLEY, and can therefore be dated to the Neolithic period (4th or 3rd millennium BC). Important concentrations of cup-and-ring marks are found in Scotland and northern England as well as other parts of Europe.

Cupisnique the style of pottery pertaining to the northern coast of Peru during the EARLY HORIZON. This style is typified by blackware jars with globular bodies, stirrup spouts and relief decoration; the iconography depicted is closely related to the styles of CHAVÍN.

Curacchiaghiu a rockshelter in Corsica, France, with Mesolithic and Neolithic occupation levels. Radiocarbon samples from this site and from Strette in the north of the island show that the colonization of Corsica can be dated to before 6500 BC. The early Neolithic levels of Curacchiaghiu, dated to c.5600 BC, contain pottery with punch-impressed decoration which may be a local development of the CARDIAL WARE found at contemporary sites on the Corsican coast.

curation an activity in which artifacts are reused, reworked and transported, to the extent that their initial locations of manufacture and use are no longer known.

curia 1 the meeting place at ROME for the Senate, located near the COMITIUM in the FORUM. The structure built by Caesar, for which work commenced in 44 BC, consisted of a hall 25.2 m (82 ft 8 inches) long and 17.6 m (57 ft 9 inches) wide. Seating consisted of marble benches across the width of the room.
 2 the meeting place for assemblies, especially the ruling bodies of Roman towns and colonies. Like their counterpart at ROME, they were usually placed adjacent to the FORUM.

cursus a Neolithic ritual monument consisting of two parallel banks with external ditches. They are usually straight, but with occasional changes of axis, and can be several kilometres long. The longest of all is the Dorset cursus which extends for 8 km (5 miles) with banks 91 m (100 yds) apart and has been dated to 2500 BC. Cursus monuments are restricted to southern and eastern England.

Cuzco or **Cusco** the capital of the INCA empire, located in the southern highlands of Peru. The name means 'navel' in Quechua, as it was the point at which the four quarters of the empire articulated, the symbolic navel of the world. Cuzco was founded in c.AD 1200 by Manco Capac, the progenitor of the Inca dynasty, and rebuilt by Pachacuti at the time of the Inca expansion. The site was built in the form of a puma, and divided into upper (*hanan*) and lower (*urin*) halves. A U-shaped central plaza, the Aucaypata, was flanked by public buildings, and contained an USNU platform. The walls of many of the principal buildings were made of stones that were carefully

CYLINDER SEAL and impression.

cut, and fitted together without the use of mortar. The site was primarily a ceremonial and political centre rather than a population centre. See also TAWANTINSUYU, CORICANCHA.

Cycladic *adj.* relating to and defining the Bronze Age culture of the Cyclades, the islands of the central-southern Aegean. The Cycladic period is divided into three phases: Early (c.3000–2000 BC), Middle (c.2000–1550 BC) and Late (c.1550–1050 BC), and there is a further tripartite subdivision of each of these phases. Renfrew has proposed, as an alternative to the traditional Early Cycladic subdivisions, a culture sequence: GROTTA-PELOS, KEROS-SYROS, and PHYLAKOPI I. Major Cycladic sites include AKROTIRI on THERA, AYIA IRINI and KEPHALA on Kea, CHALANDRIANI on Syros and Phylakopi on MELOS.

Cyclopean a style of masonry most typically used in MYCENAEAN fortifications. Large irregular blocks of stone, their surfaces roughly hammer-dressed, were laid uncoursed and the interstices between the blocks were filled with smaller rocks and stones. Later Greeks supposed that the walls had been built by the giant Cyclopes.

cylinder hammer technique see SOFT HAMMER TECHNIQUE.

cylinder seal a cylinder on which a scene, design and/or inscription is carved. This was the standard seal form of the MESOPOTAMIAN civilization, beginning with the URUK period, and was used by rolling it across the clay surface to be sealed (tablets, jar stoppers, door locks and so forth), thus producing the impression (single or repeated) of the seal's design. Dating is based on changes in the design on the seal, in the technique of cutting, and in the seal's size and proportion, while the seal's iconographic content can provide a rich source of social information. Compare STAMP SEAL.

Cypro-Minoan *adj.* relating to and defining the SYLLABIC script which was in use on Cyprus from the 15th century BC. The script recalls MINOAN LINEAR A and may have been introduced from Crete by merchants. Cypro-Minoan inscriptions appear on baked clay tablets,

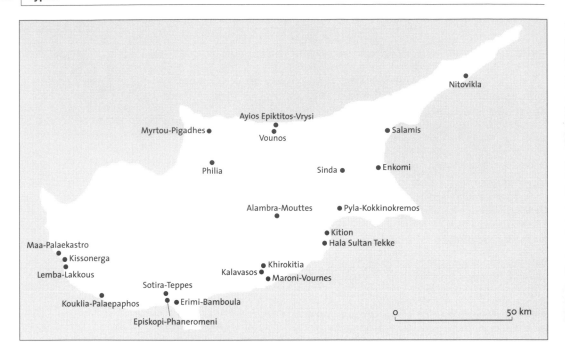

Nitovikla

Ayios Epiktitos-Vrysi

Myrtou-Pigadhes●   ● Salamis
Vounos

● Philia   Sinda ●   ● Enkomi

Alambra-Mouttes   ● Pyla-Kokkinokremos
●
● Kition
● Hala Sultan Tekke

Maa-Palaekastro
● Kissonerga   ● Khirokitia
Lemba-Lakkous   Kalavasos ●● Maroni-Vournes
Sotira-Teppes
Kouklia-Palaepaphos   ● Erimi-Bamboula
Episkopi-Phaneromeni

0   50 km

bronze votives, ivories and seals, but the script has never been deciphered. It was apparently revived in the 8th century BC and used to write Greek until the 3rd century BC.

Cyprus the third largest Mediterranean island, which was first occupied c.8000 BC. A number of Neolithic (c.6000–3500 BC) sites have been excavated, in particular KHIROKITIA, AYIOS EPIKTITOS-VRYSI and SO-TIRA. A CHALCOLITHIC phase follows (c.3500–2500 BC) which is attested at ERIMI, KISSONERGA and LEMBA.

The Early Cypriot period (c.2500–1900 BC) is known primarily from cemeteries, such as PHILIA and VOUNOUS, rather than settlements. Middle Cypriot (c.1900–1650 BC) sites include ALAMBRA and EPISKOPI. This is a period of regional diversity and the construction of fortresses suggests internal unrest. In the Late Cypriot period (c.1650–1050 BC) the main settlements were on the south and east coasts, at ENKOMI, KITION, HALA SULTAN TEKKE, KALAVASOS and MARONI.

Trade between Cyprus, Egypt and the Near East increased as the demand for Cypriot copper intensified. Cyprus may have been ALASHIYA, a state which is mentioned in Near Eastern documents. It is thought that the SEA PEOPLES were responsible for the destruction of a number of sites c.1200 BC, but the impressive architecture of Enkomi and Kition suggests that the 12th century was a period of considerable prosperity. It is possible that MYCENAEAN Greeks settled on Cyprus in the 11th century BC. They were followed by PHOENICIAN colon-

ists in the 9th century. The Iron Age city kingdoms, which include Kition, Kourion, Paphos (see KOUKLIA-PALAEPAPHOS) and SALAMIS, were dominated by Egypt and then by the Persians.

Cyrene a Greek colony in Libya founded from THERA in the late 7th century BC. Imported Greek pottery of the ARCHAIC period has been found in the extramural sanctuary of Demeter. Excavations have revealed part of the Roman city.

Cyrus II the first great ACHAEMENID king. Cyrus began his rule (around 559 BC) as a client of the MEDIAN state to the north. From his home in Fars in southwestern Iran, Cyrus managed first to defeat the Medes, and then to expand both westwards through the mountains into Anatolia (defeating Croesus of Lydia in western Anatolia; see SARDIS) and eastwards across the Iranian plateau and into Central Asia. Having largely encircled the NEO-BABYLONIAN empire, he then invaded and conquered BABYLON itself in 539 BC. Cyrus died from wounds received while campaigning against a SCYTHIAN group (the Massagetae) in Transcaucasia in 530 BC. Later Achaemenid kings extended Cyrus' empire into Egypt (Cambyses, 529–522 BC), western India (Darius, 521–486 BC) and Macedonia (Darius); the famous attempts to occupy Greece (Xerxes 485–465 BC) failed.

Czech Republic see EUROPE, CENTRAL.

Czöszhalom see HERPÁLY.

D

Dabban an early blade and burin stone industry of Cyrenaica, Libya, with dates ranging from 40,000 to 14,000 years ago (see HAUA FTEAH).

Dabki a Stone Age settlement on the Baltic coast in northern Poland, dated to the late 5th millennium BC. The inhabitants of Dabki were primarily foragers who eventually began to adopt domestic cattle and pig in the later occupation phases. Finds of pottery with pointed bases suggest connections to the ERTEBØLLE CULTURE of southern Scandinavia.

Da But an early Neolithic SHELL MIDDEN with twelve seated burials in the lower Ma River Valley, northern Vietnam. It was first excavated by E. Patte in the 1930s, and again by Vietnamese archaeologists. Dated to 4500–3700 BC, the site is intermediate between the late HOABINHIAN tradition of the inland caves such as CON MOONG, and fully agricultural Neolithic village settlements.

Dacia an early state on the territory of present-day Romania, which flourished during the final centuries BC. Dacian towns are characterized by monumental architecture, as well as by religious precincts, such as the sanctuary at SARMIZEGETHUSA. Dacia was absorbed by the Roman empire under TRAJAN in AD 106, and abandoned in AD 270.

daga puddled clay used to plaster walls and floors of houses in sub-Saharan African Iron Age settlements.

Dahshur an Egyptian royal NECROPOLIS, best regarded as a southern extension of SAQQARA. The major monuments at the site are the pyramids of SNEFRU of the OLD KINGDOM; and AMENEMHAT II, SENWOSRET III and Amenemhat III of the MIDDLE KINGDOM. The subsidiary tombs of the Princesses Khnemet and Iti near the pyramid of Amenemhat II produced the 'Dahshur Treasure' of jewellery and accoutrements, as did, to a lesser extent, the tombs of the royal ladies associated with the pyramids of Senwosret III and Amenemhat III. The main excavators at Dahshur have been de Morgan in 1894–5,

Fakhry in 1951–5, and, currently, the German Archaeological Institute.

Daima a large mound in northeastern Nigeria, which, together with neighbouring sites, provides evidence for permanent settlements of wood-walled, clay-floored houses, hunting and fishing, as well as domestic cattle and goats, extending back to the late 2nd millennium BC. Iron appeared between the 1st and 6th centuries AD. Several centuries later Daima became part of a wide-ranging trade network, which may be linked to the rise of KANEM in the late 1st millennium AD.

Daimabad a site on a tributary of the Godavari River in Maharashta, western India, that was the object of three separate investigations during the 1950s (M. Deshpande) and 1970s (S. R. Rao and S. Sali). This work revealed a stratigraphic sequence of five phases during the 3rd and 2nd millennia BC. The basal levels represent a food-producing community (including barley, rice, lentils), characterized by a coarse grey ware along with some painted pottery. The succeeding phase marks a major shift in material culture with reported HARAPPAN and Harappan-derived red wares; and the next phase represents yet another shift, to include a white-painted grey ware. Above these levels are two later phases of occupation, characterized by MALWA and JORWE wares respectively. While the architecture of the earlier levels is fragmentary, that of the later two phases is clearer, including platforming in a possible cultic complex, and domestic structures. By the last phase of occupation, subsistence included cultivation of sorghum and millet. Daimabad is perhaps best known for the chance find of a COPPER HOARD, tentatively assigned to the Jorwe phase; the hoard consists of three large figures of animals on wheels (rhinoceros, elephant and buffalo) and another of a chariot.

Dainzú a large archaeological site in central Oaxaca, Mexico, dating to c.300 BC (MONTE ALBÁN I), of which only a small portion has been excavated. It is especially known for the bas-relief carvings that are similar to the DANZANTES at Monte Albán. Those at Dainzú also include figures of ball players. The site was discovered and excavated during the 1960s by Ignacio BERNAL.

Dakhla the largest of the oases (see also SIWA and KHARGA) in Egypt's Western Desert, but still only 75 by 25 km (47 by 16 miles) in area. Occupied from the Lower Palaeolithic, Dakhla was the site of significant settlements of the dynastic period from the OLD KINGDOM until its decline in the Roman period.

Dalles, the a section of the Columbia River along the Oregon and Washington borders, USA, that is the locality of a number of important archaeological sites, presumably because of the high salmon productivity of that section of the Columbia. The Five Mile Rapids site has a sequence that goes back to approximately 10,000 BC, and other sites show similar antiquity. Later periods are also well represented. The tool assemblages and faunal remains are indicative of a heavy reliance on salmon, although other fauna are also present.

Dalton 1 a projectile point class with much internal variation, some of which is due to reuse and resharpening. It spans the transition from PALAEOINDIAN to ARCHAIC in much of midwestern and eastern North America.

2 a complex associated with the Dalton point form.

Damb Sada'at see QUETTA.

Dambwa an Early Iron Age group of the CHIFUMBAZE complex, dating to between the 5th and 8th centuries AD, distributed in the Zambezi Valley and in northwestern Zimbabwe (see KUMADZULO).

Damous el Ahmar an Algerian cave with a CAPSIAN NEOLITHIC industry and two human skeletons of the mechtoid type (see MECHTA AFALOU). Ochre staining of the skulls and associated tools and food remains indicate funerary rites. There is evidence for small stock herding from the 5th millennium bc onwards.

Dan, Tell an important TELL site of long duration (Early Bronze Age through Iron Age) in upper Galilee. The Israeli excavations begun in 1966 have uncovered portions of the Middle Bronze Age (c.2000–1550 BC) town, including the town gatehouse with its barrel-arched ceiling still intact. The excavation also uncovered a 10th–9th-century BC cult centre, where a controversial Aramaic inscription alludes to the 'house of David', the oldest such reference outside the Bible.

Danangombe or **Dhlo Dhlo** the 17th–19th-century AD capital of the Torwa state in southwestern Zimbabwe. Although smaller than its predecessor KHAMI, architectural principles are similar and include profusely decorated stone walling.

Danebury an Iron Age HILLFORT in Hampshire, England, excavated by Barry Cunliffe. In the earliest phase, the 6th century BC, the defences consisted of a single bank and ditch with two entrances. In the early 4th century a second line of ramparts was added outside the first, and the entrances were strengthened by outworks. Within the interior were traces of storage pits, rectangular four-post granary structures and round houses arranged along metalled streets. Occupation appears to have declined during the following centuries and by the 1st century BC the hillfort was probably used only as a refuge in times of danger.

Danger Cave a deeply stratified cave-site, located in extreme western Utah, USA, that has a basal occupation dated to 11,500–11,000 BP. The assemblage has possible SAN DIEGUITO affiliations. The site's latest occupations date to after 2000 BP. The excellent preservation in the cave allowed a detailed reconstruction of ARCHAIC lifestyles. The evidence from the site was instrumental in the definition of the DESERT TRADITION. See also JENNINGS.

Daniel, Glyn Edmund (1914–86) a British prehistorian whose early work concentrated on the megaliths of Europe. He is perhaps best known for developing the study of the history of archaeology as a legitimate scholarly inquiry and for popularizing the discipline through numerous books and television programmes.

Danilo culture a Neolithic culture of the Dalmatian coast of Croatia and adjacent parts of Bosnia known from both cave and open sites, dated to c.5000 BC. The Danilo culture appears to have developed from the IMPRESSED WARE cultures of the Mediterranean zone. Its fine wares are characterized by incised geometrical shapes, often decorated with red and white post-firing incrustation. Other Danilo fine ware, sometimes called RIPOLI ware, appears to have come from the Italian peninsula.

Danubian cultures a cultural tradition defined by CHILDE in his study of the Neolithic and ENEOLITHIC cultures of the Danube Basin, now outdated. Danubian I is essentially equivalent to the LINEAR POTTERY culture (c.5600–5000 BC); Danubian II to the STROKE-ORNAMENTED POTTERY, LENGYEL, TISZA and RÖSSEN cultures (c.5000–4200 BC); late Lengyel groups like BRZEŚĆ KUJAWSKI and JORDANÓW are attributed to Danubian III. Childe's Danubian sequence had an additional three phases that covered the Eneolithic and Early Bronze Ages, but these never came into common use.

Danzantes (*Sp.* 'dancers') stone slabs at MONTE ALBÁN, Mexico, carved with figures in dynamic poses once thought to resemble dancers. The figures are now considered to represent captives, some of them possibly dead, as indicated by their closed eyes; or SHAMANS who, having performed auto-sacrificial BLOODLETTING, are shown in trance-like communication with the Otherworld. Some of the carved stones are incorporated

Some of the DANZANTES slabs at Monte Albán, Mexico.

into the building of the Danzantes (structure L). Guillermo Dupaise uncovered some of the Danzantes in the early 19th century.

Dapengeng [Ta-p'en-keng] a Neolithic site near Taipei City, Taiwan, giving its name to a POSTGLACIAL culture of the 6th–5th millennia BC typified by textured pottery, extensive use of plant cordage for decorating pottery vessels (see SHENGWEN), making fish nets, etc. Compare JOMON, CHULMUN.

Dar es-Soltan or **Dar es Soltane** a Moroccan site with a long sequence spanning a final ATERIAN industry at the base, followed by IBEROMAURUSIAN and topped by CAPSIAN NEOLITHIC material.

Dart, Raymond Arthur (1893–1988) a professor of anatomy at the University of the Witwatersrand in South Africa who discovered the first australopithecine (see AUSTRALOPITHECUS) fossil in 1924 (see TAUNG). Initially scorned by other scientists, Dart was eventually vindicated. In 1955 he suggested that the faunal remains at MAKAPANSGAT were used by australopithecines as bone, tooth and horn tools, which he called the Osteodontokeratic culture. This idea has not stood the test of time, but it served to stimulate studies of TAPHONOMY.

Darwin, Charles Robert (1809–82) a British naturalist who, in 1831, embarked on a five-year, round-the-world trip studying wildlife in its natural habitat, paying particular attention to the individual species of the Galapagos Islands. His resulting book, *On the Origin of Species by Means of Natural Selection*, published in 1859, brought the theory of human evolution to a wide public audience. This theory was in direct opposition to the then current creationist view derived from biblical studies.

Darwin glass impactite formed as the result of a meteorite impact in southwestern TASMANIA. The glassy obsidian-like material is found in Pleistocene Tasmanian sites up to 100 km (60 miles) from the Darwin Crater.

Dashly an oasis in southern Bactria in northwestern Afghanistan that contains a large number of Bronze Age, ACHAEMENID and CLASSICAL sites, the first of which are extremely important. V. I. Sarianidi's work in the 1970s, which focused on the two sites Dashly 1 and Dashly 3, defined the BACTRIAN BRONZE AGE (late 3rd and early 2nd millennia BC). These settlements are focused on large, roughly square fortresses with circular towers placed at regular intervals along their sides. Other major architecture (at Dashly 3) includes a 'palace' comparable in many respects to that at SAPALLI-DEPE, and a circular double-walled building, with a complex of rooms in its interior and square towers set into its outer wall, thought to be a temple. Dashly 3 also contained residential areas, a concentration of pottery kilns and (in a late level over the 'palace') a metal-working area.

dating see ABSOLUTE DATING, RELATIVE DATING.

datum or **datum point** a point used as a reference for vertical and horizontal measurement. A site GRID, excavation units and artifactual finds are laid out or measured with reference to a site datum, preferably linked to a national standard, usually taken as sea-level.

Davis, Edwin Hamilton (1811–88) an American antiquary who collaborated with E. G. SQUIER in the description and analysis of Ohio mounds and earthen enclosures. See also ATWATER, HAVEN, THOMAS.

Dawenkou [Ta-wen-k'ou] a middle Neolithic site in Shandong Province, China, type-site of the Dawenkou culture of the eastern seaboard (c.4500–2700 BC), which is distinguished by elaborately shaped pottery deriving from the QINGLIANGANG tradition and increasingly rich burials. It is parallel to the YANGSHAO culture of the northern loess lands. Compare HONGSHAN.

Daxi [Ta-hsi] see HEMUDU.

Dazaifu a special administrative centre of the RITSURYO state of 8th-century AD Japan, located in Fukuoka Prefecture. It served as a bureaucratic gateway from Kyushu to the continent, regulating diplomatic relations with SILLA and the TANG Court (see CHINESE DYNASTIES). Several building foundations have been identified through excavation and are marked out on the present surface as a Historical Site.

Dead Sea Scrolls see QUMRAN.

Debert a CLOVIS site located in Nova Scotia, Canada, and dated to approximately 11,000–10,000 BP. There is evidence of separate concentrations of hearths and artifacts. Caribou and other animals were hunted. The site was located less than 100 km (60 miles) from the southern edge of the glacial wall of the VALDERS ADVANCE.

débitage the waste flakes and small chips produced when knapping a stone implement. Some waste flakes, such as Palaeolithic biface trimming flakes or Mesolithic TRANCHET AXE sharpening flakes, have a characteristic appearance and indicate the tools that were made or sharpened at a site even when the tools themselves are absent.

Déchelette, Joseph (1862–1914) one of the greatest French archaeologists, author of the comprehensive multi-volume *Manuel d'archéologie préhistorique, celtique et gallo-romaine* (vols. I and II, 1908–15). This was intended as a definitive synthesis of all the information then available on the prehistoric and Roman archaeology of Europe, especially France and adjacent areas. Only two volumes (prehistory and protohistory) had been prepared when Déchelette was killed in action in the first days of the First World War, but the great project was subsequently completed by Albert Grenier.

decumanus the main street in a Roman town or camp usually laid out on an east-west axis. The main street was called the *decumanus maximus*, and met the CARDO at the FORUM.

Dederiyeh Cave a prehistoric site in northwestern Syria where an apparently intentional infant NEANDERTHAL burial was discovered by a Japanese-Syrian team in 1993. Associated with a TABUN B-type Levantine MOUSTERIAN industry, the infant should probably be grouped with HOMINID remains from KEBARA and AMUD caves and sheds further light on the distribution of Neanderthals in western Asia.

deduction reasoning whereby specific outcomes can be predicted from general propositions. An example might be concluding that the aeroplanes made in a particular country are untrustworthy because the country's overall manufacturing capabilities are questionable. This deduction could then be tested with specific data. See also INDUCTION.

deductive-nomological *adj.* relating to a form of scientific reasoning, in which a general law is established, ramifications of that law are deduced and these ramifications are used to explain a specific set of data. See also POSITIVISM, NEW ARCHAEOLOGY.

deep-sea cores cores collected from ocean-floor locations that supply a more or less continuous depositional record throughout the QUATERNARY. The continuous records, in contrast to discontinuous continental records, form a potential basis for worldwide STRATIGRAPHIC correlation based on ISOTOPIC palaeontological and MAGNETIC characteristics; they can help provide a chronology for early humans and they contain a wealth of palaeoclimatic information. Changes in ocean temperature and salinity are estimated from the relative abundance of marine fossil species, fossil assemblage composition and morphological variations. Changes in *Foraminifera* assemblages (see OXYGEN ISOTOPE ANALYSIS) identified with depth in the core are compared statistically with the ecology of living species to identify these parameters.

Ages for cores are obtained by URANIUM SERIES DATING, RADIOCARBON DATING, PALAEOMAGNETISM and palaeontological extinctions. Not all methods can be applied to all cores, and there is significant interpolation between determined ages, with the assumption of uniform sedimentation rates.

deer-stones a kind of ancient megalithic art (see also KAMENNAYA BABA) of the EURASIAN STEPPES, these are stone STELAS decorated with pecked images. They represent a human (warrior) figure, but without concrete anthropomorphic features. The stela is usually divided into three zones by two horizontal lines, depicting a necklace and a belt. The upper part has earrings depicted, and three oblique lines in place of the face. The lower part has weaponry and a warrior's equipment attached to the belt (an ACINACES, a GORYTOS, a CHEKAN or pole-axe, a knife, a hone, etc.). The area between the necklace and the belt is completely covered with zoomorphic images, most often deer, executed in a very specific style – hence the name of this kind of monument. Most of them (over 500) have been found in Mongolia, with others (about 100) in the ALTAI, Tuva, Trans-Baikal and eastern Kazakhstan, and a very few (including the CIMMERIAN stelas) in

DEER-STONE: typical decoration.

Europe. They date to the Late Bronze Age–Early Iron Age (first half of the 1st millenium BC). Their cultural attribution is still unclear, but their appearance is definitely connected with the beginning of a new epoch in the history of the Eurasian steppes: the Epoch of Early Nomads.

Değirmentepe a 3 ha (7 acre) late 'UBAID site on the Euphrates River near Malatya (eastern Turkey). Wide excavations by U. Esin uncovered a settlement of closely packed houses in which appear abundant evidence of metallurgical activity and administrative use of seals. The site also contains later Bronze Age and Iron Age occupation.

Deh Luran a small plain in lowland Khuzistan, western Iran, that was the setting for the important work of Frank Hole and Kent Flannery on the origins of food production. Their excavations at Tepe Ali Kosh, Tepe Sabz, Choga Sefid and other sites produced a cultural sequence that begins around 8000 bc (?) and runs through the URUK period into historic times. In the early phases of the sequence (the Bus Mordeh, Ali Kosh and Mohammad Jaffar phases, down to about 6200 bc) can be traced the transformation of morphologically wild but herded goats and sheep into domesticated forms; domesticated cereals are present throughout, but increase in importance through time. At the same time, the settlement at Ali Kosh becomes increasingly sedentary and grows in size, and pottery appears in the Mohammad Jaffar phase.

Deir el-Bahri a locality within THEBES (EGYPT)-WEST BANK, the site of the MORTUARY TEMPLE of Nebhepetre Montuhotep (c.2044–1993 BC) of the MIDDLE KINGDOM and that of HATCHEPSUT built over 500 years later. Both buildings are remarkable for their construction on a series of terraces rising towards the cliffs of the Theban mountain of which Deir el-Bahri is a natural 'bay'. The temple of Hatchepsut contains a number of important reliefs, including those showing the transport of an obelisk and an expedition to the Land of PUNT.

Deir el-Balah a site in southern Israel, best known as a major Egyptian residency in its Levantine empire during the NEW KINGDOM.

Deir el-Medina a locality within THEBES (EGYPT)-WEST BANK, the site of the village (seventy houses) of the workmen who constructed the tombs in the VALLEY OF THE KINGS during the NEW KINGDOM. Deir el-Medina was excavated by Bruyere in 1922–51, and produced a large number of written documents, chiefly OSTRAKA, due to the atypically high level of literacy among the workers who lived there. The evidence of economic and social life provided by this documentation has made Deir el-Medina one of the best-known communities of the ancient Near East.

Dejbjerg a peatbog in western Jutland, Denmark, where, in the 1880s, two magnificent four-wheeled vehicles of the pre-Roman Iron Age were discovered. The site was

The 'bay' of DEIR EL-BAHRI, on the west bank at Thebes, looking down on the mortuary temple of Hatchepsut and, slightly beyond it, that of Nebhepetre Montuhotep.

DELPHI, Greece: view of the tholos of the temple dedicated to Athena Pronaia.

marked by stakes in the ground, and so was probably sacred. The vehicles, late CELTIC in style, were decorated with bronze bosses and masks.

Delos the island birthplace of Apollo and Artemis, and an important sanctuary which contained a colossal marble KOUROS and the 5th-century BC temple of Apollo. Elsewhere there was a sanctuary of Artemis with a temple in the IONIC ORDER. In the HELLENISTIC period the island became an important port and there are traces of houses, many of which contained portrait sculpture. The processional way was flanked by lions, one of which now stands outside the Arsenal at Venice.

Delphi an important PANHELLENIC sanctuary in Greece associated with the cult of Apollo. Inside the sanctuary were numerous THESAUROI. Victors in the associated Pythian games set up dedications, one of which was the bronze charioteer. A further dedication, set up after the Persian wars by the Greeks, was the Plataean monument consisting of twined snakes supporting a cauldron (see BYZANTIUM).

Delta the greater part of LOWER EGYPT, comprising the fan-like alluvial plain formed by the branches of the River Nile, which begin to diverge immediately to the north of CAIRO. Archaeological sites in the Delta (e.g. TANIS,

BUBASTIS) tend to be less well preserved than their UPPER EGYPTian counterparts because of their less arid natural setting.

demography the study of populations, in particular their size and composition. Its value in archaeology lies in providing information on the vital relationship between the subsistence economy, the environment and individual populations. The absolute size of a prehistoric population is extremely difficult to estimate; because of this, relative estimates based on such factors as changes in the numbers of settlements, sites and houses through time are often preferred. The study of human skeletons can give further clues as to the age and sex composition of a population, as well as to the prevalence of particular diseases or dietary patterns. See also CARRYING CAPACITY.

demotic (*Gk* 'of the people') the cursive script that succeeded the HIERATIC, from the 7th century BC to the 5th century AD, as the script used in Egyptian documents. Demotic was probably a more faithful written form of vernacular speech than hieratic, the use of which was continued for religious texts.

Denali complex a prehistoric culture or complex in Alaska containing wedge-shaped microcores, microblades, burins and bifacial points. Although most Denali sites date to c.10,500–7000 BP, microblades have recently been dated to more than 11,500 BP at the Swan Point site and represent the earliest known culture in Alaska. An even older microblade assemblage may be present in the Yukon at BLUEFISH CAVES. The Denali complex appears closely related to the Siberian DYUKTAI CULTURE, and was defined by West in 1967.

denarius a Roman silver coin, probably first struck in the late 3rd century BC. A wide range of designs were shown, and under the republic they often bore an image of the moneyer's ancestor. Under Augustus there were eighty-four denarii to the Roman pound (327.45 g [11.56 oz]).

Denbigh Flint complex a prehistoric culture or complex found in northwestern Alaska dating to roughly 4200–3000 BP. Artifacts include microblades, bipointed projectile blades, triangular harpoon heads and gravers. House plans are typically round. Coastal sites were apparently occupied during warmer months for seal hunting, and represent an early arctic maritime adaptation. The Denbigh Flint complex is considered part of the ARCTIC SMALL TOOL TRADITION, which is widespread in Arctic and Subarctic regions of North America. It may be derived from the older AMERICAN PALAEO-ARCTIC TRADITION. The Denbigh Flint complex was defined by Giddings on the basis of his discoveries at Iyatayet in 1948.

Dendera a site in UPPER EGYPT, its principal feature being the well-preserved temple of the goddess Hathor. The present temple and its subsidiary buildings (including two MAMMISI) are almost all the work of the PTOLEMYS and Roman emperors up to the reign of TRAJAN. On the desert edge behind the temple is an important cemetery of MASTABA tombs of the OLD KINGDOM to First INTERMEDIATE PERIOD.

Dendra or **Dhendra** the site of a Bronze Age cemetery in the Argolid, Greece. Greek and Swedish excavations have revealed a Middle HELLADIC tumulus, an intact MYCENAEAN THOLOS tomb of the 15th–14th centuries BC and rich CHAMBER TOMBs, one of which produced a bronze suit of armour. The associated settlement may be the Mycenaean citadel of Midea, which was fortified in the 13th century BC.

dendrochronology a biological dating method based on tree-ring sequences used to date timbers and other logs from archaeological structures and sites. Each year, trees add a ring of growth, and the age of living trees is determined by counting their growth rings. Climatic conditions affect the growth of trees as expressed by the width of these rings; during dry years ring width is relatively thin, and during moist years it is relatively thick. Hence, trees of the same species and similar age in an area affected by similar climatic conditions will exhibit similar sequences of ring widths. By finding older and younger trees that overlap in age, a relative chronology can be constructed to which the tree-ring pattern of timber finds can be compared. Absolute ages can be obtained by overlapping tree-ring sequences up to living trees. The longest (oldest) sequence to date is based on the BRISTLECONE PINE for western America and extends back 9,000 years. A sequence that is not linked to living trees is referred to as a FLOATING CHRONOLOGY and is only useful for relative chronologies in the region from which they are derived. Radiocarbon dating can provide approximate ages for the floating chronologies.

Tree-ring series are also used to identify and date palaeoclimatic changes. Statistical models that relate tree-ring width and growth rate of living trees to historic climatic parameters affecting tree growth are then applied to prehistoric changes in ring width to infer past climatic conditions. See also DOUGLASS.

dendroglyph see CARVED TREE.

dendrogram a strip chart recording the analysis of tree-ring widths for a sample or samples, which is compared to a master CHRONOLOGY in DENDROCHRONOLOGY studies.

Dene see ATHABASCAN.

Denekamp Interstadial a warm period occurring during the middle PLENIGLACIAL phase of the last (WEICHSEL) GLACIATION in Europe at c.30,000 BP.

Denisova Cave a Palaeolithic site on the Anuj River in the Altai region of Siberia. At least sixteen cultural layers have been identified in a sequence of sandy loam and clay deposits; associated faunal remains have not been studied, and only preliminary results are available concerning artifacts. The uppermost 5–6 layers are assigned to the Upper Palaeolithic and contain scrapers, burins and some typical Middle Palaeolithic tools. The lower layers contain Middle Palaeolithic assemblages (e.g. scrapers and denticulates). Presumably, most or all of the cultural layers date to the last GLACIAL. Denisova Cave appears to be one of the most important sites for the study of the Middle/Upper Palaeolithic transition in northern Asia. It was discovered and excavated by Ovodov 1977–84.

Excavations continued in the 1990s, and material was unearthed from different periods up to the Middle Ages. Among the most interesting finds are bone fragments and teeth that may tentatively be assigned to the NEANDERTHALS, dated by ^{14}C to 42,000 bp.

Dent a PALAEOINDIAN site in northern Colorado, USA, where the first CLOVIS points were found in 1932, although they were not recognized as being a new point type by their excavators. The site also provided the first unequivocal evidence for the association of stone projectile points and mammoth remains. A radiocarbon date of approximately 11,200 BP was later obtained from site material.

denticulate 1 a flake or blade tool with a series of notches removed from one edge to give a tooth-like working edge.
2 the name given by BORDES to one of the south-western French MOUSTERIAN variants, whose tool-kit contains few scrapers but a high proportion of notched and denticulate pieces.

depas or **depas amphikypellon** the Homeric term which SCHLIEMANN used to describe the two-handled cups which he found in EARLY BRONZE AGE contexts at TROY.

depositional environment the sum total of sedimentary and biological conditions, factors and processes that characterize an area and result in a deposit or series of deposits that reflect those circumstances. Archaeological debris is deposited within a depositional system and is subject to the circumstances of that system during its evolution. Conversely, understanding a depositional en-vironment implies knowledge about factors and pro-cesses that may have influenced occupation and subsequent transformations of the archaeological record. See also LITHOFACIES, LITHOFACIES ANALYSIS.

Dereivka a late Neolithic settlement and cemetery site in Ukraine, located on a tributary of the Dnieper River. Dereivka is a site of the SREDNI STOG culture. The settle-ment component covers about 3,000 sq. m (3,600 sq. yds), with several traces of dwellings as well as hearths and other features. The faunal sample from these de-posits was dominated by horse bones, probably of dom-esticated animals. Antler artifacts believed to be cheekpieces imply that the Dereivka horses were used for riding.

Desert tradition/culture the concept of an adaptation of combined hunting and gathering and incipient food production in marginal environments, representing a relatively static adaptation up to modern times. The con-cept, devised by J. Jennings at DANGER CAVE (which, it was later realized, had been a lakeshore settlement, not a desert camp), originally referred to prehistoric societies in the Great Basin and southwestern United States showing an initial dependence on agriculture. It was then extended to groups from Canada to Guatemala. Nine-teenth-century Indian groups in the Great Basin were considered modern analogues. The Desert tradition, dating from about 9000 BP to European contact, is characterized by a nomadic, wide-spectrum hunting and gathering economy; its material culture includes grinding stones, basketry, a variety of smaller projectile points than those associated with large game hunting, and an absence of ceramics.

desert varnish a chemical crust of bacterial origin, con-sisting of oxides, that is deposited on exposed rock, arti-fact and PETROGLYPH surfaces. A type of rock varnish,

desert varnish can be used in CATION RATIO DATING. It may also have incorporated organic matter that can provide an age by ACCELERATOR MASS SPECTROMETER RADIOCARBON DATING.

Developed Oldowan (A, B, C) a series of EARLIER STONE AGE industries of the OLDOWAN industrial complex rec-ognized at OLDUVAI GORGE and other African sites, dating from about 1.6 to almost 0.6 million years ago, but differing from the classic Oldowan industry in having relatively more spheroids and sub-spheroids as well as light-duty artifacts like scrapers.

Devensian see WEICHSEL.

Deverel-Rimbury a Bronze Age culture of southern Britain, known both from burial mounds with inurned cremations and from settlement sites such as the small farmsteads of Itford Hill and New Barn Down (Sussex) and from the enclosure at South Lodge (Wiltshire). The characteristic pottery form is the simple coarse Bucket urn. Deverel-Rimbury sites are found throughout southern and eastern England in the period 1400–1200 BC (Middle Bronze Age), but the origins can now be traced back several centuries to the Early Bronze Age.

Devil's Lair a limestone cave in Western Australia, exca-vated by Charles Dortch and Duncan Merrilees, with one of the longest occupation sequences in Australia, in-cluding well-defined hearths and occupation floors and a rich faunal assemblage. The cave was occupied intermit-tently from about 45,000 to about 12,000 bp. Stone arti-facts include a range of small retouched flakes and scrapers of chert or quartz and limestone artifacts. Bone points were also found, as well as several bone beads made from *macropod* (kangaroo/wallaby) fibulae. Nearby Tunnel Cave also has Pleistocene occupation.

Devil's Tower see GIBRALTAR.

Devon Downs a limestone shelter on the Lower Murray River, South Australia, with 6 m (20 ft) of rich deposits spanning the last 6,000 years, where Hale and TINDALE conducted the first scientific excavation in Australia in 1929. This provided the basis for Tindale's pioneering attempt to establish an Australian culture sequence.

Dhang Rial a mound near Wun Rok in southern Sudan with a two-phase IRON AGE sequence beginning about AD 500, overlying a ceramic LATER STONE AGE occu-pation.

Dhar Tichitt an area of southern Mauretania, Africa, which has produced evidence of grain domestication in the 2nd millennium BC from plant impressions in pottery.

Dhendra see DENDRA.

Dhimini a prehistoric settlement mound in Thessaly, Greece. In the late Neolithic period an elaborate system of walls was erected, possibly to protect a large ME-GARON. The elegant bichrome pottery in use at this time characterizes the Dhimini culture. Two THOLOS tombs date from the MYCENAEAN period when an extensive settlement developed around the mound.

Dhlo Dhlo see DANANGOMBE.

diachronic *adj.* **1** relating to development through time, as compared with SYNCHRONIC.
  2 (applied to bounding surfaces, or rock units with one or more bounding surfaces) not synchronous, but rather of different ages in different locations, or time transgressive. See also ISOCHRONOUS.

diamicton or **diamict** a sediment or soil texture comprising larger than sand-size clasts in, and supported by, a MATRIX of sand, silt and clay, regardless of origin. Many GLACIAL debris-flow and colluvial deposits are accurately described as diamictons. The term was defined to avoid confusion with the misuse of the generic term 'TILL' and its derivatives. It is now recognized that much of the material traditionally called 'till' was actually deposited by post-depositional mass movements that redeposited original till material.

Dian [Tien] a regionally distinctive Bronze Age culture centred on Lake Dian in Yunnan Province, China, dating to the late 1st millennium BC. Bronze drums resembling those from the Southeast Asian DONG SON culture reveal southward connections, while trade was active with the southern ZHOU states Shu and Ba to the north and with the HAN Dynasty thereafter. See also CHINESE DYNASTIES.

Diana a site on the Aeolian island of Lipari, north of Sicily, which gave its name to a local late Neolithic culture (*c.*3050 bc) of the islands, Sicily and southern Italy, which is characterized by red pottery (linked to Red Skorba – see SKORBA). The culture is linked to sites on Lipari where obsidian was exploited, and to early copper metallurgy here. Burials took place in oval stone-edged pits.

diaphysis the shaft of a long bone. Compare EPIPHYSIS.

diatomites sediments formed mainly from the silicate exoskeletons of DIATOMS found in lakes, for example in the Sahara and East Africa, during moist periods of the last 2 million years. Radiocarbon dating of calcium carbonate concretions on the surface of diatomites to provide terminal dates for when the lakes were at their capacity is considered problematic.

diatoms single-celled algae which grow in marine or fresh water and secrete silicious skeletons that are morphologically distinct by species. Diatom skeletons are sampled at different depth-intervals from DEEP-SEA CORES or lake cores for identification and analyses of ISOTOPIC composition, fossil assemblage composition and morphological changes, in order to determine alter-ations in PALAEOENVIRONMENTAL factors. See also DIATOMITES.

Didyma the extramural sanctuary of MILETUS, Turkey, probably dating back to the 8th century BC. During the ARCHAIC period the sanctuary attracted a number of wealthy dedications, some of which were removed during the PERSIAN sack after the Ionian revolt. The reconstructed HELLENISTIC temple included a NAISKOS inside the ADYTON.

Die Kelders a cave on the southern coast of the Western Cape Province of South Africa with a 7 m (23 ft) deposit containing MIDDLE STONE AGE remains separated from a SHELL MIDDEN, which accumulated in the first five centuries AD, by thick sterile sands. The shell midden documents the first well-described discovery of domesticated sheep in a southern Africa LATER STONE AGE context, and also contains some of the earliest Later Stone Age pottery in southern Africa. The Middle Stone Age deposits include fragmentary, arguably anatomically modern, human remains.

Dieng a complex of Hindu temples built by the rulers of MATARAM in the late 8th and 9th centuries AD around the volcanic hot springs of the mountains of northern-central Java. Most were probably CANDI.

differential fluxgate gradiometer see MAGNETO-METER.

diffusion a process whereby ideas, objects or cultural traits are transferred from one culture or society to another. It is an important explanatory concept in CULTURE HISTORY.

Dilmun see PERSIAN GULF TRADE.

Dimolit a Neolithic open settlement site in northern Luzon, northern Philippines, occupied from *c.*2500 BC, with links in pottery to later phases at MUSANG CAVE and early material at Arku Cave, both of which have yielded items paralleled in Taiwanese Neolithic sites.

ding [ting] a legged tripod first occurring in the Chinese Neolithic in ceramic (see CISHAN), then in the SHANG period in bronze. The category includes tripods and quadrapods. Bronze ding often bear TAOTIE designs.

Dingcun [Ting-ts'un] a Middle Palaeolithic site group in Shanxi Province, China, which yielded human fossil remains and large flake tools including choppers and prismatic points, with some stone balls. It is the type-site of the Dingcun culture in the Fen River area.

dingo an Australian dog, one of the few pre-European placental mammals in Australia and a Holocene introduction. The earliest secure dates are all between 3500 and 3000 bp at Wombah, New South Wales, Madura Cave and FROMMS LANDING; it is not found in TASMANIA. Its origins are unknown but its closest relatives are

Southeast Asian indigenous domestic dogs. See also THYLACINE.

dinos a Greek round-bottomed cauldron which would have been placed on a stand or tripod. Several bronze examples have survived, and clay ones are decorated in the BLACK-FIGURED and RED-FIGURED techniques. They were probably intended for the mixing of wine, and were part of the equipment for the SYMPOSIUM.

Diouwar see FABOURA.

Diprotodon a giant marsupial, a rhinoceros-sized wombat-like animal, the largest of the extinct Australian species of Pleistocene MEGAFAUNA.

direct historical approach a technique developed in the 1930s by W. D. STRONG and others for extending knowledge of the historic period into the prehistoric period. The technique consists of identifying the historic period occupants of a site through documentary evidence. The site, including its prehistoric components, is then excavated and cultural continuity is established between the two periods. This allows the use of analogy, and more importantly homology, in the study of prehistoric cultures at the site and elsewhere in the surrounding region.

Diring a prehistoric open-air site on the Lena River in northeastern Siberia at latitude 61° north. A series of late Neolithic burials assigned to the Ymyakhtakh culture were found on a high terrace in 1982. Subsequent investigation uncovered an assemblage of quartzite cores, pebble choppers and flakes buried in AEOLIAN deposits. Recent THERMOLUMINESCENCE dates on the aeolian sediment indicate that the artifacts are more than 260,000 years old. The site remains controversial, and some have suggested that the artifacts are naturally fractured rocks.

disc barrow see BARROW.

discoidal nucleus technique an efficient prepared-core-knapping technique which became relatively common during the Middle Palaeolithic. The core is worked in a manner similar to that used in the LEVALLOIS TECHNIQUE, with flaking continued until the core is too small to use.

disconformity a type of unconformity separating essentially parallel strata that can represent a significant period of non-deposition. Recognition is important for correct interpretation of archaeological site STRATIGRAPHY.

Disney, John (1779–1857) the founder of the Disney Chair of Archaeology in Cambridge University. A barrister by training, he inherited a collection of classical sculpture formed in Italy during the 18th century. Having originally displayed his antiquities in his house in Essex, Disney prepared a published catalogue of them, the *Museum*

Disneianum, and then presented them to Cambridge for display in the Fitzwilliam Museum.

Dissignac a Neolithic burial mound in Loire-Atlantique, France, containing two PASSAGE GRAVES side by side. Remains of a settlement beneath the mound yielded microliths, early Neolithic pottery and a PALAEOSOL with pollen of cultivated cereals dated by radiocarbon to c.4000 BC.

distal *adj.* remote from the point of origin. For example, distal ALLUVIAL FAN means the toe of the fan where it merges with a valley floor, well removed from the apex of the fan and adjacent mountain front, valley wall or escarpment; the finger is at the distal end of the human arm, furthest from its point of attachment to the body. Compare PROXIMAL.

distance-decay function a mathematical model that expresses the inverse ratio between the quantity of a particular substance and the distance from its source. It is especially useful in formulating models of prehistoric trade and exchange.

distributional archaeology an approach that emphasizes the collection and analysis of high-resolution spatial and attribute data of artifacts and features in order to address archaeological issues. The emphasis is on the individual pieces of archaeological deposits rather than on the unit of an archaeological site.

Diuktai see DYUKTAI CULTURE.

Divostin a Neolithic site in Serbia, with occupations of the STARČEVO (c.6500–5800 BC) (Divostin I) and VINČA (c.5500–4000 BC) (Divostin II) cultures. Divostin I features consisted of many large pits and several surface structures. Divostin II features included a number of post structures and fired clay floors, including seven late Vinča house plans.

Djebel see JEBEL.

Djeitun a 0.5 ha (1 acre) site in southern Turkmenia where excavations revealed a 6th- (and even a late 7th-) millennium BC Neolithic culture, characterized by square mud-brick architecture, a hand-made pottery only a little of which is painted, and food production based on barley, wheat, sheep, goat and cattle, together with foraging. The settlements of this culture are generally small (0.5–2 ha [1–5 acres]), and are situated along the Kopet Dagh, including sites at Togolok, Cagalli and Chopan, as well as Djeitun itself. This archaeological culture marks the earliest Neolithic of Central Asia, and may have been a centre of domestication for bread wheat. AMS dates from plant remains suggest that the site may only have been used for a few centuries.

Djenne see JENNÉ-JENO.

Djetis see JETIS.

Djoser an Egyptian king of the 3rd Dynasty, during the OLD KINGDOM. His step pyramid at SAQQARA (attributed to the architect Imhotep) represents a major technological advance on the earlier royal MASTABA tombs.

Dmanisi an open-air site in Georgia, Transcaucasia, where a human mandible and associated artifacts and faunal remains were recovered from sandy loam overlying a volcanic basalt layer. The basalt is dated to 1.8 million years ago, but the mandible and artifacts may be significantly younger. Mammal remains include Early Pleistocene taxa (e.g. *Archidiskodon meridionalis*). The human mandible has been classified as HOMO *erectus*. The artifacts are made chiefly from siliceous volcanic rock, and include cores, pebble tools and retouched flakes. Two human skulls were recovered here in 1999.

DNA see MITOCHONDRIAL DNA.

Dnepr-Donets culture a prehistoric culture of the middle and lower Dnepr basin in Ukraine, contemporaneous with the CUCUTENI A culture of Romania and the TRIPOLYE B1 culture of western Ukraine (4500–3900 BC), but with a mixed subsistence strategy in which hunted and gathered resources appear to have played a dominant role. Dolukhanov characterizes the Dnepr-Donets culture as a 'CERAMIC MESOLITHIC' group and views the presence of domestic cattle bones as due to trade.

Dniester-Bug see BUG-DNIESTER.

Dobranichevka an Upper Palaeolithic open-air site on the Supoj River (Dnepr tributary) in central Ukraine. The occupation is apparently buried in slope deposits comprising the upper FACIES of the second terrace; it yielded a single AMS radiocarbon date of 12,700 bp. The faunal remains are dominated by woolly mammoth, and the excavators uncovered a total of four MAMMOTH-BONE HOUSES with associated pits, hearths and debris concentrations. In this respect, Dobranichevka is very similar to MEZHIRICH and MEZIN.

Doc Chua a rich Bronze Age settlement and cemetery in the Dong Nai River Valley, 35 km (22 miles) north of Ho Chi Minh City, southern Vietnam, with more than thirty burials and over fifty casting moulds for bronze axes. The axe types link southern Vietnam with the KHORAT Plateau of Thailand, while thirteen bronze HALBERDS of GE (*guo* in Chinese) type show a familiarity with the weapons of WARRING STATES China, although the surface decoration is in the DONG SON tradition, as with another nineteen such weapons from nearby Long Giao. Dates suggest two phases of occupation in the late 2nd and mid 1st millennium BC.

Dodona the oracle of the god Zeus in northern Greece. Excavations in the TEMENOS have uncovered many bronze dedications including tripods. Remains include a theatre and HELLENISTIC STADIUM.

Doian see EIBIAN.

Doigahama an early-to-middle YAYOI cemetery site in Yamaguchi Prefecture, Japan, first excavated by T. Kanaseki in 1953. His analysis of the skeletal remains, which distinguishes a physical type different from the PALAEO-ASIATIC JOMON, supports the hypothesis of substantial migration from the mainland during Yayoi into western Japan.

Dölauer Heide a Neolithic hilltop settlement of the FUNNEL BEAKER culture in southeastern Germany. Fortifications, consisting of up to five bank-and-ditch systems in places, enclose a hilltop area of 25 ha (62 acres). Traces of a palisade were also identified here and there. On the spurs of the hilltop, outside the fortification, are a number of barrows.

dolichocephalic see CEPHALIC INDEX.

dolium a Roman large coarse-ware container. They could be sunk into the ground and were probably used for storing olive oil and wine. Some have been found set into the hulls of shipwrecks, making the ships an early version of 'supertankers'.

dolmen **1** a traditional French term for a megalithic tomb consisting of ORTHOSTATS and capstone, probably derived from the Cornish *tolmên*, a natural feature in which boulders support a 'capstone' to form a kind of chamber.
   2 (*East Asia*) a megalithic stone burial feature in western China (Tibet, Sichuan, Gansu) and the coastal areas of the Yellow Sea basin (the Shandong peninsula in China, the Korean peninsula and northwestern Kyushu in Japan). Mainly dated to the 1st millennium BC, these dolmens occur in three forms: raised table, low table and unsupported capstone. Polished stone implements are the characteristic grave-goods. See also BRONZE AGE.

Dolní Věstonice an Upper Palaeolithic open-air site located along the Dyje River in Moravia, Czech Republic. Artifacts and faunal remains (such as woolly mammoth

DOLMEN: a typical example, Poulnanbrone in Ireland.

[predominant], horse, reindeer) are buried in loess deposits. The main cultural layer is dated by radiocarbon and stratigraphic correlation to the beginning of the LAST GLACIAL MAXIMUM (25,000 BP). Multiple hearths and traces of a large former structure are present. The assemblage contains burins, scrapers and backed blades, and is assigned to the EASTERN GRAVETTIAN. Among the many art objects are hundreds of animal and human figurines of fired loess, including a 'VENUS' FIGURINE. Dolní Věstonice was excavated by ABSOLON and others. A number of human remains have also been uncovered, including a triple burial.

domestication the process by which species of plants and animals are transformed by deliberate human intervention from a wild form which can exist independent of humans to one which is dependent on humans for its propagation. Domesticated plants are the result of human selection for specific desirable characteristics, such as large fruits, ease of harvesting and rapid germination. Domesticated animals have been controlled and tamed, then selected for desirable characteristics as sources of meat, milk, wool, draught power and companionship. The systematic practice of intentional behaviour to change the properties of wild species lies behind the emergence of agriculture as the primary human subsistence about 10,000 years ago in the Old World and at least 5,000 years ago in the New World. This was a fundamental change in the relationship between people and their environment which had profound consequences for technology, SETTLEMENT PATTERNS and social organization.

Domica a 5 km (3 mile) long KARST cave in eastern Slovakia, continued on the Hungarian side as the Aggtelek cave. The stratified deposits in the Domica/Aggtelek cave have provided considerable information on the development of the LINEAR POTTERY culture in the upper Tisza basin in southeastern Slovakia and northeastern Hungary, particularly the BÜKK group.

Donau see GÜNZ GLACIATION.

Dongbei [Tung-pei] the northeastern region of present-day China, including the Manchurian basin and BOHAI Bay, composed of Liaoning, Heilongjiang and Jilin Provinces. This region is often treated separately from the archaeology of the North China Plain, and includes the easternmost extension of the NORTHERN ZONE.

Dong Dau a multi-period site in Vinh Phu Province in the middle Red River Valley, northern Vietnam, which has given its name to the early Bronze Age phase of the area from c.1400 to 1100 BC which was followed by the GO MUN phase. Bronze tools and weapons are quite common, as are remains of domesticated rice.

Donggou an obsolete placename for the plains of Ji'an

City in Jilin Province, China, where the state of KOGURYO made its capital in the 3rd–5th centuries AD.

Dong Son a site in the Ma River Valley of northern Vietnam, discovered in the mid 1920s and excavated many times since. It gave its name to the late Bronze and early Iron Age period (c.700 BC–AD 200) in the region. Dong Son culture is best known for its rich burials, many in log coffins, furnished with cast-bronze drums, SITULAE (buckets), bells, jewellery and other ornaments and weapons, including daggers with human figures as handles. Objects from the graves include bronze jewellery, glass beads from South Asia or other parts of Southeast Asia, Chinese items including some HAN coins, mirrors, weapons and bronze vessels. The drums of the period (classed as Heger I) were traded in large numbers west and south into the mainland of Southeast Asia, northwest into DIAN in Yunnan and by sea to the Malay peninsula, Sumatra, Java, Bali and numerous islands bordering the Java and Banda Seas. The patterns on these drums were incorporated into the design repertoire of much of island Southeast Asia. The major sites include Chao Can (eight log-coffin burials, c.600–200 BC), Viet Khe (opulent log-coffin burials with up to 100 artifacts each, including Chinese imports, c.600–200 BC), Lang Ca (314 burials), Lang Vac and CO LOA (possibly the capital of the early state of AU LAC, c.3rd century BC). The end of the period overlaps with that of early Chinese conquest, just before 100 BC.

Don Noi an open site in Kanchanburi Province, western Thailand, with an extensive CHALCEDONY workshop for flaked adzes and bracelets. It may be late Neolithic to early metal age, but dating is unclear.

Dorak a site just south of the Sea of Marmora in northwestern Anatolia, famous for the report of two looted 'royal tombs' of the Yortan culture. In the 1950s, J. Mellaart was shown the materials from the two tombs and allowed to draw and describe, but not to photograph, these objects. According to Mellaart's description, the preservation in the two cist tombs was excellent, allowing recovery of textiles, as well as an extremely rich array of objects in precious metal, stone and other materials (including turquoise, amber, lapis lazuli), vessels and weapons of gold, silver, electrum, bronze and iron. The Dorak materials vanished immediately after Mellaart's report, causing a considerable controversy, and leaving the status and even the actual existence of the Dorak tombs in doubt.

Dorian a Greek dialect spoken in the Peloponnese, the southern Aegean islands and on the southwest coast of Asia Minor. It seems likely that it was introduced into southern Greece late in the 2nd millennium BC, but the tradition that a Dorian invasion brought about the collapse of the MYCENAEAN civilization has been discredited.

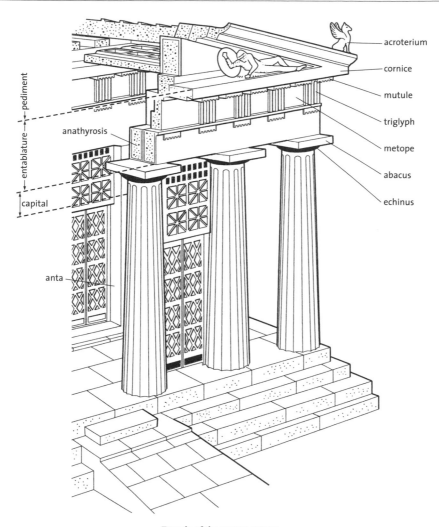

acroterium

cornice

mutule

triglyph

metope

abacus

echinus

anathyrosis

anta

pediment

entablature

capital

Temple of the DORIC ORDER.

Doric order a scheme of architecture widely used in the mainland of Greece and the Greek colonies in the western Mediterranean. The columns have no base. The CAPITAL is formed by a distinctive ECHINUS and ABACUS. The ENTABLATURE comprises a plain ARCHITRAVE, and above that alternating TRIGLYPHS and METOPES. See also PARTHENON.

Dörpfeld, Wilhelm (1853–1940) a German archaeologist who trained as an architect and excavated first at OLYMPIA, and then at TROY as SCHLIEMANN's assistant and later, in 1893–4, as his successor. Subsequently he undertook excavations on LEUKAS which he identified as the Homeric Ithaca, home of Odysseus.

Dorset a prehistoric ESKIMO culture of the eastern Arctic which originated about 1000 BC and lasted until AD 1000, when it was replaced by the THULE culture. The Dorset culture was dependent on the hunting of sea-mammals, although caribou were taken with the spear. It is noted for the development of beautiful carvings in wood, bone and ivory of human and animal forms, some realistic, others supernatural.

Dosariyah a small surface site near the coast in the Eastern Province of Saudi Arabia, perhaps the best representative of the 'UBAID interaction with the Persian Gulf. In addition to the 'Ubaid 3–4 pottery and chipped stone, the site contains a fauna that consists largely of sheep/goat, cattle and gazelle, the first two of which are probably domesticates.

Dos Pilas the largest MAYA city in the Petexbatun region of Guatemala during the late CLASSIC. It grew increasingly bellicose, and by AD 700 had absorbed several neighbouring sites such as Aguateca. Intensification of warfare (as shown by fortifications in the terminal Classic) may ultimately have caused the collapse of the Petexbatun POLITIES. The tomb of a Late Classic ruler with a spectacular head-dress ('Ruler 2', AD 698–725) was recently discovered by A. Demarest at the base of a TEMPLE MOUND.

dotaku a type of bronze bell peculiar to YAYOI period Japan. Cast from melted-down continental bronzes, the bells were originally functional with clappers, but became progressively ceremonialized and heavily decorated. Mainly limited to the SETOUCHI and TOKAI regions, they were buried in isolated caches on hilltops, and they are thought to have played a role in agricultural fertility rituals.

double axe a cutting tool which has two blades and consequently does not have to be sharpened as often as a single axe. In MINOAN CRETE the double axe was one of the most common religious symbols. Votive double axes, sometimes set between HORNS OF CONSECRATION, were frequently dedicated in shrines and sanctuaries. The cult status of double axes may have derived from their use as a sacrificial implement.

Douglass, Andrew Ellicott (1867–1962) an American astronomer who devised the DENDROCHRONOLOGY dating method as early as 1901. In 1929 he published the first continuous tree-ring sequence for the southwestern United States. It extended far enough back from modern times to be useful in dating southwestern PUEBLO villages.

Dowris a large hoard of over 200 bronzes, from Co. Offaly, Ireland, including 44 spearheads, 43 axes, 24 trumpets and 44 bells or rattles. The hoard is dated to the 8th century BC and has given its name to the Dowris phase of the Irish Late Bronze Age.

Drachenloch a Swiss Alpine cave-site at 2,245 m (7,365 ft) altitude, best known for its supposed evidence for a Middle Palaeolithic cave bear cult, including what was thought to be a stone cist containing bear skulls and piles of long bones of bears arranged along the cave walls. TAPHONOMIC studies have shown that all these features were almost certainly produced naturally by rockfalls and hibernating bears. Compare LES FURTINS.

drachma a unit of silver coinage in the Greek world. It was equivalent to six OBOLS. At ATHENS they were decorated with the motifs of Athena's head and her owl; thus they acquired the name 'owls'. At Athens they weighed 4.31 g (0.15 oz) and on Aegina 6.30 g (0.22 oz). They could be issued in multiples of a drachma, for example the *didrachm* (2 drachmas), the *tetradrachm* (4 drachmas) or the *dekadrachm* (10 drachmas). See also STATER.

Dragendorff, Hans (1870–1941) a German scholar who devised a classification scheme for shapes of TERRA SIGILLATA, published in 1895–6.

Drakensberg a South African mountain range forming the southern and eastern boundary with Lesotho, particularly known for its remarkable abundance of LATER STONE AGE rock paintings, especially those of eland. Some of these are interpreted by certain scholars in terms of the trance hallucinations of 'shamans'.

Drakhmani see ELATEIA.

Drehem ancient Puzrish-Dagan, an UR III administrative centre near NIPPUR in southern MESOPOTAMIA. Clandestine excavations brought to the antiquities market thousands of CUNEIFORM tablets that record official transactions, particularly having to do with taxation and disbursements in kind (cattle and other animals).

drift a collective term for any or all debris of all textures transported and deposited by or from GLACIAL ice and meltwater derived from the ice.

Drimolen a sinkhole containing early HOMINID fossils and faunal remains estimated to date between 2.5 and 1.6 million years ago, located about 7 km (4 miles) northwest of STERKFONTEIN in Gauteng Province, South Africa. The large collection of hominid fossils catalogued since its discovery in 1992 includes specimens of AUSTRALOPITHECUS *(Paranthropus) robustus* as well as early HOMO.

dromos the entrance passage of MINOAN-MYCENAEAN THOLOS and CHAMBER TOMBS.

Druids name given by Roman writers including Pliny and Julius Caesar to the native priesthood of Gaul and Britain, who were a focus of resistance to the expansion of Roman rule. They were noted as repositories of traditional learning, which they passed down orally from generation to generation. Hostile Roman sources make much of their presence at sacrifices, both human and animal, but they were also associated with sacred groves and mistletoe. Druidical learning died with the Druids in the 1st century AD, but the Druids became a subject of romantic interest in the 18th century, leading to the foundation of the Ancient Order of Druids in London in 1781. The modern-day Druids hold ceremonies at STONEHENGE at the midsummer solstice, though there is no evidence of any kind to link Stonehenge with the Druids described by the CLASSICAL sources.

Dry Creek a multi-component open-air site on the Nenana River in the northern foothills of the Alaska Range, southern-central Alaska, USA. Three cultural layers are buried in deposits of loess and windblown sand on the margin of an ancient terrace. The lowest layer contains a small assemblage with a bifacial point and poorly preserved remains of sheep and *wapiti* (red deer). It is dated to 11,120 bp and assigned to the NENANA COMPLEX. The middle cultural layer contains a large microblade assemblage assigned to the DENALI COMPLEX, dated to 10,690 bp and associated with remains of steppe bison and sheep. A small assemblage with side-notched points, classified as NORTHERN ARCHAIC and dated to 4670–3430 bp, was recovered from the upper layer. Dry Creek represents the most important early prehistoric site in Alaska; it was excavated by Powers in 1973–7.

Dryas a series of cold climatic phases in northwestern Europe, named after a tundra plant, when the climate of the North Atlantic returned to almost full GLACIAL conditions. Dryas I started *c.*16,000 or 14,000 BP; Dryas II (*Older Dryas*) was *c.*12,300–11,800 bp; and Dryas III (*Younger Dryas*) from *c.*11,000–10,000 bp.

Dubois, Eugène (1858–1941) a Dutch physician and palaeoanthropologist who discovered the HOMINID remains at TRINIL, Java, in 1891.

Dudeşti culture a middle Neolithic culture of southeastern Romania, contemporaneous with the VĂDASTRA immediately to the west, VINČA A/B (Vinča-Tordos) in the western Balkans, and KARANOVO III (VESELINOVO) in Bulgaria. Dudeşti pottery reflects the widespread shift in the Balkans during the late 6th millennium BC to the use of dark burnished pottery.

Dufaure see DURUTHY.

Duff, Roger (1912–78) a New Zealand archaeologist best known for his fundamental work *The Moa-hunter Period of Maori Culture*. He also excavated the WAIRAU BAR site and developed a typology for stone adzes of POLYNESIA and Southeast Asia.

Dufuna the site of an 8,000-year-old dugout canoe made from a hollowed-out tree trunk, discovered in 1987 in fluvial sediments on the Komadugu Gana, a large river system in northern Nigeria. It is the oldest known example of water craft from Africa.

Dumuzi a shepherd god, in SUMERIAN myth, who was the husband of INANNA, the union of pastoralist and agricultural production. A series of poems describe their courtship and wedding, followed by the death of Dumuzi by drowning. Inanna eventually succeeds in rescuing Dumuzi from death, but only at the cost of her own life; ENKI arranges affairs so that each lives for half the year. Dumuzi appears as Tammuz in later western Asian myth.

dun a fortified farmstead or residence, typically circular and surrounded by one or more banks and ditches. Duns (the word deriving from *dunum* or stronghold) were a common feature of the Irish landscape during the Iron Age and early Christian periods. The name is also applied to fortified sites in western and northern Britain, such as the BROCH of Dun Telve in Scotland.

Dundo a town in the Luemba Valley of northeastern Angola, where alluvial deposits of the Congo River have yielded a Stone Age sequence, mostly from secondary contexts, as well as fossil pollen assemblages.

dune a depositional landform made by mounds of sand deposited by the action of wind. Migration of active dunes can bury archaeological deposits. Relict dunes provide information for PALAEOENVIRONMENTAL reconstruction, such as general climatic conditions and prevailing palaeowind direction. Dunes are most commonly associated with deserts but also form in coastal areas and on sandy valley surfaces. Multiple dune forms are possible, depending on prevailing wind conditions, vegetation and the supply of sand. See also COVER SAND.

Dunhuang [Tun-huang] the site of the Mogao grottoes in northwestern China containing Buddhist sculptures and frescoes. The 492 surveyed caves stretch over 1.5 km (1 mile) of cliff face, all dating from the 5th–14th centuries AD (see CHINESE DYNASTIES). The artificially excavated grottoes follow two types of Indian cave temples: one with an ante-room and/or a corridor leading into the main chamber; the other with many niches or small rooms leading off the main chamber. Brightly painted frescoes cover more than 45,000 sq. m (54,000 sq. yds) of wall and ceiling space, and more than 2,000 sculptures are constructed in high relief with clay-surfaced, straw-covered wooden frames. Manuscripts and paintings obtained in 1905 by Aurel STEIN from caches at Dunhuang were brought to the British Museum.

Dura Europos a city founded around 300 BC on the right bank of the Euphrates River just north of the modern Syrian-Iraqi border. Excavations by French and American teams during the 1920s and 1930s, and renewed French work during the past decade, have traced the growth of this place from a relatively small unwalled town to a 180 ha (445 acre) walled city with a regular grid plan around 150 BC, to its destruction by SASSANIAN invaders around AD 250. A HELLENISTIC foundation in origin, the city stood in the borderlands between the Roman and PARTHIAN empires, and changed hands several times. Its frontier location exposed Dura Europos to many different traditions: excavations have found written records in Greek, Latin, Aramaic and other scripts, and temples of Greek, Roman, Parthian, western Syrian and Palmyrene gods. Particularly well preserved are sanctuaries of Mithras (an eastern cult favoured by Roman soldiers), a Christian chapel and a synagogue, the latter two created in private houses. Built during the final century of the city's existence, all three monuments have walls richly decorated with painted scenes from their respective cults.

Dur-Katlimmu see SHEIKH HAMAD, TELL.

Dur-Kurigalzu see AQAR QUF.

Dürnberg bei Hallein an Iron Age salt-mining centre in the Salzach Valley south of Salzburg in Austria. In the 5th century bc, Dürnberg eclipsed the large salt-mining complex at HALLSTATT, 40 km (25 miles) to the east, by reason of its position on the Salzach and the greater availability of land for agriculture and grazing on the flood plain. The remains of miners' settlements and graves have been found. Wealthy burials are common, and artifacts link Dürnberg with many other parts of Central Europe and the Mediterranean area.

Durrington Walls a major Neolithic HENGE monument in Wiltshire, England, with bank and ditch enclosing an oval area of 12 ha (30 acres). Within the enclosure, excavations by G. Wainwright revealed POSTHOLES of a large circular timber structure over 38 m (42 yds) across and a smaller one approximately 27 m (30 yds) across, which may have been houses or shrines. Among the pottery, late Neolithic GROOVED WARE is conspicuous. Radiocarbon tests date the henge to c.2600 BC.

Duruthy a major rockshelter in the Landes, southwestern France, excavated primarily by R. Arambourou from 1958 until the 1980s. It was occupied from at least the early MAGDALENIAN to the AZILIAN, and also contained some CHALCOLITHIC burials. The middle Magdalenian layers have been dated to the 14th millennium bp, and the late Magdalenian to the 12th millennium, when the site was a winter settlement for people exploiting reindeer and bovids. Very similar data have emerged from excavations by L. Straus at the nearby shelter of *Dufaure*. Duruthy's Magdalenian contains a wealth of PORTABLE ART, including fine carvings of horses, and a series of engraved carnivore canines.

Duvanli a 5th-century BC tumulus cemetery in Thrace (modern Bulgaria). The graves included imported ATHENIAN POTTERY, both RED-FIGURED and BLACK-GLOSSED, and several items of Greek GOLD-FIGURED silver plate.

Dvaravati an early MON state in central Thailand, for which few records have survived. It was mentioned in Chinese records of the 7th century AD and probably survived until the 11th century, when the region came under Khmer influence. The capital may have been located at NAKHON PATHOM, and such settlements as LOPBURI, U THONG and CHANSEN may have been attached to it. The term is applied to a style of Buddhist art heavily influenced by that of northern India's GUPTA Dynasty (4th–5th centuries AD) and to a lively indigenous style of terracotta modelling and stucco relief sculpture.

Dvuglazka Cave a Palaeolithic and Mesolithic site on the Tolchei River (Yenisei tributary) in southern-central Siberia. Artifacts and faunal remains are buried in a sequence of loam and rubble. The uppermost cultural layer contains a Mesolithic assemblage. A small quantity of Upper Palaeolithic artifacts was found, associated with remains of sheep and other mammals (including woolly mammoth) in an underlying cultural layer. The lower levels contain a sequence of small assemblages assigned to the Middle Palaeolithic and associated with remains of horse, woolly rhinoceros, steppe bison and sheep. The fauna appears to reflect a warm and dry climate (prior to the last GLACIAL?). The artifacts include LEVALLOIS CORES, many denticulates and some scrapers. Dvuglazka represents the northernmost Middle Palaeolithic locality in Asia; it was discovered and excavated by Abramova in 1974–9.

dyke a linear earthwork, usually a bank and ditch, that runs across country, either for defence or as a boundary (see OFFA'S DYKE).

dynasty nominally a line of hereditary rulers. The dynasties of Mesopotamia were distinguished by their places of origin, such as those of UR. In China (see CHINESE DYNASTIES), the dynasties often encompassed only regions rather than the whole country.

The dynastic divisions conventionally used to refer to periods of Egyptian history also include rulers seemingly not of the main royal line (e.g. at the end of the 18th Dynasty), but the term is nonetheless a useful point of reference.

Dyuktai Cave an Upper Palaeolithic site on the Dyuktai River (Aldan tributary) in northeastern Siberia. Five cultural layers are buried in sandy loam and rubble deposits; among the faunal remains are woolly mammoth, steppe bison, reindeer and elk. Radiocarbon estimates from the cultural layers range between 14,000 and 12,100 bp. The artifact assemblages are similar and contain wedge-shaped microcores, microblades, burins and bifacial points; they are assigned to the DYUKTAI CULTURE. Dyuktai Cave was discovered and excavated by Mochanov in 1967–70 and 1980–82.

Dyuktai culture an Upper Palaeolithic culture of northeastern Siberia dating to c.20,000–10,000 BP and possibly earlier. Diagnostic artifacts include wedge-shaped microcores, microblades, burins and bifacial points. Dyuktai assemblages have been found at DYUKTAI CAVE and a number of open-air sites in the Lena Basin, as well as open-air sites in western BERINGIA (e.g. USHKI LAKE). The Dyuktai culture appears closely related to the DENALI COMPLEX of Alaska and may be ancestral to the earliest lithic technologies, in particular the bifacially flaked points, of North America. It was defined by Mochanov in 1969.

Dzhruchula a Middle Palaeolithic cave on the Dzhruchula River in the southern foothills of the Greater Caucasus, altitude 600 m (1,970 ft), in Georgia. Two main cultural layers were distinguished in a sequence of loam and rubble. Faunal remains associated with the lower layer are predominantly of cave bear; those associated with the upper layer are chiefly of herbivores (e.g red deer). The age of the occupations is unknown, but they apparently occurred under mild climatic conditions. Tools from both layers are primarily scrapers and points; the upper assemblage reflects heavy emphasis on LEVALLOIS TECHNIQUE and blades. Dzhruchula was discovered and excavated by Tushabramishvili 1957–66.

Dzibilchaltún a large ceremonial MAYA site in northwestern Yucatán, Mexico, where about 8,400 structures have been mapped in an area of 19 sq. km (7 sq. miles). The supporting hinterland is estimated at 98 sq. km (38 sq. miles). The site is important for its almost continuous occupation from 500 BC to the present. Ninety per cent of the mapped structures were occupied during the late CLASSIC and early POSTCLASSIC, from AD 600 to 1000. The maximum population occurred in the later part of this period. From AD 1000 to 1200, the population dropped to less than 10 per cent of its former size.

The archaeological work of E. Wyllys Andrews IV and George Brainerd, begun in 1941 at this site, was interrupted by the Second World War. In 1956 and 1965 Andrews returned to resume work at the site.

Dzierzysław an Upper Palaeolithic open-air site located in Upper Silesia, Poland. Displaced artifacts are buried in loess and slope deposits. The cultural layer contains an assemblage (e.g. scrapers, laurel-leaf points) assigned to the SZELETIAN, which probably dates to the middle of the last GLACIAL.

E

Ea see ENKI.

Eanna sounding a deep test excavation in the Eanna precinct at WARKA which has a special place for studying the origins of writing and the state in southern MESOPOTAMIA. The eighteen-level sequence represents the 'UBAID (XVIII–XV), early URUK (XIV–IX), middle Uruk (VIII–VI), late Uruk (V–IV), JEMDET NASR (III) and EARLY DYNASTIC (II–I) periods (c.5000–2300 BC). The principal architectural exposures in the Eanna precinct belong to levels V–III, where a number of monumental buildings form a single complex whose function is usually assumed to be religious, but which also served a more broadly administrative purpose. The latter aspect is clearly visible in the presence in these levels of CYLINDER SEALS, scalings and written texts, all typical administrative artifacts of Mesopotamian civilization, here appearing for the first time. Economic texts first appear in Uruk IV, first with numbers only (IVb) and then with numbers together with words (IVa), and non-economic texts appear in Uruk III levels. Taken together with the rich small finds (especially of the Uruk III levels), the evidence from Warka indicates large economic organizations probably founded on religious and/or economic power over certain aspects of community life.

Earlier Stone Age or **Early Stone Age** the first stage of Stone Age technology in sub-Saharan Africa, dating from perhaps more than 2.5 million years ago to c.200,000 years ago or later (see MIDDLE AWASH). The earliest collections are considered representative of the OLDOWAN industrial complex, which was succeeded by the ACHEULIAN industrial complex shortly before 1.4 million years ago.

Early Bronze Age the period in the Levant during which towns and cities developed. The period is commonly divided into four phases: EBA I (3500–3100 BC), when Egyptian colonies appeared in the southern Levant and, late in the phase, walled towns emerged; EBA II (3100–2700 BC) and EBA III (2700–2300 BC), when walled towns were common through the region; and EBA IV (2300–2000/1950 BC), when animal herding and villages largely replaced town life. The AMORITES are traditionally thought to have been involved in the latter development.

Early Dynastic period 1 the chronological block between the JEMDET NASR and AKKADIAN periods in southern MESOPOTAMIA; the conventional date of the period is 2900–2330 BC, although calibrated radiocarbon dates for the previous periods suggest a slightly earlier beginning, and recent reconsiderations of later political chronologies may require a younger date for its end. The Early Dynastic period is divided into four phases (E.D. I, II, IIIa and IIIb, the last also called 'proto-imperial') on the basis of changes in pottery, seals and other aspects of the material culture. This archaeological definition was first achieved during the 1930s through work in the lower Diyala River (Tell ASMAR, Tell KHAFADJE); more recent work further south in Mesopotamia (ABU SALABIKH) has revealed regional differences that question the suitability of the Diyala results elsewhere in the region. Considerable development of the CUNEIFORM writing system occurred during this period, and for the first time contemporary royal inscriptions and more detailed economic texts are available for study; the period corresponds to most of the pre-Akkadian section of the SUMERIAN KING LISTS. This period thus represents the earliest conjunction of archaeological and written evidence for the social and political history of southern Mesopotamia.

2 (*Egypt*) see ARCHAIC PERIOD.

Early Horizon (800 BC–AD 100) the period during which the CHAVÍN culture, in Andean South America, flourished and culturally integrated the northern highlands and coast of Peru. After the collapse of Chavín, regional differentiation of culture areas increased, culminating in the complex cultures of the EARLY INTERMEDIATE PERIOD.

Early Intermediate period (AD 100–750) in Andean South America, a period of development of distinctive regional cultures, especially in the central Andean region. Two of the better known cultures are the MOCHE and NASCA civilizations, although numerous, less-studied (and artistically less spectacular) cultures occupied other regions of the coast and highlands. Out of this background emerged the first round of imperial expansions, in the MIDDLE HORIZON.

Early Kitchen ware see TANA WARE.

Early Later Stone Age (ELSA) an informal microlithic late Pleistocene Stone Age industry known from a few sites in South Africa. At BORDER CAVE it is characterized by minute backed pieces, bone points, ostrich eggshell beads and incised bone and wood.

Early Man shelter a site in southeastern Cape York peninsula, Australia, excavated by Andrée Rosenfeld. The lowest deposits date to about 13,000 bp and cover weathered and patinated PANARAMITEE-style engravings. The stone tool sequence is similar to MUSHROOM ROCK, while faunal remains, predominantly rock wallabies, and bone tools are preserved from deposits between 6,000 and 3,000 years old.

earth lodges structures, of varying shape and size and made of wood with an earthen covering, that served both habitation and ceremonial functions. The term is especially applied to structures found in some cultures of the American Midwest and East. Archaeologically, earth lodges are represented by hard-packed floors and/or POSTHOLES, which are the remains of wall and roof supports.

Easter Island the easternmost inhabited island of POLYNESIA, 3,700 km (2,300 miles) from South America and 2,200 km (1,370 miles) from Pitcairn Island. Now called Rapa Nui, it was christened by the Dutch commander Roggeveen, who found it on Easter Sunday 1722 and spent a few hours ashore observing the natives' way of life. After sporadic archaeological study in the late 19th and early 20th centuries, important work was done by Thor Heyerdahl's 1955 expedition, which first brought MULLOY here. The 166 sq. km (64 sq. mile) island is one huge Stone Age site, with hundreds of megalithic statues (MOAI) and platforms (AHU, and see VINAPU), house foundations, rock art, obsidian sources and stone-quarries in volcanic craters (see RANO RARAKU, PUNA PAU). Radiocarbon dates suggest a colonization by Polynesians in the first centuries AD. The island's extreme isolation led to unique cultural developments, notably the moai and the RONGORONGO 'script'. Relentless deforestation for timber and land-clearance caused soil erosion, devastated the economy and ended statue-transportation. Food shortages and probable population pressure led to a period of strife after c.AD 1600, when the MATAA were manufactured and the moai toppled, and which the birdman cult at ORONGO was designed to overcome through the choosing of an annual leader.

Eastern Anatolian Bronze Age see KURA-ARAXES CULTURE.

EASTER ISLAND: view from the ceremonial village of Orongo to the offshore islets, showing petroglyphs of birdmen.

Eastern Gravettian an Upper Palaeolithic industry or culture widely distributed across Central and eastern Europe during the LAST GLACIAL MAXIMUM (c.30,000–20,000 bp). The assemblages contain shouldered points and backed blades, and sometimes 'VENUS' FIGURINES; many sites have yielded evidence of MAMMOTH-BONE HOUSES. Compare GRAVETTIAN.

Eastern Stream see CHIFUMBAZE.

East Greek pottery pottery that was produced in numerous centres during the ARCHAIC PERIOD along the west coast of Turkey and the offshore Greek islands. Important centres include Chios (see CHIOT POTTERY), Samos, EPHESUS, MILETUS (see FIKELLURA WARE), Clazomenae and Rhodes, many of which have been recognized only as a result of chemical analysis. Related to this pottery production were painted clay SARCOPHAGI at Clazomenae.

East Spanish rock art see LEVANTINE.

East Turkana see KOOBI FORA.

Ebbsfleet see PETERBOROUGH.

Ebla a 56 ha (138 acre) site in northern Syria, some 70 km (43 miles) south of Aleppo. Now known as Tell Mardikh, it was the ancient Ebla, and Italian excavations since the 1960s have led to the discovery of a large 3rd-millennium archive, making the site one of the most important to be worked in the past generation. The multiple soundings in the site provide a sequence of six major periods, spanning the late 4th to late 1st millennia BC. The most significant discovery at the site, the archive of some 15,000 whole and fragmentary clay tablets within a palace complex (Palace G), belongs to the phase Mardikh IIB1 and is controversially dated to *c*.2400–2250 BC. These documents have generated considerable interpretative dispute, but in general reveal an unexpectedly rich and thriving urban state in Syria, interacting with neighbours to the north and east. Contemporary with the late EARLY DYNASTIC city-states and early AKKADIAN rulers in southern MESOPOTAMIA, the political and social aspects of Ebla show some similarities with the northern parts of the latter area (see KISH, ABU SALABIKH), but were nonetheless distinct.

Eboracum see YORK.

Eburran an East African obsidian industry, characterized by large backed blades, segments, scrapers and burins, formerly known as the 'Kenya Capsian'. It is restricted to a small area near Lake Nakuru in southern Kenya. Phases 1–4 are pre-Neolithic and date between 12,000 and 6000 bp; there are no dated occurrences between 6000 and 3300 bp, while phases 5A and 5B include stone bowls as well as PASTORAL NEOLITHIC pottery and date from before 2900 to well after 2000 bp.

echinus found at the top of CLASSICAL column-shafts forming part of the CAPITAL. In the DORIC ORDER it is the convex, cushion-shaped section located immediately below the ABACUS. In the IONIC ORDER it is placed between the VOLUTES of the capital and is frequently decorated with an egg-and-dart pattern.

ecofact faunal or floral material found in a site.

ed-Daba, Tell a site in the eastern Nile DELTA, Egypt. The probable location of the city of AVARIS, Tell ed-Daba, with its clear signs of Palestinian MIDDLE BRONZE AGE occupation, has been excavated by Bietak since 1969.

Edfu a site in UPPER EGYPT. Earlier religious buildings at Edfu were all but swept away by the temple of the god HORUS, which was constructed under PTOLEMAIC kings between 237 and 57 BC, and which is the most complete surviving example of an ancient Egyptian temple. To the west are tombs of the OLD and MIDDLE KINGDOM, and the TELL of the ancient town, which seems to have had continuous occupation from at least as early as the Old Kingdom until the uppermost Graeco-Roman levels. Edfu has chiefly been excavated by the French Oriental Institute in 1914–33 and by a Franco-Polish mission in 1937–9.

edge-ground stone tools 1 a tool category occurring in several sites in northern Australia and New Guinea in

The temple of EDFU is the best-preserved temple in Egypt. Although built in the Graeco-Roman period, it used traditional architectural elements, like the double-towered entrance pylon.

Pleistocene contexts. Pleistocene ground-edge hatchets were first reported at Nawamoyn and MALANGANGERR in the 1960s; flakes with ground facets have been reported from other Pleistocene sites in ARNHEM LAND, the Kimberley, southeastern Cape York and the NEW GUINEA HIGHLANDS, while a complete hatchet from Sandy Creek 1, southeastern Cape York, confirms that this technology was present in the region before 32,000 bp. Elsewhere in Australia, edge-ground tools do not appear before the late Holocene and are absent from TASMANIA.
   2 flaked stone tools, sharpened by grinding or polishing the cutting surface only, which are found in the BACSONIAN and HOABINHIAN of Southeast Asia. This may represent a transitional stage between flaked tools and the fully polished stone adzes of the Southeast Asian Neolithic.

Eemian Interglacial the last INTERGLACIAL in North Europe, following the SAALIAN and preceding the WEICHSEL GLACIATION, and spanning from *c*.125,000 to 115,000 BP. Its Alpine equivalent is RISS-WÜRM, in North America the SANGAMON and in Britain the Ipswichian, whose type-site is Bobbitshole, Ipswich.

Efate see ROY MATA.

EFEO the École française d'Extrême-Orient, founded in 1900 in Ha Noi, Vietnam, and responsible for almost all archaeological work in the former French Indochina until 1954.

Effigy mound culture a Late WOODLAND culture in the Upper Mississippi Valley, USA, characterized by BURIAL MOUNDS built in the shape of various animals, often birds.

Efimenko, Pyotr Petrovich (1884–1969) a Soviet archaeologist who was instrumental in the development of Palaeolithic archaeology during the period after 1930. Efimenko denounced traditional West European concerns with STRATIGRAPHY and TYPOLOGY, and advocated study of 'sociological issues' from a MARXIST theoretical perspective. He excavated at KOSTENKI, reporting the first discovery of a Palaeolithic LONGHOUSE (1931–6 excavations), which he linked to the social organization of its occupants. In 1938, Efimenko published a major synthesis of Palaeolithic prehistory entitled *Primeval Society*.

Egolzwil a village site on the shore of the former Lake Wauwil, Luzern, representative of the earliest phase of the Neolithic in western Switzerland. The earliest settlement is Egolzwil 3, with cereals and domestic animals and simple round-based pottery, dated to the late 5th or early 4th millennium BC.

Egtved a Middle Bronze Age burial in an oak tree trunk coffin under a circular tumulus in Jutland, Denmark. Exceptional conditions of preservation had allowed the survival of clothing including a woollen tunic and corded knee-length skirt. There were bronze bracelets on the wrists and a bronze belt-disc with a central spike. Though the body had decomposed it could be identified as that of a young woman approximately twenty years old. The coffin also contained cremated remains of a nine-year-old child. The wood has yielded a DENDROCHRONOLOGICAL date of the summer of 1370 BC.

Egypt

The predynastic era and the Archaic period
Before the construction of the Aswan Dam the River Nile, flowing northwards to the Mediterranean Sea, brought the only reliable source of water to an otherwise inhospitable corner of northeastern Africa. Flooding once a year, the Nile deposited a thick, fertile soil which allowed plants to grow.

Several hundred thousand years ago hunter-fisher-gatherer groups settled alongside the Nile. The transition to agriculture occurred during the 6th millennium BC. Cereals (wheat and barley) were grown, clay pots were manufactured and settled communities – villages, towns and then cities – emerged. The predynastic dead were buried in desert cemeteries, their flexed burials accompanied by a series of grave-goods including jewellery and pottery.

During the Archaic period (3000–2700 BC: Dynasties 1–2) the independent Nile communities formed political alliances. This was a lengthy process leading eventually to the emergence of two rival centres of power. Lower or northern Egypt included the fertile DELTA region, while upper or southern Egypt stretched as far south as the ASWAN cataracts. In c.3000 BC southern troops marched northwards to unify Egypt under one king, or PHARAOH. The newly unified land quickly became a literate state.

The Old Kingdom (2700–2160 BC: Dynasties 3–8)
The Old Kingdom was a time of inflexible feudal rule. Pharaoh, assisted by ministers chosen from his own extended family, ruled from MEMPHIS while in the prov-

inces control was delegated to the hereditary local governors. As a semi-divine being the king now occupied a position of great power; he alone could make the offerings which would satisfy the gods. Theology taught that, provided that the body was preserved, the soul might live after death. While the royal masons toiled to build the pyramids of SAQQARA and GIZA, Egypt's undertakers experimented with methods of preserving the corpse by artificial desiccation, or MUMMIFICATION.

The First Intermediate period (2160–2023 BC: Dynasties 9–11)
Egypt's long, thin geography made her an unwieldy country to rule. We do not know what caused the Old Kingdom to fail, but a series of low water levels leading to poor harvests did little to help. The First Intermediate period saw the provincial governors assuming increasing power; as the unified nation collapsed the provinces first reverted to independent units and then once again formed advantageous alliances. Eventually came the re-emergence of the two traditional power-bases. A THEBAN dynasty ruled southern Egypt while a Herakleopolitan dynasty controlled the north.

The Middle Kingdom (2023–1633 BC: Dynasties 11–13)
The Theban kings defeated their northern rivals to reunite their country under Amenenhat I. A new capital city was founded at Itj-Tawy, served by a new pyramid cemetery at LISHT. Increased foreign trade brought prosperity, while to the south a series of successful military campaigns established the foundations of the Nubian empire. As Egypt flourished, however, her eastern neighbours found themselves threatened by refugees from further east. Throughout the Middle Kingdom 'Asiatics' had been arriving in the Delta. Once well-integrated, these groups were now forming their own significant communities. With Egypt growing increasingly politically unstable, a series of high floods signalled the collapse of the Middle Kingdom.

The Second Intermediate period (1786–1550 BC: Dynasties 14–17)
Egypt emerged from the initial confusion of the Second Intermediate period as three stable, independent units. The extreme south was ruled by the NUBIAN kingdom of KERMA while southern Egypt was controlled by an Egyptian dynasty ruling from Thebes. In the north Palestinian invaders, the HYKSOS, reigned from their newly established Delta capital AVARIS.

For over a century northern Egypt thrived under Hyksos rule. The Thebans, however, grew increasingly unhappy with the situation. Suspecting collusion between the Hyksos and the Nubians – a collaboration which would pose a serious threat to those caught in the middle – the Theban kings determined to reunify their land. The victorious King Ahmose first regained control of the north and then sent his troops southwards to recapture Nubia.

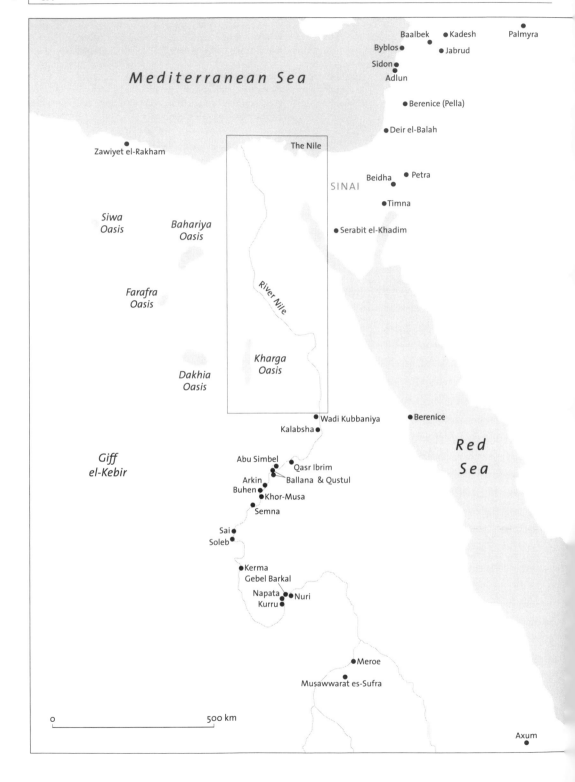

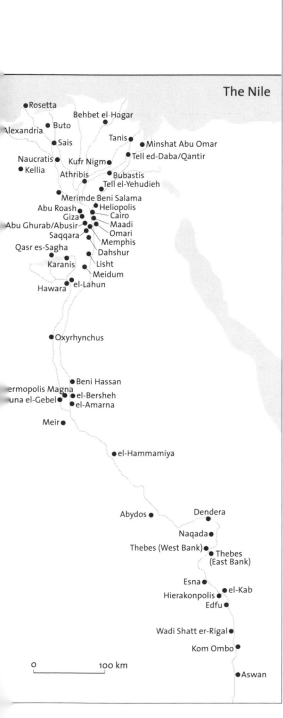

The Nile

Rosetta

Behbet el-Hagar

Alexandria ● Buto

● Sais

Tanis ●

● Minshat Abu Omar

Naucratis ● Kufr Nigm ●

● Tell ed-Daba/Qantir

● Kellia

Athribis ● ● Bubastis

Tell el-Yehudieh

● Merimde Beni Salama

Abu Roash ● ● Heliopolis

Giza ● ● Cairo

Abu Ghurab/Abusir ● ● Maadi

Saqqara ● ● Omari

Qasr es-Sagha ● ● Memphis

● Dahshur

Karanis ● ● Lisht

● Meidum

Hawara ● ● el-Lahun

● Oxyrhynchus

● Beni Hassan

ermopolis Magna ● ● el-Bersheh

una el-Gebel ● ● el-Amarna

Meir ●

● el-Hammamiya

Abydos ● Dendera

Naqada ●

Thebes (West Bank) ● ● Thebes (East Bank)

Esna ●

Hierakonpolis ● ● el-Kab

Edfu ●

Wadi Shatt er-Rigal ●

Kom Ombo ●

0   100 km

● Aswan

The New Kingdom (1550–1070 BC: Dynasties 18–20)

The Old Kingdom pharaohs had ruled by divine right. The New Kingdom monarchs were a more practical breed, whose rule was enforced by the army. Egypt, once remarkable for her insularity, quickly carved out an empire stretching from Syria to Nubia. The tribute and taxes taken from these foreign territories financed an impressive building programme back home. Now Egypt's mud-brick temples were torn down and replaced by stone monuments. The KARNAK temple complex of AMEN at Thebes was to undergo centuries of refurbishment as it became the acknowledged religious centre of the Egyptian empire. At the same time, on the west bank of the Nile, royal workmen housed at the village of DEIR EL-MEDINA started to excavate the hidden rock-cut tombs of the kings.

As the New Kingdom progressed the role of the pharaoh changed again. Warrior kings were followed by more cerebral monarchs interested in internal affairs; building, religion and the arts were now high on the royal agenda. The 18th Dynasty king Amenhotep IV, or AKHENATEN, made an ill-fated attempt to replace Egypt's traditional gods with a sole god, the sun disk or ATEN. Moving his capital city to the virgin site of Akhetaten (EL-AMARNA) Akhenaten lived in self-imposed isolation, wilfully ignorant of events outside his borders. His death saw Egypt impoverished and vulnerable, with much of her empire lost.

At the beginning of the 19th Dynasty the throne passed to a family of astute politicians and experienced soldiers from the Delta region. The RAMESSIDE era saw the restoration of much of the empire. Once again the treasury was full, and once again the masons set to work. Although Thebes retained her importance, there was increased political and religious activity in the north. Here, close to the Hyksos capital of Avaris, a new capital city, Pi-Ramesse, was built.

The late New Kingdom once again saw Egypt targeted by displaced groups. Not all these immigrants came in peace; Ramesses III was forced to beat back the SEA PEOPLES who attempted to settle in the Delta. In common with the rest of the Mediterranean world Egypt was experiencing an economic crisis with high inflation sparking outbreaks of civil disobedience and low Nile levels adding to the problem. As a confusing sequence of kings named Ramesses succeeded each other on the throne the increasingly powerful priesthood of Amen took full advantage of the situation, seizing political power for themselves.

The Third Intermediate period (1070–664 BC: Dynasties 21–25)

Egypt was once again divided. While a local dynasty ruled the north from the new Delta city of TANIS, the high priests of Amen controlled the south from Thebes. Relations between the two courts were initially cordial, and a series of royal marriages (northern princesses travelling to marry southern high priests) maintained the status quo. Eventually this good relationship collapsed, and the Tanite kings found themselves under pressure from rival dynasties based in the Delta. Now various local rulers simultaneously proclaimed themselves king.

Nubia, now fully independent, took full advantage of Egypt's collapse. In 770 BC King Kashta marched north-wards to Thebes. Kashta was proclaimed King of Upper and Lower Egypt, but it was his successor, Piye, who reached the Delta and so reunited Egypt. A century of stable rule followed. Once again, however, the Mediter-ranean world was in crisis and fertile Egypt was a prime target. In 671 BC an ASSYRIAN invasion force captured the Delta, forcing King Tanutamen to flee to Nubia. In 663 the Assyrians reached Thebes. Egypt was an Assyrian province, her Delta ruled by the Assyrian-appointed Saite kings.

The Late period (664–332 BC: Dynasties 26–31)
Once puppet kings, the Saite dynasty was able to reunite their fragmented country for over a century of indepen-dent rule. They could not resist the might of the PERSIAN army, however, and in 525 BC Egypt was defeated. The Persians, adapting to local traditions, installed their own dynasties which were interspersed by a brief period of local rule. Finally, in 332 BC, Alexander the Great con-quered Egypt.

The Ptolemaic period (332–30 BC)
Alexander appointed his general, PTOLEMY Lagus, as ruler of the new province. Following the death of Alex-ander in 323 BC Ptolemy established a dynasty of Egyp-tian-style Macedonian kings. Two centuries later ROME was the dominant force in the Mediterranean world. In 31 BC the last of the Ptolemies, Cleopatra VII, having fought and won a civil war against her brother Ptolemy, sided with Mark Antony in challenging the authority of the Roman Octavian (later known as Augustus Caesar). Cleopatra's troops fought and lost a sea battle at Actium, off the Ionian coast of Greece. The queen's subsequent suicide left Octavian free to annex Egypt. Egypt was now a Roman province.

Egyptian dynasties (with approximate dates BC)

Archaic period
Dynasty 1 3000–2840
Dynasty 2 2840–2700

Old Kingdom
Dynasty 3 2700–2600
Dynasty 4 2600–2500
Dynasty 5 2500–2350
Dynasty 6 2350–2190
Dynasty 7/8 2190–2160

First Intermediate period
Dynasty 9 2160–2106 (Herakleopolis)
Dynasty 10 (Middle Egypt) (Herakleopolis) 2106–2010
Dynasty 11 (Thebes) 2106–2023

Middle Kingdom
Dynasty 11 (Unification) 2023–1963
Dynasty 12 1963–1786
Dynasty 13 1786–1633

Second Intermediate period
Dynasty 14 (W. Delta, contemp. Dynasties 13/15) 1786–1633
Dynasty 15 (Major Hyksos) 1648–1540
Dynasty 16 (Minor Hyksos, contemp. Dynasty 15) 1648–1540
Dynasty 17 1633–1550

New Kingdom
Dynasty 18 1550–1295
Dynasty 19 1295–1186
Dynasty 20 1186–1070

Third Intermediate period (*Dynasties 22–4 Libyan, 25 Nubian*)
Dynasty 21 1070–945
Dynasty 22 945–715
Dynasty 23 818–715
Dynasty 24 727–715
Dynasty 25 715–664

Late period (*Dynasties 27 and 31 Persian*)
Dynasty 26 664–525
Dynasty 27 525–404
Dynasty 28 404–399
Dynasty 29 399–380
Dynasty 30 380–343
Dynasty 31 343–332

Ehringsdorf a Middle Pleistocene open-air site located near Weimar in eastern Germany. Artifacts and faunal remains (e.g. *Elephas antiquus, Dicerorhinus mercki*) are buried in spring deposits dated (by URANIUM SERIES) to c.225,000 bp. The artifacts, which include scrapers, points and bifaces, are typical of the Middle Palaeolithic, despite their age. Associated human skeletal remains are classi-fied as NEANDERTHALS.

Eibian an East African microlithic LATER STONE AGE industry formerly known as the 'Doian', characterized by pressure-flaked small points and other tools. It is thought to date to the Late or terminal Pleistocene.

Eight Deer (Jaguar Claw) a MIXTEC ruler of Tilantongo in Oaxaca, Mexico, during the early POSTCLASSIC who is mentioned in several CODICES as a conqueror. Under his reign Tilantongo became the largest Mixtec kingdom.

Eilsleben a fortified settlement of the LINEAR POTTERY CULTURE in eastern Germany near Magdeburg. As was the case at KÖLN-LINDENTHAL, the settled area at Eilsleben was surrounded by a rampart and ditch system which became progressively more elaborate over the dur-ation of the settlement.

Ein Gev I an open-air KEBARAN site on Lake Kinneret in the Jordan Valley, Israel, which contains semi-subterranean pit structures, about 6 m (20 ft) across and spaced roughly 20 m (22 yds) apart; the tightly flexed burial of a woman was also found in the settlement. Along with the Kebaran lithic assemblage, some of whose blades display SICKLE SHEEN, the material culture includes mortars, pestles and a few grinding stones. Together with the wild fauna (mostly gazelle), these materials are usually taken to represent an intensifying interest in wild cereals as an early step towards food production.

Ein Mallaha see EYNAN.

Ekain a MAGDALENIAN cave-site in the Basque country of northern Spain, where cave art was discovered in 1969. It contains about fifty figures, mostly paintings, including a fine panel of horses. Excavation has revealed material of the AURIGNACIAN and early Magdalenian (16,500–15,400 bp), but the art can be assigned to the later Magdalenian, dating to 12,050 bp, through stylistic analogy with an engraved stone from that layer. The occupants in this period were heavily dependent on ibex.

ekphora a funerary procession in the Greek world, that might include a cortège with chariots and mourners. Ekphorai are commonly depicted on the ceramic monumental funerary markers at ATHENS in the 8th century BC. See also PROTHESIS.

el-Ajjul, Tell a Palestinian site excavated by PETRIE in 1930–34, and including two cemeteries of the transitional EARLY to MIDDLE BRONZE AGE, one of which was remarkable for the large number of graves found to contain copper daggers. The Middle Bronze Age at Tell el-Ajjul is notable for its substantial palaces and for the quantity of gold jewellery and seals (including SCARABS) recovered from the excavations, the latter being an indication of Egyptian influence from the MIDDLE KINGDOM to the NEW KINGDOM.

Elam an early state located in southwestern Iran, an extension of the southern plain of MESOPOTAMIA. With its centres in SUSA in the Khuzistan lowlands and in Anshan in the Fars uplands of southwestern Iran (see Tal-i MALYAN), Elam represents a civilization that looked towards both Mesopotamia and the Iranian Plateau, a duality that was often expressed as an oscillation in material culture and political forms between the two. Because it was influenced at its inception by URUK-period Mesopotamia (see ACROPOLE OF SUSA, PROTO-ELAMITE), and repeatedly invaded or occupied by later Mesopotamian states, its political history is one of endemic antagonism towards its neighbours to the west, and Elam in its turn often raided southern Mesopotamia. The Elamite cultural tradition came to an end largely as a consequence of absorption into the world empires of the mid 1st millennium BC; though Susa was a principal seat of the ACHAEMENID rulers, who continued to use Elamite in some public inscriptions, the area lost much of its distinctiveness at this time.

el-Amarna a city founded on a virgin site in northern UPPER EGYPT that became the capital of Egypt during the AMARNA PERIOD. Constructed over a relatively short period (including the use of TALATAT), the central area of the city, containing the 'Great Temple' of ATEN and the 'Great Palace', was subsequently robbed of its stone masonry. The functions of some of the public buildings at el-Amarna are open to debate, but it is clear that the new city was intended to serve as the religious and administrative centre of the state (see also AMARNA LETTERS), with suburbs, villas and a workers' village on the outskirts of the central area. In the cliffs behind the city are rock-cut tombs of the officials of King AKHENATEN. The site has chiefly been excavated by PETRIE (1891–2), Borchardt (1911–14) and the Egypt Exploration Fund/Society (1901–7, 1921–36, 1977–present).

eland (*Taurotragus oryx*) the largest and fattest of all southern African antelopes, weighing up to 550 kg (87 st). It is easily hunted and can provide food for a large number of people for several days. The eland is depicted more frequently than any other animal in DRAKENSBERG rock art and was important in SAN symbolism, myth and ritual.

Elands Bay a cave on the western coast of the Western Cape Province of South Africa, excavated in the 1970s and 1980s by John Parkington. The basal layers of its 3 m (10 ft) deep stratified deposit contain early MIDDLE STONE AGE material which may be as old as late Middle Pleistocene. This is separated from LATER STONE AGE material by a break in the sequence. The faunal remains document the effects of the rise in sea-level at the end of the Pleistocene, which transformed the setting of the cave from an inland riverine to a coastal estuarine situation.

Elandsfontein an open archaeological and possibly also carnivore site originally near a waterhole, covering about 300 ha (740 acres) between shifting sand dunes in the Western Cape Province of South Africa. It contains rich collections of fossil animal bones, as well as stone artifacts and pottery. The fragmented 'Saldanha' cranium of an archaic HOMO *sapiens* was found here on an exposed surface in 1953, and is considered to be of late Middle Pleistocene age.

El Argar a rich Early Bronze Age settlement site in ALMERIA, Spain, excavated by Louis SIRET, and the type-site of the Argaric culture. Fortified Argaric villages with rectangular houses are known throughout Almeria. Burial was in stone cists or jars below the floors of the houses. At El Argar itself, 950 such burials were found. The richest Argaric burials contain gold and silver diadems, and daggers and swords of copper and bronze.

Elateia (formerly **Drakhmani**) the site of a prehistoric settlement mound in Pthiotis, Greece, which was excavated by Weinberg in 1959. Elateia has the most complete stratified sequence of central Greek Neolithic pottery deposits.

el-Bersheh a site of rock-cut tombs of Egypt's MIDDLE KINGDOM, some belonging to the NOMARCHs of that period. El-Bersheh was chiefly explored by the Egypt Exploration Fund in 1891–3.

El Beyed Vendredi a site in a deflated dune valley in central Mauretania, Africa, with rich ACHEULIAN, ATERIAN and Neolithic assemblages, discovered by Theodore Monod in 1967.

El Castillo a major cave-site discovered in 1903 by H. Alcalde del Rio in a conical hill in Santander Province (northern Spain). The 20 m (65 ft) stratigraphy at the entrance spans the entire Palaeolithic period, and has been investigated by H. Obermaier (1910–15) and by V. Cabrera (since 1980). Its earliest AURIGNACIAN material has been dated by radiocarbon (AMS) to c.38,700 bp. The Middle Palaeolithic economy was based on horse and bovid hunting, but the Upper Palaeolithic saw a shift to a specialized exploitation of deer. The cave contains engravings and paintings from different phases of the later Upper Palaeolithic (c.20,000 to 10,000 BC) including 155 animal figures, fifty red hand stencils and numerous quadrilateral forms. Charcoal in two bison figures has produced radiocarbon dates from 13,570 to 13,060 bp. The hill (Monte Castillo) also houses other decorated Palaeolithic caves: Las Chimeneas, Las Monedas and La Pasiega, the latter containing 440 animal figures.

El Ceibo a PALAEOINDIAN site in southern Patagonia (Argentina) at which extinct horse and camelid remains, along with puma and possible guanaco, were found by Augusto Cardich in association with lithic tools. While there are no radiocarbon dates from this site, the similarity of its assemblage to the earliest levels of LOS TOLDOS suggests that it represents a very early human occupation of Patagonia.

Ele Bor a Stone Age rockshelter in northern Kenya near the Ethiopian border, with evidence that hunting continued to be important even after the arrival of some small stock and camels about 5000 bp. Pottery also first appeared at the site at this time, much later than at nearby lakeside settlements.

electromagnetic surveying a geophysical surveying technique designed to locate archaeological features and sediment or soil textural discontinuities. The technique is based on the induction of an electric current flow in near-surface materials and the measurement of electrical conductivity of the current. The electric current is conducted primarily by water in pores in the soil, so the conductivity is a function of porosity, water content and water chemistry. Porosity, water retention and ion absorption in turn are affected by particle size, so that contrasting textures, such as pit fill *versus* surrounding MATRIX, will produce an anomalous reading. Electromagnetic surveying is conducted with either a PULSED INDUCTION METER or a SOIL CONDUCTIVITY METER, neither of which is as accurate as a RESISTIVITY METER or PROTON MAGNETOMETER. See also RESISTIVITY SURVEYING.

electron probe microanalysis a physical technique of chemical analysis used to determine the chemical composition of stone, ceramics, pigments, glass, metal, surface applications and stains. A highly focused electron beam bombards a point on a polished sample surface, exciting electrons which emit secondary X-rays. The wavelengths of these secondary X-rays are characteristic of the elements that emitted them, and the concentrations of elements can be calculated from the intensities of the energy spectrum.

electron spin resonance dating (ESR) a radiogenic dating method that utilizes residual effects of changing energy levels of electrons under conditions of natural irradiation of alpha, beta and gamma rays. The method is applicable to teeth, bone, heat-treated chert and flint, ceramics, archaeological sediments, shells, spring TRAVERTINE and SPELEOTHEMS. When minerals form, all electrons are in their ground state. With irradiation, the energy level of electrons can be increased temporarily, but then they return to positive charged sites near the ground state. However, some electrons are trapped in naturally occurring charge-deficit sites which can be detected by ESR spectrometry. The number of trapped electrons is a function of the amount of natural radiation and the duration of that irradiation. The age of a sample can be calculated by determining the number of trapped electrons at a given site and the dose rate of natural radiation. There are numerous factors that affect these values and they must be taken into account. The main factors that limit the effective age range of the dating technique are sample saturation and thermal stability for the upper limit, which may range up to two to three million years; and the dose rate, mineral sensitivity to radiation, and sensitivity of the ESR spectrometer for the lower limit, which can be as low as several hundred years.

Principal sources of error are post-depositional physical or chemical changes, errors in chemical analyses and reproducibility of signal intensity, and systematic errors. Because of the multiplicity of factors that may contribute to error, precision is difficult to estimate and varies with the type of sample. Precision of replicate analyses is of the order of 10 to 20 per cent for the types of samples examined.

electronic distance measuring devices (EDM) surveying and mapping instruments that utilize sophisticated electronics and infra-red or laser beams in measuring and calculating distances, locating points and determining angles. Often computer compatible, an EDM is far more accurate, time efficient and expensive than conventional surveying instruments such as a TRANSIT or THEODOLITE.

electrum a naturally occurring alloy of gold and silver, that is mined in many parts of the world, usually from quartz veins. It has similar chemical and physical properties to gold, but is paler, being a yellowish-white or pale yellow. The term is usually used if the alloy contains at least 20 per cent silver.

Elephantine an island in the ASWAN region, Egypt, regarded as Egypt's southern border during the OLD and MIDDLE KINGDOM. The town, on the southern tip of the island, has been excavated by the German Archaeological Institute since 1969; the TELL-like settlement debris seems to indicate continual occupation from the ARCHAIC PERIOD to the Graeco-Roman period.

Eleusis the site of a major Greek sanctuary in Attica, dedicated to the goddess Demeter, in whose honour the Mysteries were celebrated. The CLASSICAL Telesterion, or temple of Demeter, was constructed on the site of a MYCENAEAN MEGARON. The Romans were generous benefactors, especially Hadrian and Marcus Aurelius, who built the PROPYLAEA.

el-Fara, Tell (north) a Palestinian site chiefly excavated by de Vaux 1946–60. The CHALCOLITHIC settlement was composed of circular, semi-subterranean dwellings, while the Early Bronze Age occupation seems to have been abandoned, perhaps due to incursions by the AMORITES. The site was resettled in the MIDDLE BRONZE AGE and later became an ISRAELITE town.

el-Fara, Tell (south) a Palestinian site, excavated by PETRIE in 1928–9. The first settlement seems to have been the HYKSOS fortifications. The most impressive excavated remains of the Late Bronze Age are of a large building called 'The Residency', while the site was occupied by the PHILISTINES in the Iron Age.

El Garcel a hilltop settlement in ALMERIA, Spain, of round or oval wattle-and-daub houses with underground storage pits and simple round- or pointed-based pottery vessels. Dated to the middle Neolithic (5th millennium BC), it is the principal site of the Almerian culture, which includes a number of similar hilltop villages which may originally have been defended.

Elgin, Lord (1766–1841) a British diplomat whose removal of some of the sculpture from the PARTHENON, in part with the permission of the Turkish authorities, has been the source of much controversy. The acquisition of the sculptures by the British Museum generated a renewed interest in CLASSICAL art and in Hellenism. Elgin's collec-

tion should not be seen in isolation. It was part of a wider taste among the social elites of Europe to acquire Classical art to decorate their homes as well as to fill national museums.

El Guettar a site in Tunisia rich in animal fossils and associated with a MOUSTERIAN-type industry of over 50 per cent scrapers, probably contemporary with the ATERIAN. The excavator claims the presence of a conical 'shrine' 75 cm (29.5 inches) high and 1.3 m (4 ft 3 inches) across, filled with stone tools and bones, and constructed of limestone and flint spheroids.

el-Hammamiya a site in UPPER EGYPT remarkable for its stratified settlement sequence from the BADARIAN to the GERZEAN, excavated by CATON-THOMPSON in 1924.

el-Hesi, Tell see EL-HESY, TELL.

el-Hesy, Tell a Palestinian site, chiefly of the MIDDLE BRONZE AGE–Iron Age, important as the site where PETRIE carried out his pioneering work on the STRATIGRAPHIC aspects of TELL sites.

El Inga an Early PRECERAMIC site in highland Ecuador at which fluted stemmed 'FISHTAIL POINTS' were located. Though not well dated in absolute terms, it is clearly a PALAEOINDIAN site, and is probably roughly contemporaneous with CUEVA FELL. The fishtail point complex of South America shows technological similarities to the Clovis tradition of North America.

Elizavetovka see SCYTHIANS.

El Juyo a well-stratified Upper Palaeolithic cave-site near Santander, northern Spain, which is best known for its faunal evidence indicating intensive red deer hunting, probably by driving rather than stalking, during the SOLUTREAN and MAGDALENIAN phases. The lower Magdalenian living floors have been dated to 14,440 bp. The most recent excavations, by González Echegaray and Freeman, began in 1978, and revealed a possible 'sanctuary' with a block resembling a human face.

El-Kab a site in UPPER EGYPT on the eastern bank of the Nile, chiefly explored by a Belgian Mission since 1967. The most substantial archaeological remains at El-Kab are the massive mud-brick enclosure walls of the town, whose dilapidated contents include the temple (NEW KINGDOM and LATE PERIOD) of the patron goddess of Upper Egypt, Nekhbet. In the cliffs behind the town are rock-cut tombs, the most important being of the 18th Dynasty. El-Kab is also the type-site of the El-Kabian, a microlithic EPIPALAEOLITHIC industry, dated to c.6000 BC.

el Khiam a prehistoric site in the Judaean hills of Palestine, which gives its name to a point type characteristic of the PRE-POTTERY NEOLITHIC A lithic industry. The point is made of a truncated and symmetrically notched bladelet whose tip is usually formed by marginal retouch.

El Khril a site near Tangier in northern Morocco with evidence of pottery decorated with impressions of cardium shells, as well as bones of domesticated small stock dating from the 6th millennium bc, which may be the earliest evidence of farming from the region.

el-Lahun or **Kahun** an Egyptian site at the entrance to the FAIYUM, chiefly of the MIDDLE KINGDOM, excavated by PETRIE in 1887–8 and 1913. The major archaeological features of el-Lahun are the pyramid of SENWOSRET II, the subsidiary burial of Princess Sat-Hathor-Iunet with its rich grave-goods, the adjoining town for functionaries connected with the pyramid and the numerous HIERATIC papyri recovered from the site.

Ellerbek see ERTEBØLLE.

Elmali a town in Lycia in Turkey where painted tombs which combine both Anatolian and Greek style and iconography have been found. One tomb shows a warrior mounting a chariot and a SYMPOSIUM scene.

elm decline an episode in the pollen history of northwestern Europe c.4000 BC marked by a significant decline in the quantity of elm pollen. Once thought the result of the activities of early farming communities, it is now attributed to disease, beetles of the kind which carry Dutch elm disease having been found in a 4th-millennium context at Hampstead Heath, London.

Elmenteitan 1 a stone industry of the PASTORAL NEOLITHIC complex of early East African herders, restricted to the west side of the central Kenyan Rift Valley. It dates from about 400 bc and lasted almost two thousand years in some areas, though considerably less in others, and is characterized by large, double-edged obsidian blades, plain pottery bowls and shallow stone bowls, as well as cremation of the dead (see NJORO RIVER CAVE). Hunting, fishing and possibly cultivation were conducted in areas marginal for pastoralism.

2 a PASTORAL NEOLITHIC and Iron Age pottery tradition associated with Elmenteitan stone artifacts, confined to the west side of the Kenyan Rift Valley.

El Mirador a late PRECLASSIC site in northern Petén, Guatemala, near the Mexican border. It is one of the earliest urban centres in the Maya Lowlands, with an architectural complex perhaps larger than that of TIKAL. Its Tigre pyramid consists of more than 380,000 cu. m (500,000 cu. yds) of mud and stone, larger than many of Tikal's monuments combined. Ian Graham was the first to report on the site in the 1960s. It was joined by a causeway to nearby NAKBE, a site it rapidly eclipsed c.2300 bp, perhaps owing to a better water supply and a more defendable position.

Eloaua Island an island in the Mussau group of MELANESIA, with the two oldest LAPITA sites found in the BISMARCK ARCHIPELAGO, dated to 3450–2350 BP. One of these, Talepakemalai (ECA), is waterlogged and has extraordinary preservation of house posts and plant remains. As well as Lapita pottery, there is evidence for shell artifact manufacture and marine-oriented subsistence. Obsidian from both TALASEA and LOU occurs, with the proportion of Lou obsidian increasing over time.

elouera a triangular-sectioned backed flake resembling an orange segment, with use-polish from working bark and softwood along the straight edge. An element of the AUSTRALIAN SMALL TOOL TRADITION, its distribution is restricted to eastern Australia.

El Paraiso a large ceremonial site located in the Chillón Valley of the central coast of Peru, pertaining to the Late PRECERAMIC and the INITIAL PERIOD. It comprises a central group of six or seven mounds arranged in a U-shaped configuration. In all, the site covers some 60 ha (148 acres), and includes more than a dozen mounds. There is some question as to whether or not the U-shaped configuration was intentional; however, the predominance of such configurations in ensuing periods suggests that its presence in the Late Preceramic was not fortuitous. El Paraiso is the earliest of a series of large U-shaped ceremonial sites found on the central coast during the Initial period. Subsistence at the site was based on fishing, wild plants and cultivated plants. The growth of the site may have been related to increased cotton production in the region.

El Riego phase the occupation phase from c.7000 to 5000 BC in Mexico's TEHUACÁN VALLEY, when the society remains one of hunter-gatherers, but three plants show evidence of some domestication. These are squash (*Cucurbita mixta*), chilli peppers and avocados. They make up only a small part of the diet, however. The population in the valley at this time is estimated at three households, or twelve to twenty-four people.

ELSA see EARLY LATER STONE AGE.

Elsloo a settlement and cemetery of the LINEAR POTTERY culture in Limburg, the Netherlands, excavated by P. J. R. Modderman. The eighty houses at Elsloo could be organized into six main chronological phases, with between eleven and seventeen houses in use at any one time. The cemetery is the largest Linear Pottery burial ground known, with 113 graves, thirty-seven of which were cremations. In the inhumation burials, the bones generally were poorly preserved in the decalcified LOESS, but the grave-goods have provided important information on the Linear Pottery social order. Elsloo, together with the neighbouring settlements of SITTARD, Stein and Geleen, has been the basis for discussions of variability in Linear Pottery houses, flint tools and pottery.

Elster(ian) a North European Middle Pleistocene cold

stage including at least one GLACIAL advance; it started c.450–400,000 BP and ended with the HOLSTEINIAN INTERGLACIAL, c.300,000 BP. The British equivalent is the Anglian cold stage (formerly known as the 'Lowestoft' glaciation); its type-site is Corton in Suffolk. The Alpine equivalent is the MINDEL glaciation, and the North American equivalent is the Kansas.

Els Tudons a stone-built NAVETA ('little boat') in Menorca, Spain, a communal tomb shaped like an up-turned boat with rounded prow and squared stern. The entrance in the centre of a concave façade leads through an ante-chamber to a double-decker tomb, with the lower storey separated from the upper by a ceiling of massive stone slabs serving also as the floor of the upper chamber. Navetas were built and used in the TALAYOTIC period of the Bronze Age c.1500–800 BC.

El Tajín or **Tajín** a CEREMONIAL CENTRE in northern-central Veracrúz, Mexico, occupied from about AD 800 to 1200. The site shows influences from many other cultures, TEOTIHUACÁN, MAYA and 'TOLTEC', and there are also indications that the site influenced CHOLULA, at least. Early excavations at the site were directed by Jose Garcia Payón; recent reinterpretations of site history are the result of work by Juergen Bruggemann.

eluvial horizon a soil horizon defined by its loss of soil material in solution or suspension by PEDOGENESIS. The most common eluvial horizon is the E horizon. Eluviation and leaching are the general processes by which material is removed. Compare ILLUVIAL HORIZON.

el-Wad a prehistoric cave- and terrace-site in the MOUNT CARMEL group, Israel, first dug as a rescue excavation by Charles Lambert in 1928. His discovery of a NATUFIAN animal carving (the first prehistoric art object found in the Near East) established the group's importance. GARROD excavated El-Wad in 1929–33, identifying a stratified sequence from Natufian (Layers B1, B2) down through Upper Palaeolithic (C, D1, D2, E) to MOUSTERIAN (F, G). El-Wad is principally known for its Natufian structural and ceremonial remains and numerous human burials.

el-Yehudiyeh, Tell (*Arabic* 'Mound of the Jews') a site in the southeastern Nile DELTA, Egypt, its major feature being a rectangular enclosure of approximately 25 ha (62 acres), surrounded by a GLACIS, called the 'HYKSOS Camp'. Northeast of the enclosure is the site of the Jewish temple and town founded by the priest Onias in the reign of PTOLEMY VI.

emblema a small disc, often of silver, normally decorated with a scene or motif in relief. They were used to decorate the interior of bowls, to which they were attached by solder. Many appear to be HELLENISTIC in date.

emblem glyph a MAYA GLYPH identifying a place or POLITY. Emblem glyphs were first recognized in Maya HIEROGLYPHIC writing by Heinrich Berlin in 1958.

Emery, Walter Bryan (1903–71) an English Egyptologist, best known for his work in THEBES (EGYPT)-WEST BANK, NUBIA (especially BUHEN and BALLANA AND QUSTUL) and SAQQARA (particularly the tombs of the ARCHAIC PERIOD).

Emiran a brief early Upper Palaeolithic industry found in the Levant region and named after the Emireh cave at the northern end of the Sea of Galilee, Israel. Emiran tool-kits include backed blades and may contain MOUS-TERIAN artifact-types; this has led to suggestions that the Emiran represents a transitional industry on the Middle and Upper Palaeolithic boundary, although the possibility of contamination from an earlier archaeological occupation layer exists.

Emishi an early historical name for the farming populace of the TOHOKU region of Japan who lived outside of the 7th–9th century AD RITSURYO state's territorial administration (see JAPANESE PERIODIZATION). This populace developed from the previous YAYOI farmers of the area, who carried the JOMON genetic inheritance. It is thought the medieval EZO and later AINU population of Hokkaido developed from the Emishi.

Emory, Kenneth P. (1897–1992) American archaeologist based at the Bishop Museum, Honolulu from 1920 to 1967. His fieldwork established the basic archaeological framework for the HAWAIIAN ISLANDS. In 1950, radiocarbon dates from his pioneering excavations at Kuli'ou'ou on Oahu first demonstrated occupation older than 1,000 years.

Emporion see AMPURIAS.

'En Besor see ERANI, TEL.

encaustic portraits see FAIYUM.

Endingi a Kenyan MIDDLE STONE AGE industry characterized by flakes with faceted platforms, scrapers and *outils écaillés* (microlithic tools deliberately flaked to form a chisel-like edge), represented at ENKAPUNE YA MUTO, where it is considered to pre-date 40,000 bp.

endogamy the practice of marrying *within* one's own social unit, such as the clan or tribe. The opposite of EXOGAMY.

endscraper see SCRAPER.

Eneolithic or **Aeneolithic** a term used widely to refer to a period (primarily in the 5th, 4th and 3rd millennia BC) in many parts of the Near East and Europe (especially southeastern Europe) when copper metallurgy was in the process of being adopted by cultures which were otherwise essentially 'Neolithic' in character. The Eneolithic is also sometimes called the *Chalcolithic* (particularly in the Near East) and the *Copper Age*. North and west of the Carpathians, chronological nomenclature rarely includes this term, instead moving directly from the 'late Neolithic' to the 'Early Bronze Age'.

Engaruka an Iron Age site in northern Tanzania with remains of terraced villages and an elaborate and extensive irrigation system built mainly after the 14th century AD.

Enkapune Ya Muto or **Twilight Cave** a Stone Age rock-shelter west of Lake Naivasha in the central Rift Valley of Kenya, containing a 5–6 m (16–20 ft) deep deposit with remains from the middle Upper Pleistocene and Holocene. The basal layers pre-date 40,000 bp and contain the ENDINGI MIDDLE STONE AGE industry. Of particular interest is evidence for the LATER STONE AGE NASAMPOLAI industry with backed blades and geometric microliths, arguably pre-dating 40,000 bp, possibly the earliest known Later Stone Age occurrence. Also of interest is the presence of ostrich eggshell beads apparently dating to about 40,000 bp in the overlying Later Stone Age SAKUTIEK industry. Layers dating between about 7000 and 3000 bp contain EBURRAN material, including in the more recent of these layers pottery resembling the NDERIT, Ileret and SUSWA/SALASUN traditions, and caprine remains. Above these, ELMENTEITAN Neolithic pottery as well as cattle and caprine remains are found, and Iron Age material associated with the LANET tradition occurs at the top of the deposit. The Elmenteitan/Iron Age boundary is dated to about 1295 bp.

Enki or **Ea** the third (with AN and ENLIL) of the great SUMERIAN gods, associated with sweet water and purification (Ea was his AKKADIAN name). This god organized the world and created human beings, often interceding with the other gods on behalf of humanity. His prominent characteristics were cunning and moderate counsel, and in many myths he takes the role of trickster. Enki had a close association with the city of ERIDU, the primordial city of Sumer.

Enkomi the site of a major Cypriot settlement in eastern CYPRUS. Excavations at Enkomi began in 1890 and continued until 1974. The site, which was first occupied in the 17th century BC, profited from the copper trade. The ores were brought from the mines in the interior, smelted in the town and then exported. By the 14th century, Enkomi was clearly one of the most powerful and prosperous settlements on Cyprus and may have been ALASHIYA, the ancient capital. In c.1200 BC, however, the site was destroyed, possibly by the SEA PEOPLES. Subsequently, massive CYCLOPEAN fortifications were constructed and the town was rebuilt on a grid plan. There is fine ASHLAR architecture, in particular the sanctuary of the Horned God. Eventually, c.1050 BC, Enkomi was abandoned in favour of SALAMIS.

Enlène see VOLP CAVES.

Enlil the chief god in the SUMERIAN pantheon, who replaced his father AN in this role. He represents the ambivalent force of the wind and storms, bringing both life and destruction. In the latter aspect, Enlil was responsible for the great flood that almost destroyed humanity, having become annoyed with all the noise that the mortals made. Enlil's seat was in NIPPUR, which formed the ideological centre of Sumer.

en-Nasbeh, Tell a Palestinian site, probably the biblical Mizpah, excavated by Bade 1926–35. It was a major settlement of the early Iron Age, comprising an ISRAELITE town defended by a massive wall and well-preserved gateway. Tell en-Nasbeh has produced an important corpus of Israelite pottery from the TELL and its adjacent tombs.

Ensérune an OPPIDUM in Hérault, France, founded in the 6th century BC, replanned in the 4th century as a carefully ordered town of stone buildings arranged along roadways. A stone-built rampart enclosed both the town and a cemetery area to its west. This consisted of inurned burials, sometimes in imported Italian vessels. A further major reconstruction was undertaken in c.200 BC, when the cemetery was built over and a local script, based on Greek but hitherto undeciphered, came into use.

entablature the horizontal element of a CLASSICAL building between the column CAPITALS and the PEDIMENT or roof. In the DORIC ORDER it comprises the ARCHITRAVE above which were placed the alternating TRIGLYPHS and METOPES. In the IONIC ORDER a continuous frieze was placed above the architrave.

entasas a Greek architectural technique of exaggerating the curvature of a column shaft of buildings of the DORIC ORDER to give the optical illusion of straight sides.

Entremont an OPPIDUM in Bouches-du-Rhône, France, of roughly triangular plan with a dry-stone defensive wall of the 3rd century BC punctuated by projecting rectangular towers. Within the oppidum, dry-stone houses are arranged along a grid-plan street layout. A shrine near the centre of the settlement had human skulls nailed to the wall including one with a javelin in it; there were also sculptures depicting piles of human heads. Entremont had close trade contacts with the Greek colony of MARSEILLES (Massilia), but was destroyed in the Roman conquest of Provence in c.125 BC.

environmental archaeology a subfield of archaeology where the aim is to identify processes, factors and conditions of past biological and physical environmental systems and how they relate to cultural systems. It has been enveloped in the last decade by the broader contextual archaeology, which aims at determining the dynamic interrelationships between environment and culture by focusing on and evaluating context.

eolian see AEOLIAN.

eolith a naturally shaped or fractured stone believed by early antiquarians to be the oldest known artifact type, dating to the pre-Palaeolithic era. It is now accepted that eoliths are not human-made. See HARRISON.

Epano Englianos see PYLOS.

Ephesus a major port on the west coast of Turkey. British excavations in 1869 located the temple of Artemis (*Artemision*), and subsequent work by the Austrians has uncovered many of the important public buildings. The ARCHAIC temple in the IONIC ORDER provides a TERMINUS ANTE QUEM for the use of coinage, as a hoard of ELECTRUM coins was found in the foundation deposit. The temple, one of the SEVEN WONDERS, was burnt in 356 BC and Alexander the Great initiated its reconstruction. The bases of the columns were decorated with reliefs. Several GYMNASIA have been uncovered, including that of Publius Vedius Antoninus dedicated to Artemis and the emperor Antoninus Pius. The theatre, which belongs to the HELLENISTIC period, could have seated some 24,000 people. Near by, the Celsus Library, constructed in AD 110, has been reconstructed; it also served as a tomb. The public administrative buildings have been excavated in the vicinity of the so-called State AGORA.

Epicardial an early Neolithic pottery style of *c*.5300–4600 BC, developed from and succeeding the CARDIAL style in southern France. Decoration using the edge of a *Cardium* shell is replaced by incised decoration as the dominant mode, with great diversity of regional and local variants.

Epidauros a Greek sanctuary of the healing god Asklepios

in the Peloponnese. One of the best-preserved monuments is the theatre, which would have seated some 14,000 people. In addition to the temple, there were numerous buildings associated with the cult, including a STADIUM.

Epigravettian a term given to the late GLACIAL industries of Italy, and divided into early (20–16,000 bp), evolved (16–14,000 bp) and final phases; the latter lasts until *c*.8000 bp, evolving into the Mesolithic, and is followed by the SAUVETERRIAN and CASTELNOVIAN in the 7th millennium.

Epipalaeolithic a term used for the final Upper Palaeolithic industries occurring at the end of the final GLACIATION which appear to merge technologically into the Mesolithic. See AHRENSBURGIAN, HAMBURGIAN, AZILIAN. The term Epipalaeolithic is occasionally used instead of Mesolithic, but in the Levant it denotes the period from *c*.20,000 to 10,000 BP (see KEBARAN).

epiphysis the articulating end of a long bone. Compare DIAPHYSIS.

Epi-Pietersburg a southern African HOWIESON'S POORT-like MIDDLE STONE AGE industry which succeeds the PIETERSBURG. At BORDER CAVE it is associated with radiocarbon dates in excess of 49,000 years and is considered to date to some 80,000 years ago.

Episkopi-Phaneromeni the site of a Middle–Late Cypriot settlement in southern CYPRUS, occupied *c*.1600–1500 BC, and a Middle Cypriot CHAMBER TOMB cemetery excavated by Carpenter in 1975–8.

epistemology that element of scientific reasoning that evaluates the veracity of what is known.

ER 1470 see KOOBI FORA.

Erani, Tel an Early Bronze Age town in Israel that provides evidence for Egyptian outposts in the southern Levant during the late 4th millennium BC. Alongside materials of local tradition appear Egyptian styles of architecture, pottery, chipped stone, palettes and other artifacts. The Egyptian materials are both imported from the Nile Valley and locally made; one storage jar bears the name symbol (*serekh*) of NARMER. Other sites in southern Israel also contain impressive evidence of Egyptians living in the area, for example the administrative complex at 'En Besor with its Egyptian-style architecture, artifacts and bureaucratic procedures (clay sealings and BULLAE). The Egyptians apparently withdrew from southern Palestine around 3100 BC.

Érd a Middle Palaeolithic open-air site located near Budapest in central Hungary. Artifacts and faunal remains are buried in loess deposited in limestone hollows that may have served as carnivore dens. Cave bear predominates heavily among the faunal remains, which in general suggest human occupation prior to the last GLACIAL. The tools are chiefly composed of scrapers. Érd was excavated by Gábori-Csánk in 1963–4.

Erebuni an URARTIAN town near modern Erevan (Armenia), divided into a citadel and residential town. The place is best known for its wall paintings that clearly reveal the NEO-ASSYRIAN inspiration for much of the Urartian elite art. The Erebuni citadel was also the site of an ACHAEMENID administrative centre. See also KARMIR-BLUR.

Erech see URUK.

Erechtheion a temple on the Athenian AKROPOLIS to the north of the PARTHENON serving the cult of Erechtheus, a legendary king of ATHENS. It was built in the IONIC ORDER, construction starting in 421 BC. It housed several different cults, in addition to that of Erechtheus, and contained the old cult-statue of Athena. The CARYATID porch projected over the ruined foundations of an earlier temple, perhaps to allow continuity of the cult on the site.

Eredo a town containing one of the largest monuments in sub-Saharan Africa, a ruined 160 km-long (100 mile) earthen wall rising 20 m (66 ft) high from a moat, enclosing an area about 40 km (25 miles) from north to south and 36 km (22 miles) from east to west, constructed over three centuries from the 10th century ad in the southern Nigerian forest, east of Lagos. It is said to have been built by a childless wealthy Yoruba widow, Sungbo, who wished to be remembered for building a large monument. It apparently provided spiritual rather than physical protection, and shrines where offerings were made to protect local people from outsiders were erected on the structure.

Erevan Cave a Middle Palaeolithic site on the Razdan River in Erevan, Armenia. Artifacts were found at most levels in a sequence of loam and rubble; associated faunal remains include rhinoceros, horse, elk and red deer. The age of the occupations is unknown, but they apparently occurred during cool climatic conditions. The artifacts include many sidescrapers. Erevan Cave was excavated by Eritsyan in the late 1960s.

Eridu or **Abu Shahrain** the TELL-site at Abu Shahrain, which has been identified as ancient Eridu, the oldest city in southern MESOPOTAMIA, according to SUMERIAN mythology. The excavations by F. Safar and S. LLOYD in the 1940s revealed a long sequence of 'UBAID period (c.5000–3800 BC) occupation and provided the ceramic definition of the 'Ubaid 1 (Eridu) phase (beginning c.5500 BC). Eridu is best known for the sequence of 'Ubaid and URUK period (c.3800–3100 BC) temples, which documents the development of the tripartite arrangement of monumental architecture typical of these periods. This sequence begins with a small room fitted with an altar

(levels XVII–XVI), after which occur increasingly large multi-roomed buildings set on platforms. In this sequence, levels XI–VIII belong to the 'Ubaid 3, and levels VII–VI to the 'Ubaid 4 period; the subsequent levels (V–I) belong to the Uruk period. The usual identification of the buildings at Eridu as temples (and the comparable structures at WARKA, GAWRA and elsewhere) has recently been challenged by several French scholars, who interpret the large tripartite buildings on platforms as elite residences or, more plausibly, as audience halls, thus giving very different social implications to this architectural tradition. Other aspects of the 'Ubaid levels at Eridu include a large cemetery ('Ubaid 4 in date) and exposures of often flimsy residential architecture (in the 'Hut Sounding'). By the end of the 'Ubaid period, the Eridu settlement covered roughly 12 ha (30 acres), making it one of the known 'Ubaid towns. Architecture of the 3rd millennium is present nearer the surface, including an EARLY DYNASTIC palace (one of the few excavated so far) and a ziggurat of the UR III period.

Erim, Kenan (1921–90) a Turkish archaeologist who first worked in Sicily. His extensive excavations at APHRODISIAS started in 1961, and it is fitting that he was buried there.

Erimi-Bamboula a deeply stratified site of the 4th millennium BC in southern CYPRUS. It was excavated by Dikaios in 1973 and is the type-site for the CHALCOLITHIC I Erimi culture which is characterized by Red-on-White pottery. The settlement consisted of circular huts built of wattle and daub on stone foundations. The dead were buried INTRAMURALLY.

Er Lannic an islet in the Morbihan, France, with remains of two Neolithic STONE CIRCLES, now partly submerged by the rise in sea-level. Associated material comprises stone-built cists or hearths, polished stone axes and much pottery, including 162 decorated vase-supports. These may be remains of a cemetery which preceded the stone circles.

Erligang [Erh-li-kang] see ZHENGZHOU, SHANG.

Erlitou [Erh-li-t'ou] a site in Henan Province, China, where HANGTU foundations for two palace compounds have been excavated. Some assign the remains to the legendary XIA Dynasty, though they are included in predynastic SHANG by others (see CHINESE DYNASTIES). The four bronze JUE vessels discovered there are the earliest examples of the Shang bronze-casting tradition in piece-moulds. It is the type-site for the Erlitou culture of the HUANGHE corridor in the early 2nd millennium BC.

Erosd see ARIUŞD.

erosion a group of processes involving the physical breakdown or chemical solution, removal and transportation of materials by the actions of water, wind and ice. Erosion is capable of disrupting the context of archaeological deposits by total or partial site destruction, burial or redistribution. Some erosional processes are accelerated by the activities of people on the landscape, such as cultivation and deforestation. Some forms of erosion that can have significant impact on the archaeological record are:

(a) Soil erosion – accelerated downslope removal of soil material by various processes; more effective during heavier rainstorms, and on ground with little vegetation cover; main processes are:

(i) rainsplash erosion or raindrop erosion – direct dislodgement of material by raindrop impact and secondary displacement of larger CLASTS by undermining;

(ii) sheetwash or sheetflood erosion – removal and downslope transportation of soil material by the action of a thin sheet of water; incorporates material displaced by rainsplash erosion as well as effecting its own erosion through forces operating at the base of the sheetflow;

(iii) rill erosion – development of small channels only centimetres wide and deep at the base of sheet flows as they become locally concentrated.

(b) GULLY erosion – in stream valleys or on HILLSLOPES, gullies lengthen by upvalley migration.

(c) Wind erosion – removal of material by the wind; most effective where winds are strong, vegetation is sparse and soil moisture is lacking; main types are:

(i) deflation – loose material winnowed, picked up and carried by the wind as the wind's driving force overcomes the forces binding the particles; may create localized SAND BLOWS or scour broad areas;

(ii) abrasion – loosening and removal of material by the impact of material already picked up by the wind.

Ertebølle culture the final MESOLITHIC coastal KITCHEN MIDDEN culture of Scandinavia and the western Baltic (equivalent to the northern German Ellerbek), named after the type-site, a coastal SHELL MOUND in Jutland, Denmark, which is dated to c.3900–3250 BC. The assemblages contain introduced Neolithic artifacts, pottery and polished stone axes, while remaining Mesolithic in character although with relatively few microliths.

escarpment or **scarp** a landform consisting of a steep slope marking an abrupt change in altitude between two adjacent land surfaces. Escarpments mark geomorphic discontinuities that are usually accompanied by STRATIGRAPHIC and PEDOLOGICAL discontinuities as well. Vegetation can vary greatly on either side of an escarpment, and large-scale cliffs can be barriers to migration.

Eshnunna see ASMAR.

Esh Shaheinab the type-site for the KHARTOUM NEO-

LITHIC in the Sudan, containing bones of domestic stock dated by one of the first radiocarbon dates to 5300 bp.

Eskimo the aboriginal inhabitants of the Arctic regions of North America, characterized by great uniformity in culture, language and physical stock. Internal divisions of the Eskimo are based either on geographical location or on particular adaptive traits. The term 'Eskimo' is a derogatory Algonkin word that means 'eater of raw flesh'. The Eskimo call themselves INUIT.

Esna a site in UPPER EGYPT, chiefly known for the surviving PRONAOS of the temple to the ram-headed god Khnum, started at least as early as the joint reigns of PTOLEMYS VI and VIII (170–164 BC), but decorated mainly by Roman emperors of the 1st–3rd centuries AD. The MIDDLE KINGDOM to early NEW KINGDOM cemetery at Esna was excavated by GARSTANG in 1905–6.

ESR see ELECTRON SPIN RESONANCE.

Essenes see QUMRAN.

Es-Skhul see SKHUL.

Estaquería a late NASCA and MIDDLE HORIZON site in the Nasca Valley of the south coast of Peru. The site includes a large rectangular area in which there originally stood twelve rows of twenty upright posts, some over 50 cm (20 inches) in diameter. Investigated in 1952–3 by STRONG, it also includes a rectilinear adobe compound, and is surrounded by large cemeteries. The site may have served a ceremonial function.

etched carnelian beads South Asian carnelian beads with a decoration obtained by heating them, after a design in an alkali or metallic oxide paste has been painted on the surface; the paste design then stands out as a white or black pattern against the dull red of the stone. Developed by the Mature HARAPPAN period, the technique continues into modern times, and such beads may be widely traded, as the Harappan examples from Iranian and MESOPOTAMIAN sites illustrate.

ethnoarchaeology the study of human behaviour, and of the MATERIAL CULTURE of living societies, in order to see how materials enter the archaeological record, and hence to provide hypotheses explaining the production, use and disposal patterns of ancient material culture. Ethnoarchaeological studies, one type of ACTUALISTIC STUDY, gained importance under the NEW ARCHAEOLOGY as the need for WARRANTING ARGUMENTS in interpreting the archaeological record was stressed. It is a tool to develop MIDDLE RANGE THEORY, linking human behaviour with the archaeological record. See also TAPHONOMY.

ethnographic parallel a contemporary culture or particular behaviour that, by the process of analogy and homology, is thought to be similar to archaeologically recognizable behaviour and so can provide insights on the latter.

ethnography the description and analysis of individual contemporary cultures, using anthropological techniques such as participant observation (whereby the anthropologist lives in the society being studied) and a reliance on informants (individuals from whom specialized cultural knowledge is sought). Ethnography has provided many data of use to the archaeologist through reliance on analogy and homology. See also ETHNOLOGY.

ethnology the use of ETHNOGRAPHIC data in a comparative analysis to understand how cultures work and why they change.

ethology the study of animal behaviour, which provides hypotheses for explaining human behaviour. See also PALAEOECONOMY.

Etiolles an extensive MAGDALENIAN open-air site lying close to the River Seine, 30 km (19 miles) south of Paris, France. Excavated by Y. Taborin, it has twenty-six recognized *in situ* domestic units from successive occupations, including hearths and flint-knapping areas. Dating to 12,000 bp, the site is remarkable for the extreme abundance of its flint and débitage.

Etowah a large TEMPLE MOUND site in Georgia, USA. It comprises three individual mounds, the largest of which is over 20 m (66 ft) high, and is surpassed in volume only by CAHOKIA. It was perhaps a centre for the SOUTHERN CULT. See also MISSISSIPPIAN.

Etruria the area to the north of ROME bounded by the Rivers Tiber and Arno and the Tyrrhenian Sea. The inhabitants of the area, the Etruscans, colonized areas as far away as ALERIA, the Po Valley (see SPINA) and parts of CAMPANIA. The area is rich in mineral resources, which led to a wide range of metal products including gold, iron and bronze. The dead were buried in extensive cemeteries either in underground tombs or under tumuli (see CERVETERI). They were accompanied by a wide range of funerary goods, and the tombs themselves are an important source for ATHENIAN POTTERY. The walls of the tombs, especially at TARQUINIA, were decorated with a wide range of painted figured scenes. See also ETRUSCAN POTTERY. The twelve cities of Etruria had a focal point in the cult of Voltumna located near Orvieto. The use of inscriptions in tombs makes it clear that there was a strong family identity, including an emphasis on the maternal line.

Etruscan pottery pottery produced at various centres in ETRURIA, especially during the ARCHAIC and CLASSICAL periods. Although plain wares were particularly common (see BUCCHERO, IMPASTO), figure-decorated pottery was also produced (see CAERETAN WARE, PONTIC WARE).

Rzuczewo

Dabki

Truso

P O L A N D

f and Stellmoor

Sobiejuchy
Biskupin Osłonki
Brześć Kujawski
Chwalim Wietrzychowice
ningen Gniezno Sarnowo

Łęki Małe

ue Łęg Piekarski Janisławice Całowanie
Eilsleben Witów Swidry
Bilzingsleben Giecz
Groitzsch Senftenberg Ostrów Lednicki Gródek Nadbużny
Dölauer Heide Słupia Stara Krzemionki
Markleeberg Cmielów
Leubingen Słonowice Środa Śląska Nieptoperzowa Cave Zwoleń
Breitenbach Jordanów Bronocice Złota
s Cave Oelknitz Maszycka Cave/Wylotne
cke Kniegrotte Vikletice Dzierzysław
Postoloprty Staré Hradisko Kietrz Kraków-Spadzista/
Stradonice Homolka Olszanica Kraków-Zwierzyniec
Přezletice Závist Mamutowa
Mšecké Zehrovice Bylany
Úňetice Pohansko Oblazowa

Y CZECH REPUBLIC Tibara

Milavče Tĕšetice-Kyjovice Spišsky Stvrtok

Hluboke Mašůky Barca

Ofnet Arka
Manching Domica Bodrogkeresztúr
del Hascherkeller Istállóskö Puskaporos/Szeleta Cave
elherd Krems-Hundssteig Mad'arovce Subalyuk Tiszapolgár
ckstein Gudenus Cave Caka
Willendorf II Zillingtal Nitriansky Hrádok HUNGARY
Kamegg Jankovich
Salzofen Cave Aggsbach Budakalász Aszód
Mondsee Nové Košariská Kiskevély Pécel Tószeg
Dürrnberg bei Hallein Sopron Szelim Erd Nagyrév
Langmannersdorf Tata/ Kosziderpadlás Ocsöd-Kovashalom
Hallstatt Vértesszöllös Kisapostag Szegvár Tüzköves
Kökénydomb
A U S T R I A Repolust Cave Sagvar
Strettweg Lengyel

Zengövárkony

Euesperides a Greek city in western Cyrenaica, Libya. Although the settlement is first mentioned by the Greek historian Herodotus in the late 6th century BC, British excavations from the 1950s onwards have revealed pottery which suggests that there was occupation from at least the late 7th century BC. The city was carefully laid out in what is known as a HIPPODAMIAN PLAN, and it appears that the earliest grid on the Sidi Abeid probably dates from the 6th century BC. The city was extended in the early 4th century, taking advantage of the salt marsh, which was drying out. By the mid 3rd century BC the site was abandoned in favour of the nearby BERENICE and many of the house walls were robbed out.

Eurasian steppes a geographical zone occupying a vast territory from Mongolia in the east to the Danube River in the west. To the north it is bounded by forests, and to the south by the Black and Caspian Seas and the mountains of Central Asia. Beginning approximately from the 3rd millennium BC, with the use of pastoralism, metallurgy and wheeled-vehicles, this territory becomes an arena of important historical events: migrations of peoples, the rapid spread (in all directions) of major inventions (such as bronze metallurgy, chariots, horseriding and so on), types of tools and weaponry, art traditions and fashions, etc. It was an area where nomadic tribes had been formed, and from which they invaded areas inhabited by settled peoples, thus influencing their history. In every archaeological period there existed so-called 'historical-cultural communities', when there were local cultures with their specific peculiarities, but at the same time those cultures shared many common features. The most noteworthy example of such a community is that of the Early Nomad cultures (see GRYAZNOV), formed in the Eurasian steppes in the Early Iron Age – see SCYTHIAN TYPE CULTURES. Beginning in the last centuries BC, the Eurasian steppes served as a corridor for the movement to the west of the Central Asian nomads – HSIUNG-NU, HUNS, Turks and Mongols.

Europe, Central The prehistory of Central Europe (defined for this entry as Germany, Czech Republic, Poland, Austria, Hungary, and Slovakia) began during the initial colonization by HOMO *erectus* c.7–500,000 years ago, although the earliest evidence is very slight. The HOMINID mandible from MAUER, near Heidelberg, has been attributed to *H. erectus*, but it remains an isolated specimen. Artifacts at STRÁNSKA SKÁLA in Moravia have also been dated to this period. Somewhat later, Lower Palaeolithic sites in Central Europe, such as BILZINGS-LEBEN and STEINHEIM in Germany and VÉRTESZÖLLÖS in Hungary, have yielded human fossils intermediate between *H. erectus* and *H. sapiens*, now assigned to an archaic form of *H. sapiens*. The dating of these sites is generally between 400,000 and 175,000 years ago. Lower Palaeolithic stone tool assemblages with bifaces have been recovered from several sites, although not to the degree that they have been found in southern and western Europe. Southern and western parts of Central Europe have yielded abundant traces of *H. sapiens neanderthalensis*, including the original discovery location in the Neander valley near Düsseldorf. These are predominantly in the form of Middle Palaeolithic MOUSTERIAN stone tool assemblages that are dated between 100,000 and 40,000 years ago, found in rockshelters and caves. Sophisticated wooden spears have been found at SCHÖNINGEN and LEHRINGEN in Germany.

During the final stages of the WÜRM GLACIATION, Upper Palaeolithic settlements were widely distributed in the southern part of Central Europe. In Moravia, a series of sites dated between 30,000 and 25,000 years ago have been found, including PREDMOSTÍ and DOLNÍ VĚSTONICE, where abundant remains of mammoth, human burial and fired clay objects provide a glimpse of life during the Ice Age. At WILLENDORF in Austria, a small 'VENUS' FIGURINE is a noteworthy example of the naturalistic MOBILIARY ART of this period. In southern Poland, at KRAKÓW-SPADZISTA, traces of several MAMMOTH-BONE HOUSES were found. As the ice-sheets began to retreat, horse and reindeer were hunted by the inhabitants of sites like KNIEGROTTE and OELKNITZ in Germany and OBLAZOWA Cave in Poland. The end of the Ice Age saw the gradual warming of climate. At CAŁOWANIE and WITÓW in central Poland, groups of hunters made tanged points. Later, as forests were established, Mesolithic foragers took advantage of new animal and plant resources.

Agriculture arrived in Central Europe around 5600 BC, when LINEAR POTTERY settlements with LONGHOUSES, whose inhabitants grew wheat and barley and kept cattle, sheep, goat and pigs, were established on loess soil. Important Neolithic sites include KÖLN-LINDENTHAL, BYLANY and OLSZANICA. By 4000 BC, agriculture had been adopted throughout this area by communities of the LENGYEL, TRB, MICHELSBERG and RÖSSEN CULTURES. Ditched enclosures, either for protection or to demarcate ritual areas, are found at sites such as TEŠŠETICE-KYJOVICE in Moravia. In southern Germany and neighbouring Austria, LAKE DWELLINGS are found at sites like AICHBÜHL and MONDSEE. Later in the Neolithic, copper began to be used, first for ornaments, then for tools such as the massive axes of the TISZAPOLGÁR CULTURE of Hungary.

The development of bronze metallurgy triggered dramatic changes in Central Europe. The accumulation of wealth and status is reflected in the burials of the ÚNETICE culture of Bohemia and adjacent parts of Germany and Poland between 2100 and 1800 BC. Rich burials at LEUBINGEN in Germany and ŁĘKI MAŁE in Poland are particular examples of such wealth and status. Mining and metalworking centres became parts of larger exchange networks linking Central Europe with Scandinavia and southern Europe. Around 1200 BC there was a dramatic change in burial rite throughout this area from inhumation to cremation. Because urns with burnt bones were buried in large cemeteries such as the one at KIETRZ in Poland, the societies of this period are characterized as the URNFIELD COMPLEX.

The Late Bronze Age and Early Iron Age of Central Europe, known as the HALLSTATT period, saw many important developments. In the marshlands of northern Germany and Poland, a number of fortified sites, including SENFTENBERG and BISKUPIN, were established, although most of the inhabitants of Central Europe continued to live in small hamlets such as the one at HASCHERKELLER in Bavaria. Important commercial centres, notably the salt mines at Hallstatt in Austria, accumulated considerable wealth. By the 6th century BC, the Iron Age elite in western Central Europe had developed lively trade contacts with the Mediterranean via the Rhône Valley. Products of Mediterranean workshops and vineyards were sent north in exchange for hides, furs, food products and slaves. Exotic Mediterranean artifacts acquired by these elites appear in rich burials such as those at HOCHDORF and at hillforts such as the HEUNEBURG in southwestern Germany.

During the later Iron Age, in the last two centuries BC, immense settlements known as OPPIDA were founded in southern Central Europe. At MANCHING in Bavaria, evidence for workshops, warehouses, coin minting and iron smelting was found over an area of 380 ha (940 acres) enclosed by timber-reinforced ramparts. Along the Baltic coast, the PRZEWORSK CULTURE is known primarily from cremation burials in stone cists. Although the Romans never conquered those regions north of the Danube or east of the Rhine, the close contact with the Roman empire had a considerable impact on Central Europe. Many of its inhabitants served as mercenaries in the Roman legions and, returning home, brought Roman ideas along with pottery and weapons. With the collapse of the Roman empire in the 3rd–5th centuries AD, Germanic tribes such as the FRANKS and GOTHS assumed important roles in western and southern Europe, while ANGLO-SAXONS from northwestern Germany established footholds in the British Isles. In the 8th–10th centuries AD, as Christianity spread from western and southern Europe, several early states were established in Central Europe. These include Greater Moravia, with a centre at MIKULČICE, and the early Polish state, ruled from OSTRÓW LEDNICKI and GNIEZNO in western Poland.

Europe, eastern The prehistory of eastern Europe (defined for this entry as the modern states of Russia, Romania, Bulgaria, Moldova, Ukraine, Belarus and the Baltic states) began with the arrival of Lower Palaeolithic makers of bifaces and chopping tools. The site of KOROLEVO in the western Ukraine may be more than 700,000 years old, while a somewhat later site is located at KHRY-

ASHCHI on the Donets River. A somewhat greater number of sites can be assigned to the Middle Palaeolithic, because they have yielded MOUSTERIAN assemblages. At KIIK-KOBA and ZASKAL'NAYA in the Crimea, NEANDERTHAL burials have been found, several of which are children. Along the Dniester River, a series of Mousterian sites have been found. Perhaps the most important of these is MOLODOVA I, with its MAMMOTH-BONE HOUSE. Middle Palaeolithic occupation is also found in the Balkans, at sites like OHABA-PONOR in Romania and TEMNATA CAVE in Bulgaria.

The final stage of the WÜRM GLACIATION saw the spread of Upper Palaeolithic settlements throughout this region. Some of the earliest dates for the Upper Palaeolithic come from BACHO KIRO Cave in Bulgaria. At KOSTENKI-BORSCHEVO, a group of about twenty-five Upper Palaeolithic sites yielded abundant finds, including mammoth-bone houses and ivory 'VENUS' FIGURINES. At SUNGIR', several spectacular burials which date between 26,000 and 20,000 years ago have been found. One burial contained the skeleton of a male who was buried with numerous tools and ornaments, including 3,500 ivory beads. Far to the north, BYZOVAYA on the Pechora River is the northernmost Palaeolithic site in Europe. As the ice-sheets retreated, SWIDERIAN hunters followed the reindeer herds north. Their sites are found in Belarus and the Baltic states.

As forests established themselves across eastern Europe after the end of the Ice Age, Mesolithic societies adapted to the new environment. In addition to their campsites, large cemeteries are found. One of the most important is located at OLENEOSTROVSKI MOGILNIK on ONEGA LAKE in northern Russia, where the skeletons were sprinkled with ochre and were accompanied by artifacts of stone, antler, wood and bone. In the Baltic states and northwestern Russia, communities of the KUNDA culture hunted elk and seals. In the Balkans, important Mesolithic sites include BĂILE HERCULANE and SCHELA CLADOVEI in Romania. Along the Bug and Dniester Rivers in Moldova, inhabitants of sites at SOROCA (formerly Soroki) took advantage of the rich river resources at rapids as well as the animals of the nearby forests. They made crude pointed-base pottery and apparently obtained livestock and grain from nearby farmers.

Agriculture came to the Balkans around 6500 BC. The earliest farming communities in southern Bulgaria are known best from sites such as KARANOVO, CHEVDAR and AZMAK, where small clusters of square clay houses yielded evidence for the cultivation of wheat and barley and the bones of domestic sheep and goat. Agricultural sites were established in northeastern Romania and Ukraine by 4500 BC, where sites of the CUCUTENI-TRIPOLYE culture are found on river terraces. Their house locations are identified by timber and clay platforms known as PLOSHCHADKI. East of the Cucuteni-Tripolye

ESTONIA ↑Kunda/Narva
Zvejnieki
Novgorod/
Gubinskaya
Staraya Ladoga/↑
Onega Lake/Oleneostrovski Mogilnik
Zamostje 2
LATVIA
Luka ●
Sungir'
● Sarnate

● Šventoji
LITHUANIA
R U S S
Gnezdovo ●

BELORUSSIA
Negotino/Korshevo I & II/
Betovo/Khotylevo sites/Timonovka
● Gagarino

Berdyzh ●
● Yudinovo
● Pushkari I
Avdeevo
Yurovichi ●
Mezin ●
Kostenki-Borschevo

Rikhta ●

Shkurlat III ●

Kirillovskaya
Radomyshl' ● Kiev ●
Dobranichevka ●
Tripolye ●
Mezhirich ●
● Gontsy
Kulichivka ●
Kolomiishchina
Don River
Khryash
UKRAINE
Dnepr River

Ataki I/Ketrosy/
Korman' IV/Molodova Nezwiska
Luka Vrublevetskaya
Ripiceni-Izvor/
Stanca Ripiceni Cave
Dereivka ●
Amvrosievka ●
Korolevo ●
Vladimirovka
Kodak ●
Rozhok I ●
Polivanov Yar ●
Rashkov VII
● Sredni Stog
Soroca
Gerasimov ●
Brynzeny I/Korpach
Mikhajlovka ●
Mariupol ●
Cucuteni
Dubossary I/
Tolstaya Mogila
Tîrpeşti ● Vykhvatintsky ●
Pogrebya
Kamennaya Mogila
Otomani ●
Usatovo
Maikop
● Gura Baciului
Karbuna ●
Borodino ●
Ohaba-Ponor ●
Ceahlău-Cetăţica ●
Novye Ruseshty
Bol'shaya Akkarzha
Kul'-oba ●
Peramos
Il'skaya I ●
Turdaş ● ● Tărtăria
● Ariuşd
MOLDAVIA
Shaitan-Koba/
Semibratny ●
Sarmizegethusa ●
ROMANIA
Kabazi/
Gubs Shelter N
Adzhi-Koba/
Băile Herculane ●
Chokurcha/
● Hamangia
Kiik-Koba/
Ak-Kaya/
Mezma
Schela Cladovei
Starosel'e
Prolom II/
Syuren' I/
Coţofeni ● Cernica ● Gumelniţa
Cernavodă ●
Zaskal'naya/
● Salcuţa
Boian
● La Adam Cave
Sary-Kaya
Cascioarele
Muselievo
Ovčarovo ●
Krivodol ● Poljanica ●
Black Sea
● Střelice
● Varna
Zaminets ● Gradenitsa ● Bacho Kiro
Kremikovci ● Aibunar
● Goljamo Delčevo
Chevdar ● Karanovo
Temnata Cave Ezero
Veselinovo ●
Samuilitsa II Azmak
Duvanli
Kazanluk
BULGARIA

Yazilikaya ●

0 _____ 500 km

area, communities of the SREDNI STOG culture began their intensive use of horses at sites like DEREIVKA.

During the 5th millennium BC, copper metallurgy developed in the southern Balkans. At AIBUNAR in Bulgaria, copper was mined with antler picks. A Cucuteni-Tripolye hoard at KARBUNA in Moldova yielded a cache of early copper ornaments. Copper use was soon widespread in southeastern Europe. The opportunity for individuals and communities to accumulate considerable wealth is evident in the cemetery at VARNA in Bulgaria, where many graves have yielded considerable quantities of copper and gold ornaments. People in the Balkans continued to live in small farming communities such as OVCAROVO and POLJANICA, associated with the GUMELNIŢA culture. In northern Russia and the Baltic states, communities of the PIT-COMB and NARVA cultures, descended from the earlier hunter-gatherers of this area, continued their semi-agricultural economy. Their rock carvings are found along Onega Lake.

During the 2nd millennium BC, bronze metallurgy spread throughout eastern Europe, although use of this metal does not appear to have had the dramatic impact that it had in Central and western Europe. The transition to agriculture was consolidated further in northern Russia and the Baltic states. On the steppes north of the Black Sea and in eastern Russia near the Urals, pastoral societies, such as those of the SRUBNAYA culture, buried their dead in timber-lined graves under tumuli.

The opportunities that pastoralism offered for the accumulation of wealth reached their zenith during the 1st millennium BC in the area north of the Black Sea. Here, groups known collectively as the SCYTHIANS flourished. Scythians are known best from their graves, such as those at TOLSTAYA MOGILA, and through their contact with Greek merchants. In Bulgaria and Romania, the state of THRACIA emerged in the 5th century BC, while to the north DACIA was also established. Both were absorbed into the Roman empire during the first centuries AD. Migratory groups such as the GOTHS and HUNS caused dislocations in local communities during the 3rd–5th centuries AD. In Russia and Ukraine, traders from Scandinavia and local elites established centres at NOVGOROD and KIEV during the 9th century that eventually formed the nucleus of the Russian state.

eustasy changes in sea-level on a worldwide basis. The main factors that influence sea-level are global ice volumes, plate tectonics, changes in ocean volumes and dimensions, and movement of mantle material. During the GLACIAL-INTERGLACIAL cycles of the QUATERNARY, sea-levels fell as oceans were depleted of water and ice-sheets grew, and rose as glaciers melted returning the stored water to the ocean basins. Continental configurations were changed both by alternating exposure of land, making human and animal occupation and migration possible, altering coastal environments, and by flooding of land, subjecting any cultural remains to submarine erosional and depositional processes. Compare ISOSTASY.

eustatic *adj.* pertaining to vertical changes in worldwide sea-level. See also EUSTASY.

Eutresis a settlement site in Boeotia, Greece, which was excavated by Goldman in 1924–7 and by CASKEY in 1958. Eutresis was first occupied in the later Neolithic period and appears to have been inhabited continuously until the 13th century BC, when it was extensively fortified. Subsequently abandoned, the site was reoccupied in the CLASSICAL and HELLENISTIC periods. Eutresis is especially important because of its sequence of Early HELLADIC levels and is the type-site for the Early Helladic Eutresis culture.

Evans, Sir Arthur (1851–1941) a British scholar and archaeologist whose major contribution to Greek archaeology was his excavation of the MINOAN palace at KNOSSOS from 1899 onwards. It was Evans who first identified this early Cretan civilization and named it after the legendary King Minos.

Evans, Clifford (1920–81) an American pioneer of Amazonian archaeology, together with his wife and partner, Betty Meggers. Affiliated with the Smithsonian Institution since 1951, Evans and Meggers conducted research in Ecuador, Venezuela, British Guiana and Brazil, and provided the chronology and cultural definitions of prehistoric cultures of the northern Amazonian region.

Evans, Sir John (1823–1908) British scholar and antiquary who published important books on prehistoric stone implements, bronze implements and pre-Roman coins, and who played a vital role in supporting the claims of BOUCHER DE PERTHES.

'Eve hypothesis' see MITOCHONDRIAL DNA.

evolution a theory of biology developed by Charles Darwin, whereby an organism's degree of adaptation to the environment determines its chances of surviving, and thus successfully creating offspring and passing on its genes to the next generation. The model was first used by anthropology in the 19th century to explain the progressive and unilinear development of human societies from 'savagery' to 'civilization'; however, it was later rejected at the end of that century, largely as a result of work by Franz Boas and other anthropologists, because of its explicitly racist overtones. The work of Leslie WHITE and Julian STEWARD succeeded in reintroducing evolutionary models to anthropology and archaeology, and neo-evolutionary thought remains one of the major principles of NEW or PROCESSUAL ARCHAEOLOGY.

excavation the systematic recovery of archaeological data through the exposure of buried sites and artifacts. Excavation is destructive to any site, and is thus accompanied by a comprehensive recording of all material found and its three-dimensional locations. As much material and information as possible must be recovered from any 'dig'. A full record of all the techniques employed in the excavation itself must also be made, so that future archaeologists will be able to evaluate the results of the work accurately. Excavation is also costly. For both these reasons, it should be used only as a last resort. Excavation can be either partial, in which only a sample of the site is investigated, or total. Samples are chosen either intuitively, in which case excavators investigate those areas they feel will be most productive, or statistically, in which case the sample is drawn using various statistical techniques in order to ensure that it is representative. An important goal of excavation is a full understanding of a site's STRATIGRAPHY, which refers to the vertical layering of a site. These layers, or levels, can be defined naturally (e.g. soil changes), culturally (e.g. different occupation levels) or arbitrarily (e.g. 10 cm [4 inch] levels). See also SURVEY.

exchange a system which facilitates the transfer of goods and services between societies and/or individuals. Exchange systems can vary in size and complexity from individual, one-off bartering to complex market economies employing standardized currencies.

exogamy the practice of marrying someone *outside* one's own social unit, such as the clan or tribe. The opposite of ENDOGAMY.

experimental archaeology the controlled replication of ancient technologies and behaviour, in order to provide hypotheses that can be tested by actual archaeological data. Experiments can range in size from the reproduction of ancient tools in order to learn about their processes of manufacture and use to the construction of whole villages and ancient subsistence practices in long-term experiments.

extramural See INTRAMURAL.

Eyasi a locality in northern Tanzania with fauna, including extinct mammal species, artifacts and archaic HOMO *sapiens* remains. It was formerly thought to be of late Pleistocene age, but is now considered to date to the late Middle Pleistocene.

Eynan, Ain Mallaha or **Ein Mallaha** an extensive NATUFIAN open-air fishing settlement next to Lake Huleh in the Jordan Valley, Israel. Jean Perrot's excavations (1955–79) revealed three successive occupations, which contained perhaps fifty semi-subterranean stone-lined circular structures, 3–9 m (10–30 ft) in diameter, and often containing internal hearths and storage bins. Large storage pits and burials lie outside the structures: one 10th-millennium bc burial contained an old woman (?) with a puppy, but the best-known burial is that of a male and female found with their legs removed in an elaborately paved and walled round tomb. There is some evidence for collective burial after decomposition. In addition to its lithic industries Eynan also has a rich bone tool industry, bone and stone artwork and stone vessels.

Ezero an ENEOLITHIC and Early Bronze Age cultural complex of the lower Danube basin and the Black Sea coast of Bulgaria, named after the TELL site at Ezero in central Bulgaria. The Ezero sequence provides the most detailed chronology for southeastern Europe from the end of the Eneolithic into the Early Bronze Age. Early and Middle Ezero are contemporaneous with BADEN in Central Europe, and the intensification of sheep/goat husbandry at Ezero is taken as support for the SECONDARY PRODUCTS REVOLUTION. The Early Bronze Age level at Ezero is fortified with a stone wall.

Ezo a medieval name for the northernmost Japanese island, now called Hokkaido; by extension it designated hunter-gatherer-farmer populations that lived on the island (see EMISHI, AINU).

F

Faboura a vast accumulation of *Arca senelis* bivalve shells covering over 7 ha (17 acres) and up to 8 m (26 ft) high, southeast of Joal in Senegal, dated to between 1900 and 1300 BP and linked to the local Manding people.

fabricator 1 a stone or bone used in the manufacture of other tools. The term is usually applied to Mesolithic *plano-convex* (i.e. one side flat, one rounded) slug-shaped stone tools used in retouch.

2 (*Australia*) a small squarish or rectangular artifact with battering on opposite margins. The term has largely fallen into disuse since these objects have been shown to be bipolar cores rather than tools.

facies a part that is distinguished from the whole of a recognized unit on some basis of appearance or composition. Originally developed for geological applications, such as LITHOFACIES and biofacies, the facies concept has been widely applied, including PEDOLOGY (soil facies) and archaeology (to a culture or industry).

faience a material used in ancient Egypt, the Near East and the Aegean for glazed figurines and jewellery. It consists of a body of quartz sand, soda and lime, covered by a soda-lime glaze which is usually coloured green or greenish-blue but can be polychrome.

Faiyum a fertile depression in the Egyptian Sahara, watered by an arm of the River Nile. Important during the Neolithic (see FAIYUM 'A'), but largely undeveloped by the ancient Egyptians except during the MIDDLE KINGDOM (see HAWARA, QASR ES-SAGHA) and during the Graeco-Roman period (see KARANIS).

Many mummies from the Faiyum area, dating to the 1st/2nd centuries AD, feature lifelike portraits of the deceased on flat pieces of wood inserted into the wrappings, among the best portraits that survive from the ancient world. They were painted by using hot wax as a means of applying the pigment, and are known as 'encaustic' portraits.

Faiyum 'A' the earliest-known phase of the PREDYN-ASTIC sequence of LOWER EGYPT, represented by the (possibly seasonal) settlement sites in the northern FAIYUM explored by Gardner and CATON THOMPSON in 1924–6. Although agriculturalists, the population of Faiyum 'A' were largely dependent on the hunting of large mammals such as elephant and hippopotamus.

Fajada Butte a geological feature in CHACO CANYON, New Mexico, USA, on which is located the 'sun-dagger'. This comprises two vertical slabs of rock, through which, at the summer and winter solstices, sunlight falls on to carved spiral designs. The site has been interpreted by some as a solar observatory, but others question this function.

false colour infrared photography a photographic technique, utilizing film sensitive to infrared wavelengths, that achieves greater resolution of certain features than conventional photography because the wavelengths are unaffected by atmospheric haze and the photographic images are not represented by true colours. Differences in water absorption qualities of photographed features are also enhanced; contrasts between soil and sediment of different textures, different vegetation, and the difference between vegetation and soil are sharp.

False colour infrared photography can be used for on- and off-site soil and geomorphic mapping to help construct the geological context of sites. Archaeological features of contrasting texture and earthworks may also be expressed.

false-necked amphora see STIRRUP JAR.

Fara, Tell ancient Shuruppak, a 120 ha (297 acre) low mound in southern Babylonia, investigated by a German team in 1902 and by an American group in 1931. The city was occupied from the late 4th to the end of the 3rd millennium BC; the excavations to date are too inadequate to provide much detail about the city's character. Fara remains best known for its EARLY DYNASTIC III (c.2600–2500 BC) clay tablets that contain both economic information and literary compositions.

Fat'janovo culture or **Fatyanovo culture** a regional culture on the northeastern edge of the broader CORDED WARE complex, named after the cemetery of Fat'janovo near Yaroslavl on the upper Volga in central Russia. Fat'janovo graves are shallow shafts with no burial mounds. Vessels buried with the dead include spherical AMPHORAS with cord decoration, and Fat'janovo 'battleaxes' have distinctive drooping blades. The Fat'janovo culture appears to have been long-lived, lasting into the early part of the Bronze Age.

faunal analysis see ARCHAEOZOOLOGY.

Fauresmith, an outdated term for final ACHEULIAN collections from the southern African interior, characterized by small, well-finished pointed handaxes.

Fayum see FAIYUM.

feature a non-portable element of a larger site. Examples include fire-hearths, interior walls and ACTIVITY AREAS.

Feddersen Wierde a well-preserved TERP settlement on the German North Sea coast, dating from the 1st to early 5th centuries AD. It comprises timber buildings, especially aisled long houses with wattle walls inside, and byres and stalls. The layout of the village was like a spoked wheel, with an open area at the centre, and segments radiating outwards, with farming and dwelling areas distinct from the craft areas where leather and bones were worked.

Federmesser a small backed blade, very similar to the AZILIAN POINT, that characterizes the final GLACIAL industries of the North European Plain in the 10th/9th millennia bc and the CRESWELLIAN culture of Britain.

Fejej a 4.2 million-year-old site in southern Ethiopia which has yielded a small collection of early HOMINID teeth attributed to AUSTRALOPITHECUS *afarensis*.

Fell's Cave see CUEVA FELL.

feminist archaeology see GENDERED ARCHAEOLOGY.

fen a wetlands community, characterized by alkaline conditions, that grows in zones between fresh water and land, such as along lake margins, and rapidly evolves during a transition of infilling and shallowing. As with other types of bog, fens are locations where preservation of organic material is good, thus providing an excellent source of PALAEOENVIRONMENTAL and artifactual information.

Fengate a complex of farmsteads in England, associated with small square fields and droveways or tracks on the edge of the Cambridgeshire Fens, dating from the middle Neolithic to the end of the Middle Bronze Age. Occupation resumed in the Early Iron Age with a new layout of fields and a larger settlement, the Cat's Water village, with remains of over fifty buildings of which about ten would have been in use at once. See also PETERBOROUGH WARE.

Fengbitou [Feng-pi-t'ou] a site on the southwestern coast of Taiwan which gives its name to the Fengbitou

Neolithic culture of western Taiwan, dated to 2400–1800 BC.

Ferrières-les-Verreries a late Neolithic DOLMEN in Hérault, France, type-site of the Ferrières culture (c.3200–2800 BC), characterized by pottery decorated with incised lines and geometric motifs.

Fertile Crescent a phrase coined in the 1920s by James Breasted to describe the arc of well-watered land across MESOPOTAMIA, Syria and Palestine, bound by desert on one side and mountains and sea on the other, in which early Near Eastern civilizations thrived. Although still current in popular usage, the phrase is deceptive in several ways. The region it describes encompasses a great variety of environments, cultures, languages and paths of development. The phrase also excludes regions like Anatolia and Iran that are vital for understanding the beginnings of settled life and food production, and that were important links of trade, sources of raw materials and centres of historical empires.

fibula a pin with a catch used from the Bronze Age to the ANGLO-SAXON period. Fibulae may be highly decorated and are normally made of bronze, although examples are known in precious metal. They seem to have been used for fastening clothing.

ficron a morphological term generally used to describe a long, pointed biface with slightly concave sides and a well-made tip. BORDES specifically used the term to denote a roughly worked pointed biface, the probable forerunner of the MICOQUIAN biface form.

Fikellura ware a style of ARCHAIC EAST GREEK POTTERY using a BLACK-FIGURED technique. The name is derived from the Fikellura cemetery on Rhodes, where many examples of the fabric have been found. The fabric had at one time been attributed to Samos and Rhodes on stylistic grounds, but recent clay analyses have demonstrated that the source was in fact MILETUS.

filigree a technique used in the manufacture of jewellery whereby wire, usually gold or electrum, more rarely silver, is soldered on to metalwork.

Filimoshki a Pleistocene open-air locality on the Zeya River (Amur tributary) in far eastern Siberia, which yielded flaked quartzite cobbles of possible human manufacture. The modified cobbles were recovered from ALLUVIUM of the second terrace in 1961 by OKLADNIKOV, who classified them as Lower Palaeolithic tools. However, their age and status as artifacts remain problematic.

Filitosa a fortified promontory settlement in Corsica, France, dominated by a Bronze Age *torre* or tower, the Corsican equivalent of the Sardinian NURAGHE. The origins of the Corsican torri lie at the CHALCOLITHIC or Early Bronze Age c.2500–2000 BC. The Filitosa example is a circular dry-stone tower standing within a walled enclosure with oval houses. It dates probably from the middle of the 2nd millennium and incorporates in its construction a number of reused STATUES-MENHIRS of men armed with bronze swords and daggers.

Final Neolithic a transitional phase in which there is some use of copper or bronze but stone is still predominant. See also ENEOLITHIC.

fine orange pottery a late CLASSIC pottery type from the lowland MAYA area of MESOAMERICA. The temperless pottery comes from the region of the Usumacinta drainage near the Gulf Coast. The appearance of the pottery at such sites as ALTAR DE SACRIFICIOS and SEIBAL suggests a foreign influence in these centres during Late Classic times.

Fiorelli, Giuseppe (1823–96) one of the early directors of the excavations at POMPEII in 1860–75. The previous haphazard diggings, essentially in search of treasure and *objets d'art* to be placed on display in royal palaces, were replaced by a systematic strategy. He devised a scheme for dividing the city up into regions. He also developed a technique for taking plaster casts of the hollows in the hardened ash and cinders, thus gaining impressions of the dead and other organic material such as that used in furniture. **(See fig., p. 364.)**

fire see SWARTKRANS, CHESOWANJA.

fire hardening the exposure of a wooden tool to fire in order to dry out the wood but not to char it, which makes the tool harder and therefore more efficient. See also LEHRINGEN.

firestick farming a term coined by Rhys Jones to describe the management of the Australian ecosystem by Aborigines using fire. Aboriginal burning is well documented historically and ethnographically, and it is clear that the landscape seen by the first European settlers was cultural rather than natural. Reasons for burning include facilitating travel, creating firebreaks and encouraging the growth of food plants both for people and for animals.

'First Family' a nickname for a jumbled collection of some 200 AUSTRALOPITHECUS *afarensis* fossils found on a hillslope at Site 333 at HADAR in Ethiopia in 1975–6, dating between 3.5 and 3 million years ago. At least thirteen individuals, male and female, adult and juvenile, are represented. There is uncertainty about whether the fossils accumulated over a period of time or whether they represent a group that died simultaneously in an event like a flash flood.

Fishbourne the site of a substantial palace near Chichester (*Lat.* Noviomagus Regnensium) in England, excavated in the 1960s by the Sussex Archaeological Society under Barry Cunliffe. It started as a coastal depot with granaries to serve the Roman invasion. This was replaced by a residential structure with a bath-house, followed in *c.*AD 75 by the extensive building, covering some 4 ha (10 acres). The building was decorated with mosaics, stucco mouldings and painted wall plaster. The central square was laid out as a formal garden.

fish-hooks (*Pacific*) artifacts of two basic types: *bait* hooks, for angling; and *lure* hooks, for towing behind a moving canoe. They may be made of shell, bone, stone, tortoiseshell or wood. They are extremely varied in form, especially in eastern POLYNESIA, and act as temporal and cultural markers in the region.

fishtail point the most distinctive artifact of a stone tool tradition of South America, dating to *c.*11,000 to 8000 bc. The points are fluted and stemmed, having a roughly fish-like outline. The complex shows technical similarities to the CLOVIS tradition of North America, and thus represents the PALAEOINDIAN period in South America.

fission track dating a radiogenic dating method based on the natural and spontaneous nuclear fission of Uranium 238 and its physical product, linear atomic displacements (tracks) created along the trajectory of released energized fission fragments. Knowing the rate of fission, which is a constant, the uranium content of the material, and the number of fission tracks by counting, one can determine the age of the material. The method is most widely used to date TEPHRA BEDS and obsidian, with the tracks in glass and accessory zircon being counted. Archaeological samples such as pottery and obsidian must have been heated to anneal any previous tracks that would date the constituent mineral but not artifact. Accuracy, minimum age determinations and datable materials all depend on ^{238}U concentrations.

Five Mile Rapids site see DALLES.

Flag Fen a Late Bronze Age settlement of long rectangular timber houses on an artificial timber platform in the Cambridgeshire Fens, England. The timbers had been laid on the mud of the fen bottom in about half a metre of water. The island was reached by a timber trackway from the mainland at FENGATE. The settlement, excavated by F. Pryor since 1982, was occupied *c.*1500–700 BC, and associated artifacts include flint tools, a bronze dagger, a bracelet of Kimmeridge shale, pottery and wooden items. In 1994, England's earliest prehistoric wooden wheel, made from three planks of alderwood, was unearthed at the site.

flake a sliver of stone removed from a core during knapping, either as a planned artifact or as a waste by-product. Flakes may be retouched to make a *flake tool*, or may be used in an unmodified state. Waste flakes are those discarded during the manufacture of a tool. See also BLADE, BULB OF PERCUSSION, DÉBITAGE.

flake-blade an imprecisely defined elongated flaked stone artifact with dorsal ridges associated with sub-Saharan African MIDDLE STONE AGE collections. Unlike true blades, flake-blades do not necessarily have parallel sides, nor are they necessarily at least twice as long as they are wide. They were usually end-struck off cores, frequently taper to a point to form artifacts termed convergent or pointed flake-blades, and often have faceted platforms. Some examples were retouched to form 'knives' or denticulate or notched tools.

flint a member of the CHALCEDONY group of water-bearing silica minerals characterized by its opaqueness and dark colour, the result of included organic matter. Flint normally occurs in nodules. Its ability to fracture conchoidally made it ideal for fashioning stone implements with sharp edges. The best-known flint is from the chalk in England and northern Europe. See also CHERT, GRIMES GRAVES, KRZEMIONKI, SPIENNES, CHOCOLATE FLINT.

floating chronology a chronometrically dated chronology that is not anchored to precise time from the present, usually used in reference to DENDROCHRONOLOGY and VARVE chronologies.

Flomborn see LINEAR POTTERY.

flood a universal deluge, notions of which occur not only in the Old Testament but also in SUMERIAN and AKKADIAN texts. The SUMERIAN KING LISTS make the distinction between ante-diluvian and post-diluvian rulers. WOOLLEY's deep soundings at UR exposed a level of major flooding, and similar levels have been observed at KISH and FARA to the north; such deposits reflect the shifting of river courses in southern MESOPOTAMIA. Recent geomorphological evidence points to a catastrophic flooding of the Black Sea basin during the 5th millennium BC, an event that some have tried to connect to flood stories.

floodplain a depositional landform comprising that portion of a river valley subject to flooding. As flood waters recede, the suspended sediment load is deposited as ALLUVIUM and causes slow vertical accretion. Floodplains are usually an amalgam of secondary features including individual flood basins that may support swamps and marshes, abandoned channels, secondary flood channels, tributary stream courses and NATURAL LEVEES. With a variety of secondary landforms, floodplains can be a diverse and rich resource base. Because of the intermittent addition of organic nutrient-rich alluvium, floodplains were and are prime agricultural land. Aggradation also may cause burial and preservation of archaeological deposits in many of these subenvironments. Conversely, stream channel migration may erode large tracts of floodplain and any archaeological deposits buried below or resting upon the floodplain.

Florisbad a hot water spring deposit in the central Free State Province of South Africa, which has yielded MIDDLE STONE AGE remains, as well as a late archaic HOMO *sapiens* cranium, named *H. helmei*, which may be as old as 250,000 years, and which some researchers consider to be the immediate ancestor of modern humans in Africa. The cranium bears the impression of a hyena canine on its forehead.

flotation a water separation method for recovering small floral, faunal and artifactual remains from bulk sediment samples, originally developed by Stuart and Alice Struever at the KOSTER site. Sediment samples, with or without various pre-treatments such as air-drying, are disaggregated in water or a sodium-hexametaphosphate-water solution and passed through a fine mesh screen in the bottom of a tub or similar container, with or without mechanical agitation. Several variations of flotation machines have subsequently been developed. Floating carbonized or charred plant remains, constituting the light fraction, are recovered from the water surface by various means, and the heavy fraction of bone and lithic material is recovered from the screen. Further separation of the heavy fraction can be accomplished with heavy liquids of varying specific gravity.

fluorine dating a RELATIVE DATING technique applied to bone. Bone absorbs fluorine from groundwaters at a rate that is proportional to the time since burial, if groundwater migration rates remain constant. Fluorine concentrations are determined by CHEMICAL ANALYSIS.

flûte de Pan see PAN-PIPE LUG.

fluted point a point belonging to the early part of the PALAEOINDIAN period characterized by extreme symmetry, careful flaking and the removal of a long, parallel and shallow flake, or flute, from one or both sides of the point. The technology is peculiar to the New World, and is associated with the CLOVIS and FOLSOM point styles.

fluxgate gradiometer see MAGNETOMETER.

focus see MIDWESTERN TAXONOMIC SYSTEM.

fogou see SOUTERRAIN.

Folsom 1 a PALAEOINDIAN, fluted point type that differs from CLOVIS mainly in the length of its flute, which extends over most of the point's side. The date range for the point type is approximately 11,000–10,200 BP.

2 a complex associated with the point type, characterized by a concentration on the hunting of now extinct bison, as well as a specific lithic assemblage. The most representative Folsom complex site is LINDENMEIER.

3 the type-site in New Mexico, USA, where nineteen points were found associated with the remains of twenty-three extinct bison, close to a relict marsh.

Fontanalba see MONT BÉGO.

FOLSOM POINT.

Fontbouisse a CHALCOLITHIC settlement in Gard, France, of dry-stone houses with APSIDAL ends, type-site of the Fontbouisse culture (c.2800–2200 BC) also represented at the villages of Cambous and La Conquette, and the enclosed sites of BOUSSARGUES and LÉBOUS. Burial was in simple megalithic tombs or natural caves in the vicinity of the settlements, though INTRAMURAL burials of very young children are known. Fontbouisse pottery is characterized by complex incised and channelled decoration, and the region's earliest copper objects are sometimes found.

Fontbrégoua a cave-site in Var, southern France, with a 10 m (33 ft) sequence of EPIPALAEOLITHIC and Neolithic occupation. The earliest levels c.8000 BC have yielded evidence of hunting and gathering including carbonized hazelnuts and plant remains. The early Neolithic levels have domestic livestock and pottery and span the CARDIAL and EPICARDIAL phases. Above are deposits with middle Neolithic Chasséen (see CHASSEY), late Neolithic and BELL BEAKER remains. Pits of human bones bearing cutmarks, found amid pits of butchered animal bones, have been claimed as evidence of Neolithic cannibalism.

Font-Brunel point see TEYJAT.

Font-de-Gaume a cave near LES EYZIES, Dordogne, France, where Palaeolithic paintings were discovered by PEYRONY in 1901. About 230 figures are known, dominated by eighty-two bison, and including some polychrome work. The art is attributed to the MAGDALENIAN (c.14,000–10,000 BC).

Fontéchevade a French cave-site in the Charente region, principally excavated by Germaine Henri-Martin in 1937–54. It is dated to the RISS GLACIATION, and has yielded a Lower Palaeolithic TAYACIAN industry similar to that

recovered from CLACTON with many chopping tools. Human skeletal remains from the cave have been classed as a form of PRE- or early NEANDERTHALEr. The upper levels have produced Middle and Upper Palaeolithic material.

Forbes Quarry skull see Gibraltar.

Ford, James Alfred (1911–68) an American archaeologist who specialized in southeastern North America and made fundamental contributions to the technique of SERIATION. Ford further argued that archaeological types were imposed on the data by the classifier, and this led to a series of famous debates with Albert SPAULDING, who championed the view that types were 'discovered'.

formation processes or **site formation processes** the sum total of processes, natural and cultural, acting individually or in concert, that result in the archaeological record as it exists today. An understanding of formation processes must precede any archaeological inference because of the transformations that may have altered the original cultural and natural depositional record.

Formative period 1 a cultural stage, used in North America, that is defined by the presence of agriculture and villages. Normally, the Formative is also often accompanied by pottery, weaving, stone-carving and ceremonial architecture.

2 in MESOAMERICA, another term for the PRECLASSIC period, used in highland sequences.

3 in Andean South America, the period including both the INITIAL PERIOD and EARLY HORIZON (c.1800–1 BC), beginning with the introduction of ceramic technology. Elsewhere in South America, it also begins with the introduction of ceramics; this occurred c.7600 bp in Amazonia (see TAPERINHA), and c.5200 bp in northwestern Colombia.

Forsandmoen large complex of fifteen farmsteads dating to the Migration period, 4th–6th centuries AD, in southwestern Norway, which reflects the emergence of nucleated settlements in this area during the 1st millennium AD.

Fort Ancient a series of cultures or societies located along the Ohio River and its tributaries, USA, which date to AD 900–1600. The aspect is characterized by an increasing dependence on agriculture. PLATFORM and BURIAL MOUNDS, and palisaded houses are known. Fort Ancient has heavy MISSISSIPPIAN influence.

Fort Harrouard a promontory fort in Eure-et-Loir, France, with occupation from the middle Neolithic to the end of the Gallo-Roman period. Neolithic occupation is divided into two phases: Chasséen (see CHASSEY), with decorated VASE-SUPPORTS and terracotta female figurines, followed by ARTENACIEN. Evidence of metallurgy has been recovered in the Middle and Late Bronze Age levels, including crucibles, moulds, and a stone-filled pit interpreted as the remains of a bronze-working furnace.

Fort Rock Cave an early site in Oregon, USA, containing charcoal dated to over 13,000 BP in association with a MANO and METATE, projectile points and other stone artifacts. The validity of this association has been questioned. The occupation level above this basal component is dated to over 10,000 BP.

forum an open space in the heart of a Roman city or colony. It served a variety of functions as it was surrounded by administrative buildings (see CURIA, COMITIUM) and religious structures as well as by shops and sometimes libraries. At ROME there were several fora. The main area was the *Forum Romanum*, which included temples of Saturn, Castor and Concordia, triumphal arches and various administrative buildings. The *Forum Augustum*, some 100 m (110 yds) in length, served as a precinct to the temple of Mars Ultor built in the CORINTHIAN ORDER. The *Forum Traiani* contained Greek and Latin libraries as well as TRAJAN'S COLUMN. Compare AGORA.

fossil beach or **raised beach** a landform representing a former beach that has been elevated relative to sea- or lake-level since the time it was active. Vertical displacement may be caused by isostatic crustal changes or eustatic sea-level fluctuations, both common processes during the QUATERNARY. Lake-levels may be influenced by changes in desiccation and precipitation. The age of archaeological deposits associated with fossil beaches can be no older than the age of beach activity; archaeological surveys should be planned accordingly. See also ISOSTASY, EUSTASY.

Fourneau du Diable an open-sir site above the valley of the Dronne, in the Dordogne (France), where excavations by PEYRONY in the 1920s revealed a GRAVETTIAN occupation followed by a late SOLUTREAN established in a kind of shelter formed of fallen blocks. One large block in the Solutrean level bore auroch figures sculpted in bas-relief.

Fox, Sir Cyril (1882–1967) British archaeologist who played a major role in introducing geographical approaches to the subject, and contributed to the development of field archaeology in the 1920s and 1930s; he is best known for his classic work, *The Personality of Britain* (1932).

Foz Côa see CÔA VALLEY.

France The area now known as France was first occupied by HOMINIDs at least a million years ago, though claims have been made for occupation dating back twice as far as this. The evidence consists largely of stone tools, notably handaxes, though occupation sites are also known such as the 400,000-year-old TERRA AMATA on the Mediter-

ranean coast near Nice, with traces claimed to indicate rough brushwood or animal hide shelters. This Lower Palaeolithic phase (c.1 million–200,000 years ago) is succeeded by the Middle Palaeolithic (c.200,000–35,000 years ago) when France was occupied by NEANDERTHALS with their MOUSTERIAN stone tool industry. Neanderthals showed some of the behaviours associated with modern humans, such as burial of their dead at LA FERRASSIE. They were nonetheless supplanted around 35,000 years ago by modern humans. This change marks the beginning of the Upper Palaeolithic (c.35,000–12,000 years ago), which in France is characterized most famously by cave-art sites such as LASCAUX and CHAUVET. The Dordogne region of southwestern France is especially important during this period, with its many rockshelters giving evidence of repeated occupation by hunter-gatherers exploiting the salmon in the rivers and the migrating herds of reindeer.

At the end of the last GLACIAL period the Upper Palaeolithic gave place to the Epipalaeolithic and Mesolithic periods (from 12,000 BP/10,000 BC). Warmer temperatures promoted the establishment of Mediterranean woodland in the south and temperate forest further north. Mesolithic hunter-gatherers left evidence of their activities in the form of small flint tools known as microliths (which were the points and barbs of knives, arrows and spears), but by 6000 BC communities living on the southern coast of France had adopted domestic animals and cultivated cereals from the east, thus marking the transition to the Neolithic period. In northeastern France, the Neolithic begins c.5200 BC with a mixture of indigenous change and exogenous colonization in the form of BANDKERAMIK farmers from southern Germany who established farming settlements in the Rhineland and the eastern valleys of the Paris basin. By 4000 BC the transition to the Neolithic lifestyle was complete throughout the whole of France, though in the western regions mobile lifestyles combining small-scale cultivation with hunting and herding remained the norm for several centuries. It was these regions that saw the construction of the famous Neolithic monuments such as the BARNENEZ and GAVRINIS PASSAGE GRAVES, the CARNAC stone rows and the GRAND MENHIR BRISÉ.

The late Neolithic (c.3500–2300 BC) saw the spread of copper metallurgy among farming villages of the Mediterranean zone, and the erection of STATUE-MENHIRS depicting stylized figures. There was also the adoption of large-scale collective burial, with bones of hundreds of individuals in the caves and rock-cut tombs of southern France and in the *hypogées* and ALLÉES COUVERTES of the northeast. The Bronze Age (c.2300–800 BC) sees the spread of cremation burials, exemplified by the Late Bronze Age urnfields of the east and south. Military equipment in the form of slashing swords, helmets and sheet bronze body-armour appears towards the end of the period. It is followed by the Iron Age (c.800–50 BC),

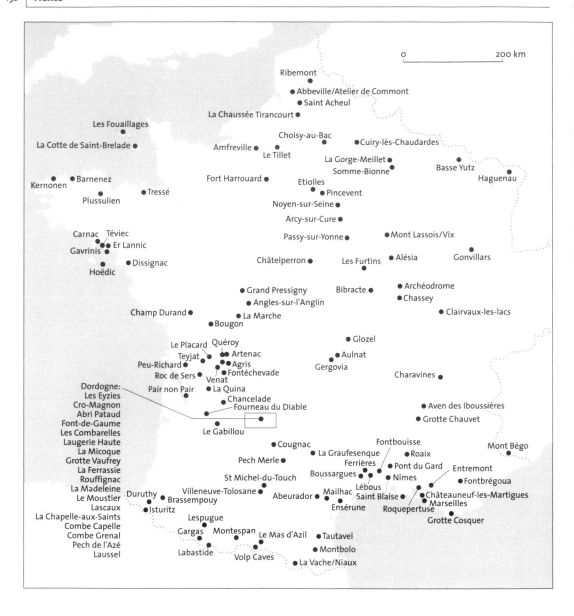

Ribemont

Abbeville/Atelier de Commont

Saint Acheul

La Chaussée Tirancourt

Les Fouaillages

La Cotte de Saint-Brelade

Choisy-au-Bac

Cuiry-lès-Chaudardes

Amfreville
Le Tillet

La Gorge-Meillet
Somme-Bionne

Basse Yutz

Haguenau

Fort Harrouard
Etiolles
Pincevent

Noyen-sur-Seine

Arcy-sur-Cure

Kernonen Barnenez
Plussulien
Tressé

Carnac Téviec
Gavrinis Er Lannic
Hoëdic
Dissignac

Passy-sur-Yonne

Mont Lassois/Vix

Châtelperron
Les Furtins
Alésia
Gonvillars

Grand Pressigny
Angles-sur-l'Anglin
Bibracte
Archéodrome
Chassey

Champ Durand
La Marche
Bougon

Clairvaux-les-lacs

Glozel

Le Placard Quéroy
Teyjat Artenac
Peu-Richard Agris
Roc de Sers Fontéchevade
Venat
Pair non Pair La Quina

Aulnat
Gergovia

Charavines

Dordogne:
Les Eyzies
Cro-Magnon
Abri Pataud
Font-de-Gaume
Les Combarelles
Laugerie Haute
La Micoque
Grotte Vaufrey
La Ferrassie
Rouffignac
La Madeleine
Le Moustier
Lascaux
La Chapelle-aux-Saints
Combe Capelle
Combe Grenal
Pech de l'Azé
Laussel

Chancelade
Fourneau du Diable

Le Gabillou

Aven des Iboussières
Grotte Chauvet

Cougnac
Fontbouisse
Mont Bégo

Pech Merle
La Graufesenque
Roaix

Ferrières
Pont du Gard
Entremont

Boussargues
Nîmes
Fontbrégoua

St Michel-du-Touch
Lébous

Villeneuve-Tolosane
Abeurador Mailhac
Saint Blaise
Châteauneuf-les-Martigues

Duruthy Brassempouy
Ensérune
Marseilles

Isturitz
Roquepertuse

Lespugue
Grotte Cosquer

Gargas Montespan
Le Mas d'Azil
Tautavel

Labastide
Montbolo

Volp Caves
La Vache/Niaux

0   200 km

when the establishment of the Greek colony of MAR-
SEILLES *c.*600 BC had a major impact on the development
of native communities in Mediterranean France. Further
north, native chiefdoms developed at hilltop centres such
as MONT LASSOIS in Burgundy, part of a late HALLSTATT
political and cultural world which extended eastwards
into southern Germany at sites like the HEUNEBERG. A
rich burial at VIX at the foot of Mont Lassois, contained a
massive bronze vessel of Greek manufacture, illustrating
how long-distance contacts extended across France at this
period. Greek contact was followed after some centuries

by Roman rule, first with the establishment of the Roman
'provincia' of Gallia Transalpina (modern 'Provence') in
122 BC, then by Caesar's brutal campaigns of conquest in
58–52 BC which carried Roman power as far as the Rhine
and the English Channel.

Despite the devastations attendant on Caesar's conquest, the provinces of Gallia or Gaul became under
Roman rule one of the most prosperous parts of the
empire. City life flourished, especially in the south, where
the remains of municipal buildings including theatres,
amphitheatres and temples indicate the status of major

centres such as Arles and Nîmes. In the mid 3rd century, disturbances on the Rhine frontier and the weakening of imperial power led to damaging raids by Germanic peoples. Gaul, along with Britain and France, broke temporarily away from Roman rule under the empire of Postumus (260–74). Archaeologically, the new uncertainty is marked by the building of city walls to protect the tempting but hitherto undefended urban centres. Roman efforts to secure the Rhine frontier ultimately failed in 406, when a confederation of Alans, Sueves and Vandals broke through; this was followed in 412 by the occupation of southern France by Visigoths from Italy. Within a century, however, control had passed to another Germanic people, the FRANKS, who ruled over a still largely Romanized population among whom Latin gradually developed into French. The major Roman cities became important Christian centres, and the alliance of church and state culminated in 800 when the Frankish ruler Charlemagne was crowned emperor by the Pope in Rome. The Frankish empire created by Charlemagne included Germany and northern Italy as well as France, but division of these territories under his successors during the 9th century led to the foundation of what came to be the medieval kingdom of France.

Franchthi Cave a prehistoric site located on the Peloponnesian coast in southern Greece. The lowest cultural layers contain late Upper Palaeolithic artifacts (e.g. small backed blades, geometric microliths) associated with the remains of wild ass, red deer, fish and other vertebrates; these layers are dated by radiocarbon to c.22,000-10,300 BP. The upper layers contain a lengthy sequence of Mesolithic and Neolithic occupations, the former including dozens of burials and some possible cremations.

Frankfort, Henri (1897–1954) a Dutch archaeologist and intellectual historian, who worked in Egypt (ABYDOS, AMARNA, Armant) and in Iraq, where he led the University of Chicago's Diyala project, which provided important information on EARLY DYNASTIC MESOPOTAMIA. While he published important studies on pottery and on CYLINDER SEALS, Frankfort's later comparative work, on kingship, religious attitudes and art in western Asia and Egypt, is perhaps more enduring.

Franks A Germanic people living east of the Rhine who first appeared in Latin sources in AD 257. During the next two centuries, they raided the Roman empire on various occasions, but some also served in the Roman army. As Roman power in northeastern Gaul diminished, the Franks extended their influence into the areas of modern northern France and Belgium. Archaeologically, the Franks are best known from the burials of their elite, which often include swords and richly ornamented jewellery. The Franks were ruled by several powerful kings, including Childeric (died AD 481) and his son Clovis (ruled

AD 481–511). Clovis consolidated Frankish power and converted to Christianity. His descendants, the Merovingians, ruled northern Gaul for the next 250 years.

Fraser Cave see KUTIKINA.

Frederick see PLANO, BLACKWATER DRAW.

Fremont a tradition, with great internal variation, found throughout much of present-day Utah, USA, between AD 400 and 1350. The tradition has some similarities to the ANASAZI in pottery types and PITHOUSE architecture. Maize, beans and squash were grown, although hunting and gathering remained an important component of their diet. Possible origins for Fremont include Anasazi immigration, movement from the Plains to the east, and a DIFFUSION of traits from the MOGOLLON.

Frere, John (1740–1807) a British antiquary who first recognized the true nature of Palaeolithic artifacts, recovered from undisturbed Pleistocene deposits in the HOXNE brickpit in association with the bones of extinct animals. Although Frere's work was published, his interpretation of the finds was largely ignored, because it contradicted the accepted Creation date of 4004 BC. See also PENGELLY.

fresco a decorative technique used on plastered surfaces. In true or *buon fresco* the pigment is applied before the plaster has dried; whereas the term *fresco secco* implies that the surface of the plaster is dry.

frigidarium the cold room in a Roman bath-house. A cold plunge-bath or a basin was provided. The frigidarium was located close to the APODYTERIUM and would have been one of the first rooms to be used by the bathers. See also THERMAE.

Frisians a barbarian people of the coastlands of Holland and northwestern Germany who raided Britain during the 3rd–5th centuries AD and later established trading networks along the southern coast of the North Sea. Their Iron Age forebears had colonized the coastal marshes. At settlements such as FEDDERSEN WIERDE (Germany) and Ezinge (Netherlands) on mounds of turf and clay called TERPEN they built houses partitioned into three sections: living quarters, a workshop and a stable for their cattle. Roman imports at these sites reflect long-distance trade, primarily in cattle and cattle products. At Feddersen Wierde, the buildings in one part of the settlement are larger and more elaborate, suggesting social differentiation. By the early 5th century, some Frisians had settled in eastern England along with other peoples from the coastal zones of northern Europe. Some have suggested that rising water-levels began to flood their settlements, causing them to seek other territories. In the 7th, 8th and 9th centuries, Frisians were active in commerce, and their town of Dorestad on the lower Rhine was a particularly important trading centre.

Fromms Landing limestone shelters in the Lower Murray Valley, Australia, excavated by John Mulvaney. The deposits span the last 5,000 years and parallel the sequence from nearby DEVON DOWNS. They include one of the earliest securely dated finds of DINGO.

frying pan the term used to describe the shallow circular vessels which are especially characteristic of the CYCLADIC GROTTA-PELOS and KEROS-SYROS cultures. Made of clay, or occasionally of stone, the frying pans often have complex designs stamped or incised on their underside and were evidently not used for cooking. However, their precise function remains obscure – suggestions include mirrors, drums and lids.

Fuchsberg a Neolithic pottery style, characterized by rich incised decoration, occupying the transition between the Danish early and middle Neolithic c.3400 BC. Fuchsberg pottery is a prominent element at the Neolithic enclosures of SARUP and TOFTUM.

Fudodo a Middle JOMON site in Toyama Prefecture, Japan, where a large oval pit-building, 8 by 17 m (26 by 56 ft) with sixteen POSTHOLES for massive pillars and four stone-lined hearths, has been excavated. The structure has been interpreted as a communal gathering- or work-place for winter tasks in the snow-laden HOKURIKU region.

Fuentenueva 3 see ORCE.

Fu Hao a consort of a late SHANG king whose tomb near Anyang City, China, contained over 400 bronze ritual vessels plus other grave-goods. Her name is known from inscriptions on the bronzes and ORACLE BONES. The Fu Hao tomb was the only royal burial among the SHAFT TOMBS at ANYANG to have survived intact.

Fujinoki a late 7th-century AD round MOUNDED TOMB in Nara Prefecture, Japan, whose stone SARCOPHAGUS yielded an eclectic but spectacular collection of horse trappings and gilt-bronze ornaments of different periods of manufacture. Some, such as the gilt-bronze shoes, are too large to be anything but ceremonial. The peninsular style of the goods indicates close relationships between the YAMATO and PAEKCHE elite.

Fujiwara a site in the ASUKA district of Nara Prefecture, Japan, comprising the first urban capital built on the Chinese CHANGAN model. Constructed in AD 694 under the late YAMATO state, it was abandoned after only twenty years when the capital was moved to HEIJO. Fujiwara is now excavated year-round by the Nara National Cultural Properties Research Institute and is documented to have covered 2 km (1.24 miles) east-west by 3 km (1.86 miles) north-south, with the palace in the north.

Fukui a Late Palaeolithic cave-site in Nagasaki Prefecture, Japan, yielding Incipient JOMON pottery together with obsidian microliths. Dated by radiocarbon to 12,700 bp, it is the earliest occurrence in the world of ceramic vessels. See also KAMIKUROIWA.

fulcrum the curved, raised structure at one end of a Roman banqueting couch which could be used as an arm rest. The edges of the fulcrum were frequently decorated with mounts, sometimes in bronze, ivory or bone.

Fumane Cave a cave-site in the Venetian Pre-Alps, Italy, where excavations by A. Broglio and M. Cremaschi since 1988 have unearthed a MOUSTERIAN and AURIGNACIAN sequence, the latter dated by AMS from c.37,000 to 32,000 bp, and containing paintings on stones.

Funan the Chinese name for an early state located in the lower Mekong region of Cambodia and south Vietnam, first recorded as a trading partner of China in the 3rd century AD, and, according to Chinese records, conquered by the KHMER state of Chenla in the 7th century. The indigenous name has been lost, but is assumed to have included the Khmer word *bnam*, 'hill'. Its main centres may have been OC ÈO and ANGKOR Borei.

funerary cones Egyptian solid pottery cones, averaging 25–30 cm (10–12 inches) long. Their dates range from the MIDDLE KINGDOM to the LATE PERIOD, but the vast majority are of the NEW KINGDOM. Rows of these cones were set into the façade of private tombs, with their outward-facing bases stamped before firing with the name and titles of the tomb-owner. Known examples come almost exclusively from THEBES (EGYPT)-WEST BANK.

Funnel(neck) Beaker a vessel with globular body and out-turned rim, characteristic of the early and middle Neolithic culture of northern Europe. See also TRB CULTURE.

Fuyu see PUYO.

Füzesabony culture the third phase of the tripartite division of the early part of the Hungarian Bronze Age (2200–1800 BC) defined by Moszolics on the basis of the sequence of the TÓSZEG TELL (see also HATVAN and NAGYRÉV). The Füzesabony culture is considered by many as the equivalent, with the same sort of settlements and material culture, of the OTOMANI culture of Transylvania. Notable Füzesabony finds include antler cheekpieces for horse-bits, found at a number of sites.

fynbos a term used for the vegetation of a major domain of the Cape Floristic Kingdom of the southwestern and southern Cape Province of South Africa. It is characterized by unusually high species richness but is treeless and somewhat grassless. It is dominated by shrubs up to 3 m (10 ft) tall, and seems to have been attractive to hunter-gatherers for long periods, especially during the last 125,000 years.

G

Gabillou, Le a cave in the Isle Valley, Dordogne (France), containing Palaeolithic PARIETAL ART in the form of over 200 engravings of animals – mostly horse, deer and bovid, but also occasionally birds and hares. There are also a couple of human figures, one with a bovid head. On the basis of style and the presence of 'grid-like' signs, they are attributed to the same period as the art of LAS-CAUX; there was an early MAGDALENIAN occupation at the entrance.

Gagarino an Upper Palaeolithic open-air site on the Don River in European Russia. The occupation horizon is buried in slope deposits comprising the upper FACIES of the second terrace. The artifact assemblage, which includes shouldered points and 'VENUS' FIGURINES, may be assigned to the KOSTENKI-WILLENDORF CULTURE or EASTERN GRAVETTIAN; radiocarbon estimates of 21,800 and 30,000 bp are broadly consistent with this dating. An oval depression with central hearth and two associated pits apparently marks the location of a former structure. The latter, found in 1927, represents the first such discovery in European Russia; its superstructure may have originally been composed of the bones of woolly mammoth, subsequently lost to weathering and erosion. Gagarino was discovered in 1926 by Zamyatnin, who conducted excavations from 1927 to 1929; further excavations were undertaken by Tarasov (1961–9).

Galgenberg see KREMS.

Galilee skull see TURVILLE-PETRE, ZUTTIYEH.

Galindo a MIDDLE HORIZON site in the Moche Valley of the north coast of Peru. The valley was largely abandoned by the MOCHE culture at this time. The site is in a strategic location near the valley neck, and is fortified. Excavations by Garth Bawden suggest that it was the centre of a small local POLITY; he finds no evidence that it was under the control of the HUARI empire, which was expanding at the time. Other researchers disagree, suggesting that Huari concentrated the remaining local population at the site after its conquest of the Moche region.

gallery grave see ALLÉE COUVERTE.

Gallery Hill a PETROGLYPH site in the Pilbara region of Western Australia. The earlier abraded linear motifs include tracks, circles, kangaroos, emus and sometimes human figures. The later pecked engravings show a much wider range of subjects including mammals, reptiles, artifacts and anthropomorphs, in dramatic compositions. Seed-grinding patches are also associated with the art.

Gallinazo the ceramic style and culture in a portion of the north coast of Peru at the end of the EARLY HORIZON and beginning of the EARLY INTERMEDIATE PERIOD, c.200 bc–ad 200. Related to the contemporaneous Recuay style of the highlands, it is the precursor of the MOCHE style, and is found from the Virú Valley to the Moche Valley.

Gambieran a distinctive local industry of large carefully retouched flake tools made of flint, confined to coastal southeastern South Australia and southwestern Victoria. Finds of Gambieran material in dated contexts at KOON-GINE and WYRIE SWAMP confirm an early Holocene age.

Gamble's Cave a cave in the central Kenyan Rift Valley, which contains a well-represented EBURRAN industry, followed by ELMENTEITAN assemblages. Several skeletons from the Eburran layers were described as Caucasoid, but they are now considered Negroid.

Gamio, Manuel (1883–1960) a Mexican archaeologist, one of the first in MESOAMERICA to excavate using metric STRATIGRAPHY, beginning in 1910. Gamio also set up a ceramic sequence for the VALLEY OF MEXICO. He began an integrated study of the TEOTIHUACÁN Valley in 1917 that extended from modern to prehistoric times, and incorporated ethnographic, historical and archaeological data. Gamio's systematic approaches set a standard among other Mesoamerican archaeologists for the investigation of Mesoamerican prehistory.

Gandhara grave culture complex a culture of the 2nd and 1st millennia BC found in the valleys of northern Pakistan, notably in Swat, that contains a large number of cemeteries composed usually of pit graves, roofed with stone and containing one or two inhumations; cremation burials appear in some graves, the ashes often held in containers of various kinds. The grave-goods found with the bodies are mostly a distinctive red or grey plain burnished pottery. Metal is present mostly as copper pins, while iron also occurs (including some horse bits); at least one horse burial is also recorded. The periodization and chronology of this grave complex is debated: some have placed the complex between the 11th and 3rd centuries BC; others prefer a shorter duration, between the 11th and 8th centuries BC.

Ganges civilization   an urban culture of the 1st millennium BC in the Ganges-Yamuna *doab*. Indian literary sources describe a situation of multiple POLITIES (*janapadas*) during the earlier 1st millennium BC, with a process of political consolidation during the middle centuries of that millennium as stronger polities absorbed their neighbours to create a smaller number of larger polities (*mahajanapadas*). By the 5th century BC, four *mahajanapadas* – Avanti, Vatsa, Kosala and Magadha – came to dominate the region, and by around 350 BC Magadha stood alone as the regional power. The subsequent MAURYAN empire (325–185 BC) can be seen as a further extension of this process. The archaeological record reveals a growth of urban centres during this same period. Kausambi in Vatsa *janapada* provides a good example of this urban growth – by 400 BC this place covered some 50 ha (124 acres) enclosed by earthen ramparts, while four secondary centres (6–12 ha [15–30 acres] in size) and sixteen villages (less than 2 ha [5 acres]) lay in its hinterland. Contemporary major centres included Rajgir (the old capital of Magadha), Campa (the capital of Anga) and Rajghat (the centre of Kasi). These places were all fortified, and the most impressive of them appeared at Ujjain, where the ramparts were 75 m (82 yds) wide at the base and stood 12 m (40 ft) high. These developments correlate with early NORTHERN BLACK POLISHED pottery.

Ganj Dareh   a site in the Kermanshah area of the Zagros Mountains, western Iran, where Philip Smith's excavations provide a long sequence of five phases that begins perhaps in the mid 9th (phase E) and runs to the early 7th (phase A) millennium bc. The earliest phase E contains only a series of pits and scattered ash lenses and debris on weathered surfaces; goats dominate the fauna, and have an age structure consistent with hunting. In the subsequent phases of occupation, mud-brick and wattle-and-daub rectilinear structures appear, in which occur a wide range of unfired clay objects (bins, very large vessels as well as small ones, rims of stone mortars, ovens, figurines and geometrics – see TOKENS). The fauna of these settlements is still focused on morphologically wild goats, which now have age patterns consistent with herding and whose hoofprints are occasionally found on mud bricks.

Gao   a site on the Niger River in Mali, capital of the SONGHAY state under Askia Mohammed in the 16th century AD. An earlier capital dating to the late 1st millennium AD was at Gao-Saney, 6 km (4 miles) to the east, where inscribed tombstones which appear to have been made in Andalusia, Spain, as well as glass beads from Fustat, Egypt, indicate the existence of contact across the Sahara by camel as well as trade routes along the Niger River at this time.

Garagay   an INITIAL PERIOD site near Lima, on the central coast of Peru. The site includes a large U-shaped temple complex and painted friezes depicting a monstrous human head. The art style is similar to other ceremonial sites on the central coast prior to the expansion of CHAVÍN influence.

Gardiner, Sir Alan Henderson (1879–1963)   an English Egyptologist whose major contribution to scholarship was his extensive work on hieroglyphic texts and historical syntheses.

Gargas   a cave in the Hautes-Pyrénées, France, first known for its richness in Ice Age fauna, where Palaeolithic art was discovered on the walls in 1906. Together with a few paintings and 148 engravings of animals, there are about 230 red or black hand stencils which often have 'missing' fingers. Sometimes seen as ritual mutilation or the result of disease, they are most probably a kind of sign-language using bent fingers. The cave was occupied from at least the Middle Palaeolithic onwards, and the animal engravings have been attributed to the GRAVETTIAN through comparison with stratified portable engravings. A bone fragment stuck into a wall-fissure close to some hand stencils, and thus possibly linked to them, has yielded a radiocarbon age of 26,680 bp, remarkably close to the direct date for hand stencils in the GROTTE COSQUER.

Garrod, Dorothy Annie Elizabeth (1892–1968)   British archaeologist and prehistorian. Having first studied and published *The Upper Palaeolithic in Britain*, she directed her first major excavation at the GIBRALTAR Devil's Tower site, finding remains of a NEANDERTHAL child. Thereafter working mainly in western Asia, she excavated at SHUKBAH cave in Palestine – identifying and naming the NATUFIAN culture – then in southern Kurdistan at the Epipalaeolithic cave at ZARZI. She is most renowned for her excavations (1928–34) in the MOUNT CARMEL cave-sites of EL-WAD, TABUN and KEBARA, where she first established an almost unbroken cultural sequence for the Levant, now known to span at least 600,000 years. From 1939 to 1952 she was Disney Professor of Archaeology at Cambridge University, the first woman professor at Oxford or Cambridge. After war service in Photographic Interpretation for the RAF, she combined professorial duties with excavation in France (ANGLES SUR L'ANGLIN), but on retirement she returned to excavation in the Levant, using the QUATERNARY sea-levels visible at the Lebanese sites of Ras el-Kelb and ADLUN to correlate her Mount Carmel sequence with that of Europe. Her pioneering work remains of great value, particularly to modern prehistoric studies in western Asia.

Garstang, John (1876–1956) an English archaeologist who excavated extensively in Egypt (e.g. BENI HASSAN, ESNA, ABYDOS), the Sudan (MEROE), Palestine (e.g. JER-ICHO), Syria (Sakje-Geuzi) and Turkey (MERSIN).

Gash a group of thirty-five sites in the Atbara region of Sudan, dating to the late 3rd or early 2nd millennium bc, with evidence of a food-producing economy post-dating the BUTANA sites. The main site of Mahal Teglinos contains 3 m (10 ft) of deposit, including human burials indicating a social hierarchy.

Gatung'ang'a a central Kenyan site which has given its name to Late Iron Age pottery ware associated with radiocarbon dates between the 12th and 14th centuries ad.

Gaudo a CHALCOLITHIC cemetery in Campania, Italy, of 3rd millennium BC rock-cut tombs, type-site of the Campanian Gaudo group. This is a variant of the central Italian RINALDONE, and is characterized by collective burial in rock-cut tombs, highly burnished pottery and occasional metalwork, including copper daggers and awls and silver beads.

Gauls see CELTS.

Gausel rich Viking burial of an elite woman in south-western Norway, dating to the early 9th century AD. In a stone burial chamber was found silver jewellery, bronze vessels, drinking horns, bridle fastenings and fragments of a reliquary. Many of the items appear to have originated in Ireland. Near by, recent excavations have revealed a large Late Iron Age settlement with about twenty buildings dating to the 6th–7th century AD. Several Viking boat burials have also been found in this area.

Gavrinis a Neolithic rectangular cairn on a small island in the Gulf of Morbihan, France, containing one of the most richly decorated megalithic PASSAGE GRAVES. The upper surface of the capstone of the chamber – invisible once the cairn was in place – has carvings of an axe or plough and two long-horned bovids; it is part of a carved MENHIR which was broken up and reused in the tomb. Twenty-nine of the ORTHOSTATs of passage and chamber carry rich non-representational decoration of meanders, zigzags and chevrons. There are radiocarbon dates of c.3400 BC.

Gawra, Tepe a TELL-site, located east of the River Tigris near KHORSABAD, Iraq, which was occupied from the 6th to the 2nd millennia BC. The STRATIGRAPHIC sequence of twenty levels produced by E. Speiser and A. Tobler in their excavation during the 1930s established one of the basic reference points for the archaeology of northern Iraq. The lowest levels reveal a transition between HALAF and 'UBAID pottery styles (see Tell AQAB), followed by a long-lasting 'Ubaid settlement. One of the best-known features here is the temple complex of the penultimate 'Ubaid level (Gawra XIII), which shows striking resemblances to the 'Ubaid temples at ERIDU and WARKA. The next set of levels form the 'Gawran' period, of the 4th millennium BC, containing (in Gawra XI-A) the famous round house as well as a sequence of temples. The later levels (Gawra VII–I) belong to the 3rd and 2nd millennia BC, terminating in a thin MITANNI settlement.

Gaymanova see SCYTHIANS.

Gaza a Palestinian site and the southernmost city of the PHILISTINE Pentapolis, which is now probably beneath the modern town of Gaza. The most impressive archaeological remains at Gaza are the mosaics of the Synagogue (probably of the 6th century AD) and the 'Great Mosque' which was originally a Crusader cathedral of the 12th century AD.

***ge* [ko]** a dagger-axe made first in bronze in the Chinese SHANG Dynasty, then in iron from the ZHOU Dynasty onwards (see CHINESE DYNASTIES). Early versions are tanged for hafting; later ones have a perforated projection extending at right angles to the blade for binding on to a haft. They might derive from jade prototypes. Often mistranslated as 'HALBERD', *ge* are, however, not thrusting but chopping implements.

Gebel Barkal a mountain in UPPER NUBIA, explored chiefly by REISNER in 1916, and by the University of Rome from 1973 to the present. It was a centre for the worship of AMEN during the Egyptian occupation in the NEW KINGDOM, and later. The temple built by RAMESSES II was extended by NAPATAN and MEROITIC rulers, who also built palaces there. A series of nearby pyramids seems to be related to the Meroitic period (see MEROE).

Gedi an early Swahili coastal town situated on a tidal inlet south of Malindi in Kenya, which enjoyed prosperity from about AD 1300 until the 16th century, as a result of trade stimulated by the exploitation of Zimbabwean gold (see GREAT ZIMBABWE, KILWA), and which has been subjected to intensive archaeological investigation.

Geissenklösterle a cave in Baden-Württemberg, south-western Germany, discovered in 1957, where excavations by E. Wagner in 1973 and J. HAHN in 1974–83 revealed possible Middle Palaeolithic, proto-Aurignacian and AURIG-NACIAN (40,200–33,100 bp), GRAVETTIAN (29,200 bp), MAGDALENIAN and Mesolithic material. The Aurignacian levels yielded bone flutes, traces of wall-painting, a BÂTON PERCÉ and a series of representations in ivory of a mammoth, bear, bison and human.

Gela a Greek colony in southern Sicily traditionally founded in 688 BC from Rhodes and Crete. It in turn went on to found AGRIGENTO. In the early 5th century BC much of its population was moved to SYRACUSE and it was refounded in 466 BC. It was again largely abandoned in 404 BC, and a new colony was established in the late 4th century. The remarkable defensive walls at Capo Soprano, which have stone bases and mud-brick upper parts, belong to this later colony.

Gelidonya a cape on the dangerous southern coast of Turkey, which is the site of a Bronze Age shipwreck excavated by Bass in 1960. The cargo included copper and tin ingots, bronze tools and pottery which indicates that the ship went down in the 13th century BC.

gelifluction the mass movement processes, both flows and slides, that take place in susceptible materials resulting from ice melt and thaw in the PERIGLACIAL environment. Gelifluction is a slightly more specific process than SOLIFLUCTION although the terms are often used interchangeably. As with other colluvial processes, gelifluction can cause destruction or redistribution of archaeological deposits.

gendered archaeology an approach to archaeological interpretation that grew out of the feminist critique of science in the 1970s and 1980s. This approach explicitly advocates the importance of females in past cultures and attempts to provide methodologies by which their roles can more adequately be recognized. Gendered archaeology also investigates the ways in which all archaeological interpretation has been – and still is – susceptible to sexist bias.

general systems theory a theory that human society can be likened to a system composed of interdependent parts or subsystems, such that change in one subsystem affects all others. The theory is very similar to the Functionalism of 1930s British anthropology, but differs in its use of terms drawn from cybernetics and engineering (the disciplines in which general systems theory was developed), in its acknowledgement of the DIACHRONIC nature of society and in its attempt to quantify the degree of change throughout the system. See David CLARKE.

geoarchaeology an ecological approach to archaeological deposits that has as its goal the understanding of the physical context of archaeological remains. Geoarchaeology is concerned with geomorphic, STRATIGRAPHIC and temporal context, site formation, post-depositional transformations of archaeological deposits and data recovery, all with emphasis on the interrelationships among cultural and land systems. Compare ARCHAEOLOGICAL GEOLOGY.

geochronology the study of earth history with respect to the timing and sequencing of geological events to which archaeological events can be correlated. Geochronology can involve both ABSOLUTE DATING and RELATIVE DATING methods. See also STRATIGRAPHY.

geoglyph a ground drawing, or drawing on the landscape. They may be chalk figures (as in southern Britain), where the white drawing stands out against the green grass on hillsides; earthen mounds of different shapes (see GREAT SERPENT MOUND); or desert intaglios, where stones on the surface, coated with a natural dark varnish, are moved aside to expose the lighter soil beneath, or the dark stones themselves are arranged to form drawings. They exist in Arizona and California, but the best-known are the huge drawings at NASCA. At least 5,000 geoglyphs exist in the Atacama Desert of northern Chile, probably dating to c.AD 600–1200, and including the 'Giant of the

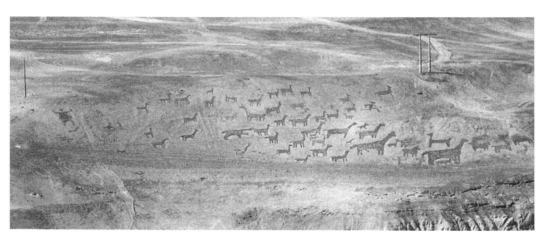

GEOGLYPHs of a llama herd plus humans, at Tiliviche in Chile's Atacama Desert, made by piling together dark stones from the surface. The electricity poles provide a scale.

Atacama', 105 m (345 ft) high, the biggest human figure ever produced in prehistory.

Geographical Society Cave a Palaeolithic site near Nakhodka in eastern Siberia. Artifacts are buried in clay and rubble deposits in a limestone cave. Associated faunal remains include woolly mammoth, woolly rhinoceros, hyena, bear and others; a radiocarbon date of 32,570 bp was obtained on one of the bones. The artifacts are confined to a small assemblage of pebble cores, flakes and a scraping tool. It is assigned to the early Upper Palaeolithic on the basis of estimated age rather than typological characteristics. The site was investigated by OKLADNIKOV in the 1960s.

Geographic Information System a software-based tool for cataloguing, organizing, mapping, analysing, querying and displaying digital geographical data. GIS is a powerful tool for determining trends, patterns, associations and other relationships among data layers that, in addition to digital spatial data, can include data held in other digital databases. Multiple scales of data are easily accommodated.

Geoksjur an oasis east of the Tedjen River (southern Turkmenistan) that contains numerous prehistoric sites. Geoksjur 1, the largest at 12 ha (30 acres), contains a sequence of ten levels spanning the later 5th and 4th millennia BC, and corresponding to the first three periods of the standard NAMAZGA sequence. Settlement in the Geoksjur oasis was tied to a former course of the Tedjen, and disappeared when the river shifted further west. The oasis gives its name to a style of painted pottery of the Namazga III period (late 4th millennium BC), characterized by densely packed repeated geometrical motifs, which appears as far away as SHARH-I SOKHTA in eastern Iran and the QUETTA region of the Indo-Iranian borderlands.

geology the study of physical, chemical and biological processes and products as they apply to the origin, history and structure of the Earth. Many of the specialized branches of geology make technical, methodological and theoretical contributions to the field of archaeology, because the Earth's surface is the platform on which all human activity has been conducted. Among the branches contributing greatly are STRATIGRAPHY, GEOMORPHOLOGY, sedimentology, PEDOLOGY, GEO-PHYSICS and GEOCHRONOLOGY. See also ARCHAEO-LOGICAL GEOLOGY.

Geometric the term used for the pottery made in Greece c.900–700 BC and, by extension, for the period as a whole.

geometric pottery the impressed pottery of southeastern China existing from c.2000 BC to the 3rd century AD, characterizing the protohistoric WUCHENG, HUSHU and Maqiao cultures of that region.

geomorphology a branch of GEOLOGY concerned with landscapes, their evolution, and the processes operating within the Earth's surface systems. Cultural remains are a part of these systems, having been deposited on, and in part resulting from, interactions with, landscapes of the past. Thus an understanding of the geomorphology of places where cultural debris was excavated is fundamental to archaeological inference.

geophysics a subfield of both GEOLOGY and physics concerned with the structure, composition and development of the Earth from a physical perspective. Many of the archaeological surveying techniques designed to identify features without excavation utilize instruments that measure physical properties of surface materials, such as RESISTIVITY SURVEYING and ELECTROMAGNETIC SURVEYING. Some dating techniques, most notably PALAEOMAGNETISM, are based on geophysical properties of the Earth.

geosol a fundamental unit in pedostratigraphic classification consisting of a sediment or rock body characterized by one or more soil horizons. A geosol is a formally recognized soil or PALAEOSOL that has a significant distribution. Recognition of geosols aids in the correlation of archaeological materials associated with them. See also STRATIGRAPHY.

Gerasimov, Mikhail Mikhailovich (1907–70) Soviet anthropologist, sculptor and archaeologist, best known for his his pioneering method of reconstructing faces on to skulls. He reconstructed more than 200 faces, including those of fossil HOMINIDS (PITHECANTHROPUS, SINANTHROPUS, the NEANDERTHAL child from TESHIK TASH and others), and portraits of some historical individuals (Ivan the Terrible, Timur/Tamberlaine, Schiller and others). He also discovered and excavated the palaeolithic site of MAL'TA.

Gergovia an Iron Age OPPIDUM, capital of the Arverni, occupying a steep-sided plateau of 150 ha (370 acres) overlooking modern Clermont-Ferrand, Puy-de-Dôme, France. The Gallic chief Vercingetorix took refuge in 52 BC and resisted all attempts by Julius Caesar to capture the oppidum. Ditches of Caesar's siege camps have been found and excavated. Vercingetorix later withdrew to ALÉSIA, where he was ultimately forced to surrender.

Germany see EUROPE, CENTRAL.

Gerzean a PREDYNASTIC culture of UPPER EGYPT, sometimes referred to as NAQADA II, dated to between c.4000–3500 and 3000 BC and which was the successor of the AMRATIAN. The most important of the Gerzean sites so far discovered are Naqada and HIERAKONPOLIS. The Gerzean displays an increasing craft-specialization, including metalworking, and ample evidence of contacts with southwestern Asia; presumably fundamental political developments also occurred in this period, culminating in Egypt becoming a unified state.

Gesher Benot Ya'aqov [Jisr Banat Yacoub] an Early/Middle Pleistocene site located in the northern sector of the Dead Sea Rift, south of Hula Valley, Israel. Recent excavations by N. Goren-Inbar have documented a 35 m (115 ft) thick sequence. The archaeological evidence is associated with a variety of environments of deposition, ranging from deep to shallow waters and margins of the palaeo Hula Lake. The archaeological data comprise lithic, palaeontological and unique palaeobotanical (wood, bark, fruits and seeds) assemblages. All lithic assemblages are assigned to the ACHEULIAN industrial complex, tools being dominated by bifaces (handaxes and cleavers). Three types of raw material were exploited: basalt (used mainly for the production of bifaces), flint (for flakes and flake tools) and limestone (mainly for chopping tools). A unique combination of techniques is found at GBY, previously unknown in the Levant at such an early date: these include soft hammer and the earliest documented LEVALLOIS TECHNIQUE.

The early age of GBY, 780,000 years, based on a PALAEOMAGNETIC reversal within the stratigraphic sequence, and the evidence of human activity in it, provide further evidence for HOMINID demographic and geographical behaviour during Early/Middle Pleistocene times. Part of the site was obliterated by drainage-bulldozing in 1999.

Getae the inhabitants of the Wallachian plain of Romania during the later part of the Iron Age. Sometimes referred to in the literature as Geto-Dacians or Thraco-Getians because of their position between the THRACIANS and DACIA, the Getae were conquered by Rome in AD 106.

Gezer a town in the western foothills of the southern Levant (Israel), reaching its greatest importance during the MIDDLE BRONZE AGE IIB–C, when it was fortified with a wall and towers and, later, a GLACIS; this occupation exended through the LATE BRONZE AGE. Gezer also has a significant Iron Age II (c.1000–600 BC) occupation, when the wall and gate (often attributed to Solomon) were renewed.

Ggantija see SKORBA.

Ghana the first of the West African empires on the border of southern Mauretania and Mali, dating from at least the 8th century to the end of the 11th century AD. It may have arisen as a result of agricultural people organizing themselves to withstand depredation by Saharan nomads. The economy was based on trade in gold, ivory and salt. See also KOUMBI SALEH.

Ghar Dalam see SKORBA.

Ghassul, Teleilat el see TELEILAT.

Ghassulian the major CHALCOLITHIC phase in Palestine, dated to the 4th millennium BC, best known from the sites of TELEILATEL EL GHASSUL and NAHAL MISHMAR. Besides the early exploitation of copper, the Ghassulian is also notable for its well-made pottery and for being the last period of large-scale use of stone tools in Palestine.

Ghirshman, Roman (1895–1979) a Ukrainian/French scholar, one of the most energetic developers of the archaeology of Iran and Afghanistan. After working at TELLO (in southern Iraq) with de Genouillac, he undertook seminal excavations at the prehistoric sites of GIYAN and SIALK in western Iran, and then worked at a number of later historic period sites in eastern Iran and Afghanistan. After the Second World War and until 1963, Ghirshman directed the French excavations at SUSA, and also excavated at CHOGA ZANBIL and at other sites near Susa.

≠Gi a pan locality in northwestern Botswana with rich MIDDLE STONE AGE remains, including an open living site, as well as LATER STONE AGE remains, such as a microlithic industry associated with pits interpreted as game traps.

Giant's Grave (It. Tomba di Gigante) the name given to the CHAMBERED TOMBS of Sardinia consisting of an elongated cairn covering a long burial chamber of CYCLOPEAN construction with CORBELLED roof. In some examples there is a horned façade. The *tombe di giganti* belong to the Bronze Age NURAGHIC culture of the 2nd millennium BC.

Gibraltar a promontory at the southern tip of Spain best known for its prehistoric cave-sites which have yielded NEANDERTHAL remains (including the Forbes Quarry skull, the first to be discovered in Europe in 1848) and Middle and Upper Palaeolithic stone artifacts. Although there had been a series of earlier explorations, the first detailed archaeological study was that of D. A. GARROD (1925–6). At Devil's Tower rockshelter she identified six levels including a stratified Neanderthal child's skull in level 4. Gorham's Cave was excavated by John Waechter in 1948–54.

New excavations by Stringer, Barton and others since 1995 at Ibex Cave, Gorham's Cave and Vanguard Cave have confirmed the late survival of Neanderthals (32,000 BP in Gorham's Cave), and provided rare evidence of an early exploitation of shellfish by Neanderthals (a mussel midden in Vanguard Cave with MOUSTERIAN artifacts in a level dating to 46,000 BP), as well as a Neanderthal exploitation of plants, including stone pine nuts in Gorham's Cave below levels dating to about 51,000 BP.

Giecz an early medieval stronghold about 25 km (16 miles) south of OSTRÓW LEDNICKI in western Poland. In the 10th century AD it was a fortified royal seat with a palace and chapel, as well as a trade centre, situated along a lake. Its timber and earth rampart, within which the stone foundations of the palace complex are found, survives to a height of 9 m (30 ft). A timber bridge about 6 m (20 ft) wide and about 150 m (160 yds) long connected this stronghold with the market settlement across the lake. Giecz was destroyed and its inhabitants deported in 1038 AD as the result of an invasion by Bretislav of Bohemia, although it was later rebuilt.

Giglio Island an island lying off the coast of ETRURIA which is the location of a possible ARCHAIC Etruscan shipwreck. Although damaged by looters, the cargo consisted of AMPHORAS carrying olives, ingots and perfumed oil contained in CORINTHIAN and Etruscan ARYBALLOI.

Gilf el Kebir a high plateau of Nubian sandstone in the Sahara Desert, southwestern Egypt, discovered by Ball and Prince Kemal el-Din in 1928 and since investigated by a variety of workers. The site has yielded surface-scatters of late ACHEULIAN artifacts, including a few bifaces, but is best known for its Neolithic material, also recovered in the form of surface-scatters, which includes stone tools made of a local sandstone, grinding stones, bone, ostrich eggshell and pottery decorated with impressed and incised designs, and for its prehistoric rock engravings in the southern part of the Gilf.

Gilgamesh a famous figure of early 3rd millennium BC MESOPOTAMIA, who belongs to both myth and history. The historical Gilgamesh remains shadowy: he is named as ruler of WARKA in the SUMERIAN KING LIST and in myths about him; and some of his contemporaries (such as Enmebaragesi of KISH) named in the myths are also known from their own inscriptions. Moreover, the Gilgamesh epic cycle seems to reflect the emergence of new kinds of (secular and military) political authority in EARLY DYNASTIC southern Mesopotamia, and in the hands of such commentators as T. Jacobsen are seen to represent a real historical process. The more mythical aspects of the Gilgamesh epic cycle address social and individual psychological confrontations of fate, social honour, friendship and death.

Gilimanuk a settlement and burial complex in western Bali of the early centuries AD, yielding extended burials, jar burials and stone SARCOPHAGI, with bronze, iron and both imported and locally manufactured glass and stone beads.

Gimbutas, Marija (1921–94) a Lithuanian-born archaeologist who specialized in the archaeology of eastern Europe. Working first at Harvard University and then at the University of California at Los Angeles, her synthesis of the archaeological data from the Neolithic and Bronze Ages led her to formulate her controversial theory of the introduction of INDO-EUROPEAN languages to Europe by

invading waves of KURGAN CULTURES from the steppes. Her excavations at ANZA in Macedonia provided important data on the early farming cultures of southeastern Europe. Her interpretations of Neolithic female figurines have found wide popular appeal, although many other archaeologists view them sceptically.

Giong Ca Vo a settlement, near the mouth of the Dong Nai River, Can Gio district of greater Ho Chi Minh City, Vietnam. It was excavated in 1993–4, together with the nearby site of Giong Phet, and more than 400 urn-burials and some inhumations were found, dating to the late 1st millennium BC. Exceptionally rich beads, pendants and bracelets made from garnet, gold, NEPHRITE, carnelian, agate, rock crystal and glass link these sites to the SA HUYNH culture to the north, as well as to the Philippines, Thailand and India.

Girsu see TELLO.

GIS see GEOGRAPHIC INFORMATION SYSTEM.

Gishi Wajinden see WEIZHI.

Giyan, Tepe a prehistoric site near Nehevand in Luristan (western Iran), where excavations by G. Contenau and R. GHIRSHMAN in the 1930s provided the cultural sequence that until recently was standard for Luristan. The five-phase sequence (Giyan I–V) begins in the mid 5th millennium BC and continues into the Iron Age, containing a series of painted pottery styles, including the Iron Age 'genre Luristan' painted pottery. Although Giyan still counts in discussions of the prehistory of western Iran, the more recent work at GODIN Tepe, Baba Jan and elsewhere has supplanted it as the anchor of regional prehistory.

Giza the site of the pyramid complexes of the Egyptian Kings KHUFU, KHAFRE and MENKAURE. The other monuments of greatest importance at the site are the Great SPHINX and its temple, and the tomb of HETEPHERES.

Gla a MYCENAEAN citadel on a rocky outcrop in what was formerly Lake Copais in Boeotia, Greece. Early in the 13th century BC Gla was massively fortified, the walls encompassing an area of 23.5 ha (58 acres). On the summit of the outcrop an L-shaped structure was built which may have had an administrative function but is not a conventional Mycenaean palace. Other structures appear to have been granaries, and it is suggested that Gla may have been fortified by the communities living around Copais, possibly under the leadership of ORCHOMENOS, when the Mycenaeans drained the lake. The citadel was burnt and abandoned late in the 13th century BC.

glacial **1** *n.* a cold climatic episode characterized in northern latitudes by the presence and growth of widespread glacial ice and cold climate processes, deposits, flora and fauna. 'Glacial' has been used as a geologic-climatic unit and as a basis for correlation of deposits. Compare INTERGLACIAL, STADIAL. See also STRATIGRAPHY, QUATERNARY.

2 *adj.* referring to cold climatic conditions.

3 *adj.* referring to or derived from a glacier.

glaciation a large-scale process whereby the land is subject to erosion and deposition by continental and alpine glacier ice. Glaciation occurred repeatedly during the QUATERNARY as glaciers expanded and contracted, modifying landscapes and affecting ice-marginal environments and the level of ocean basins.

glacis sloping ramparts with a smooth, plastered surface, used to fortify several sites in the Near East during the MIDDLE BRONZE AGE (e.g. JERICHO, LACHISH, EL-YEHUDIYEH), and associated by some scholars with the HYKSOS.

Gladysvale a cave 13 km (8 miles) north-northeast of STERKFONTEIN, Gauteng Province, South Africa, which has yielded PLIO-PLEISTOCENE fossils including specimens attributed to AUSTRALOPITHECUS *africanus*, faunal remains possibly of Middle Pleistocene age, as well as LATER STONE AGE and Iron Age material.

Glasinac a mountain valley near Sarajevo in Bosnia, in which several thousand tumuli with over 10,000 cremation burials of the Late Bronze and Early Iron Ages (contemporaneous with the HALLSTATT period in Central Europe) were found. The metal artifacts and pottery in these tumuli show connections with Greece, Italy and the Danube basin.

Glastonbury an Iron Age LAKE VILLAGE in Somerset, England, excavated by Bulleid and Gray in 1894–1914. The village consisted of some ninety circular structures within a stockaded enclosure, standing on an artificial timber and brushwood platform within the fenlands of the SOMERSET LEVELS. The circular buildings, some dwellings, others workshops or animal sheds, had thick clay floors and clay-built hearths. The settlement dates from the 3rd/2nd to the middle of the 1st century BC and yielded numerous organic remains including wooden bowls and basins, basketry and the wickerwork of the original house walls.

Glauberg a HILLFORT northeast of Frankfurt, Germany, with occupation reaching its greatest extent (20 ha [50 acres]) during the Early LA TÈNE period (5th century BC). At the foot of the hillfort, a circular burial mound 70m (77 yds) across, approached by a ditch-flanked processional way, covered the rich graves of two fully armed men. In the ditch encircling the mound a stone statue 1.86 m (6 ft) high and weighing 230 kg (507 lbs) was found in 1995. This depicted a bearded warrior in cuirass, equipped with sword and shield, and wearing a cap with projecting 'leaf crown'. Fragments of a second similar statue near by suggest that each relates to one of the burials within the mound.

glaze a type of SLIP of powdered glass applied to a pot or other object to produce a glassy appearance when fired, and to make porous materials impermeable.

gley horizon a soil horizon characterized by grey, blue or olive colours due to excessive moisture under ANAEROBIC conditions. Gley horizons and gley soils occur where the water table is high or where a hardpan or relatively impermeable horizon prevents downward passage of water through the soil profile. Gley horizons and gley soils are conducive to the preservation of plant, animal and human remains.

gleying the process whereby iron in soils and sediments is bacterially reduced under ANAEROBIC conditions. Such conditions are favoured in perennially moist environments where drainage is poor or the water table is high, such as lakes, bogs, fens, swamps, poorly drained depressions and floodplains. Gleying results in grey, blue and green soil colours and the formation of GLEY HORIZONS.

Glob, Peter Vilhelm (1911–85) a Danish archaeologist, Director General of Museums and Antiquities in Denmark, famous for his popularizing work on the bog bodies of TOLLUND and GRAUBALLE, published as *The Bog People*, and for its sequel *The Mound People*, describing the Bronze Age clothing and other remains from EGTVED, Muldbjerg and Borum Eshøj.

Globular Amphora culture a late Neolithic culture of the Vistula, Oder, Elbe and Bug drainages in northern-Central Europe, whose characteristic vessel form is a bulbous pot with a narrow neck and small handles for hanging. Cord-marked decoration is common. The origin of the Globular Amphora culture is hazy, with most linking it to the late FUNNEL BEAKER culture. It is roughly contemporaneous with, or slightly pre-dates, the CORDED WARE/SINGLE GRAVE complex, between 3200 and 2500 BC. Single burial in stone CISTS is common, and axes made from the banded flint of the HOLY CROSS MOUNTAINS are frequent grave-goods.

Glozel an assemblage of pottery, clay tablets, bricks, terracottas and glass, found in Allier, France, by Emile Fradin in 1924, that has been claimed as evidence for an indigenous literate French civilization prior to contact with Greeks and Romans. The clay tablets carry inscriptions in a hitherto undeciphered script. The find, still credited in some quarters, is now widely held to be a fraud, but scientific argument still rages about the date of the individual objects, with THERMOLUMINESCENCE indicating 700 BC–AD 100, whereas this is ruled out on ARCHAEOMAGNETIC and PALYNOLOGICAL grounds.

glyph a symbol in a writing system. In the MESOAMER-

ICAN system, a glyph may represent an idea, word, sound, syllable or some combination of these.

Gnathian ware a pottery fabric made in the 4th and 3rd centuries BC in southern Italy. It seems to have been produced initially in APULIA, although other workshops were located in CAMPANIA, LUCANIA and Sicily. The pots are decorated in a BLACK-GLOSSED technique and over-painted in white, yellow and red. The scheme of decoration is either a pattern or simple figures. Unlike other SOUTH ITALIAN POTTERY the fabric was widely exported and is especially common in North Africa.

Gnezdovo a cemetery with over 600 burials dating to the 10th century AD located in western Russia near Smolensk. Some of the richer graves contain objects of Scandinavian and Byzantine origin, which reflect the trade routes that ran through this area. A hoard of jewellery at Gnezdovo contained many silver ornaments, primarily pendants, decorated with filigree, granulation and beading. These artifacts were probably worn by women as part of their headwear.

Gniezno an early medieval stronghold in western Poland and the principal town of the Polanie tribe. Settlement began at Gniezno in the 8th century AD, and by the end of the 10th century the town had become one of the key centres of the early Polish state.

Gobedra a northern Ethiopian rockshelter with a stratigraphic sequence covering the last 12,000 years. Seeds of cultivated finger millet (*Eleusine coracana*) found in a layer initially dated to between 7,000 and 5,000 years ago have been found to be intrusive to the layer and to date to only about 1,000 years ago.

Göbekli tepe a 7th millennium BC ACERAMIC NEO-LITHIC site on a hill overlooking the northern end of the Harran plain, near Urfa in southeastern Turkey. The site contains elaborate stone architecture, much of it cultic in nature, STELAS (and slots into bedrock for their installation) similar to the Nevali Çori materials, and smaller stone figures executed in the round or in high relief. The German excavators of this ongoing project suggest that the site was a religious centre for the region as a whole.

Gobi core see WEDGE-SHAPED MICROCORE.

Godin Tepe a prehistoric site in the Kangavar Valley of Luristan, western Iran; the work of Cuyler Young here and at Seh Gabi Tepe provides a cultural sequence, running from the early 5th millennium BC to the late Iron Age, which provides the basic framework for the culture history of this section of the Zagros Mountains. Perhaps the most significant contribution of the site to wider problems of western Asian archaeology is the period Godin V, in which late URUK materials (pottery, seal styles, tablets) are concentrated, along with local materials, within the 'oval enclosure' in the centre of the

town. Godin V is prominent in discussions of the Uruk phenomenon, and presents a situation different from those at HABUBA KABIRA and ARSLANTEPE. Analysis of a stain on an AMPHORA has revealed an early wine; another example appears at late Uruk WARKA, and wine seems to have been a trade commodity during the 4th millennium.

Gogo Falls a large, complex, open site situated alongside rapids of the same name on the Kuja River near Lake Victoria in the Kanyamkago Hills of southern Kenya, which documents the beginning of food production in the region. Dating of the earlier layers, which include OLTOME pottery and evidence for a broad spectrum hunting and gathering existence, is problematic. Partially overlying the Oltome layers is an enormous ASH MIDDEN 2 m (6 ft) or more thick, formed from burnt livestock dung, associated with radiocarbon dates spanning the 1st century bc to the end of the 4th century ad. It contains quantities of well-preserved remains of domesticated cattle and caprines together with considerable numbers of hunted animals, indicating that herd management was combined with hunting, a rare occurrence in East African archaeological and ethnographic records. ELMENTEITAN pottery and obsidian artifacts are also present in the midden. The layers overlying the midden contain Early Iron Age UREWE pottery.

Gogoshiis Qabe or **Gure Makeke** a rockshelter in southern Somalia, with a continuous MIDDLE to LATER STONE AGE sequence, including a series of early Holocene burials. Some of these were associated with lesser kudu horn cores and possibly represent the earliest unequivocal evidence for the intentional placement of grave-goods with a corpse in East Africa.

Gokomere an Early Iron Age site in southeastern Zimbabwe, occupied between the 5th and 7th centuries AD, which has given its name to an Early Iron Age group (see CHIFUMBAZE). Finds include pottery, copper and iron fragments, an Indian Ocean shell and the remains of large cattle byres.

Gokstad ship one of two large CLINKER-BUILT VIKING ships found in grave mounds near Oseberg in southern Norway, preserved in waterlogged soil. The Gokstad ship, over 23 m (75 ft) long and 5 m (16 ft) wide, was built around AD 900 and contained the burial of a Viking chief accompanied by numerous bone, horn and wooden artifacts. Among the animal bones were the remains of a peacock, pointing to the very distant contacts of the Vikings. Near by, the OSEBERG ship contained the grave of two women with a cart, sleds, tools and textiles. Its prow and stern were carved with elaborate animal designs.

Golasecca an Iron Age cemetery, type-site of the Golasecca culture of Lombardy, Italy. This is characterized by cemeteries of cremation burials in urns, sometimes accompanied by wheeled vehicles, as at Ca' Morta. The burial rite and metalwork reflect influences from the HALLSTATT sphere north of the Alps. The earliest graves of the Golasecca date to c.900 BC; it becomes absorbed into the CELTIC world in the 3rd century BC.

gold-figured *adj.* denoting a technique used to decorate Greek silver plate with gold foil. Some of the more important examples of the technique, which include cups, a PHIALE and a KANTHAROS, have been found at DUVANLI and SEMIBRATNY. They show complex figured scenes such as chariot-races. Detail is incised in the gold foil. The decoration evokes the RED-FIGURED technique used particularly on ATHENIAN POTTERY. See also SILVER-FIGURED.

gold-glass *adj.* denoting a technique by which gold foil is either attached to the surface of a glass vessel or sandwiched between two layers of glass. The foil is cut to provide the decoration, which may be quite complex. The earliest examples seem to date from the 3rd century BC, although the term is often applied to vessels made at ROME in the 3rd and 4th centuries AD, which are frequently decorated with Christian themes.

Goljamo Delčevo or **Golyamo Delchevo** a TELL-site of the CUCUTENI-TRIPOLYE culture in northeastern Bulgaria, notable for its system of rectangular fortifications including palisades and a bank and ditch, within which was a series of densely packed structures separated by narrow passages. A cemetery with thirty graves was located near by.

Golo Cave a cave-site on Gebe Island in the northern Moluccas, Indonesia, with a radiocarbon sequence dating back to 32,000 BP and representing one of the earliest settlements of modern humans in eastern Indonesia. It has yielded flaked stone tools, and at c.9000 BP the inhabitants imported wallabies from western New Guinea for hunting.

Göltepe see KESTEL.

Gombe Point, previously known as **Kalina Point** a site overlooking the Congo River in Kinshasa, Democratic Republic of Congo, where the first stratigraphic succession of stone industries in Central Africa was described. However, the absence of distinct archaeological horizons and lack of consecutive order in the dates suggest to recent researchers that the archaeological deposit is mixed. The site also contains Iron Age remains.

Gomolava a double TELL-site on the Sava River in Yugoslavia, with stratified deposits from the late Neolithic to the Middle Ages. The Neolithic occupation is 1.3 m (4 ft 3 inches) thick and belongs primarily to the VINČA CULTURE (c.5500–4000 BC), with two habitation levels. The earlier, Vinča B period, has pits, presumed pit-dwellings

and above-ground houses. The later, from the Vinča C period, has multi-roomed houses. Among the botanical remains was flax, probably domesticated. The Vinča C horizon also contained a cemetery with twenty-six burials.

Go Mun a site in the middle Red River Valley, northern Vietnam, which has given its name to the second Bronze Age phase of the area from c.1100 to 700 BC, and was followed by the DONG SON culture.

Gona a locality in the Middle Awash Valley in northeastern Ethiopia, which has yielded the oldest-known stone artifacts. The collection comprises some 3,000 items, including lava cores and flakes, which are attributed to the OLDOWAN complex, and estimated to date to about 2.5 million years ago.

Gondolin a limestone quarry some 25 km (16 miles) north-northeast of STERKFONTEIN in Gauteng Province, South Africa, which has yielded a small sample of large robust australopithecine teeth, similar in size to those of AUSTRALOPITHECUS/*Paranthropus boisei* from East Africa.

Gongwangling [Kung-wang-ling] see LANTIAN.

Gönnersdorf an extensive Upper Palaeolithic open-air site on the right bank of the Rhine, northwestern Germany, excavated by Gerhard Bosinski in 1968–76. It is best known for c.400 MAGDALENIAN engraved schist plaques, some of which depict stylized females with prominent buttocks, while others depict a variety of animals. A radiocarbon date of 12,600 bp has been obtained for the late Magdalenian occupation. The site was preserved by a thick pumice layer from a volcanic eruption during the ALLERØD. Its fauna is dominated by horses. Habitation structures include a number of tents, paved with schist plaques. Seashells from the Paris Basin and the Mediterranean were present. Similar finds were made at Andernach on the left bank, opposite.

Gontsy an Upper Palaeolithic open-air site on the right bank of the Udaj River (a tributary of the Sula, in the Dnieper Basin, 20 km [12.5 miles] from the town of Lubny) in Ukraine. The remains are buried in slope deposits overlying ALLUVIUM of the second terrace. Gontsy represents one of the earliest Palaeolithic discoveries in eastern Europe in 1871–3. In 1914–15, the excavations by Scherbakivski and GORODTSOV discovered a MAMMOTH-BONE HOUSE. In 1935 a Russo-Ukrainian team led by Levitski and Brussov excavated an area of 400 sq. m (478 sq. yds), mostly involving piles of mammoth bones in ravines. From 1977 to 1980, Sergin undertook limited excavations and dismantled the house of 1915.

In 1993 a Franco-Ukrainian team led by L. Iakovleva and F. Djindjian resumed excavations and a general study of the site. Two archaeological levels have been found at between 3 and 4 m (10 and 13 ft) beneath the present surface, in a stratigraphy of loessic loams of the recent PLENIGLACIAL, resting on the pre-WÜRM terrace. The faunal remains comprise mammoth, reindeer, bison, with remains of fur-bearing carnivores (wolf, fox, bear, lynx), hares and marmots. The lithic industry can be attributed to the recent EPIGRAVETTIAN of the middle Dnieper Basin. The best known habitation structure is an oval mammoth-bone house, 6 m (20 ft) in diameter, with a central hearth, which is surrounded by numerous storage pits, hearth-clearances and traces of different activities. A second house was discovered in 1998. Major scatters of bones of mammoth, reindeer and bison with flint and bone tools and remains of ash are located at the edge of, and at the bottom of, the ravines. Gontsy is well dated with a dozen homogeneous AMS results between 14,670 and 14,110 bp for the two occupations of the site.

Gonur-depe a large site (perhaps 50 ha [124 acres]) with a central fortress and surrounding residential and craft areas, set in the Murghab delta in southeastern Turkmenia and excavated by V. I. Sarianidi in the 1970s and 1980s. The material culture defines the Gonur phase of the regional chronology, intermediate between the KELLELI and TOGOLOK phases, and showing strong continuity with both; the phase may be dated to the late 3rd–early 2nd millennia. Characteristic elements of the material inventory are the Murghab seal-amulets whose rich iconography has been compared with both MESOPOTAMIAN and Late HARAPPAN styles.

Gonvillars a cave-site in Haute-Saône, France, with a stratified sequence of Neolithic deposits. Shortly after 5000 BC a Bandkeramik group (see LINEAR POTTERY CULTURE) established an encampment at the mouth of the cave. The pottery which they used is very similar to that of the Paris Basin Bandkeramik. Hunting was important – this may have been a temporary hunting camp – but the inhabitants also had domestic sheep and dog, and cultivated cereals. They were followed shortly before 4000 BC by RÖSSEN groups, who occupied the cave for approximately 500 years.

Goodwin, Astley John Hilary (1900–1959) the first and, for a long time, the only qualified archaeologist employed in sub-Saharan Africa. His 1929 synthesis, written with C. VAN RIET LOWE, *The Stone Age Cultures of South Africa*, set out the classification of the southern African Stone Age into EARLIER, MIDDLE and LATER STONE AGE stages, which are still used today.

Gordion (*Lat.* Gordium) the PHRYGIAN capital in the 8th century BC, situated 90 km (56 miles) southwest of Ankara in central Anatolia, on the Sakarya River. The work of R. Young in 1950–74 and his successors revealed the 8 ha (20 acre) citadel within whose walls were a series of large MEGARON structures set around a courtyard; the halls of these megara had galleries along three sides,

supported by wooden pillars. Smaller megara set in rows along streets lay on terraces behind this complex. Young also investigated a series of burial mounds, including the great royal tomb, perhaps of an ancestor of Midas, which was richly supplied with grave-goods (including inscriptions on beeswax in the Phrygian script). Several deep soundings have revealed a sequence of levels from the late EARLY BRONZE AGE to the post-HITTITE period, when construction of the early Phrygian citadel complex began. Gordion was sacked by the CIMMERIANS, and though occupation at the site continued into Roman times, it had lost much of its political importance. Skeletal material from the main tumulus has been the subject of the facial reconstruction of 'King Midas'.

gorget a flat, regularly shaped artifact made from stone or other suitable material that was worn as an ornament over the chest. It is especially common in prehistoric cultures of the American Southeast and Midwest.

gorgoneion the mask of the gorgon. This mythical monster, whose glance could turn people to stone, was beheaded by the hero Perseus. The mask became a symbol to ward off evil, and one forms the centre of the PEDIMENT on the ARCHAIC temple of Artemis on Corfu. Its use may have been to instil a feeling of awe in those entering the TEMENOS. The motif was widely used on ATHENIAN POTTERY especially during the late Archaic period, as well as on Roman CINERARIA.

Gorham's Cave see GIBRALTAR.

Gorman, Chester F. (1938–81) an American prehistorian known for his work on early metallurgy and horticulture in Thailand, particularly his excavations at SPIRIT CAVE in 1965–6 and at BAN CHIANG in 1974–5.

Gornja Tuzla a Neolithic settlement of the STARČEVO CULTURE and ENEOLITHIC TELL settlement of the VINČA CULTURE in northeastern Bosnia.

Gorodtsov, Vasili Alekseevich (1860–1945) a Russian archaeologist who established the presence of, and developed a chronology for, the Bronze Age in Russia. Gorodtsov also produced several syntheses of Russian prehistory, and emphasized formal typology. He excavated at the Palaeolithic sites of GONTSY, IL'SKAYA I and TIMONOVKA.

Gorodtsov culture an early Upper Palaeolithic culture defined on the basis of several assemblages from the KOSTENKI-BORSHCHEVO sites on the Don River in European Russia, which appear to date to c.30,000–25,000 bp. The assemblages contain many endscrapers and typical Middle Palaeolithic tools (e.g. sidescrapers), and a rich inventory of bone tools (e.g. needles, awls).

Gortyn the main Roman city of the province of CRETE and Cyrenaica. Italian excavations have uncovered parts of the 400 ha (988 acre) site which lies in the Mesara plain in the south of Crete. One of the most important discoveries was the early 5th century BC 'Gortyn Law Code', one of the most extensive of the surviving Greek inscriptions.

gorytos a sheath, combining a quiver and bowcase, which was very characteristic of the SCYTHIANS in the 6th–3rd centuries BC. Splendid gorytoses, covered with golden plaques decorated with artistic relief scenes, are known from the Scythian KURGANS of the 4th century BC such as Solokha and Chertomlyk. There is a depiction of a gorytos on the famous golden Scythian vase from the KUL'-OBA kurgan.

Goths a barbarian group that first appears in the historical record in AD 238. The origin of the Goths is unclear, with some scholars locating their homeland in Scandinavia and others placing it along the lower Vistula. From here, bands of warriors moved southeast, gathering allies, creating a mixed population north of the Black Sea which Roman writers called 'Goths' and differentiated into an eastern group, the Ostrogoths, and a western group, the Visigoths. In the late 4th century AD, pressure from the Huns caused the Visigoths to move west, into the Roman empire, and they soon made their way to northern Italy. Under their leader Alaric, they sacked Rome in AD 410, before continuing on to settle in southwestern France and Spain. Later in the 5th century, the Ostrogoths under Theoderic also moved west and established a kingdom in northern Italy.

Gough's Cave a cave in Cheddar Gorge, Somerset, England, which has yielded Upper Palaeolithic (CRES-WELLIAN) flint, bone and antler artifacts, animal bones (horse and red deer) which show clear cut-marks indicating butchery, and human bones which may provide evidence, in the form of deliberate cut-marks, for prehistoric cannibalism. The site has been excavated by a number of different workers from 1927 onwards.

Gournia the site of a MINOAN town on the island of CRETE, which was excavated by Boyd-Hawes in 1901–4. The town, which dates from the Neopalatial period, c.1690–1390 BC, is dominated by the 'Palace', which imitates the major Minoan palaces in detail if not in scale, and must have been the residence of the local governor.

Gozlu Kule see TARSUS.

GPR see GROUND PENETRATING RADAR.

Gradesnitsa a late Neolithic village site of the GUMEL-NIŢA culture in northwestern Bulgaria. Similar in size and layout to other Gumelniţa sites such as POLYANITSA and OVCAROVO, with closely packed houses arranged along narrow alleyways, Gradesnitsa is known especially for a 'ritual assemblage' which includes an inscribed clay tablet similar to the ones found at TĂRTĂRIA, but dated slightly earlier.

gradiometer a geophysical instrument, used in conducting surveys, that measures the gradient in a magnetic or gravitational field. It is used to identify shallowly buried cultural features and structures. See also DIFFERENTIAL FLUXGATE GRADIOMETER, FLUXGATE GRADIOMETER.

Gradistea Muncelului see SARMIZEGETHUSA.

graffiti writing applied to walls or other objects. Commercial graffiti were scratched or sometimes painted on the underside of Greek pottery. They sometimes refer to lists of pottery vessels in a consignment, the size of batches, prices and perhaps the names of traders. Other graffiti consist of personal names and should be understood as owners' marks. Graffiti can provide important information about language; for example, in the Roman colony at CORINTH the public inscriptions tend to be in Latin, whereas the graffiti on pottery are usually in Greek.

Graig Lwyd a Neolithic stone quarry and axe factory in Gwynedd, Wales, at the eastern end of Penmaenmawr Mountain, source of the Group VII axes of the British polished axe classification. The material has been identified as augite granophyre. The factory remained in use from c.4000 to 2500 BC.

grain size analysis see PARTICLE SIZE ANALYSIS.

Gran Chichimeca the region to the north of MESO-AMERICA where the CHICHIMECS lived prior to their movement south. Originally referring to the area outside the Mesoamerican culture sphere, the term is now also used to refer to the area beyond the geographical sphere of Mesoamerica, including areas as far north as the southwestern United States.

Gran Dolina see ATAPUERCA.

Grand Menhir Brisé see CARNAC.

Grand Pressigny a complex of flint quarries, the largest in Europe, extending over several square kilometres on plateaux and valley slopes overlooking the Rivers Creuse and Claise (Indre-et-Loire, France). The flint is of exceptionally high quality and honey-coloured in appearance. In many places the flint is not far below the surface, and extraction probably took the form of surface workings and shallow pits. A number of working areas have been found on the valley floors. Grand Pressigny flint was used primarily for the production of impressive blades up to 40 cm (16 inches) in length; the distinctive blade cores are known as LIVRES DE BEURRE, after the shape of the local 19th-century butter slabs. Grand Pressigny flint was widely traded, and material of similar appearance is found in BEAKER graves in the southern Netherlands, but only petrographic analysis will demonstrate whether this is really from the Grand Pressigny source. The exploitation of Grand Pressigny flint was a FINAL NEOLITHIC and CHALCOLITHIC phenomenon in c.2800 to 2400 BC.

granulation a technique used in the manufacture of jewellery whereby grains of gold or ELECTRUM, more rarely silver, are soldered on to metalwork.

grattoir see SCRAPER.

Grauballe Man a prehistoric body found preserved in a peat bog in Jutland, Denmark, in 1952. He had had his throat cut, possibly after being knocked unconscious. Stomach contents showed that his last meal had been a gruel with sixty-three varieties of seed, including spelt, rye, clover, buttercup and black nightshade. There are radiocarbon dates of *c.*2030 bp.

Grave Creek Mound the largest conical earth mound in the New World, located in northern West Virginia, USA. The mound is about 19 m (62 ft) high, with a basal diameter of 73 m (80 yds). The mound's base was surrounded by a moat approximately 1.5 m (5 ft) deep and 10 m (33 ft) wide. The mound was the centre of a complex of smaller mounds and earthworks. It was constructed during the 3rd and 2nd centuries BC, as a mortuary mound over a high status burial. It belongs to the ADENA culture.

gravel **1** a general size-term for material greater than 2 mm (0.08 inch) in diameter. Gravel is subdivided into granule, pebble, cobble and boulder gravel.
    2 a sedimentary deposit consisting largely of gravel-size CLASTS.

Gravettian an Upper Palaeolithic industry named after the site of La Gravette, Dordogne, France. It appears to have developed in Central Europe and expanded eastwards and westwards. In France the Gravettian, also known as the Upper PERIGORDIAN, is found stratified above the AURIGNACIAN and below the SOLUTREAN, and dated to *c.*28,000–20,000 BP. The tool-kit contains backed blades, scrapers, characteristic backed points and, in some phases, NOAILLES BURINS. See also EASTERN GRAVETTIAN.

Gravisca one of the ports of TARQUINIA in ETRURIA. Recent excavations have brought to light the remains of the harbour facilities and found large quantities of Greek pottery. A stone anchor dedicated by a Sostratos to 'Aeginetan Apollo' is evidence for Greek merchants.

gravity model a model that suggests that the degree of interaction between cultures is directly proportional to their proximity to each other.

Graziosi, Paolo (1906–88) an Italian prehistorian best known for his excavations and rock art studies in Italy and North Africa. He discovered the art at LEVANZO, and published a major volume, *L'Arte dell'Antica Eta della Pietra* (1956).

Greater Peten a major architectural style of the CLASSIC MAYA Lowlands. Typical of this style is the use of polychrome painted stucco on wall surfaces. The motifs are often repeated in a variety of combinations. See also PUUC and RIO BEC-CHENES.

Great Goddess a deity represented in stone and ceramic sculpture, and in mural art, from TEOTIHUACÁN, Mexico, with dual attributes of fertility and death. Hollow ceramic figurines contain miniature figures of plants and animals as a cornucopia-like representation of natural abundance. The concept of the Great Goddess evolved into later AZTEC goddesses such as Chalchiutlicue, Xochiquetzal and Cihuacoatl.

Great Langdale a Neolithic axe factory in Cumbria, England, consisting of a number of extraction sites where high-quality stone (epidotized intermediate TUFF, the Group VI material of the British polished axe classification) was quarried in surface workings or shallow pits. The site is high in the Lake District hills, but was connected to lower-lying sites such as Ehenside Tarn where the final stages of pecking and polishing were completed. The most prominent feature today is the massive scree down the hillside at Pike of Stickle, which contains many axe rough-outs and waste flakes. This was the most productive of all the Neolithic axe factories, with products traded widely throughout Britain from *c.*4000 BC for over 1,000 years.

Great Serpent Mound a huge ritual earthen mound in Ohio, USA, which has the form of a curved serpent almost 390 m (426 yds) long, 6 m (20 ft) wide and 1.5 m (5 ft) high. The serpent holds either an egg or a frog in its jaw. A nearby BURIAL MOUND belongs to the ADENA COMPLEX, to which the serpent mound itself is dated by association.

Great Wall a monument bordering the northern loess area of China, ostensibly built to protect agriculturalists from the incursions of steppe nomads in the mid 1st millennium BC (see XIONGNU). The existing wall, over 2,000 km (1,240 miles) in length, is actually composed of a series of walls built by individual ZHOU period states; it was linked together and extended by the First Emperor of QIN. It stretches from the BOHAI Bay in the east to the Tarim Basin in the west; the portion now seen by tourists near Beijing is a Ming (see CHINESE DYNASTIES) reconstruction.

Great Zimbabwe a Late Iron Age town with impressive stone walling in southeastern Zimbabwe, the most elaborate to which the term *dzimbahwe* (see ZIMBABWE) is applied. After an Early Iron Age occupation between AD 500 and 900, not associated with building in stone, Shona speakers occupied Zimbabwe Hill from about AD 1000 and later began building stone walls. Between about AD 1270 and 1450, Great Zimbabwe was the capital of a vast Shona empire that stretched from the Zambezi River to the Northern Province of South Africa and

GREAT ZIMBABWE, Zimbabwe: the High Complex.

eastern Botswana. In contrast to most other societies of southern Africa at this time, social organization was based on class distinction between commoners and a ruling class. The kings accumulated wealth and prestige by controlling trade between the southern African interior and the East African coast. Archaeologically, this culture is recognized as the Zimbabwe tradition (formerly Ruins tradition) and is divided into MAPUNGUBWE, Zimbabwe and KHAMI phases.

Some people still cling to the outdated idea that Great Zimbabwe was built by outsiders such as PHOENICIAN traders. However, the archaeological evidence as well as historical accounts from early Portuguese traders indicate that the pottery, houses and buildings are African and are the work of the ancestors of the Shona people of modern Zimbabwe (see CATON-THOMPSON).

Grebeniki culture a late Mesolithic culture of the area between the Carpathians and the Dniester Valley in Ukraine and Moldova of about 7000 BC, succeeded by the BUG-DNIESTER complex's foraging adaptation in about 6500 BC.

Greece, Turkey, Albania and Yugoslavia Prehistoric evidence for early human habitation has been found across the region, including MOUSTERIAN activity sites at LARISA in northern Greece. In Turkey, the earliest signs of human farming activity are found in southeastern Anatolia, dating from the Neolithic period (9th millennium BC). In central Turkey, sites like HACILAR developed as small villages. The ceramic Neolithic period in western Anatolia is characterized by sites such as ÇATAL HÖYÜK near Konya. The transition from the Neolithic to CHALCOLITHIC with the use of bronze tools is found at a number of sites including BEYCESULTAN in the upper reaches of the Maeander Valley, and at MERSIN and TARUS in southern Turkey. Sites in northern Greece such as DHIMINI in Thessaly also reflect the use of settled farming patterns. As in Anatolia many of the sites continued to be occupied into the Bronze Age such as at RACHMANI in Thessaly. The site of SITAGROI in Mace-

donia is particularly important for the understanding of the use of copper in the Balkans.

Bronze Age

The Bronze Age developed across Anatolia in the late 4th millennium BC from HISARLIK (Troy) in the northwest to Tarsus in the southeast. In eastern Anatolia this phase is defined as the KURA-ARAXES CULTURE, which has links with Syria, Iran and Palestine. At the Early Bronze Age site of ALACA HÖYÜK in eastern-central Anatolia, the rich tombs include some of the earliest examples of iron objects; some archaeologists have suggested that these burials represent a group moving down from the region to the east of the Black Sea. During the Early Bronze Age a distinctive CYCLADIC culture developed in the southern Aegean. One of the key sites, which continued into the Late Bronze Age, was at PHYLAKOPI on the island of Melos.

In the Middle Bronze Age, an archive from KÜLTEPE in central Anatolia reveals contacts with the Assyrians (see ASSYRIA) from the early 2nd millennium BC. From the Late Bronze Age (c.1600 BC), central Anatolia was united under the HITTITES; the city of BOĞHAZKÖY was decorated with monumental architecture and sculpture. During the 2nd millennium BC there were developing links with the Aegean world, as indicated by sites such as THERMI on Lesbos. On CRETE a number of palaces like KNOSSOS and PHAISTOS dominated the island during the Bronze Age. LINEAR B tablets from the island provide insights into the organization of the society. Evidence for the Bronze Age in the Aegean has been provided by the discovery of a town on THERA which had been destroyed by a volcanic eruption. On the Greek mainland, palaces such as PYLOS and MYCENAE emerged; burials were often in THOLOS tombs. Around 1200 BC numerous sites throughout Greece, Anatolia and the Levant show signs of destruction, which has led to theories about invasions and the arrival of the 'Sea Peoples' who are mentioned in contemporary records.

Historic period

In eastern Anatolia there was a continuation of the Hittite kingdom, focused on sites like CARCHEMISH on the River Euphrates. In central Anatolia the PHRYGIANS appeared around the 12th century BC, with a capital established at GORDION from the 8th century BC. The Phrygians were destroyed around 700 BC by the CIMMERIANS, who probably came from the steppes to the north of the Black Sea. The western boundary of this invasion was formed by the Lydians with their capital at SARDIS, a city which was to be sacked by CYRUS II c.540 BC. The Ionian Greek cities of western Anatolia, like MILETUS, were sacked by the Persians in the early 5th century BC, though they were later rebuilt. After the collapse of the Late Bronze Age palace-orientated societies on the Greek mainland and on Crete, the Aegean world entered the Dark Ages, though evidence for settlements of this period have been discovered, such as at

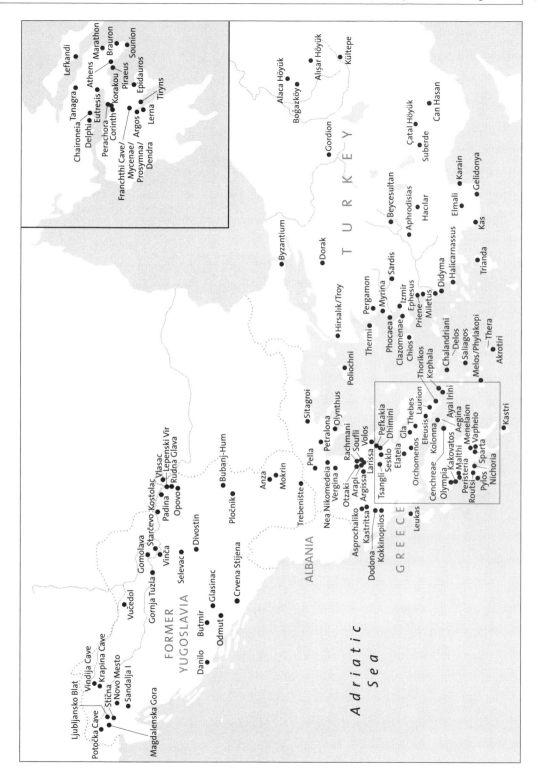

Karphi in the LASITHI mountain range of Crete. At LEF-KANDI on the island of Euboea an elaborate shrine was created c.1000 BC, apparently focused on rich burials.

From the 8th century BC onwards the city-states that become distinctive of the Greek world emerged. Social and economic factors led to the establishment of Greek colonies around the shores of the Mediterranean and the Black Sea. These independent states came together in joint festivals such as the four-yearly games held at OLYMPIA in honour of Zeus. Oracles at sanctuaries like DELPHI attracted interest from the Greek world and beyond, which is reflected in extravagant dedications discovered during the excavations. The city of ATHENS dominated the Aegean world during much of the 5th century BC; its position is reflected in the richly decorated temples like the PARTHENON.

From the 4th century BC Macedonia dominated the Greek world and much of the former Persian empire. Excavations at VERGINA may have discovered the tomb of Philip II, the father of Alexander the Great. The Hellenistic kingdoms formed in the aftermath of Alexander the Great dominated the political structure of the lands bordering the eastern Mediterranean; for example, the Attalids had their capital at PERGAMON in northwestern Anatolia.

Rome in the eastern Mediterranean

Rome started to acquire territory in the eastern Mediterranean during the 3rd century BC, initially with Epirus in northern Greece. The old Greek kingdom of Macedonia was acquired in the 2nd century BC, and CORINTH was destroyed in 146 BC, later being re-established as a Roman colony by Julius Caesar in 44 BC and becoming the centre of the new province of Achaia. The Attalid kingdom was bequeathed to Rome in 133 BC, forming the new province of Asia. The former Greek cities flourished, and their prosperity is reflected by the discoveries at EPHESUS and APHRODISIAS, with their bath-houses and facilities for sporting events. One of the most important documents of the Roman world, the *Achievements* (or *Res Gestae*) of the emperor Augustus, was cut on the walls of the temple for the imperial cult at Ankyra (Ankara). Military bases were established in eastern Anatolia to guard against incursions by the PARTHIANS. These fortresses were supplied by a network of roads which can still be traced across Turkey.

Late antiquity

The division of the Roman empire in the early 4th century BC led to the formation of a new imperial capital at BYZANTIUM, renamed Constantinople. Christianity now in effect became the official religion of the Roman empire, and BASILICAS were constructed in most of the major cities. Many of the former pagan sanctuaries such as Delphi and Olympia were abandoned.

greenstone a green-coloured, slightly metamorphosed basic igneous rock, the colour of which is due to the minerals chlorite, hornblende or epidote. The term has been adopted without differentiation for rocks including SERPENTINE, olivine, jade, jadeite and NEPHRITE, which were used for fine axes, figurines and ceremonial objects.

In southeastern Australia, greenstone (diorite) edge-ground hatchets were widely traded during the late Holocene. MOUNT WILLIAM is the best-known source. Greenstone (nephrite) was also important in NEW ZEALAND, where it was worked into a range of wood-working tools and ornaments, usually by splitting, sawing and grinding rather than flaking.

greyware ceramic ware found at MONTE ALBÁN and the VALLEY OF OAXACA, Mexico. Both common household ware and specialized ceramics are made from greyware. Specialized ceramics were of a polished greyware, and are found in high frequencies in this area.

grid a systematic array of perpendicular lines used as a frame of locational reference on an archaeological site. Elements of the grid are usually assigned some value of distance and direction with reference to a local or regional DATUM. Excavation units, recovered debris and other field observations are recorded and sometimes planned with reference to the grid. Grids are usually aligned with respect to the primary compass directions, but it is often advantageous to align them with respect either to the expected site structure, or to the primary depositional slope of the landform the site is situated upon.

Griffin, James Bennett (1905–97) influential North American archaeologist best known for his detailed ceramic studies and cultural historical syntheses of eastern North American prehistory.

Grimaldi a cave and rockshelter complex on the Italian Riviera close to the French border, which has produced Middle and Upper Palaeolithic material, most notably AURIGNACIAN and GRAVETTIAN assemblages, which have been termed Grimaldian industries. The caves have also yielded a series of seventeen elaborate HOMO *sapiens sapiens* burials, including grave-goods and evidence for partial burning of the bodies; their date remains uncertain, but they are usually assigned to the Gravettian. A series of small 'VENUS' FIGURINES, of equally uncertain date, were also found. See also GROTTE DES ENFANTS.

Grimes Graves a Neolithic flint mine in Norfolk, England, with traces of over 360 shafts surviving as shallow depressions over an area of 7 ha (17 acres). The high-quality flint was in three bands within the chalk, known as *floorstone*, *wallstone* and *topstone*. The best quality flint was the tabular floorstone. With the aid of antler picks, hour-glass shafts up to 12 m (30 ft) deep were dug in the chalk, with galleries radiating from their base. Despite the large number of shafts which were dug, exploitation was probably a small-scale, possibly seasonal, occupation, with only one or two shafts in use at any one time. The site appears to have continued in use from soon after 3000 BC to the Early Bronze Age.

Grimston see HANGING GRIMSTON.

gród (*pl.* **grody**) early medieval fortified enclosures of eastern-Central Europe. Most numerous in Poland, such strongholds also occur in eastern Germany (where they are known as *Burgwalle* or *Herrenburgen*) and the Czech Republic (where they are called *hradiste*), as well as eastwards into Russia and the Baltic states. They are characterized by earthen ramparts, often with wooden reinforcement. Some of the largest became the nuclei of urban centres, such as GNIEZNO and MIKULČICE.

Gródek Nadbużny a Neolithic settlement of the FUNNEL BEAKER culture in southeastern Poland, excavated in 1954–7. Structural remains at Gródek Nadbużny are characterized by PLOSHCHADKI. A wide variety of flint types were used, and there is evidence of copper metallurgy.

Groitzsch a group of Upper Palaeolithic open-air sites located on the Mulde River (an Elbe tributary) in eastern Germany. Artifacts are buried in sand overlying a GLACIAL MORAINE; the cultural layer probably dates to the end of the Pleistocene. Traces of two former structures with paved floors were excavated. Artifacts include endscrapers and burins, and are assigned to the MAGDALENIAN.

groma a four-armed Roman instrument used for surveying. Plumb lines were attached to each of the arms, and the groma allowed accurate alignments to be made. This was particularly useful for laying out the grid-pattern of forts and towns, for the construction of roads, and for CENTURIATION.

groove-and-splinter technique an economical method of working bone, ivory or antler developed during the Upper Palaeolithic. Two deep, parallel grooves are cut in the raw material and the splinter between them is snapped free to produce a blank for subsequent reworking.

Grooved ware a pottery style of the British late Neolithic, also known as Rinyo-Clacton ware after the sites of Rinyo in Orkney and Clacton in Essex. The typical form is the flat-based straight-walled vessel decorated with elaborate surface grooving. The pottery is found in settlement sites and CHAMBERED TOMBS, but appears to have had some special significance as it is found in especially high frequencies at major ritual sites such as HENGES.

Grotta dell'Uzzo a cave-site near the northwestern tip of Sicily, with a stratified sequence of Mesolithic and early Neolithic deposits. In the Mesolithic layers (dated to between 8000 and 6500 BC), six inhumation burials were discovered. early Neolithic levels with CARDIAL IMPRESSED WARE, bones of domestic sheep, goat and pig,

and traces of wheat and barley follow probably around 6000 BC, making this one of the earliest Neolithic sites in the central Mediterranean. The early Neolithic is followed by middle Neolithic layers with STENTINELLO and painted Masseria La Quercia ware, and finally by dark-faced wares of late Neolithic DIANA style.

Grotta di Lamalunga see ALTAMURA MAN.

Grotta Guattari a cave in the Monte Circeo, 100 km (60 miles) southeast of Rome, Italy, where the skull and jawbone of a 45-year-old NEANDERTHAL man were found in 1939, allegedly inside a ring of stones. This was interpreted by A. Blanc and others as evidence of ritual and cannibalism, since the hole at the skull's base had been widened. Recent TAPHONOMIC studies suggest strongly that the cave was a hyena den, the stone-ring was natural and there are no human-made traces on the Neanderthal bones. Dates from aurochs' teeth (ESR) and calcite (URANIUM/thorium) indicate that the bones were deposited between 57,000 and 51,000 BP.

Grotta-Pelos or **Pelos-Lakkoudes** a cultural phase, named after archaeological sites in the Cyclades, which in Renfrew's classification of the CYCLADIC culture sequence corresponds to Early Cycladic I (*c.*3200–2700 BC) in the traditional chronology.

Grotte Chauvet an Upper Palaeolithic cave at Vallon Pont d'Arc in the Ardèche, southeastern France, discovered in 1994, and containing PARIETAL ART with 420 painted and engraved figures depicting sixteen different species of animals, unusually dominated by big cats, rhinos and mammoths. The cave floor also has animal tracks and at least one human footprint. Direct AMS dating of charcoal in three paintings has yielded results of 32,410 to 30,340 bp, making these the oldest directly dated rock art in the world; however, the extreme sophistication of the Chauvet art – shading, animated scenes, full-face heads, different uses of perspective, etc. – led most specialists initially to attribute the cave to the SOLUTREAN or MAGDALENIAN, so the results remain somewhat controversial.

Grotte Cosquer an Upper Palaeolithic cave whose discovery, announced in 1991, was made by Henri Cosquer, a professional diver, since the cave's entrance – originally on dry land – was drowned by the POSTGLACIAL rise in sea-level, and is now 35 m (115 ft) beneath the surface, off the French Mediterranean coast near MARSEILLES. It contains PARIETAL ART comprising numerous paintings and engravings of animals, plus some possible Great Auks and jellyfish, and hand stencils. Direct dating of charcoal in some paintings and from fireplaces suggests two main episodes, the first around 27,000 bp, and the second around 18–19,000 bp.

Grotte des Enfants a cave in the GRIMALDI complex which has produced Upper Palaeolithic material including an adult male CRO-MAGNON HOMO *sapiens sapiens* burial lying above the double inhumation of a young man and an older woman; the latter were first thought to have Negroid characteristics, but are now seen as Cro-Magnon.

Grotte Vaufrey a cave in Dordogne, France, where excavations by J.-P. Rigaud in 1969–82 revealed a 4 m (13 ft) stratigraphy from MINDEL/RISS to early WÜRM, including a very early (pre-Würm) occurrence of the MOUSTERIAN. Dating of SPELEOTHEMS by URANIUM SERIES analysis and of burnt flints by THERMOLUMINESCENCE indicates a span from 246,000 to 74,000 BP. The cave seems to have had a series of repeated short occupations.

Ground Penetrating Radar a non-intrusive geophysical field survey technique used to detect or identify buried structures, materials, graves and other subsurface features. The technique allows for targeted excavations with minimal intrusion on the site. An antenna emits and receives pulses of relatively low-power electromagnetic energy, radar, through the ground as it is pulled along a horizontal transect over the ground surface. Objects or materials with different electromagnetic conductivity cause reflection of radar back to the antenna. Reflections are recorded, processed and displayed, creating an image of the subsurface as a *time slice*, or slice-map, where reflection time is related to depth of the discontinuity causing the reflections. Multiple parallel horizontal transects are necessary to locate buried objects precisely. Algorithms in imaging software applied to results from multiple transects allow data to be viewed as horizontal, vertical or three-dimensional images of subsurface reflections. Effective depths for the technique vary according to soil type and homogeneity: depths approaching 10 m (30 ft) may be explored in fine-grained material under optimal conditions, and 30 m (100 ft) in sand and gravel. The technique can be used to penetrate water, but is more effective in fresh water. Specifications of equipment used will also affect results. The lower the antenna frequency, the deeper the penetration, but lower the resolution.

Grubenhaus (*Ger.* pit house) early medieval house-form in northwestern Europe, comprising a rectangular pit dug into the ground to a depth of up to a metre, with a tent-like superstructure of posts and roof. The sunken area may have been a kind of cellar, with a timber floor above. Some of these structures were probably short-term dwellings, while others were workshops.

Gryaznov, Mikhail Petrovich (1902–84) a Soviet archaeologist, a specialist in the archaeology of Siberia, Kazakhstan and Central Asia. He excavated sites of the Bronze Age and of the SCYTHIAN period, particularly frozen barrows of the ALTAI MOUNTAINS such as Shibe and PAZYRYK. In 1939 he produced the first definition of the Early Nomads epoch as a special period in Eurasian history. The results of his intensive work on the archaeology of southern Siberia in the metal ages are concentrated in the monograph *Sibérie du Sud* in the series 'Archaeologia Mundi' published in 1969 in European languages. He is also well known for his excavation of an outstanding site from the early Scythian period, the ARZHAN KURGAN in Tuva, that led him to propose a hypothesis concerning the independent origin of SCYTHIAN TYPE CULTURES.

Gua Bukit Taat a cave in Terengganu, Malaya, with a HOABINHIAN assemblage dating from 9000 BP.

Gua Cawas a rockshelter in the equatorial forest in Kelantan, Malaya, with HOABINHIAN deposits dated between 12,000 and 5000 BP and rich in PHYTOLITHS of plant remains such as banana, rattan and bamboo. It contained burials of people ancestral to the non-Malay Semang and Senoi peoples.

Gua Cha a rockshelter in Kelantan, Malaya, utilized between *c.*10,000 and 1000 BP, and excavated in 1954 and 1979. Lower HOABINHIAN levels contain flaked bifacial pebble tools, many flexed burials and pig bones. Above these are extended Neolithic burials with pottery, some similar to BAN KAO. A similar sequence is found at many other caves and rockshelters in peninsular Malaysia and southern Thailand.

Gua Gunung Runtuh a cave in Perak, Malaya, with a crouched HOABINHIAN burial interred in a freshwater SHELL MIDDEN dated to 11,000–7500 BP.

Gua Kechil a rockshelter in peninsular Malaysia spanning the transitions from HOABINHIAN hunting and collecting to the Neolithic. Other sites include GUA CHA, Gua Musang, Gua Berhala, Gua Bintong, Gua Kajang, Gua Kelawak and BUKIT TENGKU LEMBU, and open sites like JENDERAM HILIR.

Guar Kepah a large SHELL MIDDEN on the west coast of Malaya, opposite Penang, which was excavated in the 1930s and yielded burials of a Melanesoid population and a Neolithic culture distinct from the BAN KAO tradition of the Thai-Malay peninsula.

Guattari Cave see GROTTA GUATTARI.

Gubinskaya Luka one of many monumental groups of conical tumuli in northwestern Russia constructed between AD 700 and 1000, not far from NOVGOROD.

Gubs Shelter No. 1 a Palaeolithic rockshelter on the Gubs River (Kuban' tributary) in the northern Caucasus of European Russia. A Middle Palaeolithic assemblage was found in the lower portion of a sequence of loam and rubble deposits; the tools are primarily sidescrapers. Two Upper Palaeolithic cultural layers overlie this assemblage. The lower layer contains a high number of endscrapers; the upper layer yielded a very different assemblage composed largely of backed blades. Faunal remains were sparse, but indicate cold climatic conditions; the entire sequence is thought to date to the last GLACIAL. The shelter was discovered and excavated by Autlev in 1961–3; further excavation was conducted by Amirkhanov in 1975–6.

Gudea a ruler of LAGASH during the post-AKKADIAN period (c.2125 BC), best known for the numerous inscribed statues of him found at TELLO, which are among the best-known objects of SUMERIAN art. The inscriptions boast of great power and extensive trading connections, though in the circumstances of the post-Akkadian period these claims are surely exaggerated.

Gudenus Cave a prehistoric cave-site located on the River Krems west of Vienna, Austria. Artifacts and faunal remains (e.g. cave bear, woolly mammoth and reindeer) are buried in stream (?) and cave deposits. The lowest cultural layer contains Middle Palaeolithic artifacts, including sidescrapers and bifaces. A small Upper Palaeolithic assemblage (MAGDALENIAN), including an animal engraving, was recovered from an overlying level. Neolithic and later remains occur in the uppermost layer.

Guilá Naquitz a PRECERAMIC site in the eastern VALLEY OF OAXACA, Mexico, dating from 8750–6670 BC. The site was discovered in 1964, and excavations were begun in 1966 by Kent Flannery. The small rockshelter was completely excavated by an interdisciplinary team, with research centred on the question of the origins of agriculture, and modelling a system of foraging and incipient cultivation. Recently, some seeds of squash (*Cucurbita pepo*), which are morphologically domesticated, from the site were directly dated by AMS to between 10,000 and 8,000 years ago, which predates other domesticates in MESOAMERICA (such as maize, beans, etc.) by several millennia. The site has recently yielded direct radiocarbon dates from corncobs of about 4300 BC. Guilá Naquitz represents one of the most thoroughly researched preceramic sites in Mesoamerica, and is part of a larger study of the preceramic settlement system in the Valley of Oaxaca.

Guitarrero Cave a site in the Callejón de Huaylas region of northern Peru, whose occupation began in the PRECERAMIC period and continued through later CERAMIC periods. Excavations by Thomas Lynch suggest that the site was a wet-season camp occupied by hunter-gatherers whose subsistence strategy was one of TRANSHUMANCE. The earliest domesticated beans known at present in South America, dating from c.8000 BC, were found here.

gully an erosional landform consisting of a trench greater than several centimetres deep and wide, characterized by steep vertical sidewalls and headwall. They form in existing valleys or on HILLSLOPES. Erosion of gullies can remove large quantities of unlithified sediment and can rapidly destroy archaeological deposits. Occurrences of settlement in deep gullies that provide shelter, particularly from winds, have been documented.

Gumanye a Late Iron Age site in southern Zimbabwe which has given its name to a FACIES of the KUTAMA tradition, which is associated with a northward spread of people from northern South Africa at the beginning of the Late Iron Age in about AD 1000, and the appearance of Shona people at GREAT ZIMBABWE in the 11th century. Gumanye sites are mainly small villages on defendable hilltops.

Gumban A see NDERIT WARE.

Gumelniţa culture a late Neolithic/ENEOLITHIC culture of the eastern Balkans, c.4600–4000 BC, roughly contemporary with Vinča D and Layer VI at KARANOVO. Many Gumelniţa settlements, such as POLYANITSA and OVCAROVO, are characterized by closely packed rectangular structures separated by narrow passages, the whole complex surrounded by a square earthwork; while others, such as CASCIOĂRELE have somewhat more dispersed layouts. Ceramics of the Gumelniţa culture are often decorated with graphite designs, reflecting a sophisticated control of firing conditions. There is considerable evidence for emergent social differentiation in the Gumelniţa culture, particularly as indicated by the finds from the cemetery at VARNA.

Gundestrup a large silver cauldron discovered in a peat bog in Jutland, Denmark, in 1891. The vessel consists of twelve separate plates of sheet silver, a round plate and two tubular fragments, which were found dismantled, stacked within the curved base. The plates of the cauldron are decorated with scenes in raised relief, representing ritual or mythological events. The figures on the outer face were originally covered in thin gold-leaf, with inlaid eyes of red or blue glass. Attempts have been made to interpret the scenes in the light of later Scandinavian mythology, but recent studies suggest that the cauldron

GUNDESTRUP, Denmark: the silver cauldron.

was manufactured not in northern Europe but in THRACE, probably in the later 2nd century BC.

Günz glaciation the first major Alpine GLACIAL advance, which started c.590,000 years ago, marking the onset of the Pleistocene phase, which lasted until the end of the MINDEL GLACIATION. The preceding Basal Pleistocene or Donau phase was a long period of alternating colder and warmer climates.

Guptas a dynasty that ruled the Indus and Ganges plains of northern India, from northern Pakistan to the Narmada River, during the period AD 320 to the early 6th century. In addition to their political power, the Guptas oversaw the establishment of the Indian tradition in the arts and sciences. Classic Hinduism began crystallizing from its Brahminical antecedents, and the rich sculptural imagery commonly associated with Hindu temples appeared during this period. The Hun invasions of the early 6th century AD disrupted Guptan stability, and may have greatly reduced urbanism in northern India for a time. See also DVARAVATI.

Gura Baciului an early Neolithic site of the CRIȘ culture in Transylvania, contemporaneous with other early farming settlements in southeastern Europe such as KARANOVO I, SESKLO and ANZA. Obsidian from sources near by in Hungary forms a major component of the lithic assemblage.

Gure Makeke see GOGOSHIIS QABE.

Gutians a people of the 3rd millennium BC whose original home was somewhere in the Zagros Mountains east of MESOPOTAMIA, perhaps Luristan. They are best known for their contribution to the fall of the AKKADIAN empire, when groups of Gutians invaded southern Mesopotamia. The Gutian, or post-Akkadian, period in Mesopotamian political history is one of extreme fragmentation, when Akkadian, SUMERIAN and Gutian dynasties ruled petty city-states; GUDEA of LAGASH (see TELLO) is the best known of these rulers. The period lasted for as little as forty years, before Ur-Nammu (2112–2095 BC) founded a dynasty at UR and began the political reintegration of the region under the UR III state.

guttae peg-like features which appear on the underside of MUTULES and TRIGLYPHS on CLASSICAL buildings of the DORIC ORDER.

Gvardzhilas-Klde an Upper Palaeolithic cave-site on the Chernula River (Kvirila tributary) on the south slope of the Greater Caucasus (altitude 600 m [1,970 ft]) in Georgia. At least two cultural layers have been defined in a sequence of rubble, clay and loam deposits. The faunal remains are chiefly of goat and woodland bison. The artifacts include many backed blades and GRAVETTIAN points, and many non-stone items (e.g. needles, harpoons); the age of the industry is unknown. Gvardzhilas-Klde was discovered and excavated by Krukovskij in 1916, and investigated in 1953 by Kalandadze and Tushabramishvili.

Gwanda see BAMBATA 2.

Gwisho a series of mounds beside hot springs in western Zambia, which contain evidence of LATER STONE AGE ZAMBIAN WILTON occupation from about 5,000 to 3,500 years ago, of particular interest because organic remains were preserved in the waterlogged deposits. About thirty-five poorly preserved KHOISAN skeletons were recovered from graves.

Gwithian a small Middle Bronze Age farming settlement in Cornwall, England, with sub-rectangular houses and associated fields. The spread of broken pottery over fields suggests the practice of manuring, and marks in the field corners indicate that wooden spades may have been in use to help make good use of land which was beyond the reach of the ARD.

gymnasium a sports-ground in a Greek city which contained a PALAESTRA. They were also centres of education.

gypsum a hydrated calcium sulphate mineral found in evaporite deposits, desert soils, and as a primary or secondary mineral in limestone, shale, marl and clay. Gypsum is usually white or colourless, but can be grey, yellow, brown, blue or red. Combined with sand, water and organic fibres, gypsum was used in the manufacture of plaster-like mixtures used as cements, coatings of architectural surfaces and in making casts, moulds and sculpture. The dense, fine crystalline variety is alabaster.

H

Ha'amonga-a-Maui a massive TRILITHON of coral at Hahake, Tongatapu, that is unique in the Pacific. The lintel rests in slots on the top of the uprights; according to tradition the monument was built in about AD 1200 by a member of the Tui Tonga dynasty. See also MU'A.

Habachi, Labib (1906–84) an Egyptian archaeologist, the most active excavator of his generation. Habachi's best-known work was at the sites of ASWAN, KARNAK and QANTIR, but he was involved in fieldwork in Egypt throughout his career.

Habuba Kabira a fortified site on the great bend in the middle Euphrates in Syria, which is the best known of several late URUK period settlements at this location. The large walled town of Habuba Kabira South seems to have been built as a planned community which existed for about fifty years. Virtually everything about it – architecture, pottery, seals, numerical tablets – is southern MESO-POTAMIAN in character. The town was part of a series of closely connected settlements on this part of the Euphrates, including Tell Qannas (the 'AKROPOLIS' of the settlement) and the nearby Jebel Aruda, perhaps a cultic centre; the settlement complex at Habuba Kabira-Tell Qannas covered at least 20 ha (50 acres), perhaps even 40 ha (100 acres). The discovery of these settlements in the 1970s caused considerable discussion of late Uruk state formation, expansionism and trade colonies.

Hacılar an important site, situated in a valley on the northern side of the Taurus Mountains in southwestern Turkey and excavated by James Mellaart in the 1950s, which presents two distinct aspects. The bulk of the settlement is a small area (under 1 ha [2.5 acres]) with occupation spanning the late Neolithic and early CHALCOLITHIC periods (roughly 5600–4500 BC), providing an important chronological anchor for this part of western Asia. The community inhabited rectangular houses, built as single rooms with internal divisions of space, set close together. Below these levels, and separated by an occupational gap, are seven ACERAMIC NEOLITHIC levels dated to the earlier 7th millennium; these levels provide evidence of morphologically domesticated barley and emmer, while the animals are not yet morphologically changed.

Hacinebi a 3 ha (7.4 acre) site on the Euphrates River just north of the Turkish-Syrian border. Excavation during the 1990s by G. Stein provided details about development of local social complexity during the 4th millennium BC (late CHALCOLITHIC) and interactions with the southern MESOPOTAMIAN world in the middle centuries of that millennium ('URUK expansion'). Later occupation includes an ACHAEMENID-HELLENISTIC period settlement and a Roman farmstead.

Hadar a locality in northeastern Ethiopia, which has proved to be one of the most abundant sources of HOMINID fossils in Africa for the period from about 3.5 to 2.5 million years ago (see 'LUCY').

Haddenham a Neolithic long barrow in Cambridgeshire, England, on an old land surface later covered by fen peat, thus preserving the original barrow in waterlogged conditions where the timber structures could survive. Many of the features usually found in megalithic chambered long mounds such as WEST KENNET were here represented by massive timberwork: a curved façade either side of the entrance; a passage; and a burial chamber containing remains of several individuals. So enormous were some of the pieces of timber that the structure has been dubbed 'megaxylic' (from Greek *megas* 'large' and *xylon* 'wood'). The great importance of the site is that it shows the kind of wooden structures which may originally have existed within many of the non-megalithic long mounds of northern Europe.

Hadra ware a type of HELLENISTIC pottery first recognized in the Hadra cemetery at ALEXANDRIA. A common shape was the HYDRIA, which was used as a burial container, often inscribed with the name of the deceased, and sometimes the date, painted or incised on the shoulder. Recent clay analysis has shown that the fabric was also produced on CRETE.

Hadrian's Wall in northern England served as the main permanent northern boundary of the Roman empire, except for short periods when the ANTONINE WALL was occupied. It was the idea of the emperor Hadrian and it lay to the north of the earlier Stanegate line (see VINDOLANDA). The wall ran from Wallsend on the Tyne to Bowness-on-Solway. However, further fortlets on the east and west coasts to the south of the wall were designed to stop infiltration. Work started in AD 122, mainly done by legionaries. In the east a stone wall was constructed, whereas in the western sector turf was used initially, although this was later replaced by a stone wall built to a narrower gauge. The wall was secured by milecastles with two turrets in between; a later plan brought the main forts on to the line of the wall.

Hafit a mountain ridge near Buraymi in southeastern Arabia on which are a number of cairns containing a JEMDET NASR-type of painted pottery, other MESOPOTAMIAN ceramic forms, bead types belonging to the same cultural configuration, as well as more locally derived materials. These late 4th–early 3rd millennium burials provide the earliest local material evidence for Mesopotamian interaction with ancient Magan (see PERSIAN GULF TRADE). Although poorly related to contemporary settlement, these burials give their name to the earliest Bronze Age cultural period in southeastern Arabia. Similarly constructed tombs and occasional pottery finds extend through the piedmont of southeastern Arabia.

Hagia Triada see AYIA TRIADHA.

Haguenau an important cemetery of Bronze Age and Iron Age BURIAL MOUNDS in the Forêt de Haguenau, Bas-Rhin, France, overlooking the Rhine. The richest of the mounds date to the Middle Bronze Age (c.1500–1350 BC), when this part of France came under the influence of the TUMULUS CULTURE of southern Germany, as shown by the metal types including heavy PALSTAVES, and the distinctive pottery with geometric excised decoration, originally filled with coloured paste.

Hahn, Joachim (1942–97) a German prehistorian who specialized in the Palaeolithic period, especially the AURIGNACIAN and its art. He is best known for his excavations at GEISSENKLÖSTERLE and Hohle Fels in southwestern Germany.

Haithabu or **Hedeby** a trading town on the Schlei estuary at the southern end of the Jutland peninsula in northwestern Germany. Haithabu was settled during the 7th century AD and over the next 200 years developed as a major commercial centre of the southeastern Baltic region. Many years of excavations have revealed evidence not only of trade but also of local industrial activities.

haji the unglazed earthenware of KOFUN period and early historic Japan, derived from the YAYOI tradition but influenced by SUE-ware shapes from the late 5th century AD. Compare SATSUMON.

Hajjar bin Humeid a small site (under 5 ha [12 acres]) in the Wadi Beihan of Yemen, which was until recently the only stratified sequence of pre-Islamic occupation in southwestern Arabia. G. van Beek distinguishes nineteen strata (lettered S–A) in a small test-pit. In addition to exposing an architectural sequence (walls and parts of houses in most levels), the excavation produced a well-controlled ceramic sequence from the beginning of the 1st millennium BC to the middle of the 1st millennium AD. This sequence thus corresponds to the emergence and florescence of the SOUTH ARABIAN CIVILIZATION.

Hajji Firuz a small ceramic Neolithic site in the Solduz Valley just south of Lake Urmia (northwestern Iran), dated to the early 6th millennium BC. M. Voigt's investigations during the 1960s indicated that the villagers occupied small two-room houses, suggesting that nuclear families formed the basic unit of labour for farming and animal herding. These families enjoyed roughly equal wealth (i.e. an apparently egalitarian society). Chemical analysis of residues in a clay vessel reveals the presence of wine, the oldest occurrence of this beverage thus far found.

Hajji Mohammad a small site near WARKA, where German soundings in the 1930s ceramically defined the 'UBAID 2 (Hajji Mohammad) period in southern MESOPOTAMIA. The German work also revealed wattle-and-daub domestic architecture of the same date.

Halaf, Tell a large TELL-site on the River Khabur in northeastern Syria, near the Turkish border, where the investigations by M. von Oppenheim between 1899 and 1929 focused on the 1st millennium BC settlement, the ancient Guzana. It was the seat of an ARAMAEAN kingdom and then a provincial capital of the NEO-ASSYRIAN empire (and the area to which many Samarians were deported in the 8th century); the Assyrian archives provide valuable details of imperial administrative affairs of the time. The foundation trenches of the Aramaean palace have dug into earlier levels that contained a previously unknown style of painted pottery, now called Halaf ware and subsequently identified at Tell ARPACHIYAH and elsewhere. Oppenheim identified another early ceramic style at the site (his *Altmonochrom*, corresponding to the 'Dark Faced burnished' ware of the AMUQ B), which perhaps represents a pre-Halaf occupation.

Halaf culture complex a range of items of material culture named after the initial discovery of its painted pottery style at Tell HALAF. The Halaf culture complex is chronologically divided into three phases (Early, Middle and Late) dating to the 6th millennium BC. The Early Halaf is found in the Balik and eastern Khabur drainages of northern Syria, while the Middle and Late Halaf have an extremely wide distribution, from Cilicia in the west to the Diyala River in the east, covering an arc against and within the inner Tauros-Zagros mountain chain; the pottery also occurs further afield to the north, as at TILKI-TEPE and some Transcaucasian sites. Halaf settlements tend to be uniformly small (generally under 4 ha [10 acres]) and classically composed of THOLOS dwellings (a round chamber with a rectilinear entrance passage). The painted pottery is decorated with geometric, floral and some naturalistic motifs (especially BUCRANIA); the Late Halaf pottery includes a polychrome painted ware. Subsistence activities focused on dry farming (of wheat and barley) and animal herds (sheep, goat, cattle, pig). Well-known Halaf sites include Tell AQAB, ARPACHIYAH and YARIM TEPE 2.

Hala Sultan Tekke the site of a major Late Cypriot town in southern CYPRUS, which is being excavated by Åström. A fine harbour and the copper trade presumably account for the wealth and cosmopolitan tastes of the inhabitants, who acquired items from the Aegean, Anatolia, Syria and Egypt. The site was eventually abandoned in the 11th century BC, possibly because an earthquake had destroyed the harbour.

Halawa Valley the site on Molokai, Hawaii, of intensive archaeological research into settlement patterns. On the coast is one of the earliest settlements in Hawaii, dating to c.AD 650 with an assemblage similar to BELLOWS BEACH. From c.AD 1200 settlement shifted inland as dependence on irrigation agriculture of taro (a root crop) increased. The pattern of taro cultivation along the valley bottom with settlements along the sides and mouth is typical of wet windward valleys in the Hawaiian Islands. Compare KAWELA, LAPAKAHI, MAKAHA VALLEY.

halberd a weapon with a pointed or V-shaped blade mounted with its long axis at right angles to the handle, yet with its flat surface in the same plane as the shaft. Halberd blades are very common among Bronze Age finds from temperate Europe.

Halfan a rich late Upper Pleistocene stone artifact tradition found in hunting and fishing camps in the Nile Valley, probably beginning in the period between 40,000 and 30,000 bp. Although it is generally identified as Upper Palaeolithic because it is characterized by tools made on small blades, it also features the persistence of the LEVALLOIS technique normally associated with Middle Palaeolithic technology.

half-life the time required for half the nuclei in a given sample of a specific radioactive ISOTOPE to decay to another isotope. The half-life value is different for each isotope, but in all cases is a critical component in the calculation of ages by RADIOMETRIC DATING methods. Also, it is the half-life that in effect determines the general age range over which a radiometric dating method is potentially useful.

Halicarnassus a Greek city on the west coast of Turkey. It became the capital of the *satrap* (Persian governor) Mausolus and it was here that his funerary monument, the Mausoleum (one of the SEVEN WONDERS), was constructed. This was decorated with sculpted friezes as well as portrait sculpture; some fragments may be seen in the British Museum.

Hallan Çemi Tepe a terminal Pleistocene site on a tributary to the Tigris River in eastern Turkey, excavated during the 1990s by M. Rosenberg. The 0.5 ha (1 acre) site contains three levels, the lowest with small U-shaped structures, the middle with circular structures and the uppermost with pit houses, the entire sequence belonging to the late 9th millennium bc. The biotic evidence indicates year-round occupation, the plant remains favouring pulses and nuts (but not cereals), the animal remains wild sheep, red deer and pig. Although the pigs retain a wild appearance, the culling patterns strongly suggest that the village maintained herds of these animals, the earliest evidence for pig domestication yet found.

Hallstatt 1 a cultural tradition of the Late Bronze Age and Early Iron Age between c.1200 and 600 bc in continental temperate Europe, named by Paul REINECKE after the cemetery and salt-mining site of Hallstatt in Austria. The beginning of the Hallstatt tradition (phases A and B) is equivalent to the URNFIELD period of the Late Bronze Age. The Iron Age begins with Hallstatt C, while a final phase, D, marks the transition to the subsequent LA TÈNE period. Within the Hallstatt tradition are a number of regional cultures, such as the LUSATIAN culture. The Hallstatt period is characterized by the emergence of centres of production and trade, such as at STIČNA in Slovenia, the HEUNEBURG and HOHENASPERG in southern Germany, and Hallstatt itself in Austria. Elsewhere, there were fortified settlements such as SENFTEN-BERG in eastern Germany and BISKUPIN in Poland. The late Hallstatt period saw the emergence of a strongly differentiated social order, in which control of trade with the Mediterranean world played a major role.

2 a site on the western side of Lake Hallstatt in the Austrian Alps, overlooking the modern town. Along an Alpine valley was a cemetery with over 2,000 graves, both cremations and inhumations, containing vast quantities of grave-goods both imported and of local manufacture. Swords with amber and ivory pommels reflect participation in an exchange network that reached from Africa to the Baltic. Further up the valley are the traces of prehistoric salt workings, in which miners' clothing and tools are often found preserved in ancient galleries.

Hallur a prehistoric site in southern India, excavated by Nagaraja Rao in the 1960s, and containing a stratigraphic sequence important to regional chronology and development. Rao defined three periods at the site (Hallur IA–B, II), which date to the 2nd and early 1st millennia BC.

The architecture, at least in Hallur IB, comprises circular structures of bamboo and daub (similar to those elsewhere in the region, e.g. TEKKALAKOTA). Copper tools (mostly axes, and also a fish hook) are present in Hallur IB, while iron appears in Hallur II. This evidence stands at the beginning of the region's megalithic grave culture, when iron becomes fairly common. The initial occupation contains bones of cattle, sheep and goat, all of which appear in the subsequent occupations. Hallur IB, however, also contains a small amount of horse bone. This suggestion of horse riding is amplified by rock art in the region, which depicts horse riders. As at similarly dated sites (e.g. Tekkalakota), Hallur IB presents evidence for cultivation of millets.

Hal Safieni a rock-cut HYPOGEUM in Malta, consisting of a system of intercommunicating underground chambers. These originally contained the remains of several thousand individuals. The earliest chambers, dating probably to the 5th millennium BC, are those of the upper level. As these became full, two further series of chambers were cut at lower levels. Also to this later phase (3rd millennium BC) belong finely cut chambers with decoration, two in relief, two in red ochre, the designs consisting of running spirals and chequers. These chambers may have been imitations of above-ground megalithic temples, of the type which originally stood over the hypogeum itself, or may be better seen at TARXIEN. See also MALTESE TEMPLES.

Halula an 8 ha (20 acre) mound on the Euphrates River in northern Syria. An on-going Spanish excavation has recorded thirty-six phases of occupation that run from PRE-POTTERY NEOLITHIC (PPNB) to HALAF times (early 7th to early 5th millennium bc). The PPNB settlement was large (some 7 ha [17 acres]), and its occupants invested considerable energy in construction – the excavations have uncovered a 3.5 m (11 ft) high stone terrace wall with a large building upon the terrace. Painted human figures decorated the floor around the hearth in the central room of one residence.

Hama a city on the middle Orontes River in Syria excavated by Danish scholars in the 1930s. The place was occupied from Neolithic to Islamic times (with some gaps), and a town exists there today. During the early 1st millennium BC Hama, ancient Hamath, was the seat of a small ARAMAEAN state; the Danish work uncovered the palace and main temple of this period.

Hamada, Kosaku (1881–1938) a Japanese art historian and archaeologist who established the first formal course in archaeology in Japan in 1913. Co-founding the Far Eastern Archaeological Society in 1925, he encouraged scholarly interchange between Japan and China.

Hamangia a late Neolithic culture of the Black Sea coastal plain of Romania and Bulgaria, contemporaneous with the early stages of the BOIAN and MARITSA cultures further inland, c.5500–4800 BC. Hamangia open settlements do not form TELLS, but rather appear to have single thick occupation layers. Burials of the Hamangia culture occur in cemeteries set apart from the settlements, as at CERNAVODĂ and CERNICA.

Hambledon Hill a Neolithic CAUSEWAYED CAMP and Iron Age HILLFORT in Dorset, England, excavated by R. Mercer. The causewayed camp yielded disarticulated human remains and may have been used for the exposure of corpses. A long barrow stood near by on the same hilltop. On another part of the hill was a palisaded settlement enclosure (the Stepleton Enclosure) which was destroyed by fire, possibly due to hostile attack. In addition to the enclosures, two series of large Neolithic dykes were also built across the arms of the promontory. The hilltop was reoccupied in the 1st millennium BC when it became the site of an impressive Iron Age hillfort, with two parallel banks and ditches enclosing traces of at least 200 hut circles.

Hamburgian a late Upper Palaeolithic reindeer-hunting culture found in northern Germany and Holland and contemporary with the late MAGDALENIAN of France. The Hamburgian is in many ways similar to the AHRENSBURGIAN, which follows it in the same area. The typical assemblages include harpoons, tanged points, endscrapers, a few microburins and specialized borers known as *Zinken*. The neighbouring northern German sites of Stellmoor and Meiendorf, excavated by A. Rust, are Hamburgian seasonal reindeer-hunting camps, preserved by waterlogged conditions and dating to 13,000–11,750 BP. They have both yielded the skeletons of young reindeer apparently deposited in a lake either as an offering or as a method of refrigeration. See also BROMMIAN.

Hammat al Qa a 7 ha (17 acre) walled Bronze Age (early 2nd millennium BC) town near Dhamar in highland western Yemen. Investigations by an American team during the 1990s have recorded the arrangement of houses, streets and open spaces within the town, and have documented contemporary agricultural terraces. The site reflects an independent trajectory towards urbanism and social complexity in highland Yemen during the Bronze Age.

hammerstone a hard stone used as a hammer during the knapping of flint and other stone. See also HARD HAMMER TECHNIQUE.

Hammurabi (1792–1750 BC) one of the best known of the ancient MESOPOTAMIAN kings. He was the sixth king of the AMORITE DYNASTY at BABYLON. Under the earlier rulers in this line, Babylon was a petty kingdom. Hammurabi changed this status by forming a succession of alliances to deal with rival kingdoms, thereby managing to conquer Babylonia and the middle Euphrates, including MARI. Although his inscriptions claim conquests into ASSYRIA, Hammurabi's effective control stopped at the Babylonian-Assyrian frontier; unlike other southern Mesopotamian empire builders, Hammurabi never attempted invasion of ELAM, although he did fight defensive wars with Elamite forces. The contraction of Hammurabi's kingdom began soon after his death.

Han 1 a term used for unrelated ethnic groups in China and Korea. In China it implies 'pure' Chinese as distinct from minority groups, and in Korea it refers to the inhabitants of the SAMHAN in the PROTO-THREE KINGDOMS period.
2 a historical period or dynasty in China (206 BC–AD 220), with the WANGMAN interregnum (AD 9–25) separating the Early (Western) and Late (Eastern) Han periods. As the first centralized state in China following unification by QIN in 221 BC, the Han court instituted iron and salt monopolies, extended territorial administration through the COMMANDERY system (see LELANG), opened commerce to the west via the SILK ROUTE and began the tradition of court histories (see HOUHANSHU). Aristocratic burials of the period are very rich (MANCHENG, MAWANGDUI), but most tombs have only LEAD-GLAZED WARE.

handaxe see BIFACE.

Hane an early eastern Polynesian (see PACIFIC) dune site at the mouth of the Hane Valley on Ua Huka Island, Marquesas, which documents settlement of the Marquesas from about AD 300 up to European contact.

Hang Gon an urn-burial and metal-working site of the 1st millennium BC in Xuan Loc Province, southern Vietnam. The large stone cist grave is unique to Vietnam, and bronzes and stone ornaments show wide-ranging contacts with SA HUYNH sites, the KHORAT Plateau of Thailand and even India.

Hanging Grimston a long barrow on the Yorkshire Wolds, England, which gave its name to the Grimston-Lyles Hill pottery style of the British earlier Neolithic of the 4th millennium BC. The characteristic vessel shape is the round-based CARINATED bowl with everted rim.

hangtu [hang-t'u] the Chinese technique of pounded-earth construction of walls and foundation platforms for buildings; first developed in the terminal Neolithic (LONGSHAN) period and subsequently used for monumental architecture. See also ERLITOU, QISHAN, XIAOTUN. Compare PISÉ.

haniwa the unglazed earthenware funerary sculptures of KOFUN period Japan, erected on MOUNDED TOMB surfaces either to outline and protect the burial precincts or as sumptuary display.

Harappa one of the great cities of the Mature HARAPPAN

civilization, located in the Punjab region of Pakistan, and excavated by M. S. Vats in the 1920s and 1930s, by M. WHEELER in the 1940s and more recently by G. Dales, M. Kenoyer and R. Meadow. Although the Mature Harappan occupation is the best explored aspect of the city, both Early Harappan (the 'pre-defence' levels) and Late Harappan ('Cemetery H' and related habitation levels) are also documented. The Mature Harappan city, covering about 80 ha (200 acres), presents the common Harappan form of a citadel with monumental architecture, and with a larger zone of residential architecture to the east; the excavations at MOHENJO-DARO provide a clearer picture of Harappan urbanism.

Harappan civilization one of the great civilizations of antiquity, located in Pakistan and northwestern India. A development of the 3rd millennium BC in the greater Indus Valley, and named after the site of HARAPPA, the civilization represents one of world archaeology's great traditions. It is divided into three phases – Early, Mature (or Urban) and Late (or Post-Urban). The Early Harappan phase includes several regional cultural provinces in the Punjab, Sind and neighbouring Baluchistan regions of the northwestern Indian subcontinent (see AMRI, KOT DIJI, KALIBANGAN) early in the 3rd millennium. Around 2600–2500 BC the Mature Harappan abruptly coalesced from these antecedents. The Mature Harappan is typified by urban centres and massive 'public' architecture, the use of characteristic 'administrative' devices (a still undeciphered writing system, square STAMP SEALS and metrical standards, especially for weight), technological sophistication and wide contacts with surrounding regions (from Central Asia to southeastern Arabia and southern MESOPOTAMIA). Covering an enormous area (some 800,000 sq. km [309,000 sq. miles]), many aspects of the material culture (in architecture, pottery, metal and bead forms, seals) are present throughout the Harappan region, though significant regional variation does exist (see ALAMGIRPUR, MITATHAL, RANJPUR). Around 2000–1800 BC, this urban expression of the Harappan tradition collapsed, leaving regional Late Harappan cultures in villages and small towns whose continuity with the Mature Harappan is evident principally in pottery, but which had lost many of the artifacts that were central to Mature Harappan society (especially seals and writing). Late Harappan cultures existed through most of the 2nd millennium BC.

Harare see KUTAMA.

hard hammer technique the use of a hammerstone to remove flakes during the knapping of flint and other stone. Hard hammer flakes are short and deep with a prominent BULB OF PERCUSSION. Compare SOFT HAMMER TECHNIQUE.

hard water effect a potential source of contamination and error in radiocarbon dating. Hard water is water enriched in dissolved salts of calcium and magnesium which may derive from older or dead carbon in some reservoirs. $^{14}C/^{12}C$ ratios of aquatic plants and organic and inorganic carbonate precipitates will reflect the reservoir ratio. If old or dead carbon is present, the resultant radiocarbon ages will be too old. Typically these reservoirs are in areas of limestone terrain or other carbonate rocks where carbonate dissolution leads to the introduction through ground water of old or dead carbon. Other factors affecting reservoir $^{14}C/^{12}C$ ratios include exchange with the atmosphere, introduction of humus, the amount of soil carbonate, and temperature and precipitation. If the hard water effect is suspected and corrections are not made, ages should be reported as maximums only.

Hargeisan a stone industry of northern Somalia characterized by the production of large blades from prismatic cores, which precedes the appearance of microlithic assemblages. The Hargeisan was originally proposed by J. D. Clark in 1954, but the existence of this industry is not supported by more recent research.

Harifian a hunting/gathering culture in the Negev and Sinai, whose members lived in seasonal encampments with permanent architecture. These communities represent a specialized desert adaptation with a late NATUFIAN-derived lithic industry which was largely contemporary with the PRE-POTTERY NEOLITHIC (PPNA, c.8500–7600 BC) communities further north in the Levant. The characteristic tool type of the Harifian is the Harif point, which is an obliquely truncated bladelet with a pointed base formed by the microburin technique and steep retouch. The designation was defined by Antony Marks's work in the Negev.

Harmal, Tell a tiny administrative centre (1.7 ha [4.7 acres] in area) belonging to the kingdom of Eshnunna (see Tell ASMAR) during the OLD BABYLONIAN period, lying just outside Baghdad in central Iraq. T. Baqir excavated a large proportion of the site in the 1950s, revealing a walled settlement with administrative, cultic and residential buildings. Despite its small size, it contained a large number of literary and 'scholarly' texts in addition to administrative archives; a pair of life-size lion figures in terracotta found here are famous examples of Old Babylonian art.

harpoon technically, a spear-like implement with a detachable head which is used in hunting or fishing. However, archaeologists use the term to refer to all barbed bone or antler points. Harpoons are particularly associated with the MAGDALENIAN and the Mesolithic of Europe.

Harrison, Benjamin (1837–1921) an English grocer and amateur archaeologist who collected hundreds of Palaeolithic stone tools from northern Kent, and who excavated at the OLDBURY rockshelter site. Harrison is best remembered for his strong belief in EOLITHS as genuine stone tools.

Hasanlu a prehistoric site in the Urmia basin, south of Lake Urmia (northwestern Iran), which was the focus of a large project conducted by Robert Dyson from the 1950s to the 1970s. In addition to Hasanlu itself, the project excavated at Pisdeli, HAJJI FIRUZ, Dalma, Dinkha and others, to produce a ten-phase chronological sequence that begins in the late 7th millennium BC and continues (with breaks) into Islamic times. The regional project has also shed considerable light on early ceramic Neolithic adaptations (the Hajji Firuz phase, late 7th to mid 6th millennia BC), on the chronology and origins of the Iron Age in western Iran, on early 1st-millennium BC upland communities under pressure from ASSYRIAN imperial expansion (Hasanlu IV, from which the famous gold bowl derives), and on regional interactions during other periods (e.g. Dalma pottery of the 5th millennium, Dinkha pottery of the 2nd millennium BC).

Hascherkeller a Late Bronze Age/Early Iron Age site of the HALLSTATT period in Bavaria, Germany, near the city of Landshut on the Isar River. Settlement remains consisted of three farmsteads enclosed by earthworks, within which was evidence for the manufacture of pottery and for bronze casting. Hascherkeller has been interpreted as typical of the rural farmsteads that dotted Central Europe in the first part of the last millennium BC, prior to the emergence of centres of production and commerce such as HALLSTATT, STIČNA and the HEUNEBURG.

Hassi Mouilah an important Algerian EPIPALAEOLITHIC (dated to c.8600 bp) and Neolithic (c.5300 bp) site. Finds include many pointed-base pots with overall impressed decoration, projectile points and geometric microliths, as well as ostrich eggshell and amazonite beads.

Hassuna, Tell a prehistoric site on the Tigris near the confluence of the Upper Zab, in northern Iraq, where the excavations by S. LLOYD and F. Safar in the 1940s defined a sequence of a previously unknown pre-SAMARRAN culture in northern MESOPOTAMIA, now named after the site. The seventeen levels defined fall into four cultural phases. At the bottom (level Ia) is an ephemeral occupation, perhaps by a semi-sedentary community whose material culture is similar to that at UMM DABAGHIYAH. Following this phase are three architectural levels (Ib–c, II), now identified as 'Archaic Hassuna', and then three levels (III–V) of 'Standard Hassuna' (6200–5500 BC). The subsequent occupations consisted of five HALAF (6th millennium BC) levels (VI–X) and three 'UBAID (5000–3800 BC) levels (XI–XIII); two much later occupations (levels XIV-XV) cap the mound. In this sequence, Samarran painted wares occur in levels III to VIII, indicating a considerable chronological overlapping of Hassuna, Samarran and Halaf ceramic styles. Lloyd and Safar's excavations provided the type-site for the

HASSUNA CULTURE COMPLEX, and defined its two developmental phases; these are still used today.

Hassuna culture complex a late Neolithic culture that is roughly and uncertainly dated to the late 7th and into the 6th millennium BC, and has its distribution in the Jezirah of northern Iraq, running from the Tigris River in the area of the Upper Zab towards the Khabur triangle; it seems to be derived from the earlier Neolithic found at such sites as UMM DABAGHIYAH and the basal level of HASSUNA. The culture complex, best known from the sites Hassuna and YARIM TEPE 1, is divided into two phases, the 'Archaic' and 'Standard' Hassuna, according to changes in the painted and incised decoration of the pottery. The architecture of these settlements forms complexes of small rooms set around open spaces. Subsistence was focused on the cultivation of a variety of wheats and barley, and on herding sheep, goat and cattle; the material culture incorporates a variety of exotic materials, including copper, turquoise and carnelian beads. Although once considered representative of early agricultural colonization in northern MESOPOTAMIA, a number of earlier sites are now known (see MAGHZALIA, NEMRIK, QERMEZ DERE).

Hastinapura a site of some 30 ha (74 acres) on the upper Ganges in northern India, where B. B. Lal's excavations revealed a cultural sequence from the 2nd millennium BC to medieval times, though with major breaks. The earliest evidence of occupation is a few OCHRE COLOURED POTTERY SHERDS beneath a PALAEOSOL, over which are levels of fragmentary wattle-and-daub and mud-brick architecture, together with PAINTED GREY WARE and other wares. These people cultivated rice and kept a wide variety of animals, including horse, and also used iron as well as copper. Following major flooding and erosion, the site was reoccupied by people using NORTHERN BLACK POLISHED WARE in a community of brick architecture laid out on regular drained streets, who habitually used iron and employed coinage. The later levels belong to the late 1st millennium BC and to medieval times. Lal's work at Hastinapura provided the first good stratigraphic context for Painted Grey ware, which marks the trend towards urbanism and the GANGES CIVILIZATION, fully expressed in the Northern Black Polished ware horizon.

Hatchepsut an Egyptian queen, reigning in c.1473–1458 BC, during the 18th Dynasty. Her reign is a rare example of a woman assuming the monarchy in Ancient Egypt. The best-known monuments of Hatchepsut are the 'Red Chapel' at KARNAK and her MORTUARY TEMPLE at DEIR EL-BAHRI.

Hatnub (*Egyptian* 'House of Gold') a site in UPPER EGYPT, 18 km (11 miles) southeast of EL-AMARNA, the location of alabaster quarries worked from at least as early as the OLD KINGDOM until the Roman period. Hatnub has provided inscriptional material left by expeditions sent to the quarry, in the form of loose STELAS and GRAFFITI on the quarry walls.

Hattusha see BOĞHAZKÖY.

Hatvan culture the second culture in the tripartite sequence of the Hungarian Early Bronze Age defined by Moszolics on the basis of the STRATIGRAPHY at TÓSZEG, where the Hatvan culture occurs between NAGYRÉV and FÜZESABONY. Cremation burial in pits was practised. Hatvan settlements are also known, characterized by fortifications and long post structures. The Hatvan culture is believed to have originated in eastern Hungary and spread westwards.

Haua Fteah a very large cave in northern Libya, excavated by MCBURNEY, and containing remains dating from Lower Palaeolithic to historical times, including the most complete sequence of Upper Pleistocene and Holocene stone industries known from North Africa. The lowest layers are as yet unexcavated and the earliest industry so far described is the Libyan AMUDIAN (pre-AURIGNACIAN) blade industry. It was succeeded at least 60,000 years ago by the LEVALLOISO-MOUSTERIAN, which was in turn replaced about 40,000 years ago by the DABBAN industry. This continued until about 18–16,000 years ago, when it was followed by the Eastern ORANIAN, and later by LIBYCO-CAPSIAN material. Pottery as well as domestic sheep and/or goats are present by about 7,000 years ago. It has been suggested that the Eastern Oranian and Libyco-Capsian be considered part of a single industry similar to the IBEROMAURUSIAN.

Haury, Emil (1904–92) North American archaeologist, often referred to as the 'Dean of Southwest archaeology', through his excavations at Point of Pines and SNAKETOWN in Arizona, as well as many theoretical contributions, Haury helped establish the intellectual framework of archaeology in that region.

Hau Xa an urn burial cemetery of the late SA HUYNH culture, located in sand dunes near Hoi An, central Vietnam.

Haven, Samuel Foster (1806–81) an American antiquary whose monograph *Archaeology of the United States* (1856) did much to debunk many of the wilder speculations on North American prehistory, in particular the origins of the Midwestern mounds. See also ATWATER, DAVIS, SQUIER, THOMAS.

Hawaiian Islands the northern tip of the Polynesian triangle and the largest islands in POLYNESIA outside NEW ZEALAND. There are two alternative views of the dating of first settlement; either the islands were first occupied between AD 200 and 600, or slightly later, AD 600–800. The first settlers probably came from the Marquesas, bringing with them a range of domestic plants and animals. One important theme in Hawaiian archaeology is environmental change, both natural and as a result of forest clearance. Intensive agricultural systems and population growth supported the development of highly stratified chiefdoms. See also PI'ILANI-HALE HEIAU.

Hawara site in Egypt of the second pyramid of King AMENEMHAT III, dated to *c.*1844–1797 BC, possibly a later and more elaborate replacement for that at DAHSHUR. The particularly large MORTUARY TEMPLE attached to the pyramid seems to have been identified by some Greek and Roman authors as the 'Egyptian labyrinth' of legend.

Hawkes, Christopher (1905–92) Professor of European Archaeology at the University of Oxford and a specialist on the Iron Age archaeology of Britain. He set new research directions for the study of the British Iron Age in the 1930s with his A-B-C scheme invoking successive migrations or invasions from the Continent. This scheme, though now abandoned, was widely influential. Hawkes also conducted major excavations at several Iron Age sites including the pre-Roman and Roman settlement of Camulodunum (COLCHESTER) in Essex.

Hayonim Cave a well-stratified prehistoric site in western Galilee, Israel, excavated 1965–79 and 1992–9 by O. Bar-Yosef and associates. Bedrock was not attained: the earliest occupational horizons in the cave yielded MOUSTERIAN artifacts and animal bones. The oldest (layer F) has produced a particular Mousterian industry known as the Abu Sifian, rich in blades and elongated Mousterian points. It is overlain by layer E, characterized by increasing amounts of LEVALLOIS flakes with rare points, reminiscent of the QAFZEH assemblages. THERMOLUMINESCENCE and ESR dates indicate a range of 220–100,000 bp. Following an erosional gap, there is a Levantine AURIGNACIAN layer (29–27,000 bp) with flint, bone and antler tools including one split-base point. KEBARAN deposits, rich in non-geometric microliths, were found only near the cave entrance. Finally, three phases of NATUFIAN occupation, mostly attributed to the earlier period of this culture, include six built-up stone structures and seventeen graves.

Hayonim Terrace in front of HAYONIM CAVE, Israel, was excavated by D. Henry and later by F. Valla. It contained a thin layer of Geometric KEBARAN (rich in narrow trapeze-rectangles) and a series of NATUFIAN structures dated to the middle phase of this culture. Among the important finds was a grave in which both dogs and humans were jointly buried.

Hazleton a Neolithic chambered long barrow of Severn-Cotswold type in Gloucestershire, England, with two megalithic chambers reached by passages entered from near the middle of the long sides. Careful excavation allowed the construction sequence of the mound to be studied, consisting of a number of dry-stone cells filled with rubble. Remains of around forty persons were found in the burial chambers. Radiocarbon dates indicated a short period of construction and use in *c.*4700 BC.

Hazor a Palestinian site, the most important CANAANITE town excavated so far, explored by YADIN in 1955–8 and 1968. The central part of Hazor, a natural spur termed the 'upper city', was occupied in the EARLY BRONZE AGE. In the MIDDLE BRONZE AGE the 'upper city' was defended by a substantial (8 m [25 ft] thick) brick wall, while a GLACIS seems to have enclosed an area of approximately 80 ha (200 acres) to the north termed the 'lower city'. Canaanite Hazor flourished from the 18th century BC, but was destroyed by the ISRAELITES in the late 13th century BC. The 'upper city' was later fortified by SOLOMON and Ahab, prior to its sacking by the ASSYRIANS in 732 BC.

Head-Smashed-In a KILL-SITE in southern Alberta, Canada, in which bison were killed by stampeding them *en masse* over a cliff. The site has evidence of almost continuous use going back to about 3700 BC.

Healy Lake a prehistoric open-air site in the Tanana Valley, central Alaska, USA. Four cultural layers have been defined in shallow loess deposits. The lowest layer appears to date to *c.*11,000–10,000 bp and contains CHINDADN POINTS and microblades. It was investigated by Cook and McKennon in 1962–7.

hearth the fire site, a feature of many domestic habitation sites. The hearth is often centrally located, and has a variety of shapes and sizes. The burnt earthen rims of some hearths provide suitable oxidized material for ARCHAEOMAGNETIC DATING.

Heathery Burn a cave-site, in Co. Durham, England, with remains of Late Bronze Age occupation. Discovered during quarrying in the late 19th century, the cave held an extensive deposit of pottery, animal bones and bronzes, sealed under stalagmite. The finds included horse-riding equipment and evidence of metalworking. The cave may have been used as a hunting shelter by local chieftains in the 8th century BC.

Heavenly Horse tomb a 5th-century AD MOUNDED TOMB of the SILLA Kingdom in Kyongju City, Korea. A mound of pebbles covered with a layer of earth, 57 m (187 ft) in diameter, enclosed and protected from robbers an internal WOODEN-CHAMBER containing the lacquered wooden coffin of a male dressed in a gold crown and a girdle decorated with curved beads (see MAGATAMA). Grave-goods included horse trappings, glass cups, lacquer ware and ox horns. The tomb's intact interior has been restored as a display area for a site museum within the mound.

heavy mineral analysis heavy minerals are those of relatively high SPECIFIC GRAVITY, such as garnet, tourmaline, epidote and zircon, which usually occur as accessory detrital mineral grains in sedimentary deposits. The heavy minerals in pottery temper and matrix, or any other material produced from a sedimentary deposit, can be examined to help identify the geological PROVENANCE or source of the material. Different sources within a region may be characterized by contrasting heavy mineral suites. Heavy minerals are separated from the light minerals of lesser specific gravity by pouring the sample into a column of heavy liquid with relatively high density. The most commonly used is bromoform with a specific gravity of 2.85. The heavy minerals sink and are siphoned off, whereas the lighter minerals will float on the heavy liquid. The heavy mineral fraction is then identified and counted using low-power microscopy and compared to heavy mineral analyses from potential sources. Although the analysis is routine, the heavy liquids utilized are generally toxic and extreme care must be taken.

Hedeby see HAITHABU.

van Heekeren, H. Robert (1902–74) Dutch prehistorian best known for his important work in Indonesian archaeology, including the first excavation there of a Neolithic village (Kendeng Lembu, eastern Java); while working on the infamous Thailand–Burma railway under the Japanese in 1942, he found prehistoric stone tools along the banks of the Kwai Noi, the first evidence for Pleistocene occupation in Thailand. In later years he developed our knowledge of the 'TOALIAN' culture, and found the first evidence for Pleistocene man at Cabenge (southwestern Sulawesi). He also undertook important excavations at Anyar Lor (western Java), of sarcophagus burials in Bali, and caves in Flores and central Java. He produced two fundamental books, *The Stone Age of Indonesia* (1957) and *The Bronze-Iron Age of Indonesia* (1958).

Heger I see DONG SON.

heiau a Hawaiian stone temple, equivalent to the MARAE of eastern POLYNESIA. Most are complex arrangements of walls, terraces and platforms. See also AHU.

Heidelberg jaw see MAUER JAW.

Heijo the site of the 8th-century AD palace and capital of the RITSURYO state in Nara Prefecture, Japan, also known as the Nara Palace and Capital. Excavated continuously since 1952, the palace site was bought in 1961 and established as a historical site and museum. Plans of excavated palace buildings are reproduced in surface landscaping, and samples of buildings and the palace wall have been reconstructed. Occupied 710–84 (see JAPANESE PERIODIZATION), the 4.3 by 4.8 km (2.7 by 3 mile) capital followed the Chinese gridded-city plan as established at CHANG'AN (see also FUJIWARA). The discovery at Heijo of inked MOKKAN has added a documentary

HEI TIKI of jade, from New Zealand.

perspective to the information given in the 8th-century court histories, the KOJIKI and NIHON SHOKI.

Heine-Geldern, Robert (1885–1968) an Austrian ethnographer and historian who interpreted much of Southeast Asian and Pacific prehistory within a DIFFUSIONist framework.

hei tiki a MAORI neck pendant of stylized human form, often of GREENSTONE.

Heliopolis a once-important ancient Egyptian city, major cult centre of the god RE. Little remains of it apart from the still-standing obelisk of King SENWOSRET I. It is now a northern suburb of Cairo.

Helladic the Bronze Age culture of central and southern Greece. The chronological system devised by WACE and BLEGEN has three main divisions: Early (c.3000–2000 BC), Middle (c.2000–1550 BC) and Late (c.1550–1050 BC), each of which is further subdivided into three phases designated by Roman numerals. Late Helladic is the period of the MYCENAEAN civilization.

hellenistic *adj.* relating to a period of time dating from the death of Alexander the Great (323 BC) to the establishment of the Roman empire in the 1st century BC. The hellenistic world consisted of the kingdoms carved out from the former Persian empire as well as the Greek mainland. The term *hellenistic art* can be applied to post-CLASSICAL material outside this geographical area, such as in ETRURIA or southern Italy. See also ARCHAISTIC.

Hell Gap 1 a deeply stratified site in eastern Wyoming, USA, which provides virtually a complete PALAEO-INDIAN sequence for the Plains of North America. The site was occupied from about 11,200 to 8000 BP.

2 a PLANO tradition complex dated 10,000–9500 BP.

3 a projectile point type belonging to the Plano tradition.

Hembury a Neolithic CAUSEWAYED CAMP in Devon, England, partly overlain by a later Iron Age HILLFORT. POSTHOLES of a circular Neolithic house were found beneath the Iron Age west gate. The causewayed camp yielded WINDMILL HILL pottery and radiocarbon dates indicating occupation in c.4200–3900 BC.

Hemudu [Ho-mu-tu] an early Neolithic site in Zhejiang Province, China. Located on the coast of Hangzhou Bay, it has wet-preserved wooden raised-stilt architecture and abundant plant and animal remains, notably thick deposits of rice grain, husks and straw. It is the type-site of the southern rice-growing regime in contrast to the northern millet regime represented at CISHAN. Marshland species are well represented, indicating broad-spectrum collecting and aquatic domesticate experimentation. Dog, pig and water buffalo were the main domesticated animals. It is dated to the late 6th and early 5th millennia BC, and is succeeded by the QINGLIAN-GANG culture in the early Neolithic; and by the Daxi, Qujialing and LIANGZHU cultures in the middle Neolithic (c.3800–2800 BC).

henge a ritual enclosure, usually circular or nearly so, consisting of a bank and ditch with one or two opposing entrances. The bank is usually outside the ditch, and excavations at major henges such as DURRINGTON WALLS and Mount Pleasant have shown that substantial circular timber buildings once stood in the interior. Henges are especially common in the lowland south and east of England, but are also found in the further west and north where they sometimes enclose a stone setting. In recent years much attention has been paid to the special deposits of polished stone axes and other materials deposited at the henges – placed either in the enclosing ditch, or in pits dug within the interior. Henges differ from STONE CIRCLES in that the height of the surrounding bank will in most cases have created an enclosed space, hidden from the outside world, to which entry might have been allowed only to special individuals or on special occasions.

Hengelo Interstadial a continental middle PLENIGLA-CIAL INTERSTADIAL occurring during the final GLACI-ATION between the Moershooft and DENEKAMP interstadials and starting at c.39,000 BP.

Hengistbury Head a promontory jutting into the Solent estuary in Dorset, England, with an Upper Palaeolithic (CRESWELLIAN) open-air site which has yielded a well-defined scatter of flint artifacts proved by CONJOINING to belong to one assemblage; THERMOLUMINESCENCE dates around 12,500 bp have been obtained. A nearby Mesolithic site has evidence for on-site flint-knapping. The site rose to prominence in the Iron Age, c.100 BC, as a trading centre with connections to continental Europe. Roman wine AMPHORAS and luxury goods were among the imports. The entrepôt fell into decline in the mid 1st century BC.

heqin [ho-ch'in] the system of reverse tribute employed by the HAN Dynasty court in China for pacifying surrounding populations. As a reward for voluntary submission of tribute and acknowledgement of Han hegemony, lavish gifts of precious goods were bestowed on embassies from regions such as YAYOI Japan or the XIONGNU.

Herculaneum (Gk Herakleion) a small coastal town in CAMPANIA in Italy, buried under volcanic mud after the eruption of Vesuvius in AD 79. It probably started as an ARCHAIC Greek foundation. First attempts at exploration were made in the 18th century through tunnels around the theatre, but systematic excavations were conducted only in the 19th century and then again from the 1920s. Some of the houses have yielded important finds, such as the villa of the papyri containing important portraits as well as a library including works of Epicurus. The mud has allowed many timber items such as furniture to survive.

herm a low stone shaft on the top of which may be carved a portrait or the head of a deity. On some examples two heads are carved back-to-back (janiform). Although herms are found in the Greek world, for example in the AGORA of CLASSICAL ATHENS, they were particularly popular as decorative elements in the gardens of Roman houses.

Hermopolis Magna (Arabic el-Ashmunein) a site in northern UPPER EGYPT, with its NECROPOLIS at TUNA EL-GEBEL. Hermopolis Magna has chiefly been excavated by Roeder in 1929–39, and by the British Museum in 1980–90. The site is a substantial TELL, largely composed of the remains of the buildings erected within the sacred enclosure of this important city. The fragmentary stone structures on the tell, the earliest of which date to the MIDDLE KINGDOM, are mostly the remains of various phases of building at the great temple of THOTH. The most important standing building is the remains of a Roman basilica.

Herodium a Palestinian site, chiefly excavated in 1962–7 by Corbo. An impressive fortress constructed by Herod the Great (37–4 BC), it consisted of a circular fortified palace on the summit of a conical hill. Herodium also served as the site of Herod's tomb, and was a stronghold for Jewish rebels in the revolts against Roman rule.

Herpály a late Neolithic TELL site near Berettyóújfalu in the Tisza Valley of eastern Hungary, one of the type-sites of the Herpály-Czöszhalom culture group, together with the Czöszhalom tell further north. Contemporaneous with the TISZA CULTURE, Herpály and Czöszhalom date to the 5th millennium BC. Closely spaced timber-and-clay houses at Herpály are three-roomed structures which are interpreted as having had two storeys. Copper rings, pendants and beads were obtained from copper-producing areas elsewhere in the Carpathians.

Hetepheres a queen of the Egyptian OLD KINGDOM, the wife of SNEFRU and mother of KHUFU. Her unmarked tomb, within her son's pyramid complex at GIZA, was discovered by REISNER in 1925. This seems to have been a reburial of the funerary equipment (but without Hetepheres' MUMMY) from her original tomb, the location of which is unknown.

Heuneburg an Early Iron Age fortified site of the HALLSTATT period in Baden-Württemberg, Germany, which flourished c.600–440 BC. The fortifications at the Heuneburg enclosed an area of 3 ha (7.4 acres) near the headwaters of the River Danube. In most phases, they were built from rubble-filled timber cribs, but in period IV they were built on a Mediterranean-style plan from mud-bricks on a stone foundation. The settlement deposits at the Heuneburg contain considerable evidence for local manufacturing activity and trade with the Mediterranean. Imported objects include coral, fine pottery and Greek AMPHORAS from Massilia (modern MARSEILLES), presumed to have contained wine.

'hiatus palestinien' following the ACERAMIC NEO-LITHIC in the southern Levant, the archaeological evidence for settlements declines precipitously. Once this situation was seen as a region-wide depopulation and abandonment. However, recent evidence, especially the identification of the PRE-POTTERY NEOLITHIC C period (6200–5900 BC) and more numerous radiocarbon dates have essentially eliminated this gap in regional occupation.

Hierakonpolis a site in southern UPPER EGYPT, a major settlement of the PREDYNASTIC and ARCHAIC PERIOD. The town-enclosure at Hierakonpolis (the 'Kom el-Ahmar') was excavated by Quibell and Green in 1897–9, particularly a series of successive shrines, the earliest of which dates to the early Archaic/late Predynastic, as does a famous cache of votive objects, mainly of Kings NARMER and 'Scorpion'. Hierakonpolis was also explored by Fairservis and Hoffman in 1969–88.

hieratic (*Gk* 'sacred') a cursive form of HIEROGLYPHIC script, developed for everyday use in handwritten documents, and used in varying forms throughout Egyptian history until replaced for widespread non-religious use by DEMOTIC.

hieroglyphic (*Gk* 'sacred carved writing') a pictorial script employed by the ancient Egyptians from the beginning of the 3rd millennium BC until the end of the 4th century AD. It was primarily used for religious purposes and on public monuments, surviving in these contexts even after it had been superseded in more vernacular contexts by the cursive scripts HIERATIC and DEMOTIC

which evolved from it. Pioneering work in the decipherment of hieroglyphic texts was carried out by CHAMPOLLION.

Higgs, Eric Sidney (1908–76) a British archaeologist who conducted innovative work on the origins of agriculture. Higgs pioneered the technique of SITE CATCHMENT ANALYSIS and also initiated a school of archaeological thought called PALAEOECONOMY.

High Cliffy Island an island off the Kimberley coast, northwestern Australia, with evidence of occupation over the last 3,000 years, including many circular stone structures with walls up to a metre high forming the foundations of huts. See also LAKE CONDAH.

High Lodge a British Palaeolithic site in Suffolk. The original interpretation, based on artifact typology, was that it had yielded three separate industries: a slightly worn ACHEULIAN OVATE biface industry, a rather crude flake industry and a MOUSTERIAN industry with finely made tools but no prepared-core flaking technique. Recent excavation suggests that High Lodge may be c.450,000–500,000 years old, and that the entire assemblage may be similar to material from CLACTON and SWANSCOMBE.

Hili 8 one of a number of scattered small settlements in the Buraymi district of southeastern Arabia. It provides the key architectural and ceramic sequence for the Bronze Age of the region (c.3000–1800 BC). Here S. Cleuziou exposed a mud-brick tower (a typical architectural form in settlements of the period) that underwent a sequence of rebuilding. These excavations also provided important evidence for the emergence of Arabian oasis farming and water management, a component of which was domesticated sorghum (*Sorgo bicolor*) from the beginning of the sequence; this occurrence of domesticated sorghum is among the earliest known, and may point to a non-African centre of its domestication. As part of the project several UMM AN-NAR-type tombs were also excavated, one of which contained the remains of around 100 individuals together with many ceramics, stone vessels and other small finds.

hill figure see GEOGLYPH.

hillfort any hilltop fortress, though the term now most commonly refers to sites of the Late Bronze Age or Iron Age. The earliest hillforts of c.1000 BC were followed in the 7th and 6th centuries BC by sites with increasingly elaborate fortifications, including timber-framed ramparts and long, heavily defended entrance corridors. These gave way to massive multiple-dump ramparts and intricate entrances with outworks in the 3rd and 2nd centuries BC, a form which sees its fullest expression at MAIDEN CASTLE. In upland Britain, earth and timber defences were replaced by dry-stone walling. Some hillforts may have been permanent settlements, but many were merely temporary refuges. See also CRICKLEY, DANEBURY, HAMBLEDON, MONT LASSOIS.

hillslope a nearly ubiquitous sloping landform that ascends to higher GEOMORPHIC surfaces and descends to lower geomorphic surfaces. Hillslopes are the products of both erosional and depositional processes and are inherently unstable, thus presenting a potentially complex context for archaeological deposits. Hillslopes can be segmented into the following geomorphic components, listed in descending order, all of which need not be present to form a hillslope:

(a) *summit* – more or less level upland position at a drainage divide;

(b) *shoulder* – convex surface immediately below the summit where erosional processes dominate;

(c) *backslope* – more or less linear slope segment where both erosional and depositional processes occur; the backslope may have an associated thin surface veneer of material in transit downslope;

(d) *footslope* – concave segment where depositional processes dominate;

(e) *toeslope* – slightly concave, flattening segment where depositional processes dominate; the toeslope may represent all or part of a valley ALLUVIAL surface.

Footslopes and toeslopes are areas where archaeological deposits may be buried and preserved, and where cultural debris eroded from upslope may be redeposited. The shoulder and backslope are areas where archaeological deposits may be eroded. Material in these positions may be *in situ*, or temporarily redeposited while in transport downslope. The summit is subject to AEOLIAN deposition which may bury cultural deposits, and localized sheetflood EROSION and deposition which may differentially redistribute cultural debris locally.

Himiko see YAMATAI.

hinge fracture a fracture which occurs by error during flint knapping, producing a characteristic flake with a smooth, almost rounded end. It is either caused by a misdirected hammer blow allowing the fracture force to escape to the outside of the core, or is a direct result of the conchoidal nature of the stone itself.

Hippodamian planning the rectangular type of town layout which was practised, though not exclusively, by Hippodamos of MILETUS in the 5th century BC. Miletus, a harbour city in western Turkey, received a new layout after its destruction by the Persians in 494 BC, consisting of some 400 blocks. Public buildings and spaces were fitted into this grid, sometimes requiring multiples of the basic blocks. Hippodamos is said to have planned the PIRAEUS. See also PRIENE.

hippodrome see CIRCUS.

hiri an ethnographically documented Papuan coastal exchange system linking the Motu of the Port Moresby area with the Elema and Naman of the Papuan Gulf, through exchange of clay pots for sago and of shell valuables for canoe logs. Like the MAILU system, the hiri seems to have operated for about the last 400–500 years and is archaeologically documented from sites such as Popo and MOTUPORE.

Hisarlık/Troy a tiny site (the mound is about 2 ha [5 acres] in area), first excavated by J. von Hahn in 1864, and then, famously, by H. SCHLIEMANN in 1871–90, by W. DÖRPFELD in the 1890s, by C. BLEGEN in the 1930s, and again by a joint German-American project in the 1990s. A recently discovered lower town probably held most of the inhabitants, the TELL serving as a citadel. Hisarlık has a far greater historical importance than would be expected from its size. Set on a plain overlooking the southern entrance to the Dardanelles in northwestern Anatolia, it contains a series of walled Bronze Age settlements (Troy I–VII, with subphases), as well as later CLASSICAL period occupation on its surface; in absolute dates the Bronze Age settlement began in the late 4th millennium and continued to the 12th century BC. This sequence defines a key reference for comparative chronologies, especially for pottery, but also for metal types and architectural forms. In the occupation history of the site, Troy II and VII are most widely discussed. The famous 'treasure of Priam' (a hoard of objects in precious metals and semi-precious stones) came from one of the Troy II (EARLY BRONZE AGE II) levels. Troy II was a small fortified town whose interior at one point (Troy IIc) was dominated by a large MEGARON complex (courtyard, storerooms and ancillary buildings in addition to the three megara themselves); at other times Troy II was composed of regular blocks of rooms separated by streets. Troy VIIa is the best candidate for the Troy of Homer's *Iliad*, though considerable controversy surrounds this issue. At this time, the area enclosed by the town walls

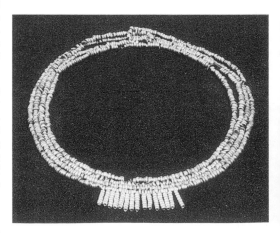

HISARLIK/Troy, Turkey: gold necklace of the Early Bronze Age, *c*.2300 BC.

was filled with small houses densely packed together, most of which contained large storage jars sunk into floors; finds of MYCENAEAN painted pottery reflect contact with that world. The settlement ended in massive fires.

Hissar, Tepe an important site in the Damghan plain of northeastern Iran, excavated by Erich Schmidt in the 1930s and re-examined by Robert Dyson in the 1970s. Schmidt defined eight occupational phases at the site (Hissar I–III, with subdivisions), which may be dated to between the late 5th and early 2nd millennia BC. Evidence from Hissar II (later 4th to early 3rd millennia BC) suggests that this community was involved in the PROTO-ELAMITE phenomenon, manifested in a number of pottery forms, seals and tablet blanks. The material culture at the end of the sequence (Hissar IIIC) marks the appearance of a burnished grey ware that figures prominently in discussions of Indo-Aryan movements and the origins of the western Iranian Iron Age. A mid-1990s Iranian salvage project recovered several CUNEIFORM texts on clay, as yet unpublished, from late 3rd millennium contexts.

historic period any period in the past that can be studied by using contemporary written documents. See also PREHISTORIC PERIOD, PROTOHISTORIC PERIOD.

Hittites a people of obscure origin who settled in Anatolia and the Levant in the later 3rd millennium BC, like other speakers of INDO-EUROPEAN languages such as the Luwians. The Hittites settled in the area of BOĞHAZKÖY by the beginning of the 2nd millennium. Their subsequent history, down to around 1200 BC, is one of cycles of integration and expansion followed by collapse, a process that is reflected in the division of Hittite political history into Old Kingdom (perhaps 1700–1600 BC) and empire (roughly 1450–1200 BC). In the latter period, the Hittites were major players in the military and diplomatic struggle for Syro-Palestinian client states, usually in opposition to the Egyptians, as reflected in the AMARNA archives. The Hittite state collapsed during the regional upheavals at the end of the LATE BRONZE AGE, notably the movements of the SEA PEOPLES and pressures from Anatolian groups from the north. During the Iron Age, some petty states in northern Syria continued certain aspects of the Hittite cultural tradition (variously named Neo-Hittite, Syro-Hittite, Neo-Luwian), before being swept away by ASSYRIAN empire-building.

Hivaoa see PUAMAU VALLEY.

Hjortspring a boat or war canoe, deposited as a ritual offering in a bog at Als, Denmark, in c.200 BC. The boat, the earliest known CLINKER-BUILT vessel, was 19 m (62 ft) long and was powered by oars with no mast. It was part of a larger offering consisting of hundreds of spears, swords and shields, as well as chain mail and domestic items. The Hjortspring hoard may have been an offering of war booty in thanksgiving for victory.

Hluboke Mašůky a fortified Neolithic settlement of the LENGYEL culture in southern Moravia. The fortifications consisted of a ditch about 1 km (0.6 mile) in circumference and 1.8 to 2.8 m (6 to 9 ft) deep, reinforced by a two-row palisade through which four gates opened into the interior of the ramparts.

Hoabinhian a loosely related group of early-to-mid Holocene stone tool industries (a 'techno-complex') of mainland and parts of maritime Southeast Asia, first identified in cave-sites of Hoa Binh Province in northern Vietnam, bordering the Red River Valley. Dates range from c.10,000 to 2000 BC, depending upon the area. Many of the occupation sites of this period are thought to have been lost with the flooding of SUNDALAND during the POST-GLACIAL sea-level rise. Three broad phases have been recognized in the Vietnamese and related sites: the 'archaic', characterized by massive unifacially worked pebble tools; the 'intermediate', recognized by the reduction in size of pebble tools and the appearance of bifacial working and occasional edge-grinding (see also BACSONIAN); and 'late', characterized by smaller scrapers, knives, grinding stones, piercers, rare sawn and polished stone tools, shell artifacts and, towards the end, pottery. The relative crudeness of tools in earlier phases may have been due to greater reliance upon bamboo, wood and rattan than upon stone. Debate continues concerning when during this sequence the transition occurred from broad-spectrum hunting and gathering to horticulture and then rice agriculture (see SPIRIT CAVE).

Hochdorf an Iron Age tumulus located near Stuttgart in Baden-Württemberg, Germany, dated to the final quarter of the 6th century bc (late HALLSTATT period). Discovered in 1978, the Hochdorf tumulus was about 30 m (100 ft) high and surrounded by a stone wall. It contained a burial chamber built of alternating layers of planks and stones. The occupant of the burial chamber was a tall (1.83 m [6 ft]) high-status male, between thirty and forty years old. His grave-goods were extraordinarily rich, many the products of Mediterranean workshops, and include a Greek bronze cauldron with reclining lions on its rim, gold-covered shoes and a bronze couch.

Hoëdic a Mesolithic cemetery and settlement on a small island off the southern coast of Brittany, France. The cemetery consists of burials in shallow depressions in the bedrock, beneath the base of the settlement MIDDEN. Nine graves (two double, one triple) contain remains of fourteen individuals, in four graves accompanied by red-deer antlers. Near by was a circular paved area which may have been used in funerary rituals. Though formally Mesolithic, Hoëdic has also yielded remains of domestic sheep, probably adopted from early farming groups on

HOCHDORF, Germany: bronze human figure, 30 cm (1 ft) high, from the couch.

the Atlantic coast of France further to the south. AMS dates span a range from 7165 to 5080 bp. See also TÉVIEC.

Hohenasperg an Iron Age fortified site of the 6th century bc dated to the HALLSTATT D period. The Hohenasperg is one of a number of Early Iron Age commercial centres that includes the HEUNEBURG and MONT LASSOIS. As was the case at other such commercial centres, finds at the Hohenasperg and the nearby tumulus at Kleinaspergle include many luxury items of Greek origin.

Hohlenstein-Stadel a cave in Baden-Württemberg, southwestern Germany, containing occupation of the MOUSTERIAN, AURIGNACIAN, MAGDALENIAN (specifically 14th millennium bp) and Mesolithic. In the Aurignacian levels, a 28 cm (11 inch) ivory statuette of an anthropomorph with a feline head has been found, dating to 31,750 bp.

Hohmichele an Iron Age tumulus with primary burial of an elite individual and retainers in southwestern Germany dating to the HALLSTATT period. The Hohmichele tumulus lies not far from the HEUNEBURG and reflects the local wealth which resulted from trade with the Mediterranean area. Major grave-goods included a bronze cauldron and a four-wheeled wagon. Exceptional preservation in the timber burial chamber resulted in the find of a piece of silk, which perhaps found its way to this area through trade from China.

Hohokam a prehistoric tradition located in southern Arizona, USA, which may be culturally antecedent to the contemporary Pima and Papago Indians. The term comes from a Pima Indian word that means 'all used up'. Both indigenous and external origins for Hohokam have been proposed. The tradition is divided into the Pioneer (AD 150–550), Colonial (AD 550–900), Sedentary (AD 900–1100), Classic (AD 1100–1450) and Post-Classic (AD 1450–1700) periods. The tradition is characterized by changes in house and pottery styles, and the early use of irrigation agriculture. Main crops were maize, beans and squash, with a variety of lesser plants. The Hohokam also built 'BALL COURTS' – oval depressions about 60 m (197 ft) long – which are very similar to those used by the MAYA. Their function amongst the Hohokam is not clear, however, and they may have served as ceremonial dance courts, rather than for a ball-game itself. The Sedentary period is marked by a strong MESOAMERICAN influence in the form of PLATFORM MOUNDS, cotton fabric, copper bells and other items. See also SNAKETOWN.

hokei shukobo literally 'square-moated burial precincts' of YAYOI and KOFUN period Japan. Within each precinct, measuring 6–25 m (20–82 ft) per side, occur coffin or pit burials of adults, and jar burials of children – giving rise to their interpretation as family burial grounds. Variations without moats or with round shapes are also known.

Hokule'a an experimental replica of a POLYNESIAN double-hulled canoe built by Ben Finney and sailed from Maui in the Hawaiian Islands to Tahiti and back in 1976 by traditional navigation methods. The voyage has thrown considerable light on ancient Polynesian voyaging.

Hokuriku a pre-modern administrative district of Japan (see RITSURYO) along the northern Japan Sea coast of Honshu Island, Japan – often used in archaeological writings; it consists of modern Niigata, Toyama, Ishikawa and Fukui Prefectures. See also FUDODO.

Holmes, William Henry (1846–1933) an American archaeologist who did much to debunk many of the wilder claims about the antiquity of humans in North America, and whose 1903 monograph on ceramics laid the foundations for the subsequent CULTURE HISTORY of the eastern United States.

Holocene **1** a chronostratigraphic unit (see STRATIGRAPHY), either the latest stage of the Pleistocene series or the latest series of the QUATERNARY system, the hierarchical usage varying regionally. In either case, the Holocene was never formally defined, but is accepted to replace the term 'Recent'. The Holocene stage (series) encompasses all deposits younger than the top of either the WISCONSINIAN STAGE of the Pleistocene series in North America and the WÜRM/WEICHSEL in Europe. The Holocene follows the last Pleistocene GLACIATION and is typically characterized by INTERGLACIAL conditions and processes. Its lower boundary is generally assigned an age of 10,000 bp, although clearly the transition from GLACIAL to interglacial conditions was globally time-transgressive and differed in character regionally. Many technological, economic and social advances took place during the Holocene, evidence of which is preserved in the archaeological record in Holocene deposits.

2 a geochronological unit (see STRATIGRAPHY), either the latest age of the Pleistocene epoch or the latest epoch of the Quaternary period, the hierarchical usage varying regionally. The lower boundary is generally assigned an age of 10,000 bp.

Holsteinian Interglacial a North European Middle Pleistocene warm phase occurring between the ELSTERIAN and SAALIAN cold stages, starting c.300,000 BP and ending c.200,000 BP. The Alpine equivalent is the MINDEL-RISS, the American the YARMOUTH, and the British the Hoxnian, after its type-site at HOXNE, Suffolk (see FRERE).

Holy Cross Mountains a range of low mountains in central Poland, important in prehistory both as sources of flint (including CHOCOLATE FLINT) during the Mesolithic, Neolithic and Early Bronze Age and as a centre for iron metallurgy during the Iron Age, at sites like SZUPIA STARA.

hominid an abbreviated or popular form of *Hominidae*, the family of bipedal primates with relatively large brains, to which humans (HOMO) and australopithecines (see AUSTRALOPITHECUS) belong.

hominin 1 An abbreviated or popular form of *Homininae*, to which members of the genus HOMO belong, the zoological nomenclature for a subfamily of the *Hominidae* (see HOMINID).

2 In more recent literature, an abbreviated or popular form of the zoological tribe *Hominini*, species more closely related to humans than to great apes, which includes the genera ARDIPITHECUS, AUSTRALOPITHECUS, *Homo*, KENYANTHROPUS, ORRORIN, *Paranthropus* and *Praeanthropus*.

Homo the HOMINID genus to which humans belong. Although the details of the evolutionary roots of *Homo* are not well understood, the genus is generally considered to have evolved in Africa from an australopithecine ancestor (see AUSTRALOPITHECUS) in the period between 3 and 2 million years ago (but see KENYANTHROPUS, ORRORIN). In comparison with australopithecines, *Homo* has a larger brain, a more modern postcranial skeleton better adapted to bipedal locomotion, smaller jaws and teeth, and, especially among more recent species, increasing reliance on culture.

Until recently, it was thought that the oldest *Homo* species was *H. habilis* ('handy man'), first described from OLDUVAI GORGE in Tanzania in 1964, the first early *Homo* identified in Africa. 'Habiline' fossils assigned to this species date to the period between 1.9 and 1.6 million years ago and are known from sites in East and South Africa (see KOOBI FORA, Olduvai Gorge). *H. habilis* had a small and light apelike build like gracile australopithecines, but with a larger brain. Its presumed link with stone tools resulted in it being credited with being the OLDOWAN toolmaker. *H. habilis* was once considered to represent the evolutionary link between australopithecines and later species of *Homo*, but further discoveries indicate that the early stages of the development of *Homo* include several species and are more complex than previously believed.

Some researchers suggest that a skull fragment from LAKE BARINGO in Kenya and a jaw from Uraha in Malawi, dated to about 2.5 million years ago, may be *Homo*. A 2.3 million-year-old upper jaw and teeth from HADAR, Ethiopia, have been described as a species of *Homo*, *Homo* sp. This specimen, A.L. 666-1, was found together with simple stone artifacts and provides the oldest known evidence of a direct association between hominids and stone tools.

Two additional early African *Homo* species that have been identified are *H. rudolfensis*, best known from fossils dating between 1.9 and 1.8 million years ago from Koobi Fora, with KNM-ER 1470 the type specimen, and *H. ergaster* (the 'workman'), or 'early African *H. erectus*', best known from 1.9–1.5 million-year-old fossils from Koobi Fora.

The taxonomy of early species of *Homo* is currently under revision. Some researchers suggest that *H. habilis* and *H. rudolfensis* should be reclassified as australopithecines, and propose that the earliest *Homo* is *H. ergaster*. Some of the older African fossils now ascribed to *H. ergaster* were previously known as *H. erectus* ('upright man'), a name originally given to fossils with a muscular, stocky build and heavy face with thick brow ridges found in Java in 1891, the first early human fossils recognized outside Europe (see DUBOIS, JAVA MAN). *H. erectus* was considered to have been the first hominid to spread out of Africa about 1 million years ago, and to have represented a stage in human evolution between *H. habilis* and *H. sapiens*. However, new evidence (see DMANISI, LONGGUPO) suggests that Asia may have been occupied by hominids more primitive than *H. erectus* by as early as 2 million years ago. Some palaeoanthropologists now regard *H. erectus* as too specialized to have been an ancestor to modern humans (but see JINNIUSHAN, MABA).

Hominid fossils dating to the period between about 800,000 and 200,000 years ago are loosely named 'archaic' *H. sapiens*. They were powerfully built creatures who had brain sizes gradually increasing to approach that of the modern average, but with backward-sloping foreheads behind large brow ridges, as well as large faces with big teeth positioned in front of rather than directly below the braincase. The diversity of hominids during this time is currently unclear (see also BROKEN HILL, FLORISBAD, NDUTU, STEINHEIM). A distinct species of this period known from Europe (see TAUTAVEL, MAUER, PETRALONA), Africa (see BODO), and possibly China (Dali) is H. heidelbergensis. This species is sometimes regarded as the ancestor of both modern H. sapiens and the extinct H. sapiens neanderthalensis or H. neanderthalensis, as are 800,000-year-old hominid remains from Gran Dolina (ATAPUERCA) in Spain, ascribed to H. antecessor.

NEANDERTHALS, named after the Neanderthal site near Düsseldorf, Germany, made Middle Palaeolithic stone artifacts, at least occasionally buried their dead and supported the disabled, had a brain as large as our own, but had massive brow ridges, a receding chin, as well as a heavy muscular build. They appear in the fossil record between 200,000 and 150,000 years ago, although Neanderthal features have been identified in some 300,000-year-old fossils (see Atapuerca's Pit of the Bones). Comparisons between Neanderthal and modern human DNA suggest that Neanderthals were an evolutionary dead-end and did not contribute genetic material to modern humans. Although Neanderthals and modern humans may have coexisted or alternated in occupation in the Near East for some 50,000 years, their relatively abrupt replacement by modern humans in Europe some 30,000 years ago is the subject of much speculation and debate.

The oldest known anatomically modern H. sapiens or H. sapiens sapiens fossils come from sites in Africa and the Near East (see BORDER CAVE, KLASIES RIVER MOUTH, QAFZEH), where they are respectively associated with MIDDLE STONE AGE and Middle Palaeolithic artifacts, and date to between 130,000 and 80,000 years ago. Some researchers suggest that modern people spread from Africa to other parts of the world (the 'Eve' or 'OUT OF AFRICA' hypothesis), but see Jinniushan, Maba.

Homo antecessor see ATAPUERCA.

Homolka a late Neolithic fortified site in Bohemia of the RIVNAČ culture. The hilltop settlement of Homolka was enclosed by two, apparently successive, palisade systems, within which were a number of small rectangular huts. Some of the huts appear to have been burnt, and despite the fortifications the duration of the Neolithic settlement at Homolka is thought to have been brief.

homology a specific form of reasoning by analogy, whereby two temporally separate phenomena are similar to each other because of their historical and/or genetic connection to each other.

Honam the district of South Korea comprising North and South Cholla Provinces in the southwestern peninsula. This name is used in categorizing regional archaeological finds.

Hongshan [Hung-shan] a site in Liaoning Province, China, giving its name to a precocious northeastern Neolithic culture of surprising complexity. Outstripping the YANGSHAO and early DAWENKOU cultures of northern and central China, the Hongshan has elaborate jade ornaments of different animals (totems?), substantial temple sites of stone enclosures and altars, and female figurines and mask representations. It is dated to c.3500–3000 BC. The recently discovered site of NIUHELIANG has life-size female statues in painted clay, high-status burials and many fine jade ornaments: this 'goddess temple' was probably a ceremonial centre.

Hopewell a WOODLAND stage complex dated to approximately 100 BC to AD 500, and centred in southern Ohio, USA, but which spread beyond this core area throughout much of the American Midwest. Hopewell BURIAL MOUNDS were often constructed in groups that were enclosed by earthworks. Some earthworks represented effigies. Yellowstone obsidian, distinctive platform pipes and mica sheets carved into mythical animals are also characteristic of the phase. Hopewell seems to represent some form of Interaction Sphere based on the exchange of raw and finished materials, such that Hopewell traits were adopted by existing cultures. Although the cultivation of maize, beans and squash was practised, Hopewell sites seem to have relied heavily on hunting and gathering.

Horgen a Swiss middle/late Neolithic culture, dated c.3400–2800 BC, that follows PFYN and, in western regions, the CORTAILLOD, but sees a decline in the use of copper. Its type-site is a settlement site on Lake Neuchâtel.

horizon any artifact or element of cultural behaviour found in numerous cultural units over a relatively wide area that was introduced to those cultures in a relatively brief period of time, which is thus indicative of a rapid dissemination of ideas. An example is the spread of the bow-and-arrow technology through prehistoric North America. Horizons, like the horizon-style concept used in South American archaeology from which it was derived, allow the archaeologist to link together separate cultural units for the purposes of reconstructing CULTURE HISTORY. See also SOIL HORIZON.

horns of consecration or **sacral horns** one of the most common MINOAN religious symbols, being most plausibly interpreted as the horns of a sacrificed bull. In pictorial representations, horns of consecration often crown the façade of a shrine or sanctuary, presumably to indicate the sanctity of the structure concerned.

horreum a Roman granary. The floors were usually raised to allow air circulation and prevent the entry of rodents. Horrea were an integral part of Roman military encampments. Extensive examples remain at OSTIA.

horsehoof core a high-domed single platform core, usually very large, with stacked step fractures forming an undercut striking platform. They were originally thought to be chopping tools for wood working, and were a defining type of the AUSTRALIAN CORE TOOL AND SCRAPER TRADITION. However, they are also found in more recent sites, and most archaeologists now believe that they are discarded cores.

Horus an Egyptian deity depicted as a falcon or falcon-headed man. The son of OSIRIS and ISIS, Horus was particularly associated with kingship and worshipped in local manifestations, e.g. at EDFU.

Horvat Teiman see KUNTILLET AJRUD.

Hoshino a deeply stratified Palaeolithic site in Tochigi Prefecture, Japan, that provides the stone tool chronology for the KANTO region. The lower eight cultural strata producing lithics lie under a volcanic pumice layer dated by radiocarbon and FISSION TRACK to 40–50,000 bp. This was the oldest Palaeolithic site known in Japan until those discovered around Sendai City. See also NISHIYAGI, BABADAN A, NAKAMINE, TAKAMORI.

Hottentot see KHOIKHOIN.

Houhanshu the *Chronicles of Later Han* compiled in AD 398–445 from the WEIZHI. They contain the court histories of the later HAN Dynasty as well as ethnographic accounts of peoples in the peripheral regions of East Asia (see YAMATAI).

Housesteads one of the Roman garrison forts built along the line of HADRIAN'S WALL, in northern England. Excavations have revealed the standard features of garrison headquarters, granaries, barracks and latrines. Outside the south gate lies the civilian settlement. An earlier turret lies under the northern part of the fort, showing that the strategy of having a garrison on the line of the wall was not part of Hadrian's original plan.

Howieson's Poort a MIDDLE STONE AGE industry of southern Africa, characterized by the production of small blades, standardized backed artifacts such as segments, and, in some collections, both unifacial and bifacial points in addition to typical Middle Stone Age flake-blade forms. It is linked to radiocarbon dates greater than 40,000 BP and a date of about 70,000 or more BP enjoys support (see EPI-PIETERSBURG, KLASIES RIVER MOUTH). The presence of small blades and backed artifacts are taken by some to indicate the existence of 'modern' behaviour in Middle Stone Age times.

Hoxne a Lower Palaeolithic site in Suffolk, England, where in 1797 John FRERE first recognized as tools the shaped flints which workmen were finding in the brickpit; to him they were 'weapons of war', today they are bifaces. The site has yielded ACHEULIAN material traditionally divided into three distinct industries; these include OVATE, CORDATE and pointed bifaces, hammer-stones and scrapers and associated floral and faunal remains. Hoxne has become the type-site for the British Hoxnian INTERGLACIAL occurring between the Anglian and Wolstonian GLACIALS.

Hoxne was also the site of a hoard of gold jewellery, silver plate and coins that was probably buried in the early 5th century AD and discovered in 1992. One bracelet was decorated with the name of its presumed owner, Juliana.

Hoxnian see HOLSTEINIAN.

hradiste see GRÓD.

Hsiung-nu an ethnonym for nomads who, at the end of the 3rd century BC, headed an alliance of pastoralist tribes in Inner Asia (central Mongolia and the steppes of Trans-Baikal, Russia). By the 2nd century BC the Hsiung-nu had grown in strength and carried out a campaign of conquest, which ended the SCYTHIAN epoch in this region. Their military successes were assisted to a considerable extent by use of iron weaponry and the invention of a long-range bow. In the 1st century BC feuds arose among the Hsiung-nu, and caused the migration of part of the 'Northern Hsiung-nu' to the west. The 1st century AD was a time of decline in Hsiung-nu power; they suffered a number of defeats at the hands of their neighbours. The main Hsiung-nu archaeological monuments are the NOIN-ULA barrow-cemetery (northern Mongolia), the Major and Minor Ivolga forts, the Ivolga barrow-cemetery and the settlement of Dureny in Trans-Baikal, Siberia.

Huaca de la Luna see MOCHE.

Huaca de los Reyes see CABALLO MUERTO.

Huaca del Sol see MOCHE.

Huaca La Florida a large U-shaped monumental site near Lima, on the central coast of Peru, pertaining to the early INITIAL PERIOD (c.1700 bc), with construction beginning perhaps as early as the Late PRECERAMIC. The site includes a central platform over 17 m (56 ft) high, flanked by long narrow wings, 3–4 m (10–13 ft) high and 500 m (547 yds) long; the site exceeds 1 million cu. m (1.3 million cu. yds) of artificial fill, according to Thomas Patterson. The site was probably used for only a few centuries and then abandoned.

Huacaloma an INITIAL PERIOD and EARLY HORIZON site in the Cajamarca region of the northern highlands of Peru. In the Early Huacaloma period, a rectangular structure with a central hearth is found, reminiscent of structures at KOTOSH. In the Late Huacaloma period, the early buildings were buried and others built over them. At the contemporaneous site of Layzón, a series of six platforms was built up the side of a hill. The ceremonial architecture reached its climax in the Layzón period, of the late Early Horizon and early EARLY INTERMEDIATE PERIOD.

Huaca Prieta a Late PRECERAMIC site (*c*.2300 bc) in the Chicama Valley on the north coast of Peru. Excavations by Junius B. BIRD revealed elaborate twined textiles made of cotton, depicting images of birds and other designs. The site represented a sedentary occupation by Preceramic people, whose subsistence was based primarily on fishing and some domesticated squash and beans. Most agriculture was devoted to the production of industrial plants such as gourds and cotton.

Huachichocana a series of stratified caves and rockshelters in Jujuy Province, northwestern Argentina, between 3,200 and 3,800 m (10,500 and 12,470 ft) altitude, some of them containing PICTOGRAPHS. Nine have been studied so far. Excavations by A. Fernández Distel in cave III revealed PRECERAMIC occupation extending back to 10,200 bp in layer E3, with material including not only lithics but also fragments of textiles of plant and camelid-wool, basketry, wooden and bone implements, and plant remains, among which were specimens of pumpkin, bean, chili and maize which are claimed to be domesticated – this claim remains highly controversial. This level, dated to the 9th millennium bp, also contained the secondary inhumation of the lower part of a young man accompanied by a basket with feathers. His head was burnt and destroyed in a nearby hearth. Other funerary remains in other layers include a burial in layer E2 which Fernández Distel considers may have been a SHAMAN. Analyses of camelid fibres suggest the appearance here of domestic forms around 3400 bp. Ceramics start occurring in layer E1, dated to 1420 bp.

Huanghe [Huang-ho] the Chinese name for the Yellow River of northern China. The Huanghe corridor connects the North China Plain in the east with the Wei River Valley in the west (see ERLITOU).

Huánuco Pampa an INCA city located in the northern-central highlands of Peru. It covers some 2 sq. km (0.8 sq. miles), and is arranged around a central plaza measuring 550 by 350 m (600 by 383 yds). The site includes functionally specialized sectors including high-status residence, large-scale food preparation, a military garrison and a compound with restricted access in which probably lived the Chosen Women. Hundreds of storage buildings, with a storage capacity totalling 37,000 cu. m (48,400 cu. yds), were built along the hillside above the site. Excavations by Craig Morris suggest that the site had no large permanent population, but rather was occupied by people brought in temporarily to render their labour service to the empire.

Huari **1** an empire pertaining to the first half of the MIDDLE HORIZON (*c*.ad 750–900) in Peru. Huari iconography shares some symbols, especially the Staff Deity, with the contemporaneous TIAHUANACO culture of the Lake Titicaca Basin. Huari styles of architecture and artifacts are found throughout most of highland and coastal Peru. Because of their stylistic similarity to Tiahuanaco stone carving, Huari artifacts were initially termed 'Tiahuanacoid' or 'Coast Tiahuanaco'. Eventually the site of Huari was identified as the source of the style, first by excavations by Julio C. TELLO, and later by investigations by John H. Rowe, Donald Collier and Gordon R. Willey.

Large planned orthogonal complexes probably served as Huari provincial administrative centres, indicating imperial control of the highlands. While Huari artifacts are found widely distributed on the coast of Peru, no administrative centres have been identified yet, so the nature of the Huari presence remains unclear. Offering deposits of intentionally smashed ceramics have been found both in the highlands and on the coast. The expansion of the empire followed a period of climatic deterioration and widespread political upheaval at the end of the EARLY INTERMEDIATE PERIOD. The causes of its collapse are unknown. See also CONCHOPATA, GALINDO, JINCAMOCCO, PACHECO, PIKILLACTA, TIAHUANACO, MARCA HUAMACHUCO.)

2 the capital of the Huari empire, a large urban site located in Ayacucho, Peru. The architectural core of the site covers 3 sq. km (1.2 sq. miles), and the total extent of the occupation may have been as much as 10 sq. km (3.9 sq. miles); the site had a large resident population numbering probably in the tens of thousands. In addition to diagnostic planned orthogonal architecture, there are tombs and ceremonial structures of cut stone. The site was occupied from the Early Intermediate period, Huarpa times, but did not coalesce into a large political centre until the Middle Horizon. It was abandoned at the time the empire collapsed.

Huaricoto a ceremonial site in the Callejón de Huaylas region of the northern highlands of Peru, pertaining to the Late PRECERAMIC, INITIAL PERIOD and EARLY HORIZON. The site, excavated by Richard Burger and Lucy Salazar-Burger, includes a small artificial mound comprising thirteen superimposed constructions. Offerings were burned in hearths in ritual chambers, and periodically the structures were ritually interred, in a manner similar to other sites pertaining to the KOTOSH religious tradition of the Late Preceramic and Initial periods.

Huashan a site in southwestern China, near the Vietnamese border, which has the world's biggest rock art panel. A limestone cliff along the Zuojiang River has over 1,800 red paintings covering an area 200 m (220 yds) wide and 40 m (130 ft) high. They comprise mainly anthropomorphs together with a few zoomorphs and motifs interpreted as bronze drums (see DONG SON) and ring handled swords. These motifs, together with radiocarbon dates of stalactites, place the art between 2370 and 2115 years ago, the period between the early Warring States (see ZHOU) and the Eastern HAN Dynasty.

Huasteca a subarea on the northern frontier of MESOAMERICA in northern Tamaulipas, Mexico, and the Texas coast of the United States. This area was occupied by hunter-gatherers who served as a buffer between the high cultures of Mesoamerica and the southeastern United States. The area is named after a linguistic branch of the MAYA who separated from the main Maya group by about 2000 BC, and who were culturally distinct at the time of the Spanish conquest in AD 1520. The area has an archaeological sequence extending from the early PRECLASSIC to the AZTEC conquest and Spanish contact.

Hudson, Kenneth (1916–99) a British social historian and museologist who coined the term INDUSTRIAL ARCHAEOLOGY, and was the first editor of the *Journal of Industrial Archaeology*. He wrote prolifically on industrial and modern social history, and was a pioneer of new approaches in presenting the past in museums.

Huelva a large hoard of bronzes from Andalusia, Spain, dating to the 8th century BC, including Central European types and CARP'S TONGUE SWORDS of the ATLANTIC BRONZE AGE.

human evolution see HOMO.

humus **1** decayed organic compounds in the soil that impart brown and black colours, particularly to the A horizon. Humus does not include the living soil biomass, undecayed plant and animal parts and tissues or their partial decomposition products. It is a source of nutrients for plant and crop growth. See SOIL HORIZON.
 2 organic material and leaf litter on the forest floor.

Hunam-ri [Hunamni] a MUMUN pottery site in Kyonggi Province, Korea, at which one of the nineteen excavated pit houses yielded carbonized rice, foxtail millet, barley, sorghum and soybeans – thought to be the earliest agricultural remains on the peninsula, dated by radiocarbon to between 3280 and 2520 bp (see KOREA).

hunebed (literally 'Hun's grave') a traditional name for megalithic tombs of the Neolithic of northern Germany and the northern Netherlands, comprising an elongated rectangular central burial chamber, usually with a short entrance passage in the middle of one side and surrounded by a kerb of large stones. They are associated with TRB C material (TIEFSTICHKERAMIK phase) of the 4th millennium BC. Some believe that the name is derived from the Old German 'hune' meaning 'huge', for they are often 50 m (164 ft) or more in length.

Hungary see EUROPE, CENTRAL.

Huns (*Gk* Hunnoi, *Lat.* Chunni, Hunni) a nomadic people, formed in the 2nd–4th centuries AD in the Pre-Urals from the Central Asian tribes of HSIUNG-NU and the local Ugrian and SARMATIAN tribes. The late 4th century saw the beginning of the mass movement of the Huns to the west, which gave a spur to the so-called Great Migration of peoples. Under their great leader Attila, the Huns settled on the shores of the Danube from where they attacked Gaul and Italy. In 451 a combined army of Romans, Goths and Franks defeated the Huns at Châlons in Gaul. When Attila died in 453 the Hunnish empire disintegrated, but their movement westwards had, in turn, dislodged other barbarian peoples from their homes. After their defeat in 455 in Pannonia, the Huns went to the Black Sea littoral and gradually disappeared as a people. But the name remained in use for some time as a collective term for the nomads of that area.

hunter-gatherer a type of society in which subsistence is based on the hunting of wild animals and the gathering of wild plants. It is most commonly associated with a band level of social organization. Over the past 3 million years of human evolution, hunting and gathering has been the single most practised form of economy, although currently there is probably not one true hunter and gatherer society anywhere in the world, as a result of pressure from industrialized and agricultural societies.

Huon Peninsula part of the northeast coast of Papua New Guinea, containing uplifted coral-reef formations spanning much of the Pleistocene. WAISTED AXES have been found in stratified contexts sealed beneath volcanic ashes dating to *c*.40,000 bp.

Hureidah a site near the modern town of Hureidah, on the Wadi 'Amd in the Hadramaut region of Yemen (southwestern Arabia), where G. CATON THOMPSON excavated a temple of the god Sin, together with a small group of tombs and a farmstead, in 1937; this work was the first systematic excavation in SOUTH ARABIA. The rectangular temple, of dressed stone blocks on a plastered rubble platform, shows several episodes of modification; it is usually assigned a 7th–6th century BC date, but the evidence for this remains tenuous.

Hurrian(s) a non-Semitic, non-Sumerian language whose speakers appeared in northern MESOPOTAMIA during the later 3rd millennium BC. These people seem to have come from the mountainous regions to the north, perhaps from the Caucasus, and some scholars suggest a connection with the KURA-ARAXES culture. Hurrian speakers established a number of small kingdoms in northern Mesopotamia, Syria and southwestern Anatolia; during the 2nd millennium people with Hurrian names represented large proportions of the populations in some of these areas. By the mid 2nd millennium, the elites in many of the Hurrian states such as that of MITANNI bore INDO-EUROPEAN (Indo-Aryan) names and/or titles, e.g. *mariyanna*.

Hushu a site in Jiangsu Province, China, giving its name to the Hushu culture in the area around Nanjing City. The culture is characterized by GEOMETRIC POTTERY and bronze implements, tools and vessels. It is contemporaneous with the SHANG and early ZHOU bronze cultures (see CHINESE DYNASTIES).

Huxley's Line see WALLACE'S LINE.

hxaro the name used by the Ju/hoansi or !Kung SAN of the Kalahari Desert in Botswana for an institutionalized system of sharing and gift exchange. It serves to strengthen networks of social and economic relationships which play a role in survival in marginal habitats. The giver of a gift to a *hxaro* partner can expect to receive one in exchange or be able to ask for something when in need. A young adult typically has between 10–16 *hxaro* partners, many of which live in areas with complementary resources up to 100 km (60 miles) or more away. The gifts exchanged are not necessarily of the same value and the exchange can take place within a long or short period, but never immediately. Beads are one of the most important items of exchange and the word for sewn beadwork is synonymous with that for *hxaro* gifts. Some archaeologists suggest that the presence of quantities of ostrich eggshell beads in LATER STONE AGE archaeological sites in southern and East Africa may indicate an antiquity for this exchange system extending back to at least 40,000 years ago (see ENKAPUNE YA MUTO).

hydria a Greek jar used to carry or store water. A hydria should have two horizontal loop handles on the body and a single vertical handle from the rim to the shoulder.

Hyksos the foreign rulers who seized control of a substantial area of northern Egypt during the Second INTERMEDIATE PERIOD. They were probably derived from the Palestinian immigrants who infiltrated the eastern DELTA during the MIDDLE KINGDOM, eventually becoming powerful enough to form the 15th Dynasty. Their capital in Egypt was the Delta city of AVARIS, from where they were ultimately expelled by AHMOSE.

hypocaust the Roman means of heating buildings. The floor was supported on low pillars of tile. Hot air from a furnace would be drawn into this space and up through

HYDRIA.

vertical flues built into the walls. Hypocausts are found in both houses and THERMAE.

hypogeum a rock-cut CHAMBER TOMB, often used for a series of inhumations.

hypostyle hall part of an Egyptian temple, situated between the sanctuary and the open court behind the PYLON, whose name refers to the densely packed columns contained between screen-walls at its front and rear.

hypothetico-deductive reasoning a form of scientific reasoning, in which a hypothesis is set up, predictions are deduced from the hypothesis, and these predictions are tested for their accuracy against empirical data. See also POSITIVISM, NEW ARCHAEOLOGY.

Hyrax Hill a site on the shores of Lake Nakuru in central Kenya with LATER STONE AGE material, a PASTORAL NEOLITHIC settlement of at least 500 sq. m (600 sq. yds) associated with a cemetery containing nineteen stone-covered flexed burials and Iron Age remains, including a series of so-called SIRIKWA HOLES.

Iberia Divided from the remainder of Europe by the Pyrenean mountain chain and flanked by the Atlantic Ocean to the west and north and by the Mediterranean to the south and east, the relative isolation of Iberia has given a distinctive character to its prehistoric and historical development.

Stone tools and bone fragments discovered at ORCE near Granada may date to 1.6 million years ago, but the earliest secure evidence of HOMINID presence in Iberia is provided by the caves of Sierra de ATAPUERCA, notably the GRAN DOLINA, where human remains have been dated to 780,000 BP. These were succeeded by populations of HOMO *heidelbergensis*, represented also in other regions of Europe, who manufactured ACHEULIAN handaxes and at TORRALBA AND AMBRONA were associated with evidence interpreted as the hunting of large mammals including elephants. By 200,000 years ago the Iberian peninsula was occupied by NEANDERTHALS, and its location at the western margin of Europe made it one of the last surviving enclaves of Neanderthal population as modern humans spread westwards across Europe. The Iberian Neanderthals appear to have become extinct by 27,000 BP but a skeleton of a four-year-old child from LAGAR VELHO in Portugal, dated to 26,000 BP, has been claimed to show both Neanderthal and modern human features and to indicate interbreeding between the two populations.

During the Upper Palaeolithic period (27,000–10,000 BP) the Iberian peninsula was a relatively warm refuge within GLACIAL age Europe. In the north, the Cantabria region is famous for its Upper Palaeolithic cave art, represented above all by the spectacular polychrome paintings at ALTAMIRA. Whereas cave art was concentrated in northern Spain and southwestern France, discoveries of open-air engravings in the CÔA VALLEY of Portugal indicate that Palaeolithic art was far from restricted to caverns or rockshelters, though much of the evidence has been destroyed by erosion.

During the POSTGLACIAL period, communities of hunters and gatherers flourished along the Atlantic coasts of Iberia, exploiting marine resources. The results of their activities are visible in the large SHELL MIDDENS which accumulated at favoured locations, as for example around the estuaries of the Tagus and Sado Rivers in southern Portugal. These middens contained numerous human burials, suggesting a close connection between feasting and mortuary rituals. The latest of the shell middens are probably contemporary with the earliest farming settlements of southern Iberia which date to the 6th millennium BC. Debate continues as to the relative contributions of colonization and indigenous acculturation in the adoption and spread of the new economy. In addition to domesticates, the first farmers also began the construction of monumental tombs, notably PASSAGE GRAVES represented by the impressive examples of the Portuguese Alentejo or the ANTEQUERA tombs of Andalusia. Megalithic chambered tombs on the Iberian uplands illustrate the intensification of occupation of formerly marginal areas, and many of those in western Iberia are decorated with carved or painted motifs (the only area within western European megalithic art where painted designs have survived).

By the end of the 4th millennium BC, complex societies had developed in the arid region of ALMERIA in southeastern Spain and around the Tagus Estuary in southern Portugal. Fortified centres at Los Millares and Zambujal illustrate the rise of elites, who are also represented by prestige goods deposited in the graves. Iberian metal resources began to be exploited during the 3rd millennium BC and remained a source of social and commercial power up to the present day, notably in the Rio Tinto exploitations of southwestern Spain. Early Iberian metal working may have played a part in the spread of copper and gold metallurgy to other regions of Atlantic Europe, through maritime connections already demonstrated in the distribution c.2500 BC of distinctive BEAKER pottery. During the 2nd millennium BC, these Atlantic connections brought western and northern Iberia within the scope of the Atlantic Bronze Age.

It was in the south of the peninsula, and partly as a result of contact with other Mediterranean regions, that the first Iberian states arose. PHOENICIAN contacts with the HUELVA area may have been associated with the rise of the kingdom known in classical sources as TARTESSOS

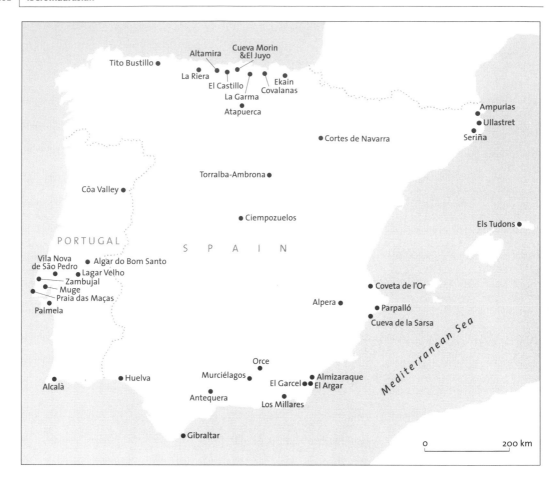

as early as the 9th century BC. Greek and Phoenician colonies followed, notably Gades (Cadiz) (8th century BC) and EMPORION (Ampurias) (6th century BC). Colonies gave place to conquest in the 3rd century when the Carthaginian generals Hamilcar and Hannibal annexed the southern part of the peninsula before embarking on a war with Rome. Hannibal's defeat in the Second Punic War (218–202 BC) resulted in Iberia becoming a province of the Roman empire, though centuries of warfare, marked above all by the famous siege and capture of Numantia, a city of the Celtiberians in 133 BC, were only ended by the campaigns waged by the emperor Augustus in the mountainous north and west from 26 to 19 BC. Thereafter Iberia was divided into three Roman provinces, Baetica, Tarraconensis and Lusitania. The peninsula flourished under Roman rule and the prosperous and highly Romanized cities of the south produced Roman emperors Trajan (r. 98–117) and Hadrian (r. 117–18).

The breakdown of Roman control in western Europe during the 4th and 5th centuries AD saw Iberia invaded by a confederation of Germanic peoples (Alans, Vandals and Sueves) in 409. From the confusion which followed, the Christian kingdom of the Visigoths emerged as the major power and had won control of the entire peninsula by the middle of the 5th century. Visigothic control was undisputed for a century and a half until, in 711, Arab armies from North Africa crossed the Straits of Gibraltar. From 714 all except the far north of Iberia became an Islamic (Moorish) state, first as a province of the great Umayyad empire, then as separate kingdoms, until the Christian *Reconquista* of the 12th century, culminating in the suppression of the last Moorish kingdom of Granada by the Christian monarchs Ferdinand and Isabella in 1492.

Iberomaurusian, Mouillian or **Oranian** a stone industry characterized by small backed bladelets, and widespread in North African coastal areas from south of Rabat in Morocco as far east as Tunis, from at least 20,000 to 10,000 years ago. Remains of the makers of Iberomaurusian artifacts of the MECHTA-AFALOU type of HOMO *sapiens sapiens* have been discovered in large cemeteries at COLUMNATA, TAFORALT, as well as Afalou bou Rhummel on the coast of eastern Algeria. See also TAMAR HAT, HAUA FTEAH).

Iblis, Tal-i a prehistoric mound in the Kirman district of Iran, discovered by Aurel STEIN in the 1930s and excavated by Joseph Caldwell in the 1960s. Caldwell's work reveals a long (but interrupted) sequence from the early 4th to 1st millennium bc (uncorrected radiocarbon dating). The importance of the site rests on the documentation of early copper smelting operations within the context of a village architectural sequence; metallurgical activity seems particularly important in the mid 4th millennium, but extends into the early 3rd, when some ceramic evidence indicates contacts with the PROTO-ELAMITE world to the west.

ice age a general term for periods characterized by the expansion of continental and alpine glaciers. It is often used to refer to the last GLACIATION of the QUATERNARY.

ice-free corridor an area of land between the Cordilleran and LAURENTIDE GLACIAL systems of North America, which was never glaciated. The corridor ran down the east slope of the Rockies and provided access to the continental interior for early humans entering the New World at the end of the Pleistocene. Sonic geologists argue that the corridor may have been open from 55,000 BP.

Iceman see SIMILAUN MAN.

ice wedge a vertical, narrow and deep wedge-shaped vein of ground ice that penetrates the soil or sediment mass with only minor disruption of the mass on either side of the wedge. Ice wedges form where there is PERMA-FROST in the PERIGLACIAL environment. Casts of fossil ice wedges are one of the few true indicators of former permafrost conditions.

idiographic *adj.* pertaining to individual, idiosyncratic or unique events. Idiographic explanation, which is the opposite of NOMOTHETIC explanation, is concerned with the specific histories of people, and was considered to be unscientific by the NEW ARCHAEOLOGY.

Idojiri a group of over fifty site localities in Nagano Prefecture, Japan, which is representative of the dense mountain settlement of the Middle JOMON period in the CHUBU region. Abundant stone QUERNS and starchy biscuit remains indicate the processing of plant foods in a possible horticultural exploitation pattern.

Ife an important town in southern Nigeria, with courtyards paved with pieces of pottery set on edge. It has yielded a remarkable series of near life-size terracotta and 'bronze' (actually brass) representations of human heads in a naturalistic style, probably of religious importance and used during rituals. Ife art had its 'classic' period

between the 11th and 15th centuries AD, and is thought to be derived, perhaps indirectly, from the earlier NOK tradition.

Igbo Laja see OWO.

Igbo-Ukwu a remarkable southeastern Nigerian site, apparently dating to some time between the 8th and 11th centuries AD, which indicates that the centralization of social authority and the concentration of wealth seen in later times were already taking place at the end of the 1st millennium AD. The finds include a shrine full of ritual 'bronze' (brass) vessels and regalia, a disposal pit with quantities of 'bronze' and copper items as well as pottery, and a burial of an important person. The CIRE PERDUE 'bronzes' are unique, being exceptionally delicate and intricate, and unlike those from BENIN and IFE.

Ignateva Cave, Ignatiev or **Yamazy-Tash** a prehistoric cave-site located along a tributary of the Belaya River in the southern Urals of European Russia. The lower cultural layer contains artifacts (e.g. microliths) and faunal remains (e.g. cave bear, reindeer), and is assigned to the late Upper Palaeolithic. During the early 1980s, numerous schematic cave paintings (extinct animals, a human female and abstract signs) were reported from Ignateva Cave, some of which may be Palaeolithic. The upper cultural layer contains Iron Age remains.

Ilgynly-Tepe an ENEOLITHIC TELL settlement in southern Turkmenistan about 240 km (150 miles) southeast of the modern town of Ashkhabad. Numerous building levels contain a sequence of occupation between about 5000 and 3000 BC. Compounds that consist of dwelling rooms, courtyards, workshops and sanctuaries were separated by streets. Artifacts include stone female figurines, stone mortars, copper tools (including a cast axe-adze with a shaft hole) and clay animal figurines. Large clay BUCRANIA and wall paintings of snakes and trees in the sanctuaries reflect symbolic behaviour. A considerable amount of charcoal from the wood of trees indicates that the desert area in which this site is located was once an oasis.

'Ili'ili'opae one of the largest HEIAU in the Hawaiian Islands, on Molokai.

Illahun see EL-LAHUN.

Illinoian see SAALIAN.

illuvial horizon a soil horizon defined by accumulation, or illuviation, of material derived from one or more overlying soil horizons either by deposition of fine particles from suspension, precipitation from solution, or by both. The most common illuvial horizon is the B horizon. Compare ELUVIAL HORIZON.

Illyria an area of the western Balkans, described by CLASSICAL writers as lying to the west of the Vardar and

Morava Rivers, and extending to the Adriatic Sea and the eastern edge of the Alps. The inhabitants of Illyria during the last centuries BC, the Illyrians, resisted Greek influence but later were absorbed into the Roman empire.

Ilsenhöhle see RANIS CAVE.

Il'skaya I a Middle Palaeolithic open-air site on the Il' River (Kuban' tributary) in the northern Caucasus, European Russia. As many as twelve occupation horizons are buried in slope deposits overlying ALLUVIUM of the third terrace. The faunal remains are dominated by steppe bison; although the age of the occupations is unclear, the large body-size of some of the carnivores suggests a cold interval (early last GLACIAL?). Sidescrapers predominate among the tools. The site was excavated by Zamyatnin in 1926/1928, GORODTSOV in 1936–7 and Praslov in 1963 and 1967–9.

Imgur-Enlil see BALAWAT.

impasto a type of early pottery made in ETRURIA especially during the VILLANOVAN PERIOD. It was made from unrefined clay and fired to a dark brown or black colour. Common shapes include biconical urns and hut models which were used for cremations.

impluvium a water tank placed in the centre of the ATRIUM under the COMPLUVIUM in a Roman house.

Impressed ware the earliest Neolithic pottery of Mediterranean Europe, with decoration impressed into the clay using wooden sticks, combs, fingernails or seashells. The most characteristic early Neolithic Impressed ware is that decorated with the edge of a cockle (*Cardium*) shell, and known as CARDIAL WARE.

Inamgaon an important site in Pune, excavated by the Deccan College during the 1960s and 1970s, which provides a detailed view of the 2nd millennium MALWA and JORWE cultures of the northern Deccan (Maharastra, western-central India). The Malwa phase at the site contains large rectangular domestic structures of wattle and daub, often with internal divisions, and with circular platforms, storage bins and jars. The community cultivated, possibly with some irrigation, wheat, barley, sorghum and various legumes, kept cattle, sheep, goat and pig, and also hunted and fished. The Jorwe community lived in structures similar to those built earlier, though now some differences in size of structure are apparent, perhaps reflecting some social differentiation. Subsistence also continued much in accordance with earlier patterns, now definitely with irrigation. At Inamgaon by late Jorwe times the settlement was smaller, and constructed of small, round wattle-and-daub huts.

Inanna the 'queen of heaven', a SUMERIAN deity, roughly equivalent to the AKKADIAN Ishtar, the daughter of NANNA/Sin; she was the goddess both of love and of war, as well as of the storehouse and rain, and was closely associated with WARKA.

Inca or **Inka** an extensive empire occupying most of Andean South America at the time of the Spanish conquest in AD 1532. Its expansion began in the mid 15th century when Pachacuti defeated the Chankas, the traditional enemy of the Inca, and began to conquer regions beyond CUZCO, the capital city. Most of the extent of the empire was conquered by his son Topa Inca Yupanqui. The empire was torn by a bloody war of succession between the brothers Atahuallpa and Huascar. The war ended at about the time that Francisco PIZARRO arrived in Peru; he took Atahuallpa captive in Cajamarca and ended Inca rule.

The Inca incorporated regions into their empire through a combination of diplomacy and military conquest. Lands and animals in subject regions were divided into three parts: one for the Inca, one for the cult of the sun god, and the rest for the people of the region. Tribute, *mita*, was collected in the form of labour, provided in rotation by each household. Normal *mita* requirements included working the lands of the Inca and the Sun, and producing textiles. Some villages provided special services, such as serving as litter-bearers of the Inca, or as *chaski*, the runners who carried messages along the Inca road system, *capac ñan*, that tied together the far-flung empire. The Inca left local religious beliefs intact, but decreed that the worship of the sun god be added to local religions. When possible, the Inca also left local political control intact, and ruled through alliance with local rulers; where this was not possible, local systems were reorganized, and sometimes Inca rulers were installed. Particularly hostile groups were moved to new locations; these *mitmag* settlements were sometimes placed in friendly regions to diffuse conflict. *Mitmag* were also used to exploit natural and agricultural resources of particular interest to the Inca. A special class of retainers, *yanakuna*, was created by the Inca to serve as lower-level bureaucrats and as personal servants to the royal Inca nobility.

Anyone directly related, within five generations or less, to the Inca ruler was considered to be Inca. Non-Incas could also be raised to the status of Inca-by-privilege by the emperor. The Inca dynasty was begun by Manco Capac, the legendary founder of Cuzco; Atahuallpa was the 13th ruler of the dynasty. The Inca were said to be direct descendants of Inti, the sun god, and his sister-wife, Quilla, the moon god.

Inca Cueva a group of caves and rockshelters, many of them containing PICTOGRAPHs, and open-air sites in Jujuy Province, northwestern Argentina, between 3,700 and 3,900 m (12,140 and 12,800 ft) altitude; excavations have revealed occupation by hunter-gatherers from c.11,000 bp onwards. Inca Cueva 7 yielded lithic material as well as remains of textiles, ropes and basketry of plant or animal fibres (camelid and human hair); remains of decorated or painted leather objects; reed pipes; varied objects of wood or bone; and remains of a hallucinogenic plant from the eastern forests in a pipe of puma bone – this was all thought originally to be from a ritual deposit, and has been dated to *c.*4030 bp (final PRECERAMIC). Current thinking is that there are three different layers here, and that the cave may have served as a corral for camelids in a period before 4000 bp. Inca Cueva 4 contains geometric paintings on the wall, fallen fragments of which have been dated to at least 10,620 bp. The earliest ceramics at this location come from Alero 1, dating to 2900 bp.

index fossil a fossil that has a widespread geographical range but is temporally restricted to a brief period of existence. These fossils are useful in biostratigraphic classification of rock or sediment units (see STRATIGRAPHY). The concept is used for cultural artifacts referred to as 'diagnostic'. Artifacts that share the attributes of index fossils are useful in the CROSS-DATING and correlation of deposits that contain them, and construction of chronologies. See also TYPE.

India India is defined here as the region south of the Himalaya, Karakorum and Hindu Kush Mountains, from the Brahmaputra drainage on the east to the Indus drainage and its bordering hill country (Baluchistan) on the west. Other important divisions include the Doab (the Ganges and Yamuna Rivers) in northern India, and peninsular India to the south (including the Narmada drainage, and the Deccan Plateau).

While traces of Palaeolithic occupation are common, with a core-tool industry (SOAN) preceeding a flake industry, the Pleistocene record does not yet match in global significance that for other parts of the Old World; remains of archaic HOMO *sapiens* are reported from Narmada. Terminal Pleistocene–Holocene microlithic industries are also common, and spectacular rock art sites (BHIMBETKA) of early-mid Holocene date also occur; hunting-foraging groups using a microlithic technology persisted well into the 1st millennium in parts of peninsular India. Food production first appeared during the 8th–7th millennia in Baluchistan, at least partly as an indigenous process (see MEHRGAHR); over the next three millennia village cultures in Baluchistan achieved a degree of social complexity (see DAMB SADAAT, QUETTA, RANA GHUNDAI).

In the Indus Valley proper several regional cultures emerged late in the 4th millennium, distinctive in their material culture but sharing enough similarities to be grouped as Early HARAPPAN (see AMRI, KOT DIJI, KALIBANGAN); these towns and villages prefigure the Mature Harappan civilization, which formed abruptly around 2600–2500 BC and endured until 2000–1800 BC. Harappan (or Indus) settlements appear throughout the Indus drainage, into the western Doab (e.g. AL-AMGIRPUR), and along the coast on either side of the Indus delta. While the cities (MOHENJO-DARO, HARAPPA) attract attention, most people continued to live in towns (LOTHAL, CHANHU-DARO) and villages (ALLAHDINO). The Indus civilization presents characteristics of a complex society, like a hierarchical SETTLEMENT PATTERN, craft specialization, administrative technologies (writing, seals, standardized weights and measures), but it lacks clearly identifiable palaces or temples and notable accumulations of weath in burials or other contexts; the social and political character of this civilization remains enigmatic. Harappan artifacts appearing as far away as Mesopotamia and Central Asia attest to wide-reaching commercial connections (see GULF TRADE, MELUHHA, SHORTUGAI). Elsewhere in India, relatively simple societies based on hunting/gathering, pastoralism or 'Neolithic' village farming (see BARZAHOM) prevailed during the 3rd millennium BC.

The Late Harappan horizon, a family of descendant cultures in the Indus region (see CEMETERY H, JHUKAR, PIRAK, CHANHU-DARO, RANGPUR, ROJDI), extended the Harappan tradition shorn of cities and writing. Evidence for peoples moving south from Central Asia (see BMAC, QUETTA HOARD, NAUSHARO) in the early 2nd millennium BC may correlate with the historical tradition of Aryan invasions. Farming villages also took firm root in the Doab and across large portions of northern peninsular India; the diverse material culture, and especially the pottery, of these villages sometimes recalls Harappan styles (BLACK-AND-RED POTTERY, JOWRE, MALWA; see AHAR, DAIMABAD, HALLUR, NAVDATOLI, PIKLIHAL, TEKKALKOTA). In the Doab a sequence of pottery styles spans the mid 2nd to mid 1st millennia BC. OCHRE COLOURED POTTERY is associated with ephemeral settlements and with hoards of copper weapons and other artifacts (COPPER HOARD; see also DAIMABAD). PAINTED GREY WARE followed, found in a village context in which iron technology made its appearance (see HASTINAPURA). NORTHERN BLACK POLISHED WARE marked the second Indian urbanization during the middle third of the 1st millennium BC. This development occurred across northern India, from GANDHARA in the northwest (see TAXILA), through the Doab (see MATHURA, KAUSAMBI, PATALIPUTRA) and into the Narmada drainage (see UJJAIN); these walled cities emerged in tandem with Gangetic state formation. Buddhism and Jainism took form in this context (traditionally placed in the 6th century, but perhaps a century or more later). The roots of Indian literacy also belong to this time, with several Indian scripts emulating the Aramaic alphabet which the ACHAEMENID Persians introduced to the region when it absorbed Gandhara (late 6th century BC). Peninsular India lagged somewhat behind these northern changes. Pastoralism remained an important economic orientation well into the 1st millennium BC (see ASH MOUNDS). The diverse

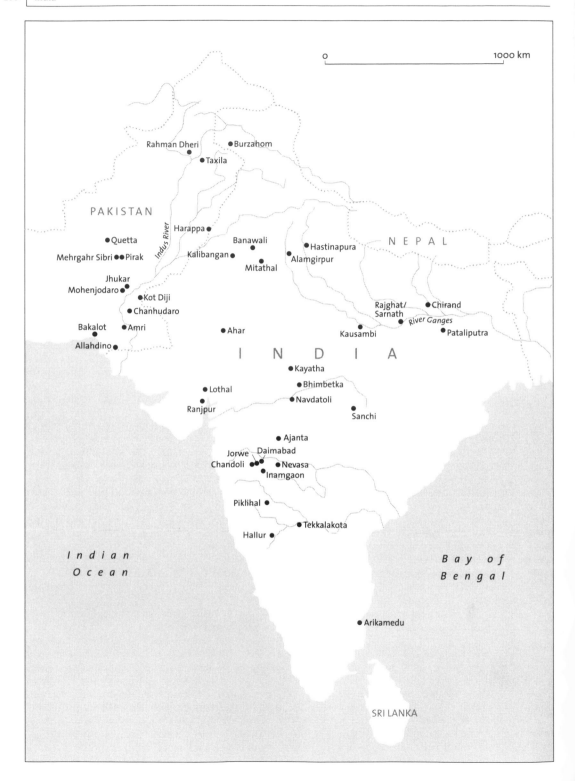

0   1000 km

Rahman Dheri
Burzahom
Taxila

PAKISTAN

Quetta
Harappa
Banawali
Hastinapura
NEPAL
Mehrgahr Sibri Pirak
Kalibangan
Alamgirpur
Mitathal
Jhukar
Mohenjodaro
Kot Diji
Rajghat/ Chirand
Chanhudaro
Sarnath
River Ganges
Bakalot Amri
Ahar
Pataliputra
Allahdino
Kausambi

INDIA

Kayatha

Lothal
Bhimbetka
Navdatoli
Ranjpur
Sanchi

Ajanta
Jorwe Daimabad
Chandoli Nevasa
Inamgaon

Piklihal

Tekkalakota
Hallur

Indian
Ocean

Bay of
Bengal

Arikamedu

SRI LANKA

monumental burials of the megalithic culture also belong to the 1st millennium BC; pottery and iron artifacts are associated with these monuments (see BRAHMAGIRI).

In the aftermath of Alexander's campaign in northwestern India, the MAURYAN empire arose from its Gangetic centre to control territories from Afghanistan through much of peninsular India; under royal patronage Buddhism spread widely through the empire (see AJANTA, ASOKA, SANCHI, KANDAHAR, STUPA). The Mauryan empire dissolved during the 2nd century BC into local kingdoms (including those of the invading Saka SCYTHIANS), and these conditions lasted until the emergence of the KUSHAN; based in Afghanistan (see BAMIYAN, BEGRAM, SURKH KOTA) and gaining domination over northern India in the first centuries AD, Kushan commercial activities on the Silk Road helped introduce Buddhism to China. Under the Gupta Dynasty (4th–6th centuries AD) in northern India, Hinduism emerged from the earlier Brahmanism of Vedic tradition, and widely displaced Buddhism; early Hindu temples appear at SANCHI and elsewhere. In southern peninsular India, states developed late in the 1st millennium, at least partly in response to expansionary pressures from the north. Roman traders in the Indian Ocean included Indian and Sri Lankan ports of call (see ARIKAMEDU, MANTAI), and hoards of Roman coins are widespread in the south; such foreign commercial contacts also stimulated state formation.

Indianization the process by which Southeast Asian states of the 1st millennium AD borrowed, adapted and assimilated aspects of South Asian political, religious and literary culture; it should not be confused with colonization or wholesale copying, since the end result was distinctively Southeast Asian.

Indian Knoll an ARCHAIC site in Kentucky, USA, comprising a SHELL MOUND and the possible remains of living floors. Most significantly, the remains of over 1,100 burials were also found, many of them accompanied by exotic grave-goods, suggestive of some degree of social ranking.

indigenous archaeology an approach to archaeological interpretation which recognizes that traditional archaeology, because it is the product of Western science, has often been insensitive to the concerns and needs of Native peoples. This new approach, which is becoming particularly important in the Antipodes and North America, tries to strike a balance between scientific (i.e. Western) constructions of the past and the legitimate desire of Native peoples to have a say in how their past is archaeologically constructed and presented. See also NAGPRA.

Indo-European a large language group that includes most of the modern European languages (e.g. Romance, Germanic, Slavic, Baltic, Greek, Albanian) except Basque, Finnish and Hungarian; modern Indo-Iranian (e.g. Persian, Hindi) and other tongues (e.g. Armenian); and also numerous dead languages (e.g. HITTITE, Tocharian, PHRYGIAN). Various attempts have been made to explain this pattern of languages as a result of migrations or invasions in prehistoric and early historic times. The most widely accepted solution places the Proto-Indo-European homeland in the southern Russian steppes in the broad zone north of the Black and Caspian Seas during the 5th millennium BC, but the problem of identifying language groups from archaeological remains makes it difficult to assess the conflicting hypotheses.

Indonesia see ASIA, SOUTHEAST.

induction the process of reasoning whereby general propositions are derived from an analysis of individual events. An example might be concluding that a country's total manufacturing ability was poor based on its inability to produce efficient cars. Compare DEDUCTION.

Indus civilization see HARAPPAN.

industrial archaeology a branch of Historical Archaeology that specializes in studying the processes of Western industrialization.

industry a frequently repeated assemblage of restricted content, such as stone tools only. Industry is occasionally used as a synonym for assemblage.

infrared absorption spectrometry a physical technique used to determine mineralogy or chemical composition of artifacts and organic substances, particularly AMBER. A sample is bombarded by infrared radiation which causes the atoms in the sample to vibrate at frequencies characteristic of the atom species present. That part of the radiation spectrum vibrating at the same frequencies is absorbed; the amount of transmitted radiation at each wavelength is detected, forming the basis for identification.

Ingaladdi a rockshelter in Australia's Northern Territory. The upper deposits, from 3000 bp, contained TULAS and points from the AUSTRALIAN SMALL TOOL TRADITION. The lower layers, mainly rock rubble, contained flake scrapers, small HORSEHOOF CORES and engraved sandstone fragments, and accumulated between 7000 and 5000 bp.

Ingapirca an INCA site in highland Ecuador at which is found a large oval platform, 37 by 12 m (121 by 40 ft) in extent and 3–4 m (10–13 ft) high, faced with cut stone. On the summit was a gable-roofed building that was divided lengthwise into two rooms. Although the structure has been called a castle or guardhouse, it more likely served a more ideological function, symbolizing the Inca occupation of the northern Andes, and its subjugation of the Cañari peoples.

Ingombe Ilede an Iron Age site in southern Zambia, occupied in the 14th and 15th centuries AD by people who traded extensively with the East African coast as well as the interior. A series of elaborate graves contained metal bangles, woven cotton cloth, marine gastropod shells, gold beads, large quantities of imported glass beads, bundles of copper wire, bars and cross-shaped ingots, as well as iron hoes and gongs.

ingot a quantity of a resource (usually metal) of standardized form and weight, used as currency and for trade: e.g. the Bronze Age Mediterranean had copper ingots in the form of an oxhide and weighing approximately 30 kg (66 lbs). See also KAŞ.

inhumation see BURIAL.

Initial period the period 1800–800 BC in Andean South America, during which ceramics were introduced, and agriculture and animal husbandry formed the subsistence base for most cultures. Monumental ceremonial architecture became widely distributed on the coast of Peru, where centres followed a U-shaped plan on the central coast, and a linear plan with PLATFORM MOUNDS and sunken circular courts in the north. In the northern highlands of Peru the KOTOSH religious tradition was widespread. A period of cultural heterogeneity, the Initial period ended with the abandonment of many of the coastal centres, and the beginning of the CHAVÍN cult.

Inka see INCA.

insula (*Lat.* island) The term is normally applied to a block within the grid-pattern of a Roman city. See also CARDO, DECUMANUS.

intaglio 1 *n.* a gem-stone in which the decoration is cut into the surface.
2 *adj.* relating to a technique by which the decoration is cut into the surface. The technique is widely used on gems as well as on glass vessels.

'Intercultural'-style carved chlorite the name given to a group of vessels and other objects that appear in western Asia during the 3rd millennium BC, which are made of chlorite, STEATITE, SERPENTINE and other soft stones, and which share a rich iconography. Such objects are distributed from the middle Euphrates to Central Asia, the Indus and southeastern Arabia, though most come from southern and western Iran, southern MESOPOTAMIA and the western Persian Gulf. The discovery of a production centre at Tepe YAHYA provoked considerable interest in this style, especially with respect to inter-regional exchange and shared beliefs in western Asia of the mid and later 3rd millennium.

interglacial 1 *n.* a relatively warm climatic episode, between GLACIAL episodes, characterized by little or no glacial ice, warm climate processes, deposits, flora and fauna, and increased soil-forming processes in some areas. In reference to the QUATERNARY, interglacials were considerably briefer than glacials. Compare INTERSTADIAL. See also STRATIGRAPHY.
2 *adj.* referring to relatively warm climatic conditions.
3 *adj.* referring to or derived from non-glacial processes and conditions.

Intermediate period one of three particular periods of Egyptian history when the central cohesion of the state collapsed, resulting in the country being ruled by a number of regional potentates (i.e. between OLD KINGDOM / MIDDLE KINGDOM / NEW KINGDOM / LATE PERIOD).

interrupted ditch enclosure see CAUSEWAYED CAMP.

interstadial 1 *n.* a relatively brief and warmer climatic episode within a longer, cooler GLACIAL episode. An interstadial is usually characterized by some degree of glacier recession, climatic amelioration with attendant changes in flora and fauna, and increased expression of PEDOGENESIS. However, the expression of an interstadial is likely to be more variable regionally than an INTERGLACIAL.
2 *adj.* referring to relatively brief and warmer climatic conditions within a glacial episode.

intramural *adj.* (of graves) located within the confines of a settlement, as opposed to those outside, which are *extramural*.

Inuit the name by which the Eskimo call themselves. It means 'The People'.

involution a structure formed by contortion of saturated sediment or soil material resulting from seasonal freezing accompanied by high pore-water pressures. Soil involutions are most commonly found associated with the active layer of PERMAFROST, but can form where permafrost is not present and are not diagnostic. Churning action that creates involutions may also cause disturbance or mixing of any archaeological deposits that are present in affected areas. Involutions may also be confused with archaeological features. See also CRYOTURBATION.

Inyanga or **Nyanga** a highland region in eastern Zimbabwe, with evidence of Stone Age, Early Iron Age (see GOKOMERE) and, particularly, Late Iron Age occupation. In the 17th and 18th centuries AD, Barwe/Tonga people built substantial fortified stone-walled settlements covering some 8,000 sq. km (3,100 sq.miles).

Iolkos see VOLOS.

Ionic order a scheme of architecture usually found in the cities of western Turkey as well as in the islands of the eastern Aegean. The CAPITAL is formed by two sets of VOLUTES, between which there is an ECHINUS decor-

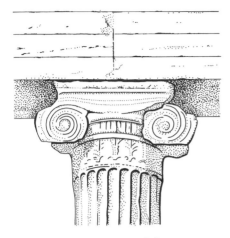

IONIC ORDER capital.

ated with an egg-and-dart pattern. The columns rest on elaborately carved, often horizontally fluted, bases. The ENTABLATURE allowed for a continuous frieze, which could be decorated in relief. Ionic columns could be used as internal columns for a STOA as they tended to be taller. See also ERECHTHEION.

Ipiutak see NORTON.

Ipswichian see EEMIAN.

iron a ductile, malleable, magnetic metallic element, used in the manufacture of functional and decorative artifacts that commonly occurs in oxide form, such as *haematite*. Iron metallurgy characterized the cultural period termed the Iron Age.

Iron Age the third stage in THOMSEN'S THREE-AGE SYSTEM, a period of antiquity in the Old World in which iron metallurgy superseded the use of bronze for tools and weapons. In *Europe*, the earliest iron appears around 1100 bc, but conventionally the transition from the Bronze Age to the Iron Age is placed in the early part of the 1st millennium bc. In temperate Europe, this is during the second half of the HALLSTATT period. The Iron Age continues through the LA TÈNE period in Central and western Europe. The appearance of the Romans ends the Iron Age in western Europe, while beyond the Roman frontier, the Iron Age continues until the so-called migration period in the 4th to 6th centuries AD.

In *East Asia*, iron came into use in China *c*.500 BC in the middle ZHOU period. It was introduced to the Korean peninsula *c*.400 BC, making the Late Bronze Age in Korea contemporaneous with the Early Iron Age, and the Late Iron Age contemporaneous with the PROTO-THREE KINGDOMS period (see KOREA). Both bronze and iron were first used by the YAYOI peoples in Japan (see

JAPANESE PERIODIZATION). Iron is dated from *c*.700–500 BC in Southeast Asia.

Iron smelting apparently spread from western Asia to North *Africa* by the 8th century BC. According to one viewpoint, it may have been introduced to sub-Saharan Africa from PHOENICIAN or Greek colonies on the North African coast, or via the Nile Valley (see MEROE), or by other routes. However, some suggest iron metallurgy could have developed independently in West Africa from indigenous pre-Iron Age copper metallurgy (see AKJOUJT, AGADEZ). The earliest occurrences of iron technology in West Africa have been found at Do Dimi (2628 bp), AZELIK (2490 bp) and Ekne Wan Ataran (2400 bp) in Niger, and at TARUGA (2541 bp) in Nigeria. Iron-smelting sites in Buhaya, Tanzania (see KATURUKA) date to the late 1st millennium bc or possibly earlier. The spread of iron technology over much of Central, eastern and southern Africa was at one time linked with the spread of Negroid BANTU-speaking peoples from their homeland in the Nigeria-Cameroon border area, but some archaeologists now believe that the Bantu dispersal may have begun before the advent of iron technology. Bantu-speaking Iron Age peoples reached southern Africa in the first few centuries ad. They were farmers who lived in settled village communities and brought not only knowledge of metal working, but also pottery as well as domestic plants and animals.

The southern African Iron Age is divided into the Early Iron Age, dating from about AD 200 until AD 1000, and the Late Iron Age, dating from AD 1000 until the 19th century. The date of AD 1000 is an arbitrary division. The Early Iron Age includes the first metal-using agriculturalists and their immediate descendants (see CHIFUMBAZE). The period from the late 1st millennium AD, as well as the Late Iron Age, saw the development of wealthy states with stratified societies in many parts of sub-Saharan Africa (see GHANA, GREAT ZIMBABWE, MALI, MAPUNGUBWE, SONGHAY).

IRSL see LUMINESCENCE DATING.

Isaac, Glynn Llywelyn (1937–85) a palaeoanthropologist who played a pivotal role in the post-1960s florescence of knowledge about early Pleistocene culture in East Africa. His work at OLORGESAILIE is regarded as a classic and he is particularly credited with developing new approaches to the interpretation of very early archaeological remains, including the formulation of the 'food-sharing model' and the concept of 'home bases'.

Isbister a Neolithic CHAMBERED TOMB on the island of South Ronaldsay, Orkney, Scotland, consisting of a passage leading to a main chamber of long rectangular plan with four irregular oval side chambers. Remains of some 342 people were found within the chambers, mostly as disarticulated bones. There was some evidence of sorting, with long bones and skulls placed in different parts of the tomb. Radiocarbon dates indicate construction in c.3150 BC.

Ischia (*Gk* Pithekoussai) an island off CAMPANIA, southern Italy. Some MYCENAEAN pottery has been found, but the island is best known for the Euboean colony which was founded in the 8th century BC before CUMAE. Evidence for iron smelting has been discovered, perhaps reflecting the exploitation of the mineral resources of ETRURIA and Elba.

Isernia or **La Pineta** a well-stratified Lower Palaeolithic open-air site in the Volturno Valley, central Italy, which is not yet fully excavated, but which has produced many disarticulated animal bones associated with thousands of stone tools including limestone choppers and chopping tools and flint flakes. POTASSIUM ARGON dates place the campsites at c.730,000 BP, and the fauna (bison, rhinoceros, etc.) indicates a steppe environment.

Ishango a series of sites on or near the shore of Lake Rutanzige (formerly Lake Edward) in the northeastern Democratic Republic of Congo with a long LATER STONE AGE occupation sequence. A level dated to as much as 25,290 bp contained fragmentary human skeletons, abundant faunal remains, microlithic cores and double-row barbed bone harpoon points.

Ishtar see INANNA, ASTARTE.

Isimila a site in riverine deposits near Iringa in southern Tanzania, rich in ACHEULIAN stone artifacts including huge handaxes and picks, thought to date to the late Middle Pleistocene. See also OLORGESAILIE.

Isin a city on the palaeo-Euphrates near NIPPUR. The mound of Isin covers about 150 ha (370 acres). Although investigated early in the 20th century, systematic excavation began in the mid 1970s with B. Hrouda's work on the 2nd and 1st millennium BC levels. Earlier occupation is also apparent in late 4th and 3rd millennium sherds from disturbed contexts, and in 'UBAID sherds recovered from surface contexts; the German team also excavated a building of EARLY DYNASTIC I date. Isin takes its importance from its political history, as the seat of a major kingdom of the OLD BABYLONIAN period and as the origin of the dynasty (the Isin II, 1157–1026 BC) that ruled BABYLONIA after the KASSITE period.

Isin/Larsa period see OLD BABYLONIAN PERIOD.

Isis an Egyptian anthropoid goddess, the wife of OSIRIS and mother of HORUS. The most important cult centres at which she was worshipped as the principal deity are PHILAE and BEHBET EL-HAGAR. During the Roman period the cult of Isis became popular in parts of the Roman empire outside Egypt, including a substantial temple to the goddess in ROME itself.

Isle Royale an island in northwestern Lake Superior, North America, that is the location of ten sunken ships, ranging in age from the mid 1800s to the present. The cold fresh water of the lake has preserved the wrecks to a degree unknown in salt water, and has thus provided UNDERWATER ARCHAEOLOGY with almost unprecedented opportunities for research. See also PADRE ISLAND SHIPWRECKS.

isochronous *adj.* formed during the same span of time; for example, one sediment unit having upper and lower boundaries that are SYNCHRONOUS with a second sediment unit would be isochronous with the second unit. See also DIACHRONIC.

isostasy a process by which the distribution of mass within the Earth's crust is balanced by large-scale topography. Changes in crustal mass that affect ISOSTATIC equilibrium can occur through stripping by erosion, loading of GLACIAL ice, loading of sediments derived from erosion into basins and tectonic changes. In response, equilibrium in part is restored by vertical movements of crustal blocks. During the QUATERNARY, crustal loading by continental glaciers caused crustal depression beneath the ice and crustal forebulge beyond the ice margin. As mass decreased with melting of the ice and was transferred to ocean basins, crustal readjustments caused uplift in some areas and downwarping in others. In coastal areas, isostatic crustal adjustments, always in interaction with EUSTASY, had considerable impact on land exposure or submergence, with attendant archaeological implications for settlement, migration and changing environmental resources. In some regions, isostatic and EUSTATIC sea-level changes resulted in flights of FOSSIL BEACH ridges.

isostatic *adj.* pertaining to changes in altitude of the Earth's crust in response to shifts in the crustal mass as compensation for loading and unloading of the crust. Isostatic adjustments have considerable impact on the preservation and location of archaeological sites along coastal areas and lakes, and on strategies for identifying them. See also ISOSTASY.

isotope atoms of the same element that have different atomic masses due to different numbers of neutrons in the nuclei, but that have similar chemical properties. Many isotopes are naturally unstable, or radioactive, because of the composition of the nuclei, and tend to change spontaneously to stable configurations, or stable isotopes. This process forms the basis for RADIOMETRIC DATING.

isotopic replacement a chemical process, a source of contamination in RADIOMETRIC DATING, whereby an ISOTOPE within a sample used for dating is exchanged with an isotope of the same element that is a different age. For example, the ^{14}C isotope in carbonate material, such as shell or bone, may be replaced during recrystallization by 'younger', 'older' or 'dead' carbon isotopes dissolved in surrounding ground water; the sample will yield an inaccurate age.

Israelites the Semitic people of the Old Testament, identified archaeologically by the numerous dispersed small villages that replaced LATE BRONZE AGE towns after 1200 BC in the central hill country of the southern Levant (biblical Samaria and Judea); these villages present characteristic house forms, pottery and other features. Explanations for this transformation include nomadic invasion (cf. biblical accounts in Exodus and Joshua), settlement of indigenous nomads and brigands and social revolution by the urban lower classes at the end of the Bronze Age. The Israelite displacement of CANAANITE culture brought them into confrontation with the PHILISTINES and ARAMAEANS. Walled towns re-emerged after 1000 BC with the appearance of the united kingdom of Israel (see SOLOMON), and expanded under the divided kingdoms of SAMARIA (Israel) and Judah (see JERUSALEM). The ASSYRIANS destroyed Samaria in the late 8th century BC, and the BABYLONIANS took Judah into exile early in the 6th century BC.

Issyk mound a so-called 'royal' KURGAN of the SCYTHIAN period, which was constructed in the 4th–3rd centuries BC by one of the SAKA tribes. The site is 50 km (31 miles) east of Almaty, in Kazakhstan. It was excavated in 1969–70 by K. Akishev. The kurgan was 6 m (20 ft) high and 60 m (66 yds) in diameter. When the mound was removed, two graves appeared: the central one had been completely ravaged in ancient times, but the lateral one (to the south) had remained intact. The lateral grave's chamber (3.3 by 1.9 by 1.5 m [10 by 6 by 5 ft]) was constructed of logs. In the southern and western parts of the chamber were found thirty-one ceramic, wooden, bronze and silver vessels, while the northern part contained the remains of a deceased nobleman, seventeen–eighteen years old, lying on his back on a board floor with his head to the west. The discoveries also included more than 4,000 golden plaques that decorated his costume, footwear and a tall conical head-dress. Many of the adornments are executed in the SCYTHIAN-SIBERIAN ANIMAL STYLE. Because of these incredibly rich adornments, the grave's occupant was dubbed the 'Golden Man' by archaeologists. There was also iron weaponry (an ACINACES and a sword inlaid with gold-plating) and a bronze mirror lying by the man's belt.

Istállóskö an Upper Palaeolithic cave-site located in the Bükk Mountains of northeastern Hungary. Artifacts and faunal remains (e.g. reindeer, red deer and steppe bison) are buried in loess and rubble. The lower cultural layer contains an AURIGNACIAN assemblage which includes numerous split-base bone points, but few stone tools (e.g. burins). This layer yielded a radiocarbon date of 42,350 bp, and apparently represents one of the oldest Aurignacian occupations in Europe. The upper cultural layer contains a younger Aurignacian assemblage (c.31,000 bp) including a bone 'flute', burins, endscrapers and bone points. Istállóskö was excavated by Hillebrand in 1913–25, VÉRTES in 1947–51, and others.

Isturitz a cave-system in the Pyrénées-Atlantiques, southwestern France, comprising three superimposed tunnels. The uppermost, Isturitz, excavated by E. Passemard in 1912–22 and by R. de Saint-Périer in 1928–50, is enormously rich in occupation material from the MOUSTERIAN to the late MAGDALENIAN, and in PORTABLE ART from the later Upper Palaeolithic. It also houses some deep wall-engravings of animals. Below it is *Oxocelhaya* (or Haristoy) which contains some PARIETAL ART. The lowest tunnel, *Erberua*, is protected by the underground river which was first breached in 1973. It houses paintings and engravings on its walls, and intact Magdalenian hearths on its floor.

Italy The Italian peninsula is separated from the rest of Europe by the arc of the Alpine mountains in the north, and connections by sea have long been as important as those by land. Its first human residents, however, must have arrived overland via the Alpine passes. Italy was occupied along with the rest of Europe around a million years ago. Populations of HOMO *heidelbergensis* were succeeded c.200,000 years ago by classic NEANDERTHALS, whose remains were found in GROTTA GUATTARI at Monte Circeo. The transition to the Upper Palaeolithic (c.35,000–10,000 BP) marked the replacement of the Neanderthals by modern humans. At the GRIMALDI caves in the Italian Riviera a sequence of elaborate modern human burials has been found which illustrate the behavioural complexity and funerary practices of the new species.

The end of the last GLACIAL and the improvement in temperature allowed modern humans in the EPIPALAEOLITHIC (or Mesolithic) period to exploit a widening range of resources. They are represented by long cave sequences at sites such as ARENE CANDIDE and GROTTA DELL'UZZO, which continue into Neolithic and later periods when pottery and domesticates were introduced. The early Neolithic in southern Italy c.6000 BC may have been associated with colonist farmers from the eastern side of the Adriatic, who lived within multiple-ditched enclosures on low-lying plains including PASSO DI CORVO on the Tavoliere. Farming also became established in northern Italy, notably in the Po Valley, and spread into the Alpine foothills. Lake-edge settlements such as MOLINO CASAROTTO (with Middle Neolithic BOCCA QUADRATA material) mark the beginnings of a 'lake village' tradition which continued into the Iron Age, and which is common to the entire Alpine region (including France, Germany, Switzerland and Austria).

Towards the end of the 4th millennium BC societies became more complex with the introduction of prestige

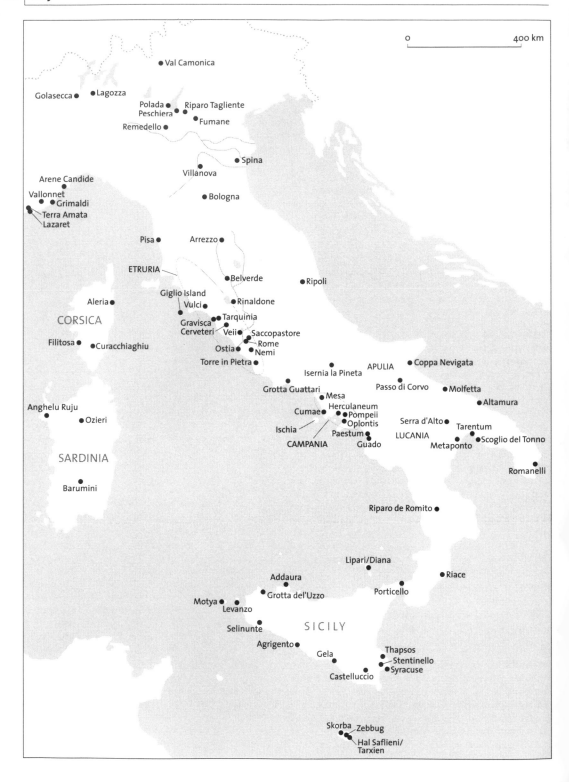

0   400 km

- Val Camonica
- Golasecca
- Lagozza
- Polada
- Riparo Tagliente
- Peschiera
- Remedello
- Fumane
- Spina
- Villanova
- Bologna
- Arene Candide
- Vallonnet
- Grimaldi
- Terra Amata
- Lazaret
- Pisa
- Arrezzo
- ETRURIA
- Belverde
- Ripoli
- Giglio Island
- Rinaldone
- Vulci
- Aleria
- Tarquinia
- Gravisca
- Cerveteri
- Veii
- Saccopastore
- Rome
- Filitosa
- Curacchiaghiu
- Ostia
- Nemi
- CORSICA
- Torre in Pietra
- Isernia la Pineta
- APULIA
- Coppa Nevigata
- Grotta Guattari
- Passo di Corvo
- Molfetta
- Mesa
- Altamura
- Anghelu Ruju
- Herculaneum
- Cumae
- Pompeii
- Ozieri
- Oplontis
- Serra d'Alto
- Tarentum
- Ischia
- Paestum
- LUCANIA
- Scoglio del Tonno
- CAMPANIA
- Guado
- Metaponto
- SARDINIA
- Romanelli
- Barumini
- Riparo de Romito
- Lipari/Diana
- Riace
- Addaura
- Porticello
- Motya
- Grotta dell'Uzzo
- Levanzo
- SICILY
- Selinunte
- Agrigento
- Gela
- Thapsos
- Stentinello
- Syracuse
- Castelluccio
- Skorba
- Zebbug
- Hal Saflieni/Tarxien

materials including copper. Metal daggers and other artifacts appear in Copper Age cemeteries at RINALDONE and REMEDELLO SOTTO in northern and central Italy; they are also represented in Alpine rock art in the VALCAMONICA, and on carved STELAS such as those of the Val Venosta. The most striking insight into the period is provided by the discovery of the 'Iceman', a preserved human body at SIMILAUN in the Tirolean Alps, equipped with bow and arrows and a copper axe. The Copper Age of southern Italy, by contrast, was characterized by collective burials such as those of the CASTELLUCCIO rock-cut tombs of Sicily. The importance of maritime contact is suggested by the early metal-working evidence from the acropolis of LIPARI, dated to the 4th millennium BC, but becomes considerably clearer in the late 2nd millennium, when trade with Mycenaean Greece is attested by finds of characteristic Mycenaean pottery and metal work at this and other sites in southern Italy and Sicily.

From the 8th century BC, the south was drawn more closely into the Mediterranean world by the foundation of PHOENICIAN colonies in western Sicily (notably MOTYA), and by Greek colonies on both Sicily and the mainland, chief among them being SYRACUSE, CUMAE and Neapolis (Naples). Commercial and territorial competition led to a series of wars between Greeks and Carthaginians in which both sides endeavoured to seize control of the whole island of Sicily. On the mainland, indigenous state formation in ETRURIA led to the emergence of the Etruscan city-states in the 8th century BC. The Etruscans extended their control to the Po Valley in the north and Campania in the south, though their dominance was broken in the 4th century by the settlement of Celtic peoples in the Po Plain and by the rising power of Latium and the city of ROME in the south. The major Etruscan cities have left few architectural remains, but are known above all for their cemeteries, notably the rock-cut CHAMBERED TOMBS of CERVETERI and the painted tombs of TARQUINIA, which contained large numbers of Attic painted vessels imported from Greece.

During the 3rd century BC the city-state of Rome in a series of wars took control of the entire Italian peninsula, wresting control of Sicily from the Carthaginians (First Punic War 264–241 BC) and defeating the Carthaginian invasion of Italy (Second Punic War 218–202 BC) to become the dominant power in the central Mediterranean. Roads were constructed to enable Roman armies to move quickly to different parts of the peninsula. The wealth derived from imperial possessions abroad fuelled the construction of municipal buildings and luxury villas, though there was also widespread use of slaves and large estates developed at the expense of small independent farms. Stable government under the early empire (1st and 2nd centuries AD) promoted continued prosperity, which is illustrated by the well-preserved cities of POMPEII and HERCULANEUM. By the end of the 2nd century, however, Italy was losing its prominence as political and economic centre of the empire, and the imperial capital was moved to Constantinople (modern Istanbul) in AD 330. Within Italy, northern centres of Milan and Ravenna became the principal seats of government, though Rome retained its importance as the centre of the western Christian church and residence of the popes.

The political and military weakness of the western Roman empire culminated in the sack of Rome by the Ostrogoths in 410 and (more savagely) by the Vandals (a Germanic people settled in North Africa) in 455. Ostrogothic, Byzantine and Lombard rule followed over much of the Italian peninsula during the succeeding period. Links with northern Europe were strengthened during the Carolingian period (Charlemagne was crowned emperor by the Pope at Rome on Christmas Day 800), while Sicily and the south were contested between Arabs, Byzantines and Normans. The revival of the north Italian cities in the 12th century marked a new phase, with Pisa, Genoa and Venice profiting from overseas trade (notably in the eastern Mediterranean) and laying the cultural and economic foundations of the Italian Renaissance.

Itazuke the type-site in Fukuoka Prefecture, Japan, for early YAYOI pottery. Itazuke is also important for its extensive early Yayoi period paddyfield remains of canals, embankments, etc., which for a long time were evidence of the first agriculture in Japan (compare TORO). Recent excavations at Itazuke, Nabatake and Magarita sites document the beginnings of rice-growing in the previous JOMON period (compare TORIHAMA).

ivory the enlarged teeth of certain mammals utilized as a resource. The most important sources were the tusks of elephants and mammoths (upper incisor teeth) and of walruses (upper canines). It formed a highly prized resource in prehistory, used for carving, engraving and the manufacture of tools from the early Upper Palaeolithic onwards.

Iwajuku the first Palaeolithic site discovered in Japan, in 1949. Layers I and II are assessed to be 20,000 and 15,000 years old, respectively. They contained elongated blades, scrapers and choppers in I and thin, small blades in II. Iwajuku 0, below I, has yielded crude 'tools', estimated to be over 50,000 years old, that are similar to those at SOZUDAI with the same problems of manufacture recognition.

Iwanowice–Babia Góra an Early Bronze Age settlement and cemetery of the MIERZANOWICE CULTURE in southern Poland, dated to the late 3rd and early 2nd millennia BC. Concentrations of pits, including distinctive bell-shaped storage pits, mark the locations of households. The cemetery contained about 300 skeleton burials in oval or rectangular pits.

Iwo Eleru a rockshelter in the now forested area of southwestern Nigeria, with the longest dated sequence of microlithic artifacts known from West Africa. The oldest layers date to about 12,000 years ago and include a burial of the oldest Nigerian skeleton yet uncovered, which is considered to have Negroid features. Layers post-dating 5,000 years ago may contain evidence for the beginning of agriculture in the forests of West Africa.

Ix Chel see COZUMEL.

Iximché a highland MAYA site in Guatemala with strong Mexican influence. Its easily defensible position on a hill surrounded by ravines is typical of the POSTCLASSIC PERIOD. In one burial, dating to less than 100 years before the Spanish conquest, was found the largest cache of gold items in the Maya area, excluding that dredged from the Sacred CENOTE at CHICHÉN ITZÁ. At the time when it was conquered by Pedro de Alvarado in 1524, Iximché was the capital of the Cakchiquel Maya. Various archaeologists have worked at Iximché, including Jorge F. Guillemín, supported by the Guatemalan government, and Robert Wauchope, who analysed the ceramics from the site.

Izapa a PRECLASSIC site in the Pacific coastal plain of Chiapas, Mexico, where monumental sculpture indicates influence from the OLMEC, while also incorporating pre-cursors to later MAYA iconographic elements, including scenes relating to the POPOL VUH.

Izbet Sarteh a small Early Iron Age (12th–11th century BC) village in the western foothills of central Israel. Israeli excavations in the 1970s exposed a large proportion of the village, uncovering remains of three distinct phases. The earliest village was arranged as a circle of rooms enclosing a central courtyard containing multiple storage pits. This kind of circular arrangement around an open space is often considered a typical village plan of this period, when the material culture associated with the Israelites took shape in Palestine. The second phase, belonging to the late 11th century BC, was a more open scatter of small buildings and silos around a larger central building. A sherd incised with five lines of writing (including the alphabet) in proto-CANAANITE script was found in one of these silos. The final phase was a brief reuse of the second-phase central building.

Izmir a city on the west coast of Turkey. The earliest settlement dates to the 3rd millennium BC. The ARCHAIC city lay at modern Bayrakli, where a temple of Athena has been found. The Roman state AGORA, including a basilica, has been uncovered. In the HELLENISTIC period the city seems to have been a centre for the production of terracotta figurines.

Jabrud or **Yabrud** a group of three prehistoric rock-shelter sites in Syria excavated by A. Rust, producing Palaeolithic, NATUFIAN and Neolithic occupation levels and giving its name to the Palaeolithic Jabrudian industry. Typical Jabrudian tool-kits contain scrapers made on thick flakes with unfaceted striking platforms associated with Upper Palaeolithic-style blades, and often yield many bifaces. The Jabrudian dates to *c.*150,000 BP, and is a kind of final ACHEULIAN.

jacal see ADOBE.

jade a reddish-brown, green or whitish hard, semi-precious stone (NEPHRITE, JADEITE) used in East Asia from the Neolithic period onwards (see HONGSHAN, LIANGZHU) for ornamental and ritual objects (see BI, ZONG, MAGATAMA). It cannot be cut or flaked but must be worked through abrasion. See also MANCHENG.

jadeite a stone carved by MESOAMERICANS into ornaments and statuary. The OLMEC are widely known for their jadeite carvings, which include masks and WERE-JAGUARS. Jadeite and jadeite objects were traded throughout Mesoamerica, from Olmec times to the Spanish Conquest. Known sources of jadeite include the Balsas Valley in Guerrero and the Motagua River Valley in Guatemala, but a number of sources have not yet been identified. Jadeite had ritual significance, symbolizing water. Mesoamerican nobles were buried with a piece of jadeite in their mouths, representing their heart. Mesoamerican jadeite is often, erroneously, called jade, which does not exist in the region: it varies from colourless to white, green and greenish-blue; emerald to light green stones are considered the most precious. See also GREENSTONE.

Jaguar Cave **1** a cave in Tennessee, USA, containing aboriginal footprints in wet clay. A radiocarbon date on associated torch charcoal of approximately 4700 BP is the earliest evidence of a visit to a deep cave in North America.
2 a cave-site in Idaho, USA, dating to the 9th and 10th millennia BC, which is important for its very early evidence of the dog.

Jamestown the site of the first permanent English settlement in America, founded in Tidewater, Virginia, in AD 1607. Archaeological excavations at the site added immensely to the existing historical documentation on early colonial life. See also MARTIN'S HUNDRED.

Janisławice a single Mesolithic burial with numerous grave-goods from central Poland, dated to *c.*5500 BC during the ATLANTIC climatic period. Janisławice is the type-site of the Janisławice culture, the late Mesolithic group inhabiting the GLACIAL outwash of eastern-Central Europe. Assemblages of the Janisławice culture typically contain raw materials from distant sources, especially CHOCOLATE FLINT.

Jankovich a prehistoric cave-site located near the River Danube in northern-central Hungary. Artifacts and faunal remains are buried in rubble and 'cave earth' deposits. The lower cultural layer yielded a Middle Palaeolithic assemblage ('Jankovichian'), containing bifacial foliates and sidescrapers and associated primarily with remains of cave bear. The overlying cultural layer contains an Upper Palaeolithic assemblage (probably GRAVETTIAN) associated primarily with remains of reindeer. Neolithic and Bronze Age artifacts were found in the uppermost level and floor of the cave. Jankovich was excavated by Hillebrand in 1913–25, VÉRTES in 1956, and others.

Janse, Olaf R. T. (1895–1985) a Swedish archaeologist who worked in France, Indochina and the Philippines. He excavated DONG SON and many early HAN sites in northern Vietnam.

Japan Japan has a history of conducting Western-style archaeology since 1872, with the first stratigraphic excavation carried out at KOU in 1919. The 1872 excavations of OMORI shell mound defined JOMON pottery (of the Jomon period, *c.*10,000–300 BC), and soon thereafter YAYOI pottery (of the Yayoi period, *c.*300 BC–AD 300) was discovered at Yayoi-cho, Tokyo. The KOFUN period (AD 300–710), known to the early historic NARA court by its imperial mausolea such as OJIN and NINTOKU, was the period of state formation and urbanization, with

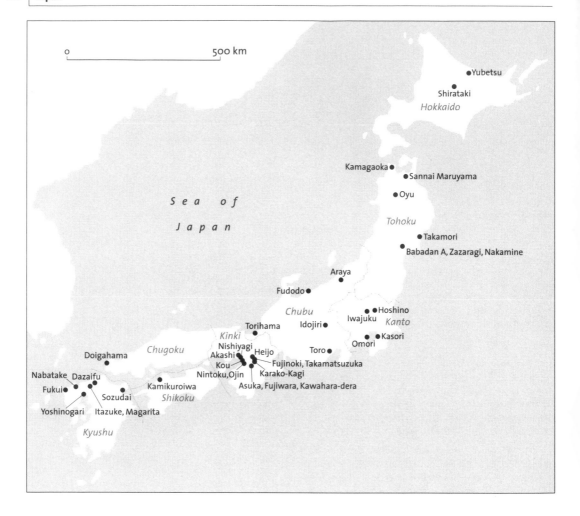

successive capitals established at ASUKA, FUJIWARA and finally HEIJO with its diplomatic outpost of DAZAIFU.

The Palaeolithic was a postwar discovery, at IWAJUKU in 1949. Excavations at SOZUDAI resulted in early dates proposed for the occupation of the Japanese Islands, and HOSHINO provided a standard Palaeolithic chronology and tool typology. Unique tool types (ARAYA burins) and techniques (YUBETSU microblades) are regional characteristics. Dates for the Palaeolithic are constantly being pushed back, as at BABADAN A, ZAZARAGI and NAKAMINE, bringing the initial occupation of Japan close to the HOMO *erectus* occupation of China. However, because of the general non-survival of bone and other organics in Japan – MINATOGAWA, AKASHI and NISHIYAGI being the exceptions – it is not yet known if *H. erectus* existed there.

The beginning of the Jomon period is marked by discoveries of pottery and PORTABLE ART within micro-

blade and Late Palaeolithic subsistence systems, as at FUKUI and KAMIKUROIWA. Early horticulture is attested at TORIHAMA and thought to have supported the Middle Jomon mountain culture, exemplified by IDOJIRI. However, the period was generally one of hunting, gathering and fishing – as known at large shellmound sites such as KASORI. A rich material culture, as in the late KAMEGAOKA culture, focused on personal ornamentation and ritual (cf. OYU stone circle), but rich burials indicating social stratification are unknown. Large house structures as at FUDODO are interpreted as communal work places or incipient chief's houses.

The Yayoi period is characterized by the adoption of wet rice agriculture (known at MAGARITA, NABATAKE and ITAZUKE) and metal working. The cemetery at DOIGAHAMA reveals that these innovations were accompanied by migration from the Korean Peninsula. The use of bronzes – shown at TORO to be unknown in eastern

Japan – was confined to western Japan, where contacts with the peninsula were maintained. Stimulated by the Chinese presence on the Korean Peninsula from 108 BC, local chieftains emerged to rule small 'countries' within Japan, with moated and/or palisaded village sites (YOSHI-NOGARI, KARAKO) as central settlements.

Mounded tomb construction began in the mid 3rd century AD, with a Kofun period elite establishing relations with emerging peninsular states in the 4th century. The adoption of peninsular prestige goods from the 5th century is indicated in the grave-goods, as at FUJINOKI, and in tomb chamber decoration, as at TAKA-MATSUZUKA. The adoption of Buddhism from the mid 6th century caused temple-building, as at KAWAHARA-DERA, to replace mounded-tomb construction. In the 7th century, Japan turned its attention to China as the model for administrative development.

Japanese periodization the artificial classification of prehistoric and historic eras used by archaeologists and historians for Japan. The major chronological divisions after the Palaeolithic are: JOMON (10,000–300 BC); YAYOI (300 BC–AD 300); KOFUN (300–710); Nara (710–94); Heian (794–1183); Medieval (= Kamakura, Muromachi, Momoyama, 1183–1603); Feudal (Edo/Tokugawa, 1603–1868); Meiji (1868–1914); Taisho (1914–25); Showa (1925–88); Heisei (1989–present). See also NEOLITHIC, BRONZE AGE, IRON AGE.

Jarlshof a settlement in the Shetland Islands, Scotland, named after a house in a Walter Scott novel. Preserved by wind-blown sand, it was uncovered by violent storms in the 19th century AD. Early 2nd millennium BC houses of SKARA BRAE type were followed by Bronze Age occupation, and then Iron Age structures – SOUTERRAINS, WHEEL-HOUSES and a BROCH. There was a VIKING farmstead in the 9th century AD, and a medieval fortified farm.

Jarmo a small ACERAMIC NEOLITHIC to ceramic Neolithic village site in the Zagros foothills of northwestern Iraq that was a central focus of Robert Braidwood's interdisciplinary project on the beginnings of domestication in the 1950s. Although now superseded by subsequent work, the Jarmo project largely defined the task of explaining the origins of food production. The site dates to the later 7th millennium BC, and exhibits many of the characteristics now recorded in other prehistoric localities of the 'hilly flanks' of the Zagros.

Jastorf culture an Iron Age culture of the southern Baltic region during the late HALLSTATT period, extending from Lower Saxony through Pomerania, representing some of the earliest iron metallurgy of the North European Plain.

Java Man remains of HOMO *erectus* (once *Pithecanthropus erectus*) found in 1891 by DUBOIS at TRINIL in Java, probably dating to *c*.1 million–500,000 BP, less robust than the *H. erectus* of JETIS (MOJOKERTO child). See also SANGIRAN.

Jayavarman II a Khmer ruler (*c*.AD 802–50) who unified many petty kingdoms and founded the KHMER empire based at ANGKOR.

Jayavarman VII the last great Khmer ruler (AD 1181–*c*.1218), who extended the empire from Vietnam and westwards to the borders of Burma. He imposed BUDDHISM as the main state cult, and was the builder of ANGKOR Thom, the BAYON and many other immense religious monuments, leading to the decline of the KHMER empire after his death.

Jażdżewski, Konrad (1908–85) a leading figure in Polish archaeology during the mid 20th century. After the Second World War he served as director of the Museum of Archaeology and Ethnography in Łódz. He excavated sites from many different periods, including BRZEŚĆ KUJAWSKI (Neolithic) and ŁĘG PIEKARSKI (Iron Age).

Jebel Irhoud a site in Morocco containing a nearly complete skull, a skull cap and a partial mandible, once thought to be NEANDERTHAL, but now regarded as archaic HOMO *sapiens*, together with LEVALLOISO-MOUSTERIAN artifacts, dated by ESR to at least 106,000 bp.

Jebel Moya a mountain in the southern Gezira of Sudan with many graves, and large settlements based on mixed farming. Occupation at about 4000 BP has pottery like that of the NUBIAN C-GROUP. Later occupation has MEROITIC traits.

Jebel Uweinat a mountain in southeastern Libya near the frontier where Sudan, Libya and Egypt meet. It is rich in rock art depicting domestic animals and was a focal point for Neolithic herders around 6200 BP. Of particular interest are depictions of giraffes tethered and led by halters.

Jefferson, Thomas (1743–1826) an early president of the United States of America, famous in archaeology for what amounts to one of the first scientific and controlled excavations in the discipline. In 1784, Jefferson excavated a BURIAL MOUND on his Virginia estate, in order to recover specific information on its construction and use.

Jelling one of the most remarkable groups of monuments in Denmark, including the two largest barrows in that country – 78 m (85 yds) across and 11 m (36 ft) high, traditionally seen as the resting places of the last pagan monarchs, Gorm (died *c*.AD 950) and his queen Thyra. They may have been buried together in one mound, since the other had no burial chamber. Between them stands a Romanesque church, with two very fine RUNE-stones outside, one of which bears the oldest crucifixion scene in Denmark. There are also fifty stones forming a boat-shaped outline.

Jemdet Nasr a site near KISH in the northern end of the MESOPOTAMIAN alluvial plain, where Stephen Langdon's excavations in the 1920s revealed a style of painted pottery which now defines the Jemdet Nasr period in the southern Mesopotamian sequence. This period (equivalent to the URUK III of the EANNA SOUNDING sequence) is dated to the last few centuries of the 4th millennium and represents a basic continuation of the preceding late Uruk period, with some important developments, most notably in the application of writing to lists (professions, places, objects). The site of Jemdet Nasr itself was occupied from late Uruk to EARLY DYNASTIC I times; a substantial building of Jemdet Nasr date may represent the earliest-discovered palace in southern Mesopotamia. A re-examination of the site underway in the late 1980s was cut short by the political problems of 1990.

Jenderam Hilir an open-air Neolithic site in Selangor, Malaya, which has yielded many tripod bowls like those from BAN KAO, Thailand, and dating to c.2000 BC.

Jenné-jeno or **Djenne** a large mound of occupation debris on the Inland Niger River Delta, about 3 km (1.9 miles) southeast of Jenné in Mali. It was first occupied by iron-using herders and fishermen in about 250 bc, and expanded into a walled town with craft specialists and an economy based on herding, fishing and the cultivation of millet, sorghum and African rice, as well as craft specialists and traders, between ad 300 and 800. During its height in about ad 800, it was encircled by a mud-brick wall 4 m (13 ft) or more high and almost 2 km (1.2 miles) in circumference, and, together with smaller neighbouring sites within a 1 km (0.6 mile) radius, formed a population concentration of some 27,000 people. It was abandoned by at least ad 1468, probably about ad 1400, apparently when the economic centre moved to a new neighbouring site on which modern Jenné stands.

Jenness, Diamond (1886–1969) a pioneering Canadian ethnologist and archaeologist, who established much of the groundwork for understanding the archaeology of the Arctic. In 1925 Jenness first described the DORSET culture, which pre-dated the THULE culture.

Jennings, Jesse (1909–97) a North American archaeologist whose work concentrated on the Southwest and Great Basin. His excavations at DANGER CAVE, augmented by detailed ethnographic modelling, provided the essential framework for understanding Great Basin prehistory.

Jerf el-Ahmar a large village of well-preserved circular and rectangular houses on the Middle Euphrates in north-eastern Syria, which is destined to be drowned by a dam. It dates to the PRE-POTTERY NEOLITHIC A (9th millennium BC), locally known as Mureybitian, after MUREYBIT. Excavations in the 1990s by Danièle Stordeur have uncovered about thirty houses, including some monumental subterranean dwellings, and a rich flint and bone industry, as well as figurines of humans and animals, decorated stone vessels and long polished-stone batons. The site was occupied at a time of transition from hunting and gathering to agriculture; its occupants ate mostly cereals and legumes, and cultivated at least some of these plants. A series of stone plaques bear schematic depictions and abstract symbols which epigraphers consider to be 'pictograms', 4,000 or 5,000 years earlier than those of the URUK period, and forming an intermediate stage in an evolution from Palaeolithic art to true writing such as CUNEIFORM.

Jericho (*Arabic* Tell es-Sultan) a 4 ha (10 acre) site in the Jordan Valley, Israel, chiefly excavated by GARSTANG in 1930–36 and KENYON in 1952–8, with a long and virtually uninterrupted sequence from the NATUFIAN period to the LATE BRONZE AGE. Kenyon's work provided information on the origins of food production (with botanical and faunal evidence of early domesticates) and the subsequent developments towards urban life in Palestine. The site is famous for its Neolithic settlement: during the PRE-POTTERY NEOLITHIC A phase, there were stone fortifications including a large tower against the inner face of the town wall. The most notable feature of PPNB Jericho are the PLASTERED SKULLS. During the MIDDLE BRONZE AGE Jericho was defended by a GLACIS, but little archaeological evidence has survived of the Late Bronze Age to corroborate the biblical account of its destruction by Joshua and the ISRAELITES; in any case, any falling walls were more probably caused by one of the area's frequent earthquakes.

Jerusalem a city in the Judaean hills, Israel, which was occupied for thousands of years and which has been excavated virtually continuously since the 1860s. Comparatively little remains of ancient Jerusalem, chiefly because of the repeated destructions suffered by the city (e.g. that of Titus in AD 70) and later BYZANTINE and Islamic overbuilding. The first major construction at Jerusalem seems to have been the stone fortifications of the LATE BRONZE AGE. Jerusalem was captured by the ISRAELITES under David in c.996 BC and extended to the north by SOLOMON, who built a temple and palace in an area later overbuilt by the Herodian temple platform, and by Hezekiah, whose water tunnel is still visible. Jerusalem was patronized by the Byzantine emperors because of its Christian associations and by Islamic caliphs as a holy city. Most of the walls to be seen at Jerusalem are the work of Suleiman the Magnificent (AD 1538–41) on top of Herodian and Roman foundations, while the octagonal 'Dome of the Rock' (AD 685–92) is the most striking of the Islamic buildings in Jerusalem.

Jerzmanowice see NIETOPERZOWA CAVE.

Jerzmanowician an early Upper Palaeolithic industry of Poland characterized by bifacial foliates, retouched blades and denticulates. The Jerzmanowician was defined by Chmielewski in 1961 on the basis of artifacts from NIETOPERZOWA CAVE.

jet lignitic fossil wood that is dense, hard and black. An ability to accept a strong polish and workability made it desirable in jewellery manufacture. Jet is found in geologically young shales and other fine-grained rocks.

Jetis or **Djetis** a geological formation (bed) along the Brantas River in eastern Java which has yielded remains of early Pleistocene (pre-TRINIL) fauna apparently adapted to open forest environment, and HOMO *erectus* remains referred to as the MOJOKERTO child; date *c*.1.5 million years BP and before.

Jevišovice a stratified late Neolithic site in Moravia of the FUNNEL BEAKER and BADEN cultures. Although excavated in the early part of the 20th century, Jevišovice continues to provide the basic chronological yardstick for the late Neolithic and ENEOLITHIC in this part of the Carpathian Basin.

Jhukar a site in the Sind, Pakistan, excavated by N. G. Majumdar in the 1920s, that gives its name to the Late HARAPPAN culture of the region, also represented at AMRI and CHANHU-DARO. The Jhukar is characterized by considerable continuity with the Mature Harappan in its pottery but a loss of many other typical Harappan elements (notably writing, seals, urbanism). At the same time, several metal forms appear that relate to northeastern Iran and Central Asia (see SIBRI).

Jia Lanpo (1908–2001) Chinese archaeologist best known for his work at the site of ZHOUKOUDIAN, where he directed excavations from 1935; he also investigated other important sites such as DINGCUN, LANTIAN and SHIYU. He was a strong believer that the modern Chinese could be traced back to their Pleistocene ancestors in China.

Jincamocco a MIDDLE HORIZON site located in the central highlands of Peru. The site comprises a large rectangular enclosure of HUARI style architecture, measuring 128 by 256 m (140 by 280 yds), and an additional 12 ha (30 acres) of rectilinear architecture. Excavations by Katharina Schreiber indicate that the site functioned as a regional administrative centre of the Huari empire (AD 750–900), and that the empire extensively reorganized the region in which it was located in order to provide centralized political control, and to increase local production of maize.

Jingdezhen [Ching-te-chen] a city in Jiangxi Province, China, forming the focus of an ancient kiln works centre. Porcelains were produced here from the end of the Tang Dynasty (late 10th century AD) until 1911. Before the 14th century, the Song and Yuan courts (see CHINESE DYNASTIES) were supplied with the best products from the larger kilns; then imperial kilns were built for the direct supply of the Ming court. The type of kiln used was the sloping long kiln until the Qing Dynasty, when an egg-shaped kiln was invented. Documents of the 13th century count 300 kilns in production. Compare STONEWARE, YUE, CELADON.

Jinmium a rockshelter in the Northern Territory of Australia. In 1996 the excavators claimed dates of at least 116,000 years for the oldest human occupation, based on THERMOLUMINESCENCE. These startling results, which more than doubled the known antiquity of human occupation in Australia, were received with scepticism and it has since been shown that the original TL dates were incorrect. OSL and radiocarbon dates suggest that the site is actually less than 20,000 years old.

Jinniushan [Chin-niu-shan] a site in Liaoning Province, China, dating to the Early and Late Palaeolithic. The lithics in the lower strata, including scrapers and bipolar flakes, resemble those from ZHOUKOUDIAN locality 1, and the upper levels have yielded HOMO *sapiens* remains. These fossils have transitional characteristics between *H. erectus* and modern Asians and comprise primary evidence for refuting the 'Eve hypothesis' of population replacement by incoming *H. sapiens sapiens*. These remains of an archaic *H. sapiens* comprise a well-preserved skull and other bones; analysis of associated animal teeth by ELECTRON SPIN RESONANCE and URANIUM SERIES DATING has produced results of 195–165,000 years ago and *c*.200,000 years ago respectively, making these the oldest known *H. sapiens* remains in China. See also MABA.

Jomon the POSTGLACIAL period of hunting and gathering in Japan (10,000–300 BC), divided into six phases: Incipient (10,000–7500 BC), Earliest (7500–5000), Early (5000–3500), Middle (3500–2500/2000), Late (2500/2000–1000) and Final (1000–300). The period coincides with the existence of Jomon pottery (see FUKUI Cave),

JOMON pottery vessel, Japan.

succeeded by YAYOI pottery in 300 BC (see JAPANESE PERIODIZATION). It is characterized by marine resource utilization and settled village living from Early Jomon; the development of widespread trading networks and ritual development in Middle Jomon in the CHUBU and KANTO regions; collapse of settlement in these regions in Late Jomon; and the development of deep-sea fishing communities in TOHOKU in Final Jomon. Also, during the last millennium BC, rice agriculture was adopted by northern Kyushu Jomon groups, setting the stage for the Yayoi expansion (see ITAZUKE). To what extent horticulture was practised in other Jomon phases and areas is uncertain (but see TORIHAMA). See also FUDODO, IDOJIRI, OYU, KAMIKUROIWA, KAMEGAOKA, KASORI, OMORI, SANNAI MARUYAMA. The PALAEOASIATIC Jomon peoples are morphologically related to the ancestors of the modern AINU, also of Palaeoasiatic stock. The term Jomon means 'cord-marked'.

Jones-Miller a HELL GAP COMPLEX site located in northeastern Colorado, USA. The site is a KILL- and/or butchering SITE. A POSTHOLE and associated artifacts at the site have been interpreted as the remains of a 'medicine post' similar to those used by some historic Plains tribes as locations or offerings to ensure a successful kill.

Jordanów or **Jordanów Śląski** a cemetery of a late phase of the LENGYEL culture in Silesia in southwestern Poland, excavated by Seger at the beginning of the 20th century when the locality was known as Jordansmühl. (Jordanów, and the regional group of the Lengyel culture named after it, are often mistakenly called 'Jordanova' in some literature.) Of particular importance are the Jordanów copper ornaments, which include binocular spirals and beads resembling those from BRZEŚĆ KUJAWSKI and OSŁONKI. These copper ornaments are among the earliest-known from north of the Carpathians.

Jorvik see YORK.

Jorwe a small single-period site, where excavations by H. D. Sankalia provided the initial definition of the material culture of Maharashtra, western-central India, during the second half of the 2nd millennium BC. Together with the evidence of additional excavated sites, the Jorwe culture is characterized by a fine black-on-red ware decorated with painted registers of geometric mo-

tifs, a rich copper tool industry in addition to equipment in stone, the cultivation of barley, wheat and various legumes, the keeping of cattle, buffalo, sheep and goat, as well as hunting.

Juan knife a long flake with abrupt blunting retouch along one margin. Ethnographic specimens have hand-grips of skin or resin and are documented from western, central and eastern Queensland, Australia. They are very rare in archaeological contexts and are only known from the last few hundred years.

Judds Cavern see WARGATA MINA.

Judeideh, Tell a 30 m (100 ft) high mound at the eastern edge of the AMUQ plain in southeastern Turkey. Excavations by the University of Chicago during the 1930s exposed large areas of Iron Age architecture on the mound summit, while work on the mound slopes and base traced occupation into ceramic Neolithic times. The latter evidence provided a major part of the Amuq sequence.

jue **[chueh]** a bronze wine vessel characteristic of the SHANG bronze tradition of China (see CHINESE DYNASTIES), and used for heating wine in ancestral rituals.

Jutes a historically known Germanic people of the 5th and 6th centuries AD who arrived in England alongside ANGLO-SAXONS and other continental groups, but whose archaeological traces are elusive. St Bede the Venerable (673–735) in his *Ecclesiastical History of the English Nation* wrote: 'Those who came over were of the three most powerful nations of Germany – Saxons, Angles and Jutes. From the Jutes are descended the people of Kent, and of the Isle of Wight, and those also in the province of the West Saxons who are to this day called Jutes, seated opposite to the Isle of Wight.' The location of the Jutish homeland is controversial. Many associate it with Jutland, although it is probable that many of the Jutes left this area and settled among FRISIANS, FRANKS and Saxons before crossing to England.

Juxtlahuaca Cave a cave-site in Guerrero, Mexico, known for its polychrome cave paintings in the OLMEC style. Dating to c.3,000 years ago, these paintings are some of the oldest documented in the New World, and are located nearly 2 km (1 mile) inside the mountain.

K

K2 a LATE IRON AGE site in the Northern Province of South Africa, which accumulated to a depth of more than 6 m (20 ft) during the period between about ad 1030 and 1220. K2 has given its name to the southern FACIES of the initial phase of the LEOPARD'S KOPJE complex. It dominated the Limpopo Valley, developed specialized craftsmen in bone and ivory working, and traded these products locally and with the East African coast, in exchange for items such as glass beads. More than seventy human skeletons were previously described as of KHO-ISAN physical type, but are now considered Negroid. At about AD 1200, the centre of the state moved to the nearby MAPUNGUBWE Hill (see BAMBANDYANALO).

Kabáh a MAYA late CLASSIC centre in western-central Yucatán, Mexico, that peaked from the 8th to the 10th century AD and was then virtually abandoned. A paved causeway (*sacbe*) runs from the arch at Kabáh to the PUUC city of UXMAL. Although it was one of the larger cities of the region, little is known of Kabáh beyond its ceremonial architecture. Its most famous construction is the Kodz Pop, a range-type building whose façade is covered with long-nosed masks. The site was first explored by various archaeologists through the Peabody Museum, Harvard University.

Kabambian an Iron Age group which succeeds the KIS-ALIAN in the southeastern Democratic Republic of Congo from the 14th to the 18th centuries AD. Its development is linked to the growth of interregional trade in croisettes (cross-shaped copper ingots) as well as the expansion of long-distance trade with the East African coast.

Kabri a MIDDLE BRONZE AGE (c.2000–1550 BC) centre on the coastal plain, north of MOUNT CARMEL in Israel. As in many other settlements of this period, massive ramparts surrounded the 32 ha (80 acre) city. Excavation inside the walls has uncovered remains of the palace, one hall and corridor of which were ornamented with frescoes that resemble MINOAN art and may be the work of foreign craftsmen. Kabri also contains the remains of a late Neolithic settlement.

Kabwe see BROKEN HILL.

Kadero an early Neolithic site on the eastern side of the Nile River in central Sudan, some 20 km (12.5 miles) north of Khartoum, consisting of two settlement MIDDENs and a separate burial area covering about 3 ha (7.4 acres), radiocarbon dated to between 5960 and 5030 bp. Large quantities of bones of domestic stock, especially cattle, were recovered. Impressions of sorghum and other tropical grasses found on pottery indicate the processing of these cereals, but it is not known whether they were domesticated. Most of the substantial collection of grindstones found are thought to have been used for purposes other than preparing grain, such as grinding ochre or fashioning bone and stone tools. Some of the fifty-five human burials contained rich grave-goods including stone mace heads, palettes, necklaces of carnelian beads, ivory bracelets, pottery and quantities of ochre, and suggest the existence of elite social groups (see ESH SHAH-EINAB, KHARTOUM NEOLITHIC).

Kadesh (TELL Nebi Mend) a site on the River Orontes in Syria, excavated by Pézard in 1921–2 and by Parr in the 1970s. Kadesh, being in a strategic position, was a relatively important city during the LATE BRONZE AGE, and was the site of the inconclusive battle between RAMESSES II and the HITTITES in c.1275 BC.

Kafiavana a rockshelter in the NEW GUINEA HIGH-LANDS, excavated by Peter White. The deposits span the last 11,000 years and contain amorphous stone artifacts, bone tools and a rich faunal assemblage. Marine-shell ornaments and ground axe-adzes appear c.9000 bp, and pig remains occur from about 6500 bp.

Kaghanate or **Khanate** (*Turkic* 'kagan': prince, ruler) a name for the early medieval nomad states (empires) of the Old-Turks (late 6th century to early 8th century AD), of the UIGHURS (AD 744–840), of the KHAZARS (late 7th century to mid 10th century) and others. The biggest was the Old-Turks empire. The First Turkic Kaghanate was founded in AD 552 after the Turks' victory over the Jou-Jans. The Turks carried out a dynamic campaign of conquest, and the frontiers of the Kaghanate extended to Manchuria in the east and the Amu-Darya River (Oxus) to the west. Internal strife within the Turkic aristocracy eventually caused, in the final 6th to early 7th centuries, a partition of the empire into two enemy states: the Western and the Eastern Turkic Kaghanates. The Eastern was conquered in 744–5 by the Uighurs, and the Western was ravaged in 740. The Turkic Kaghanate played an important role in the consolidation of the Turkic population in Eurasia, and contributed to the development of ethnic groups which became a base for the modern Turkish-language peoples.

Kahun see EL-LAHUN.

kaizuka literally 'SHELL MIDDEN' in Japanese; a characteristic feature of the JOMON and early YAYOI periods.

Kakovatos the site of a MYCENAEAN settlement in Messenia, Greece, which DÖRPFELD erroneously identified as the Homeric PYLOS. The three THOLOS tombs which he excavated do, however, suggest that this was a regional centre.

Kalabsha the original site in Egypt of an unfinished Graeco-Roman temple dedicated to the Nubian god Mandulis, and re-erected at ASWAN during the NUBIAN RESCUE CAMPAIGN.

Kalambo an Early Iron Age group in northern Zambia, with distinctive pottery, which takes its name from a large 4th-century AD village site at KALAMBO FALLS. Several deep pits at this site are thought to have been graves, although no bones have been preserved.

Kalambo Falls a Zambian site near the southeastern corner of Lake Tanganyika, excavated in the 1950s by J. Desmond Clark. Deposits of ancient lakes have preserved traces of occupation spanning the Stone and Iron Ages. The earliest remains recovered are late ACHEULIAN, dating to the late Middle Pleistocene, but older material may lie below the modern water-table. The late Acheulian layers are of particular interest, since many contain plant remains and worked wood (see KALAMBO, KAPOSWA).

Kalanay a cave-site in Masbate, central Philippines, with metal period jar burials of the late 1st millennium BC or later, which has given its name to a pottery complex or 'culture' thought to date to c.400 BC–AD 1500, and exhibiting some similarities with the SA HUYNH pottery of coastal Vietnam.

Kalasasaya see TIAHUANACO.

Kalavasos a site in southern CYPRUS that has, since 1976, been the focus of a series of excavations directed by Todd. At Tenta there is an ACERAMIC NEOLITHIC 1 (7th-millennium BC) settlement surrounded by an enclosure wall. The houses were circular two-storey structures built of stone and mud-brick. Human figures were painted in red ochre on the wall of one house. Ayious, a CHALCOLITHIC (early 4th-millennium BC) site, consists of a warren-like arrangement of pits, some of which were connected by tunnels. Their function is obscure but may have involved specialized processing activities. Ayios Dhimitrios, occupied c.1325–1225 BC, is one of the most extensive Late Cypriot towns. A large ASHLAR structure is thought to have served as an administrative centre and a number of rich CHAMBER TOMBS have been discovered.

Kalemba a rockshelter near Chadiza in southeastern Zambia, containing a succession of Stone Age industries, including a MIDDLE STONE AGE sequence of BAMBATAN succeeded by TSHANGULAN material, LATER STONE AGE NACHIKUFAN I collections, and a series of fragmentary human skeletons post-dating 8000 bp, which have features generally falling within the range of variation of recent Negro people.

Kalhu an imperial ASSYRIAN city on the River Tigris, south of NINEVEH, Iraq, best known for the extensive excavations on the citadel (Nimrud) and arsenal ('Fort Shalmaneser') conducted by LAYARD, MALLOWAN and others. The oldest discovered materials at the site are NINEVITE 5 pottery sherds at Nimrud, and Middle Assyrian texts and materials establish the existence of a town in the later 2nd millennium BC. It was established as the imperial seat by AŠŠURNAṢIRPAL II (883–859 BC), and later Assyrian kings also built extensively in the city; Sargon II (721–705 BC) moved the imperial seat to KHORSABAD, and after this time Kalhu was a provincial capital. The rectangular city wall enclosed about 360 ha (890 acres), with Nimrud and 'Fort Shalmaneser' set in corners of the wall and separated from the rest of the city as walled compounds containing a massive temple, palace and other administrative buildings. The excavations of the Assyrian city produced abundant monumental art, important administrative archives, a large corpus of carved ivories, an example of a folding ivory 'book' with beeswax-coated leaves on which is written a CUNEIFORM text, and many other small objects. Recent Iraqi work revealed several intact royal graves of Sargon's time, containing a spectacular array of gold jewellery, glass and other objects within vaulted CHAMBER TOMBS. Later post-Assyrian occupation, on a reduced scale, continued until the HELLENISTIC period.

Kalibangan a major site on the extinct Ghaggar/Hakra River in northern Rajastan, India, containing both Early and Mature HARAPPAN settlements. The Mature Harappan settlement lies in two separate walled sections, covering some 15 ha (37 acres), in the familiar Harappan urban form. The Early Harappan levels (spanning the first half of the 3rd millennium BC) occur below the Mature Harappan citadel. The pottery of this earlier walled place, though showing some similarities with the KOT DIJI style, is characteristic of this region. As in other regional expressions of Early Harappan, some formal antecedents to Mature Harappan ceramics occur. Similar pottery occurs further east in Haryana, India. Kalibangan is also well known for the plough scars discovered outside the settlement, and dated to this Early Harappan phase.

Kalina Point see GOMBE POINT.

Kalomo a variously interpreted Late Iron Age facies or tradition of southern Zambia, variously dated from the end of the 9th or early 11th centuries ad, with 'late' Kalomo material identified by some in mid 12th- and 14th-century ad contexts, best known from Isamu Pati. Many Kalomo villages were repeatedly reoccupied, resulting in accumulations of deposit up to 3 m (10 ft) thick. Circular houses were arranged around open areas apparently used as cattle byres. There was some iron-working, especially of items like arrowheads and knives, while copper for bangles was obtained by trade. Cattle and small stock outnumber hunted animals, and sorghum was cultivated. Glass beads as well as conus and cowrie shells indicate contact with East African coastal trade.

Kalumpang a Neolithic site in western-central Sulawesi which, together with the related site Minanga Sipakko, has produced undated late Neolithic assemblages including POLISHED STONE ADZES, ground slate projectile points, possible stone reaping knives and pottery, some aspects of which have been related to the Taiwanese Neolithic and to LAPITA wares of Oceania.

Kalundu a southern Zambian site which has given its name to an Early Iron Age group or tradition represented on the Batoka Plateau of southern Zambia, associated with occupation mounds up to 3 m (10 ft) high, dating from the 5th–9th centuries ad, also synonymous with the Western Stream of the CHIFUMBAZE COMPLEX. Faunal remains from Kalundu show the gradual replacement of hunted with domestic animals. Small numbers of iron and copper objects were found, but no glass beads, although cowrie shells indicate at least indirect contact with the East African coast during this period.

Kamabai a rockshelter in the Guinea Highlands of Sierra Leone with three cultural horizons dated between 4500 and 600 BP, showing a sequence from the LATER STONE AGE through the 'Guinea Neolithic' to the Iron Age.

Kamares a MINOAN cave sanctuary on the slopes of Mount Ida in CRETE. The finds from the cave included Middle Minoan pottery with white, red, crimson and orange decoration on a dark ground, which became known as Kamares ware.

Kambuja the KHMER state centred on Cambodia, the pre-14th-century phase of which is often referred to as ANGKOR. The name is borrowed from SANSKRIT.

Kamegaoka a waterlogged Final JOMON site in Aomori Prefecture, Japan, which has yielded abundant wooden, ceramic and basketry vessels, many painted with lacquer; stone and bone personal ornaments; ceramic figurines and engraved plaques, etc. The Final Jomon assemblage of sophisticated ritual and finely made objects spread throughout TOHOKU is often assigned to the 'Kamegaoka culture' but is also known as the 'Obora culture'.

Kamegg a Neolithic enclosure and settlement of the LENGYEL culture in eastern Austria dating to the early part of the 5th millennium BC. The enclosure consists of two concentric ditches with diameters of 140 m (153 yds) and 76 m (83 yds) respectively. Four breaks in the ditches, located approximately at the cardinal points, provide access to the interior of the enclosure. The outer ditch appears not to have been finished completely. As with contemporaneous Lengyel enclosures, such as the one at TĚŠETICE-KYJOVICE in Moravia, this site may have been planned as a ritual location for settlements in the surrounding countryside but never completed. Afterwards, it seems to have served as an ordinary Neolithic settlement.

kamennaya baba (*Russian*, 'stone woman') a collective term for anthropomorphous stone statues of the EURASIAN STEPPES. It is a folk name that was borrowed by archaeologists in the 19th century, when the statues became a subject of special scientific interest. Nowadays the term 'stone statues' is used more often. The anthropomorphous statues of the Eurasian steppes belong to different cultures and periods. The most ancient are statues of the YAMNAYA culture (northern Black Sea littoral, Crimea) and of the OKUNEVO culture (MINUSINSK BASIN), dating to the Early Bronze Age. The so-called DEER-STONES were erected in the Late Bronze Age and the Early Iron Age over a vast territory (Mongolia, Trans-Baikal, Tuva, ALTAI, etc.). The Early Iron Age also saw related SCYTHIAN statues (western and northern Black Sea littoral, Crimea, northern Caucasus) and sculptures of the Scythian-Sarmatian period from the Ustyurt Plateau in western Kazakhstan (see also BAITE). The most numerous are the medieval stone statues of Turkic-language nomads: those of the Old-Turks (Mongolia, Tuva, Altai, Xinjang, Kazakhstan and Kyrgyzstan) and those of the POLOVCIANS (steppes of southern Russia and of southern Ukraine).

Kamennaya Mogila a Mesolithic or ACERAMIC NEOLITHIC site in southern Ukraine, near the coast of the Sea of Azov. Claims have been made for the occurrence of very early domesticated cattle and sheep/goat at Kamennaya Mogila, but these have been disputed on grounds of uncertain dating. Situated on a river floodplain, the settlement resembles those of the BUG-DNIESTER culture (e.g. at SOROKI).

Kamid al Loz, Tell a 6 ha (15 acre) site in the Biqa' Valley of Lebanon, investigated by German groups between the 1960s and 1980s, that represents the seat of a petty state during the LATE BRONZE AGE, the Kumidi mentioned in the AMARNA archive. The archaeological work traces a settlement history from the late Neolithic to BYZANTINE times. Through most of this sequence, Kamid al Loz was an unfortified village. The exposed MIDDLE BRONZE AGE and Late Bronze Age levels, in contrast, indicate a walled town within which were significant palace and temple constructions as well as domestic architecture. Kumidi lay on both the north-south route through the Biqa' Valley and on the route connecting the Damascus basin with the Mediterranean, a setting that helps explain its strategic importance in periods of competing regional powers during the Bronze Age.

Kamikuroiwa an Incipient JOMON rockshelter site in Ehime Prefecture, Japan, which has yielded early ceramics (10,700 bp) as at FUKUI. Small cobbles bearing incised drawings of female features from Kamikuroiwa are the earliest PORTABLE ART recovered in Japan.

Kamilamba the earliest-known Iron Age tradition in the Upemba Depression of the southeastern Democratic Republic of Congo, dated to about the 6th–8th centuries AD, named after the Kamilamba site where an Iron Age layer succeeds LATER STONE AGE material.

Kaminaljuyú a MAYA centre in the southern highlands of Guatemala, best known for the strong TEOTIHUACÁN influence during the early CLASSIC. Evidence for this influence lies in ceremonial and ritual objects, and in locally produced items with Teotihuacán form and decoration. The relationship between Teotihuacán and Kaminaljuyú was probably commercial and religious. Contacts between central Mexico and Teotihuacán were directed through Kaminaljuyú.

Kaminaljuyú controlled the obsidian production on the Pacific slopes. During the late Classic, Kaminaljuyú shows less evidence of Mexican influence, probably owing to the collapse of Teotihuacán.

Kamoa the first site in Central Africa in which ACHEULIAN material was identified, thus extending the known antiquity of human occupation in this region to the EARLIER STONE AGE. It is located on the banks of the Kamoa River in the southeastern Democratic Republic of Congo and contains a succession of industries from Earlier to LATER STONE AGE. No bone is preserved, but pollen collections have provided information on past environments.

Kampong Sungei Lang the site, near Klang, in peninsular Malaysia, of a metal age 'boat burial', the gravegoods of which include two DONG SON bronze drums, MUTISALAH beads and iron implements (see TULANG MAWAS), dated c.300 BC. Related sites include TEMBELING, Kuala Trengganu (burial with two drums and beads), Kampong Pencu (bronze bell with Dong Son-style decoration) and Klang (bronze drum, three bells, iron hoard). It is probably contemporary with the BERNAM-SUNGKAI slab graves.

Kampong Sungei Mas see ŚRIVIJAYA.

Kanapoi a locality between the Kalabata and Kakurio Rivers southwest of LAKE TURKANA in northern Kenya, which in 1965 yielded a 4 million-year-old early HOMINID humerus of ambiguous genus, and, in 1994, nine dental, cranial and postcranial fossils described as AUSTRALOPITHECUS *anamensis*, the earliest known australopithecine species, dated to 4.2 million years ago (see ALLIA BAY).

Kandahar the capital of ancient Arachosia in southern-central Afghanistan. British excavators in the 1970s traced occupation from the 18th century AD back to the earlier 1st millennium BC. Holding a strategic position on communication routes, Kandahar was an important centre for ACHAEMENID, Greek, MAURYAN, KUSHAN and other powerful kingdoms.

Kaneaki a HEIAU in the MAKAHA VALLEY, Molokai, Hawaii, now reconstructed. One of the few heiau ever excavated, it has been shown to have six construction phases beginning about AD 1460.

Kanem a West African state adjacent to and north of Lake Chad, which became established in the late 1st millennium AD as a result of trade with areas to the north, particularly Tunis, and the establishment of a ruling house which controlled tribute-paying peoples. Under King Salma (AD 1194–1221), the state converted to Islam and mosques were built. After a long period of warfare in which cavalry played an important role, the former Bornu Province southwest of Lake Chad rose to prominence as the new centre of the state in the 16th century AD. See also DAIMA.

Kangaroo Island an island off the South Australian coast which, although uninhabited at European contact, is rich in KARTAN sites attesting to previous Aboriginal occupation. Kartan surface sites on Kangaroo Island are thought to be late Pleistocene and were replaced by an amorphous small tool industry known from Seton Cave. The most recent work at CAPE DU COUEDIC, however, where Kartan material has been found associated with a wider range of artifacts and dated to around 7000 bp, has cast doubt on this interpretation.

Kanish see KÜLTEPE.

Kansai an early medieval administrative district of western-central Japan (see JAPANESE PERIODIZATION) corresponding roughly to the modern KINKI district; often used in discussions of Japanese archaeology.

Kansas see ELSTERIAN.

Kansyore ware a distinctive highly decorated pre-Iron Age pottery which characterizes the Kansyore phase of the Oltome tradition in the Lake Nyanza (formerly Lake

Victoria) basin of East Africa. Dating is problematic, but an age in the last few millennia bc is indicated. See also GOGO FALLS.

Kantarawichai a large late prehistoric/early historic moated settlement (see MOATED SITES) lying between NON CHAI and BAN CHIANG HIAN in the Chi Valley, KHORAT, Thailand. Buddhist remains of the mid 1st millennium AD are similar to those of DVARAVATI sites.

kantharos or **cantharus** a type of CLASSICAL drinking cup with two vertical handles which can project above the rim. Early examples are often stemmed, although in the 5th century BC a stemless version was produced. In the 4th and 3rd centuries BC it became one of the most popular types of drinking vessel in the Greek world.

Kanto a modern administrative district of eastern Honshu Island, Japan – often used in archaeological writings – comprising Tokyo Metropolitan District and Kanagawa, Saitama, Gunma, Tochigi, Ibaragi and Chiba Prefectures. See also HOSHINO.

Kaposwa a late Holocene microlithic LATER STONE AGE industry represented at KALAMBO FALLS in northern Zambia.

Kapova, Kapovaya or **Shul'gantash** a cave located on the upper Belaya River in the southern Ural Mountains, European Russia, containing rare examples of eastern European Palaeolithic cave art. Approximately forty naturalistic and stylized paintings (monochrome and bichrome) of extinct mammals (woolly mammoth, woolly rhinoceros) are preserved on the walls and ceiling of the cave; many abstract designs (e.g. geometric figures) are also present. A cultural layer (comprising stone artifacts, ornaments, former hearths and faunal remains [primarily mammoth] was excavated within the cave, and yielded radiocarbon dates of 16,010 to 13,930 bp. Kapova was investigated during the 1960s and 1970s by BADER and during the 1980s by Shchelinskij.

Kapthurin a 250,000-year-old formation of sedimentary and volcanic deposits near LAKE BARINGO in central Kenya, below which occur long, thin MIDDLE STONE AGE blades some researchers consider arguably reminiscent of more recent Upper Palaeolithic examples. The blades feature in debates about the origins of modern human behaviour (see BLOMBOS, KATANDA).

Kapwirimbwe an Early Iron Age village in eastern Lusaka, Zambia, occupied in the 5th century ad, which has given its name to a tradition of the CHIFUMBAZE COMPLEX. POSTHOLES indicate the existence of structures, and collapsed DAGA debris is interpreted as the remains of iron smelting furnaces. Animal bones of domestic cattle were recovered. Of particular interest are potsherds with small holes bored into them, identified as strainers used in salt-making.

Kara-Bom a Palaeolithic open-air site located near the confluence of the Semisart and Kaerlyk Rivers in the Altai region of Siberia. Artifacts and isolated faunal remains

KAPOVA Cave, Russia: view of the entrance from inside, showing winter icicles.

(including woolly rhinoceros) are buried in loam, clay and rubble deposits at the base of a bedrock cliff. The lowermost horizons contain Middle Palaeolithic assemblages with LEVALLOIS cores, sidescrapers and points, and remain undated. An Upper Palaeolithic industry containing retouched blades, endscrapers and burins was found in overlying layers and dated by radiocarbon to 43,000 BP. Kara-Bom was discovered and initially excavated by OKLADNIKOV in 1980.

Karain a huge collection of caves in the flanks of the Anti-Taurus (Mount Katran), near Yenikoy, in Antalya Province, southern Turkey. Excavations were first undertaken by Kökten, and more recently by Yalcinkaya and Otte. Cave E contains a long sequence (over 12 m [40 ft]) in which the Lower Palaeolithic is represented by an industry of denticulated CLACTONIAN flakes (around 350–400,000 BP). Above this, abundant deposits contained various Middle Palaeolithic industries such as a 'Charentian' overlain by LEVALLOISIAN of 'Karain' or 'Zagros' type. Human bones have been found in different deposits including a jaw fragment of HOMO *erectus* type and several apparently NEANDERTHAL teeth. Cave B nearby has yielded a long EPIPALAEOLITHIC sequence (18–12,000 BP), with an AURIGNACIAN industry above a recent MOUSTERIAN. Close to Karain, the cave of Ökuzini contained a long, rich sequence spanning the final Palaeolithic and the Mesolithic.

Karako-Kagi a YAYOI period site in Nara Prefecture, Japan, which serves as the type-site for the western Yayoi pottery chronology. The first excavation in 1938 revealed a series of storage pits; recent excavations have recovered a double moat around the presumed village site, which includes the separately discovered remains at Kagi, and a fragment of a bronze bell (see DOTAKU) casting mould indicates craft production on site.

Karakol a cemetery of the Early Bronze Age (the beginning of the 2nd millennium BC) in the ALTAI MOUNTAINS (Ongudai district), Russia, excavated in 1985 by V. Kubarev. The burials were in stone chambers constructed in pits. The most interesting features are some unique pecked, engraved and painted images discovered on the stone slabs which were used for the construction of the cists. The images are anthropomorphic deities, masked figures, elks and ibexes, and some of them are definitely related to the burials. Later, through comparison with other materials, the Karakol culture was distinguished, which is similar to, and SYNCHRONOUS with, the OKUNEVO CULTURE of the neighbouring MINUSINSK BASIN.

Karanis the Classical name for the site of Kom Aushim, situated in the northeastern FAIYUM, Egypt. Excavations by archaeologists from Michigan University in 1924–35 yielded over 5,000 papyri and OSTRAKA, which are a major source of evidence for the economy and administration of Roman Egypt during the 2nd–4th centuries AD.

Karanovo a stratified TELL site in eastern Bulgaria which has provided the basic chronological sequence for the Neolithic and much of the ENEOLITHIC of the eastern Balkans. The 12 m (40 ft) of deposits at Karanovo contain seven major phases of occupation. Karanovo I gives its name to the earliest Neolithic occupations north of Greece, and forms part of the complex of cultures that include STARČEVO, CRIŞ and KÖRÖS. Karanovo II continues this tradition. Karanovo III is an occupation of the middle Neolithic VESELINOVO culture, while levels IV and V are contemporaneous with the late Neolithic VINČA CULTURE of the western Balkans. The very thick Karanovo VI level represents perhaps several centuries of occupation by the Eneolithic GUMELNIŢA culture. The final level, VII, is a very early stage of the Bronze Age.

Karari an EARLIER STONE AGE industry of the OLDOWAN industrial complex found in the upper layers of the KOOBI FORA formation on the east side of Lake Turkana in northern Kenya, dating to about 1.5–1.25 million years ago. It is characterized by more artifact types than in the underlying KBS industry, as well as the appearance of bifaces.

Karasuk culture a Bronze Age culture of the Central Asian steppe of Kazakhstan and Russian Siberia, which developed from the ANDRONOVO culture. The typical Karasuk artifact is a short knife or dagger, bent at the point where the handle joins the blade. Remains of Karasuk bridles mark the beginning of horse riding on the Siberian steppe.

Karatepe an 8th-century BC Neo-HITTITE fortified palace on the Ceyhan River in the Adana plain, southwestern Anatolia, whose architecture was documented by H. Bossert and the subject of recent research by H. Çambel. Of particular importance are the reliefs and inscriptions on the two monumental gateways, which carry the bilingual PHOENICIAN-Luwian HIEROGLYPHIC texts that were instrumental in the decipherment of the Luwian writing system.

Karaz see KURA-ARAXES CULTURE.

Karbuna a hoard of the CUCUTENI-TRIPOLYE culture found in Moldova between the Prut and Dniester Rivers. Eight hundred and fifty-two stone, bone, shell and copper artifacts were found in a 34 cm (13 inch) high decorated vessel. Of the 444 copper items, 87 per cent were beads, while the remainder were bracelets, discs, plaques, pendants and two axe-adzes. Among the shell ornaments were several made from SPONDYLUS.

Karkarichinkat (Nord and Sud) two mounds in the TILEMSI Valley of Mali, Africa, occupied by herder-fishers between c.3900 and 3300 BP. Occupation may have been the result of the southward retreat of tsetse belts as the Sahara Desert expanded.

Karmir-blur an URARTIAN town near modern Erevan (Armenia), comprising a citadel and walled residential area that together cover some 40 ha (100 acres). B. B. PIOTROVSKY's excavations reveal the citadel to be a strongly fortified dense array of storerooms (especially for cereals, wine and weapons) beneath residential suites. The lower town contained blocks of buildings of varying size and complexity. Karmir-blur was occupied largely in the 7th century BC (though some pre-Urartian graves also occur, and the place was again used in HELLENISTIC times), and seems to have replaced the 8th-century complex at EREBUNI as the Urartian seat near Erevan.

Karnak a vast complex of religious buildings in the northern part of the Egyptian city of THEBES. The central part of the site is the temple enclosure of the god AMEN, containing his main temple together with a series of subsidiary religious structures, the whole complex covering an area of approximately 120 ha (300 acres). From the NEW KINGDOM this was the most important religious establishment in the Egyptian empire with considerable economic and political power, but Karnak (called in Egyptian 'the Most Select of Places') was the site of a temple from at least as early as the MIDDLE KINGDOM. To the south of the Amen enclosure is the smaller complex of the goddess Mut, consort of Amen, while to the north is that of the god Montu, the predecessor of Amen as pre-eminent deity at Thebes. A processional route runs south from Karnak to the LUXOR temple.

Karolta 1 a PETROGLYPH site in the Olary region of northwestern South Australia with PANARAMITEE-style engravings. Controversial CATION RATIO dates have been obtained from twenty-four motifs ranging from 31,600 to 1400 bp, but these are not widely accepted.

karst a terrain with a unique set of landforms and drainage patterns characterized by formation and enlargement of cavities resulting largely from chemical weathering and erosion, primarily by the solution process, in regions of carbonate and evaporite rocks. Caves, collapse features, sinkholes (dolines), deranged and disrupted surface drainage, springs and an active subterranean drainage system are some of the more common characteristics of karst topography.

Kartan a variant of the AUSTRALIAN CORE TOOL AND SCRAPER TRADITION found on KANGAROO ISLAND and in neighbouring areas of mainland South Australia, and comprising HORSEHOOF CORES, unifacial pebble choppers, large steep-edged flake scrapers and waisted axes, but very few flakes or flake tools. Originally defined by TINDALE, it was previously thought to be Pleistocene in age. However, recent research on Kangaroo Island suggests that Kartan assemblages date to the early Holocene and reflect the flaking properties of local quartzite.

Kar-Tukulti-Ninurta a city near ASSUR which was a new foundation by the MIDDLE ASSYRIAN king Tukulti-Ninurta I (1243–1207 BC) as a cultic and royal residential centre, and which provides a good illustration of the Assyrian habit of founding new capitals. The settlement forms a walled square of about 60 ha (148 acres), divided into two sections by a canal; the western section contained a large palace complex, a temple of Assur and domestic architecture, while the eastern section remained unbuilt.

kārum 1 an AKKADIAN term denoting the 'harbour' of a city, usually set apart from the rest of the community, in which trade occurs; in this sense, the kārum may be a harbour proper (as at UR) or simply a section of the town in which commercial exchange takes place (as at Kanish; see KÜLTEPE).
2 an Akkadian term for the organization of merchants residing in the physical kārum, where the merchant community is largely self-governing (though with specified legal, economic and social obligations to the larger community); the best-known example of this organization comes from the Old ASSYRIAN trading colony at Kültepe in Cappadocia.

Kaş see Ulu Burun.

Kasori a Middle/Late JOMON SHELL MIDDEN site in Chiba Prefecture, Japan, now a historical park. At least forty-seven pit-houses have been excavated in a circular village plan with shell deposits around its rim. It is the type-site for Kasori-type Jomon ceramics and representative of plaza-type Jomon village sites.

Kassala a pre-AXUMite cultural phase from the eastern Sudan comprising the BUTANA, GASH and MOKRAM groups.

Kassites a mountain people of the Zagros, with a distinctive language and culture, who began infiltrating MESOPOTAMIA in the early 2nd millennium BC. After the sack of BABYLON by the HITTITE king Mursili I (conventionally dated to 1595 BC), a Kassite dynasty established itself in Babylonia and by the mid 15th century controlled all of the region. Lasting until 1158 BC, the Kassite rule represents the longest episode of political integration in the history of southern Mesopotamia (though interrupted by the invasion of the MIDDLE ASSYRIAN king Tukulti-Ninurta I in 1225 BC). Although it maintained political stability, brought economic prosperity, and encouraged artistic and literary achievement in Babylonia, the Kassite period is relatively little studied and therefore comparatively unknown. Important sites of the Kassite period include AQAR QUF, WARKA and, especially for the texts, NIPPUR.

Kasteelberg a shelter of granite boulders near St Helena Bay on the west coast of the Western Cape Province, South Africa, whose occupants may have been ancestral to the

KHOEKHOEN, containing material of Stone Age herders dating between about 1800 and 800 bp.

Kastri 1 a site on the island of Kythera, off the southern coast of mainland Greece, which was excavated by Coldstream and Huxley in 1963–5. Originally an Early HELLADIC settlement, Kastri was colonized *c.*2500 BC by MINOANS, apparently from the west of Crete. As trade between Crete and Laconia intensified in the 2nd millennium, Kastri prospered, but the collapse of the Minoan palace economy led to the abandonment of the site.

2 a site on the island of Syros; see CHALANDRIANI.

Kastritsa an Upper Palaeolithic cave-site located on Lake Ioannina in northwestern Greece. A series of occupation levels dating between *c.*22,000 and 11,000 bp are buried in silt, sand and rubble; the faunal remains are heavily dominated by red deer, together with aurochs and steppe ass. The Upper Palaeolithic artifacts include backed blades, shouldered points, bone points and decorated pebbles. Traces of a structure partially surrounding a former hearth were encountered near the entrance of the cave. Kastritsa was investigated by HIGGS and others in the 1960s.

Katanda a locality in the Semliki Valley of northeastern Democratic Republic of Congo, where three sites with MIDDLE STONE AGE artifacts as well as barbed and unbarbed bone points have been dated by ELECTRON SPIN RESONANCE, OSL and THERMOLUMINESCENCE, together with sedimentary and faunal analyses, to older than 90,000 bp. However, some researchers consider that the points may be anomalous because their contexts are complex and other well-dated sites of similar age have not produced such artifacts. The systematic fashioning of tools from organic materials is often considered a modern behavioural trait, hence the Katanda bone points feature in debates about the origins of modern human behaviour (see BLOMBOS).

Katotan see KATOTO.

Katoto an Iron Age cemetery with collective graves in the southeastern Democratic Republic of Congo, probably dating to the 13th century AD, which has given its name to an Iron Age tradition contemporaneous with the KISALIAN. Kisalian pots are often found in Katotan graves and vice versa. Many of the Katotan burials were multiple, comprising a man buried with women and children. Ceremonial axes, anvils and a large iron gong were found in one of the graves. This bell is the oldest known symbol of hierarchically structured political authority in Central Africa. Cowrie shells and glass beads indicate contact with East African coastal trade.

katun a period of time in the CLASSIC MAYA LONG COUNT equalling 7,200 days, or about twenty years. The celebration of katuns was a major ritual of kingship in the Classic period. The katun is the chronological unit used in the SHORT COUNT.

Katuruka an Early Iron Age site in the Buhaya region of northeastern Tanzania, with evidence of sophisticated iron-smelting technology dating to the last few centuries BC and associated with UREWE pottery. This is the oldest-known evidence for iron-working in Central and southern Africa.

Kauri Point a PA in Tauranga, North Island, that was the site of one of the first major systematic excavations in NEW ZEALAND. First occupied about 500 years ago, it had three phases of fortification interspersed with periods of undefended settlement. The nearby swamp has excellent preservation of artifacts, including a remarkable series of wooden combs.

Kausambi a site on the Yamuna River near its confluence with the Ganges in Uttar Pradesh, northern India, that was subject to intensive investigation in the 1940s to 1960s by G. R. Sharma, providing important evidence of the origins and development of the Gangetic Iron Age urban civilization. The earliest documented levels of the site, Kausambi I, contain a pottery related to the OCHRE COLOURED POTTERY horizon and dated to the middle of the 2nd millennium BC. These are followed by levels of the Kausambi II period, which contain black-and-red, red, grey and black wares, that relate to the cultural province of the lower Ganges to the east; iron objects appear at this time, dated roughly to the second quarter of the 1st millennium BC. The first defensive walls of the settlement were constructed during this period. The following Kausambi III period is characterized by NORTHERN BLACK POLISHED WARE, beginning perhaps around 500 BC, when the palace complex of the town was first built. Some 50 ha (124 acres) in area early in this period, the city walls came to enclose as much as 250 ha (620 acres). These levels are followed by those belonging to the early 1st millennium AD.

Kawahara-dera see ASUKA.

Kawakiu Bay a site in western Molokai, Hawaiian Islands, with large MIDDEN deposits and stone structures indicating the presence of a permanent fishing community. The site has been dated by obsidian HYDRATION to AD 1750.

Kawela a dry leeward valley in southern Molokai, Hawaiian Islands. The pre-European settlement pattern is well preserved, and most features date to the last one or two centuries before European contact. Agriculture was largely limited to some irrigation cultivation of root-crops (sweet potato and taro) and large fishponds were the main focus of production. See also HALAWA VALLEY, LAPAKAHI, MAKAHA VALLEY.

Kaya the name of a confederation of small POLITIES on

the southern Korean coast during the THREE KING-DOMS period (see KOREA). The coastal (Pon-Kaya) polity in KIMHAE was active during the 3rd to early 5th centuries AD. In the late 5th century, power shifted inland to Tae-Kaya. Kaya territory was flanked on the west by the state of PAEKCHE and on the east by SILLA. Silla conquered Pon-Kaya in 532 and Tae-Kaya in 562 in its efforts to unite the peninsula. Kaya remains consist mainly of wood- or stone-chamber burials with or without large mounds (as at POKCH'ONG-DONG); the tombs have yielded much iron armour and grey STONE-WARE, the first to be produced in Korea and which stimulated SUE ware production in Japan.

Kayatha a site on the Malwa Plateau of central India, where excavations have defined a sequence of three CHALCOLITHIC cultures, as well as Iron Age and early historic levels. At the base of the Chalcolithic sequence, dated to the second half of the 3rd millennium BC (and therefore contemporaneous with the Mature HARAPPAN to the north), is a culture complex characterized by Kay-atha ware (violet paint on a brown slip) as well as incised and red-painted buff wares. The community inhabited small huts, and used both lithic and copper equipment. The second phase marks the appearance of pottery similar to that of the Banas culture, typified by a white painted black-and-red ware (see AHAR) and dated to the early 2nd millennium. The last Chalcolithic phase, dated to the second quarter of the 2nd millennium, belongs to the MALWA culture as seen at NAVDATOLI.

Kayenta a regional variant of the ANASAZI TRADITION, located in northeastern Arizona, USA, and most clearly defined during the PUEBLO II stage. Kayenta is recognized by specific pottery types and architectural construction techniques.

Kazanluk or **Kazanlik** a large Neolithic, ENEOLITHIC and Early Bronze Age TELL in the Valley of Roses in southern Bulgaria with a 6 m (20 ft) stratigraphy. The bottom 2 m (6.5 ft) are of the early Neolithic KARANOVO I culture, above which was a VESELINOVO (Karanovo III) layer, a Karanovo V–VI occupation enclosed by a stone wall, and an Early Bronze Age occupation. As at CHEVDAR, careful sieving produced a large sample of faunal and botanical remains, indicating a subsistence strategy based on emmer wheat and sheep/goat in the early Neolithic settlement.

KBS 1 an EARLIER STONE AGE industry of the OLDOWAN industrial complex found in the lower layers of the KOOBI FORA formation on the east side of Lake Turkana in northern Kenya, dating to about 1.8 million years ago.

2 a TUFF layer at the Koobi Fora site. The dating of this layer was formerly controversial, but the current consensus places it at about 1.9 million years ago.

3 a site at Koobi Fora from which stone artifacts and animal bones are an important source of information on early HOMINID behaviour.

Kebara Cave a Palaeolithic site at the southern end of MOUNT CARMEL, Israel, occupied from the Middle Palaeolithic to EPIPALAEOLITHIC. Soundings were first made by Stekelis (1927) and GARROD and McCown (1928) who identified a previously unknown microlithic industry later named KEBARAN by Garrod. TURVILLE-PETRE (1931) excavated the upper levels at Kebara: B (Lower NATUFIAN), C (Kebaran) and D (AURIGNACIAN). Stekelis' excavations (1951–65) mainly addressed the Middle/Upper Palaeolithic transition. Bar-Yosef and associates (1982–9) used newly available techniques for absolute dating and the study of site formation processes to clarify the problematic chronology of the Levantine Middle Palaeolithic. MOUSTERIAN HOMINID remains include a deliberately buried and well-preserved adult male NEANDERTHALer (Kebara 2), whose neck and hyoid bones provoked intense debate on Neanderthal capacity for speech and language. The burial was dated by THERMO-LUMINESCENCE to 61–59,000 BP and by ESR to 64–60,000 BP.

Kebaran a culture identified at KEBARA CAVE which forms the earliest phase of the Levantine EPIPALAEO-LITHIC (c.20–14,500 BP) which succeeded the local Upper Palaeolithic and was followed by the Geometric Kebaran complex, and then the NATUFIAN. The Kebaran was produced by nomadic hunter-gatherers with an increasing reliance on wild cereals, and marks an early step towards sedentism, domestication and food production (see EIN GEV I and OHALO II). Its flint industry is characterized by bladelets and microliths modified to form backed and pointed pieces and groundstone implements for food processing.

Kehe [K'o-ho] an early Palaeolithic site in Shanxi Province, China, belonging to the heavy tool tradition with LANTIAN and DINGCUN, as opposed to ZHOUKOUDIAN with mainly flake tools.

Keilor a site near Melbourne, Victoria, Australia, where a fully modern cranium was found in 1940 in ALLUVIAL sediments and dated to c.13,000 bp. Artifacts have been found throughout the sequence. The earliest levels have been estimated to be more than 30,000 years old.

Kelleli a group of Bronze Age sites in the lower Murghab Delta (southeastern Turkmenistan), whose material culture defines the Kelleli phase of the regional chronology, dated to the late 3rd millennium BC; Kelleli settlements are generally very small (up to about 6 ha [15 acres]).

Kellia a site on the desert fringe of the western Nile DELTA, Egypt. Excavated since 1964 by a Franco-Swiss mission, Kellia is an extensive Coptic monastic settlement with continuous occupation from the 4th to 8th centuries AD. The pottery recovered from the excavations at Kellia comprises one of the most important ceramic assemblages of the late Roman period from Egypt.

Kel'taminar or **Kel'teminar** a culture complex, found in the desert steppe of Khoresmia and the Kyzyl Kum southeast of the Aral Sea in Kazakhstan, Uzbekistan and Turkmenia, defining a pottery-using, foraging/herding adaptation that appears to be a response to the Holocene wet phase when more surface water was available in this desertic landscape. In some areas, these groups also worked copper and turquoise, presumably for exchange with agricultural neighbours to the south (reflected in stylistic echoes of NAMAZGA II–III in Kel'taminar pottery). The culture complex is poorly dated, but seems to belong in the 5th–3rd millennia BC, spanning the Mesolithic to the Early Bronze Age. Most sites comprise unstratified surface remains and are difficult to date: some (e.g. Djanbas 4) have evidence of reed and wood structures. The culture is thought to have played a role in the subsequent development of the SRUBNAYA and ANDRONOVO cultures.

kendi a spouted water container of Southeast Asia of the 1st and 2nd millennia AD. The name is derived from the Sanskrit *kundika*.

Kennewick Man the skeleton of a middle-aged man, found by the bank of the Columbia River at Kennewick, Washington (USA) in 1996. The remains have been dated to *c*.9500 BP, but exhibit numerous Caucasoid (i.e. non-North American aboriginal) features. The skeleton has become a *cause célèbre* in pitting the needs of scientists who wish to examine the skeleton in detail to understand its biological origins against those local Indian groups who wish to have it reburied with no analysis under the terms of NAGPRA.

Kenniff Cave a sandstone shelter in southern-central Queensland, Australia, with stencilled art and over 3 m (10 ft) of occupation deposits going back 19,090 years. Excavated in 1962 by John Mulvaney, this site provided the first evidence of Pleistocene occupation of Australia, and established the foundations of the two-phase sequence in current use throughout the continent.

Kent's Cavern a British prehistoric cave-site on the South Devon coast, first excavated by Father MacEnery in 1825 and since investigated by Goodwin-Austen, PENGELLY, and at least twelve other workers. MacEnery's recognition of Palaeolithic artifacts and associated fauna in situ beneath a stalagmite floor was one of the first indications of the true age of British stone tools. The site has yielded Upper Palaeolithic implements (including CRESWELLIAN blade tools and bone artifacts), Middle Palaeolithic bifaces and rather crude Lower Palaeolithic implements including bifaces and a chopper. The upper layers have produced some Mesolithic, Neolithic and more recent material.

Kenya Capsian see EBURRAN.

Kenyanthropus a genus of early HOMINID, known from a 3.5 million-year-old partial skull (catalogue number KNM-WT-40000) of the species *Kenyanthropus platyops* (meaning 'flat face'), found in 1999 in sediments of the Lomekwi River on the western shore of LAKE TURKANA in northern Kenya. It is characterized by a tall, flat face and other features which distinguish it from its hominid contemporary, AUSTRALOPITHECUS *afarensis* (see 'LUCY'), from which it probably differed in diet. *Kenyanthropus* indicates that other early hominids coexisted with australopithecines, probably in different ecological niches, and that the relationships among early hominids, and between early hominids and the emergence of HOMO, are unresolved (see 1470, p. 333).

Kenyon, Dame Kathleen Mary (1906–78) a British archaeologist who worked extensively in Britain up to the early 1950s, but is best known for her work at JERICHO in 1952–8 and JERUSALEM in 1961–7. The work at Jericho firmly established the existence of a PRE-POTTERY NEOLITHIC (PPNA/B) and an EPIPALAEOLITHIC subsistence focused on wild cereals (NATUFIAN).

Kephala the site of a FINAL NEOLITHIC settlement and CIST GRAVE cemetery on the Cycladic island of Kea, excavated by CASKEY and Coleman in 1961–6. The close links between Kephala and sites in Attica, such as ATHENS and THORIKOS, have led to the recognition of an Attica-Kephala culture.

Kerameikos one of the main cemetery areas of ATHENS and the location for some of the pottery workshops. German excavations have revealed extensive remains of the cemeteries outside the Dipylon and Sacred Gates. Some are private, although a multiple burial for the Spartans killed at the end of the 5th century BC has been located. Many of the tombs were marked by STELAS with relief decoration, and through inscriptions it has been possible to identify family plots.

Kerinci a highland volcanic-lake area of western-central Sumatra, which has produced many surface finds of obsidian microliths, and a prehistoric bronze urn similar to other such finds from Lampung (Sumatra), Madura and Cambodia.

Kerkenesdağ an Iron Age city covering over 300 ha (740 acres) on a mountain top in central Turkey at a great bend of the Kızılırmak (Halys) River. A British programme of detailed geophysical mapping and excavation during the 1990s has revealed the layout and contents of the entire city. The place may be identified as ancient Pteira, which CLASSICAL authors mention as occupied by MEDES and destroyed by Croesus of Lydia in 547 BC.

Kerma a Sudanese site, a major centre of the Kingdom of KUSH, excavated by REISNER in 1913–16. The only

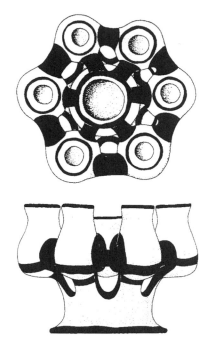

KERNOS.

substantial surviving building associated with the settlement is a massive mud-brick structure, the 'Western Deffufa', a castle containing a series of apartments. To the east is a large cemetery of tumulus graves, including the royal NECROPOLIS of the kings of Kush, probably dating to the Second INTERMEDIATE PERIOD (see EGYPT). These tumuli, the most impressive of which are as large as 90 m (98 yds) in diameter, were elaborately built with internal mud-brick reinforcing walls; in addition to the main burial chamber some of the larger tombs also contained sacrificial human interments (over 300 in one case).

Kerma ware distinctive handmade pottery with very thin walls and a black-and-red lustrous finish, found in a range of elegant shapes; a product of the KERMA culture.

Kernonen a burial mound of the Armorican Early Bronze Age Tumulus culture c.2000–2500 BC, in Finistère, France. The circular stone cairn covered a rectangular dry-stone chamber containing the remains of a single individual accompanied by exquisitely flaked flint barbed-and-tanged arrowheads, originally held in a quiver, amber beads, four bronze axes, and three fine bronze daggers with wooden hilts decorated with thousands of tiny gold nails.

kernos a composite Greek cult vessel, made of clay or stone.

Keros-Syros a cultural phase, named after two islands in the Cyclades, which in Renfrew's classification of the CYCLADIC culture sequence corresponds to Early Cycladic II (c.2700–2300 BC) in the traditional chronology.

Kesslerloch a Swiss MAGDALENIAN reindeer-hunting cave-site, first excavated by K. Merk in 1874, and occupied during a cold phase of the final GLACIATION, with reindeer bones representing about 80 per cent of the recovered fauna. The site is best known for its bonework including harpoons and spearthrowers, and art objects including a famous engraving of a rutting reindeer. The stone tool-kit includes many borers.

Kestel a mining site in the Toros Mountains, some 30 km (19 miles) southeast of Niğde in southern-central Turkey. Investigation by A. Yener in the 1980s and 1990s documented 3rd-millennium BC (and early medieval) tin mining here. The nearby 3rd-millennium BC hilltop settlement at Göltepe contains pit houses, metallurgical industrial MIDDENS, and crucibles incrusted with high-tin residues. Although controversial, these sites indicate Anatolian tin production during the Early Bronze Age.

Ketrosy a Middle Palaeolithic open-air site on the Dniester River in western Ukraine. The occupation horizon is buried in ALLUVIAL and slope deposits on a low terrace, and is thought to date to an INTERSTADIAL preceding the early cold LAST GLACIAL MAXIMUM. Faunal remains include woolly mammoth and steppe bison. Sidescrapers and denticulates predominate among the tools. Ketrosy was discovered and excavated by Anisyutkin during 1972–9.

keyhole tombs MOUNDED TOMBS of KOFUN period Japan, with a ground plan shaped like an old-fashioned keyhole. They are assumed to be the tombs of the rulers and highest-ranking elite. The symbolism of the shape is unknown and generally unrepresented in other East Asian mounded tomb traditions. In the 4th–5th centuries AD, two sizes are found, their lengths averaging approximately 100 and 200 m (110 and 220 yds). Compare OJIN, NINTOKU.

Kfar Samir see ATLIT DROWNED SITES.

Khafadje a site on the lower Diyala River in eastern-central Iraq, and excavated as part of FRANKFORT's Diyala project in the 1920s and 1930s. Khafadje has a stratified ceramic sequence from JEMDET NASR to late EARLY DYNASTIC times which, together with the results from Tell ASMAR, provided the yardstick for the archaeological periodization of 3rd-millennium BC southern MESOPOTAMIA. The excavation exposed a long succession of Sin temples (Jemdet Nasr to Early Dynastic III), a three-phase Temple Oval (E.D. II–III), and an extensive

KEYHOLE TOMB, Japan.

residential district which contained a large number of burials beneath floors.

Khafre or **Chephren** an Egyptian king of the 4th Dynasty (during the OLD KINGDOM), and owner of the second pyramid complex to be built at GIZA; this includes the still-impressive Valley Temple and the Great SPHINX, whose features are presumably a portrait of Khafre.

Khami **1** a capital of the Torwa state in southwestern Zimbabwe, built in the 15th century AD after the decline of GREAT ZIMBABWE, and occupied until the mid 17th century, when the capital moved to DANANGOMBE. The site has distinctive architecture consisting of house platforms and low walls often decorated with ornate herringbone and chequered stone arrangements. Imported goods and considerable quantities of gold found by early treasure hunters indicate that trade with the East African coast was important.

2 the third phase of the ZIMBABWE tradition, dating from about ad 1450–1820.

3 a former name for a microlithic LATER STONE AGE early to mid Holocene industry from the Matopo Hills of southwestern Zimbabwe, also formerly known as the Rhodesian WILTON or Matopan industry, now named the NSWATUGI industry, in which five phases dating between about 9400 and 5000 bp have been recognized.

Khanate see KAGHANATE.

Khania see CHANIA.

Khao Jamook an Iron Age burial site near the Thai-Burmese border, whose decorated high-tin bronze bowls,

like those from BAN DON TA PHET, provide evidence for early contacts between India and Southeast Asia in the 4th century BC.

Kharga the easternmost of Egypt's Western Desert oases, Kharga was occupied from c.400,000 BP until the Graeco-Roman period.

Khartoum Neolithic a central Sudanese industry with radiocarbon dates between 6000 and 5000 bp, characterized by microlithic tools, grinding implements, fish hooks and distinctive stone adzes and 'gouges', associated with domestic stock and pottery (see ESH SHAHEINAB, KADERO).

Khazars one of the nomadic Turkish-language tribes that was left in eastern Europe after the demise of the Hunnish empire. In the early 7th century AD, in the steppes of the northern Pre-Caucasus (territory of modern Dagestan), they created the Khazar KAGHANATE. In the 8th century they waged war with the Arabs, were defeated, and after that went north to the Volga and Don steppes. Part of the Khazar aristocracy adopted Judaism. At the end of the 9th century the nomad Pechenegs invaded the territory of the Khazars. Eventually in the 10th century the Russian Prince Svyatoslav smashed the Khazar Kaghanate and destroyed its capital Itil' (on the Volga River). Archaeologically the Khazar Kaghanate (which also included the Alans and Bolgars) is represented by monuments of the Saltovo-Mayatskaya culture – forts, settlements and cemeteries.

Kheit Qasim three adjacent sites (I, II and III) in the Jebel Hamrin area of eastern-central Iraq (on the upper Diyala drainage and the edge of the Zagros foothills), which were excavated by J.-F. Forest as part of rescue work. Kheit Qasim I is a large EARLY DYNASTIC cemetery of brick tombs with multiple inhumations. This funerary tradition, unusual for southern MESOPOTAMIA, is duplicated at another Hamrin site of similar date (Tell Ahmad al-Hattu), and may reflect a connection with communities in the Zagros. Kheit Qasim II is a contemporary village settlement; a larger fortified Early Dynastic I settlement occurs near by at Abu Qasim. Kheit Qasim III is a small 'UBAID period site, the excavation of which revealed an elaborate dwelling with a tripartite floor plan focused on a large 'T'-shaped central hall; similar to SAMARRAN house forms (e.g. at Tell es-SAWWAN), this plan also appears at other sites in the Hamrin (e.g. Tell ABADA, Tell Madhur), and probably housed extended families as the basic social and economic units of 'Ubaid society.

Khipu see QUIPU.

Khirbet Kerak (also called TELL Beth Yerah) a Palestinian site on the southwestern shore of the Sea of Galilee. It was settled from the EARLY to MIDDLE BRONZE AGE and again in the HELLENISTIC to BYZANTINE periods. It is the type-site for 'Khirbet Kerak ware', a class of Early

Bronze Age burnished pottery vessels with incised or ribbed decoration, probably of Anatolian origin.

Khirokitia the site of a prehistoric settlement in southern CYPRUS, which was excavated by Dikaios in 1936–46 and more recently by Le Brun. Khirokitia was first occupied in the ACERAMIC NEOLITHIC I phase (7th millennium BC), abandoned and then reoccupied in Neolithic II (later 5th millennium BC). The settlement, which was surrounded by a massive enclosure wall, consists of circular houses built of stone and mud-brick. The roofs were apparently flat, not domed as was once believed. The dead were buried INTRAMURALLY.

Khmer an ethno-linguistic group once occupying Cambodia, southern Vietnam and adjacent parts of Thailand, and, at the height of the power of the state of ANGKOR, dominating most of Thailand and southern Laos. They were linguistically related to the MON.

Khoekhoen, Khoekhoe, Khoe, Khoikhoin, Khoikhoi or **Khoi** (various spellings in current usage, though Khoekhoen [singular Khoe, adjective Khoekhoe], the currently recognized English spelling for the self-appellation meaning 'people' among the Nama of Namibia, is sometimes preferred. Khoe is pronounced somewhat like the first three letters of the word 'question' in English, but with more of an 'h' sound at the beginning) a Stone Age pastoral people with pottery, cattle, sheep and goats, who lived in the western parts of southern Africa during the last 2,000 years, known to European colonial inhabitants as 'Hottentots'. Cattle, sheep and goats have no wild progenitors in southern Africa and must have been introduced into the region from further north, probably from northern Botswana, from where several possible routes of introduction have been proposed. The mechanism of introduction, whether by migration of herding peoples, diffusion through existing hunter-gatherer communities, or a more complex scenario, is the subject of ongoing research, as is the possibility that pottery spread before the introduction of domestic animals.

KHIROKITIA, Cyprus.

Historical accounts from the 17th and 18th centuries record that these people lived in hierarchically structured, territorially based clans based on cattle ownership, and between which power struggles occurred. A camp consisted of 500 or more individuals who were related, as well as 'clients' working for them. Sometimes larger hordes occurred. Chiefs were not hereditary but selected on the basis of leadership skills and seniority. This social organization may have developed only in recent centuries. Houses were made from a framework of poles covered with mats, a 'matjieshuis', a practice that has been traced archaeologically back to at least 1,300 years ago. In order to provide sufficient grazing for their animals, camps were often transported to new locations on the backs of oxen, which were also used in battle during frequent raids between groups. This society disintegrated rapidly in the 18th century when grazing lands were lost to Dutch settlers, stock exchanged for goods like metal, tobacco and liquor, and the people succumbed to alcoholism, drought, as well as human and animal epidemic diseases. Only a few people who had Khoekhoe ancestors still live as herders in Namaland in Namibia and in the Namaqualand National Park in northwestern South Africa. The Nama language is still used in Namibia. See also CAPE COASTAL WARE, KHOISAN.

Khoisan or **Khoesaan** a collective term for the indigenous hunter-gatherer and herding peoples of southern Africa (see KHOEKHOEN, SAN). Although the term masks variability and was never used by the indigenous people themselves, it is widely used as a convenient shorthand reference. It was coined in 1928 by Leonhard Schultze, originally spelled Koïsan, and shortly thereafter anglicized as Khoisan.

Khok Charoen a late prehistoric cemetery with over fifty inhumations in the upper Pa Sak Valley, central Thailand, provisionally dated to c.1000 BC.

Khok Phanom Di a 5 ha (12 acre) prehistoric mound near Chonburi on the east coast of the Gulf of Thailand. Over 150 burials arranged in 'family clusters' were excavated by Higham and Thosarat from the 7m (23 ft) deep deposit. The burials, dated between 2000 and 1400 BC, show increasing differentiation of wealth towards the middle of the sequence. Pottery-making was a local specialization, and the 'pottery princess' had a burial with richly decorated ceramics, pottery-making equipment and over 120,000 shell beads. Although the site was contemporary with bronze-making communities in central and northeastern Thailand, no metal was found despite the wealth of grave furnishings.

Khok Phlap a late Neolithic–Bronze Age burial site near Ratchaburi, western Thailand, roughly contemporary (c.800 BC) with NONG NOR across the Gulf of Thailand.

Khorat an extensive sandstone plateau in northeastern

Thailand, drained by the Songkhram, Chi and Mun Rivers flowing east to join the Mekong. Little is known of hunter-gatherer settlement, but hundreds of archaeological sites ranging from the Neolithic (late 3rd millennium BC), Bronze Age (c.1700–500 BC), Iron Age (c.500 BC–AD 200), early historic (c.AD 200–1000) and KHMER (c.AD 1000–1400) periods have been located, and many have been excavated. Bronze and Iron Age sites are especially well represented, with exceptionally rich burials appearing in the late 2nd millennium BC in moated mounds, which mark the increasing power of local chiefs. In the mid 1st millennium AD, Buddhism spread through the plateau as independent DVARAVATI kingdoms were formed, and later the region was incorporated into the Khmer empire until the late 14th century AD, when the expansion of the Thai kingdom of Ayutthaya brought the area into the cultural sphere of central Thailand.

General period A (c.3600–2000 BC) refers to the period of initial settlement of known early sites, most of which are in the northern (Songkhram) basin (see BAN CHIANG, PHU WIANG, NON NOK THA). The period is characterized by subsistence based upon rice cultivation and rearing of pigs and dogs, supplemented by broad-spectrum hunting and gathering; use of polished stone adzes and stone and shell jewellery indicates a degree of regional trade, as well as incipient social ranking.

General period B (c.2000–800/400 BC) covers the period of transition to the use of tin-bronze, dispersed small-scale production of bronze using metals imported from mining and processing sites in the mountains bordering the plateau (PHU LON, NON PA WAI), the presence of cattle and increases in population, number of settlements and degree of social ranking. Many of the sites in the north were occupied by this period (see BAN NADI), and some of those in the southern Chi-Mun basin (BAN CHIANG HIAN) as well.

General period C (c.800/400 BC–AD 300/500) was when iron replaced bronze in tools and weapons, water buffalo became prominent and wet-rice cultivation appears to have been established, as settlement spread down from low terraces into the floodplains. Rapid population growth occurred, and clusters of small villages formed about larger settlements, suggesting that small political units were developing, particularly in the Chi-Mun basin (see NON CHAI, KANTARAWICHAI, MUANG FA DAET, NON DUA, PHIMAI, MUANG SIMA).

General period D (c.AD 300/500–1300) occurred when larger settlements of the previous period expanded and those of the Chi-Mun basin acquired encircling moats (see MOATED SITES). The period is that of formation of small states, later absorbed into larger ones, long-distance trade relations and a degree of INDIANIZATION.

Khor-Musa a group of five stratified Middle Palaeolithic occupation sites in the Second Cataract of the southern Nile Valley, Egypt. The recovered artifacts include LEVAL-LOIS flakes, denticulates and burins, accompanied by well-preserved faunal remains. The term Khormusan was coined by Marks to describe technologically similar extensive late Middle Palaeolithic sites lying close to the River Nile and contemporary with, or following, the ATERIAN.

Khorramabad a valley in the Luristan section of the Zagros Mountains in western Iran, which contains a series of Middle and Upper Palaeolithic sites, some of which (Kunji, Gar Arjeneh, Yafteh, Ghamari and Pa Sangar) were excavated by Frank Hole and others during the 1960s. The combined results of this work provide a sequence of MOUSTERIAN, Baradostian and ZARZIAN industries that span the Late Pleistocene, a sequence replicating that of SHANIDAR.

Khor Rori a port town on the Dhofar coast of southern Oman, involved in the maritime trade of South Arabian incense and other goods between India, East Africa and the Mediterranean world during the first few centuries AD.

Khorsabad a city in Iraq which was a short-lived capital of ASSYRIA. It was one of the first MESOPOTAMIAN sites to be excavated by Emile BOTTA, beginning in 1843; the excavation was continued by V. Place, and the site was re-examined by G. Loud in the 1920s and 1930s. Khorsabad is the location of Dur-Sharrukin, built over an existing village by the NEO-ASSYRIAN king Sargon II (721–705 BC) as a new capital north of NINEVEH, and used as a fortified place by his successors. The nearly square walls of Sargon's city enclosed roughly 325 ha (803 acres); the palace complex and arsenal formed separate compounds set in the city walls. The early French work focused on Sargon's palace, and uncovered a fabulous series of wall reliefs and monumental sculpture, much of which was lost in the Euphrates while being transported to France.

Khotylevo sites two Palaeolithic localities on the Desna River in Ukraine. At Khotylevo I, Middle Palaeolithic artifacts are buried in ALLUVIUM at the base of the second terrace. The molluscan fauna suggests that the alluvium is of last INTERGLACIAL age, although the mammalian remains include reindeer. LEVALLOIS cores and bifaces are common among the artifacts. At Khotylevo II (700 m [766 yds] upstream), an Upper Palaeolithic horizon is buried in slope deposits overlying a low bedrock promontory; both the STRATIGRAPHIC context and radiocarbon dates (23,660 and 24,960 bp) indicate an early LAST GLACIAL MAXIMUM age. The faunal remains are primarily of woolly mammoth. Features include hearths, pits and debris concentrations. The artifacts, which include 'VENUS' FIGURINES, permit assignment to the KOSTENKI-WILLENDORF CULTURE or EASTERN GRAVETTIAN. The Khotylevo sites were discovered by Zavernyaev, who conducted excavations at

Khotylevo I during 1958–9, and Khotylevo II during 1969–75.

Khryashchi a Palaeolithic locality on the northern Donets River in the south of European Russia. Artifact assemblages were recovered from ALLUVIUM of the third terrace, and from the middle of a series of three buried soils overlying the alluvium. The lower, and possibly the upper, assemblage dates to the late Middle Pleistocene, and represents one of the few firmly dated pre-Late Pleistocene sites on the Russian Plain. (The nearby locality of Mikhajlovskoe, also on the northern Donets, is another example.) The artifacts comprise archaic flake and core tools; no handaxes were found. Khryashchi was investigated by Goretskij in 1952, and by Praslov in 1964–6.

Khuan Lukpad the site of a protohistoric industrial and trading settlement near Khlong Thom, Krabi, on the west coast of peninsular Thailand, specializing in the production of glass and stone beads and tin. Imports found at the site (Roman and Indian seals, fragments of Middle Eastern glass, and a Chinese mirror and some glazed stonewares) date to the early–mid 1st millennium AD.

Khufu or **Cheops** an Egyptian king of the 4th Dynasty, during the OLD KINGDOM, the successor of SNEFRU. Owner of the Great Pyramid at GIZA, the largest of the ancient Egyptian pyramids, he is otherwise relatively poorly attested in the archaeological record.

Kibiro an Iron Age salt-working site on Lake Mutanzige (formerly Lake Albert) in northwestern Uganda.

Kidder, Alfred Vincent (1885–1963) a pioneering American Southwest archaeologist, perhaps best known for his extensive excavations of the prehistoric PUEBLO at Pecos, close to Santa Fe, New Mexico. Kidder intensively analysed the artifacts, and was able to provide a new framework for Southwest CULTURE HISTORY. Kidder convened the first Pecos Conference in 1927, from which emerged the PECOS CLASSIFICATION. Perhaps less well known are his intensive archaeological surveys and excavations in MAYA archaeology for the Carnegie Institution, and his early use of interdisciplinary techniques.

Kietrz one of the largest URNFIELD cemeteries of the LUSATIAN culture in Central Europe, with over 3,000 graves, located in Silesia, southwestern Poland. Most of the burials consist of one or more urns filled with cremated bones and placed in pits, but some appear to have had mortuary structures with upright posts erected above them.

Kiev one of the major towns of medieval Russia, located on the eastern bank of the Dnieper River in Ukraine. Kiev began in the 10th century AD with the establishment of a fortified town with churches and palaces on a bluff overlooking the river. This town was expanded during the 11th century. Subsequent construction took place both on the bluff and on the riverbanks below. Kiev continued as one of the centres of commerce in medieval eastern Europe until it was sacked by the Mongols in the 13th century AD.

Kiik-Koba a Middle Palaeolithic cave-site in the Crimea, Ukraine. Two occupation levels were identified by the excavator. The age of the occupations is unknown, but the remains of arctic fox and choughs in the upper level indicate cold climatic conditions (early last GLACIAL?); MEGALOCEROS and saiga remains are common. Artifacts from the lower level are crude and battered in appearance, containing few defined tool types. The upper level yielded an assemblage rich in sidescrapers and bifacial foliates. Two burials were also found in the cave, but it is unclear with which level(s) they are associated. One burial contained the remains of a robust adult NEANDERTHAL. The second burial contained the poorly preserved remains of a young child. Kiik-Koba was excavated by Bonch-Osmolovskij in 1924–6.

Kili Gul Mohammad see QUETTA.

Killke the ceramic style pertaining to the CUZCO region of Peru, in the LATE INTERMEDIATE PERIOD, the antecedent to INCA-style ceramics. First identified by John H. Rowe, Killke vessels have globular bodies, a white or buff SLIP, and simple geometric designs painted usually in black, and sometimes in black and red.

kill-site an archaeological site, whose primary function was the killing of single or multiple animals. The site is recognized by its particular location, tool assemblages or TAPHONOMY.

kiln sites centres in a number of mainland Asian states where glazed stonewares were manufactured during the early 2nd millennium AD, the best-known wares being produced at Phnom Kulen and Buriram (ANGKOR), Go Sanh (CHAMPA), Kalong and the SUKHOTHAI sites in Thailand, sites in northern Vietnam and probably in Burma.

Kilu a limestone shelter on Buka Island, northern Solomons, MELANESIA. There are three main phases of occupation, one about 28,000–20,000 bp and a second about 9000–6500 bp; the upper levels of the site contain plain calcareous-tempered pottery dated elsewhere to c.2500 bp. The flaked stone artifacts are primarily undiagnostic scrapers and flakes, on some of which plant residues have been identified. Kilu establishes Late Pleistocene occupation of islands off the SAHUL shelf, implying the capacity for regular open-sea voyaging. See also BISMARCK ARCHIPELAGO.

Kilwa an important trading centre on the island of Kilwa Kisiwani, 1.5 km (1 mile) off the coast of Tanzania, with the ruins of many centuries of occupation by Islamic merchants. It was first occupied in the 9th century AD and later became a major mercantile centre on the East African coast, until trade passed into Portuguese hands from the end of the 15th century. The major period of Kilwa's prosperity began after about AD 1200 with the founding of the so-called 'Shirazi' dynasty of rulers who, according to tradition, came from the Persian Gulf. They were Muslims who issued coins and constructed elaborate stone buildings, including a mosque and a magnificent palace. Large quantities of goods were imported from Arabia and the east, such as Islamic glazed ceramics, Chinese porcelains and glass. These were exchanged for ivory, skins and, especially, gold from the African interior.

Kimberley point a pressure-flaked bifacial point sometimes with a serrated edge, found mainly in the Kimberley region of Western Australia, but also traded widely in northern and central Australia. Their antiquity is unknown, but point industries in northern Australia generally belong to the AUSTRALIAN SMALL TOOL TRADITION. Kimberley points were still made at European contact and new raw materials such as glass and porcelain were quickly adopted.

Kimhae a city on the southern Korean coast housing the Kimhae SHELL MIDDEN of the PROTO-THREE KINGDOMS period (see KOREA). The midden is the type-site for Kimhae pottery, a category now hotly contested as to its composition. It traditionally included both earthenware and stoneware of the 1st–4th centuries AD, but is now confined by some archaeologists to stoneware alone (compare WAJIL). Kimhae region was also the centre of one of the KAYA polities in the THREE KINGDOMS period.

kin a period of time in the CLASSIC MAYA LONG COUNT equalling a single day.

Kinai a pre-modern district in western-central Honshu Island, Japan, consisting of the original 'five home provinces' of Japan: YAMATO, Kawachi, Izumi, Settsu and Yamashiro (see RITSURYO) – now comprising parts of Nara, Osaka and Kyoto Prefectures. The term is widely used in archaeological writings.

Kinki a modern administrative district in Japan comprising Hyogo, Kyoto, Shuga, Mie, Nara, Osaka and Wayakama Prefectures. It is one of the regional designations often used in archaeological work.

Kintampo a mid 2nd-millennium bc complex associated with the beginning of food production in West Africa. In comparison with preceding Stone Age societies, it is characterized by evidence for intensification in village settlement, subsistence, food processing, art and decoration, as well as exchange networks. The economy was based on domesticated sheep and goats, although hunting continued to be important, and possibly also involved oil-palm management and yam cultivation. Abundant grindstones are thought to attest to increased plant-food processing. There is a dramatic increase in the

quantity of ceramics, which probably reflects more use of ceramics for cooking and storage. Artifacts also include shell and stone beads, stone bracelets and clay figurines, as well as a unique but characteristic scored stone slab or 'Kintampo cigar' of unknown function (see SONGON DAGBE). Recent excavations at Birimi, a Kintampo site in northern Ghana, have produced grains of pearl millet in sub-Saharan Africa.

Kirillovskaya an Upper Palaeolithic open-air site in the city of Kiev on the Dnieper River in Ukraine. The remains are buried in slope deposits on the second terrace. The site was discovered in 1893 by Khvojko, who conducted the first large-scale excavations (more than 7,000 sq. m [8,370 sq. yds]) of an open-air Palaeolithic site here in 1894–1900. Woolly mammoth predominates among the faunal remains, and as many as four MAMMOTH-BONE HOUSES may have been unearthed by Khvojko without being recognized as such. A recently reported AMS radiocarbon date of 19,200 bp supports earlier assignment of the occupation to the late Upper Palaeolithic.

Kisalian an extraordinarily rich Iron Age complex in the southeastern Democratic Republic of Congo, which succeeded the KAMILAMBIAN towards the 8th century AD. The Classic Kisalian reached its peak in the 10th century AD, and is associated with graves containing numerous objects in iron, copper and ivory as well as items suggesting contact with the East African coastal trade, and finely made pottery. Kisalian funerary practices indicate the beginning of a hierarchical society in Central Africa at the turn of the 1st millennium AD (see SANGA).

Kisapostag an Early to Middle Bronze Age culture of western Hungary and Slovenia characterized by cemeteries with cremation burials. Although typologically contemporaneous with late ÚNETICE and HATVAN, the use of the cremation burial rite in open cemeteries by the Kisapostag culture in the early 2nd millennium bc foreshadows that of the URNFIELD period several centuries later.

Kisese a series of sites with impressive rock paintings in the Kondoa region of central Tanzania, including naturalistic animals and anthropomorphs. Kisese II rockshelter has a transitional MIDDLE STONE AGE/LATER STONE AGE industry containing small convex scrapers and ostrich eggshell beads associated with a radiocarbon date of 31,480 bp, above which there is a long sequence of Later Stone Age microlithic assemblages.

Kish an important EARLY DYNASTIC city on a former channel of the Euphrates. The site is composed of several separate large mounds that together define an occupation sequence from 'UBAID to medieval times. Excavation at Kish occurred as early as the 1850s, but the most informative investigations were those of Ernest Mackay and L. Watelin in the 1920s and early 1930s. Evidence for the earliest occupations is confined to several 'Ubaid sherds; good occupation contexts begin with the JEMDET NASR and run through early Islamic periods. The most significant contributions of Kish to the archaeology of southern MESOPOTAMIA belong to the Early Dynastic periods at the Ingharra group of mounds. The discoveries here include the 'Y' settlement (Early Dynastic I–II) with its rich burial evidence (including cart burials of the sort also found at UR and SUSA), and the 'A' complex of palace and ziggurat (Early Dynastic I–II) and cemetery (Early Dynastic IIIb and AKKADIAN); major flood deposits separated the 'Y' and 'A' occupations. The importance of Kish to the 3rd-millennium history of southern Mesopotamia is reflected in the textual sources, where it plays a pivotal role in the regional political affairs of competing city-states, and the city may have been the centre of a cultural tradition distinct from that further south in Mesopotamia (see ABU SALABIKH).

Kiskevély a prehistoric cave-site located near Budapest in northern-central Hungary. Artifacts and faunal remains are buried in clay and rubble. The lower cultural layer contains Middle Palaeolithic tools (chiefly side-scrapers), apparently dating to the early part of the last GLACIAL. GRAVETTIAN (?), Neolithic and younger remains occur in the upper layers.

Kissonerga-Mosphilia one of the largest CHALCOLITHIC (mid 4th- to mid 3rd-millennium) settlements on CYPRUS, being excavated by Peltenburg. The houses are circular stone structures. Floors and walls were plastered and sometimes painted.

Kissonerga-Mylouthkia an early CHALCOLITHIC (mid 4th-millennium BC) site in western CYPRUS, investigated by Peltenburg in 1976–80, consists of a dense cluster of hollows which contained occupational debris but may not actually have been inhabited.

kitchen-garden agriculture a form of cultivation where garden and tree crops are grown in plots adjacent to dwellings. This form of agriculture is currently an important component of MAYA households' subsistence. Recent work in the Maya area suggests that the clear areas near prehistoric residential mounds, previously identified as plazas, may be kitchen gardens. This idea has implications for understanding the demographics and the agricultural practices of the Maya.

kitchen midden 1 *n.* a mound formed by the accumulation of domestic refuse.
   2 *adj.* relating to the people who created the MIDDEN. In Scandinavia, particularly Denmark where mounds of shellfish debris (*Kjökkenmöddings*) of up to 2,000 cu. m (2,600 cu. yds) have been found, the name 'SHELL MIDDEN' is given to some of the Mesolithic groups. See also ERTEBØLLE, OBANIAN.

Kition the site of a major Late Cypriot settlement in southern CYPRUS, which has been excavated by Karageorghis. The site was first occupied in the 13th century BC. The settlers evidently profited from the copper trade and built two temples. In *c.*1200 BC Kition was destroyed, possibly by the SEA PEOPLES. CYCLOPEAN fortifications replaced the earlier mud-brick enceinte (enclosure) and the sanctuary was enlarged. The industrial installations constructed alongside the temples suggest that metallurgy and religion were closely linked. In the 11th century BC, possibly as a result of an earthquake, Kition was abandoned but was recolonized in the 9th century BC by the PHOENICIANS, who rebuilt the temples and remained until 312 BC.

kiva a ceremonial chamber, often semi- or completely subterranean and of varying shape, used by contemporary PUEBLO groups of the American Southwest. Prehistoric kivas are thought to have evolved out of earlier PITHOUSE structures.

Kivik Bronze Age cairn on the Baltic coast of Scania, southern Sweden, dated to approximately 1000 BC. In 1748, several large stone slabs with engravings were discovered to line its interior. The engravings depict what appears to be a funeral procession – mourners, chariots and people blowing horns and beating drums. Some of these images are echoed in rock art at other sites in Scandinavia.

Kjökkenmöddings see KITCHEN MIDDEN.

Klasies River Mouth a series of caves and overhangs on the Tsitsikama coast of the Eastern Cape Province of South Africa, which has provided 20 m (66 ft) of clearly stratified deposits forming one of the most complete sequences available for studying the archaeological record and sea-level changes of the Late Pleistocene. Of particular interest are some of the oldest-known remains of anatomically modern HOMO *sapiens*, considered to date to some 100,000 years ago; arguable indications of CANNIBALISM in the Late Pleistocene; and evidence for the systematic exploitation of marine resources such as shellfish by 120,000 years ago. The detailed MIDDLE STONE AGE artifact sequence shows that the HOWIESON'S POORT industry is part of the Middle Stone Age rather than transitional between the Middle and LATER STONE AGE as previously thought. The Middle Stone Age HOMINID remains and artifacts play an important role in debates about the origins of modern humans and modern human behaviour. The extensive Middle Stone Age sequence is capped by Later Stone Age deposits containing painted stones and burials with numerous shell beads dating to the last 5,000 years.

Klein Afrika one of the earliest Early Iron Age sites in the Northern Province of South Africa, with pottery associated with dates from the 4th–6th century AD.

klepsydra 1 a spring located on the slopes of the AKRO-POLIS at ATHENS.

2 a water clock. In the law courts at ATHENS one basin containing two choes (see CHOUS) would drain into a second basin at a lower level. They would have timed a speech of six minutes.

kleroterion an allotment machine used to decide who would serve on the jury in the law courts. Surviving examples, such as the one from the AGORA at ATHENS, are made of marble, although it is likely that others were of wood. The front face was divided into several columns, into which a potential juror placed a ticket which would identify him. A bronze tube attached to the side of the machine would allow balls to drop and, depending on their colour, would decide which groups of jurors would be accepted or rejected.

Klimá, Bohuslav (1925–2000) a Czech archaeologist who carried out important fieldwork at the Upper Palaeolithic sites of DOLNÍ VĚSTONICE, PAVLOV, Petrkovice and PREDMOSTI, and did seminal work on the Pavlov culture, a Central European variant of the GRAVETTIAN industry.

kline a couch used widely in the Greek world. It normally has a head-board, and occasionally a foot-board. The kline was often used to recline on during the SYMPOSIUM. Dining-rooms may be easily recognized on an archaeological site, as the layout of the couches arranged around the walls required that the entrance door to the room had to be offset to one side. See also TRICLINIUM.

Klisoura Gorge, Cave 1 a Palaeolithic cave-site in the eastern Peloponnese, Greece, with an important sequence from the AURIGNACIAN (dating from 34,000 to 24,000 bp) to the EPIGRAVETTIAN and Mesolithic. The Aurignacian contains several basin-like structured hearths, lined with daub. The fauna is dominated by fallow deer and hare.

knapping the working of stone to produce a tool by applying force to its surface, either by percussion (direct or indirect) or by pressure. The hard but brittle nature of flint and its homogeneous structure made it the preferred knapping material in prehistoric Europe and North Africa. See also BULB OF PERCUSSION, HARD HAMMER, SOFT HAMMER, PRESSURE FLAKING, PRIMARY FLAKING, SECONDARY FLAKING, STRIKING PLATFORM.

knapping floor see CHIPPING FLOOR.

Kniegrotte an Upper Palaeolithic cave-site located on the Orla River in eastern Germany. Artifacts and faunal remains (chiefly horse and reindeer) are buried in loam and rubble dated by radiocarbon to 13,582–10,175 bp. Artifacts include burins, borers and a harpoon; they are assigned to the late MAGDALENIAN.

Knorosov, Yuri Valentinovich (1922–99) a Soviet linguist who 'cracked' the MAYA hieroglyphic code by relating

KNOWTH, Ireland: satellite passage graves.

phonetic symbols recorded in the 16th century by Bishop Diego de Landa to existing Maya languages. His insights were initially rejected by Western Mayanists, but eventually proved to be crucial and have generated tremendous advances in decipherment.

Knossos a site on Crete that has been occupied more or less continuously since 6000 BC when the first Neolithic settlers arrived. Neolithic Knossos was discovered by EVANS during his excavation of the MINOAN palace. This was constructed c.1900 BC, destroyed by an earthquake c.1700 BC, and then completely rebuilt. Like MALLIA, PHAISTOS and ZAKRO, Knossos was a multi-storey structure, planned around a central court and designed to serve a range of different functions: political, economic, cultural and religious. As the largest of the Minoan palaces, Knossos is likely to have governed much of Crete. This was certainly the case c.1450–1370 BC when the MYCENAEANS were in control. Even after the final destruction of the palace, Knossos remained prosperous and powerful, emerging as one of the foremost Greek city states on Crete.

Knovíz culture a Bronze Age URNFIELD regional group of Bohemia and parts of Thuringia and Bavaria between 1400 and 900 bc. A characteristic Knovíz vessel form is the *Etagengefäss*, in which a large bulging vessel has a smaller bottomless pot fused on top of it to form a neck. Essentially similar is the neighbouring MILAVČE group. Knovíz settlements appear to have been small rural farmsteads.

Knowth a large circular Neolithic burial mound over 60 m (65 yds) in diameter in Co. Meath, Ireland, containing two PASSAGE GRAVES entered from opposite sides of the mound. The passages and chambers are richly decorated with megalithic art, as are many of the stones in the kerb which encircles the mound. Around it lies a series of smaller satellite passage graves. Knowth is one of the three principal elements of the BOYNE VALLEY megalithic cemetery and dates probably from the 4th millennium BC.

Koban culture a Late Bronze Age/Early Iron Age culture centred on northern Ossetia in the Caucasus, Russia, dated between 1100 and 400 BC. The Koban culture is known primarily from burials in stone cists grouped into small cemeteries. These have yielded many large bronze objects, particularly figurines with animal motifs and shaft-hole axes, which reflect considerable metallurgical skill and the local abundance of copper.

Kobystan a low plateau in Azerbaijan west of Baku and set against the eastern end of the Caucasus mountain range, which is perhaps best known for its corpus of rock art, some of which is Mesolithic and Neolithic in date (the rest being Bronze Age and medieval). The earlier series show human and animal figures, often in hunting scenes (drives, bow and arrow). Excavations at rockshelters in the area (e.g. Kjaniza) indicate hunting-gathering communities using a microlithic (including geometrics) tool-kit, who at some point started using pottery without a change in lithic technology or subsistence. The fauna recovered from these sites corresponds well to the animals depicted in the rock art (cattle and onager, with fewer mountain goat and gazelle).

Kodak a Middle Palaeolithic locality on the lower Dnieper River in Ukraine. A small assemblage of artifacts, including several sidescrapers, was recovered from sediment filling an ancient ravine. Among the associated faunal remains are early forms of woolly mammoth and reindeer. Kodak was excavated by Teslya in 1934–5.

Kodiak tradition a long-lasting tradition (5000 BP to the historic period) that was centred on Kodiak Island and the adjacent mainland of Alaska, and which was characterized by a heavy use of polished slate for artifacts. Subsistence practices concentrated on the hunting of sea-mammals. Towards the end of the period, it was influenced by elements of the THULE culture.

kodj or **kodja** a flaked stone hammer-hatchet unique to southwestern Australia, comprising two semi-discoidal flakes of igneous rock hafted in a ball of Xanthorrhoea resin mounted on a thin handle. One stone is usually blunt for pounding, while the other is sharpened for chopping.

Koenigswald, Gustav H. Ralph von (1902–82) a Dutch-German palaeoanthropologist, best known for his discoveries of HOMINID remains in Java at NGANDONG in 1933 and SANGIRAN in 1937–9.

Kofun literally 'old mound'; the name of the protohistoric 'Tomb' period in Japan (AD 300–710) featuring YAMATO and RITSURYO state formation and development. Characterized by HAJI ware, SUE ware and MOUNDED TOMBS, the Kofun period is divided into Early

(4th century), Middle (5th century) and Late (terminal 5th–7th centuries) phases which are illuminated by the KOJIKI and NIHON SHOKI texts. See also JAPANESE PERIODIZATION.

Koguryo a protohistoric people of eastern Manchuria related to the PUYO, known from HAN Dynasty texts as horse-riders, who became a strong state power in the 4th century AD (see PROTO-THREE KINGDOMS, THREE KINGDOMS). They are famous for their MURAL TOMBS (see ANAK, DONGGOU).

Kojiki the earliest surviving chronicle of Japan, compiled in AD 712 under the RITSURYO state. Together with the NIHON SHOKI, it provides protohistoric data for the preceding KOFUN period.

Kökénydomb a Neolithic settlement of Hungary's TISZA culture in which small rectangular houses stood in close parallel rows with narrow alleys between them. Fragments of plaster from the Kökénydomb houses were found; these had been decorated with elaborate incised decoration. Notable ceramic artifacts include what have been called 'altars' – enigmatic rectangular or triangular clay pedestals.

Ko Kho Kao a port site on the west coast of peninsular Thailand near TAKUAPA, from which have been recovered fragments of Middle Eastern glass and Chinese glazed stonewares of the late 8th and 9th centuries AD; it was probably linked by an overland route to the port of LAEM PHO.

Kokkinopilos a group of Palaeolithic open-air sites along the Louros River in northwestern Greece. Artifacts were recovered from the surface and from fill deposits. At one locality, Middle Palaeolithic LEVALLOIS cores and flakes in the fill deposits were dated by THERMOLUMINESCENCE to more than 150,000 BP. Bifacial foliates are also present, and may be of comparable age. Kokkinopilos was investigated by HIGGS in 1963–4.

Kokorevo a group of six Upper Palaeolithic open-air sites on the Yenisei River in southern-central Siberia. At each locality, artifacts and faunal remains are buried in ALLUVIUM of the second terrace; among the fauna, reindeer and hare are the most common species. Nine radiocarbon estimates from Kokorevo I–IV range between 15,900 and 12,940 bp. The artifacts include wedge-shaped microcores, microblades, sidescrapers and retouched blades. At Kokorevo I, two bone points with microblades set into their sides were found, one embedded in the shoulder-blade of a steppe bison. Assemblages from Kokorevo I are assigned to the KOKOREVO CULTURE, but those from Kokorevo II and III are assigned to the AFONTOVA CULTURE. The Kokorevo sites were initially excavated by Sosnovskij in 1925–8; later excavations were undertaken by Abramova from 1961–6.

Kokorevo culture an Upper Palaeolithic culture of southern-central Siberia, dating to c.20,000–10,000 BP. Diagnostic artifacts include wedge-shaped microcores, microblades, sidescrapers and endscrapers. The Kokorevo culture was defined by Abramova in 1979.

Koldewey, Robert (1855–1925) a German architect who established the German participation in the archaeological investigation of MESOPOTAMIA. After working in Anatolia and the eastern Mediterranean, he began excavation in Mesopotamia, where he investigated AL HIBA, Fara, ASSUR and, over an eighteen-year period, BABYLON. In the latter site, he uncovered the famous ISHTAR Gate, and also the temple of MARDUK, palace of NEBUCHAD-NEZZAR and other monuments. This work is published in a series of reports that still form the basis for understanding the archaeology of Babylon.

Köln-Lindenthal a site of the LINEAR POTTERY CULTURE near Cologne, in the Rhineland, western Germany, c.4300–4100 bc. Excavated by Buttler in 1929–34, Köln-Lindenthal was one of the earliest attempts to expose a settlement plan. The excavator initially interpreted the large pits as subterranean dwellings and the post structures as granaries. Subsequently, the post structures were identified as LONGHOUSES, with the pits serving as the sources of mud plaster for the house walls. Köln-Lindenthal is unusual among Linear Pottery settlements in that it is encircled by a ditched enclosure in its later phases.

Kolomiishchina one of the best-known village sites of the CUCUTENI-TRIPOLYE culture, in western Ukraine. Kolomiishchina is estimated to cover 2.7 ha (6.7 acres), about half of which has been excavated. The excavator identified the traces of thirty-nine complete or partially preserved structures, from 4 m (13 ft) to over 22 m (72 ft) in length. Most of the buildings were arranged in a circle approximately 100 m (110 yds) in diameter, in the centre of which were two structures. While the presence of ovens suggests that most buildings were houses, others may have been used for storage or as shrines.

Kolomoki a large site in Georgia, USA, covering over 4,000 sq. km (1,550 sq. miles), that comprises numerous BURIAL MOUNDS, as well as a PLATFORM MOUND, and dates to the latter half of the 1st century AD. The size of the complex is indicative of a CHIEFDOM level of social organization, unlike other less socially complex contemporary cultures.

Kolonna a site on the island of Aegina in the Aegean that has been occupied almost continuously since the late 4th millennium. The Bronze Age settlement, which was protected by a series of fortifications, is an extraordinary amalgam of the HELLADIC, CYCLADIC and MINOAN cultural traditions. The site derives its name from the single intact column of the 6th-century BC temple of Apollo.

Kommos the site of a MINOAN settlement on the south coast of Crete, excavated by Shaw. It would seem that Kommos served as the harbour town for the palace of PHAISTOS. One monumental structure may have been built so that ships could be kept in dry dock over the winter. In the 10th century BC, after a period of abandonment, a temple was built on the ruins of the Minoan town. This sanctuary remained in use until the Roman period.

Kom Ombo the site of a TEMPLE in southern UPPER EGYPT constructed by Ptolemaic kings and early Roman emperors. The Temple is unusual in having a double axis, a result of its dedication to two principal deities, Haroeris (a form of HORUS) and the crocodile-headed Sobek. To the south of Kom Ombo itself is a substantial tract of agricultural land where, in the 1920s, Vignard excavated a series of Upper Palaeolithic sites which produced a series of chronologically overlapping industries now termed the Sebekian, Silsillian and Sebillian (c.15,000 to 9500 BC).

Komornica culture the name applied to the early Mesolithic assemblages of the area lying between the Oder and Bug drainages in central and northern Poland, roughly contemporaneous with the MAGLEMOSIAN culture in Denmark during the 9th and 8th millennia BC.

Kondoa see KISESE.

Kongemose a Mesolithic culture of southern Scandinavia and Denmark, whose type-site is the lake-settlement of Kongemosen in Zealand. Dating to the late BOREAL and early ATLANTIC (c.5600–5000 bc), the culture lies between the MAGLEMOSIAN and ERTEBØLLE. Known primarily from summer coastal sites devoted to the exploitation of forest species and marine resources, it features large blades, axes, bone points and a mainly geometric art.

Königsaue a Middle Palaeolithic open-air site located northwest of Halle in eastern Germany. Artifacts and faunal remains (e.g. woolly mammoth, reindeer) are buried in a lengthy succession of lake deposits (former Aschersleben Lake); Middle Palaeolithic occupation is dated to the early GLACIAL. The artifacts include sidescrapers and small handaxes.

Konso-Gardula a rich site in southern Ethiopia where early ACHEULIAN stone artifacts, dating to shortly after 1.4 million years ago, were found in 1991 in association with a mandible of HOMO *ergaster*.

Kon-Tiki the replica of a balsa raft of the type observed in the 16th century AD along the coasts of Ecuador and northern Peru, built in 1947 for Thor Heyerdahl. With a crew of five, he sailed the raft from South America to the Tuamotu Archipelago to demonstrate that South American Indians could have reached POLYNESIA. Archaeological evidence, however, suggests that such contact could only have been minor.

Koobi Fora an area along the northeast shore of LAKE TURKANA in northern Kenya which is one of the richest known depositories of early HOMINID fossils and stone artifacts from the period between about 2.5 and 1 million years ago. Of particular interest are the fragmentary remains of more than 150 hominids, including specimens attributed to a robust australopithecine (*A. aethiopicus* or *A. boisei*), a possible gracile australopithecine and several species of early HOMO, including *H. habilis*, *H. ergaster* as well as *H. rudolfensis*, for which the 1.9 million-year-old cranium KNM-ER 1470 was the type specimen used to name this species (see KBS 2). See also KARARI, OLDOWAN.

Koolan 2 a rockshelter in the Buccaneer Archipelago off the West Kimberley coast, Western Australia, with evidence of use of marine resources in the Late Pleistocene and early Holocene. A minimum age of 27,300 bp makes this the oldest coastal site in Australia. See also MANDU MANDU CREEK, MATENKUPKUM.

Koonalda Cave a limestone sinkhole on the Nullarbor Plain, South Australia. Excavations by Alexander Gallus, and later by Richard Wright, showed that the cave was visited between about 24,000 bp and 14,000 bp to mine flint nodules. Finger markings deeper in the cave in complete darkness are presumed to be contemporary with the quarrying. They comprise random meandering lines, together with a few more definite designs such as grids or lattices and concentric circles. Charcoal from the floor dated to about 20,000 bp may be from torches.

Koongine a limestone cave in southeastern South Australia, excavated by David Frankel. Most of the 2 m (6.5 ft) of deposit relates to a 1,000–2,000 year period of occupation about 9000 bp. The site was only reoccupied within the last 1,000 years. The stone assemblage confirms an early Holocene date for the GAMBIERAN industry. Like other caves in the region, Koongine has finger markings similar to those at KOONALDA CAVE.

Koori or **Koorie** the name preferred by non-traditional Aboriginal people over much of southeastern Australia to refer to themselves. Other names are in use by Aboriginal groups elsewhere.

Korakou a site in the Corinthia, Greece, which was excavated by BLEGEN in 1915–16 and proved to have been occupied more or less continuously throughout the Bronze Age. It was largely on the basis of the Korakou stratigraphy that WACE and Blegen devised their classification of the HELLADIC pottery sequence. This is also the type-site for the Early Helladic II Korakou culture.

kore a statue, usually draped, of a female figure. Korai are usually found as dedications in Greek sanctuaries, although some have been found in funerary contexts. An important series have been found in the temple of Hera on Samos as well as on the AKROPOLIS at ATHENS. The clothes of some of the Athenian examples have retained extensive traces of bright colours. Inscriptions show that many of these female statues were set up by men, and thus the choice of sex may be related to the nature of the deity in whose sanctuary the statues were placed. Compare KOUROS.

Korea Korean archaeology is a relatively new discipline which is actively pursued through excavations by universities, museums and strategically located national research institutes. The Palaeolithic period was only discovered in 1962. KULPO-RI site in the north and SOKCHANG-RI in the central peninsula are thought, on faunal and stratigraphic evidence, to date to up to 400,000 years ago. Finds of HOMO *erectus* fossils at JINNIUSHAN – north of the Korean border with China – raise the possibility that the pensinsula might have seen occupation by human ancestors.

The Holocene saw the development of coastal and riverine occupation, such as at the TONGSAM-DONG SHELL MOUND on the south coast and AMSADONG village site on the Han River. The subsistence regime was characterized by riverine fishing, collecting of shellfish and processing of gathered plant foods. The prehistoric period (8000–700 BC) is known by the name of the textured-surface pottery produced – CHULMUN, meaning 'comb-marked' – earliest known from the OSAN-RI site.

From c.2000 BC, millet cultivation was introduced from northeastern China, and, slightly later, rice from southern China. HUNAM-RI shows the new colonization of hilly areas for crop growing. The pottery changed at this time to plain surfaces (MUMUN). It is thought that the basis of village life became sufficiently stabilized in this period to support hierarchical social development with the adoption of bronze working from 700 BC.

Despite proximity to the early Chinese states, the Korean Bronze Age (700 BC–AD 0) shows clear affiliations with the northeastern Asian bronze tradition – as evidenced by the lute-shaped daggers discovered at SONGGUK-RI and DOLMEN building.

From the 4th century BC, the northern peninsula was influenced by the Chinese state of Yan, a notable producer of iron. The northern peninsula entered the Iron Age (400 BC–AD 300) as much as four centuries before iron was known to southern Korea. In 108 BC, the Han Dynasty conquered the northern peninsula and established military commanderies in the region. During the commandery period (108 BC–AD 313) the southern peninsula acquired iron and stoneware technology, as known from the KIMHAE shell mound.

With the collapse of the commandery system, the regional polities of KOGURYO, SILLA and PAEKCHE

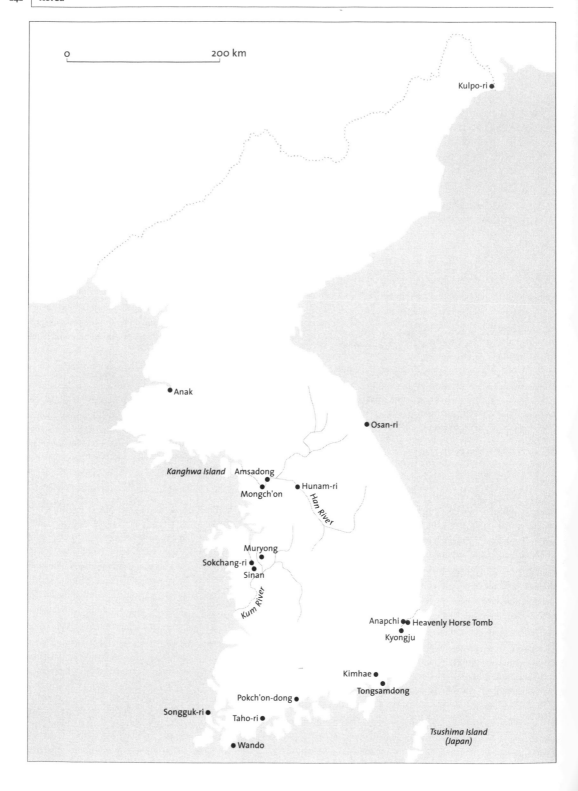

0   200 km

Kulpo-ri ●

● Anak

● Osan-ri

Kanghwa Island   Amsadong ●
           ● Hunam-ri
Mongch'on ●

Han River

Muryong ●
Sokchang-ri ●
Sinan ●

Kum River

Anapchi ●● Heavenly Horse Tomb
          ● Kyongju

Kimhae ●
      ● Tongsamdong

Pokch'on-dong ●
Songguk-ri ●   Taho-ri ●

● Wando

*Tsushima Island
(Japan)*

developed in the THREE KINGDOMS period (AD 300–668). These polities were characterized by walled site construction, such as at MONGCH'ON, and monumental tomb construction: for example, the HEAVENLY HORSE TOMB and MURYONG tomb.

The adoption of the TANG administrative style by Silla in the 7th century resulted in the construction of a gridded city on the CHANG'AN model. The ANAPCHI pond and pavilions have recently been reconstructed to illustrate the new urban style. Silla conquered its rivals in 668, leading to the establishment of a bureaucratic state on Confucian principles. United Silla (AD 668–918) was succeeded by Koryo (AD 918–1392), and ties with China were maintained into the historic period – both diplomatically and through trade, as known at the shipwreck sites of SINAN and WANDO. Buddhism, introduced in the Three Kingdoms period, provides the context for much other historical archaeology.

Korman' IV a Palaeolithic and Mesolithic open-air site on the Dniester River in western Ukraine. A total of sixteen occupation horizons are buried in a thick bed of slope deposits overlying ALLUVIUM on the second terrace. The four lowest horizons contain Middle Palaeolithic artifacts, are associated with buried soils, and appear to date to warm intervals preceding and/or following the early cold LAST GLACIAL MAXIMUM. A sequence of younger horizons, dated by radiocarbon estimates and stratigraphic correlation, spans the early and late Upper Palaeolithic (30,000–10,000 bp). Two Mesolithic horizons are contained in the modern soil. Korman' IV, in conjunction with the MOLODOVA sites, provides a key to the succession of Palaeolithic industries of the Dniester region. The site was discovered and initially studied by Botez in 1930–31; Chernysh conducted large-scale excavations 1948–61.

Korolevo a Palaeolithic open-air site located on the Tisza River in the eastern Carpathian basin, Ukraine. Thirteen artifact layers occur in a sequence of loams containing numerous buried soils; stream gravels underlying the loams also contain artifacts. Faunal remains are absent. The lowest two layers are dated by THERMOLUMINESCENCE and PALAEOMAGNETISM to the late Lower Pleistocene (i.e. 730,000 bp). Both these and the five overlying layers are assigned to the Lower Palaeolithic, and contain chopping tools, bifaces, sidescrapers and other tools. Except for the uppermost layer, which is assigned to the Upper Palaeolithic, the remaining layers contain Middle Palaeolithic assemblages (e.g. LEVALLOIS cores, sidescrapers). Korolevo appears to represent one of the oldest occupations, and provides one of the most important Palaeolithic cultural sequences in Europe.

Körös an early Neolithic culture of southern Hungary, part of the complex that includes KARANOVO I, CRIŞ and STARČEVO (sometimes seen in literature as STARČEVO-KÖRÖS). Körös settlements do not form TELLS but rather tend to occur on river levees in this low-lying region. The most common species in Körös faunal assemblages are sheep and goats. The Körös culture is believed to have been the precursor of the LINEAR POTTERY culture that subsequently developed on the Hungarian Plain.

Korpach an Upper Palaeolithic open-air site on the Prut River in Moldova. The lowest occupation level has yielded a radiocarbon date of 25,250 bp, and contains an assemblage rich in tool types characteristic of both the Middle and Upper Palaeolithic. The upper levels presumably date to the late Upper Palaeolithic. The site was excavated by Grigor'eva in 1975–6.

Korucu Tepe a small (3 ha [7 acre]) mound on the Altinova plain of eastern Anatolia, in the upper Euphrates drainage, where M. van Loon's work provides a cultural sequence of 140 levels divided into twelve phases that begins with the early CHALCOLITHIC (around 4500 BC) and runs largely unbroken to the Early Iron Age (to c.800 BC); a medieval occupation caps this sequence. The Korucu sequence, a standard for regional comparative chronology, also reflects some of the broader interregional patterns of western Asian prehistory, including some connection with the HALAF phenomenon in the early occupations, and a strong connection with the KURA-ARAXES culture during the 3rd millennium.

Koryo see KOREA.

Kosipe an open site in the NEW GUINEA HIGHLANDS, dating back to c.26,000 bp. The sparse artifacts include WAISTED AXES and tanged tools.

Kossinna, Gustaf (1858–1931) a professor of German prehistory, beginning in 1902 at the University of Berlin. Kossinna developed a method for the study of prehistoric cultures, which he called 'settlement archaeology', involving the mapping of characteristic finds to establish the boundaries of their distribution. His interpretation of these distributions had a distinctly nationalistic character, particularly when applied to the artifacts which he identified as 'Germanic', found between the Oder and Vistula Rivers in Central Europe.

Kostenki-Borshchevo a group of twenty-five Upper Palaeolithic open-air sites on the Don River in European Russia. The sites are located on the first and second terraces, adjacent to side-valley ravines, on the west bank of the river. The remains are buried in slope deposits containing humic layers and a thin volcanic ash layer, which permit cross-correlation among many sites. Early Upper Palaeolithic occupations (more than 25,000 bp), associated with remains of horse and other mammals, were found on the second terrace. At five sites, cultural layers underlie the volcanic ash and apparently date to c.36,000–32,000 bp or earlier; these cultural layers contain assemblages assigned to the STRELETS CULTURE and

SPITSYN CULTURE. Cultural layers were found in humic horizons above the volcanic ash dating to c.32,000–26,000 bp at eight sites; they contain assemblages of the Strelets culture and the GORODTSOV CULTURE. Younger cultural layers assigned to late Upper Palaeolithic industries (c.25,000–10,000 bp), and often associated with large quantities of woolly mammoth remains, occur at shallower depths on the second terrace and on the first terrace. Complex feature arrangements, including MAMMOTH-BONE HOUSES, traces of other types of dwelling structures, debris-filled pits, hearths and debris concentrations, were found at some sites; many items of PORTABLE ART, including ivory animal and 'VENUS' FIGURINES, were also recovered. Excavations were initiated at Kostenki in 1879 by Polyakov; in subsequent years, investigations were undertaken by Spitsyn, EFIMENKO, ROGACHEV, BORISKOWSKIJ, Praslov and others.

Kostenki-Willendorf culture an Upper Palaeolithic culture defined on the basis of assemblages from sites distributed across Central Europe and the Russian Plain dating to c.30,000–20,000 bp. The assemblages contain backed blades, shouldered points and art objects including 'VENUS' FIGURINES. It may be generally equated with the EASTERN GRAVETTIAN industry.

Koster a thick, well-stratified multi-component site in Illinois, USA. The site was excavated under the direction of Stuart Struever and James Brown in the 1970s and was one of the first major multi-disciplinary endeavours of the 'NEW ARCHAEOLOGY'. Twenty-three cultural horizons, stratigraphically separated over a thickness greater than 10.5 m (34.5 ft), range in age from greater than 8700 bp to protohistoric times. The site has served as a benchmark for defining the ARCHAIC period cultural chronology in the American Midwest. Focusing on the interrelationships between people and their changing environment, the site has yielded information on the emergence of sedentism, the rise of broad-based subsistence patterns and the origins of wild plant cultivation, all during the Archaic period. The site also contributed to the methodology of excavation, including pioneering approaches to deeply buried sites and the application of the flotation technique of recovering fine-grained remains.

Kostienki see KOSTENKI.

Kostolac an ENEOLITHIC site in Serbia that has given its name to the Kostolac group, often considered a late variant of the BADEN culture of the Carpathian Basin.

Kostrzewski, Józef (1885–1969) a central figure in Polish archaeology during the first half of the 20th century. Kostrzewski founded the department of archaeology at the University of Poznań and was responsible for the excavation of a number of significant sites, including BISKUPIN.

Kosziderpadlás a settlement of the TUMULUS CULTURE of the Middle Bronze Age about 70 km (43 miles) north of Budapest, Hungary, famous for three large hoards that define the range of bronze artifacts found in similar hoards across Central Europe about 1500 BC. Such hoards – with axes and swords decorated in spiral and geometric patterns, spiral bracelets and anklets with rolled ends, and similar elaborate bronze artifacts – mark what is known as the 'Koszider horizon' throughout this region.

Kota Batu see SANTUBONG.

Kota Cina see ŚRIVIJAYA.

Kota Tampan an open site in peninsular Malaysia, yielding remains of a pebble and flake stone industry, once thought to be very early but now dated to 31,000 BP or later, and classed as Upper Palaeolithic.

Kot Diji a small, walled site in the upper Sind of Pakistan, excavated in the 1950s by F. Khan, that provides a sequence of Early and Mature HARAPPAN levels. The Early Harappan painted ceramics, similar to later products of the AMRI culture, present several decorative motifs later typical of the Mature Harappan, and characteristic Harappan vessel forms also appear; radiocarbon dates indicate an early 3rd millennium BC date for these levels at Kot Diji. Following extensive burning, the overlying levels of the site are Mature Harappan in character. The Kot Diji pottery style appears over large areas of the Punjab to the north (e.g. HARAPPA, RAHMAN DERI).

Kotosh a major ceremonial site in the northern-central highlands of Peru, first utilized during the Late PRECERAMIC period, and whose occupation continued until after the demise of the CHAVÍN culture of the EARLY HORIZON. A series of temples was constructed in sequence up a hillside at Kotosh; each temple was filled in and covered over, and the subsequent temple built above it. The lowest temple, the Temple of the Crossed Hands, is the best known. Square in plan, the single doorway is flanked on the interior wall by two small rectangular niches, one on either side. Below each niche, modelled in bas-relief in the mud plaster covering the wall, is a pair of crossed human forearms. One pair is larger than the other, suggesting male-female duality. Around the perimeter of the structure is a low bench, and a fire pit is found in the centre of the floor. This style of religious architecture, and evidence of ritual burning of offerings, is found elsewhere in the northern Peruvian Andes, suggesting the existence of what has been termed by Richard Burger and Lucy Salazar-Burger the Kotosh religious tradition. This tradition ended with the expansion of the Chavín cult in the Early Horizon. See also HUARICOTO, LA GALGADA.

kotyle 1 a unit of Greek measure that varied from city to city, ranging from 0.21 to over 0.33 litre (0.37 to 0.6 pint).

2 a type of drinking cup with two horizontal handles more usually called a SKYPHOS.

Kou see SETOUCHI.

Kouklia-Palaepaphos a site in southern CYPRUS that has been the focus of excavations since 1869. There was evidently activity on the site as early as the 3rd millennium BC, but it was in the Late Cypriot period that Palaepaphos became a major centre as the rich tombs in the Evreti cemetery testify. In c.1200 BC a magnificent ASHLAR temple was built, presumably in honour of Aphrodite. This was certainly the centre of her apparently licentious cult in the CLASSICAL period. In 498 BC Palaepaphos, then capital of one of the Cypriot kingdoms, was attacked by the PERSIANS, whose massive siege ramp was never demolished and has been excavated.

Koumbi Saleh or **Kumbi Saleh** a site in southern Mauritania, thought to have been the capital of the GHANA empire, and occupied from at least the 6th century ad, until its apparent abandonment in the 15th century ad. Partial excavations have uncovered the remains of a large urban settlement with a wide central avenue and market lined by two-storey stone buildings, as well as two extensive cemeteries and a mosque, for which the foundations were laid in the 9th century ad. The royal quarter has apparently not yet been excavated. Artifacts indicate the importance of long-distance trade in commodities including gold and salt.

kouros (*Gk* 'a youth') a Greek statue produced in the ARCHAIC period showing a naked striding figure. The two main uses of such statues were as funerary markers or as dedications in sanctuaries; in both cases related inscriptions seem to indicate that they should be associated with members of the social elites. They are usually larger than lifesize although small examples were made. Their medium is often marble, although there are also bronze and alabaster examples. Stone examples could be painted and an example from the AKROPOLIS at ATHENS was given fair hair. The type is thought to have been influenced by Egyptian sculpture. Compare KORE.

Kourounkorokale a cave close to the Niger River in western Mali, containing a microlithic and harpoon industry, with an economy based on fishing, molluscs and hunting. A later phase, featuring microliths, grindstones and decorated pottery, had an economy of hunting and gathering, with little evidence of fishing.

Kow Swamp a cemetery site in the Murray Valley, Victoria, Australia, dating from 15,000 to 9000 bp and documenting a range of burial practices. The fossil material is robust and archaic-looking, and is crucial to Thorne's hypothesis of a dual origin for the Australian Aboriginal population. Brown has shown that some archaic features in skeletal material from Kow Swamp and COOBOOL CREEK can be accounted for by artificial deformation. The Kow Swamp collection is the largest single Late Pleistocene population in the world. It has now been returned to the local Aboriginal community and reburied.

Kradenanrejo a burial site of the early 1st millennium AD near Lamongan, northeastern Java, with a child's burial inside a PEJENG-type bronze drum and covered by a HEGER I drum, together with carnelian, agate, glass and gold beads, bronze containers with DONG SON decoration and a gold umbrella.

Kraków-Spadzista three Upper Palaeolithic sites located on the Rudawa River in Kraków, southern Poland. At Kraków-Spadzista B, EASTERN GRAVETTIAN artifacts (e.g. backed blades, shouldered points) are buried in loess deposits dating to the beginning of the LAST GLACIAL MAXIMUM (23,040–20,600 bp); associated faunal remains are chiefly woolly mammoth, and traces of three MAMMOTH-BONE HOUSES were found. At Kraków-Spadzista A, an AURIGNACIAN assemblage underlies the Eastern Gravettian level.

Kraków-Zwierzyniec a Palaeolithic open-air site located near the confluence of the Rudawa and Vistula Rivers in Kraków, southern Poland. Artifacts and some faunal remains (e.g. woolly mammoth, reindeer) are buried in loess and slope deposits. The lower cultural layers contain Middle Palaeolithic assemblages, apparently dating to the last INTERGLACIAL and subsequent cooler periods. Above a sterile layer, several Upper Palaeolithic assemblages (e.g. endscrapers and burins), assigned to the AURIGNACIAN and dating to the INTERSTADIAL preceding the LAST GLACIAL MAXIMUM, were found.

Krapina Cave a Middle Palaeolithic site located north of Zagreb in Croatia, first excavated by D. Gorjanović-Kramberger in 1899. Artifacts and faunal remains (including red deer, cave bear and rhinoceros [*Dicerorhinus mercki*]) are buried in deposits of sand and rubble, dated by ESR and URANIUM-SERIES to 130,000 BP (last INTERGLACIAL). The Middle Palaeolithic industry is predominantly composed of sidescrapers. Krapina has yielded over 850 skeletal remains representing several NEANDERTHALS (HOMO *neanderthalensis*).

Krasnyj Yar an Upper Palaeolithic open-air site on the Angara River in southern-central Siberia. Seven cultural layers are buried in sand and sandy loam on the third terrace; the age of the occupations is unclear, but they probably date to the LAST GLACIAL MAXIMUM (25,000–14,000 bp). Among the associated faunal remains are reindeer, horse and woolly rhinoceros. The artifact assemblages from the various layers are similar and include wedge-shaped microcores, microblades, points and endscrapers. Krasnyj Yar was initially investigated by OKLADNIKOV in 1957; subsequent excavations were conducted by Abramova in 1957–9, and Aksenov and Medvedev in 1964–5.

krater a large Greek vessel made of clay or metal, in which wine and water were mixed.

Kremikovci an early Neolithic culture of the southern Balkans, centred on the highlands of Macedonia and neighbouring parts of Bulgaria and Yugoslavia. The Kremikovci culture is contemporaneous with, and bears similarities to, the KARANOVO I culture of southern Bulgaria, the STARČEVO culture of Serbia and Bosnia, the KÖRÖS culture of southern Hungary and the CRIŞ culture in Romania. Kremikovci ceramics are characterized by white-on-red or black-on-red painted decoration. Kremikovci settlements, such as Vrsnik, Slatina and Kremikovci itself, tend to be low mounds with thick early Neolithic cultural deposits.

Krems-Hundssteig an Upper Palaeolithic open-air site located on the Danube in northeastern Austria. Artifacts and faunal remains (e.g. woolly mammoth, woolly rhinoceros) are buried in loess deposits. The assemblage, which includes endscrapers and retouched blades and is dated to 35,200 bp, is assigned to the AURIGNACIAN. At the nearby Galgenberg hill, in 1988, a remarkable female figurine of green serpentine was found in an Aurignacian level dated to 31,790 bp.

krepidoma the base or foundations of a CLASSICAL building, usually stepped.

Krivodol group an ENEOLITHIC regional group of northwestern Bulgaria broadly correlated with layer VI at KARANOVO, c.4200–4000 BC, and known largely from settlements such as ZAMINETS.

Kroeber, Alfred Louis (1876–1960) an American anthropologist known primarily for his work in North America, where he supervised NELSON's initial work on California SHELL MOUNDS. He advocated the efficacy of SERIATION, by applying the technique to Zuni POTSHERDS in 1915. Later he conducted fieldwork in Peru, summarized the ceramics collected there by UHLE, and used them to develop regional sequences. He excavated in the NASCA region, including the sites of CAHUACHI and ESTAQUERIA. He was also responsible for formally defining the HORIZON style concept.

Kromdraai a site in Gauteng Province, South Africa, with PLIO-PLEISTOCENE cave fillings containing early HOMINID and associated animal fossils as well as early stone artifacts, which yielded the first robust australopithecine (see AUSTRALOPITHECUS), *Paranthropus robustus*, in 1938. See also STERKFONTEIN, SWARTKRANS.

krotovina a soil feature consisting of an animal burrow filled with soil or sediment that is usually, but not necessarily, in contrast with the surrounding material into which the burrow was excavated. The filling material is derived from overlying soil horizons or sediment strata. Different animals produce burrows of different size, shape and orientation; identification of the animals responsible can provide supplementary environmental information based on habitat requirements or restrictions.

Krzemionki a flint mine in the HOLY CROSS MOUNTAINS of central Poland, in use primarily during the middle and late Neolithic by the FUNNEL BEAKER and GLOBULAR AMPHORA cultures. Axes made from the grey and white 'banded' flint from Krzemionki were widely exchanged throughout the Vistula and Oder drainages. At Krzemionki, in a belt 4 km (2.5 miles) long by about 100 m wide, over 1,000 shafts were sunk to depths of between 4 and 15 m (13 and 49 ft). Galleries reaching 30 m (98 ft) in length connected many of the shafts. The Funnel Beaker settlement of CMIELÓW is located 9 km (6 miles) from Krzemionki.

kshemenitsa a term of Russian derivation used in eastern Europe to refer to a dense scatter of flint artifacts and débitage on a Late Palaeolithic or Mesolithic open site. Within a kshemenitsa, a number of flakes can be refitted to cores, suggesting that these areas were the locations of flint working and related activity.

Kuala Selinsing or **Tanjong Rawa** a port site in peninsular Malaysia, in use for most of the 1st millennium AD, the finds from which include the remains of a bead industry pottery similar to PONTIAN; and Indian seals and Chinese stonewares from surface layers.

Ku Bua a moderately large (2,000 by 800 m [2,190 by 875 yds]) settlement of the DVARAVATI period near the mouth of the Mae Klong River, southern-central Thailand; its roughly rectangular moat possibly dates to the KHMER period of domination, after c.AD 1000. A late Roman lamp from the eastern Mediterranean was found here in the 1920s.

Kückhoven see LINEAR POTTERY.

Kudaro two cave-sites located on the south slope of the Greater Caucasus Mountains (1,600 m [5,250 ft] above sea-level) in Georgia. Artifacts and faunal remains are buried in loam and rubble. At Kudaro I, the three lowest cultural layers are assigned to the ACHEULIAN, and are associated with the remains of Middle Pleistocene vertebrates (e.g. *Dicerorhinus*, *Macaca*). The artifacts include bifaces, choppers and sidescrapers. Small quantities of Middle Palaeolithic artifacts, associated with remains of Late Pleistocene vertebrates including cave bear and salmon, were found in overlying levels; the tools include points and sidescrapers. The uppermost layers contain late Upper Palaeolithic, Mesolithic and younger remains. Both Kudaro I and III were discovered and excavated by Lyubin in 1955–87.

kudurru (literally 'boundary') a term applied to carved stone documents that record land grants or sales during the KASSITE and post-Kassite periods in southern MESO-

POTAMIA. These monuments, often placed in temples, are decorated with the symbols of the various gods whose protection guaranteed the land transfers. The term is also applied, anachronistically, to 3rd-millennium CUNEIFORM documents in southern Mesopotamia that also deal with land transfers.

Kufr Nigm a site in the eastern Nile DELTA, Egypt, excavated by Zagazig University since 1984. Kufr Nigm contains a cemetery which has yielded material of the ARCHAIC PERIOD, including ceramic jars incised with the name of NARMER.

Kujavian see KUYAVIAN.

Kuk a site in the Wahgi Valley near Mount Hagen, which has been studied intensively by Jack Golson and documents the development of agricultural systems in the NEW GUINEA HIGHLANDS. The archaeological evidence includes a probable 30,000-year-old hearth, evidence for clearance and features suggesting cultivation of crops such as taro at about 9000 bp, a sequence of field systems from about 6000 bp to the present, and evidence of sweet potato cultivation from about 250 years ago. Pollen and sediment analyses from elsewhere in the highlands confirm a long history of human impact on the environment extending back into the Late Pleistocene.

Kukuba a limestone shelter excavated by Ron Vanderwal, and the oldest known site in lowland mainland New Guinea. The lower of the two cultural horizons has a date of c.4000 bp.

Kulichivka an Upper Palaeolithic open-air site on the Ikva River (Styr' tributary) near Kremenets in western Ukraine. Two occupation levels are buried in slope deposits on a bedrock hill overlooking the valley. The lower level is associated with a buried soil and apparently dates to the INTERSTADIAL preceding the LAST GLACIAL MAXIMUM; the artifact assemblage contains tool types characteristic of the Middle and Upper Palaeolithic. The upper level presumably dates to the late Upper Palaeolithic (i.e. 25,000–10,000 bp). Kulichivka was excavated by Savich in 1968–73.

Kůlna Cave a prehistoric cave-site located northeast of Brno in Moravia, Czech Republic. Artifacts and faunal remains are buried in deposits of loam and rubble. The lower levels, which are correlated with the last INTERGLACIAL and early GLACIAL, contain a Middle Palaeolithic industry with bifacial foliates and denticulates. A younger Middle Palaeolithic industry (e.g. sidescrapers and bifaces), probably dating to the early last GLACIAL, was found in overlying levels. Late Upper Palaeolithic (MAGDALENIAN), Neolithic, Iron Age and later remains occur in the upper layers. Kůlna Cave was excavated by Valoch in 1961–76 and others.

Kul'-Oba a KURGAN of a SCYTHIAN chief of the 4th century BC, discovered in 1830 near Kerch (Crimea, Ukraine). Under the cairn there was a stone vault built in Greek style. The deceased was buried in a wooden SARCOPHAGUS, wearing clothes and a head-dress that were all embroidered with golden plaques, a golden neck-ring with images of equestrian Scythians and golden bracelets on his hands. A complete set of weaponry was found in different parts of the burial. The man's body was accompanied by that of his wife or concubine. The golden adornments of her ritual attire and a famous ELECTRUM vase decorated with scenes of Scythian life are wonderful examples of work by Greek jewellers. Other discoveries included the body of a servant or slave, AMPHORAS, bronze cauldrons and bronze and silver utensils.

Kulp'o-ri a site in North Hamgyong Province, Korea, attributed to the Middle Palaeolithic based on tool typologies. Rocks for supporting a hut structure 11.5 by 8 m (37 by 26 ft), excavated in 1964, provided the first evidence of Palaeolithic dwellings in Korea.

Kültepe an important site in Cappadocia near Kayseri in central Anatolia, the best documented of the Old ASSYRIAN KĀRUM, or lower city, in this case the ancient Kanish. First excavated in the late 19th century, and best known from the work of T. Örgüç begun in 1948, Kültepe consists of a 20 ha (50 acre) mound with an associated settlement outside it; the latter represents the location of the kārum and was settled only during the late 3rd and early 2nd millennia BC. Occupation in the mound began in EARLY BRONZE I times and continued (interrupted at several points) to the CLASSICAL period. During the period of the kārum, the city was dominated by a fortified palace (covering over 1 ha [2.5 acres]), and also contained residential structures of varying sizes within a city wall. The kārum was a residential and commercial district also enclosed by a wall (defining an area perhaps 3 km [1.9 miles] in diameter). Divided into five phases (IV–II, Ib, Ia), the period of the Old Assyrian CAPPADOCIAN TRADE corresponds to levels II and Ib (dated to the 19th–18th centuries BC), when Assyrian merchants representing commercial firms in ASSUR resided in the kārum, largely adopting the local material culture. The many documents (c.15,000) from Kanish provide the richest available picture of a MESOPOTAMIAN trading community. The post-kārum levels on the city mound include an early 1st-millennium occupation that shows strong material connections both to the 'Syro-Hittite' kingdoms to the southwest (ORTHOSTATS with reliefs) and with the PHRYGIAN kingdom to the west (much 'Phrygian' painted pottery).

Kulupuari a site on the Kikori River, Gulf Province, Papua New Guinea. Excavations by Jim Rhoads produced the earliest direct evidence for sago palm exploitation and evidence for coastal trading systems preceding the HIRI and MAILU networks, both about 1300 bp.

Kumadzulo a large Early Iron Age village of the DAMBWA tradition in southern Zambia, occupied between the 5th and 7th centuries AD. It contains remains of remarkably small rectangular pole-and-DAGA structures with large corner posts. Cattle and small stock were herded, while grindstones and iron hoes suggest grain cultivation. Small cross-shaped copper ingots and a glass fragment attest to trading activity.

Kumbi Saleh see KOUMBI SALEH.

Kunda culture a Mesolithic culture of the BOREAL and ATLANTIC climatic periods of the eastern Baltic littoral, named after the site of Kunda-Lammasmagi on the Gulf of Finland in Estonia. Kunda settlements often contain traces of an elaborate bone and antler industry associated with the emphasis on fishing and seal-hunting in the economy. Among terrestrial mammals, elk (*Alces alces*) appears to have been particularly important. The Kunda culture is succeeded by the NARVA culture with the appearance of pottery and the first traces of food production.

Kuntillet Ajrud (or **Horvat Teiman**) a fortified way-station in eastern Sinai, belonging to the Judaean kingdom in the early 8th century BC. One of many small fortified places in Negev and eastern Sinai, Kuntillet Ajrud is remarkable for paintings, and ink drawings and inscriptions on some walls and storage vessels. The inscriptions name the CANAANITE gods BAAL and El, and also Yahweh and (controversially his consort) ASHERAH, indicating a degree of polytheism that the Old Testament masks.

Kura-Araxes culture, Eastern Anatolian Bronze Age, Transcaucasian Early Bronze Age or **Karaz** a culture complex characterized by a type of black or red highly burnished, handmade pottery that occurs in EARLY BRONZE AGE sites of Transcaucasia (drained by the Kura and Araxes Rivers, hence the designation), eastern Anatolia and northwestern Iran; closely related pottery also occurs in western Syria (the Red-Black Burnished ware of AMUQ H–I) and northern Palestine (the KHIRBET-KERAK ware). Other typical features of the complex are portable hearths and frequently circular houses. In Transcaucasia and adjacent regions, the culture complex exhibits minimal differentiation of settlement sizes and provides little indication of social hierarchy (by grave-goods, architectural variation). At the same time, many settlements are fortified, and intensified agricultural production is evident in field terracing and large water management works. The culture complex appears during the mid later 4th and continues to the later 3rd millennia BC.

Kurban Höyük a 7 ha (17 acre) site on the banks of the Euphrates River in Turkey, now under the lake behind the Ataturk dam. American excavations during the 1980s identified six occupation periods from late HALAF through the Early Bronze–Middle Bronze transition, as well as early Islamic and medieval settlements. The associated pottery provides a key chronological sequence for southeastern Anatolia.

kurgan (from an Old-Turkic term for a fortress) a term which was primarily used for any hill, including big BURIAL MOUNDS, but is now used in Russian archaeology as a term for any barrow, burial mound or tumulus. The best known, due to their enormous size, are the so-called 'royal' kurgans of the SCYTHIAN period (see ARZHAN, ISSYK, KUL'-OBA, PAZYRYK, SALBYK, TOLSTAYA MOGILA).

Kurgan cultures an outdated term for a complex of cultures defined by M. GIMBUTAS as a key element in a model of cultural development and dispersal in the steppe zone of southern Russia and Ukraine. The Kurgan cultures are distinguished by their use of KURGANS or burial mounds and are differentiated by the subterranean architecture of the burials. The first Kurgan culture is the YAMNAYA, or Pit-Grave, culture, the second the CATACOMB GRAVE culture, and the third the SRUBNAYA, or Timber-Grave, culture. In Gimbutas' model, there were several incursions of the INDO-EUROPEAN-speaking Kurgan cultures into eastern Europe.

Kurru a site in UPPER NUBIA, the NAPATAN royal cemetery from the late 9th to mid 7th centuries BC. The early tumulus tombs, probably the legacy of the KERMA CULTURE, were replaced by steep-sided pyramids after the conquest of Egypt by the Napatan kings. See also NURI.

Kurtén, Björn (1924–88) a Finnish palaeontologist who specialized in the study of Pleistocene mammals of the Holarctic, and contributed significantly to knowledge of Pleistocene environments and human palaeoecology.

Kush an Egyptian term for UPPER NUBIA generally, and for any independent state which established itself in this region during periods of Egyptian weakness (e.g. during the Second INTERMEDIATE PERIOD). See also KERMA, NAPATA.

Kushans or **Kushanas** an ancient tribe that became a core of the Kushana Kingdom. This political dynasty and people of East Asian origin arose in the final centuries BC and the first centuries AD. At its zenith their state controlled a vast area from the Ganges Plain through eastern Iran, part of modern Central Asia, Afghanistan and, probably, Xinjiang. Despite its great role in the history of the Ancient World, the Kushana Kingdom has been poorly studied. The most famous Kushana king is Kanishka. Archaeologists have established trading connections between the Kushana Kingdom and China, the PARTHIANS and Rome that were implemented through the SILK ROUTE. In the Kushana period Buddhism began to spread from India to Central Asia and the Far East. Kushana art can be characterized as a HELLENISTIC art of the Middle East.

Kutama a southern African Late Iron Age tradition which clusters the GUMANYE, Harare, K2, LEOPARD'S KOPJE, MAMBO, MAPUNGUBWE and WOOLANDALE pottery groups, and which is identified with the transition from the Early to the Late Iron Age at the end of the 1st millennium AD. Some researchers have suggested that the makers of Kutama pottery moved north from southeastern South Africa and introduced the Shona language to modern Zimbabwe.

Kutei a region of eastern Borneo which has yielded several 5th-century AD SANSKRIT inscriptions of a vaguely Hindu character, but written for local rulers, as well as 9th–10th-century statuary related to that of Java.

Kutikina formerly **Fraser Cave** a limestone cave in southwestern TASMANIA, with extraordinarily rich occupation deposits 20,000–15,000 years old sealed beneath a stalagmite layer. The excavation of Kutikina in 1981 first established the Pleistocene occupation of southwestern Tasmania, now confirmed at numerous other sites. See also NUNAMIRA CAVE, WARGATA MINA.

Kuyavian long barrow an earthen long barrow of the FUNNEL BEAKER CULTURE in northern Poland about 4000 BC. Kuyavian barrows are characteristically surrounded by a kerb of large erratic boulders and are sometimes called 'megalithic', even though they lack true megalithic architecture. In addition, they normally have a very characteristic trapezoidal plan and often occur in groups. Despite their large size, they normally contain single primary burials, rarely more than two. Key sites are SARNOWO and WIETRZYCHOWICE. They are related to the HUNEBEDs of northern Germany and Holland.

Kwale a site in southeastern Kenya which has given its name to a branch of the Eastern Stream or UREWE

KYLIX.

tradition of the CHIFUMBAZE Early Iron Age complex. This tradition appeared in southeastern Kenya and northern Tanzania in the 2nd century AD.

kyathos 1 a Greek measure of capacity, six to a KOTYLE.
   2 a dipper consisting of a small bowl at the end of a long handle. Silver, bronze and clay examples are known from both the Greek world and ETRURIA.

kylix a Greek stemmed drinking cup usually made of clay or metal.

Kyongju a basin and city in southeastern Korea which housed the historic capital of the SILLA kingdom and United Silla state (see KOREA). The original Silla capital is thought to be a walled site on a river levee, Panwol-song (Half-moon fortress). Later, a gridded city on the model of CHANG'AN was laid out north of the fortress. The basin was protected by fortresses on the surrounding mountaintops, and the southern mountain of Namsan was a Buddhist sanctuary of hundreds of temples and sculptures in its forty valleys.

L

La Adam Cave a Mesolithic cave-site on the Black Sea coast of Romania. Claims have been made for the presence of early domesticated sheep or goats at La Adam, but the context of these finds is not securely dated and has been called into question.

Laang Spean a prehistoric cave-site in western Cambodia, occupied between *c*.7000 and 500 BC, with evidence of reuse in *c*.AD 900. By *c*.4000 BC the occupants were using a late HOABINHIAN tool-kit and cord-marked and paddle-impressed pottery; succeeding layers contain increasingly elaborate pottery associated with flaked stone tools. Subsistence appears to have been based upon broad-spectrum hunting and gathering.

Labastide a MAGDALENIAN decorated cave in the Hautes-Pyrénées, southern France, containing numerous engraved figures on its walls, as well as a huge polychrome horse painting. Rich in hearths and engraved stones, the cave's occupation has been dated to 12,310 bc.

La Brea see RANCHO LA BREA.

La Chapelle-aux-Saints a MOUSTERIAN cave-site in Corrèze, southwestern France, where the burial of an almost complete NEANDERTHAL male adult with severe osteoarthritis was discovered in 1908 by the abbé Bouyssonie. The bones were studied in detail by Boule in 1911–13, and were for a time regarded as a type-skeleton for Neanderthal man. They are now generally considered to represent an extreme form of Neanderthaler. Middle Palaeolithic stone tools and numerous animal bones were also recovered from the cave.

La Chaussée-Tirancourt a late Neolithic ALLÉE COUVERTE constructed in *c*.2900 BC in Somme, France, and used for several centuries until infilled and destroyed in *c*.2000 BC. Remains of over 350 individuals were preserved in two separate deposits divided by a chalk fill, sixty in the lower, almost 300 in the upper. The discovery that genetic abnormalities present in the lower layer recurred directly above at the same location in the upper layer suggested that individual families or kin groups each had rights to a different part of the tomb.

Lachish (*Arabic* TELL ed-Duweir) a Palestinian site, chiefly excavated by Starkey 1932–8. In the CHALCOLITHIC period natural caves at Lachish were adapted for use as dwellings. During the MIDDLE BRONZE AGE the natural defensive hill was supplemented by a GLACIS. The destruction levels attributed to the Egyptian kings of the early NEW KINGDOM were followed by rebuilding during the LATE BRONZE AGE, including the construction of a major building at the foot of the earlier rampart, termed the 'Fosse Temple'. Lachish seems to have been again destroyed in the 12th century BC and possibly deserted until the 10th century BC when it was occupied by the ISRAELITES. Biblical evidence suggests that Rehoboam constructed the substantial Iron Age fortifications. Lachish was sacked in 701 BC by the ASSYRIANS, an event commemorated in the palace-reliefs from NINEVEH.

Laconian pottery pottery made at SPARTA largely in the 6th century BC. BLACK-FIGURED and BLACK-GLOSSED was produced. Laconian pottery was once thought to have been made in Cyrenaica, Libya, because one well-known cup showed the king of CYRENE, Arkesilas, of *c*.568–550 BC. The fabric was widely exported and is common in Cyrenaica (see TOCRA), in ETRURIA and in the Greek colonies in Italy.

La Cotte de Saint-Brelade a Palaeolithic ravine-site on Jersey, Channel Islands, principally excavated by MCBURNEY in 1961–78, which has produced some ACHEULIAN-style bifaces, many thousands of MOUSTERIAN artifacts, animal bones including mammoth and rhinoceros concentrations, and thirteen teeth attributed to a NEANDERTHALer. Jersey was linked to the continent during periods of low sea-level.

lacquer (*East Asia*) the resin of the sumac tree (*Rhus verniciflua*) used as a coating to harden and strengthen cloth, paper, wood, baskets, leather or ceramic objects. Often the lacquer, coloured red or black, is applied directly to the object's surface in many layers; however, objects themselves can be constructed, for example, of layers of cloth or paper, each lacquered as they are added to the form. The term 'lacquer ware' in archaeological contexts (see SINAN, TORIHAMA) usually refers to lac-quered wooden vessels.

Laem Pho the site of a port on the east coast of peninsular Thailand, near CHAIYA, from which have been recovered fragments of Middle Eastern glass vessels and Chinese glazed stonewares of the late 8th and 9th centuries AD; it was probably linked by an overland trade route across the peninsula to KO KHO KAO.

Laetoli formerly **Laetolil** a site in northern Tanzania where fieldwork between 1974 and 1981 yielded some thirty early HOMINID fossils attributed to AUSTRALOPI-THECUS *afarensis*, dating to about 3.8–3.6 million years ago, as well as an archaic HOMO *sapiens* skull, known as the Ngaloba skull, probably dating to some 150,000 years ago. Of particular interest was the 1976 discovery by Andrew Hill of 3.7 million-year-old animal tracks in-cluding impressions of monkeys, antelopes, elephants, two species of rhinoceros, three-toed horses, a small cat, birds and perhaps dung beetles, made in wet ash, which later dried and hardened, from the nearby volcano Sa-diman. Even more astounding was the 1978 discovery by Paul Abell of a 27 m (30 yds) long trail of 3.7 million-year-old hominid footprints, also made in hardened wet volcanic ash, which are the oldest hominid tracks known and confirm the existence of bipedal hominids at that time, excavated by a team directed by Mary LEAKEY in 1978–9.

La Ferrassie a well-stratified rockshelter in Dordogne, France, excavated by PEYRONY and, more recently, by Delporte, which has yielded Middle Palaeolithic material including the burials of two NEANDERTHAL adults and five children and babies; one infant lay beneath a slab with cup marks on it. The site has given its name to a subdivision of the CHARENTIAN MOUSTERIAN tradition. The Upper Palaeolithic material forms a 10 m (33 ft) stratigraphy including CHÂTELPERRONIAN, AURIGNA-CIAN and GRAVETTIAN stages, and has proved one of the keys to understanding the Upper Palaeolithic sequence in France. Crude engravings on blocks in the Aurignacian level include animals and possible 'vulvas'.

La Galgada a site in the western slopes of the northern highlands of Peru, pertaining to the Late PRECERAMIC and early INITIAL PERIOD. Similar to KOTOSH, the site comprises a series of sequentially built temple structures. Each structure was circular to roughly square with rounded corners, with a bench around the interior per-imeter, and a vented fire pit in the centre of the floor. Analysis of the fire pit ash has revealed remains of chilli pepper seeds. Each temple structure was filled, some-times used as a tomb, and covered over prior to the construction of the subsequent temple. In addition to the ceremonial architecture, domestic architecture indicates a resident population numbering in the thousands. The latest ceremonial constructions at the site no longer have a central hearth, and are laid out in a U-shaped configur-ation. See also HUARICOTO.

Laga Oda a rockshelter in the Chercher Mountains of southeastern Ethiopia, containing a series of microlithic stone artifact industries, the earliest of which appeared at least 16,000 bp. Damage on artifacts from the 2nd millennium bc suggests they were used to harvest grasses, but it is not known if these were cultivated or wild.

La Garma an Upper Palaeolithic cave-site in Cantabria, northern Spain, discovered in 1995, which, in addition to PARIETAL ART comprising paintings, engravings and hand stencils of the MAGDALENIAN, also has intact occupation floors of at least 500 sq. m (600 sq. yds), with thousands of animal bones, sea-shells and tools of flint, bone and antler, including BÂTONS PERCÉS and MOBILIARY ART objects. There are also areas of charcoal, deposits of bones and stalagmites, and enigmatic rectangular stone structures on the cave floor.

Lagar Velho, abrigo do a rockshelter in central Portugal where, in 1998, the burial of a young GRAVETTIAN child (known as the Lapedo child) was excavated, dating to c.24,500 bp. The skeleton, accompanied by red ochre, a perforated sea-shell and pierced red deer canines, is claimed to display a mixture of NEANDERTHAL and modern features, as a consequence of the extensive ad-mixture between the local Neanderthal populations and anatomically modern humans dispersing into Iberia c.28,000 bp; this interpretation remains highly contro-versial.

Lagash see AL HIBA.

Lagoa Santa a series of sites in Minas Gerais, Brazil, which display evidence of occupation in the Late Pleisto-cene, with human remains and stone tools found associ-ated with extinct animals such as mastodon and sloth. The rockshelter of Lapa Vermelha IV, excavated by A. Laming-Emperaire in the 1970s, has a 13 m (43 ft) stra-tigraphy with occupation back to 15,300 bp, and an in-dustry of quartz flakes. The Cerca Grande complex, of 10,000–8000 bp, features small flakes of rock-crystal, as well as axes, bone projectile points and burials, especially in the cemetery of Santana do Riacho with its fifty flexed inhumations. This site also has hundreds of rock paint-ings, including hunting scenes, from the Planalto tra-dition (7000–3000 bp).

La Gorge-Meillet the richest Iron Age chariot burial of the so-called 'Marnian' culture, Marne, France. On the chariot lay the body of a youth equipped with sword, spearheads, bronze helmet, gold bracelet and toilet set of tweezers, ear scoop and nail cleaner. There were also wheel-made pottery vessels and an ETRUSCAN bronze flagon. Above this principal interment was the body of an older man, possibly a retainer. The burial dates to LA TÈNE Ia, *c.*475–450 BC.

Lagozza di Besnate a late Neolithic settlement in Lombardy, Italy, dated to *c.*3600 BC, consisting of remains of wooden pile dwellings in a peat-filled basin. It is the type-site of the Lagozza culture, characterized by finely made black-burnished CARINATED bowls. At ARENE CANDIDE it succeeds the BOCCA QUADRATA (Square Mouth pottery) assemblage. Copper axes found at Lagozza sites are among the earliest copper objects from northern Italy.

La Graufesenque see SAMIAN WARE.

La Gravette see GRAVETTIAN.

Laguna de Bay a lake area east of Manila, Philippines, where a copper plate was found in 1990 inscribed with ten lines in the Kawi (Old Javanese) script. Dated in SANSKRIT to 892 in the Saka era (AD 900), the inscription records the acquittal of a debt by a high-status person and his descendants. The language includes Old Tagalog, Old Malay and Old Javanese words, and mentions locations in the modern Bulacan Province, north of Manila. This is by far the oldest evidence of writing from the Philippines, and firmly links the region to the Indianized world 1,000 years ago.

lagynos a type of HELLENISTIC jug produced in various centres in the eastern Mediterranean. It has a low, squat body with a vertical neck with rounded mouth; there is a single strap handle.

Lake Baringo a central Kenyan lake in a region with deposits containing early HOMINID and archaeological remains. See also CHESOWANJA, KAPTHURIN.

Lake Besaka a central Ethiopian locality west of Harar with a backed microlith industry and evidence for the exploitation of aquatic resources from early Holocene times (see 'AQUALITHIC'). The 2nd millennium bc saw the production of large quantities of scrapers and the appearance of domestic cattle. A fragment of a stone bowl, similar to those associated with PASTORAL NEOLITHIC sites further south in East Africa, has also been found.

Lake Condah a complex of stone structures in southwestern Victoria, Australia, studied in detail by the Victoria Archaeological Survey, which includes hut foundations and fish traps. The fish traps exploit small variations in topography to control water flows. The complex post-dates the Late Pleistocene volcanic activity in the area which formed the swamps, and analysis of lake levels suggests that the fish-trap system in its present form could not have operated before about 4000 bp. Fish-trap systems are a feature of Holocene southwestern Victoria and may have facilitated large ceremonial gatherings. See also TOOLONDO.

lake dwelling or **lake village** a settlement formerly on the edge of a lake, now usually buried by lake-shore sediments or drowned beneath the lake waters. The most famous examples are the pile-dwellings of Switzerland and northern Italy, villages built on wooden stilts to keep them above the damp ground of the lake shore; some may indeed have stood above the lake waters, as ethnographic examples from West Africa illustrate. The Swiss pile-dwellings first came to scholarly notice when lake levels fell in 1853. Other famous lake villages are known in northern Italy (POLADA) and eastern France (CLAIRVAUX-LES-LACS, CHARAVINES), and in southwestern England (GLASTONBURY). See also MONDSEE.

Lake George a lake in southeastern New South Wales, Australia, that has yielded a continuous pollen sequence covering the whole of the Pleistocene. An increase in charcoal and expansion of fire-tolerant eucalypts at an inferred date of 120,000 BP has been claimed to indicate the arrival of humans in Australia. This interpretation remains controversial, while the date has been questioned by Wright, who suggests about 60,000 BP as more likely, on the basis of age-depth regression analysis.

Lake Hauroko the site of a 17th-century AD cave burial on an island in this lake on South Island, NEW ZEALAND. The female skeleton was found seated on a bier of sticks and wrapped in a cloak of woven flax with a dogskin collar and feather edging.

Lake Jasper an underwater site in southwestern Western Australia. It comprises a scatter of stone artifacts in a woodland landscape, inundated when the lake was formed about 4000 bp.

Lake Mangakaware a lakeside PA in the Waikato District, North Island, NEW ZEALAND, with good preservation of artifacts and structural remains. The site covers about 0.2 ha (0.5 acres) and comprises an artificial mound with a semicircle of houses around an open space (MARAE) and defended by palisades. The site was occupied about AD 1500–1800.

Lake Mungo a now-dry lake with a LUNETTE dune in the WILLANDRA LAKES area of western New South Wales, Australia. The area is rich in archaeological sites, including surface scatters, hearths and shell middens, spanning at least 40,000 years. Assemblages from Lake Mungo formed the basis for the original definition of the AUSTRALIAN CORE TOOL AND SCRAPER TRADITION. In 1969, the remains of a cremated human female (WLH 1) dated to *c.*26,000 bp were found, the oldest evidence of cremation in the world. Pleistocene human remains continue to be found, including, in 1974, the extended inhumation of a man covered in red ochre (WLH 3). In 1999 Alan Thorne announced a new age for WLH 3 of 60,000 ± 6,000 years, based on ESR, URANIUM SERIES and OSL analyses, although the date remains controversial. More recently, the oldest DNA so far found has been successfully recovered from WLH 3. Analysis has shown that it contains a genetic sequence that does not occur in modern human populations.

Lake Ngaroto pa a lakeside fortified settlement in the Waikato District, North Island, NEW ZEALAND, comprising an artificial mound built up as a result of repeated construction of sandy living floors, but with little evidence of substantial structures.

Lake Nitchie a shaft burial of a large robust male in western New South Wales, Australia, about 6500–7000 bp. The man wore a necklace of pierced teeth from at least forty-seven Tasmanian devils, an animal now extinct on the Australian mainland.

Lake Rudolf see LAKE TURKANA.

Lake Sentani a lake in Irian Jaya, northern New Guinea, where metal objects, including bronze socketed axes and spearheads, were found in a burial mound. The objects are undated, but may relate to the activities of recent Indonesian traders.

Lake Turkana formerly **Lake Rudolf** a lake in the East African Rift Valley in northern Kenya and southern Ethiopia, in a basin containing the most productive early HOMINID deposits known, dating to over 4 million years ago. The lake has undergone cycles of expansion and drying up. See also ALLIA BAY, AUSTRALOPITHECUS, HOMO, KANAPOI, KOOBI FORA, LOTHAGAM, NARIO-KOTOME.

Lake Victoria the site of the largest cemetery known from the Murray River, Australia. The southern end of the lunette dune is estimated to contain about 10,000 burials. Cemeteries are a distinctive feature of the Holocene archaeological record in the Murray Valley. Colin Pardoe has argued that their appearance reflects substantial increases in population size and density and associated social change. See also COOBOOL CREEK, KOW SWAMP, ROONKA.

lake village see LAKE DWELLING.

Lala a Tunisian site containing a CAPSIAN industry typified by geometric-shaped backed microliths, as well as an abundant bone industry.

Lalibela 1 an Ethiopian cave with evidence of the Near Eastern domesticates barley, chickpeas and legumes, in association with stone artifacts, pottery and bones tentatively identified as cattle and small stock, dating to the mid 1st millennium BC. This evidence supports the view that agriculture developed at an early date in Ethiopia, but unfortunately does not indicate its exact antiquity.

2 The capital of the Zagwe Dynasty east of Lake Tana in Ethiopia, noted for early 12th-century ad churches cut from solid rock, with architectural features that may be traced to AXUM.

Lal-lo a series of estuarine shell middens dating from c.2000 BC along the CAGAYAN River in northern Luzon, Philippines, with incised, dentate-stamped and red-slipped pottery, stone adzes, probably related to early AUSTRONESIAN settlement of the area.

La Madeleine see MAGDALENIAN.

Lamalunga Cave see ALTAMURA MAN.

La Marche a Palaeolithic cave-site in the Vienne region of France, only 30 km (19 miles) from ANGLES-SUR-L'ANGLIN, which yielded over 1,500 engraved stone slabs, studied primarily by L. PALES. They include figures of humans, carnivores, horses, deer, bison, mammoths, etc. The site has been dated to 14,280 bp, the early mid MAGDALENIAN. In 1990 the Réseau Guy Martin, a cave above La Marche, was found to contain both parietal and portable engravings and has produced a radiocarbon date of 14,240 bp.

Lamb, Winifred (1894–1963) a British archaeologist who was appointed as Honorary Keeper of Greek and Roman Antiquities at the Fitzwilliam Museum in Cambridge in 1920. She was one of the first women to reside at the British School at ATHENS and joined the British excavation of MYCENAE in 1921. After work at SPARTA she completed a study of Greek and Roman Bronzes (1929). She conducted a major excavation at THERMI on the island of Lesbos and subsequently excavated at Kusura in Turkey to investigate the link between Anatolia and the Aegean. With John GARSTANG after the Second World War she helped to found the British Institute of Archaeology at Ankara.

Lamb Spring a PALAEOINDIAN site in Colorado, USA, with possible culturally modified camel bones dated to approximately 13,000 BP. Other bones present include mammoth, horse and bison. The site also contains later Palaeoindian components.

La Micoque see MICOQUIAN.

lamina a sheet-like unit layer of sediment defined by STRATIFICATION planes less than 1 cm (0.4 inch) apart. Horizontal laminae are parallel to bedding planes and CROSS LAMINAE are at an angle to bedding planes. Laminae are a fundamental sedimentary structure used in interpretation of depositional environments of which cultural debris may be a part.

La Mojarra a site in southeastern Veracruz, Mexico, where a STELA with a long hieroglyphic text was found. The text is written in the Mixe-Zoque language, and includes LONG COUNT dates of AD 143 and AD 156. Since La Mojarra is located within the OLMEC territory, this stela supports the argument that the Olmec invented hiero-glyphic writing and the long count calendar.

Lancefield Swamp a site in southern-central Victoria which was the first in Australia where contemporaneity of extinct MEGAFAUNA and artifacts was established. *Macropus titan*, a giant kangaroo, was the dominant species in the bone bed, dated to c.26,000 bp. There is no evidence that humans were responsible for the deaths of these animals, though there was some scavenging by *Thylacoleo*, an extinct marsupial carnivore.

landform a configuration of the earth's surface created by a distinct erosional or depositional process or set of processes. Landforms are the principal components that collectively comprise a landscape, whether at the scale of mountains and plains, or at the scale of individual valley features. Different landforms have different archaeological implications regarding settlement, resources and site visibility, preservation and destruction.

landnam a Danish term, meaning literally 'land taking', used to describe episodes of land clearance for cultivation identified in the pollen record. The usual *landnam* episode begins with a drop in tree pollen, then a rise in the level of grass and plantain pollen, and then a return of higher levels of tree pollen. The Danish palaeoecologist Iversen argued that such episodes represented the arrival of farmers practising SHIFTING CULTIVATION, in which a short period of cultivation was followed by a regeneration of the forest.

landscape the collection of landforms particular to a region at a particular time. Identifying former landscapes is a key component in understanding archaeological context, because it is upon landscapes that human occupation and activities occur.

landscape archaeology see OFFSITE.

Lanet a site in southern Kenya which has given its name to a widespread Iron Age pottery ware which appeared about 1185 bp. This has elongated gourd-like or bag-like pots with handles, spouts and a twisted cord roulette decoration. It is often associated with SIRIKWA HOLES.

Lang Ca a cemetery of the DONG SON culture with 314 burials on the Red River, northern Vietnam, upriver from Ha Noi. Some graves were exceptionally rich in bronze ornaments and weapons, as at VIET KHE, and indicate the appearance of an elite chiefly class in the mid 1st millennium BC.

Langebaan a site on the shore of the Langebaan Lagoon along the southwest coast of the Western Cape Province of South Africa, where a trail of footprints made in wet sand, arguably by an anatomically modern HOMO *sapiens* individual some 117,000 years ago, have been preserved in an ancient dune deposit. The site is not to be confused with the nearby 4.5 million-year-old palaeontol-ogical site of Langebaanweg (or Langebaan), which has yielded an extraordinary collection of PLIOCENE fauna.

langi tombs burial mounds of the Tui Tonga dynasty on Tongatapu, Tonga. The rectangular mounds are faced with slabs of coral limestone. Some contain burial chambers, also built of coral slabs. Most are associated with the ceremonial centre at MU'A on Tongatapu.

Langkasuka an early historic state in the Pattani region of peninsular Thailand, first mentioned in Chinese records of the 6th century AD and still extant early in the 2nd millennium, incorporating YARANG.

Langmannersdorf an Upper Palaeolithic open-air site located in Austria. Three cultural layers are contained in loess deposits dating to the LAST GLACIAL MAXIMUM (radiocarbon dates of 20,580–20,260 bp). The assemblage includes burins and endscrapers, and is assigned to the AURIGNACIAN.

Lang Rongrien a cave in Krabi Province, peninsular Thailand, which was occupied intermittently between 38,000–27,000 BP by hunters using chert flake tools. Above a sterile rock fall there is an early Holocene HOAB-INHIAN occupation with bifacial pebble tools like those from Malaya; and then, in the 3rd–2nd millennium BC, a cemetery of Neolithic farmers with pottery related to the BAN KAO tradition.

Lang Vac a cemetery of the late DONG SON culture on the Ca River, Nghe Tinh Province, Vietnam, dated to the late 1st millennium BC. The 100 burials contained several bronze drums, a large number of daggers with human figures as handles, bronze swords and a Chinese bronze crossbow trigger mechanism.

Langweiler see LINEAR POTTERY.

L'Anse-Amour a burial site on the coast of southern Labrador, Canada, which contains the remains of an adolescent skeleton, dated to between 7,000 and 7,500 years ago. The body had been placed face down, with a rock slab on its back. Various grave-goods, including a walrus tusk, stone spear points, a bone whistle, an antler harpoon head, a bone pendant and ochre-covered graphite pieces together with an antler pestle were found with the skeleton. The body had been laid in a deliberately excavated pit, which had then been filled and covered with a mound of stones. The site is one of the earliest of this complexity in the world, and the oldest BURIAL MOUND in North America.

L'Anse aux Meadows a VIKING site in northern New-foundland, Canada, that was founded at the end of the 10th century AD. The site contains the remains of Scandi-navian-style houses and other artifacts of European origin (including an iron smithy). See also VINLAND, SKRAELINGS.

Lantian [Lan-t'ien] an Early Palaeolithic site in Shaanxi Province, China, where HOMO *erectus* remains have been found at two localities, Gongwangling and Chenjiawo, dated to *c.*700,000 bp in the Middle Pleistocene. The core tools from Lantian have been used to characterize a heavy-tool tradition in Palaeolithic China, in contrast to a flake-tool tradition typified by the ZHOUKOUDIAN finds.

Lanzón see CHAVÍN.

Laoguantai [Lao-kuan-t'ai] see PEILIGANG.

Laos see ASIA, SOUTHEAST.

Lapakahi an area on the main island of Hawaii with a settlement pattern typical of dry leeward valleys, with a belt of uncultivable land separating the coastal settlement, established *c.*AD 1300, from the dry-land agricultural areas. Compare HALAWA VALLEY, KAWELA, MAKAHA VALLEY.

La Pasiega see EL CASTILLO.

Lapedo child see LAGAR VELHO, ABRIGO DO.

La Pineta see ISERNIA.

Lapita an Oceanic culture complex defined by distinctive dentate-stamped pottery (i.e. stamped with a toothed implement), appearing first in island MELANESIA (ELOUA) *c.*3500 bp and distributed as far east as Fiji and Samoa. Most Lapita sites occur on offshore islands or strandlines and assemblages also include shell artifacts, stone adzes and obsidian from TALASEA and LOU, with material from Lou predominating in later phases. The distinctive pottery style and obsidian suggest long-distance trade. The origins of the complex are controversial. Some researchers propose rapid spread into the Pacific from island Southeast Asia, while others see Lapita as an indigenous development in island Melanesia. Lapita is thought to be associated with the spread of AUSTRONESIAN speakers into the western Pacific and the settlement of POLYNESIA. See also BISMARCK ARCHIPELAGO, NENUMBO, WATOM.

La Quemada a site on the northern frontier of MESOAMERICA, in the modern state of Zacatecas, Mexico, and on an important north-south trade route. It was occupied in the late CLASSIC (*c.*AD 600–900), after the fall of TEOTIHUACÁN but before the rise of TULA. It was probably involved in turquoise trade with central Mexico.

La Quina a Middle and Upper Palaeolithic site complex in the Charente, southwestern France, which has given its name to one of the sub-divisions of the CHARENTIAN MOUSTERIAN tradition identified by BORDES. It was excavated primarily by the Henri-Martins in 1906–36 and 1953–65. Fragments of twenty-seven NEANDERTHALers were found.

L'Arbreda see SERIÑA.

La Riera a well-stratified prehistoric cave-site in Asturias, northern Spain, which has yielded over 55,000 stone artifacts and a large amount of faunal evidence, which indicates intensive red deer and ibex hunting during the Upper Palaeolithic (SOLUTREAN and MAGDALENIAN) phases of occupation. This is followed by an AZILIAN SHELL MIDDEN layer with associated harpoons, flint bladelets and microliths, and then clearly distinct ASTURIAN levels with characteristic *conchero* (shell midden) deposits and a tool-kit including quartzite choppers, picks and sidescrapers. The cave was first excavated by the Conde de la Vega del Sella in 1917–18 and has since been investigated by a variety of workers, notably G. Clark and L. Straus in 1976–9. Its occupation began *c.*20,500 and ended *c.*6500 bp.

Larisa or **Larissa** a site in northern Greece where MOUSTERIAN industries have been found. Milojcic defined a FINAL NEOLITHIC Larisa culture characterized by the black polished pottery found at ARAPI, ARGISSA, OTZAKI and SOUFLI, but the belief that this represents a distinct chronological phase would appear to be mistaken. Typical Larisa pottery has in fact been identified in late Neolithic contexts.

larnax 1 a closed box. A gold example was found in the royal tomb at VERGINA. In art, examples are seen being carried by women in scenes which are often linked to the preparation of textiles in the home.

2 a MINOAN-MYCENAEAN clay coffin which usually resembles a rectangular wooden chest. The painted decoration on the sides of larnakes sometimes includes religious or funerary scenes.

3 a bath-tub. Such tubs are made of a special fabric which contained straw.

Larnian a Mesolithic industry found along the coast of western Scotland and eastern Ireland, named after Lough Larne, and characterized by the presence of SHELL MIDDENS. The early Larnian tool-kits include leaf-shaped points and scrapers; the later Larnian assemblages contain more flakes than blades and include tranchet axes and very small scrapers made from beach pebbles.

Larsa the most prominent city in the history of southern MESOPOTAMIA during the early OLD BABYLONIAN period, when it was the political seat of a kingdom that controlled a large part of the region, and contending with the kingdom of ISIN. Archaeological remains of the city form a group of TELLS within an area of about 350 ha (865 acres), located about 20 km (12 miles) east of WARKA. First explored by Loftus in the mid 19th century, Larsa has been the object of a French investigation, initiated by A. PARROT in 1933, then again in 1967 and after, which concentrated on the palace of Nur-Adad (1865–1850 BC) and the temple complex known as the E.babbar, dedicated to the god SHAMASH, and used between Old Babylonian and NEO-BABYLONIAN times. The documented settlement history of the site spans the late 3rd millennium (UR III) to mid 1st millennium (Neo-Babylonian) BC.

Lartet, Edouard (1801–71) a French scholar, known as the founder of the science of palaeontology, who proposed a classificatory scheme for the Palaeolithic based entirely on recovered animal bones. He worked with CHRISTY, excavating many of the well-known rockshelter sites of southern France (AURIGNAC, LE MOUSTIER, LA MADELEINE), and was one of the first to recognize *in situ* MOBILIARY ART.

Lascaux a MAGDALENIAN cave in the Dordogne, France, discovered by four boys in 1940, which houses the most spectacular collection of Palaeolithic wall-art yet found. Best known for its 600 magnificent paintings of aurochs, horses, deer and signs, it also contains almost 1,500 engravings dominated by horses. A shaft features a painted scene of a bird-headed man with a wounded bison and a rhinoceros. Stone tools for engraving were found in the cave's engraved zones. Many lamps were recovered, as well as 158 fragments of pigment, and colour-grinding equipment. Scaffolding was used in some galleries to reach the upper walls and ceiling. Much of the cave floor was lost when the site was adapted for tourism, but it was probably never a habitation, being visited briefly for artistic activity or ritual. Charcoal has provided radiocarbon dates around 15,000 bp and in the 9th millennium bp. The cave was closed to tourists in 1963 owing to pollution, but a facsimile, Lascaux II, is now open near by.

Las Chimeneas see EL CASTILLO.

Las Haldas a large ceremonial site on the north-central coast of Peru, pertaining to the INITIAL PERIOD. The site has a stepped pyramid at one end, and a series of smaller mounds and sunken courts extending along a linear axis.

Lasithi an upland plain on the island of Crete, which has been inhabited since the Neolithic period and which was intensively exploited by the MINOANS.

Las Monedas see EL CASTILLO.

Last Glacial Maximum or **Late Pleniglacial** the geological period dating between 25,000 and 14,000 bp, during which global temperatures achieved the lowest levels of the Upper Pleistocene (127,000–10,000 bp). Massive continental ice sheets developed in the northern hemisphere, and a corresponding fall in sea-levels occurred worldwide. Despite harsh climatic conditions, human populations (represented by anatomically modern people and industries of the Upper Palaeolithic) occupied most unglaciated portions of the Old World.

Late Bronze Age a period in the Levant which encompasses the gradual decline of CANAANITE culture after its MIDDLE BRONZE AGE apogee, under conditions of Egyptian military colonization. In the first phase, LBA I (c.1550–1400 BC), the Egyptians expelled the HYKSOS, campaigned through the southern Levant and raided as far as the Euphrates, gaining control over large sections of the Levant. In the following phases (LBA IIa, or Amarna Age, c.1400–1300 BC, and LBA IIb, c.1300–1200 BC) the Egyptians tightened administrative control, under which condition Canaanite urban life withered. See also ISRAELITES.

Late Horizon (AD 1476–1533) the period in Andean South America during which the INCA empire expanded to gain political control over the entire Andean region.

Late Intermediate period (AD 1000–1476) the period in Andean South America following the collapse of the MIDDLE HORIZON empires, during which distinctive regional cultures emerged on the coast and in the highlands of the central Andes. The best known, and most extensive, was the CHIMÚ culture. The various POLITIES that developed during the Late Intermediate period were conquered by the INCA empire. See also CHANCAY.

La Tène a site on the shore of Lake Neuchâtel, Switzerland, with remains of a timber double-bridge spanning a former river bed and a settlement on its southern bank. Abundance of Iron Age metalwork suggests a place where votive offerings were thrown into the water. The material includes over 150 swords, many with decorated scabbards, as well as FIBULAE, spearheads and other bronze and iron tools and weapons. The site has given its name to the second major division of the European Iron Age (succeeding the HALLSTATT phase) and to the La Tène style of CELTIC art. The La Tène period is customarily subdivided into three parts: La Tène I, c.480–220 BC; La Tène II, c.220–120 BC; La Tène III, c.120–Roman conquest.

Late period an era of Egyptian history (c.664–332 BC) comprising the 26th to the 30th Dynasties, plus the second Persian occupation sometimes called the 31st Dynasty. A period of alternating foreign rule and native kings, ended by the invasion of Alexander the Great.

Late Pleniglacial see LAST GLACIAL MAXIMUM.

lateral-chambered tomb see SEVERN-COTSWOLD.

Later Stone Age or **Late Stone Age** the third and final stage of Stone Age technology in sub-Saharan Africa, dating from about 30,000 or more years ago until historical times in some areas. In southern Africa, it is known as the Later Stone Age and is particularly associated with the ancestors of the Bushman or SAN and KHOEKHOEN people known from historical and ethnographic records. Characteristics include abundant evidence for art and personal decoration, burials, and in some, but not all, assemblages, microlithic stone tools such as bladelets, segments and small scrapers, which were hafted on handles, and specialized hunting and gathering equipment. Pottery and stone bowls appear at various times and places in the last three millennia, when some Later Stone Age societies also acquired stock and switched to a herding way of life (see KHOEKHOEN).

Before the appearance of stock, all Later Stone Age people were nomadic hunter-gatherers who did not live in settled communities. A great variety of game as well as plant foods, shellfish, fish, birds and insects were consumed. Their societies were probably egalitarian with great emphasis on sharing and reciprocity. The arrival of stock, which involved the maintenance of personal wealth, transformed the social relations of some Later Stone Age people. See also ALBANY, EARLY LATER STONE AGE, EBURRAN, GOODWIN, KHAMI, LOCKSHOEK, MATOPO, NACHIKUFAN, OAKHURST, PASTORAL NEOLITHIC OF EAST AFRICA, PFUPI, POMONGWE, ROBBERG, ROCK ART, SAN, SMITHFIELD, WILTON, ZAMBIAN WILTON.

Lathrap, Donald Ward (1927–90) an American archaeologist specializing in the study of South and Middle America. His most important contribution was the proposal that the lowland Amazon regions were able to support complex societies, in all probability civilizations, long before they arose elsewhere on the continent.

latte rectangular settings of large stone pillars with hemispherical CAPSTONES which formed the basis of structures. Burials sometimes occur between the uprights. Latte appear in the Mariana Islands, Micronesia, about 1,000 years ago.

Laugerie Haute a well-stratified French rockshelter in the Dordogne near LES EYZIES, and excavated by LARTET, PEYRONY, BORDES and others. The site has yielded AURIGNACIAN, GRAVETTIAN, SOLUTREAN and MAGDALENIAN occupation levels, and is one of the type-sites used in the classification of the French Upper Palaeolithic. Laugerie Basse is a nearby rockshelter with a wealth of Magdalenian material including many art objects.

laurel-leaf point a long, thin and elegantly worked leaf-shaped SOLUTREAN flake tool with delicate invasive retouch. The largest laurel leaf found, recovered from Volgu in eastern France, measured approximately 35 cm (14 inches) long but less than 1 cm (0.4 inch) thick. See also WILLOW-LEAF POINT.

Laurentian an important late ARCHAIC tradition in northern New York and Vermont, and the upper St Lawrence Valley (5200–4400 BP). The tradition comprises such phases as Vergennes, Brewerton and Vosburg. It is characterized by specific scrapers, slate points or knives, ground stone gouges and stone plummets used as weights for fishing lines.

Laurentide a continental ice-sheet that originated in northeastern Canada during the WISCONSIN GLACIAL episode, and subsequently spread south and west. The system began to recede about 14,000 BP. The timing of its expansion and retreat, and the dating of its coalescence with Cordilleran glaciers originating in the Rocky Mountains, is crucial to dating the entry of humans into the New World. See also ICE-FREE CORRIDOR.

Lauricocha a region of the highlands of central Peru in which several PRECERAMIC cave-sites have been excavated by Augusto Cardich. The sites represent seasonal hunting camps, and include remains of deer and camelids. In the Lauricocha I period (c.8000–6000 bc), projectile points were triangular in form. In Lauricocha II (c.6000–4000 bc), willow-leaf-shaped points were typical. Later occupations have also been identified, extending up to and into the INITIAL PERIOD.

Laurion the silver mines in Attica, Greece, which were operating from the Bronze Age. Numerous shafts have been sunk exploiting the deep layers of ore. Above ground were extensive processing areas. A washery at Agrileza has recently been excavated by the British School. There were several other mining settlements including Thorikos.

Lausitz culture see LUSATIAN.

Laussel a rockshelter near LES EYZIES, Dordogne (France), where, in 1911, Dr Lalanne unearthed several bas-relief carvings of humans on large blocks, including the famous 'Venus', 44 cm (17 inches) high, holding what seems to be a horn in her right hand. They were partly covered by GRAVETTIAN deposits, but could be older.

La Vache a MAGDALENIAN cave-site in Ariège, French Pyrenees, containing a series of occupation layers and hearths rich in PORTABLE ART. Some of the art objects feature the same pigment-recipes as at nearby NIAUX, and come from layers dating to the 13th millennium bp. The economy was based heavily on ibex and reindeer exploitation.

La Venta one of the major CEREMONIAL CENTRES of the OLMEC, and one of the largest sites in this region of Mexico. There has been some difficulty in establishing the chronology at La Venta, which radiocarbon dates have been unable to resolve. La Venta reached its maximum population and height of power during the Middle FORMATIVE, c.850–750 BC. Evidence like the large, parabolically concave mirrors at the site and the appearance of elite residences and public building indicate a shift from the pan-MESOAMERICAN trade network of the Early Formative to increased regionalization, accompanied by social and political evolution. La Venta rose to power after the collapse of SAN LORENZO in c.1150 BC, and as the impact of Olmec ritual in the VALLEY OF MEXICO lessened. As with most Olmec sites, the end of the occupation was violent, indicated by the mutilation of the monumental sculpture. Archaeologists suggest La Venta's collapse was caused by the conflict between the apparent CARRYING CAPACITY of the immediate area and the large numbers of workers postulated to construct and maintain the structures at the site.

La Venta is well known for the arrangement of sixteen stone figures and six jadeite axes, in reddish-brown sand under the courtyard floor near the Northeastern Platform. Although this cache is recognized as being placed in a ritual context, its further meaning is unknown. La Venta has four giant Olmec stone heads. The first was discovered by F. Blom and O. LaFarge in 1925. In 1940, STIRLING located three more heads, in a row, at the northern end of the site.

Layard, Sir Austen Henry (1817–94) a Paris-born British lawyer who, along with BOTTA, began archaeological excavation in MESOPOTAMIA, each working in competition around Mosul in northern Iraq. Layard became interested in western Asian antiquities while making a trip through Anatolia and Syria. Thinking he had discovered NINEVEH, he began excavation at the NEO-ASSYRIAN city of KALHU in 1845, then in 1849 moved to Nineveh itself. His work unearthed massive palace complexes with associated winged bulls at the gates and extensive archives, then undecipherable, inside. The former now stand in the British Museum. Layard also made soundings at ASSUR, BABYLON and NIPPUR. He produced an extremely popular account of his research, *Nineveh and its Remains*.

layers see STRATA.

Layzón see HUACALOMA.

Lazaret an ACHEULIAN cave-site near Nice, France, excavated by a variety of workers, principally Octobon and de Lumley. Possible evidence has been found for a large hut-like construction, 11 m (12 yds) long, illuminated by two fires, within the cave. The assemblage, dated to RISS, includes pointed bifaces and choppers. Human remains corresponding to two children and one adult have been found. The fauna is dominated by red deer and ibex.

LBK see LINEAR POTTERY CULTURE.

Lchashen a Bronze Age site near Lake Sevan in Armenia, where a group of pit graves under stone cairns has yielded traces of seven wagons and six carts, with tripartite disc wheels, and two spoked-wheel chariots. The Lchashen finds have provided some of the most complete evidence of early wheeled vehicles beyond that available from models.

lead-glazed ware a soft-fired earthenware of HAN Dynasty China with a greenish-grey lead glaze, made specifically for funerary deposits. Not only vessels but miniature ceramic sculptures of daily scenes and architectural forms occur among this ware. Compare STONEWARE, CELADON.

Leakey, Louis Seymour Bazett (1903–72) a pioneer East African archaeologist, anthropologist and human palaeontologist with wide-ranging interests, especially known for his work at OLDUVAI GORGE in Tanzania, and as an inspirational lecturer and research fundraiser. The 1959 discovery of ZINJANTHROPUS at Olduvai Gorge by his wife, Mary LEAKEY, led to intensive early HOMINID research in East Africa.

Leakey, Mary Douglas (1913–96) the second wife and colleague of Louis LEAKEY, an archaeologist in her own right renowned for her research at East African sites including OLDUVAI GORGE, where her painstaking studies and beautiful drawings of OLDOWAN artifacts and 'living floors' were a pioneering contribution which set new standards in fieldwork and analysis of early archaeological sites, and where she discovered ZINJANTHROPUS in 1959. She also discovered HOMINID fossils and footprints at LAETOLI, and had wide-ranging archaeological interests including rock art and the establishment of field museums. She was known as a breeder of Dalmatian dogs, which invariably feature in photographic records of her excavations.

Leang Buidane a jar-burial cave of the 1st millennium AD on Salebabu Island in the Talaud group, between Sulawesi and the Philippines. Glass, etched agate and CARNELIAN BEADS, fragments of iron, a socketed copper axe and bivalve clay axe-casting moulds demonstrate the wide contacts of the peoples of the Sulawesi Sea in later prehistory.

Leang Burung 1 a rockshelter site in southwestern Sulawesi, Indonesia, with deposits post-dating ULU LEANG (c.2000 BC and later); its assemblage includes late TOALIAN microliths and Maros points and pottery.

2 a rockshelter site in southwestern Sulawesi, Indonesia, which has yielded a late Pleistocene (c.29,000–17,000 bc) stone industry characterized by unretouched flakes, a few similar to the LEVALLOISian of Europe. The industry appears in the lowest levels of Ulu Leang, underlying the Toalian assemblages.

Leang Tuwo Manee a cave on Karakallang, an island of the Talaud group between Sulawesi and the Philippines. Excavated in 1975, it has two phases: in the lower, c.4000–2000 BC, there is an unretouched chert flake-blade assemblage, with some edge gloss. Above this appears pottery, with cruder nodular brown chert flakes.

Lébous a CHALCOLITHIC enclosed settlement in Hérault, France, excavated by J. Arnal, consisting of a dry-stone wall with circular huts or towers attached. Some have interpreted the site as a fortified settlement with towers, others as a livestock enclosure with shepherds' huts. The associated material is of FONTBOUISSE type. A number of similar sites are known, including BOUSSARGUES.

Lefkandi a settlement on the Aegean island of Euboea,

which has been the focus for British and Greek excavations since 1965. The Xeropolis headland seems to have been occupied continuously from the later 3rd until the end of the 2nd millennium BC. The earliest level contains the Anatolian-inspired pottery which characterizes the Lefkandi I phase. Late in the MYCENAEAN period the settlement was twice destroyed by fire and then abandoned, presumably in favour of the site associated with the three PROTOGEOMETRIC cemeteries. The Toumba cemetery developed around an artificial tumulus covering a large APSIDAL structure, approximately 45 m (50 yds) long, enclosed by a PERISTYLE of wooden columns. Built c.1000 BC, this contained the rich graves of a man and a woman, and may have been a shrine for a hero-cult. Objects from the cemeteries suggest links with the eastern Mediterranean. See also AL MINA.

Łęg Piekarski a richly furnished burial site located in western-central Poland and dated to the 1st or 2nd century AD. Referred to as 'princes' graves', the burials at Łęg Piekarski yielded elaborate silver and bronze vessels and a variety of other high-status items. Burials such as those at Łęg Piekarski and elsewhere in eastern-Central Europe are regarded as evidence for the emergence of local hereditary CHIEFDOMS at the beginning of the 1st millennium AD.

lehm see loam.

Lehringen a Middle Palaeolithic site near Bremen in Lower Saxony, Germany, best known for the discovery of a broken yew wood spear with a sharpened and FIRE-HARDENED tip recovered from between the ribs of a straight-tusked elephant skeleton. The spear was originally 240 cm (nearly 8 ft) in length, and has been interpreted as a 'thrusting' spear, as it would probably have been too long to throw accurately.

Leilan, Tell a 90 ha (222 acre) site on the Wadi Jarrah in the Khabur triangle in northwestern Syria. The work of H. Weiss in the 1980s and 1990s identified this city as Shubat Enlil, the capital of SHAMSHI-ADAD I (1813–1781 BC). While a few HALAF sherds appear on the surface of the site and at the base of the stratigraphic sounding, the documented occupation of the site extends from the early 4th to the first half of the 2nd millennium BC, defining a sequence of northern 'UBAID (Leilan VI), URUK-related (Leilan V–IV), NINEVITE 5 (Leilan III), a later 3rd-millennium BC occupation (Leilan II) and an early 2nd-millennium occupation with Khabur ware (Leilan I). Urbanization of the earlier village began with Leilan III, culminating in Leilan II times in a walled lower town covering some 75 ha (185 acres), an upper town of 15 ha (37 acres), and possibly a 10 ha (25 acre) enclosed KĀRUM appended to the lower town wall. The important continuing excavations at Tell Leilan are throwing considerable light on the social and political developments in northern Syria during the 3rd and earlier 2nd

millennia BC, and especially on the emergence of urban states in the region and on Shamshi-Adad's empire, documents from which have already been recovered at the site.

leilira a large pointed or rectangular blade which may be retouched to form a point, or a rectangular scraper-like tool, associated with point industries of the AUSTRALIAN SMALL TOOL TRADITION in northern Australia. They were hafted as spearheads or fighting picks, or as knives.

Leisner, Georg (1870–1957) and **Leisner, Vera** (1885–1972) a husband and wife team of German archaeologists who devoted their lives to the first comprehensive survey and analysis of the megalithic tombs of Iberia; it was a massive undertaking, the results of which were published in a major series of monographs *Die Megalithgräber der Iberischen Halbinsel* in 1942–65.

leister a two-pronged fork-like spear used in fishing by the present-day ESKIMO. Some Mesolithic and Neolithic barbed bone points were probably used as leister prongs.

lekane an open large basin usually with two horizontal handles. It is often found in Greek domestic contexts and seems to have been an essential household item. It was probably multi-purpose in function, but may have been used for storing liquids.

lekanis a shallow Greek basin normally with two horizontal handles. It is usually fitted with a lid which could be reversed to form a stemmed plate. RED-FIGURED examples are often decorated with scenes of women, and it is possible that the shape was used as a trinket box.

Łęki Małe a complex of tumulus burials of the ÚNETICE culture in western Poland near Poznań. The central burials in the Łęki Małe tumuli lie in stone cists with wooden ceilings, covered by stone pavements. Grave-goods include bronze axes, daggers and HALBERDS; gold ornaments; amber ornaments; and pottery vessels. Łęki Małe is comparable with the Únetice burial at LEUBINGEN and the burials of the WESSEX CULTURE.

lekythos a Greek vessel, usually made of clay, which has a narrow neck and was used for perfumed oil.

Lelang [Lo-lang] the name of a HAN Dynasty COMMANDERY founded in 108 BC on the northern Korean peninsula near modern P'yongyang. As an outpost in the HEQIN (tributary) system of controlling border populations, Lelang became a regional trading centre, distributing Han and succeeding Wei court gifts to foreign embassies (e.g. YAYOI, PUJO, YAMATAI) and securing raw materials for central court use. Lelang existed until destroyed by KOGURYO in AD 413 (see CHINESE DYNASTIES, PROTO-THREE KINGDOMS, THREE KINGDOMS). The commandery compound and many of the MOUNDED TOMBS of the Han elite and later Koguryo MURAL TOMBS were excavated by Japanese teams in the 1930s.

Le Lazaret see LAZARET.

Lelesu a less well-known Early Iron Age tradition of the CHIFUMBAZE complex in central Tanzania, dating to about ad 200. Lelesu pottery suggests connections with both KWALE and UREWE wares.

Le Mas d'Azil a massive river-tunnel and cave-system in Ariège, French Pyrenees, containing occupation deposits from the AURIGNACIAN to the Bronze Age. Its MAGDALENIAN layers are phenomenally rich in cultural material and PORTABLE ART, producing dates in the 12th millennium bc. On the river's left bank, PIETTE first recognized AZILIAN material in 1887 – including perforated barbed points, and the painted pebbles of which this site contained more than all other sites combined – and thus filled the hiatus between the Palaeolithic and Neolithic.

Lemba-Lakkous the site of a CHALCOLITHIC (mid 4th to mid 3rd millennium BC) settlement in western CYPRUS, which was excavated by Peltenburg in 1976–83. The houses were circular huts built of stone and PISÉ. The dead were buried INTRAMURALLY in pit graves.

Le Moustier see MOUSTERIAN.

Lengyel culture a broadly distributed culture in eastern Europe, considered to be late Neolithic in Hungary, the Czech Republic and Austria, and early Neolithic in Poland. Named after the type-site of Lengyel in western Hungary, the culture is characterized by a variety of vessel forms including bowls, small AMPHORAS, biconical pots and pedestalled bowls. The earliest Lengyel pottery (c.5000–4500 BC) retains many decorative elements that appeared at the end of the LINEAR POTTERY culture, including painted and incrusted designs, but through time decoration virtually disappeared. Late Lengyel (4500–4000 BC) pots have small appliqué bosses. The Lengyel culture saw some of the earliest use of copper in temperate Europe. Settlements of the Lengyel culture vary considerably. Many (e.g. POSTOLOPRTY, BRZEŚĆ KUJAWSKI and OSŁONKI) are characterized by trapezoidal LONGHOUSES, while others are surrounded by defensive works (e.g. Osłonki, HLUBOKE MAŠŮKY). Enigmatic circular ditched enclosures, called 'rondels' in Austria, the Czech Republic and Slovakia (e.g. TĚŠETICE-KYJOVICE, Friebritz and Svodin) appear to have had a ritual function. Lengyel burials are largely contracted inhumations, either in cemeteries (e.g. JORDANÓW) or in settlements (as at Brześć Kujawski). The Lengyel culture has affinities with the RÖSSEN and TISZA cultures.

Leopard's Hill a southern Zambian cave, some 60 km (37 miles) southeast of Lusaka, containing a long succession of microlithic LATER STONE AGE collections which first appear between 24,000 and 21,000 bp, very fragmentary Holocene human remains, carnivore accumulations, as well as some Early Iron Age pottery. Of particular interest is the find of a 22,000-year-old bored stone of a size suitable to have been a digging stick weight.

Leopard's Kopje a Late Iron Age complex of southwestern Zimbabwe and adjacent areas of northern South Africa, named after the Leopard's Kopje or Nthabazingwe site in southwestern Zimbabwe. The Leopard's Kopje initial or A phase dates to the 10th and 11th centuries AD. It is represented in the Limpopo Valley by the K2 FACIES and further north in southwestern Zimbabwe by the MAMBO facies. The second or B phase of the Leopard's Kopje tradition continues as the MAPUNGUBWE facies in the Limpopo Valley and the WOOLANDALE facies in southwestern Zimbabwe in the 12th and 13th centuries AD. Societies in this phase are characterized by trade with the East African coast, gold mining and working, the construction of stone walling, class distinction and the development of sacred leadership. These processes led to the ZIMBABWE culture. See also KUTAMA.

Lepcis Magna or **Leptis Magna** a harbour town in the Roman province of Africa, now Libya. The site seems to have been settled by the PHOENICIANS during the 6th century BC. Under the emperor Augustus it seems to have been Romanized and it gained the status of a colony under the emperor Trajan. Excavations have uncovered the FORUM, remodelled under the emperor Septimius Severus, and related administrative buildings. The hunting baths are particularly well preserved.

Le Pech de l'Azé see PECH DE L'AZÉ.

Lepenski Vir a settlement of complex hunter-fishers, and later farmers, in the Djerdap Gorge of the River Danube in Yugoslavia, excavated by D. SREJOVIĆ between 1965 and 1971. Eight habitation levels have been divided into three main phases, although the idiosyncratic nature of their contents has led to disagreements over their chronological position. Phases I and II apparently had an economy based on red deer, boar, aurochs and fish. The phase I and II settlement had a total of about twenty-five trapezoidal structures with wide ends facing the river. Most had a limestone sculpture near the hearth with features reminiscent of fish, with bulging eyes and piscine mouths. Fish bones were quite common in the faunal sample from Lepenski Vir. Among terrestrial species, red deer, aurochs and boar comprise most of the sample from phases I and II. Phase III is an occupation of the STARČEVO culture, with domestic cattle, pigs, sheep and goats. Interpretations of Lepenski Vir vary. Typically, it is seen as a complex foraging adaptation that emerged in the 7th millennium BC. A dissenting point of view places phases I and II later, in the late 7th/early 6th millennia BC, contemporaneous with early farming communities of the Starčevo culture near by.

Le Placard a cave-site in the Charente region of France which has yielded abundant SOLUTREAN and MAG-

DALENIAN material including seventy-four well-carved BÂTONS PERCÉS and numerous decorated and carved objects. Engravings were recently discovered on its walls, and some fallen engraved fragments were stratified between two Upper Solutrean layers. Le Placard was a major industrial and artistic site in both periods.

Lepsius, Karl Richard (1810–84) a German Egyptologist, chiefly known for the Prussian survey of Egyptian monuments of 1842–5.

Leptis Magna see LEPCIS MAGNA.

leptolithic *adj.* literally 'of small stones', occasionally used to describe industries with many blades and blade tools, without any particular dating connotation.

Lerma point a projectile point type found before 7000 BC in Tamaulipas and Puebla, Mexico, including the site of SANTA ISABEL IZTAPÁN. This laurel leaf-shaped point is similar to those found in the Great Basin in the United States, and is thus suggestive of an adaptation commonly defined as the DESERT TRADITION.

Lerna a site on the coast of the Argolid, Greece, which was excavated by CASKEY in 1952–8. Lerna was first occupied in the Neolithic period, subsequently abandoned and then reoccupied in Early HELLADIC. The site was fortified and the House of Tiles was built. This impressive two-storey structure, 25 by 12 m (27 by 13 yds), appears to have served an administrative function and may have been a proto-palace, but it was burnt down *c.*2200 BC. Although Lerna never entirely recovered from this setback, archaeologically the Middle Helladic levels have proved extremely informative.

Leroi-Gourhan, André Georges Léandre (1911–86) a French prehistorian best known for his revolutionary work on Palaeolithic art (*Préhistoire de l'art occidental*, 1965), seeing it as structured and composed rather than as a random collection of images, and for his excavations at LES FURTINS, ARCY-SUR-CURE and especially PINCEVENT, where he pioneered techniques of horizontal excavation, the minute study and moulding of occupation floors and ethnological reconstruction of prehistoric life.

lesche an enclosed space in the Greek world where people could sit and talk, with perhaps also a dining area. Compare STOA.

Les Combarelles a long narrow cave near LES EYZIES (in Dordogne, France), where hundreds of Palaeolithic engravings were discovered on the walls in 1901. They are dominated by horses, together with bison, bear, reindeer, mammoth and anthropomorphs, and are assigned to the mid MAGDALENIAN (*c.*14,000–12,000 BC).

Les Eyzies a village at the centre of the French Dordogne's distribution of Palaeolithic cave and rockshelter sites.

The cave of Les Eyzies has yielded MAGDALENIAN and AZILIAN material. See also CRO-MAGNON, ABRI PATAUD, LAUGERIE HAUTE, FONT DE GAUME, LES COMBARELLES.

Les Fouaillages a triangular Neolithic cairn on Guernsey, Channel Islands, covering a megalithic cist towards the narrow end, a closed megalithic cist in the centre, and a PASSAGE GRAVE entered from the middle of the widest end. Pottery of CERNY type was found and radiocarbon dates suggested construction in *c.*4300 BC. In the 3rd millennium BC the monument was buried beneath a large oval mound.

Les Furtins a MOUSTERIAN cave-site in Saône-et-Loire, eastern France, excavated by LEROI-GOURHAN, where six bear skulls were thought to be deliberately arranged on a limestone slab, and hence evidence of a cave bear cult. It is now clear that hibernating bears and fallen ceiling fragments produced these finds. Compare DRACHENLOCH.

Lespugue a series of small cave-sites in the Save Gorge, Haute-Garonne, in the French Pyrenees, where R. de Saint-Périer encountered material from the AURIGNACIAN to the MAGDALENIAN. In the Grotte des Rideaux, in 1922, he discovered the famous ivory 'VENUS' of Lespugue. Damaged during extraction, it was found beneath a rock, but seems to have been associated with GRAVETTIAN material.

Les Trois Frères see VOLP CAVES.

Le Tillet a gravel pit at Seine-et-Marne in northern France, with a well-defined loess stratigraphy recorded by BORDES, which has yielded a clear sequence of Palaeolithic industries including ACHEULIAN and a MOUSTERIAN assemblage with BOUT COUPÉ-style bifaces.

Le Tuc d'Audoubert see VOLP CAVES.

Leubingen an Early Bronze Age high-status burial of the ÚNĚTICE culture located in southeastern Germany. At Leubingen, a timbered mortuary house under a barrow was erected over the burial of an adult male and an adolescent, probably female. Elaborate grave-goods include not only bronze daggers, chisels, axes and HALBERDS, but also a gold armlet, beads, pins and earrings.

Leukas or **Levkas** one of the Ionian islands, in Greece, that was the focus of lengthy and detailed investigations by DÖRPFELD, SCHLIEMANN's collaborator, who believed but could never prove that this was the Homeric Ithaca, home of Odysseus. In the Nidhri plain he discovered a richly furnished Early HELLADIC tumulus grave cemetery and two Middle Helladic tumuli.

Levalloiso-Mousterian the name given to MOUSTERIAN industries in which the artifacts are made on flakes

LEVALLOIS flake and core.

knapped using the LEVALLOIS TECHNIQUE rather than the more efficient DISCOIDAL NUCLEUS TECHNIQUE.

Levallois technique a prepared-core knapping technique which allows the removal of large flakes of predetermined size and shape. The top and sides of the core are trimmed to form a *tortoise core*, a striking platform is prepared, and one or two flakes are struck from the core. The flakes show characteristic preparation scars on the dorsal surface and a faceted striking platform. See also DISCOIDAL NUCLEUS TECHNIQUE.

Levantine art rock art found primarily in rockshelters of eastern Spain, comprising small red-painted figures of deer, ibex, humans, etc., including hunting scenes. Traditionally assigned to the Mesolithic, it is now thought to date primarily to the Neolithic period.

Levanzo a small island lying to the west of Sicily, Italy, where GRAZIOSI discovered fine engravings of horses, deer, humans and cattle in the Grotta Genovese, dating to the Upper Palaeolithic (ROMANELLIAN), c.10,000 bc.

level an instrument used in surveying to take vertical measurements for constructing maps and identifying the height of individual artifacts. A level is less sophisticated than a TRANSIT or THEODOLITE, consisting of a focusing or non-focusing telescope for sightings, some form of level-bubble to level the scope, and a set of cross-hairs. Vertical readings are taken by sighting the level on a graduated stadia rod or levelling staff, to gain a reading of the difference between instrument height and ground surface at the base of the rod. Subtracting the stadia rod reading from the height of the level above the ground surface gives the difference in height between ground surface at the instrument station and ground surface at the shot point.

Levkas see LEUKAS.

Lhokseumawe a series of marine SHELL MIDDENS on the mid Holocene coastline of northeastern Sumatra, containing HOABINHIAN stone tools, a high proportion of which are SUMATRALITHS.

Lhote, Henri (1903–91) a French naturalist, geographer and ethnogapher, best known for his work on the rock art of the western and central Sahara, particularly that of the TASSILI, made famous by his book *A la découverte des fresques du Tassili* (1958).

Liangzhu [Liang-chu] a site in Jiangsu Province, China, giving its name to one of the middle and late Neolithic rice-growing cultures of HEMUDU lineage in the central Yangtze River basin. It is distinguished by jade artifacts (see ZONG) with intricate incising and relief carvings of the TAOTIE motif. The late Liangzhu culture is contemporaneous with the LONGSHAN cultures of the late Neolithic further north.

Liaodong [Liao-tung] the peninsula in Liaoning Province, China, between the BOHAI Bay and the Yellow Sea.

Liaoning see SONGGUK-RI.

libation a Greek or Roman offering of wine to the gods poured from a PHIALE or PATERA which had been filled from an OINOCHOE.

Libby, Willard Frank (1908–80) an American chemist who devised and reasoned the fundamentals of the radio-carbon dating method in the early 1950s, for which he won a Nobel prize.

Libyco-Capsian see CAPSIAN.

Li Chi [Li Ch'i] (1895–1979) a Chinese archaeologist from Hubei Province who took his Ph.D. from Harvard in 1928. Upon returning to China, he conducted the excavations at ANYANG. Moving to Taiwan in 1949, he established the first archaeology department of any Chinese university, at the National Taiwan University in Taipei.

lienzo a large document similar to a CODEX, made of an animal skin or cloth. The major difference between the two is that a lienzo is either rectangular or irregular, while a codex is a folded scroll. In MESOAMERICA the lienzo is frequently, but not always, a map showing elite land holdings. Its name comes from the Spanish for 'linen', and all surviving specimens are post-conquest.

Lie Siri a rockshelter on the north coast of eastern Timor, which was excavated in 1967 and yielded a sequence from c.7000 to 1500 BC. The site is rich in biological remains, and contains evidence for the arrival of agriculturalists bringing domesticated pigs, goats, dogs, monkeys and a marsupial from the Melanesian region.

Lijiacun [Li-chia-t'sun] see PEILIGANG.

Lima culture the culture located on the central coast of Peru during the EARLY INTERMEDIATE PERIOD. A major population centre was the site of CAJAMARQUILLA, and Lima-style ceramics show influence from the MOCHE culture of the north coast. Stylistic influences in ceramic design during the MIDDLE HORIZON indicate either conquest by, or interaction with, the HUARI empire.

limes the technical name for the frontier zone of the Roman empire. The name is applied to permanent fixed structures such as HADRIAN'S WALL as well the line of forts and towers which protected the Rhine and Danube frontiers.

Lime Springs, Tambar Springs and Trinkey Springs are all open sites in the Liverpool Plains area of New South Wales, Australia, where artifacts and MEGAFAUNA have been found. The Lime Springs sequence dates from c.19,000 to c.6000 bp and is claimed to show that megafauna survived into the Holocene. However, both the association and the dating have been questioned and have not been confirmed.

Lindenmeier a FOLSOM site in northern Colorado, USA. ARCHAIC and late prehistoric COMPONENTS are also present; the date for the Folsom occupation is approximately 11,000 BP. It was used as a KILL-/butchering and camp SITE, and contained a wide variety of artifacts and animal bones. It has been suggested that the site served as a seasonal meeting-place for individual hunting groups or bands.

Lindisfarne an island off the northeastern coast of England where St Aidan and other monks from the Scottish island of Iona founded a monastery in AD 634. It became a centre for producing illuminated manuscripts such as the *Lindisfarne Gospel* of c.700, a sumptuous blend of CELTIC and Germanic art. The island was raided by Danes in 793.

Lindner Site see NAUWALABILA.

Lindow Man a bog body discovered in 1984 in Cheshire, England, during peat cutting. One leg is missing but the rest of the body is relatively well preserved and is that of a young man around twenty-five years old who had been twice struck violently over the head, garotted and finally had his throat cut. Like the famous TOLLUND and GRAUBALLE bodies from Denmark, this may have been a ritual sacrifice. Radiocarbon dates show that Lindow Man met his untimely end in the 1st or 2nd century AD. Parts of between one and three other bodies have also been found at Lindow.

Linear A a SYLLABIC script devised by the MINOANS which was in use throughout CRETE and on a number of other Aegean islands in Greece in the Neopalatial period (c.1690–1390 BC). The script, which has never been deciphered, was inscribed on clay tablets, evidently administrative documents, on stone vases and bronze DOUBLE AXES.

Linear B a SYLLABIC script, in use in MINOAN CRETE and MYCENAEAN Greece in the period 1450–1200 BC, which Michael VENTRIS deciphered as an early form of Greek. It would appear that the script was devised at KNOSSOS when the Mycenaeans took control and spread to mainland Greece but was effectively restricted to the major palace sites: MYCENAE, PYLOS, THEBES and TIRYNS. Most Linear B inscriptions are on clay tablets and document the economic transactions of the palace administration.

Linear Pottery culture or **Linearbandkeramik** the earliest Neolithic culture of Central Europe, distributed broadly from the western Ukraine to eastern France, between c.5600 and 5000 BC. The Linear Pottery culture is frequently called by its German name, *Linearbandkeramik* (LBK), as well as a variety of local names, and V. G. CHILDE referred to it as 'DANUBIAN I'. The Linear Pottery culture takes its name from the incised lines on its fine pottery, beginning with simple meander and spiral patterns and developing into complex designs, often including punctates (small depressions or pits) and stroked ornamentation. The characteristic vessel form is a ¾-spherical bowl. Late variants of Linear Pottery include the ZELIEZOVCE STYLE of Slovakia and southern Poland and the SARKA STYLE of Bohemia.

The best available evidence indicates that the Linear Pottery culture is derived from the KÖRÖS culture of the northern Balkans. It spread across northern-Central Europe relatively rapidly in several stages. Among the earliest Linear Pottery sites are Brunn and Neckenmarkt in Austria and Schwanfeld and Bruchenbrücken in Germany. Linear Pottery settlements are concentrated in the loess-filled basins of Central Europe and are situated primarily on the margins of floodplains. They are characterized by many LONGHOUSES with rectangular ground plans, the largest freestanding structures in the world at the time. Such houses have been found at many sites, including CUIRY-LÈS-CHAUDARDES, KÖLN-LINDENTHAL, Langweiler, BYLANY, ELSLOO, SITTARD and OLSZANICA. Analysis of ceramics indicates that these settlements were occupied over long periods, possibly even several centuries. At a number of sites, including Köln-Lindenthal, EILSLEBEN, Darion and Vaihingen/Enz, the settled area was enclosed by fortification ditches and ramparts. Eventually, Linear Pottery settlement spread to the North European Plain, at sites like BRZEŚĆ KUJAWSKI and Zollchow, while in the karst uplands of Slovakia, caves such as DOMICA were inhabited. At NEZVISKA in Ukraine, settlement remains included a large surface structure 12 by 7 m (40 by 23 ft) with several hearths.

The economy of the Linear Pottery culture was based on grain cultivation and on domesticated livestock, primarily cattle. Ceramic sieves suggest the use of milk to make cheese. Another characteristic Linear Pottery artifact is the SHOE-LAST ADZE (or celt), a long, thin chisel-shaped ground-stone tool, probably used for woodworking. A well at Kückhoven in Germany, constructed from wooden planks, was dated by means of DENDRO-CHRONOLOGY to between 5089 and 5087 BC, and contained a bowstave and arrowshaft made of elmwood.

Linear Pottery burials are generally found in a contracted position and frequently are grouped in cemeteries of several dozen or more graves. Well-known Linear Pottery cemeteries include those at NITRA, Rixheim, Flomborn, Elsloo, Niedermerz, Wandersleben, Schwetzingen and SONDERSHAUSEN. In some cemeteries, such as Elsloo and Niedermerz, the acidic loess has destroyed the bones, leaving only stains in the soil and grave-goods to indicate the location of a grave. Some cremations are also known. At Sondershausen, Nitra and Rixheim, bracelets, discs and beads made from SPONDYLUS, a marine shell from southeastern Europe and the Aegean, were found in several graves. At Talheim and Asparn, many of the skeletons in mass graves bear signs of traumatic injury.

lingling-o a type of knobbed earring, made of jadeite, glass or metal, which is characteristic of SA HUYNH in Vietnam and related sites in the islands (TABON CAVES, KALANAY), and found as a trade item elsewhere in Southeast Asia.

Lipari an AKROPOLIS site on the island of the same name in the Aeolian group (Italy). Beneath the Castello of Lipari, excavations have revealed a long sequence of occupation stretching back to the Neolithic c.4000 BC. In the Bronze Age, Lipari became an important trading centre, and MYCENAEAN pottery has been found dating to the period 1500–1250 BC. Remains of HELLENISTIC buildings show that the Castello was also important in CLASSICAL times. The volcanic deposits of the island of Lipari were exploited in the Neolithic as an important source of obsidian used by the farming settlements of southern Italy.

Lisht the royal NECROPOLIS of Egypt's early 12th Dynasty, which was probably close to the now unknown capital of the time, Iti-Tawy. The poorly preserved pyramid of King AMENEMHAT I, excavated in 1920, seems to have been the first royal tomb at Lisht. It was followed by the better preserved example of King SENWOSRET I, 2.5 km (1.5 miles) to the south, which was excavated by Gauthier and Jéquier in 1894 and the Metropolitan Museum of Art in 1908–34. A notable discovery in the MORTUARY TEMPLE of Senwosret's pyramid complex was ten fine statues of the king, bigger than life-size.

lithics stone artifacts and tools. Because such MATERIAL CULTURE preserves so well, lithic analysis constitutes an important component of archaeological investigation.

lithofacies part of a recognized sediment or rock unit that is differentiated by some aspect of composition or character such as grain size or SEDIMENTARY STRUCTURES. Because characteristics of sedimentary units are closely related to their DEPOSITIONAL ENVIRONMENT, recognition and description of lithofacies and lithofacies associations is integral to interpretation of depositional environments and the context and integrity of related archaeological deposits in those environments.

lithofacies analysis a technique used to identify and interpret DEPOSITIONAL ENVIRONMENTS in which archaeological deposits are found. Sediment bodies are subdivided into constituent LITHOFACIES which are examined in terms of geometry, vertical sequences and lateral associations. Although arrays and sequences of lithofacies are interpretable in their own right, qualitative or quantitative comparisons are made to lithofacies models, which are generalized summaries of sedimentary characteristics of specific depositional environments developed from work in modern as well as ancient depositional environments that serve as interpretative guides and predictors.

lithophone a naturally occurring stone, stalactite or stalagmite which may have been struck by Palaeolithic people to create musical notes. In addition, many sets of carefully tuned lithophone bars have been found in late Neolithic and metal age contexts in central and southern Vietnam.

'Little Foot' see STERKFONTEIN.

Little Salt Spring a site in Florida, USA, adjacent to a flooded basin and sinkhole, which is famous for the excellent preservation of prehistoric materials. The earliest components at the site belong to the PALAEO-INDIAN period (12,000–8500 BP) and contain hearths, a well-preserved non-returning oak BOOMERANG, a socketed antler projectile point and the shell of an extinct giant land tortoise with a wooden stake still stuck in it. The succeeding ARCHAIC (6800–5200 BP) comprised an extensive burial, and excavations have recovered a minimum of twenty individuals dated to c.6180 bp. The peat in which the burials were found allowed excellent preservation – one skull had the remains of the brain inside. Wooden, bone, shell and stone tools were found, as well as a wealth of PALAEOENVIRONMENTAL data. See also REPUBLIC GROVES, WINDOVER.

Little Woodbury an Iron Age farmstead in Wiltshire, England, excavated by Gerhard BERSU in 1938–9, consisting of an oval ditched enclosure within which were found POSTHOLES of one large round house together with a smaller circular structure, four-post granaries and storage pits. It was occupied from the 4th to the 2nd century BC.

Liu Sheng see MANCHENG.

livre de beurre the name of the distinctive blade cores of GRAND PRESSIGNY flint, so called from their yellowish colour and their resemblance in shape to the slabs of butter common in the area in the 19th century.

Ljubljansko Blat a wetland area near Ljubljana in

Slovenia, in which a number of late Neolithic and ENEO-LITHIC sites have been found, primarily of the VUČEDOL culture, including traces of copper working and casting.

Llano Estacado a large plateau in eastern New Mexico and the Texas Panhandle, USA. During the PALAEO-INDIAN period, it was much wetter and more hospitable than it is today, the indigenous fauna including antelope, badger, bison, camel, coyote, fox, horse, jackrabbit, mammoth, muskrat, peccary, prairie dog, racoon, skunk and wolf. The area contains many Palaeoindian sites, including BLACKWATER DRAW, and has attracted numerous archaeological investigations, which have been able to recover detailed information on Palaeo-indian settlement patterns. Llano Estacado is Spanish for the 'Staked Plain', and the region received its name because early Spanish explorers were forced to stake out their line of march in order to be able to return safely.

Llano tradition see CLOVIS.

Lloyd, Seton (1902–96) a British archaeologist of the Near East. An architect by training, Lloyd was drawn into archaeology when he worked at Tell EL-AMARNA and then in Iraq and Turkey. He was named adviser to the General Directorate of Antiquities in Iraq in 1939, in which capacity he conducted important excavations at HASSUNA, ERIDU, UQAIR, AQAR QUF and Tell HARMAL. In 1948 Lloyd became the director of the British Institute in Ankara; while in Turkey he worked at Harran and BEYCESULTAN. He then held a position in the Institute of Archaeology (London) during the 1960s. In addition to his professional reporting, Lloyd produced numerous books for a lay audience.

loam, loehm or **lehm** a texture class used in describing sediment and soil consisting of a mixture of sand, silt and clay that contains 7–27 per cent clay, 28–50 per cent silt, and less than 52 per cent sand. Other loamy textures exist that have differing percentages of sand, silt and clay constituents. Loams tend to be agriculturally productive soils because of their generally good drainage qualities.

Lobo Tuwa see ŚRIVIJAYA.

Lockshoek a term sometimes used for a 12,000–8000 BP non-microlithic LATER STONE AGE industry of the OAK-HURST complex in the interior of South Africa (replacing the term SMITHFIELD A). It is contemporary with and equivalent to the ALBANY industry of the southern and eastern Cape Province.

loehm see LOAM.

loess an AEOLIAN deposit of massive to horizontally bedded silt. During GLACIAL times, meltwater streams carried large sediment loads including large amounts of silt derived from glacial abrasion. These streams were mostly braided with barren expanses of floodplains. Prevailing winds preferentially winnowed silt from exposed flats and fans at the glacial front and redeposited the silt as a blanket deposit in upland areas downwind from the source valleys. It is not uncommon to have beds of sand interbedded with silt close to source valleys (see COVER SAND). Extensive loess bodies are present in North America, Europe and Asia. Archaeologically, loess is significant for several reasons. Soil erosion in loess-covered regions during the Holocene has caused substantial redeposition of this silt in colluvial slopes, ALLUVIAL FANS and as valley fill, potentially burying, sometimes deeply, and preserving archaeological sites in these settings. Loess is a deposit rich in nutrients for plants and is excellent for agricultural purposes. The ability of loess deposits to maintain stable vertical walls has been exploited, in China for example, by people who have built dwellings in the thick loess. In Central and eastern Europe, loess soil was favoured by the earliest farming communities, especially the LINEAR POTTERY culture in Slovakia, the Czech Republic, Germany, Poland and the Netherlands, and the CUCUTENI-TRIPOLYE culture in Ukraine and Moldova.

Lolang see LELANG.

London (*Lat.* Londinium) an important port during the early years of the Roman occupation of Britain. Like COL-CHESTER it suffered during Boudicca's revolt, but subsequently became the centre of government for the province. The monumental tombstone of the procurator Julius Classicianus who took over in the aftermath of the revolt has been found. Traces of the palace, dating to AD 80–100, have been discovered. Around AD 100 the city received a large basilica, forming one side of the FORUM. A fort was incorporated into the layout of the city, presumably for the permanent garrison attached to the procurator's staff. A MITHRAEUM has been excavated at Walbrook, which contained various pieces of marble sculpture.

long barrow see BARROW.

Long Count a means of counting time devised during the MESOAMERICAN PRECLASSIC period. Using the day (KIN) as the basic unit of measure, the Long Count includes a series of increasingly large units of measure (i.e. UINAL = 20 kin; TUN = 18 uinal; KATUN = 20 tun; BAKTUN = 20 katun). In the most widely accepted correlation, the MAYA began their count in the year 3113 BC, with most recorded dates falling in the CLASSIC period (8th–10th baktun). The Long Count cycle will conclude in AD 2012, though some carved monuments allude to other cycles both before and after the current era.

Longgupo or **Wushan hominid site** a cave in eastern Sichuan Province, central China, 20 km (12 miles) south of the Yangtze River, which was discovered in 1984. Excavations in the 1980s yielded crudely fashioned lithic artifacts of OLDOWAN technology, and HOMINID remains.

PALAEOMAGNETIC analysis suggested an early Pleistocene age, and ELECTRON SPIN RESONANCE dating has confirmed this, indicating an age of 1.96 to 1.78 million years. The hominid remains, initially thought to be HOMO *erectus*, have been ascribed to *H. ergaster* or even *H. habilis*.

longhouse 1 (*Neolithic*) an elongated wooden post structure typical of the early Neolithic (*c*.5500–4000 BC) and the later Iron Age (*c*.500 BC–AD 500) of northern-Central Europe (as well as late WOODLAND cultures of northeastern North America, particularly the Huron and Iroquois tribes, *c*.AD 1300–1600, and the peoples of the northwest coast of North America, *c*.AD 1000–1800, such as the Haida). The North American longhouses were divided into living quarters for a number of residential groups, while the European structures may have been multi-purpose buildings that served both as dwellings and as stables for livestock.

2 (*Palaeolithic*) a type of dwelling structure attributed to the Upper Palaeolithic by Soviet archaeologists. The dwelling is reconstructed as an elongated above-ground structure up to 100 m (110 yds) in length, with a central line of interior hearths and, in some cases, an arrangement of debris-filled pits. The walls and roofing are thought to have been supported by wooden poles and large mammal bones. Remains of supposed longhouses were described from KOSTENKI I and IV, and PUSHKARI I during the 1930s; another possible example was reported at AVDEEVO in the 1950s. The interpretation of these features is controversial; they may actually represent several small structures.

long **kiln [*lung* kiln]** see JINGDEZHEN.

long mound see BARROW.

Longquan [Lung-ch'üan] see CELADON.

Longshan [Lung-shan] the collective name of the prominent regional cultures of the late Neolithic in northern China dating to the 3rd millennium BC. The Longshan period encompasses the trends towards the emergence of civilization (walled sites of HANGTU construction, first metal use, warfare, etc.) and is distinguished by delicate black polished ceramics of complicated shapes. Compare LIANGZHU, MACHANG, QIJIA.

Lopburi a major settlement occupied from the late prehistoric to the historic period, located near the confluence of the Chao Phraya and Pa Sak Rivers in central Thailand, adjacent to major copper deposits. Lopburi and smaller sites in its catchment region (e.g. BAN THA KAE, NON PA WAI, Lopburi Artillery Centre, Huai Yai and others) produced copper and bronze during the 2nd and 1st millennia BC, and some sites continued to produce copper and iron into the KHMER period of occupation. Already an important town during the DVARAVATI period, Lopburi became the major centre in central Thai-

land in the 11th–13th centuries, and it has given its name to the Khmer-influenced art of the region during that period.

Los Millares a CHALCOLITHIC settlement and cemetery of *c*.2400 bc in ALMERIA, Spain. The settlement stands on a spur between the River Andarax and a seasonal stream, and is protected by a series of dry-stone walls with circular bastions running across the neck of the promontory. Within the settlement were a series of circular houses, and immediately outside it to the west was a cemetery of some eighty PASSAGE GRAVES. The tombs were of circular 'THOLOS' type with ORTHOSTATIC walls and CORBEL-VAULTED roofs, and were used for communal burial. The rich grave-goods included an ivory sandal, bone 'idols', copper axes and daggers, and pottery decorated with double 'eye' motifs. See also SIRET.

Los Toldos a PALAEOINDIAN rockshelter in southern Patagonia (Argentina), excavated by Augusto Cardich. The lowest levels of the site contained extinct horse and camelid, and guanaco associated with unifacially retouched tools. A radiocarbon date of 12,600 bp has recently been called into question, and its association with the artifacts is unclear. However, a subsequent stratum also contains extinct horse, and guanaco associated with retouched tools; this level is dated minimally to 8700 bp.

lost wax or ***cire perdue*** a method of casting awkwardly shaped objects in metal. A wax model of the object is coated in clay and baked, and the melted wax allowed to escape. Liquid metal, poured into the resulting cavity in the mould, assumes the model's shape, and is released when hard by breaking the terracotta surround – hence each mould can be used only once. First developed in the 4th millennium BC in the Near East, it was used primarily for bronze in the Old World (especially in Southeast Asia), and for gold in South America and MESOAMERICA.

Lothagam a site southwest of LAKE TURKANA in northern Kenya, where a piece of a HOMINID mandible containing a molar tooth too fragmentary to identify genus or species, considered to date between 6–5 million years ago, was found. It may represent the earliest known hominid. The locality has also yielded a few fragmentary HOMO *sapiens* skeletons of Holocene date.

Lothal a HARAPPAN town (covering about 7 ha [17 acres]) on an extinct course of the Sabarmati River near the Gulf of Cambay in Gujerat, northwestern India, where S. R. Rao's excavations in the 1950s revealed a walled settlement. This contained residential and craft (especially stone beads and copper working) areas, a citadel on a platform in the southeastern corner of the town, and a large dock along the eastern town wall. Rao has argued from this last feature that Lothal was a Harappan sea port, perhaps engaged in the PERSIAN GULF TRADE (a Dilmun seal was a surface find on or near the site), though the 'dock' is more plausibly identified as a water tank. Lothal is also remarkable for the presence of local non-Harappan pottery in Mature Harappan levels, and for the subsequent post-Harappan occupation that shows a strong continuation of the Harappan tradition but with the loss of many salient characteristics. See also RANJPUR.

Lough Gur a series of sixteen Neolithic and Early Bronze Age settlement sites on the Knockadoon peninsula on the shores of Lough Gur, Co. Limerick, Ireland. Excavations here have revealed plans of several rectangular Neolithic houses, some associated with BEAKER pottery. More unusual are the enclosures around some of the houses, consisting of a double ring of stones, the revetment or facing of a turf bank which protected the houses against the depredations of livestock. These are dated to c.2600 bc. Near by are a number of megalithic CHAMBERED TOMBS and STONE CIRCLES.

Lou Island an island in the Manus group, Admiralty Islands, that is an important source of obsidian in the BISMARCKS and the western Pacific. Lou obsidian first appears at Pamwak at about 12,000 bp, but only travels beyond the Manus group with the arrival of LAPITA. It increases in importance over time in Lapita sites at the expense of TALASEA obsidian. There are a series of short-lived occupation sites and obsidian workshops on Lou, buried by volcanic ash layers which provide good chronological control. Excavation at the Sasi site, dated to c.2100 bp, produced a unique bronze artifact.

loutrophoros a type of container with an ovoid body, long neck, flaring mouth and two long handles. From the iconography of Athenian RED-FIGURED examples it seems to be linked with women and may have been used for carrying water as part of the marriage ceremony. The shape also appears either in relief or in the round on Attic grave STELAS.

Lovčičky a Late Bronze Age settlement in southern Moravia of the URNFIELD period, belonging to the VELATICE group. At Lovčičky, in the centre of an open area surrounded by smaller post houses stood a larger building with the appearance of a 'hall'.

Lovelock Cave a cave in Nevada, USA, with evidence for human use and occupation from 9,000 to 150 years ago. The arid and constant temperature preserved an amazing array of organic artifacts, such as baskets, clothing, sandals and nets. The site is particularly famous for duck decoys made from tule (march bulrush). These beautifully preserved objects date to 3500–1000 BP.

Lowasera a fishing settlement site, apparently semi-permanently occupied, southeast of LAKE TURKANA in northern Kenya, containing evidence of an aquatic life-style between about 9000 and 4500 bp. Food remains comprise fish, crocodile and hippopotamus, while artifacts include backed microliths, scrapers, choppers and grindstones, pottery with 'wavy-line' decoration, as well as bone harpoons (see 'AQUALITHIC').

Lower Egypt the northern part of Egypt, chiefly comprising the Nile DELTA and the area around MEMPHIS. The boundary between Lower and UPPER EGYPT was somewhere between LISHT and MEIDUM on the west bank of the Nile; on the east bank the second NOME of Upper Egypt extended slightly further to the north.

Lower Nubia that part of the Nile Valley extending southwards from the traditional border of Egypt at ASWAN as far as the Second Cataract of the Nile.

Luangwa 1 a Late Iron Age complex identified with the main pottery style in eastern and most of central and northern Zambia during the 2nd millennium AD. It appeared as a sudden break from the CHIFUMBAZE complex in the 11th century and is considered to have originated in Zaire.

2 EARLIER STONE AGE SANGOAN collections from secondary contexts in river gravel deposits in eastern Zambia, which are characterized by large picks and other core tools.

Lubang Angin a cave in the Gunung Mulu National Park, Sarawak, eastern Malaysia, containing burials wrapped in bark cloth, paddle-stamped, NIAH three-colour ware and double-spouted water jars, glass beads and iron fragments. The site is dated between 700 BC and AD 500.

Lubbock see AVEBURY, LORD.

Lucania an area of Italy to the south of CAMPANIA adjoining the Tyrrhenian Sea. It contained several Greek colonies including PAESTUM. See also LUCANIAN POTTERY.

Lucanian pottery a type of RED-FIGURED pottery produced in LUCANIA from the late 5th and through the 4th century BC. One of the initial centres of production was located at METAPONTO, and there are clear links with APULIAN POTTERY. See also SOUTH ITALIAN POTTERY.

'Lucy' a famous, small 3.18 million-year-old australopithecine (see AUSTRALOPITHECUS), attributed to A. afarensis, found at HADAR in Ethiopia in 1974. Forty per cent of the skeleton was recovered, which makes this one of the most complete specimens of an australopithecine ever found. The name 'Lucy' was inspired by the Beatles' song 'Lucy In The Sky With Diamonds', which was playing on a tape in the field camp shortly after the remains were found.

Luka Vrublevetskaya an ENEOLITHIC settlement of an early phase of the CUCUTENI-TRIPOLYE culture in Ukraine. Luka Vrublevetskaya provides good evidence for the development of the Cucuteni-Tripolye culture. Eight pit-dwellings were excavated at Luka Vrublevetskaya, contrasting with the PLOSHCHADKI found in later

Cucuteni-Tripolye settlements, and one was exceptionally large (43 m [47 yds] long) with eleven hearths arranged down the middle. Numerous female figurines were also found.

Lukenya Hill a southern Kenyan boulder-hill containing material from the MIDDLE STONE AGE to the Late Iron Age. Of particular interest is a long sequence of LATER STONE AGE backed microlith industries, linked to a radiocarbon date on bone apatite of 29,950 bp and a series of radiocarbon dates on bone apatite and collagen ranging from 21,500 to 12,000 bp, and which are associated with a late Upper Pleistocene fragmentary modern human skull claimed to show features similar to those of modern Negroid people.

luminescence dating a series of radiogenic dating techniques developed for dating fired archaeological material; suitable for dating QUATERNARY sediments laid down in a range of depositional environments, particularly loess, other AEOLIAN deposits and COLLUVIUM; and still undergoing refinement and experimentation. Sediments and materials buried in them are exposed to ionizing radiation from decay of radioactive ISOTOPES which causes energy in the form of displaced electrons to be stored in electron traps within mineral crystal lattices. Trapped electrons accumulate through time. When stimulated, trapped electrons in the crystal lattice are freed, releasing energy in the form of light, referred to as luminescence. The intensity of the signal is a measure of the accumulated radiation exposure, or equivalent dose; the longer the exposure or the stronger the radiation level, or dose rate, the greater the emitted luminescence of a sample. When archaeological material such as pottery is fired, any stored energy in mineral grain inclusions is released and the thermoluminescent clock is reset. Upon burial, the mineral inclusions begin to store energy anew. Electron stimulation can take a number of forms, giving rise to different types of luminescence dating. THERMOLUMINESCENCE dating utilizes heat; optical stimulated luminescence dating (OSL) visible light; and infrared stimulated luminescent dating (IRSL) infrared light.

lunette see WILLANDRA LAKES.

Lung Hoa a prehistoric settlement and cemetery in the Red River Valley, northern Vietnam, belonging to the late Neolithic PHUNG NGUYEN culture of the mid 2nd millennium BC. Some graves contained stone and jade GE (*guo* in Chinese) HALBERDS imported from SHANG China.

Lungshan see LONGSHAN.

Luni see APENNINE CULTURE.

lunula a sheet gold collar of Early Bronze Age date, sometimes with incised geometric decoration similar to that on BELL BEAKERS. Lunulae are of Irish or western

British origin but are found also on adjacent parts of the continent. They may have been worn as ritual equipment.

Lupemban a post-SANGOAN stone industry of parts of Central and eastern Africa, which overlies the Sangoan levels at KALAMBO FALLS, and is dated to more than 30,000 years ago, or considerably earlier, characterized by bifacially worked core tools as well as large sidescrapers and long double-ended bifacial points which may have been spear points (see MWANGANDA). Lupemban artifacts are abundant in the river gravels of the Dundo area of northern Angola, where pollen suggests vegetation and climate in Lupemban times were similar to those of today.

lur a Late Bronze Age bronze horn from southern Scandinavia. *Lurer* consist of a long curving tube, cast in sections and expertly fitted together, ending in a circular plate decorated with raised bosses or similar design. Lacking a proper mouthpiece, *lurer* are capable of producing only a limited range of sounds. They are often found in pairs of similar size and tone and were sometimes deposited in bogs as votive offerings.

Luristan bronzes a heterogeneous group of metalwork styles found in the mountains of western-central Iran, spanning the two millennia between about 2600 and 600 BC. Until c.1000 BC this metalwork is essentially indistinguishable from that of other areas of western Asia; after that time (i.e. during the Iron Age) the style becomes more regionally distinctive, especially for weapons and horse equipment. Even in the latter period, however, the Luristan bronzes do not seem to be the products of a single regional or ethnic community. Thus, while denoting the broad region of this metalwork, the term has very little cultural historical meaning.

Lusatian culture or **Lausitz culture** a Late Bronze Age/Early Iron Age (HALLSTATT period) culture of Poland and eastern Germany. The Lusatian culture is known from both URNFIELD cemeteries (e.g. KIETRZ) and settlements. Many larger settlements, such as BISKUPIN, SENFTENBERG and SOBIEJUCHY, are fortified. Cattle were the primary Lusatian livestock species, and Ostoja-Zagórski has suggested that the herds were large.

lustral basin a sunken room in MINOAN architecture, entered by a short flight of steps and usually screened off by a parapet. EVANS believed that lustral basins were used for ritual purification but, in certain contexts, they are more plausibly interpreted as bathrooms.

Luxor the modern town which now covers most of what was the ancient city of THEBES (EGYPT)-EAST BANK. In the southern part of the town is the temple of Luxor, largely constructed under AMENHOTEP III and RAMESSES II, and connected with KARNAK via a processional route.

Lydenburg an Early Iron Age village in Mpumalanga Province in eastern South Africa, occupied in the mid 1st millennium ad, which has given its name to an Early Iron Age group. Of particular interest are seven unique, hollow, fired-clay sculpted heads, which are among the oldest surviving examples of Iron Age art in southern Africa. These are thought to have been used in rituals, such as initiation ceremonies, after which they were deliberately broken and the pieces discarded into deep pits. The presence of similar fragments at other contemporary southern African Iron Age sites suggests the practice may have been widespread.

lydion a form of pot containing perfumes. The name is derived from Lydia, an area where numerous examples have been found. Many examples were made in western Turkey (see EAST GREEK POTTERY) as well as at ATHENS.

Lyles Hill a Neolithic settlement site, in Antrim, Ireland, type-site together with GRIMSTON in Yorkshire of the Grimston-Lyles Hill pottery style of the British middle Neolithic (4th millennium BC). The site was enclosed within a continuous bank but no ditch.

Lyngby see BROMMIAN.

M

Maadi an Egyptian PREDYNASTIC site to the south of CAIRO, chiefly excavated by Menghin and Amer in 1930–35. The settlement debris at Maadi is up to 2 m (6 ft) thick and covers an area of approximately 18 ha (45 acres). The community was probably centrally organized with defined areas for houses and for the large pottery jars and pits which comprised storage areas. The economy of Maadi seems to have relied less on hunting than did MERIMDE. The presence of imports of the GERZEAN of UPPER EGYPT and of EARLY BRONZE AGE Palestine suggests that Maadi may have been an important trading centre. Its period of occupation has been dated to c.3200–3000 BC, immediately preceding the ARCHAIC PERIOD.

Maa-Palaekastro a promontory on the west coast of CYPRUS. It is the site of a fortified settlement excavated by Karageorghis in 1979–86, and was first occupied late in the 13th century BC, possibly by the SEA PEOPLES. A fine ASHLAR structure may have been their sanctuary. Early in the 12th century BC this settlement was destroyed by fire, and it would appear that Maa was then taken over for a brief period by MYCENAEAN Greeks who subsequently moved on to KOUKLIA-PALAEPAPHOS.

Maba [Ma-pa] a site in Guangdong Province, China, where transitional fossils between HOMO *erectus* and *H. sapiens sapiens* have been discovered in the Middle Palaeolithic period. See also JINNIUSHAN.

Macassans Indonesian traders, mainly from Sulawesi,

MACHU PICCHU, Peru.

who visited tropical Australia to collect and process *trepang*, also known as *bêche-de-mer* or *sea cucumber*, an important ingredient in Chinese cooking. The trade seems to have begun about AD 1700 and continued until the end of the 19th century. Archaeological evidence of the trade is common in northern Australia. The Macassan influence on local Aboriginal society can be seen in artifacts, including dug-out canoes and metal tools, art motifs, language and ritual, while Macassan sailing vessels, or *praus*, were depicted in rock art and rock arrangements.

MacEnery see KENT'S CAVERN.

Machang [Ma-ch'ang] a late Neolithic culture in north-western China of YANGSHAO descent, contemporaneous with the LONGSHAN cultures of the east, dating to 2800–1800 BC.

Machu Picchu an INCA site northwest of CUZCO, Peru. Situated on a sharp ridge between a large and a small mountain peak, it includes agricultural terraces, habitation structures, religious architecture and tombs. The site was abruptly abandoned at the time of the Spanish conquest, and the Spanish seem to have shown little interest in it. 'Discovered' by Hiram Bingham in 1911, it has been interpreted as many different things: an Inca fortress, a convent, the lost site of VILCABAMBA, the location of the origin of the Inca dynasty, and ever more fanciful things. John H. Rowe has noted that Spanish documents list a place named 'Picchu' as still belonging to the descendants of the Inca Pachacuti in the 16th century; he argues that the site functioned as a royal estate belonging to Pachacuti.

MacNeish, Richard Stockton (1918–2001) An American archaeologist best known for his major excavations in Latin America, particularly those in the TEHUACÁN VALLEY, Mexico, in the 1960s, which focused on the origins of maize agriculture in the New World, and at PIKIMACHAY, Peru. Towards the end of his life he worked on an alleged pre-CLOVIS occupation at Pendejo Cave in New Mexico, and on the origins of rice cultivation in China.

Macorijes or **Macorix** the name given to the indigenous groups on the island of Santo Domingo in the Caribbean whose ceramics correspond to the MEILLACOID style of the 9th century AD onwards. They spoke a language different from that of the TAINOS, and occupied the northern-central parts of Hispaniola or Dominican Republic, and part of eastern Cuba.

macrofauna large animals (compare MICROFAUNA).

macrolith a large stone tool (compare MICROLITH). See also ASTURIAN.

Madai Caves a series of caves in Sabah, northern Borneo, Malaysia, yielding prehistoric remains dating to *c*.9000 BC and later. Agop Atas, the largest, and Agop Sarapad were inhabited from *c*.9000 to 5000 BC by hunters using pebble and flake tools. After a 3,000-year gap, the caves (particularly Agop Atas) were reused between *c*.2000 and 500 BC by people using stone flake tools and pottery similar to that at LEANG TUWO MANEE in Talaud. The caves were again abandoned, then reused early in the 1st millennium AD.

Mad'arovce an Early Bronze Age regional culture of the central Danube basin, centred on the Váh drainage in western Slovakia. The Mad'arovce culture emerged towards the end of the neighbouring ÚNĚTICE culture and is sometimes considered a late sub-group of Únětice. As in the case of the OTOMANI culture to the east, Mad'arovce settlements often occur on fortified hilltops, although others occur in lowland valleys.

Maes Howe the most splendid of the PASSAGE GRAVES in Orkney, Scotland. A long passage with floor, walls and ceiling of massive stone flags leads to a rectangular main chamber with CORBEL-VAULTED roof, the stones of each course sloped to make a smooth-faced vault. Though the top of the vault has been lost, it is estimated that it would originally have been approximately 4.5 m (15 ft) in height. To either side of the main chamber and in the rear wall facing the entrance, small square openings, originally with removable closing blocks, lead to rectangular side chambers. Of the tomb contents nothing now remains, and VIKING RUNIC inscriptions of the 12th century AD within the tomb, which refer to the discovery of a treasure, can probably be discounted. A series of radiocarbon dates averaging 2700 BC was obtained from the ditch which surrounds the cairn.

Maeva an impressive complex of twenty-five MARAE on Huahine, Society Islands, POLYNESIA. Many have now been restored.

Magadha see GANGES CIVILIZATION.

Magallanes (Magellan) chronological sequence of the prehistoric occupation of Patagonia, divided into five phases; elaborated by Gordon Willey in 1971. Phase I (*c*.10,000 bp) is typified by FISHTAIL POINTs, such as those found at CUEVA FELL. Phase II was left undefined. Phase III (*c*.6000 bp) includes willow-leaf and stemless triangular points. Phase IV (*c*.5000 bp) is defined by triangulate points with broad, basally indented stems. The final phase (*c*.1500 bp) includes fairly recent hunter-gatherer occupations. The very early occupation of Patagonia, by Magallanes I, if not earlier (see LOS TOLDOS), suggests that the initial occupation of the New World, via the Bering Land Bridge, may have taken place much earlier than currently accepted dates. See also MONTE VERDE.

Magan see PERSIAN GULF TRADE.

Magarita see ITAZUKE.

magatama (*Jap.* 'curved bead') a jade or jasper pendant produced in the JOMON, YAYOI and KOFUN periods. During the Kofun period, it attained the status of an imperial emblem, together with the BRONZE MIRROR and sword. Many such curved beads also decorate the gold crowns of SILLA.

Magdalenian the final West European Upper Palaeolithic industry, best known for its art, which seems to have originated in southwestern France and spread out to adjacent areas, lasting from c.16,000 to 10,000 BC. The Magdalenian people hunted primarily deer or ibex, and fished for salmon. Their assemblages include practical but unremarkable stone tools, and well-made bone and antler implements including spearthrowers, BÂTONS PERCÉS and barbed harpoons. The type-site is the Dordogne rockshelter of La Madeleine, France, first excavated by LARTET and CHRISTY, and extremely rich in MOBILIARY ART. See also PALAEOLITHIC ART, PARIETAL ART.

Magdalenska Gora an Early Iron Age (HALLSTATT period) complex of tumuli in Slovenia, near STIČNA. Excavated by the Duchess of Mecklenburg in 1905–14, the graves at Magdalenska Gora have yielded a broad range of artifacts from the 7th century BC. Of particular significance are the SITULAE, but also numerous weapons, helmets and body armour. Magdalenska Gora is one of a number of Hallstatt tumuli complexes which include NOVO MESTO in Slovenia and NOVE KOSARISKA in Slovakia.

Maghzalia, Tell a small ACERAMIC NEOLITHIC site in the Sinjar region of northern Iraq, excavated by N. I. Merpert and R. M. Munchaev. It provides important evidence for early sedentary communities and probably farming in the northern MESOPOTAMIAN piedmont. The architecture features rectilinear structures with stone foundations, and a stone wall surrounded the village. The excavation produced indirect indications of cultivation as well as more direct evidence of hunting. The lithic industry contains similarities with aceramic sites in the Zagros (e.g. JARMO) and also with ACERAMIC NEOLITHIC industries of Syro-Palestine.

Maglemosian (from *Danish* for 'big bog') the first Mesolithic culture of northern Europe found in Scandinavia, the northern Balkans, northern Scotland and northern England, and lasting from c.8000 to 5000 BC. The assemblages reflect the exploitation of the POSTGLACIAL forest and riverside environments, with evidence of increased woodworking provided by stone axes and faunal remains indicating the wide variation in diet which included fish and birds. Microliths, picks and bone and antler fishing and hunting tools such as barbed points are characteristic Maglemosian artifacts.

magnetic *adj.* **1** pertaining to magnetism, the ability to be magnetized or affected by a magnet.

2 relating to the earth's magnetic field. See also ELECTROMAGNETIC SURVEYING, MAGNETIC SUSCEPTIBILITY, ARCHAEOMAGNETIC DATING, PALAEOMAGNETISM.

magnetic susceptibility a property of sediment and soil, measured as a ratio of intensity of magnetization of the material to the strength of an applied magnetic field. It is an indication of the concentration of magnetic minerals in the material, such as the magnetite family minerals and haematite. In QUATERNARY LOESS-PALAEOSOL sections, the magnetic susceptibility profile serves as a substitute for climatic data, although the relationship is not fully understood.

Concentrations tend to be greater in palaeosols and less in unaltered loess.

magnetometer a geophysical instrument that measures the Earth's magnetic field strength, used in ELECTROMAGNETIC SURVEYING to identify changes in the field within soil or sediment that might be caused by subsurface features, hearths or metal objects. The proton magnetometer takes intermittent measurements of absolute field strength. The fluxgate, differential fluxgate and proton magnetometers take continuous measurements of relative vertical change in intensity of field strength.

Magosian a term formerly widely used in eastern and southern Africa for stone industries containing microliths and small blades as well as MIDDLE STONE AGE artifacts, which were thought to be transitional between the Middle and LATER STONE AGE. The original sample from the Magosi site in Uganda has been shown to be mixed and the term is no longer used.

magoula see TOUMBA.

Mahaiatea the largest MARAE ever constructed in Tahiti, Society Islands, POLYNESIA. It was built in AD 1767 by the chieftainess Purea of Papara and described in 1769 by Joseph Banks. Now largely destroyed, it comprised a platform 81 by 22 m (89 by 24 yds) at the base, rising in eleven steps to a height of about 13.5 m (44 ft). The platform was faced with squared volcanic stone over a basal course of coral blocks, and stood at one end of a walled court 115 m (126 yds) long.

Mahal Teglinos see GASH.

Mahan see SAMHAN.

Maiden Castle an impressive Iron Age HILLFORT in Dorset, England, with several concentric lines of huge chalk ramparts following the contours of the steep-sided hill. Excavations by WHEELER, in 1934–7, showed that beneath the hillfort were traces of a Neolithic CAUSEWAYED CAMP overlain by a later Neolithic long mound over 500 m (550 yds) in length. The first hillfort, c.500 BC, was a relatively simple affair occupying only the eastern part of the site. The hillfort was considerably extended and strengthened c.250 BC, with highly elaborate entrances at east and west. Traces of round houses and streets have been found in the interior. The fort was besieged and captured by the Romans in AD 43.

Maikop ENEOLITHIC KURGAN burials in the northern Caucasus Mountains, Russia, dating to the late 4th millennium BC. Under the main Maikop barrow was a tripartite mortuary structure. In the central part was the burial of a male, characterized as a 'royal' individual, under a canopy with gold and silver supports. Gravegoods included silver vessels with animal designs (including horses), gold figurines of a lion and two bulls, copper tools and textiles with elaborate designs. The Maikop burials have given their name to the Maikop culture of the Caucasus, with walled settlements.

Mailhac a settlement site and cemetery of the Late Bronze Age and Iron Age near Narbonne in the Aude, southern France, excavated by O. and J. Taffanel in the 1930s. The occupation site, a hilltop OPPIDUM called Le Cayla, dominates the present-day village, and has five phases of superimposed occupation spanning the period from the end of the Bronze Age to the Roman period. The first phase, Cayla I, the same age as the NECROPOLIS of Moulin, is located 800 m (875 yds) from the settlement, on the plain. There are about 1,000 cremation graves in the necropolis, 367 of which have been excavated or localized, and they are dated from c.870 to 700 BC. The cemetery is divided into three stages – Le Moulin, Grand Bassin I and Grand Bassin II – which together span the Late Bronze Age to the mid Iron Age. They form the type-series for the chronology of this period in the Languedoc region of southern France. The latest phase, Grand Bassin II, is marked by the appearance of Greek and ETRUSCAN imports.

The Mailhac culture (or Mailhacian) is a late URNFIELD group of Languedoc, and has its own pottery style, with a decoration comprising double parallel incisions that form anthropomorphous, zoomorphic and geometric motifs. The 6th-century BC phase known as Cayla II has imported ceramics from Italy and Greece, while Cayla III (5th–4th centuries BC), the first village of the sequence to be built with stone and brick rather than timber, has Attic wares. Cayla IV, constructed in the same way, has many CELTIC characteristics (ceramics, coins, weapons, headsculptures), and seems to have been destroyed, and had its rampart overthrown, in 75 BC, probably by the Romans. Cayla V, built on its ruins, was gradually abandoned during the 2nd century AD.

Mailu an island about 15 km (9 miles) off the southeast coast of New Guinea that was a significant centre in coastal Papuan trading systems. The islanders were middle-men in local and long-distance ceremonial exchange systems and linked such networks from the Papuan Gulf (the HIRI) to the Massim region (the

kula), manufactured shell valuables and held a monopoly on local pottery manufacture. Archaeological evidence documents some 1,500 years of growing regional specialization, culminating in the development of the ethnographic system about 400–500 years ago.

Majninskaya an Upper Palaeolithic open-air site on the Uj River near its confluence with the Yenisei in southern-central Siberia. Nine cultural layers are buried in sandy ALLUVIUM of the second terrace; they are dated (radiocarbon and PALAEOMAGNETISM) to c.19,000–9000 bp. Among the associated faunal remains are horse, red deer, aurochs and birds. The artifacts include wedge-shaped microcores, sidescrapers and endscrapers, laterally grooved bone points and a crude anthropomorphous figurine of fired clay.

Makaha Valley a valley in Oahu, Hawaii, that was first settled c.AD 1100. Agricultural terraces, habitation sites and HEIAU have been documented in the course of a detailed archaeological survey. The lower part of the valley was used for dryland cultivation while the much wetter upper valley allowed irrigation of root-crops (taro). Compare HALAWA VALLEY, KAWELA, LAPAKAHI.

Makapansgat see MAKAPAN VALLEY.

Makapan Valley or **Makapansgat Valley** a valley on the farm Makapansgat some 19 km (12 miles) east-northeast of Potgietersrus in the Northern Province of South Africa, in which many caves preserve an archaeological record from australopithecine times, about 3.32 million bp to the present. The oldest site is the Makapansgat Limeworks site (and adjacent Horse Mandible Cave), dating between about 3.32 and 1.6 million bp, which has produced important samples of AUSTRALOPITHECUS africanus as well as large collections of fossil animal remains (see DART).

The *Cave of Hearths* (and adjacent Hyaena Cave) contains a long record of human habitation. Its ACHEULIAN artifacts date from about 400,000 bp. The site seems to have been unoccupied between about 200,000 and 110,000 bp, after which it was intermittently occupied from about 110,000 to 50,000 bp, again from about 10,000 to 5,000 bp, and once more from Iron Age times until the 1900s. A mandible fragment found with the Acheulian material is described as early or archaic HOMO sapiens or *H. rhodesiensis* (see BROKEN HILL). Some of the Acheulian layers probably contain hearths, but comprise mainly burnt bat guano, which may have been ignited naturally or accidentally.

The *Historic Cave* or *Makapansgat* preserves Iron Age remains and is particularly famous as the location of a battle between a Boer Commando and local Langa and Ndebele people in 1854, when Chief Makapan together with many of his tribe and livestock were besieged in the cave for nearly a month, and many hundreds died of hunger and thirst or were shot. *Rainbow Cave* is a limeworkers' excavation which has yielded MIDDLE STONE AGE artifacts, *Peppercorn's Cave* contains Iron Age and historical artifacts as well as fossiliferous breccia, *Ficus Cave* and *Ficus Iron Age site* contain Iron Age and 19th-century material, and *Buffalo Cave* has Pleistocene animal remains.

Makarovo a group of four Upper Palaeolithic open-air sites on the Lena River in southern-central Siberia. At Makarovo 2, two cultural layers are buried in ALLUVIAL deposits of the second terrace, and have yielded radiocarbon dates of 11,400–11,950 BP. Both layers contain microblades and other artifacts typical of the Siberian late Upper Palaeolithic. At Makarovo 3, redeposited artifacts are buried in slope sediments on the third terrace along with remains of woolly mammoth, reindeer and other mammals. The assemblage includes sidescrapers and endscrapers and choppers, and is thought to date to the early Upper Palaeolithic. At Makarovo 4, weathered artifacts were found in slope deposits on the fourth terrace, including points, sidescrapers and endscrapers. This assemblage has been dated by radiocarbon to more than 39,000 BP and represents one of the earliest Upper Palaeolithic occupations in Siberia. Makarovo was first discovered and investigated by OKLADNIKOV in 1941; subsequent work at these sites was undertaken by Aksenov in 1966–75.

Makwe a rockshelter with a long LATER STONE AGE sequence near Katete in southeastern Zambia. Contemporary with NACHIKUFAN III material in adjacent regions is a distinct late microlithic industry named the Makwe industry, which persisted even after the arrival of Iron Age farmers in the area. It is characterized by the gradual replacement of backed flakes and blades by segments and other geometric microliths during the 4th and 3rd millennia bc, until the final stages were characterized almost exclusively by segments. The artifacts also include bone points and beads made on bone or shell. Of particular interest is the retention of mastic on many microliths, allowing archaeologists to reconstruct hafting methods.

malachite a green copper carbonate mineral that is an alteration product of copper ore deposits. It was used as a source of copper and, when powdered, as a cosmetic.

malacology the study of aquatic and terrestrial molluscs as indicators of past environmental conditions and diet. Certain land snails are good microenvironmental indicators, having very restrictive environmental tolerances for ground cover, vegetation and moisture regimes. Calcareous sediment and soils in which carbonate mollusc shells are preserved are sampled in a vertical column, the sediment is wet-sieved, and snails are dried, identified and counted. Percentages of species are plotted versus depth, and environmental changes are interpreted from changes in the snail assemblage.

Edible species of marine and aquatic molluscs give an indication of diet and the subsistence economy. See also SHELL MIDDEN.

Malakunanja a sandstone shelter in ARNHEM LAND, northern Australia, first excavated by Johan Kamminga and re-excavated by Rhys Jones and Mike Smith. The sequence is similar to that of NAUWALABILA. THERMOLUMINESCENCE dates suggest that the lowest artifacts are about 50,000 years old, but these remain controversial.

Malangangerr a rockshelter in ARNHEM LAND, northern Australia, excavated in 1964–5 by Carmel Schrire. The two-part sequence extends back about 25,000 years. Hatchet heads of ground stone between 18,000 and 23,000 years old from here and Nawamoyn first established the presence of edge-ground tools in Pleistocene Australia.

Malaya Sya an Upper Palaeolithic open-air site on the Belyj Iyus River (Chulym tributary) in western Siberia. Artifacts and faunal remains are buried in loam and clay deposits on the slope of a side-valley ravine. Among the faunal remains are reindeer, sheep, steppe bison and woolly mammoth. Three radiocarbon estimates, ranging from 34,500 to 20,370 bp, are reported, and seem generally consistent with the view that the occupation predates the LAST GLACIAL MAXIMUM. The artifacts include large retouched blades and endscrapers, and are considered to be representative of the early Upper Palaeolithic, which remains poorly known in Siberia. Malaya Sya was discovered and excavated by Ovodov in 1974.

Malaysia see ASIA, SOUTHEAST.

Mali the West African empire which followed GHANA two centuries later. About AD 1230, a group of Kangaba under their leader Sundiata founded an empire which a century later extended over much of sub-Saharan West Africa under the unifying effect of Islam, until its overthrow by SONGHAY by the end of the 15th century. Mali's prosperity was based on trans-Saharan and local trade, especially in gold and salt. During the reign of Sundiata's grandson, Mansa Musa (1307–32), Mali became famous throughout the Mediterranean world and Europe, and the city of Timbuktu became renowned as a centre of learning.

Malia or **Mallia** the site of a MINOAN palace, on the island of Crete, constructed c.1900 BC, destroyed by an earthquake c.1700 BC, and then completely rebuilt. The final destruction is dated c.1450 BC. Malia lacks the refinement of the palaces at KNOSSOS and PHAISTOS. More space proportionately is set aside for the storage of agricultural produce, in particular oil and grain. Much of the town around the palace has been uncovered by the French excavators. Of particular interest are two large PROTO-PALATIAL complexes, known as the AGORA and Quartier Mu.

Mallowan, Sir Max Edgar Lucien (1904–78) a British archaeologist who worked in the Near East. Beginning as an assistant to C. L. WOOLLEY at UR, Mallowan's career in northern MESOPOTAMIAN archaeology encompassed work at NINEVEH, ARPACHIYAH, CHAGAR BAZAR, Tell BRAK and Nimrud (KALHU) in the 1930s and 1950s. In addition to field work, he served as director of the British School of Archaeology in Baghdad and also presided over the British Institute of Persian Studies, in both capacities promoting archaeological investigation of western Asia. Mallowan was married to Agatha Christie, who used her excavation experiences as the setting for *Murder in Mesopotamia* and other mysteries.

Mal'ta, an Upper Palaeolithic and Mesolithic open-air site on the Belaya River (Angara tributary) near Irkutsk in southern-central Siberia. The Mesolithic layer is buried under the modern soil on the third terrace; the more deeply buried Upper Palaeolithic layer overlies a buried soil and is believed to date to the beginning of the LAST GLACIAL MAXIMUM (c.24,000–23,000 bp). Faunal remains associated with the lower layer include reindeer, arctic fox, woolly mammoth and woolly rhinoceros. Excavation uncovered traces of former dwellings, partly constructed with limestone slabs, and a child burial. The artifact assemblage contained prismatic cores, retouched blades and endscrapers. Many ornaments and art objects, including human and animal figurines were found. Mal'ta was excavated by GERASIMOV, Sosnovskij and others in 1928–37 and 1956–8.

Maltese temples a series of some eighteen stone-built structures of multi-lobed plan, scattered either singly or in small clusters across the Mediterranean islands of Malta and Gozo. Constructed during the period 3600–2500 BC, these monuments have yielded carved stone panels and corpulent and sometimes colossal statues. They incorporate two distinct varieties of local limestone, hard coralline and softer globigerina, with individual blocks weighing up to 20 tonnes. Among the most remarkable of the Maltese sites is the group of four interlinked temples at TARXIEN, distinguished by the richness of their carved decoration. Adjacent to Tarxien is the underground HYPOGEUM of HAL SAFLIENI, a contemporary three-storey burial complex.

Malthi a precipitous Bronze Age AKROPOLIS in Messenia, Greece, which was excavated by Valmin in 1927–36. Unlike most Middle HELLADIC sites, Malthi was fortified and the houses, although rather ramshackle, appear to have been built to an integrated plan. MYCENAEAN remains are unimpressive except for two THOLOS tombs at the foot of the akropolis.

Maluquer de Motes, Juan (1915–88) a Spanish archaeologist best known for his studies of megaliths in Navarre and his excavations at CORTES DE NAVARRA.

Malwa a plateau in northwestern Madhya Pradesh in western-central India, which gives its name to a CHALCOLITHIC culture of the earlier 2nd millennium BC, best known from sites such as NAVDATOLI. The ceramics of the culture include a characteristic fine red-slipped ware with elaborate black-painted decoration (Malwa ware), as well as black-painted cream-slipped, black-and-red-painted, JORWE and Lustrous Red wares which appear and disappear during the history of the culture. These people were cultivators (wheat, rice, legumes, oil seed plants, fruits) and animal keepers (cattle, sheep, goat, pig) and hunters; while copper objects are relatively frequent, lithic industries are strongly represented. Sites with a material culture related to the Malwa culture complex occur well to the south (e.g. NEVASA) and east of the Malwa plateau, marking a wide distribution of the central Indian Chalcolithic.

Malyan, Tal i- an important site, the ancient Anshan, in the Kur River drainage of Fars, southwestern Iran, which represents the upland centre of the succession of POLITIES (ELAM, SUSA) that traditionally warred with southern MESOPOTAMIAN states. The sequence at Malyan spans the later 5th millennium BC to the early 1st millennium AD, with its most important occupation occurring during the Banesh (c.3400–2800 BC) and Kaftari (c.2200–1600 BC) periods. During the Banesh period, the city wall at Malyan enclosed nearly 200 ha (495 acres), of which 50 ha (124 acres) was filled with architecture; at this time, a strong PROTO-ELAMITE connection is evident. Kaftari period Malyan occupied some 130 ha (320 acres), as the centre of a hierarchically integrated settlement system.

Mambo a Late Iron Age phase of the LEOPARD'S KOPJE complex in southern Zimbabwe, dated to the 10th and 11th centuries AD. At Nthabazingwe in southwestern Zimbabwe, Mambo remains which overlay a Zhizo layer included evidence for DAGA-plastered circular houses, iron tools, copper bangles and some glass beads, which suggest contact with East African coastal trade. Food remains included sorghum, finger millet, ground beans, cowpeas, cattle, as well as some sheep and goats. The importance of cattle is suggested by clay cattle figurines; female figurines were also found. 'Mambo' is a Shona word for 'leader', and also appears in this context in Iron Age publications.

mammisi or **birth-house** an independent religious building found associated with the larger cult temples of the LATE PERIOD/Graeco-Roman period in Egypt. The mammisi was connected with the mythological birth of the god of the temple concerned, or with giving birth where the deity concerned was female (e.g. the goddess Hathor at DENDERA).

mammoth a genus of elephant (*Mammuthus*) which became adapted to the conditions of the Ice Age in the

MAMMISI or 'birth-house' at the temple of Dendera, Egypt, erected during the Roman period at a site famous since the Old Kingdom for the worship of the goddess Hathor.

northern hemisphere. Up to 3.5 m (11 ft) tall with a domed head, sloping back, long shaggy fur and large curving tusks (see IVORY), mammoths were frequently depicted in Palaeolithic art, and are best known from complete carcasses occasionally unearthed in Siberia and Alaska. Their massive molars comprised a series of vertical, flattened plates which wore to produce a flat but ridged grinding surface. The two main species were the woolly mammoth, *M. primigenius* (northern Eurasia and northern North America), and the Columbian mammoth, *M. columbi* (southern North America). Both subsisted largely on open grassy vegetation, and became extinct between 11,000 and 10,000 BP, except for a population on Wrangel Island in the Siberian Arctic Ocean which survived until *c.*3500 BP. See also MAMMOTH-BONE HOUSE.

mammoth-bone house/hut a type of dwelling structure thought to have been built by the inhabitants of Upper Palaeolithic sites in Central and eastern Europe between *c.*25,000 and 12,000 bp. Remains of these structures typically comprise a circular or oval arrangement of woolly mammoth bones and tusks (*c.*4–8 m [13–26 ft] in diameter), containing a central interior hearth and much occupation debris. The bones and tusks are believed to have provided structural support in regions where wood was scarce. Pits, hearths and debris concentrations are often found immediately adjacent to the bone arrangement (i.e. presumably external to the former structure). One or more mammoth-bone houses have been uncovered at KRAKOW-SPADZISTA in Poland, at DOBRANICHEVKA, MEZHIRICH and KOSTENKI XI in the former Soviet Union, and elsewhere.

Mamutowa a Palaeolithic cave-site located on the Kluczwoda River north of Kraków in southern Poland. Artifacts and faunal remains (primarily cave bear) are buried in clay and rubble. Middle Palaeolithic artifacts (e.g. sidescrapers) occur in the lowest cultural layers, while overlying levels contain evidence of two early

Upper Palaeolithic industries, AURIGNACIAN (e.g. split-base bone points) and JERZMANOWICIAN (e.g. laurel-leaf points) probably dating to the INTERSTADIAL preceding the LAST GLACIAL MAXIMUM. The upper layers contain GRAVETTIAN artifacts probably dating to the Last Glacial Maximum. Mamutowa was excavated principally by ZA-WISZA in 1873–81 and Kowalski in 1957–74.

Mancheng [Man-ch'eng] a city in Hebei Province, China, where two early HAN Dynasty tombs were cut into a rock cliff. They consist of several chambers totalling almost 200 cu. m (262 cu. yds) of space in which 2,800 funeral objects were deposited, including bronze vessels; gold, silver, iron, glass and jade articles; earthenware; lacquer ware and silk fabrics. The deceased, identified as Prince Liu Sheng and his wife, wore suits of jade platelets sewn together with gold thread. Compare SHAFT TOMBS, MOUNDED TOMBS.

Manching a very large OPPIDUM of the Late Iron Age near Ingolstadt in Bavaria, Germany, dated to the LA TÈNE period of the last few centuries BC. Adjacent to the Danube during this period (although now some distance away from the river), Manching is situated on a low river terrace. A 7 km (4 mile) MURUS GALLICUS rampart enclosed 380 ha (940 acres), of which a fraction (about 7 ha [17 acres]) has been excavated. These excavations have yielded thousands of features and hundreds of thousands of artifacts and animal bones. Manching appears to have been a commercial settlement, perhaps a regional market. Skeletal remains with injuries inflicted by metal weapons reflect a violent end to the settlement around 50 BC.

Manchuria an old name for northeastern (DONGBEI) China, comprising the Sungari and Liao River basins – the latter draining into BOHAI Bay; now parts of Heilongjiang, Jilin and Liaoning Provinces. It derives from the Manchu peoples, speakers of a non-Chinese, ALTAIC language.

Manda a trading city of the East African coast which has been the subject of extensive archaeological investigation, located on the Lamu Archipelago off the Kenyan coast, where African products such as ivory, horns and skins were exchanged for imports such as beads, pottery, glass and cloth from Arabia and further east. It extended over 3.8 ha (9.4 acres) during the 9th century AD, expanded to over 7 ha (17 acres) by the 10th century AD, and covered at least 10 ha (25 acres) by the 11th–13th centuries AD, after which its importance diminished. Construction materials included both wattle and daub as well as coral rubble and baked brick. A huge 'sea-wall', which was greatly enlarged during the 11th–13th centuries AD, protected substantial stone-built houses. Faunal remains comprise domestic stock including camel, as well as fish, shellfish and sea turtle. Evidence of iron working and bead manufacture has been uncovered.

Mandu Mandu Creek a rockshelter at Northwest Cape, Western Australia, where the first episode of occupation began about 32,000 years ago and includes evidence for the use of marine resources. The site was abandoned about 20,000 years ago and only reoccupied in the late Holocene. Twenty-two cone shell beads were recovered from the base of the sequence. These demonstrate that the antiquity of personal adornment in Australia is comparable to that in Europe. See also KOOLAN 2, MATENKUPKUM.

Manetho an Egyptian priest active in the early 3rd century BC. Manetho's history of the kings of ancient Egypt, preserved in the writings of later authors, provides the basis of the relative chronology of Egypt before the invasion of Alexander the Great.

Mangaasi a pottery tradition in Vanuatu, MELANESIA, characterized by incised and applied relief, dating from about 700 BC to about AD 1600. It is quite distinct from LAPITA pottery, but similar wares are found in the northern Solomons and New Caledonia.

Mannalargenna Cave a cave on Prime Seal Island in Bass Strait, Australia, with evidence of occupation from about 20,000 bp to about 8000 bp. This site, and the broadly contemporary Beeton Shelter on Badger Island, document occupation on the Pleistocene land-bridge that connected TASMANIA to the Australian mainland.

mano a one- or two-handed ground stone tool, used with the METATE to grind vegetable material for food. Manos have a variety of shapes and sizes and have some degree of usefulness in constructing CULTURE HISTORY. This term is most often used in MESOAMERICA and the American Southwest.

Mantai a port on the north coast of Sri Lanka, active from the late 1st millennium BC to the 13th century AD. A massive double moat encloses about 30 ha (74 acres) of settlement, which has built up 11 m (36 ft) of archaeological deposits above a mid 2nd-millennium BC Mesolithic encampment. Several investigations during the 20th century have recorded extant late monuments and lapidary art, and the outline of occupation history. The place seems to have been most prosperous during the centuries before 1000 AD, during the active SASSANIAN and Abbasid maritime trade in the Indian Ocean.

manuport any object transported and deposited by humans.

Maori the descendants of POLYNESIANS who settled NEW ZEALAND early in the 2nd millennium AD.

Mapungubwe a Late Iron Age site built on and around a hill in the Northern Province of South Africa, near the confluence of the Limpopo and Shashi Rivers, where South Africa, Botswana and Zimbabwe meet. It has given its name to the southern FACIES of phase B of the

MARAE, Tahiti.

LEOPARD'S KOPJE complex. Mapungubwe was occupied between c.AD 1220 and 1270 and is a forerunner of developments at GREAT ZIMBABWE. It seems to have been the capital of a state which controlled trade with the East African coast, and represents a period during which a highly stratified society developed and the wealth and status of ruling chiefs increased greatly. A hilltop graveyard contained an extraordinary collection of gold objects, including rhinoceros figurines, a headrest, a bowl and a sceptre, all covered with thin sheets of gold foil hammered on to wooden or mastic models with small gold tacks.

Maqiao [Ma-ch'iao] see GEOMETRIC POTTERY.

marae an eastern POLYNESIAN stone temple, very variable in design, but basically a rectangular enclosure with upright stones and a stone platform or AHU. Marae are especially characteristic of the later period of eastern Polynesian prehistory AD 1200–1800. In Tonga, Samoa and NEW ZEALAND, the word also refers to an open space within a village. See also HEIAU.

Marajó Island the large island, some 39,000 sq. km (15,000 sq. miles) in extent, at the mouth of the Amazon River, Brazil, extensively investigated by Clifford EVANS and Betty Meggers. Especially at the eastern end of the island are numerous sites comprising artificial mounds, built as platforms upon which villages were located. The largest centre, Os Camutins, includes some forty mounds. Excavations by Anna C. Roosevelt at the site of Aterro dos Bichos indicate that some twenty large multi-family houses were arranged around an open space and surrounded by a wide earthen wall. The island is characterized by savanna vegetation, not tropical rainforest, and the prehistoric population subsisted on maize, seeds and fish. The site was occupied from 400 BC until about AD 1300.

Marakanda see AFRASIAB.

Marathon a site in Attica, Greece, that is rich in tombs: an

Early HELLADIC CIST GRAVE cemetery, Middle Helladic tumuli and a MYCENAEAN THOLOS tomb, in which two horses had been buried as grave offerings. ATHENS' defeat of the Persian army in 490 BC is commemorated by the Soros, the large mound in which the Athenian casualties were buried, and by the tomb of the Plataeans which, if correctly identified, is the communal grave of their Greek allies.

Marca Huamachuco a large EARLY INTERMEDIATE PERIOD and MIDDLE HORIZON site in the northern highlands of Peru, the centre of a major POLITY. During the Middle Horizon the HUARI empire extended its influence into the Huamachuco region, and began construction of the planned centre at Viracochapampa, but never completed the site. Huari materials at Marca Huamachuco suggest interaction between the local polity and the empire, but whether or not the polity came under imperial control is unclear.

Mardikh, Tell see EBLA.

Marduk a BABYLONIAN god who came to take the place of the SUMERIAN deity ENLIL, now as the ruler of the gods rather than simply their head; this shift in the relationship between the gods reflected the shift towards the less encumbered power of MESOPOTAMIAN kingship. Marduk's seat was at BABYLON itself.

Mari a city of 6 sq. km (2.3 sq. miles), on the middle Euphrates in southeastern Syria, which seems to have been founded in the early 3rd millennium and continued to be occupied to the late 1st millennium BC. Within this long settlement history, two periods may be singled out: the third quarter of the 3rd millennium and the early 2nd millennium, when kings of Mari played significant roles in the political affairs of MESOPOTAMIA. André PARROT's work at Mari, begun in the 1930s and continued by a later generation of French archaeologists, has revealed major temple and palace complexes and also major archives belonging to these two periods. The most important of these is the palace of Zimri-Lim (1782–1759 BC), composed of 300 rooms over a 2.5 ha (6 acre) area and containing extremely rich archives informative of many aspects of the early 18th-century BC (OLD BABYLONIAN PERIOD) Mesopotamian world; this palace was famous for its size and splendour, and the king of UGARIT expressed a wish to visit it.

Marib a site on the Wadi Dhana in northern Yemen, southwestern Arabia, associated with the Sabaean kingdom of the SOUTH ARABIAN civilization. Marib is widely known for the dam constructed there across the *wadi*; the first hydraulic installations in the *wadi* may belong to the 2nd millennium BC while the famous 1st-millennium AD dam itself was in use until the 6th century, when it ruptured for the last time. The city at Marib covered about 120 ha (297 acres); the famous temples of Mahram Bilqis and Awwam lie on the opposite bank of the *wadi*. Explored by the Wendell Phillips group in the 1950s, Marib was more recently the object of a German investigation which greatly elucidated the environmental and hydrological aspects of the area.

Mariette, François Auguste Ferdinand (1821–81) a French Egyptologist. His main contribution to archaeology, besides an extensive programme of excavation (e.g. SAQQARA), was the founding of the Egyptian Antiquities Service and what was to become the CAIRO Museum.

Marinatos, Spyridon (1901–74) a Greek archaeologist who, in 1939, first put forward the theory that the end of the MINOAN civilization in the Aegean could have been caused by the volcanic eruption of the island of THERA. His long career in archaeology culminated in the discovery of the buried Bronze Age city at AKROTIRI on Thera.

Maritsa culture a late Neolithic culture of the eastern Balkans, characterized by the materials from layer V at KARANOVO, approximately contemporaneous with VINČA C, between c.4700 and 4400 BC. Maritsa pottery reflects the general Balkan trend towards dark pottery, although a special characteristic of it is a tendency for the surface of the vessel to be covered by either incised (narrow) or excised (wide) lines, which are filled with white paint applied after firing.

Mariupol a Neolithic cemetery of the DNIEPER-DONETS culture on the coast of the Sea of Azov in southern Ukraine. The burials at Mariupol were furnished with large numbers of flint tools, pendants and beads made of animal teeth, bone and shells, but no pottery. A number of beads of non-local stone were also found.

Markleeberg a Lower Palaeolithic open-air site located on the Pleisse River near Leipzig, eastern Germany. Artifacts and faunal remains (e.g. *Mammuthus trogontherii*) are buried in riverine gravels, probably deposited during the late Middle Pleistocene. The artifacts include flakes, sidescrapers and occasional handaxes.

Marlik tepe an Early Iron Age (14th–10th century BC) cemetery in northwestern Iran. Iranian excavations during the early 1960s identified fifty-three tombs constructed among the boulders of a natural hill; gravegoods included gold, silver and bronze vessels often decorated with raised (repoussé) or engraved scenes, as well as jewellery, weapons and other riches. These finds, dated by art historical criteria, are important for discussions of INDO-EUROPEAN movements at the beginning of the Iron Age.

Marnian an Iron Age culture of northeastern France characterized by chariot burials, c.475–325 BC. See also ARRAS, LA GORGE-MEILLET, SOMME-BIONNE.

Maroni-Vournes the site of a major Late Cypriot settlement in southern CYPRUS, which is being excavated by Cadogan. The site was first occupied c.1600 BC. An impressive ASHLAR structure dates from the 13th century BC.

Maros group an Early Bronze Age group that inhabited the marshy areas along the Maros River in southeastern Hungary and neighbouring areas of Yugoslavia and Romania between 2700 and 1500 BC. The Maros group is known from settlements such as Popin paor and Klárafalva-Hajdova, which were small, self-contained communities of five to eight households living in small rectangular houses, and inhumation cemeteries, such as MOKRIN and Szöreg.

Maros point see TOALIAN.

Marquis of Dai [Marquis of Tai] see MAWANGDUI.

Marseilles (*Gk* Massilia) a city on the coast of southern France, close to the mouth of the River Rhône, which was traditionally founded in either c.600 or 540 BC as a colony of Phocaea in western Turkey. An earlier trading settlement may have been located further west at SAINT-BLAISE. Excavations have revealed remains of the Roman port, including a well-preserved merchant-ship, and the defences.

Marshall, Sir John (1876–1958) a British archaeologist, originally trained in CLASSICAL archaeology, who devoted most of his career to the ancient past of India, where he was Director General of Archaeology during the 1920s and 1930s. Marshall built upon his initial interests by researching Indian connections with the HELLENISTIC world, excavating at sites like Bhita (a late 1st-millennium BC town) and TAXILA. He announced the discovery of the HARAPPAN CIVILIZATION in 1921, and spent the rest of that decade excavating at MOHENHO-DARO.

Martin's Hundred the tract of land on the James River close to JAMESTOWN and Williamsburg, Virginia, USA, which was settled by English colonists in AD 1619. The centre of the plantation was Wolstenholme Towne. The settlement was attacked by Indians in 1622, and at least fifty-eight settlers were killed. Excavations have revealed evidence for the massacre, as well as a detailed cross-section of early colonial life in North America. The area was later resettled as Carter's Grove plantation in the 1700s.

Martkopi a set of extremely large KURGAN burials in eastern Georgia (Transcaucasia), associated with rich funerary goods and a characteristic style of pottery derived from KURA-ARAXES types. These burials date to the later 3rd millennium BC, and provide a bridge between the Kura-Araxes culture complex and the TRIALETI materials; excavations at SOS HÖYÜK in north-eastern Anatolia supply a rare example of settlement during this period.

Marxist archaeology the use of principles drawn from Marxist political theory to understand past societies. Social organization and change are explained in terms of conflicts between segments of society, such as those based on class, sex or age. Because of its emphasis on the importance of the economy in determining the particular form of a society, Marxism has proven to be a popular and robust source of archaeological inference, even in non-communist countries. Since Marxist archaeology does not consider other explanations, it is often criticized as being unscientific, especially by PROCESSUAL ARCHAEOLOGISTS, although in fact many of their own assumptions about society are similar to those made by Marxists. Marxist archaeology's evolutionary basis has been criticized by POSTPROCESSUAL ARCHAEOLOGY, although the latter remains very sympathetic to the Marxist notion that an understanding of who has power and how that power is exercised is a vital element in explaining social change. See also CHILDE.

Mary Rose the flagship of England's Tudor king Henry VIII's fleet, which sank on its maiden voyage in AD 1545 in the Solent, off the south coast. A major project of UNDERWATER ARCHAEOLOGY led to its exploration and excavation, and eventually its raising in 1982. The wreck has yielded huge quantities of finds which shed light on military equipment of the time, such as bows, as well as everyday objects.

Masada a Palestinian site, excavated chiefly by YADIN in 1963–5. A fortress-palace complex built by Herod the Great (37–4 BC), Masada was used as a stronghold by the zealots of the Jewish revolt of AD 66–73 and was the scene of their last stand against the Romans, who subsequently garrisoned the fortress.

Mas d'Azil see LE MAS D'AZIL.

Mashkan-Shapir see ABU DUWARI, TELL.

Maspero, Gaston Camille Charles (1846–1916) a French Egyptologist, MARIETTE's successor as Director of the Egyptian Antiquities Service.

massebah a standing stone (or group of stones) similar in form to a DOLMEN, but erected in the Levant. It seems to have possessed a cultic purpose (e.g. in CANAANITE contexts as at GEZER and HAZOR) or, when set up by the ISRAELITES, to have commemorated a particular event.

Massilia see MARSEILLES.

mastaba (*Arabic* 'bench') a superstructure of Egyptian tombs, chiefly of the ARCHAIC PERIOD and OLD KINGDOM, including the royal tombs of the 1st and 2nd Dynasty. It was a low, rectangular building with a flat roof and vertical or inward-inclined walls, which enclosed

MASADA, Israel: the ruins of Masada; in the background the Dead Sea; the Roman camp (73 BC) can be made out as a dark line in the top right hand corner of the photograph.

the shaft to the subterranean burial chamber. Early mud-brick mastabas were replaced by more elaborate stone structures, often with numerous internal rooms.

mastodon a group of large mammals related to elephants. The most celebrated species, the American mastodon *Mammut americanum*, was utilized by PALAEOINDIANS before becoming extinct about 10,000 BP. Resembling a stocky and slightly elongated elephant, it had a hairy coat and shorter, straighter tusks than its contemporary the mammoth. The word mastodon means 'breast-tooth', and refers to the large hemispherical cusps, about eight in number, that form the crushing surface of each molar. The American mastodon subsisted on spruce and pine forests.

mastos a breast-shaped drinking-cup, usually fitted with one horizontal and one vertical handle. BLACK-GLOSSED and figure-decorated Athenian examples have been found.

Maszycka Cave a prehistoric cave-site located on the Pradnik River near Kraków in southern Poland. Artifacts and faunal remains (e.g. woolly mammoth, reindeer) are buried in loess deposits. The main cultural layer contains an Upper Palaeolithic assemblage (e.g. retouched blades, endscrapers and bone points) assigned to the MAG-DALENIAN and dated by radiocarbon to c.17,500–

16,500 BP. It is associated with human skeletal remains of at least sixteen individuals. The uppermost layer contains Neolithic remains.

MAT see MOUSTERIAN OF ACHEULIAN TRADITION.

mataa a large-stemmed obsidian flake used hafted as a dagger or spearhead on EASTER ISLAND, and associated with the period of internal conflict of the 18th and 19th centuries AD.

Matacapan a site in the region of the Tuxtla Mountains of the southern Gulf Coast of Mexico, whose sequence begins in the early PRECLASSIC. The site is best known for its early CLASSIC settlement, when it was under the influence of TEOTIHUACÁN. Matacapan contains a Teotihuacán *barrio*, or neighbourhood, in the central Mexican architectural style. Like KAMINALJUYÚ, Matacapan played an important role in Teotihuacán's trade network.

A University of New Mexico-Universidad de Veracrúz archaeological project, begun in the 1980s, has conducted extensive research at the site. This study has incorporated a number of ETHNOARCHAEOLOGICAL projects to address issues of subsistence and ceramic production.

Mata Menge an early Pleistocene locality in the Soa River Basin in central Flores, Indonesia, where bones of *Stegodon* and flaked stone tools have been found in volcanic ash deposits dating to c.800,000 years ago. Together with Boa Lesa and Dozu Dhalua, the region provides the best dated evidence for HOMO *erectus* in Southeast Asia, and for the ability of *H. erectus* to cross major water barriers.

Mataram the name of the state which dominated central and eastern Java during the 8th–10th centuries AD. Major sites include the STUPA of BOROBUDUR, the temple complex of DIENG, and numerous CANDI (funerary temples), the most prominent being the PRAMBANAN complex.

Matarrah a HASSUNAN village of 3 ha (7.4 acres) located south of Kirkuk in northern Iraq. R. Braidwood's work in 1948 revealed small-roomed houses, alleys and open spaces within the village; the appearance of SAMARRAN painted pottery in upper parts of the sequence at Matarrah helped demonstrate the chronological relationship and interaction between these two cultures.

Matenbek a limestone shelter near MATENKUPKUM, in the BISMARCK ARCHIPELAGO, Melanesia, with two episodes of occupation. The earlier occurred about 20,000 bp, while the later began about 8500 bp. The occurrence of *phalanger* (possum) in the oldest levels suggests a Pleistocene human introduction of this species to New Ireland. Obsidian from TALASEA also appears in the basal deposits.

Matenkupkum a cave in an uplifted coral terrace on New Ireland, BISMARCK ARCHIPELAGO, Melanesia, excavated by Chris Gosden. The site was first occupied about 35,000 years ago. Fish and shellfish remains from the oldest levels provide the earliest evidence for use of marine resources in SAHUL. The site seems to have been unused between 20,000 and 16,000 bp and may have been abandoned finally about 10,000 years ago although the recent deposits have been disturbed. The stone assemblage comprises mainly unretouched flakes from pebbles; obsidian from TALASEA first appears c.16,000 bp. See also KOOLAN 2, MANDU MANDU CREEK.

material culture the physical remains of humanly made traces of past societies, which constitute the major source of evidence for archaeology.

mathematics see VIGESIMAL MATHEMATICS.

Matola a coastal SHELL MIDDEN site near Maputo in southern Mozambique, whose pottery is used to define the Matola unit of the first Iron Age farmers in eastern-southern Africa. Matola sites date from the 3rd–5th centuries AD (1720–1470 bp) and the pottery is similar to KWALE ware from East Africa, which suggests a rapid southward spread of Iron Age farmers down the East African coast at the beginning of the 1st millennium AD.

Matopan see NSWATUGI.

matrix 1 grains in sediments or rocks that collectively

are relatively finer than the coarsest material in the sediment or rock. Matrix is the material within which cultural debris, a fossil or any item of note is contained or embedded.
2 the main metal constituent in an alloy.

Matt-painted pottery Middle HELLADIC pottery which has simple decoration in a manganese-based purple-black paint on a pale ground. Although quite common, Matt-painted pottery has a more restricted distribution than MINYAN.

Matupi a cave in the northeastern Democratic Republic of Congo, with a long sequence of microlithic LATER STONE AGE collections dating from more than 40,700 to 3000 bp, representing one of the earliest such occurrences in sub-Saharan Africa. The levels dating to 21,000–12,000 BP contain unusual decorated bored stones and drills used in their manufacture.

Matuzka a large Palaeolithic cave in the northwestern Caucasus (Russia). A long sequence of cultural layers is buried in a succession of rubble and loam deposits that date from at least the beginning of the Late Pleistocene to the early last GLACIAL (130,000–40,000 BP?). Over 90 per cent of the associated mammal remains are cave bear, and appear to have accumulated through natural mortality. Most of the cultural layers are assigned to the Middle Palaeolithic, and contain sidescrapers.

Mauer jaw or **Heidelberg jaw** a large broken human mandible with small teeth and a receding chin, recovered in 1907 by workmen in a sandpit at Mauer, southern Germany, in association with elephant and rhinoceros bones but no artifacts. The jaw has been attributed to an adult male HOMO *erectus* or PRE-NEANDERTHALer, and dated either to the MINDEL GLACIATION, or the GÜNZ-Mindel INTERGLACIAL.

Mauna Kea a basalt ADZE quarry complex on Hawaii, located at an altitude of 3,350–3,780 m (10,990–12,400 ft) above sea-level and extending over about 20 sq. km (7.7 sq. miles). It comprises a series of extraction areas and workshops with religious shrines and habitation sites. It has been the subject of detailed field research and experimental replication by Patrick McCoy.

Maungaroa Valley a valley on Raratonga, southern Cook Islands, which, like the OPUNOHU VALLEY, has a well-preserved example of POLYNESIAN settlement pattern, and has been surveyed in detail by Peter Bellwood. The MARAE and paved house-platforms were clustered into four settlements, dating between about AD 1600 and 1823.

Maupiti burial ground a site on an islet in the lagoon on Maupiti, Society Islands, POLYNESIA, which yielded sixteen flexed and extended burials dating to AD 800–1200. Grave-goods included pearl-shell fish-hooks, adzes and ornaments of early eastern Polynesian type (see PACIFIC), all paralleled closely at HANE in the Marquesas.

Mauriwi a name attributed in the 19th and early 20th centuries to the earliest inhabitants of NEW ZEALAND, thought to have been conquered by the later MAORI. The 'Mauriwi myth' has now been discredited. They were sometimes confused with the MORIORI of the Chatham Islands.

Maurya an imperial dynasty of northern India between 325 and 185 BC. The first Mauryan king moved into the power vacuum that Alexander the Great created in the southeastern provinces of the ACHAEMENID empire, and his immediate successors expanded across much of peninsular India. Inscriptions of Asoka give some idea of the extent of the empire during the mid 3rd century BC, being found from KANDAHAR in Afghanistan to Karnataka in southern India.

Mauryan pillars see ASOKAN PILLARS.

Mawangdui [Ma-wang-tui] the location near Changsha City, China, of two early HAN Dynasty tombs constructed with features of both SHAFT TOMBS and MOUNDED TOMBS. The eastern tomb had a mound 50 m (55 yds) in diameter and 20 m (65 ft) high; underneath was a rectangular shaft with a northern approach ramp leading into the large WOODEN-CHAMBER 16 m (52 ft) underground. The last of three nested lacquer coffins with painted designs contained a female corpse that was so well preserved that an autopsy was carried out on it, resulting in the discovery of tubercular nodules in the left lung. The deceased was identified through inscriptions on the grave-goods as the wife of one of the three generations of men bearing the title of Marquis of Dai. Among the sumptuous grave-goods were three rare musical instruments and an important painting on silk.

Maxton an 11th-century AD Early Iron Age site in northeastern Zimbabwe, which has given its name to a late phase of the period. Maxton sites are frequently on hilltops and are associated with stone walling.

Maya one of the high cultures of MESOAMERICA, and one of its major CLASSIC civilizations from about AD 200 to 850. The Maya practised SWIDDEN AGRICULTURE, as well as intensive agriculture, terracing and raised fields, growing maize and other crops, as well as arboriculture, especially of ramon nuts (see CHULTUN). Maya culture is well known for its CEREMONIAL CENTRES, STELAS and accomplishments in HIEROGLYPHIC writing (see GLYPH), CALENDRIC SYSTEMS and MATHEMATICS. The term Maya also refers to a culture area, and is typically divided into the Lowland and Highland Maya. The descendants of the Maya still occupy the region.

POLYCHROME POTTERY is a hallmark of Lowland Maya CLASSIC culture. Maya society supported craftsmen skilled in creating luxury goods as well as monumental buildings. Maya society had an aristocracy, full-time specialists, a government in which religion and ritual played a critical role, and a peasant population to support the elites.

Maya ceremonial centres were associated in some fashion; major centres were linked to minor, as well as to the surrounding rural populations. Probably, major centres were also grouped into larger POLITIES. Kinship played an important role in elite-ranked activities, including political power. The internal organization at different centres implies variable levels of political organization. The ceremonial centres were constructed and supported by the outlying population of farmers. Religion was a central part of Classic Maya culture, but POSTCLASSIC Maya centres appear to have a more secular focus.

Many of the southern Lowland Maya cities collapsed between AD 800 and 850, probably due to a combination of factors including soil depletion through intensive cultivation, and the inadequate management of urban, military and subsistence issues. However, during the period of collapse in the southern Lowlands, centres in the northern Lowlands began to grow (AD 800–1000). The South's decline may have played a role in the North's prosperity, but the subsequent decline of the latter is not yet well understood.

Mayapán a late POSTCLASSIC MAYA centre in western-central Yucatán, Mexico, with a wall 8 km (5 miles) long and up to 2 m (6 ft) high encircling the city. Within these walls, in an area of approximately 4 sq. km (1.5 sq. miles), 3,600 mostly residential structures have been mapped. Population estimates range from 6,000 to 15,000, but are generally given as 10,000 at its peak. Mayapán is in a relatively infertile part of the Yucatán, and the site was supported through tribute from neighbouring areas. Nobles from these regions were held as hostages at Mayapán to ensure their families and towns would pay the tribute.

Although built over an earlier city, Mayapán held most of northern Yucatán under its control from the time of its founding by the Cocoms lineage (AD 1200 or 1250) until it was sacked c.AD 1400 during a local uprising led by the rival Tutul Xiu family.

Characteristic of Mayapán is the large number of elaborate residences and their close proximity to the main ceremonial structures. The relative lack of religious structures has been explained in terms of the construction of Mayapán at a relatively late date; the prominence of religion in Maya culture had given way to the importance of secular and militaristic issues. The first archaeological investigations at the site were sponsored by the Carnegie Institution of Washington in the 1950s.

Mayor Island the most important source of obsidian in NEW ZEALAND in the Bay of Plenty, North Island. Mayor Island obsidian was exchanged throughout New Zealand

and may have been the first source to be found and used by the original settlers.

Maysar or **Samad** a district of the Omani piedmont in southeastern Arabia, where German work focused on excavating an UMM AN-NAR period settlement that contained abundant information on Bronze Age copper smelting, the chief product for which ancient Magan was known (see PERSIAN GULF TRADE). Other work in the district also provides evidence for Bronze Age agricultural production and burial patterns, as well as Iron Age settlements, fortifications and burials.

McBurney, Charles Brian Montagu (1914–79) a British prehistorian, best known for his excavations, at the HAUA FTEAH Cave in North Africa and at LA COTTE DE ST BRELADE, Jersey.

McCarthy, Frederick David (1905–97) a pioneering Australian archaeologist based at the Australian Museum in Sydney and from 1964 to 1971, the first Principal of the Australian Institute of Aboriginal Studies. His excavations at Lapstone Creek and Capertee formed the basis of the Eastern Regional Sequence, which remains in use with modifications in southeastern New South Wales. With his wife, Elsie Bramell, and H. V. V. Noone he completed a typological classification of Australian stone tools.

Meadowcroft Rockshelter a stratified rockshelter in Pennsylvania, USA, that spans the PALAEOINDIAN, ARCHAIC, late prehistoric and historic periods, and has revealed a vast array of artifactual, botanical and faunal data. The early dates for the initial occupation of the site have generated much controversy. The lowest level, stratum I, has only charcoal and some radiocarbon dates that pre-date 32,000 bp. The overlying level, IIa, which lasts into the Archaic, does contain stone artifacts and radiocarbon dates that might take cultural occupation back to 19,000 bp or earlier. Recent summaries of the available radiocarbon dates by the site's principal excavator, James Adovasio, conservatively place early occupation of the site at c.14,500 BP and possibly as early as c.16,700 BP.

me'ae ceremonial structures in the southern Marquesas Islands, POLYNESIA. They comprise complex and irregular groups of terraces with platforms (PA'EPA'E) for priests' houses. There are two types: *mortuary me'ae* were built in secluded places and had stone-lined pits for burials; *public me'ae* were associated with TOHUA.

Mechta Afalou a robust, large-brained type of modern HOMO *sapiens* which has a long ancestry in North Africa extending back to Middle Palaeolithic times. It was once thought to be restricted to the Magreb, but is now known to have been widely distributed throughout northern Africa in the Late Pleistocene and to have been present in Egypt about 20,000 bp. Mechta Afalou cranial remains

of three individuals from DAR ES-SOLTAN as well as remains from other Moroccan sites are associated with ATERIAN artifacts, remains from COLUMNATA and TAFORALT are associated with IBEROMAURUSIAN artifacts, and the physical type is also associated with CAPSIAN artifacts (see MECHTA-EL-ARBI). The close resemblance between Mechta Afalou and CRO-MAGNON people has prompted researchers to speculate whether the Cro-Magnons were descended from a group present in the Magreb in the Middle Palaeolithic.

Mechta-el-Arbi one of the most important Upper CAPSIAN sites located west of Tebessa in Algeria. It contained the remains of a number of humans of MECHTA AFALOU type.

Medes an Indo-European speaking people, related to Persians, who moved southwards through the Zagros from a still undetermined region (perhaps in Central Asia) during the Iron Age. The Persians eventually settled in Fars in southwestern Iran, while the Medes were present in the region of Hamadan in western Iran by the 9th century BC. The disparate Median groups were unified into a kingdom by Cyaxares in the late 7th century, when an alliance between the Medes, the SCYTHIANS and the newly resurgent BABYLONIAN kingdom attacked and overthrew the NEO-ASSYRIAN empire (between 614 and 612 BC). In the mid 6th century BC, the Persian king CYRUS overran the Medes.

medicine wheel a type of site located in the northwestern portion of the North American Plains, which comprises stone alignments in the form of radiating spokes, often with central and peripheral cairns. Although their exact purpose is unclear, medicine wheels may have functioned as memorials to important people, played a role in vision quests and other ceremonies, served as boundary or navigation markers, or served as calendars for the observation of the summer solstices and other celestial events. Some medicine wheels may be as old as 5500 BP.

Medinet Habu part of the site of THEBES (EGYPT)-WEST BANK. The most substantial monument at Medinet Habu is the relatively well-preserved MORTUARY TEMPLE of RAMESSES III, the scenes on whose walls include representations of that king's campaigns against the SEA PEOPLES. Medinet Habu eventually became the most important administrative centre in the Theban area.

Megaceros see MEGALOCEROS.

megafauna large-bodied animals like the bison, mammoth, mastodon and camel, many of which disappeared during the Pleistocene extinctions, and which served as major food sources for late Pleistocene hunters. Conventionally, the division between mega- and microfauna is often placed at 40 kg (88 lbs) bodyweight.

megalith (*Gk* megas 'large', lithos 'stone') a large stone. Compare MICROLITH. The term is sometimes used to refer to a megalithic monument.

megalithic art Neolithic engravings found on the megalithic stones of CHAMBERED TOMBS and MENHIRS. The motifs include representational elements such as axes, oxen and human breasts, as well as abstract designs such as spirals, concentric circles, zigzags and triangles. Megalithic art is particularly associated with PASSAGE GRAVES, GAVRINIS in Brittany and KNOWTH and NEWGRANGE in Ireland being among the most notable examples.

megalithic culture (*India*) an Iron Age culture of southern India where the burials present a heterogeneous phenomenon that is nonetheless grouped together under the terms 'megaliths' and 'megalithic culture'. The grave forms include several kinds of urn burials and various forms of cist, pit and rock-cut graves; stone ALIGNMENTS are also associated with the Iron Age. The disposition of bodies is equally variable: simple inhumation, secondary burial (both single and multiple), and occasionally cremation burial. These variations may correspond to caste differences, as also described in early Tamil writings and found in contemporary practice. Despite their heterogeneous forms, the graves generally contain a burnished black-and-red ware (also found in settlements) and a fairly uniform series of iron tools, weapons, horse equipment and other household equipment. This funerary complex appears to have developed by the beginning of the 1st millennium BC (and perhaps somewhat earlier) and to have endured into the early 1st millennium AD.

megalithic monument a construction made of large stones. The term is commonly applied to any CHAMBERED TOMB, even if built with small stones. Megalithic monuments are particularly numerous and most thoroughly studied in the Neolithic and Bronze Age of western and northwestern *Europe*. See ALIGNMENT, ALLÉE COUVERTE, CROMLECH, DOLMEN, HUNEBED, MENHIR, PASSAGE GRAVE, STONE CIRCLE.

In *West Africa*, on the other hand, the dates of megalithic monuments are uncertain. Upright standing stones have been found in two areas: the largest number are in the Casamance region of eastern Senegal, and consist of circles of laterite blocks, some over 3 m (10 ft) long, used as funerary monuments (see TIEKENE-BOUSSOURA). Megalithic monuments are also found at Tondidiaro in the central delta of the Niger River floodplain in Mali. In Central Africa, near BOUAR in the west of the Central African Republic, there are over 100 funerary monuments consisting of rubble mounds with walls and large stones dating to the last millennium bc.

In the *Far East*, the term is used in relation to DOLMENS (mostly of the 1st millennium BC) and the later MOUNDED TOMBS.

In *Southeast Asia*, megalithic monuments likewise date to the last millennium BC and later, and include 'menhirs' and 'dolmens' analogous to those of Europe, stone pavements and terraces, large carved stones, stone slab or cist graves and stone SARCOPHAGI. Apart from the stone burial vats of XIANG KHOUANG in Laos, most large stone remains are found on the Malay peninsula and in the islands, and they appear to be related to burials or ancestor cults. Some (including those of PASEMAH in Sumatra, the BERNAM-SUNGKAI area of the peninsula, and Pasir Angin on Java) date to the last four centuries BC, others (the slab graves of Kidangan, Besuki, Gunung Kidul, and Kuningen on Java) probably date to the 1st millennium AD, and yet others (Tlaga Mukmin and other sites in Sumatra, the Niah pavements, and stones of the peninsula and Sarawak) are more recent still.

In the *Pacific*, megalithic structures are found in parts of POLYNESIA and include anthropomorphous statues (MOAI) and religious structures (MARAE). See also EASTER ISLAND, HA'AMONGA-A-MAUI, PUAMAU VALLEY, TAIPIVAI VALLEY, TAPUTAPUATEA.

Migration theories based on megalithic remains are now discounted in Southeast Asia as they are in Europe. It is now accepted that the practice of erecting such monuments arose independently in many different times and places, and for a wide variety of purposes.

megalithic yard a unit of measurement corresponding to 0.829 m (2.72 ft) considered by some to underlie the layout of STONE CIRCLES and ALIGNMENTS in Britain and Brittany.

Megaloceros a group of large Pleistocene deer, also known as the 'giant deer'. The best-known species, *M. giganteus*, has been erroneously termed the 'Irish elk'. Although abundant in Ireland, it also occurred widely across Europe and western Asia. Standing up to 1.8 m (6 ft) at the shoulder, the males carried huge palmated antlers spanning up to 3 m (10 ft). Its remains are occasionally found in Palaeolithic assemblages, and there are rare depictions in cave art (see COUGNAC). It became extinct c.9000 BP.

Megarian bowl a type of handleless Greek drinking-cup made in moulds. The bowls tend to be decorated in relief, for example with scenes of Dionysos or acting, and finished in the BLACK-GLOSSED technique. They were in widespread use in the HELLENISTIC period from the 3rd century BC, and they merge into the red-glossed ARRETINE WARES. The type was first recognized at Megara, although they were produced in other centres such as ATHENS and CORINTH.

megaron a rectangular or APSIDAL-ended structure in Aegean architecture, usually entered through a shallow porch at one end.

Megiddo a Palestinian TELL on a natural hill, the subject of large-scale excavations by Chicago University in 1925–39. First occupied during the late Neolithic, Megiddo was a well-defended town of the EARLY to MIDDLE BRONZE AGE, wealthy even after its capture by TUTHMOSIS III, as shown by the important series of ivories recovered from the site. In the Iron Age Megiddo was strongly fortified by ISRAELITES during the early 9th century BC, when a casement wall and gateway, large stables (or storehouses) and an elaborate water-system were constructed.

Mehrgahr an important site in the Kachi plain of Baluchistan in western Pakistan occupied from some time before 6000 BC until the beginnings of the Mature HARAPPAN in the 3rd millennium BC. The excavations of J.-F. Jarrige have revealed ACERAMIC NEOLITHIC occupations in which occur mud-brick domestic architecture and a massive funerary platform. This community cultivated wheats, barley and other plants, some of which were in transitional stages of domestication; the animals initially are mostly wild, but by the end of the Aceramic occupation are almost all domesticated sheep, goat and cattle, and seem to have been domesticated locally. The later phases of occupation provide important evidence of social differentiation and craft specialization in this region, contributing to the early 3rd millennium milieu in which the Harappan civilization was formed.

Meidum the site of the remains of the first true Egyptian pyramid, probably started by King Huni of the 3rd Dynasty, but completed by his successor SNEFRU. Associated with the pyramid are MASTABAS of the early 4th Dynasty.

Meiendorf see HAMBURGIAN.

Meillacoid a kind of pottery that characterizes the MACORIJES groups in the Caribbean from the 9th century AD onwards. The name comes from the site of Meillac in northern Haiti, and denotes thin, decorated ceramics, sometimes with appliquéd strips, and with depictions of turtles and bats. Archaeological study shows that from the 13th century the Macorijes or Meillacoids became fused with the TAINOS, not only in the Dominican Republic but also in eastern Cuba and the Bahamas.

Meir the site of an important series of rock-cut tombs of the local NOMARCHs of the late OLD-MIDDLE KINGDOM in Egypt. The relief decoration of these tombs was recorded by Blackman in five seasons between the years 1912 and 1950.

Melanesia the ethnographic and geographical region which comprises New Guinea, the BISMARCK ARCHIPELAGO, the Solomons, Vanuatu, New Caledonia and Fiji. It is characterized by great cultural diversity. New Guinea was occupied by 40,000 bp, when it was joined to Australia, and the Bismarcks and Solomons (KILU) seem to have been occupied by about 30,000 bp. There may have been an independent development of horticulture in the NEW GUINEA HIGHLANDS in the early Holocene. Certainly, pollen analyses show a long history of human impact on the environment going back into the Late Pleistocene. The appearance of LAPITA pottery in the region seems to document the expansion of AUSTRONESIAN speakers into the Pacific.

Melka Kontoure or **Melka Kunturé** a site near Addis Ababa in Ethiopia particularly noted for its long stone artifact sequence, which dates from more than 1.5 million years ago. It includes OLDOWAN, ACHEULIAN, MIDDLE STONE AGE and microlithic LATER STONE AGE collections, as well as various HOMINID fragments, including a HOMO jaw fragment, originally attributed to *Homo erectus*, associated with Acheulian artifacts.

Melkhoutboom a cave in the Eastern Cape Province of South Africa with LATER STONE AGE material spanning the last 15,000 years. Of particular interest is one of the largest and best-studied collections of well preserved plant remains dating to the last 7,500 years, which indicates that plant foods formed an important component of the diets of Holocene Later Stone Age people. Unusually well-preserved string and netting items made from plant fibres, as well as leather, wood and bone artifacts, were found.

Melos the principal source of the obsidian in the Cyclades, which was extensively used for chipped stone implements in the prehistoric Aegean. Although obsidian was being acquired from Melos as early as the 10th millennium BC, it would appear that the island was not inhabited on a permanent basis until the 4th millennium. In the Bronze Age the main settlement was at PHYLAKOPI. The CLASSICAL POLIS, devastated by ATHENS in 416 BC, centred on the fortified AKROPOLIS of Ancient Melos.

Meluhha see PERSIAN GULF TRADE.

Memphis the capital of Egypt in the ARCHAIC PERIOD and OLD KINGDOM, and thereafter one of the most important cities of the ancient Near East. Very little remains of the city of Memphis, although impressive mortuary/religious structures associated with the capital may be seen on the desert fringe to the west, from ABU ROASH to DAHSHUR, especially at GIZA and SAQQARA.

Menelaion, the remains that appear to have been the principal MYCENAEAN site in Laconia, Greece. The two mansions, built in the 15th and 14th centuries BC, foreshadow the later palaces in their layout. In the 8th century BC the cult of Menelaus and Helen was established, and the remains of their CLASSICAL shrine dominate the site.

menhir (*Old Breton* men 'stone', hir 'long') a single standing stone. Menhirs are especially characteristic of Britain and Brittany in the Neolithic and Early Bronze

Age, though they are also known in more recent periods from other parts of the world, such as Ethiopia and Madagascar.

Menkaure or **Mycerinus** an Egyptian king of the 4th Dynasty (during the OLD KINGDOM), and owner of the smallest of the three pyramids of the Old Kingdom at GIZA.

Merimde Beni Salama a site in the western Nile DELTA, Egypt, excavated by Junker in 1928–39. This settlement of small dwellings seems to have been occupied for about 600 years (probably c.4900–4300 BC), perhaps with a population as large as 16,000. The Merimde culture largely overlaps with FAIYUM 'A', and with the BADARIAN/AMRATIAN groups of UPPER EGYPT.

Meroe a site in UPPER NUBIA, the capital of a state of the early 3rd century BC to the early 4th century AD, until its conquest by AXUM. Meroitic civilization seems to have owed much to the preceding NAPATAN state in its use of ancient Egyptian models for its state architecture, including the royal pyramids and temples such as that at MUSAWWARAT ES-SUFRA. Meroe has mainly been excavated by GARSTANG in 1910–14, REISNER in 1922–5 and, since 1965, by Shinnie.

Mersin the location of the small but high TELL-site of Yümük tepe, in coastal Cilicia, southwestern Anatolia, which was excavated by J. GARSTANG, who defined thirty-three major levels. The bulk of this sequence represents Neolithic (levels XXXIII–XXIV) and CHALCOLITHIC (XXII–XII), which bear strong similarities to the AMUQ periods A–B and C–F respectively. This sequence contains Halaf ceramics (see HALAF TELL) in levels XIX–XVII, and painted pottery of the 'UBAID style (levels XVI–XV). The architecture of the late Neolithic settlement (level XXIV; the earlier levels presented only traces of walling and floors) comprises large enclosures with many attached silos. During the Chalcolithic, the place was fortified (starting with level XVI), with complexes of rooms set against the walls on either side of a massive gateway. After a long break, occupation at the site resumed with MIDDLE BRONZE AGE to Iron Age settlements (levels XI–III), the last three of which contain ceramic evidence for contacts with the Aegean world (MYCENAEAN to late ARCHAIC Greek pottery). The final two occupations belong to the BYZANTINE and medieval periods. An Italian project reopened work on prehistoric sections of the mound during the 1990s.

Merv an oasis city on the Murghab River in eastern Turkmenistan. Because successive inhabitants built in different areas, the site sprawls over an enormous area, and contains many distinguishable parts. The earliest settlement, of ACHAEMENID times, was at the 20 ha (49 acres) Erq Qala. After the Greek conquest of the Achaemenids, the SELEUCIDS built Antiocha Margiana, rep-

MESA VERDE, USA: Cliff Palace.

resented by the site of Gyaur kala, the wall of which encloses some 340 ha (840 acres) with Erq Qala acting as a citadel set into the wall. Subsequent occupations expanded to the west, with the early Islamic city being even larger than the HELLENISTIC. Merv was the object of long-term Soviet investigation, and during the 1990s of an on-going collaborative British project.

Mesa an early prehistoric open-air site located in the northern slope of the Brooks Range in Alaska above latitude 68° north. Artifacts are buried in shallow AEOLIAN sediment overlying bedrock, and are dated by radiocarbon to roughly 10,000 BP. The assemblage includes lanceolate points, bifaces, gravers and scrapers. Although microblades were also found at the site, they are believed to represent a separate occupation. The points exhibit similarities to early prehistoric forms of the North American Plains, and are assigned to the PALAEOINDIAN tradition.

Mesara the largest and most fertile plain on the island of CRETE, which has been intensively exploited since the later Neolithic period. The MINOAN palace of PHAISTOS, and Gortyn, the capital of the Roman province of Crete and Cyrenaica, are the two principal archaeological sites.

Mesa Verde a large flat-topped mountain (or *mesa*) in southwestern Colorado, USA, which is the location of some of the most spectacular ANASAZI structures in the American Southwest. Mesa Verde is especially famous for its cliff-dwellings, which are large PUEBLO III multi-roomed apartment dwellings built into large rock overhangs on the sides of cliffs. Most famous of these is CLIFF PALACE. The *mesa* was abandoned, along with the rest of the northern Southwest, about AD 1300. The archaeological remains of Mesa Verde were first brought to the attention of European Americans by Richard WETHERILL in 1888.

Mesoamerica 'Mesoamerica' is a term used by archaeologists to define the culture area of central, southern and eastern Mexico, Belize, Guatemala and portions of Honduras, El Salvador, Nicaragua and Costa Rica. It is more of a cultural definition than a geographical one, since 'Mesoamerica' implies a set of shared cultural traits. Thus, the boundaries of 'Mesoamerica' shift through time as culture groups on the frontiers variably incorporate core traits that unify more central Mesoamerican cultures.

The concept of 'Mesoamerica' was first proposed by culture historian Paul Kirchhoff in the 1940s, and was quickly adopted as the label for the field of study that included such diverse groups as the AZTECS, MAYA, ZAPOTECS and OLMECS. As defined by Kirchhoff, Mesoamerica was a multi-ethnic, multilingual area that was nevertheless unified by a number of cultural characteristics, including use of a 260-day ritual calendar, a 52-year cycle, monumental pyramidal architecture, a ceremonial BALL GAME, ritual importance of heart sacrifice, and a diet comprising maize, beans and squash. This list is not comprehensive, and not all cultures considered 'Mesoamerican' necessarily shared all of the traits. As with most models, it does not hold up well to rigorous scrutiny but does capture important similarities shared by diverse groups throughout the defined region, and it distinguishes them from adjacent groups which generally lack these traits.

How could such a common set of cultural traits come to be found throughout a multicultural and multilingual mosaic? Archaeologists in the later half of the 20th century debated this issue, especially in relation to the historical development of the region. One leading paradigm has been that of the 'Olmec mother culture', in which the Olmec of the early and middle FORMATIVE PERIOD developed the Mesoamerican culture traits and, through conquest and colonization, spread the characteristics as a pan-Mesoamerican culture. In support of this, religious symbolism with roots in the Olmec heartland of the southern Gulf Coast have been discovered in a wide variety of sites and regions, including Costa Rica, Guatemala, OAXACA, Guerrero, Morelos, Puebla and the VALLEY OF MEXICO. Historical linguists provide additional evidence based on loan words from proto-Mixe-Zoquean (the language spoken in the Olmec heartland) into other Mesoamerican language families, presumably as an indication of the influence of Olmec culture.

Opponents of the 'mother culture' paradigm argue that other contemporary sites such as SAN JOSÉ MOGOTE in Oaxaca and CHALCATZINGO in Morelos were already evolving complex social structures when they came into contact with the Olmec. Instead of being overwhelmed by Olmec culture, the argument is that exchange networks linked elites from dispersed sites to Olmec elites in a reciprocal relationship. Local elites chose to adopt selected traits, especially those relating to legitimation of authority, and in exchange traded exotic materials such as jade and iron-ore mirrors to the Olmec. In this scenario Olmec culture was not passed down along a vertical axis (i.e. mother to child) so much as between relatively equal partners.

However the actual transmission took place, it is generally accepted that the Olmec were the first Mesoamerican civilization, and subsequent groups shared to varying degrees elements of Mesoamerican culture that were first prominent among the Olmec. This transformation is well documented at the Zapotec capital of MONTE ALBÁN, where over the course of 1,300 years (500 BC to AD 800) the iconography depicts the emergence of a distinctive culture while still retaining such Mesoamerican diagnostics as the calendar, ball game and sacrifice. Similar processes took place throughout Mesoamerica, so that by the late Formative period numerous regional styles can be identified, though underlying similarities all link them as 'Mesoamerican'.

A relative latecomer to this process may be found in the Maya lowlands, where recent discoveries at middle Formative sites such as Nakbe and EL MIRADOR indicate the development of social complexity featuring monumental earthworks and a religious programme unrelated to Olmec culture. Mesoamerican influences infiltrate Maya culture during the late Formative, and recent decipherments of the Maya hieroglyphic writing system supports artifactual evidence for trade and political interaction with central Mexico during the early CLASSIC PERIOD. The Maya established numerous autonomous polities at sites such as TIKAL, CALAKMUL, COPÁN and PALENQUE, where noble lineages recorded their dynastic histories on hieroglyphic-covered monuments. The beautiful art and architecture of the Maya provide important insights into their religion and world-view.

The Classic period city of TEOTIHUACÁN, located in the northern BASIN OF MEXICO, reached remarkable heights as an urban and religious centre. Through its monopoly over important obsidian sources, Teotihuacán established a vast trade network reaching distant lands, including the Gulf Coast, the Maya and northern Mexico. As a pilgrimage centre, Teotihuacán was able to project claims of legitimacy to nobles who carried icons of their authority back to their homelands. More than the actual trade goods, this elite ideology was likely the most significant 'export' available at Teotihuacán.

Teotihuacán's empire came to a violent end about AD 650, when the ceremonial centre was apparently

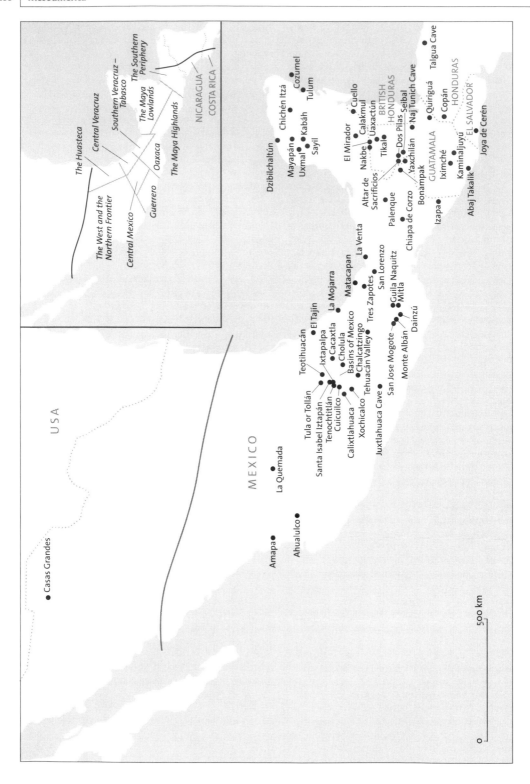

The West and the Northern Frontier

Central Mexico

Guerrero

Oaxaca

The Maya Highlands

The Huasteca

Central Veracruz

Southern Veracruz – Tabasco

The Maya Lowlands

The Southern Periphery

NICARAGUA

COSTA RICA

USA

MEXICO

Casas Grandes

Amapa

La Quemada

Ahualulco

Tula or Tollán

Santa Isabel Iztapán

Tenochtitlán

Cuicuilco

Calixtlahuaca

Xochicalco

Juxtlahuaca Cave

Teotihuacán

Ixtapalpa

Cacaxtla

Cholula

Chalcatzingo

Basins of Mexico

Tehuacán Valley

San Jose Mogote

Monte Albán

Dainzú

Guila Naquitz

Mitla

El Tajín

La Mojarra

Matacapan

Tres Zapotes

San Lorenzo

La Venta

Palenque

Chiapa de Corzo

Bonampak

Izapa

Abaj Takalik

Altar de Sacrificios

Dzibilchaltún

Mayapán

Uxmal

Kabáh

Sayil

Chichén Itzá

Cozumel

Tulum

Cuello

Calakmul

Uaxactún

El Mirador

Nakbe

Tikal

Dos Pilas

Seibal

Yaxchilán

Naj Tunich Cave

Quiriguá

Copán

Talgua Cave

BRITISH HONDURAS

HONDURAS

GUATEMALA

Iximché

Kaminaljuyú

EL SALVADOR

Joya de Cerén

500 km

0

burned and abandoned. Beginning at this time central Mexico features a number of competing cities employing an eclectic artistic style with Maya and Gulf Coast elements. This new formulation is best demonstrated at the site of CHOLULA, in the Puebla/Tlaxcala Valley. Cholula was a contemporary of Teotihuacán during the Classic period, but while Teotihuacán became stagnant and declined in power, Cholula drew upon its ceremonial importance and multi-ethnic composition. It is characterized by a new religious cult featuring the Feathered Serpent god, QUETZALCÓATL; long-distance trade organized around the pochteca merchant guild; and a colourful art style known as Mixteca-Puebla found on ceramics, murals and textiles. Cholula's ceremonial centre was built around its Great Pyramid, Tlachihualtepetl ('artificial mountain'), which grew to become the largest pyramid ever built, covering more than 16 ha (40 acres) at its base. The fusion of highland and lowland cultural patterns resulted in an 'internationalism' that again united Mesoamerica, and was the basis for POSTCLASSIC cultural practices.

The most powerful empire of Postclassic Mesoamerica was again located in the Basin of Mexico, where the Aztecs founded their island capital of TENOCHTITLÁN. Because of the extensive documentary accounts recorded by the Spanish, historians know considerably more about the Aztecs than about previous Mesoamerican groups. Aztec archaeology has focused on the Great Temple, dedicated jointly to the patron deity Huitzilopochtli and the rain god TLALOC. The Aztec empire received tribute from a vast hinterland, and maintained control by means of a well-organized army. This severe control ultimately backfired, however, as subjugated groups allied themselves with the conquering Spanish to break away from the Aztec empire and thereby bring an end to pre-Columbian Mesoamerica.

Mesoamerica was never united into a single political unit, but shared cultural traits that linked diverse cultures into a complex but interconnected mosaic. Millions of indigenous Mesoamericans still maintain cultural practices developed thousands of years earlier with the Olmec. Ethnographic studies of traditional groups provide fresh insights into the archaeological remains of ancient Mesoamerica.

mesocephalic see CEPHALIC.

Mesolithic the 'middle Stone Age', a period of transition in the early Holocene between the Upper Palaeolithic hunter-gatherer existence of the last GLACIATION and the development of farming and pottery production during the POSTGLACIAL Neolithic. The Mesolithic was a response to changing climatic conditions following the retreat of the glacial ice at c.8500 BC. It was of relatively short duration in the Near East, where farming started about 7000 BC; in Britain it lasted until the arrival of Neolithic technology from the Continent during the 4th millennium. Mesolithic tool-kits reflect the need to adapt to the changing environment, and are characterized by the presence of microliths and stone axes or adzes used in woodworking.

Mesopotamia (Gk '[the land] between the rivers') This region of the NEAR EAST is defined by the Euphrates and Tigris Rivers together with their tributaries (especially the Khabur and Balik for the Euphrates, the Diyala/Hamrin and Upper Zab for the Tigris). Although both rivers have their headwaters in Anatolian mountains to the north, these highlands are normally excluded from Mesopotamia proper. The latter is further divided into the northern piedmont, where rainfall agriculture is widely possible (ASSYRIA to the Syrian middle Euphrates) and the southern ALLUVIAL zones where irrigation is required for farming (BABYLONIA or SUMER and AKKAD); the Karun drainage of southwestern Iran (see SUSA, ELAM) might also be considered a part of Mesopotamia.

ACERAMIC NEOLITHIC village life appeared in Syrian Mesopotamia (e.g. ABU HUREYRA) somewhat earlier than in northeastern Mesopotamia (e.g. MAGHZALIYA, QERMEZ DERE); the latter area is still poorly known during this period. Development of irrigation techniques by the late (ceramic) Neolithic (beginning c.6000 BC) permitted farming communities to colonize central and southern Mesopotamia (SAMARRAN and 'UBAID cultures respectively; see also CHOGA MAMI); the parallel northern Mesopotamian sequence includes HASSUNA and HALAF cultures, with 'Ubaid material culture supplanting the Halaf around 4500 BC. Already in the 6th millennium BC at least some communities were using TOKENS and seals to record transactions (SABI ABYAD).

During the 4th millennium BC the URUK culture of southern Mesopotamia marked the emergence of cities (WARKA), writing (CUNEIFORM), sophisticated administrative technologies (BULLA, CYLINDER SEAL), massive public buildings (EANNA), and social complexity – the foundation of the Mesopotamian tradition of civilization. Important elements of this culture also appeared in ELAM, northern Mesopotamia, and the adjoining mountains (see URUK EXPANSION, PROTO-ELAMITE). The Mesopotamian tradition developed significantly during the 3rd millennium BC (EARLY DYNASTIC period) of SUMERIAN city-states (see also ROYAL CEMETERY of UR, KISH, ASMAR, KHAFAJE, TELLO). Although northern Mesopotamia lagged behind the south (see NINEVITE 5), cities eventually (2600 BC) appeared here as well (see ASSUR, LEILAN, TAYA). When the AKKADIANS emerged as a political force in the south (c.2300 BC) they imposed themselves on the north as well (BRAK, EBLA). The UR III kingdom (2050 BC) also controlled northern territories, although many northern cities had declined by this time. The ziggurat, a characteristic Mesopotamian architectural feature, took its final form during Ur III times, as did many pieces of classic Mesopotamian literature.

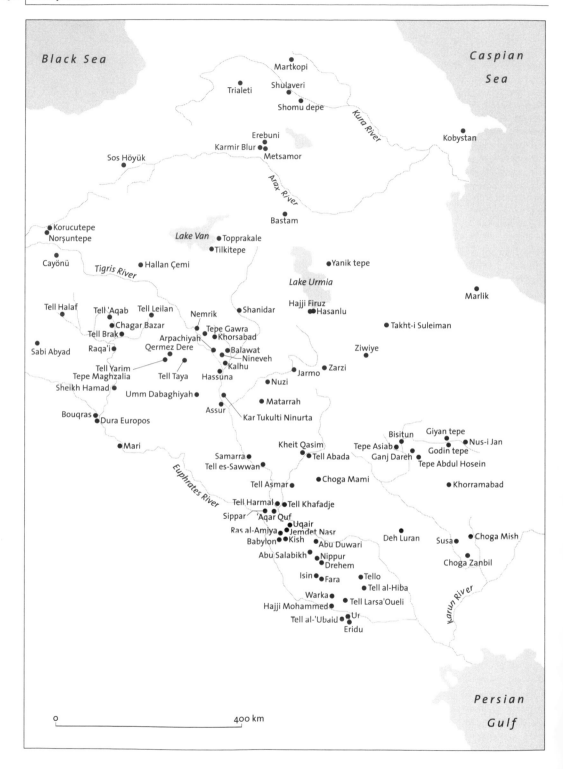

Black Sea

Caspian

Sea

Martkopi

Trialeti   Shulaveri

Shomu depe

Kobystan

Erebuni
Karmir Blur
Metsamor

Sos Höyük

Arax River

Kura River

Bastam

Korucutepe
Norşuntepe

Lake Van   Topprakale

Tilkitepe

Çayönü

Hallan Çemi

Tigris River

Yanik tepe

Lake Urmia

Marlik

Tell Halaf

Tell 'Aqab   Tell Leilan

Chagar Bazar

Tell Brak

Nemrik   Shanidar

Tepe Gawra
Khorsabad

Hajji Firuz
Hasanlu

Takht-i Suleiman

Sabi Abyad

Raqa'i

Arpachiyah
Qermez Dere

Ziwiye

Balawat
Nineveh

Tell Yarim
Tepe Maghzalia

Kalhu

Tell Taya   Hassuna

Sheikh Hamad

Umm Dabaghiyah

Nuzi

Jarmo   Zarzi

Matarrah

Assur

Bouqras
Dura Europos

Kar Tukulti Ninurta

Bisitun   Giyan tepe

Mari

Kheit Qasim

Tepe Asiab   Nus-i Jan

Samarra
Tell es-Sawwan

Tell Abada

Ganj Dareh   Godin tepe
Tepe Abdul Hosein

Tell Asmar

Choga Mami

Khorramabad

Tell Harmal
Tell Khafadje

Sippar   'Aqar Quf

Ras al-Amiya
Babylon
Uqair
Jemdet Nasr
Kish

Deh Luran   Susa   Choga Mish

Abu Duwari

Abu Salabikh
Nippur
Drehem

Choga Zanbil

Isin   Fara   Tello

Warka   Tell al-Hiba

Hajji Mohammed
Tell Larsa'Oueli

Tell al-'Ubaid   Ur
Eridu

Euphrates River

Karun River

Persian

Gulf

0   400 km

Two centuries of competing kingdoms, often under the rule of AMORITE kings, followed in the south (ISIN-LARSA), MARI and further west (ALEPPO, QATNA); merchant families of ASSUR operated a system of trading colonies in Anatolia (KĀRUM, KANESH), and the GULF TRADE was active (see DILMUN, MAGAN). HAMMURABI of BABYLON then bested his rivals to create a large empire around 1760 BC, but the entire region soon entered a period of decline (a 'dark age'); a HITTITE raid on Babylon in 1595 BC brought Hammurabi's OLD BABYLONIAN Dynasty to a close.

A KASSITE dynasty then imposed itself on BABYLONIA (see AQAR KUF), governing a revitalized regional kingdom for some five centuries; the region went into an extended decline after the 11th century BC. To the north, HURRIAN kings assembled the MITANNI kingdom, which stretched across northern Mesopotamia to the Mediterranean (see NUZI, ALALAKH), and came into conflict with Egyptians and Hittites. ASSUR revolted and then destroyed Mitanni by the early 13th century BC, creating a small empire in northern Mesopotamia (see MIDDLE ASSYRIAN). This empire retracted under the pressure of ARAMAEAN incursions, but then expanded beyond its former frontiers in the 9th century BC, reaching its greatest extent in the mid 7th century BC when the NEO-ASSYRIAN kings ruled all Mesopotamia and ELAM to the Mediterranean and Egypt (see also NIMRUD, KHOR-SABAD, NINEVEH).

When the NEO-BABYLONIAN king, in alliance with the MEDES, overthrew the Assyrian yoke late in the 7th century, BABYLON established its own suzerainty over much of the former Assyrian territory. Perhaps best remembered for NEBUCHADNEZZAR's sacking of JERUSALEM and the deportation into exile of its inhabitants in 586 BC, this empire collapsed in its turn when the ACHAEMENID Persians conquered Babylon in 539 BC. The Achaemenids created an empire on a far vaster scale than previously attempted, controlling lands from Central Asia and northwestern India to Egypt and Thrace. Although PARSAGADAE and then PERSEPOLIS were its dynastic seats, the Persians exercised administrative rule from SUSA and BABYLON. Mesopotamia then passed into the hands of other empires – the SELEUCIDS, PARTHIANS, SASSANIANS and Moslems. Unable to withstand these waves of foreign domination, the Mesopotamian tradition gradually dissolved, the last dated cuneiform text falling around AD 75.

metal detector a GEOPHYSICAL instrument used in ELECTROMAGNETIC SURVEYING to detect metal artifacts hidden by vegetation or shallowly buried in sediments or soil. Sophisticated metal detectors can be programmed to detect only those artifacts above a certain depth, and to detect only those artifacts of a given alloy.

metallographic examination or **metallographic microscopy** a method of analysing the manufacturing tech-

niques of metal artifacts. A cross-sectional slice of a metal artifact is polished, etched to highlight internal structures, and examined under a metallurgical microscope. Reflected light from the microscope enhances uneven surfaces revealing grain size, shape and boundaries, inclusions, fabric, defects and other detail.

metallurgical analysis the study of metal artifacts and waste products to determine their material source, manufacture techniques and technology, and uses. Analysis may involve METALLOGRAPHIC EXAMINATION and a variety of CHEMICAL ANALYSIS methods.

metallurgy the art of working metals; it includes various techniques used to improve the practical and aesthetic qualities of metals, including ANNEALING, REPOUSSÉ, soldering, welding and the creation of alloys. See also LOST WAX.

Metaponto (*Lat.* Metapontum) a Greek colony in southern Italy with HIPPODAMIAN PLANNING. Two temples in the DORIC ORDER may have been dedicated to Hera and Apollo Lycaeus. Recent field-surveys in its hinterland have revealed a pattern of small rural establishments. See also LUCANIAN POTTERY.

metate a flat, ground-stone slab, used as a plate for the grinding of vegetable material, in conjunction with the MANO. Like the mano, they have a variety of shapes and sizes, and have some utility in the construction of CULTURE HISTORY. This term is most often used in MESOAMERICA and the American Southwest. See also QUERN.

methodology the assumptions and theories that determine the methods of archaeological investigation, and the procedures by which archaeological statements are tested.

metope part of the ENTABLATURE of a building of the DORIC ORDER, placed between TRIGLYPHS. The 7th century BC temple of Apollo at Thermon had clay metopes decorated with mythological scenes and other motifs. However, later temples had metopes which were either plain or sculpted (see PARTHENON).

Metsamor a site near Yerevan in Armenia at the edge of the Ararat plain, which contains both KURA-ARAXES and LATE BRONZE to Early Iron Age occupations. The latter settlement reveals the existence of pre-URARTIAN states in Transcaucasia. The city covered as much as 100 ha (247 acres), and contained a fortified citadel and attached 'cultic' area, residential zones, and industrial areas (especially of metallurgical production). Two elite graves discovered within the city suggest burial of retainers with the principal interments (a practice reminiscent of other early states, such as the ROYAL CEMETERY at UR or those of SHANG China): one of the graves contained fifty people, mostly women, in addition to the two central bodies. Moreover, each of these graves contained an inscribed object (in Mesopotamian CUNEIFORM and Egyptian HIEROGLYPHIC), which not only provides chronological evidence (15th–14th centuries BC) but also implies long-distance contacts with the civilizations to the south.

Mezhirich an Upper Palaeolithic open-air site located at the confluence of the Rosava and Ros' Rivers (Dnieper tributary system) in Ukraine. The occupation horizon is buried in slope deposits overlying mixed ALLUVIUM/COLLUVIUM on the second terrace; radiocarbon dates range between 17,855 and 12,900 bp. Woolly mammoth predominates among large mammalian remains; small vertebrates, including hare, rodents and birds, are also common. At least four MAMMOTH-BONE HOUSES, with associated pits, hearths and debris concentrations, were uncovered. In addition to the stone artifacts, a large number of non-stone tools, ornaments and art objects were found, including painted mammoth bones. Mezhirich was discovered in 1965, and excavated by Pidoplichko and Shovkoplyas in 1966–74, and by Gladkih and Korniets in 1976–81.

Mezin, an Upper Palaeolithic open-air site on the Desna River in Ukraine. The occupation horizon is buried in slope deposits overlying bedrock in a side-valley ravine; an AMS radiocarbon date of 15,100 bp supports earlier assignment (on the basis of artifacts and features) to the late Upper Palaeolithic. Woolly mammoth predominates among the fauna, but horse, reindeer, wolf and arctic fox are also common. At least two MAMMOTH-BONE HOUSES, with associated pits, hearths and debris concentrations, were uncovered. In addition to the stone artifacts, a number of non-stone tools, ornaments, art objects and painted mammoth bones (musical instruments?) were found. Mezin was discovered and initially excavated by VOLKOV in 1908–16; subsequent investigation was conducted by Shovkoplyas in 1954–61 and others.

MEZHIRICH, Ukraine: reconstruction of hut made of mammoth bones.

Mezmaiskaya Cave a cave located in the northwestern Caucasus containing MOUSTERIAN artifacts (bifaces, sidescrapers) and a NEANDERTHAL infant burial dating to roughly 40,000 years ago or earlier. Associated bones of bison and sheep reveal evidence of Neanderthal hunting of large mammals. An overlying layer yielded Upper Palaeolithic artifacts (blades and bone awls) dated by radiocarbon to 32,000 years BP. Mezmaiskaya Cave was investigated by Golovanova in 1987–97.

Miaodigou II [Miao-ti-kou] a middle Neolithic culture of China in the YANGSHAO tradition, chronologically falling between Yangshao and LONGSHAN of the central loess highlands at c.2800 BC. It is known for its painted pottery with spiral designs.

Michelsberg a middle Neolithic hilltop enclosure in Baden-Württemberg, Germany, type-site of the Michelsberg culture found in the Rhineland, Belgium and eastern France in the period 4500–4000 BC. Pottery forms include pointed- and round-based vessels with flaring rim, and flat pottery discs known as *plats à pain*, which probably served as lids.

Micoqulan 1 (*morphology*) a pointed-pyriform (pear-shaped) or *lanceolate* (tapering) biface with a well-made tip.
   2 a final ACHEULIAN phase occurring on the Lower-Middle Palaeolithic borderline and contemporary with or just slightly older than the biface MOUSTERIAN. Although originally defined by Hauser in 1916 on the basis of the assemblages from the French site of La Micoque, near LES EYZIES, most Micoquian sites are found in Central Europe (e.g. KŮLNA CAVE, KRAKÓW-ZWIERZYNIEC, MUSELIEVO) and some occur in European areas of the former USSR (e.g. KIIK-KOBA, STAROSEL'E).

microblade a small stone BLADE, typically several centimetres in length, often produced from a conical or wedge-shaped microcore. Microblades are found in Upper Palaeolithic industries of Eurasia (e.g. EASTERN GRAVETTIAN), but are especially common in the Upper Palaeolithic of Siberia (e.g. DYUKTAI CULTURE). They are also characteristic of Mesolithic and later industries in the circumpolar regions (e.g. ARCTIC SMALL TOOL TRADITION).

microburin technique a method of producing a microlith by notching and snapping a blade. The waste product, which shows characteristic traces of the manufacturing process, is known as a *microburin*.

microfauna small animals such as rodents or insectivores as compared with macrofauna.

microlith 1 a small later Upper Palaeolithic or Mesolithic stone artifact varying in size from approximately 1 to 5 cm (0.4 to 2 inches), and used as the tip of a bone or wooden implement or as an arrow-point. Microliths were either struck as blades from very small cores, or were made from fractured blades using the MICROBURIN TECHNIQUE.

2 (*Australia*) small backed implements made on blades or flakes, characteristic of the AUSTRALIAN SMALL TOOL TRADITION. The range of shapes is wide and includes geometric forms and BONDI POINTS. Microliths are widely distributed in southern Australia but are rare or absent in the tropical north. They are thought to be spear barbs.

Micronesia an ethnographic and geographical region comprising the Palau, Marianas, Caroline and Marshall Islands and Kiribati. The archaeology of the region is poorly understood, but western Micronesia, comprising the Palau and Marianas, was settled within the last 4,000 years. The islands of eastern Micronesia are mainly atolls and were settled more recently, probably from eastern MELANESIA. As in POLYNESIA, pottery production ceased in eastern Micronesia soon after first settlement.

microwear see USEWEAR ANALYSIS.

midden a concentration of cultural debris. The term is sometimes used to include the material in which the debris is encapsulated, and modifications of this MATRIX, but can also be used solely for the debris concentration.

Middle Assyrian a term denoting an important phase of the ASSYRIAN empire. In the LATE BRONZE AGE 'game of nations' expressed in the AMARNA archives, Assyria had long been dominated by the MITANNI state, but in the 14th century BC this relationship was reversed. Starting at the end of the 14th century, thanks to a series of vigorous Assyrian kings, the empire expanded rapidly through northern MESOPOTAMIA and the mountainous region to the north, and briefly occupied BABYLONIA (in 1225, under Tukultia-Ninurta I, 1243–1207 BC). This empire then weakened considerably during a period of dynastic troubles but Tiglath-pileser I (1114–1076 BC) restored Assyrian dominion over largely the same regions (and briefly reached the Mediterranean coast). Questions of succession weakened Assyria in the late 11th century, as did severe nomadic disruptions throughout Mesopotamia (see ARAMAEANS, CHALDEANS), and the empire retracted to its core area for several centuries.

Middle Awash a section of the valley of the Awash River in northeastern Ethiopia, which has yielded sites containing a rich HOMINID fossil, archaeological, mammalian and environmental record, dating from the MIOCENE to the Holocene. Of particular interest are the finds of australopithecine (see AUSTRALOPITHECUS) fossils of the period between about 3.5 and 2.5 million years ago, which are generally attributed to *A. afarensis* (see HADAR, 'LUCY'), as well as some of the oldest-known stone artifacts in the world. These are of the flaked cobble technology of the OLDOWAN complex and date to about 2.5 million years ago. See also GONA.

Middle Bronze Age a period in the Levant associated with the sophisticated urban civilization of the CANAANITES, characterized by towns surrounded by massive ramparts, symmetrical temples and elaborate palaces. The period is conventionally divided into two or three phases, each with several names: MBA I (or MBA IIA; *c.*1950–1800 BC), when walled towns reappeared after urban collapse at the end of the EARLY BRONZE AGE; and MBA II–III (or MBA IIB–C; *c.*1800–1550 BC), when CANAANITE society thrived (see LATE BRONZE AGE).

Middle Horizon (AD 750–1000) in Andean South America, the period during which the first large-scale imperial expansions took place, politically uniting portions of the central Andean region. In central Peru, the HUARI empire came to control the highlands and possibly the coast. In the Titicaca Basin, the TIAHUANACO state controlled the altiplano, and established colonies in, or trade relations with, adjacent regions in Bolivia, extreme southern Peru and northern Chile. These complex POLITIES pertain to the first centuries of the Middle Horizon. The latter century or so of the Middle Horizon was a period of political and economic collapse.

Middle Kingdom a period of Egyptian history comprising the 11th to the 13th Dynasty (*c.*2023–1633 BC).

Middle Missouri tradition see PLAINS VILLAGE INDIAN.

middle-range theory a set of theories that allow the construction of accurate statements of past behaviour based on the analysis of the contemporary archaeological record. Middle-range theory is considered by some archaeologists to be the essential key to a scientific understanding of the archaeological record. See also BRIDGING ARGUMENT, PROCESSUAL ARCHAEOLOGY.

Middle Stone Age the second stage of Stone Age technology in sub-Saharan Africa, first identified and named by GOODWIN in the 1920s, and described as having a number of 'variations' by Goodwin and VAN RIET LOWE in 1929. Some of these terms, including HOWIESON'S POORT, Mossel Bay, Still Bay, EPI-PIETERSBURG and PIETERSBURG, are still used, but with different meanings. Dates of about 250,000 and 230,000 years ago have been obtained for Middle Stone Age artifacts from northern Kenya and Zambia respectively, and the period postdating about 125,000 years ago in southern Africa is particularly rich in Middle Stone Age remains. The southern African Middle Stone Age ended at some time between about 27,000 and 20,000 years ago, with the youngest reliable date being 22,000 years ago for a Middle Stone Age occupation associated with exceptionally well-preserved plant remains from Strathalan B Cave in the Eastern Cape Province of South Africa. It is roughly equivalent to the Middle Palaeolithic found elsewhere in the Old World. Middle Stone Age assemblages lack handaxes and cleavers, and are characterized by flakes, typically produced by preparing the core from which the flake was to be struck. The flakes vary in size and shape, some being triangular and others long, elongated forms termed 'flake-blades'. A few were retouched into denticulates, points and scrapers, or even bifacial points.

A 20 m (65 ft) thick accumulation of Middle Stone Age layers at KLASIES RIVER MOUTH in the Eastern Cape Province of South Africa was subdivided by John Wymer into five chronological divisions: MSA I (characterized by long, thin flake-blades, a few of which were retouched to form points and denticulates, and many of which had platforms crushed during flake manufacture), MSA II (with higher counts of convergent or pointed flake-blades), the Howieson's Poort (with backed microliths and high percentages of artifacts made on fine-grained materials), MSA III (similar to the MSA II with points and 'knives') and MSA IV (with fewer flake-blades). Thomas Volmán later used these divisions to subdivide the Middle Stone Age into MSA 1, MSA 2a and 2b, Howieson's Poort and MSA 3 stages. However, apart from the Howieson's Poort, the differences between these industries are negligible and difficult to quantify, in comparison with their similarities.

Middle Stone Age assemblages in southern Africa are associated with anatomically modern HOMO *sapiens* (see BORDER CAVE, Pietersburg). Whether or not Middle Stone Age humans behaved like modern humans is the subject of on-going debate.

Midea see DENDRA.

Midland 1 a PALAEOINDIAN point type that is essentially an unfluted FOLSOM point.

2 a Palaeoindian complex found in the North American Plains that is very similar to Folsom, the major difference being in the point type. The two complexes are roughly contemporaneous, although at some sites they are vertically separated, with either being found above the other. The relationship between the two complexes is unclear, some archaeologists seeing the point type simply as a variant of Folsom. The type-site for the complex is the Scharbauer site, near Midland, Texas. The Midland complex is best represented at the HELL GAP site. The Midland component at this site contained possible evidence for structures, indicated by circular patterns of POSTHOLES.

3 From the Scharbauer site was recovered the skeleton (Midland 'Man') of a young woman, one of the earliest acceptable human remains on the North American continent. It dates to over 10,000 BP.

midwestern taxonomic system a hierarchical TAXONOMY devised by William McKern in 1939 and intended to unify archaeological classification in North America. The taxa have no temporal implications. The focus is a complex of TRAITS found in a number of sites. It is the elemental taxon and is implicitly similar to the ethnographic TRIBE. An ASPECT comprises similar foci in a larger region, and a PHASE is defined as a grouping of similar aspects. Other hierarchically larger taxa include the pattern and the base.

Mierzanowice culture an Early Bronze Age culture of southern Poland, contemporaneous with the ÚNĚTICE CULTURE of Silesia and Bohemia, dating to the late 3rd and early 2nd millennia BC. The Mierzanowice culture evolved from late CORDED WARE, and its pottery continues to use cord-marking as its primary means of decoration. Settlements, as at IWANOWICE-BABIA GÓRA, are located in upland areas and comprised small clusters of dwellings and related structures, with a cemetery near by. Mierzanowice burials are somewhat less richly furnished than the Únětice tombs and occur in flat cemeteries.

Mikhajlovka a stratified ENEOLITHIC settlement in the lower Dnieper Valley of Ukraine, which has yielded important data on subsistence, including faunal remains of sheep, goat and cattle, along with horses. Three main settlement horizons occur at Mikhajlovka. The first is an occupation of the CUCUTENI-TRIPOLYE culture, the second an occupation of the SREDNI STOG culture, and the final occupation is of the CATACOMB GRAVE culture.

Mikulčice a focal urban settlement of Greater Moravia, the earliest SLAVIC state-level POLITY in eastern-Central Europe just prior to AD 900. The core of Mikulčice was a stronghold with five APSIDAL churches and a princely residence. Around this fortified area were suburbs with houses and workshops of craftsmen. Greater Moravia fell in AD 907.

Milavče a Middle Bronze Age site in southeastern Bohemia, the type-site of the Milavče group (related to KNOVÍZ), which used a tumulus burial rite but which shifted from inhumation burial to cremation. Most of the cremations are urnless, but in one richly furnished grave, the ashes were contained in a wheeled bronze cauldron, about 30 cm (1 ft) in diameter.

Mildenhall the site in Suffolk, England, of a major hoard of late Roman (4th-century AD) silver plate now in the British Museum. Some pieces bear the Christian *chi-rho* monogram, though some of the relief ware shows scenes of the god of wine, Bacchus.

Miletus a Greek city at the southern mouth of the Meander Valley in Turkey, built on a narrow spit of land. The city was destroyed by the PERSIANS in 494 BC and the new layout reflects HIPPODAMIAN PLANNING. Excavations have revealed administrative buildings (BOULEUTERION, PRYTANEION) as well as the theatre. The harbour mouth was guarded by statues of lions. Its extramural sanctuary was located at DIDYMA. See also EAST GREEK POTTERY, FIKELLURA WARE.

millefiori a type of multi-coloured glass, literally meaning 'a thousand flowers'. The effect is created by fusing together slices from cores of different coloured glass giving a mosaic effect.

Millennium Man see ORRORIN.

milpa agriculture the cultivation of maize fields, often for only a few years, by SWIDDEN AGRICULTURE. *Milpa* is a Spanish corruption of an AZTEC term meaning 'in the fields'.

Mimbres a regional variant of the MOGOLLON culture, centred in southern-central New Mexico, USA. It is most famous for its magnificent ceramic tradition, composed of animal and human figures drawn on black-on-white vessels. The rise of Mimbres may have been partly due to the development of a CHACO-Mexican trade, with Mimbres serving as trading middle-men.

Mimi figures thin, stick-like human figures which are a feature of ARNHEM LAND rock art in northern Australia. They are earlier than X-RAY ART and are disclaimed by contemporary Aboriginal people, who attribute them to Mimi spirits.

mina a unit of Greek weight, the equivalent of the Near Eastern *manah*. It was formed by 100 DRACHMAS, which on the standard at ATHENS weighed 431 g (15 oz), or on AEGINA 630 g (22 oz). It has been recognized that items of silver plate could be made to weigh 1 mina: for example, the GOLD-FIGURED PHIALE from DUVANLI.

Mina Perdida a ceremonial PLATFORM MOUND site located in the Lurín Valley on the central coast of Peru, dating to the early part of the INITIAL PERIOD. Like the contemporaneous HUACA LA FLORIDA, it was probably used for only a few centuries and then abandoned.

Minatogawa a Late Palaeolithic site in Okinawa Prefecture, Japan, consisting of a limestone fissure in which skeletal remains dating to *c.*16–18,000 bp have been found.

Mindel Glaciation the second Alpine Pleistocene GLACIAL advance which ended with the onset of the HOLSTEINIAN INTERGLACIAL. See also ELSTERIAN.

Ming tombs the burial sites of the Ming emperors (see CHINESE DYNASTIES) near modern Beijing, one being now open as a site museum. The SPIRIT PATH leading to the tombs includes animal sculptures and bureaucrats in classical pose, nearly double life-size.

Minoan a term devised by Arthur EVANS for the Bronze Age civilization of Crete – from Minos, legendary ruler of KNOSSOS. On the basis of his excavations, Evans divided the period into three chronological phases, Early (*c.*3000–2000 BC); Middle (*c.*2000–1550 BC); and Late (*c.*1550–1050 BC). He then subdivided these so that each phase has three divisions designated by Roman

MING TOMBS, China: statue on the Spirit Path.

numerals. An alternative system, proposed by Platon, took more account of major architectural developments: Prepalatial (Early Minoan I–III), Protopalatial (Middle Minoan I–II), Neopalatial (Middle Minoan III–Late Minoan IIIA1) and Postpalatial (Late Minoan IIIA2–IIIc). MYRTOS and VASILIKI are two of the most informative Prepalatial sites.

At the start of the Protopalatial period, palaces were constructed at KNOSSOS, MALIA and PHAISTOS. These were administrative, economic and religious centres. An additional palace was built at ZAKRO in the Neopalatial period. There were towns at CHANIA, GOURNIA, KOMMOS, MOCHLOS and PALAIKASTRO, and villas at sites such as AYIA TRIADHA and TYLISSOS. Widespread destruction *c.*1450 BC has been attributed to MYCENAEAN Greeks, who subsequently took control and ruled much of Crete from Knossos.

Minshat Abu Omar a site in the northeastern Nile DELTA, Egypt, which has been investigated by a team from Munich Museum since 1977. Archaeologically, the most important part of this site is the cemetery dating to the PREDYNASTIC/ARCHAIC PERIOD transition, a period which is relatively poorly attested in the Delta. Among the objects found in these graves (which include ceramic and stone vessels, slate palettes, jewellery and copper tools) are imports from Palestine and UPPER EGYPT.

Minusinsk Basin a geographical area in southern Siberia; it comprises steppes and forest-steppes in the basin of the middle course of the Yenisei River, and is naturally isolated by the Sayan Mountains from the east and south, by the Kuznetsk Alatay chain from the south, and by taiga from the north. It includes the Republic of Khakasia, the southern part of the Krasnoyarsk region and the eastern part of the Kemerovo region. This area has the biggest concentration of archaeological sites in Siberia (and perhaps in the whole of Russia), and also has the longest history of archaeological investigation, since the first excavation in Siberia was carried out here in 1721 by D. G. Messerschmidt on the orders of Peter the Great. All periods and all kinds of archaeological sites and monuments are represented here; its periodization is now well established; and the sites here have been excavated quite intensively. Of particular importance is the very rich rock art of the Minusinsk Basin: there are more than 100 rock art sites on the banks of the Yenisei and other rivers, while petroglyphs are also represented on stone slabs and MENHIRS used for the construction of numerous KURGANS. The Minusinsk Basin was sufficiently open to witness all the new trends that arose on the EURASIAN STEPPES, and it was isolated enough to avoid occasional invasions and influences. The classification and periodization of Minusinsk antiquities, created by S. TEPLOU-KHOV, has become a standard for the whole of Siberian archaeology. See also the AFONTOVA, KOKOREVO, AFANASIEVO, OKUNEVO, ANDRONOVO, KARASUK, TASHTYK cultures.

Minyan the term which SCHLIEMANN devised for the distinctive Middle HELLADIC pottery which he found during his excavations at ORCHOMENOS, whose legendary ruler was King Minyas. Grey Minyan is particularly common, whereas Yellow Minyan has a more restricted distribution.

Miocene the epoch preceding the PLIOCENE and dating between about 25 and 5 million years ago.

Miriwun a rockshelter on the Ord River, Kimberley, Western Australia, now submerged by Lake Argyle, which was first occupied c.18,000 bp. Like many Australian sites, it has strong continuity in economy throughout the sequence, with a wide range of aquatic and terrestrial species represented. Small tools occur in the upper levels from about 3000 bp, while larger notched and denticulated flakes and adzes characterize the lower levels.

Mississippian a series of related complexes located in the southeastern part of North America (especially along that section of the Mississippi and its tributaries south of St Louis), from approximately AD 800 to the historic period. Mississippian influence was also found outside this 'core-area'. The precise nature of the Mississippian is still debated, some archaeologists defining it by the presence of particular types of MOUNDS or pottery of particular styles and/or temper. There is an increased dependence in the Mississippian on the growing of maize, beans and squash, which supplemented hunting-and-gathering, and there is evidence for greater redistribution of resources and centralized political control. See also CAHOKIA, SOUTHERN CULT.

Mitanni the most important of the 2nd-millennium BC HURRIAN kingdoms with INDO-EUROPEAN elements in elite circles. Mitanni was a player in the game of international power politics in the LATE BRONZE AGE. Of roughly equal status to the HITTITES, Babylonians and Egyptians, Mitanni initially dominated ASSYRIA, and controlled most of northern MESOPOTAMIA and Syria during the 16th and 15th centuries BC. During the 14th century, Assyria rose to prominence, destroying Mitanni in the process.

Mitathal a prehistoric site west of Delhi in Haryana in northern India, excavated by S. Bhan in 1968. It consists of a double mound with two periods of occupation whose ceramic and architectural traditions show a continuous development. The earlier period (Mitathal I) contains pottery similar to that belonging to the Early HARAPPAN settlement at KALIBANGAN. In the later period (Mitathal IIA–B), this pottery continues, but with strong Mature Harappan additions, which are also evident in the town layout and other artifacts. These cultural developments indicate that this part of northern India was involved in the milieu from which developed the Harappan civilization, but with a distinctive regional flavour.

Mithraeum a Roman temple, often in the form of a basilica, to the Persian mystery god Mithras. The cult seems to have been particularly popular with soldiers. An example has been excavated at Walbrook in LONDON.

Mitla a site in central Oaxaca, Mexico, with ceramics dating from MONTE ALBÁN I (900–300 BC), but without structural evidence until Monte Albán III A–V (AD 200–1521). The earlier structures on the site are ZAPOTEC, the later ones are MIXTEC or a Mixtec-Zapotec blend. Some structures were still occupied into the 16th century. Alfonso CASO and Daniel F. Rubín de la Borbolla conducted the first modern excavations in the mid 1930s.

mitochondrial DNA or mtDNA genetic instructions inherited through the maternal line. Deoxyribonucleic acid (DNA) is a molecule that carries genetic instructions from parents to offspring. Most of it is found in the nucleus of cells, and, in sexually reproducing species, each individual inherits approximately equal amounts of nuclear DNA from both parents. A small quantity of DNA is also found in another structure within cells, known as the mitochondrion, which generates energy for the cell, but this mitochondrial DNA is inherited only from the mother. Studies of mtDNA in modern human populations indicate that the greatest genetic diversity and hence antiquity occurs in Africans and that other populations diverged more recently.

It was initially suggested that a 'founding mother', dubbed 'Eve' after the biblical character and also known as 'mitochondrial Eve', lived in Africa between about 140,000 and 280,000 years ago, but more recent studies have expanded this estimate to between 100,000 and 1 million years ago, rendering the so-called 'Eve hypothesis' of a relatively recent African origin for modern humans more controversial. Studies of the male sex chromosome, the Y chromosome, have proved that 'Adam' is equally elusive, and suggest an origin of the order of 200,000 years ago or less, while those based on nuclear DNA also support a relatively recent origin of modern humans. Some researchers contend that the dating and distribution of skeletal remains of modern humans (see KLASIES RIVER MOUTH, QAFZEH, SKHUL) supports the initial mtDNA study suggesting that the founding population of modern humanity lived in Africa some 200,000 years ago (see 'OUT OF AFRICA' HYPOTHESIS).

Mixtec a linguistic and cultural affiliation in the Mexican state of Oaxaca, especially in the Mixteca Alta region in the northwestern part of the state. Linguistic affiliations are today shared by a highly diverse cultural group. The prehistoric Mixtec shared pan-Mesoamerican culture traits with other groups throughout MESOAMERICA.

During the Mesoamerican POSTCLASSIC, the Mixtecs and ZAPOTECS struggled for power in Oaxaca. Early Mixtec dynasties date back to the 7th century AD. The occurrence of Zapotec settlements on top of Mixtec GREYWARE ceramics suggests a certain amount of blending of the two cultures, probably during MONTE ALBÁN V (AD 1250–1521). Mixtec POLYCHROME POTTERY was famous for its lacquer-like polish and brilliant colours. Mixtec CODICES are among the most important native pictorials produced in Mesoamerica.

Mixteca-Puebla style an artistic tradition found during the POSTCLASSIC period throughout MESOAMERICA, characterized by use of bright colours and religious iconography. It appears on murals, POLYCHROME POTTERY and CODICES. CHOLULA was one of the centres for the development of this stylistic tradition, which is linked to the spread of the cult of QUETZALCÓATL.

Mladeč point a type of point manufactured from bone, antler or ivory, with an elongated oval shape. It is found in AURIGNACIAN sites of Central Europe.

Mlu Prei a cluster of late prehistoric sites in northern-central Cambodia, which includes the small sites of O Yak, O Pie Can and O Nan. They were occupied during the transition period from the Neolithic (polished stone adzes of several types along with a few flaked sidescrapers and bone projectile points) to the Bronze Age (armlets, axes, axe-chisels, sickles, stone bivalve moulds and clay crucibles, possibly linked technologically to HANG GON

in southern Vietnam), and then to the Iron Age (axes, etc.).

moa a species of giant flightless birds (order: Dinornithiformes), once common in NEW ZEALAND, which were hunted to extinction by the MAORI between first settlement and the 16th century AD. There were about thirteen species in six genera with varying regional distribution. The largest, *Dinornis giganteus*, could be up to 4 m (13 ft) high, while *Euryapteryx geranoides* was the most commonly hunted. As well as meat, moas provided raw material for bone artifacts and their eggs were used as water containers. At one time, moas were thought to be a key resource and the earliest phase of New Zealand prehistory was defined as the 'moa-hunter period'. It is now clear, however, that moa-hunting was only regionally important, particularly in the South Island.

moai a colossal stylized stone human figure of a type found on EASTER ISLAND. Most of the 800 to 1,000 known were quarried from volcanic TUFF at RANO RARAKU and carved between c.AD 600 and 1500. They are up to 10 m (33 ft) high and weigh up to 82 tonnes. Many were transported to the AHU located around the coast, and placed on top, facing inland; some of those on major ahu wore a huge cylindrical red stone head-dress from PUNA PAU and had white coral eyes fitted. All the moai, probably ancestor figures, were eventually toppled during internal strife.

moated sites a complex class of protohistoric and early historic sites in Thailand and Cambodia. The best known of these are the settlements encircled by one or more irregular (roughly circular) moats, a large number of which have been found in the Chi-Mun basin of the KHORAT Plateau of northeastern Thailand. Although many of these sites had late prehistoric phases of occupation, the moats themselves appear to have been added during phases of settlement growth after about AD 300–500, probably acting as source of both dry-season water and edible aquatic flora and fauna. These settlements, many of which were metal- and pottery-producing centres, appear to have dominated surrounding clusters of smaller, unmoated settlements. By AD 600–700 large settlements of the MON states in central Thailand were moated. Rectangular moats and tanks mark some KHMER settlements. The chronology in Cambodia has yet to be established; in Thailand these moats date to the period of Khmer dominance in the 11th–13th centuries AD.

mobiliary art or **chattel art** a term used to describe portable art, usually carved or engraved stone, bone, ivory or antler or small crudely fired clay models, produced during the Upper Palaeolithic. See also BÂTON PERCÉ, 'VENUS' FIGURINE; compare PALAEOLITHIC ART, PARIETAL ART.

Moche/Mochica the major culture of the north coast

of Peru during the EARLY INTERMEDIATE PERIOD. The religious and political focus of the Moche POLITY was centred at the Huaca del Sol and the Huaca de la Luna in the Moche Valley. Moche influence extended as far south as at least the Nepeña Valley, and as far north as Lambayeque, as documented by the distribution of Moche art and architecture. An outgrowth of the earlier GALLINAZO style, Moche ceramics were often modelled to depict realistically all manner of animal and plant life, and possibly portraits of Moche rulers. Other vessels were painted in fine-line drawings depicting elaborate themes such as the presentation of a ritual goblet and others. Christopher Donnan suggests that most Moche art can be seen to reflect perhaps only fifteen or so major themes. The Moche culture has been divided into five phases, the last of which pertains to the MIDDLE HORIZON. In Moche V times, the southern portion of Moche territory was abandoned by the Moche, and they established a new capital in the north, at PAMPA GRANDE. In 1987 the tomb of the so-called Lord of SIPÁN was discovered, in the far northern portion of Moche territory. Huaca de la Luna is a large artificial platform, 95 by 85 by 20 m tall (104 by 93 yds by 66 ft tall), built against the slope of Cerro Blanco, and it probably served a ceremonial function. The Huaca del Sol is a large stepped pyramid (342 by 159 by 40 m tall [374 by 174 yds by 130 ft tall]) with a cross-shaped plan, made of some 143 million adobe bricks. Makers' marks on the bricks suggest the existence of a labour tax, similar to that of the later INCA empire. Evidence of structures on the summit suggests that the huaca served a political function within the Moche polity. It is perhaps the largest single construction ever built in the prehistoric Andean region.

Mochlos an island, formerly a peninsula, on the north coast of Crete. An Early MINOAN cemetery of house tombs contained rich offerings, the gold jewellery and stone vases being particularly impressive, and there is also a large Middle-Late Minoan settlement.

mode single or multiple ATTRIBUTES whose frequencies change through time and space, and thus are useful in constructing CULTURE HISTORY.

model a simplified version of reality that allows that reality to be better understood. Models can vary in complexity from a simple distribution map to complex mathematical formulae, and can be both physical representations and purely literary descriptions. Models provide hypotheses which can then be tested with archaeological data.

Modjokerto see MOJOKERTO.

Moesia a Roman province of the lower Danube region, extending from Serbia to the mouth of the Danube. In its eastern part, Moesia lay between DACIA to the north and THRACIA to the south. During the 1st century AD, the Romans built a series of defensive walls and forts in southern Romania to guard the Moesia-Dacia frontier. Later, the GETAE came to settle in Moesia.

Mogao [Mo-kao] see DUNHUANG.

Mogollon a prehistoric tradition in the Mogollon Highlands of eastern Arizona and western New Mexico, USA, which was heavily influenced by both the ANASAZI and the HOHOKAM. As with the Anasazi and Hohokam, the Mogollon tradition is chronologically divided on the basis of architectural and pottery changes. After AD 1000, Mogollon became so heavily influenced by the Anasazi that it is no longer recognizable as an independent tradition and indeed by AD 1450, the term Western Pueblo is often applied to these late manifestations. Maize, bean and squash agriculture was practised, although their reliance on hunting and gathering always remained great, compared to the other two Southwest traditions. The tradition has a number of regional variants: MIMBRES, Pine Lawn, Upper Little Colorado, Forestdale and Point of Pines.

Mohammad Jaffar see DEH LURAN.

Mohenjo-daro the best known of the Mature HARAPPAN cities. Mohenjo-daro lies in the Sind region of Pakistan, and was excavated by J. MARSHALL and E. Mackay in the 1920s and 1930s, with later work conducted by M. WHEELER, G. Dales and, very recently, by Italian, French and German workers. The city covers some 80 ha (198 acres), divided into a smaller citadel to the east and a larger residential area to the west. The walled citadel, built on a baked-brick platform, contained a number of massive structures (including the Granary, Great Bath, the 'College', among others). The lower settlement was laid out on a regular grid of major and secondary streets, defining residential blocks; most of the individual dwellings in these blocks fall into one of five floor plans. Numerous craft installations were also present in the lower town, including potting, bead making, shell working, dyeing and metal working. The artifacts recovered in the Marshall/Mackay excavations still provide the basic definition of the Mature Harappan material culture, especially pottery styles, seals, weights, bead forms, figurines and metal forms.

'Moi forts' or **'Cham forts'** a series of small circular earthen-walled enclosures in eastern Cambodia and Vietnam. One site, Mimot, was excavated by B.-P. Groslier in the 1960s, and more recent work by German and Cambodian archaeologists has confirmed that they belong to a late Neolithic–early metal age culture.

Mojokerto or **Modjokerto** a town near JETIS, Java, which has given its name to the remains of a HOMO *erectus* child (once called *Pithecanthropus robustus*, *P. modjokertensis* or *H. modjokertensis*), dating to *c*.1.5 million years BP or before. ARGON-ARGON dating of volcanic

MOHENJO-DARO, Pakistan: the granary, with baths in the foreground.

pumice and minerals at the site has produced an age of 1.8 million years.

mokkan literally 'wooden tablets' in Japanese; administrative artifacts known from HAN Dynasty Chinese sites. Their bureaucratic use was adopted by United SILLA in Korea and the RITSURYO state in Japan in the 8th century AD. In Japan, *mokkan* used as tax tallies, work records, task evaluations, etc. have been excavated by the tens of thousands at the HEIJO Palace and other administrative offices around the country; in Korea, many are known from ANAPCHI pond.

Mokram a group which succeeds the GASH group in eastern Sudan about 3300 BP. There is evidence for a settlement hierarchy and sites contain domestic stock and sorghum.

Mokrin an Early Bronze Age cemetery in northeastern Yugoslavia belonging to the MAROS GROUP. Over 300 graves contained flexed inhumations in which males had their heads pointing north, females to the south, and the bodies all faced east. Male graves contained weapon and head ornaments, while female graves contained head ornaments, beaded sashes and bone needles.

Molfetta a middle Neolithic settlement in the 'Pulo di Molfetta', Puglie, Italy, originally a curious circular cave over 100 m (110 yds) across, but now open to the sky owing to the collapse of the cave roof. On the floor of the former cave are remains of several oval huts with stone footings and wattle-and-daub walls. The pottery consists of red-on-buff painted ware, together with a late variety of IMPRESSED WARE related to the Sicilian STENTINELLO style. A Neolithic cemetery near by held some fifty crouched burials.

Molino Casarotto see BOCCA QUADRATA.

Molodova a group of Palaeolithic and Mesolithic open-air sites on the Dniester River in western Ukraine. The two most important localities are Molodova I and V, where multiple occupation levels are buried in slope deposits overlying ALLUVIUM on the second terrace. At both sites, Middle Palaeolithic artifacts and associated faunal remains (primarily woolly mammoth) are contained in humic loams that appear to represent redeposited buried soils; both sites also yielded evidence of MAMMOTH-BONE HOUSES, which are otherwise unknown from the Middle Palaeolithic. The artifacts include many tools made on blades (retouched blades, points and sidescrapers). Most of the Middle Palaeolithic levels apparently date to INTERSTADIALS prior to the beginning of the last GLACIAL. Molodova V also contains at least ten levels that span the full duration of the Upper

Palaeolithic; associated faunal remains are chiefly of horse and reindeer. The lower levels (c.30,000–25,000 bp) yielded a distinctive early Upper Palaeolithic industry (MOLODOVA CULTURE); the upper levels (c.23,000–12,000 bp) contain late Upper Palaeolithic assemblages with large numbers of burins. The Molodova sites, in conjunction with KORMAN' IV, provide the most complete and best-dated sequence of Upper Palaeolithic occupation in Ukraine. Molodova I was discovered and first investigated by Botez in 1927–31; subsequent discoveries and excavations at these sites were undertaken by Chernysh in the period 1948–84.

Molodova culture an Upper Palaeolithic culture of western Ukraine, represented principally at MOLODOVA V. It spans much of the duration of the Upper Palaeolithic and is divided into phases. The early phase (c.30,000–25,000 bp) is characterized by burins, large retouched blades and endscrapers. The later phases (c.23,000–12,000 bp) have a continuing predominance of burins, along with backed blades and points. Non-stone tools and art objects are less common than among other Upper Palaeolithic cultures of Europe.

Moloko a Late Iron Age complex which appears in Gauteng Province and adjacent areas of the Mpumalanga and North-West Provinces of South Africa at c.AD 1200–1300. A second phase of the complex starts c.AD 1600 with a dramatic increase in the number of stone-built settlements on the grasslands of the southern high-veld of South Africa (see SOUTHERN HIGHVELD Types N, V, Z).

Mon an ethno-linguistic group, related to the KHMER and to various hill groups of mainland Southeast Asia, who formed the earliest states in the lower Irrawaddy Valley of Burma, and in the Chao Phraya Valley, KHORAT and peninsular regions of Thailand, most dating to the 1st millennium AD (see DVARAVATI).

Mondsee culture an ENEOLITHIC culture of the Alpine foothills of northeastern Austria, named after a LAKE DWELLING site on the Mondsee, 30 km (19 miles) east of Salzburg. Mondsee ceramics are often ornamented with incised geometrical shapes with white incrustation. An important dimension of the Mondsee culture is its involvement with the mining of local Alpine copper sources and the manufacture of copper artifacts on a scale larger than hitherto practised.

Mongch'on an irregularly shaped walled site on the south bank of the Han River in Seoul, Korea. Dating from the late 3rd to late 5th centuries AD, it was probably an important economic and administrative centre of the early PAEKCHE state. Excavated mainly by the Seoul National University Museum from 1985, several pithouses, storage pits, iron horse-trappings and much bone-plate armour have been recovered from the interior.

Monk's Kop see MUSENGEZI.

Montagu Cave a Stone Age cave-site some 180 km (112 miles) east-northeast of Cape Town in the Western Cape Province of South Africa. It is one of only a handful of southern African cave-sites containing EARLIER STONE AGE ACHEULIAN material and in which the MIDDLE STONE AGE overlies the Acheulian (see CAVE OF HEARTHS in Makapansgat Valley). The Middle Stone Age layers include the HOWIESON'S POORT industry and include a concentration of rocks perhaps artificially arranged. The LATER STONE AGE layers include a grindstone found on top of an oval pit containing carbonized plant remains.

Mont Bégo a complex of glaciated valleys on the slopes of Mont Bégo, Alpes-Maritimes, France, rich in protohistoric rock art. The principal concentrations are those in the so-called Vallée des Merveilles and at Fontanalba. Representations include stylized figures, abstract shapes and artifacts, including daggers of Early Bronze Age type. Some of the engravings may be still older; but others are as recent as the Middle Ages or later. The 150,000 engravings are scattered over 40 sq. km (15.5 sq. miles) at between 2,000 and 2,600 m (6,560 and 8,530 ft) altitude.

Montbolo, Balma de a small cave in the Pyrénées Orientales, France, excavated by J. Guilaine; halfway up a rock face, very difficult of access, it has Neolithic and CHALCOLITHIC deposits. The Neolithic assemblage is characterized by simple globular vessels with tubular lug-handles and is transitional between early Neolithic CARDIAL WARE and middle Neolithic Chasséen (see CHASSEY). There is a single radiocarbon date of 4500 bc for this layer, and others of c.2100 bc for a series of Chalcolithic burials.

Monte Albán a large CEREMONIAL CENTRE located on top of an artificially flattened mountain, 400 m (1,300 ft) above the city of Oaxaca, Mexico. The CHRONOLOGY developed at this site is the basis for dating all other sites in the VALLEY OF OAXACA.

Monte Albán I (500–200 BC), the first period of occupation, already shows a well-developed culture, influenced by the OLMEC ('Olmecoid'), with a knowledge of calendrics, and having the earliest-known form of HIEROGLYPHIC writing. Most of the DANZANTES were carved during this period, as was the inner, or first, building in which they were placed.

During the Monte Albán II, II–III and IIIA, the site continued to grow, as well as to be influenced by other MESOAMERICAN groups. In Monte Albán IIIB (AD 600–800) the centre was also influenced by TEOTIHUACÁN. It is this later period that is seen as a 'true ZAPOTEC' period, and also when Monte Albán reached its peak population of 50–60,000 (in the city and surrounding 8 sq. km [3 sq. miles]).

During the subsequent period, Monte Albán IV (AD 800–1200), the construction of large buildings at

Monte Albán ceased, and the emphasis of the region moved to the valley. Monte Albán was essentially abandoned. The MIXTEC entered the area at this time, and throughout this and the overlapping period of Monte Albán V (AD 1200–1521) Monte Albán was used as a sacred mountain relating to ancestral spirits. One CLASSIC tomb, tomb 7, was reused at this time as an oracular shrine dedicated to a Mixtec earth/fertility goddess. Most of our information from the site comes from Alfonso CASO and his collaborators, who spent many years there, beginning in 1931.

Monte Alegre see CAVERNA DA PEDRA PINTADA.

Monte Circeo see GROTTA GUATTARI.

Montelius, Oscar (1843–1921) a distinguished Swedish prehistorian famous for his typological schemes for the European Neolithic and Bronze Age. His detailed subdivision of the Northern Bronze Age (1885) into five successive phases was based on close study of the changing styles of bronze artifacts. He later adapted it to other parts of Europe. Montelius was also a strong adherent of the *ex oriente lux* view, which held that all European culture in later prehistoric times was derived from the ancient civilizations of Egypt and the Near East.

Monteoru culture a Middle Bronze Age culture of eastern Romania and Moldova, c.1800–1500 BC. The type-site of Monteoru is a fortified hilltop near Bucharest. In a nearby inhumation cemetery are four large clusters of graves.

Montespan a Palaeolithic cave-site in Haute-Garonne in the French Pyrenees, where N. Casteret, in 1923, discovered engravings on the walls as well as a series of clay statues and bas-reliefs, most notably a sphinx-like headless bear, over a metre long, made of approximately 700 kg (14 cwt) of clay. It seems to guard the cave's low 'sanctuary' where many engravings are found. The site's art is assigned to the middle MAGDALENIAN.

Montet, Pierre (1885–1966) a French Egyptologist, best known for his work at TANIS and BYBLOS.

Monte Verde an Early PRECERAMIC (c.13,000 bp) site in southern Chile, one of very few sites that may represent a pre-CLOVIS occupation in the New World. Excavated by Tom D. Dillehay, the site includes remains of eleven or twelve residential huts, roughly rectangular with shallow clay-lined pits used as braziers, and built of wood frames possibly covered with animal hides. Another structure, whose foundation is compacted sand and gravel, has a wishbone shape and a protruding rectangular platform. Tools were of wood, bone or stone; stone tools were naturally fractured, or sometimes shaped through percussion flaking. There may be stratigraphic evidence for an even earlier occupation of the site with a date of c.33,000 bp from deeper strata.

Mont Lassois an Iron Age HILLFORT dominating the upper valley of the River Seine, Côte-d'Or, France, and commanding an easy land route from the Seine to the Rhône-Saône corridor leading to the Mediterranean. Principal occupation is dated to the second half of the 6th century BC (HALLSTATT D), when Mont Lassois was probably the residence of a powerful CELTIC chieftain. Trade with the Greek colonies of southern France is demonstrated by finds of Massiliote wine AMPHORAS and Attic BLACK FIGURE WARE. Immediately below the hillfort is the rich contemporary burial of VIX.

Moore, Clarence Bloomfield (1852–1936) an American archaeologist, noted for his detailed and intensive investigations of numerous sites in the southeastern part of North America. His most famous work was conducted at the MOUNDVILLE and POVERTY POINT sites.

Moose Mountain a MEDICINE WHEEL, located in southern Saskatchewan, Canada. The site comprises a central cairn approximately 10 m (33 ft) in diameter, which is surrounded by an ellipse of stones. Radiating from the central cairn are five stone lines, each of which ends in a small stone cairn. A radiocarbon date of approximately 2600 BP indicates an initial construction of the site, although a later date of 1700 BP has also been proposed. It has been suggested that the site was aligned with reference to the summer solstice.

Mootwingee see MUTAWINTJI.

Mopir an obsidian source on New Britain. Less well known than nearby TALASEA, Mopir seems to have been buried by ash from the eruption of Mount Witori in 3500 bp and remained inaccessible for up to 1,000 years.

moraine a term for a family of depositional landforms directly resulting from the action of glacier ice. The morphology and origin of the more common moraine types are as follows:

(a) end or terminal moraine – linear ridge transverse to flow of glacial ice, marking maximum extent of ice advance. The ridge forms as the result of a balance between ice advance and ablation of the ice which causes the ice front not to fluctuate for some period of time;

(b) recessional moraine – linear ridge forms due to a pause in the ice front during retreat. End and recessional moraines may form natural dams which support lakes;

(c) ground moraine – plain formed by deposition in the wake of a steadily retreating glacier that may be relatively featureless, have subtle linear rises or minor moraines transverse to glacial flow, or consist of streamlined landforms parallel to ice flow such as flutes or drumlins;

(d) hummocky or ablation moraine – chaotic low-relief

plain resulting from stagnation and downwasting of glacial ice;

(e) lateral moraine – linear ridges along valley walls parallel to ice flow of valley glaciers.

Moraines usually offer different drainage conditions from surrounding terrain so that different vegetational communities might be supported.

Morgan, Lewis Henry (1818–81) one of the founders of American anthropology, whose unilinear scheme of human development – from savagery to barbarism to civilization – greatly influenced future archaeological models of CULTURE HISTORY and the application to the discipline of models drawn from the theory of evolution.

Moriori the POLYNESIAN inhabitants of the Chatham Islands, the furthest limit of Polynesian dispersal. Archaeological evidence suggests that the islands were settled from NEW ZEALAND during the Archaic phase, but became isolated after about AD 1400.

Morley, Sylvanus Griswold (1883–1948) an American archaeologist who studied MAYA civilization. From 1908 to 1914 he recorded Maya GLYPHS. Morley synthesized his own work and that of his peers and, with Sir J. E. S. THOMPSON, proposed an interpretation of Maya civilization which remained accepted and virtually unquestioned for years. This interpretation was based on a study of the large Maya CEREMONIAL CENTRES, proposing that the Classic Maya were not urban dwellers, but farmers who occupied 'vacant centres' only during religious holidays.

In 1915 Morley became a research associate of the Carnegie Institution of Washington. At this time he began surveying the southern Maya lowlands. He also directed the huge Carnegie project at CHICHÉN ITZÁ 1921–40. Morley's contact with modern-day Maya greatly influenced his interpretations of the prehistoric Mayan civilization.

Morse, Edward Sylvester (1838–1925) an American zoologist credited with the introduction of the modern discipline of archaeology to Japan with his excavation of the OMORI SHELL MIDDEN in 1877 while teaching at Tokyo (Imperial) University.

mortar a vessel, usually of stone, on or in which food or other materials can be ground or crushed by a pestle or grinder. Some rock-types particularly suitable for this purpose might be traded over large distances.

mortarium a Roman grinding bowl.

Mortillet, Gabriel de (1821–98) a French prehistorian who proposed an alternative to LARTET's classificatory scheme for the Palaeolithic, based on archaeological remains rather than palaeontology. De Mortillet's scheme used type-names such as MOUSTERIAN, AURIGNACIAN and SOLUTREAN, which are still used today, but divided the Palaeolithic into time-periods, not cultures or traditions.

Mortlake see PETERBOROUGH WARE.

mortuary temple an Egyptian temple, usually situated close to a royal tomb. The specialized purpose of the mortuary temple was to provide a centre for the performance of rites for the benefit of the dead king. Compare CULT TEMPLE.

mosaic 1 a technique using TESSERAE, especially in the Roman world.

2 a TESSELLATED area often with complex designs and even inscriptions. See also COLOGNE, FISHBOURNE, OSTIA.

Moshebi's Shelter a site in eastern Lesotho containing a MIDDLE STONE AGE sequence including the HOWIESON'S POORT industry, as well as LATER STONE AGE remains, including pottery.

Mossbauer spectroscopy a technique of analysis used to determine the presence and type of iron-bearing minerals in ceramics, and to interpret firing conditions. Iron is one of the few ISOTOPES in which the Mossbauer effect, the recoil-less fluorescence of gamma rays, occurs. Samples are bombarded with gamma rays; the detected amount of absorption by iron nuclei provides information regarding the iron-bearing minerals present.

Motupore an island in Bootless Bay, near Port Moresby, Papua New Guinea, investigated by Jim Allen. Archaeological material from Motupore, especially the evidence for manufacture of shell valuables and pottery, documents the development of a coastal trading centre, which supplied goods to Papuan Gulf communities between about 500 and 250 years ago. See also HIRI.

Motya a PHOENICIAN harbour town situated on a small offshore island reached from the Sicilian mainland by a causeway. The earliest activity seems to date from the 8th century BC. Extensive excavations by the British and Italians have revealed a *cothon* (artificial dock), the walls, houses, cemeteries and the *tophet* (sanctuary). Although the site is Phoenician, large quantities of Greek pottery, both fine and domestic, have been found. The site provides an important TERMINUS ANTE QUEM of 397 BC, when it was destroyed by the Syracusans and largely abandoned.

Mouillian see IBEROMAURUSIAN.

mound (*Australia*) a series of low earth mounds found in southwestern and central Victoria, the central Murray, Riverina and Northern Territory of Australia. They are mostly less than 1 m (3 ft) high, and seem to have been formed primarily through the heaping up of refuse from earth ovens. They are normally interpreted as dry camping places in poorly drained areas, although it has recently been speculated that they might have originally been garden mounds. They often contain burials. The oldest mounds date from c.4000 bp along the Murray River, while they appear in southwestern Victoria from c.2500 bp.

mounded tombs a form of elite burial in East Asia constructed with monumental earthen or stone-piled mounds containing various burial facilities such as a WOODEN-CHAMBER, clay enclosure, brick or megalithic stone chamber. Round and square mounds are common; KEYHOLE TOMBS are exclusive to Japan. The tombs and their contents provide the major sources of data for the THREE KINGDOMS period in Korea and the KOFUN period in Japan (see MURYONG, HEAVENLY HORSE TOMB, FUJINOKI, POKCH'ON-DONG, TAKAMATSU-ZUKA). One of the earliest mounded tombs in China was that of the First Emperor of QIN, and the MING TOMBS are some of the latest. The tombs contain a variety of prestige goods differing in time and space, but including such items as BRONZE MIRRORS, lacquer vessels, iron swords and armour, funerary pottery (LEAD-GLAZED WARE, SUE ware), gold jewellery, silk, jades and horse trappings. HANIWA or a SPIRIT PATH were constructed outside the tombs. Compare SHAFT TOMBS, MA-WANGDUI, MANCHENG.

Moundville an important MISSISSIPPIAN site in Alabama, USA, that reached its zenith approximately 300 years before European contact. It comprised about twenty mounds, mostly PLATFORM MOUNDS. Over 3,000 burials, of varying social status, have been uncovered at the site, and it is likely that it was part of a CHIEFDOM. Moundville has much evidence for the SOUTHERN CULT, and was first investigated by C. B. MOORE.

Mount Camel an Archaic midden site covering about 1.5 ha (3.7 acres) at the north end of the North Island, NEW ZEALAND, and dating to AD 1150–1260. The excavations by Wilfred Shawcross revealed earth-ovens and evidence for a range of activities, including butchering, fish scaling and manufacture of bone and ivory ornaments.

Mount Cameron West the most complex art site in TASMANIA, Australia. It features a range of non-figurative engravings on slabs fallen from the cliff. The motifs compare with those of PANARAMITEE ART. However, the space behind the slabs was used as a camp-site in 1350–850 bp, suggesting the engravings are recent.

Mount Carmel a low limestone coastal range in Israel, running some 32 km (20 miles) southeast from Haifa. Numerous caves and wadis have formed along its length, notably the prehistoric sites EL-WAD, TABUN, SKHUL, KEBARA and NAHAL OREN.

Mount Sandel an Irish Mesolithic site in County Londonderry, which has yielded a series of circular wooden hut-foundations with central hearths, and a distinctive lithic

industry including microliths, tranchet axes and the early appearance of polished stone axes. The site was first excavated by Collins and later by Woodman.

Mount William a GREENSTONE (diorite) axe quarry and workshop in central Victoria, Australia, and the centre of an exchange network through most of Victoria and into South Australia and southern New South Wales. First documented in the late 19th century by the anthropologist, A. W. Howitt, it has since been the subject of detailed study by Isabel McBryde.

Mount Yengo a rockshelter in the Sydney Basin, Australia, with both paintings and engravings. The paintings are mostly hand stencils. The panel of engravings is buried under the floor deposits and comprises circles and animal tracks reminiscent of the PANARAMITEE tradition. The excavator, Jo McDonald, has argued that the engraved art is about 5,000–6,000 years old and represents a regional survival of Panaramitee.

Mousterian a term first used for Middle Palaeolithic artifacts recovered from the lower rockshelter at Le Moustier, Dordogne, France, excavated by LARTET and CHRISTY. The term was then extended to include assemblages showing a high proportion of flakes, racloirs, points, occasional bifaces and the use of prepared-core-knapping techniques. The Mousterian has a wide geographical distribution, stretching across Europe and Asia, and from Britain to North Africa. Three major regional variants have been identified: West, East and LEVAL-LOISO-Mousterian, each with clear sub-groups based mainly on typological differences in tool forms. Mousterian occurrences have been dated between the late RISS and the late middle WÜRM GLACIATIONS (c.180,000 to 30,000 BP). They are frequently associated with the occupation of caves or rockshelters and with NEANDERTHAL remains. See also CHARENTIAN.

Mousterian of Acheulian tradition (MTA[French] or MAT [English]) the name given by BORDES to one of the MOUSTERIAN variants identified in southwestern France on the basis of artifact typology. The MAT has two recognized sub-types: Type A, with bifaces, backed knives, denticulates and scrapers; developing into Type B, with fewer bifaces and a higher frequency of Upper Palaeolithic tool-types such as burins and awls.

Movius, Hallam Leonard (1907–87) an American prehistorian best known for his field work in Northern Ireland and Southeast Asia, and for the excavation of the Upper Palaeolithic rockshelter of ABRI PATAUD, France, in 1958–64.

Moxeke see PAMPA DE LAS LLAMAS.

Mrs Ples see STERKFONTEIN.

Mšecké Zehrovice an Iron Age settlement in Bohemia, dated to the LA TÈNE C–D period (c.150–50 BC). Mšecké

Zehrovice has been termed an 'industrial village' at which both iron and sapropelite (a type of shale) were worked. Two large contiguous rectangular enclosures, each about 100 m (110 yds) per side, delimited an area which may have had a ritual purpose. The best-known find from Mšecké Zehrovice is the stone bust of a CELT with a curling moustache and wavy hair.

MTA see MOUSTERIAN OF ACHEULIAN TRADITION.

Mu'a a ceremonial centre of the ruling dynasties on Tongatapu, Tonga. The ditched and banked earthworks enclose an area of 400 by 500 m (440 by 550 yds) with many house-platforms and LANGI TOMBS. It has never been excavated but, according to tradition, became the residence of the ruling Tui Tonga dynasty about AD 1200, the defences being built about AD 1400.

Muang Fa Daet a large (approximately 170 ha [420 acre]) late prehistoric/early historic settlement in the upper Chi Valley, KHORAT, Thailand. It is the largest MOATED SITE in the Khorat, the rectangular outermost of its three concentric moats and the 15 ha (37 acre) reservoir dating to the period of KHMER domination late in the 1st millennium AD. It was a major farming, trading and bronze- and iron-working site. Material culture of the mid 1st millennium AD resembles that of the state of DVARAVATI, and much of the moated site was sacred Buddhist space.

Muang Sima a large (over 150 ha [370 acre]) late prehistoric/early historic settlement upstream from PHIMAI in the Mun Valley, KHORAT, Thailand, occupied by the early 1st millennium AD. By the 7th and 8th centuries AD, the twice-enlarged MOATED SITE appears to have been the centre of a small indianized (see INDIANIZATION) state called, according to the inscription from the site, Srî Canāsa. Buddhist remains of the period are similar to those of DVARAVATI.

Muara Jambi see ŚRIVIJAYA.

mud-brick a brick dried in the sun, used for construction in dry climates. See also ADOBE, SEBBAKH.

Mud Glyph Cave a site located in Tennessee, USA, which comprises a series of almost inaccessible 'galleries' containing a rich collection of prehistoric art, constructed from incisions cut into the natural mud of the cave walls. Designs are mostly anthropomorphous, but zoomorphs as well as abstract designs identical to ones on contemporary artifacts (including the SOUTHERN CULT) are also present. The cave was used from AD 420 to 1750, with heaviest use between the 12th and 16th centuries. See also MISSISSIPPIAN, WOODLAND.

Muge the location of Mesolithic *concheiros* (SHELL MOUNDS) near the mouth of the Tagus, Portugal, excavated in the 1880s and 1950s. Their dates lie between 7350 and 5150 bp, the ATLANTIC period, and they contain a microlithic industry together with quartzite pebbles and grindstones, as well as bone points and axes of red deer antler like those of Lyngby (see BROMMIAN). The three *concheiros* of Muge yielded over 230 burials, the most important European Mesolithic funerary assemblage.

Mulloy, William Thomas (1917–78) an American archaeologist who developed the cultural chronology of the northwestern Plains, USA, especially at Pictograph Cave, Montana. He is best known for his important work on EASTER ISLAND from 1955 onwards, especially the excavation and restoration of ORONGO and several AHU with their MOAI.

Multiregional Hypothesis see 'OUT OF AFRICA' HYPOTHESIS.

Mumba-Höhle or **Mumba** an impressive rockshelter near Lake Eyasi in northern Tanzania, first dug by Margit Kohl-Larsen in 1938, and one of a very few excavated deeply stratified sites in East Africa. Its 9 m (30 ft) deposit spans much of the last 125,000 years and contains material from the MIDDLE STONE AGE to the Iron Age. Of particular interest is a transitional Middle/LATER STONE AGE industry called the Mumba industry containing backed microliths and ostrich eggshell beads, associated with dates of more than 37,000 bp, while the overlying Middle/Later Stone Age NASERA industry, associated with dates of 33,200 and 27,000 bp, contained rare backed microliths but several hundred ostrich eggshell beads and two bored stones.

Mumbwa a cave in the Kafue Valley of southern Zambia, containing a MIDDLE STONE AGE sequence similar to that of KALEMBA, including a collection of skeletons apparently placed within piled stones against the cave wall. Unfortunately, the excavations were conducted in 1930 and some of the material has been lost. Much of what remains is very fragmentary, and the context of the skeletons is not well established. The cave also contains LATER STONE AGE and Iron Age material.

mummification the artificial treatment of a cadaver, with the aim of preserving a life-like appearance, a body that has been treated in this way being popularly known as a mummy. The earliest attempts at mummification by the Egyptians were during the OLD KINGDOM, but only in the NEW KINGDOM were techniques developed (major removal of internal organs, effective use of desiccating agents, subcutaneous padding) which made mummification possible on a reasonably large scale. Not only people but also sacred animals and birds were treated in this way. All stages of the procedure were accompanied by elaborate rituals.

It is thought that the practice was inspired by the natural desiccation of bodies in the desert sand, and the term is often extended to bodies preserved accidentally in this way in other parts of the world, such as Peru. See also CHINCHORRO.

Mummy Cave a deeply stratified site in the mountains of western Wyoming, USA, with thirty-eight distinct levels, the earliest dating to before 7300 BC, and the latest dating to the 16th century AD.

Mumun literally 'no decoration' in Korean; the tradition of 'plain pottery' of the Korean peninsula, succeeding CHULMUN pottery in c.1500 BC and lasting to AD 300 in the PROTO-THREE KINGDOMS period. It was the dominant pottery type from the Bronze Age through the Proto-Three Kingdoms period. Mumun-pottery sites without bronze fit unconformably between the Chulmun and Bronze Age (e.g. HUNAM-RI). See also KOREA.

Mundigak a prehistoric site northwest of Kandahar in the upper Helmand drainage in southern Afghanistan, where the excavations of J.-M. Casal in the 1950s provided an important cultural sequence (Mundigak I–VII). The first five of these periods form a succession of occupations from the 5th to the early 2nd millennium BC. By the Mundigak IV period (later 3rd millennium), the settlement had grown from a village to a town covering some 7 ha (17 acres) and containing a large colonnaded 'palace' building and other monumental structures within a walled citadel. At the same time (especially in Mundigak III–IV), the pottery and various small finds indicate increasing interaction with surrounding regions, including Turkmenistan (GEOKSJUR, NAMAZGA III), Baluchistan and the Early HARAPPAN Indus region. The later two periods (Mundigak VI–VII) belong to the Iron Age.

Mungo see LAKE MUNGO.

Munsell colour chart a widely used colour identification system with a standardized method of description and notation of colours of sediment, soil, chert, pottery and rock. The method facilitates communication of colours to those familiar with them but unable to see samples at first hand. It consists of an atlas of charts of colour chips which are numerically graduated scales with visual increments of hue, value and chroma. Components of value and chroma correspond to the perceptual attributes of lightness and saturation, respectively. *Hue* refers to the range of perceptions from red to blue, and back to red. *Value* refers to the degree of darkness or lightness of the colour. *Chroma* refers to brightness of the colour, or to the degree to which a colour differs from a grey of the same lightness.

Münsingen-Rain an Iron Age cemetery near Bern, Switzerland, of 170 flat graves dating from early LA TÈNE to the beginning of middle La Tène c.200 BC. Grave-goods include swords, spears, FIBULAE and in one instance a necklace of amber beads. Careful analysis of the grave-goods has allowed the individual burials to be placed in chronological order by SERIATION.

Munyama a Ugandan cave on Buvuma Island in Lake Victoria with an early backed microlith industry dating to c.15,000 BP.

mural tombs MOUNDED TOMBS of East Asia with painted frescoes on the walls of the interior stone chamber; particularly associated with KOGURYO but also occurring in China and Japan (see ANAK, TAKAMATSU-ZUKA). Koguryo murals can be divided into genre paintings, portraits and directional deities of the Chinese tradition.

Murciélagos, Cueva de los a Neolithic cave near Albuñol, Granada, southern Spain, which in the mid 19th century was found to contain about sixty naturally mummified human bodies, including twelve laid out in a semi-circle around a woman dressed in a leather tunic and a necklace of esparto grass from which hung seashells and a boar's tusk. The bodies were accompanied not only by lithic and bone tools, and ceramic fragments, but also some wooden tools and a quite exceptional collection of well-preserved baskets, bags, bowls, sandals and mats of woven esparto grass. Some of the baskets were decorated with dyed red and green geometric motifs. The esparto has yielded radiocarbon dates between 5200 and 4600 BC. Two of the bags contained blackish earth, while others held locks of hair, seashells or poppy seeds.

Mureybet an important late EPIPALAEOLITHIC (NATUFIAN) and PRE-POTTERY NEOLITHIC (to PPNB) settlement on the middle Euphrates excavated by Maurits van Loon and Jacques Cauvin. It is a key site for understanding the emergence of food production in northern Syria. The architectural sequence shows the transition from circular to rectilinear structures during the PPNA, during which time the community was heavily involved in morphologically wild cereals (especially einkorn) which were probably being cultivated. Together with ABU HUREYRA, Mureybet provides a detailed picture of the origins of food production and village life on the middle Euphrates between 8500 and 6800 BC.

Murray Black Collection a large collection of skeletal material collected between 1937 and 1950 by George Murray Black in the central Murray Valley, Australia. None of the material was properly excavated and thus lacked contextual data, though most was mid to late Holocene in date. It included the COOBOOL CREEK material. The collection has now been returned to Aboriginal communities in the Murray Valley for reburial.

murus gallicus a term used by Julius Caesar in his account of the Gallic Wars to describe the defences of the CELTIC OPPIDUM of Avaricum (Bourges). This was a timber-laced rampart, with heavy beams in the front face tied to similar beams in the rear face by cross-members and held in place by iron nails. The spaces between the beams were filled by regular courses of stone walling. Evidence of *murus gallicus* defences has been found at a number of late Celtic oppida.

Muryong an early 6th-century AD king of PAEKCHE, whose MOUNDED TOMB is near Kongu City, Korea. Chinese-style bricks bearing moulded decoration were used to construct the chamber, whose contents were intact upon excavation in 1971. They included a bronze chopstick and spoon set, precious toiletry goods, small glass sculptures and an inscribed plaque identifying the deceased.

Musang Cave a cave in northern Luzon, northern Philippines. Its early phase is represented by a flake industry dated c.12,000 to 9000 bc. Following a gap there is a Neolithic assemblage dated to c.3500 BC or later, with links to DIMOLIT and Arku Cave, and possible Taiwanese Neolithic connections.

Musawwarat es-Sufra a MEROITIC site in UPPER NUBIA, excavated by Hintze in 1960–70. A colonnaded temple is the central building in a complex of monumental stone structures, which also include large enclosures identified as elephant pens.

Muselievo a Palaeolithic open-air site on the Osm River near its confluence with the Danube in Bulgaria. The main cultural layer is buried in rubbly loess overlying a limestone promontory. The artifacts, which appear to have been partly redeposited, include bifacial foliates and sidescrapers; this layer may date to the early cold LAST GLACIAL MAXIMUM.

Musengezi a Late Iron Age tradition of northern Zimbabwe, which overlaps in time with the GREAT ZIMBABWE tradition, and is associated with radiocarbon dates from the end of the 13th–16th centuries ad. It is best known for burials in rock clefts and caves, such as the Monk's Kop site, which yielded about seventy skeletons buried sitting upright and wrapped in bark cloth and palm fibre matting, surrounded by clay pots.

Mushroom Rock a painted sandstone shelter near Laura, southeastern Cape York, Australia, with 4 m (13 ft) of deposit. The site was first occupied in the Late Pleistocene. The sequence falls into the two phases common in Australia, with the earlier AUSTRALIAN CORE TOOL AND SCRAPER TRADITION giving way to the AUSTRALIAN SMALL TOOL TRADITION. Ochre was found throughout the deposits.

Mutawintji an area of western New South Wales, Australia, which is rich in archaeological remains. There are many figurative and non-figurative engravings on rocky slopes and in shelters, as well as a wide range of stencils of body parts, natural objects and artifacts, including some European items, in shelters. Some of the engravings

MYCENAE, Greece: the Lion Gate.

are of PANARAMITEE type. There are also many surface camp-sites. Mutawintji was also a significant focus for Aboriginal ceremonial activity.

mutisalah literally 'false pearl', a kind of small opaque red glass bead found in late prehistoric and early historic sites in Southeast and East Asia. They were first made in southeastern India, and later in many parts of Southeast Asia such as KHUAN LUKPAD, Palembang and OC ÈO, and were traded as far north as Korea and Japan. Also referred to as a type of Indo-Pacific monochrome drawn glass bead, they remained in use as primitive valuables in eastern Indonesia, especially Timor and Flores.

mutule a projecting flat slab found under the CORNICE in CLASSICAL buildings of the DORIC ORDER.

Mwanganda an undated elephant butchery site in northern Malawi, comprising the bones of a single elephant together with numerous scrapers and a few core axes attributed to the LUPEMBAN industry. It is of interest because it apparently preserves a discrete episode of activity.

Mwitu another name for the Early Iron Age of eastern and southern Africa, also known as the CHIFUMBAZE complex, represented by sites with related pottery styles, dating to the 1st millennium AD.

Mwulu's a cave near Potgietersrus in the Northern Province, South Africa, which provided the type sample for the MIDDLE STONE AGE PIETERSBURG industry. This is succeeded by deposits containing the Middle Stone Age BAMBATA-like Mwulu industry.

Myanmar see ASIA, SOUTHEAST.

Mycenae the site, in the Argolid, Greece, of the first major MYCENAEAN excavations, initiated by SCHLIEMANN in 1876. He was followed by TSOUNTAS, WACE, MYLONAS and TAYLOUR. Mycenae appears to have been a relatively insignificant Middle HELLADIC site, but it rose to prominence at the end of the period when the two SHAFT GRAVE CIRCLES were built for the members of a royal family which must have controlled much of the northeastern Peloponnese. Subsequently the elite were buried in the nine THOLOS tombs which include the magnificent Treasury of Atreus. The citadel of Mycenae was first fortified in the 14th century BC, and the defences were strengthened in the 13th century when the Lion Gate was constructed. On the summit of the AKROPOLIS stood the palace of the ruler. Late in the 13th century Mycenae was devastated, possibly by an earthquake, and suffered a further destruction in the 12th century. Mycenae never recovered and emerges from the Dark Ages as a minor Argive town.

Mycenaean *adj.* relating to the civilization of Late Bronze Age Greece. The SHAFT GRAVE CIRCLES at MYCENAE constitute one of the earliest manifestations of the Mycenaean civilization, which originated in the Peloponnese in the 16th century BC and spread to central Greece and subsequently across the southern Aegean. In the 14th and 13th centuries palaces were built at Mycenae, PYLOS, THEBES and TIRYNS. Their role as administrative and economic centres is evident from the LINEAR B documents written by the palace scribes. The dead were splendidly buried in THOLOS tombs and CHAMBER TOMBS. A spate of destructions c.1200 BC apparently precipitated the decline and eventually the collapse of the civilization.

Mycerinus see MENKAURE.

Mylonas, George (1898–1988) a Greek archaeologist who excavated at Ayios Kosmas, ELEUSIS, MYCENAE and OLYNTHUS. He was Secretary-General of the Archaeological Society of Athens in 1979–88.

Myrina a city on the west coast of Turkey, where excavations in the cemeteries during the 19th century revealed hundreds of terracotta figurines, mainly HELLENISTIC in date.

Myrtos a site on the southern coast of Crete. An Early MINOAN settlement, occupied c.2600–2200 BC, was excavated on the hill of Fournou Korifi by Warren, and at Pyrgos Cadogan uncovered a Neopalatial country house, built c.1550 BC and destroyed by fire c.1450 BC.

Myrtou-Pigadhes the site of a Late Cypriot settlement and sanctuary in northern CYPRUS, excavated by du Plat Taylor in 1949–51. The sanctuary, which was built c.1400 BC and remained in use until c.1175 BC, contained a magnificent ASHLAR altar crowned by HORNS OF CONSECRATION.

Myshtulagty lagat a cave-site (also known as Weasel Cave) located in North Osetia in the northern-central Caucasus region (Russia) containing a deep sequence of rubble and loam deposits. Large mammal remains include deer, goat and cave bear. The lowest cultural layers date to the late Middle Pleistocene (c.200,000 BP) and yielded assemblages of Middle Palaeolithic artifacts, including denticulates, scrapers and LEVALLOIS blades. Overlying layers date to the last INTERGLACIAL, and contain a similar industry. Higher levels yielded Middle Palaeolithic assemblages without blades that date to the last GLACIAL. The uppermost levels contain Bronze Age, Iron Age and medieval artifacts. Myshtulagty lagat was discovered and excavated by Hidjrati in 1981–97.

N

Nabatake see ITAZUKE.

Nabonidus the last king of the NEO-BABYLONIAN empire (555–539 BC) and the last independent indigenous king of Babylonia. Nabonidus is notorious for his ten-year withdrawal from BABYLON to the city of TAYMA in northwestern Arabia, possibly because of a quarrel with the entrenched power of the MARDUK priesthood at Babylon. His neglect of affairs of state made CYRUS's conquest of Babylonia both easier and more welcomed by certain factions in Babylon.

Nabta Playa one of the largest playas in the Western Desert of Egypt. Two early Neolithic occupations of site E-75–6 are of particular interest. The lower of these dates to about 8800–8500 bp and is of the early Neolithic of El-Kortein type. The upper dates to about 8100 bp and is of the early Neolithic of El-Nabta type. Excavations of the latter have revealed a laid-out village of houses, hearths, storage pits and walk-in wells, which is interpreted as evidence for growing social control in these societies. Sorghum was an important food plant, but it is not clear whether it was gathered from the wild or under cultivation; previous reports of the presence of cultivated barley have not been confirmed. Remains tentatively described as domestic cattle dating to 8840 bp have been identified at site E-75–3, while cattle and small domestic livestock are found in middle and late Neolithic contexts in the playa.

Nachikufan Zambian LATER STONE AGE microlithic industries named after Nachikufu Cave in northern Zambia. These industries were originally regarded as a single local tradition, the 'Nachikufan industrial complex', which was divided into several phases, labelled I, IIA, IIB and III, but the supposed continuity of these is no longer upheld. The 'Nachikufan I' is now regarded as a more widespread industry dating to between c.20,000 and 12,000 BP, characterized by very small pointed backed bladelets and various scrapers, as well as relatively early examples of bored stones (see MATUPI). Later phases of the Nachikufan are more restricted geographically. The Nachikufan IIA and IIB are associated with radiocarbon

dates between c.9720 and 7200 BP and c.5630 and 4830 BP respectively, while the Nachikufan III is linked with dates in the final millennia of the Holocene.

naga long walled avenues divided by crosswalls into separate rectangular enclosures, found only in the central part of Viti Levu, Fiji. Similar structures, but without crosswalls, occur on Vanua Levu. They were associated with male initiation ceremonies.

Nagada see NAQADA.

NAGPRA (Native American Graves Protection and Repatriation Act) signed into law by President George Bush in 1990, this is one of the most important pieces of US government legislation concerning the treatment and ownership of antiquities. The law gives Native American tribes the right to reclaim (or repatriate) aboriginal human remains, associated grave-goods and certain other items such as sacred objects from museums, universities and other institutions that have received federal support. The law has fundamentally changed how archaeology is conducted in the USA, and has given Native Americans a much greater say in how their past is constructed and presented. See also INDIGENOUS ARCHAEOLOGY.

Nagyrév the initial culture in the tripartite sequence of the Hungarian Early Bronze Age defined by Moszolics on the basis of the stratigraphy at TÓSZEG, where the Nagyrév culture precedes the HATVAN and FÜZESABONY. In its earlier stages, Nagyrév shows connections with the VUČEDOL group (c.2500 BC), while later it reflects contemporaneity with ÚŇETICE (c.2000 BC). Nagyrév vessels are characterized by extremely high constricted necks.

Nahal Hemar a cave-site west of the southern end of the Dead Sea, Israel, which seems to have been used as a storage depot during PRE-POTTERY NEOLITHIC B (PPNB) times (7th millennium BC). The arid climate has preserved exceptional examples of articles made from linen, straw, wood and other organic materials. The cave also contained several skulls plastered with asphalt, a stone mask with painted stripes presumably used for rituals, and fragments of clay statues of the type found at 'AIN GHAZAL.

Nahal Mishmar a Palestinian site discovered in 1960. It consists of a cave containing a cache of 630 CHALCO-LITHIC copper objects of the GHASSULIAN culture, with incised and solid decorative elements, including 240 mace-heads, eighty 'sceptres' and ten crowns.

Nahal Oren a site on the western slope of MOUNT CARMEL, Israel, excavated by Stekelis in 1941 and 1954–60, and by Noy and HIGGS in 1969–71. The stratified deposits revealed occupation from KEBARAN to early PRE-POTTERY NEOLITHIC A (PPNA) times. The PPNA settlement consisted of many circular stone structures set along the *wadi* terraces, and contained a rich material culture of chipped stone, ground stone tools, bone tools, stone vessels and some art objects. The NATUFIAN settlement also contained circular stone structures, and an important group of thirty-six burials. The Kebaran levels (16,300–13,850 BC) are less well known.

Nahua a group of tribes in central Mexico, originally from the north, the last and best-known of which were the AZTECS.

Nahuatl a Uto-Aztecan language. Groups speaking Nahuatl migrated into MESOAMERICA from its northern frontier, GRAN CHICHIMEC. The name Nahuatl is commonly used for the language of the AZTECS.

naiskos a small Greek temple or shrine.

Naj Tunich a cave in southeastern Guatemala where 8th-century AD MAYA cave art was discovered in 1980. It comprises almost 100 paintings and a few PETROGLYPHS, mostly HIEROGLYPHIC texts and human figures. Many of the major paintings were vandalized in 1989.

Nakamine a Palaeolithic site in Miyagi Prefecture, Japan, which has yielded stone tools sandwiched between layers dated to 150,000 and 300,000 bp. These argue for Early Palaeolithic occupation of the Japanese islands.

Nakbe a MAYA urban centre in northern Guatemala, 13 km (8 miles) from EL MIRADOR, to which it was joined by a causeway. The site, whose name means 'by the road' in Yucatec Maya, was seen from the air in 1930, but first visited in 1962 by Ian Graham. It comprises two main clusters of platforms and mounds, including a pyramid 50 m (164 ft) high. Occupied between c.3000 and 1000 BP, Nakbe was a major centre only in the middle PRECLASSIC (c.3000–2300 BP) when maize and squash were already being grown here. It may have been eclipsed by the rise of El Mirador, and was abandoned for a millennium until reoccupied in the late CLASSIC by small communities.

Nakhon Pathom a very large (3.7 by 2 km [2.3 by 1.2 miles]) protohistoric and early historic settlement in the lower Chao Phraya Valley, central Thailand, which is thought to have been the capital of the state of DVARA-VATI for a time. The first three phases of the Phra Pathom CHEDI may date to this period and earlier. The rectangular moat may have been added during the period of KHMER power, after c.AD 1000.

Nakhon Si Thammarat a city on the east coast of peninsular Thailand, known as Ligor to early colonial traders. The pre-modern phases of its occupation are represented by three sites: Muang Nakhon Si Thammarat, of the 15th–18th centuries AD; Muang Phra Wieng, a moated settlement and Buddhist centre, probably the capital of TAM-BRALINGA; and the c.8th–15th-century site Ban Tha Rua, apparently the port associated with the capital.

Nama see KHOEKHOEN.

Namazga-depe a site in Turkmenia on the north slope of the Kopet Dagh, where excavations by B. A. Kuftin and I. N. Khlopin in the 1950s to 1970s produced the standard chronological framework for the CHALCO-LITHIC and Bronze Age of western-Central Asia. This sequence contains six phases, numbered Namazga I (earliest) to VI (latest), which span the ENEOLITHIC (i.e. Chalcolithic; NMZ I–III, c.4800–3000 BC) and Bronze Age (NMZ IV–VI, c.3000–1500 BC); the sequence thus covers the time from the ANAU IA Neolithic culture to the beginning of the Iron Age (Yaz I, see YAZ-DEPE). The site of Namazga-depe itself grew from the size of a small town (about 15 ha [37 acres]) in its early occupation to that of a small city (about 50 ha [124 acres]) during the Namazga IV–V times (most of the 3rd millennium), before collapsing in its final 'tower' phase (about 2 ha [5 acres]) in the late 3rd/early 2nd millennium BC.

Nämforsen see SCANDINAVIA.

NAN languages see PAPUAN LANGUAGES.

Nana Mode a 7th-century AD Iron Age site in the Central African Republic, containing pottery decorated with a carved wooden roulette.

Nan Madol a town and ceremonial centre on Ponape in the Caroline Islands, MICRONESIA. Built in a tidal lagoon, it covers about 70 ha (173 acres) and comprises ninety-two artificial rectilinear platforms built of coral rubble with basalt facings, surrounded by channels. The complex is protected by two breakwaters. It is divided into two sections: the southern part was mainly for houses of the nobility and public and ceremonial activities; while the northern part was for priests' houses, and includes the chiefly burial enclosure of Nan Douwas. The complex was never finished and is assumed to have been built within the last few centuries at a time when the CHIEF-DOMS of Ponape were unified under a single dynasty.

Nanna the SUMERIAN god, equivalent to the AKKADIAN god Sin, who was the oldest son of ENLIL, and was

connected to the moon and to fertility; his principal city
was UR.

naos **1** a shrine, usually monolithic, within which the
image of an Egyptian deity was housed. The largest naoi
are those where a temple's main cult-statue was kept, in
the sanctuary.

2 a Greek temple which may be placed within a TE-
MENOS. See, for example, PARTHENON.

Napata a district in UPPER NUBIA, including the sites of
KURRU, GEBEL BARKAL, NURI and Sanam. Napata was
the seat of a kingdom (called KUSH by the Egyptians) to
which it gives its name, which flourished between the
late 9th and early 3rd centuries BC.

Naqada a site in UPPER EGYPT, where PETRIE and Quibell's 1894 excavations produced the first substantial evidence of the Neolithic in Egypt and provided the basic
framework for the PREDYNASTIC sequence of Upper
Egypt. See AMRATIAN and GERZEAN.

Nara see JAPANESE PERIODIZATION, HEIJO.

Naram-sin the grandson of SARGON and the last great
ruler of the AKKADIAN empire, who, conventionally in
2254–2218 BC, managed to sustain his grandfather's conquests, putting down a series of rebellions, and campaigned against foreign enemies in Syria and to the east.
The Akkadian empire began to fall apart under the rule
of his son Sharkalishari. Even so, Naram-sin became identified with this collapse in CUNEIFORM literature: in the
poem 'Curse of Akkad', Naram-sin takes the part of the
unjust king whose impious acts invite divine retaliation
in the form of invasion and disaster. Just as Sargon provided the positive paradigm of kingship, so Naram-sin
supplied the negative.

Nariokotome a locality on the western side of LAKE
TURKANA, Kenya, where a virtually complete skeleton
of an adolescent boy, equivalent in age to a modern
eleven-year-old, dating to between 1.56 and 1.51 million
years ago, was found at site N3 in 1984–8. Only the feet
and a few other pieces are missing, a rare occurrence in
skeletons of this period. It is thought he could have died
from septicaemia caused by gum disease and that his
remains fell into or were washed into a marsh before
being covered rapidly by mud and volcanic ash. Also
known as the 'Turkana Boy' or by the catalogue number,
KNM-WT 15000, he had long limbs and would have been
about 1.82 m (6 ft 1 inch) tall had he survived to maturity,
indicating that early humans reached their present
height by 1.5 million years ago. Although the skeleton
looks remarkably modern in many respects, its brain
capacity is estimated at only 900 cc (55 cu. inches), about
two-thirds that of modern humans, which implies considerable behavioural differences in comparison with
people today. Originally described as HOMO *erectus*, the
skeleton is now widely assigned to *H. ergaster*.

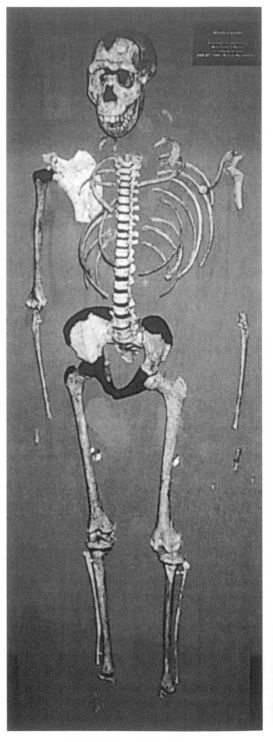

NARIOKOTOME skeleton, Kenya.

Narmer an Egyptian king, ruling in UPPER EGYPT in the late PREDYNASTIC period, and possibly to be equated with the legendary King Menes, who united Egypt at the beginning of the ARCHAIC PERIOD. Narmer is best known from the 'Main Deposit' of ritual objects at HIERAKONPOLIS.

Narosura an important southern Kenyan PASTORAL NEOLITHIC site covering at least 8,000 sq. m (9,600 sq. yds), dating to between the 9th and 5th centuries BC. The stone industry is characterized by obsidian geometric backed microliths and burins, as well as ground stone axes and stone bowls. The abundant pottery, decorated with incisions and comb-stamping, is frequently burnished and is known as Narosura ware. Most of the animal bones represent domestic stock, but there is no evidence for cultivated crops.

Narva culture a Neolithic culture of the eastern Baltic littoral, in the 5th, 4th and 3rd millennia BC, occurring in Lithuania, Latvia, Estonia and portions of Poland and Belarus. At two key sites, Osa and Narva-town, Narva assemblages occur deposited over those of the Mesolithic KUNDA culture. Many artifact categories show continuity from Kunda to Narva, with the addition of pottery in the form of pointed-base pots with straight or S-profiles and oval bowls. Other important sites include SARNATE in Latvia and SVENTOJI in Lithuania.

Nasampolai a blade-based LATER STONE AGE industry dominated by very large backed blades, several of which have traces of red ochre placed to suggest they were hafted, as well as geometric microliths, thought to pre-date 40,000 bp at the Kenyan site of ENKAPUNE YA MUTO.

Nasca or **Nazca** the major culture of the south coast

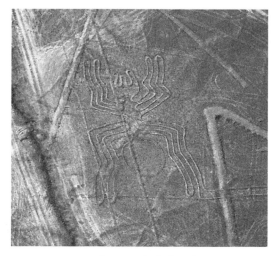

NASCA, Peru: geoglyph of a spider.

of Peru during the EARLY INTERMEDIATE PERIOD. An outgrowth of the earlier PARACAS culture, Nasca ceramics are painted in up to sixteen colours, depicting plants, animals, humans, supernatural creatures and elaborate geometric designs. Stylistically the ceramics have been divided into nine phases, the first of which is an extension of terminal Paracas culture. During phases 2–4 (c.ad 200–500), which can be termed Early Nasca times, ceramics were depicted with fairly realistic designs. CAHUACHI served as the central ceremonial focus of the culture, and construction of the site continued through most of this period. There is little evidence of complex political organization at this time, and people lived in small villages adjacent to arable land. The dead were buried in large cemeteries, many of them located near Cahuachi.

In Nasca phase 5, a transitional phase, new design elements were added to ceramic designs, and designs were increasingly abstract. New constructions at Cahuachi had ceased, and a system of horizontal wells, PUQUIOS, may have been established. New settlements were established in previously unoccupied portions of the valleys. In phases 6 and 7 (c.ad 600–750), Late Nasca times, ceramic designs became extremely abstract and complex, and warriors were depicted with increasing frequency. Most small villages were abandoned, and population aggregated into large settlements, some of them in defensible locations. The dead continued to be buried in cemeteries near Cahuachi, suggesting that the site continued to serve as a ceremonial centre, but no new constructions were made there. Nasca came under the control of the HUARI empire in the MIDDLE HORIZON; Nasca 8 ceramics are a local style, while what has been called the Nasca 9 style is a style introduced by Huari.

Nasca lines or **geoglyphs** straight lines, geometric shapes and representational designs found on the desert plain in the NASCA region of the south coast of Peru. The lines were created by clearing the surface of the ground of small red-brown stones, exposing the lighter coloured soil beneath. Many of the straight lines radiate outwards from points located at small hills or the end of low ridges, suggesting a largely ceremonial function. Various living forms are depicted as well, including birds, whales, a monkey, a spider, an anthropomorphous owl and others. The figures are mostly concentrated along one edge of the plain, and some are stylistically similar to designs painted on Early Nasca ceramics (c.ad 100–500).

The straight lines have a much wider geographic distribution, and seem to date not only to the EARLY INTERMEDIATE PERIOD, but also to earlier and later periods. Known to outsiders since at least the early 19th century, the lines were first scientifically recorded by Alfred KROEBER in 1926. Paul Kosok saw them in 1941, and was able to interest one of his students, Maria REICHE, in studying them; she devoted the rest of her life to this work. She believed that the figures represent constellations, and that many straight lines have astronomical significance. Other researchers have suggested that the lines were ceremonial pathways, and may have pointed towards sacred places, especially mountains. See also CEQUE.

Nasera an impressive boulder-hill in northern Tanzania, originally excavated in 1932 by L. S. B. LEAKEY, who called it Apis Rock. It contains a 9 m (20 ft) deep deposit of MIDDLE and LATER STONE AGE remains. Of particular interest are stone artifact collections which appear to document the transition from the Middle to the Later Stone Age in the period between 30,000 and 20,000 bp, apparently later than suggested from other East African sites (see ENKAPUNE YA MUTO, MATUPI, MUMBA-HÖHLE). The Middle/Later Stone Age Nasera industry at this site is associated with radiocarbon dates between 26,000 and 18,500 bp, while the overlying Later Stone Age Lemuta industry is associated with radiocarbon dates between 21,600 and 14,800 bp.

Native American Graves Protection and Repatriation Act see NAGPRA.

Native Americans the past and contemporary aboriginal inhabitants of North America. The term is used to differentiate these peoples from North Americans of European or other descent.

Natufian the terminal EPIPALAEOLITHIC culture complex of the Levant, dated to c.12,500–10,000 BP, and named after the site of Wadi en-Natuf in Palestine. Natufian assemblages contain geometric microliths, bone artifacts such as points, spearheads and fish-hooks, and tools such as flint sickle-blades, pestles and mortars, which indicate the harvesting of cereals. As yet there is no clear evidence of the deliberate sowing of crops, and faunal remains suggest that the Natufian people were primarily settled or semi-settled hunters with relatively elaborate burial rituals. A number of large settlements contain substantial permanent architecture, food storage facilities, a large amount of fixed and portable grain-pounding and -grinding equipment, and cemeteries, which indicate differential wealth and status within communities. Initially confined to a central Levantine core area, Natufian groups later appear in the middle Euphrates Valley, southern Jordan and the Negev. They were the first settled occupants of JERICHO. See also EYNAN, MOUNT CARMEL.

natural levee a depositional landform consisting of low linear ridges adjacent to and paralleling either side of ALLUVIAL channels. Natural levees form as channels overflow their banks; flow velocity and depth of flood waters decrease immediately outside channel boundaries, depositing the coarser material of the suspended load adjacent to the channel. Repeated overbank flooding leads to levee growth. Natural levees in alluvial valleys are slightly better-drained landscape positions than other floodplain landforms, and archaeological material is often on and buried within them, reflecting their utilization.

Naucratis a Greek trading settlement in the Nile Delta, Egypt, excavated by PETRIE and others. The finds are dominated by Greek fine pottery. Many of the sherds are inscribed with the names of Greek deities and they seem to have been dedicated in the sanctuaries. The earliest pottery from the site is Transitional CORINTHIAN POTTERY which is traditionally dated to c.630–620 BC.

Nauwalabila a painted sandstone shelter in ARNHEM LAND, northern Australia, with nearly 3 m (7 ft) of deposit, going back more than 20,000 years. The lowest levels contain artifacts typical of the AUSTRALIAN CORE TOOL AND SCRAPER TRADITION. This is succeeded by an amorphous industry of scrapers and utilized flakes. Elements of the AUSTRALIAN SMALL TOOL TRADITION such as points begin to appear from about 6000 bp. The earliest edge-ground tools date to about 14,000 bp. Claims based on OSL dating of a maximum age of up to 59,000 for the oldest cultural levels remain controversial. See also MALAKUNANJA.

Navan an Iron Age enclosure and royal residence in Co. Armagh, Ireland. Earliest remains are of a round house with associated stockade occupied from 700 to 100 BC; the skull of a Barbary ape from North Africa indicates the special nature of this first Navan settlement. In c.100 BC the site was transformed by the construction of a massive circular timber building, 43 m (47 yds) across, standing within a great circular banked and ditched enclosure. The timber building was later burned down and covered by a monumental cairn. Iron Age Navan is identified with the historical Emhain Macha, royal seat of the Ulaid, the pre-Christian kings of Ulster.

Navdatoli an important site on the Narmada River in western Madhya Pradesh in western-central India. Sankalia's investigation of Navdatoli together with Maheshwar on the opposite bank of the river provides evidence of Lower and Middle Palaeolithic, CHALCO-LITHIC, Iron Age and medieval occupations. The Chalcolithic occupation, dated to the 2nd millennium BC, presents four phases distinguished by changes in the pottery: a painted black-and-red ware and a black-painted cream-slipped ware occur in the first phase, while JORWE ware appears in the third and fourth phases; the painted MALWA ware occurs throughout this sequence. In all these levels the architecture consists of rectilinear or circular huts of bamboo and daub. The Chalcolithic levels present important information on subsistence in this part of India during the 2nd millennium BC (a focus on wheats and a wide variety of legumes, with addition of rice in the second phase). After a flood deposit, this occupation is followed by several periods belonging to the late 1st millennium BC and early 1st millennium AD, during which architecture shifts from single room dwellings in smaller settlements to monumental architecture and towns, correlated with the ceramic sequence NORTHERN BLACK POLISHED to RED POLISHED wares.

naveta (*Lat.* 'little boat') a stone-built CHAMBERED TOMB shaped like an upturned boat with rounded prow and squared stern. Navetas are found on the Balearic Islands and date from the later Bronze Age (*c.*1500–800 BC). See also ELS TUDONS.

Naville, Henri Edouard (1844–1926) a Swiss Egyptologist who excavated at ABYDOS, DEIR EL-BAHRI, and in the DELTA (e.g. BUBASTIS).

Nazca see NASCA.

Nderit ware formerly **Gumban A** one of several distinct pottery wares associated with PASTORAL NEOLITHIC sites in Kenya and northern Tanzania, but not well defined chronologically or spatially. It is characterized by wedge-shaped impressions over large areas of the pot's surface, and often has deep scoring inside the pot. Now subsumed within the OLMALENGE tradition.

Ndondondwane an important mid 8th-century AD Early Iron Age village in the Thukela River Valley of central KwaZulu-Natal Province, South Africa. Of particular interest are the remains of structures interpreted as stockades, nearly 2,000 fragments of waste from the manufacture of ivory bangles, and pieces of large ceramic sculpture. These include large eyes, horns and crocodile-like jaws on a scale larger than the LYDENBURG heads. Also of interest is the earliest date for domestic chicken in southern Africa as well as the remains of the black rat, domestic dog, goats and sheep.

Ndutu a lake in northern Tanzania where a fragmentary human skull, variously assigned to early archaic HOMO *sapiens* or *H. heidelbergensis*, thought to date between about 400,000 and 200,000 bp, was found.

Neanderthal(er)s or **Neandertal(er)s** an archaic form of humans that inhabited Europe, Central Asia, and the Near East during the Late Pleistocene. They are generally classified as a separate species of HOMO (*H. neanderthalensis*), and are named after the river valley in Germany where their first widely recognized remains were discovered in 1856. The earliest Neanderthal remains are found in western Europe at Biache (France) and EHRINGSDORF (Germany) and date to the late Middle Pleistocene (roughly 200,000 BP). The most recent remains have been dated by radiocarbon to *c.*30,000 BP at Zafarraya (Spain) and VINDIJA CAVE (Croatia). The Neanderthals are widely believed to have been replaced by modern humans (*H. sapiens*) between 40,000 and 30,000 BP, but may have interbred with the latter in some areas.

Neanderthals evolved a highly characteristic skeletal morphology that includes a low and receding frontal bone with large browridge and long braincase with high cranial volume (averaging over 1,500 cc [230 cu. inches]). Their faces exhibit pronounced forward projection (prognathism), an enlarged nasal cavity and inflated cheeks. Their jaws usually lack a chin, and display a gap between the last molar and ascending ramus (retromolar space). Their front teeth were relatively large, and typically exhibit heavy wear, apparently reflecting routine use for gripping objects and materials. The post-cranial skeleton is characterized by a broad, thick chest and relatively short distal limb segments, which are thought to reflect adaptation to cold climates. The post-cranial bones are thick and exhibit large muscle attachments, indicating a very robust and powerful frame.

The Neanderthals inhabited caves and rockshelters in Europe and the Near East, and they also occupied open-air sites (especially in eastern Europe). They are closely associated with the MOUSTERIAN stone tool industry (Middle Palaeolithic), which entailed production of a variety of flake tools (including scrapers, points, and bifaces) from LEVALLOIS and other types of cores. There is little evidence for production of bone, antler or ivory implements, although USEWEAR ANALYSIS of Mousterian tools reveals heavy working of wood and animal hide. There are also few traces of ornament or art in their sites, but substantial evidence of burial of the dead. Some burials contain flexed skeletons and may contain grave goods, although the latter are controversial. Neanderthal sites often contain large quantities of large mammal remains, and many of these reflect evidence of hunting, although some believe that they may have depended more heavily on scavenging than modern humans.

Nea Nikomedeia or **Nea Nikomidhia** a site in Macedonia which was excavated by Rodden in 1961–4 and proved to be one of the earliest Neolithic sites in Greece, occupied in the early Neolithic period only. A large structure in the centre of the mound contained a number of female figurines and is thought to have served a ritual purpose.

Near East This area is defined as the region of Southwest Asia from Iran to the Mediterranean coast in which numerous ancient civilizations rose and flourished. The Near East encompasses several broad subregions distinguished by environmental characteristics: the Iranian Plateau, southern and northern MESOPOTAMIA, northern Syria, southern Levant, Anatolia and Arabia.

The region was the bridge across which HOMO *erectus* moved out of Africa to colonize Asia and Europe, leaving their traces at sites like UBEIDIYEH and DMANISI well over 1 million years ago. Middle Palaeolithic sites, some accompanied by NEANDERTHAL remains (SHANIDAR, MOUNT CARMEL Caves), are common. Several sites in the Levant (notably the Mount Carmel Caves) provide

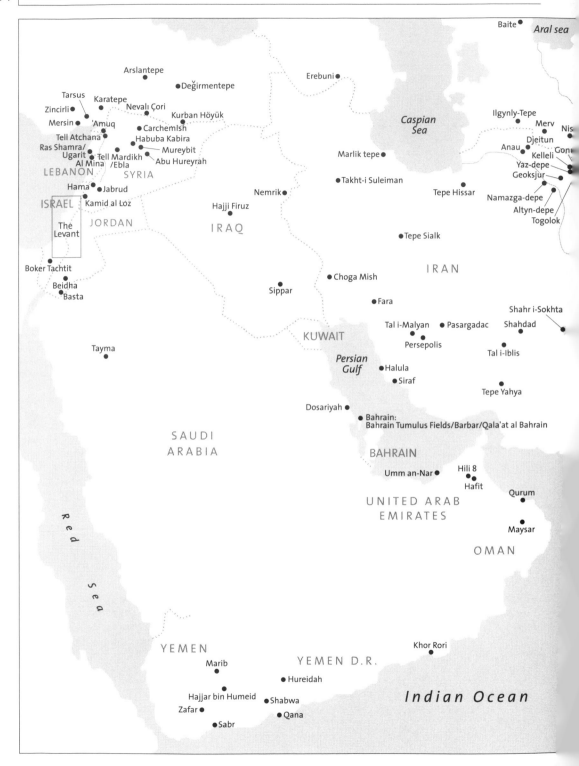

Baite

Aral sea

Arslantepe

Erebuni

Değirmentepe

Tarsus
Zincirli
Karatepe
Nevalı Çori
Kurban Höyük
Mersin
'Amuq
Carchemish
Tell Atchana
Habuba Kabira
Ras Shamra/
Ugarit
Mureybit
Al Mina
Tell Mardikh
/Ebla
Abu Hureyrah

*Caspian
Sea*

Ilgynly-Tepe
Merv
Nis
Djeitun
Anau
Gon
Kelleli
Marlik tepe
Yaz-depe
Geoksjur
Namazga-depe
Altyn-depe
Togolok

LEBANON
SYRIA

Hama
Jabrud
ISRAEL
Kamid al Loz
The
Levant

JORDAN

Nemrik

Takht-i Suleiman

Tepe Hissar

Hajji Firuz

IRAQ

Tepe Sialk

IRAN

Boker Tachtit
Beidha
Basta

Sippar

Choga Mish

Fara

KUWAIT

Tal i-Malyan
Pasargadac
Shahdad
Persepolis
Shahr i-Sokhta
Tal i-Iblis

Tayma

*Persian
Gulf*

Halula
Siraf

Tepe Yahya

Dosariyah

Bahrain:
Bahrain Tumulus Fields/Barbar/Qala'at al Bahrain

SAUDI
ARABIA

BAHRAIN

Umm an-Nar
Hili 8
Hafit

Qurum

UNITED ARAB
EMIRATES

Maysar

OMAN

R
e
d

S
e
a

Khor Rori

YEMEN

Marib

YEMEN D.R.

Hureidah

Hajjar bin Humeid
Shabwa
Zafar
Qana
Sabr

Indian Ocean

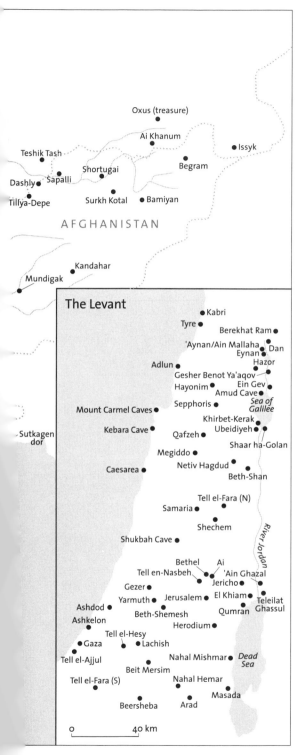

Oxus (treasure)

Ai Khanum

Teshik Tash

Issyk

Shortugai

Begram

Dashly Sapalli

Tillya-Depe

Surkh Kotal ● Bamiyan

AFGHANISTAN

Kandahar

Mundigak

Sutkagen dor

The Levant

Kabri

Tyre

Berekhat Ram

'Aynan/Ain Mallaha Dan
Eynan
Hazor

Adlun

Gesher Benot Ya'aqov

Hayonim Ein Gev
Amud Cave

Sepphoris Sea of
Galilee

Mount Carmel Caves

Khirbet-Kerak

Kebara Cave Ubeidiyeh
Qafzeh

Shaar ha-Golan

Megiddo

Netiv Hagdud

Caesarea Beth-Shan

Tell el-Fara (N)

Samaria

Shechem

Shukbah Cave

River Jordan

Bethel Ai

Tell en-Nasbeh 'Ain Ghazal
Jericho

Gezer

Yarmuth El Khiam
Jerusalem Teleilat
Beth-Shemesh Qumran Ghassul

Ashdod

Ashkelon Herodium

Tell el-Hesy

Gaza Lachish

Tell el-Ajjul

Nahal Mishmar Dead
Beit Mersim Sea

Tell el-Fara (S) Nahal Hemar

Masada

Beersheba Arad

0   40 km

important skeletal remains of early anatomically modern *H. sapiens*.

The Near East was the setting for the earliest known emergence of food production. NATUFIAN hamlets appeared around 12,000 bp in the southern Levant, and other groups settled down in uplands to the north soon after (e.g. HALLAN ÇEMI), subsisting on abundant wild foods but manipulating some plants and animals in ways that led to the domestication of cereals and legumes by 10,000 bp in the Levant and, shortly after, that of sheep, goat, pig and cattle in Anatolia. This new economy supported farming villages and small towns of ACERAMIC NEOLITHIC cultures in the Levant, Anatolia, northern Mesopotamia, and western Iran (see JERICHO, AIN GHAZAL, ABU HUREYRA, ÇAYÖNÜ, AŞIKLI, ZAWI CHEMI SHANIDAR, ALI KOSH, GANJ DAREH). Although these cultures presented significant regional differences in material culture, exchange of obsidian and other goods over long distances provided linkages between them. By 6000–5500 BC farming villages based on a common suite of plants and animals were common across the Near East, partially excepting Arabia (see MESOPOTAMIA, SHULAVERI-SHOMU, DJEITUN, MEHRGAHR).

The URUK period (3800–3100 BC) saw the appearance of cities and complex societies in southern Mesopotamia; the PROTO-ELAMITE phenomenon marked a related development at SUSA and MALYAN. Town life was not widespread elsewhere until around 2600 BC, when it emerged not only in northern Mesopotamia and northern Syria (e.g. EBLA) but also on the Iranian Plateau (e.g. Malyan, SHAHR I-SOKHTA), Central Asia (e.g. NAMAZGA, ALTYN, MUNDIGAK) and the HARAPPAN region. In central Anatolia the rich graves at ALACA also represent a movement towards complex societies. These regions were in contact with each other during the 3rd millennium BC, exchanging valuable materials like LAPIS LAZULI and finished goods like INTERCULTURAL STYLE carved stone vessels (also see PERSIAN GULF TRADE); Mesopotamian imperialism affected political contacts (AKKADIANS, UR III). The southern Levant followed a separate trajectory, with well-developed settlement (e.g. GHASSUL) and important metallurgical advances (MISHMAR). Egyptian contacts, perhaps colonization, were strong during the EARLY BRONZE AGE I (3500–3100 BC), followed by the emergence of walled towns of the Early Bronze Age II–III (3100–2300 BC). The KHIRBET KERAK aspect of this period reflects movement of peoples into the Levant from Transcaucasia.

Town life weakened in many areas late in the 3rd millennium, when important shifts of ethno-linguistic populations occurred, notably of AMORITES and HURRIANS, who both seized political power in Mesopotamia. Elements of the Central Asian BMAC appearing on the Iranian Plateau and the fringes of Pakistan (SHAHDAD) may represent INDO-EUROPEAN movements.

City life strengthened again during the MIDDLE

BRONZE AGE (2000–1600 BC) in the Levant (CANAAN-ITES), Anatolia (KANESH, BOĞAZKÖY), Syria and northern Mesopotamia (Ebla, MARI, LEILAN) and western Iran (Susa, Malyan). HAMMURABI'S BABYLON is the best known of the Mesopotamian kingdoms in this period. The OLD ASSYRIAN KĀRUM trading colonies were but one of the interlinking trading systems of the time (see Persian Gulf trade). The LATE BRONZE AGE (c.1600–1200 BC) witnessed imperial rivalries: Egypt, MITANNI, HITTITES and ASSYRIA struggling over Syria. An interregional upheaval, involving the SEA PEOPLES, brought the Bronze Age to a close.

In the immediate aftermath of this catastrophe (early Iron Age, 1200–1000 BC), the NEO-HITTITES retained control of cities like CARCHEMISH and HALAF, and the PHOENICIANS prolonged the Canaanite culture, but new peoples emerged in many places (PHILISTINES and ISRAELITES in the southern Levant, ARAMAEANS in Syria, PHRYGIANS in Anatolia). BABYLONIA experienced a decline, but beginning in the late 10th century BC the ASSYRIANS extended their grasp over a large portion of the Near East, creating an empire that reached its pinnacle in the early 7th century BC, when it included both ELAM and Egypt; URARTU to the northeast successfully resisted. In central Asia the YAZ culture re-established town life.

The NEO-BABYLONIAN empire (612–539 BC) replaced the Assyrians, soon followed by the Achaemenid PERSIAN empire (550–330 BC); the latter stretched from central Asia to Thrace and Egypt. The invasion of Alexander's Macedonians supplanted Persian with Greek dominion, the SELEUCID dynasty ruling Asian territories (see AI KHANUM). The PARTHIANS (150 BC–AD 220) and then SASSANIANS (AD 220–640) governed large Asian empires, battling ROME for control of western Mesopotamia. The Moslem conquests of the 7th century AD then placed the Near East within an even wider political world.

nearest-neighbour analysis a method of determining the extent to which two-dimensionally located points are randomly distributed. The technique has been especially useful to archaeologists studying the distribution of sites over the landscape and their relationship to each other.

Nebuchadnezzar II (604–562 BC) the great royal figure of the NEO-BABYLONIAN empire, well known from the biblical accounts of his activities in Judaea and Samaria. At the beginning of his rule, Babylonia controlled much of MESOPOTAMIA proper, but was under pressure from a resurgent Egypt and its allies in Palestine. Nebuchadnezzar defeated the Egyptians and, famously, conquered the petty states of the Levant, including JERUSALEM, many of whose inhabitants were deported to BABYLON. Most of the monumental buildings at Babylon are his work. The Neo-Babylonian empire did not long survive his death. See also NABONIDUS.

Neckenmarkt see LINEAR POTTERY.

Necker Island a small barren island off the Hawaiian chain; despite being uninhabited at European contact, it is rich in remains of houses, cultivation terraces and thirty-three HEIAU of an unusual and standardized form. It is not known whether these result from occasional visits from the main Hawaiian islands or a resident population.

necropolis a cemetery, literally a 'city of the dead'.

Nefertiti an Egyptian queen, the chief wife of AKHENATEN. Nefertiti seems to have played a more prominent role in public life than was usual among consorts of Egyptian kings, and is identified by some scholars with the monarch named Smenkhkare, who briefly succeeded Akhenaten.

Nelson, Nels (1875–1964) an American archaeologist who worked in both California and the American Southwest. He is famous for his substantial contribution to the archaeological interpretation of stratigraphy in his work in the Galisteo Basin of New Mexico, especially at the site of San Cristobal Pueblo. He was influenced in this by his earlier excavations of California SHELL MOUNDS, under the direction of Alfred KROEBER and Max UHLE, as well as by innovations in the excavation of various European Palaeolithic sites.

Nelson Bay a coastal cave, containing a 6 m (20 ft) deep deposit, on the Robberg Peninsula in the southeastern Western Cape Province, South Africa. A sterile deposit separates basal MIDDLE STONE AGE material from the upper layers, which contain successive LATER STONE AGE ROBBERG, ALBANY, WILTON and post-Wilton industries. The faunal remains document habitat changes caused by sea-level rise and vegetation changes at the end of the Pleistocene.

Nemi the site of a grove of Diana in the Alban Hills just outside ROME. In 1929 remains of two ships were found in the lake, perhaps those used by the emperor Caligula. These were subsequently destroyed during fighting in the Second World War.

Nemrik a multi-phase 2 ha (5 acre) early Neolithic site near the Tigris River, north of Mosul in Iraq. A Polish team excavating during the 1980s uncovered semi-subterranean houses with mud-brick walls and interior pillar bases to support a roof. The settlement dates to the 8th and into the 7th millennium bc, with domesticated plants and animals appearing only towards the end of the occupation.

Nenana complex a prehistoric culture or complex in southern-central Alaska dating to c.12,000–10,500 bp, characterized by small bifacial projectile points (including CHINDADN POINTS) and a lack of microblade technology. It represents the earliest firmly dated set of archaeological remains in Alaska. The complex was defined by Powers and Hoffecker in 1989.

Nene Valley ware a type of Roman pottery, formerly known as Castor ware, produced near Peterborough in England from the 2nd to the 4th centuries AD. The different shapes, which include tumblers, were decorated with a dark SLIP and had added decoration in white; some show elaborate hunting scenes.

Nenumbo a LAPITA site dating to c.3000 bp in the Main Reef Islands, Santa Cruz group. Excavations by Roger Green identified several structures including a substantial rectangular wooden building, several other smaller less permanent structures, earth ovens and storage pits, and a possible fence. Faunal remains include pig, chicken, fish, dugong and sea turtle. Artifacts include shell ornaments and obsidian, mainly from TALASEA. The Lapita pottery shows a particularly wide range of motifs.

Neo-Assyrian the famous political period of the Assyrian empire in the Iron Age. It was basically an extension of the MIDDLE ASSYRIAN patterns of empire building. After the troubles that produced the collapse of the earlier Assyrian empires, the next expansionary episode belonged to the 9th century BC, identified with AŠŠURNA-ṢIRPAL II (883–859 BC) and his immediate successors. This empire was not long lived, as the question of succession to the throne again weakened the Assyrian expansionary impulse. The intervening period of military mediocrity lasted until the reign of TIGLATH-PILESER III (744–727 BC), who began the creation of the famous Assyrian empire that is reflected in the Old Testament, and among whose rulers are the well-known Sargon (721–705 BC), Sennacherib (704–681 BC), Esarhaddon (680–669 BC) and Assurbanipal (668–627 BC). The Assyrian empire, which at its largest extent stretched from ELAM to Egypt, was destroyed by an alliance of BABYLONIANS and MEDES in 612 BC.

Neo-Babylonian period a long period of political weakness, social disruption (see ARAMAEANS, CHALDEANS) and economic decline through the first part of the 1st millennium BC culminating in the absorption of BABYLONIA into the NEO-ASSYRIAN empire (by 688 BC). After several unsuccessful attempts, a rebellion in the 620s managed to evict the Assyrians, and Nabopolassar (625–605 BC) took the throne of Babylonia. In alliance with the MEDES, Nabopolassar managed to destroy the Assyrian state (between 616 and 612 BC), and the Babylonians occupied much of northern MESOPOTAMIA and Syria. This empire was consolidated by NEBUCHADNEZZAR II but lasted only until 539 BC, when the Persian CYRUS invaded and occupied Babylon.

Neolithic a term introduced by Sir John LUBBOCK in 1865 to describe the period of antiquity in which people began to use ground stone tools, cultivate plants and keep domestic livestock (in contrast to the Palaeolithic), yet still used stone instead of metals for tools. In a number of parts of the world, such as western Europe, the appearance of pottery was also added as a hallmark of the Neolithic. The dating of the Neolithic is quite variable, beginning in the Near East in the 9th millennium BC and lasting into the 2nd millennium BC in the more northerly parts of Europe. Over the last century, the term has become progressively more equivocal. For instance, in the Near East, the first food production occurs before pottery (see PRE-POTTERY NEOLITHIC); in Japan, pottery appears among foraging populations without food production (see FUKUI, KAMIKUROIWA). Copper metallurgy appears at the end of the Neolithic, leading some to designate this transition to the Bronze Age as the ENEOLITHIC. In the minds of most Old World archaeologists, the term retains a basic utility as a convention of scholarly communication, which serves to differentiate a society with evidence of food production from those without it on the one hand and from those with bronze metallurgy on the other.

In *East Asia* the Chinese Neolithic (6000–2000 BC) includes all social development from the beginning of agricultural society to social stratification; the late Neolithic is often referred to as the LONGSHAN period. It is succeeded directly by the SHANG period of state formation, known also as the early Chinese Bronze Age. In Japan and Korea, the POSTGLACIAL ceramic hunter-gatherers (JOMON, CHULMUN) are also termed Neolithic for their possible horticultural activities, though cultivation of domesticates occurs later. See also CHINESE DYNASTIES, KOREA, JAPANESE PERIODIZATION.

Neolithic of Capsian tradition see CAPSIAN NEOLITHIC.

Neolithic Revolution see BROAD SPECTRUM.

Neopalatial see CRETE.

nephrite iron calcium magnesium silicate of the amphibole mineral group, which occurs in low-grade metamorphic rocks and is widely distributed. Nephrite is the more common of the two varieties of jade; the other variety is the tougher, more compact, jadeite. Nephrite ranges from white to dark green but can be blue and black, and was used for jewellery and ornamental carvings. See also GREENSTONE.

Netiv Hagdud an early PRE-POTTERY NEOLITHIC (PPNA, 8th millennium BC) site at the western edge of the Jordan Valley in Israel. Excavation has uncovered circular rooms that are sometimes joined together to form a larger complex. Burial, mostly secondary interments that lacked skulls, occurred in and around the houses. Other finds include obsidian from central Anatolian sources, remains of basketry, cordage and wooden objects, and clay figurines. Subsistence relied on hunting and on collection of wild barley along with emmer wheat, oats, legumes and acorns; some of the barley presents characteristics of domesticated grain, but this evidence remains equivocal.

network analysis the study of interconnected sites or points. Analysis is aimed at understanding the reasons for the particular configurations of the network, whether they be economic, social or geographical.

neutron activation analysis a physical technique of CHEMICAL ANALYSIS used to determine the composition of a wide range of materials found in archaeological contexts. A specimen is bombarded with neutrons which interact with nuclei in the sample to form radioactive ISOTOPES that emit gamma rays as they decay. The energy spectrum of the emitted rays is detected with a counter, and constituent elements and concentrations are identified by the characteristic energy spectrum of emitted rays and its intensity.

Nevalı Çori a prehistoric site near Samsat on the Euphrates River in southwestern Turkey. The work of H. Hauptmann in the 1980s and 1990s revealed a PRE-POTTERY NEOLITHIC settlement that contains significant new information on cultic activities of the PPNB complex. The excavations reveal a series of buildings with stone foundations, one of which differs from the others in architectural detail and accoutrements. Here the floor is paved with stone slabs and in the middle of one room is an upright stone STELA. Broken stelas occur elsewhere in the site, one of which (incorporated into the wall of a structure) bears a human face in high relief. Later occupation at the site includes HALAF period circular dwellings, and EARLY BRONZE AGE I walling and pits with which are associated copper slags and crucibles.

Nevasa a locality in the headwaters of the Godavari River, on the northern Deccan Plateau of Maharashtra in western-central India, which presents a rich prehistory studied by M. D. Deshpande and H. D. Sankalia. Palaeolithic materials occur within the river sediments, and Sankalia has proposed the name 'Nevasan' to refer to the Middle Palaeolithic industry of central India. The next reported occupation is identified by JORWE ware, and belongs to the regional CHALCOLITHIC of the later 2nd millennium BC; the Jorwe pottery at Nevasa displays some idiosyncratic characteristics. The levels of this culture contain remains of houses constructed with wooden posts and plastered floors. Double urn burials (mostly of children) occur under floors; beads strung on a thread of silk and cotton were in one of these burials. Following the Jorwe period settlement is one belonging to the late 1st millennium, where in multi-roomed structures occur black-and-red wares, 'Russett Coated Painted' ware, other wares of the Late Iron Age in southern India and some sherds of NORTHERN BLACK POLISHED WARE. The next phase represents a basic continuation of the latter, but now with an introduction of RED POLISHED WARE and

NEWGRANGE, Ireland: the entrance and roof box, with megalithic art in front.

of AMPHORAS, ROULETTED WARE and other products of the Mediterranean world, indicative of a connection with Rome by the maritime trade early in the 1st millennium AD (hence the designation 'Indo-Roman' for this period).

new archaeology a development in the 1960s aimed at making archaeology more scientific, now more often referred to as PROCESSUAL ARCHAEOLOGY. It proposed that archaeology should openly state its assumptions and use specific scientific procedures derived from POSITIVISM. Some new archaeologists believed that laws of human behaviour were obtainable by using the correct METHODOLOGIES. Key elements in new archaeology were cultural evolution and GENERAL SYSTEMS THEORY. See also DEDUCTION, DEDUCTIVE-NOMOLOGICAL, HYPOTHETICO-DEDUCTIVE REASONING, INDUCTION.

New Forest ware a type of Roman pottery produced in the New Forest area of southern England especially in the 3rd and 4th centuries AD. Various shapes were produced including cups, flagons and MORTARIA. The plain surface is decorated with added white decoration. The fabric has a limited distribution, with most of the fine-wares travelling no further than 80 km (50 miles) from the kilns.

Newgrange the most famous of the Irish PASSAGE

GRAVES, part of the BOYNE VALLEY cemetery, Co. Meath. The large kidney-shaped mound, dated to *c*.3100 BC, is over 100 m (110 yds) in diameter and 13 m (43 ft) high. A kerb of large stones carved with wavy lines, lozenges, triangles and similar motifs encloses the base of the mound. Megalithic art is also represented on several of the ORTHOSTATS of the passage and chamber. The chamber itself is of cruciform plan and is roofed by a tall CORBELLED VAULT. Above the outer entrance to the passage is the roof box, a small opening designed to allow sunlight to shine along the passage and into the chamber for seventeen minutes at sunrise on 21 December, the winter solstice. The current appearance of the Newgrange mound, with a near-vertical façade of white quartz blocks above the kerb, is a result of a contentious modern reconstruction.

New Guinea Highlands an area between 1,300 and 2,300 m (4,265 and 7,545 ft) above sea-level which was unknown to Europeans until the 1930s. The population comprises MELANESIAN speakers of PAPUAN LANGUAGES and is characterized by small-scale acephalous political organization, although it has some of the most intensive agricultural systems and highest population densities in the Pacific. The prehistory of the Highlands goes back at least 26,000 years (see KOSIPE) and a long sequence of development of agricultural systems has been documented in areas like the Wahgi Valley (see KUK) beginning in the early Holocene.

New Kingdom a period of Egyptian history comprising the 18th to the 20th Dynasty (*c*.1550–1070 BC), an era of imperial expansion and subsequent decline.

Newstead the location of the Roman fort of Trimontium on the River Tweed in Scotland. It seems to have been built under the initial invasion by Agricola *c*.AD 81 and then reoccupied after the establishment of the ANTONINE WALL.

New Zealand New Zealand was the last major land mass to be colonized by humans. Dating the colonization has been controversial, but the Polynesian ancestors of the MAORI probably arrived in the 12th or 13th century AD. They encountered an environment which would have been very unfamiliar to them. New Zealand is larger than the rest of POLYNESIA put together and its climate is mainly temperate rather than tropical. The land was rich in game, including marine mammals and large flightless birds, of which the MOA is the best known. The moa lacked native predators and within a few centuries had been hunted to extinction. Seal colonies also disappeared in many areas.

The first settlers introduced dogs and rats, but do not seem to have brought pigs and chickens. They also introduced Polynesian tropical food crops such as taro and kumara, or sweet potato. These, however, were at the very limit of their range and could not be grown in much of the South Island. The development of storage facilities was an important innovation that allowed kumara to be grown in temperate conditions as far south as the north coast of the South Island. Some indigenous species were also brought into cultivation. How important cultivated plants were to the economy is controversial, but horticulture seems to have been marginal in many areas. Loss of soil through clearance and erosion led to abandonment of some settlements (see, for example, PALLISER BAY). The bulk of the population lived on the North Island, while the South Island had only small numbers of hunter-gatherers.

New Zealand also has a wider range of rock types than island Polynesia. New stone raw materials were quickly discovered, and traded over long distances. MAYOR ISLAND obsidian seems to have been particularly valued. GREENSTONE (nephrite) was also highly prized and widely traded, particularly in more recent times. It was usually worked by polishing and used for adzes and a range of personal ornaments, such as HEI TIKI.

Many early settlements, such as WAIRAU BAR and SHAG RIVER MOUTH, are found near the mouths of estuaries. Their economy was mainly based on hunting and gathering. There were significant changes in Maori society from about AD 1500. Population increase seems to have led to competition for resources and major increases in warfare. This can be seen in the archaeological record by a shift to fortified settlements or PA. Some pa were hillforts, such as OTAKANINI or TE AWANGA.

Others, such as LAKE MANGAKAWARE or LAKE NGA-ROTO, were built in swamps or by lakes and defended by palisades.

The archaeological sequence has commonly been divided into two phases. The earlier Archaic phase is associated with an early eastern Polynesian (see PACIFIC) artifact assemblage. DUFF coined the term 'moa hunter' to characterize this culture, based on his finds at Wairau Bar. The later Classic Maori phase corresponds to the elaborate stratified society described by 18th-century European voyagers such as COOK. Elaborate traditions of wood carving, tattooing and personal adornment developed during this period and continue to characterize contemporary Maori culture.

Nezwiska a site of the LINEAR POTTERY CULTURE in Ukraine, on the eastern fringe of Linear Pottery distribution. Settlement remains included a large surface structure 12 by 7 m (13 by 8 yds) with several hearths. Although it is elongated, the structure at Nezwiska is different in its construction and proportions from the large timber LONGHOUSES that characterize Linear Pottery settlements in Central Europe.

Ngaloba see LAETOLI.

Ngamuriak a Neolithic open-air site in southwestern Kenya where extensive excavations revealed stone tools and pottery of the ELMENTEITAN tradition, dating to c.2000 BP. The animal bones and teeth belong almost exclusively to domestic cattle and sheep/goats. The former represent the earliest evidence for humped cattle in eastern Africa. Features at the site include one or two house floors, several MIDDENS and accumulations of animal dung. Obsidian used in tool manufacture was obtained from the Rift Valley, more than 100 km (62 miles) away.

Ngandong a site in the SOLO River Valley in eastern Java, excavated by Dutch archaeologists in 1931–3, who unearthed remains of Pleistocene fauna (later than TRINIL) and twelve skulls of advanced HOMO *erectus* (SOLO MAN), with which a stone industry of choppers and retouched flakes has been traditionally associated (see CHOPPER/CHOPPING TOOLS), but these may have been washed down from higher terraces. The human remains were variously estimated to be 500,000 or 100,000 years old, but analysis (both here and at SAM-BUNGMACHAN) of supposedly associated bovid teeth by ELECTRON SPIN RESONANCE and URANIUM SERIES DATING has produced a highly controversial result of between 53,000 and 27,000 years ago, long after *H. erectus* was thought to be extinct. See also von KOENIGSWALD.

Ngaro see NDERIT.

Ngarrabullgan Cave a cave in northern Queensland, Australia, with a shallow cultural deposit with evidence of occupation from before 37,000 bp to about 32,500 bp. Then the site seems to have been abandoned and not reused until the mid Holocene. Paired radiocarbon and OSL determinations for Ngarrabullgan confirm the reliability of OSL dates. Dates based on THERMO-LUMINESCENCE and OSL methods have generated considerable controversy in Australia.

Ngilipitji a quartzite quarry in eastern ARNHEM LAND, whose products, including LEILIRA blades, were key items in traditional exchange in northern Australia. Techniques of quarrying and point manufacture have recently been studied with the traditional owners.

Ngoc Lu a locality in Ha Niam Ninh Province, southeast of Ha Noi, Vietnam, which has given its name to the finest Heger I type of bronze drum found there in 1983; it is 63 cm (2 ft) high and decorated with scenes of dancers and village ceremonies including drum playing, deer and birds.

Nguom a rockshelter in Vo Nhai Province, 100 km (62 miles) north of Ha Noi, Vietnam, excavated in 1982, with HOABINHIAN occupation and three burials in the upper levels, underlain by tools of the SON VI tradition and, at the base, dated to c.23,000 BP, a flake tool assemblage, also found at the nearby Mieng Ho Cave, but otherwise unique in Vietnam.

Nhunguza a site about 40 km (25 miles) north-northeast of Harare in northern Zimbabwe, one of the northern-most centres of the GREAT ZIMBABWE state, where five structures within a stone enclosure have been excavated: three are considered to have been used for sleeping, another as a living area, and the last, containing three sections, possibly as a ceremonial centre of the ruler.

Niah Cave the West Mouth site at Niah in Sarawak, northern Borneo, which is one of the major prehistoric deposits of island Southeast Asia containing human remains, the best known of which is the 'deep skull', a HOMO *sapiens* skull recovered from a depth associated with radiocarbon dates of c.38,000 bc, which would make it among the earliest in the region. However, excavation of the site was not carried out by archaeological strata, and the carbon and the skull were recovered from different parts of the cave, making it more likely that the skull represents a much later inhumation cut into earlier levels. Other deposits include a series of flexed, seated and fragmentary burials more securely dated to 12,000–1500 bc; extended burials in wooden coffins or mats of the last two millennia BC; and jar burials and cremations ranging in date from c.?1500 BC to after AD 1000. Distinctive pottery appears by c.2500 BC along with Neolithic polished stone adzes, and metal appears by the 1st millennium AD.

Niaux a huge cave in Ariège, in the French Pyrenees, where Palaeolithic drawings were discovered on the walls in 1906. Prehistoric visitors had explored all 2 km (1 mile) of galleries, and left some footprints. No trace of occupation has been found. The 'Salon Noir' houses six panels of black animal figures (bison, horse, ibex, deer) of different sizes. Figures are sparser elsewhere, but include some engravings in the clay floor. Recent analysis has shown that some black figures were first sketched in charcoal, and it has been claimed that six different pigment 'recipes' have been detected. Dates for the same recipes at nearby LA VACHE assign much of Niaux's art to the late MAGDALENIAN of the 13th millennium bp and this is partially confirmed by radiocarbon dates of 13,850 and 12,890 bp from charcoal in Salon Noir bison figures. If valid, these results suggest that the Salon Noir was not a single, homogeneous composition, as was thought, but was decorated in at least two separate phases.

Nichoria or **Nikhoria** the site of a MYCENAEAN settlement in Messenia, Greece, excavated in 1969–73. A substantial 15th-century BC structure, rebuilt in the 14th century, may be an early palace, and there were at least two THOLOS tombs.

Niedermerz see LINEAR POTTERY.

niello powdered sulphides of copper and silver, heated to produce a bluish-black plastic substance which was used to decorate metalwork, in particular the inlaid daggers from the SHAFT GRAVE circles excavated at MYCENAE.

Nietoperzowa Cave or **Jerzmanowice** a prehistoric cave-site located on the Bêdkówka River, northwest of Kraków in southern Poland. Artifacts and faunal remains (primarily cave bear) are buried in loam and rubble deposits. The lower cultural layers contain Middle Palaeolithic assemblages (e.g. sidescrapers and bifaces) dated by stratigraphic correlation to the end of the Middle Pleistocene, last INTERGLACIAL and early GLACIAL. Above a sterile layer lie several early Upper Palaeolithic layers containing laurel-leaf points, which are assigned to the JERZMANOWICIAN industry; the lowest of these layers yielded a radiocarbon date of 38,500 bp. Neolithic and later remains occur in the uppermost layer. Nietoperzowa was excavated by Roemer in 1878–9, Chmielewski in 1956–63 and others.

Nihewan [Ni-ho-wan] a basin and stratigraphic formation in Hebei Province, China. The sands and clays of the Nihewan formation were originally dated to between 3 and 1.52 million years ago; now they are thought to be 1 million years old, but they still include some of northern China's earliest Palaeolithic tools (quartzite choppers and flakes). The mammalian fauna of the Nihewan formation belongs to the Lower Pleistocene and is characterized by an early form of horse.

Nihon Shoki or **Nihongi** the second-earliest surviving chronicle of Japan, compiled in the 8th century AD as

NINEVEH: relief from the palace of Sennacherib in Nineveh, showing the siege of the Jewish town Lachish by Sennacherib in 701 BC. Detail: defence tower.

part of the RITSURYO state's effort at legitimizing the ruling dynasty. These political documents include imperial genealogies, legendary events and reign chronicles; their use in archaeology provides data for the protohistoric KOFUN period. See also KOJIKI.

Nikhoria see NICHORIA.

Nikiniki a cave-site in western Timor excavated by Bühler in 1935, the first professionally excavated and reported prehistoric site from present-day Indonesia.

Nîmes (*Lat.* Nemausus) a colony founded by the emperor Augustus in France. Extant remains include the mid 1st-century AD AMPHITHEATRE designed by Titus Crisius Reburrus. It could hold some 21,000 people. The Maison Carrée is a temple dating from the 1st century BC. Water brought by aqueduct to the town (see PONT DU GARD) was redistributed from the *castellum*.

Nimrud see KALHU.

Nineveh a walled city covering some 750 ha (1,850 acres) at the time of the NEO-ASSYRIAN empire, which has provided its steady stream of excavators (beginning with Emile BOTTA in 1842) with a wealth of Neo-Assyrian art, architecture and texts, including the famous winged bulls that grace the British Museum and the library of

Assurbanipal. The city walls incorporate two mounds, Kuyunjik (the citadel) and Nebi Yunus (the arsenal), which correspond to the separate citadel and arsenal compounds that were standard in Neo-Assyrian cities. Most attention has been paid to the Kuyunjik mound, beginning with H. LAYARD's and H. Rassam's work on the palaces of Sennacherib (704–681 BC) and Assurbanipal (668–627 BC). The Kuyunjik mound was also the setting of Max MALLOWAN's deep sounding at the ISHTAR temple. This work established a long sequence whose earliest levels begin with a HASSUNA occupation (Nineveh 1). The regional implications of the Nineveh sequence have been overtaken by later work, though the term 'NINEVITE 5' is still current in the archaeological literature. Mallowan's deep sounding also recovered one of the most famous pieces of later 3rd-millennium art work, the life-size bronze head of a king, often identified as the AKKADIAN king SARGON.

Ninevite 5 1 a style of painted pottery and the accompanying incised and excised decorated wares; the term is derived from Max MALLOWAN's deep sounding at NINEVEH.
 2 an archaeological period or horizon in northern MESOPOTAMIA. Recent work (at Telul Thelathat, LEILAN, Tell Mohammad 'Arab) has firmly dated this pottery to c.2900–2500 BC, and has defined stylistic changes within the period, notably the chronological priority of the painted over the incised wares.

Ninstints the finest *in situ* example of North American northwest coast architecture and monumental art. This large multi-lineage village site is located on Anthony Island, off the coast of British Columbia, Canada, and comprises standing superstructures of buildings, living floors, roof beams and twenty-one standing mortuary poles, some of which date to the early 1800s. The earliest occupation of the site is dated to approximately AD 360, and the village was abandoned in 1888. The village was occupied by the prehistoric and historic Haida.

Nintoku the 17th emperor of Japan, as given in the traditional list for the 5th century AD and the name of the KEYHOLE-shaped MOUNDED TOMB, the largest in Japan, measuring over 485 m (530 yds) long, specified as his mausoleum in Osaka Prefecture.

Nippur a city of southern MESOPOTAMIA, one of the great cultural centres of the Mesopotamian world, which has been the object of successive American excavations, beginning with those of John Peters in 1889 and continuing to McGuire Gibson's work until 1990. The city, covering some 75 ha (185 acres), was first occupied by late 'UBAID times, and continued to be inhabited into the 1st millennium AD. Nippur was a religious and scribal centre, though never a political capital; in SUMERIAN myth, Nippur was the city of the god ENLIL and the meeting place of the divine assembly. The archaeological investigations of the city have provided an extremely detailed sequence of pottery which covers most of the pre-Islamic periods of southern Iraq, much of which comes from a deep sounding in the INANNA temple precinct. Excavations at the site have also produced a wealth of CUNEIFORM archives (particularly cultic texts of various periods and economic texts of the KASSITE and ACHAEMENID periods). And in addition to the religious architecture of EARLY DYNASTIC and UR III dates (e.g. the Inanna precinct, the Enlil ziggurat), the Nippur excavations have recently exposed OLD BABYLONIAN residential architecture, the social and economic history of which can be interpreted with the aid of contemporary documents.

Nisa the capital city of the PARTHIANS (Old Nisa), located south of Ashkhabad in modern Turkmenistan. Soviet investigation documented several large public buildings of the 2nd century BC, notably the Square and Round Halls, ornamented with Greek-style sculptural figures executed in clay and stucco over a wooden framework and set into wall niches. The Square Hall acted as a depository for a rich treasure, among the items in which were Greek figurines in marble, silver and other materials, and more than sixty ivory drinking horns richly carved in a manner which adopts Greek images into an Iranian arrangement.

Nishiyagi a site in Hyogo Prefecture, Japan, where a 5 cm by 27 cm (2 by 11 inch) wooden board dating to the Palaeolithic period has been excavated. Preserved by waterlogging and bearing whittling scars, it is dated to 50,000–70,000 bp. See also HOSHINO.

Nissan Island a MELANESIAN island, halfway between the BISMARCK ARCHIPELAGO and the Solomons, where recent work at several sites has identified a sequence of LAPITA stratified above earlier material. The pre-Lapita deposits date back to c.5000 bp and are ACERAMIC NEOLITHIC; they do, however, contain TALASEA obsidian, indicating long-distance sea voyaging in the pre-Lapita period.

Nitovikla the site of a fortress in eastern CYPRUS, which was excavated by Sjöqvist in 1929. The fortress was built in the Middle Cypriot period, presumably to defend the Karpass peninsula against sea raids from Anatolia and Syria; it was destroyed, and then rebuilt in the Late Cypriot period.

Nitra a large cemetery of the LINEAR POTTERY culture in southern Slovakia which has provided a considerable amount of data on mortality, age and sex ratios, and differential burial treatment during the early Neolithic. Seventy-five per cent of the male burials, particularly those of older individuals, had grave-goods, including SPONDYLUS shell ornaments and SHOE-LAST axes.

Nitriansky Hrádok a multi-period ENEOLITHIC and Bronze Age hilltop site in Slovakia. A bell-shaped pit of the BADEN culture, 4 m (13 ft) deep, contained ten kneeling skeletons with hands held to their faces. Later, the hilltop was a fortified site of the MAD'AROVCE culture of the Early Bronze Age in Slovakia during the 3rd millennium BC. The fortifications at Nitriansky Hrádok are characterized by a double ditch and timber-framed rampart, with elaborate 'inturned' gateway construction. Numerous artifacts include antler cheekpieces for horse-bits.

nitrogen dating a RELATIVE DATING technique applied to bone. In the burial environment, bone collagen decomposes, releasing nitrogen, a major component, at a fairly uniform slow rate. The relative ages of bones in similar burial environments can be compared by examining the remaining nitrogen content, assuming bones initially have similar amounts of collagen. Nitrogen concentrations are determined by CHEMICAL ANALYSIS.

nitrogen isotopes different groups of plants and kinds of soil as well as modern herbivore bone collagen from arid or wet areas differ in the ratio between two nitrogen isotopes, 15N/14N, relative to that in standard atmospheric N2. Bone COLLAGEN in suitably preserved archaeological samples may be used to reconstruct certain aspects of past diets and/or climates and habitats, depending on factors which include the degree to which protein is preserved.

Niuheliang a Neolithic site in Liaoning Province, China, near the Inner Mongolian border. It consists of fifteen locations of MOUNDED TOMBS, most with inner stone pit-chambers and stone kerbs, and one semi-subterranean cruciform-shaped pit-building which is thought to have functioned as a 'Goddess Temple' from the ritual goods discovered there. The burials have yielded HONGSHAN jades, and the partially excavated 'temple' yielded fragments of clay sculptures of female forms, including a face inlaid with talc eyes and possibly ivory teeth. The site has no known settlements associated with it.

Njoro River Cave one of the earliest sites of the ELMENTEITAN industry of the PASTORAL NEOLITHIC in Kenya, dated to about the 12th century BC. It functioned as a cemetery for cremated burials, each of which was accompanied by a stone bowl, pestle and mortar. An elaborately decorated wooden vessel, thought to be associated with milking, and a gourd were also recovered, as were quantities of stone beads.

Nkhudzi a Late Iron Age cemetery on the southwestern shore of Lake Malawi, dating to the late 18th–early 19th centuries AD. Abundant grave-goods attest to a period of trade with the East African coast, as well as slave raiding. The site has given its name to Nkhudzi ware, which was introduced into Malawi in about the 18th century ad, and

NOIN-ULA BARROWS, Mongolia: fragment of the felt carpet.

of which variants are still in use in parts of southern Malawi.

Nkope an Early Iron Age first millennium ad site in southern Malawi which has given its name to an Early Iron Age pottery ware of the Eastern Stream or UREWE tradition of the CHIFUMBAZE or MWITU complex. Nkope ware has a wide distribution throughout Malawi as well as in adjacent areas of Zambia and Mozambique, and is closely related to other Early Iron Age pottery wares such as KWALE and LELESU in East Africa, GOKOMERE and ZIWA in Zimbabwe, and DAMBWA in Zambia. Of particular interest are fish bones, rarely preserved in this context.

Noailles burin an Upper Palaeolithic flake tool retouched to give several chisel-like edges. Named after the cave of Noailles in Corrèze, France, it characterizes a FACIES of the Upper PERIGORDIAN (the 'Noaillian') dating to c.27,000 bp. See also BURIN.

nodule a rounded to irregular relatively hard mass of mineral matter formed in a soil that exhibits massive internal structure formed by the localized deposition of minerals from solution. Nodules that formed under differing environmental conditions may differ mineralogically, isotopically and radiometrically. These characteristics may aid PALAEOENVIRONMENTAL reconstruction and age determination of the conditions under which they formed. Compare CONCRETION.

Noen U-Loke an Iron Age mound near BAN PRASAT, NON MUANG KHAO and BAN LUM KHAO on the KHORAT Plateau, northeastern Thailand, excavated in 1997–8. Evidence was found for bronze, iron and glass working, house structures, pits with carbonized rice remains, and 126 burials spanning five mortuary phases dated between 200 BC and c.AD 300. Associated ornaments including agate, carnelian, gold and bronze ornaments were exceptionally fine, and one burial had four bronze belts; another was accompanied by 400 bronze ornaments and a silver-coated spiral head ornament.

Noin-Ula barrows a cemetery of the HSIUNG-NU

nobility (end of the 1st century BC–beginning of the 1st century AD), located in the Noin-Ula Mountains in northern Mongolia. It has more than 200 large KURGANS, square in plan, about 2 m (6 ft) high, with burial chambers made of logs and containing wooden coffins. The site was primarily excavated in 1924–5. Among the finds are Hsiung-nu material (weaponry, utensils, objects of art) as well as numerous Chinese goods made of bronze, jade, wood, lacquer and silk fabrics. The rich material characterizes a culture of the Hsiung-nu from the time of the HAN Dynasty in China, when close cultural and kinship ties existed between the Hsiung-nu nobility and the Chinese court. Of special interest are the woollen fabrics of great artistic value from Bactria, PARTHIA and Asia Minor, which came to the Hsiung-nu as a result of lively trade via the SILK ROUTE. The most famous find is an embroidered felt carpet bearing the scene of a griffin attacking an elk. Most of the finds from Noin-Ula are housed in the Hermitage in St Petersburg.

Nok a valley in central Nigeria which has given its name to an Early Iron Age culture limited to the Jos Plateau area and associated with early evidence for iron smelting in West Africa. It is characterized by distinctive broken terracotta human and animal figurines, associated with radiocarbon dates from the latter half of the 1st millennium bc to the first few centuries ad, some of which may be altar figures associated with an agricultural fertility cult. Nok settlement sites at TARUGA and Samun Dukiya date to between the 5th and 3rd centuries bc.

nomarch the chief official of an Egyptian NOME. The power of a nomarch, usually most pronounced during an INTERMEDIATE PERIOD, may be seen in the often lavish tombs they built for themselves (e.g. BENI HASSAN, EL-BERSHEH).

Nombe a rockshelter in the NEW GUINEA HIGHLANDS with evidence of occupation going back 25,000 years. Extinct species, including THYLACINE and PROTEMNODON, occur in the Pleistocene levels with WAISTED AXES.

nome an administrative district of ancient Egypt. By the Graeco-Roman period, whose temples are the major source of surviving lists of nomes, there were twenty-two in UPPER EGYPT and twenty in LOWER EGYPT.

nomothetic adj. pertaining to general laws and principles of human behaviour. It is the opposite of IDIOGRAPHIC.

Non Chai a large (approximately 38.5 ha [95 acre]) late prehistoric settlement on the edge of the modern city of Khon Kaen, in the upper Chi Valley, KHORAT, Thailand, apparently settled c.600–500 BC. Iron appears in basal layers. Peak economic activity occurred between c.200 and 100 BC, at which time local pottery was traded to the Songkhram basin sites about 100 km (62 miles) to the

north. The site was abandoned by about AD 300. The early date of abandonment may explain the lack of moats (see MOATED SITES).

Non Dua a late prehistoric moated settlement (see MOATED SITES) in southern KHORAT, Thailand, occupied from c.600 to 500 BC to c.AD 800. The local economy included rock-salt extraction and trade.

Nong Nor lies close to the coast on the Bang Pakong River, Thailand, south of KHOK PHANOM DI, and was excavated in 1991–3. The first period of occupation is basically a SHELL MIDDEN with a single crouched burial dating to about 2500 BC, then situated on a marine embayment at a time of higher sea-level. The second phase of occupation is dated to between 1100 and 600 BC, with 166 burials cut into the earlier midden. Stone jewellery was made from serpentine, talc, jade and carnelian (perhaps the oldest found in Thailand), and in addition to bronze ornaments and small chisels, some pure tin bangles were found.

Non Muang Khao a 55 ha (136 acre) double settlement mound, 20 km (12.5 miles) east of BAN PRASAT on the KHORAT Plateau of northeastern Thailand. Excavations in 1996–7 revealed many superimposed plastered floors, some with wooden posts in situ. Dated to c.50 BC–AD 400, the floors, often covering burials packed with rice chaff, resemble those of NON YANG to the east. Pottery in the graves includes very fine PHIMAI black ware, and there are also bronze, glass and agate ornaments.

Non Nok Tha an extensively excavated prehistoric settlement on the KHORAT Plateau of northeastern Thailand, occupied from the mid 3rd millennium to about 500 BC, and again in the 1st millennium AD. Finds of bronze tools and casting materials in the 1960s and some erratic early dates prompted claims that bronze metallurgy had developed independently in Thailand before China, and as early as anywhere in the Near East. Later AMS dates have shown the early dates to be unreliable.

Non Pa Kluay a Bronze–Iron Age settlement and cemetery in the Phu Wiang region of the KHORAT Plateau of northeastern Thailand, close to NON NOK THA.

Non Pa Wai one of a cluster of metal smelting sites in the Khao Wong Prachan Valley of central Thailand, northeast of LOPBURI, dated to the late 2nd millennium BC. Finds include thousands of crucibles, tuyères, cup moulds for casting copper ingots and slag of bivalve moulds for casting such items as axe-, spear- and arrow-heads, and bracelets. These are underlain by Neolithic burials dated to c.2300 BC.

non-site archaeology see OFF-SITE ARCHAEOLOGY.

Non Yang a large Iron Age site (300–1 BC) in the eastern Mun Valley, northeastern Thailand, which was excavated

1981–90, and yielded evidence for clay-plastered rectangular houses or rice barns built on the ground. This is unusual in Southeast Asia, where structures are generally raised on wooden piles.

Noricum an Iron Age POLITY (sometimes referred to as a 'kingdom') in the eastern Alps, with its seat at Magdalensberg in Austria. Noricum flourished during the last centuries BC and was linked to the Italian peninsula by close trading connections. Mining and iron working were significant economic activities. Around 15 BC, Noricum was absorbed by the Roman empire.

normative *adj.* relating to a view of culture, whereby an individual society has a uniform and standard way of doing things, so that these social norms are represented by particular homogeneous patterns in the archaeological record.

Norşuntepe a 10 ha (25 acre) prehistoric site in the Keban plain on the upper Euphrates River in eastern Anatolia, where H. Hauptmann's excavations have revealed a sequence of occupation from CHALCOLITHIC to Iron Age times. The earliest levels show connections with the HALAF and 'UBAID horizons, but are not well known. During the occupation contemporary with the late URUK period, architecture becomes more elaborate and contains a probable copper foundry. Copper workshops continue to be present in the subsequent EARLY BRONZE levels, whose ceramics reveal connections both to the south (pottery comparable to 'AMUQ G materials) and to the northeast (KURA-ARAXES culture). At the end of the Early Bronze period, the multiple-building architecture is replaced by a single large complex, perhaps a rural manor house. The later occupations are less substantial. The evidence for copper production at Norşuntepe during the late 4th millennium BC has added significance when combined with similar evidence at the nearby site of Tepecik, where the late Uruk phenomenon is more strongly represented. In both cases, the copper production was based on the important Ergani copper sources, and was arguably stimulated by demand in southern MESOPOTAMIA.

Northern Archaic tradition a cultural tradition of the North American Arctic and sub-Arctic dating to *c.*6000–4000 bp. The most characteristic artifact type is the side-notched point, although assemblages also contain oval bifaces, endscrapers and notched pebbles (net-sinkers?); microblades have been recovered from some sites, but may represent mixture of materials from other traditions. The Northern Archaic tradition is widely thought to reflect a population intrusion from more southerly latitudes; it was defined in 1968 by Anderson.

Northern Black Polished ware a very fine grey ware with a lustrous black surface (actually ranging from silvery-white to brown) produced by coating the surface with an alkali flux and firing in a reducing atmosphere. This ware was made from 500 BC (or slightly earlier) until the 1st century BC, and had a distribution from the lower Ganges in the east into the Punjab in the west. NBPW characterizes the urban kingdoms of early historical India, the social setting of the Buddha.

Northern Maritime tradition a late prehistoric cultural tradition of the Arctic and sub-Arctic coastal regions from northeastern Siberia to Greenland. It dates from at least 2100 BP to the 20th century, and includes the OLD BERING SEA/OKVIK, BIRNIRK and THULE cultures as well as others (and is considered ancestral to modern Eskimo and Inuit culture). Material components include toggle HARPOON heads, kayaks and umiaks, and ground slate knives. The economy was heavily based on the hunting of marine mammals, including whales. The Northern Maritime tradition was defined by H. B. Collins.

Northern zone the steppe region south of the Gobi Desert along the northern edge of agricultural China, comprising Inner Mongolia, the ORDOS and southern DONGBEI regions. Within this zone developed several local Bronze Age cultures with nomadic connections in the 1st millennium BC.

Norton a series of Arctic Alaska cultures, essentially coastal in orientation, dating from approximately 1000 BC to AD 1000, which contain the first evidence for the use of ceramics in the region. The CHORIS CULTURE, which is the earliest manifestation of the tradition, is characterized by pottery that is Asiatic in origin, is fibre-tempered and has linear-stamp decorations. The IPIUTAK CULTURE, dated to the end of the tradition, lacks 'classic' Norton forms, such as pottery.

Nové Košariská an Early Iron Age complex of tumuli near Bratislava in Slovakia, dated to the HALLSTATT C and D periods. Of the seven tumuli at Nové Košariská, five have been excavated to reveal elaborate central timber-lined chambers with cremation burials in many different vessels (between twenty and eighty in each tumulus), but relatively few bronze weapons or luxury items.

Nové Mesto an Upper Palaeolithic open-air site located on the Váh River in western Slovakia. Artifacts were found at many levels in a deep succession of loess and slope deposits. The lowest buried soil, correlated with the final warm phase of the Middle Pleistocene, yielded isolated flakes. Middle Palaeolithic artifacts (e.g. sidescrapers) were recovered above the last INTERGLACIAL soil, while an overlying soil (corresponding to the early GLACIAL?) yielded a laurel-leaf point (SZELETIAN?). The uppermost buried soil contains artifacts assigned to the EASTERN GRAVETTIAN.

Novgorod an early urban centre in northwestern Russia 160 km (100 miles) south of St Petersburg, excavated from 1932 by ARTSIKHOVSKY, V. Yanin and others. Founded in the 9th century AD, Novgorod came to control a vast territory in the 14th and 15th centuries, extending to the Arctic Ocean and beyond the Ural Mountains. Excavations at Novgorod have revealed evidence of extensive craft production and involvement of the city's merchants in a vast trading network. Among the most interesting finds from Novgorod are over 900 letters and documents written on BIRCH-BARK between the 11th and 15th centuries. Extensive waterlogged deposits account for the good preservation. A well-developed programme of DENDROCHRONOLOGY has produced very precise dating for the city.

Novo Mesto an Early Iron Age settlement and complex of tumuli in Slovenia, dated to the HALLSTATT D period in the 5th century BC. A stone wall enclosed a 2.5 ha (6.2 acre) settlement centre. Near by, ten large tumuli, averaging 30 m (33 yds) in diameter, have been excavated. The number of inhumation burials in each ranges from twenty to thirty-five. Finds include bronze SITULAE, breastplates and helmets, as well as ornaments of Baltic amber.

Novye Ruseshty or **Novi Ruseşti** a multi-period Neolithic and ENEOLITHIC site in Moldova. The first occupation at Novye Ruseshty was of the LINEAR POTTERY culture, while later layers belong to the CUCUTENI-TRIPOLYE culture. Near by was the location of the KARBUNA hoard, and a number of copper objects have been found in Cucuteni-Tripolye contexts at Novye Ruseshty itself.

Noyen-sur-Seine a middle Neolithic enclosure consisting of a system of palisades cutting across a meander of the River Seine, Seine-et-Marne, France. In a later phase the enclosure was replaced by an interrupted ditch enclosure, smaller in area and cutting across the first. Within the enclosures domestic debris indicates a settlement-site including hearths, storage pits, pottery and stylized female terracotta figurines. To the east of the enclosure in peat deposits of an old arm of the Seine, Mesolithic organic remains have been found (*c.*7000–5000 BC), in particular a dugout canoe and basketry fish-traps.

Nswatugi a microlithic LATER STONE AGE early to mid Holocene industry from the Matopo Hills of southwestern Zimbabwe, in which five phases dating between about 9400 and 5000 bp have been recognized. Former names include southern Rhodesian WILTON, Rhodesian Wilton, Matopan and KHAMI industry.

Ntereso a problematic Neolithic open site of the KINTAMPO culture in northern Ghana. Evidence of sedentism is seen in POSTHOLES, which trace the remains of 4 sq. m (4.8 sq. yds) rectangular houses, probably built from wooden poles, mud and grass. Bones of domesticated sheep, goats and cattle were found.

Nthabazingwe see LEOPARD'S KOPJE, MAMBO.

Ntusi the capital site of a 2nd millennium ad Central African interlacustrine state in central Uganda with extensive earthworks and impressive water-storage dams. See also BIGO, BWEYORERE.

Nubia that part of the Nile Valley stretching from ASWAN in Egypt as far south as the Khartoum district in the Sudan, and conventionally divided into UPPER and LOWER NUBIA. See also A-GROUP, C-GROUP, KERMA, NAPATA and MEROE.

Nubian Rescue Campaign an international effort, coordinated by UNESCO between 1960 and 1980, to limit the loss of archaeological data as a result of the building of the ASWAN High Dam and the subsequent flooding of much of LOWER NUBIA by the newly created Lake Nasser. The campaign had two main objectives: the survey and excavation of as many as possible of the archaeological sites which would be destroyed by Lake Nasser; and the dismantling and re-erection of the most important temples in the affected area (e.g. ABU SIMBEL, PHILAE, KALABSHA).

nucleus see CORE.

Nunamira Cave formerly **Bluff Cave** one of several recently excavated limestone caves in southwestern TASMANIA, Australia, which have particularly rich Pleistocene occupation deposits. The site was first occupied *c.*30,500 bp and abandoned about 12,000 years ago. Red-necked wallaby was the main hunted species. The variety of stone types used includes a small quantity of DARWIN GLASS which must have been transported at least

NOVGOROD, Russia: the Kremlin.

100 km (60 miles). See also KUTIKINA, WARGATA MINA, WARREEN.

nuraghe (*pl.* **nuraghi**) a circular stone defensive tower with CORBEL-VAULTED internal chambers dating from the Middle and Late Bronze Ages on Sardinia (*c.*1500–800 BC). Some, such as BARUMINI, were strengthened by the addition of substantial outer fortifications with further stone towers in the 1st millennium BC. The later part of the Nuraghic period is noted also for its bronze figurines and votive models.

Nuri a site in UPPER NUBIA, the successor to KURRU as the main royal pyramid cemetery of the NAPATAN kings during the mid 7th to early 3rd centuries BC.

Nus-i Jan one of the few excavated plausibly MEDIAN sites. It lies in the Malayer Valley of Luristan in western Iran. D. Stronach's work revealed a small fortified settlement of the late 8th century BC which contained a columned hall, a fort and several shrines; one of the latter is identified as a fire-temple which was intentionally filled with shale when the place was abandoned. This architectural reminder of Median cultic practices may not be directly associated with Zoroastrianism, but surely belongs to the general cultural background of this important religious system. A later PARTHIAN settlement also exists on the site.

Nuzi the small (4 ha [10 acre]) site of Yorgan Tepe near Kirkuk in northeastern Iraq where the excavations by Edward Chiera and others in the 1920s and 1930s recovered evidence for occupation from 'UBAID to Sassanian times. Many of the earlier levels of the site are poorly understood, and Nuzi takes its importance from a collection of Old AKKADIAN texts (when the place was named Ga.sur) of the 23rd century BC and from the wide exposure of mid 2nd-millennium occupation associated with the kingdom of Arrapkha and with the MITANNI. The abundant texts recovered from the latter occupation provide the richest available documentation of the Mitanni empire and for the sociopolitical character of 2nd-millennium petty kingdoms in northeastern Iraq. Nuzi also gives its name to a style of painted pottery strongly associated with Mitanni domains but widely distributed in mid 2nd-millennium western Asian sites.

Nyanga see INYANGA.

nymphaion an elaborately decorated semicircular monumental CLASSICAL fountain-house, often with niches filled with sculpture. The name is derived from Caves of the Nymphs.

O

Oakhurst a cave in the southeastern Western Cape Province of South Africa containing over 3 m (7 ft) of LATER STONE AGE material. The basal layers dating to c.12,000–8000 BP preserve material ascribed to the ALBANY or Oakhurst industry (formerly SMITHFIELD A). Some researchers include this industry together with the LOCKSHOEK and POMONGWE industries in an Oakhurst complex. This is characterized by quadrilateral flakes larger than those in preceding or succeeding assemblages. Microliths are very rare and there are few formally patterned artifacts other than scrapers more than 2 cm (0.8 inch) long, although there are numerous bone tools at some sites.

oasis a fertile patch in a desert. The five major oases of the Western Desert of Egypt (Siwa, Bahariya, Farafra, Dakhla and Kharga) were considered as peripheral border regions by the ancient Egyptians. Kharga Oasis has produced industries of the Lower and Middle Palaeolithic discovered by Gardner and CATON-THOMPSON in 1930–33. Apart from the settlements of the OLD KINGDOM and First INTERMEDIATE PERIOD in Dakhla Oasis, the oases do not seem to have been substantially occupied in the historic period until the 1st millennium BC.

Oaxaca see VALLEY OF OAXACA.

Obanian *adj.* denoting a group of KITCHEN MIDDEN settlements found along the western Scottish coast and dating to the late Mesolithic, between c.3065 and 3900 bc. The sites have yielded rather poor stone implements but well-preserved bone and antler artifacts designed to exploit the coastal environment, including harpoon heads and finger-shaped objects identified as 'limpet scoops'.

obelisk an ancient Egyptian monolithic monument, consisting of a tall, thin, square shaft tapering to a pyramidal peak. Obelisks were usually cut from a hard stone, particularly granite from ASWAN, and were typically erected in pairs before the PYLON of a temple. The sides of an obelisk were inscribed with columns of HIEROGLYPHIC text referring, in a self-laudatory manner, to the king who caused it to be erected. This form of monument was used from the OLD KINGDOM onwards, but the largest surviving examples (up to 30 m [98 ft] in height and 450 tonnes in weight) were products of the NEW KINGDOM.

Oblazowa an Upper Palaeolithic cave-site located along the Bialka River in southern Poland. Artifacts and faunal remains (e.g. reindeer, arctic fox) are buried in cave deposits, apparently dating to the beginning of the LAST GLACIAL MAXIMUM. The artifacts include an endscraper, blades and a polished fragment of a woolly mammoth tusk which represents a BOOMERANG. The latter has been dated to 18,160 bp, but bones from the same layer have yielded dates of 31–32,000 bp, so the boomerang may be contaminated in some way.

Ob Luang a rockshelter in northwestern Thailand, excavated in 1985–8, with HOABINHIAN-like flaked cobble tools and traces of wall painting.

obol a small unit of Greek coinage, derived from the word for a spit. Six obols were the equivalent of one DRACHMA, literally a handful. Iron spits, probably an early form of currency, have been excavated in the sanctuary of Artemis Orthia at SPARTA. At ATHENS the silver obol weighed c.0.72 g (0.025 oz), and on AEGINA it weighed 1.05 g (0.037 oz). Multiples of the obol could be issued such as the *triobol* (three) and the *tetrobol* (four).

Obora see KAMEGAOKA.

Obre a complex of Neolithic settlements on the Bosna River near Sarajevo in Bosnia. The settled area at Obre I covered an area of about 1.5 ha (3.7 acres), with rectangular houses similar to those at KARANOVO I and ANZA arranged in rows. Obre II was occupied somewhat later, by the BUTMIR culture, related to VINČA. Situated halfway between the Adriatic coast and the inland Morava corridor, Obre has yielded pottery from both areas, which has been interpreted as reflecting possible TRANSHUMANT pastoralism.

obsidian a naturally occurring volcanic glass, easily chipped to form extremely sharp (though brittle) edges; this makes it a desirable raw material for tools. In western Asia, important obsidian sources occur in central and

Obsidian was also an important trade item in MESOAMERICA, and many of the basic tools of prehistoric households there were made of this material. See also OBSIDIAN HYDRATION DATING.

Obsidian was an important resource in the Pacific and was widely exchanged. The most important sources are in MELANESIA, where obsidian from TALASEA and Mopir on New Britain was exploited as far back as 20,000 years ago at MATENBEK, with obsidian from LOU coming into use in the late Holocene. There are also many sources in NEW ZEALAND, the most important being MAYOR ISLAND, and obsidian was widely used from first settlement. It was also important on EASTER ISLAND (see MATAA).

obsidian hydration dating a chemical dating method used to date obsidian artifacts. It is based on the diffusion of atmospheric and soil water into fresh surfaces of obsidian, beginning immediately after they are exposed. A distinct hydration rind grows inwards and it thickens with time. The rate of thickening, or hydration rate, is also a function of temperature and to a lesser degree chemical composition of the obsidian. This rate can be calibrated for a region and composition, by CROSS-DATING and FISSION TRACK DATING methods. In regions where hydration rates have been determined, ages in excess of 100,000 years have been calculated.

Oc Èo the most famous protohistoric site in Southeast Asia, located in the Mekong delta, southern Vietnam, and once connected with the state of FUNAN. The urban enclosure comprises five rectangular ramparts and four moats, covering 450 ha (1,112 acres), and bisected by a canal linked to other sites and waterways giving access to the sea. Structural remains and finds at this early port site date mainly to the 1st millennium AD, the heaviest use of the site being between the 2nd and 7th centuries. Imports include Chinese bronzes, Indian beads, seals and other jewellery, Roman medallions of the 2nd century AD, and jewellery from the Mediterranean. Local manufactures include glass and stone beads, and jewellery of tin, bronze and gold. The canals linked the town to docks at Ta Kev, and to inland sites like Angkor Borei and Da Noi.

ochre soft varieties of the iron oxide minerals haematite, limonite and goethite, widespread weathering materials of iron-bearing minerals, used as a pigment for painting and pottery SLIPs, personal decoration and on skeletons. Red ochre is haematite, whereas limonite and goethite produce brown, yellow and black colours.

Ochre Coloured Pottery a distinctive ceramic of post-HARAPPAN northern India. OCP is a poorly fired ware to which a red wash or SLIP has been applied. The ware belongs to a family of Late Harappan ceramics (e.g. Late Siswal, Bara, Cemetery H of HARAPPA) which are poorly systematized or understood, and OCP tends to be an elastic term. Generally speaking, these Late Harappan

Granite OBELISK, 22 m (72 ft) high, of King Senwosret I, one of a pair erected in the city of Heliopolis, Egypt.

eastern Anatolia, the neighbouring Transcaucasus and southwestern Arabia. Chemical characterization studies of these flows and of obsidian artifacts from ancient sites (through TRACE ELEMENT ANALYSIS) have pinpointed sources and documented traffic in obsidian through western Asia, both within regions nearer to the sources and in those much further away; as in the Aegean (see MELOS) this traffic seems to begin with the Neolithic.

ceramics belong to the 2nd millennium BC. They may be grouped with similar pottery as a style derived from the Harappan tradition, and are broadly dated to most of the 2nd millennium BC.

Ocsöd-Kovashalom a late Neolithic site of the TISZA culture, located on the Körös River in eastern Hungary. Neolithic finds and settlement features are spread over an area of 21 ha (52 acres), concentrated on three small elevations. These settlement nuclei yielded traces of a number of small rectangular post structures that had undergone several episodes of rebuilding over the occupation span of the settlement. Associated with these were a number of household features, including ovens, storage pits, rubbish pits and burials.

oculus (*Lat.* 'eye') the central opening at the top of a dome, such as that in the Pantheon at ROME.

odeum or **odeon** a Roman covered concert hall usually with tiered seating. A good example is that of Agrippa in the AGORA at ATHENS.

Odmut a cave-site in the Montenegran Alps, on the Piva River, in Yugoslavia. The lower layers at Odmut resulted from a long Mesolithic occupation during the 8th and 7th millennia BC. Sixty-five per cent of the Mesolithic faunal sample consisted of ibex, 25 per cent of red deer, and the remainder of roe deer, pig and bear. Fish bones and antler harpoons were also found. Later layers contained an early Neolithic IMPRESSED WARE occupation, above which were late Neolithic, ENEOLITHIC and Early Bronze Age deposits.

Oelknitz an Upper Palaeolithic open-air site located on the Saale River in eastern Germany. Artifacts and faunal remains (e.g. horse, reindeer) are buried in deposits dated by radiocarbon to 12,542–11,750 bp. Among the tools are backed blades, endscrapers, burins and bone points; art objects include stylized 'VENUS' FIGURINES. The assemblage, which is assigned to the MAGDALENIAN, is considered typical of this region ('Oelknitz Group').

Offa's Dyke a linear earthwork of ANGLO-SAXON England, c.192 km (120 miles) in length, and built by King Offa of Mercia in the late 8th century AD as a frontier between his kingdom and that of Powys. This large earthen bank and quarry ditch lies close to the modern border of England and Wales.

off-site archaeology, non-site archaeology or **landscape archaeology** an approach, especially in archaeological survey, where the unit of analysis is the artifact rather than the site. Off-site archaeology recognizes that many of the material consequences of human behaviour are ephemeral and will not conform to standard definitions of sites, and documents the distribution of humanly modified materials across the landscape.

Ofnet a cave-site in Bavaria in which concentrations of human skulls were found in two pits. Recent AMS radiocarbon dates have established that these are of Mesolithic date, approximately 6500 BC.

ogam or **ogham** a CELTIC script of northwestern Europe comprising about twenty letters represented by tally marks on either side of or crossing a horizontal baseline. Of uncertain origin, it is thought to have been created in the 2nd or 3rd century AD. Most inscriptions are found in Ireland and Wales (in ancestral Gaelic), but the script is also found in Scotland by the 8th century (in an unknown tongue). Claims have been made for ogam inscriptions in many parts of the New World, especially North America, but most scholars treat these with extreme scepticism.

Ohaba-Ponor a Palaeolithic cave-site located on a tributary of the Mureş River in the southern Carpathian Mountains of western Romania. Artifacts and faunal remains are buried in deposits of loess and clay: among the faunal remains are woolly mammoth and reindeer. Most of the cultural layers contain assemblages dominated by sidescrapers and points, and are assigned to the Middle Palaeolithic. The uppermost layer apparently contains a small Upper Palaeolithic assemblage. Ohaba-Ponor was excavated by Nicolăescu-Plopşor in 1954–5 and others.

Ohalo II an EPIPALAEOLITHIC site on the southwest shore of the Sea of Galilee, Israel, exposed during periods of exceptionally low water-levels. Excavations (1989–91) by D. Nadel have revealed a KEBARAN campsite (radiometrically dated to 19,400 BP) with extensive microlithic and bone tools and ground stone pestles and mortars, numerous animal and fish bones and a human adult male burial. Anaerobic conditions have preserved *in situ* burnt remains of brushwood huts (the earliest yet known), and enabled identification of c.100 species of seeds and fruits, many edible, suggesting year-round occupation. Twisted plant fibres are interpreted as cordage used in bags or nets associated with fishing.

oinochoe a Greek jug made from precious metal, bronze or clay. It seems to have been used for pouring wine at the SYMPOSIUM and it is often shown in conjunction with a PHIALE during the pouring of LIBATIONS at an altar. See also CHOUS.

Ojin the 16th emperor of Japan as given in the traditional list for the 5th century AD, and the name of a KEYHOLE-shaped MOUNDED TOMB, 415 m (454 yds) long, specified as his mausoleum in Osaka Prefecture.

Okhotsk a deep-sea fishing culture of Northeast Asia, between the 8th and 14th centuries AD, on coastal areas of northeastern Hokkaido, Japan, and southern Kurile and Sakhalin Islands. Compare SATSUMON.

Okladnikov, Aleksei Pavlovich (1908–81) a Soviet archaeologist and specialist in Siberian and Central Asian prehistory. Okladnikov discovered and excavated the

NEANDERTHAL burial at the site of TESHIK TASH in Uzbekistan, and investigated many important Siberian Palaeolithic sites, including UST'-KAN CAVE, ULALINKA, MAKAROVO, KRASNYJ YAR, BURET' and others. He also carried out important work on the rock art of Siberia (e.g. Shishkino, Tomskaya Pisanitsa) and Mongolia (e.g. Khoit-Tsenker-Agui), and was a pioneer of the complete recording of rock art sites.

Okunevo culture one of the most spectacular and most mysterious cultures of the Bronze Age. It arose in the mid 2nd millennium BC in the MINUSINSK BASIN through the symbiosis of the local Neolithic cultural traditions and foreign groups of pastoralists. The most characteristic feature of the Okunevo culture is its unique art, which shows an astounding diversity in its imaginative products: decorated STATUE-MENHIRS (a kind of KA-MENNAYA BABA), images on stone slabs (from graves and sanctuaries), rock art including petroglyphs, ochre paintings and very fine engravings, as well as superb objects of portable art.

Okvik see OLD BERING SEA/OKVIK.

Ökuzini see KARAIN.

Olbia see SCYTHIANS.

Old Babylonian period a chronological designation, roughly dated between 2000 and 1600 BC, for a time of competing kingdoms in southern MESOPOTAMIA which were eventually conquered by HAMMURABI of BABYLON. During the first half of the period, the political landscape of southern Mesopotamia was composed of multiple kingdoms, many ruled by AMORITE dynasties; ISIN and LARSA were two of the more important kingdoms, and these two cities supply the term 'Isin-Larsa period' in referring to the first quarter of the 2nd millennium BC. The second half of the Old Babylonian period contained the large kingdom that Hammurabi created, his successors gradually lost, and Murshili I the HITTITE king destroyed in his raid on Babylon (in 1595 BC according to the conventional chronology). Archaeological work on Old Babylonian settlements is well represented throughout southern Mesopotamia.

Old Bering Sea/Okvik a prehistoric Arctic and sub-Arctic culture found in the Bering Strait region and adjacent areas, and dating to 2100–1250 BP. It is considered part of the NORTHERN MARITIME TRADITION and ancestral to the BIRNIRK and THULE cultures. Artifacts include toggling harpoons, sealing darts, polished slate knives (ulus), snow goggles, lamps, and linear and check-stamped pottery. Elaborate ivory carvings of animals and people, as well as 'winged objects', have also been found in many sites. Houses were semi-subterranean with entrance tunnels. The economy was based primarily on the hunting of marine mammals, including seal, walrus and whale.

Oldbury a rockshelter located in Kent, in one of the few areas of Britain with caves suitable for occupation during the Palaeolithic period. The site, which has yielded many typologically Middle Palaeolithic artifacts including bifaces and well-made flake tools, was excavated by HARRISON in 1890.

Old Copper culture a related series of late ARCHAIC complexes in the upper Great Lakes area of Canada and the United States which shared the use of beaten native copper. The metal was shaped into a wide variety of utilitarian tools. The copper tools may have also carried some degree of social prestige.

Old Cordilleran a tradition, recognized most easily by a distinctive leaf-shaped, bi-pointed lanceolate point (Cascade type), which is found throughout Pacific North America. The tradition is best recognized at the FIVE MILE RAPIDS SITE in levels dated to about 9800 BP, with earlier dates possible. The tradition has a terminal date of about 7000 BP. The Old Cordilleran tradition may have cultural ties to such southerly located complexes as SAN DIEGUITO.

Old Crow a series of locales along the Old Crow River in the Yukon, Canada, which were once thought to contain the earliest indisputable artifact in the New World, a piece of caribou leg-bone that had been worked into a tool used to de-flesh animal hides. A radiocarbon date obtained from the tool in the 1960s was approximately 27,000 bp, although the tool was very similar to ones made by recent DENE peoples. In 1986, a new and more accurate technique of radiocarbon dating was applied to the bone, and this gave a date of only 1350 bp, thus destroying claims to the tool's antiquity.

Older Dryas see DRYAS.

Oldishi a Kenyan PASTORAL NEOLITHIC pottery tradition. In southwestern Kenya, it dates to between about 1000 and 400 bc, and is associated with bones of domesticated cattle and caprines, chert-backed microliths and obsidian stone artifacts.

Old Kingdom a period of Egyptian history comprising the 3rd to the 8th DYNASTIES (c.2700–2160 BC), sometimes referred to as the 'Pyramid Age' from the monumental tombs of its more powerful kings.

Oldowan an EARLIER STONE AGE industry and complex, named and defined by Mary LEAKEY, and represented at OLDUVAI GORGE and other African sites, dating from about 2.5 to 1.4 million years ago and later, traditionally presumed to have been made by HOMO habilis, but probably also made by other early Homo species such as H. rudolfensis, and possibly also australopithecines (see AUSTRALOPITHECUS). It is characterized by the production of small flakes removed from alternate faces along the edge of a cobble. Many Oldowan flaked cobbles

or 'choppers' show signs of use and were probably oppor-
tunistic tools, but the purpose of the flaking seems to
have been the production of small, sharp flakes which
could be used as cutting or scraping tools. The utility
of such flakes for cutting even elephant hide has been
confirmed by experiments. Other tool types include hammerstones, heavy- and light-duty scrapers and spheroids.

Olduvai Gorge an important locality in northern Tanzania containing a series of sites in sediments in an
ancient lake basin, from which the longest cultural sequence in the world has been recorded. Research by Louis
and Mary LEAKEY, and other workers, has uncovered
numerous HOMINID remains and large collections of
animal bones as well as stone artifacts dating from *c.*1.9
million years to less than 10,000 years ago. Of particular
interest are the finds of ZINJANTHROPUS in 1959, and
the first fossils to be named HOMO *habilis* in the early
1960s. These finds sparked intensive studies of early
hominids at sites throughout East Africa, on which a great
deal of current knowledge of early humans is based. See
also DEVELOPED OLDOWAN, OLDOWAN.

Oleneostrovski Mogilnik a large Mesolithic cemetery
located on Lake Onega in northern Russia. One hundred
and seventy burials (out of an estimated 400) have been
excavated, yielding more than 7,000 artifacts. Variation
in grave-goods has indicated the existence of differential
access to wealth and of inherited status positions.

Ollantaytambo an INCA site in the Urubamba Valley,
near CUZCO, Peru. The site comprises a planned town,
trapezoidal in outline, and a ridge-top 'fortress' which
includes both domestic and ceremonial architecture.
Originally a royal estate belonging to the Inca Pachacuti,
it was used as a fortress by Incas rebelling against the
Spanish.

Olmalenge a Kenyan PASTORAL NEOLITHIC pottery
tradition, formerly known as NDERIT WARE, which is
divided into a northern FACIES in the Turkana region
and a southern facies in the Nakuru Basin.

Olmec the first complex civilization to emerge in ME-
SOAMERICA, and a distinctive art style. The Olmec civilization began during Mesoamerican early PRECLASSIC (at
least 1200 BC) and ended *c.*400 BC. This culture was
marked by CEREMONIAL CENTRES, beautiful art work in
jadeite and shell, and monumental sculpture. The Olmec
culture represents a shift to a village-and-centre, rather
than a village, social order. The earliest of the ceremonial
centres is SAN LORENZO, located near the Gulf of Mexico
coast.

The Olmec also produced an art style expressed primarily through sculpture, and realistic in its rendition of
natural and supernatural forms. The WERE-JAGUAR is a
central theme of this style. Elements of Olmec style and
iconography are found throughout Mesoamerica during

OLMEC culture, Mexico: giant stone head.

the middle Preclassic period. Sculptures range from small
jadeite figures to huge stone heads standing almost 2 m
(6.5 ft) tall.

Olmeca-Xicallanca a cultural group from the southern
Gulf Coast of Mexico who played an important role in
transforming MESOAMERICA during the transitional
period between the CLASSIC and POSTCLASSIC
(*c.*AD 600–1200). They were probably non-CLASSIC
MAYA (Putun), and are mentioned in ethnohistorical
texts as occupying the highland centres of CHOLULA and
CACAXTLA, and are therefore responsible for introducing
Maya stylistic and cultural elements. Under the name
Nonoalca they also helped create the TOLTEC POLITY at
TULA.

Olorgesailie an informative EARLIER STONE AGE
ACHEULIAN locality in southern Kenya, discovered by
Mary LEAKEY in 1944, with remarkable accumulations of
thousands of HANDAXES, CLEAVERS and other stone
artifacts, now dated to between 900,000 and 700,000
years ago. Most of the assemblages have probably experienced some post-depositional sorting or movement from
water action. This probably also played a role in the accumulation of the remains of many extinct giant gelada
baboons found at one site, which some archaeologists
interpret as the result of HOMINID hunting (see ISAAC).

Olsen-Chubbuck a KILL-SITE in Colorado, USA, in which
at least 200 bison were driven into an *arroyo* (a deep, dry
stream cutting). The site is approximately 8,500 years
old and dates to the Firstview complex of the PLANO

tradition. Its analysis by WHEAT was one of the first aimed at providing information on the specific strategies of PALAEOINDIAN hunting and butchering techniques.

Olszanica a settlement of the LINEAR POTTERY culture in southern Poland near Kraków, located on a loess-covered plateau. Excavations revealed thirteen LONG-HOUSES of varying dimensions. House 6, measuring 41.5 m (136 ft) long, has been interpreted as the dwelling of a high-status individual, while in a smaller house imported obsidian and sherds of BÜKK pottery from Hungary were found. Radiocarbon dates point to the late 5th millennium bc.

Oltome a pre-pastoralist Kenyan pottery tradition of problematic date, within which KANSYORE ware represents a phase (see GOGO FALLS). Domestic animals are not associated with Oltome ceramics as once thought.

Olympia a major PANHELLENIC sanctuary in the western Peloponnese of Greece. Athletic events were part of the festival associated with the TEMENOS of Zeus. German excavations have uncovered remains of the temple of Zeus, in which was placed the CHRYSELEPHANTINE statue of the god, one of the SEVEN WONDERS; the workshop of Pheidias in which it was created has also been found. The temple was decorated with architectural sculpture. Inside the *temenos* was a temple of Hera and other buildings including THESAUROI. There were also numerous private dedications; only the bases for the now lost bronze statues remain. Traces of the STADIUM have been uncovered.

Olynthus a city in northern Greece destroyed in 348 bc. It provides a TERMINUS ANTE QUEM for the development of BLACK-GLOSSED pottery. Excavations have revealed houses fitting into HIPPODAMIAN PLANNING.

Omari a cluster of settlements/cemeteries to the south of CAIRO, Egypt, excavated by Debono in 1943–52. Omari seems to represent a community of a transitional phase between the two major PREDYNASTIC sites of LOWER EGYPT, MERIMDE and MAADI.

Omo a river in southern Ethiopia which has exposed a complex series of riverine and lake shore deposits laid down at intervals during the last 4 million years. Of particular interest is the 1 km (0.6 mile) thick Shungura formation dating between 3 and 1 million years ago, which contains a rich fossil vertebrate sequence, including gracile and robust australopithicenes (see AUSTRALOPITHECUS) as well as early HOMO. Layer F of this formation, dating to between 2.4 and 2 million years ago, contains concentrations of flaked and battered quartz pebbles, which differ from OLDOWAN collections of this period. Detailed dating with POTASSIUM-ARGON, PALAEOMAGNETISM and faunal comparisons makes Omo a valuable reference sequence for comparisons with other sites of this age in East Africa. A skull and partial

adult skeleton known as Omo I, found in the Kibish formation and thought to date to some 130,000 years ago, are among the oldest known modern human remains. However, a partial cranium known as Omo II, although presumably of comparable age, is more archaic in appearance.

Omori a Late to Final JOMON SHELL MIDDEN site near Tokyo, Japan, where the first formal archaeological excavation in the Western sense was carried out in 1877 by Edward S. MORSE.

Ondratice a group of Middle Palaeolithic open-air localities situated northeast of Brno in Moravia (Czech Republic). Artifacts are buried in the modern soil (formed on loess); no faunal remains are preserved. The cultural layer contains a mixture of Middle and Upper Palaeolithic tool types (e.g. endscrapers and sidescrapers and retouched blades); its age is unknown. Ondratice was investigated by ABSOLON in 1928, Valoch in 1965 and others.

1470 the catalogue number given to more than 150 fragments comprising an early HOMINID cranium, KNM-ER 1470, found below the KBS tuff layer at KOOBI FORA, Kenya, by Bernard Ngeneo in August 1972. In the initial description, Richard Leakey ascribed it to an indeterminate species of HOMO, and it was thought to date to 2.9 million years ago. However, current estimates date the KBS tuff to about 1.9 million years ago. The fossil is now generally ascribed to, and is the type specimen for, the species *Homo rudolfensis*, a name proposed by Valerii Alexeev in 1986. It has been suggested that the fossil might be reassigned to the genus KENYANTHROPUS, but to a species different from *K. platyops*, which had a smaller brain.

Onega Lake a lake basin in northwestern Russia and its environs where the granite outcrops have been decorated with petroglyphs, a form of rock art. Figures of people, elk, birds, boats with people in them, circles, and semicircles were pecked into the rock outcrops during the 4th and 3rd millennia bc.

Ongbah Cave a badly disturbed site in western-central Thailand near the Three Pagodas Pass, close to a major trade route to Burma, and a source of lead. While there appears to have been HOABINHIAN period occupation (*c.*9000 bc), the best-known remains from the cave come from later (3rd–2nd-century bc) burials: iron implements, bronze bangles similar to those from BAN DON TA PHET, stone beads and fragments of at least five DONG SON cast-bronze drums.

Onion Portage a deeply stratified coastal site in northwestern Alaska. The site has evidence for occupation from at least 8500 BP and possibly earlier, and contains complexes belonging to the AMERICAN PALAEOARCTIC, NORTHERN ARCHAIC, ARCTIC SMALL TOOL TRADITIONS, as well as later prehistoric INUIT cultures.

opaline a fine-grained siliceous rock type widely used for stone artifact manufacture in the southern African Stone Age, variously named CHALCEDONY, chert and agate by archaeologists.

opisthodomos a shallow room which served as an entrance for the ADYTON of a CLASSICAL temple. It is found at the rear of a temple, and is often entered through two columns placed between two stub walls (see ANTA). Compare PRONAOS.

Oplontis or **Torre Annunziata** an extensive seaside villa destroyed during the eruption of Vesuvius in AD 79 (see also HERCULANEUM, POMPEII) and excavated from the 1960s. The building seems to have been undergoing reconstruction at the time of the destruction, with some of the walls stripped for redecoration. However, the remaining wall paintings were in good condition and show architectural settings including columns in the CORINTHIAN ORDER.

Opovo an ENEOLITHIC settlement of the late VINČA CULTURE located in northeastern Yugoslavia along the Tamis River, dating to the early 5th millennium BC. Opovo is a low mound with three major occupation levels. Its rectangular one-room houses were built of poles and clay. Most had been burned, probably deliberately. Among the animal bones from Opovo are many from wild species such as red deer and roe deer.

oppidum a term used by Caesar to denote the fortified native towns he encountered in his campaigns in Gaul in 58–51 BC, now by extension used for all fortified CELTIC towns; they are distinguished from HILLFORTS by their combination of residential, industrial, market and administrative functions. See also ENSÉRUNE, ALÉSIA, BIBRACTE, ENTREMONT, GERGOVIA.

optical dating see LUMINESCENCE DATING.

optical emission spectrometry a physical technique used to identify trace elements in stone and metal artifacts and ceramics that may aid in identifying the material source. A sample is bombarded with a laser beam or other energy source, exciting the atoms; as the atoms relax they emit light of a wavelength characteristic of the constituent atoms. The wavelength spectrum and intensity are analysed for the type and concentrations of constituent elements present.

Opunohu Valley the site of a detailed survey by Roger Green on Moorea, Society Islands, POLYNESIA. About 500 structures were recorded, including terraces, houses, MARAE and shrines, most dating to the 18th century AD. The analysis successfully related settlement organization to ethnographically recorded social structure.

opus caementicium Roman concrete work.

opus incertum a Roman construction technique by which irregular blocks of stone were attached to a concrete core.

opus quadratum a Roman construction technique consisting of squared blocks. It is the equivalent of ASHLAR masonry.

opus reticulatum a Roman construction technique where blocks are laid on a concrete core so that the edges are placed on a diagonal, thus forming a criss-cross pattern.

opus sectile a Roman construction technique using marble of different colours laid in a geometric or other ornamental pattern, as part of the decoration for floors or walls.

opus signium a Roman construction technique for flooring, consisting of crushed brick set in mortar.

oracle bones divination bones – usually shoulder blades (*scapulae*) or tortoise under-shells (*plastrons*) – of the SHANG culture region of northern China. Used in scapulomancy to divine messages from the ancestors, they are inscribed variously with the charge, answer and name of the diviner. They have been discovered at the ZHOU site of QISHAN and the Shang site of ANYANG, dating to the late 2nd millennium BC. The inscriptions are the earliest examples of coherent Chinese script (compare WUCHENG), and those deciphered from Anyang allow reconstruction of the Shang kinship system and some aspects of the economic and political systems. Oracle bones are preceded in the Chinese Neolithic period by uninscribed divination bones, and the pottery marks on YANGSHAO, LONGSHAN and some other ceramics have been interpreted as incipient writing systems.

ORACLE BONE from the Shang Dynasty, 16th–11th centuries BC.

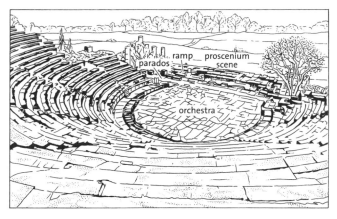

ORCHESTRA.

Orangia a MIDDLE STONE AGE open site in the southern Free State Province, South Africa, now inundated by a dam, which has given its name to an early Middle Stone Age PIETERSBURG-like flake-blade industry, the Orangian.

Oranian see IBEROMAURUSIAN.

Orce an open-air site by a former lake near Orce, 97 km (60 miles) northeast of Granada, southern Spain, where excavations by J. Gibert have unearthed what is claimed to be Europe's oldest known occupation. The main excavation site, Venta Micena, also has abundant, well-preserved animal bones, dated by PALAEOMAGNETISM and microfauna (rodents) to about 1.6 million years ago. Some bones display marks of artificial breakage and cutmarks made by stone tools, and the bones are associated with fractured stones including artifacts and MANU-PORTS. The white flint core and flakes found at the site of Fuentenueva 3 since 1993 are also indisputably of human manufacture. A series of human fragments have also been recovered, all assigned to 1.6 or even 1.8 million years ago, though the species is still uncertain (possibly HOMO *habilis*).

orchestra an area which served as the dancing-floor for Greek religious events. With the construction of permanent theatres, the orchestra became the area at the foot of the tiers of seats in the semicircular auditorium where acting took place. Actors gained access to the orchestra by means of a PARADOS. With the advent of the SKENE, the function and size of the orchestra diminished.

Orchestra Shell Cave a cave near Perth, Western Australia, with occupation deposits dating back at least 6,500 years. Finger markings resemble those from KOONALDA CAVE and from a number of sites such as KOONGINE CAVE in the Mount Gambier district of South Australia.

Orchomenos the home of the legendary King Minyas in Boeotia, Greece, after whom SCHLIEMANN named the distinctive Middle HELLADIC MINYAN pottery which he found during his excavations. A large frescoed Late Helladic structure is tentatively identified as a palace and the magnificent THOLOS tomb, known as the Treasury of Minyas, is proof that Orchomenos was a major MY-CENAEAN centre. Later remains include the impressive fortifications of the CLASSICAL city and a fine 4th-century BC theatre.

Ordos the desert region in the 'hook' of the Yellow River in northern China, location of a Palaeolithic 'Ordos culture' (see SHUIDONGGOU). Small bronze animal sculptures produced in this region during the 1st millennium BC have been referred to as 'Ordos bronzes' (compare SHANG, ZHOU). Both these terms have fallen out of use; the area is now referred to as the NORTHERN ZONE.

ore a mineral, or mineral aggregate, from which a prized constituent, usually a metal, can be profitably exploited.

orientalizing 1 a decorative scheme found especially on Greek pottery. Motifs and images, such as sphinxes, lions, PALMETTES and lotus plants from the countries bordering the eastern Mediterranean, appear from the late 8th century BC. The style is probably the result of renewed contact with Syria, PHOENICIA and Egypt. See also AL MINA.
2 a chronological period in Greece forming the link between the Early Iron Age and the ARCHAIC. It spans the late 8th century BC and continues through the 7th; it saw the rise of narrative in Greek art.

Orongo a ceremonial village of about fifty stone houses with CORBELLED roofs standing 300 m (1,000 ft) above the ocean at the edge of the Rano Kau volcanic crater on EASTER ISLAND. Some houses contain PICTOGRAPHS, while one enclosed a richly carved MOAI. Rich in PETRO-

GLYPHS of vulvas and of birdmen holding eggs, Orongo was the site of the annual birdman ritual, which involved obtaining the first sooty-tern egg from a nearby islet, and which persisted until c.AD 1878. Probably built in the 16th century AD, it was excavated and restored by MULLOY and others.

Oronsay a small island in the Inner Hebrides, Scotland, best known for a series of at least six coastal late Mesolithic SHELL MIDDEN sites dated to c.3700–3200 bc, which have provided abundant well-preserved faunal remains, including large numbers of coalfish bones. Excavations by Mellars in 1970–79 revealed that small groups of people moved seasonally from site to site.

Orrorin a genus claimed to be of the earliest bipedal hominid yet found, known from a collection of 6 million-year-old fossil bones from at least five individuals, both male and female, of *Orrorin tugenensis*, discovered in 2000 in the Tugen Hills in the Baringo District of Kenya, and nicknamed 'Millennium Man'. '*Orrorin*' means 'original man' in the local dialect. Some researchers argue that these remains represent the earliest known human ancestor and that australopithecines (see AUSTRALO-PITHECUS), some species of which are widely considered to be human ancestors, instead represent a side branch in human evolution (see AFRICA, ARDIPITHECUS, *Australopithecus*, HOMO, KENYANTHROPUS).

orthostat a large upright stone supporting the capstone or roof of a chamber or passage in a megalithic tomb.

Osan-ri [Osanni] an early Neolithic site in Kangwondo Province, Korea. It has produced the earliest radiocarbon dates yet for CHULMUN pottery, in the 7th millennium BC.

oscillum an ornament, normally made of marble, suspended from the ARCHITRAVE of a PERISTYLE in a Roman house. Some are circular with reliefs cut on both faces, whereas others may be in the form of theatrical masks.

Oseberg see CLINKER-BUILT.

Oshara see PICOSA.

Osiris an Egyptian deity, depicted as an anthropoid figure with MUMMIFIED body, plumed crown and the crook and flail emblems of kingship. He was primarily the god who ruled the Underworld after his murder by his brother SETH. Osiris was the brother and husband of ISIS and the father of HORUS. He was especially revered at ABYDOS, where his tomb was thought to be situated.

OSL see LUMINESCENCE DATING.

Osłonki a settlement of the LENGYEL culture (c.4500–4000 BC) in northern-central Poland, 8 km (5 miles) west of BRZEŚĆ KUJAWSKI. Like Brześć Kujawski, Osłonki is characterized by trapezoidal LONGHOUSES and

numerous burials scattered among them. The burials are striking for the number of copper artifacts they contain. In one, the skull of a woman was decorated with a 'diadem' in which copper strips had been wrapped around a belt of perishable material, presumably leather or cloth. A deep fortification ditch protected the settlement.

ossuary or **osteotheke** a charnel house used for multiple, typically secondary, inhumations.

osteoarchaeology a branch of archaeology which deals with human anatomy, especially bony structure or organization, in the context of archaeological deposits.

osteodontokeratic see DART.

osteotheke see OSSUARY.

Ostia a major port at the mouth of the Tiber serving ROME. It seems to have been established in the 4th century BC. In AD 42 its facilities were increased by the construction of breakwaters under the emperor Claudius at a site slightly removed from the actual mouth of the Tiber. The emperor Trajan constructed a hexagonal inner harbour in which over 100 ships were able to moor. This was surrounded by warehouses, and was connected to the river by a canal. Its international relations are underlined by the Square of the Corporations, where merchants from various parts of the Mediterranean had offices; their origins, such as SABRATHA in Tripolitania or Narbonne in Gaul (France), were stated by inscriptions set in MOSAICS. Substantial remains include tenement houses, baths and a synagogue.

Ostionoid groups or **Ostiones** the name given to a ceramic series originating in western Puerto Rico, and denoting cultures which developed on that island from the 7th century AD and emigrated to Santo Domingo, Cuba and Jamaica, eventually giving rise to the TAINOS and MACORIJES and other cultures.

ostrakon a POTSHERD. At ATHENS, names could be incised on the ostraka, and these pieces could be cast to expel a citizen from the city for a period of ten years (hence 'ostracize'). One well contained 190 ostraka inscribed with the name of Themistokles, and it is possible that they were prepared before the vote for the illiterate. Ostraka could also be used for making lists or even practising the alphabet.

In Egypt, ostraka (potsherds or a flake of stone, typically limestone) were used as a cheap and readily available vehicle for short texts, usually in HIERATIC or DEMOTIC, of a semi-permanent nature such as letters. Ostraka were also used for artists' sketches and preliminary drawings. Ostraka from the NEW KINGDOM are especially numerous, the site most associated with them as a source of evidence for the life of a community being the workmen's village of DEIR EL-MEDINA.

ostrich eggshell ostrich eggshells were used as containers for water and pigments, such as ochre and specularite, and fragments were made into beads by LATER STONE AGE people in southern and East Africa. They are still used for bead manufacture and for storing water in the Kalahari Desert (see HXARO). They were sometimes decorated with incisions and are often found buried near springs and streams.

Ostrich eggshell fragments are found in MIDDLE and Later STONE AGE sites, but the earliest indubitable evidence for the use of ostrich eggshells as containers comes from 14,000-year-old fragments with ground openings at BOOMPLAAS CAVE in South Africa. Early examples of ostrich eggshell beads have been found in Later Stone Age deposits dated to about 40,000 bp at ENKAPUNE YA MUTO in Kenya and in 38,000-year-old Early Later Stone Age layers at BORDER CAVE in South Africa.

Ostrów Lednicki an early medieval stronghold in western Poland located on an island in Lake Lednica about 12 km (7.5 miles) west of GNIEZNO. Archaeological research on the island has revealed the remains of a mortared stone chapel and palace complex, surrounded by an earth and timber rampart. This enclosure is believed to have been the seat of the Piast dynasty in the mid 10th century AD. The island was connected to the mainland by two timber bridges. Workshops which specialized in precious metals have been discovered on the lake shore by one of the bridges.

Otakanini a PA of ring-ditch type on an island in Kaipara Harbour, North Island, NEW ZEALAND, excavated by Peter Bellwood. Like KAURI POINT, the site shows a sequence of fortifications beginning about AD 1500.

Otomani an Early Bronze Age culture of eastern Slovakia and Transylvanian Hungary and Romania, essentially the equivalent of the FÜZESABONY culture in the central Hungarian sequence. Otomani ceramics feature large, pointed bosses, and bronze artifacts, especially weapons, are also elaborately ornamented. A number of Otomani settlements are known, particularly fortified ones at BARCA and SPIŠSKY STVRTOK, which also provide evidence for social differentiation.

Otrar a medieval city in southern Kazakhstan, at the centre of the Otrar Oasis. First mentioned in written sources of the 8th century AD, Otrar was an important trading-point on the way from Iran and Central Asia to Siberia, Mongolia and China. In 1218 the so-called 'Otrar catastrophe' occurred, when a merchant caravan sent to Otrar by Genghis Khan was wiped out by Otrar's ruler. This caused the Mongol invasion of Central Asia. In 1220, after five months of siege, Otrar's fortifications were destroyed and the city was taken by the Mongols. In 1405 Tamerlane (Genghis Khan's descendant) died at Otrar. The city was abandoned in the 16th century.

The ruins of the city are situated on the middle course of the Syrdar'ya River, and they comprise a pentagonal hill which covers some 20 ha (50 acres) and is 18 m (60 ft) high. Remains of the fortifications are preserved: walls with towers and a ditch. The suburbs, also bound by a wall and a ditch, cover an area of about 150 ha (370 acres). Excavations have been carried out at the site since 1969 by the Kazakhstan archaeologists K. Akishev, K. Baipakov and L. Erzakovich.

Otzaki the site of a Neolithic–Early Bronze Age settlement mound in Thessaly, Greece, excavated by Milojcic in 1953–5. Otzaki has been a key site in defining the Thessalian cultural sequence, but the stratigraphy is not as clear as Milojcic believed.

Ötzi see SIMILAUN MAN.

'Oueli a small mound near LARSA, excavated by the French group working at the latter site, which provides a deep sequence of 'UBAID culture deposits, the base of which is earlier than the 'Ubaid 1 (ERIDU) period. The excavators have proposed the label 'Ubaid 0 for these earliest levels, and have provisionally assigned a dating of c.5800–5500 BC to them. Although some surface pottery collections had previously been tentatively identified as pre-'Ubaid 1, 'Oueli provides the first stratigraphic confirmation of such an early settlement on the southern MESOPOTAMIAN ALLUVIUM. The decorated ceramics show similarities with SAMARRAN pottery.

Ounan Point or **Ounanian Point** a pointed bladelet with basal stem, found in North African Late Pleistocene and Holocene industries, such as the Ounanian and early Neolithic of the eastern Sahara. See also SHAMARKIAN.

'Out of Africa' Hypothesis also known as the 'Eve', 'Garden of Eden', 'Single Origin' or 'Out of Africa 2' Hypothesis, a model of the origins of modern humans, based on MITOCHONDRIAL DNA data and fossil evidence (BORDER CAVE, SKHUL, KLASIES RIVER MOUTH, OMO, QAFZEH), that HOMO *sapiens* evolved first and relatively recently in Africa, perhaps some 200,000 years ago, before spreading to the rest of the world and displacing archaic human species already living there. This model therefore does not regard East Asian *H. erectus* as a direct ancestor of modern humans. A competing model, the Multiregional Hypothesis, argues that there was no single origin of modern humans, but rather continuity in human evolution in the many regions into which humans dispersed after leaving Africa for the first time ('Out of Africa 1') at least a million years ago (but see DMANISI, LONGGUPO). Advocates of the latter model argue that fossils like those from Dali, JINNIUSHAN and MABA provide a link between earlier *H. erectus* and later *H. sapiens* populations in the Far East, and therefore regard East Asian *H. erectus* as ancestral to modern *H. sapiens* in the region.

ovate a refined ACHEULIAN biface with an oval or elliptical outline and a flat or deliberately twisted profile. Many ovates have a tranchet finish.

Ovčarovo a TELL of the ENEOLITHIC GUMELNIŢA CULTURE dating to the 5th millennium BC. In the thirteen habitation levels, 112 rectangular houses have been excavated. Ovčarovo is one of many small farming communities in northeastern Bulgaria (such as POLJANICA) whose inhabitants may have contributed to the wealth found in the contemporaneous cemetery of VARNA located near by on the Black Sea coast.

Owo the most easterly Yoruba kingdom in Nigeria, where an excavation at Igbo Laja revealed a concentration of terracotta sculptures dated to the early 15th century AD. Many of the terracottas of human heads have a striking resemblance to those from IFE, while others are stylistically similar to those from BENIN.

Oxus treasure a very large group of valuable objects, which originated from the River Oxus (Amydarya) on the territory of modern Tadjikistan (ancient Bactria). It is not known exactly where the treasure was found, who found it, and why such a collection should have been put together. It was first mentioned in 1880, when Mohammedan merchants carrying the treasure were robbed on their journey from Kabul to Peshawar. Part of the treasure was successfully retrieved from the robbers, part of it disappeared into Indian bazaars, and some pieces were acquired later. The British Museum now has some 180 objects, known as the Oxus treasure: most are of gold, others of silver and copper, and there are also a few CYLINDER SEALS together with a hundred coins said to come from this hoard. They form a perplexing mixture of coins and objects whose dates range from at least 550 to 175 BC. The coins are from mints in Greece, Phoenicia, Asia Minor and Bactria. The objects are mostly from the great ACHAEMENID empire; some show Greek influence, while others display the contorted style of the SCYTHIANS. The most famous among them are a gold model of a chariot drawn by four horses, a silver statuette probably representing a Persian King of the Achaemenid dynasty, a pair of gold armlets, and golden plaques with images of people and animals.

oxygen isotope analysis isotopic analysis that examines the $^{18}O/^{16}O$ ratio of materials; changes in ratio are often interpreted as having palaeoclimatic significance, particularly in the analysis of DEEP-SEA CORES. Such cores preferably sample ocean bottom sediment rich in carbonate skeletons of *Foraminifera*, small benthic and planktonic marine organisms. The isotopic ratio in the marine fossils is the same as that of the water in which they lived. *Foraminifera* sampled from cores have revealed cyclic fluctuations in the $^{18}O/^{16}O$ ratio, which are interpreted as evidence primarily for continental ice volume change in response to GLACIAL-INTERGLACIAL cycles. The isotopic fluctuations arise as isotopically

OXUS TREASURE, Bactria: image of a warrior wearing an acinaces.

lighter ^{16}O is preferentially evaporated from oceans. During glacial episodes, the ^{16}O is preferentially stored in glacial ice, and oceanic $^{18}O/^{16}O$ ratios are relatively low in response to the addition of the isotopically lighter enriched water that was stored in glaciers. At least eleven cycles have been recognized, and formed the basis for re-evaluating the classical model of four glacial episodes.

Because temperature variations are correlated with changes in atmospheric $^{18}O/^{16}O$ ratios, oxygen isotopic analysis has also been used to identify seasonal changes in ice cores, interpret temperature variations during SPE-LEOTHEM precipitation, and examine isotopic variations in tree ring climatic relationships.

Oxyrhynchus (*Arabic* Bahnasa) a site in Middle Egypt. The activities of SEBBAKH-diggers and the excavations of Grenfell and Hunt in 1897 and 1903–7 produced many thousands of fragments of literary and non-literary papyri from the rubbish-dumps of the Graeco-Roman town.

Oyu a town in Akita Prefecture, Japan, where two Late JOMON period STONE CIRCLE sites are located. Both have two nested circles, the outer 135–50 m (148–64 yds) across and the inner 35–47 m (38–51 yds) across, and associated 'sundial' arrangements of a standing stone and surrounding pavement to the northwest. Such stone circles have been found to contain burials in shallow pits under the alignments.

Ozette a village site located in Washington State, USA, which was occupied from about the 15th century AD to the historic period, and consists of a row of LONG-HOUSEs and individual dwellings. Excellent preservation at the site allowed recovery of houses as well as wooden boxes, baskets and various artifacts, some of which were beautifully carved and decorated with shells and teeth.

Ozieri a late Neolithic culture of Sardinia, named after the cave-site of San Michele near Ozieri. Ozieri material is known from caves, village settlements and rock-cut tombs. It is characterized by the high-quality pottery, with a polished or burnished surface incised with flamboyant designs including zigzags, hatched triangles, arcs, festoons and stars. The CARINATED shapes recall Chasséen (see CHASSEY) and LAGOZZA pottery, but the decoration is unique. Classic Ozieri decorated ware has been dated to c.4100–3500 BC at the Grotta di Filiestru (Bonu Ighinu).

P

pa a MAORI term meaning fortified place. The best-known *pa* are ditched and banked enclosures of various types, but some were built in swamps and defended by palisades. Relatively few have been excavated, but most are Classic Maori in date. There is often evidence of occupation before defences were constructed. See also KAURI POINT, LAKE MANGAKAWARE, LAKE NGAROTO, OTAKANINI, TE AWANGA.

Pacariqtambo a region to the south of CUZCO, Peru, the place of origin of the INCA royal dynasty according to oral tradition. The original Inca ancestors, the four brothers Ayar and their four sister-wives, were said to have emerged from a cave with three windows on the mountain called Tambotoco. They organized the people into ten groups, and thence migrated north. The last remaining brother, Manco Capac, founded Cuzco.

Pacatnamú a large MIDDLE HORIZON and LATE INTERMEDIATE PERIOD site in the Jequetepeque Valley on the north coast of Peru, excavated by Christopher Donnan. The site is located on a promontory, bounded by the ocean on one side and steep cliffs on another. Large defensive walls impede access along the remaining side. Within the walled portion of the site are more than fifty truncated pyramid complexes – mounds, courtyards and enclosures. The site was occupied first in the Middle Horizon, and it may represent the southernmost extent of the MOCHE V POLITY. The site was abandoned near the end of the Middle Horizon, and reoccupied later in the Late Intermediate period; it was abandoned again at about the time that the CHIMÚ polity expanded into the region.

Pachacamac a large ceremonial site on the central coast of Peru, first established during the MIDDLE HORIZON, when it may have been under the control of the HUARI empire, or it may have been an independent POLITY. The site, excavated by UHLE, was a major pilgrimage centre, and still functioned as such at the time of the Spanish conquest. People from throughout the Andean region came to consult the oracle at Pachacamac. Branch oracles were established in other regions as well, these being considered 'wives' of Pachacamac. When the INCA conquered the region they allowed the centre to continue to function, and added their own Temple of the Sun to the site, along with other constructions.

Pachamachay a PRECERAMIC cave-site at 4,300 m (14,100 ft) altitude, in the central highlands of Peru. Excavated by John Rick, the site was a base-camp located in the high PUNA zone, occupied year-round by a small group who made infrequent trips out to other resource zones, and who subsisted almost entirely on meat. The site has a very early date of 11,800 bp, but most of the occupation seems to date to between 9000 and 2000 bp.

Pacheco a MIDDLE HORIZON site in the Nasca Valley on the south coast of Peru at which a major HUARI offering-deposit was found. The deposit, excavated by Julio C. TELLO, comprised hundreds of intentionally smashed polychrome vessels, buried in a large unstructured pit. There were remains of other structures as well, but details are unknown; the site was destroyed in the early 1950s.

Pacific The exploration and settlement of the scattered islands of the Pacific Ocean was a remarkable human achievement. Culturally, the Pacific is now commonly divided into three regions: POLYNESIA, MELANESIA and MICRONESIA. Its thousands of islands range from relatively large volcanic islands to tiny coral atolls. Settlement of the western Pacific rim occurred in the Late Pleistocene, with a rapid dispersal of primarily maritime people throughout the relatively protected waters and intervisible islands of western Melanesia and into northern AUSTRALIA. Australia was certainly settled by 40,000 years ago. In Melanesia, there are several Pleistocene sites in the BISMARCK ARCHIPELAGO, including MATENKUPKUM and YOMBON, which are more than 30,000 years old (see also MATENBEK, PAMWAK, BALOF). By 29,000 years ago evidence from KILU suggests that humans had reached the Solomons. Obsidian from TALASEA is found in many sites in the region, suggesting ongoing contact and exchange. The colonization of the

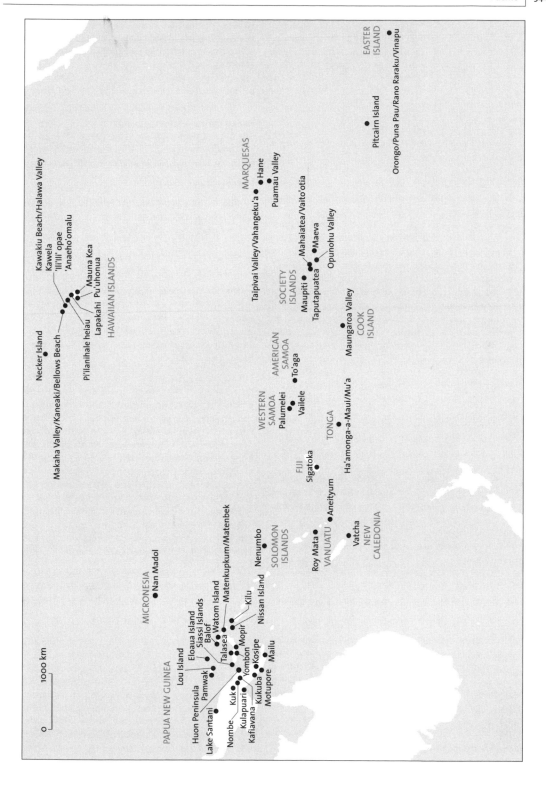

EASTER
ISLAND

Orongo/Puna Pau/Rano Raraku/Vinapu

Pitcairn Island

Puamau Valley
Hane
MARQUESAS

Kawakiu Beach/Halawa Valley
Kawela
'Ili'ili' opae
'Anaeho'omalu
Mauna Kea
Lapakahi   Pu'uhonua
Pi'ilanihale heiau
HAWAIIAN ISLANDS

Mahaiatea/Vaito'otia
Maeva
Opunohu Valley
Taipivai Valley/Vahangeku'a
Maupiti
SOCIETY
ISLANDS
Taputapuatea

Maungaroa Valley
COOK
ISLAND

Necker Island

Makaha Valley/Kaneaki/Bellows Beach

AMERICAN
SAMOA
To'aga

WESTERN
SAMOA
Palumelei
Vailele

TONGA
Ha'amonga-a-Maui/Mu'a

FIJI
Sigatoka

VANUATU   Aneityum

Vatcha
NEW
CALEDONIA

MICRONESIA
Nan Madol

Nenumbo
SOLOMON
ISLANDS

Roy Mata

Matenkupkum/Matenbek
Kilu
Nissan Island
Watom Island
Mopir
Eloaua Island
Siassi Islands
Balof
Talasea
Yombon
Kosipe
Mailu
Lou Island
Kuk
Kulapuari
Kukuba
Motupore
PAPUA NEW GUINEA
Huon Peninsula
Pamwak
Lake Santani
Nombe
Kafiavana

0   1000 km

remote Pacific was an explosive and rapid expansion of settlement, probably reaching as far as South America. The capacity to undertake long-distance return voyaging in the deep ocean was critical to the successful colonization of the region. Computer simulation studies and the available archaeological evidence suggest that the pattern of spread is consistent with a deliberate strategy of sailing upwind in search of new islands. This was a safe strategy, as it ensured the ability to return.

Experimental voyages, such as those of the HOKULE'A, demonstrate the skills of traditional Pacific navigators. The development of the double-hulled Polynesian sailing canoe allowed the transport of sufficient numbers of people, together with the necessary domestic animals and plants, to establish viable colonies.

About 3,500 years ago, the LAPITA cultural complex first appeared in the western Pacific and spread very rapidly from the Bismarck Archipelago, in Papua New Guinea, as far east as Fiji and Samoa. The origins of Lapita are controversial, but it is believed to be associated with the spread of AUSTRONESIAN speakers from Southeast Asia into the Pacific. Lapita was a maritime culture with an economy based on marine resources and domesticated plants and animals. Obsidian from Talasea and LOU is found throughout the region, suggesting continuing contact between widely separated communities. Lapita lasted for about a thousand years. In Melanesia, it was followed by other pottery-making traditions such as MANGAASI. In the Fiji-Tonga-Samoa triangle, pottery making seems to have declined and was finally abandoned about 2,000 years ago.

Expansion of settlement into eastern Polynesia began about 2,000 years ago. The HANE dune site in the Marquesas, the MAUPITI BURIAL GROUND and VAITO'OTIA in the Society Islands, and the early Hawaiian sites of BELLOWS BEACH on Oahu and HALAWA dune on Molokai are all examples of early eastern Polynesian sites. The remote EASTER ISLAND was probably settled soon after. Reaching NEW ZEALAND was considerably more difficult and dangerous, and it was the last major land mass to be colonized. The presence of sweet potato in eastern Polynesia suggests that Polynesian voyagers also reached South America.

The settlement of Micronesia is poorly understood, but the western islands were probably settled from the Philippines, while the atolls of eastern Micronesia seem to have been occupied more recently from Melanesia. Pacific societies are very diverse. The more densely populated island groups in Polynesia and Micronesia developed highly stratified CHIEFDOMS. Megalithic monuments are a feature of the Pacific archaeological record. The PULEMELEI stone mound on Samoa is one of the most spectacular of these (see also HA'AMONGA-A-MAUI, NAN MADOL). Some islands, like PITCAIRN and NECKER, were colonized, but abandoned before the arrival of Europeans.

Pacitan or **Patjitan** a region of southern-central Java where, along the Baksoko River, stone tools were found which MOVIUS classified as chopper/chopping tools of assumed Middle and Late Pleistocene date. Recent work indicates that these large tools formed only part of a pebble and flake industry of the Late Pleistocene and early Holocene.

Padah Lin cave-sites in the mountains of eastern Burma, not far to the west of SPIRIT CAVE, with early hunter-gatherer remains dating to c.11,000 BC, amongst the earliest-known HOABINHIAN assemblages.

Padang Lawas see ŚRIVIJAYA.

Padina a multi-period site in Serbia, located on the River Danube several kilometres upstream from LEPENSKI VIR. The two major occupations of the site are a 'pre-Neolithic' level contemporaneous with Lepenski Vir I and II, and a Neolithic layer with STARČEVO pottery. Burials occur in both phases, among the houses.

Padre Island the site, off the coast of Texas, of the remains of three Spanish treasure ships (out of a fleet of four) that were wrecked in AD 1554. The site is especially important because it contains some of the few such treasure ships that have been scientifically excavated, documented and published.

Paekche an early historic state succeeding Mahan (see SAMHAN) on the Korean peninsula (c.AD 300–662) which was in competition with KOGURYO and SILLA and had diplomatic and military relations with YAMATO in Japan. Its first capital was in or near MONGCH'ON Fortress near modern Seoul, thence removed to Ungjin (modern Kongju) and Sabi (modern PUYO), both in southern Ch'ungch'ong Province. Its remains mainly consist of stone-stepped or earthen MOUNDED TOMBS in these areas (see MURYONG), although excavations and survey in modern Puyo have determined the positioning of the gridded city constructed in the 7th century on the Tang model (see CHINESE DYNASTIES), including the locations of several Buddhist temples. Compare CHANG'AN, HEIJO, ANAPCHI.

pa'epa'e elaborate, well built, rectangular house-platforms in the Marquesas Islands, POLYNESIA.

Paestan pottery a type of SOUTH ITALIAN POTTERY produced at PAESTUM perhaps under the influence of SICILIAN POTTERY (see also CAMPANIAN POTTERY). It is unlike the other types of South Italian pottery in that some of the craftsmen signed their work; at the moment Asteas and Python are known. Production seems to have started near the middle of the 4th century BC.

Paestum (Gk Poseidonia) a coastal Greek colony in LUCANIA, Italy, founded c.600 BC. It is notable for a major series of temples in the DORIC ORDER which were rediscovered in the 18th century. They were dedicated to

PAESTUM, Italy: the temple of Poseidon.

Argive Hera (the 'Basilica'), Poseidon and Athena ('Ceres'), and range in date from the mid 6th century to the mid 5th century BC. A Roman FORUM was inserted over some of the sanctuary areas in the 3rd century BC; buildings include a shrine to the emperor and a temple of peace. There are also traces of an AMPHITHEATRE within the walled city. Some of the local tombs were decorated with murals, one of the more famous being the 5th-century BC 'Tomb of the Divers'. See also PAESTAN POTTERY.

Pagan an urban and Buddhist religious centre in upper Burma, capital of the Burman state formed in the mid 9th century AD and conquered by Mongol armies late in the 13th century, famous for the *c*.5,000 large and small temples and STUPAs built there over the centuries, the best known of which are the Kyanzittha, Ananda, Shwezigon and Nanpaya of the 11th century, the Sapada, Thatbinnyu and Shwegugyi of the 12th, and the Mahabodhi, Kondawgyi, Mingalazedi and Tilominlo of the 13th.

Pager, Harald (1923–85) a Czechoslovak-born graphic artist who emigrated to South Africa, where he became interested in rock art and developed a technique of reproducing paintings accurately by using black-and-white actual-sized photographs which he coloured in paint in the field. He is particularly acclaimed for his studies of paintings in the Ndedema Gorge in the DRAKENSBERG Mountains of South Africa, and in the BRANDBERG Mountains of Namibia.

Paglicci an Italian prehistoric cave-site on the Adriatic coast with a detailed stratigraphy, best known for its GRAVETTIAN material dating from *c*.24,700 to 20,000 bp, including two burials covered in ochre, and its cave art.

Paiján a PRECERAMIC tradition found in the north and central coast and highlands of Peru. Characteristic points are triangular, with a long narrow stem; they are never fluted. The Paiján tradition probably post-dates the PALAEOINDIAN FISHTAIL POINT tradition, and may have developed out of the EL INGA complex. The Paiján tradition may represent the first adaptation to the exploitation of maritime resources on the coast of Peru.

Painted Grey ware a pottery type characteristic of Iron Age sites in northern India, from the eastern Punjab and northern Rajasthan to the central Ganges. Of a fine, thin and well fired grey fabric, its decoration is black- or red-painted geometric designs. The ware, dated roughly 900–500 BC, is commonly associated with Indo-Aryan movements into northern India, though this is far from proven.

Pair-non-Pair a cave, whose name means 'Heads or Tails', near Bordeaux, southwestern France, in which François Daleau spotted Palaeolithic PARIETAL ART in 1883, though without at first realizing its significance. It contains a series of deep animal engravings, some of which were covered by GRAVETTIAN, and could therefore be AURIGNACIAN in age – the cave's occupation spanned a period from the MOUSTERIAN to the Gravettian.

palaeoanthropology a multi-disciplinary approach to the study of human evolution.

Palaeoasiatic a postulated early 'race' of HOMO *sapiens sapiens* of northeastern Asia, including the POSTGLACIAL CHULMUN and JOMON inhabitants of the Korean peninsula and Japanese islands, and the modern AINU. It is thought to have been replaced in the former area by TUNGUS-speaking migrants.

palaeoeconomy a school of archaeological thought, headed by E. S. HIGGS, concerned with the long-term determinants of human behaviour, specifically those concerned with the relationship between humans and their environments. Palaeoeconomy was strongly influenced by concepts drawn from animal ETHOLOGY.

palaeoenvironment the ancient environment. Palaeoenvironments can be reconstructed using a variety of techniques, such as ARCHAEOZOOLOGY and PALYNOLOGY. This kind of information is invaluable to an archaeologist, since it is assumed that the environment plays a fundamental role in determining many aspects of behaviour.

palaeoethnobotany or **archaeoethnobotany** the recovery and identification of plant remains from archaeological sites. This information helps the archaeologist reconstruct ancient environments, ancient diets, and human use and impact on ancient plant communities. See also ARCHAEOZOOLOGY.

Palaeoindian of late Pleistocene and early Holocene cultures of North America, with a terminal date of approximately 7000 BP, depending on the precise area.

Palaeoindian groups were mobile hunters and gatherers, often of now-extinct MEGAFAUNA, and probably used a spear technology, although use of the ATLATL is not impossible.

Palaeolithic literally the 'old Stone Age', the technological division of prehistory covering the period from the first appearance of tool-using humans to the retreat of the GLACIAL ice in the northern hemisphere at c.8500 BC and the emergence of the Mesolithic. Palaeolithic people lived as hunter-gatherers without agriculture and without formal pottery production. The Palaeolithic has traditionally been subdivided into three successive phases based mainly on artifact typology, although there is a growing awareness that such a classificatory approach may not be entirely valid, considering the vast time-span and the varying climatic and geographical conditions involved. The Lower Palaeolithic is the period of early HOMINID pebble tool and core tool manufacture. More technologically advanced tools appear in the Middle Palaeolithic, with a developing aesthetic and religious awareness and the appearance of NEANDERTHALERS. The Upper Palaeolithic is the period of fully modern humans, HOMO *sapiens sapiens,* a period of delicate stone and bone tool manufacture and the development of Palaeolithic art.

These terms have been used throughout the Old World, though primarily within Eurasia. The New World equivalent is PALAEOINDIAN.

In *East Asia,* the subdivisions are somewhat different from those farther west. The Palaeolithic period in China divides into Early (1,000,000–73,000 BC), Middle (c.73,000–40,000 BC), and Late (40,000–10,000 BC), typified by the remains at ZHOUKOUDIAN locality 1 and Upper Cave. Some dates by PALAEOMAGNETISM suggest a 1.7 million-year bp start to the Chinese Palaeolithic (see YUANMOU), but these are under review. In Korea and Japan, sites have been attributed up to 600,000 bp, as a new group of sites around Sendai City are substantiating the Early Palaeolithic in Japan (see SOZUDAI, SOKCHANG-RI, BABADAN A, ZAZARAGI, KULP'O-RI, HOSHINO, NISHIYAGI, NAKAMINE, TAKAMORI). The majority of sites in Korea and Japan belong to the Late Palaeolithic. The dual tool traditions of China (see LANTIAN) are joined by blade technologies c.30,000 bp, with small blades appearing at 28,000 bp. Heavy flakes (see SETOUCHI) and blades in Late Palaeolithic Japan are replaced by microblades (see YUBETSU) at 14,000 bp, and overall bifacial flaking at 12,000 bp. Ceramics appear in the terminal Palaeolithic record of Japan (see FUKUI). See also AKASHI, ARAYA, DINGCUN, IWAJUKU, JINNIUSHAN, KEHE, MABA, MINATOGAWA, NIHEWAN, SHIYU, SHUIDONGGOU.

Palaeolithic art the art of the last Ice Age, usually divided into four groups: (a) portable or MOBILIARY ART, comprising a wide variety of forms, from engraved stones to carvings in antler or ivory – thousands of such pieces are known from Spain to Siberia; (b) deep engravings or bas-reliefs on large blocks of stone in rockshelters, known from southwestern France; (c) art on rocks in the open air, either deeply pecked figures or engravings (see CÔA); (d) cave-art or PARIETAL ART, known primarily in Spain, France and Italy. It includes a range of techniques from finger-markings and engravings to bas-relief sculpture and painting. It comprises animal figures (mostly adults drawn in profile, and dominated by horse and bison), much rarer anthropomorphs and abundant non-figurative motifs and 'SIGNS'. Some is on open view, but much is hidden or inaccessible. Art in Europe appears early in the Upper Palaeolithic (see VOGELHERD, HOHLENSTEINSTADEL, GEISSENKLÖSTERLE, GROTTE CHAUVET), and becomes abundant in the SOLUTREAN and especially MAGDALENIAN periods. Art of similar antiquity is also known on other continents (see PEDRA FURADA, APOLLO 11, KOONALDA, EARLY MAN, KAMIKUROIWA, etc.). Much of the European art appears linked to a complex mythology and incorporates a distinct set of rules: early interpretations such as 'art for art's sake' ('shamanism') or hunting magic are now recognized as far too simplistic.

palaeomagnetism the magnetic polarization of magnetic particles in rocks and sediment in alignment with the Earth's magnetic field at the time of rock formation and sediment deposition. Palaeomagnetism can be used in STRATIGRAPHY for correlation. Past reversals in the earth's magnetic field are recorded in susceptible deposits and independently dated by other methods; the youngest reversal dates to about 700,000 bp. With time, the magnetic poles also wander on a smaller scale, which causes regional variations in declination (angle between magnetic and true north) and inclination (angle of vertical inclination from a horizontal plane). Measurement of these parameters on materials of different ages can be used to build regional chronologies that can be independently dated. See also ARCHAEOMAGNETISM.

palaeontology the study of the remains, origin and evolution of life forms through time. Fossils may provide PALAEOENVIRONMENTAL information based on habitat restrictions. The unique sequencing and non-repeating nature of evolution provides a biostratigraphic tool for RELATIVE DATING and CORRELATION. See STRATIGRAPHY.

palaeopathology a branch of pathology which deals with anatomical and physiological abnormalities in humans in ancient contexts. Sometimes used in determining the cause of death in individuals, palaeopathology is also useful in studies of nutrition, exercise and disease in ancient populations.

palaeopedology the study of the genesis, character, STRATIGRAPHY and geomorphic, temporal and PALAEO-

ENVIRONMENTAL significance of buried fossil soils (PALAEOSOLS) formed on landscapes of the past, all of which affect the interpretation of any associated archaeological record. Palaeopedology can help identify features, characteristics and processes that resulted from, or were influenced by, people and their manipulation and exploitation of landsystems.

palaeoserology a branch of serology which deals with serums and their reactions and properties, primarily in humans, in ancient contexts. Such studies generally require the preservation of body tissue, which is rare except in the case of some mortuary practices or in unusual MATRICES.

palaeosol BURIED SOIL formed on a landscape of the past or under different extrinsic and intrinsic factors, processes and conditions than the present day, which has temporal significance and is a source of PALAEOENVIRONMENTAL information. Palaeosols are preserved in a variety of DEPOSITIONAL ENVIRONMENTS including Pleistocene loess sequences, where they aid in interpretation of GLACIAL-INTERGLACIAL sequences, and alluvial river valleys, colluvial HILLSLOPE and ALLUVIAL FAN environments, where sedimentation also tends to be episodic. See also PALAEOPEDOLOGY.

Palaepaphos see KOUKLIA-PALAEPAPHOS.

palaestra an open exercise area often surrounded by PORTICOS. In the Greek world it might form part of a GYMNASIUM complex which would include a STADIUM. Alternatively it might be connected to THERMAE.

palafitta (*pl.* **palafitte**) an Italian term (*pala*, post, and *fitta*, driven in) for a dwelling built on wooden posts fixed in the sediments at the edge of a lake, of the kind known in Italy, Switzerland and France in the Neolithic and Bronze Age. See also LAKE DWELLING.

Palaikastro the site of a MINOAN settlement on the island of CRETE. The Neopalatial town is particularly impressive, the blocks of houses laid out on either side of paved streets, but despite the fact that Palaikastro was a populous and evidently prosperous settlement, no palace has as yet been discovered. On Petsophas, above Palaikastro, a PEAK SANCTUARY has been excavated.

Palenque a MAYA centre on the western frontier of the Maya Lowlands in the state of Chiapas, Mexico. It reached its height during the late CLASSIC, coming to power as TEOTIHUACÁN was in its decline. Palenque collapsed between AD 810 and 830.
In 1952 the archaeologist Alberto Ruz discovered the burial chamber of Pacal, the greatest ruler of Palenque, who died in AD 683 at the age of eighty. The spectacular burial was beneath the floor in the Temple of Inscriptions.

Paleo-Indian see PALAEOINDIAN.

Palermo Stone a diorite STELA, one fragment of which is now in Palermo, with others in London and Cairo. The complete monument was a year-by-year record of the reigns of the kings of Egypt from the 1st to the 5th Dynasty, and is a major source of information regarding the chronology of the OLD KINGDOM.

Pales, Léon (1905–88) a French prehistorian best known for his pioneering work on PALAEOPATHOLOGY, his studies of footprints in caves, and especially for his 25-year decipherment of the hundreds of engraved slabs from LA MARCHE.

Palli Aike see CUEVA PALLI AIKE.

Palliser Bay an area at the south end of the North Island of NEW ZEALAND which has been the subject of a detailed regional study by archaeologists from the University of Otago. The sites include settlements, burials and fields for sweet potato cultivation, but no storage pits. The area is today at the limit of sweet potato cultivation, but was first occupied as early as AD 1100. It was abandoned about AD 1400 as a result of environmental degradation and climatic change.

Palmela a cemetery of four CHALCOLITHIC rock-cut tombs near the Tagus estuary in Setubal, Portugal. The tombs have a passage leading to a 'man-hole' entrance, originally closed by a fitted door slab, beyond which is a kidney-shaped chamber, originally used for collective inhumation. The tombs were rich in BEAKER material, including over fifty beakers along with copper knives and fragments of gold foil. Also present was the distinctive leaf-shaped copper blade known as the Palmela point, which is found in beaker assemblages throughout Iberia and along the Mediterranean and Atlantic coasts of France.

palmette a stylized palm-frond often used as a decorative motif in Greek and Roman art. They were used in a variety of ways and in different media, which included architecture (see ANTEFIX) and pottery (see BLACK-GLOSSED).

Palmyra a city dependent on trade between Syria and the east. Under the emperor Septimius Severus it gained the status of a Roman colony. Remains of the city include colonnaded streets and the temple of Bel. Communal tombs in towers were marked by plaques in high relief showing the deceased.

palstave a bronze axe type in which the blade is divided from the heel by a ridge, with shallow grooves on either side of the heel to facilitate hafting. In Europe, the palstave was a Middle Bronze Age development from the flat and flanged axes of the Early Bronze Age, the new design being intended to improve the efficiency of hafting, but ultimately giving way to the still more efficient socketed axe of the Late Bronze Age.

PALENQUE, Mexico.

palynology or **pollen analysis** the study of fossil and living pollen and spores including their production, dispersal and applications. Palynology, developed by Norwegian geologist Lennart von Post, is utilized in PALAEOENVIRONMENTAL reconstruction, identifying natural and human-induced vegetation changes, and developing relative CHRONOLOGIES. The resilient *exine* (outer coating) of the pollen and spores of plants, mosses and ferns is preserved in ANAEROBIC environments, such as lakes and bogs, and some acidic and dry soils, such as in caves.

Samples are preferably collected in a core, and the pollen is concentrated by chemical treatments and fine mesh wet SIEVING, then stained, mounted on slides, examined and counted under a microscope. Identification is aided by unique combinations of morphological features on the exine. A pollen diagram is constructed, which consists of the pollen count data, expressed as percentages for each taxon and plotted versus depth, which represents relative time. An absolute pollen diagram illustrates the numbers of pollen grains of a given taxon deposited on a unit area per unit measure of time, and requires numerous radiocarbon ages. Diagrams are zoned, based on changes in pollen assemblages or influx rates. Inferences about past environments and environmental change are made from sequential changes in zone composition and are based primarily on studies of modern pollen production, dispersal, SEDIMENTATION, reworking, preservation and relationships to modern environments.

Pollen zonation can be used as a RELATIVE DATING tool. Pollen zones may be recognized and correlated regionally, although they may well be DIACHRONIC. In some circumstances, pollen zones may be related to archaeological deposits, thus providing some indication of age. See also ABSOLUTE POLLEN COUNTING.

Pampa de las Llamas or **Moxeke** a major INITIAL PERIOD ceremonial centre in the Casma Valley of the northern-central coast of Peru. The site follows a linear axis, with the large mound of Moxeke near one end, and Huaca A at the other. Parallel to the central axis are rows of small, contiguous U-shaped structures. Huaca A, excavated by Thomas and Shelia Pozorski, is built according to a rigid, bilaterally symmetrical plan, and may have served as a storage facility.

Pampa Grande a MIDDLE HORIZON, MOCHE V site in the Lambayeque region on the far north coast of Peru. After the abandonment of the Huacas del Sol and Luna, and the southern portion of Moche territory, a new capital was established at Pampa Grande. The site covers over 4 sq. km (1.5 sq. miles), and includes truncated pyramids, residential architecture and storage facilities.

Pampa Ingenio see NASCA LINES.

Pamwak a limestone rockshelter on Manus, Admiralty Islands, with nearly 4 m (13 ft) of very rich cultural deposits. The age of the first occupation is unknown, as the lowest layers lack organic material and have not yet been dated. The earliest date so far is about 13,000 bp at a depth of about 1.7 m (5.5 ft). Most of the artifacts from the older layers are chert. Obsidian from LOU ISLAND replaced chert about 12,000 years ago.

Panaramitee art widely distributed in Australia, but best known from the arid centre. The tradition is characterized by pecked figures depicting a limited range of motifs, mostly bird and animal tracks, and circles. Crescents, dots, spirals, lines, mazes and human figures also occur. Panaramitee art has long been thought to be ancient, but, like all rock art, is difficult to date. The lowest deposits at EARLY MAN SHELTER, c.13,000 bp, covered Panaramitee-style engravings. The CATION RATIO dates of 30,000 from KAROLTA are no longer accepted. However, the survival of the tradition into the Holocene has been claimed at Mount Yengo and Panaramitee-type motifs feature in contemporary Aboriginal art in central Australia. See also CLELAND HILLS, MUTAWINTJI, STURTS MEADOWS.

HMS Pandora a shipwreck discovered in 1983 on Australia's Great Barrier Reef and the subject of a long term archaeological research programme by the Queensland Museum. The *Pandora* sank in 1791 on her return voyage from pursuing the *Bounty* mutineers. Unlike most historic wrecks on the reef, the *Pandora* sank virtually intact after being refloated by her crew and was rapidly sealed under a layer of sand. Consequently, the ship and its contents are unusually well preserved.

pan-grave culture a semi-nomadic cattle-herding people of the Eastern Desert of Egypt who flourished during the Second INTERMEDIATE PERIOD (1633–1550 BC) and were so called because of their distinctive round or oval shallow graves, which have been found throughout UPPER EGYPT and LOWER NUBIA. Their material culture has much in common with the C-GROUP. The pan-grave people served as mercenaries during this turbulent period of Egyptian history and continued in a similar role as the police force of NEW KINGDOM Egypt, when they were called the Medjay.

Panhellenic *adj.* literally 'all Greek'. It is applied to regional, rather than local, sanctuaries which attracted dedications from across the Greek world. See DELPHI, OLYMPIA.

Panjikent an ancient Sogdian (see SOGD) fort, situated on the right bank of the Zeravshan River in Tadzhikistan, 40 km (25 miles) east of Samarkand. It is unique monument of the Pre-Islamic culture of Central Asia. Excavation of the site was begun in 1946 by Soviet archaeologist A. Yakubovski and continued by A. Belenitski. The fort existed from the 5th century AD up to the 8th, when it was destroyed by Arabs. The ruins of Panjikent encompassed a citadel, while suburbs and cemeteries lay outside the town wall. Two temples, the ruler's palace and the dwellings of townspeople have also been discovered. Numerous Sogdian inscriptions on potsherds, slabs and walls have been found at the fort. Panjikent is especially famous for its monumental art: murals, wooden sculptures and wooden and clay bas-reliefs. The walls of many excavated houses were decorated with clay and stucco figures (executed in a manner seen earlier at sites like NISA). The subjects of the murals are, mostly, cult and epic scenes. Images of some deities provide evidence of the influence of Hindu iconography. In style and content the Panjikent art is connected with some other Central Asian cities (such as AFRASIAB, Varakhsha, etc.) as well as with those of Iran, Afghanistan and India.

Panlongcheng [Pan-lung-ch'eng] an early SHANG period site in Hubei Province, China, thought to be the southernmost outpost of the Shang political system in the 15th–13th centuries BC. A walled town of 7.5 ha (18.5 acres) was accompanied on the outside by numerous elite burials containing ERLIGANG-style bronzes (see ZHENGZHOU), poor burials, pottery and stone tools and bronze manufacturing.

Pannonia an area of modern-day Hungary west and south of the River Danube incorporated into the Roman empire as a province in AD 10. Pannonia became one of the more prosperous Roman frontier provinces in Central Europe and was the location of numerous VILLAS. Its principal town was Aquincum, on the site of the Buda section of modern Budapest.

pan-pipe lug or **flûte de Pan** a kind of handle, comprising a series of vertical cylindrical lugs side by side, found on either side of Neolithic pots of the CHASSEY, CORTAILLOD and LAGOZZA cultures of France, Switzerland and northern Italy. Its name is derived from its

PANARAMITEE ART, at Sturts Meadows, Australia.

resemblance to a set of Pan pipes, and such lugs were probably a means of suspending the vessels.

Panticapaion see SCYTHIANS.

Papuan languages a group of over 700 languages spoken mainly in New Guinea, but also elsewhere in MELANESIA and the islands of eastern Indonesia. They are widely believed to be descended from the languages of the first people to migrate into Melanesia. They are also referred to as Non-Austronesian (NAN) languages.

papyrus the flexible writing material produced from the marsh plant *Cyperus papyrus*. The pithy stem of the papyrus plant was cut into thin slivers and laid out in two overlying rows running vertically and horizontally, which were then pounded, forming a homogeneous whole as the starch present in the released sap dried. Papyrus was produced on a relatively large scale in Egypt, from at least as early as the 1st Dynasty until the extinction of the plant in Egypt during the Middle Ages, and was used for a wide range of documents from letters and administrative records to religious texts.

Paquimé see CASAS GRANDES.

Paracas the major EARLY HORIZON culture on the south coast of Peru, showing direct influence from the religious centre at CHAVÍN. The Paracas culture is known primarily from tombs and associated funerary artifacts. The type-site, the Paracas NECROPOLIS, was discovered by KROEBER and excavated by TELLO. Paracas textiles are some of the finest prehistoric textiles known anywhere in the world. Tapestries were woven and embroidered with elaborate depictions of mythical creatures, and then used as mummy wrappings (see MUMMIFICATION). Painted cotton textiles with pure Chavín designs have also been found. Paracas ceramics were typically incised with geometric or representational designs, especially felines, and painted after firing with resin-based paints. The Paracas style is the direct antecedent of the NASCA tradition.

paradigm a set of assumptions, objectives and METHODOLOGIES which determine the specific procedures of scientific investigation. Examples of paradigms in archaeology include BEHAVIOURAL ARCHAEOLOGY, CULTURE HISTORY, PROCESSUAL (NEW) and POSTPROCESSUAL ARCHAEOLOGY.

parados an entrance or exit used by actors entering an ORCHESTRA **(see fig., p. 335)** of a theatre. It lies between the seats and the SKENE.

Paranthropus see AUSTRALOPITHECUS.

Parhae see BOHAI.

parietal art literally 'art on walls'; the term is extended to cover prehistoric works of art on any non-movable surface, including blocks, ceilings and floors. See also LEVANTINE ART, PALAEOLITHIC ART. Compare MORTUARY ART.

Parmana a region of the Middle Orinoco drainage, Venezuela. Research by Anna C. Roosevelt has documented a shift in subsistence from root crops, especially manioc, to the cultivation of seed crops, particularly maize, roughly 800–400 bc. Maize cultivation in turn led to a sharp increase in population density, and provided the basis for the later emergence of CHIEFDOM-level societies.

Parmerpar Meethaner a rockshelter in northern-central TASMANIA with a long occupation sequence from about 34,000 bp to about 780 bp. It is one of the oldest sites in Tasmania (compare WARREEN); Richard Cosgrove's excavations document human adaptation to an increasingly forested environment during the Pleistocene-Holocene transition. The artifacts include thumbnail scrapers in the Pleistocene levels. There is evidence of increasing occupation intensity over the last 3,000 years.

Paroong Cave one of several limestone caves in the Mount Gambier district, South Australia, with deeply incised, pounded or abraded motifs, especially circles. The style has been termed the Karake style, and is thought by some to be Pleistocene in age.

Parpalló Cave a well-stratified prehistoric cave situated near Gandia, on the Valencia coast, Spain, and excavated by PERICOT in 1929–31. The site has a characteristic GRAVETTIAN layer including backed blades, burins and endscrapers, followed by a sequence of SOLUTREAN levels featuring barbed and tanged points, and then four MAGDALENIAN levels with typical stone, bone and antler artifacts including microliths, needles and harpoons. Over 5,000 small stone plaques, engraved and painted with animal motifs, and scores of decorated bones were found in the Palaeolithic levels of the cave. The Mesolithic occupation phase includes typical microburins, and is followed by Neolithic and later-period material.

Parrot, André (1901–80) a French theologian, one of the great formative generation of MESOPOTAMIAN archaeologists. Parrot's major contribution to the field was his long-term project at MARI. In the 1920s he worked at several sites (including BAALBEK and BYBLOS) in the French protectorates in the Levant. In the early 1930s he shifted to Mesopotamia, where he concluded the French work at TELLO and began exploration at LARSA; in 1933 Parrot began his excavation at Mari, which continued under his direction for the next forty years. Also involved in the government museum service (eventually becoming director of the Louvre), Parrot produced numerous books for a popular audience, and his history of Mesopotamian archaeology remains one of the best ever written.

Parsagadae the ancestral seat of the ACHAEMENID dynasty and the first imperial capital of CYRUS the Great, located north of PERSEPOLIS in Fars. The site contains remnants of several palaces, cult buildings and other structures; investigation of one palace discovered 3rd century BC (i.e. post-Achaemenid) occupation. The tomb of Cyrus still stands largely intact.

Parthenon a highly decorated temple on the AKROPOLIS at ATHENS dedicated to Athena. The building in the DORIC ORDER was started in 447 BC as part of a programme of construction by the statesman Perikles, although it overlies an earlier temple which was either destroyed by the Persians in 480 BC or started by the general Kimon in the 460s and later abandoned. The Parthenon contained an elaborate CHRYSELEPHANTINE statue of the goddess. The PEDIMENTS were filled with scenes of the conflict between the deities Athena and Poseidon over Attica, and the Birth of Athena. The METOPES show battles between Lapiths and Centaurs, the gods and the giants, Greeks fighting Amazons, as well as events at TROY. Although the temple was of the Doric order, a continuous frieze was placed along the upper walls of the CELLA (a feature of the IONIC ORDER), and was thus partially obscured by the outer colonnade. It showed a procession of horsemen, chariots, sacrificial animals and officials which moved along both sides of the Cella to meet at the eastern end with the gods seated on Olympus and the folding of the dress for the goddess. Many of the sculptures were removed by ELGIN and are now in the British Museum.

Parthians the inhabitants of Khorasan in northeastern Iran, who removed themselves from BACTRIAN Greek domination in the mid 3rd century BC, and then during the 2nd century BC formed an empire that incorporated Iran and most of MESOPOTAMIA. The Parthians are perhaps best known historically for their intermittent wars with the Romans, including the defeat of Crassus at Carrhae in 53 BC and the temporary loss of Mesopotamia to TRAJAN (in AD 115–17). The Parthian empire was overthrown early in the 3rd century AD by the SASSANIANS in southern Iran. The English phrase 'Parthian shot' derives from the typical Parthian military tactics of mounted bow-men, who could fire at the enemy while retreating.

particle size analysis or **grain size analysis** the analysis of the grain size distributions used to characterize and describe archaeological sediments or soils, identify subtle depositional trends, and address specific research questions. Particle size distributions are not diagnostic of a particular depositional agent, process or environment, but may aid in characterization and interpretation of these parameters. For determining sand, silt and clay percentages, various SEDIMENTATION methods are utilized that are based on laws of settling velocity of particles. Microscopy methods are also available. For determining size distribution of fine gravel and sand, SIEVING is performed. Particles greater than pebble size are measured directly.

Pasemah a plateau in southwestern Sumatra famous for its 'megalithic' remains, including stone slab graves and large sculpted boulders bearing figures of animals and warriors wearing metal armour, swords and beads similar to those found in Iron Age burials of the last centuries BC, and carrying DONG SON bronze drums. Sites include Tegurwangi, Tanjungara, Pagaralam, Gunungmegang, Pematang and Batugajah.

Paso a lakeshore SHELL MIDDEN in northern Sulawesi, Indonesia, containing obsidian flake tools and bone points pre-dating the TOALIAN (c.6500 BC); similar forms appear in basal ULU LEANG and Agop Sarapad (MADAI CAVES).

passage grave a type of CHAMBERED TOMB in which the chamber is reached from the edge of the covering mound via a long passage.

Passo di Corvo a middle Neolithic enclosure in Puglie, Italy, surrounded by concentric ditches. Within the ditches are traces of approximately 100 circular hut compounds. These contained rectangular houses on low stone footings associated with red painted pottery. There is a single radiocarbon date of c.5200 BC. Several hundred enclosures of this type are known on the Tavoliere plain.

Passy-sur-Yonne a cemetery in Yonne, France, of middle Neolithic long mounds, up to 300 m (330 yds) in length, represented today only by their surrounding ditches. From a broad eastern end, interrupted by a central 'entrance' gap, the monuments tail away to a narrow western extremity. Individual burial in a deep pit near the eastern end of the structure is the general rule. Associated pottery includes early middle Neolithic CERNY and indicates a date of c.3800 BC. Similar cemeteries are now also known from the Caen area of Normandy.

Pastoral Neolithic of East Africa a general term for pre-Iron Age food-producing societies in East Africa. Although the term refers only to pastoralism, it is in fact uncertain whether or not crops were cultivated as well. The route by which food production reached East Africa may have been from Ethiopia or the Sudan. The earliest Pastoral Neolithic sites are on the plains of northern Kenya and date to the middle 3rd millennium BC. Southern Kenyan Pastoral Neolithic sites date from the end of the 2nd millennium BC and the tradition continues until the appearance of iron working in the last few centuries BC and first centuries AD. The Pastoral Neolithic is not found south of northern Tanzania. Several Pastoral Neolithic traditions have been recognized, but are generally not well defined chronologically. See ELMENTEITAN, GOGO FALLS, NAROSURA, NDERIT, NGAMURIAK, NJORO RIVER CAVE, OLDISHI, OLMALENGE.

Pataliputra (modern Patna) the capital city of the Magadha kingdom and then the imperial centre of the MAURYAN kingdom, set along the south bank of the Ganges River in northeastern India. The place was first settled as a village in the 5th century BC, and quickly grew to become the largest South Asian city of its time. The Greek diplomat Megasthenes described it (around 300 BC) as a long narrow city, some 14 km (9 miles) long and 3 km (2 miles) wide, protected by a broad moat and surrounded by a timber palisade with 570 towers and sixty-four gates. Limited archaeological work has recorded several aspects of the city. Survey and soundings have revealed a large moated area of 340 ha (840 acres) within a sprawling palisaded 22 sq. km (8.5 sq. mile) district; these observations largely substantiate Megasthenes' description. The palisade was a double line of timbers set 4 m (13 ft) apart and probably filled with earth. The only other reported monument inside the city is a hall fitted with eighty pillars and set upon a 1 m (3 ft) high podium, around which ran a canal. The construction of this is reminiscent of ACHAEMENID architecture, and probably reflects Mauryan borrowings of imperial display from the southeastern provinces of the somewhat earlier Persian empire.

patera a rounded bowl, often bronze, of the Roman period usually attached to a long handle. Its shape probably made it suitable for the pouring of LIBATIONS.

patina **1** the outermost surface of an artifact which differs in colour, texture, lustre or composition from the remainder of the artifact, resulting from chemical, physical or biological alteration in response to surrounding soil environmental conditions. Numerous processes may obscure or destroy surface detail including corrosion, dissolution, precipitation, abrasion and replacement.
 2 a porous bluish or white weathering, caused by alkaline conditions which slowly affect the surface of flint when exposed to the atmosphere or to rainwater. A green patina caused by corrosion can affect bronze objects.

Patjitan see PACITAN.

Patna see PATALIPUTRA.

patu a short MAORI fighting club made of wood, bone or stone. Finds of whalebone and wooden clubs comparable to Maori patu at VAITO'OTIA, Society Islands, suggest they may have been part of the early eastern Polynesian (see PACIFIC) assemblage introduced to NEW ZEALAND by the first settlers.

Paviland Cave the Goat's Hole Cavern at Paviland, Gower Peninsula, in Wales, which has yielded early Upper Palaeolithic material of *c.*38,000 to 10,000 years ago (AURIGNACIAN and CRESWELLIAN), including the earliest-known British ceremonial burial, identified by Buckland in 1823 as the 'Red Lady of Paviland' but which was actually an ochre-covered male burial; dating to 26,350 bp, it was accompanied by ivory objects.

Pavlov an Upper Palaeolithic open-air site located near the Dyje River in southern Moravia in the Czech Republic. The cultural layer is contained in loess deposits, and yielded radiocarbon dates of 26,730–26,000 bp; among the faunal remains are woolly mammoth, horse and reindeer. Traces of over a dozen former structures with central hearths were encountered. The artifacts include small retouched blades, Gravette points and animal figurines of fired loess, and are assigned to the EASTERN GRAVETTIAN.

Payne, Humfry G. G. (1902–36) the director of the British School at Athens from 1929 to his death. While Assistant Keeper in the Coin Room at the Ashmolean Museum in Oxford he prepared what is considered to be a definitive study of ARCHAIC Corinthian art, *Necrocorinthia* (1931). See CORINTHIAN POTTERY. After fieldwork on Crete, which included one of the post-Bronze Age cemeteries near KNOSSOS, his interest in archaic Corinthian art led him to conduct work in the archaic sanctuary at PERACHORA. With G. M. Young he prepared an illustrated catalogue of the archaic sculpture from the Athenian AKROPOLIS. See also KOUROS, KORE.

Pazyryk a complex of Iron Age tumuli in the ALTAI Mountains of southwestern Siberia, dating to the 5th to 3rd centuries BC, many of which were excavated by RUDENKO and GRYAZNOV. The Pazyryk burials are the graves of high-status individuals among the nomadic pastoralists of this region, and they are characterized by exceptional preservation of their contents. Timber burial chambers were covered by stone cairns, under which the ground was permanently frozen to a depth of 7 m (23 ft). Not only were artifacts of wood, leather, skin and wool preserved, but also the mummified bodies of the occupants of the tombs and the horses buried with them also survived. The frozen tombs of Pazyryk, UKOK and many other cemeteries belong to the Pazyryk culture, one of the SCYTHIAN TYPE CULTURES.

peak sanctuary a MINOAN cult place in the mountains of CRETE. The sacred status of peak sanctuaries was indicated by deposits of votive offerings rather than by monumental architecture.

peat a sedimentary body of dark brown or black partially decomposed organic matter preserved under ANAEROBIC conditions in an environment containing excessive moisture. Peats are important sources of PALAEOENVIRONMENTAL information; macrobotanical remains, pollen, beetle parts, gastropods and even human remains are usually well preserved and can be radiocarbon dated. Peat could also have been used as a fuel source when dried. See also LINDOW, TOLLUND, GRAUBALLE.

pebble a size subdivision of gravel clasts that ranges

between 4 and 64 mm (0.16 and 2.5 inches) in diameter, according to the Wentworth-Udden classification system. Crude, early tools were often made from pebble-size clasts and are referred to as pebble tools.

Pécel a Late ENEOLITHIC regional variant of the BADEN culture in southwestern Hungary, known primarily from cemeteries.

Pech de l'Azé a well-stratified Palaeolithic tunnel-cave in the Dordogne, France, with six distinct ACHEULIAN levels dating to the RISS GLACIATION, followed by six MOUSTERIAN levels dating to the WÜRM glaciation. Excavated principally by BORDES, it contains numerous hearths of various kinds. ESR dating of animal teeth shows occupation between 232,000 and 53,000 years ago.

Pech Merle a major cave in the Quercy region, France, where Palaeolithic paintings and engravings were first discovered in 1922. About sixty animal figures (dominated by mammoth) are known, together with numerous dots and signs. The most famous figures are a frieze of black drawings, and the 'spotted horse' panel. The art was assigned to three phases, from 20,000 to 10,000 BC, and a radiocarbon date of 18,400 bp was obtained from a butchered reindeer bone left in front of the horse panel, but charcoal from the right-hand spotted horse has produced a radiocarbon result of 24,640 bp. The cave was never inhabited by Palaeolithic people, and their scant traces (including footprints) suggest a series of brief visits.

Pecos Classification a culture stage sequence devised by the first Pecos Conference of 1927 to organize prehistoric material from the American Southwest. It was later restricted to the ANASAZI tradition of the northern part of the region. Architecture and ceramics are the primary elements defining the stages. The individual stages are Basketmaker I–III and PUEBLO I–V, and show increasing social, architectural, subsistence and technological complexity.

pectoral (*Lat.* 'pectus', breast) a piece of jewellery that was worn on the chest. One of the most famous pectorals is that from the TOLSTAYA MOGILA barrow.

pediment a triangular recess usually found at both ends of CLASSICAL temples and treasuries, often filled with sculpture. It is located above the ENTABLATURE. See also TYMPANON.

pedogenesis the total interaction of physical, chemical and biological factors, processes and conditions that cause a soil to evolve, as expressed by SOIL HORIZONS. Through pedogenesis, archaeological deposits can be displaced, mixed, sorted or buried. Pedogenic processes continuously interact with depositional and erosional processes, which result in the SOIL PROFILE. If SEDIMEN-

TATION processes overwhelm pedogenesis, the former land surface soil is buried and becomes a PALAEOSOL.

pedology the study of the genesis, characteristics, distributions and uses of soils. Proper interpretation of the context and integrity of archaeological deposits associated with soils requires identification and understanding of the soils, or the pedology. See also PALAEOPEDOLOGY, PALAEOSOL.

pedoturbation a general term applied to the set of processes by which soils are disrupted, mixed, sorted or materially cycled to different degrees of homogenization by a variety of physical, chemical and biological agents. Both the land surface and layers within the soil, and any associated cultural debris, may potentially be affected, including total or partial destruction of feature boundaries and interiors.

Pedra Furada or **Toca do Boqueirão do Sítio da Pedra Furada** a huge painted sandstone rockshelter in the Piauí region of eastern Brazil, excavated by Niè017;de Guidon in the 1970s and Fabio Parenti in the 1980s, at which a long sequence of possible hearths have yielded radiocarbon dates back to c.47,500 bp. Fallen painted wall-fragments have been found STRATIFIED in layers dating to 12,000 and possibly 17,000 bp, indicating the presence of rock art by that period. While the upper layers of the site represent an undisputed post-PALAEOINDIAN occupation, some researchers have questioned the identification of crude quartzite pebble and flake tools and hearths in lower levels.

Pedra Pintada, Caverna da a sandstone cave in the equatorial lowlands of the Lower Amazon in Brazil, where excavations by A. Roosevelt in the early 1990s revealed a PALAEOINDIAN occupation spanning a period from c.11,200 to 10,000 bp. Lithics included stemmed, triangular spearpoints, and the fauna was primarily big fish, rodents, turtles and birds. Woodworking tools were also recovered, as well as the remains of tropical fruits, Brazil nuts, palm seeds and other starchy, oily, vitamin-rich plants. Samples of pigment in PICTOGRAPHs have been found to be similar to samples from hundreds of lumps and drops of red pigment, as well as two small fragments of painted wall, stratified only in the oldest Palaeoindian level.

Pefkakia the site of a late Neolithic–Bronze Age settlement mound in Thessaly, Greece, excavated by Theocharis in 1957 and by Milojcic in 1967–77. Pefkakia has been a key site in defining the Thessalian cultural sequence, and the presence of CYCLADIC, MINOAN and Trojan imports has made it possible to link this securely into the Aegean chronological framework.

Peiraeus see PIRAEUS.

Pei Wenzhong [Pei, Wen-chung] (1904–82) a Chinese

Palaeolithic archaeologist who graduated from the Geology Department of Beijing University and joined the ZHOUKOUDIAN excavations in 1928. From 1935 to 1941 he studied in France, returning with a Ph.D. from the University of Paris to become the Director of the Cenozoic Laboratory of the Geological Survey of China. In the post-war period, he was a Research Fellow of the Laboratory of Vertebrate Palaeontology of the Chinese Academy of Sciences. Pei was a pioneer of TAPHONOMIC studies of bone breakage.

Peiligang [P'ei-li-kang] a cluster of Neolithic sites in Henan Province, China, and namesake of the earliest millet-based culture of northern China which includes, or is parallel to, CISHAN, Laoguantai and Lijiacun.

Pejeng a locality in central Bali, Indonesia, whose temple contains a giant (1.68 m [4 ft 6 inches] tall) bronze drum named 'Bulan' (Moon) of Pejeng, dating to the early 1st millennium AD, a locally made variant of the DONG SON drum tradition, ancestral to the recent *moko* drums of eastern Indonesia. The name Pejeng is now given to a distinctive type of tall, slender drum with an overhanging tympanum, widely found in eastern Java and Bali.

Pekárna a prehistoric cave-site located east of Brno in Moravia, Czech Republic. Artifacts and faunal remains (e.g. reindeer, arctic fox) are buried in rubble and loam. The lower cultural layers contain assemblages assigned to the EASTERN GRAVETTIAN, with some associated Middle Palaeolithic artifacts. Above these lie two MAGDALENIAN cultural layers containing endscrapers, borers, bone/antler points and a harpoon; art objects include bones engraved with depictions of animals. Neolithic and later remains occur in the upper layers. Pekárna was excavated by ABSOLON and others.

Peking Man see ZHOUKOUDIAN.

pelike a large container with two vertical handles probably used for water or wine at a Greek SYMPOSIUM. The term is of modern, not ancient, usage and refers to a type of AMPHORA where the greatest diameter is below the mid-point.

Pella 1 the royal city of the kingdom of Macedonia in northern Greece. The palace, dating from the early 4th century BC, has been located in the northern part of the city. It contained a gymnasium and bathing complex. Pella was the birthplace of Alexander the Great. The excavations have uncovered a number of fine pebble mosaics, among the earliest known from the Greek world. They include a late 4th-century BC mosaic of a stag-hunt 'signed' by the artist Gnosis. The city itself was laid out in a grid plan.

2 (Jordan) see BERENICE.

Pelos-Lakkoudes see GROTTA-PELOS.

Pendlebury, John Devitt Stringfellow (1904–41) an Eng-lish archaeologist who started his career at the British School at ATHENS and excavating on prehistoric sites in Macedonia. In 1929 he was appointed Curator of KNOSSOS, a post he held until 1934. His interest in the link between Egypt and Greece led him to join the excavation of Armant in 1928, and in 1930 he was appointed Director of Excavations on the British excavations at EL-AMARNA in Egypt. From 1935 he excavated at several sites around the Lassithi plain in Crete, notably at Karphi. He published the *Archaeology of Crete* (1939). Pendlebury was killed during the German invasion of Crete in April 1941.

Pendzhikent see PANJIKENT.

Pengelly, William (1812–94) one of the first British archaeologists to demonstrate the true antiquity of British Palaeolithic artifacts by showing that stone tools clearly made by humans were contemporary with the remains of extinct animals. This contradicted the then widely accepted chronology of Archbishop Ussher (1581–1656) which dated the Creation to 4004 BC. Pengelly excavated in Devon at KENT'S CAVERN and WINDMILL CAVE, BRIXHAM.

Pengkalan Bujang see ŚRIVIJAYA.

Peninj a locality next to Lake Natron in northern Tanzania, which has yielded horizons containing ACHEULIAN handaxes as well as an almost complete lower jaw of a robust australopithecine, AUSTRALO-PITHECUS or *Paranthropus boisei*, dated to some 1.4 million years ago.

Pentelic marble a white marble quarried from Mount Pentelikon in Attica, Greece. It was widely used for public buildings, such as the PARTHENON.

Peoples of the Sea see SEA PEOPLES.

Perachora a Greek sanctuary located on a promontory jutting into the Bay of CORINTH and excavated by PAYNE. In the Early Iron Age a sanctuary of Hera was established which attracted a wide range of offerings including ivories. Round the harbour were found traces of a STOA and a temple of Hera Akraia.

percussion technique the group of methods used to strike a flake from a core. *Direct* percussion means simply hitting a core with a hammer, either hard or soft. *Indirect* percussion involves the use of a punch placed between the core and the hammer to direct the force of the blow precisely to the striking platform, a method probably used to produce blades. *Anvil* percussion, or 'block on block' percussion, is the striking of a core against a fixed hardstone anvil; while the *bipolar* technique involves resting the core on a stationary anvil and striking it with a hammer, producing a flake with a BULB OF PER-CUSSION at each end.

PERGAMON, Turkey: the Asklepieion.

Pergamon the capital of a HELLENISTIC kingdom in Turkey dating to 283–133 BC. The steep-sided AKROPOLIS was decorated with a range of elaborate buildings. The focus is the theatre which lay above a long terrace, itself dominated by a temple of Dionysos. Remains of the library, once containing some 200,000 volumes (many written on parchment), have been found. One of the most spectacular monuments is the Altar of Zeus, which was decorated with a continuous sculpted relief showing a *Gigantomachy* (battle between gods and giants); parts are now in Berlin. In the Roman period a temple of Trajan was constructed. In the lower city a sanctuary of Asklepios was reached by a ceremonial way.

Pericot García, Luis (1899–1978) a Spanish archaeologist, best known for his meticulous excavation over three seasons in 1929–31 and subsequent publication of the PARPALLÓ cave, as well as his work on northeastern Spanish megaliths.

periglacial environment an environment characterized by severe frost action in non-GLACIAL conditions and dominated by processes and features influenced by cold climates, including ground ice, mass movements, production of relatively large amounts of weathered debris, often strong wind activity at times, resulting in substantial AEOLIAN deposits of silt and sand, and valleys with bedload-dominated streams. It is often associated with

the area fringing modern and Pleistocene glaciers and areas of PERMAFROST, but conditions vary widely with altitude, latitude and climatic parameters.

Perigordian a classificatory division of the French Upper Palaeolithic proposed by PEYRONY and named after the French Périgord region. It viewed the CHÂTELPERRONIAN as the 'Lower Perigordian' developing into the GRAVETTIAN or 'Upper Perigordian'. This scheme is not now widely accepted, as it is based on artifact typology rather than STRATIGRAPHIC evidence, and it assumes the contemporary parallel development of the Perigordian and AURIGNACIAN cultures.

Periplus of the Erythraean Sea an anonymous Greek guide to trading centres and the exchange of goods along the Red Sea, in East Africa and in India, written in about AD 40–70. However, indisputable archaeological evidence for the existence of trading voyages along the East African coast before the 8th century AD was lacking before the 1997 discovery of Roman beads at Mkukutu in the Rufiji Delta of Tanzania. The beads are of a type made on the island of Rhodes between 100 BC and AD 400, and the archaeological layer in which they were found is associated with radiocarbon dates calibrated to between AD 200 and 400.

Peristeria one of the most prosperous and powerful Early

MYCENAEAN (c.1550–1400 BC) settlements in Messenia, Greece. The four THOLOS tombs, although disturbed, contained splendid offerings and the East House may have been a palatial residence.

peristyle a colonnade which is found (a) on the exterior of buildings such as temples, and (b) within the courtyard of a HELLENISTIC or Roman house.

Perjamos or **Periam** a TELL site near Arad in western Romania, the type-site of the Early–Middle Bronze Age Periam culture, largely contemporaneous with the OTOMANI or FÜZESABONY culture to the north and northeast. Stratified sites like Periam and Pecica, as was the case at TÓSZEG, provide a detailed chronological sequence for the first half of the Bronze Age in this part of the Carpathian Basin.

permafrost continuous or discontinuous perennially frozen ground, overlain by the active layer, a surface zone up to about 3 m (10 ft) thick which undergoes seasonal freezing and thawing, formed under cold climatic conditions. During QUATERNARY GLACIAL episodes, permafrost extended to lower latitudes in North America, Europe and Asia. Amelioration of climatic conditions left relict landforms, such as PINGO scars, ICE WEDGE casts and patterned ground, as indicators of former permafrost in these areas.

Persepolis the ACHAEMENID ceremonial centre, situated on a wide plain within the Zagros Mountains of Fars in southwestern Iran, one of the great architectural

PERSEPOLIS: carved relief on the eastern stairway of the Apadana showing Persian and Median officers on their way to the reception held at Nawruz (New Year).

treasures of world history. Darius I (521–486 BC) moved the Achaemenid seat from Pasargadae (where stands the tomb of CYRUS the Great [559–530 BC]) to Persepolis. Here he and the kings that followed built, on a large terrace, a series of columned buildings (the Persian *apadana* refers to a columned hall) which are today identified as palaces, treasury, harem and Apadana proper. Perhaps the most famous of the Persepolis monuments is the terrace staircase, on the stone walls of which are depicted the bearers of tribute from all the parts of the Achaemenid empire. While the tombs of several later kings are at Persepolis itself, the nearby cliff face at Naqsh-i Rustam contains the rock-cut burial chambers of Darius I and his three successors; Naqsh-i Rustam also presents some Middle ELAMITE (late 2nd millennium BC) and SASSANIAN (earlier 1st millennium AD) inscriptions. Alexander the Great, following his victory over the last Achaemenid king, burnt Persepolis in 330 BC.

Persian Gulf trade the active maritime trading of the 3rd and early 2nd millennia BC between MESOPOTAMIA – especially Lagash (TELLO) and UR – and three places whose names appear at various times in the CUNEIFORM texts of southern Mesopotamia: Dilmun, Magan and Meluhha. The combination of textual evidence and archaeological analysis indicates that Dilmun corresponds to the BARBAR culture area in the Persian Gulf, and that Magan probably relates to the UMM AN-NAR and related cultures in southwestern Arabia (possibly extending to the southern coast of Iran); less certainly, Meluhha is usually identified in the HARAPPAN culture area. To southern Mesopotamia, the Persian Gulf trade was a principal source of copper produced in Magan (see MAYSAR), as well as a variety of semi-precious stones and other goods shipped from the Iranian Plateau and elsewhere; the chief products exported from Mesopotamia were textiles and grain. Owing to the commercial wealth generated by this trade, and to the abundant artesian water of the place, Dilmun also held an important place in SUMERIAN mythology, as a sort of Eden.

Persians see ACHAEMENIDS, MEDES.

Peschiera a Bronze Age LAKE DWELLING at the foot of Lake Garda in Veneto, Italy. Dredging operations in the 19th century recovered a mass of Late Bronze Age metalwork (c.1250–1100 BC) along with pottery and other artifacts, and the remains of the timber piles which supported the houses. Among the bronzes are FIBULAE of violin-bow form, the world's oldest safety-pins.

Petén a part of the MAYA Lowlands, MESOAMERICA. The Petén is a geographical and cultural area including the southern two-thirds of the Yucatán; it is also a modern department of Guatemala. The environment is that of a lowland rain forest. TIKAL and UAXACTÚN in the northeastern Petén, and ALTAR DE SACRIFICIOS in the southwestern part of the region, have materials dating from the PRECLASSIC to the late CLASSIC.

Peterborough ware a Neolithic pottery tradition of southern Britain comprising successive Ebbsfleet, Mortlake and FENGATE styles. Poorly made and crudely decorated, the vessels were principally intended for everyday domestic use.

Petersfels a southern German cave-site lying to the northwest of Lake Constance, near Baden, excavated most recently by G. Albrecht (1974–9). It shows evidence of MAGDALENIAN occupation during a cold period including some jet artifacts which may represent figurines, harpoon-heads, burins, awls, backed bladelets and decorated BÂTONS PERCÉS. The remains of at least 1,200 reindeer dominate the fauna, exploited primarily in the autumn.

Petit-Chasseur, Sion a late Neolithic and CHALCOLITHIC burial complex in the Valais, Switzerland, consisting of one large megalithic chamber (M VI) and several smaller tombs. The large chamber stands within a triangular stone pavement, with large engraved anthropomorphous stone STELAS in front. Despite much later disturbance, M VI can be dated to the late Neolithic period. Twenty-six of its stelas have been found reused in smaller tombs of slightly later date containing BEAKER material, and it is clear that the original megalith M VI was also emptied of its primary contents and reused at that period. The figures on the stelas are equipped with triangular daggers of a form paralleled in 3rd-millennium BC contexts in northern Italy, and thus testify to transalpine contacts at this early period.

Petra a city in modern Jordan which rose to importance during the HELLENISTIC period. It is best known for its temples and tombs cut in the rock faces.

Petralona a Middle Palaeolithic cave-site located near Thessalonika in eastern Greece. A series of occupation levels are contained in clay, loam and rubble deposits. Among the faunal remains are giant deer (see MEGALOCEROS), red deer and cave bear. The dating is problematic; estimates range from the early last GLACIAL to the early Middle Pleistocene. Artifacts include scrapers, chopping tools and spheres, and have been characterized as 'early MOUSTERIAN' 22. They are associated with a human skull that is widely assigned to a very archaic form of HOMO *sapiens*; dating by URANIUM and PALAEOMAGNETISM suggests a minimum date of 160,000–200,000 years for the skull.

Petreşti culture an ENEOLITHIC culture of Transylvania in northwestern Romania, contemporaneous with the early stages of the CUCUTENI-TRIPOLYE culture to the east and the GUMELNIȚA culture to the southeast. Petreşti pottery is decorated with brown parallel lines in elaborate patterns prior to firing.

Petrie, Sir William Matthew Flinders (1853–1942) an English Egyptologist, a major figure in the development of the science of archaeology. His insistence on the importance of all material recovered from a site was in marked contrast to the excavation techniques of most of his predecessors and contemporaries, as was his use of these data (e.g. SEQUENCE DATING). An energetic excavator of Egyptian sites (e.g. KAHUN, NAQADA, ABYDOS, MEMPHIS), he concentrated his activities after 1926 on Palestine, where he carried out pioneering work (e.g. at Tell EL-AJJUL).

petroform a line of rocks or boulders placed on the ground in the shape of an animal, mythological figure or other shape.

petroglyph see ROCK ART.

petrological analysis or **petrological microscopy** a technique utilizing a petrological microscope for identifying mineral constituents of artifacts based on the optical behaviour of polarized light as it passes through a THIN SECTION. Minerals refract the light in different diagnostic ways because of differences among crystal lattice characteristics that allow their identification.

Peu-Richard a late Neolithic enclosure in Charente, France, with concentric rock-cut ditches and out-turned entrances, type-site of the Peu-Richardien culture of western France, which is characterized by pottery with flamboyant incised or channelled decoration including so-called *oculi* or double-eye motifs, *c.*3500–2800 BC.

Peyrony, Denis (1869–1954) a French schoolteacher who became the foremost prehistorian in the Dordogne region. He discovered the CAVE ART at FONT DE GAUME, Bernifal and Teyjat, and carried out pioneering excavations at major sites such as LA FERRASSIE and LAUGERIE HAUTE. He proposed the two-stage PERIGORDIAN system, and created the prehistory museum of LES EYZIES.

Pfupi a Zimbabwean rockshelter, which has given its name to the Pfupian, a term previously used for a little-known LATER STONE AGE industry from northeastern Zimbabwe, characterized by ground stone axes, bored stones, geometric microliths and small bifacial points.

Pfyn a middle Neolithic culture of northeastern Switzerland related to the MICHELSBERG culture of the Rhineland. Typical pottery includes round and flat-based vessels, and simple copper objects and crucibles are occasionally found. The Pfyn culture is represented at a number of Neolithic LAKE DWELLINGS, including the well-preserved village of Thayngen-Weier.

Phaistos the site of a MINOAN palace on the island of CRETE, constructed *c.*1900 BC, destroyed by an earthquake *c.*1700 BC, and then rebuilt. The final destruction is dated *c.*1450 BC. Although not as large a palace as

KNOSSOS, Phaistos shares the same basic layout and is in some respects superior architecturally, the residential block being particularly impressive. It is assumed that Phaistos controlled the fertile MESARA plain.

Phalaborwa a copper and iron ore mining town in the eastern Northern Province, South Africa, where a long Iron Age sequence dating back to the 8th century AD has been investigated. There are hundreds of sites where the ore was smelted to extract copper and iron, which were then worked into a variety of tools and ornaments, as well as numerous shafts and tunnels of ancient copper mines.

pH analysis a technique for measuring the hydrogen ion concentration, the pH, of a soil or sediment, which is an indication of acidity or alkalinity. The pH in part governs, but is also influenced by, what chemical processes occur, and gives an indication of the likelihood of preservation of some types of cultural remains. Bone, shell and carbonate lithic debris may dissolve where pH is acidic, whereas preservation is likely in calcareous material where pH values are relatively high.

Pharaoh a title used today as a synonym for the king of ancient Egypt, derived from the Egyptian term 'Great House', which originally referred to the palace but came to be applied to the royal personage during the NEW KINGDOM.

phase a term whose specific definition varies depending on who is using it and where it is being used, but which generally refers to an archaeological unit defined by specific artifacts and other cultural traits that make the unit distinguishable from other similarly defined units. The phase is fairly restricted in time and space. It is similar in conception to the FOCUS (with the addition of a temporal dimension) of the MIDWESTERN TAXONOMIC SYSTEM and the Old World culture, and is often implicitly used to represent a distinct prehistoric people.

phiale a shallow Greek dish which could be used either as a drinking vessel or for pouring LIBATIONS (see OINOCHOE). The name frequently appears in temple inventory lists of plate, and, since extant examples in silver seem to have been made to a round number of units, they were probably a convenient way to stack and count bullion.

Philae an island in the Nile near ASWAN, on the southern border of LOWER EGYPT. The most important of the complex of temples built on Philae is that of the goddess ISIS, to whom the island was considered sacred; the nearby island of Biga was the preserve of her mythological husband OSIRIS. The earliest standing monument from Philae dates from the reign of Nectanebo I (380–362 BC) but most of the building on the site was initiated by the PTOLEMAIC kings and early Roman emperors (e.g. the Kiosk of Trajan). The temples of Philae were dismantled and re-erected on the nearby island of Agilkia during the NUBIAN RESCUE CAMPAIGN.

Philia the type-site for the CHALCOLITHIC III (mid 3rd millennium BC) Philia culture in northern CYPRUS, which is characterized by red polished pottery. The Philia culture may have been introduced by settlers from Cilicia.

Philippines see ASIA, SOUTHEAST.

Philistines one of the SEA PEOPLES, referred to in Egyptian texts from the reign of RAMESSES III as the Peleset. Unsuccessful in their attempts to establish themselves in Egypt, they settled on the coast of the southern Levant, especially around GAZA, ASHKELON and ASHDOD, with inland enclaves at Gath and Ekron. These five cities (the 'pentapolis') made up a military confederation which caused substantial difficulties for the early ISRAELITE kingdoms until Philistine dominance in the southern Levant was effectively broken by King David. Philistine material culture seems to be influenced, especially in pottery types, by that of MYCENAEAN Greece, while iron-working seems to be a significant industry.

Phillips, Philip (1900–1994) one of the most distinguished of all North American archaeologists. His area of specialization was the MISSISSIPPIAN culture and the Lower Mississippi Valley, but he is best known as the co-author (with Gordon Willey) of the classic *Method and Theory in American Archaeology*.

Phimai a large late prehistoric/early historic moated settlement in the middle Mun Valley, KHORAT, Thailand, occupied before 600 BC. Between *c*.200 BC and AD 300 it was a major regional iron-working and trading centre. Phimai Black pottery of this period is found throughout the upper Mun Basin, in large quantities within a radius of 50 km (30 miles), and in smaller quantities further afield. Although perhaps overshadowed by MUANG SIMA in the mid 1st millennium AD, it became a major regional commercial, administrative and sacred centre under KHMER rule in the 11th to 13th centuries. See also ANGKOR.

Phnom Kulen a mountain 45 km (28 miles) northeast of ANGKOR sacred to Indra, with important temples and the River of 1,000 Vishnus, where JAYAVARMAN II and most succeeding Khmer monarchs went to be crowned as Cakravartin or Universal Ruler. The site was also a major quarry for sandstone for temple building.

Phnom Rung a major temple of the 11th–13th centuries AD, in Buriram Province, northeastern Thailand; it is situated high on the Dangkrek Mountains, overlooking the Cambodian plains, and was built by the Narendraditya family, which ruled much of present-day Thailand on behalf of the ANGKOR monarchs.

Phocaean ware a type of Roman red-glossed pottery produced especially from the 4th to the 7th centuries AD.

It was made on the west coast of Turkey and its products have a wide distribution, especially in the eastern Mediterranean.

Phoenicians a Semitic people along the central-eastern Mediterranean coast during the 1st millennium BC, and the cultural heirs of the CANAANITES. Best remembered for their extensive trading from ports like BYBLOS, SIDON and TYRE, the Phoenicians also produced distinctive and elegant metal and ivory work, glass, purple (murex) dye, and other valuable commodities. They founded colonies on Cyprus and then on the coast of North Africa, Spain and the western Mediterranean islands; CARTHAGE is the best remembered of these foundations. The Phoenicians adopted a version of the Canaanite alphabet which they transmitted to the Greeks. Their lucrative trading activities made the Phoenician cities valuable to foreign rulers like the ASSYRIANS and Greeks, in whose empires the Phoenicians often enjoyed a special status.

phosphorus survey or **phosphate analysis** a technique used to identify, through the analysis of soil phosphorus concentrations by various methods, human settlements and activity and burial areas within sites. Excrement and bone are relatively high in phosphorus content, so that human activity and remains tend to produce comparatively large concentrations of phosphates. Identification of such areas implies a need to understand the distribution and range of naturally occurring phosphorus because variations may occur with vegetational abundance and type, and with SOIL HORIZON.

photogrammetry a technique of constructing maps, making scale drawings of sites and structures, or determining measurements, over a range of scales, from photographs, aerial or otherwise. Maps are made, usually from aerial photographs, from multiple projections with distortion of the photographs taken into account.

photomicrograph a photograph of anything that can be viewed in magnification through a microscope taken for permanent documentation and to facilitate communication. It is taken by a camera built in or mounted on any type of microscope, including a SCANNING ELECTRON MICROSCOPE, PETROLOGICAL MICROSCOPE, optical microscope or binocular microscope. Items of archaeological interest might include palaeobotanical remains, THIN SECTIONS, USE-WEAR on artifacts and structures of metals.

Phra Viharn a group of KHMER temples on the Dangrek range at 730 m (2,395 ft), between Thailand and Cambodia, built under Suryavarman I in the early 11th century AD.

Phrygians a people who, at the collapse of the HITTITE empire and the attendant movements of peoples, moved into central Anatolia, probably from a region east of the Black Sea, by the middle of the 12th century BC. Here they founded a kingdom that encompassed most of Anatolia,

bordering URARTU and ASSYRIAN client states to the east. They are best remembered, via Greek literature, for two kings whose names have become bywords, Midas and Gordias. The Phrygian kingdom was destroyed by the CIMMERIAN invasion at the end of the 8th century BC, though Phrygian traditions continued into CLASSICAL times in Anatolia.

Phu Lon a copper-mining and ore-processing site near the Mekong River on the northern fringes of KHORAT, Thailand. It is one of a number of metal-extracting and working sites in the hills ringing the plateau, and was in use intermittently between c.1750 and 275 BC.

Phung Nguyen a site in northern Vietnam which has given its name to the late Neolithic–early Bronze transition period in the region, tentatively dated to c.2300–1500 BC, and preceding DONG DAU, characterized by polished stone adzes and traces of bronze.

Phu Wiang a circular sandstone outcrop in the upper Chi basin, KHORAT, Thailand, immediately south of NON NOK THA, which encloses many prehistoric sites including Nong Nong Chick, Don Sawan, Don Wat Kao and Don Kok.

Phylakopi the site of a Bronze Age settlement on the Aegean island of MELOS, excavated by British archaeologists in 1896–9, 1911 and 1974–7. The remains of three successive 'cities', respectively Early (= Phylakopi I), Middle and Late CYCLADIC, were discovered. The third city had close cultural ties, initially with MINOAN CRETE and subsequently with MYCENAEAN Greece. The administrative centre appears to have been the MEGARON. The Mycenaean cult centre has also been identified.

phytoliths microscopic biogenic opal silica bodies secreted by or deposited in plants, which are incorporated into the soil upon decay of plants and often preserved. Different plants produce phytoliths with different characteristic shapes and sizes, although not all morphologies are unique to individual species; identification of phytoliths collected from stratified sections may indicate the character of past vegetation.

Picosa culture a late ARCHAIC CULTURE, often called the elemental Southwestern culture, which emerged about 3000 BC in the American Southwest. Its name comes from an amalgamation of the previously defined Pinto Basin culture of southern California, southern Nevada and western Arizona, the Cochise culture of southeastern Arizona and southwestern New Mexico and the Oshara tradition of the Four Corners region. It is considered by some archaeologists to be ancestral to the later ANASAZI, HOHOKAM and MOGOLLON traditions.

pictograph see ROCK ART.

Picts the 'Picti' or 'painted people' who occupied northeastern Scotland during the post-Roman period; they are first mentioned in Roman texts of the late 3rd century AD, although they were probably direct descendants from the local Bronze and Iron Age tribes. Their best known archaeological traces are the Pictish symbol stones, memorial blocks or pillars carved with creatures such as fish and birds, as well as geometric shapes, mirrors, combs and, later, new Christian elements.

Piedmont tradition a late ARCHAIC tradition in northeastern North America which is characterized by particular stemmed projectile points and lithic assemblages.

Pietersburg a term sometimes applied to South African early MIDDLE STONE AGE artifact assemblages dating to the late Middle Pleistocene or early Late Pleistocene, and characterized by numerous long parallel-sided flakeblades, many of which have minimal retouch or utilization damage on the sides. See also MWULU'S, ORANGIA.

Piette, Edouard (1827–1906) a pioneering French prehistorian who excavated some major sites in southwestern France (see LE MAS DAZIL, BRASSEMPOUY). The first person to bridge the gap between the Palaeolithic and the Mesolithic through his discovery of the AZILIAN, he was also extremely open-minded, being one of the very few scholars to accept ALTAMIRA's authenticity from the start, and a staunch believer in animal control before the Neolithic period. He amassed the greatest collection of Palaeolithic PORTABLE ART, and gave it to the nation. He also introduced H. BREUIL to prehistory.

Piggott, Stuart (1910–94) distinguished British prehistorian who excavated several major Neolithic sites in southern England, working with Richard ATKINSON at STONEHENGE, WEST KENNET and WAYLAND'S SMITHY. Posted to India during the Second World War he also wrote about Indian archaeology. After his retirement as Professor of European Archaeology at Edinburgh in 1977 Piggott turned to a long-term interest and published two books on the origins and spread of wheeled vehicles in early Eurasia. His most influential writings, however, were on British prehistory, notably his 1938 study of the 'WESSEX CULTURE' (exploring the nature and international links of the Early Bronze Age) and his major 1954 survey of the Neolithic cultures of the British Isles, which established the groundlines for all future work on the subject.

Pi'ilanihale heiau the largest temple in the HAWAIIAN ISLANDS, located on Maui. It is a complex structure built in four phases, beginning about AD 1400. The final additions were made about AD 1778. It served as a chiefly residence as well as for ceremonial activity.

Pikillacta a MIDDLE HORIZON site near CUZCO, Peru, which served as a HUARI administrative centre. The site measures over 800 m (875 yds) square, and comprises planned architecture of Huari style. Portions of the site were never completed, but excavations by Gordon McEwan demonstrate an extensive Huari occupation, and MIDDEN area. A sector of the site comprises small, ovoid, contiguous structures thought by some to be storehouses, although McEwan argues that they were habitation structures.

Pikimachay a large PRECERAMIC cave-site in Ayacucho, central highland Peru. Its excavator, Richard S. MAC-NEISH, argued that he had identified very early, pre-CLOVIS phases dating to between 20,000 and 11,000 bc, associated with the bones of extinct sloth. However, these phases have been largely discounted as representing human occupation. Other levels in the cave demonstrated a long preceramic occupation, beginning about 9000 bc.

Piklihal a prehistoric locality in eastern Karnata in southwestern India, where F. Allchin's work defined a series of Neolithic and megalithic grave period occupations. The Neolithic settlements, beginning around 2100 BC and continuing through much of the 2nd millennium, contain a series of circular beaten-earth floors ringed with stone (presumably to support a perishable superstructure). The earliest of these settlements, which may be associated with the Deccan ASH MOUNDS, has a fauna of cattle, sheep and goat; creation of small farm plots by terracing on hillsides also belongs to this early Neolithic phase. The late Neolithic occupations (later 2nd and early 1st millennia BC) continue along much the same lines, and are similar to other sites in the southern Deccan (e.g. HALLUR, TEKKALAKOTA). The pottery, which in the early Neolithic was handmade, is now turned on a slow wheel and some of it bears a resemblance to late JORWE pottery to the north. The subsequent megalithic to early historic occupations present a sequence of pottery that covers most of the 1st millennium BC and continues into the early 1st millennium AD; this sequence contains various BLACK-AND-RED WARES, white-painted black-and-red wares, 'Russet Coated' ware, Indian ROULETTED WARE and RED POLISHED WARE. Iron appears throughout this latter sequence.

pile dwellings see LAKE DWELLINGS.

pillar crypt a basement room in MINOAN architecture which contains one or two pillars. Their primary function was clearly structural but the fact that some were incised with sacred symbols, such as the DOUBLE AXE, led EVANS to speculate that they were also the focus for cult activities.

Piltdown Man skeletal remains recovered from Piltdown, Sussex, England, by Charles Dawson in 1912–15, which were believed to represent the 'missing evolutionary link' between ancient and modern humans. In 1953 the bones underwent a stringent examination which revealed them to be a deliberate forgery, consisting of fragments of a modern human skull and a female orangutan mandible. The identity of the perpetrator(s) of the hoax is still uncertain.

Pincevent an extensive late MAGDALENIAN open-air site in Seine-et-Marne, northern France, which was discovered during commercial sand quarrying in 1964, and excavated by LEROI-GOURHAN until 1985. The project pioneered large-scale horizontal excavation in the western European Palaeolithic and new techniques such as latex moulds of living-floors, and was a training school for generations of archaeologists. Around 9–10,000 BC there were at least fifteen occupations here, interspersed with the Seine's flood loams. Over 100 habitation structures (tents) and twenty large hearths have been found. The fauna, almost entirely reindeer, points to occupation from early summer to early winter. The site has provided many examples of CONJOINED FLINTS.

pingo a landform that consists of a conical mound formed by a buried body of ground ice up to 40 m (130 ft) high and 600 m (650 yds) wide. Open-system pingos form under discontinuous PERMAFROST in lowland areas underlain by permeable gravel and sand. Closed-system pingos form under continuous permafrost when shallow lakes freeze under certain conditions. Relict pingos, identified by a circular ridge with a central basin, often filled with peat, are used as indicators of the extent of permafrost and the PERIGLACIAL environment.

pintaderas a Portuguese term for small stone or terra-cotta objects with a design cut into them in relief, which are thought to have been used to apply paint to the body. Some are flat, others cylindrical, and the stamping surface may be flat, concave or convex. They are common in the Antilles, MESOAMERICA and the north of South America, as well as in the Canaries, Africa, and Central and south-eastern Europe from the Neolithic period onwards (e.g. in the KÖRÖS culture).

Pinto Basin see PICOSA CULTURE.

Piotrovski, Boris Borisovich (1908–90) a Soviet archaeologist and orientalist, Director of the State Hermitage 1964–90, best known for his excavations (1939–71) at, and research on, the URARTIAN town and fortress of KARMIR-BLUR in Armenia. His main work concerned the history, culture and art of the Caucasus and Ancient East, particularly the URARTU state, and the problem of the origin and history of the Armenians. He is also known as an Egyptologist; in 1961–3 he led the Soviet expedition as part of the NUBIAN RESCUE CAMPAIGN, and in particular investigated the ancient gold mines of Wadi-Allaki.

Piraeus the main port of ATHENS, to which it was linked by the construction of the 5th-century BC Long Walls, which ran for more than 6 km (4 miles). The city itself was laid out in HIPPODAMIAN PLANNING. Traces of *trireme* (warship) sheds have been found. Extant remains include a small HELLENISTIC theatre.

Pirak a 9 ha (22 acre) prehistoric site on the Kachi plain of Baluchistan in western Pakistan, where J.-M. Casal's excavations revealed a post-HARAPPAN cultural sequence of six phases (Pirak IA–B, II, IIIA–C) which covers most of the 2nd millennium and the early 1st millennium BC; although Mature Harappan pottery occurs on the surface of the site, none exists in stratigraphic context. In addition to a succession of mud-brick architecture (which includes a large platform in the first period, and large rooms with niches in the later periods), the Pirak sequence is characterized by a painted pottery of a dense geometric style seemingly derived from the earlier painted pottery of the QUETTA tradition, without a hint of Harappan survivals. In the earlier phases, the painted decoration is monochrome, but becomes bichrome (black and red on buff) in later phases. The Pirak sequence revealed several regionally important 'events'. Beginning with the lowest levels (perhaps 1800 BC), rice, sorghum and millet occur among the cultigens at the site, marking their early appearance in the Indus region, and indicative of intensified agricultural production. At the same time, both horse and camel bones appear among the fauna, as do figurines of these two animals. And beginning in Pirak II (in the third quarter of the 2nd millennium BC), and becoming more common in later levels, iron appears.

Pi-Ramesses see QANTIR.

pirri graver an Australian tool type, with a moderate to pronounced underside curvature, extensive flaking on the opposite face, and a retouched cutting edge on the narrow end of the tool. Pirri gravers are up to 80 mm (3.15 inches) long, 40 mm (1.6 inches) wide and 25 mm (1 inch) high. Ethnographic examples were hafted for use as engraving tools for making grooves on wooden artifacts. Their distribution is not well known, but seems to correspond broadly to that of the TULA.

pirri point a symmetrical leaf-shaped or triangular point up to 60 mm (2.4 inches) long, unifacially worked, with invasive flaking, sometimes by pressure, on the dorsal surface. The striking platform may be removed by trimming the butt. Pirri points belong to the AUSTRALIAN SMALL TOOL TRADITION and are widely distributed in arid Australia, mainly in South Australia and the Northern Territory. The Aboriginal term *pirri* refers to wood-engraving tools. It has been mistakenly applied to unifacial points which were sometimes reused for engraving. See also PIRRI GRAVER.

Pisa a Roman naval base in northern Italy for the Tyrrhenian Sea. Excavations in 1999 revealed eleven Roman ships in the silted-up harbour of the port. One of the ships was found to contain the remains of several species of animals including a lion, perhaps indicating that the beasts were destined for an animal show somewhere in Italy.

pisé *adj.* (of walls) formed from mud or clay. Compare MUD-BRICK and WATTLE AND DAUB.

Pitcairn Island one of a number of isolated islands in the Pacific which had prehistoric occupants at some time but were uninhabited at European contact. Evidence of occupation from Pitcairn and neighbouring islands goes back to *c*.AD 1100 and includes stone platforms with anthropomorphous statues, PETROGLYPHS, stone fish-hooks and adzes, and domestic pig remains. The material resembles NEW ZEALAND Archaic assemblages. See also NECKER ISLAND.

Pit-Comb Ware culture a complex of incipient agricultural groups of the forest zone around the southern Baltic and GLACIAL outwash of central and eastern Poland, named for their pottery, which is characterized by comb-stroked decoration and pronounced pits. Related groups are the PITTED-WARE CULTURE of central Sweden and Finland, and the NARVA culture of Estonia. The makers of Pit-Comb ware are poorly known, largely from surface finds and a few sites. Few data are available on subsistence, and some have referred to Pit-Comb Ware as a 'ceramic Mesolithic' or 'paraneolithic' culture.

Pit-Grave culture see YAMNAYA CULTURE.

Pithecanthropus see JAVA MAN, MOJOKERTO.

Pithekoussai see ISCHIA.

pithos a large Greek storage jar, used for items such as olive oil, wine and grain. In the Aegean the dead were sometimes buried in pithoi.

pithouse a subterranean or semi-subterranean chamber used by prehistoric inhabitants of the American Southwest as their primary habitation structure. The pithouse was most popular in the period AD 200–900, and is thought to have been used primarily by individual families. It evolved into the KIVA.

Pit of the Bones see ATAPUERCA.

Pitted-Ware culture pottery-using foraging and incipient agricultural groups in Sweden and Finland of the 4th to 1st millennia BC. Pitted-Ware communities of the northern Baltic region relied to a large degree on seal hunting and pig raising. In addition, ornaments of amber were manufactured extensively.

Pitt-Rivers, General Augustus Lane-Fox (1827–1900) a pioneer of scientific excavation and recording. After a military career he inherited the Rivers estates in south-western England in 1880, and over the following twenty years excavated a series of prehistoric and Romano-British sites on his estates, including Wor Barrow, South Lodge and Bokerly Dyke, which he published in the four-volume report *Exavations in Cranborne Chase* (1887–98). In these works he stressed the importance of STRATIGRAPHY and the precise recording of the location of all finds. Pitt-Rivers was also the first Inspector of Ancient Monuments in England and Wales.

Pizarro, Francisco (1475–1541) a Spanish adventurer who, impressed by the gold of Peru in the 1520s, returned there in 1532 with 180 men and destroyed the empire of the INCAS, who thought the Spaniards were gods returning as prophesied in legends. The founder of modern Lima, he was assassinated in 1541.

Plain of Jars see XIANG KHOUANG.

Plain Pottery see MUMUN.

Plains Village Indian a collection of archaeological cultures found on the central and eastern Plains of North America in the period AD 900–1850. Despite regional variation, Plains Village Indians were characterized by large habitation structures in permanent or semi-permanent settlements that were often fortified; pottery; and some degree of reliance on corn horticulture. Along the Missouri River in present-day North and South Dakota, there developed the Middle Missouri tradition. In the 1400s, drought forced an abandonment of the central Plains, and its former occupants moved into the Middle Missouri area to form the Coalescent tradition.

Plainview 1 a PLANO projectile point, distinguished by parallel sides and a concave base, although much internal variety exists. A variant named Firstview was identified at the OLSEN-CHUBBUCK site.

2 a site in Texas which is the type-site for the complex.

3 a Plano complex associated with the Plainview point and characterized by non-diagnostic stone and bone tools.

plane table a drawing board that is mounted on a tripod used in conjunction with an ALIDADE. Drafting paper is attached to the table, which is then levelled with an alidade. A map is constructed directly on the drafting paper by sighting through the alidade the point to be mapped, while aligning the alidade straight edge so that it intersects the point on the map representing the mapping station, drawing a line along the straight edge, and scaling the calculated distance along the line to the measured point. The technique is somewhat dated, being replaced by PHOTOGRAMMETRY and other methods.

Plano a PALAEOINDIAN tradition in North America, characterized, in the west, by the hunting of bison and the development of diverse projectile point styles and complexes, such as AGATE BASIN and HELL GAP, Cody and Frederick. The Plano tradition dates from approximately 10,000 to 7000 BP.

plano-convex brick a characteristic brick-form of the EARLY DYNASTIC (and especially of the E.D. II–III) period in southern MESOPOTAMIA, this term refers to bricks that are flat on one face and domed on the other, often with thumb-impressed holes on the latter surface. These bricks were used, with a great deal of mud mortar, in vertical courses inclined in alternating directions to create a 'herringbone' pattern.

plastered skulls a series of prehistoric skulls which are among the most famous discoveries at JERICHO, Israel. They had been covered in plaster and then painted to render the visage of the dead individual, usually with cowry shells set in the orbits. Such skulls occur in PRE-POTTERY NEOLITHIC B (PPNB) contexts at several sites in Syro-Palestine (e.g. Ramad, Beisamun). This practice seems to be an elaboration of the common practice of separating head from body of the dead for separate burial, a custom already present in PPNA times, when groups of skulls were buried together.

platform mounds earthen flat-topped mounds that were surmounted by buildings, which served as habitation and/or ceremonial structures. See also CAHOKIA, MIS-SISSIPPIAN.

Plawangan a late prehistoric cemetery in northern-central Java where one flexed child burial was found inside an upturned HEGER I drum with a bronze spear, pottery, glass beads and a gold eye-and-mouth cover.

playa a low-relief dry lake basin in arid or semi-arid regions where runoff collects, forming a temporary lake which eventually evaporates. When dry, the playa is sub-jected to AEOLIAN erosional and depositional processes. FOSSIL BEACH ridges around playa lakes sometimes have associated archaeological deposits that may become either deflated lags, or buried as the result of aeolian activity.

Pleistocene 1 a geochronological division (*Pleistocene epoch*) of geological time, following the PLIOCENE. The Early or Lower Pleistocene begins c.1.8 million years ago; the Middle c.780,000 years ago; and the Late or Upper c.127,000 years ago. It is regarded as either coterminous with the QUATERNARY, or as ending c.10,000 bp to be followed by the Holocene.

2 the chronostratigraphic division (*Pleistocene series*) (see STRATIGRAPHY) of the Quaternary system defined by deposits, overlying Pliocene deposits, containing evi-dence of humans and their development and resulting from alternating GLACIAL and INTERGLACIAL processes and conditions in response to multiple major environ-mental changes. In some classification systems, the Pleis-tocene series is equivalent to the Quaternary system, being its only series. In other classification systems, the Quaternary system is divided into the Pleistocene series and Holocene series, the rank accorded the Holocene series varying regionally. In this case the division is usu-ally taken to be 10,000 bp.

Pleistocene extinctions the extinction of fauna (in-cluding the mammoth) in North America and elsewhere at the end of the Pleistocene. Explanations for the extinc-tions range from massive environmental change or human over-hunting to a combination of both.

In *Australia*, there were several species of giant mar-supial, among them DIPROTODON, the macropods PRO-TEMNODON and *Sthenurus*, a flightless bird *Genyornis* and the predator *Thylacoleo*, which became extinct during the Late Pleistocene. The timing of extinctions seems to have varied throughout the continent, with late survival claimed in better-watered areas at sites such as LIME SPRINGS, while at Tandou in arid western New South Wales extinctions were complete by 27,000 bp. CUDDIE SPRINGS has provided the strongest evidence yet for association between MEGAFAUNA and artifacts. See also LANCEFIELD.

Pleniglacial see LAST GLACIAL MAXIMUM.

Pliocene the epoch dating between c.5 million years ago and the beginning of the Pleistocene at 1.8 million years ago.

Plio-Pleistocene the latter part of the PLIOCENE and the early part of the Pleistocene, i.e. the period between about 3 and 1 million years ago.

Pločnik a stratified flat settlement in southern Serbia, whose name is often used in connection with the late phase of the VINČA culture, 4600–4000 BC. In the 3 m (10 ft) deposits at Pločnik, three occupation layers were distinguished. The bottom two are late Vinča, while the uppermost is of the BUBANJ-HUM group. In the Bu-banj-Hum levels, four hoards of copper tools include cast shaft-hole axes.

Plog, Fred (1944–92) North American archaeologist whose theoretical writings, linked with numerous field projects in the Southwest, helped establish PROCESSUAL ARCHAEOLOGY's dominance in North America.

ploshchadki a Russian term for house floors consisting of a clay layer covering a base of horizontal logs, usually hardened by fire. Such house remains are characteristic of the CUCUTENI-TRIPOLYE culture, but also occur in the GUMELNIŢA, PETREŞTI and VINČA cultures, reflecting a widespread construction practice in southeastern Europe during the late Neolithic.

ploughmarks or **plough scars** scars, identified by sharp physical discontinuities in soil colour or texture in upper SOIL HORIZONS, seen in excavation profiles or plan view, which mark the location, depth and type of previous agricultural practices. Ploughmarks associated with the modern soil indicate cultivation and possible displace-ment of associated archaeological deposits.

Plussulien a Neolithic quarry in Côtes-du-Nord, France, used for approximately 2,000 years (4000–2000 BC) for the production of polished stone axes of 'type A' dolerite. The site consists of outcrops of dolerite, remains of hearths used in fire-setting, and massive accumulations of debris. Among this were found many hammerstones and grinders for crushing the blocks of dolerite and shaping the axes. Polished stone axes of Plussulien dolerite are found as far away as the Alps, the Pyrenees and southern Britain.

pluvial **1** *n.* a wet climatic episode, marked by high lake-levels as indicated by various lines of evidence, including FOSSIL BEACHES. These moist episodes apparently were not SYNCHRONOUS worldwide but rather varied somewhat in age with latitude. High lake-levels and other favourable ecological changes accompanying these periods of increased precipitation led to increased human occupation and activity in areas that otherwise were of limited attraction.

2 *adj.* pertaining to or due to rain.

pochteca a class of long-distance merchants in AZTEC society. These traders travelled to foreign lands, and often acted as spies during their expeditions.

Pod Hradem an Upper Palaeolithic cave-site located northeast of Brno in Moravia, Czech Republic. Artifacts and faunal remains are buried in rubble and 'cave earth' deposits. The lower layers contain some artifacts, including a laurel-leaf point, assigned to the SZELETIAN, and a younger early Upper Palaeolithic industry (e.g. retouched blades) was found in overlying layers; both industries are associated primarily with cave bear remains and dated to the middle of the last GLACIAL. Late Upper Palaeolithic artifacts, associated with reindeer remains, occur in the upper layers.

Pohansko an early medieval settlement and hillfort in Moravia, Czech Republic, near the town of Břeclav. Pohansko was occupied continuously from the 6th to the 10th centuries AD. Between the 6th and the 8th centuries, Pohansko was a small agricultural settlement with at least seventy-nine structures divided into several precincts. A nearby cemetery contains fifty-five cremation burials, most in urns. In the 9th century, a large fortified enclosure was built. Its ramparts consisted of an outer stone wall and an inner timber wall with earth fill between them. In the northwestern corner of the fort, a rectangular compound, interpreted as a royal manor, contained a church with cemetery, a residential area with multi-room houses built on mortared stone foundations, and a working area with stables and granaries.

point a broad category of stone artifacts, including a variety of pointed tools flaked on one or both sides. See also SIDE-NOTCHED, SHOULDERED, LAUREL-LEAF, WILLOW-LEAF and SWIDERIAN POINTS.

point bar a depositional alluvial landform located on and just behind the convex bank of meandering streams which is a series of accretionary ridges and swales, formed and modified as the stream floods and the meander bend migrates. The slightly better-drained ridges were often loci of human activities related to exploitation of aquatic and wetland resources.

Pokch'on-dong a THREE KINGDOMS (see KOREA) cemetery site in Pusan City, southeastern Korea, built on a hillock overlooking the coastal valleys. Burials consist of large pits equipped with wooden chambers and coffins. Much iron armour has been excavated here, indicating the site's affiliation with the KAYA POLITIES. It later acquired SILLA cultural affiliation as known through its ceramic repertoire.

Pokrovka a complex of Iron Age cemeteries in central Russia along the Khobda River near the border with Kazakhstan, dating from the 6th century BC to the 3rd century AD. Numerous KURGANS contain multiple burials in deep pits, often with side niches. Some of the burials contained skeletons of women buried with weapons such as iron swords and daggers and bronze arrowheads.

Polada an Early Bronze Age LAKE DWELLING in Lombardy, Italy, type-site of the Polada culture (*c.*2200–1600 BC). This includes cultural features directly derived from BEAKER assemblages, such as WRISTGUARDS and v-perforated buttons, alongside features of indigenous origin. Many Polada sites are waterlogged and have revealed a wide range of organic remains, including long bows, crook ARDS, dug-out canoes and spoked wheels.

Poland see EUROPE, CENTRAL.

Polesini an Upper Palaeolithic site near Rome, Italy, excavated by RADMILLI in 1952–6 which yielded thousands of stone tools and faunal remains dominated by red deer, primarily exploited in winter. The site is best known for its engraved MOBILIARY ART, dating to the 11th millennium bp.

Poliochni the site of a prehistoric settlement on the Aegean island of Lemnos, which was excavated by della Seta in 1931–6 and by Bernabò BREA in 1951–6. Poliochni was first occupied in the FINAL NEOLITHIC period. The Early Bronze Age settlement, one of the largest in the Aegean, had fine houses, wide streets and massive stone fortifications, but eventually suffered a catastrophic destruction. After a period of abandonment Poliochni was reoccupied, but the Middle and Late Bronze Age levels have largely been eroded.

polis a Greek state incorporating a city, smaller towns and villages, and its territory.

polished stone adze a chopping/cutting tool, bevelled on one side, characteristic of the Neolithic of much of Southeast Asia. It seems to have developed from earlier edge-grinding techniques, in some places appearing as early as 6000 BC and continuing in use in metal-poor regions into the 1st millennium AD. The adzes were generally flaked to shape from a large core, then ground and polished over most or all surfaces. Many were traded as roughed-out forms ('blanks') to be polished by the recipient. The basic adze form, common to most areas and phases, is the simple quadrangular shape (rectangular or trapezoidal), probably ancestral to other forms. It appears early in Thailand (SPIRIT CAVE) and Taiwan. Differences between rectangular and oval/lenticular cross-sections appear to relate to the hardness of stone used rather than, as once believed, to different cultures. Three major groupings have been suggested: one in southern China, characterized by Duff's type 2A, stepped 1A and slightly shouldered 1B, which are associated with southern LUNG-SHANOID and other contemporary cultures, and which seem to connect with forms in Taiwan, the Philippines and Polynesia; the northern Indochinese focus is characterized by simple types which frequently have oval or lenticular cross-sections (see SAI YOK, BAN KAO); the third focus encompasses the Malay peninsula and much of western Indonesia. The development sequence and migration model proposed by Heine Geldern on the basis of adze types are no longer accepted.

polity a term used by Renfrew to describe small-scale but politically autonomous early states found, for instance, in MYCENAEAN Greece and ETRUSCAN Italy.

Polivanov Yar a Neolithic settlement of the CUCUTENI-TRIPOLYE culture in Ukraine, located on a high promontory across which a ditch and bank were constructed to complete the defences. Ingots of smelted copper at Polivanov Yar point to trade contacts with the Carpathian-Balkan region to the west.

Poljanica or **Polyanitsa** a TELL site of the ENEOLITHIC GUMELNIȚA culture in northeastern Bulgaria. Excavation of eight habitation levels has revealed densely packed rectangular houses, many with party walls or separated by narrow alleys, set within a rectangular palisade. The living quarters appear to have been relatively uniform in size, consisting of a basic module of a large room with a hearth. Interior posts supported a roof.

pollen analysis see PALYNOLOGY.

Polovcians (also known as Kipchaks, Comans) an ethnonym for Turkish-language nomads who, at the beginning of the 11th century AD, arrived in the steppes of eastern Europe. The Polovcian army consisted of light and heavy cavalry and was characterized by its mobility. They carried out raids on Byzantium, Hungary and, especially often, on Russian lands. Some states used the Polovcians as a military force in the struggle with the Pechenegs (as Byzantium did), the Selijuks (Georgia) and the Mongols (Russia). The Polovcians were allies of the Russians in the important battle against the Mongols in 1223. Archaeologically the Polovcians are represented by burials with a horse and ANTHROPOMORPHOUS stone or wooden statues, known as KAMENNAYA BABAS.

Polyanitsa see POLJANICA.

polychrome pottery *sensu stricto,* pottery that is decorated with more than two colours, but very often applied to any pottery that has more than one colour in its decoration.

Polynesia a region of widely scattered islands in the central Pacific, distributed roughly in a triangle with the HAWAIIAN ISLANDS, EASTER ISLAND and NEW ZEALAND at its corners. It is fairly homogeneous in terms of ethnicity, language and social organization. It is divided into two regions, with some differences in material culture and religion: western Polynesia includes Tonga, Samoa and Tuvalu; while eastern Polynesia includes the Society, Cook, Austral, Marquesas, Tuamotu and Hawaiian Islands, as well as Easter Island and New Zealand. Pottery production seems to have ceased in western Polynesia about AD 300, and the only pottery found in eastern Polynesia seems to have been imported from the west.

Polynesian outliers nineteen small islands with Polynesian-speaking populations in MELANESIA, to the east of the Solomons, New Hebrides and New Caledonia, and on the southern fringes of MICRONESIA.

Pomongwe 1 a LATER STONE AGE industry of southwestern Zimbabwe, dated to between about 11,000 and 9400 bp, and characterized by large circular or convex scrapers as well as smaller scrapers, rare backed artifacts, abundant bone needles and the presence of tortoiseshell bowls. Some researchers view it as a regional industry within the OAKHURST complex.

2 a cave with many fine rock paintings, especially of giraffe, in the Matopo Hills of southwestern Zimbabwe, which has a long sequence of stone industries and faunal remains.

Pompeii a town in CAMPANIA, Italy, buried under ASH after the eruption of Vesuvius in AD 79. The site was rediscovered in the mid 18th century and a large part of its *c.*65 ha (160 acres) has been excavated. The oldest part of the city lay in the FORUM area, and the street layout has a different orientation to the rest of the city. Extensive remains include houses, workshops, an AMPHITHEATRE, a PALAESTRA and various civic buildings. Many of the private houses had decorated wall plaster which has been categorized into four styles. Outside the gates were cemeteries, and beyond them large residential establishments such as the Villa of the Mysteries. See also FIORELLI.

pond barrow see BARROW.

Pong Tuk on the Mae Klong River in western-central Thailand, the find-place of a late Roman bronze lamp (*c.*5th–6th century AD) similar in form to ceramic lamps found at other sites in the vicinity: U THONG, KU BUA and NAKHON PATHOM.

Pont du Gard part of the 40 km (25 mile) long aqueduct taking water to NÎMES. Where the line crossed the River Gard a three-stage aqueduct was constructed, taking the water some 49 m (158 ft) above the river. The present length of the upper storey is 275 m (300 yds).

Pontian a site in peninsular Malaysia of a boat burial of the early centuries AD associated with pottery similar to that from KUALA SELINSING, with decorative motifs also noticed at OC ÈO. The boat is of Southeast Asian type (see SHIPWRECKS).

Pontic ware a type of BLACK-FIGURED pottery produced in ETRURIA in the ARCHAIC period. The style seems to have been influenced by techniques used in Attica, CORINTH and Ionia.

Pontnewydd Cave a cave-site in North Wales which has yielded Middle Pleistocene HOMINID remains representing at least three individuals, an important series of dates (170–230,000 BP) and an industry once believed to be atypical MOUSTERIAN, but now accepted as Upper

POMPEII, Italy: plaster cast of one of the victims of the volcanic eruption.

ACHEULIAN with the use of prepared-core-flaking techniques. The lithic artifacts are made from local hard stones which are difficult to knap, and which give all the tools a rather primitive appearance. The cave has been investigated since the end of the 19th century, most recently by H. S. Green.

Popol Vuh the origin myth of the MAYA, dating back at least to the CLASSIC period. It was recorded from an oral tradition in the early colonial period, though Classic Maya POLYCHROME POTTERY reproduces scenes from the narrative. The story describes the relationship between natural and supernatural realms of the cosmos, and the relationship between mortals and deities. One important segment describes a BALL GAME played between the Hero Twins, Hunahpu and Xbalanque, and the Lords of the Underworld, resulting in their emergence to form the Sun and Moon.

porphyry a type of stone quarried in the eastern Egyptian desert. There are three main types: red (*rosso antico*), green and black. Many sculptures in this medium seem to be linked to the Roman imperial family; therefore it is thought that the quarries were under direct control of the emperor.

portable art see MOBILIARY ART, PALAEOLITHIC ART.

portal dolmens or **portal tombs** megalithic tombs with above-ground chambers consisting of a heavy capstone, supported on three or more uprights in such a way that the capstone slopes markedly downwards from front to back. Whether these distinctive monuments were originally hidden within a covering mound is unclear. Portal dolmens are found in Wales and Cornwall, but are most common in western Ireland, especially in the Burren area (e.g. Poulnabrone, Co. Clare – **see picture, p. 121**).

Port Arthur a penal settlement on the Tasman Peninsula, south of Hobart, TASMANIA, Australia. The complex was begun in AD 1830 and finally closed in 1877 after a brutal history. A range of structures survives at Port Arthur itself, while other buildings associated with the penal colony occur elsewhere on the peninsula. From 1979 to 1986, Port Arthur was the subject of an intensive archaeological programme associated with the management of the site, and therefore occupies a key place in the development of historical archaeology in Australia.

Port aux Choix the site of an ARCHAIC cemetery of over 100 burials located in northwestern Newfoundland, Canada, which is dated between the late 3rd and late 2nd millennia BC. The burials were accompanied by gravegoods, which included ochre, polished slate artifacts, barbed bone points, toggled bone harpoon heads, shell beads and combs, needles, knives and scrapers made variously from bone, ivory and antler.

Portchester a late Roman fortress on Portsmouth harbour, in southern England, which formed part of the defensive system known as the SAXON SHORE forts. A later Norman castle was built into one corner of the substantial Roman walls.

Port Essington a site on the Cobourg Peninsula, north-east of Darwin in Australia's Northern Territory, which was excavated by Jim Allen in 1966 and is a pioneering example of historical archaeology in Australia. The Victoria military settlement lasted from AD 1838 to 1849 and was the third unsuccessful attempt by the British to settle tropical Australia. The surviving structures include Cornish round chimneys, while artifacts of bottle-glass are evidence of Aboriginal presence at the site.

Porticello a shipwreck site in the Straits of Messina between Italy and Sicily. Although the site had been looted, the cargo is known to have consisted of life-size bronze statuary, AMPHORAS, ingots, ink-pots and fine pottery. It dates to c.440–430 BC.

portico a colonnade, usually forming part of a building such as PALAESTRAE. Porticos often bordered gardens in Roman houses.

Portland Vase see CAMEO GLASS.

Portugal see IBERIA.

positivism a school of philosophy initially associated with Auguste Comte in the 18th century. There is an emphasis on the 'testability' of statements and the separation of data from the theories that explain them, especially as propounded in a variant of positivism termed *logical positivism*. Positivism has become somewhat *passé* in contemporary philosophical theory, but it became, and remains, the primary theoretical basis of NEW ARCHAEOLOGY.

Postclassic period (AD 750/900–1520) the period following the collapse of CLASSIC PERIOD civilizations in MESOAMERICA. This collapse did not occur simultaneously throughout Mesoamerica, hence the variable beginning date for the period. Mesoamerican cultures during the Postclassic tended to be more secular than those of the Classic period.

Postglacial The present INTERGLACIAL period (i.e. the Holocene); the term is sometimes used to refer to the period of time following a GLACIAL episode.

posthole a hole dug into the ground and into which the base of an upright post is placed. Even after the post itself has rotted away, the posthole remains archaeologically recognizable, because the sediment with which it is filled is often of a different texture or colour from the surrounding soil. The pattern of postholes in a site can provide invaluable evidence on the size and shape of houses and other structures. The American term for posthole is *postmold*.

Postoloprty a Neolithic site of the LENGYEL culture in Bohemia, in which a 33 m (36 yd) long trapezoidal LONGHOUSE with bedding trenches (similar to those at BRZEŚĆ KUJAWSKI and OSŁONKI) had four features interpreted as hearths spaced down its centre. B. Soudský argued that these represented the habitation areas of four separate families, by analogy with LONGHOUSE divisions among the Iroquois of North America.

Postpalatial period see CRETE.

postprocessual archaeology a school of archaeological thought which rejects most of the tenets of the NEW or PROCESSUAL ARCHAEOLOGY. It is based on the notions that culture must be understood as sets of symbols that evoke meanings, and that these meanings vary depending on the particular contexts of use and the specific histories of both artifacts and the people who use them. MATERIAL CULTURE is also vital to the control and exercise of social power over individuals. Explanation of human behaviour cannot be reduced to ecological factors, but rather must be sought within the cultures themselves, as specific, often idiosyncratic, responses to particular conditions.

potassium-argon dating an isotopic dating method based on the radioactive decay of ^{40}K to the stable ISOTOPE ^{40}Ar. The method is used primarily to date lava flows and TUFFS, both of which could be in STRATIGRAPHIC sequences with archaeological deposits, and the PALAEOMAGNETIC reversal timescale by dating ocean floor basalts. When originally formed, these deposits have no ^{40}Ar because the heat at time of emplacement has driven it away. The age is based on the known HALF-LIFE of ^{40}K, the constant proportion of ^{39}K and ^{40}K in rocks, and the $^{40}K/^{40}Ar$ ratio with both isotopes being measured in the sample. The method is routinely applied from about 100,000 to 30 million years; the theoretical upper limit is several orders of magnitude greater.

Potočka Cave an Upper Palaeolithic site located in the mountains of Slovenia (c.2,000 m [6,500 ft] altitude). Artifacts and faunal remains (chiefly cave bear) are buried in cave deposits dating to the last GLACIAL. The small Upper Palaeolithic assemblage includes sidescrapers (rare) and endscrapers, and retouched blades, and is assigned to the AURIGNACIAN. Potočka Cave was excavated by Brodar.

potsherd a fragment of a pot. See also OSTRAKON.

Poverty Point a site in northern Louisiana, USA, which belongs to the WOODLAND STAGE. The site comprises a huge octagonal earthwork, approximately 1.8 km (1 mile) in diameter. The earthwork itself is composed of six individual ridges that surround a central plaza. There is no evidence of agriculture at the site. Poverty Point objects are small irregularly shaped baked clay pieces, the precise function of which is unknown. They may have been used as an equivalent of boiling stones to facilitate the heating of water. The associated Poverty Point complex dates from 1300 BC to at least 400 BC.

pozzolana a volcanic dust found in central Italy, especially at Pozzuoli (*Lat.* Puteoli). It was used to strengthen Roman concrete, as well as for lining water channels.

PPNA, PPNB, PPNC see PRE-POTTERY NEOLITHIC.

Praeanthropus see AUSTRALOPITHECUS.

Praia das Maças a pair of CHALCOLITHIC CHAMBERED TOMBS near Lisbon, Portugal, the first rock-cut, the second with dry-stone superstructure roofed by a COR-BELLED VAULT. The rock-cut tomb contained decorated slate plaques, an alabaster comb, and other material of late Neolithic or earliest Chalcolithic type, with a radiocarbon date of 2300 bc. The later tomb, blocking the entrance to the earlier monument, was over twice as large and contained c.150 burials, with BEAKER pottery, PALMELA points and a tanged dagger. It has a radiocarbon date of 1690 bc.

Prambanan a complex of Hindu and Buddhist temples, many of them CANDI, near Yogyakarta in central Java, built by the rulers of MATARAM in the late 8th and 9th centuries AD. Best-known temples include Loro Jonggrang, Candi Sewu and Plaosan. Kalasan and Ratu Baka are near by.

Prasat Muang Singh a 13th-century AD KHMER town on the Kwae Noi River in western Thailand. Constructed under JAYAVARMAN VII, the temples were built from laterite with superb stucco decoration maintaining the local DVARAVATI tradition. The city marks the westernmost extent of the Khmer empire.

Preceramic see PRE-POTTERY NEOLITHIC, ACERAMIC NEOLITHIC.

Preceramic period (*c.*9000[?] to 1800 BC) the period in Andean South America beginning with the first human occupation of the region and ending with the introduction of ceramic artifacts; the Preceramic is sometimes divided into six phases on the coast of Peru. The general date at which human occupation first took place is a matter of dispute, with some researchers claiming to have found evidence for late Pleistocene occupations, prior to 9000 bc (see MONTE VERDE, PEDRA FURADA). Very few such sites stand up to close scrutiny. But there is little dispute that in the Early Preceramic a PALAEO-INDIAN tradition spread through South America, evidenced by lithic complexes including fluted stemmed 'FISHTAIL' POINTS at such sites as EL INGA and CUEVA FELL. This is followed by a long period, termed by some the Archaic period, during which foraging populations occupied much of the continent. Both domestic architecture and ceremonial architecture emerged at this time (see ASANA). The Late Preceramic (sometimes called the

Cotton Preceramic, or Preceramic VI in coastal Peru) was a period in which sedentary villages began to appear with some regularity on the coast, and agriculture began to supply an increasing portion of the diet. Monumental ceremonial architecture and widespread religious traditions also occurred in the Late Preceramic (see KOTOSH, EL PARAISO). The period ends with the introduction of pottery and the start of the INITIAL PERIOD. In other parts of South America, pottery was adopted much earlier: in Amazonia c.7600 bp (see TAPERINHA), and in northwestern Colombia c.5200 bp. See also FORMATIVE.

Preclassic period (2000 BC–AD 250) the period in which most traits of MESOAMERICAN culture which distinguish it from South American and North American cultures appear. The OLMEC is the first of the Mesoamerican cultures to appear in the Preclassic, early in the period. In the MAYA area, the later portion of the Preclassic is often referred to as the PROTOCLASSIC PERIOD. The earliest writing (GLYPHS) in Mesoamerica occurs in this period.

Předmostí a Palaeolithic open-air site on the Bečva River in northeastern Moravia, Czech Republic. Artifacts and faunal remains are buried in loess and slope deposits; many details are obscured by missing data. Middle Palaeolithic artifacts, probably dating to the early GLACIAL, are associated with a buried soil in the lower part of the sequence. Upper Palaeolithic cultural layers (AURIGNACIAN and EASTERN GRAVETTIAN) were found in the upper levels, associated with numerous woolly mammoth bones (about 1,000 individuals) and dated by radiocarbon to 26,870 bp. A mass grave containing the remains of twenty individuals, apparently associated with the main Eastern Gravettian layer, was discovered in 1894. The site is rich in bone and ivory tools, pendants and PORTABLE ART including female figurines, a mammoth carving and a remarkable stylized female figure engraved on a tusk.

Pre-Dorset a series of early Arctic cultures and complexes characterized by microblades, knives, scrapers and burins. The Pre-Dorset economy was based on the hunting of seal and walrus, and also of land animals in some areas. It originated in the western part of the continent in the 5th millennium BP and spread east to northern Greenland. It is part of the ARCTIC SMALL TOOL TRADITION and, as its name implies, is the basis of the later DORSET CULTURE which emerged about 3000 BP.

Predynastic *adj.* relating to Egypt before it became a unified state in c.3000 BC. See also BADARIAN, AMRATIAN, GERZEAN, MERIMDE BENI SALAMA, OMARI and MAADI.

prehistoric period or **prehistory** any period for which there is no contemporary documentary evidence. It constitutes the major segment of the human past, and is the major object of study in archaeology. See also HISTORIC PERIOD, PROTOHISTORIC PERIOD.

pre-Neanderthal a name given to the makers of the ACHEULIAN industry, believed by some to develop into classic NEANDERTHALers.

Prepalatial period see CRETE.

Pre-pottery Neolithic an early phase of the Neolithic of the Near East, during which agriculture was practised (presumably as a consequence of the intensive use of wild cereals by the preceding NATUFIAN communities) but pottery, the other major innovation of the period, was not yet produced. Domesticated animals also appear in the later phases of this period. The term was coined by KENYON. Its two subdivisions, based on the excavations at JERICHO, are Pre-pottery Neolithic A (PPNA, c.8500–7600 BC) and Pre-pottery Neolithic B (PPNB, c.7600–6000 BC). Recent work at 'AIN GHAZAL suggests the existence of a third, terminal phase, the PPNC, dated to 6200–5900 BC. See also ACERAMIC NEOLITHIC.

pre-projectile point complex a complex proposed by Alex Krieger which encompasses the earliest archaeological evidence for humans on the North American continent. Its most important characteristic is that it lacks time-diagnostic stone projectile points.

pressure flaking a secondary retouch technique involving the use of a compressor of antler, bone, hard wood or stone to apply direct pressure to the edge of a primary flake. Fine flat flakes may be detached with great precision by this method, which is particularly associated with some tools in the later SOLUTREAN of France, as well as with some New World points. Heating flint can be helpful to the technique.

Přezletice a Lower Palaeolithic open-air site located near Prague in the Czech Republic. Artifacts are buried in lake deposits that apparently pre-date the Middle Pleistocene (over 730,000 BP) on the basis of PALAEOMAGNETISM and associated fauna, especially mammoth; the assemblage includes chopping tools, crude bifaces and flakes.

Priene a Greek city located on the north side of the Meander Valley in Turkey. Its original site is unknown but in the 4th century BC it was refounded on a rocky spur of Mount Mykale opposite MILETUS. The lower city was laid out in a grid pattern (see HIPPODAMIAN PLANNING). The AGORA and surrounding public buildings (e.g. BOULEUTERION, PRYTANEION), the STADIUM, the theatre, the temple of Athena and some houses have been excavated. The AKROPOLIS is situated on top of a sheer cliff above the lower city.

primary cremation the cremating of a corpse on a pyre in the grave. Compare SECONDARY CREMATION.

primary flake a mechanically struck unretouched stone flake produced during knapping. Compare RETOUCH.

primary inhumation see BURIAL.

probe or **soil probe** a tool used for exploring subsurface STRATIGRAPHY or the presence of archaeological debris which is similar to a core but less expensive and incapable of penetrating more than several metres. A probe may consist of a short hollow tube, or a rod of spring steel with a ball-bearing welded to the tip and a handle on the opposite end, both of which are pushed by hand into the ground.

processual archaeology see NEW ARCHAEOLOGY.

profile 1 n. a vertical section which exposes lateral relationships and vertical STRATIGRAPHY of sediments, soils and rocks, soil horizonation, and, if present, archaeological features, structures and relationships.
2 n. the graphic representation of a profile.
3 vb to draw a profile.

proglacial adj. of or pertaining to landforms, deposits, processes and environments beyond the margin of GLACIAL ice, such as lakes, streams, loess and PERIGLACIAL features.

projectile point a generic term for the tip of a projectile. It can be made of bone, stone, metal or any other suitable material. See ATLATL, BOW-AND-ARROW and SPEAR-POINT. The tool changed in shape through time and so is invaluable in the reconstruction of CULTURE HISTORY.

Prolom II a Middle Palaeolithic cave-site in the Crimea, Ukraine, containing four occupation levels. The age of the occupations is unclear, but the remains of reindeer and arctic fox indicate cold climatic conditions (early last GLACIAL?); saiga is the most common species. The artifact assemblages are primarily composed of side-scrapers, but include some bifacial foliates and possible worked bone; they are assigned to the AK-KAYA CULTURE. Prolom II was discovered in 1973 by Kolosov, who conducted excavations during 1981–2.

pronaos a shallow porch through which the CELLA of a Greek temple was entered and the cult-statue approached. Compare OPISTHODOMOS.

prondnik a type of stone artifact representing an asymmetrical scraping tool flaked on both sides. Prondniks are found in some late Middle Palaeolithic sites of Central Europe (MICOQUIAN).

propylon the entrance gate to a CLASSICAL TEMENOS. On the AKROPOLIS at ATHENS a simple gate was replaced in 437 BC by the monumental Propylaia built on the same orientation as the PARTHENON. It included a *pinakotheke* (picture gallery) which also served as a dining-room.

Prošek, František (1922–58) a Czech archaeologist and

Palaeolithic specialist who was instrumental in establishing the stratigraphic position and significance of the SZELETIAN in the Palaeolithic of Central Europe.

proskenion or **proscenium** a single-storeyed structure placed in front of the SKENE and protruding into the ORCHESTRA of a CLASSICAL theatre. It was often faced with half-columns and was probably used as a raised stage.

Proskouriakoff, Tatiana (1909–85) a Siberian-born MESOAMERICAN archaeologist, epigrapher and artist. Proskouriakoff focused on deciphering the historic content of MAYA GLYPHS. Before her work, the emphasis on understanding Maya glyphs was limited to more esoteric (e.g. astronomy and religious) matters. With that of Heinrich Berlin, Proskouriakoff's research established the use of STELAS to document dynastic sequences. She also deciphered glyphs relating to conflict. These two types of glyphs added substantial depth to the understanding of Maya civilization.

Prosymna see ARGOS.

Protemnodon an extinct species of giant kangaroo, found at several sites in Australia and New Guinea including LANCEFIELD and NOMBE. See also MEGAFAUNA.

prothesis the lying-in-state of a corpse in the Greek world. The scenes on pottery are usually located in the home, and the deceased is normally shown surrounded by mourners. The scenes are particularly common on the ceramic monumental funerary markers at ATHENS in the 8th century BC. See also EKPHORA.

Protoclassic period (*c.*50 BC–AD 250) that period at the end of the PRECLASSIC PERIOD, and immediately preceding the CLASSIC PERIOD, in MESOAMERICAN culture. Cultures of this period have transitional styles between the Preclassic and Classic cultures, occurring contemporaneously with other Preclassic cultures and earlier than Classic period cultures. The term is generally limited to the MAYA area.

Protocorinthian see CORINTHIAN POTTERY.

Proto-Elamite *adj.* denoting the earliest texts written in a language that can be identified as ELAMITE during the 3rd millennium BC. These texts are of two distinct kinds, separated in time. The earlier is analogous to the texts from the URUK IVa period in the EANNA SOUNDING at WARKA, but using a very different sign list; these date to the very late 4th/early 3rd millennia BC. The later texts are composed in the so-called 'linear script', which dates to the late 3rd millennium BC. The first kind of texts appear at SUSA in the ACROPOLE 1 level 16, and also in a number of sites on the Iranian Plateau (SIALK, Tepe MALYAN, Tepe YAHYA, SHAHR-I SOKHTA), usually associated with a distinctive ceramic assemblage and style of seal. This constellation of material traits, and especially the writing system, is called Proto-Elamite in the archaeological literature. The distribution of these materials seems to reveal a concern for control over critical routes of communication and access to traded exotic materials, and the Proto-Elamite phenomenon is often seen as analogous to the slightly earlier late Uruk expansion.

Protogeometric the pottery made in Greece *c.*1050–900 BC and, by extension, the period as a whole.

protohistoric period or **protohistory** **1** the period following prehistory and preceding the appearance of written records in the historic period. In parts of Europe, the term denotes the period between the Bronze Age and the Roman conquest when writing was already in use in other areas of the world.

2 a period when non-literate aboriginal peoples had access to European goods, but had not yet entered into actual face-to-face contact with them.

3 period(s) during which some historical documentation is available but fragmentary, or not directly from the society under examination. In East Asia, the ORACLE BONES and bronze inscriptions respectively make the SHANG and ZHOU periods protohistoric. The Late Bronze Age (for East Asia) and PROTO-THREE KINGDOMS and THREE KINGDOMS periods of the Korean peninsula and the YAYOI and KOFUN periods of the Japanese islands, are variously illuminated from Chinese sources (see HOUHANSHU, WEIZHI) and later local historic records (see KOJIKI, NIHON SHOKI, SAMGUK SAGI) of those societies. See also CHINESE DYNASTIES, KOREA, JAPANESE PERIODIZATION.

4 the period AD 1250–1519 following the POSTCLASSIC in MESOAMERICA, in which the reorganization of that period becomes solidified. Historical and native documents and eyewitness accounts exist for this period, which ends immediately before the Spanish conquest of 1521.

protome the forepart or upper part of a figure. The term is often applied to griffins mounted on the rim of bronze cauldrons as well as to terracotta figurines.

proton gradiometer see MAGNETOMETER.

proton magnetometer see MAGNETOMETER.

Protopalatial period see CRETE.

Protosesklo a term sometimes used for the Greek early Neolithic period, or an early Neolithic phase, in Thessaly. See also SESKLO.

Proto-Three Kingdoms the PROTOHISTORIC period of the Korean peninsula (*c.*AD 0–300), also known as the Late Iron Age or LELANG period, which led into the THREE KINGDOMS period of KOGURYO, SILLA and PAEKCHE state formation. The archaeology of the Proto-Three Kingdoms period is mainly that of Lelang and KOGURYO in the north and the SAMHAN in the south, the latter consisting of MUMUN, WAJIL and KIMHAE pottery finds, stone cist and jar burials, and a few settlement sites – mainly SHELL MIDDENS and (ditched) villages on hill-tops. Both bronze and iron were in use, with iron being produced at many shell midden sites along the southern Korean coast. See also KOREA, TAHO-RI.

provenance or **provenience** the source, place of origin, or location of something. Debris collected in site survey or excavation, sites and raw material sources are usually assigned a provenance within a three-dimensional reference system. The horizontal reference system is usually some form of grid tied to a reference datum. The vertical dimension is usually referenced to a vertical datum.

proximal *adj.* close to the centre or to the point of origin or attachment. For example, a proximal ALLUVIAL FAN is the apex area of the fan just beyond a valley mouth, and adjacent to a mountain front, valley wall or escarpment; the proximal end of a long bone is the end at which it is attached to the body. Compare DISTAL.

prytaneion a building in which the *prytaneis*, effectively an inner executive council of a Greek city, could meet. Compare BOULEUTERION.

Przeworsk culture a Late Iron Age culture over much of the Vistula and Bug drainages, named after a site in southeastern Poland and dated to the LA TÈNE period. The Przeworsk group is known primarily from graves, which have yielded a number of characteristic FIBULAE and other metal artifact types.

psalia ancient accessories of horse-bits, or cheek-pieces. They comprise a pair of vertical rods which were attached perpendicularly to the ends of bits and served for attaching the reins and as a stop piece. Psalia of bone, wood, bronze and, later, of iron were used everywhere that horseriding was adopted. Their shapes are very varied, and are useful for chronological and cultural attributions. At the beginning of the 2nd millenium AD, when the size of bridle rings increased and curb-bits and snaffles were invented, psalia gradually went out of use.

psephoperibombetrios a type of Greek drinking cup with a hollow rim into which pellets were inserted. When shaken, a rattling sound was given, either to attract attention for more wine or perhaps to accompany music during the SYMPOSIUM. Many of the examples are 4th-century BC KANTHAROI.

pseudo-isodomic *adj.* denoting a Greek masonry style, with squared blocks placed in alternating wide and narrow layers. See also ASHLAR.

Ptolemy a name borne by all the kings who ruled Egypt between 304 and 30 BC. The founder of the dynasty, Ptolemy Lagus, was a general of Alexander the Great who established himself in Egypt on the fragmentation of the Macedonian empire following Alexander's death. Although, in many ways, Egypt functioned as a HELLENISTIC state during the Ptolemaic period, the traditional forms of art and architecture were continued, especially in the building of temples to Egyptian gods which were inscribed with HIEROGLYPHIC texts.

Puamau Valley the site on Hiva Oa, Marquesas, POLYNESIA, of a group of large stone anthropomorphous statues up to 2.5 m (8 ft) high. These are the largest such statues in Polynesia outside EASTER ISLAND. See also TAIPIVAI VALLEY.

public archaeology a generic term for that branch of archaeology that deals with the impact of contemporary construction and other developments on archaeological sites, and the various laws enacted to mitigate the threat. It has spawned an industry aimed at preserving archaeological sites, which is known in Great Britain as Rescue Archaeology, and in the United States as Salvage Archaeology or CULTURAL RESOURCE MANAGEMENT. In some countries, such as the United States, the protection of antiquities is extended to shipwrecks in both fresh and salt water.

Pucara an EARLY INTERMEDIATE PERIOD culture of the Peruvian altiplano. The site of Pucara includes a monumental sunken court surrounded by structures, and walls made of dressed stone slabs. Pucara ceramics are elaborate, including painted and incised designs, and may be related to ceramics of the late PARACAS culture. The iconography of Pucara ceramics anticipates that of the MIDDLE HORIZON styles of TIAHUANACO and HUARI.

Pueblito see TAIRONA.

pueblo 1 a Spanish term for village applied to the historic and contemporary town sites of American Southwest Pueblo Indians. The pueblos are 'apartment-like'

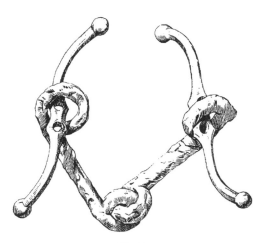

PSALIA.

complexes of small interconnected rooms, up to four storeys high, made of wattle and daub. See also ADOBE.

2 a culturally homogeneous, linguistically diverse group of NATIVE AMERICANS who inhabit the American Southwest. They are believed to be the successors of prehistoric ANASAZI, HOHOKAM and MOGOLLON groups. See also KIVA, PITHOUSE.

3 specific stages in the Anasazi cultural tradition.

Pueblo Bonito a major site in CHACO CANYON, New Mexico, USA, comprising a large prehistoric PUEBLO, constructed by the ANASAZI in two main building periods: 1) the early part of the 10th century AD; 2) the latter half of the 11th century. The site was first excavated by George Pepper and Richard WETHERILL of the Hyde Expedition in 1897–9, and later in 1921–7 by Neil Judd and the National Geographic Society. The site comprises over 300 ground-floor rooms (with an estimated 650 in total), and at least thirty-two KIVAS (including two great kivas).

Pujo an early historical place-name occurring on silver seals excavated from tombs near the HAN Dynasty LELANG COMMANDERY on the Korean peninsula. The seal inscriptions *Pujo Yegun* and *Pujo Chang* are interpreted as titles given to men of Pujo (eastern Korea?) prior to and just after the establishment of Lelang, indicating the co-operation of peninsular natives in territorial acquisition and administration by the Han.

pulsed induction meter a GEOPHYSICAL instrument used in ELECTROMAGNETIC SURVEYING to detect primary metals and, under favourable conditions, other shallow or shallowly buried features. A magnetic field is generated and induced as pulses to the ground which produces eddy currents in metal objects and responsive soils. The currents are detected by a receiver.

Pulumelei a site on Savai'i, Samoa, which is one of the most spectacular monuments in the Pacific. It is a flat-topped stone mound, 12 m (40 ft) high and 60 by 50 m (66 by 55 yds) at the base. A sunken ramp at either end leads to the top, where there are remains of structures. It is undated, but surrounded by other structures, and may have been the focus of ceremonial activity.

puna the highest Andean ecozone, devoted to herding of camelids and hunting of wild camelids and other game. Because of the danger of frost, agriculture is rarely practised, and few permanent settlements are found on the puna. Remains of PRECERAMIC hunter-gatherer cultures have been found widely here. Work by John Rick suggests that groups in central Peru lived in sedentary settlements, subsisting on a diet of mostly meat. Other researchers suggest that such groups practised TRANSHUMANCE, and occupied puna sites on a scheduled, seasonal basis.

Puna Pau a quarry on EASTER ISLAND, source of a soft red *scoria* (volcanic rock) used to make the huge cylindrical head-dresses (*pukao*) placed as late embellishments on some major MOAI.

Punt an area on the coast of eastern Africa, possibly close to the Sudan/Eritrea border, to which the ancient Egyptians sent naval trading expeditions for exotic products. The best-known expedition to Punt is that depicted in the reliefs at DEIR EL-BAHRI.

puquio one of a series of semi-subterranean AQUEDUCTS found in the NASCA region, Peru. Each puquio functions as a horizontal well, tapping groundwater and directing it through a subterranean tunnel and/or an open trench to a small reservoir. While some believe the puquios to have been built by the Spanish during the colonial period, archaeological evidence indicates construction in *c.*6th century AD, by the Nasca culture. Thirty-five puquios remain in use at present; their original number may have been forty.

Purépecha see TARASCANS.

Puritjarra a sandstone shelter in the CLELAND HILLS, central Australia. The first substantial use of the site occurred 22,000–18,000 bp, though it was sporadically used from about 30,000 years ago. The stone assemblage includes small elongated flakes and large flakes. Puritjarra clearly demonstrates occupation of the Australian arid zone prior to the LAST GLACIAL MAXIMUM.

Purron phase a phase (2300–1500 BC) during the period of food collecting and incipient plant cultivation in the TEHUACÁN VALLEY, Mexico. During this phase there is a substantial increase in the amount of agricultural products in the diet, and a concomitant decrease in reliance on meat. Dates for this phase are difficult to establish, and derive more from knowing the end of the ABEJAS and start of the AJALPAN phases than from firm dates associated with Purron phase materials.

Pushkari I an Upper Palaeolithic open-air site located on a bedrock promontory above the Desna River in Ukraine. The occupation horizon is buried in loess, and has yielded radiocarbon dates of 21,000 and 19,010 bp. Woolly mammoth predominates among the fauna. According to BORISKOWSKIJ, a small LONGHOUSE is represented by a linear arrangement of three hearths and associated small pits and debris. Pushkari I was excavated by Rudinskij in 1932–3 and by Borsikowskij in 1937–9.

Puskaporos a prehistoric rockshelter located along the Szinva River in the Bükk Mountains of northeastern Hungary. Artifacts and some faunal remains (including cave bear and woolly rhinoceros) are buried in clay and rubble deposits. The lower cultural layer contains a Middle Palaeolithic assemblage (age unknown) with laurel-leaf points and sidescrapers. Late Upper Palaeolithic, Neolithic and younger remains occur in the upper layers.

Putnam, Frederic Ward (1839–1915) an important figure in the development of professional archaeology in North America. He made major contributions to the study of the mounds of midwestern North America and of the antiquity of humans on the continent (which he believed to pre-date the end of the last GLACIATION).

Putun see CHICHÉN ITZÁ, COZUMEL.

Puuc a region in the northern-central part of the MAYA area of Mexico, with a distinctive architectural style. Puuc architecture is characterized by mosaic façades carved in stone: usually the decorations are rain-god masks and earth-god façades. Typically, the mosaics are contrasted with areas of minimal or no decoration. UXMAL is one of the best-known Puuc centres. The Puuc architectural style spread beyond the Puuc region itself, throughout the northern plains of the Yucatán. See also RIO BEC-CHENES and GREATER PETEN.

The Puuc region was slow in reaching CLASSIC Maya status. It was the last variant of Classic Maya culture. The Classic Maya collapse was delayed in the Puuc region for about 100 years. During this time, Puuc cities probably took advantage of the instability of the cities in the southern lowlands. The Puuc collapse was probably caused by a combination of factors, including those that brought down the rest of the Maya centres.

Pu'uhonua or 'city of refuge' the best-preserved example of such a refuge, now reconstructed, at Honaunau on the west coast of Hawaii. It comprises an enclosure built by walling off a peninsula, with three HEIAU. By tradition, the complex was first built in AD 1450 and was still in use in the early 19th century.

Puyo 1 the Korean pronunciation of Chinese 'Fuyu', an ethnic group in the northern Manchurian basin known to the HAN Chinese, with whom the political elite of both PAEKCHE and KOGURYO states claimed ancestral affiliations.

2 the name of a modern city in South Korea, known earlier as Sabi and serving as the last Paekche capital, remodelled on CHANG'AN.

Pyla-Kokkinokremos the site of a Late Cypriot settlement in southern CYPRUS, excavated by Dikaios in 1952 and by Karageorghis in 1981–2. The site was occupied in the late 13th century BC, possibly by the SEA PEOPLES who built massive fortifications but then abandoned Pyla for KITION.

pylon a monumental gateway, the usual entrance to an Egyptian temple from the MIDDLE KINGDOM onwards. The pylon consisted of two wide, massive towers flanking a comparatively small gateway into the temple. Large grooves down the front of each tower would be used for insetting tall wooden flagpoles, while pairs of colossal statues and obelisks were often erected in front of the pylon.

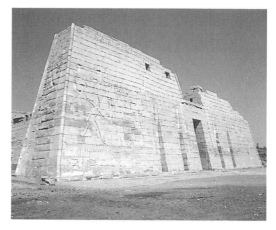

The massive PYLON entrance to the Medinet Habu mortuary temple, built for King Ramesses III on the west bank at Thebes.

Pylos the best-preserved of the MYCENAEAN palaces, located on the hill of Epano Englianos in Messenia, Greece, and revealed by BLEGEN's excavations between 1939 and 1952–66. The 'Palace of Nestor' was built in the 14th century BC and destroyed by fire late in the 13th century. The large archive of LINEAR B tablets recovered from the palace indicates that the ruler of Pylos exercised political and economic control over much of Messenia.

P'yonhan see SAMHAN.

pyramid 1 (*Egypt*) a structure of stone or brick with a square base and four straight sides converging to a point at the apex, having evolved from the step pyramid. It is the central monument of a pyramid complex. The pyramid was the preferred form of tomb for the kings of the OLD KINGDOM and MIDDLE KINGDOM, the royal burial being in a chamber within or below the pyramid itself. The largest Egyptian pyramid is that of KHUFU at GIZA, its base being 230 m (250 yds) long and with an original height of 146 m (480 ft). The use of the pyramid as a royal tomb was revived by the kings of NAPATA and MEROE. Compare ZIGGURAT.

2 (*New World*) one of a wide range of religious or funerary mounds throughout the Americas. At first they were merely constructed of earth or rubble; later examples were given facings of mud-brick or stone. In most cases they were truncated pyramids, with religious structures placed on a flat platform at the top (hence TEMPLE MOUND, PLATFORM MOUND). See TEOTIHUACÁN, CAHOKIA, CHICHÉN ITZÁ.

pyramid complex the structures associated with royal pyramids of the OLD KINGDOM and MIDDLE KINGDOM in Egypt. The major elements were: (1) the Valley Temple, often with a quay on the River Nile, and probably used

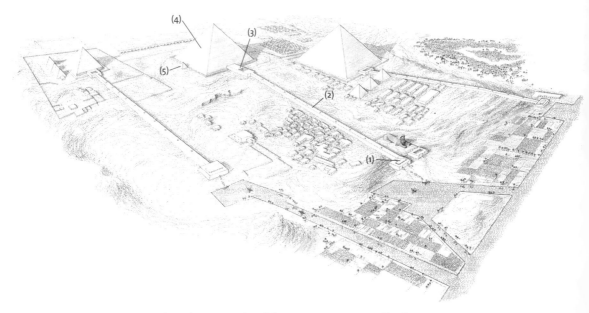

Artwork reconstruction of the PYRAMID COMPLEX at Giza, Egypt.

for ceremonies connected with the MUMMIFICATION of the king; (2) the Causeway, an enclosed passageway from the Valley Temple to the Mortuary Temple, used as the approach to the tomb during the royal funeral and probably the slipway for transporting blocks used in the construction of the pyramid; (3) the MORTUARY TEMPLE; (4) the royal pyramid itself; (5) a subsidiary pyramid, of uncertain function. Satellite pyramids, for the burials of important female members of the immediate royal household, were often located close to or within the royal pyramid complex; (6) subsidiary burials of members of the extended royal family and officials of the king, often in regular rows of MASTABA tombs; (7) pits containing full-sized boats (e.g. like those associated with the Pyramid of KHUFU).

Pyu an ethno-linguistic group once dominant in central Burma, whose language was probably related to Burmese.

pyxis a lidded box in Greek archaeology.

Qafzeh a prehistoric cave-site near Nazareth, Israel, first excavated by R. Neuville (1933–6) who found remains of five individuals in Middle Palaeolithic levels. B. Vandermeersch (1965–79) found a further fourteen adults and children, also in the cave entrance area; at least six are considered deliberate burials. At first described by Vandermeersch as 'Proto-CRO-MAGNONS' the Qafzeh population is now accepted as early anatomically modern HOMO *sapiens*, apparently preceding later NEANDERTHAL populations in western Asia.

THERMOLUMINESCENCE dates on flints average 92,000 BP, while ESR dates on animal teeth range from 96,000 to 115,000 BP. Compare SKHUL, TABUN, KEBARA.

Qala'at al Bahrain a low TELL, covering about 18 ha (44 acres) on the north coast of Bahrain, which provides the key archaeological sequence for the central portion of the Persian Gulf, spanning the mid 3rd millennium BC to medieval periods. The lowest levels (I–II) belong to the BARBAR culture, and represent one of its best-known settlements. The town was walled and its gate contained a concentration of seals, sealings, Indus weights, occasional CUNEIFORM texts and exotic raw materials, all reflective of the PERSIAN GULF TRADE. Later occupations include a KASSITE period settlement (period III) and several towns of the 1st millennium BC; a SASSANIAN to Islamic fortress lies on the northern edge of the site.

Qana modern Bir Ali, a port town on the coast of southern Yemen which served as an outlet for South Arabian frankincense and myrrh during the first half of the 1st millennium BC. Soviet excavations here during the 1980s recovered Mediterranean and Indian pottery and other goods.

Qantir a site in the eastern Nile DELTA where excavations by the Pelizaeus-Museum Hildesheim have revealed the city of Pi-Ramesses. This city was established by RAMESSES II as the capital of the Egyptian empire and its cosmopolitan nature is confirmed by strong evidence of HITTITE and MYCENAEAN presence at the site, perhaps particularly associated with the extensive industrial area.

Qaryat al-Faw a caravan station in southwestern Saudi Arabia, on the incense route northwards from South Arabia. Saudi excavations revealed a fortified caravanserai, residences and tombs; well-preserved wall paintings are especially noteworthy. The place was in use during the final centuries BC and the first centuries AD.

Qasr es-Sagha an Egyptian site in the northern FAIYUM, with an unusually undecorated temple, probably of the MIDDLE KINGDOM.

Qasr Ibrim a site in LOWER NUBIA, now partially submerged by Lake Nasser. Archaeological evidence indicates an almost continual, and chiefly military, occupation of this fortified cliff from at least as early as the NEW KINGDOM to its abandonment in AD 1812. Qasr Ibrim has been the focus of a major series of excavations by the Egypt Exploration Society since 1963.

Qermez Dere a late EPIPALAEOLITHIC to early ACERAMIC NEOLITHIC site just southeast of Jebel Sinjar in northern Iraq, where T. Watkins' excavations in the 1980s defined seven phases of occupation. Structures are evident only in the later phases, with a succession of semi-rectangular pit dwellings with plastered walls and floors, each of which contains a plastered STELA in its centre; the last house, deliberately destroyed and filled, also had six human skulls placed within it. The lithic industry bears strong resemblances to that found further west on the Euphrates River, especially in the earliest phases of MUREYBET; this westward connection had already been noticed at later sites such as Tell MAGHZALIA. The community's subsistence was focused on cereals, legumes and nuts, and on cattle, equids, gazelle, sheep/goat and many small animals and birds; these all seem to be wild. Qermez Dere stands at the beginning of documented habitation on the northern MESOPOTAMIAN plain.

Qijia [Ch'i-chia] a protohistoric culture of northwestern China contemporaneous with the LONGSHAN and early SHANG cultures at c.2000 BC. It is distinguished by Neolithic traditions of painted pottery, animal husbandry (sheep?) and use of copper artifacts.

Qilakitsoq a site on the west coast of Greenland where the mummified remains (see MUMMIFICATION) of eight humans were found, dating to between AD 1425 and 1525. The bodies, buried in two adjacent graves, ranged in age from a six-month-old baby to three females of about fifty. All the bodies were the remains of children or women. Not only was their clothing still preserved, but the last meal could be identified in the stomach of one mummy, and facial tattoos on five of the adults were visible. The bodies belonged to members of the archaeologically defined THULE culture. See also SKRAELING.

Qin [Ch'in] one of the ZHOU states in protohistoric China, whose last ruler unified all Zhou states in 221 BC and became the first emperor (*Qin Shihuangdi*) of a united China (see CHINESE DYNASTIES). He was buried in a large MOUNDED TOMB near Xian City, roughly 440 m (480 yds) square, which allegedly contains a scale-version of the palace, rivers of mercury and cocked crossbows to deter plunderers. A terracotta army of over 7,000 life-size soldiers, discovered in 1974, was made at his instigation and buried in three long pits near his tomb for eternal protection. Though the Qin Dynasty was short-lived, the standardization of weights and measures, coinage and the development of a state infrastructure by Qin Shihuangdi laid the basis for a stable, centralized state in the HAN Dynasty.

QIN, China: head of a member of the terracotta army.

Qingliangang [Ch'ing-lien-kang] a Neolithic culture of the 5th millennium BC on the eastern seaboard of China, succeeding HEMUDU and merging with DAWENKOU. It is distinguished by its unpainted, openwork pedestalled ceramics (compare YANGSHAO pottery). A major site is Songze.

Qishan [Ch'i-shan] a site in Shaanxi Province, China, identified with the capital of the predynastic ZHOU peoples prior to their takeover of the SHANG in 1027 BC (see CHINESE DYNASTIES). Excavations in 1979 revealed inscribed ORACLE BONES and HANGTU foundation platforms for palace buildings.

QSR-44 see SODMEIN.

Quanterness a PASSAGE GRAVE in Orkney, Scotland, of MAES HOWE or Quanterness/Quoyness type, dated to c.3000 BC. A long, low passage leads to the principal chamber, which is of rectangular plan with a tall CORBEL-VAULTED roof. Six smaller side chambers, also corbel-vaulted, are arranged around the main chamber. Excavations by C. Renfrew in the main chamber and one of the side chambers yielded remains of 157 individuals, giving an estimated total for the whole tomb of 394 individuals. Construction is dry-stone throughout, and the tomb is covered by a large circular cairn.

Quanzhou [Ch'üan-chou] a late 13th-century AD Song (see CHINESE DYNASTIES) shipwreck at Houzhu, Fujian Province, China. The ship, 24 m (78 ft) long, was keeled, with thirteen internal compartments, constructed shell-first (compare SINAN). See also SHIPWRECKS.

quartz a hard silicon dioxide mineral which is an important constituent in most igneous, metamorphic and sedimentary rocks. Quartz is typically colourless to white, but with traces of other oxide impurities it takes on nearly a full spectrum of colours. Quartz sand is sometimes used as temper in pottery.

quartzite a metamorphic rock consisting mostly of quartz. Most quartzites are altered quartz sandstones. It is a dense, hard rock that is able to fracture conchoidally; flaked tools were made from quartzite, when available, in the absence of chert or flint. Quartzite was also used as a heavy monumental building stone. Small rounded quartzite cobbles made ideal hammerstones and handaxes.

Quaternary 1 a major GEOCHRONOLOGICAL subdivision (*Quaternary period*) (see STRATIGRAPHY) of geological time.
2 a major chronostratigraphic subdivision (*Quaternary system*) (see stratigraphy) of GEOLOGY, characterized by deposits resulting from alternating GLACIAL and INTERGLACIAL processes and conditions in response to

multiple major environmental changes. The base of the Quaternary system is defined by basal deposits that overlie PLIOCENE deposits. Much of the evidence for the history of humans is preserved in deposits of the Quaternary system. The base has been variably taken to be about 1.8 to 2.45 million years, but is now placed at the top of the OLDUVAI PALAEOMAGNETIC event at *c*.1.88 million years.

Quechua 1 the language of the INCA empire, called *Runa Simi* by them. Several dialects of the language are still widely spoken in the Andean region, especially in Peru and Bolivia.

2 the Andean ecozone in which grains, especially maize, are grown in hillside plots. The quechua zone is typically extensively terraced.

quern a large grindstone (see also METATE). The most common forms are: the *saddle-quern*, where material was ground on an immobile concave stone, and the *rotary quern*, where one stone is rotated on another by hand, animal, water or wind power.

Quéroy a cave-site in Charente, France, with stratified deposits from the beginning of the middle Neolithic to the LA TÈNE Iron Age. The Late Bronze Age levels (*c*.800 BC) yielded several sherds bearing incised symbols, some representational (zoomorphic or anthropomorphous), others abstract (geometric). Similar signs have been found on potsherds in other parts of central and southern France and constitute a form of proto-writing, probably for religious use. Beneath the occupation deposits are remains of tundra species which accidentally fell into the cave towards the end of the last Ice Age, including horse, reindeer and saiga antelope.

Quetta a valley of Baluchistan in western Pakistan where the survey and excavations by W. Fairservis produced a standard chronological sequence for the region. The sounding at Kili Gul Mohammad indicated four periods (KGM I–IV) and that at Damb Sada'at three (DS I–III), which dovetail (KGM IV just prior to DS I); the combined results provide a cultural sequence that begins around 5000 BC and continues to the later 3rd millennium BC. A number of distinctive pottery styles appear in this sequence, which thus provides a valuable framework for relative chronology. In the 1980s a hoard of metal vessels and other materials associated with the BACTRIAN BRONZE AGE turned up during hotel construction.

Quetzalcóatl a principal deity of POSTCLASSIC ME-SOAMERICA. The word means 'Precious Feather Serpent' in NAHUATL. The deity took a number of forms, including the wind god (*Éhecatl*) and the morning star (*Tlahuizcal-pantecuhtli*). Many circular buildings in Mesoamerica are associated with Quetzalcóatl in his various forms: the centre of his cult in the late Postclassic was CHOLULA. The Yucatec Maya term for Feathered Serpent is *Kukulkán*.

Depictions of feathered serpents on temple columns in the Yucatán have been used to suggest central Mexican influence among the MAYA.

Quetzalcóatl played a significant role in the Spanish conquest. CORTÉS arrived in the BASIN OF MEXICO during a period in which diviners predicted the return of Quetzalcóatl. This prophecy greatly influenced the way in which Moctezuma II initially received and treated Cortés.

Quimbaya a late prehistoric culture (AD 300–1600) in western Colombia, South America, known especially for its goldwork, representing some of the most advanced metallurgical techniques in the prehistoric New World. Quimbaya ceramics were sometimes modelled, and decorated with negative painting and incision.

quipu or **khipu** a mnemonic device used by the INCA, made of a thick cord from which descended a series of strings, sometimes of different colours. Knots were placed in the string, their size and position denoting numerical value. A special class of bureaucrats, called *quipucamayoq*, were charged with keeping the imperial records, and 'reading' the quipu.

Quiriguá a small MAYA centre in the southern Lowlands of Guatemala, one of the first Maya sites to be studied thoroughly, having been discovered shortly before it was visited in 1840 by Frederick CATHERWOOD. Some of the first excavations at the site were by Alfred P. Maudslay in 1881, and by Edgar Lee Hewitt in 1910. Evidence of conflict between COPÁN and Quiriguá strengthened arguments of warfare and capture as important aspects of CLASSIC Maya art and culture. The largest STELA ever erected by the Maya, Stela E, almost 11 m (36 ft) tall, was found here.

Qujialing [Ch'ü-chia-ling] see HEMUDU.

Qumran the site close to the Dead Sea, Israel, of a community of the Essenes, a Jewish sect who lived there from the *c*.1st century BC to the 1st century AD. Their religious writings seem to have been hidden in nearby caves during the period when the Romans put down the Jewish Revolt, events which probably led to the end of the community. These documents, known as the Dead Sea Scrolls, were discovered in 1947, and were recently dated by AMS/radiocarbon to the last two centuries BC and the 1st century AD.

Qurum or **Ras al Hamra** the area in which the long-term Italian project on the coast near Muscat in Oman in south-eastern Arabia revealed evidence for mid-Holocene hunting and gathering maritime adaptations on the Indian Ocean. Several of these sites also contain extensive cemeteries, which provide important documentation of the pathologies and gene pools of these populations.

Qustul see BALLANA.

Quynh Van a SHELL MIDDEN in Nghe Tinh Province, 50 km (31 miles) north of Vinh, central Vietnam. Excavated in 1963–4, the site is dated to the mid 3rd millennium BC, and yielded over thirty flexed and seated burials, as at DA BUT, with distinctive pointed-base coarse, coil-built pottery. All the stone tools are flaked and not polished, as is common elsewhere in Vietnam at this time.

R

Ra see RE.

Rabel Cave a cave in the CAGAYAN VALLEY of northern Luzon, Philippines, with red-slipped pottery dated to c.2800 BC, possibly marking early AUSTRONESIAN settlement of the Philippines.

Rachmani or **Rakhmani** the site of a Neolithic–Bronze Age settlement mound in Thessaly, Greece, excavated by WACE and Thompson in 1910. The FINAL NEOLITHIC Rachmani culture is characterized by crusted red, pink and white pottery.

racloir see SCRAPER.

Radial-Decorated Pottery culture see BADEN CULTURE.

radiate a coin on which the Roman emperor wears a pointed solar crown, particularly from the 3rd century AD. Although once thought to be the equivalent of two DENARII, the coin's weight in silver suggests an equation of 1.5 denarii.

radiocarbon an unstable, or radioactive, ISOTOPE of carbon with atomic mass 14 which is produced in the atmosphere and assimilated into living plants and animals in equilibrium with the atmospheric ^{14}C content. Radiocarbon is the basis for radiocarbon dating, the method most frequently used by archaeologists. ^{14}C has a HALF-LIFE of 5,730 years; it was originally calculated by Willard F. LIBBY to be 5,568 years, and this value is utilized in calculating radiocarbon ages.

radiocarbon dating a RADIOMETRIC DATING technique for determining the age of late QUATERNARY carbon-bearing materials, including wood and plant remains, bone, peat and calcium carbonate shell. The method is based on the radioactive decay of the ^{14}C ISOTOPE in the sample to nitrogen, with the release of β particles that is initiated when an organism dies and ceases to exchange ^{14}C with the atmosphere. After death the ^{14}C content is a function of time and is determined by counting β particles with either a proportional gas counter or a liquid scintillation counter for a period of time. The method yields reliable ages back to about 50,000 bp and under extreme conditions to about 75,000 bp. See also RADIOCARBON, LIBBY, ACCELERATOR MASS SPECTROMETRY, ISOTOPIC REPLACEMENT, HARD WATER EFFECT, CALIBRATION.

radiography or **x-radiography** a physical technique of analysis in which a sample is bombarded by small-wavelength, high-energy electromagnetic radiation, usually x-rays, to study its composition and structure. The specimen is placed on a radiosensitive surface, usually photographic film, and is irradiated by x-rays. The structure and composition of the sample affects the passage of x-rays by differential absorption. An image is recorded on the film consisting of darker and lighter tones reflecting the intensity of x-rays that passed through the sample, and therefore the structure. Radiography is particularly applicable to metals such as iron that are subject to corrosion; the weathering products and uncorroded material absorb the x-rays differentially, as do some decorative materials that may have been added to the metal object. Radiography has also been applied successfully to the examination of SEDIMENTARY STRUCTURES in slab samples of fine-grained sediment, rocks and ceramic sections, as well as to mummies and other biological remains. Microradiographic techniques have been developed to examine the atomic structure of crystalline substances (see X-RAY MICROSCOPY).

CT or CAT (computed axial tomography) is a technique using x-rays to identify internal anatomical structures nondestructively, not only in soft tissues (such as tumours in human brains), but also in fossil bones and teeth. It has been used successfully to obtain three-dimensional records of internal anatomical details in early HOMINID fossils.

radiometric dating or **radiometric assay** dating using a method based on the decay of radioactive ISOTOPES and yielding absolute age estimations, usually reported with a standard error. These methods include RADIOCARBON DATING, URANIUM SERIES DATING and POTASSIUM-ARGON DATING.

Radmilli, Antonio Mario (1922–98) a leading Italian

prehistorian who excavated many Palaeolithic sites such as POLESINI and Castel di Guido (a Lower Palaeolithic site with an ACHEULIAN bone industry), and also Neolithic sites. He was professor of Human Palaeontology at the University of Pisa.

Radomyshl' an Upper Palaeolithic open-air site located in the upper reaches of a side-valley ravine which empties into the Teterev River (a tributary of the Dnieper) in European Russia. The occupation horizon is buried in loam near the ground surface (recently eroded by local deforestation). The faunal remains are almost exclusively of woolly mammoth, and are mostly grouped into concentrations; a pit and several hearths were also uncovered. It has been suggested that the site is of early Upper Palaeolithic age, because the artifacts include tool types characteristic of the Middle and Upper Palaeolithic; however, an AMS radiocarbon date of 19,000 bp has recently been reported. Radomyshl' was excavated by Shovkoplyas between 1957 and 1963.

Rahman Dehri a 22 ha (54 acre) site in the western Punjab (the Derat Jat region of Pakistan) at which F. A. Durrani's investigations greatly illuminate the millennium (roughly 3400–2500 BC) leading up to the Mature HARAPPAN civilization. Here the early levels contain a regional style of painted pottery, while the ceramic assemblages of subsequent phases are increasingly dominated by the KOT DIJI style. Throughout this pottery sequence occur a large number of GRAFFITI on sherds, which, it has been suggested, may be an antecedent to the Harappan script. By its later phases, the settlement is walled and divided into two sections by a major thoroughfare, with a clear orthogonal street plan which may also be a precursor to Mature Harappan urbanism.

Raimondi stela see CHAVÍN.

raised beach see FOSSIL BEACH.

Rajghat the site of Old Banaras on the River Ganges in eastern Uttar Pradesh, India, where A. K. Narain's excavations provided an eight-phase periodization (Rajghat IA–VI), representing the time between c.800 BC and the mid 2nd millennium AD. Rajghat IA contains a variety of pottery characteristic of this formative period in the middle Ganges: black-and-red and black-slipped wares, both sometimes white painted, as well as red wares. NORTHERN BLACK POLISHED WARE appears in Rajghat IB (beginning around 500 BC), a time when a number of embankments were constructed against flood waters and a major channel dug between the Barna and Ganges Rivers. NBPW continues in Rajghat IC (though in a coarse version) and a grey ware appears, as do cast coins. The first baked-brick architecture and large multi-room buildings appear in Rajghat II, perhaps 200 BC, and red wares begin to replace the earlier pottery; these characteristics are further emphasized in later periods belonging to the 1st

millennium AD (Rajghat III–IV). The Rajghat sequence presents a separate cultural milieu or the emergence of urban life in the middle Ganges Basin from that found further west in the Ganges-Yamuna doab (alluvial plain) represented by HASTINAPURA; this regional cultural distinction endured until the NBPW horizon spanned the Gangetic drainage (by about 500 BP).

Rakhmani see RACHMANI.

Ramesses a name borne by eleven Egyptian kings of the NEW KINGDOM. The most renowned was Ramesses II, who reigned between c.1279 and 1213 bc and was probably the most active builder of new monuments, and usurper of existing ones, of all the monarchs of Ancient Egypt. The major political event of the reign of Ramesses II was the much-commemorated, though probably indecisive, battle with the HITTITES at KADESH.

Rancho La Brea a late QUATERNARY faunal locality and prehistoric site located near Los Angeles, California, USA. Large numbers of vertebrate remains dating between c.40,000 and 11,000 BP are buried in asphalt deposits representing ancient tar seeps. Younger deposits contain a human skull dated to c.9000 BP and some artifacts (including MANOS and wooden spear points).

Ranis Cave or **Ilsenhöhle** a prehistoric and historic site located near the River Saale in eastern Germany. Artifacts and faunal remains (of e.g. woolly mammoth, reindeer) are buried in clay, silt, sand and rubble. The lowest layer contains a small assemblage assigned to the Middle Palaeolithic. Overlying layers contain assemblages with both Middle and Upper Palaeolithic elements (e.g. end-scrapers and bifacial foliates) dating to the middle of the LAST GLACIAL MAXIMUM. Late Upper Palaeolithic (GRAVETTIAN, MAGDALENIAN), Bronze Age and historic remains occur in the upper layers. Ranis Cave was excavated by von Breitenbuch in 1926–32 and by Hulle in 1932–9.

Ranjpur a prehistoric site just south of LOTHAL in coastal Gujarat in northwestern India which provides clear evidence for the Mature and Late HARAPPAN succession in this part of the Harappan world. S. R. Rao's excavations in the 1950s defined five periods (Ranjpur I, IIA–C, III). Ranjpur I is an occupation containing a microlithic industry (perhaps dated to 3000 BC), and separated from later levels by a silt deposit. The Mature Harappan settlement of Ranjpur IIA includes many of the typical artifacts of this civilization (e.g. baked bricks and drains, GRAFFITI on pottery, stone weights, triangular terracotta cakes, beads); the pottery is also Harappan but does show some regional variation. Ranjpur IIA provides evidence for rice cultivation in the Mature Harappan; Lothal provides similar evidence, and this may represent an economic variation of Mature Harappan civilization. Harappan characteristics diminish in Ranjpur IIB–C: some disappear entirely (e.g. some typical pottery forms, stone weights, terracotta cakes); others are modified, in that the technological qualities of the pottery deviate from the Mature Harappan standards, and construction becomes less substantial. At the same time, new elements appear in the material culture (e.g. new animal motifs on painted pottery, the class of red burnished pottery named 'Lustrous Red ware'). In Ranjpur III the Lustrous Red ware becomes common, and a black-and-red ware (often decorated with white paint) also appears. This sequence of Late Harappan materials is repeated in other sites of the region (e.g. Lothal, Rodji).

Rano Raraku a volcanic crater on EASTER ISLAND where most of the MOAI were quarried in the soft TUFF. One of the world's most remarkable sights, it is filled with almost 400 unfinished statues in all stages of completion, in its inner and outer wall, with many finished moai erected either facing the crater-lake or outside on the plain. Thousands of flaked basalt hand-held picks lie discarded at the site. Most quarrying occurred between c.AD 1000 and 1500.

Rapa Nui see EASTER ISLAND.

Raqa'i a 0.4 ha (1 acre) site on the middle Khabur River in eastern Syria. Excavations by a joint American-Dutch team recovered a sequence of village buildings which cover the first half of the 3rd millennium BC (NINEVITE 5 and immediately after). The most striking feature of the site is a large round building, about 20 m (22 yds) across, with internal divisions and deep vaulted silos that indicate grain storage that far exceeded the village population; comparable concentrations of storage capacity appear at nearby sites (e.g. Tell Atij). Proposed interpretations of this phenomenon include long-term storage for a seasonally pastoralist-agrarian economy, and surplus grain production for shipment to a large consumer city like MARI.

Ras al-Amiya a 'UBAID period site in southern MESOPOTAMIA, just north of KISH. Discovered during modern canal cutting, the site lies beneath 1–2 m (3–7 ft) of silts and demonstrates that small prehistoric sites are underrepresented in southern Mesopotamia. Limited examination in 1960 detected four building levels, with additional deposits below. The associated pottery assigns the site to the HAJJI MOHAMMAD ('Ubaid 2) phase of this culture.

Ras al Mawra see QURUM.

Ras Hafun a trading site in northern Somalia which provides evidence of early 1st-millennium AD pre-Islamic occupation in the form of green glazed ceramics originally from SOHAR on the Omani coast, which are dated from the 1st century BC to the 5th century AD (see PERIPLUS OF THE ERYTHRAEAN SEA).

Ras Shamra see UGARIT.

rath a type of ring fort found in Ireland and southwestern Wales; in Wales dated to the Late Iron Age/Roman period (1st century BC–4th century AD); in Ireland mainly to the early Christian period, c.5th–10th centuries AD.

Rawlinson, Sir Henry Creswicke (1810–95) a British army officer and diplomat, whose work on the trilingual inscription at BISITUN in western Iran was instrumental in the decipherment of the CUNEIFORM languages of western Asia. Beginning in the 1830s, he produced a translation of the Persian text by 1851, and that of the BABYLONIAN by 1857. Although Rawlinson did produce several academic publications on his work in the mid 19th century, he subsequently returned to politics and diplomacy, and among other things sat in Parliament and was minister to the Iranian court.

Raymonden see CHANCELADE.

Re or **Ra** an Egyptian deity chiefly associated with the sun, and usually depicted as a hawk-headed man with a sun-disc on his head. Re's chief cult centre was the city of HELIOPOLIS and he was especially important during the OLD KINGDOM, being closely associated with the kings of the 4th and 5th Dynasties. In the NEW KINGDOM Re is most importantly attested in the composite deity AMEN-RE, state god of the Egyptian empire.

Real Alto a site of the VALDIVIA culture located near the coast of Ecuador, at which the emergence of early complex social organization has been documented. In its earliest occupation (Valdivia I–II, roughly 3500–3200 bc), the site comprised a small village laid out in a U-shaped configuration. Later, the site included public architecture, and evidence of social inequality (Valdivia III, 3200–3000 bc).

Reclau Viver see SERIÑA.

Redcliff a complex series of fossiliferous cave fillings at a limestone quarry in central Zimbabwe, containing MIDDLE and LATER STONE AGE assemblages, Iron Age GOKOMERE pottery and carnivore accumulations.

red-figured adj. denoting a technique used to decorate pottery. During the decoration of the pot, the area of the figure is left empty ('reserved') and the detail is painted in (contrast BLACK-FIGURED). The red of the clay, which was sometimes heightened by a wash, would contrast with the black gloss. The technique appeared at ATHENS in the late 6th century BC (see ATHENIAN POTTERY) and it remained popular down to the 4th century BC. It was produced in smaller quantities at CORINTH, although in Italy there were several centres from the late 5th century (see SOUTH ITALIAN POTTERY).

Red Lady of Paviland see PAVILAND.

Red Polished ware a pottery type produced in South

Asia during the first three centuries AD. It is a fine red ware with red or orange SLIP which is highly burnished. This pottery is most commonly found near the coast of northwestern India (in and around Gujarat), but is also found in the Gangetic plain and in the interior further south. Because the ware is comparable in many respects (but very different in vessel forms) to Roman products, it is often thought to represent an imitation of SAMIAN pottery from the Mediterranean, but it can now safely be regarded as a local Indian (Gujarati) product and probably derived from a black polished ware antecedent.

Red Skorba see SKORBA.

refitting see CONJOINING.

Reiche, Maria (1903–98), a German mathematician who devoted her life to the study of the NASCA LINES (Peru). She went to Peru in 1932 and worked there as a teacher. In 1941 the American archaeologist Paul Kosok took her to Nasca and showed her the network of lines in the desert he had seen from the air. After being interned in Lima as a German national during the war, she returned to Nasca in 1946 and began the work that would last the rest of her life. Minutely studying the lines and animal figures on the desert plain, her measurements and plans led her to posit an astronomical explanation for the GEOGLYPHS, and also to suggest a standardized system of measurements used by their prehistoric builders. Her solitary pursuit of knowledge was at first regarded with scepticism on the part of the local residents, but her perseverance earned her the respect of local residents and many honours bestowed by the Peruvian government.

Reinecke, Paul (1872–1958) a German archaeologist in Munich who defined the basic periodization of the Bronze and Iron Ages in Central Europe between 1902 and 1911. Largely on the basis of typology in hoard finds from southern Germany, Reinecke divided the Early and Middle Bronze Age into four periods, A to D. He also recognized the continuity of the Iron Age from the Late Bronze Age, particularly on the basis of burial finds, and applied the term HALLSTATT to this whole period. His scheme is still used in modified form.

Reisner, George Andrew (1867–1942) an American Egyptologist. A prolific excavator, his best-known sites are GIZA (including the pyramid of MENKAURE and the tomb of HETEPHERES), Naga ed-Der, SAMARIA and in NUBIA (especially KERMA and NAPATA).

rejoining see CONJOINING.

relative dating dating methods that measure differences in age utilizing an ordinal scale. For example, relative dating methods would include sequencing of events or materials relative to another but without linkage to ages in years before present (bp) or calendar years. Principal relative dating techniques include STRATIGRAPHY and stratigraphic correlation. Compare ABSOLUTE DATING.

relict soil soil which formed on a pre-existing landscape or under extrinsic and intrinsic factors, processes and conditions different from today, but which was not buried, so that it has been subjected to later PEDOGENESIS, possibly under different conditions from those under which it acquired its original properties and characteristics. Because relict soils may represent a relatively large amount of time, archaeological debris of widely different periods may be superimposed, with little if any STRATIGRAPHIC separation, and a greater chance of mixing of components.

Remedello Sotto a cemetery in Lombardy, Italy, of 117 flat graves holding individual inhumations, type-site of the CHALCOLITHIC Remedello culture of the Po Valley and Veneto in the 3rd millennium BC. Typical grave-goods include fine bifacially flaked daggers of flint (possibly imitating metal types), as well as triangular copper daggers, copper axes and awls. See also RINALDONE.

Repolust Cave a Palaeolithic cave-site located on the Mur River in southeastern Austria. Artifacts and faunal remains (e.g. cave bear [predominant], woolly mammoth) are buried in cave deposits, apparently dating to a warm interval (last INTERGLACIAL?). The lowest two layers contain an undated assemblage of Lower or Middle Palaeolithic character (e.g. sidescrapers and denticulates).

repoussé adj. denoting a technique used in the manufacture of jewellery whereby a design is embossed on the back of a sheet of metal with a hammer and punches. The term is also used of decoration worked on the front, although this technique is more correctly called *chasing*.

Republic Groves an ARCHAIC cemetery in Florida, USA, which produced remarkably well-preserved human and animal bone (dating to c.6520–5745 bp), stone artifacts, wooden stakes and other burial goods. Human brain tissue was recovered from some of the skulls. See also LITTLE SALT SPRING, WINDOVER.

rescue archaeology see PUBLIC ARCHAEOLOGY.

resistivity meter a GEOPHYSICAL instrument used in RESISTIVITY SURVEYING to identify buried features and structures based on differences in resistance in the soil. The instrument detects resistance offered by the soil as an electric current is passed through it. Anomalous readings may indicate the presence of archaeological disturbances.

resistivity surveying a reasonably inexpensive GEOPHYSICAL SURVEY method used to locate buried features and structures with a RESISTIVITY METER. An electrical current is passed through the soil between electrodes, and the resistance is recorded. Differences in registered ground resistance are in response to the differing conducting capabilities of the soil and features. A decrease in resistance is facilitated by an increase in soil moisture. Limitations arise in distinguishing natural from cultural features if the GEOLOGY or soils of an area are highly variable. Also, the survey should be conducted under as uniform conditions as possible: any changes in soil moisture content, for example over the course of a day, or from rainfall, will affect the results. Compare ELECTROMAGNETIC SURVEYING.

retouch or **secondary flaking** the working of a primary flake, usually by the removal of small fragments of stone, to form a tool.

Rhodesian Man see BROKEN HILL.

rhythmite a SEDIMENTARY STRUCTURE consisting of rhythmically bedded couplets of LAMINAE or BEDS that have no temporal implications or connotation. If it can be demonstrated that couplets were deposited annually, they are referred to as VARVES.

rhyton a Greek vessel, made of metal, clay or stone, sometimes in the form of an animal head, which was used to pour LIBATIONS.

Riace a coastal resort in southern Italy where two life-size bronze statues of naked warriors were found. A date in the 5th century BC seems likely. No traces of a shipwreck have been found and it is possible that they were jettisoned when their ship ran into trouble. They may have formed part of a cargo of booty looted from Greece.

Ribemont-sur-Ancre a Belgic (Late Iron Age) sanctuary in the Somme *département* of northern France with striking arrangements of human remains. Within a rectangular enclosure defined by ditch and bank were two ossuaries. One took the form of a box formed from more than 200 horse and human long bones framing a pit filled with human ash. The ossuaries date to *c*.200 BC and were followed by further deposits in the enclosure ditch during the 1st century BC, then by the construction of a Gallo-Roman temple during the Roman period. It is unclear whether the ossuary bones were those of community members or belonged to prisoners or enemies.

Richey-Roberts Clovis Cache a CLOVIS site, located in Washington State, USA, comprising thirty artifacts and bone and antler fragments. Of special interest is the recovery of fourteen Clovis points, some of which are 23 cm (9 inches) long, all recovered from a 2 sq. m (2.4 sq. yd) excavation unit. The points showed wear patterns and signs of use-breakage, which counters arguments that because of their length they may have been purely ceremonial. Hypotheses for the site's function include a tool cache, a flint-knapper's hut, a hunting shrine, a shaman's hut, or even the burial of a high-status individual.

Richmond, Sir Ian Archibald (1902–65) director of the British School at Rome. He later excavated Roman sites

RHYTON.

in Britain, which led to the publication of *Roman Britain* (1948).

Riemchen a German term referring to a brick form typical of the late URUK period in MESOPOTAMIA. The brick is long and thin with a roughly square cross-section, and was used both to construct bonded walls and to produce patterns on the façades of public buildings of the time. The term gives its name to one of the buildings in the Eanna precinct at WARKA, the *Riemchengebäude*.

Rikhta a Middle Palaeolithic open-air site on the Rikhta River in central Ukraine. Artifacts were recovered from shallow depths in sand overlying redeposited TILL; no faunal remains were found. The age of the artifacts, which may include material from different time periods, is unknown. Numerous bifacial foliates are present among the tools. Rikhta was excavated by Smirnov during 1974.

Rillaton cup a gold cup found in a WESSEX CULTURE

grave in Cornwall, England, in 1837. The burial consisted of a stone cist beneath a burial mound, and along with the cup there was a bronze dagger and pottery. The cup is of BEAKER shape but dates several centuries later to the late Wessex culture, c.1650–1400 BC. The cup was given to King William IV after its discovery, and for many years was used by King George IV to hold his collar studs, but was eventually given to the British Museum in 1936.

Rim an open site in northern Burkino Faso, Africa, from which a sequence of three archaeological phases dating between 12,000 and 1,000 years ago has been recognized. Although no organic remains were found, it is believed that a date of 3600 bp for the start of the second phase is associated with a food-producing society. See also KINTAMPO.

Rinaldone a cemetery in Lazio, Italy, consisting of eight flat graves with individual inhumations, type-site of the CHALCOLITHIC Rinaldone culture of Tuscany and Lazio, related to the northern Italian REMEDELLO culture. Burials include both single graves in flat grave cemeteries and collective inhumations in rock-cut tombs. Richest in metal of all the Italian Chalcolithic groups, Rinaldone graves contain copper flat axes, daggers and HALBERDS, as well as flaked flint daggers. Rinaldone material is also found at the village site of Luni sul Mignone. It dates from c.3000 to 2200 BC.

Ringkloster a Danish late Mesolithic (ERTEBØLLE) site which is unusual in being situated over 10 km (6 miles) inland. However, the recovery of a piece of whalebone in the upper layers of the site indicates contact with the coast.

Rinyo-Clacton see GROOVED WARE.

Rio Bec-Chenes a regional architectural style during the Lowland CLASSIC MAYA period. The style included mosaic façades rather than the modelled stucco of the GREATER PETEN group. See also PUUC.

Riparo de Romito, Papasidero an Italian cave-site, near Cosenze, Calabria, discovered in 1961 and excavated by GRAZIOSI in 1963–8. Its 8 m (26 ft) stratigraphy contained GRAVETTIAN, EPIGRAVETTIAN (18,700 bp) and ROM-ANELLIAN (10,960 bp) material; the Romanellian level yielded three graves, each containing a male and female. One male was a seventeen-year-old dwarf, the earliest known in the world (11,150 bp). A large block beside the graves bore engravings of bulls.

Riparo Tagliente a rockshelter in the Verona region of Italy, whose 3 m (10 ft) stratigraphy contains material from the MOUSTERIAN, early AURIGNACIAN and final EPIGRAVETTIAN (13,330–12,000 bp). The latter period yielded a number of animal and abstract engravings on stones.

Ripiceni-Izvor a prehistoric open-air site on the Prut River in eastern Romania, located 200 m (220 yds) north of STANCA RIPICENI CAVE. Cultural levels are contained in loess and ALLUVIAL gravel overlying a bedrock terrace; associated faunal remains include woolly mammoth and wild ass. The lowest level is buried in the gravel and comprises flakes assigned to the Lower Palaeolithic. The six overlying levels are assigned to the Middle Palaeolithic and contain sidescrapers and bifacial foliates; radio-carbon dates of 46,400–40,200 bp should be treated as minimum estimates. The upper levels contain AURIG-NACIAN (?), GRAVETTIAN and post-Palaeolithic assem-blages. Ripiceni-Izvor was excavated by Moroşan in 1929–30 and Nicolăescu-Plopşor in 1961–4.

Ripoli a Neolithic ditched settlement in Abruzzi, Italy, which has given its name to the Ripoli Trichrome Painted ware of the central Italian middle Neolithic (c.4500–3500 BC). Typical decoration is a band of triangles in dark brown and red paint on a buff background. Ripoli pottery is one of a series of Italian trichrome painted wares, which includes the Capri style of southwestern Italy and Sicily and the Scaloria style of APULIA.

Riss Glaciation the penultimate Alpine GLACIAL ad-vance which started c.250,000 years ago and lasted over 100,000 years. See also SAALIAN.

Ritsuryo a Japanese term referring to the code of laws adopted in AD 702, thus marking the shift from YAMATO to Ritsuryo state administration. The Ritsuryo state of the Nara period utilized the Tang Dynasty model of capital city (see CHINESE DYNASTIES, JAP-ANESE PERIODIZATION, CHANG'AN, FUJIWARA, HEIJO) from which emanated several trunk routes (-do), e.g. the Hokkai-do, HOKURIKU-do, TOKAI-do, SAN'IN-do, SAN'YO-do, Saikai-do. These formed the foci of regional administrative districts, known by the route names, which were further divided into provinces containing a provincial capital with attached Buddhist monastery and nunnery, and county seats; many of these early historic administrative sites including DAZAIFU have been ex-cavated throughout Japan, some yielding MOKKAN. The names of some of the road-districts are still used in the archaeological literature for discussing regional cultural development.

river terrace see TERRACE.

Rivnač culture an ENEOLITHIC culture of Bohemia, known primarily from a number of small ditched and palisaded sites such as HOMOLKA in the early 3rd millennium BC. The Rivnač culture is related to the BADEN culture slightly to the southeast.

Rixheim see LINEAR POTTERY.

Roaix a rock-cut tomb or HYPOGEUM in Vaucluse, France, containing remains of several hundred individuals in two distinct layers. The burials in the lower layer of *c*.2150 bc were accompanied by daggers and arrowheads of flint, simple round-based pots and almost 2,500 beads of shell, greenstone, turquoise, copper and glass paste. The upper layer of *c*.2090 bc was more poorly furnished, and from the position of the skeletons, and the presence of flint arrowheads embedded in them, has been interpreted as a war grave.

Robberg a LATER STONE AGE microlithic industry of the Western and Eastern Cape Provinces of South Africa, generally dated to between *c*.18,000 and 12,000 BP, although recent research at ROSE COTTAGE Cave indicates that it persisted there until 9560 ± 70 BP, and characterized by bladelet cores yielding numerous bladelets less than 25 mm (1 inch) long. The few formally patterned artifacts include various scrapers and some backed bladelets, as well as worked bone and ostrich eggshell beads.

Robinson, George Augustus (1788–1866) a London-born Hobart bricklayer who was employed in Australia by Lieut.-Governor Arthur between 1829 and 1834 to undertake a series of expeditions to establish friendly relations with the Tasmanian Aborigines and later to induce them to settle at WYBALENNA on Flinders Island in Bass Strait. From 1835 to 1839 he presided over the Wybalenna settlement. In 1839 he became Chief Protector of Aboriginals in Victoria, a post he held until 1849. The daily journals Robinson kept during his travels in TASMANIA and Victoria provide valuable information about Aboriginal culture shortly after the European invasion.

Roc de Sers a rockshelter in Charente, France, where, in 1927, Dr Henri-Martin discovered series of SOLUTREAN bas-relief sculptures on a score of limestone blocks; they depict horses, bovids, deer, ibex and a bison, as well as a human apparently fleeing a musk-ox or bison. The blocks are now thought to be the fallen fragments of an originally parietal frieze.

rock art prehistoric or historic graphic markings on suitable cliff, cave or rock surfaces, made for a variety of purposes such as religious rites, the depiction of historical or mythological narratives, as territorial markers, or simply as decoration. The term encompasses *petroglyphs*, which are carvings made into the rock face, *engravings* (incisions) and *pictographs*, which are made of pigments derived from a variety of mineral or organic substances.

rocker jaw a distinctive anatomical feature of POLYNESIAN populations, where the lower edge of the mandible is convex and thus does not sit firmly on a flat surface.

rockshelter or **abri** a natural concavity or hollow in a rock wall, usually along a valley, large enough for occupation or activities and providing its occupants with some shelter from the elements. The hollows can form in a variety of ways depending upon the type of rock; these include rock fall, spalling, grain by grain attrition, solution, river valley flooding and scour, or a combination of these.

rock-temple an Egyptian temple cut into a solid outcrop of rock, rather than built as a free-standing masonry structure, particularly in the sandstone cliffs of NUBIA. See also ABU SIMBEL.

Rocky Cape a site in northern TASMANIA which provides the longest continuous sequence from a coastal MIDDEN anywhere in Australia. The main chamber of the South Cave has 3.5 m (11.5 ft) of occupation deposit and was used 8000–3800 bp. The deposits seal an inner chamber, also with occupation, the surface of which is an intact living floor dating to 6800 bp. The North Cave was used from 5500 bp. The sequence documents, from about 3500 bp, the loss of bone tools and fish remains, and increasing replacement of local raw materials with exotic fine-grained cherts.

Rogachev, Aleksandr Nikolaevich (1912–84) a Soviet archaeologist and Palaeolithic specialist who excavated at AVDEEVO, but devoted most of his attention to the study of the stratigraphy and remains (including former structures) at the KOSTENKI-BORSHCHEVO sites on the Don River.

Rök location of one of Sweden's largest RUNE stones, 2.5 m (8ft) high, on which every face is covered with a total of 760 runic characters. The text was inscribed by a chieftain named Varin in memory of his dead son, Vämod.

Romanelli a coastal cave-site near Lecce, Italy, with a sparse lower industry which has been classified as either MOUSTERIAN or Upper Palaeolithic, followed by an Upper Palaeolithic '*Romanellian*-type' industry which is dated to *c*.12,000 BP and includes geometric microliths and artwork, including *c*.200 plaquettes with engravings of animals and geometric motifs. There are meanders and abstract designs engraved on the walls.

Romania see EUROPE, EASTERN.

Rome a major urban settlement in Italy beside the River Tiber. Early traces of settlement, dating back to the 9th century BC, have been found on the hills. These include traces of huts, some of which have recently been excavated on the Palatine. Down to the 6th century Rome was under the influence of the Etruscans (see ETRURIA), but afterwards became an important centre in its own right. Historical events led to its expansion and its conquests were reflected in the richness of the architecture.

The focus for the city was the FORUM, which was surrounded by political (see COMITIUM, CURIA) and religious buildings. The emperor Augustus played a major part in beautifying the city with structures such as the ARA PACIS, his family mausoleum and the forum Augustum. Later emperors also added to the city with further markets and civic amenities (see TRAJAN'S COLUMN). The large population was catered for by gladiatorial events and chariot-racing, which required specialized structures (see CIRCUS, COLOSSEUM). Further recreational facilities were provided by THERMAE, which required substantial quantities of water (see AQUEDUCT). Burials were outside the city (see CATACOMB, COLUMBARIUM). Extensive warehousing facilities were required to feed the population; food was brought upriver from OSTIA.

Rongorongo an abbreviated term for the enigmatic 'script' from EASTER ISLAND, surviving on twenty-nine pieces of wood, and comprising parallel lines of engraved characters, each alternate line being upside down. Possibly a post-European contact phenomenon, the characters seem to be symbols or 'cue-cards' expressing ideas, rather than a true phonetic writing system.

roomblock a single or double row of rooms, in sites of the American Southwest, made either from wattle and daub or masonry slabs. The roomblock partially surrounded either a PITHOUSE or KIVA. Individual rooms were used as living quarters, storage areas, or for specialized activities like corn grinding.

Roonka a complex of open sites on the Lower Murray River, South Australia, some of which date back to 18,000 bp. The area seems to have been exclusively a cemetery 7000–4000 bp. From about 4000 bp the area was more intensively used both for habitation and for burials. The Roonka burials show a wide diversity of mortuary practices and many individuals were buried with grave-goods.

Rop a central Nigerian rockshelter with two horizons of microlithic stone artifacts, the upper of which dates to about 2000 BP and is associated with ceramics. Of particular interest is a horse tooth dated on stratigraphic grounds to more than 2000 bp, which may be evidence for the antiquity of these animals in West Africa. Early Iron Age remains are associated with a radiocarbon date of 1975 bp.

Roquepertuse a Late Iron Age sanctuary in Bouches-du-Rhône, France, perched on a small rocky outcrop, the site of a skull or severed-head cult. Three stone pillars supported a lintel carved with a frieze of horses' heads in low relief. Niches in the pillars held human skulls, all male and under forty years old. Other sculpture included a fine double-head and figures squatting cross-legged. The sanctuary is probably of late 3rd or 2nd century BC date, and was destroyed by the Romans during their conquest of Provence in 123 BC.

Rose Cottage Cave a cave protected by a giant boulder

near Ladybrand in the eastern Free State Province of South Africa. Its long Stone Age sequence was first investigated in the 1940s and 1960s, and it has recently been the subject of a decade-long research programme investigating changing culture and environments during the past 100,000 years. Its sequence comprises pre-HOWIESON'S POORT, Howieson's Poort and post-Howieson's Poort MIDDLE STONE AGE collections, a possible Middle/LATER STONE AGE transitional industry, and a Later Stone Age sequence including ROBBERG, OAKHURST, WILTON and post-classic Wilton assemblages. The study of variation in the spatial distribution of remains suggests the existence of aggregation camps, like those where modern Kalahari SAN bands come together periodically to socialize, exchange gifts, arrange marriages, etc., as early as 13,000 bp.

Rosetta Stone a basalt STELA discovered in 1799 at Rosetta, a town in the extreme northwest of the Nile DELTA, during the Napoleonic occupation of Egypt. The trilingual inscription on the stone, a decree issued in 196 BC by King PTOLEMY V, is written in Egyptian HIEROGLYPHIC, DEMOTIC and Greek script, and was instrumental in the important early work on the decipherment of hieroglyphs by CHAMPOLLION. The Rosetta Stone is now in the British Museum.

Roskilde a fjord in Denmark where, in 1962, UNDERWATER ARCHAEOLOGY was carried out to remove a number of sunken VIKING-age ships, dating to AD 1000–1050, which had been sunk as a protective barrier against enemy raids. A coffer dam was built around the site, which was then drained to facilitate the work. The waterlogged timbers were solidified and preserved, and the ships are now on show in a special museum at the site. They form a varied collection, from warships to cargo vessels and merchant ships.

Rössen culture a Neolithic culture of central and southern Germany and the Rhineland which developed from the LINEAR POTTERY culture. Named after a cemetery near Halle with seventy burials, the Rössen culture is characterized by pottery with complex incised geometrical motifs, particularly 'hanging chevrons', zigzags and diamonds. A number of Rössen settlements are characterized by trapezoidal LONGHOUSES, some of which are extremely long (e.g. 50 m [55 yds] at Deiringsen-Ruploh, 60 m [66 yds] at Bochum-Hiltrop).

Rouffignac a huge cave-site in the Dordogne, France, with important Mesolithic (SAUVETERRIAN) occupation layers at the entrance, dating from 9150 to 8370 bp. MAGDALENIAN engravings were first discovered inside by speleologists in 1947. The further discovery of hundreds of painted and engraved figures in 1956, heavily dominated by over 100 mammoths, caused a major controversy. There is no doubt whatsoever that the vast majority of the cave's figures are authentically

Palaeolithic, but legitimate suspicion still hangs over a small handful of those in the main galleries.

rouletting a technique used to decorate pottery.

(a) On Greek pottery it appears in the early 4th century BC. It seems to have been applied by a strip of metal as the pot was turned on the wheel, leaving a band of even decoration normally on the inside. A more accurate term would be *chattering*.

(b) On Roman pottery the decoration was applied by a wheel. It is often found on the exterior of vessels, especially on the rim.

(c) On pottery from peninsular India it was made of a coarser fabric than the Mediterranean product. It is found also on forms derived from the NORTHERN BLACK POLISHED WARES of northern India. This ROULETTED ware is usually considered an imitation of Roman products, but at ARIKAMEDU it first appeared during the final centuries BC before the arrival of Roman imports.

round barrow see BARROW.

Routsi the site of a MYCENAEAN THOLOS tomb in Messenia, Greece, which was excavated by MARINATOS in 1956–7. The lavish grave-offerings included bronze weapons, gold, amber and glass jewellery, and fine pottery.

Royal cemetery the most famous discovery of WOOLLEY's excavation at UR in southern MESOPOTAMIA. It consists of a group of some 2,500 tombs ranging from the later EARLY DYNASTIC to the UR III period, mostly belonging to the Early Dynastic III (c.2600–2300 BC). The size, structure and wealth of these graves varies tremendously. The richest, belonging to the king Meskalamdug and his immediate successors (roughly 2500 BC), are multiple vaulted chambers with access by ramps; these burials contained an immense amount of precious materials (gold, silver, lapis lazuli, exotic shell, ETCHED CARNELIAN BEADS) and provide many of the famous artifacts of the SUMERIAN civilization (the 'royal standard of Ur', inlaid stringed instruments, the ELECTRUM helmet of Meskalamdug, the female attendant's head-dress, the gold figure of a ram caught in a thicket, etc.). Other prominent features of the royal burials were the accompanying soldiers and servants (up to seventy-four individuals, often women), and the presence of carts drawn by equids, a feature matched in roughly contemporary burials at KISH, SUSA and other places.

Roy Mata a chief of Efate Island, New Hebrides, South Pacific, who was buried in c.AD 1265 on Retoka Island together with about thirty-five other individuals, twenty-two of whom were male-female pairs. The collective burial was excavated in 1967 and suggested that, when buried, the males had been alive but unconscious, while the females had been conscious. Rich ornaments accompanied many of the burials.

Rozhok I a Middle Palaeolithic open-air site on the coast of the Sea of Azov in European Russia. Six cultural levels are buried in slope deposits representing an ancient ravine fill. The occupations appear to date to the earlier part of the last GLACIAL. Steppe bison predominates among the faunal remains. The artifacts include side-scrapers and many typical Upper Palaeolithic forms (e.g. endscrapers). Rozhok I was discovered and excavated by Praslov during 1961–2.

Ruanga a site of the GREAT ZIMBABWE period in north-eastern Zimbabwe, containing evidence of separation between elite and commoners: the walled upper part of the town contained gold, copper and iron ornaments, as well as imported glass beads, while the lower part of the settlement had plaster and wood houses containing utilitarian items.

Rudenko, Sergei Ivanovich (1885–1969) a Soviet archaeologist, anthropologist and ethnologist, a specialist in the antiquities and peoples of Siberia, Kazakhstan and the Volga basin. One of his monographs was devoted to the Eskimo Problem. He is best known for his excavations and publications concerning the large KURGANs of the ALTAI MOUNTAINS, of the SCYTHIAN period, such as Bash-Adar and Tuekta, and especially for his spectacular finds in the frozen tombs at PAZYRYK.

Rudna Glava the site of prehistoric copper mining in eastern Serbia. The shafts at Rudna Glava, sometimes 20 m (66 ft) or more in depth, following veins of malachite, contained pottery of the VINČA culture. The extent of the shafts at Rudna Glava indicates that early copper metallurgy in southeastern Europe required significant investment in the extraction of raw material.

Ruins tradition see GREAT ZIMBABWE.

runes a script created in northern Germany or Scandinavia around the 4th century AD, comprising twenty-four characters. The runic script, based on Latin, was developed in the ANGLO-SAXON and VIKING kingdoms, and is found primarily on memorial stones, as well as on artifacts. See also MAES HOWE.

Runnymede a settlement site on the banks of the River Thames in Surrey, England, with occupation levels of the middle Neolithic (c.3700–3300 BC) and Late Bronze Age (c.900–700 BC), well preserved beneath riverine ALLUVIUM. The Neolithic deposits are notable for their high density of material including intact hearths. Remains of the Late Bronze Age settlement include a large round-house and parts of two sub-rectangular buildings.

Russia see EUROPE, EASTERN.

Ryzhanovka see SCYTHIANS.

Rzuczewo a settlement site on the Bay of Gdańsk in

northern Poland, which gives its name to a sub-group of the broader CORDED WARE/SINGLE GRAVE complex of the late Neolithic. Settlements of the Rzuczewo culture (known in German as the *Haffkustenkultur*) have post dwellings erected on terraces along the shoreline. The Rzuczewo culture had a maritime economy, relying to a large degree on fishing and sealing, as well as on the use of domesticated livestock.

Saalian cold stage the penultimate cold stage in North Europe, spanning c.200,000 to 125,000 BP, following the HOLSTEINIAN and preceding the EEMIAN. Its Alpine equivalent is the RISS, in North America the Illinoian, and in Britain the Wolstonian, named after the type-site of Wolston in Warwickshire.

Saar a Bronze Age town on the island of Bahrain, belonging to the BARBAR culture. A British team has uncovered large areas of residential architecture, streets and other facilities that give the clearest available picture of town life of this period.

Sabatinovka culture a Late Bronze Age culture along the lower Dnieper River and the northeast Black Sea coast. In contrast to the neighbouring pastoralists of the SRUB-NAYA CULTURE, Sabatinovka settlements are those of sedentary farming peoples who cultivated wheat and barley and kept herds of cattle.

Sab Champa a late prehistoric and early historic moated settlement in the Pa Sak Valley, central Thailand, adjacent to copper deposits, and the site of a bronze-working industry.

Sabi Abyad a late Neolithic site in the Balikh drainage of northern Syria. Dutch excavations since the 1980s have uncovered multiple architectural levels that span the 6th and into the 5th millennia BC. The ceramic sequence provides important evidence for the emergence of the HALAF CULTURE complex. Perhaps the most important aspects of the site belong to level VI, the well-preserved 'burnt village' of large multi-room buildings. Concentrations of sealings, TOKENS and containers in several rooms imply a sophisticated monitoring system for portable property already in the 6th millennium BC. The site also contains a garrison outpost of the MIDDLE ASSYRIAN kingdom.

Sabr an extensive site on the southern coastal plain east of Aden in Yemen. Current excavations by a joint German-Russian team are uncovering large mud-brick buildings, one of which is interpreted as a temple. Some rooms contain a wealth of ivories, copper/bronze arti- facts and other imported goods. The pottery and other items at the site identify a culture that extended along the Red Sea coast as well, and interacted with East African groups during the period 1400–800 BC.

Sabratha a coastal city in the Roman province of Africa, now Libya. It seems to have been settled by the PHOE-NICIANS by the mid 5th century BC. Excavations by KENYON revealed substantial remains of the Roman civic and religious buildings.

Saccopastore a Palaeolithic site in a quarry near Rome, Italy, which has yielded two small NEANDERTHALOid skulls, associated with a few MOUSTERIAN tools and dated to the last INTERGLACIAL.

sacral horns see HORNS OF CONSECRATION.

Sacsayhuaman the INCA 'fortress' located on a hilltop adjacent to CUZCO in Peru. The site constituted the head of a puma, the planned shape of the site of Cuzco. One side of the hilltop is flanked by three parallel zigzag walls made of huge blocks of cut and fitted stone. On the summit are the remains of various structures, including the foundations of a round tower that was dismantled by the Spanish. Probably originally planned as a Temple of the Sun, the site was used as a fortress by the Incas during the siege of Cuzco, when they tried to defeat the Spanish invaders.

Sagvar an Upper Palaeolithic open-air site in Hungary. Artifacts and faunal remains (e.g. reindeer) are buried in loess deposits. The two cultural layers yielded radio-carbon dates of 18,900–17,760 bp. The artifacts (e.g. end-scrapers) are assigned to the GRAVETTIAN.

Sagvardzhile an Upper Palaeolithic and Neolithic cave-site on the Shavitskhali-Dzevrula River in western Georgia. Artifacts and faunal remains are buried in rubble, clay and loam layers that overlie ALLUVIUM. The lowest cultural layer (V) contains redeposited artifacts and remains of red deer, bison and horse. The assemblage includes many typical Middle Palaeolithic tools (e.g. points and scrapers) and is thought to date to the early Upper Palaeolithic (30,000–25,000 bp?). Four *in situ*

SACSAYHUAMAN, Peru.

cultural layers overlie level V; little information is available on their contents. Above these layers lie more redeposited Palaeolithic remains, some of which are mixed with Neolithic material. Sagvardzhile was excavated by Kiladze in 1951–2.

Sahagún, Bernardino de a 16th-century Franciscan friar who recorded extensive information on Aztec culture, religion and natural history. Published as the *Florentine Codex: The General History of the Things of New Spain*, this has become a primary source for interpreting POST-CLASSIC MESOAMERICA.

Sahel an Arabic word meaning 'shore' and used to refer to the grassland zone on the southern fringes of the Sahara Desert, occupied by pastoral people.

Sahul shelf the continental shelf which comprises Australia, including TASMANIA, and New Guinea. At times of low sea-level, the Sahul shelf has been exposed as dry land, Australia and New Guinea forming a single land mass with a common prehistory. By extension, the term 'Sahul' is often used for this land mass.

Sa Huynh a site on the central coast of Vietnam which has given its name to a culture thought to be proto-CHAM, active c.600 BC–AD 200, with widespread sea trading links (see KALANAY). Most assemblages known are from jar burials, which are closely paralleled by those in the Philippines, northern Borneo and Sulawesi. Characteristic artifacts associated with this iron-using culture are the LINGLING-O earrings and double-headed animal pendants of NEPHRITE and glass found at a number of sites in Vietnam, Palawan (in the Philippines), Sarawak

and Thailand (BAN DON TA PHET). Major sites include HANG GON urnfield, Phu Hoa, Tam My; Long Thanh and Binh Chau represent formative phases.

Sai an island in UPPER NUBIA, containing an important cemetery of the KERMA CULTURE.

Saint Acheul see ACHEULIAN.

Saint-Blaise a settlement close to the mouth of the Rhône in France. Greek pottery from as early as the 7th century BC has been found, as well as quantities of Etruscan BUCCHERO. It may have been the site of an early trading post taking advantage of the route up into central France, and was later replaced by the colony at Massilia (see MARSEILLES). Extant remains of the HELLENISTIC town include substantial stretches of wall.

Saint-Césaire a prehistoric rockshelter in the Charente-Maritime, France, which was excavated by F. Lévêque in 1976–87 and yielded AURIGNACIAN, CHÂTELPERRONIAN and MOUSTERIAN layers. A NEANDERTHAL skeleton found in the Châtelperronian and dated to c.36,300 BP (by THERMOLUMINESCENCE on burnt flints) may represent one of the latest dated Neanderthalers.

Saint-Michel-du-Touch a Neolithic enclosure consisting of a series of successive palisades and interrupted ditches across a promontory between the Rivers Garonne and Touch, Haute-Garonne, France. Within were large rectangular pits, possibly for ritual use, and over 300 smaller rectangular and circular structures, originally interpreted as hut bases but now thought to be cooking hearths. There was also a large rectangular pit containing two richly furnished burials. The material associated with all these structures was of Chasséen (see CHASSEY) type, and a sequence of radiocarbon dates indicates occupation c.4500–3400 BC.

Sais (*Arabic*: Sa el-Hagar) a site in the western Nile DELTA, capital of Egypt during the 26th Dynasty (in the LATE PERIOD). The attempts of the Saite kings to recreate Egypt's magnificent past must have made Sais an impressive city, but little now remains of this much denuded site. The numerous sculptural masterpieces to have come from Sais are largely the product of the digging for SEBBAKH, which caused the destruction of the TELL.

Sai Yok a cave-site in western-central Thailand on the upper Khwae Noi River, utilized during three broad periods: a preceramic phase with pebble tools of a broadly HOABINHIAN type (c.?10,000–8000 BC); a Neolithic phase with parallels at BAN KAO; and an historic period phase. The term is occasionally attached to the pebble tools of the region.

Sakazhia a Palaeolithic cave-site on the Tskhaltsitela River in western Georgia. Middle Palaeolithic artifacts were found in a sequence of loam and rubble layers in one portion of the cave; faunal remains are predominantly of cave bear. The assemblages (generally small) contain many points, scrapers and denticulates. One of the lower levels of the sequence produced some human skeletal fragments that are classified as NEANDERTHAL. An Upper Palaeolithic assemblage was excavated from another portion of the cave. Associated faunal remains are primarily of steppe bison; the artifacts include backed blades and points. The age of the occupations is unknown. Sakazhia was discovered and excavated by Shmidt and Kozlowskij in 1914; subsequent investigations were conducted by Nioradze in 1934–7 and 1974–80.

Sakkara see SAQQARA.

Sakutiek a Kenyan early LATER STONE AGE stone artifact industry characterized by small scrapers and *outils écaillés* (tools flaked to form a chisel-like edge), a few backed microliths and pieces typical of MIDDLE STONE AGE industries such as flakes with faceted platforms, as well as ostrich eggshell beads, represented at ENKAPUNE YA MUTO, where it is associated with radiocarbon dates of the order of 40,000 bp.

Salamis a coastal city in eastern CYPRUS occupied from the Bronze Age. CHAMBER TOMBS of the Early Iron Age contained the cremated remains of members of the social elites which evoked the heroic burials recorded by Homer.

Salasun see SUSWA.

Salbyk a valley in the MINUSINSK BASIN (60 km [37 miles] north of Abakan in Khakasia, Russia) where four-

teen enormous, so-called 'royal' KURGANS of the Tagar culture (see SCYTHIAN TYPE CULTURES) are concentrated. The biggest – the Big Salbyk kurgan – was excavated in 1954–6 by S. Kiselev. Originally the mound was pyramidal in shape, and 25–30 m (80–100 ft) high. It was made of turf layers and clay, and bounded by a 70 m (77 yd) square perimeter of gigantic slabs of Devonian sandstone. On the corners, along the sides and by the entrance, twenty-three huge vertical stone slabs were set up, which weighed several tonnes each. Under the corner-stones, skeletons of adults and children were found, presumably 'building offerings'. The chamber (5 m [16 ft] square, at a depth of 1.8 m [6 ft]) was located in the western part of the kurgan. It was a complicated construction of logs, birch-bark and clay. The DROMOS connected the western walls of the tomb and the perimeter. The tomb had been ravaged, but the remains of seven bodies were left. The only find was a bronze knife dating to the 5th–4th centuries BC. The construction of this kurgan entailed a huge effort by many people. In particular, the vertical stones for the perimeter had to be brought from the banks of the Yenisei River, 70 km (43 miles) from Salbyk. S. Kiselev calculated that the mound had been constructed by 100 people working for seven years.

Salcuţa a stratified site in southwestern Romania, important for its ENEOLITHIC levels which have made it the type-site for the Salcuţa culture, c.4200 bc, in layers II and III. Salcuţa pottery is characterized by dark burnished ware similar to that of contemporaneous Balkan cultures such as GUMELNIŢA. Layer IV at Salcuţa contained unpainted pottery with affinities to COŢOFENI and BADEN.

Saldanha Man see ELANDSFONTEIN.

Saliagos an islet off Antiparos in the Aegean, the site of a late Neolithic settlement which was excavated by Evans and Renfrew in 1964–5. The quantity of fish bones recovered suggests an economy based on maritime resources.

Salvage archaeology see PUBLIC ARCHAEOLOGY.

Salzgitter-Lebenstedt a northwestern German open-air MOUSTERIAN hunting site near Hanover dated to c.50,000 BP, which has yielded an eastern Mousterian assemblage with some typical western Mousterian artifact-forms.

Salzofen Cave a prehistoric cave-site located in the mountains (2,000 m [6,560 ft] altitude) of northwestern Austria. Artifacts and faunal remains (chiefly cave bear) are buried in loess and rubble deposits. The lower cultural layer contains several artifacts (scraper, flakes) assigned to the Middle Palaeolithic. Neolithic remains occur in the uppermost levels.

Samad see MAYSAR.

Samaria a Palestinian site, excavated by Harvard University in 1908–10 and Crowfoot in 1931–5, best known as the capital of the northern Kingdom of Israel. Samaria was founded by King Omri (c.882–871 BC), who built the 'upper city' consisting of a palace defended by walls of ASHLAR masonry. Samaria was captured by the ASSYRIANS in 721 BC, but was later an important HELL-ENISTIC city. Objects of the ISRAELITE period found at Samaria include OSTRAKA and ivory plaques similar to those from NIMRUD.

Samarkand see AFRASIAB.

Samarra an Islamic city of the Abbasid Dynasty (mid 8th–mid 10th century AD, a golden age of Islamic civiliz-ation), founded as the new capital in AD 836 on the River Tigris, north of Baghdad in central Iraq. Among its many monuments, the most famous is the spiral mina-ret of Mutawakkil's (AD 847–861) great Congregational Mosque. The explorations of the city have provided a rich source of information on early Islamic architecture, public monuments and town planning. In addition, E. Herzfeld's work early in this century revealed a prehis-toric cemetery with inhumations containing a distinctive type of painted pottery, subsequently named *Samarran ware*.

Samarran culture complex an archaeological culture of eastern-central Iraq (along the middle Tigris River) dating to the second half of the 6th (and early 5th) millennium BC. It is best known from the sites of Tell es SAWWAN and CHOGA MAMI. These two sites provide the strati-graphic and stylistic basis for distinguishing three phases of the culture, of which the Early contains a coarse ware decorated only by incision, the Middle a painted style that incorporates dynamic naturalistic scenes as well as dense geometric designs, and the Last more open geo-metric painted designs and an absence of naturalistic motifs. Middle Samarran painted pottery appears as im-ports on many sites belonging to the Standard HASSUNA and Middle HALAF cultural periods. The subsistence economy of Samarran communities involved irrigation agriculture, a significant step towards the formation of MESOPOTAMIAN civilizations, and also herding of sheep, goat and cattle.

sambaqui term for a SHELL MIDDEN in Brazil, where they are found along the littoral between 20 and 30 degrees latitude, close to mangroves. They vary in diam-eter from a few dozen to a few hundred metres, and can be more than 10 m (33 ft) high. They often contain burials, as well as hut floors. Most of them were formed between 4500 and 2000 BP, but they may date back to the 8th millennium BP. Fishing was also important at these sites, but hunting and plants appear to have played only a minor role. The polished stone industry is rich, including axes, net weights, and zooliths of birds or fish, often with a basin-like depression in the back, perhaps used for crushing palm nuts, or for ritual snuff-taking ceremonies.

Sambor Prei Kuk an early historic urban centre to the southeast of ANGKOR in Cambodia, apparently the capital of the pre-Angkor KHMER state of Isanapura of the 7th–8th century AD, probably referred to by the Chinese as ZHENLA.

Sambungmachan a locality on the Solo River, central Java, which yielded a rather complete skull of a late form of HOMO *erectus* dated to the late Middle Pleistocene, possibly associated with two flaked pebble tools. See NGANDONG.

Samguk Sagi Records of the THREE KINGDOMS, the earliest surviving history for Korea, compiled by Kim Pu-sik in AD 1185.

Samhan literally 'three HAN' in Korean, the collective name of the Mahan, P'yonhan and Chinhan groups of protohistoric peoples in the southern half of the Korean peninsula during the PROTO-THREE KINGDOMS period, as known from the Chinese dynastic histories (see WEIZHI, HOUHANSHU). Small POLITIES among the Samhan are thought to have given rise to the protohis-toric states of PAEKCHE, KAYA and SILLA.

Samian ware a type of Roman red-glossed pottery mis-takenly thought to have been produced on Samos. Numerous production centres have been identified. The earliest were in southern Gaul (France) at sites such as La Graufesenque, but the production spread northwards into central and eastern Gaul as well as to Britain (see COLCHESTER). The forms, type of decoration and stamps have allowed a detailed chronology to be established and the ware is thus important when found in a stratified context. See also TERRA SIGILLATA.

Sampung a village in eastern-central Java which has given its name to a mid Holocene industry characterized by bone tools and stone points similar to the Maros points of the TOALIAN of Sulawesi. Sites include Gua Lawa, Gunung Cantalan, Petpuruh, Sodong, Marjan.

Samrong Sen a late prehistoric (c.1000 BC) freshwater SHELL MIDDEN and burial site in central Cambodia, the finds of which indicate occupation during the transition from the use of polished stone adzes to bronze (stone bivalve moulds for sickles, axes, arrowheads, fish hooks, bells). Similar moulds have been found at a series of small sites near the Laotian border in the vicinity of MLU PREI and at Long Prao in the south.

Samuilitsa II a Middle Palaeolithic cave-site located on the Iskr River in central Bulgaria. Ten cultural layers are contained in a succession of clay, sand and rubble, which apparently dates to the earlier last GLACIAL; the upper-most levels yielded a radiocarbon estimate of 42,780 bp. The artifact assemblages are relatively homogeneous, and include scrapers and bifacial foliates.

Samun Dukiya see NOK.

San or **Bushmen** indigenous hunter-gatherer people of southern Africa who formerly lived throughout the region and spoke a variety of languages. Many have become absorbed into agricultural societies since the arrival of KHOEKHOEN herders and Iron Age BANTU-speaking peoples during the last two millennia. Their territories were further diminished by the arrival of European colonists, and after about AD 1850 many were exterminated by settlers in the interior of South Africa. Traditionally, they lived a nomadic hunting and gathering existence in an egalitarian society comprising small bands of about twenty people which amalgamated at certain times of the year. Men hunted game with bows and arrows, while women gathered their staple diet of plant foods. Although the small groups of San still living in the Kalahari no longer live a traditional way of life, sensitive use of their historical and ethnographic record can provide valuable insights into the interpretation of LATER STONE AGE archaeological remains and rock art from southern Africa.

There is unfortunately no term in the vocabularies of indigenous southern African hunter-gatherers to describe groups larger than linguistic units. The terms 'San' and 'Bushmen' are problematic as both have developed derogatory connotations. The term San (pronounced 'Saan') is a word used by the Nama herding people to describe their hunter-gatherer neighbours. It translates as 'forager-people', but has taken on a connotation of 'rascals' or 'tricksters'. The term 'Bushmen' (in many variations), which was used by European colonists for several hundred years, unfortunately also became derogatory and implied an uneducated, backward person. Some archaeologists therefore prefer to use economic terms like 'hunter-gatherer', but even these are not always suitable.

San Agustín a region of highland Colombia, South America, in which are found numerous large (about 30 m [33 yds] in diameter) artificial mounds, containing stone-lined chambers which probably served as tombs or shrines. The region is best known for the stone sculptures, sometimes found inside the chambers. A common depiction is a human form with feline features; other animals and birds are also depicted. The dating of the sculptures is debated, with estimates all falling in the period between 500 BC and AD 1500.

Sanchi an early Buddhist monastery complex outside Vidisia in central India. The place is best known for its elaborate STUPA, which was probably originally constructed during MAURYAN times and then enlarged during the subsequent Sunga Dynasty (185–73 BC) of Magadha. Also noteworthy are two early caitya halls (oblong halls with a rounded end used for Buddhist worship), probably also Mauryan foundations.

sanctuary see TEMENOS.

sand **1** a size term for sediment or soil particles, from 0.05 to 2 mm [0.02 to 0.04 inch] in diameter. As a particle size term, the definition of sand-size particles is independent of mineral composition or other properties other than size. See also CLAY, SILT.

2 a texture term used in describing sediment and soils, defined, depending on the classification system used, as containing a certain percentage of sand-size particles relative to silt- and clay-size particle content. Sand is sometimes used as temper in pottery manufacture.

3 a descriptive term for a sediment body (deposit) composed primarily of sand-size particles.

Sandai (*Chinese* 'three periods') the XIA, SHANG and ZHOU of PROTOHISTORIC China (see CHINESE DYNASTIES).

Šandalja I a Lower Palaeolithic site located on the Istrian Peninsula in Croatia. Artifacts and faunal remains (e.g. macaque) are contained in a BRECCIA filling an ancient KARST cavity which probably dates to the Lower Pleistocene. The artifacts include chopping tools.

San Dieguito complex a late PALAEOINDIAN complex, located in California, southwestern Nevada and western Arizona, USA, which comprises leaf-shaped bifaces (either points or knives), choppers, scrapers and hammerstones. It post-dates CLOVIS in local sequences. See also OLD CORDILLERAN, VENTANA CAVE.

Sandy Creek a rockshelter in northern Queensland, Australia, first excavated in 1969 by Percy Trezise and re-excavated in 1989–91 by Mike Morwood. The site was first occupied about 32,000 bp. A ground-edge waisted hatchet was recovered from the base of the sequence. Pecked engravings on the shelter wall are partially covered by the cultural deposits and an engraved fragment, apparently detached from the wall, was excavated from a layer dated to 14,400 bp.

Sanga an important Iron Age cemetery in the southeastern Democratic Republic of Congo, dating from the end of the 1st millennium AD to the last two centuries. Considerable wealth in the form of KISALIAN iron and copper objects and pottery is associated with the main period of usage dating to the 11th and 12th centuries AD. These included flange-welded iron gongs, like those known to have been royal symbols in later times. Some researchers suggest that differentiation in the graves indicates the development of a social hierarchy based on control of local trade from about ad 800.

Sangamonian Age a major North American geochronological subdivision (see STRATIGRAPHY) of the Pleistocene epoch ranging from about 125,000 to 75,000 bp. See also SANGAMONIAN STAGE.

Sangamonian Stage a major chronostratigraphic subdivision (see STRATIGRAPHY) of the Pleistocene series encompassing deposits of the last INTERGLACIAL episode defined, in the upper American Midwest, as those occurring above TILLS of the preceding GLACIAL episode (Illinoian Age) and buried by loesses of WISCONSINAN AGE. The stage is based on a well-expressed warm climate PALAEOSOL, the Sangamon Geosol. Although the boundaries are recognized to be time-transgressive, they are placed at about 125,000 and 75,000 bp. See also EEMIAN.

Sangiran the key site in the SOLO River Valley of Java for the study of faunal and human evolution in the region, which has also given its name to a stone small-flake industry identified by Von KOENIGSWALD as Middle Pleistocene. More recently it has been suggested that many of the 'flakes' are natural, and that those which are human-made are from the High Terrace Gravels, and are thus of late Pleistocene or Holocene date. The skull cap of a young HOMO *erectus* child was estimated to be 900,000–700,000 years old, but ARGON-ARGON DATING of volcanic pumice and minerals at the site has produced an age of 1.6 million years.

Sangoan a stone industry or complex named after Sango Bay on Lake Victoria in Uganda. The name is applied to some EARLIER STONE AGE assemblages from forested areas of equatorial and southeastern Africa. Most Sangoan samples are selected or collected from secondary contexts and they may have been produced over a long period in the Middle Pleistocene. Handaxes and cleavers are relatively rare in the Sangoan, which is characterized by light-duty tools as well as crude pick-like tools called *core axes*. A suggestion that the Sangoan represents an adaptation to wooded areas has not been supported by recent evidence.

San'in a pre-modern district (see RITSURYO) along the western north coast of Honshu Island, Japan, widely used in archaeological writings. It comprises portions of modern Kyoto and Hyogo Prefectures, and Tottori and Shimane Prefectures.

San José Mogote an important FORMATIVE, or PRE-CLASSIC, site in the VALLEY OF OAXACA, Mexico. The large nucleated village was involved in the manufacture and trade of shell ornaments and magnetite mirrors. Kent Flannery's research at San José Mogote was most important for the systematic investigation of MESO-AMERICAN culture at the household and community level.

San Lorenzo a major OLMEC centre in the Gulf Coast Lowlands of Veracruz, Mexico; it was a large nucleated village with a population estimated at 1,000. The centre flourished during the early FORMATIVE. The collapse of San Lorenzo *c.*1150 BC was abrupt and violent: monuments and sculptures, including Olmec heads, were defaced and architecture dismantled. LA VENTA came to power after San Lorenzo collapsed.

The labour requirements to build and maintain the centre necessitated a large population, but at the same time this population was forced to maintain agricultural fields farther away from the site. The collapse of San Lorenzo is thought to have resulted from these conflicting pressures.

Sannai Maruyama, an Early to Middle JOMON site (see JAPANESE PERIODIZATION) in Aomori Prefecture, Japan, which has survived virually intact and has yielded over 500 pit-buildings; up to 30,000 ceramic vessels; objects of wood, bark, bone, antler; clay and stone figurines; jadeite and amber pendants, and lithics of obsidian. Ten pit-buildings exceed 10m (11 yds) in length and are thought to be communal workshops or winter dwellings. An enigmatic structure consists of six chestnut tree trunks, 80 cm (30 inches) in diameter, set in two sets of three POSTHOLES. Imaginative reconstructions make it rows of totem poles or a watchtower, storehouse, or ritual building.

Sanskrit a language in the Indo-Aryan branch of INDO-EUROPEAN, and the literary language of Hindu religious texts. The oldest of these texts, the *vedas* and including the *Rigveda*, were written down by the mid 1st millennium BC, following an oral tradition that originated perhaps during the mid 2nd millennium BC in north-western India. Standardized by grammatical treatises of the 5th century BC, classical Sanskrit was used in Brahminical writings up to around AD 1000, and a form of Sanskrit continues in use as a vehicle for learned writings. The oral tradition behind Vedic Sanskrit provides the basis for arguments about the migration of Indo-Aryan speakers into the subcontinent, and specifically about possible archaeological reflections of this migration (e.g. the GANDHARA GRAVE CULTURE COMPLEX, PAINTED GREY WARE, COPPER HOARD).

Santa Ana a district of Manila, Philippines, south of the Pasig River, where over 300 burials were excavated in the 1960s. Abundant quantities of glazed Asian trade wares were found as grave-goods, predominantly Sung-Yuan (11th–13th centuries) and some early Ming wares (14th–15th centuries).

Santa Isabel Iztapán a mammoth KILL-SITE in the VALLEY OF MEXICO, dating to 9,250 years ago. Straight-based and slightly stemmed, lanceolate and leaf points were found in association with the two imperial mammoths (*Mammuthus imperator*). Other tools at the site include an obsidian blade, sidescrapers and a semilunar knife. Based on these tools, a combination of hunting techniques (lance-ambushing and dart-stalking) are inferred.

Santorini see THERA.

Santubong a complex of sites on the coast of Sarawak, northern Borneo, the remains of a major port of the 10th–

13th centuries AD, probably connected with the state the Chinese called Po-ni. Local industries included iron, processed from the iron-rich slag-like lateritic clays of the area; and exports, like those of the contemporary ports of KOTA CINA and LOBO TUWA on Sumatra, included gold and forest products.

sanukite a type of andesite produced in the Inland Sea region of Japan by now-extinct Miocene volcanoes; it is named after the old province of Sanuki. It was used extensively in this region during the Palaeolithic and POSTGLACIAL periods (JOMON, YAYOI) for stone tools. See also SETOUCHI.

Sanxingdui a Bronze Age site consisting of two pits (3.5 by 4.6 by 1.6 m [11.5 by 15 by 5 ft] deep, and 2.3 by 5.3 by 1.5 m [7.5 by 17.5 by 5 ft] deep) discovered in a brickyard in Guanghan, Sichuan Province, China. The pits were filled with discarded artifacts, which had been ritually burned then buried: gold, bronze, jade, stone, pottery, discs, beads, tools, cowry shells, elephant tusks and burnt animal bones. Most outstanding were bronze sculptures, the tallest over 2.5 m (8 ft), of human-like figures and faces with unusual facial features. The pits were contemporaneous with late SHANG (13–12th centuries BC) but the artifacts display a unique regional cultural style separate from the Shang.

San'yo a pre-modern district bordering the Inland Sea on western Honshu Island, Japan (see RITSURYO), widely used in archaeological writings. It comprises modern Yamaguchi, Hiroshima and Okayama Prefectures and a portion of Hyogo Prefecture.

Sanz de Sautuola, Marcelino (1831–88) a Spanish landowner who excavated in ALTAMIRA and, with his daughter, discovered the Palaeolithic paintings there. Unable to persuade the scholarly establishment of their authenticity, he died a broken and bitter man, his honour and honesty still in question. He was not vindicated until 1902.

Sao an industry from the Chari Basin in Chad, Africa, associated with sites on mounds above flood-waters of the river. It is poorly documented, but is probably contemporary with DAIMA and is thought to date to the late 2nd millennium BC.

Saoura a basin in the northwestern Sahara with a long sequence, including OLDOWAN, ACHEULIAN and ATERIAN remains. Good PALYNOLOGICAL and GEOMORPHOLOGICAL data have provided useful information on past environments.

Sapalli-depe a 4 ha (10 acre) site in southern Uzbekistan, excavated by A. Askarov, containing three periods of Middle to Late Bronze Age occupation, the lower two of which define the Sapalli phase in the regional chronology (at some time in the mid to later 3rd millennium BC). The

site contained a central square fortification (82 m [90 yds] to a side) with internal blocks of rooms. Askarov recovered a large number of INTRAMURAL burials which have excellent preservation of organic materials; at least four of the graves contained silk textiles, indicating contacts to the east with China.

Saqqara or **Sakkara** a site in LOWER EGYPT, the largest of the cemetery-sites associated with MEMPHIS. Saqqara contains a vast array of monuments including royal MASTABA tombs of the ARCHAIC PERIOD; fifteen royal pyramids, chiefly of the OLD KINGDOM, the first and most important being that of DJOSER; the SERAPEUM and other animal galleries; and large numbers of important private tombs from the Archaic period to the Graeco-Roman period, but especially of the Old Kingdom associated with the royal pyramids of that date.

sarcophagus (*Gk* 'flesh-swallowing') a kind of stone which was reputed among the Greeks to consume the flesh of dead bodies, and hence was used for coffins. The term is now applied in archaeology to any stone chest used to contain a corpse. In Egypt, the sarcophagus held the MUMMY. Large rectangular sarcophagi often contained at least one wooden coffin. Most sarcophagi of the LATE PERIOD are notable for their anthropoid shape, their outer form being modelled with the contours of the human body and features of the face/head.

In the CLASSICAL world, the term denotes a container of clay or marble that held a corpse. In the Greek cities of western Turkey, such as CLAZOMENAE, in the ARCHAIC and Classical periods, they could be decorated in a technique closely related to pottery painting. In the Roman period elaborately carved sarcophagi were produced in several centres and exported over long distances.

Sardis a city on the Gediz Cay plain, some 90 km (60 miles) inland from Izmir in western Anatolia, associated with Croesus and the Lydians. Although earliest evidence for settlement in the region belongs to the EARLY BRONZE AGE, the first documented occupation of the city occurred in LATE BRONZE AGE times (the evidence of the stratigraphic sounding in the 'House of the Bronzes'); later occupation extends through the 1st millennium BC up to late CLASSICAL times. The Lydian city, of the 7th and 6th centuries BC, contained an AKROPOLIS and walled lower settlement covering perhaps as much as 250 ha (620 acres). Other salient aspects of the city are gold works (at 'Pactolus North', where areas of furnaces and cupellation are documented) and the grave mounds of the 'royal cemetery' (at Bin Tepe). After the conquest by CYRUS the ACHAEMENID (in the early 540s BC), the city became a *satrapal* (provincial) capital.

Sargon (c.2330–2280 BC) the founder of the AKKADIAN empire in the late 24th century BC, who was the first successful empire builder of MESOPOTAMIA. Originally associated with KISH, Sargon founded a new capital at AGADE.

Sarka style a late variant of LINEAR POTTERY which occurs in western Bohemia, c.3900 bc, parallel to the development of the ZELIEZOVCE STYLE in Slovakia and southern Poland. Sarka vessels are painted in black spirals on buff fabric before firing.

Sarmizegethusa a Late Iron Age town in eastern Romania, seat of the DACIAN state founded by Burebistas in the 1st century BC, also known by its modern name of Gradistea Muncelului. Sarmizegethusa was composed of several separate precincts over an area 3 km (2 miles) long. Next to a hilltop citadel is a sanctuary area with several shrines or temples. At the foot of this hill is an industrial area where bronze and iron products and pottery were manufactured.

Sarnate a site of the NARVA culture on the coast of Latvia, on the edge of a swampy lagoon. Large lenses of shells of the water chestnut *Trapa natans* have been found at Sarnate, some covering several square metres up to 40 cm (16 inches) thick, around hearths within houses. Some preserved wooden mallets still had fragments of water chestnut shells embedded in their faces. A variety of other wooden artifacts have also been found at this waterlogged site. A similar site is that of Šventoji on the coast of Lithuania.

Sarnath a Buddhist centre outside Benaras on the Ganges River, India, where the Buddha delivered his first sermon. Sarnath contains several important MAURYAN monuments, among them a pillar capped with four lions, the magnificent Dharmarajika STUPA and a caitya hall (a Buddhist ceremonial structure).

Sarnowo the site of KUYAVIAN long barrows of the FUNNEL-BEAKER CULTURE in northern-central Poland, c.4000–3500 bc. The nine trapezoidal-plan barrows at Sarnowo arc oriented with the narrow ends facing northwest. Features earlier identified as ARD-marks beneath one have recently been reinterpreted as the traces of a structure.

Sarsa see CUEVA DE LA SARSA.

sarsen a type of sandstone from the Marlborough Downs of northern Wiltshire, England. Sarsen was used in several Neolithic monuments of the region including the AVEBURY STONE CIRCLE and the WEST KENNET long barrow, and at STONEHENGE, where the principal circle and its lintels, the five great TRILITHONs and the Heel Stone are of this material.

Sarup two overlapping Neolithic enclosures in Funen, Denmark, with interrupted ditches. The earlier and larger enclosure, Sarup I, belongs to the FUCHSBERG phase at the transition from the Danish early to middle Neolithic, c.3400 BC. A substantial palisade with only a single main

entrance stood behind two parallel lines of interrupted ditches. This was followed c.120 years later by Sarup II, a smaller enclosure of similar but slighter construction. Some twelve Neolithic enclosures of this type are now known from southern Scandinavia, other examples being TOFTUM and Büdelsdorf.

Sasanian or **Sassanian** a Persian empire established in AD 224 after a revolt against PARTHIAN rule. The Sassanians controlled much of western Asia until the Arab Islamic invasion in AD 651. At its largest, the empire extended from Transcaucasia and western-Central Asia in the north to the Indus and southern Arabia in the east and south, and to the frontier with the Romans and BYZANTINES in the west. This large region was controlled by a relatively centralized political and military apparatus, and the Sassanian intensification of economic production induced considerable settlement growth in regions such as southern MESOPOTAMIA.

Satingpra a region on the east coast of peninsular Thailand, with sites, including Kok Moh, which span the later 1st and early 2nd millennia AD, possibly associated with LANGKASUKA.

Satruper Moor a wetland region in Schleswig-Holstein in northern Germany, containing a complex of sites representing the transition from foraging to sedentism in northern Europe c.4500–4000 BC. A number of sites can be attributed to the ERTEBØLLE/ELLERBEK culture, with pointed-base pots. Claims for bones of domestic animals and cereal pollen from these sites have not been substantiated.

Satsumon a type of incised-motif pottery related to HAJI ware on early historic Hokkaido, Japan. The Satsumon culture existed between the 4th and 14th centuries AD. Compare OKHOTSK.

sauceboat a vessel, usually made of clay but occasionally of metal, which is extremely common in mainland Greece and in the Cyclades in mid–late 3rd-millennium BC contexts. It seems likely that sauceboats were used for drinking rather than pouring, but their precise function is unclear.

saucer barrow see BARROW.

Sautuola see SANZ DE SAUTUOLA.

Sauveterrian a Mesolithic culture which follows the AZILIAN in France in c.9000 bp, and whose influence spread into Britain, where it is contemporary with the later MAGLEMOSIAN. The assemblages contain many geometric microliths, but axes are rare. The culture is named after rockshelters in Sauveterre-la-Lémance, Lot-et-Garonne, France.

Sawwan, Tell es a prehistoric site, 2–3 ha (5–7 acres) in size, on the Tigris River near Samarra, which is the best-known SAMARRAN period site. B. Abo al-Soof's work there established this class of painted pottery as more than a luxury ware and provided a developmental sequence for it. Excavations during the 1960s revealed the greater part of the village, divided into five architectural levels. From its beginning the community was enclosed by a ditch, and later by a ditch and wall. The later phases of occupation are famous for their 'T'-shaped buildings, a floor plan that also occurs, in modified form, in 'UBAID sites further south (see KHEIT QASIM). A large group of burials occur under the floor of a building in the initial settlement. The crops include (in addition to emmer and einkorn) six-rowed barley, bread wheat and flax, all correlated with early irrigation; domesticated sheep and goat appear, while the other fauna (including cattle) is morphologically wild. The radiocarbon dates (uncalibrated) span the second half of the 6th millennium bc.

Saxon Shore a defensive system of forts built in the late 3rd century AD along the south and east coasts of England to defend the province of Britannia against seaborne raids. The walls of substantial fortresses can still be seen at Burgh Castle in East Anglia, Richborough in Kent, Pevensey in Sussex and PORTCHESTER in Hampshire.

Sayil a Lowland MAYA site located in the PUUC region in Yucatán, Mexico, which reached its peak during the late CLASSIC period. Work by an American archaeological team in 1983–8, under the co-direction of Jeremy Sabloff and Gair Tourtellot, involved both extensive and intensive survey, as well as excavation, at Sayil and the surrounding area. The resulting data are often quite different from those traditionally gained from excavations. At the site, CHULTUNS under residences and palaces were used as reservoirs. PHOSPHATE tests of the soils in the 'plazas' associated with raised residential platforms suggest that these areas were KITCHEN-GARDENS instead. The findings of the Sayil Project challenge some of the traditional interpretations of Maya culture.

Scandinavia Human settlement in Scandinavia began substantially later than elsewhere in Europe. Ice covered this area until about 13,500 years ago, when it began to disappear from southwestern Sweden. Over the next 3,000 years, southern Sweden up to the area of Stockholm became deglaciated, as did much of southern Finland and parts of southern and western Norway. The Scandinavian glacier had retreated to its modern extent by about 8,500 years ago. The melting of the ice triggered major coastline changes, through both rising sea-levels (EUSTASY) and the uplift of land (ISOSTASY) freed from its weight. These changes were not uniform throughout Scandinavia. In southern Scandinavia, higher sea-levels inundated coastal regions, while in northern Scandinavia, isostatic rebound is as much as 250 m (820 ft) in places.

Late Palaeolithic hunters followed reindeer herds northwards as soon as the tundra could be inhabited.

Their characteristic tanged points have been found at several sites in southern Sweden, particularly around Lake Finjasjön. After the onset of warmer conditions beginning about 9,000 years ago, the forests of Scandinavia were populated by bands of Mesolithic foragers. Coastal communities exploited rich resources in lagoons and estuaries. At SKATEHOLM on the Baltic coast, burials of both people and dogs reflect complex mortuary customs. The Mesolithic period is also characterized by the preservation through waterlogging of organic remains normally lacking at sites of this period. These include fishtraps and a decorated paddle from the small coastal settlement of Tybrind Vig in Denmark, illustrating the importance of marine resources in the hunter-gatherer lifestyle. Watercraft permitted the settlement of seal hunters on rocky islands of the Stockholm archipelago.

During the 5th millennium BC this lifestyle became increasingly complex, as revealed by cemeteries such as VEDBAEK and Skateholm, and by the adoption of pottery which suggests a more settled existence than appears to have been common among most European Mesolithic groups. The transition to the Neolithic is placed late in the 5th millennium (c.4100 BC) and was marked by new pottery types, by the construction of burial monuments and by limited cultivation and stock rearing. Farming appeared in southern Sweden around 4000 BC, when Neolithic communities descended from Mesolithic hunters integrated wheat, barley, cattle, sheep, goat and pigs into their economy. In southern Sweden, the farmers of the TRB CULTURE, with its distinctive funnel-necked pottery, used CHAMBERED TOMBS as communal graves. In Norway, central and northern Sweden and Finland, the PITTED-WARE CULTURE emerged from local Mesolithic populations who relied on seal hunting and pig raising. At AJVIDE on Gotland, rich Pitted-Ware burials have been found with ornaments of bone and shell. Later, sites of the SINGLE GRAVE and BOAT AXE CULTURES reflect a developed Neolithic society throughout much of Scandinavia. Both LONG MOUNDS and PASSAGE GRAVES were built during the 4th millennium BC, and CAUSEWAYED CAMPS such as SARUP on the island of Funen served as centres for ceremonial gatherings, perhaps on a seasonal basis. Individual burials with items of personal display such as battleaxes mark a changed social order at the beginning of the late Neolithic (c.2800 BC).

Southern Sweden, notably the regions of Scania and Västergotland, shares in many of the Danish developments, and the large numbers of megalithic tombs built in these regions during the middle Neolithic are particularly notable. Further north, however, conditions were unsuitable for cereal agriculture but POSTGLACIAL climatic warming allowed the expansion of hunting and gathering groups ancestral to the modern Saami. These groups executed rock engravings at ritually important locations, such as the Nämforsen rapids in northern Sweden.

Borg

400 km

SWEDEN

FINLAND

NORWAY

Vendel
Valsgärde
Anundshög   Birka

Gokstad
Oseberg   Tanum
Gausel   Tureholm
Forsandmoen   Timboholm
                                    Rök

                                             Vallhagar
                                                  Uggarde rojr
                                             Ajvide

Ertebølle
Gundestrup   Tustrup   Eketorp
DENMARK   Grauballe   Barkaer   Ringkloster
           Tollund   Vätteryd
Dejbjerg   Bygholm   Trundholm   Lake Finjasjön
     Jelling   Toftum   Roskilde   Kivik
     Egtved   Trelleborg   Uppakrå
Tybrind Vig   Skateholm
Hjortspring   Sarup   Vedbaek Bøgebakken

Hedeby (Haithabu)

The Scandinavian Bronze Age (c.1700–500 BC) can be illustrated by a series of sophisticated metal artifacts, which are all the more remarkable in that southern Scandinavia (where the bulk of the material is concentrated) possesses no metal resources of its own. They include the bronze trumpets known as LURS, and the famous sun-chariot from TRUNDHOLM in Denmark. The amount of metal required for these ritual objects is small, and was probably obtained in part in exchange for Baltic amber, which is found as far south in Europe as MYCENAE. The first bronze objects to appear in Scandinavia came from workshops in Central Europe. Bronze Age finds in Scandinavia are known primarily from burials. Some tombs were elaborate, such as the enormous cairns at KIVIK in Scania and Uggarde rojr on Gotland. Later in the Bronze Age, elite burials were outlined with upright stones in the form of ships, a pattern that persisted into subsequent periods. Rock art, particularly petroglyphs such as those at TANUM, depicts boats, warriors, feet and hands, and abstract designs. Much of Finland and Norway remained outside the range of these developments, however.

From the 1st millennium BC (Pre-Roman Iron Age c.500–50 BC and Roman Iron Age 50 BC–AD 400) field systems and small farming villages make their appearance, such as VALLHAGAR on Gotland and FORSANDMOEN in Norway. Central places such as Uppåkrå in Scania and Eketorp on Öland became important trade centres. During the first centuries AD, a warrior elite emerged in coastal areas of Norway and Sweden, and trading was complemented by raiding. Craft production under elite patronage resulted in the production of elaborate jewellery and weapons, such as those found in tombs at Vendel and Valsgärde near Uppsala. Gold coins from mercenaries who had served in Roman legions were melted down to make the magnificent ornaments found in the TUREHOLM and Timboholm hoards. There is new evidence of ritual activity in the form of the famous 'bog bodies' such as TOLLUND MAN. The placement of offerings in bogs and lakes is a tradition which in Scandinavia goes back to the Mesolithic period but became particularly pronounced during the last centuries BC and the first centuries AD; in addition to the bog bodies there is the GUNDESTRUP cauldron (possibly war booty from southeastern Europe) and the entire ship and its contents from HJORTSPRING. The importance of ships and boats is also reflected in the 'ship settings' of standing stones of the Germanic Iron Age (AD 400–700). Lying beyond the limits of the Roman empire, southern Scandinavia underwent indigenous social and political development during this period until advances in maritime technology and the development of early states brought it into wider international contact at the beginning of the VIKING age.

During the Viking period (8th–11th century AD) the peoples of southern Scandinavia engaged in widespread raiding and commercial activity. Trading emporia were established at sites like BIRKA on Lake Mälaren, while chiefs lived in longhouses such as the one at BORG in northern Norway. Vikings erected stones with RUNES, such as the one at RÖK in central Sweden, to commemorate dead relatives and important events. Their single-masted, clinker-built wooden ships were able to cope with long-distance voyages across open sea and opened up the settlement not only of Ireland, Britain and Normandy, but also Iceland, Greenland and North America. The discovery of the Viking settlement at L'ANSE AUX MEADOWS on Newfoundland confirms the testimony of the Icelandic sagas that Vikings did indeed reach North America and settled there for a short period. Viking ships preserved in ship burials at OSEBERG and GOKSTAD in Norway, and recovered from the seabed at ROSKILDE in Denmark, demonstrate the technical sophistication of these vessels, while the tremendous wealth of the Gokstad burial reflects distant connections. In Ireland, Scandinavian commercial activity laid the foundations of the first towns at sites such as Dublin and Waterford. To much of northwestern Europe, however, the Vikings had a reputation as traders and warriors, and substantial groups of armed Viking colonists settled in eastern England and northern France. Danes and Norwegians were dominant in these western ventures, while Swedish Vikings exploited the trade routes of the Russian rivers and may have been instrumental in the foundation of the Russian state of Kiev.

Viking activity overseas was closely related to the foundation of trading towns and centralized states in southern Scandinavia. Excavations at HEDEBY in northern Germany have revealed the timber buildings and craft activities of one such town, and these can be paralleled at Viking overseas centres such as Jorvik (YORK) and Dublin. During the 10th century Christianity spread to south Scandinavia, and was adopted by the ruling elites. The royal centres of Old Uppsala (Sweden) and JELLING (Denmark) had large royal burial mounds of the pre-Christian tradition, but at Jelling these were succeeded in the late 10th century by a Christian church. The Christianization of Scandinavia was essentially complete by the 12th century, and together with the decline of overseas activity this marks the transition from the Viking age to the medieval kingdoms of Norway, Sweden and Denmark.

scanning electron microscopy a technique used to examine the microscopic and submicroscopic structure, relief and morphology from about 20X to 50,000X and greater magnification, as well as to determine the chemical identity, of nearly any material for which a sample can be prepared. A scanning electron microscope (SEM) forms an image of a sample as it is scanned at an adjustable angle by a high-energy electron beam. Backscattered and secondary electrons and x-rays emitted from the sample have differing wavelengths that vary with surface topography and elements present. The

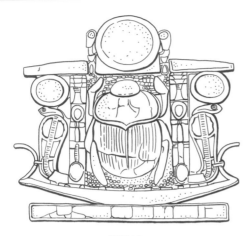

SCARAB.

signal from these emissions is processed and an image of the object is displayed on a television-like screen. Emitted x-rays are characteristic of the elements present. They can be analysed for chemical composition and spatial distribution under the coverage of the electron beam (see BETA-RAY BACKSCATTERING). In addition to the great advantage of magnifying power, the SEM is capable of a great depth of field, which makes it more useful than a light microscope in many cases.

scapulomancy see ORACLE BONES.

scarab an Egyptian STAMP SEAL, in use from the MIDDLE KINGDOM, whose oval base carried an incised design or the name and titles of the owner. The back of the seal was in the form of the dung beetle *Scarabaeus sacer.*

scarp see ESCARPMENT.

scarred tree a eucalypt from which a slab of bark has been removed to make a shelter, container, shield or canoe, or which has toeholds cut into it for climbing. The bark was cut with a hatchet and stone or wooden wedges were used to prise it off. Several species were used. Scarred trees are common in southeastern Australia. Compare CARVED TREE.

Scharbauer see MIDLAND.

Schela Cladovei a late Mesolithic/Neolithic site in western Romania, along the River Danube about 40 km (25 miles) downstream from LEPENSKI VIR. Twenty Mesolithic burials of adults and children at Schela Cladovei were arranged with their feet towards a hearth. Two of the burials contained red ochre. A later layer contained materials of the Neolithic CRIŞ culture.

Schele, Linda (1942–98) an American art historian who combined translations of MAYA HIEROGLYPHIC texts with architecture and iconographic interpretations to dramatically transform understanding and popularity of CLASSIC Maya. She brought leading epigraphers together in University of Texas GLYPH workshops to greatly facilitate decipherment. In numerous co-authored publications Schele reconstructed the significance of Maya religion, including BLOODLETTING as a means of summoning ancestors, and the Maya perception of their relationship to the cosmos.

Schliemann, Heinrich (1822–90) a German businessman who was convinced that the cities described by Homer had once existed. His excavations at TROY in 1874–90, MYCENAE in 1874–8 and TIRYNS in 1881–5 proved that he was essentially correct, but his desire to fit the finds to his theories, and his sometimes unscientific approach, have led modern archaeologists to criticize him. There is no doubt, however, that Schliemann pioneered the study of the MYCENAEAN civilization.

Schönfeld group a late Neolithic group of southeastern Germany whose origin has been a matter of debate. Some have seen it as a regional group of CORDED WARE, while another point of view links it to the TIEFSTICHKERAMIK of the late FUNNEL BEAKER culture. The Schönfeld ceramics are distinctive in that the shallow, parabolic bowl is the dominant vessel form, often with patterns of incised zigzag lines.

Schöningen a Lower Palaeolithic open-air site in eastern Germany, located along the shore of an ancient lake, and dating to roughly 400,000 BP. The site yielded rare specimens of wooden (spruce and fir) artifacts, including eight spears, three of which are 1.8–2.3 m (6–7.5 ft) in length. The wooden artifacts were found associated with flint tools (scrapers and points) and numerous mammal remains (horse, elephant, rhinoceros and others). Stone tool cut-marks are reported on many bone fragments. Schöningen may have yielded some of the earliest evidence of hunting in Europe. The site has been investigated by Thieme since 1982.

Schroda a 9th-century AD capital and religious centre of some importance, 12 ha (30 acres) in extent and occupied by about 300–500 people. It is located a few kilometres northeast of MAPUNGUBWE, adjacent to the Limpopo River, in the Northern Province of South Africa, and is attributed to the ZHIZO phase of the Early Iron Age. It documents the initiation of trade between the southern African interior and the East African coast, which later led to the rise of Mapungubwe and GREAT ZIMBABWE. Ivory, probably exchanged for the quantities of imported glass beads recovered, was worked in one area, while several caches of small human and animal clay figurines were found in another section of the site.

Schwanfeld see LINEAR POTTERY.

Schwetzingen see LINEAR POTTERY.

SCRAPER.

Scoglio del Tonno a headland projecting into Taranto harbour, Puglie, Italy, site of Middle and Late Bronze Age settlement with sherds of Late HELLADIC III pottery, indicating contact with MYCENAEAN traders from the Aegean *c*.1300 BC.

scraper a prehistoric retouched flake tool with a thick working edge, probably used to scrape skins or for wood-working. *Sidescrapers*, or *racloirs*, have the retouched working edge along the long edge of the flake; an *end-scraper*, or *grattoir*, has a rounded retouched end and is often made on a blade.

Scythians an ethnonym attached to the horse-riding nomads of the steppes of southern Russia and Ukraine during the 1st millennium BC by Greek writers such as Herodotus. The Scythians were predominantly pastoral-ists, whose wealth lay in vast herds of livestock, and they had much in common with many other such groups of nomads across Eurasia at this time. In the late 7th century BC, Greek trading colonies were established along the north coast of the Black Sea, including Olbia at the mouth of the Bug River, Chersonesos on the tip of Crimea and Panticapaion at the entrance to the Sea of Azov.

Scythian tombs typically consist of a central shaft, 10–15 m (33–50 ft) deep, dug into the loess subsoil. At the base of the shaft, a burial chamber, often reinforced with timbers, was hollowed out. After the body of the deceased Scythian (along with those of servants and relatives) and the grave-goods were placed in the chamber, the shaft was filled with earth and rocks. A tumulus, which could reach a height of 20 m (66 ft), was heaped up over the top of the shaft. Additional burials were sometimes added by digging adjacent shafts and then either tunnelling into the original burial chamber or hollowing out another.

A gold PECTORAL from the tomb at TOLSTAYA MOGILA is perhaps the finest example of Scythian goldwork, the product of a Greek colonial workshop in which Scythian themes were interpreted by Greek artisans. A side grave contained five burials: a young woman and infant laid side-by-side with rich burial-goods, a young man with a bow-and-arrow, a young woman next to a niche with food offerings, and a male next to a complete wagon and several horses. A ditch around the perimeter of the mound contained bones of horses, boar and deer, as well as POTSHERDS of wine vessels, presumably the remains of a funeral feast.

Scythian gold and silver ornaments and vessels are often decorated with images of animals and humans.

Wild animals and battling warriors are two common themes, but some motifs are more peaceful. A silver bowl from the Gaymanova tumulus was decorated with a gold-plated frieze with two elderly warriors wearing tunics of fur-trimmed leather engaged in conversation.

Scythian contact with Greeks led to the emergence of permanent settlements, such as Elizavetovka at the mouth of the Don, which developed into a centre of craft production and trade in the second half of the 4th century BC and was surrounded by ramparts and ditches. The late Scythian tomb at Ryzhanovka, south of Kiev in Ukraine, provides additional hints of sedentism. The layout of the tomb resembles that of a two-room house. One chamber is like a kitchen with a mock hearth with bronze kettles containing boiled horse and lamb bones. The other resembles a bedroom, in which the chief's body lay on a wooden platform. The 'domestic' nature of this grave and its late date have led to the hypothesis that the late Scythians were in transition from nomadic to settled life.

Scythian-Siberian Animal Style the name for a very specific style in the ancient art of the EURASIAN STEPPES, which spread widely in the 8th–3rd centuries BC in the SCYTHIAN TYPE CULTURES. It was one of the main signs determining the Scythian-Siberian cultural-historical community. The characteristics of this style are an acute observation of nature, a realism in the execution of ani-mals' shapes and movements, a dynamism in compo-sitions, and the depiction of fighting animals. The most

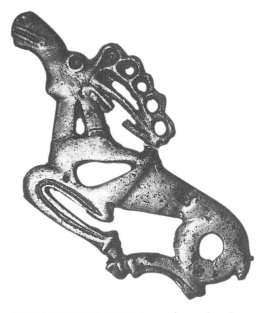

SCYTHIAN-SIBERIAN ANIMAL STYLE: a bronze deer plaque of the Tagar culture (see SCYTHIAN TYPE CULTURES).

popular images were those of herbivorous animals (deer, goats, horses, elks), of predators (panthers, tigers, wolves), boars and fantastic creatures (griffins and others). The style is implemented in various categories of art: TOR-EUTICS, wooden and bone carving, rock art, images on DEER-STONES, leather and felt applications, and tattooing. The realism of the images is combined with a definite conventionality: the animals' figures were arranged in accordance with the shape of the object which they decorated; there were some canons for depicting animals (kneeling deer, curled-up predators, etc.) and special ways of depicting parts of their bodies (curled antlers, ringed eyes, etc.).

Scythian type cultures on the territory of the EURASIAN STEPPES in the Early Iron Age (8th–3rd centuries BC) a number of archaeological cultures arose and converged, which shared many features. The mobile lifestyle of the nomads helped spread these features into Central Europe and China. The community that was formed in this way is now known as 'The Scythian-Siberian World', or 'The Scythian-Siberian cultural-historical community'. Its best-known culture is that of the SCYTHIANS. All of the community's numerous cultures can be divided into two groups: the main cultures, which determined the content of the Scythian-Siberian World and the trends in its development; and those cultures which developed under the influence of the main cultures. This division probably also reflects ethnic differences: the principal bearers were ancient Indo-Iranians. The main cultures of the Scythian type are: the culture of the Scythians proper (Black Sea littoral), the Savromatian culture, the culture of the Saka (Central Asia), the PAZYRYK culture (ALTAI MOUNTAINS), the Tagar culture (MINUSINSK BASIN), the Uyuk culture (Tuva) and the culture of Ordos (Mongolia). All these cultures have three components in common: weaponry, horse-harnesses and the SCYTHIAN-SIBERIAN ANIMAL STYLE. This is the so-called Scythian Triad which determines the community of the Scythian type cultures.

Seacow Valley or **Zeekoei Valley** a river valley in the southeastern Northern Cape Province of South Africa, which has been the subject of intensive archaeological survey by C. Garth Sampson, resulting in the identification of over 14,000 Stone Age sites. Of particular interest are detailed studies of the ceramic sequence dating to the millennium prior to the arrival of European settlers in the 1760s. This has provided unique information on the spatial and territorial organization of Stone Age SMITH-FIELD hunter-gatherers, as well as on hunter-gatherer/herder interactions.

seal a device of stone, bone, ivory or wood with an INTAGLIO design, which was impressed upon nodules of wet clay in order to identify, secure or authenticate the object to which the clay had been attached. In this respect

the role of seals in the development of writing systems was clearly fundamental. Because of their use by those in authority, seals were a powerful status symbol and were sometimes accorded talismanic properties. See also CYLINDER SEAL, STAMP SEAL.

sealing see BULLA.

Sea Peoples a collective term for various population groups in the eastern Mediterranean, at least some of whom seem to have been of Aegean origin, who migrated into the Levant in c.1200 BC. They appear to have been responsible for the destruction of cities such as UGARIT and ALALAKH, but were repulsed from Egypt by Kings Merenptah and RAMESSES III, a victory illustrated on the walls of MEDINET HABU. See also PHILISTINES.

sebbakh (*Arabic*) a term used to refer to the degraded mud-brick of ancient buildings, utilized as a cheap source of fertilizer by Arab peasants. The practice of digging for sebbakh in the nineteenth century, and the early years of the twentieth, produced many of the objects now in museums and private collections, albeit with little record of their archaeological provenance.

Sebekian see KOM OMBO.

Sebillian see KOM OMBO.

Sechín Alto a large INITIAL PERIOD ceremonial site in the Casma Valley of the northern-central coast of Peru, perhaps the largest site occupied at that time. The site comprises a series of PLATFORM MOUNDS and plazas, arranged along a linear axis. The largest pyramid measures 40 m (130 ft) in height. See also PAMPA DE LAS LLAMAS.

secondary cremation the practice of removing the cremated remains of the dead person from the pyre to the grave. Compare PRIMARY CREMATION.

secondary flaking see RETOUCH.

secondary inhumation see BURIAL.

Secondary Products Revolution a series of changes in late Neolithic material culture and subsistence data, interpreted by Andrew Sherratt and others as indicating a shift from flood plain horticulture to a greater reliance on domestic livestock, particularly for their 'secondary products': traction power for wheeled vehicles and the plough, wool and milk.

sediment individual grains or aggregate grains of mineral and organic material which have been or are in the process of being eroded and transported from site of origin, and deposited by water, wind, ice or people. Sediment provides part of the physical context of archaeological deposits. As soon as material is culturally deposited, archaeological artifacts are fundamentally sediment grains subjected to the same surface or near-surface physical, chemical and biological processes as surrounding natural grains. In an archaeological site, sediment may be created and deposited directly by people, redeposited by people, or derived from the decay of humanly made structures. Material moved, modified or otherwise related to human activity in the past is sometimes referred to as 'archaeological sediment'. Sediment characteristics and layering (see STRATIGRAPHY) are studied both on and off archaeological sites to reconstruct palaeoenvironments and to identify physical context.

When affected by soil-forming processes, or PEDOGENESIS, sediment is altered and may take on soil properties such as SOIL HORIZONS.

sedimentary structure fundamental observable properties of sediments, defined by composition, size, shape, orientation and grain packing, generated by physical, biological, chemical and diagenetic processes. Many sedimentary structures are generated by the movement and SEDIMENTATION of particles in a fluid medium at or near the interface of that medium with a substrate, such as a riverbed. In these cases, the type and scale of sedimentary structure are a function of the conditions of flow, fluid properties and sediment properties. As such, sedimentary structures are sources of process and environmental information. When examined with reference to a vertical series of sediments or deposits over an area, the succession of sedimentary structures provides information about past depositional environments and environmental change, both of which can have an impact on the integrity and interpretation of archaeological deposits (see LITHOFACIES ANALYSIS).

sedimentation a process whereby transported sediment is deposited by agents such as water, wind or ice. Depending on the conditions of sedimentation, pre-existing surface archaeological deposits may be buried intact, or with considerable redistribution of material.

segment or crescent a small stone tool made on a blade or bladelet, shaped like a portion of a circle, with backing along a curved arc opposite a straight unretouched edge (see RETOUCH), which was hafted, possibly as a projectile tip or as part of a cutting implement. They occur typically in some sub-Saharan African HOWIESON'S POORT and LATER STONE AGE assemblages (see WILTON), and are widespread in North Africa, especially in Sudanese Neolithic sites. The term *crescent* is now outdated.

Sehonghong a large rockshelter in eastern Lesotho, with a sequence of periodic Stone Age occupation dating from about 70,000 BP MIDDLE STONE AGE HOWIESON'S POORT-like material to LATER STONE AGE hunter-gatherer remains as late as AD 1872. Some 20,000-year-old stone artifacts, previously considered Middle Stone Age, are now regarded as belonging to a Later Stone Age ROBBERG-like microlithic tradition.

Seibal a MAYA Lowland centre in southern-central Petén, Guatemala, which peaked from AD 770 to 900 while other cities in the Southern Lowlands were declining. Archaeologists suggest the influx at the site of non-CLASSIC Maya (Putun) from the Gulf Coast prompted its development at this time.

Seima-Turbino bronzes bronze objects with very characteristic forms, which in the mid 2nd millennium BC were spread over a vast territory of northern Eurasia from the ALTAI MOUNTAINS to the eastern Baltic area. They include splendid, large heavy weapons: CELT-axes, spearheads, knives and daggers with handles decorated with figurines, etc. These bronzes were found in graves and hoards. The main sites – the cemeteries of Seima, Turbino and Reshnoye in European Russia, and Rostovka in Siberia – are thousands of kilometres apart, and yet contain objects of the same type. The mobile Seima-Turbino tribes were not numerous: over a territory of more than 3 million sq. km (1.2 million sq. miles) only some 450 bronze artifacts and thirty casting moulds have been found. They used an innovative casting technology, and produced closed thin-walled shafts and high-quality tin-bronzes of a kind previously unknown in this area. This type of highly developed metallurgy emerged in the Altai, and then the migration of its bearers to eastern Europe contributed to the development of local metallurgy. The so-called 'Seima-Turbino trans-cultural phenomenon' existed for a very short period of 150–200 years; its chronology is still problematic, but this period lies somewhere between the 17th and 13th centuries BC, most likely the 16th–15th centuries.

Seine-Oise-Marne (SOM) culture a late Neolithic culture of the Paris basin area of northeastern France (3400–2800 BC). The culture is known best from collective burials in rock-cut *hypogées*, semi-subterranean funerary houses and ALLÉES COUVERTES such as LA CHAUSSÉE-TIRANCOURT. The typical SOM pottery type is the coarseware flat-based flower pot. There are few associated settlement sites.

selectionist theory this offshoot of evolutionary theory proposes that cultural change can most adequately be explained by seeing all human behaviour as a series of adaptive responses operating in the same way as biological change.

Seleucids a dynasty of Greek rulers of western Asia (from Anatolia and Syria into Central Asia), from the end of the 4th century into the 1st century BC. Seleucus, one of Alexander the Great's lieutenants, founded the dynasty after extended struggles with rivals following Alexander's death in 323 BC. His successors abandoned some eastern provinces to the MAURYANS and to independent Greek dynasties (notably in Bactria) during the 3rd century, and then lost BABYLONIA to the expanding

PARTHIAN kingdom by 130 BC, before succumbing entirely to Roman and continued Parthian pressures. The Seleucids founded or greatly enhanced many cities across their empire, and oversaw the creation of new cultural identities which combined Greek and western Asian traditions.

Selevac a late Neolithic site of the VINČA culture (B–C phases) located in the Morava Valley of Serbia. Selevac is a large settlement, with archaeological material covering an area of 53 ha (131 acres). Within the 3 m (10 ft) of archaeological deposits, the lower levels indicate the vertical replacement of structures, while the later levels show horizontal displacement. The houses were constructed of timber posts, with wattle-and-daub walls. The faunal assemblage indicates that wild animals were more common in the lower levels, scarcer in the upper ones.

Selinunte (*Gk* Selinous, *Lat.* Selinus) a Greek colony in southwestern Sicily traditionally founded by the Sicilian city of Megara Hyblaea in 651 or 628 BC. A series of temples of the DORIC ORDER have been found; Temple E had relief METOPES on mythological themes. A complex series of fortifications have been found on the AKROPOLIS. Some of the earliest material from the site has been found in the TEMENOS of *Malophoros* ('apple-carrier') to the west of the city. The foundation of the colony provided a fixed point for the dating of Early CORINTHIAN POTTERY on the scheme devised by PAYNE. Recent excavations have now revealed earlier pottery.

SEM see SCANNING ELECTRON MICROSCOPE.

Sembiran an extensive port site in northern Bali, Indonesia, with remains ranging from the 1st to the 12th centuries AD. Early remains include Indo-Roman ROULETTED WARE (see ARIKAMEDU), a sherd bearing an early Indian script, imported glass beads and fragments of a mould for casting a bronze drum of the PEJENG variety. It was a major Indonesian port on the spice trade route. See also BUNI.

Semenov, Sergei Aristarkhovich (1898–1978) a Soviet archaeologist who first developed the technique of microscopic analysis of wear patterns on artifacts in order to determine their function(s). Although Semenov devoted particular attention to the analysis of wear on Palaeolithic stone and bone tools, he also studied artifacts from later time periods.

Semibratny the Seven Brothers' tumuli in the Kuban, Georgia. These rich SCYTHIAN burials, mostly of the 5th century BC, were accompanied by numerous horses. Although containing fine examples of Scythian craftsmanship, the burials included important examples of Greek GOLD-FIGURED silver plate.

Semna a site at the southern end of the Second Cataract of the Nile in NUBIA, comprising two major forts (Semna on the west bank, Kumma on the east) and a forward observation post (Semna South). Semna, like BUHEN, was part of the elaborate frontier system constructed by the Egyptians to defend their southern frontier during the MIDDLE KINGDOM.

Senftenberg a Late Bronze Age fortified site of the LUSATIAN culture in eastern Germany. Surrounded by a bank-and-ditch enclosure, the interior of Senftenberg is occupied by rectangular-plan post structures in irregular rows, although not as densely packed as at the roughly contemporaneous site of BISKUPIN.

Senwosret or **Sesostris** the name of four of the monarchs of Egypt's MIDDLE KINGDOM who, with the four kings named Amenemhat, constitute the majority of the 12th Dynasty, a period of Egyptian strength from *c.*1963 to 1786 BC.

Sepphoris a classical city in Lower Galilee, Israel, lying on the road between Tiberias and the Mediterranean. The site appears to have been occupied from the Iron Age and was destroyed by Rome in 4 BC. The city was then rebuilt in a classical form with facilities such as a theatre. The late antique city was equipped with colonnaded streets. The site has been excavated by both American and Israeli archaeologists.

septal slab an upright stone slab across the floor of a megalithic CHAMBERED TOMB, dividing it into separate segments.

Sepulcros de Fosa cemeteries of individual crouched inhumations in simple pits or stone cists, found in the Catalonia region of northeastern Spain in the middle Neolithic period (5th–4th millennia BC).

sequence dating a method developed by PETRIE to date AMRATIAN and GERZEAN graves at the Egyptian site at Hu (Diospolis Parva). The system employed was a SERIATION based on the overlapping lifespans of artifact types to produce a relative chronology of the graves by their contents.

Serabit el-Khadim the chief ancient Egyptian site in an area of the southwestern Sinai exploited for its deposits of turquoise and copper ore. The major monument at Serabit el-Khadim is the temple of the goddess Hathor, 'Mistress of Turquoise', which was active from the 12th until the 20th Dynasty, and which contains STELAS erected both by kings and by the officials connected with the mining expeditions which worked in the area.

Serapeum a funerary complex at SAQQARA in Egypt where the APIS bulls were interred after MUMMIFICATION. Before the reign of RAMESSES II the bulls were buried in individual tombs, surmounted by small chapels; subsequently a series of underground galleries was constructed with side chambers for the great stone SARCOPHAGUS of each bull. The Serapeum, discovered by MARIETTE, was a place of pilgrimage, and the votive STELAS left by worshippers (c.1,200 of which have been recovered, from the NEW KINGDOM to the PTOLEMAIC period) are an important source of information.

serdab (*Arabic* 'cellar') a chamber found within some Egyptian MASTABAS of the OLD KINGDOM, appearing during the reign of DJOSER and relatively widespread in the cemeteries at GIZA and SAQQARA after the reign of MENKAURE. The serdab contained a statue of the tomb-owner which magically benefited from the produce brought to the adjoining offering-room, through an eye-level slot in the dividing wall. The use of the serdab declined with a change in mortuary practices towards the end of the Old Kingdom.

Sered'-Mačanské vršky a Mesolithic dune site in the Váh Valley near Nitra in Slovakia, the type-site of the Sered' group, the name given to the Mesolithic assemblages of western Slovakia. The Sered' group is distinguished by the extremely small size of its geometrical microlithic tools. Unusually for dune sites, there is good preservation of bone at Sered', and a faunal assemblage of red deer, roe deer, wild pig, bison and hare is reported, as well as fish bones.

seriation a RELATIVE DATING technique, in which artifacts are temporally organized, according to their relative popularity. *Evolutionary seriation* is based on changes that represent essentially technological improvements. An example of this is the THREE AGE SYSTEM. *Similiary* or *stylistic seriation* is based on gradual changes in the frequencies of stylistic attributes, so that the greater the similarity in style, the closer in age artifacts are to each other.

Seriña or **Serinya** a series of cave-sites in Girona, north-eastern Spain, comprising occupation in the MOUSTERIAN and the Upper Palaeolithic. The MAGDALENIAN is best represented at Bora Gran d'En Carreras, and the SOLUTREAN at Reclau Viver. Excavations by N. Soler at L'Arbreda since 1972 have uncovered a detailed sequence at the transition from Middle to Upper Palaeolithic, with radiocarbon (AMS) dates of 40,400 bp for the Upper Mousterian and c.38,500 bp for the start of the AURIGNACIAN.

serpentine a group of relatively common water-bearing magnesium silicate minerals which principally occur in altered ultrabasic rocks rich in olivine and pyroxenes. Serpentine-rich rocks are referred to as *serpentinites*. The most common are green and greenish-blue. Serpentine minerals were used in the manufacture of fine stone tools, vessels, jewellery and architectural decorations.

Serpent Mound see GREAT SERPENT MOUND.

Serpents Glen a rockshelter in Western Australia with two distinct episodes of occupation. The older is more

than 23,000 years old and is the first evidence for Pleistocene occupation of the Western Desert region. The site was reoccupied about 4700 bp and continued in use to the present.

Serra d'Alto a Neolithic village in Basilicata, Italy, defended by three concentric ditches, which has given its name to the Serra d'Alto pottery style (c.4500–3500 BC). This attractive pottery has decoration of rectangular meanders in black or dark purple paint on a buff surface, and though commonest in APULIA was traded widely, reaching even Lake Garda in the north and Malta in the south.

Sesklo a site in Thessaly, Greece, which was first occupied late in the 7th millennium BC, in the ACERAMIC NEOLITHIC period. By the middle Neolithic, the period of the Sesklo culture characterized by elegant red-on-cream decorated pottery, the site had grown to a considerable size and the large MEGARON complex on the AKROPOLIS suggests a central authority. Subsequently destroyed by fire, Sesklo was reoccupied in the late Neolithic period and remained a substantial settlement throughout the Bronze Age.

Sesostris see SENWOSRET.

sestertius a Roman bronze coin, four of which made a DENARIUS.

Seth an Egyptian god, the mythological brother and murderer of OSIRIS, and contender with HORUS for the vacant kingship. Generally regarded as a deity with negative connotations he was, however, occasionally revered; for example, in the eastern DELTA during the HYKSOS period, because of Seth's identification with the god BAAL. Seth was represented as an anthropoid deity with the head of an unidentified mammal.

Setouchi 1 the Japanese name for the Inland Sea region of western Japan.
  2 a Late Palaeolithic stone-working technology for producing side-blow flakes using local SANUKITE. Such flakes were used for fashioning Kou knives among others, a tool type named after the Kou site in Osaka Prefecture, other types of knives being produced on classic blades.

settlement pattern study a type of archaeological study to record all human-made features of the landscape, relating them to their natural topographic setting and locating them in time. The importance of these studies is the broad regional perspective of cultures and how they change through time, incorporating population estimates, and the distribution of population centres across time and space. In MESOAMERICA, settlement pattern studies enable the archaeologist not only to link regional centres together, but to observe the distribution of archaeological materials from non-elite contexts.

Seven Brothers' Tumuli see SEMIBRATNY.

Seven Wonders a HELLENISTIC list, probably drawn up in the 2nd century BC, of monuments considered the most outstanding ever created. The compilation, which reflected the Greeks' confidence about comprehending the world and the works of humankind following the campaigns of Alexander the Great, comprised: the Egyptian pyramids, the Hanging Gardens of BABYLON, the Mausoleum of HALICARNASSUS, the Artemision of EPHESUS, the CHRYSELEPHANTINE statue of Zeus at OLYMPIA, the Pharos at ALEXANDRIA and the Colossus of Rhodes.

Severn-Cotswold a group of Neolithic burial monuments in southwestern Britain consisting of a long mound, tapering towards one end, with one or more PASSAGE GRAVES. The two principal varieties are: the *axial-chambered tombs* such as WEST KENNET, where the passage entrance opens from the centre of the broader end of the mound; and the *lateral-chambered tombs* such as HAZLETON, where two megalithic chambers are entered from opposite sides of the mound midway along its length.

Sevso treasure a hoard of Roman silver treasure, which appeared on the art market with rumoured find-spots in both Yugoslavia and the Lebanon. The name is taken from the owner's inscription on one of the dishes.

Shaar ha-Golan a Palestinian site excavated by Stekelis from 1943 to 1952. It is the type-site of a Neolithic culture of the Jordan Valley termed the YARMOUKIAN, the most distinctive artifact of which is a schematic pebble or clay figurine.

shabti or **ushabti** a figurine found in Egyptian tombs of the MIDDLE KINGDOM onwards, often in large numbers, and usually in the form of a mummy bearing agricultural implements. The shabti was intended to serve as a magical replacement should the deceased be called upon to perform tasks of manual labour in the netherworld.

Shabwa the capital city of the South Arabian Hadramawt state, located at the western end of Wadi Hadramawt in Yemen. French excavations during the 1970s and 1980s documented major architectural elements of the early 1st millennium AD city, like the city wall and the citadel/ palace. A deep sounding produced a pottery sequence that extended nearly to 2000 BC, one of few long chronological sequences in the region.

Shaft Grave Circles A and B sites at MYCENAE which were excavated by SCHLIEMANN in 1876 and by Papadhimitriou *et al.* in 1952–4. The circles were enclosed by a low stone parapet and contained approximately thirty graves altogether, most of which were shaft graves. The spectacular offerings suggest that the rulers of Mycenae must have been buried in the grave circles, which were in use in the later 17th and 16th centuries BC.

shaft straightener see BÂTON PERCÉ.

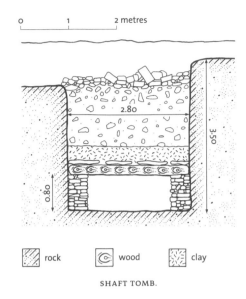

rock   wood   clay

SHAFT TOMB.

shaft tombs a type of monumental burial structure used by the SHANG elite of northern China (see XIBEIGANG), consisting of a deep central shaft at the bottom of which was constructed a WOODEN-CHAMBER for holding a wooden coffin and grave-goods. One to four sloping ramps led into the chamber, producing in the last instance a cruciform tomb plan. Compare MAWANGDUI, MANCHENG, MOUNDED TOMBS.

Shag River Mouth one of the largest and most complex archaic settlement sites in southern NEW ZEALAND. It has a long history of investigation from the late 19th century to the most recent excavations in 1987–9. The site is rich in cultural material and includes evidence of several dwellings. The most recent excavations have shown that it was occupied for about fifty years in the middle of the 14th century AD.

Shahdad a complex of settlements in the Kirman Province of Iran, dated from the late 4th millennium BC to Islamic times, which is important for its three excavated cemeteries. These graveyards document the emergence of stratified societies during the 3rd millennium of southern Iran, whose elites amassed material wealth in styles that reflect wide-ranging contacts with surrounding civilizations. Surface survey on the settlement itself reveals areas of semi-precious stone workshops and of a major copper-smelting industry; some excavation of the latter area has taken place, revealing complexes of furnaces and workshops dated to the second half of the 3rd millennium BC.

Shahr-i Qumis a PARTHIAN city in Khorasan (northeastern Iran), probably to be identified with the ancient Hecatompylos. British investigation of the site during the

1970s uncovered buildings of the Parthian period, among them courtyard houses with a central room surrounded by a corridor, a typical Iranian design of the period. In addition to the Parthian city, the place contains occupation from Iron Age to medieval times.

Shahr-i Sokhta a site located in the Seistan district of Iran, and excavated by M. Tosi during the 1960s and 1970s, containing a sequence spanning the late 4th to early 2nd millennium BC. Beginning with a size of under 20 ha (50 acres), the settlement grew to cover nearly 100 ha (250 acres) by the late 3rd millennium, before collapsing to under 10 ha (25 acres) in the early 2nd millennium BC. The site is a fundamental reference for understanding urbanization and complex societies in the Bronze Age of eastern Iran and Afghanistan, and provides a wide range of evidence for subsistence and craft production, social stratification, interregional exchange and other relations, and other social questions.

shaman a term of multiple uses, primarily denoting the agent of a type of world-view, to which it gave its name (see SHAMANISM). The term comes from the Tungus people of Siberia, and was subsequently applied to other Siberian peoples, and then to hunter-gatherer peoples elsewhere. It means the person, male or female, who is charged by the community with carrying out rituals involving the spirits of the wild animals they wish to kill and eat, as well as other functions linked to the community's survival and well-being (healing the sick, communing with the dead or solving a variety of problems). Shamans' actions are based on the idea that they are in direct contact with the spirits, and must therefore act out this relationship during the ritual, in an atmosphere of high drama. Contrary to popular ideas derived from the vocabulary of world religions, Siberian shamans' performance of this direct contact is playacting; it does not involve trance or ecstasy, and hallucinogens are rarely used. The term shaman has been indiscriminately extended to a whole variety of healers, witchdoctors, sorcerers, diviners, rainmakers, etc., in other parts of the world, becoming so vague and all-encompassing that it has virtually lost all precise meaning outside of Siberia, though some shamanic elements can be found in other contexts.

shamanism the world-view of Siberian hunting societies is based on a relationship of 'exchange' between the human community and the spirits of the wild animal species they and kill and eat. It is a symbolic system, often characterized as 'animism', which is expressed during rituals by gestures and vocalization that imitate animals. These actions have often been mistaken as signs of an altered state of consciousness (trance, ecstasy, etc.) rather than correctly understood as culturally prescribed performance. The occurrence among hunter-gatherers of cosmologies incorporating wild animals as other kinds of 'people' related to humans through exchange has led many archaeologists and historians of religion to postulate 'shamanistic' cosmology as universal among prehistoric peoples, but this cannot be demonstrated since the attributes of a SHAMAN (clothing, drum) are perishable and the performance leaves no material traces. The terms 'shamanic' and 'shamanistic' are often applied uncritically to indigenous non-Western small societies and to prehistoric societies, especially those of hunter-gatherers, although the characteristics of Siberian shamanism are not found among hunter-gatherer societies in the southern hemisphere and in the north reflect extensive contacts through the fur trade. One thus has absolutely no way of knowing whether prehistoric societies had any kind of shamanism, since it is by no means a universal, even among hunter-gatherers, and cannot be reduced to a simplistic equation with a particular state of mind, with 'trance' or 'hallucination' or even a shaman's equipment.

Shamarkian a microlithic stone industry, including OUNAN POINTS, found in 8,000–6,000-year-old sites in the Sudanese Nile Valley. The 7,000-year-old Shamarkian-like stone artifacts from Catfish Cave in southern Egypt are associated with bone fishing-harpoon heads.

Shamash see UTU.

Shamshi-Adad I (c.1813–1781 BC) the first of the great rulers of ASSYRIA, who originated in a tribal group located near MARI on the River Euphrates. By undetermined means, he created an empire in northern MESOPOTAMIA which stretched from the middle Euphrates in the west to the mountains in the east; although he did not directly control northern BABYLONIA, some of the kingdoms there (including that of HAMMURABI of Babylon) were his clients. With his capitals at ASSUR and Shubat-Enlil (Tell LEILAN), Shamshi-Adad placed as governors his elder son at Ekallatum (opposite Assur) and his younger son at Mari, the source of most of the textual evidence about this ruler. On his death, the brothers could not control their inheritance, and the empire collapsed.

Shang the second of the CHINESE DYNASTIES in the PROTOHISTORIC SANDAI period, 16th–11th centuries BC. Shang originated as the name of a Bronze Age people, who are now said to have ruled the Shang state – known by a characteristic set of bronze weapons (e.g. GE), ritual vessels (e.g. JUE, DING) of the Erligang and Anyang styles and ORACLE BONE inscriptions. The major Shang sites are ZHENGZHOU, PANLONGCHENG and ANYANG. Compare WUCHENG, XIAJIADIAN, SANXINGDUI.

Shanga a trading settlement on the south side of Pate Island in the Lamu Archipelago off the Kenyan coast, briefly occupied before overseas trade, marked by the appearance of imported pottery from the Arabian Gulf region, which was initiated at the beginning of the 8th century AD. It probably reached its greatest extent of 5 occupied ha (12 acres) containing houses built of coral and mud in the 13th century AD. Conversion to Islam occurred by the 12th century AD, if not before, when a small wooden building thought to have been a mosque was replaced with a much larger structure built of coral, and silver coins with Islamic inscriptions were in circulation. Cemeteries of the 12th and 13th centuries AD have Islamic interments.

Shanidar a cave in the Zagros foothills near Erbil in northeastern Iraq, where excavations by Ralph Solecki in the 1950s and 1960s revealed a Palaeolithic sequence including MOUSTERIAN, Baradostian (the Upper Palaeolithic blade industry of the Zagros region) and Mesolithic levels. The site provides the type assemblage for the Baradostian industry (33,000–27,000 BP), but is best known for the burials of NEANDERTHALS recovered from the Mousterian levels dating to 60,000–44,000 BP. One may have had flowers placed in the grave, although some specialists believe that their presence may instead be attributed to the habits of a burrowing rodent.

Shaqadud a complex of Sudanese sites in the western Butana, 50 km (30 miles) east of the Nile River. Site S1, the main site, consists of two localities: S1-A, a large cave, and S1-B, a MIDDEN in front of the cave. Small surface sites are found on top of the surrounding plateau. The cave and midden together comprise a cultural sequence nearly 7 m (23 ft) deep. The lower deposits of the midden contain a Khartoum Mesolithic microlithic industry with pottery, which lasted for about 2,500 years, and which in the period between about 6800 and 5700 bp was gradually replaced by artifacts typical of the Khartoum Neolithic, which lasted little more than a thousand years. The cave deposits accumulated during a relatively short period of time about 4000 bp and contain material that is the subject of ongoing study. Faunal remains include domestic stock, but floral remains indicate only wild forms.

shard see POTSHERD.

Shechem a Palestinian site excavated by Sellin in 1913–34 and WRIGHT in 1956–64. Building works of the MIDDLE BRONZE AGE resulted in a massively fortified site, including a GLACIS of the HYKSOS period, at which time Shechem seems to have controlled the territory from MEGIDDO to GEZER. The subsequent destruction level has been attributed to the campaigns of AHMOSE. The rebuilding of Shechem in the LATE BRONZE AGE included fortifications and a temple containing a MASSEBAH, while ISRAELITE Shechem was, before the founding of SAMARIA, the short-lived capital of the Kingdom of Israel.

Sheikh Hamad, Tell the ancient Dur-Katlimmu on the middle reaches of the Khabur River in eastern Syria, the object of a German excavation project since the late

1970s. First settled as a village in the late 4th millennium, the place was a 15 ha (37 acre) town during the 2nd millennium BC. In the 13th century BC Dur-Katlimmu was the seat of an ASSYRIAN provincial governor; excavations have uncovered the governor's palace and an important archive of CUNEIFORM tablets. NEO-ASSYRIAN kings expanded the town, its 9th-century BC walls enclosing 55 ha (136 acres), and created an elaborate irrigation system to feed the urban population. Settlement retracted again after the 7th century BC, the site hosting a village until early Islamic times.

Sheikh Hassan, Tell a town on the Euphrates River in northern Syria where German excavations of the 1980s and 1990s uncovered deeply stratified 4th-millennium BC deposits beneath HELLENISTIC remains. The 4th-millennium town presents a southern MESOPOTAMIAN character, and together with BRAK and HACINEBI places the initial northward spread of URUK period culture around 3600–3500 BC (Middle Uruk).

shell midden or **shell mound** an archaeological deposit consisting primarily of mollusc shells resulting from food procurement activities. Shell middens are important sources of information on diet, subsistence economy, aquatic harvesting patterns and techniques, and seasonality. See also KITCHEN MIDDEN, SAMBAQUI.

shengwen [sheng-wen] (*Chinese* 'cord motif') coarse pottery with textured surface decoration in early POST-GLACIAL Chinese sites, predating the Neolithic wares of CISHAN and HEMUDU. It is comparable though not similar to JOMON pottery in Japan, CHULMUN pottery in Korea, and corded ware in the DAPENGENG culture of Taiwan.

sherd see POTSHERD.

shifting cultivation a method of cultivation, very common in tropical forests where soils are thin, in which a field site, or swidden (see SWIDDEN AGRICULTURE) is cleared and then used for a very short period of time until its fertility is depleted, whereupon the cultivation site is relocated to fresh soil. Shifting cultivation is often associated with slash-and-burn, a method of land clearance in which standing vegetation is cut, allowed to dry, and then burned prior to the planting of crops. Evidence for land clearance from LANDNAM episodes in pollen diagrams from temperate Europe led to the hypothesis that shifting cultivation was practised there during the Neolithic, but evidence of long-term settlement and thick fertile soils contradicts such a model.

Shilla see SILLA.

ship setting burial type common in Scandinavia beginning in the Late Bronze Age and continuing through the Iron Age in which the burial, usually a cremation, is surrounded by an oval setting of upright stones in the shape of a ship, often 10–20 m (33–66 ft) long. The stones are usually graded in height so the highest are at the prow and the stern, echoing the profile of vessels seen in the rock art of this period.

shipwrecks the remains of sunken ships; those in Southeast Asian waters, dating to the 1st and early 2nd millennia AD, indicate that most shipping in the region was carried in locally built sewn-plank and lashed-lug vessels built with layered hulls and incorporating no iron. Small sea-going vessels had double outriggers, but the larger ones, despite the illustrations on BOROBUDUR, probably did not. Those in the Gulf of Siam and off Vietnam, dating to the 13th–15th centuries AD (Koh Khram, Phu Quoc, etc.) have established the contemporaneity of some Thai and Vietnamese ceramics. Two wrecks, one in QUANZHOU (Ch'uan chou) Bay and one off the Paracel Islands, indicate that by the 13th–15th century Chinese vessels were also carrying cargoes to and from Southeast Asia. No Indian vessels have yet been found in Southeast Asian waters.

Shirataki see YUBETSU.

Shishur a small fortified town in the interior uplands of Dhofar (southern Oman), built around a sink-hole which has now partly collapsed the site. Excavation during the 1990s by an American team revealed Late Iron Age to medieval remains. The place is popularly identified with Ubar, a semi-legendary caravan town.

Shiyu [Shih-yu] a Late Palaeolithic site in Shanxi Province, China, yielding a fossil human occipital bone and fourteen animal species, primarily horse and donkey, giving a radiocarbon date of c.28,000 bp. The lithics include small scrapers and points, and microlithic cores and blades.

Shizhaishan [Shih-chai-shan] a cemetery site in Yunnan Province, China, where the distinctive regional DIAN bronze culture was documented in 1956. Contemporaneous with the HAN Dynasty, the grave-goods consisted primarily of bronze and iron weapons and tools, with unique representational motifs of animals and ethnic peoples of the region. Bronze cowrie containers and drums, the latter related to those of DONG SON, are the characteristic types of Dian.

shoe-last adze or **celt** a long, thin chisel-shaped ground-stone tool characteristic of the LINEAR POTTERY culture. The function of the shoe-last adzes is the subject of some discussion. While the majority of scholars believe them to have been woodworking tools, some have argued that the shoe-last adzes served as ARD-shares or hoes for cultivation.

Short Count a 256-year cycle in the MAYA system, based on a sequence of thirteen KATUNS. See also CALENDAR ROUND.

Shortugai a prehistoric settlement on the Amu Darya (Oxus River) in northeastern Afghanistan discovered in the 1970s by H. Francfort in an extension of the French work at the Graeco-Bactrian town of Ai Khanum. In its lower two levels it contained a Mature HARAPPAN settlement. Located 600 km (370 miles) from the northern edge of the Indus ALLUVIUM, it contains a typically Harappan material culture (dated to the second half of the 3rd millennium BC) and has an associated irrigation system. The Badakshan source of lapis lazuli is accessible from the site, and a considerable amount of lapis occurs in the site; for these reasons, Shortugai is often identified as a Mature Harappan trading colony. The subsequent two periods of occupation belong to the 'Beshkent' culture, a probably semi-nomadic culture of southern Tadjikistan/eastern Bactria, best known from cemeteries and dated to the first half of the 2nd millennium.

Shoshong see TOUTSWE.

shouldered point a category of stone point manufactured on a blade, exhibiting a notch on one side of the base, and sometimes flaked partially or wholly on both sides. Shouldered points are especially characteristic of some Upper Palaeolithic industries of Europe (SOLUTREAN and EASTERN GRAVETTIAN).

Showlow a prehistoric PUEBLO ruin in Arizona, USA, which provided timbers enabling the modern DENDROCHRONOLOGY sequence to be tied to the prehistoric sequence for the first time.

Shriver a site in Missouri, USA, containing a WOODLAND occupation, what appears to be a FOLSOM occupation and, underlying that, an assemblage of chert flake tools. Neither of the levels can be reliably dated, except by THERMOLUMINESCENCE of the chert itself, which gave dates of approximately 10,700 BP and 13,000 BP. The 'pre-Folsom' materials are similar to other hypothetically contemporary assemblages.

Shu see ZHOU, DIAN.

Shubat Enlil see LEILAN.

Shuidonggou [Shui-tung-kou] a Late Palaeolithic site in Ningxia Hui Autonomous Region, China, yielding bison remains, numerous ostrich eggshell fragments and classic blade artifacts. Originally assigned to the 'ORDOS culture', the assemblage is characterized by prepared-platform NUCLEI highly varied in shape, marginally retouched flakes and pebble tools.

Shukbah Cave a prehistoric site in the Judaean desert, Israel, where GARROD directed her first excavation in Palestine in 1928, and unexcavated since. The cave's location in the Wadi en Natuf suggested to her the name NATUFIAN for the EPIPALAEOLITHIC culture she identified in layer B. A Levantine MOUSTERIAN level underlies the Natufian, separated by an erosional gap of unknown length.

Shulaveri-Shomu culture a culture, named after two Neolithic sites on the Kura River in eastern Georgia and western Azerbaijan (Transcaucasia), which represents a local Neolithic to early CHALCOLITHIC phenomenon, characterized by small sites (never more than 5 ha [12 acres]) containing usually small, round domestic structures, and by a hand-made coarse pottery decorated only by incision or applied knobs and other elements; at the bottom of some sites (e.g. Shulaveri) pottery is uncommon, perhaps implying a recent adoption of this technology. Subsistence focused on cultivation of a variety of cereals (wheats, barleys, millet), as well as legumes and grapes; irrigation seems to have been practised from the earliest phases of the culture. The fauna concentrates on domesticated cattle and sheep/goat, while hunting is minimally represented. The Shulaveri-Shomu culture seems to date (on the basis of a few calibrated radiocarbon determinations) to the mid 6th to early 5th millennia BC.

Shul'gantash Cave see KAPOVAYA.

Shulgi (2094–2047 BC) the successor to Ur-Nammu, the founder of the UR III dynasty. Shulgi created the Ur III empire. Quiescent until halfway through his reign, he undertook a bureaucratic reform that greatly centralized state control over economic life, and at the same time undertook a series of campaigns that brought into his administrative control a large area extending up the Tigris River and through the adjacent sections of the Zagros Mountains down to SUSA. This small empire endured only half a century, collapsing in the reign of Shulgi's third successor Ibbi-sin (2028–2004 BC).

Shum Laka an impressive rockshelter, about 15 km (9 miles) southeast of Bamenda in Cameroon, with deposits spanning at least the last 30,000 years, including microlithic and macrolithic stone artifact assemblages of Holocene date, as well as Early and Late Iron Age material. Of particular interest are eighteen human skeletons, the first prehistoric human remains discovered in western-Central Africa. Four date to about 7000 bp, and the others postdate 3000 bp.

Shuruppak see FARA.

Sialk, Tepe an important prehistoric site near Kashan on the Iranian plateau which provides an interrupted cultural sequence that spans from the Neolithic to the Iron Age. R. GHIRSHMAN's excavations in the 1930s defined six major phases, the last two represented chiefly by cemeteries A and B of Iron Age date. The earlier four phases (Sialk I–IV, each divided into two or more subphases) form an unbroken succession from the early 6th to the early 3rd millennium BC, the various subphases of which all exhibit external connections. Most of these connections are to other upland sites of Iran, and provide a stratigraphic anchor for regional chronologies. In Sialk IV, on the other hand, the two subphases indicated involvement in the late URUK and PROTO-ELAMITE phenomena. Since Sialk lies on the Great Khorasan Road (connecting MESOPOTAMIA with Central Asia and ultimately with East Asia), these connections with the Mesopotamian world are often understood as reflecting trading ventures.

Siassi Islands islands in the Vitiaz Strait between New Guinea and New Britain which were occupied by traders with exclusive control over exchange westwards of pottery and eastwards of obsidian and sago. As in southern coastal Papua, the ethnographically documented system appears within the last few hundred years, but ancestral versions date back 1,500–2,000 years. See also HIRI, MAILU.

Siberia and Central Asia The territory of Siberia and adjacent regions is very rich archaeologically, and humans have settled there despite the cold climate for hundreds of thousands of years. Much of its prehistory has been studied through the personal efforts of the pioneer of Siberian archaeology A. P. OKLADNIKOV, although in the last two decades many new research projects have been undertaken. One of the earliest Siberian sites is DIRING YURIAKH on the Lena River, where Lower Palaeolithic artifacts have been found on gravel terraces. The dating of the Diring finds is controversial. Some initial THERMOLUMINESCENCE dates were as early as 1.8 million years, but more recent dating places the site between 400,000 and 200,000 years ago. Middle Palaeolithic sites have been found in several localities in Central Asia. TESHIK TASH in Tadjikistan yielded a NEANDERTHAL child burial, the easternmost find of a Neanderthal known. At UST'-KAN Cave in the ALTAI region, the most common animal species are mountain sheep and hare.

The Upper Palaeolithic is especially well represented in Siberia. The northernmost Palaeolithic site in the world is found at BERELEKH at 71° north latitude. On the headwaters of the Lena and the Yenisei Rivers near Lake Baikal, many Upper Palaeolithic sites are known. Among the most important are TOLBAGA, dated between 35,000 and 27,000 years ago, and MAL'TA, where dwellings, ornaments and a large sample of animal bones reflect life between 24,000 and 20,000 years ago. Eastern Siberia was a jumping-off point for the colonization of the New World, so Upper Palaeolithic sites of the DYUKTAI CULTURE have been the subject of considerable interest recently. One of the most important is USHKI on Kamchatka, where bifacial points presage finds in the New World, and DYUKTAI CAVE, where microblades bear a resemblance to the DENALI COMPLEX of Canada.

The POSTGLACIAL foragers of Siberia adjusted to the warmer climate and forested conditions. Elk hunting was their major pursuit. Pottery manufacture marks the beginning of the Neolithic period, although change in subsistence from foraging to farming was very gradual. In

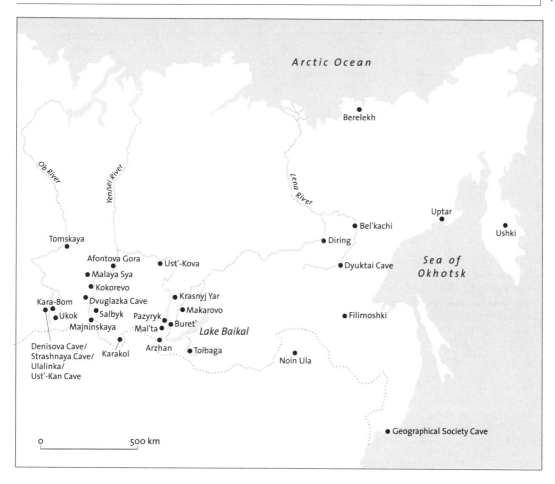

southern parts of Central Asia, the KELTA'MINAR culture is characterized by a mix of hunting and herding over the course of several millennia. In the Lena basin, the site of BEL'KACHI has yielded Neolithic sand-tempered pottery with net or mat impressions dating to about 4000 BC. The copper-using AFANASIEVO CULTURE of western and southern Siberia herded cattle, sheep and horses, and buried their dead under low mounds surrounded by a low circular stone wall. At BOTAI in northern Kazakhstan, wear on horse teeth suggests that they were tamed for riding around 3500 BC.

Bronze Age metallurgy took advantage of the rich mineral resources of this region, particularly in the ALTAI Mountains. Settlements of the ANDRONOVO CULTURE of western Siberia and Kazakhstan between 1500 and 800 BC consist of large semi-subterranean log houses. Its successor, the KARASUK CULTURE, was widespread across Siberia. During the Bronze Age, patterns of nomadic pastoralism that continued into later millennia were established. In the final millennium BC, the herds of these pastoralists generated tremendous wealth, which is reflected in their tombs. The frozen burials of the Altai at PAZYRYK and UKOK contained well-preserved bodies of people and horses, along with gold and silver artifacts, and textiles of felt and silk. During the 1st millennium AD, the caravan tracks of the SILK ROUTE led across southern-Central Asia between China and the eastern Mediterranean.

Sibri a small settlement near MEHRGAHR in the Kachi plain of eastern Baluchistan in Pakistan, investigated as part of J.-F. Jarrige's Mehrgahr project, which contains many artifacts with very strong similarities to Central Asian cultures to the north. This connection is reinforced by the South Cemetery at Mehrgahr, where much of the material culture is virtually identical with Central Asian forms. A recently discovered burial near QUETTA repeats this pattern, while earlier discoveries in Baluchistan and parts of the Sind had hinted at this northern connection. Considerable controversy exists over the precise dating of these materials, and how they should be interpreted in the prehistory of the northern subcontinent.

Sicilian pottery a type of SOUTH ITALIAN POTTERY decorated in the RED-FIGURED technique which seems to have been produced from the late 5th century BC. There appear to have been several production centres including SYRACUSE, Himera and possibly Centuripe. The style seems to have had an impact on PAESTAN and CAMPANIAN POTTERY.

sickle sheen a silica deposit or polishing that may occur along the working edge of flint tools during the harvesting of many soft plant types, including the Gramineae (cereals and grasses). The resulting 'sickle sheen' or gloss is often used to infer subsistence patterns, namely the consumption of wild or cultivated cereals. The inference is a weak one, however, since harvested plants may be non-dietary.

side-notched point a type of stone point, chipped on both faces and exhibiting notches on both sides near the base; in some cases, the notches are shallow and wide, forming a stemmed base. Side-notched points are diagnostic of the NORTHERN ARCHAIC TRADITION in North America.

sidescraper see SCRAPER.

Sidi Abderrahmane a series of beach and cave deposits in a quarry near Casablanca in Morocco, which have yielded a sequence of abundant ACHEULIAN stone artifact collections linked to sea-level changes, as well as a mandible fragment attributed to HOMO *erectus*.

Sidon a city situated on the Mediterranean coast of Lebanon, which was a major centre of the PHOENICIANS. Little archaeological work has been undertaken on the ancient city, which lies beneath the modern town.

sieving a technique of PARTICLE SIZE ANALYSIS used to determine the size grades of pebble gravel, sand and coarse silt in sediment, soils and archaeological deposits. A weighed sample is placed on the top sieve of a series of nested sieves, stacked with progressively smaller mesh size towards the bottom. Sieve mesh sizes are standardized so that the sized sample fractions are amenable to statistical analysis. The stack is mechanically agitated, and the material retained in each sieve, representing a size fraction, is weighed and its percentage of the total calculated. Wet sieving, sometimes as part of a flotation technique, is performed to recover small cultural remains from sites.

Sigatoka a stratified dune site on Viti Levu, Fiji, which has produced a discontinuous pottery sequence. The lowest levels, *c.*500 BC, contain LAPITA material, with some unusual forms. Above this, paddle-impressed pottery dated to *c.*AD 200 occurs.

Signal Butte a stratified site located in western Nebraska, USA, which has a discontinuous occupation sequence stretching from approximately 4500 BP to the historic period. It provided an invaluable initial CULTURE HISTORY for the Great Plains of North America.

signs apparently non-figurative representations found either engraved or painted in Palaeolithic PARIETAL ART, including certain often-repeated forms such as *tectiforms* ('hut shapes') or *claviforms* ('club-shapes') which are regionally restricted and may be 'ethnic markers'.

Silbury Hill a huge conical chalk mound, 40 m (130 ft) high and 160 m (175 yds) in diameter, surrounded by a broad, deep quarry ditch. Located in Wiltshire, England, it is part of the AVEBURY complex of Neolithic monuments. Excavations, most recently by R. Atkinson, have failed to reveal any trace of a burial within or beneath the mound, and its purpose and significance are unclear, though the effort required to build it *c.*2600 BC would have surpassed even that for the great Avebury HENGE.

Silk route the collective name for several overland and ocean routes of trade between China and the Mediterranean between the 1st and 8th centuries AD. From CHANG'AN, capital of China's HAN Dynasty, the primary route led west through the Gansu corridor into the Tarim basin at DUNHUANG. Separate routes ran around the northern and southern edges of the Takla Mahan desert, meeting in the west at Kashgar to continue into Turkmenia in Central Asia.

Silla a PROTOHISTORIC state on the Korean peninsula (*c.*AD 300–935) which was in competition with KOGURYO and PAEKCHE until 668 and had diplomatic and military relations with YAMATO in Japan. In 668 it unified the peninsula under the rule of United Silla. The capital remained in Kyongju, where large MOUNDED TOMBS of the 5th and 6th centuries have produced much fine gold work (see HEAVENLY HORSE TOMB). In the 7th century the capital was redesigned on the Chinese gridded-city plan (see CHANG'AN, compare HEIJO), and the ANAPCHI pond was constructed.

Silsillian see KOM OMBO.

silt **1** a size term for sediment or soil particles, from 0.002 to 0.05 or 0.06 mm (0.00008 to 0.0002 inches) in diameter. As a particle size term, the definition of silt-size particles is independent of mineral composition or other properties apart from size. See also SAND CLAY.
2 a TEXTURE term used in describing sediments and soils, defined, depending on the classification system used, as containing a certain percentage of silt-size particles relative to sand- and clay-size particle content.
3 a descriptive term for a sediment body (deposit) composed primarily of silt-size particles which is typically soft and plastic when moist. Loess deposits consist

primarily of silt-size particles, and would be described as silt.

silver-figured *adj.* denoting a technique used to decorate Greek and Etruscan bronze and gold. Either silver figures were attached to the other metal, or silver foil was placed over relief decoration.

Silver Leaves one of the earliest-known Iron Age sites south of the Zambezi River, located in the eastern Northern Province, South Africa, and dated to the 3rd–4th centuries AD with pottery similar to that from MATOLA. Of particular interest are seed impressions of cultivated bulrush millet, *Pennisetum americanum*, representing the earliest evidence for crop cultivation in the region.

sima a row of vertical tiles placed at the edge of a CLASSICAL roof above the CORNICE, forming a gutter. It was normally made of clay which could be painted. Water was thrown clear of the building by the use of elaborate spouts often in the form of lions' heads. See also ANTEFIX.

Sima de los Huesos see ATAPUERCA.

Similaun Man the oldest complete human body ever recovered from prehistory, this CHALCOLITHIC man, aged in his mid-to-late forties, was found in the Similaun Pass in the Tyrolean Alps, Italy, in 1991. The corpse, which seems to have become air-dried at high altitude before being enveloped by a glacier *c*.5,300 years ago, was clothed in leather leggings, a coat of tanned goat hide, a bearskin cap and a cape of woven grass; his shoes of bearskin and deerskin were filled with grass for insulation. Among the seventy everyday objects he had with him were a stone necklace, a wooden-framed backpack, a copper-tipped axe, a bow with a quiver of fourteen arrows, and a leather pouch containing flints and tinder. Tattooed marks on his torso, back and inner knees may be therapeutic, to relieve his arthritis, or tribal markings. Traces of meat have been found in his colon. Analysis suggests that he was prone to a crippling disease which recurred several times in the month before he succumbed to the elements on the mountain. •

Sin see NANNA.

Sinai the Sinai Peninsula has always been an important land-bridge between Africa and Eurasia, but with little to encourage substantial settlement in its own right. For Ancient Egypt, the occupation of Sinai was limited to mining stations in the southeast of the peninsula, as at SERABIT EL-KHADIM and a scatter of way-stations and forts between the eastern Nile DELTA (*Pelusium* for the Late and Graeco-Roman periods) to GAZA, including the forts at Haruba and Bir el-Abd.

Sinan the site of an early 14th-century AD Yuan ship (see CHINESE DYNASTIES) wrecked off the southwestern Korean coast at Mokpo, South Cholla Province, and discovered in 1976. It has seven compartments, constructed shell-first, with a V-shaped cross-section. Its cargo was enormous, including nearly 17,000 ceramics, half of them CELADON; 18.5 tonnes of coins; and many metal, stone, wooden and lacquer objects.

Sinanthropus see ZHOUKOUDIAN.

Sinda the site of a Late Cypriot settlement in eastern CYPRUS, excavated by Furumark in 1947–8. The site, which was first occupied in the 13th century BC, was massively fortified but nevertheless experienced two major destructions, possibly inflicted by the SEA PEOPLES, and was eventually abandoned early in the 12th century BC.

Single Grave culture a Danish Neolithic culture dated *c*.2800–2400 BC, part of the North European CORDED WARE complex. The Single Grave culture is characterized by single inhumations (predominantly male) under round barrows, accompanied by stone battleaxes and Corded Ware BEAKERS. The burial mounds are sometimes multi-phase, with a primary mound at the base covered over by later heightenings, each with a central burial. This gives rise to the typical three-phase Single Grave sequence of *under-grave, bottom-grave* and *over-grave*. Few settlement sites are known.

Sintashta a complex of sites (a fortified settlement, five cemeteries and a mortuary-temple construction) from the Middle Bronze Age (18th–16th centuries BC) in the southern Urals (Russia). It belongs to the so-called 'Land of Cities', along with the ARKAIM complex, and is presumably connected with the ancient Indo-Iranians (Aryans). Sintashta is especially famous for its cemetery, which is one of the richest funeral complexes of the EURASIAN STEPPES. In the graves warriors were buried in their chariots and with their horses. The grave-goods include tools, weapons and an abundance of jewellery. Sintashta has been excavated since the 1970s by the Russian archaeologists V. F. Gening and G. B. Zdanovich.

Sion see PETIT-CHASSEUR.

Sipán a complex of tombs in the Lambayeque region of the far north coast of Peru, pertaining to the MOCHE culture of the EARLY INTERMEDIATE PERIOD. Discovered by looters in 1987, the site contains an unknown number of intact royal, or at least incredibly lavish, tombs. Excavations are being carried out by Peruvian archaeologist Walter Alva. The tomb of the Lord of Sipán, the excavation of which has been completed, included a central personage buried in a wooden box, filled with a spectacular variety of artifacts, including a necklace of large gold beads in the form of peanuts. He was surrounded by four other individuals and a dog, and numerous ceramic vessels. Another human, presumably meant to guard the tomb, was buried above the main chamber with his feet cut off. These tombs are perhaps the first intact, elaborate Moche burials excavated by professional archaeologists.

sipapu a small hole in the floor of some KIVAS that gives access to the lower world in PUEBLO mythology. Sipapus have been identified, by homology, in some prehistoric kivas.

Sipontian see COPPA NEVIGATA.

Sippar an important city in southern MESOPOTAMIA, some 30 km (19 miles) downstream from Baghdad. Excavated during the 1880s by H. Rassam on behalf of the British Museum, and again at several times during the 20th century by French, German and Iraqi teams, Sippar is best known for the large number of CUNEIFORM texts found there. These texts illuminate important details of town organization and administration during the OLD BABYLONIAN PERIOD, and religious affairs during the NEO-BABYLONIAN period.

Siraf a major early Islamic port on the Persian Gulf coast of Iran, near Bushire. The place was already settled during SASSANIAN times but expanded greatly during the 9th–10th centuries AD, when the Abbasid maritime trade with China brought great wealth. British excavations during the 1960s and 1970s uncovered remains of the main mosque, palatial and more ordinary residences, shops and craft quarters.

Siret, Henri (1857–1933) and **Siret, Louis** (1860–1934) Belgian engineers working in the ALMERIA region of Spain from 1880; keen amateur archaeologists, the Siret brothers were the first to reveal the amazing richness of the CHALCOLITHIC and Bronze Age of southeastern Spain, with their excavations at many key sites including LOS MILLARES, EL ARGAR and Tabernas.

Sirikwa Holes circular depressions, 5–10 m (16–33 ft) in diameter, sometimes with stone walling around the circumference, which functioned as cattle byres in Iron Age sites of the Western Highlands of Kenya during the first half of the 2nd millennium AD. Many Sirikwa Holes have also been found in the Kenyan Rift Valley, for example at HYRAX HILL and LANET, where they are dated to about the 16th–17th centuries AD, and probably reflect an eastward movement of cattle-keepers from the highlands at that time.

Si Satchanalai an early historic city on the Yom River in northern-central Thailand, with walls several kilometres long. Undated prehistoric burials are followed by brick-built Buddhist structures and the establishment of a major industrial centre of the SUKHOTHAI kingdom (13th to 14th century AD). It is famous for its stoneware ceramic industry, and hundreds of kilns have been located, and many excavated, along the right bank of the Yom at BAN KOI NOI and BAN PA YANG. The best known of the wares (the brown-glazed Chalieng wares, under-glaze black-on-

cream Sukhothai wares and the green-glazed CELADONS), collectively called 'Sawankhalok' after the present name of the district, date to the 14th–16th centuries AD but earlier phases of production at the Ban Koi Noi site may date to the period of MON domination before the mid 13th century.

Sitagroi a prehistoric settlement mound in Greek Macedonia investigated by Gimbutas and Renfrew in 1968–9. The excavations at Sitagroi made it possible to correlate the Neolithic and Early Bronze Age sequences of the Balkans and the Aegean, and proved that copper metallurgy was an independent development in the Balkans.

site any place where there is evidence for past human behaviour. A site can be as small as an isolated find, which is either a single artifact or a small number of artifacts from which few inferences can be drawn, or as large as an ancient city. Sites are classified according to their function, although different regions of the world tend to have different terms for specific types of site. Major types include a domestic/habitation site (the primary residential locus); a KILL-SITE; and a processing/butchering site (where animal carcasses were stripped of their meat and other useful resources). There are, however, many other types.

site catchment analysis the definition of the site catchment, the total area from which the contents of a site have been derived, and an assessment of the catchment's economic potential, according to the principles of PALAEOECONOMY. See SITE EXPLOITATION TERRITORY.

site exploitation territory the territory surrounding a site which is habitually exploited by the site's inhabitants. It was a central concept in PALAEOECONOMY, which proposed a model for site exploitation territories of a one-hour walking distance for farmers, and a two-hour walking distance for hunter-gatherers.

site formation processes see FORMATION PROCESSES.

site structure the arrangement of the various components at a place, including the distribution of artifacts, features, facilities and activities. The concept of site structure applies to both behavioural and archaeological contexts. Often done in the context of ETHNO-ARCHAEOLOGICAL studies, site structural analysis identifies how the organization and use of space relate to other aspects of the cultural system.

The space required for most activities depends on the physical constraints of the human body. Because the proportions of the human body have remained relatively constant through time, we can develop an understanding of the constant relationship between activity types and the space needed to perform those activities. This knowledge can then be taken to the archaeological record. Additional ethnoarchaeological studies of site structure identify other factors influencing the organization and use of space. These factors include length of occupation, number of people at the site, types of facilities necessary for a given activity, and the nature of the materials resulting from the activity. Site structural analyses from contemporary or ethnographic contexts are then used to make WARRANTING ARGUMENTS in the context of the archaeological record.

Sittard a LINEAR POTTERY settlement in Limburg, the Netherlands, excavated by P. J. R. Modderman. Over thirty houses, many of them LONGHOUSES, were excavated, and it is estimated that between three and six were occupied at any one time, somewhat fewer than at the contemporaneous site of ELSLOO near by.

situla a CLASSICAL bucket-shaped container, with a single swinging handle across the rim. Silver and bronze examples are often found in burials in Macedonia and Thrace.

Siwa the most inaccessible of the major oases in Egypt's Western Desert, Siwa was occupied between 9000 and 7000 BP, but unknown to dynastic Egypt until the 26th Dynasty (664 BC). It was famous in the Graeco-Roman period as the site of a noted oracle, visited by Alexander the Great.

Six's technique a technique used to decorate 6th-century BC ATHENIAN POTTERY, and first discussed by Jan Six in 1888. The black surface of the pot was overpainted in red or white, and the detail was cut through, showing the black surface of the pot (contrast BLACK-FIGURED).

Skara Brae a Neolithic village of stone-built houses preserved beneath a later sand dune on Orkney, Scotland. The houses are of sub-rectangular internal plan and are linked together by covered passageways. Built-in furnishings of stone included dressers, beds, wall cupboards and limpet tanks. The villagers kept cattle and sheep, but cereal farming and fishing with limpet bait were also important. Two phases of occupation have been identified, spanning six centuries, c.3100–2500 BC.

Skateholm a group of southern Swedish Mesolithic fishing sites on the coast of Scania which used to be on small islands in a lagoon. They were discovered and excavated by Lars Larsson in 1980–84, and include domestic areas and over eighty graves of men, women and juveniles. The site of Skateholm 4 is dated to 6000–5500 BP.

skene 1 a Greek temporary shop or building.
2 a permanent stage-building, of several storeys, for a theatre placed behind the ORCHESTRA **(see fig., p.335).** It could be used as a backdrop for a play, as well as for storing equipment. In the Roman period the skene could be decorated with statues. See also PROSKENION.

Skhul (Es-Skhul) a small rockshelter and terrace site in the MOUNT CARMEL group, Israel. T. D. McCown (working under GARROD's direction in 1931–2) found remains of ten individuals (seven adults and three children) apparently deliberately buried on the terrace and associated with a Middle Palaeolithic LEVALLOISO-MOUSTERIAN industry. The Skhul population are now considered to be early anatomically modern HOMO *sapiens*. THERMOLUMINESCENCE dates average 119,000 BP; ESR dates range from 81,000 to 101,000 BP. Compare QAFZEH, TABUN.

Skorba a Maltese temple complex with earlier deposits beneath. A four-apse temple with a central apse of the TARXIEN phase (c.3000–2600 BC) has been added to a three-apse temple of the preceding *Ggantija* phase (c.3600–3000 BC). Excavations beneath the temples revealed an oval hut of the *Ghar Dalam* (IMPRESSED WARE) phase (c.5000 BC), and near by was an oval-roomed building of the *Red Skorba* phase (c.4300–4000 BC), thought from the presence of figurines to be a shrine, precursor of the later temples.

Skraeling a term applied to the aboriginal inhabitants of Greenland by Norsemen who settled the island in the late 10th century AD. The Skraelings are probably represented archaeologically by the THULE culture. See also QILAKITSOQ.

skyphos a type of Greek drinking vessel, normally a deep cup with two horizontal handles mounted near the rim. See also KOTYLE.

slash-and-burn see SHIFTING CULTIVATION, SWIDDEN AGRICULTURE.

Slavs a complex of ethnic groups speaking related languages which emerged during the second half of the 1st millennium AD in eastern Europe, although some have traced their roots to antecedents like the VENEDIANS. The emergence of state-level POLITIES in the lands of the Slavs began with Greater Moravia, centred on MIKULČICE, in the 9th century AD and in western-central and southern Poland in the 10th century. Further east, nodes of trade and commerce emerged at localities like NOVGOROD and KIEV. The basic unit of all these communities was the stronghold the GRÓD or *hrad*.

slip a mixture of clay and water which is applied to the surface of a pot before firing to improve the pot's smoothness and decrease its porosity. See also CERAMICS.

Słonowice a Neolithic mortuary structure of the TRB CULTURE and settlement of the Bronze Age TRZCINIEC CULTURE in southern Poland. The TRB mortuary structure consisted of an elongated trapezoidal palisade, about 120 m (131 yds) long and oriented east-west, consisting of timbers set upright in a bedding trench, which is believed to have outlined a low mound. A single primary burial was found in the wider end. This structure may represent a southern variant of the KUYAVIAN LONG BARROWS found in northern Poland, which date to roughly the same period.

slopewash a general term for COLLUVIUM consisting of a typically, but not necessarily, poorly sorted deposit located on and at the base of hillslopes. Slopewash is the result of soil erosion upslope, downhill sediment transport and final SEDIMENTATION. Soil erosion may result from a number of processes, some human-induced. Erosion and transport may result in the incorporation and displacement of archaeological deposits. Deposition at the base of the slope may include cultural debris redeposited from upslope locations, and it may result in the burial of intact and previously redeposited artifacts.

Slovakia see EUROPE, CENTRAL.

Słupia Stara an Iron Age metallurgical site of the VENEDIAN people in the HOLY CROSS MOUNTAINS of central Poland, dated to the 1st and 2nd centuries AD. At Słupia Stara, the neighbouring site of Słupia Nowa, and several other sites in the vicinity, clusters of several hundred iron-smelting furnaces about a metre in diameter are found in parallel rows.

smelt *vb* to separate metal from ore, usually by heating in a hearth or furnace.

Smenkhare see NEFERTITI.

Smith, Sir Grafton Elliot (1871–1937) an Australian-born anatomist who, along with his student and later colleague W. J. Perry, unswervingly advocated a hyper-diffusionist view that all civilizations, if not all cultures, including those in the New World, originated as a result of influences from Ancient Egypt.

Smith, Worthington George (1835–1917) a British amateur archaeologist who pioneered the scientific excavation and detailed recording of Palaeolithic sites and exposed sections. He is best known for his illustrations of flint artifacts and his CONJOINING of flint flakes.

Smithfield a LATER STONE AGE industry of the South African interior, named by VAN RIET LOWE after a series of open sites near Smithfield in the Free State, originally thought to be contemporaneous with the WILTON and initially described as having several variations, the A, B, C, N and P, each identified by distinctive tool types. The designation is now applied to a complex post-dating the Wilton in the South African interior between AD 1300 and 1700. Smithfield stone artifacts tend to be associated with hunter-gatherer pottery containing grass temper. See also SEACOW VALLEY.

Smyrna see IZMIR.

Snaketown a large site in Arizona, USA, excavations of which provided much basic information for the formula-

tion of the HOHOKAM sequence. The site covers over 1 sq. km (0.4 sq. mile) and has sixty refuse mounds. At its peak of use, the site contained a BALL COURT, a large habitation area comprising PITHOUSES built around a central plaza, and extensive irrigation ditches. Craft specialization was also apparent, not only in pottery but also in shell. Such items as copper bells and distinctive pottery figurines are highly suggestive of contact with MESOAMERICAN cultures. See also HAURY.

Snefru an Egyptian king, founder of the 4th Dynasty. Building works which should probably be ascribed to him are the two pyramids at DAHSHUR and at least the completion of that at MEIDUM.

Snettisham a location in Norfolk, England, where a single field has yielded nine hoards of Iron Age treasure comprising almost 200 gold, silver and bronze TORCS or neckrings, as well as bracelets and coins, dating to *c*.70 BC. The most spectacular object is one massive torc of gold-rich electrum.

Soan the name given to a Lower Palaeolithic industry of the Punjab (Pakistan and northwestern India) which was encountered in a group of sites by de Terra and Patterson during their geological and archaeological explorations of the region in the 1930s. The term encompassed both handaxes and chopper/chopping tools. Much of this material, together with the GEOMORPHOLOGICAL units from which it was gathered, has been redated to Middle Palaeolithic times, and the Soan seems to have no archaeological validity.

soapstone see STEATITE.

Sobiejuchy a lakeside settlement of the Late Bronze Age/Early Iron Age (HALLSTATT period [*c*.1200–600 bc], LUSATIAN culture), in northern-central Poland, 12 km (7.5 miles) north of BISKUPIN. Sobiejuchy was surrounded by a double palisade filled with stones and earth, and was occupied for about seventy-five years. The settlement of Sobiejuchy was destroyed by fire, as was the case at Biskupin, and skeletons were found in the settlement debris with arrowheads embedded in the bones.

Sodmein Cave or **Wadi Sodmein Cave** or **site QSR-44** a cave located in the Red Sea Mountains of the Egyptian Eastern Desert, about 40 km (25 miles) north-northwest of Quseir, which is the first deep stratified Palaeolithic site recorded in Egypt, providing stone artifacts and environmental information extending back to at least 45,000 bp. The remains include Middle Palaeolithic, Upper Palaeolithic and Neolithic material.

soft hammer, bar hammer or **cylinder hammer technique** the use of a hammer made of bone, antler, wood or some other relatively soft material, to remove flat flakes during flint knapping. Flakes struck with a soft hammer have a characteristic appearance, being relatively long and thin with a diffuse BULB OF PERCUSSION. Compare HARD HAMMER TECHNIQUE.

Sogd or **Sogdiana** a historical region located in the basin of the Zeravshan and Kashkadarya Rivers (in modern Uzbekistan and Tadzhikistan). On this territory were situated such cities as Samarkand (Marakanda), Cyropolis and others. Sogd was inhabited by Sogdians – an ancient Iranian people formed from the Saka tribes. In the 6th–4th centuries BC Sogd belonged to the ACHAEMENID empire. In 329–328 BC the Sogdians put up sustained resistance to Alexander the Great. After his death the country belonged successively to the SELEUCID kingdom, to the Graeco-Bactrian kingdom and to the KUSHANS. In the 6th–7th centuries AD it was conquered by the Turkic KAGHANATE, and in the beginning of the 8th by Arabs. Sogd played a great role in the economical and cultural life of the East. Its merchants controlled all of the silk trade. In the 5th–8th centuries there was a rapid growth of cities with fortified citadels, suburbs and necropolises. Palaces, temples and houses of nobles were decorated with murals and carvings on wood, clay and alabaster. Especially famous are the wonderful murals of such sites as PANJIKENT and AFRASIAB. There are also numerous objects of applied art made of silver, such as decorated dishes and vessels, known as Sogdian Silver.

Sohar a port on the Arabian Sea coast of Oman, still occupied today but most flourishing during early Islamic times (8th–10th centuries AD). French soundings at the site indicate that the place already operated earlier in the 1st millennium AD, and enjoyed connections with the Persian Gulf, India and southern Arabia.

soil **1** unconsolidated mineral or organic matter at and near the land surface which is the product of and influenced by PEDOGENESIS: the interacting pedogenic, depositional and erosional processes and factors along with environmental factors that have through time physically, chemically, biologically and morphologically altered pre-existing material from its original conditions. The alterations form differentiated layers (see SOIL HORIZON) with respect to the land surface that comprises a soil.

Archaeological deposits are often associated with soils because, for a soil to form, some type of dynamic balance of the land surface is implied, since it takes time for pedogenic processes to be expressed; the longer a favourable 'stable' surface on which a soil is forming is exposed, the greater the likelihood of occupation and discard of debris. Archaeological deposits associated with soils are subject to the same environmental conditions, processes and factors as the soil.

Soils also have temporal significance because it takes time for pedogenic alterations to occur. Although not all soils may be ISOCHRONOUS across a landscape, they are often a useful means of correlation. See also PALAEOSOL.

2 *(engineering)* all unlithified material, whether it has

been altered or not. Often any available engineering drilling records are consulted for subsurface information about an archaeological site or area prior to archaeological investigations, making the distinction between this and the foregoing definition important.

soil conductivity meter a GEOPHYSICAL instrument used in ELECTROMAGNETIC SURVEYING to identify metal objects and shallow pit features with different conductivity from the surrounding soil.

soil geomorphology the study of the interaction of PEDOGENIC and GEOMORPHIC processes as applied to interpretation of old and new landscapes. By definition, archaeological debris was deposited on former landscapes. After deposition, it was then subject to alteration by both pedogenic and geomorphic processes, potentially resulting in burial, mixing, redistribution or removal. The physical context of archaeological material is best determined and evaluated by an integrated soil geomorphic approach. See GEOMORPHOLOGY, PEDOGENESIS.

soil horizon a layer in a soil or soil material, developed through PEDOGENESIS, which differs from overlying or underlying genetically related layers in chemical, physical or biological properties and characteristics. Sequences of genetically related soil horizons make up the SOIL PROFILE which reflects the environmental conditions under which it formed.

soil probe see PROBE.

soil profile **1** a vertical sequence of SOIL HORIZONS expressed as a result of PEDOGENESIS acting over time. Different soil profiles with different soil horizons evolve under different extrinsic and intrinsic factors, processes and conditions. The soil profile therefore provides environmental or, in the case of PALAEOSOLS, palaeoenvironmental information, such as clues to vegetation type and prevailing climate.

2 a vertical section, exposed either in excavation or naturally, which reveals soil horizons. Ideally, the excavation should be deep enough to expose the entire succession of soil horizons. See also PROFILE.

soil stratigraphy a specialized branch of STRATIGRAPHY concerned with identification of soils as stratigraphic units (pedostratigraphic units) and their chronological ordering. A pedostratigraphic unit is a formally defined three-dimensional, laterally traceable, buried sediment or rock body, consisting of one or more SOIL HORIZONS (e.g. PALAEOSOLS), and is not to be confused with the sequencing of soil horizons within a SOIL PROFILE. In stratigraphic sequences where multiple palaeosols occur, soil stratigraphic study provides information for palaeoenvironmental reconstruction, monitoring environmental change, and dating pedological and depositional episodes.

soil structure the physical arrangement of sediment into secondary aggregations referred to as *peds* as the result of PEDOGENESIS. Soil structure is defined by the size and shape of peds, and the degree to which cohesive forces bind sediment particles within and between peds. Soil structure is a principal soil property noted in describing and interpreting soils.

Sokchang-ri [Sokchangni] a Palaeolithic site in South Ch'ungch'ong Province, Korea, with twelve cultural layers, dug by Sohn Pow-key (Son Bo-gi) from 1962. Layer 1 yielded obsidian scrapers, rhyolite burins, prismatic cores and an occupational floor dated to *c*.20,000 bp. Layer 6 gave a radiocarbon date on charcoal to *c*.30,000 bp, and heavy quartzite tools in the lower layers are dated to the Middle Pleistocene by comparison with ZHOUKOUDIAN artifacts.

Soleb a site in UPPER NUBIA, capital of KUSH under TUTANKHAMEN. It is notable for the temple of AMEN-HOTEP III (*c*.1391–1353 BC) and a cemetery of the NEW KINGDOM. The site was extensively examined by Pisa University 1957–77.

solifluction the process of mass movement of water-laden soil and sediment material as the result of the thawing of frozen ground. Solifluction can cause disruption or displacement of archaeological deposits, as well as result in burial in downslope landscape positions. COLLUVIUM deposited as the result of solifluction can be found as hillslope veneers, colluvial wedges and fans at the base of hillslopes, and as valley fill.

Solo a river in central and eastern Java, the terraces of which have yielded remains of early humans, PLIOCENE, Pleistocene and early modern fauna, and stone tools of uncertain association. The geological beds of archaeological interest, clearly exposed at SANGIRAN, are: *Pucangan* (Lower–Middle Pleistocene, *c*.3–2 million years BP at base, containing pre-modern JETIS fauna with which the earliest HOMINID remains, the MOJOKERTO child, are linked); *Kabuh* (Middle Pleistocene, *c*.1.4–0.7 million years BP at base, containing pre-modern TRINIL fauna and JAVA MAN HOMO *erectus* remains); *Notopuro* (volcanic soil formation marking the transition to Upper Pleistocene); and *High Solo Gravels* or *High Terrace* (Upper Pleistocene, *c*.?0.5 million years BP at base, containing modern NGANDONG fauna associated with SOLO MAN and *H. sapiens*, and stone tools distinctly different from the ACHEULIAN).

Solo Man (HOMO *erectus soloensis*) an advanced HOMINID, somewhat more archaic than European NEANDERTHALS, found at NGANDONG and Sambung-macan in the Solo Valley of Java; it may possibly be later than PEKING MAN but is at a similar evolutionary level. See also DUBOIS.

Solomon king of the united kingdom of Israel and Judah.

His reign (*c*.965–928 BC) saw a good deal of building activity at many sites including JERUSALEM.

Solutrean or **Solutrian** a western European Upper Palaeolithic industry which appears to have developed in the Rhône Valley area of France, following AURIGNACIAN influence at about 19,000 BC, and which lasted approximately 3,000 years. The type-fossils are the laurel-leaf point (Earlier Solutrean) and the shouldered point (Later Solutrean). Solutrean flint artifacts represent some of the best examples of Palaeolithic knapping technology, and the assemblages also contain some fine bone work. Many decorated caves in France can be assigned to this period. The name is derived from the French open-air site of Solutré, Saône-et-Loire, excavated most recently by J. Combier; it has material from the MOUSTERIAN to the late MAGDALENIAN, and specialized in the exploitation of horse herds, rounded up against the foot of a craggy hill.

SOM see SEINE-OISE-MARNE.

Somerset Levels a wetland region of southwestern Britain, famous for its preserved prehistoric organic remains. These include the Neolithic SWEET TRACK and the Iron Age villages of GLASTONBURY and Meare.

Somme-Bionne a Marnian chariot burial in Maine, France, equipped with an ETRUSCAN bronze beaked flagon and Attic RED-FIGURE KYLIX, dating to LA TÈNE Ia, *c*.450–420 BC.

Somme-Tourbe see LA GORGE-MEILLET.

Sondershausen a cemetery of the LINEAR POTTERY culture in eastern Germany. Twenty-eight inhumation burials were found at Sondershausen, with the skeletons in a contracted position lying on their sides. Ornaments of SPONDYLUS shell occurred in both male and female burials.

Songguk-ri [Songgungni] a Bronze Age site in South Ch'ungch'ong Province, Korea, where a stone cist burial yielded in 1974 the first Liaoning-type dagger found on the peninsula. Excavation of the associated village site in 1985 revealed two pit-houses dated to the 5th century BC.

Songhay a 15th–16th century AD West African empire, which controlled virtually the entire great bend of the River Niger from its capital at GAO by means of wealth based on Saharan trade. A warlike and ambitious Songhay king, Sanni Ali, came to the throne in about AD 1464 and set about conquering neighbouring towns and consolidating his kingdom. After his death, an army general, later known as Askia Mohammed, took control of the throne and developed a very efficient administrative and taxation system, including the use of uniform weights and measures. Trade and learning flourished and the university at Timbuktu became renowned all over the Islamic world. However, in 1589 the empire was overthrown by a Moroccan army under El Mansur, whose soldiers were armed with guns and easily defeated the Songhaians, who could defend themselves only with spears and swords.

Song Keplek and **Song Terus** two cave-sites in the Southern Mountains (Punung-Pacitan district) of eastern Java belonging to the SAMPUNG culture. Excavated by an Indonesian/French team, they were occupied by hunter-gatherers between 8000 and 5000 years BP.

Songon Dagbe one of more than 100 large SHELL MOUNDS at the Ebrie Lagoon in the Ivory Coast dating to c.2400 bp. Contact with areas further north is suggested by the presence of several KINTAMPO 'cigars'.

Songze [Sung-tse] see QINGLIANGANG.

Son Vi type-site of a pre-HOABINHIAN stone tool industry located at river terraces and cave-sites around the Red River Valley in northern Vietnam, dating to c.18,000–9000 BC, and characterized by unifacially flaked pebbles, rare bifacially worked pebbles, choppers, sidescrapers and 'round-edged' pebbles. The industry precedes Hoabinhian phases at Con Moong and Hang Pong 1, the transition occurring c.10,000–9000 BC.

Sopot Lengyel an ENEOLITHIC culture of northwestern Yugoslavia, viewed as a regional variant either of the LENGYEL or of the VINČA cultures in the 5th millennium BC.

Sopron an Early Iron Age cemetery (HALLSTATT C period) located in western Hungary, 60 km (37 miles) southeast of Vienna. In the cremation burials found under barrows at Sopron were a number of unusual urns with incised human figures which depict people spinning, weaving on an upright loom, playing the lyre, dancing, and riding on horseback. Other individuals lead horse-drawn wagons, herd animals and hunt. Male figures are depicted wearing trousers, the earliest known representation of this garment in temperate Europe.

Soroca formerly **Soroki** a complex of sites in the middle Dniester Valley of Moldova which have provided most of the data on the late Mesolithic/early Neolithic BUG-DNIESTER culture. Located on a low terrace, the earliest occupations at Soroca (c.6500 BC) are ACERAMIC and have an exclusively hunting and fishing economy. Later levels (c.5800 BC) have much the same sort of economy, but include pointed-base vessels unlike those of the CRIȘ culture near by. Claims have been made for evidence of local domestication, particularly of pigs, at Soroca, although the data are equivocal.

Soroki see SOROCA.

soros a Greek burial mound. One of the best known contained the Athenian dead from the battle of MARATHON in 490 BC. See also MAGOULA, TOUMBA.

Sos Höyük a roughly 2 ha (5 acre) mound east of Erzurum (northeastern Turkey) in the interfluve between the Euphrates and Araxes River drainages. Excavations during the 1990s by A. Sagona have recorded an occupation sequence that spans the late 4th to the late 1st millennia BC. The site belongs to the Transcaucasian world, and represents one of the few excavated settlements of the later 3rd and earlier 2nd millennia BC. The sequence also provides important chronological details, especially for dating the MARTKOPI and TRIALETI pottery styles.

Sotira-Teppes a site in southern CYPRUS which was excavated by Dikaios in 1947–54 and is the type-site for the Neolithic II (later 5th millennium BC) Sotira culture, which is characterized by combed ware. The settlement, which was surrounded by an enclosure wall, consists of circular and oval stone and mud-brick houses. The dead were buried in a simple pit-grave cemetery at the foot of the hill. At Sotira-Kaminoudhia Swiny has excavated an Early Cypriot settlement and cemetery.

Soufli the site in Thessaly, Greece, of a Neolithic–Bronze Age settlement mound and a cremation cemetery.

Sounion the promontory in Attica, Greece, on which was constructed the temple of Poseidon. This dated to the mid 5th century BC.

souterrain a long stone-built chamber sunk into the ground and roofed with stone slabs, usually beneath a house or settlement and intended for cold storage. Souterrains are found in Scotland, Ireland, Cornwall (where they are known as *fogous* and date to the 2nd and 1st centuries BC) and Brittany, where the earliest belong to the mid 1st millennium BC.

South Arabian civilization a group of kingdoms which developed during the 1st millennium BC and lasted until the mid 1st millennium AD, in the region of southwestern Arabia roughly corresponding to modern Yemen. The most famous of these kingdoms include the Minaeans, Qatabanians, Sabaeans and Himyar. Sharing a system of writing, and further united by many common cultural attitudes and materials, these states were based both on exploiting the agricultural potential of this mountainous area and, more famously, on producing and exporting incense (frankincense and myrrh). The attention paid to these groups by Greek and Roman writers as well as in several biblical episodes (especially the 'Queen of Sheba') is due almost entirely to the commercial aspect of the southern Arabian states, which were proverbially wealthy.

South Cadbury see ARTHUR.

Southeastern Ceremonial complex see SOUTHERN CULT.

Southern Cult a complex of motifs and objects, also

known as the Southeastern Ceremonial complex, found throughout the southeastern part of North America during the MISSISSIPPIAN, which appears to be almost a true horizon in the 13th century AD. The 'cult' was probably not a religious cult in the modern sense of the word, and was probably tied into widespread exchange networks. Distinctive motifs include the cross, 'sun circle', swastika and an eye-and-hand motif.

Southern Highveld Settlements Iron Age farms of the early 2nd millennium AD, located on the extensive grasslands of the southern highveld area of the Free State and Gauteng Provinces, South Africa. The farmers built numerous stone walls to enclose cattle byres and courtyards around houses. Many of these structures still stand today and have been classified as Types N, V and Z settlements, which are associated with the MOLOKO complex and the dispersal of the ancestors of the modern Sotho-Tswana people.

Southern Rhodesian Wilton see KHAMI, MATOPO.

South Italian pottery a type of pottery that was produced in the Greek colonies in southern Italy and Sicily, particularly from the late 5th century BC. There were various centres of production: see APULIAN, CAMPANIAN, GNATHIAN, LUCANIAN, PAESTAN and SICILIAN POTTERY.

Sozudai a controversial Palaeolithic site in Oita Prefecture, Japan, excavated by C. Serizawa, who claims a date of 400,000 bp on geological grounds and tool comparisons with ZHOUKOUDIAN. Many archaeologists do not accept that the tools are of human manufacture; some accept a date of only 70,000 bp.

spacer-plate a flat rectangular or sub-rectangular plaque of amber or jet, with a complex arrangement of through-borings to serve as a separator for the strings of a multi-strand necklace. Amber spacer plates are found as components of necklaces of amber beads in graves of the Early Bronze Age WESSEX CULTURE, and contemporary examples of jet are known from burials in eastern Yorkshire, England.

Spain see IBERIA.

spall see BURIN.

Spanish Levantine art see LEVANTINE.

Sparta the main urban centre of Laconia on the banks of the River Eurotas in Greece. An important sanctuary, dating from the Early Iron Age, was that of Artemis Orthia where numerous ivory, bone, lead and ceramic offerings have been found. In the Roman period the sanctuary was remodelled by the construction of a theatre. Another sanctuary was that of Athena Chalkioikos, a structure decorated with bronze plates. See also LACONIAN POTTERY.

spatial archaeology a theoretical approach to the study of the distribution of archaeological sites, artifacts and technologies.

Spaulding, Albert Clinton (1914–90) an American archaeologist who contributed much to the development of modern archaeological theory, especially PROCESSUAL ARCHAEOLOGY. He engaged in a famous series of debates with James FORD on the nature of the archaeological type, and also advocated the adoption of explicitly scientific and quantitative methods by the discipline.

Spear Hill a complex of twenty-eight sites in the Pilbara region of Western Australia with a wide range of PETRO-GLYPHs similar to those of GALLERY HILL.

spearpoint the tip of a projectile used for throwing or stabbing. See also PALAEOINDIAN, PROJECTILE POINT.

spearthrower a long stick with a hooked end designed to hold a spear. The implement is used to extend the reach of the arm, producing a stronger and longer throw. In Europe antler spearthrowers, often beautifully carved, developed during the MAGDALENIAN phase. See also ATLATL.

specific gravity a physical property of all solids and liquids defined by the ratio of the mass of a body to the mass of an equal volume of distilled water at prescribed temperature conditions. Knowing the specific gravity of the pure metals can help in calculating by means of a simple non-destructive analysis the composition of a metal artifact if it is a two-component alloy, and preferably if one of the alloy components is known. The property is also utilized in preparations for HEAVY MINERAL ANALYSIS.

speleothem a secondary mineral deposit, usually carbonate, precipitated in air-filled caves from seeping waters enriched in carbonate. Geographically widespread periods of speleothem growth (as *stalagmites* and *stalactites*) and ISOTOPIC composition of speleothems may provide palaeoclimatic information. They can be dated by the URANIUM SERIES DATING method. Periods of speleothem growth near coastal or river valley areas of carbonate rock can provide information on past sea-level or river-level fluctuations. Speleothem deposition can potentially bury earlier archaeological deposits.

sphinx a mythological beast usually with a lion's body and a man's head or face. As a motif in Egyptian art the sphinx was used as a depiction of royal power, and therefore only the king was shown in this form. The largest representation of an Egyptian sphinx is also one of the earliest, the Great Sphinx at GIZA, associated with the pyramid complex of King KHAFRE. Representations of ram-headed lions termed *crio-sphinxes*, and associated with the god AMEN, are found from the NEW KINGDOM, most notably as statues flanking the roads between the temple of LUXOR and the complex at KARNAK.

sphyrelaton a bronze statue made by the technique of hammering bronze plates over a core. The plates were secured by nails. The technique is a precursor to the LOST WAX technique, and three statues dating to the 8th century BC have been found in the temple of Apollo at Dreros on Crete. The technique was also used to produce colossal statues, some of which survived into the Roman period.

Spiennes Neolithic flint mines in Belgium covering an area of 60 ha (150 acres). The earliest are opencast pits, but deep shafts with underground galleries later became necessary as the more accessible deposits were exhausted. A second less extensive flint mine series at Petit-Spiennes c.1 km (0.6 mile) to the west became the site of a double-ditched enclosure in the MICHELSBERG period, running across the shafts and dumps of the earlier mining complex.

Spina a harbour town located at the mouth of the River Po in Italy. It seems to have been occupied by the Etruscans and was probably founded in the early years of the 5th century BC. Its extensive cemeteries (Valle Trebba and Valle Pega) have yielded large quantities of imported ATHENIAN POTTERY. The site may have served as an outlet for agricultural produce from the Po Valley and slaves from Central Europe which could be shipped down the Adriatic to the urban centres of the Greek world. Its rise in fortune contrasts with the decline of Massilia (see MARSEILLES), perhaps seeing a new emphasis on the Alpine Passes rather than on the Rhône Valley.

Spirit Cave one of numerous limestone rockshelters in the KARST uplands of northern Thailand, occupied intermittently from before 9000 BC until c.5500 BC. Stone implements of the lower layers fall within the range associated with the HOABINHIAN. Some publications claim that after c.6000 BC these are mixed with cord-marked and burnished pottery and with flaked and edge-ground or polished stone adzes and small slate knives similar to those later used to harvest rice in the region. But it is possible that the pottery was intrusive and derived from later Iron Age log-coffin burials situated at a higher level in the same cave. While no rice remains were found at the site, rice husks were recovered at the site of Banyan Valley Cave, 30 km (19 miles) to the east, along with small slate knives. This site was occupied by c.3500 BC and continued in use into the 1st millennium AD. A third rockshelter in the region, Steep Cliff Cave, utilized between c.5500 and 3500 BC, appears to have been used as a seasonal hunting campsite.

spirit path the rows of stone sculptures arranged facing the path up to Chinese MOUNDED TOMBS from the HAN Dynasty onwards. Their function was to guard or honour the deceased. The sculptures often include people and animals, of three-quarters to double life-size. Decadent examples are seen at the MING TOMBS outside Beijing.

Spiro a site, located in eastern Oklahoma, USA, which comprises eight mounds of varying size, one of which had served as both a TEMPLE MOUND and BURIAL MOUND. The largest of these, the Craig mound, was 11 m (36 ft) in height. Much of the site has been destroyed by pot-hunting. It contained a rich assemblage of artifacts associated with the SOUTHERN CULT. See also ETOWAH, MISSISSIPPIAN, MOUNDVILLE.

Spišsky Stvrtok a Bronze Age fortified site of the OTO-MANI culture in eastern Slovakia. The hilltop settlement of Spišsky Stvrtok is surrounded by a stone and earth rampart 170 m (186 yds) in circumference, plus an outer stone wall. One part of the site is termed the 'acropolis', in which the houses had stone foundations and in one of which was a hoard of gold and bronze artifacts. The houses outside the 'acropolis' were of simpler construction. This distinction has been interpreted as indicating social differentiation, with the members of the elite living in the 'acropolis'.

Spitsyn culture an early Upper Palaeolithic culture defined chiefly on the basis of the lowest level of KOSTENKI XVII on the Don River in European Russia, dating to c.40,000–30,000 bp. It is characterized by burins, retouched blades and scrapers; some bone tools and ornaments (e.g. perforated fox teeth) are also present. The Spitsyn assemblages represent a very early but fully developed Upper Palaeolithic industry which contrasts sharply with the contemporaneous STRELETS CULTURE.

Spondylus gaederopus a species of marine shell found in the eastern Mediterranean, widely used in Neolithic Europe for ornaments, including bracelets, discs and beads. These ornaments are found in many sites from southeastern to northwestern Europe, including those of the LINEAR POTTERY culture in Slovakia, Germany, the Netherlands and eastern France.

Spring and Autumn period see ZHOU.

Springbok Flats or **Tuinplaas** a broken cranium, mandible and assortment of damaged appendicular bones comprising a partial skeleton of HOMO *sapiens*, discovered during roadworks in the Springbok Flats region, about 130 km (80 miles) northeast of Pretoria in South Africa, and described by Robert BROOM in 1929, shortly after the discovery. The remains have a curious combination of gracile and robust anatomical structures: they are essentially modern but the tibia is considered suggestive of archaic affinity. The dating remains unresolved but could be older than 30,000 bp. Broom suggested a MIDDLE STONE AGE date on the basis of associated extinct fauna and the occurrence of Middle Stone Age artifacts at nearby sites. Attempts to provide radiocarbon dates have been unsuccessful because of insufficient collagen preservation.

Spy a prehistoric cave-site near Liège, Belgium, best known for the late 19th-century discovery of three damaged NEANDERTHAL skeletons, the first ever found associated with MOUSTERIAN artifacts. The upper layers of the cave yielded Upper Palaeolithic material.

square-mouth see BOCCA QUADRATA.

Squier, Ephraim George (1821–88) an American antiquary who, with Edwin H. DAVIS, described and analysed hundreds of mounds and enclosures in the Ohio and the Mississippi Valley. Their resulting book, *Ancient Monuments of the Mississippi Valley*, was a remarkable volume for its time, and still stands as a pioneering work in American archaeology, even though they concluded that the mounds were too sophisticated to have been constructed by the ancestors of contemporary Indians. As part of his research on Mound Builder origins, Squier also conducted archaeological work in Central America, Peru and Bolivia. See also ATWATER, HAVEN, THOMAS.

Sredni Stog culture an ENEOLITHIC culture of the Dnieper basin of Ukraine of the 4th millennium BC. It is seen as the precursor of the YAMNAYA culture of the late Eneolithic and is known from a number of settlements and cemeteries including DEREIVKA. The Sredni Stog culture is particularly important for its role in the domestication of the horse.

Srejović, Dragoslav (1931–96) a Yugoslav archaeologist and professor of archaeology at the University of Belgrade. Srejović is best known for his excavation of two important settlements, LEPENSKI VIR and VLASAC, between 1965 and 1971. Located in the Iron Gates gorges where the Danube cuts through the Carpathian Mountains, these sites provide key data for understanding the transition from foraging to farming in southeastern Europe.

Śri Kṣetra an early name for the town of Prome in lower Burma, capital and Buddhist religious centre of the state of the same name in the early–mid 1st millennium AD, later absorbed by PAGAN.

Śrivijaya a major trading state in the Malacca Straits in Southeast Asia, resembling the later Malacca Sultanate, and controlling ports in Sumatra and the Malay Peninsula during the 7th–8th centuries AD and again in the 10th–13th centuries, periods of booming trade in Asian waters. The capital has long been assumed to be at present-day Palembang in South Sumatra Province, and recent excavations by French and Indonesian archaeologists confirm this. Some twenty Śrivijayan sites, mostly temples, have also been investigated outside Palembang, and other locations, mainly along the coast, have also been investigated. These include *Kota Kandis* in Jambi Province, a trading settlement downstream from Muara Jambi which has yielded large quantities of 12th- to 14th-century Chinese ceramics, a short inscription palaeographically dated to the 9th century and a 12th-century Cola bronze statue; and *Pugungraharjo*, a large site in Lampung Province with a megalithic complex, large stepped earthen mounds, 12th–14th-century Chinese ceramics, and a Buddhist statue (12th–13th century).

In South Sumatra Province, the following major sites have been identified:

Kota Kapur, on the west coast of the island of Bangka, a pre-Śrivijayan site taken over in AD 686 by Śrivijaya, as attested by a dated Old Malay inscription. It includes two late 6th-century temples with 'mitred Visnu' statues, and is surrounded by a 1.5 km (1 mile) earthen wall. Under the temples, an iron-working site has been dated to *c.* 3rd–5th centuries AD.

Ulu Musi two sites, with many jar burials.

Candi Tingkip a medium-sized brick temple site with a 7th–8th century standing Buddha statue in Sri Lankan style, on the upper reaches of the Musi Rawas, not far from the border with Jambi.

Bumi Ayu a vast Hindu complex with Saivite statues dated to the 10th–12th century AD, 80 km (50 miles) upriver from Palembang.

Bingin a brick temple with 8th–9th-century Buddhist statues on the bank of the Musi Rawas, and a surrounding earthen wall.

Elsewhere in the region, other large sites linked to late Śrivijaya are Kota Cina (northeastern Sumatra, 11th–14th century), Lobo Tuwa (northwestern Sumatra, 11th–12th century), Kampong Sungei Mas (Kedah, Malaysia, 10th–11th century) and Pengkalan Bujang (Kedah, Malaysia, 10th–14th century), all of which have yielded large quantities of Chinese stoneware, Middle Eastern glass and some ceramics.

Środa Śląska a late medieval buried hoard in southwestern Poland which contained many pieces of jewellery and coins. An important element in the hoard is a gold crown decorated with almost 200 precious stones and topped by seven eagles. A circular FIBULA with a cameo of an eagle cut from blue CHALCEDONY and set with garnets, emeralds, sapphires and pearls was probably made in Italy. Over 4,000 gold and silver coins found in the Środa Śląska hoard date from the second half of the 13th and the first half of the 14th centuries.

Srubnaya culture or **Timber Grave culture** a Bronze Age culture of the steppes of the Volga and Don basins in southern Russia, succeeding the YAMNAYA culture. Srubnaya burials contain remains of horse trappings, and settlements have significant percentages of horse bones in their faunal samples, leading to the belief that mounted pastoralism was the dominant form of subsistence and settlement.

stadial a climatically cold episode of relatively short duration represented by deposits and processes characteristic of GLACIAL conditions. Compare INTERSTADIAL. See also STRATIGRAPHY.

stadium a long narrow running track, often surrounded on three sides by banks, sometimes tiered with seating. The name is derived from the term for the measurement of 600 (ancient) feet (452 cm [178 inches]). An elaborate starting-gate has been excavated at Isthmia near COR-INTH. Stadia were normally attached to major sanctuaries where athletic games took place (see DELPHI, OLYMPIA), but they were also among the public buildings of a Greek city.

stage a general level of cultural development, which can be regional, continental or even global in distribution. *Sensu stricto*, the concept has no temporal implications, but in practice it is often used as an integral part of the CHRONOLOGICAL sequencing of CULTURE HISTORY. Examples are the ARCHAIC, WOODLAND and FORMATIVE.

stalactite/stalagmite see SPELEOTHEM, TRAVERTINE.

St Albans (*Lat.* Verulamium) a Roman town (*municipium*) in England built on the site of an earlier Iron Age capital. The early town was laid out in a grid pattern and traces of timber-framed shops have been found lining Watling Street. The town was destroyed by Boudicca (see COL-CHESTER), but was rebuilt with a monumental FORUM which was opened in AD 79 by the governor Agricola. In addition to temples linked to strictly Roman cults, buildings apparently dedicated to native deities have been found. In the 2nd century a theatre was constructed. See also WHEELER.

stamnos a round-mouthed jar, with two horizontal handles mounted on the upper part of the body. It is a shape often decorated in the RED-FIGURED technique at ATHENS.

stamped decoration a technique normally used to decorate plain wares (see BLACK-GLOSSED). It first appears on ATHENIAN POTTERY in the middle of the 5th century BC, and frequently consists of patterns of PAL-METTES. From the 4th century it was used in conjunction with ROULETTING. Figured stamps were also occasionally used. The stamp was cut on to the end of a rounded stick and applied by a circular motion.

stamp seal a seal which is pressed into the sealed material, rather than rolled as is a CYLINDER SEAL. In Bronze Age western Asia, the form as well as iconography of stamp seals tends to be correlated with culture areas; thus, it is square in the Indus, round in the Persian Gulf (BARBAR) and COMPARTMENTED in Central Asia (BACTRIAN BRONZE AGE).

Stanca Ripiceni Cave an Upper Palaeolithic site on the Prut River in eastern Romania, located 200 m (220 yds) south of RIPICENI-IZVOR. Four cultural layers occur in the succession of cave deposits; among the associated faunal remains are horse, reindeer and steppe bison. The lowest assemblage includes bifaces, scrapers and burins, and probably dates to the earlier Upper Palaeolithic (i.e. 25,000 bp). The three overlying levels apparently date to the late Upper Palaeolithic; the uppermost assemblage includes geometric microliths.

Stanton Drew a megalithic complex in Avon, southwestern England, comprising three circles of standing stones respectively 110, 44 and 30 m (120, 48 and 33 yds) in diameter, two of them with attached stone avenues. In 1997 a MAGNETOMETER SURVEY of the Great Circle (largest of the three) revealed traces of nine concentric rings of POSTHOLES within the stone circle, as well as the presence of an encircling ditch outside. This suggests that the stones which are visible today are all that remains of a much more elaborate structure of concentric timber circles incorporating between 400 and 500 substantial timber posts. It may be compared with the evidence for a timber phase preceding the erection of the SARSENs at STONEHENGE.

Stanwick an extensive Late Iron Age enclosure in Yorkshire, England, consisting of ditches and banks defining an area of some 300 ha (740 acres) around a small central nucleus. Originally interpreted as an encampment built by the CELTIC Brigantes in the 1st century AD in their resistance to the Romans, and the largest HILLFORT in Britain, it is now thought to be no more than an enclosed private estate or demesne containing a number of residential compounds.

Staraya Ladoga a VIKING settlement in northwestern Russia. Known in Norse as 'Aldeigjuborg', the settlement at Staraya Ladoga was a node in a trading network that extended from the Baltic to the Black Sea. Workshops at Staraya Ladoga have yielded important information on iron working and other local crafts, including bone and woodworking. Staraya Ladoga later developed into a major medieval town with a fortress, monasteries and churches.

Star Carr a waterlogged earlier MAGLEMOSIAN lake-side settlement in Yorkshire, England, excavated by J. G. D. CLARK in 1949–51 and originally dated to the 8th millennium bc. The damp conditions have led to the preservation of wooden tools and a large number of bone and antler artifacts, including 187 barbed points, 'mattock heads' of elk antler, and a group of twenty-one perforated red deer frontlets which may have been worn as ceremonial or hunting masks. The faunal remains, primarily red deer, indicated summer occupation, possibly by people based on the coast. New excavations in the late 1980s revealed that there had been repeated deliberate burning of the reedswamp over a long period, perhaps to attract grazing animals. Radiocarbon dates proved the occupation to be 1,000 years older than previously thought, starting c.8700 BC, and involving at least 250 to 300 years of repeated visits. At the base of the lake-edge occupation was a wooden platform or trackway of large split timbers. Work in the surrounding area has confirmed that Star Carr was merely one of a series of at least a dozen activity areas distributed around the shores and islands of this ancient lake.

Starčevo culture the earliest Neolithic culture of the western Balkans, named after a settlement site north of the Danube near Belgrade in Yugoslavia, part of a broadly distributed complex of cultures that includes KARANOVO I, KREMIKOVCI, KÖRÖŞ and CRIŞ, c.6500–5800 BC. Starčevo settlements in southern Yugoslavia are generally TELLS, but further north in Serbia they are usually flat sites, reflecting an adaptation to the temperate continental environment. At the more northerly Starčevo sites, cattle bones exceed those of caprines in quantity, suggesting a shift from the pattern seen in the earliest Neolithic sites in the Near East, Greece and the southeastern Balkans. At LEPENSKI VIR, a Starčevo occupation lies over the settlement of complex foragers.

Staré Hradisko a Late Iron Age OPPIDUM in Moravia, first occupied in the mid 2nd century BC and abandoned about a century later. Staré Hradisko has provided important information on manufacturing, including pottery production using kilns. The interior of Staré Hradisko is subdivided by palisades into smaller units, possibly separate farmsteads.

star mound a stone or earth structure in Samoa, about 2 m (6.5 ft) high and 10–15 m (11–16 yds) in diameter, with several projecting arms. Their function is unknown, but was probably religious. They are apparently recent in date.

Starosel'e a Middle Palaeolithic cave-site in the Crimea (Ukraine). Four cultural layers containing artifacts and faunal remains were found in a sequence of loam and rubble deposits. The presence of arctic fox and reindeer indicates cold climatic conditions, and the upper levels have yielded radiocarbon and ESR/URANIUM SERIES dates of 40,000–50,000 BP. The tools include scrapers, points and bifacial foliates. A mass of wild ass remains (at least 287 individual animals) was found in possible association with the occupation, and may or may not reflect hunting of large herds. The skeleton of an anatomically modern human child was originally reported from the Middle Palaeolithic levels but is now widely believed to be intrusive and of relatively recent age. Starosel'e was excavated by Formozov during 1952–6, and by Marks in 1993–5.

state a type of society, characterized by a strong, centralized government, socio-economic class divisions and a market economy. Populations are normally very large, and have cities and monumental architecture. It represents the most complex form of social organization.

stater the Greek electrum and silver coin equivalent to the Near Eastern *shekel*. It was also the same as a *didrachm* (see DRACHMA).

statue-menhir a standing stone with carving of schematic human figures, some in relief, others simply engraved lines. Found in southern France, northern and eastern Italy, and on Corsica and Sardinia, they include female figures with breasts and necklaces, and heavily armed male warriors. Most statue-menhirs are of late Neolithic to Early Bronze Age date, but Iron Age examples are also known, e.g. in northern Corsica.

status an individual position or rank in society, and the responsibilities and privileges that go with it. Status can be either *achieved*, whereby an individual works to gain a particular status in the course of his/her lifetime, or *ascribed*, in which status is gained by being born into a particular class or family.

steatite or **soapstone** a soft, white to green massive rock consisting mostly of the clay mineral *talc*, a magnesium silicate which forms by hydrothermal alteration of ultrabasic rocks or by low-grade metamorphism of siliceous dolomites. The softness of steatite lends itself to carving and it was used to produce figurines and other carvings, jewellery, vessels, seals and decorative stone works. Steatite is fire resistant and was used to make moulds for metal casting.

Steenbokfontein a Stone Age cave on the western coast of the Western Cape Province of South Africa, containing a sequence of which the upper layers dating to the last 8,500 years have been excavated, as well as rock paintings of handprints, human figures and fat-tailed sheep. Of particular interest is the occurrence of painted slabs which apparently exfoliated from the cave wall and became covered with subsequent archaeological deposits in at least 3600 bp. This is the oldest known parietal art in southern Africa.

Steep Cliff Cave see SPIRIT CAVE.

Stein, Sir Mark Aurel (1862–1943) an archaeologist, Hungarian by birth and British by choice, who was perhaps the greatest archaeological explorer of Central and western Asia. His early training in SANSKRIT took him to India, where he developed an interest in antiquities to the north. Beginning in 1892 and continuing until 1930, Stein made four trips through western China and Khotan, where he documented a great many medieval monuments and caravan routes. Stein was made Superintendent of the Indian Archaeological Survey in 1910, a post he held until 1929, and he made a number of exploratory archaeological tours through Baluchistan and many parts of Iran, in which he located many important sites and made soundings in a number of them.

Steinheim a German site near Stuttgart where a female HOMINID skull with prominent brow-ridges and certain similarities to the SWANSCOMBE skull was recovered in 1933 from gravels dated to the HOLSTEINIAN INTERGLACIAL. The skull belongs to an early form of HOMO *sapiens* with specific NEANDERTHAL characteristics.

stela or **stele** an upright stone slab, often inscribed or carved in relief, and sometimes painted. In Egypt, the term denotes an upright slab (of stone or other durable material), usually with a rounded or flat top, upon which texts and illustrations intended to be of a permanent nature were inscribed. Funerary stelas were located in the publicly accessible superstructures of tombs; their subject matter related to the wellbeing of the deceased. Commemorative stelas were, typically, erected in temples as a record of a particular event, such as an endowment made to the temple by the king. Votive stelas recorded an individual's veneration of a particular deity or deities.

In MESOAMERICA, carved stone shafts are usually found with temples. Work by PROSKOURIAKOFF and others in deciphering them demonstrated that they are historical monuments recording the exploits and genealogy of rulers (see e.g. QUIRIGUÁ).

Stellmoor see AHRENSBURGIAN, HAMBURGIAN.

Stentinello a Neolithic village site near Syracuse in Sicily, Italy, enclosed by rock-cut ditches, type-site of the Sicilian Stentinello culture (*c.*5600–4400 BC). The characteristic pottery is a development of CARDIAL or IMPRESSED WARE, with exuberant decoration covering the whole surface of the pot, sometimes with white chalky incrustation.

Stephens, John Lloyd (1852–1905) an early explorer of the MAYA Lowlands. A New York lawyer, Stephens travelled with the Englishman Frederick CATHERWOOD in 1841 and 1843, and documented a number of little-known or unknown Maya sites. The accounts of these explorations, along with Catherwood's extraordinary drawings, provided an introduction to the ancient Maya Lowlands civilization.

step pyramid a transitional form of Egyptian royal tomb, between the MASTABA of the early ARCHAIC PERIOD and the true pyramid of the OLD KINGDOM. The only known completed step pyramid is that of DJOSER.

Sterkfontein a series of fossiliferous cave fillings dating from at least 3.3 million years ago, perhaps as old as 3.5 million years ago, in dolomite hills in western Gauteng Province, South Africa, which has produced some 600 HOMINID fossils, most of which comprise the largest collection of australopithecine (see AUSTRALOPITHECUS) fossils in southern Africa, as well as fossil bones

STERKFONTEIN, South Africa.

and teeth of many other animals. Between 1936 and 1947, Robert BROOM, later assisted by John Robinson, recovered many fossil remains of fauna and of gracile australopithecines, including in 1947 a complete adult skull some 2.5 million years old, described by Broom as *Plesianthropus transvaalensis* and nicknamed 'Mrs Ples' (now attributed to *Australopithecus africanus*; the possibility that it may be male is under investigation).

A subsequent ongoing excavation programme initiated by Phillip Tobias from 1966 continues to uncover early hominid fossils, including the discovery announced by Ron Clarke in 1997 of a 3.3 million-year-old australopithecine foot, dubbed 'Little Foot', which, while indicating bipedalism, also exhibits a mix of ape and human features including a big toe that could grasp objects like tree branches. In 1998, Clarke announced the discovery of the skull and associated rest of the skeleton of this creature, which is the most complete australopithecine skeleton yet discovered, and is currently still being excavated and studied.

Both *A. africanus* and a heavier flat-faced species, *Paranthropus robustus*, lived at Sterkfontein between about 3 and 2.5 million years ago, while a remarkably complete cranium found in 1976 and attributed to *Homo habilis* indicates the presence of this species at the site at least 1.8 million years ago. Some 3 million-year-old fossilized wood (of vines) indicates that the Sterkfontein environment was forested at that time. Stone artifacts include OLDOWAN collections dating to between 2 and 1.7 million years ago, ACHEULIAN assemblages some 1.5 million years old, as well as MIDDLE STONE AGE tools (see KROMDRAAI, MAKAPAN VALLEY, SWARTKRANS, TAUNG).

Steward, Julian Haynes (1902–72) an American archaeologist and ethnographer who worked on South American and Great Basin cultures, and was a major proponent of the re-emergence of evolutionary and ecological thought in American anthropology and archaeology. He argued that culture was heavily influenced by the specific local environment, and that regularities could thus be sought to explain cultural change.

Stichbandkeramik see STROKE-ORNAMENTED POTTERY CULTURE.

Stična an Early Iron Age fortified settlement with an associated group of BURIAL MOUNDS near Ljubljana in Slovenia, dated to the later part of the HALLSTATT period. The hilltop settlement at Stična was fortified by earth and stone walls which enclosed an area of about 32 ha (80 acres). Over 6,000 graves are known from the cemeteries, found primarily in about 140 burial mounds. Stična is located amidst iron deposits and a number of iron-smelting sites, which resulted in the development of this locality as a commercial centre.

Still Bay or **Stillbay** a MIDDLE STONE AGE industry named by A. J. H. GOODWIN after a holiday resort south of Riversdale in the southern Western Cape Province of South Africa, where early collections were made in eroded sands on a hill overlooking the resort, and characterized by thin pressure-flaked bifacial leaf-shaped points made on fine-grained raw materials like silcrete. See also BLOMBOS.

Stirling, Matthew Williams (1896–1975) an American archaeologist, best known for his extensive work on the OLMEC, including the sites of LA VENTA, SAN LORENZO, TRES ZAPOTES and Cerro de las Mesas.

stirrup jar or **false-necked amphora** a ceramic container used to transport oil or perfume. First found in MINOAN CRETE but more typical of MYCENAEAN Greece, they were widely exported.

stoa a Greek multipurpose colonnaded building, single- or double-storeyed. Stoas could serve as a seat for magistrates, as house shops and as dining-rooms. They are often found lining the edge of an AGORA or a TEMENOS, where they would have provided shade from the sun or protection from the rain. The stoa adjoining the agora at ATHENS was decorated with painted plaques showing scenes from the battle of MARATHON (see SOROS).

Stone Age 1 the oldest and longest division of the traditional THREE AGE SYSTEM devised by THOMSEN to

STIRRUP JAR.

classify the prehistoric period on the basis of technology. The Stone Age covers the period from the first production of stone artifacts to the first use of metals, and is of varying length in different areas of the world. It may be further subdivided into the Palaeolithic (Old), Mesolithic (Middle) and Neolithic (New) Stone Age.

2 (*sub-Saharan Africa*) the first and longest stage of human technology, beginning some 2.5 million years ago, and continuing in some areas until the 19th century AD, characterized by the production of tools made from stone as well as from other materials such as bone and wood. It is equivalent to the term Palaeolithic used in Europe and elsewhere. See also ACHEULIAN, GONA, GOODWIN, EARLIER, MIDDLE and LATER STONE AGES, MIDDLE AWASH, OLDOWAN.

stone circle a ring of standing stones, sometimes surrounded by a ditch. In Britain and Ireland, almost 1,000 stone circles are known, dating from the Neolithic and Early Bronze Age, famous examples being those of CALLANISH, AVEBURY and STONEHENGE. The earliest stone circles appear to be those of northern and western Britain, such as Stenness in Orkney and Castlerigg in the Lake District, which date to before 3000 BC. In some cases (notably at Callanish and Avebury) they are associated with avenues of stones which framed a ceremonial or processional approach to the circle itself. Much effort has been applied to the geometry and astronomy of stone circles. Earlier claims that a universal unit of measurement (the so-called 'MEGALITHIC YARD') was used in laying out these stone circles are now generally discounted. Claims that stone circles incorporate astronomical alignments on the rising and setting of the sun and moon at certain seasons of the year have received some support (notably the famous midsummer solstice alignment at Stonehenge), but arguments relating them to movements of the stars or planets are unconvincing. Though especially characteristic of Britain and Ireland, stone circles are also found in other regions of western Europe (such as the Pyrenees), and the arcs or horseshoe settings of standing stones in Brittany should probably be considered a related phenomenon.

Stonehenge a major Neolithic and Early Bronze Age ritual monument in Wiltshire, England. In its form (phase 1, c.2900 BC) Stonehenge was a circular monument surrounded by a bank with internal ditch c.100 m (110 yds) in diameter, and a ring of fifty-six AUBREY holes (originally holding timber posts, but later used for cremation burials) immediately inside the ditch. In phase 2, c.2900–2400 BC, a series of internal timber settings were raised in the interior, though the disturbance caused by subsequent modifications makes it impossible to establish the plan of this timber phase. At the beginning of phase 3 (c.2550–1650 BC) some eighty BLUESTONES were brought to the site from the Preseli Hills of southwestern Wales and set up in a double horseshoe arrangement. At the same time, the first section of the Avenue was built, flanked by banks and ditches and running over 500 m (550 yds) downhill from the entrance to the monument. A little later, these bluestones were removed and the present SARSEN circle with lintels enclosing a horseshoe arrangement of five massive sarsen TRILITHONS was put in place. The bluestones were subsequently re-erected in a circle and horseshoe shadowing the sarsens.

Further modifications to Stonehenge were made down to the end of phase 3 in c.1650 BC. Well known for its summer solstice orientation, Stonehenge has been interpreted as the temple of a sun or sky cult. Its social importance is reflected in the high density of Early Bronze Age burial mounds of the WESSEX CULTURE in the vicinity, including the Winterbourne Stoke and Normanton Down

STONEHENGE, England: some of the trilithons.

cemeteries, the latter including the famous BUSH BARROW.

stone line a descriptive term for a subsurface sheet of stones one layer thick within a soil which, when cut in vertical profile, appears as a line. Stone lines may consist wholly or in part of archaeological debris. Stone lines have various origins, including buried residual lag deposits on erosion surfaces, stony strata inherited from stratified material, and PEDOTURBATION with selective size-sorting. The contextual interpretation of any archaeological debris in stone lines depends upon proper interpretation of stone line genesis. See also STONE ZONE.

stoneware a ceramic fired above 1,000 °C and distinguished from earthenware by the formation of the mineral *mullite* in the ceramic body during firing. It is usually grey in colour, owing to firing in a reducing atmosphere in a kiln. In East Asia, stoneware was sporadically produced from the SHANG Dynasty onwards, but mass production did not begin until the 3rd century AD, when the technique was transferred to the Korean peninsula and then to Japan from KAYA. See also SUE.

stone zone a descriptive term for a subsurface BED of stones or stony material within a soil that is greater than one layer of stones thick. Stone zones may consist wholly or in part of archaeological debris. As with STONE LINES, stone zones have multiple origins, the correct assessment of which is necessary for the interpretation of any archaeological debris contained within the zone.

Stradonice a large Iron Age OPPIDUM in Bohemia, settled in the 2nd century BC during the LA TÈNE period. Stradonice was a production centre, particularly of fine painted ceramics. In addition, it contained a mint for coins, which are found within a 30 km (19 mile) radius.

Strandloper 1 'beachcomber'. A term originally used by European writers to refer to a small group of about fifty to eighty KHOEKHOE former herders, who called themselves the Goringhaicona ('Watermen'), and who settled near Cape Town in the 17th century ad. The term was last used in Dutch records in 1681. The innumerable SHELL MIDDENS along the southern African coast are sometimes popularly and incorrectly attributed to 'Strandlopers', who were erroneously thought to have subsisted exclusively on a marine diet. The middens represent regular or occasional visits to the coast to exploit marine resources by different groups of LATER STONE AGE people who lived at or near the coast as well as further afield, and whose diet comprised a wide variety of other foods as well.

2 (not widely used) a South African coastal LATER STONE AGE industry of the last 2,000 years, characterized by pottery, large flakes, flaked cobbles and rare retouched stone artifacts.

Stránská Skála a Lower Palaeolithic former cave-site

located near Brno in Moravia, Czech Republic. Artifacts are buried in cave, slope and loess deposits that apparently antedate the Middle Pleistocene (over 730,000 BP) on the basis of PALAEOMAGNETISM and associated fauna (e.g. sabre-tooth cat). The artifacts include chopping tools and flakes.

Strashnaya Cave a Middle Palaeolithic site in the Altai region of Siberia. Redeposited artifacts and faunal remains are buried in a deep sequence of loam and rubble. Among the faunal remains are woolly mammoth, steppe bison, red deer, horse and many others; the absence of arctic species indicates occupation during a mild climatic interval (prior to the last GLACIAL?). The artifacts include LEVALLOIS cores, scrapers and some denticulates. Strashnaya was excavated in 1969 and 1970 by OKLADNIKOV and Ovodov.

strata (*sing.* **stratum**) or **layers** informal SEDIMENTATION units greater than 1 cm (0.4 inch) thick, usually incorporated in BEDS.

stratification a structure in sedimentary rocks or sediment produced by deposition of more or less tabular units such as BEDS, STRATA and LAMINAE. Changes in depositional conditions and sediment supply cause changes in sediment composition, texture and internal sedimentary structures, resulting in deposition of a unit contrasting with the immediately underlying unit, and thereby giving rise to stratification. Stratification is the basis for STRATIGRAPHY, which has archaeological implications regarding environmental interpretation, sequencing of events and construction of CHRONOLOGIES.

stratigraphy the study of the formation, composition, sequence and correlation of statified sediment, soils and rocks. Stratigraphy is the principal means by which the context of archaeological deposits is evaluated, chronologies are constructed and events are sequenced. It is governed by a number of stratigraphic principles developed to help order materials and events in time and space. Among the underlying principles are:
(a) law of superposition – older BEDS or STRATA are overlain and buried by progressively younger beds or strata;
(b) law of cross-cutting relationships – a feature that cuts across or into a bed or stratum must be younger than that bed or stratum;
(c) included fragments – fragments, material or debris from an older bed may be incorporated in a younger bed, but not vice versa;
(d) correlation by fossil inclusions – strata may be correlated based on the sequence and uniqueness of their floral and faunal content.
These principles carry no implications for absolute age or age differences, although CHRONOMETRIC DATING techniques may aid in establishing temporal relationships.

Stratigraphy applied to archaeological concerns has variously been called 'archaeostratigraphy' or 'archaeological stratigraphy'. The stratigraphy of an archaeological site is invaluable for interpreting the sequence of deposition of the site, and thereby the relative ages of artifacts, features and other phenomena in the site.

Straubing group an Early Bronze Age regional group of Lower Bavaria, Germany, during the early 2nd millennium bc, sometimes classified as a regional variant of the ÚNĚTICE culture.

Strelets culture an early Upper Palaeolithic culture defined on the basis of several assemblages from the Oka-Don Lowland of the European Russia dating to c.40,000–25,000 bp; it exhibits some geographic and temporal variation. The earliest Strelets assemblages (e.g. lowest level of KOSTENKI I) reflect heavy emphasis on Middle Palaeolithic tools and techniques of production; the former include scrapers, points and bifaces. Later assemblages (e.g. SUNGIR') contain a higher percentage of typical Upper Palaeolithic forms such as scrapers and burins, as well as some non-stone tools and art objects. The most diagnostic tool type throughout the sequence is a small triangular bifacial point with a concave base.

Střelice a settlement of the LENGYEL culture in Moravia, Czech Republic, best known for the find of a clay model of a timber house with a gabled roof. This model provides our only direct glimpse of house construction in Neolithic Central Europe, otherwise known only from stains of POSTHOLES and bedding trenches in the soil.

Strettweg the findspot near Graz in Austria of an elaborate bronze model wagon, made up of a four-wheeled platform on which a female figure holds a bowl above her head, surrounded by male figures including four men on horseback wearing conical helmets and carrying shields and spears. The Strettweg 'cult wagon' belongs to the HALLSTATT cultural tradition, dated to the 6th century BC.

strigil a rounded bronze or silver scraper used in the Greek and Roman worlds to remove olive oil which was applied after bathing or taking exercise in the GYMNASIUM. On ATHENIAN POTTERY strigils are shown in the hands of athletes, often in conjunction with an ARYBALLOS.

striking platform the part of a core which is struck to produce a flake, and which becomes partially detached from the core with the flake. The striking platform may be plain, or it may be prepared or flattened by removing small facets to produce a longer and thinner flake.

Stroke-Ornamented Pottery culture an early/middle Neolithic culture of West-Central Europe (Bohemia, southwestern Poland, eastern and southern Germany) which follows the LINEAR POTTERY culture in this area between *c.*5000 and 4700 BC. On Stroke-Ornamented pottery, the continuous incised lines that characterize Linear pottery disappear and are replaced by lines of small stroke-like jabs or depressions. LONGHOUSES of the Stroke-Ornamented Pottery culture (often called by its German name, *Stichbandkeramik*) are often slightly trapezoidal in plan.

Strong, William Duncan (1899–1962) an American who was a pioneer in Plains archaeology. He helped develop the Direct Historical Approach of working back through archaeological sequences from the known historical past, and made significant contributions to the development of a distinct archaeological theory in the years between the two world wars.

structural archaeology a branch of archaeology, closely linked to POSTPROCESSUAL ARCHAEOLOGY, which studies culture as a set of symbols and codes that determine how individuals act in a society. Culture must be viewed as more than just an adaptation to the environment. These structural codes connote particular meanings to members of society, meanings that can change depending on their particular context. Thus, a safety pin used in association with a baby has one set of meanings, but connotes an entirely different meaning if used as decoration by a punk rocker. Structural archaeology is concerned with how individuals manipulate the meaning of MATERIAL CULTURE, as embedded in structural codes, in order to make new statements and to create new meanings. Because of its concern with the meanings evoked by the symbolic nature of material culture, structural archaeology is virtually synonymous with what is often called *symbolic* or *cognitive* archaeology.

stucco a lime plaster, especially that used for creating interior architectural elements such as masks or for providing a surface for walls.

stupa a Buddhist monument, usually built to contain relics associated with the Buddha or other holy people or sacred texts; miniature stupas might also be built as votive offerings, and Hindus of the Jainist sect built stupas in commemoration of saints. They occur throughout the Buddhist world, and tend to be constructed in places sacred to Buddhism, but the architectural form varies in different regions (domed in northern India, multi-stage pagodas in China, Japan and Korea, terraced temples in Java). One of the best-known Indian stupas is the 2nd-century BC complex at Sanchi (in Madhya Pradesh), which comprises domed stupas on circular bases, enclosed by stone railings ornamented with carved reliefs showing events in Buddha's life and mythological figures.

Sturts Meadows a PANARAMITEE site in western New South Wales, Australia, about 40 km (25 miles) from MUT-AWINTJI. The engravings occur on a series of mudstone

outcrops extending for over a kilometre (0.6 mile). Radiocarbon dating of carbonate DESERT VARNISH on the engravings has yielded a minimum age of 10,000 bp.

Subalyuk a Middle Palaeolithic cave-site located in the Bükk Mountains of northeastern Hungary. Artifacts and faunal remains are buried in clay and rubble deposits; ibex predominates in the lower levels, but cave bear predominates in the upper. Middle Palaeolithic tools (chiefly scrapers) occur in both lower and upper levels, and appear to pre-date the last GLACIAL. Human skeletal remains, exhibiting classic NEANDERTHAL characteristics, were found in the upper levels.

Sub-Atlantic climatic period the last of five POST-GLACIAL climatic periods of northern Europe defined on the basis of POLLEN ANALYSIS by Blytt and Sernander, beginning *c.*1500 bc. The Sub-Atlantic period is characterized by a continuation of the trends towards dampness and coolness that began during the preceding SUB-BOREAL period.

Sub-Boreal climatic period one of five POSTGLACIAL climatic and vegetational periods defined by Blytt and Sernander on the basis of POLLEN ANALYSIS, dated between *c.*5000 and 3500 bp. In northern Europe, the Sub-Boreal has been thought of as a cooler and drier period, especially in contrast to the preceding warmer and more humid ATLANTIC period, but it now appears that in Central and southern Europe the climate became moister because of the southward displacement of the polar air masses and the resultant climatic perturbation.

Suberde a small ACERAMIC NEOLITHIC settlement near Lake Sugla in southern Turkey, excavated by Jacques Bordaz in the 1960s and 1970s. It presents a later 7th-millennium BC example of a relatively permanent community which seems to have relied heavily on hunting (sheep, goat, cattle, pig) and some harvesting of possibly wild cereals (an inference based on SICKLE SHEEN and grinding equipment). The case of a possibly specialized hunter's village in a landscape of farming communities is also presented at MUREYBET and UMM DABAGHIYAH.

Submycenaean the transitional phase which bridges the Late HELLADIC and PROTOGEOMETRIC periods in mainland Greece. Although characterized on the basis of the pottery from cemeteries in Attica, Submycenaean is also attested stratigraphically on sites in central Greece and the Peloponnese. It would appear to have been a relatively short phase and is dated *c.*1050–1020 BC.

subsistence that part of the overall economy of a society concerned with the acquisition, production and distribution of food resources.

Sue a Japanese grey, unglazed stoneware of the late 5th–14th centuries AD, derived from the KAYA stoneware traditions on the Korean peninsula. Originally imported and then centrally produced in Japan for funerary use, it was deposited in MOUNDED TOMBS of the KOFUN period for containing food offerings. Within the RITSURYO state it became a standardized court service ware, and production sites were decentralized to the provinces to supply additional regional administrative headquarters. Compare HAJI.

Sukhaya Mechetka or **Volgograd** a Middle Palaeolithic open-air site on the Volga River at Volgograd in European Russia. The occupation horizon rests on the surface of a buried soil thought to be of last INTERGLACIAL age, underlying a thick bed of slope deposits. Among the heavily weathered faunal remains, steppe bison is the most common species. The artifacts include both scrapers and bifacial foliates. Along with KHOTYLEVO I, Sukhaya Mechetka represents one of the few last Interglacial sites on the Russian Plain. The site was discovered by Grishchenko in 1951, and excavated by Zamyatnin from 1952–4.

Sukhothai the capital of the first Thai kingdom (AD 1290–*c*.1350) in northern-central Thailand, founded by King Ramkhamhaeng and comprising a walled enclosure, 1.7 by 1.3 km (1.1 by 0.8 miles), with many brick temples and water tanks within and outside the enclosure. The Ramkhamhaeng inscription of AD 1292 on a square stone column, written in KHMER, MON and Thai, is said to provide the first evidence of Thai as a written language, although its authenticity has since been questioned. The city expanded outwards from its core towns of Sukhothai and SI SATCHANALAI late in the 13th century, then coming under the influence of the state of Ayuthya in the 15th century. Its best-known remains include a collection of Buddha images of a distinctive style (to which the state has given its name), and a range of glazed stoneware vessels (characterized by under-glaze decoration in black/brown on a cream SLIP) produced by kilns in the town during the 14th–15th centuries, and forming part of the repertoire of the much larger industry at Si Satchanalai.

sumatralith a unifacially flaked discoid stone tool, often formed on a thin slice of the CORTEX of a large pebble, characteristic of some HOABINHIAN assemblages in Southeast Asia, particularly in coastal SHELL MIDDENS in northern Sumatra..

Sumerian king lists a group of CUNEIFORM documents assembled in the early 2nd millennium BC in southern MESOPOTAMIA which offer a partly mythical and partly historical summary of ruling dynasties. Beginning with the lowering of kingship from the heavens, the list begins with a series of kings, first at ERIDU and then at other cities, who ruled for tens of thousands of years; this series ends with the flood. Afterwards, kingship was once again lowered, first at KISH and then at other cities; the earlier

of these kings reigned for hundreds of years but regnal spans soon became biologically plausible and some of these rulers (especially at Kish) are known from contemporary EARLY DYNASTIC documents (see GILGAMESH). The list continues to the early 2nd millennium. In addition to its mythical aspects, the king list is not an attempt at history, as it presents contemporary rulers as sequential in time, and does not include many important dynasties (e.g. that of Lagash; see TELLO). Rather, the variations of list have a political purpose, namely to validate contemporary royal authority by lineally tracing kings at the time of their composition to the beginnings of kingship in southern Mesopotamia.

Sumerian question the traditional academic question of Sumerian origins, in both a cultural and, especially, a linguistic sense. The Sumerian language has no known relatives, and is poorly understood, making impossible the kinds of comparative analyses found in INDO-EUROPEAN studies. To the extent that the archaic CUNEIFORM texts of southern MESOPOTAMIA (i.e. those of the late URUK and JEMDET NASR periods, in the later 4th millennium BC) are comprehended, the language is already Sumerian. Some elementary Sumerian vocabulary (some place names, terms in basic economic activities) is often argued to be adopted from some pre-Sumerian population, implying a movement of Sumerian speakers into a southern Mesopotamia that was already occupied by settled agriculturists. However, this linguistic argument is contested, and the archaeological record reveals no perceptible break in a continuous cultural development. In short, the Sumerian question is a problem not at present open to solution.

Sumerians people speaking and writing Sumerian who are the earliest documented inhabitants of southern MESOPOTAMIA. Sumerian is unrelated to any other known language, and considerable controversy surrounds the question of Sumerian origins (see SUMERIAN QUESTION). The Sumerians, along with AKKADIAN-speaking elements in southern Mesopotamia, created in the late 4th and 3rd millennia BC a tradition of social and political organization, art, literature and religious observation that greatly influenced neighbouring cultures and provided many of the central features that defined the Mesopotamian world until the end of its existence.

sun-dagger see FAJADA BUTTE.

Sundaland the enlarged Southeast Asian continental region created by the drop in sea-levels during periods of GLACIATION, which connected much of western Indonesia to the mainland.

Sungir' an Upper Palaeolithic open-air site on the Klyaz'ma River (Oka tributary) near Vladimir in European Russia. After the Pechora Basin sites (e.g. BYZOVAYA), it is the northernmost Palaeolithic site in Europe. The occupation horizon is associated with a buried soil in slope deposits overlying a bedrock promontory, and appears to date to c.25,000 bp, although radiocarbon estimates range between 25,500 and 14,600 bp. Reindeer is the most common species among the fauna. The site is best known for its spectacular burials, which contain three complete skeletons and numerous associated ornaments and art objects, including ivory spears, bracelets, brooches, ivory beads (c.10,000) and over 200 perforated fox teeth. The artifacts, which include small triangular bifacial points and many typical Middle Palaeolithic forms, have been compared to the STRELETS CULTURE assemblages from KOSTENKI. Sungir' was discovered in 1955, and excavated by BADER during 1956–70.

sun temple a religious structure built by kings of the 5th Dynasty of Egypt for the worship of the sun-god RE. Architecturally the sun temple resembles the pyramid complexes of the same period, with valley temple and causeway leading to the Upper Temple. The main elements of the Upper Temple were a large open court, containing an altar, which stood before a monumental, squat, masonry-built obelisk. Of the six sun temples known to have been built, only those at ABUSIR and ABU GHURAB have so far been located.

Surkh Kotal an imperial seat of the KUSHAN, located in northeastern Afghanistan. French excavations here focused on the 2nd-century AD dynastic shrine of the great Kushan king Kanisha (perhaps AD 78–142), an impressive hill-slope monument of multiple levels connected by staircases, at the top of which sat a fire temple.

survey or **surveying** 1 the examination of the surface of the earth for archaeological SITES, and their recording and preliminary analysis. Because of constraints of time and money, many surveys are sample surveys, in which only a portion of the total area under consideration is actually examined. Samples can be drawn either intuitively, in which the archaeologists only look at those areas in which they feel sites will be found; or they can be statistically generated using a variety of techniques. The latter type of sample is more representative of the total area, and thus more accurate.
2 the three-dimensional plotting of a site, its features and artifacts, using a variety of techniques borrowed mostly from civil engineering. Techniques can range in sophistication from a hand-held compass and hand-drawn map, to computer- and satellite-assisted location systems. See also EXCAVATION, TRANSIT, THEODOLITE, PLANE TABLE, ALIDADE.

Susa one of the great sites of western Asia, a capital of ELAM lying in the Khuzistan lowlands in southwestern Iran, at the southeastern edge of the MESOPOTAMIAN alluvial plain. Systematic excavation here began in the 1880s, and has been continued over the past century by a succession of French teams. These efforts reveal an unbroken succession of occupation from the late 5th millennium BC to early medieval times. The archaeology of Susa does not present a single encompassing cultural sequence, but rather a series of sequences from separate excavation areas loosely tied together by ceramic parallels and periods in the city's history (see ACROPOLE OF SUSA). The cultural and political history of Susa traces multiple cycles of alternately looking towards the civilizations of southern Mesopotamia to the west and integrating with peoples in the mountains to the east; in the latter connection, Susa was traditionally associated with Anshan (Tepe MALYAN) in Fars. Susa was frequently controlled or deeply influenced by a succession of Mesopotamian neighbours, but just as frequently was the centre of autonomous Elamite states, and often invaded BABYLONIA. Susa's success in the latter regard is reflected in the numerous pieces of famous Mesopotamian art that have been recovered there (including the Victory STELA of NARAM-SIN, HAMMURABI's law code, and many KASSITE KUDURRU).

Susquehanna tradition a late ARCHAIC TRADITION in northeastern North America which is characterized by particular stemmed points and knives. Some of the earliest point styles may have evolved from earlier PIEDMONT TRADITION forms.

Suswa/Salasun an early PASTORAL NEOLITHIC pottery tradition found only in highland Kenya, dating to 4860 bp at ENKAPUNE YA MUTO.

Sutkagen-dor a Mature HARAPPAN settlement and presumed port on the coast of Makran, western Pakistan. Limited investigation indicates the town was divided into citadel and lower town areas, a common pattern of INDUS CIVILIZATION urbanism.

Sutton Hoo a group of 6th- and 7th-century AD burial mounds in Suffolk, England, marking the royal cemetery of the Wuffingas, early ANGLO-SAXON kings of East Anglia. The fame of the site rests on the discovery in 1939 of a richly furnished ship-burial beneath mound 1, with sword, shield and decorated helmet of Swedish style, large gold belt buckle with intricate animal interlace, and purse and cloak clasps with designs in multi-coloured glass. There were also Merovingian gold coins from France and silver vessels from BYZANTIUM, providing further testimony to the importance of the deceased, who may have been the powerful East Anglian ruler Raedwald (d. 625). The site has been excavated by C. W. Phillips and, more recently, by M. Carver.

Šventoji a group of sites near the Baltic coast in western Lithuania of the NARVA CULTURE, dated to the late 4th millennium BC, and the RZUCZEWO CULTURE, dated to the 3rd millennium BC. At Šventoji 23, the Narva population lived in timber houses and lived by fishing, hunting and gathering, supplemented with some domestic plants and animals. Later, the Rzuczewo community at Šventoji 6 cultivated cereals and collected hazelnuts and water chestnuts.

Swahili ware see TANA WARE.

Swanscombe, Barnfield Pit a well-stratified British Lower Palaeolithic site by the River Thames which has yielded a fragmented skull belonging to an early form of HOMO *sapiens* with strong NEANDERTHAL characteristics. Typical CLACTONIAN artifacts have been recovered from the Lower Gravel, an ACHEULIAN pointed biface assemblage has come from the Middle Gravel, and the Upper Loam has produced a refined OVATE Acheulian assemblage.

Swarling see AYLESFORD.

Swartkrans a fossiliferous cave filling, thought to date between 1.8 and 1 million years ago, 1 km (0.6 mile) northwest of STERKFONTEIN, in western Gauteng Province, South Africa. Since 1948, the site has produced many fossils of the heavily built australopithecine, AUSTRALOPITHECUS *robustus*, as well as less abundant remains of early HOMO (previously named *Telanthropus capensis* and more recently *H. erectus*, but whose species identification is the subject of ongoing study), as well as large collections of faunal remains. The deposits contain DEVELOPED OLDOWAN as well as MIDDLE STONE AGE artifacts.

Of particular interest are 1.8–1 million-year-old polished and scratched bones, which replication experiments by C. K. 'Bob' Brain suggest were used to dig up edible bulbs and roots. It has also been suggested that they may have been used to extract termites from their nests. They may even have been carried around in skin bags or bundles. Brain and Andrew Sillen have argued that the chemical analysis of carbon residues and the spatial distribution of 1 million-year-old burnt bones indicates that they were burnt in camp fires and may be early evidence for the use of controlled fire. Brain's analysis of how australopithecine and other animal bones were deposited in the cave, through predation by large cats such as leopards and sabre tooths, is a classic pioneering study in the field of TAPHONOMY.

Sweden see Scandinavia.

Sweet Track a Neolithic timber trackway preserved in the waterlogged peat deposits of the SOMERSET LEVELS, England, and excavated by J. and B. Coles. The track was an ingenious raised plank walkway running for 1,800 m (1,970 yds) across wet reed swamp from the southern end of the Levels to Westhay Island. DENDROCHRONOLOGY has dated the construction precisely to the winter of 3807/3806 BC, making it Europe's oldest road.

swidden agriculture a system of farming in which fields are prepared by cutting down the natural vegetation,

letting it dry and burning it off. This technique serves to clear the field and enrich the soil with nutrients from the ash. Swidden fields are generally productive for no more than a few years, after which the farmer moves to a new area and repeats the process. Swidden agriculture is common throughout much of MESOAMERICA. See also SHIFTING CULTIVATION.

Swiderian a late Upper Palaeolithic industry of Poland characterized by burins, scrapers and SWIDERIAN POINTS. Swiderian sites are associated with dune deposits dating to the end of the Pleistocene (c.11,000–9000 BP). See also BROMMIAN.

Swiderian point a type of stone point manufactured on a blade, with a stemmed base flaked on both sides. It is found in sites of the SWIDERIAN industry in Poland.

Swidry a group of Upper Palaeolithic open-air sites located along the Vistula River in Poland. Concentrations of artifacts (including scrapers, burins and SWIDERIAN POINTS) are deposited on sand dunes thought to date to the end of the Pleistocene (c.11,000 BP). These sites are assigned to the SWIDERIAN culture.

Swieciechów flint a variety of flint from the HOLY CROSS MOUNTAINS of central Poland (compare CHOCOLATE FLINT, CMIELÓW). It is dark grey to black in colour with flecks of white or light grey. It was exploited primarily by communities of the FUNNEL BEAKER culture and was distributed over a broad area in the Bug, Vistula and Oder drainages. Swieciechów flint is commonly found in the form of very large blades up to 30 cm (1 ft) long, and axes.

Sydney Cove a well-preserved wreck found in 1977 on Preservation Island in the Furneaux Group, Bass Strait, Australia, and the subject of detailed archaeological research since then. Wrecked in 1797, she was the first merchant ship to founder in Australian waters after the settlement of New South Wales; her cargo of spirits attests to the importance of the rum trade in the colony. Expeditions mounted after the wreck established the existence of Bass Strait.

syllabic *adj.* denoting scripts such as LINEAR A and B in which each of the signs represents a syllable.

symbolic archaeology see STRUCTURAL ARCHAEOLOGY.

Symbolkeramik CHALCOLITHIC pottery of ALMERIA found at LOS MILLARES and similar sites, decorated with incised *oculi* or 'rayed sun' motifs, sometimes in pairs.

symposium a male drinking-session held at the end of a Greek meal. Scenes of the symposium frequently appear as the decoration on Greek pottery. These show the wide range of activities which took place in addition to drinking, such as music, singing, games and sexual intercourse. Many of the vessel forms of Greek pottery are connected to the symposium either as cups or for containing or mixing the wine and water. See also AMPHORA, KRATER, PELIKE, KLINE.

synchronic or **synchronous** *adj.* occurring simultaneously or at the same time. The term is often used in correlation of events or bounding surfaces of STRATIGRAPHIC units, or to characterize the equivalency of age across a widespread bounding surface. Compare DIACHRONIC. See also ISOCHRONOUS.

Syracuse a Corinthian colony in southeastern Sicily, traditionally founded *c.*734 BC. The city took advantage of the fine natural harbour. The earliest settlement was on the island of Ortygia, whereas later settlement was on the mainland in the area known as Achradina. A series of temples were constructed in the 6th century BC in both the DORIC and IONIC ORDERS. The temple of Athena was later incorporated into the cathedral. On the mainland are remains of the theatre, as well as the quarries which also served as a prison in the late 5th century BC. The city was defended by the Euryalus fort. In 21 BC the city became a Roman colony. Roman remains include a substantial AMPHITHEATRE constructed in the 3rd century AD.

systems theory see GENERAL SYSTEMS THEORY.

Syuren' I an Upper Palaeolithic cave-site in the Crimea, Ukraine. Three occupation horizons are buried in a thick bed of sand and rubble. The most common species among the faunal remains are saiga and arctic fox, the latter indicating cold climatic conditions. The age of the occupations is unclear; they are thought to date to the earlier Upper Palaeolithic on typological grounds. Many elements typical of the Middle Palaeolithic (e.g. points) and AURIGNACIAN industry (e.g. keeled endscrapers) are present. Along with ADZHI-KOBA, Syuren' I represents one of the rare Upper Palaeolithic sites of the Crimea. The site was investigated by Merezhkovskij in 1879–80, and by Bonch-Osmolovskij in 1926–9.

Szakalhát-Lebo group a middle Neolithic culture of the Tisza River Valley in eastern Hungary, succeeding the Alföld variant of the LINEAR POTTERY CULTURE south of the Körös River, and preceding the TISZA culture between

*c.*5000 and 4800 BC. Settlements of this group, such as Csóka, have small rectangular single-room structures. The figurines resemble those of the early phases of the VINČA culture immediately to the south, but the pottery is decorated in patterns associated with the Alföld Linear Pottery variant.

Szegvár-Tűzköves a settlement of the TISZA culture in eastern Hungary at which a stratified TELL is flanked by a contemporaneous single-layer settlement. Szegvár-Tűzköves is famous for its human figurines, both male and female, which are depicted as seated on a 'throne'. Small groups of burials, of which a total of seventy-seven have been excavated, are found within the settlement. Skeletons are contracted, with males lying on the right side and most females on their left.

Szeleta Cave a prehistoric cave-site located on the Szinva River in the Bükk Mountains of northeastern Hungary. Artifacts and faunal remains (cave bear [predominant], reindeer and woolly mammoth) are buried in rubble and 'cave earth' deposits. The lowest cultural layer comprises a small quantity of Middle Palaeolithic (?) artifacts. The overlying layer contains an assemblage (including laurel-leaf points and scrapers) assigned to the early Upper Palaeolithic SZELETIAN industry; it yielded a radiocarbon date of 41,700 bp. Szeletian assemblages also occur in the upper layers, the youngest of which yielded a date of 32,620 bp, and Neolithic remains were found near the surface. Szeleta Cave was excavated by Hillebrand in 1906–13 and VÉRTES in 1966.

Szeletian an early Upper Palaeolithic industry of Central Europe characterized by bifacial foliates and sidescrapers; later assemblages contain more endscrapers and retouched blades. The industry dates to the middle of the last GLACIAL, and appears to develop from the local Middle Palaeolithic (MICOQUIAN). The Szeletian was defined by PROŠEK in 1953.

Szelim a prehistoric cave-site located near the River Danube in northern-central Hungary. Artifacts and faunal remains (including cave bear [predominant], reindeer, and woolly mammoth) are buried in loess and clay. The lower cultural layer contains a Middle Palaeolithic assemblage (e.g. sidescrapers) which probably dates to the beginning of the last GLACIAL. Late Upper Palaeolithic, Neolithic and younger remains occur in the upper layers.

T

taap knife a saw-knife, known only from the southwest of Western Australia, comprising small stone chips mounted in a row on a wooden handle. In ethnographic specimens, the chips are unretouched and irregular in shape, but backed microliths may have been used in the past.

Tabarin a northern Kenyan site which has yielded an early HOMINID mandible fragment dated between 5.15 and 4.15 million years ago and ascribed to AUSTRALOPI-THECUS *praegens*.

Tabon Caves a series of caves on Palawan in the Philippines which have produced remains ranging in date from *c*.22,000 bc to the late metal age. The skeletal material of Tabon Cave (*c*.22,000–20,000 bc) is younger than dates at NIAH, but perhaps more securely dated, and it falls within the same date range as LEANG BURUNG 2 in Sulawesi. Later remains at the caves include jar burials of the 1st millennium BC and later, related both in form and in contents (LINGLING-O, double-headed animal pendant) to SA HUYNH on the Vietnamese coast and KALANAY in the islands.

Tabun Cave a Palaeolithic site in the MOUNT CARMEL complex, Israel, with the thickest accumulation of cultural deposits, excavated by GARROD 1931–4, by Jelinek (1967–72) and by Ronen since 1975. Garrod established that EL-WAD and Tabun together comprised the longest stratigraphic sequence in the Near East. According to recent estimates based on ESR, THERMOLUMINESCENCE and PALAEOMAGNETIC dates, Tabun may span some 800,000 years or more. It remains the archaeological yardstick for the Early and Middle Palaeolithic of the Levant. Using Garrod's STRATIGRAPHY, layer G contains the earliest occupational horizon, with a flake industry too poor to be characterized. Layer F (upper ACHEULIAN) has abundant and fine handaxes, scrapers, and other flake tools; layer E, subdivided a–d by Garrod, contains an Acheulo-Yabrudian industry with (close to the top of the layer) an AMUDIAN horizon; layers D, C, B and the Chimney are LEVALLOISO-MOUSTERIAN. An adult female NEANDERTHAL skeleton was recovered by Garrod in 1932 from an uncertain provenance in layer C, B or the Chimney, and a mandible from layer C, similar to the archaic modern human populations of SKHUL and QAFZEH.

Taforalt a large Moroccan cave, excavated by J. Roche, with a long sequence from MOUSTERIAN, through ATERIAN to an IBEROMAURUSIAN SHELL MIDDEN on top. A large Iberomaurusian cemetery of 185 people, including 100 children, of MECHTA-AFALOU type, is dated to 11,900 bp. The site's lowest Iberomaurusian layers have been dated to *c*.22,000 bp.

Tagalagal an open-air Neolithic site at the foot of an inselberg in the northern Bagzanes massif of the Aïr of northeastern Niger, associated with radiocarbon dates of 9330 and 9370 bp, which are the oldest dates for a site with ceramics in the Sahara. Stone tools include burin-like flakes and delicate arrowheads, as well as much grinding equipment.

Taho-ri a cemetery of jar and coffin burials on the southern Korean coast, spanning the PROTO-THREE KINGDOMS to THREE KINGDOMS periods (see KOREA). One burial had a separate pit for grave-goods: bronze and iron spearheads, Star-and-Cloud bronze mirrors of mid-early HAN date, an animal buckle, a small bronze bell, and wushu coins; organic remains coated with lacquer included a brush handle, sword hilt and sheath, and wooden container. These goods indicate a higher literate and skilled craft society than was previously thought to have co-existed with the LELANG COMMANDERY in the north.

taiga see BOREAL FOREST.

Taima-Taima a site in Venezuela at which were found mastodon bones and a small quantity of stone tools. It has been suggested by R. Gruhns and A. L. Bryan that the site represents a pre-CLOVIS occupation, between 12,000 and 15,000 years ago. Other scholars question whether the tools were truly associated with the bones.

Taínos an ARAWAKAN group encountered by Columbus on his arrival in the Antilles in AD 1492. They flourished between the 12th and 15th centuries AD on the islands of Santo Domingo and Puerto Rico, where there are remains of ceremonial plazas (some possibly ball courts), and permanent villages of up to 1,000 houses. The Taínos appear to have developed from earlier cultures such as the OSTIONOID groups, and were organized into chiefdoms. They were farmers, and expert navigators who crisscrossed the Caribbean. They produced works of art in wood, bone, shell and stone, and are particularly noteworthy for their highly developed CHICOID wares, named after Boca Chica, in the southern Dominican Republic. They also left PARIETAL ART throughout the Antilles. The Spanish conquest led to their disappearance: by 1550, scarcely 500 survived on Santo Domingo. See also MEILLACOID.

Taipivai Valley a site on Nuku Hiva in the Marquesas Islands in Polynesia, with many stone structures. These include VAHANGEKU'A, and anthropomorphous stone statues of a type also known from the PUAMAU VALLEY.

Tairona a late prehistoric culture in northeastern Colombia, organized at the level of a CHIEFDOM. One of the larger sites is Pueblito, which includes as many as 3,000 houses, as well as public architecture. Most sites are villages, with a central PLATFORM MOUND.

Tajín see EL TAJÍN.

Takamatsuzuka a MOUNDED TOMB of the KOFUN period dating to the late 7th century AD. Located in Nara Prefecture, Japan, the small round mound, 18 m (59 ft) in diameter and 5 m (16 ft) high, contains a stone chamber with plastered walls bearing painted murals of the Chinese directional symbols (see MURAL TOMBS). These were first assigned to KOGURYO influence, but recent opinion favours a Tang attribution (see CHINESE DYNASTIES). The tomb belonged to an aristocrat of the YAMATO state with continental connections.

Takamori the earliest date for the Palaeolithic period in Japan currently stands at c.500,000 bp with the discovery of the Takamori II site. Unlike initial Palaeolithic datings at HOSHINO, which were based on radiocarbon and pushing to the limits of the technique, the recent determinations by the Sekki Bunka Danwakai (Stone-tool Culture Discussion Group) have been made with a suite of dating techniques all generally conforming to each other. TEPHRA 1 overlying the tool layer at Takamori II was dated to 430,000–610,000 bp by ELECTRON SPIN RESONANCE (ESR) and to 460,000–490,000 by PALAEOMAGNETISM; Tephra 5, directly above 1, was dated by THERMOLUMINESCENCE (TL) to 380,000–520,000. Materials for ESR were not very suitable at Takamori II, and although the ESR dates for five strata were consistently older the deeper they were buried, a difference of 10,000 was noted between ESR (older) and TL (newer) datings of the strata.

The lithics at Takamori, estimated at c.500,000 bp, are mainly small flakes (c.3 cm [1.2 inches]) of CHALCEDONY and jasper – worked bifacially into knives and scrapers – and a few larger picks and axes (c.8 cm [3 inches]) made of coarser crystalline TUFF and shale. These attributes, together with the fact that the tools are irregular as regards striking platform and working edge, are also common to the ZHOUKOUDIAN 1 assemblages in China between 200,000 and 500,000 bp. The makers of the Zhoukoudian tools are known through fossil finds to have been HOMO *erectus*, but no fossils of ancient HOMINIDs have yet been found in Japan. Some archaeologists assume the date of the Takamori II site indicates *H. erectus* occupation of the mountainous edge of Palaeolithic East Asialand (now the Japanese Islands), but this line of thinking is clearly being suppressed in the face of lack of fossil finds.

Takht-i Suleiman a sanctuary and pilgrimage destination of PARTHIAN, SASSANIAN and early Islamic date in Iranian Azerbaijan. The original structure (3rd century BC) consisted of several MESOPOTAMIAN-style temples set upon an ACHAEMENID style platform.

Takuapa an early historic settlement and religious centre in peninsular Thailand, connected to the port at KO KHO KAO, with remains indicating contact with South India from the late 1st to the early 2nd millennia AD.

Talasea an obsidian source on the north coast of New Britain, BISMARCK ARCHIPELAGO. Talasea obsidian first occurs in Late Pleistocene contexts at MATENKUPKUM and MATENBEK, and is widely distributed in early LAPITA sites throughout MELANESIA; in later Lapita sites, it tends to decline in importance relative to LOU obsidian.

talatat stone blocks of relatively small size (the Arabic term refers to three hand-breadths) used in Egypt for the rapid construction of temples of the AMARNA PERIOD.

talayot a massive Bronze Age dry-stone tower, usually with central chamber, found on the Balearic Islands. Roughly equivalent to the Sardinian NURAGHE, talayots display a broader range of forms with circular, square and stepped examples. Many later became the centre of a small village of dry-stone houses.

talc see STEATITE.

talent a unit of Greek and Near Eastern weight. It was the equivalent of sixty MINAS; at ATHENS it would have weighed 25.86 kg (57.01 lbs), and on AEGINA 37.80 kg (83.33 lbs).

Talepakemalai see ELOAUA ISLAND.

Talgai the site in southern Queensland of the first human fossil skull found in Australia, in 1886. The cranium is robust and archaic-looking, resembling the KOW SWAMP material. It has not been firmly dated, but the deposits in which it was found have a minimum age of 14,000 to 16,000 bp.

Talgua Cave a cave-site in the Olancho Valley, northeastern Honduras, in which a burial chamber was discovered in 1994, containing numerous 3,000-year-old skeletons, together with offerings of jade, marble and ceramics. Most were secondary burials, the bones painted with red ochre. Some bones had become covered with glistening calcite, so that initial reports of the site called it the 'cave of glowing skulls'.

Talheim see LINEAR POTTERY.

Tallgren, Arne Michael (1885–1945) a Finnish archaeologist who specialized in the prehistory of Russia and Siberia, specifically of the Bronze Age of the Ural and the Altai Mountains. In 1923 he was appointed to the chair of archaeology at Helsinki University. Tallgren founded the journal *Eurasia Septentrionalis Antiqua*, which provided a forum for archaeologists working in northern Eurasia during the 1920s. Although stripped of his honorary membership of the Academy for the History of Material Culture for his denunciation of the ideological purges of Soviet archaeologists in the early 1930s, Tallgren was instrumental in promoting contact between Soviet and Western prehistorians during this era.

Tamar Hat a small, but very rich Algerian cave, probably a camp for hunting Barbary sheep, with 3 m (9ft) of IBEROMAURUSIAN remains. These show only gradual change through time, indicating reuse of the site by people and their descendants for nearly 5,000 years. This is the only Iberomaurusian sequence excavated to bedrock, where it is dated at c.20,600 bp. It has been suggested that the Barbary sheep herds may have been 'managed' by culling animals selectively. See also AR-AMBOURG.

Tamaya Mellet one of several sites in the Tamesna of Niger in Africa, containing bone harpoons associated with lacustrine fauna at c.9400 bp although this date has been questioned. See also 'AQUALITHIC'.

tambo or **tampu** a waystation along the INCA road system. Tambos were located a day's travel apart, and equipped with storehouses and rest houses. More elaborate tambos were established every four or five days' travel apart. Stationed at each tambo were runners, *chaski*, who carried messages in relay fashion throughout the empire.

Tambo Colorado an INCA administrative centre located in the Andean foothills in the Pisco Valley of south coastal Peru. The site is well preserved, including red-painted walls which give the site its name. It lies along an important Inca road connecting the coast with VILCAS GUAMAN.

Tambo Viejo a large site in the Acarí Valley of the south coast of Peru. It was occupied during early NASCA phases of the EARLY INTERMEDIATE PERIOD, and represents an extension of Nasca culture to the south. A part of the site was reoccupied during INCA times, when it served as a TAMBO along the royal highway of the Inca.

Tambralinga an early historic state located in peninsular Thailand in the later 1st and early 2nd millennium AD, centred probably on NAKHON SI THAMMARAT, and possibly encompassing CHAIYA.

Tampanian the stone tool industry of KOTA TAMPAN.

tampu see TAMBO.

Tana ware or **Early Kitchen ware** or **Swahili ware** the pottery of early Swahili communities of the late 1st millennium AD, found from the Lamu Archipelago off the Kenyan coast as far south as Vilanculos Bay in Mozambique, as well as on the islands of Zanzibar, Pemba, the Comoros and Madagascar.

Tanagra a town in Boeotia, Greece, best known for the discovery in the late 19th century of numerous terracotta figurines in its cemeteries. Many date from the HELLENISTIC period. More recently MYCENAEAN CHAMBER TOMBS have been excavated in the area.

Tang see CHINESE DYNASTIES.

tang a projection at the base of a tool or weapon which could be attached to a handle or shaft.

Tanis probably the most important archaeological site in the Nile DELTA of Egypt, the chief excavations being carried out by PETRIE in 1883–6 and by MONTET in 1929–51. It is best known for the rich, and largely intact, royal tombs of the 21st and 22nd Dynasties (c.1070–715 BC) which were constructed within the precincts of the great temple of the god AMEN. It seems likely that much, if not all, of the large quantity of comparatively early material excavated at Tanis (e.g. of the OLD KINGDOM, MIDDLE KINGDOM, RAMESSES II) was transported there by kings of the 21st and 22nd Dynasties to adorn their building works at the site.

Tanjay a coastal site on Negros Island, southern Visayas, Philippines, containing habitation debris, craft production areas and burials dating from AD 500 to Spanish colonial times. It is one of the few sites with systematic typologies of locally produced plain and decorated earthenwares.

Tanjong Rawa see KUALA SELINSING.

Tanum a major concentration of Scandinavian prehistoric rock art in Bohuslän, Sweden. The designs are pecked on glacially smoothed rock surfaces and depict ships, ploughing scenes, warriors armed with spears and battle axes, carts and possible sun discs. The many-oared ships, sometimes with fighting warriors, are particularly

The central temple area at TANIS, built during the Third Intermediate period, largely from stone blocks, statues and obelisks removed from the Ramesside city of Pi-Ramesses.

characteristic. Dating is difficult but the Tanum art is attributed mainly to the later Bronze Age.

taotie [t'ao-t'ie] a Chinese Neolithic design motif first occurring on jade objects of the LIANGZHU culture, then adapted to bronze in the SHANG period. In its earlier form it is thought to represent a person wearing a cap of rank; later, it evolved to form a mythic animal figure with claws, horns, etc. See also ANYANG.

Taperinha a prehistoric riverine SHELL MIDDEN of several hectares near Santarem, northern Brazil, where investigations by Anna Roosevelt have proved that this part of the lower Amazon has the oldest pottery in the New World, dated by AMS and THERMOLUMINESCENCE to the 8th millennium BP. See also PRECERAMIC, FORMATIVE.

taphonomy the study of the transformation of materials into the archaeological record. Originally the term was limited to the examination of these processes for living organisms (i.e. processes affecting the composition and completeness of a skeleton after the animal's death). Unlike ETHNOARCHAEOLOGY, the focus of taphonomic studies is the understanding of the processes resulting in the archaeological record *per se*. See also ACTUALISTIC STUDY.

Taputapuatea a MARAE on Raiatea, Society Islands (Polynesia), which was a centre for the worship of the god Oro. The surviving platform (AHU) is 40 by 7 m (130 by 23 ft) and faced with coral slabs up to 4 m (13 ft) high. Shell from the platform fill is dated to the 17th century AD.

Tara the Hill of Tara, Co. Meath, seat of the pre-Christian and early Christian High Kings of Ireland. It is encircled by the RATH na Riogh, the 'Fort of the Kings', a large enclosure like that at NAVAN with ditch inside bank and therefore non-defensive in nature. At the centre of the enclosure are two conjoined raths or ringforts probably of early Christian date, with a third rath just outside the enclosure. The earliest monument on the Hill, within the Rath na Riogh, is the Mound of the Hostages, a small Neolithic PASSAGE GRAVE dated *c*.2800 BC.

Tarascans or **Purépecha** a people of central Mexico, contemporaries of the AZTECS but not under their subjugation. Their capital was *Tzinzunzan*; later it was *Pátzcuaro*.

Tardenoisian the final Mesolithic culture identified in southwestern France following the SAUVETERRIAN and characterized by the presence of geometric microliths but few woodworking tools. The Tardenoisian is found in Iberia and Central Europe but did not spread to Britain, possibly because of the newly formed English Channel. The Tardenoisian shows definite Neolithic influences. It is named after the French site of Fère-en-Tardenois, Aisne.

Tarentum (*Gk* Taras) a colony of SPARTA in southeastern Italy founded in the late 8th century BC. It takes advantage of a fine natural harbour. There is also some MYCENAEAN pottery. The earliest city was located on the peninsula now occupied by the Citta Vecchia. Tombs of the ARCHAIC period have yielded large numbers of imported Greek pots. In the CLASSICAL period Tarentum may have been a production centre for some APULIAN POTTERY as well as terracotta figurines.

Tarquinia the greatest of the ETRUSCAN cities, in Tuscany, Italy, with remains of a powerful wall and the base of the great central temple, the Ara della Regina, which had terracotta winged horses in its PEDIMENT; both

TANUM, Sweden: rock art figures at Vitlycke, known as 'the couple'.

were built in the 4th/3rd century BC. To the east the important VILLANOVAN cemetery of Selciatello (10th–7th centuries BC) relates to the earliest period of the city's development; the principal Etruscan cemetery, with burial mounds covering frescoed rock-cut tombs, is at Monterozzi to the south. Tarquinia was absorbed into the Roman confederacy in 353 BC and enjoyed several more centuries of prosperity before post-Roman decline and destruction by Arab raiders in the early Middle Ages. The city was served by the port of GRAVISCA.

Tarsus a prehistoric site in coastal Cilicia, southwestern Anatolia, where H. Goldman's excavations in the 1930s and 1950s at a location called Gözlü Kale produced a sequence which complements that of MERSIN; together they provide the basic framework for the region. Although the Tarsus excavation reached late Neolithic and CHALCOLITHIC levels, these are contained in a very small exposure and are more fully known at Mersin. The subsequent levels, opened over larger areas, contained a series of EARLY BRONZE AGE occupations not evident at Mersin. During this time the settlement changed character several times, with the first fortification appearing in Early Bronze Age II level; the pottery and small finds, which previously had correlated with the AMUQ sequence (up to Amuq F), now find more similarity with Anatolian forms to the northwest (as far away as TROY II–IV). The MIDDLE BRONZE AGE levels contain a painted pottery similar to that at Tell ATCHANA, followed by

LATE BRONZE AGE occupations which include a walled HITTITE temple compound and a large Hittite administrative building. The site also contains an important series of Iron Age deposits, as well as later (to the early medieval period) occupation.

Tărtăria a late Neolithic site in western-central Romania where in a VINČA pit were found three unbaked clay tablets with incised signs, which some have claimed bear a resemblance to signs from JEMDET NASR and URUK in MESOPOTAMIA. There is about a 1,000-year discrepancy between the Tărtăria tablets and the later Mesopotamian symbols, suggesting that the resemblance is coincidental. Since then, similar tablets have been found in a slightly later context at GRADESNITSA in Bulgaria.

Tartessos an early trading state at the mouth of the River Guadalquivir in southern Spain, referred to by eastern Mediterranean writers of the 8th century BC as a source of gold, silver, tin and lead.

Taruga a central Nigerian Iron Age site where terracotta figures of the NOK culture were found in association with large quantities of domestic pottery and iron smelting debris and furnaces. These are dated between the 5th and 3rd centuries BC and are among the oldest so far discovered in West Africa.

Tarxien a late Neolithic temple complex in Malta, comprising remains of four temples. The first, of which little survives, was built in the Ggantija phase c.3300 BC. Two further temples of four-apse type (the South and East Temples) were built at the beginning of the following Tarxien phase c.3000–2500 BC. The South Temple is particularly fine, with carved running spirals and the lower part of a large standing statue originally c.2.75 m (9 ft) tall. A door in the right-hand rear apse leads into the Central Temple, of six apses with central niche, the fourth and last in the sequence. The temples were abandoned c.2500 BC and the area became a cemetery of

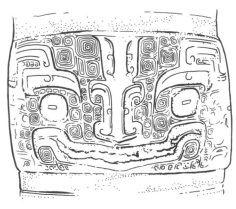

TAOTIE.

TASHTYK CULTURE, Siberia: clay funerary masks.

inurned cremation burials in the so-called Tarxien Cemetery phase c.2500–1500 BC. See also MALTESE TEMPLES.

Tashtyk culture a culture, primarily of pastoralists, which flourished in the MINUSINSK BASIN of southern Siberia from the 1st century BC to the 6th century AD. It is most noteworthy for the fact that its dead, buried in vaults and graves, were often transformed into MUMMIES, with their organs and ashes inside them. They were then given individualized clay masks. Only women and teenagers seem to have received this treatment – men were cremated, and their ashes sometimes inserted into a mannequin or 'funerary doll', which was then given a mask. The bodies had pillows of wood, stone or wool, and were accompanied by numerous wooden vessels containing meat and drink.

Tasian an early phase of the BADARIAN. The term was coined by Brunton, from the site of Deir Tasa, but it is not now generally regarded as a valid description of a distinct cultural group.

Tasmania an island which, during the Pleistocene, was part of SAHUL but was cut off from mainland Australia by rising sea-levels about 12,000 years ago. Evidence of human occupation in Tasmania goes back about 35,000 years (see PARMERPAR MEETHANER, WARREEN). Numerous extraordinarily rich sites in the area document the adaptation of the southernmost humans during the Pleistocene to the PERIGLACIAL EVIRONMENT (see KUTIKINA, NUNAMIRA, WARGATA MINA). Tasmania did not share in the developments associated with the AUSTRALIAN SMALL TOOL TRADITION on the mainland, and edge-ground tools, microliths and the dingo are all absent. The simplicity of the Tasmanian material culture at European contact has long been fascinating to anthropologists and archaeologists. Changes did, however, occur in Holocene Tasmania and are well documented at sites such as ROCKY CAPE. Previously unoccupied or rarely used areas begin to be colonized 4,000–3,000 years ago, and at the same time there is evidence for wider distribution of fine-grained chert from quarries along the west coast. Fish seem to have disappeared from the diet about 3500 bp. Bone tools also fall out of use at about the same

time. The reasons for these changes are unclear and have generated much debate. The arrival of Europeans was disastrous for the Tasmanians, who were almost exterminated during the 18th century. See also ROBINSON, WYBALENNA.

Tasmanian tiger see THYLACINE.

Tassili n'Ajjer a rugged massif in southeastern Algeria, famous for its rock art, which covers most of the Saharan sequence and includes wild animals, human figures, domesticated cattle and chariots.

Tata a Middle Palaeolithic open-air site located near the River Danube in north-central Hungary. Artifacts and faunal remains (e.g. woolly mammoth [predominant], extinct horse, and wild ass) are buried in loess deposited between layers of spring sediment; the cultural layer apparently dates to the early last GLACIAL. The tools include sidescrapers, bifaces and some Upper Palaeolithic types. Tata was excavated by VÉRTES in 1958–9 and others, and yielded a carved and polished segment of mammoth molar, and a fossil with an engraved line on it, both dating to c.100,000 bp.

taula a Bronze Age ritual monument found on the Balearic Islands, consisting of two carefully cut stone slabs balanced one on top of the other, sometimes with mortise-and-tenon joint, to form a 'T'. The largest taula, at Trepuco, is 4 m (13 ft) high.

Taung a fossiliferous deposit at a limestone quarry in the North-West Province, South Africa, currently thought to date to at least 2.4 and possibly as much as 2.8 million years ago, which produced the first australopithecine (see AUSTRALOPITHECUS) fossil in 1924. The site of the discovery has since been blasted away and is marked by a plinth. This so-called 'Taung baby' consisted of the face and endocranial (brain) cast of a young child, named *Australopithecus africanus* ('southern ape of Africa') by DART in 1925. It was initially dismissed as a human ancestor by many because its small brain and human-like teeth did not correspond with then current opinion on human evolution, but Dart was later vindicated by the discovery of many more australopithecines from southern and East African sites. Growth lines in the teeth suggest it was between 2.7 and 3.7 years old when it died. It is thought that the child may have been killed and dismembered by a carnivore, and then the skull taken to an eagle's nest, as scratch marks on the skull could be the claw marks of a large bird of prey like the crowned eagle, and the fauna found with it corresponds with that typically found below eagle nests.

Tautavel or **Caune de l'Arago** a cave-site in the Pyrénées-Orientales, in southern France. Excavations by H. de Lumley since 1964 have revealed a 10 m (33 ft) stratigraphy containing Middle Pleistocene/Lower Palaeolithic material. Associated with an archaic

TAYACIAN industry on quartz were a number of human remains, notably the front part of a skull. Opinions are divided about classing these as HOMO *erectus* or as archaic NEANDERTHALers; dating is also complex, but it is thought they lie between 320,000 and 200,000 BP.

Tawantinsuyu the name given by the INCA to their empire; usually translated as 'the four quarters', its more precise meaning is 'the parts that in their fourness make up a whole'.

Taxila a great city in northwestern Pakistan, explored by J. MARSHALL and later by others, which contains three major settlements, Bhir, Sirkap and Sirsuleh. Bhir is an unplanned walled town whose earliest levels date to around 500 BC and which continued in use up to the founding of Sirkap. Sirkap is a planned settlement founded in the 2nd or 1st century BC and lasting into the 2nd century AD; here blocks of buildings are laid out on a regular grid of streets, and an interior wall divides the place into upper and lower cities. Sirsuleh was an early Kushan foundation (perhaps 1st or 2nd century AD), and continued this succession of cities. At Sirkap, the upper city contains the Hathial mound group, where recent excavation has revealed earlier settlements. Hathial A contains at least two phases of occupations, the earlier with ceramic parallels to the KOT DIJI tradition (dated perhaps 2000 BC) and the later a settlement belonging to the middle phase of the GANDHARA GRAVE culture (dated around 1000 BC). Hathial B (the 'citadel' of Sirkap), on the other hand, contains a sequence that spans the range 700 BC to AD 100.

taxonomy a system of classifying artifacts or other cultural material into discrete units or taxa, based on their similarities to each other. Taxonomy is the basis of the organization of archaeologically recovered MATERIAL CULTURE.

Taya, Tell a site in the northwestern Sinjar area of northeastern Iraq containing extensive stone architecture which is largely visible on the surface. Julian Reade's programme in the late 1960s to early 1980s of excavation and extensive mapping indicates that the site was occupied from very late EARLY DYNASTIC times into the early 2nd millennium BC (Khabur ware), with later NEO-ASSYRIAN, PARTHIAN and Islamic settlement also present. Most of the visible architecture belongs at the beginning of this sequence, and formed a walled inner area of dense architecture covering 65 ha (160 acres) and an outer zone of more scattered buildings over another 90 ha (222 acres). The mapping project presents one of the clearest pictures of town layout yet available for a large settlement in 3rd-millennium MESOPOTAMIA.

Tayacian a rather nebulous term which has been used to describe probably unconnected Lower and Middle Palaeolithic industries which have no bifaces and no well-made flake tools. The name was derived from material at LA MICOQUE in LES EYZIES-de-Tayac. See also FONTÉ-CHEVADE.

Taylor, Walter W. (1913–97) influential North American archaeological theorist, whose book *A Study of Archaeology* (1948), which encouraged North American archaeologists to return to their anthropological roots, presaged the NEW ARCHAEOLOGY.

Taylour, Lord William (1904–89) a British archaeologist whose principal excavations were at MYCENAE, where he uncovered the cult centre, and at Ayios Stefanos in Laconia.

Tayma an Iron Age city in the Hejaz region of northwestern Arabia, best known as the place where NABONIDUS, the last king of the NEO-BABYLONIAN empire, resided for ten years. A contiguous series of large walled compounds, one of them enclosing a small mound, form the centre of the town, with large walls extending from these to enclose 9 sq. km (3.5 sq. miles). Set in one of the latter walls is an excavated cultic area, formed as a linear series of rooms set on a natural rock outcrop; one of these rooms contains a stone block, on two sides of which are carved cultic scenes with an iconography derived from the MESOPOTAMIAN world (probably ACHAEMENID). STELAS with Aramaic inscriptions also belong to this part of the 1st millennium BC.

Te Awanga a fortified ridge PA, at Tiromoana, Hawkes Bay, NEW ZEALAND. Excavations by Aileen Fox revealed remains of palisades, a large rectangular house and distinctive raised-rim sweet potato storage-pits. Unusually early dates from storage pits suggest that these features may date back to the earliest settlement, although old timber may have been used. See also KAURI POINT, OTAKANINI.

Tegdaoust see AWDAGHAST.

Tehuacán Valley a semi-arid highland valley in Puebla, Mexico. The valley, about 1,800 m (5,900 ft) above sea-level, has one of the longest continuous archaeological sequences in MESOAMERICA (7000 BC–AD 1520). Research in the valley was conducted mainly by Richard S. MACNEISH in the 1960s. His work, primarily in cave and rockshelter sites, documented changes in subsistence from a period of hunting and gathering and incipient agriculture (AJUEREADO and EL RIEGO PHASES) to a major reliance on domesticated foods (ABEJAS and PURRON PHASES). Archaeological materials from the earlier phases are considered part of the DESERT TRADITION. The Tehuacán Valley research represents significant findings in the origins of agriculture, and the shift to dependence on agriculture, in Mesoamerica.

Tekkalakota a prehistoric site of the southern Deccan in Karnataka, southwestern India. Nagaraja Rao's excavations here in the 1960s revealed two successive occupations (Tekkalakota I–II) dated to the 2nd millennium BC. Both occupations contain the mud or stone floors of circular (sometimes rectilinear) huts in which were various pieces of household equipment; these dwellings are scattered on a hill-slope. Around and in the settlement are burials, which in Tekkalakota I are secondary and in Tekkalakota II are usually extended or in urns. Metal objects, though rare, occur in both periods; mostly copper tools, although gold is also present in the earlier period. The fauna emphasizes domesticated cattle, while finger millet and *horse gram* (a legume) exist in Tekkalakota I. This cultural configuration, found also in other sites of the region (e.g. Bramagiri, HALLUR, PIKLIHAL), represents a food-producing adaptation to the hill country of southern India.

Telanthropus a genus previously used for early HOMO fossils from SWARTKRANS.

Telarmachay a PRECERAMIC (9000–2000 bp) rock-shelter located on the PUNA of central Peru, at an altitude of 4,420 m (14,500 ft). Excavations by Danièle Lavallée indicate that the site was seasonally occupied, and that *in situ* camelid domestication took place there. She argues that structured mobility was a more likely subsistence adaptation than the sedentary occupation suggested by Rick in the case of PACHAMACHAY.

Teleilat Ghassul the Palestinian type-site of the GHASSULIAN, chiefly excavated by Mallon and Koppel in 1929–38 and by the British School of Archaeology in 1967–78. Teleilat Ghassul is particularly known for its polychrome geometric and figurative mural paintings on the walls of the rectangular mud-brick houses, which were often lime-plastered.

Tell for sites beginning 'Tell', see under other element of name.

tell (*Arabic* 'mound' or 'hill') a major archaeological feature of settlement sites in the Near East. A tell is an artificial mound created by the accumulation over centuries of stratified layers of disintegrated mud-brick walls and cultural debris, brought about by new phases of occupation being built upon the ruins of their predecessors on the same site. The terms *tal*, *tepe*, *depe* and *höyük* refer to the same phenomenon in areas adjacent to MESOPOTAMIA. As a site type, tells are variable in size, comprising the extremely low mounds of villages as well as those of major cities, and may refer to a single mound or a series of connected mounds. In many places in western Asia ancient tells are still being occupied, that at Erbil in northern Iraq being a famous example.

Tellem a pre-Dogon society with large NECROPOLISes in the Bandiagara escarpment of Mali, Africa, dated between the 11th and 16th centuries AD.

Tello, Julio Cesar (1880–1947) a Peruvian archaeologist of mostly native ancestry, educated in science and medicine in Peru, and in anthropology at Harvard. He excavated at many of the major sites in Peru, including CHAVÍN, PARACAS, HUARI, PACHECO and PACHACAMAC. He argued that Chavín was the first major civilization in the Andes, a view that has only recently fallen from favour. Tello founded what is today called the National Museum of Anthropology and Archaeology in Lima; he is buried in a courtyard in the museum grounds.

Tello a site identified as Girsu, the capital of the Lagash city-state in early southern MESOPOTAMIA; the French work at Tello, begun by Ernst de Sarzec in 1887 and continued by various others until 1933, revealed for the first time the character of SUMERIAN civilization. Although poorly executed by modern standards of stratigraphic control, de Sarzec's work recovered many important pieces of Sumerian art (e.g. the 'STELA of the Vultures', the silver vase of Entemena, the statues of GUDEA) and also a significant corpus of EARLY DYNASTIC III and UR III CUNEIFORM texts. The latter represent the richest available body of written evidence for the social, political and economic affairs of the Early Dynastic III Mesopotamian city-states, and also provide valuable evidence for the GUTIAN 'dark age' and Ur III administrative practices. The rulers of Lagash include the line of Enannatum, which fought a protracted border war with Umma, the later Uruinimgina (Urukagina) who is known for his administrative and religious reforms, and the post-AKKADIAN Gudea famous for his statues and building programmes. Girsu was occupied from late 'UBAID to OLD BABYLONIAN times, and also has a late 1st-millennium BC palace.

Tembeling a river valley of the interior of peninsular Malaysia with sites yielding Neolithic and metal age remains. The former include the curved stone 'Tembeling knife' from such sites as Nyong, and the latter include iron tools (see TULANG MAWAS) and a DONG SON bronze drum from Batu Pasir Garam.

temenos a Greek sanctuary or sacred precinct at a cult centre (see AKROPOLIS, DELPHI, OLYMPIA). It could contain numerous buildings such as the NAOS, housing the main cult, and a series of THESAUROI, STOAS, as well as dedications from worshippers.

Temet a Neolithic site at the foot of Mount Grèboun in northeastern Niger, containing a cultural layer covered by more than 6 m (20 ft) of diatomite deposits, which are dated to 8565 bp just above the cultural layer. The stone industry is of particular interest since it indicates an association of blades and bladelets as well as a microlithic component with many geometric pieces, elsewhere considered indicative of different industries.

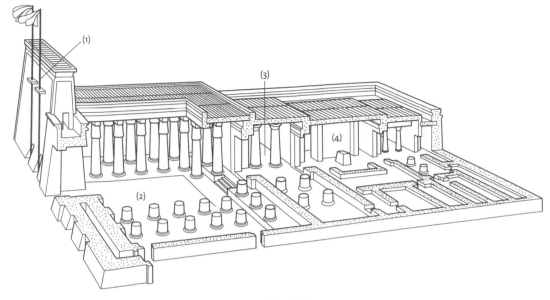

TEMPLE (Egyptian).

Temnata Cave a Palaeolithic site located in central Bulgaria. Artifacts and faunal remains (e.g. woolly mammoth, bear) are buried in deposits of clay and rubble. The lowest cultural layer contains a Middle Palaeolithic assemblage (sidescrapers predominate among tools), which may date to the early cold LAST GLACIAL MAXIMUM. A younger Middle Palaeolithic assemblage with bifacial foliates was found outside the cave. The upper levels in the cave contain AURIGNACIAN and GRAVETTIAN assemblages. Temnata Cave was investigated by Kozłowski and others, who obtained radiocarbon dates between 38,000 and 21,000, with THERMOLUMINESCENCE dates of 46,000–45,000 bp.

temper crushed material added to a clay to improve its firing qualities. Temper may be stone, various organic materials or broken pottery. See also CERAMICS.

temple a building with a religious function. The structure of the many imposing temples of the CLASSICAL world has been studied in particular detail (see ADYTON, ANTA, CELLA, OPISTHODOMOS, PRONAOS).

In *Egypt*, archaeological evidence, especially the well-preserved examples of the Graeco-Roman period (e.g. EDFU), indicates that from at least as early as the NEW KINGDOM the basic layout of an Egyptian temple was composed of a number of well-defined elements: (1) the PYLON; (2) an open *courtyard*, with colonnades on at least the lateral sides and often also at the front and rear; (3) the HYPOSTYLE HALL; (4) the *sanctuary*, which was the central element of a CULT TEMPLE, containing the image of the deity, usually housed within a NAOS.

The number of these elements within any individual temple, especially pylons, courtyards and hypostyle halls, was largely the result of additions and alterations by successive kings. The sacred precinct of a town, including the temple and its associated buildings, was surrounded by a massive mud-brick enclosure wall.

temple mound an artificial hill constructed of earth and stone on which stands a temple or some other ceremonial building. In MESOAMERICA these structures are terraced, or stepped. In some cases, as in the Temple of Inscriptions at PALENQUE, temple-mounds served as tombs.

Temple Mound period the period following the BURIAL MOUND period, when many cultures in eastern North America built large PLATFORM MOUNDS. It begins approximately AD 800 and continued to the time of European contact. It is often used synonymously with the MISSISSIPPIAN.

Temple of the Crossed Hands see KOTOSH.

Templo Mayor see TENOCHTITLÁN.

Tenerian a Neolithic industry of the Tenere Desert and surrounding areas of Niger, well represented at ADRAR BOUS and ARLIT, and extending eastwards into Chad, dating between 6500 and 4500 bp, and associated with a pastoral economy possible in the Sahara at that time, as well as evidence that hunting was important. Artifacts include pottery, ground stone axes and backed microliths, as well as bifacially flaked triangular stone knives and projectile points.

Tenochtitlán the great AZTEC capital, located where Mexico City now stands. The city was founded in AD 1325 on an island in Lake Texcoco. The Aztecs reclaimed the swampland in this part of the lake, building artificial islands on which houses and other structures were placed, and constructing CHINAMPAS and other agricultural plots. It was linked to the mainland by three causeways.

Tenochtitlán was an excellent example of planned urban growth. Through the city ran six major north-south and two major east-west canals, with smaller canals feeding into them. Houses along streets and canals were on stone-faced platforms. The city had between sixty and seventy wards, corresponding to kinship units. Each ward had communally constructed public buildings. The wards were divided between four principal districts. The district of Tlatelolco held a large market.

At the centre of Tenochtitlán was the major ceremonial precinct. Palaces, temples, BALL COURTS and other public buildings were arranged around plazas. The *Templo Mayor* (Great Temple) dominated the precinct. It comprised a truncated pyramid, on which were two temples, one dedicated to the Aztec patron god, Huitzilopochtli, and the other to the rain god, TLALOC. Recent excavations under the direction of Mexican archaeologist Eduardo Matos Moctezuma have discovered the multi-stage construction sequence of the Templo Mayor, including hundreds of offertory caches which reveal Aztec concepts of the cosmic order.

Tenochtitlán fell to CORTÉS in 1521, while under the rule of Moctezuma II, and later of Cuauhtémoc. By 1522, the city had virtually disappeared. The ruins of residences filled the canals, and the Spaniards disassembled buildings and used the stone in the construction of their own city.

Teotihuacán ('place of the gods' in NAHUATL) a major site in the northeastern part of the BASIN OF MEXICO, in the Teotihuacán Valley. Outstripping CUICUILCO, located at the southern end of the Basin, in power, size and population, by AD 100 Teotihuacán had about 40,000 inhabitants. At its peak, between AD 450 and 650, Teotihuacán was one of the largest cities in the world, with a population of 150,000. It was a planned urban centre with streets laid out on a grid pattern around blocks of multi-family 'apartment complexes'.

Teotihuacán's rise to power is attributed to its advantageous position on a trade route, its monopoly over an important obsidian source, the favourable conditions for intensive agricultural production in the Basin, and the religious significance of the site. Teotihuacán controlled much of the obsidian manufacture and trade throughout MESOAMERICA, and its position on a natural trade route to both the south and east allowed it to control the trade of other goods also. Both KAMINALJUYÚ and MATACAPAN, as well as other centres, were under the domination of Teotihuacán. Evidence for this influence is seen in the predominance of Teotihuacán art and architectural styles. Other sites (e.g. TIKAL, MONTE ALBÁN and CHOLULA) also show evidence of interaction with Teotihuacán. At some times, military strength was involved in Teotihuacán's occupation of these centres; but at others, it appeared limited to commercial or religious influence.

At the heart of the city's 20 sq. km (7.7 sq. miles) is a complex of major structures including the huge pyramids of the Sun and Moon (that of the Sun is 210 m [230 yds] square at the base, and 64 m [210 ft] high), distributed along a central road called 'The Street of the Dead'.

In 1971 a ceremonial cave was discovered under the Pyramid of the Sun. It has been suggested that the location of the temple, as well as the city as a whole, may be related to the cave. Teotihuacán was probably an important religious site, to which many made pilgrimages. This aspect of the city probably also increased its influence throughout much of Mesoamerica.

After AD 650, the population of Teotihuacán began to decline. By 750 the city had been destroyed. Currently, there are no satisfactory explanations for the demise of Teotihuacán. Climatic deterioration and invasion by semi-nomadic groups are the two commonly given reasons for its fall. The archaeologist George Cowgill has also suggested that the inefficiencies of the bureaucratic system played a role in its end.

Leopoldo Batres carried out the first major excavations at Teotihuacán in 1905. More recently, Ignacio BERNAL undertook excavations at the site, René Millon conducted a detailed mapping project of the city, and William T. Sanders carried out a settlement pattern survey of the Basin of Mexico.

Tepe for sites beginning 'Tepe', see under other element of name.

tephra a general term for all air-borne volcanic ejecta emanating from a volcanic vent during eruption. Tephra includes volcanic dust, ash, cinders, lapilli, scoria, pumice, bombs and blocks, any of which can cause rapid burial of cultural debris. Tephra beds cover a broad area and are deposited essentially instantaneously, making them ideal STRATIGRAPHIC markers. Furthermore, most tephra can be dated by POTASSIUM-ARGON DATING and FISSION TRACK DATING methods. See also TEPHROCHRONOLOGY.

tephrochronology a dating method utilizing ages, widespread distribution, and correlation of TEPHRA layers and the application of the results. Ages can be determined radiometrically by POTASSIUM-ARGON DATING and RADIOCARBON DATING, and radiogenically by FISSION TRACK DATING. Because tephra BEDS are essentially ISOCHRONOUS they provide throughout their extent limiting ages on overlying and underlying material, including archaeological deposits. Identification of multiple tephra beds may provide bracketing ages for intervening strata. Tephrochronology has also been used to date and correlate GLACIAL advances, sea-level changes and ALLUVIAL FANS.

tepidarium a warm room in a Roman bath-house. Attached to it was a plunge-bath, which would have made the atmosphere of the room humid. See also THERMAE.

Teploukhov, Sergei Alexandrovich (1888–1933) a Soviet archaeologist, and researcher in Siberia. He investigated archaeological sites from different periods in the basin of the Yenisei River in southern Siberia, on the Issyk-Kul Lake in Kirghizia, and took part in the excavations of the NOIN-ULA barrows in Mongolia. He is best known for the first classification of the archaeological cultures of the MINUSINSK BASIN in southern Siberia, which remains basically valid.

terminus ante quem (*Lat.* 'the end before which') a term used to provide fixed points in the STRATIGRAPHY of a site or in the relative dating of artifacts, *before* which something occurred. For example, the presence of Early Ripe CORINTHIAN POTTERY at SELINUNTE, thought to have been founded in 629/8 BC, provides a *terminus ante quem* for the production of that style of pottery. The presence of datable material such as pottery or coins above a destruction layer would provide a *terminus ante quem*. Compare TERMINUS POST QUEM.

terminus post quem (*Lat.* 'the end after which') a term used to provide fixed points in the STRATIGRAPHY of a site or in the relative dating of artifacts, *after* which something occurred. For example, the lack of pottery decorated with ROULETTING at MOTYA, a site destroyed in 397 BC, is thought to be a *terminus post quem* for the introduction of the technique. The presence of datable material such as pottery or coins STRATIFIED under a destruction layer would likewise provide a *terminus post quem*. Compare TERMINUS ANTE QUEM.

Ternifine see TIGHENIF.

terp a type of settlement found in the lowland coastal regions of the Netherlands and Germany bordering the North Sea during the later Iron Age (1st–5th centuries AD). The accumulation of settlement debris over a period of decades or centuries forms a low mound, similar in some respects to the TELLS of the ancient Near East. The raised character of the terp provided refuge in times of flooding. The most famous terp settlement is FEDDERSEN WIERDE in the coastal salt marshes south of the River Elbe, where waterlogging had preserved the remains of timber LONG-HOUSES with wickerwork panels and partitions.

Terra Amata a French Lower Palaeolithic site located in Nice and excavated by de Lumley in 1966, who dates it to the MINDEL GLACIATION (*c.*380,000 BP). It has been claimed that the site may have been used annually for fifteen successive years by ACHEULIAN hunter-gatherers who built fires and erected tent-like constructions during the late spring or early summer.

terra sigillata a type of Roman pottery, normally red-glossed, to which were applied stamps often bearing the name of the potter. It was produced in several centres, especially in the western Mediterranean. See also ARRE-TINE WARE, SAMIAN WARE.

terrace **1** a landform consisting of a level to gently sloping former alluvial surface, restricted to a valley, elevated above the active floodplain, and bordered on one side by a valley wall or scarp ascending to a higher terrace, and on the other side by a scarp descending to a lower terrace or the modern valley floor. Terraces form as the result of changes in stream regimen, caused by numerous factors, and can be either erosional or depositional in origin. Terraces may exhibit relict floodplain landforms, providing the basis for interpreting former valley conditions, processes and environments. Terraces are often favoured loci for human activity because of their intermediate position between upland and bottomland resources, and their relatively well-drained landscape situation. Archaeological deposits associated with terraces are equal in age or younger than the terrace. Older archaeological deposits may be buried in alluvial fill beneath the terrace. Where multiple terraces exist in a valley, successively lower terrace levels are progressively younger, a fact that can be used to advantage in archaeological surveying, tempered by the possibility that younger terrace veneer deposits may be present and obscure the archaeological record. See also BENCH.
2 a landform consisting of a level to gently sloping former platform elevated above current sea-level, lake-levels or dry lake beds. This type of terrace can have associated beach ridge (see FOSSIL BEACH) landforms and wave-cut platforms (see BENCH). Marine terraces form as a result of oscillations of sea-level, common during the QUATERNARY, caused by the interaction of vertical changes in sea- and land-levels. Archaeological materials associated with this type of terrace are no older than the activity that created the terrace. Marine terraces, and associated archaeological deposits, may be submerged as the result of later, higher sea-level stands.

terracotta 'baked earth', or fired clay, which is still quite porous; artifacts are mostly in the form of figurines, simple vessels, tablets or loom weights. See also CERAMICS.

terracotta army see QIN.

terramara (*pl.* **terremare**) the name given to Middle Bronze Age settlements in the Emilia region of northern Italy, on account of their rich black organic occupation deposits, used as fertilizer by local farmers.

Tešetice-Kyjovice a site of the LENGYEL culture in southern Moravia, which includes a circular enclosure with a ditch about 60 m (200 ft) in diameter with four entrances oriented approximately to the cardinal points of the compass. Within the enclosure were two concentric palisades, with gates at the points where entrances break the ditch. Traces of settlement occur outside the enclosure, the function of which is uncertain.

Teshik Tash a Middle Palaeolithic cave-site with five levels of a MOUSTERIAN industry, located at 1,800 m (5,900 ft) altitude in Tadjikistan in Central Asia, and excavated by A. P. OKLADNIKOV in 1938–9. Teshik Tash, dated to c.44,000 BP, is best known for its NEANDERTHAL child burial. Subsequent work in the region has revealed a large number of Mousterian sites whose industries have been divided into several distinct FACIES.

tessellated *adj.* (of Roman mosaic floors) formed by TESSERAE.

tessera a small cube of stone, glass or tile set in concrete and used to form part of a Roman mosaic.

tetrastyle **1** four columns forming the façade of a CLASSICAL building such as a NAISKOS.
2 four columns placed in a square pattern, such as at the four corners of an IMPLUVIUM within the ATRIUM of a Roman house.

Teufelsbrücke an Upper Palaeolithic site located on the Saale River in eastern Germany. Five cultural layers, apparently dating to the end of the Pleistocene, are buried in sediments at the entrance of a nearly collapsed rockshelter. Faunal remains include horse, reindeer and arctic fox. The assemblages contain bone points and harpoons, and are assigned to the late MAGDALENIAN. A radiocarbon date of 13,025 bp has been obtained.

Téviec a small island off the coast of Brittany, France, containing a SHELL MIDDEN excavated by the Péquarts in 1928–34. It has a Mesolithic cemetery of ten graves which have yielded twenty-three burials, some accompanied by stag antlers, shell jewellery and red ochre, and associated with 'ritual' hearths. AMS dates for the site span a range from 6740 to 5680 bp.

texture 1 a property of sediment and soils defined by the relative proportions of gravel-, sand-, silt- and clay-size particles which is in part a function of DEPOSITIONAL ENVIRONMENT. Soil texture class names are assigned to soil or sediment with specific ranges of percentages of sand, silt and clay. Boundary percentages and class names vary according to which of the several recognized texture classification systems is used.
2 the size, shape and arrangement of constituent grains in igneous, metamorphic and sedimentary rocks. Rock texture is an important criterion in various rock classification schemes. The texture of artifacts is one property

that in combination with others may help to identify material source. Ceramics can be described by texture defined by the geometrical aspects of its constituents, which may provide clues to the origin and manufacturing techniques and technology.

Teyjat La Mairie, Teyjat, Dordogne, France is a late MAGDALENIAN cave-site which has yielded engravings of aurochs, horses, reindeer, bison and bears. A bow was reportedly recovered but inadvertently destroyed during the excavation of Teyjat; if correct, this would represent the earliest known evidence for the use of the bow and arrow. Teyjat has given its name to the Teyjat point, also known as the Font-Brunel point, a tanged point made on a blade.

Thailand see ASIA, SOUTHEAST.

Thames pick a term occasionally used for a large and crudely made Mesolithic tranchet axe.

Tham Khuong a cave in Lai Chau Province, 150 km (93 miles) west of Ha Noi, Vietnam, excavated in the 1970s, with Late Pleistocene occupation at the base dated to c.30,000 BP, an overlying HOABINHIAN occupation with two burials, and some later metal age use in upper layers. Abundant animal and plant remains were collected.

Thapsos a Middle Bronze Age cemetery of c.400 rock-cut tombs in Sicily, Italy, mostly reached by a vertical shaft and used for collective inhumations. Type-site of the Thapsos culture of eastern Sicily, it is characterized by decorated pottery, bronze swords and daggers, and MYCENAEAN imports including pottery and FAIENCE beads.

Thebes the site of a MYCENAEAN palace in Boeotia, Greece, identified on the basis of the frescoes, jewellery and in particular the LINEAR B tablets which have been discovered in excavations under the modern town. The layout of the palace remains uncertain, and investigation of CLASSICAL and medieval Thebes, the most powerful city in Boeotia, is equally problematic.

Thebes (Egypt)-East Bank the city of Waset in UPPER EGYPT, called Thebes by the Greeks, was one of the most important cities of ancient Egypt. On the east bank of the Nile was the main part of the city itself; it is now mostly overbuilt by the modern town of Luxor, apart from the temple largely constructed by AMENHOTEP III and RAMESSES II, while a short distance to the north was the temple of KARNAK.

Thebes (Egypt)-West Bank the NECROPOLIS of the ancient city of Waset, and the largest concentration of standing monuments in Egypt. These fall into two major categories: MORTUARY TEMPLES and royal/private tombs, the latter being dug chiefly into the cliffs and valleys of the Theban mountain, while the former are mostly sited on the narrow desert plain between the mountain and the cultivated land close to the Nile. Both types of monument are best represented by examples of the NEW KINGDOM. The most important mortuary temples are those of Nebhepetre Montuhotep and HATCHEPSUT (both at DEIR EL-BAHRI), RAMESSES III (at MEDINET HABU), Ramesses II ('the Ramesseum'), Seti I, and the COLOSSI OF MEMNON. The largest concentrations of royal tombs are at el-Tarif (11th Dynasty), Dra Abu el-Naga (17th Dynasty) and the VALLEY OF THE KINGS, while the burials of several members of the royal families of the 19th–20th Dynasties are to be found in the Valley of the Queens.

theodolite a surveying instrument consisting of a focusing telescope which is able to pivot on both horizontal and vertical planes; scales for measuring vertical and horizontal angles; and some type of levelling device. It is used to survey and map sites and surrounding environments, to plot excavation units and debris, and for topographic mapping. See also TRANSIT.

Thera or **Santorini** the volcanic island in the Cyclades which erupted cataclysmically c.1500 BC, burying the prehistoric settlement at AKROTIRI under a thick layer of TEPHRA. MARINATOS suggested that it was this eruption which caused the collapse of the MINOAN civilization, but the destruction of sites on Crete appears to have occurred at least a generation later.

therianthrope a part-human/part-animal figure, as found in rock art.

Thericleian ware a form of decoration described in literary sources and essentially belonging to the late 5th, 4th and 3rd centuries BC. Silver, *terebinth* wood (from pistachio trees) and clay seem to be the three main media used. Various characteristics are noted which include ribbing and a black colour (see PSEPHOPERIBOMBETRIOS). Extant candidates seem to be the BLACK-GLOSSED pottery. The name is derived from the name of Therikles, a Corinthian potter, who is said to have developed the technique.

thermae a bath-complex in the Roman world which contained not only rooms of different temperatures (see FRIGIDARIUM, CALDARIUM, TEPIDARIUM) but also exercise areas (see PALAESTRA). See also APODYTERIUM.

Thermi the site of a Bronze Age settlement on the Aegean island of Lesbos, excavated by LAMB in 1929–33. Thermi was colonized early in the 3rd millennium BC by settlers who had close links with sites in northwestern Anatolia and who also traded with the Cyclades. The settlement grew to a considerable size and was eventually fortified before being abandoned. After several centuries Thermi was resettled and was finally destroyed by fire, apparently in the 13th century BC.

thermoluminescence see LUMINESCENCE DATING.

thesauros a treasury resembling a NAISKOS located in

a TEMENOS as a store for the valuables of distant states. An elaborate series of thesauroi have been excavated leading up the sacred way at DELPHI. Many were highly decorated with sculpture, and thus served to make a statement about the importance of the city which had dedicated them. For example, the so-called Siphnian treasury had CARYATIDS on the porch, and a continuous sculpted frieze.

Thiessen polygons polygons constructed around sites (or features) on the landscape in such a way that the area enclosed by each polygon is nearer to the site used to define the polygon than it is to any other site. The resulting pattern serves as a model for understanding, amongst other things, the exploitation territories of individual settlements. The areas so defined can be tested against archaeological data for their closeness of fit.

thin section a sample chip that has been ground down to a paper-thin (0.03 mm [0.001 inch] thick) sheet and mounted on a glass slide beneath a cover slip. It is used in PETROLOGICAL ANALYSIS of the mineralogical composition of ceramics, stone artifacts and soils.

13 carbon/12 carbon the ratio between the two stable ISOTOPES of carbon, reported as d13C, measured relative to a marine carbonate standard (the Chicago PDB standard), against which most natural materials have negative values, used as an indicator of past diets and environments. The ratio between these two isotopes changes during chemical reactions (a process called isotopic fractionation), including photosynthesis, of which three different pathways are known, each with characteristic stable carbon isotope ratios: C3 (associated with temperate grasses such as wheat), C4 (tropical plants like maize), and CAM (succulents). When plants are eaten by animals, their stable carbon isotope ratios are passed along the food chain and, after further fractionation, are stored in various human or animal tissues, including bone. Measurement of the $^{13}C/^{13}C$ ratio of such archaeological remains can thus provide a basis for the interpretation of past diets and environments. The ratio is also used in the CALIBRATION of RADIOCARBON (^{14}C) dates.

tholos a round chamber with attached rectilinear entrance passage in Greek architecture, in particular the CORBEL-VAULTED MYCENAEAN tombs, also known as *beehive* tombs, exemplified by the Treasury of Atreus at MYCENAE.

Thomas, Cyrus (1825–1910) an American scholar famous for his pioneering studies of the mounds of the American Midwest. After careful and detailed analysis, Thomas was able to demonstrate that these mounds had been built by the ancestors of contemporary NATIVE AMERICANS. See also ATWATER, DAVIS, HAVEN, SQUIER, POWELL.

Thompson, Homer Armstrong (1906–2000) a Canadian archaeologist who was involved in the excavation of the

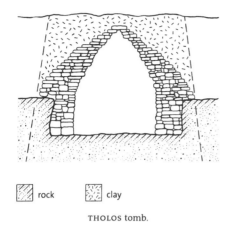

▨ rock   ▨ clay

THOLOS tomb.

Athenian AGORA by the American School of Classical Studies at Athens, serving as Field Director (1947–67). His work uncovered the buildings associated with Athenian democracy. The agora excavation served as a training ground for North American classical archaeologists and has been called 'the exemplary dig of all time'.

Thompson, Sir John Eric Sidney (1898–1975) an English ethnographer and archaeologist who worked in the MAYA area. In 1926, Thompson joined the Carnegie Institution excavations in the Yucatán. He was a pioneer in the study of Maya HIEROGLYPHIC writing. Thompson also studied the contemporary Maya, suggesting that aspects of Precolumbian culture had persisted to modern times. Thompson was the first New World archaeologist to be knighted.

Thomsen, Christian Jurgensen (1788–1865) a Danish antiquary and curator of the National Danish Museum of Antiquities, most famous for devising the THREE AGE SYSTEM. The first *ethnoarchaeologist* (using modern people's stone tools to explain the uses of prehistoric artifacts), he also called for osteological studies, chemical analysis of pot-residues, and study of the mutual relationships of artifacts in graves.

Thorikos an area in Attica, Greece, which lies just north of the Laurion hills and is a rich source of metallic ores from which copper, silver and lead were being extracted as early as the 3rd millennium BC. In the MYCENAEAN period, Thorikos evidently prospered since two THOLOS tombs were constructed on the AKROPOLIS. In the 5th and 4th centuries BC, ATHENS exploited the Laurion mines intensively and a number of ore washeries were built, but the most impressive CLASSICAL structure is an unusual elliptical theatre. See also LAURION.

Thoth an Egyptian deity, usually depicted as an ibis-headed man, although the baboon was also an animal sacred to this god. Thoth was particularly associated with

the activities of scribes and was later identified with the Greek god Hermes. His main cult-centres were at HERMO-POLIS MAGNA, and Hermopolis Parva in the DELTA.

Thracia or **Thrace** the eastern part of the Balkan peninsula north of the area of Greek settlement, extending to the shores of the Black Sea. In the 5th century BC Thracia encompassed the territory of modern Bulgaria and Romania. In the 4th century, its leader Seuthes established a state-level POLITY on Greek and Macedonian models, with a capital at Seuthopolis, but this state was short-lived. By the 2nd century AD. Thracia had become a province of the Roman empire, territorially equivalent to the southern part of modern Bulgaria.

Three Age System a model devised by Christian THOMSEN for organizing the artifacts on display at the National Museum in Copenhagen. The system was first publicized with the opening of the museum in 1819, and was later expanded in a formal guidebook written by Thomsen in 1836 (the first English translation appeared in 1848). The system has become the primary organizational framework for the whole of European prehistory. The model proposes that European prehistory can be broken into three successive stages, each one marked by changes in the dominant technology: Stone Age; Bronze Age; Iron Age.

Three Kingdoms 1 in China, the Wei (AD 220–265), Shu Han (AD 221–263) and Wu (AD 222–280) Kingdoms of the Three Kingdoms/Six Dynasties period, which succeeded the HAN Dynasty (see CHINESE DYNASTIES). **2** on the Korean peninsula, the PROTOHISTORIC kingdoms of KOGURYO, PAEKCHE and SILLA, existing independently from c.AD 300 until 668, when the peninsula was unified under Silla. The KAYA POLITIES coexisted with the larger Three Kingdoms during this time. See also KAYA, KOREA.

Thulamela a stone-walled Late Iron Age settlement near Pafuri in the northern Kruger National Park of South Africa, close to the meeting point of the borders of South Africa, Zimbabwe and Mozambique, occupied between the 13th and 17th centuries AD, and located at the southeastern limit of the extent of the Zimbabwe tradition. Of particular interest are two burials of high-ranking individuals that in 1996 were found to contain the first gold grave-goods excavated under controlled conditions from a South African Iron Age site. A male dating to the 15th century AD was buried with gold bracelets, rolls of iron wire clamped with small pieces of gold and ostrich eggshell beads. The bones were not in their anatomical positions and were interred some time after decomposition had occurred. A female burial dating to the late 15th–16th century AD included a triple-stranded gold wire bracelet and 291 gold beads apparently forming a double bracelet.

Thule a prehistoric ESKIMO culture which originated in Alaska about AD 900, and spread eastwards as far as Greenland about AD 1000 as a result of climatic improvement, although it retreated westwards again after AD 1300. The culture was dependent on the hunting of sea-mammals, although caribou and other land animals were also taken. Western Thule used a coarse pottery which was later replaced by soapstone vessels. Stone was not commonly used for artifacts, the preferred media being bone, ivory and antler. The Thule were the SKRAEL-INGS encountered by the VIKINGS in the 10th century AD. See also QILAKITSOQ.

thumbnail scraper a small convex scraper, the size and shape of a thumbnail, found in both Pleistocene and Holocene contexts in Australia. Their functions are poorly understood. Finely worked thumbnail scrapers have been seen as part of the AUSTRALIAN SMALL TOOL TRADITION. However, they are increasingly reported from Pleistocene sites and are a distinctive feature of southwestern TASMANIAN Pleistocene assemblages from about 24,000 years ago. They are also reported from sites of comparable age in Victoria.

Thunderbird site a PALAEOINDIAN and ARCHAIC campsite in Virginia, USA, which is part of a series of sites known as Flint Run. The Thunderbird site includes both processing and hunting sites. POSTHOLE may be the remains of the oldest structures in North America (approximately 11,000 BP), although their association with the CLOVIS level is not certain, and they may date to the succeeding Archaic.

thylacine or **Tasmanian tiger** a flesh-eating marsupial predator which became extinct on the Australian mainland about 3000 bp, possibly as a result of competition with the dingo, but which survived in TASMANIA until the 20th century.

Tiahuanaco or **Tiwanaku** a major MIDDLE HORIZON site located on the altiplano of the central Andes in Bolivia, the capital of a large regional state. The central core of the site comprises a ceremonial district, 500 by 1,000 m (550 by 1,100 yds) in extent. This includes a large sunken rectangular plaza, the Kalasasaya, as well as the Akapana, a large U-shaped mound surrounding a spring. Near the Kalasasaya is the monumental Gate of the Sun. Originally a single slab of andesite (it is presently broken into two pieces), it was cut to form a large doorway, with niches on either side. Above the doorway is an elaborate bas-relief frieze depicting a central deity, the Staff Deity, a human standing on a low stepped platform, wearing an elaborate head-dress with appendages ending in the heads of animals, and holding a staff in each hand. He is flanked by rows of anthropomorphous birds. Along the bottom of the panel are a series of anthropomorphous faces, much like the face of the Staff Deity.

TIAHUANACO, Bolivia: the Gate of the Sun.

The site had a substantial population numbering probably in the tens of thousands. Investigations by Alan Kolata indicate that Tiahuanaco reorganized agriculture in the altiplano, building systems of raised fields to bring marshy land under cultivation and to increase production of potatoes. The distribution of Tiahuanaco artifacts and architecture suggests that it was the capital of a state that controlled the Titicaca Basin of Peru and Bolivia. Tiahuanaco colonies have been found in the Moquegua Valley of Peru, and trade relations were established with regions as far away as San Pedro de Atacama, Chile. Although Tiahuanaco shared some aspects of its iconography with HUARI, especially the Staff Deity and associated figures, the two cultures are geographically distinct, only overlapping in the region of Moquegua in southern Peru, where the Tiahuanaco site of Omo lies within sight of the Huari site of Cerro Baul. The relationship between the two POLITIES, whether amicable or not, is yet unclear.

Tianko Panjang a cave-site in the interior of central Sumatra, yielding an obsidian microlith industry characterized by unretouched flakes and chips of c.9000 bc and later; upper levels contain pottery.

Tiaret a region of Algeria where many CAPSIAN sites are found.

Tibava an ENEOLITHIC cemetery and settlement of the TISZA CULTURE in eastern Slovakia, dating to the 5th millennium BC. Tibava is located at the entrance to a pass through the Vihorlat Range of the Carpathians which formed an important route between the Tisza and Vistula drainages. Copper axe-adzes which were manufactured further south in the Balkans found their way north to this site through trade. Rich graves in the cemetery contained up to thirty-two pottery vessels and objects of stone, flint, copper and gold.

Tiefstichkeramik a style of pottery decoration which characterizes the FUNNEL BEAKER culture of the North European Plain in Germany and Holland between *c*.4000 and 3700 BC. *Tiefstich* decoration consists of short, deeply incised strokes in bands and zigzag patterns. It is closely associated with the HUNEBED tombs of the North European Plain.

Tiekene-Boussoura a funerary megalithic site in eastern Senegal, dating to the 6th–8th centuries AD. Thirty monuments with nine circles of upright stones enclosing multiple burials with pottery were found, suggesting a highly stratified society contemporaneous with GHANA.

Tiemassas a Senegalese site with an undated microlithic industry containing geometric microliths as well as leaf-shaped and hollow-based projectile points.

Tievebulliagh a Neolithic axe factory in Co. Antrim, Northern Ireland, source of many of the Group IX porcellanite axes; a second source is the small offshore island of Rathlin some 24 km (15 miles) to the north. Group IX axes are widespread in Ireland and are also found in mainland Britain.

Tighenif (formerly **Ternifine**) an ACHEULIAN site next to a spring in northwestern Algeria, from which three well-preserved human mandibles, some teeth and a small skull fragment were recovered by ARAMBOURG in the 1950s, initially described as belonging to *Atlanthropus mauritanicus*, and later attributed to HOMO *erectus*. They were associated with handaxes and flaked cobbles, as well as abundant faunal remains indicating an early Middle Pleistocene date.

Tiglathpileser III a king of ASSYRIA, founder of the later Assyrian empire. After the 9th-century NEO-ASSYRIAN empire collapsed (following the reign of Shalmaneser III – see AŠŠURNAṢIRPAL II), the next great king was Tiglathpileser III (744–727 BC), who restored and extended the empire, and reorganized provincial administration. During his reign, BABYLONIA was effectively brought within the empire as a client state. Sargon II (721–705 BC) further enlarged the empire, campaigning extensively in Syro-Palestine and in URARTU and other mountainous regions around Assyria, and engaged in a protracted war with the CHALDEAN king Merodach-baladan in southern Babylonia. These two kings established the 'classic' Assyrian empire that provided later western Asian empires with the model of imperial rule.

Tikal one of the largest of the Southern Lowland MAYA centres, located in Guatemala. The earliest buildings at the site date to 800 BC, from which time construction continued for over 1,000 years. At its height, its central core covered 16 sq. km (6 sq. miles). Evidence of influence from TEOTIHUACÁN is thought to have come from the ruler Curl Nose, and later his son, Stormy Sky. Curl Nose who may have been from KAMINALJUYÚ, married into the ruling dynasty at Tikal.

The site is most significant for the results of an extensive mapping project carried out by the University Museum of the University of Pennsylvania, 1956–70, under the direction first of Edwin Shook and then of William R. Coe. During the course of the project, the substantial number of domestic structures mapped made Maya archaeologists re-evaluate the notion that Maya ceremonial centres were non-urban, occupied only during certain events. The residences identified implied a substantial population for the centre, estimated at between 45–75,000. To accommodate such a population, archaeologists had to reconsider their assumptions about the agricultural system of the Precolumbian Maya. Work by Dennis Puleston suggests that the very nutritious ramon nut was an important food source, in addition to corn, beans and squash. Puleston found an association between the distribution of housemounds, ramon trees and CHULTUNS. Chultuns provide an effective place to store the ramon nuts.

tiki see HEI TIKI.

Tilemsi a north-south-oriented valley that ends at the River Niger at GAO in Mali. It was probably one of the main routes followed by pastoralists who moved southwards after the desiccation of the Sahara after about 4,500 BP. See also KARKARICHINKAT.

Tilkitepe a prehistoric site to the southeast of Lake Van in eastern Anatolia, which represents the northernmost well-documented representation of the HALAF culture. Excavated principally in the 1930s by E. Reilly and K. Lake, the stratigraphic and contextual control of the Halaf material is poor, and allows only a typological approach to the recovered materials. Later occupations also occur, represented by later CHALCOLITHIC and some EARLY BRONZE AGE (KURA-ARAXES culture) pottery. Tilkitepe lies near some of the obsidian sources by Lake Van, and many commentaries on the Halaf phenomenon invoke this proximity as an example of controlled access to this widely traded material.

till an aggregate of material, consisting typically but not necessarily of massive, unsorted or poorly sorted DIAMICTON, deposited directly by GLACIAL ice, and not significantly resedimented after original deposition. Till is direct evidence of GLACIATION, and is often associated with MORAINE landforms. Much of the material in the environment directly in front of a glacier is descriptively diamicton, but not all diamicton is till, and much of it may be series of debris and sediment flow deposits, caused by the reworking of till in this water-rich environment. Several types of till are recognized, deposited in the supraglacial or subglacial environment, based on associated sediment types, landforms and STRATIGRAPHIC sequence.

Tillya-Depe a small (1 ha [2.5 acre]) site in southern Bactria in northwestern Afghanistan, excavated by V. I. Sarianidi in the 1970s. It consists of a series of Iron Age (Yaz complex) levels (see YAZ-DEPE) dated to the first half of the 1st millennium BC, the early levels containing a central fortified architectural platform. The site is perhaps most famous for the group of 'royal tombs' dug into its surface after abandonment; these had extremely rich contents, including many gold vessels and jewellery, and are dated to the early 1st millennium AD (seemingly KUSHAN).

Timbaktu see SONGHAY.

Timber Grave culture see SRUBNAYA CULTURE.

time slice see GROUND PENETRATING RADAR.

Timna a series of copper-smelting sites in southern Israel, exploited from the CHALCOLITHIC to the Roman period and excavated by Rothenberg in 1964–77. The most remarkable structure located at Timna is a small temple of the goddess Hathor, showing Egyptian interest in the area during the NEW KINGDOM.

Timonovka two Upper Palaeolithic open-air sites on the Desna River near Bryansk in European Russia. The occupation horizons at each locality are buried in loess and slope deposits overlying a bedrock promontory. Collectively, the sites have yielded radiocarbon dates of 15,110–12,200 bp. The heavily weathered faunal remains are predominantly woolly mammoth. Timonovka I was originally reported to contain evidence of large semi-subterranean dwellings, but these features have been revealed as ICE-WEDGE casts; however, the remains of at least two MAMMOTH-BONE HOUSES may be represented. Timonovka I was discovered and initially excavated by Voevodskij in 1927; subsequent excavations were conducted by GORODTSOV in 1928–33 and ROGACHEV in 1955. Timonovka II was discovered and excavated by Grekhova during 1965–7.

tin a malleable metallic element typically added to other metallic elements to form alloys, most notably bronze, for the manufacture of artifacts. Most tin is extracted from the tin oxide mineral *cassiterite*.

Tindale, Norman Barnett (1900–1993) a pioneering Australian archaeologist who conducted the first scientific excavations in Australia at DEVON DOWNS in 1929. His cultural sequence has not survived the test of time, but his tribal map of Australia remains a key reference.

Tingkayu a series of sites in Sabah, northern Borneo, near the edge of an ancient lake, yielding a sophisticated pebble and flake industry based on local chert, characterized by bifacially flaked lanceolate knives and large tabular bifaces, dating c.28,000–17,000 BP, preceding the industry of the BATURONG CAVES.

Tintan a Holocene site in northern Mauretania, Africa, which yielded fifty individuals highly reminiscent of the MECHTA-AFALOU type.

Ti-n-Torha two rockshelter sites in the ACACUS of southwestern Libya. Ti-n-Torha East and Two Caves are two rockshelters with radiocarbon dates between 9350 and 7730 bp with evidence for fishing, fowling and hunting, especially of Barbary sheep. Ti-n-Torha North has radiocarbon dates between 7440 and 5260 bp and was occupied by pastoralists with cattle and small stock, especially sheep.

tipi ring a circle of stones found in the northern Plains of North America, thought to be the remains of weights used to keep in place the wall of a skin lodge or *tipi*. There are probably millions of these sites in the northern Plains.

Tîrpeşti a stratified site of the CUCUTENI-TRIPOLYE culture in northeastern Romania. Surrounded by a ditch, it is relatively small, but shares many characteristics with the larger Cucuteni-Tripolye sites in terms of location, organization and presence of figurines.

Tiryns a site in the Argolid, Greece, which was once coastal but has since been stranded some distance from the sea. The German excavations, initiated by SCHLIEMANN in 1884, have revealed a large, circular, Early HELLADIC structure which may have served as a communal granary. The massive CYCLOPEAN fortifications and the MYCENAEAN palace, built in the 14th–13th centuries BC, indicate that Tiryns remained a major centre but may have been dominated by MYCENAE politically.

Tisza culture a late Neolithic culture of eastern Hungary, centred on the Tisza River, contemporaneous with the LENGYEL culture of eastern-Central Europe and sharing many of its characteristics, between c.4800 and 4200 BC. Both TELL and horizontal settlements are known. Tisza ceramics are characterized by a wide variety of forms, including footed and pedestalled bowls. They are frequently decorated with incised lines in complicated geometrical patterns that cover their entire surface. Red, yellow and white paint is applied after firing.

Tiszapolgár culture an ENEOLITHIC culture of eastern Hungary, successor to the TISZA CULTURE between 4200 and 3800 BC, named after the large cemetery site at Tiszapolgár-Basatanya. The pottery continues the Tisza tradition of pedestalled bowls and other similar forms, but is characterized by an almost total lack of decoration save for small lugs and bosses, a phenomenon similar to the late phase of the LENGYEL culture to the northeast. At Tiszapolgár-Basatanya, 156 contracted inhumations occurred in individual pits with a vessel and often a copper shaft-hole hammer-axe or other tool.

Tito Bustillo a cave-site in Asturias, northern Spain, named after one of its discoverers in 1966 and containing a wealth of PORTABLE and PARIETAL ART of the Upper MAGDALENIAN. It is especially notable for a polychrome panel of horses and deer, for the westernmost depictions and bones of reindeer, and for a number of engraved stones dating to the Upper Magdalenian (14,250 bp). The cave was blocked immediately after this period.

Titriş Höyük a Bronze Age town located at the edge of a plain near the Euphrates in southeastern Turkey. The site focuses on a 3 ha (7 acre) mound, in which appear Early Bronze Age through medieval occupations. A walled lower town covers another 32 ha (79 acres), with extramural suburbs also present. The lower town was a rapid and planned development around 2600/2500 BC, and was abandoned just as abruptly around 2200/2100 BC (mid–late Early Bronze Age). A programme of MAGNETOMETRY survey provides an unusually detailed plan of the houses, streets and city wall; excavation has corroborated and extended the magnetometry results. Investigation of one extra-mural suburb revealed a workshop for making CANAANEAN BLADES.

Tiwanaku see TIAHUANACO.

TL see LUMINESCENCE DATING.

Tlaloc the rain and storm god of POSTCLASSIC central Mexico, characterized by goggle eyes and long fangs. Similar rain deities originate in the PRECLASSIC among the OLMEC, indicating a long sequence of cultural continuity and the importance of rainfall to the agricultural societies of MESOAMERICA. Depictions of Tlaloc at sites outside the region, in the centres of KAMINALJUYÚ and COPÁN, are used as further evidence of TEOTIHUACÁN's influence at these places.

Tlapacoya and Tlatilco see BASIN OF MEXICO.

tlatoque the ruler of a city-state in the BASIN OF MEXICO during AZTEC rule. These petty kings were supported by produce cultivated on communal land and by tribute in labour and service. The tlatoque generally claimed descent from QUETZALCÓATL through the 'TOLTECS', thus strengthening his right to rule through his divine lineage.

To'aga a deeply stratified coastal site on Ofu Island, Samoa, with evidence of occupation spanning the entire Samoan sequence, and unusual preservation of shell and bone. The oldest deposits date to 3700–3300 BP and may be LAPITA. The succeeding assemblage dates to 2500–1900 BP and is characterized by plain ceramics, and shell fish-hooks and ornaments, some of which are comparable to early eastern Polynesian material (see PACIFIC) from the Marquesas and Society Islands.

Toalian a mid Holocene (6000 BC and later) stone flake and blade industry of Sulawesi, Indonesia, characterized by backed flakes and microliths, including Maros points.

Toca de Esperança a PRECERAMIC site in eastern Brazil, whose earliest level yielded a date of 295,000 bp. The bones of extinct Pleistocene fauna were associated in this level with what have been claimed to be very crude chipped stone tools. Most scholars are very sceptical of the early date; if accurate, the site would represent a HOMO *erectus* occupation in the New World, which is regarded as extremely unlikely.

Toca do Boqueirão see PEDRA FURADA.

Tocra (*Gk* Taucheira) a Greek city in Cyrenaica, Libya, probably founded in the late 7th century BC. Imported ARCHAIC Greek pottery was found in votive deposits in the sanctuary of Demeter and Kore.

Toftum a Neolithic enclosure in Jutland, Denmark, consisting of a causewayed ditch, double on the west side. Material recovered was of the transitional early/middle Neolithic FUCHSBERG phase, c.3400 BC. See also SARUP.

Togolok **1** a group of Late Bronze Age sites in the Murghab delta in southeastern Turkmenistan. Togolok sites are generally smaller than those of the GONUR phase, though Togolok I is perhaps 15 ha (37 acres), and some others are equally large. As with the Gonur phase, many aspects of the material culture are similar to the BACTRIAN BRONZE AGE.
2 a chronological phase (dated perhaps to the second quarter of the 2nd millennium BC) which shows considerable continuity with the preceding Gonur phase.

togueres habitation areas above the floodplain of the interior delta of the Niger River in Mali which have yielded rich archaeological material of agricultural fishing people. Excavated sites include Toguere Dowpil, occupied between 1000 and 500 BP, and Toguere Galia, with dates between 1000 and 800 BP.

Tohoku a modern district of northern Honshu Island, Japan, often used in archaeological writings. It comprises Aomori, Iwate, Akita, Yamagata, Miyagi and Fukushima Prefectures. See EMISHI, JOMON, KAMEGAOKA.

tohua ceremonial dancing grounds unique to the Marquesas Islands, Polynesia, comprising rectangular flat earthen areas, surrounded by raised platforms used either for temples or as seating for spectators. One of the largest tohua is VAHANGEKU'A in the TAIPIVAI VALLEY.

Tokai a pre-modern district of Japan (see RITSURYO) bordering the Pacific seaboard, often used in archaeological writings. It comprises modern Tokyo Metropolitan District and Chiba, Ibaragi, Saitama, Kanagawa, Shizuoka, Aichi and Mie Prefectures (see TORO).

tokens small clay geometric objects (spheres, discs, cones, ovoids, cylinders and so forth) found in many early Neolithic sites of western Asia (Levant, the Taurus and Zagros Mountains and their piedmont zones). The work of

TOLLUND MAN, Denmark.

D. Schmandt-Besserat suggests that these clay geometrics give rise ultimately to writing. Similarly shaped clay 'counters' occur within hollow clay BULLAE (envelopes), which are sealed by a CYLINDER SEAL impression, a characteristic of late URUK southern MESOPOTAMIA. These same bullae might also bear impressions of the tokens themselves, representing the content of the bulla. From this form of accountancy to writing numbers on a tablet (i.e. the flattened bulla) is a short step; soon thereafter, words were added to the numbers to clarify the accountancy. This progression is observed at the ACROPOLE of SUSA and (with some stratigraphic circularity) at WARKA (EANNA SOUNDING).

Tolbaga an Upper Palaeolithic open-air site on the Khilok River near Lake Baikal in southern-central Siberia. The main cultural layer is buried in slope deposits on a TERRACE of medium elevation. Associated faunal remains include woolly rhinoceros, steppe bison and reindeer; two of the bones yielded dates of 34,860 and 27,210 bp. Among the artifacts are retouched blades, sidescrapers and endscrapers, points, burins and a piece of carved bone representing the head of a bear. Redeposited artifacts and faunal remains were found in overlying sandy loam layers. Tolbaga is an important Siberian early Upper Palaeolithic locality; it was discovered and excavated in the 1970s by OKLADNIKOV and others.

Tollund Man an Iron Age bog body discovered in the Tollund Fen, central Jutland, Denmark, in 1950. Naked except for a pointed leather cap, he lay in the bog on his right side with a noose around his neck. Stomach contents showed that his last meal had been a gruel containing barley, linseed, knotweed, dock and camomile but no meat. Possibly a ritual sacrifice or an executed criminal, Tollund Man has been radiocarbon dated to c. 2100 bp.

Tolstaya Mogila one of the so-called 'royal' SCYTHIAN KURGANS, situated on the Lower Dnieper, Ukraine, and

excavated in 1971 by B. Mozolevski. The burial mound was 8.6 m (28 ft) high and 70 m (77 yds) in diameter, and outlined by a ditch. In the ditch and around it there were lots of animal bones and AMPHORA sherds, the traces of a grandiose funeral feast. The central tomb consisted of an entrance-pit, two catacombs and a chamber, connected with a DROMOS. It belonged to a representative of the highest Scythian nobility. All the chambers had been ravaged. Among the very few preserved items found in the dromos are an iron sword in a golden scabbard and a famous golden PECTORAL – both are top-class works of art made by Greek artists and ordered by the Scythians. The relief images on the pectoral depict scenes of animals fighting, and scenes from Scythian life. Next to the central construction were two tombs with horses in rich harnesses, as well as the graves of the grooms. A later lateral chamber contained the burial of a young woman with her servants. Her clothes and head-dress were amply decorated with golden plaques and adornments (a total of 600). Shortly afterwards, a child was buried next to the woman, also in rich clothes. The combination of burials shows that this kurgan was a burial vault for one noble family.

'Toltec' one of the important cultures of MESOAMERICA, whose influence lasted from AD 900 to 1100. The AZTECS claimed to be descended from the 'Toltecs'; and, to date, much of our understanding of the 'Toltecs' comes from ethnohistoric sources. These sources contain legend and myth, as well as fact. Archaeologists are currently reassessing their understanding of the 'Toltecs', and are using the archaeological record to supplement other sources. The 'Toltecs' have been depicted as spreading their influence throughout Mesoamerica through military conquest and coercion, but the archaeological evidence for this is not clear. At TULA, the 'Toltec' capital, symbols of militarism, death and blood are prevalent. Nearly identical architecture and symbolism occur at the MAYA site of CHICHÉN ITZÁ, fuelling speculation of 'Toltec' interaction in the Yucatán.

Tomba di Giganti see GIANT'S GRAVE.

Tomskaya an Upper Palaeolithic open-air site on the Tom' River (Ob' tributary) in Tomsk, western Siberia. A small assemblage of artifacts was found in association with the disarticulated skeleton of a woolly mammoth, buried in loess-like loam overlying ALLUVIUM of the third terrace. The remains have yielded a date of 18,300 bp. The artifacts include burins and retouched blades. Tomskaya apparently represents a KILL-SITE, which is rare among Palaeolithic sites in Russia. It was excavated by the zoologist Kashchenko in 1886.

Tondidiaro see MEGALITHIC MONUMENT.

Tongsamdong a Neolithic SHELL MIDDEN site in South Kyongsang Province, Korea, dating to c.4500–1500 BC.

JOMON pottery and obsidian from Kyushu among the CHULMUN remains document overseas interaction with Japanese island inhabitants.

tool an artifact used for a specific task.

Toolondo the remains of a fish-trap system, in southwestern Victoria, Australia, comprising earth-cut channels. Excavations by Harry Lourandos established that the system fell out of use about 200 years ago. As in the case of LAKE CONDAH, the antiquity of the system remains unknown.

Toolumbunner an ochre quarry in northern TASMANIA, visited in the 1830s by ROBINSON. The site was relocated in 1982 and subsequently investigated by a team from Melbourne University. Excavation showed that the site was in use for at least the last 500 years.

topography the physical configuration of the landscape, usually expressed with particular reference to relief and contour. A detailing of site topography is fundamental in archaeological site description. Often this includes construction of a topographic map, where three-dimensional relief is expressed in two dimensions by the use of contour lines, representing intersections of a set of imaginary equally spaced horizontal planes at prescribed altitudes with the land surface. Contour lines are identified by altitude, preferably relative to a formally recognized sealevel, but sometimes to a relative local DATUM. Several surveying instruments can be used to construct local topographic maps, including the TRANSIT, THEODOLITE and LEVEL.

Toprakkale **1** a site on the eastern shore of Lake Van in eastern Anatolia, which, together with the related monuments around the lake, represents the centre of the URARTIAN state (roughly 850–600 BC). Toprakkale itself contains a large temple complex and associated storerooms and residential area which were subject to 'excavation' in the 19th century, yielding a great many bronzes, carved ivory, and possibly silk. Elsewhere in the Van area are a series of fortified sites with the typically Urartian extensive storerooms; temples at various places, including that at Adilcevas, which retains some of its wall paintings; the rock-cut tomb of Argishti I (786–764) at Tushpa; and monumental inscriptions in various localities. Urartian texts also refer to a large number of irrigation works in the Van area. Recent Turkish work at Van has focused on the citadel and palace of Argisti I; excavation in the mound of Van Kalesi has exposed Urartian levels overlying a sequence that begins in the EARLY BRONZE AGE.
2 a class of burnished fine red ware characteristic of the Urartian period.

torc or **torque** a neckring, usually of gold, worn by CELTIC warriors and sometimes found in Late Iron Age hoards or graves. One of the finest examples is the SNETTISHAM torc.

Tordos see TURDAŞ.

toreutics (*Gk* toreutikos, carving or chiselling) the art of working in relief on artistic objects in metal. The term is most often used for the refinement of wares by embossing or stamping, but it sometimes also means the finishing of moulded wares.

Torihama an early JOMON site in Fukui Prefecture, Japan, where waterlogging has preserved evidence of horticultural practices, as well as many bone and wood artifacts such as a dugout canoe, paddles, hunting bows, tool hafts, wooden bowls and a lacquer comb. Remains of gourds and beans at 5000–3500 BC suggest mid Holocene extension of control over garden crops in western Japan well before the adoption of rice agriculture (see ITAZUKE).

Toro a late YAYOI site in Shizuoka Prefecture, Japan, known for its unbounded village plan and wet-preserved wooden tools and architectural remains. Excavated in 1948 as the first interdisciplinary project of the Japanese Archaeologists' Association, it has long served as the type-site for the rice-growing Yayoi period despite being in the marginal TOKAI region (compare ITAZUKE). Several pithouses and raised granaries have been reconstructed as a historical park; excavated paddy-field systems adjoin the village, but the cemetery has not been recovered. Compare YOSHINOGARI.

Torralba and Ambrona two large Lower Palaeolithic Spanish lake-side sites, 2 km (1.2 miles) apart, 150 km (90 miles) northeast of Madrid, which have been excavated by numerous workers, most recently Howell, Aguirre, Butzer and Freeman. The sites have yielded ACHEULIAN tools and the remains of many partially dismembered animals, particularly straight-tusked elephants and horses. Many of the bones are water-transported, but it is possible that some artifacts were used to kill or at least butcher some of the animals. The sites belong to the Middle Pleistocene, somewhere between 700,000 and 300,000 BP.

torre a circular dry-stone tower of Bronze Age date (2nd millennium BC) found in southern Corsica. Though in some ways equivalent to the Sardinian NURAGHE, the Corsican torre was capped by a CORBELLED VAULT covering the principal chamber, and was not topped by a fighting platform. A torre is the central feature of the FILITOSA promontory fort.

Torre Annunziata see OPLONTIS.

Torre in Pietra a Palaeolithic site approximately 25 km (16 miles) to the south of Rome, Italy, which has yielded an ACHEULIAN industry of probable RISSIAN age with associated faunal remains, and an early dating MOUSTERIAN assemblage.

tortoise core see LEVALLOIS TECHNIQUE.

Torwa see KHAMI.

Tószeg a TELL site in eastern Hungary near Szolnok on the Tisza River, where a stratigraphy several metres in depth has defined the chronological sequence of the Early Bronze Age in this region. A variety of periodizations have been proposed during the mid 20th century by CHILDE, Tompa and Moszolics. Moszolics' chronology from the early 1950s is generally still used, with the settlement layers at Tószeg providing the NAGYRÉV-HATVAN-FÜZESABONY sequence between c.2500 and 1500 BC.

toumba or **magoula** in Greek archaeology an artificial mound or TELL.

Toutswe an Iron Age tradition in eastern Botswana, named after the large settlement of Toutswemogala, which achieved prominence at the same time as K2 and MAPUNGUBWE. About 300 sites, which were organized in a hierarchy to correlate with size and location, dating between about ad 680 and 1300, have been identified. These are clearly visible on aerial photographs because they are identified by concentrations of *Cenchrus ciliaris* grass, which grows abundantly on such mounds. Massive vitrified deposits at sites such as Toutswemogala, Bosutswe and Shoshong are accumulations of animal dung which caught fire in the past and which testify to herding on a substantial scale.

trace elements elements that occur naturally in minor amounts in minerals in soils and sediment. Trace element suites can be identified by various analyses and may serve as 'fingerprints' for some artifact raw material sources. Source identification can lead to further interpretations of trade and economic systems.

trademarks see GRAFFITI.

tradition 1 long-term continuity in either individual technologies or attributes.

2 a temporally ordered series of archaeological phases or cultures that show cultural similarities to each other.

trait an element of an archaeological culture or technology.

Trajan's column a column at ROME, some 38 m (125 ft) high, decorated with a continuous spiral relief frieze, surmounted by a statue of the emperor, celebrating the DACIAN wars in the Balkans conducted by the emperor Trajan (AD 98–117). It formed part of the FORUM of Trajan, and the ashes of the emperor and his wife Plotina were placed in its base. The frieze provides a narrative of the campaigns and is an invaluable source of information on Roman and Dacian armour, weapons and other military matters.

tranchet axe a large Mesolithic axe with a cutting-edge formed by the intersection of two flake scars removed by the TRANCHET TECHNIQUE.

tranchet technique 1 the precise removal of a large flat flake from the tip of a biface, so that the edge of the tranchet flake scar forms a straight cutting-edge.

2 a northern and northwestern Mesolithic technique used to create or resharpen the cutting-edge of an axe or adze, by striking a thick flake from the tip. The resultant tranchet flakes have a highly distinctive appearance.

Trang Kenh an early metal age settlement and important NEPHRITE (jade) ornament workshop, excavated in 1968 and 1986, and dated to c.1200 BC, with later DONG SON period burials, near the Bach Dang River, north of Hai Phong, Vietnam. Jade working locations are rare in East Asia, and the site of Bai Tu in Hai Bac Province is the only other one known from Vietnam.

Transcaucasian Early Bronze Age see KURA-ARAXES CULTURE.

transhumance a subsistence strategy, in which human groups copy the seasonal or periodic movement, between fundamentally different environmental zones, of the animals on which they rely for food. This movement is often altitudinal and is determined by seasonally changing climate and resource availability. In Europe and the Old World, the term is usually restricted to pastoralist farmers and their livestock, whereas in the New World the term is often used more generally for any well-defined animal/human migration. The identification of prehistoric transhumance patterns was one of the principal aims of many studies of PALAEOECONOMY.

transit a surveying instrument capable of measuring horizontal and vertical angles and horizontal distances. Similar to a LEVEL, ALIDADE and THEODOLITE, it consists of a focusing telescope for long sightings. Unlike the level and alidade, however, the telescope is mounted on a graduated base used to measure horizontal angles. It also has a striding level to level the scope, either a bull's-eye level or two bubble levels perpendicular to one another to level the instrument on the tripod on which it rests, a vernier scale for measuring vertical angles, stadia and cross hairs for determining distances with measurements taken from a stadia rod, and a compass for determining magnetic north and taking compass bearings. The telescope can also pivot on a horizontal transverse axis to reverse its line of sight. The transit is used for the same purposes as a theodolite. It cannot, however, be used to construct a map in the field simultaneously, as can be done with a plane table and alidade.

transmission electron microscopy a technique used to examine the internal and surface structure and morphology of a wide range of materials. An extremely thin sample is prepared either by grinding it to a fine powder which is mounted on a carbon film, or by reproducing the surface of the sample in one of several ways. A high-energy electron beam is focused so that it passes through the sample. An image of the sample is enhanced by magnification and projected so that it can be photographed if desired. Unlike in SCANNING ELECTRON MICROSCOPY, the sample must be extremely thin for the beam to penetrate it and reveal internal structures. Otherwise, many of the same tasks can be performed with both instruments.

travertine or **tufa** a light-coloured, compact calcite deposited from solution in ground and surface waters at springs, seeps and in caves. Porous varieties may be referred to as calcareous tufa, calcareous sinter or spring deposits. Banded varieties are often referred to as onyx or onyx marble, although onyx is actually a CHALCEDONY. Cave stalactites and stalagmites are formed of travertine. Travertine deposits are potential sources of palaeoenvironmental information, as fossils and organic remains may be incorporated and preserved. Dense travertine with little or no detrital contamination is a candidate for URANIUM SERIES DATING and ISOTOPIC analysis.

TRB culture an early and middle Neolithic culture of northern Europe characterized by the use of a funnel-necked BEAKER (*Trichterrandbecher*) with globular body and out-turned rim. Five regional groups can be distinguished, with largely separate development: the western group in the Netherlands, sometimes associated with Hunebedden (see HUNEBED); the southern group in Germany with Baalberge and Salzmünde variants; the southeastern group in the Czech Republic; the eastern group in Poland; and the northern group in Denmark and Sweden, sometimes found in megalithic tombs and at enclosures such as SARUP and TOFTUM. Copper was worked in the southeastern group, and products distributed among the eastern and southern groups, reaching even the northern group as shown by the BYGHOLM hoard.

Trebenište an Iron Age burial site of the HALLSTATT D period (*c.*600 BC) in southern Yugoslavia, where a large KRATER of Greek origin, resembling the one from VIX, was found. Trebenište represents the most northerly penetration of Greek goods into lands adjacent to Greece during this period (although in western Europe there is ample evidence of trade with Greece at this time).

tree-ring dating see DENDROCHRONOLOGY.

Trelleborg a VIKING fortress in Zealand, Denmark, of *c.*AD 1000, comprising a central circular fortification, 13.6 m (45 ft) in diameter, with four gates. These serve two main streets dividing the interior into four quadrants, each containing four barrack buildings arranged in a square. Each building was boat-shaped, 30 m (33 yds) long and 8 m (9 yds) wide.

trephination or **trepanation** a surgical technique whereby small sections of cranial bones were removed. The cuts were made by scraping or sawing, or, less com-monly, by drilling a series of adjacent round holes. After removal of the bone piece, the head was wrapped, and in many cases the patient survived the operation and the bone grew back. Trephination is found especially in the south coast PARACAS culture of Peru, dating to the EARLY HORIZON, but the practice was also used elsewhere in the world and in other periods.

Tressé a late Neolithic ALLÉE COUVERTE in Ille-et-Vilaine, France, with a paved chamber over 10 m (33 ft) long roofed by seven capstones. ORTHOSTATS of the terminal chamber were carved with four pairs of small breasts. Material recovered included late Neolithic coarse ware pottery and blades of GRAND PRESSIGNY flint.

Tres Zapotes an OLMEC CEREMONIAL CENTRE in southern Veracruz, Mexico. The site is poorly known except for its sculptures, including Olmec heads. Occupied from 1000 to 600 BC, Tres Zapotes became the most important centre after LA VENTA was destroyed. Matthew STIRLING excavated here, beginning in 1938.

Treugol'naya Cave a small cave located near the town of Pregradnaya in the northwestern Caucasus region of Russia. The lower and middle levels contain mammals of the early Middle Pleistocene (e.g. *Stephanorhinus hundsheimensis*), and the occupation layers are dated to roughly 500,000–400,000 BP. The artifact assemblages are small and include choppers, scrapers and limaces. A large quantity of red deer and bison remains were found associated with the artifacts, but probably were accumulated by carnivores. Treugol'naya Cave is the earliest known site in eastern Europe, and was excavated by Doronichev in 1986–91.

Trialeti a high plateau region south of Tbilisi in southern Georgia (Transcaucasia), where B. A. Kuftin's exploration of KURGANS during the 1930s produced one of Georgia's most widely known archaeological cultures. Of variable size and internal structure, the Trialeti Bronze Age kurgans contain single burials, often accompanied by a four-wheeled cart. The grave-goods include a range of painted wares and an extremely rich inventory of metal objects (cups, buckets, weapons, jewellery in gold, silver, tin, bronze, copper), sometimes with an extremely rich iconography. Kurgans in other parts of central Transcaucasia have since been found with a comparable cultural inventory; however, the corresponding settlements are very rarely reported. The date of the Trialeti, conventionally 'Middle Bronze Age', is debated and may be pushed back into later Early Bronze times, but certainly begins by around 2000 BC and lasts to the mid 2nd millennium BC.

Trianda the site of a MINOAN colony, on the Aegean island of Rhodes, founded in the 16th century BC, presumably to facilitate trade between CRETE and CYPRUS. After the destruction of the Minoan palaces in the 15th century,

MYCENAEANS may have settled at Trianda, but the site was abandoned in the 14th century.

triangulation a surveying technique in which a network of triangles is laid out, and an unknown point is located by measuring the angles and distances formed by the lines of sight between the point in question and two known points of a triangle. A base line of known length is established between two control points that serves as one side of one of the triangles. Calculation of distances to other points is then a matter of trigonometric calculations using angles shot with a TRANSIT or other surveying instrument.

tribe a form of social organization which comprises a centrally organized collection of bands. See also BAND, CHIEFDOM, STATE.

Trichterrandbecher see TRB CULTURE.

triclinium the dining-room of a Roman house. The name is derived from the three couches (see KLINE) placed around the walls of a square room. Tables with food would be placed in front of the couches. Some large houses might have several triclinia.

triglyph part of the ENTABLATURE of a Greek building of the DORIC ORDER, alternating with a METOPE. The triglyph had three elements separated by two vertical grooves.

trilithon two upright stones supporting a third to form a kind of arch or doorway. A horseshoe arrangement of five huge SARSEN trilithons is the central feature of STONEHENGE. The island of Tonga has a massive coral trilithon, c.5 m (16 ft) high, of AD 1200 (see HA'AMONGA).

Trimontium see NEWSTEAD.

Trinil a site in the SOLO River Valley of Java. It has given its name to the Pleistocene fauna of c.1.3 million to 500,000 BP, which succeeds that of JETIS, apparently adapted also to an open forest environment. HOMO *erectus* (JAVA MAN) remains are less robust than those of Jetis, and have an estimated age of 900,000 years.

Triple Alliance an alliance formed in AD 1428, when the Aztec-Mexica of TENOCHTITLÁN joined with the Texcoco and the state of Tacuba to overthrow the city-state of Azcapotzalco. Eventually, the AZTECS came to dominate the alliance. The rise of the Triple Alliance ended the competition between city-states in the BASIN OF MEXICO that had begun with the fall of TEOTIHUACÁN.

Tripolye see CUCUTENI-TRIPOLYE.

trireme see PIRAEUS.

Trou Magrite a cave-site near Dinant in the Ardennes, Belgium, first excavated in the 1860s by Edouard DU-PONT, who found an ivory statuette (probably of a man), and an engraved reindeer antler, both now attributed to the AURIGNACIAN. The deposits also contained MOUS-TERIAN, GRAVETTIAN and MAGDALENIAN material. Fresh excavations in the 1990s by L. Straus and M. Otte focused on the transition from the Mousterian to the Aurignacian, and produced controversial dates of c.40,000 for the latter. The cave's abundant Gravettian industry led Dupont to define an 'Upper PERIGORDIAN' stage, between the Aurignacian and Magdalenian, long before PEYRONY's French scheme of the 1920s.

Troy see HISARLIK.

Trundholm a bronze wheeled model of a horse pulling a disc, covered with gold leaf probably to represent the sun. The model, dated to c.1650 BC, was found in 1902 in the Trundholm bog, Zealand, Denmark, where it may have been deposited as a ritual offering.

Truso an early medieval trading town on the shore of Lake Drużno in northern Poland near the mouth of the Vistula River. Truso was described in the 9th century AD by the ANGLO-SAXON traveller Wulfstan, who reported arriving there after a seven-day voyage from HAITHABU, but its actual location was only discovered in 1982. Excavations over the next few years revealed its port area and its workshops. The remains of at least nine boats were found along the lakefront. The workshops in timber houses along streets contain traces of craft production in glass, gold, amber and horn.

Trzciniec culture an Early/Middle Bronze Age culture of the Vistula and Bug drainages in eastern Poland. It continues many cultural traits which emerged at the end of the Neolithic in the CORDED WARE culture, including both the ceramic forms and flint industry. At the same time, there appear a small number of bronze artifacts, primarily imports from areas to the west and south. Trzciniec graves are primarily under tumuli, although cremations are also known. Dating is somewhat uncertain, but generally thought to be between 1800 and 1500 BC.

Tsangli the site of a Neolithic–Bronze Age settlement mound in Thessaly, Greece, excavated by TSOUNTAS in 1905 and by WACE and Thompson in 1910. The late Neolithic Tsangli culture is characterized by grey-on-grey and matt-painted pottery.

Tshangula a cave in the Matopo Hills of southwestern Zimbabwe, containing a sequence of MIDDLE STONE AGE and LATER STONE AGE assemblages, which has given its name to a late Middle Stone Age industry post-dating 30,000 BP, also known as the Umguzan. It contains backed microliths and ostrich eggshell beads as well as Middle Stone Age artifacts, but is not well documented, and may contain more than one industry.

Tshitolian a LATER STONE AGE industry named after the Tshitolo Plateau in the southern Democratic Republic of Congo, dating from c.14,000 to 5000 BP and distributed in Angola, DRC, Gabon and Cameroon in equatorial Africa. It is characterized by backed microliths, small core axes, picks and foliate points.

Tsodilo Hills an important rock art region with many painted LATER STONE AGE rockshelters as well as Iron Age sites near the Okavango swamp in northwestern Botswana. The rock art includes red paintings of a variety of animals, including scenes with domestic animals, grids, spoked circles and handprints, as well as cupmarks.

Tsountas, Christos (1857–1934) a Greek archaeologist who excavated at MYCENAE from 1877 to 1902. He investigated a number of settlement sites in Thessaly, in particular DHIMINI and SESKLO, and he also excavated extensively in the Cyclades.

Tuc d'Audoubert see VOLP.

Túcume a monumental site in the Lambayeque Valley of northern Peru, built c.AD 1100. It covers over 2.2 sq. km (0.85 sq. miles), and includes twenty-six major pyramids arranged around the La Raya Mountain. Recent investigations of the site, led by Thor Heyerdahl, have found that it was a vibrant urban settlement of the Lambayeque culture. The site survived conquest, first by the CHIMÚ culture and later by the INCA empire, but was abandoned early in the Spanish colonial period. Excavations revealed numerous human burials, with grave-goods including textiles and silver artifacts. A frieze apparently depicting reed boats supports Heyerdahl's suggestion that people from Túcume engaged in deep-sea navigation and long-distance ocean trade.

tufa see TRAVERTINE.

Tufariello see APENNINE CULTURE.

tuff a clastic sedimentary rock consisting of compacted volcanic ash. Tuff may bury and preserve archaeological deposits, and can usually be dated by the POTASSIUM-ARGON DATING method.

Tuinplaas see SPRINGBOK FLATS.

Tula a modern town in the state of Hidalgo, Mexico, which has been identified with Tollán, the legendary capital of the 'TOLTECS', by Wigberto Jimenez Moreno and Jorge Acosta in the 1940s. The site began gaining importance in AD 800, after TEOTIHUACÁN fell. Tula reached its greatest extent between AD 900 and 1100. Military symbols are a major theme at the site. It is famous for the Atlantean statues, standing nearly 5 m (16 ft) tall, that supported the roof of pyramid B. Tula was destroyed in AD 1156. After its decline, central Mexico had no central power until the appearance of the AZTECS.

tula or **tula adze** a hafted chisel used in arid central Australia primarily for working the intractable hardwoods of the region. It is made on a thick flake with a prominent bulb and a convex bulbar surface. It could be hafted on a short handle or on a spearthrower. Tulas mounted on spearthrowers were generally smaller, and functioned as light-duty wood scrapers. Repeated resharpening of the semicircular working edge opposite the obtuse-angled striking platform results in a distinctive 'slug'. The oldest archaeological examples date back to 3,600–2,700 years ago in central Australia; steel replaced them in the 20th century. See also ADZE.

tulang mawas ('monkey bone') a long-shafted, socketed iron axe unique to the Iron Age (c.300 BC) of peninsular Malaysia, normally found in hoards and perhaps used as units of value rather than as tools. Other socketed tools of the industry are distantly related to those from BAN DON TA PHET.

Tule Springs a site near Las Vegas, Nevada, USA, which was originally considered to have evidence for human occupation, in the form of hearths and artifacts, which pre-dated 28,000 BC. More recent work at the site has suggested that the earliest date for human use of the site is no greater than 11,000 BP.

Tulúm a POSTCLASSIC MAYA site on the east coast of Yucatán, Mexico. It is a fortified site, facing the sea and surrounded on three sides by a wall 6 m (20 ft) thick and between 3 and 5 m (10 and 16 ft) high. The city, an important trading centre, has a planned design in a concentrated pattern with residences around the CEREMONIAL CENTRE. The buildings at Tulúm are architecturally inferior to those of the CLASSIC Maya.

tumbaga an alloy of gold and copper, developed in the northern Andes by the MOCHE culture of Peru, during the EARLY INTERMEDIATE PERIOD. This alloy is both hard and flexible, making it especially suitable for producing very thin sheets of metal. Its relatively low melting point makes it suitable for cast artifacts. When washed with acid and then hammered, the surface of tumbaga artifacts could be made to look like pure gold.

tumulus a mound of earth or stones, usually covering a burial or burials. The TUMULUS CULTURE is a Middle Bronze Age culture of southern Germany known mainly from inhumations beneath round barrows; it is not to be confused with the Armorican Tumulus culture of Brittany, represented at KERNONEN, with close parallels to the WESSEX CULTURE of southern Britain. See also TOUMBA, SOROS, BURIAL MOUNDS.

Tumulus culture a Middle Bronze Age culture of the central Danube region of the Czech Republic, Slovakia, Austria and Bavaria, following the ÚNĚTICE culture, c.1800–1400 BC. Named after the prevalent burial rite under round mounds of earth and stone (a practice obviously not limited to this period), the Tumulus culture reflects the continuation of a number of earlier trends in ceramics and metalwork, with greater elaboration of

TULA, Mexico: the Atlantean statues.

forms and decorative techniques. The Tumulus burial rite was followed by the URNFIELD burial pattern.

tun the basic unit in the CLASSIC MAYA LONG COUNT equalling 360 days.

Tuna el-Gebel the site of a major cemetery in Middle Egypt, the NECROPOLIS of the site of HERMOPOLIS MAGNA. Foremost among the mortuary monuments are the LATE PERIOD/Graeco-Roman tombs, especially that of the High Priest of THOTH, Petosiris, and the underground galleries containing the burials of sacred ibises and baboons. Near by is a rock-cut STELA marking the boundary of the city of Akhetaten (see EL-AMARNA).

tundra the region between ice-caps and tree-line of lower arctic latitudes, characterized by treeless vegetation consisting of mosses, lichens, sedges, grasses and stunted shrubs growing on PERMAFROST. During the QUATERNARY, tundra and tundra-like conditions were translated southwards during GLACIAL episodes as continental ice-sheets expanded.

Tungus an ethno-linguistic group of eastern Eurasia, especially in the Siberian region. Speakers of Tungusic languages, belonging to the ALTAIC language family, are thought to have infiltrated the Korean peninsula in the Bronze Age (1st millennium BC), resulting in a replacement of the PALAEOASIATIC population of the earlier CHULMUN Neolithic period. This migrational hypothesis has yet to be confirmed.

Turdaş or **Tordos** a site in Transylvania, northwestern Romania, which has given its name to a variant of the

VINČA culture, roughly equivalent to Vinča A/B, sometimes differentiated as the 'Turdaş culture'.

Tureholm largest gold hoard of the Migration period in Scandinavia, containing about 12 kg (26.5 lbs) of gold. Similar remarkable hoards include the one from Timboholm, which consisted of 7 kg (15.5 lbs) of gold in the form of ingots and interlinked gold rings, and the three-ringed collar from Ålleberg, which has tiny human faces separated by crouching animals as its principal motif. The gold in these finds came primarily from Roman coins that had been melted down and reworked by local craftsmen.

Turkana Boy see NARIOKOTOME.

Turkey see GREECE, TURKEY, ALBANIA AND YUGOSLAVIA.

Turville-Petre, Francis Adrian Joseph (1901–42) an English archaeologist whose brief but important career was confined to British mandated territory in western Asia. After extensive surveys in the Galilee area, he excavated in Emireh and ZUTTIYEH caves in 1925, finding in Zuttiyeh the fragmentary GALILEE SKULL: with a relative date of 300–350,000 BP, this remains the oldest human fossil yet found in the Levant. He accompanied GARROD to the southern Kurdistan caves of ZARZI and Hazar Merd in 1928, then joined her expedition at MOUNT CARMEL to direct the first detailed investigation of the NATUFIAN, KEBARAN and AURIGNACIAN levels at KEBARA cave in 1931. His career ended abruptly with retirement to Greece and early death in Cairo.

Tustrup a Neolithic mortuary house of *c.*2900 BC at the centre of a cemetery of megalithic tombs in Jutland, Denmark. The sub-rectangular structure, open on one side, was of dry-stone construction but boarded internally with a combination of split oak trunks and megalithic ORTHOSTATs. On the floor were twenty-eight highly decorated pottery vessels and beneath one of the walls was a sand-filled pit which may have held a burial.

Tutankhamen a comparatively minor Egyptian king of uncertain parentage of the 18th Dynasty, ruling *c.*1336–1327 BC, and whose reign saw the end of the AMARNA PERIOD. Tutankhamen is best known for the discovery of his virtually undisturbed burial in the VALLEY OF THE KINGS by CARTER in 1922. The splendid contents of this remarkable tomb are now housed in the CAIRO Museum.

Tuthmosis the name of four of the monarchs of Egypt's 18th Dynasty (early NEW KINGDOM). Tuthmosis I and III were both active military campaigners who extended the Egyptian empire in Palestine and NUBIA.

tuyère a clay nozzle or pipe through which air is forced into a forge or furnace, fragments of which are often found on African Iron Age metal smelting sites.

12 carbon see 13 CARBON/12 CARBON.

Twickenham Road see KAPWIRIMBWE.

Twilight Cave see ENKAPUNE YA MUTO.

Twin Rivers a late Middle Pleistocene site near Lusaka in central Zambia, containing stone artifacts associated with one limonite and three haematite pieces of pigment thought to be at least 200,000 years old. Iron oxide pigments feature in debates on the origin of symbolism in the archaeological record.

Tybrind Vig see SCANDINAVIA.

Tylissos the site of a MINOAN settlement on the island of CRETE. The impressive Neopalatial houses excavated by Hazzidakis in 1909–13 suggest that Tylissos must have been a local administrative centre.

tympanon or **tympanum** a vertical face which forms the rear of a PEDIMENT. The 7th-century BC temple of Artemis on Corfu has the tympanon carved in high relief.

type a specific artifact, which serves to represent the *taxon* of which it is a member. Types are very often 'idealized' versions, from which actual specimens deviate to a lesser or greater extent. See also INDEX FOSSIL.

typology the classification of a contemporary series of artifacts by dividing them into types and sub-types based upon a consideration of qualitative, quantitative, morphological, technological and functional attributes. Typologies are often constructed to help in the formation of chronologies and CULTURE HISTORY.

Tyre a site on the coast of Lebanon, a little-excavated city of the PHOENICIANS. See also SIDON and BYBLOS.

tzolkin the sacred almanac, having 260 days, that was part of the CALENDAR ROUND used in MESOAMERICA. It consists of twenty named days combined with thirteen numbers. The almanac is referred to as the tzolkin by MAYA scholars, although this may not have been the name used by the Maya themselves. NAHUATL-speakers call the almanac the *Tonalpohualli*.

U

Uai Bobo 1 and **2** cave-sites in eastern Timor excavated in 1967, with combined sequences from c.13,000 BC into the 1st millennium AD, spanning the end of hunting and gathering and the introduction of agriculture, probably by AUSTRONESIAN immigrants, about 2500 BC. The two sites contained rich faunal and botanical remains.

Uan Afuda a cave with rock paintings in the ACACUS Mountains of Libya, with evidence for control over wild Barbary sheep by Mesolithic hunters about 9000 BP.

Uan Muhuggiag a cave in the ACACUS Mountains of southwestern Libya, well-known for its rock art. It has been suggested that rock paintings of cattle, which are buried below archaeological deposits, date from before 5400 bp. A skull of domestic cattle dating to 5950 bp is one of the earliest known from the central Sahara. Excavations revealed two occupations by pastoral people: the first dates to about 7500 bp, and the second, which included pottery, is associated with radiocarbon dates of 4730 and 3770 bp.

Uaxactún a MAYA centre of moderate size in the southern Maya Lowlands, about 40 km (25 miles) north of TIKAL. It was one of the most extensively studied Maya sites in the first half of the 20th century. Much of the work at the site was done for the Carnegie Institution of Washington by Oliver Ricketson in 1926–30 and by A. Ledyard Smith in 1931–7. This research focused on an increased understanding of elite Maya culture. The ceramic sequence at Uaxactún provides the basis for the whole of Lowland Maya chronology.

'Ubaid culture complex a set of items of material culture associated with the 'Ubaid culture. The initial settlement of southern MESOPOTAMIA by food-producing communities is identified archaeologically by this culture. Although still not fully understood, the date of the 'Ubaid seems to cover the second half of the 6th and most of the 5th millennia BC. The culture is characterized by a style of painted pottery that changes through time, giving rise to a four-part division, 'Ubaid 1–4 (the first two of these are also called ERIDU and HAJJI MOHAMMAD respectively); excavations at 'OUELI contain a long pre-'Ubaid 1 sequence that is tentatively being named 'Ubaid 0. During the 'Ubaid period, towns coalesced within clusters of villages along river and irrigation channels, and contained massive architecture, usually identified as temples (see ERIDU). While the earlier phases of the 'Ubaid are restricted to the southern Mesopotamian ALLUVIUM, the later phases appear through a large region of western Asia, from the Persian Gulf in the south to coastal Syria in the northwest. North and west of southern Mesopotamia, the cultural horizon is often called the Northern 'Ubaid; several sites (e.g. Tell AQAB, Tepe GAWRA) indicate a gradual rather than abrupt transition to 'Ubaid pottery styles from HALAF antecedents, while the CHOGA MAMI Transitional pottery represents a geographical or chronological transition between SAMARRAN and 'Ubaid styles. See also 'UBAID, TELL AL-.

'Ubaid, Tell al- a site in the far south of MESOPOTAMIA excavated as part of the British work at UR in the early 20th century. 'Ubaid provided the initial material definition of the 'UBAID period (corresponding to the 'Ubaid 3–4 periods in the modern terminology). Although the site provided the first archaeological identification of this culture, the subsequent excavations at Ur and elsewhere provided the stratigraphic basis for its chronological divisions. The site was occupied from 'Ubaid 1 to EARLY DYNASTIC I times, and again during the Early Dynastic III. In addition to the 'Ubaid pottery, the site is best known for the Early Dynastic temple oval, an architectural type also found at KHAFADJE and AL HIBA.

Ubar see SHISHUR.

Ubeidiyeh an Early Pleistocene site located 10 km (6 miles) south of Lake Kinnereth in the Jordan Valley, Israel, assigned to an OLDOWAN early ACHEULIAN culture due to its close similarity to the technology of OLDUVAI GORGE (upper bed II). It thus represents one of the earliest sites known outside Africa. The assemblages include choppers, core-scrapers, proto-bifaces, trihedral picks, discoids, spheroids and polyhedrons, made from boulders, cobbles and pebbles derived from gravel deposits. Some fragments of HOMO *erectus* have been found, and the whole site is dated to *c*.1.4 million years BP.

Ugaritb (*mod.* **Ras Shamra**) an important Bronze Age city of coastal Syria. Excavations at Ugarit by C. Schaeffer and his successors, begun in the 1920s, provide the most detailed picture of petty kingdoms of Syro-Palestine during the LATE BRONZE AGE, in this instance a client state of the HITTITE empire. This picture is based both on archaeological remains (architecture, art work and small finds) and on texts, the latter revealing social, political, economic and cultic affairs. Excavation at Ras Shamra also gives important information on earlier periods. The place was first settled by an ACERAMIC NEOLITHIC community in the late 7th millennium BC, and deep soundings have traced a largely unbroken cultural sequence (with strong parallels to the 'AMUQ sequence) through the MIDDLE BRONZE AGE (earlier 2nd millennium BC), when Ugarit was a small kingdom involved in the interregional politics of the time (see MARI, OLD BABYLONIAN PERIOD).

Uhle, Max (1856–1944) a German archaeologist, one of the first to use artifact style and stratigraphic associations to establish a chronological sequence. He undertook excavations in the major coastal valleys of Peru, and his collections were taken to the Lowie Museum at Berkeley, California. He is perhaps best known for his excavations at PACHACAMAC, and for his synthesis of the first broad regional chronology for the central Andean region.

Uighurs an ethnonym for Turkish-language nomads (ancestors of modern Uighurs) who in AD 744 smashed the eastern Turkic KAGHANATE and created the Uighur Kaghanate in inner Asia, with its capital at Karabalghasun on the Orhon River (Mongolia). The Uighurs adopted Manichaeism (a widespread religion originating in the Near East) from Sogdian (see SOGD) missionaries. In 840 the Uighurs were routed by the Yenisei Kirghizs and migrated in different directions. A sizeable portion of them went to eastern Turkestan, where they created the Kocho State and adopted Buddhism. The Kocho State existed until the middle of the 13th century when it became part of the Mongol empire.

uinal a period of time in the CLASSIC MAYA LONG COUNT equalling twenty days.

Ukok a plateau in the ALTAI MOUNTAINS where, between 1990 and 1995, frozen tombs were excavated inside some KURGANS. They date to about 400 BC, and contained not only superbly preserved bodies of people and horses, but also lavish textiles and leather objects. In 1993 N. Polosmak discovered the famous 'Frozen Princess', a tattooed woman of about twenty-five, in a log coffin, with fine clothing and leather items, and a remarkable tall wooden head-dress; six horses had been killed and placed outside her burial chamber, and there were wooden salvers bearing cuts of mutton and horsemeat. In 1995 the

tomb of a man, the 'Warrior' or 'Horseman', also 2,500 years old, was found on the plateau at an altitude of 2,200 m (7,220 ft). Like the 'princess', he was buried in a wooden coffin in a log-lined chamber; aged about twenty-five to thirty, he seems to have been killed in battle, and has a wound in his stomach. He has two long braids of hair, and a spectacular large tattoo of a deer on his right shoulder.

Ukraine see EUROPE, EASTERN.

Ulalinka a Palaeolithic open-air site on the Ulalinka River in the Altai region of Siberia. Upper Palaeolithic artifacts are buried in loess-like loam overlying clay and coarse gravel deposits. The gravels yielded an assemblage of fractured rocks that are purportedly artifacts; both the status of the artifacts and the dating of the gravels are problematic. Some researchers believe that the assemblage represents a chopping tool industry of early Pleistocene age. The site was discovered by OKLADNIKOV in 1961.

Ullastret an Early Iron Age town in Girona, northeastern Spain, consisting of a triangular hilltop enclosure protected by a stone wall with circular towers. Within the defences were rectangular stone-built houses, cisterns, paved streets and a market place. Abundant finds of Greek pottery and coins testify to close contacts with Greek colonies near by on the Mediterranean coast. The town was founded in the 6th century BC and destroyed by fire shortly after 200 BC.

Ulu Burun the site of the wreck of a Bronze Age ship which went down off Cape Ulu Burun, just east of Kaş on the southern coast of Turkey, in the late 14th century BC, and which has been investigated by Bass and Pulak since 1984. The ship was presumably en route from a Cypriot or Near Eastern port to the Aegean, and carried 10 tonnes of copper ingots, 1 tonne of tin ingots, terebinth resin, glass ingots, hippopotamus and ivory tusks, ebony logs, Cypriot pottery, bronze weapons and jewellery from the Near East, Egypt and the Aegean.

Ulu Leang 1 a rockshelter site in southwestern Sulawesi, Indonesia, the basal layers of which date to the early Holocene (*c*.8000–6000 bc) and contain flake tools similar to those of LEANG BURUNG 2, with additional types of stone and bone tool which were further elaborated in the TOALIAN assemblages of succeeding layers of the site and at Leang Burung 1. Ulu Leang 2 is a small cave higher in the cliff with metal age jar burials related to the KALANAY tradition.

Uluzzian a lithic industry recognized in 1963, and found in a score of Palaeolithic caves and open-air sites in Italy. Comprising abundant scrapers, denticulates, small curved backed points and characteristic crescents, it occurs after the final MOUSTERIAN and ends as a contemporary of the early AURIGNACIAN. The oldest radiocarbon dates for the industry exceed 33,000 bp.

Umguzan see TSHANGULA.

Umm an-Nar a small coastal island in Abu Dhabi in the Persian Gulf on which is a Bronze Age settlement together with a series of contemporary tombs. Excavated by a Danish group in the 1950s and 1960s, the settlement and more particularly the tombs established the archaeological character of the Bronze Age in southeastern Arabia. The settlement and the burials defined an archaeological culture (funerary architecture, pottery and small finds), dated roughly 2500 to 2000 BC, which is distributed through much of southeastern Arabia, and which may be identified with the ancient CUNEIFORM place-name Magan (see PERSIAN GULF TRADE).

Umm Dabaghiyah a small prehistoric site in the Jezirah in northern Iraq which provided one of the first indications of a pre-HASSUNA occupation of MESOPOTAMIA. Diana Kirkbride's excavations revealed an architectural sequence composed of small rooms in long blocks arranged around a central space. This community kept some domesticated animals, but relied heavily on hunting (especially onager); some domesticated cereals are present, but these are often argued to have been imported (perhaps in exchange for animal skins) and not locally cultivated, since the region of the site is not suited to dry farming. The material culture of Umm Dabaghiyah includes a range of painted, incised, burnished and plain wares, some of which bear resemblances to 'archaic' Hassuna materials. The same material culture occurs at Tell Sotto and at Telul Thalathat.

umu ti large earth-ovens, common in Canterbury and Otago, South Island, NEW ZEALAND, used for cooking the roots of the cabbage tree *Cordyline australis.*

unconformity a surface of non-deposition that appears as a break between two rock or sediment units in a sequence. Unconformities arise from changes in depositional conditions to conditions of erosion or non-deposition. Recognition of unconformities on and off archaeological sites is significant because they may represent substantial periods of time for which a depositional record is lacking.

underwater archaeology the survey, excavation and analysis of submarine archaeological remains, most often the remains of sunken ships. Underwater archaeology was pioneered in the Mediterranean, but is now used in many other places where such techniques are suitable.

Únetice or **Aunjetitz** an Early Bronze Age culture of Bohemia and adjacent areas of Bavaria, southeastern Germany and southwestern Poland, whose name is taken from a cemetery north of Prague. Its origin is uncertain, although the NAGYRÉV culture and BELL BEAKER culture

are often mentioned as playing a role. Únetice burials, particularly the rich inhumations at LEUBINGEN and ŁĘKI MAŁE, have been compared with those of the contemporaneous WESSEX CULTURE in their opulence and indications of social differentiation. Únetice is generally dated between 2100 and 1800 BC.

unguentarium a container for perfumed oil. In the HELLENISTIC period the name is usually applied to a small ceramic container, often found in tombs. In the Roman period the name is applied to glass containers of a variety of shapes.

Upper Egypt a geographical term for that part of the Nile Valley stretching to the south of LOWER EGYPT as far as ASWAN.

Upper Nubia a geographical term for that part of the Sudanese Nile Valley from the 2nd Cataract as far south as Khartoum.

Upper Republican an aspect located in the central Plains of North America, which dates to AD 1000–1450, and is characterized by cord-roughened pottery, semi-subterranean earth lodges, and an equal dependence on the growing of corn, beans and squash, and on hunting and gathering. Abandonment of western Upper Republican sites may have been caused by a widespread drought.

Upper Swan an open site on an ALLUVIAL terrace of the Swan River, Western Australia. Dated to 38,000 bp, it is one of the oldest firmly dated sites in Australia. The assemblage of quartz and quartzite flakes and flake tools is not typical of the AUSTRALIAN CORE TOOL AND SCRAPER TRADITION.

Uptar an early prehistoric open-air site near the city of Magadan in northeastern Siberia. Artifacts were recovered from a layer of sand underlying a volcanic ash dated to 8260 BP. The assemblage includes lanceolate bifacial points and microblade fragments. One of the points exhibits unifacial fluting similar to PALAEOINDIAN points of the North American Plains and northern Alaska, and represents the only reported fluted point from Siberia.

Uqair, Tell a double mound about 50 km (30 miles) south of Baghdad in southern MESOPOTAMIA. Excavations on the northwest mound by S. LLOYD in 1940–41 uncovered the Painted Temple, of late URUK date. The temple building itself has the tripartite arrangement typical of early public Mesopotamian architecture, in which a row of rooms run along each side of a long central hall, and was set upon a 5 m (16 ft) high platform. The mud-brick walls of the temple were preserved up to 3.8 m (12.5 ft) high, their interior faces plastered and painted with animal and human figures and geometric designs. The temple was deliberately filled when the platform was enlarged, probably during JEMDET NASR times; a small group of early clay tablets are to be associated with this later phase. Lloyd also found multiple layers of 'UBAID period residential architecture at the edge of the mound, and traces of 3rd millennium BC occupation.

Ur a site in southern MESOPOTAMIA, already popularly known by its identification with Abraham and the CHALDEANS, which was established by the excavations of Leonard WOOLLEY and others during the 1920s and 1930s as one of the most important in the region. Occupation at Ur began during 'UBAID times, in the 6th–5th millennia BC, when the town covered up to 10 ha (25 acres); it grew in size and importance during the 3rd millennium, reaching 50 ha (124 acres) by the late EARLY DYNASTIC period when the city was an important factor in regional affairs. In the last century of the 3rd millennium BC the city was the ceremonial centre of the UR III empire, which briefly controlled much of Mesopotamia and the adjacent zones of the Zagros. The city lost its political importance in the following centuries, though it remained an important trading centre of the PERSIAN GULF TRADE and grew slightly in size (to 60 ha [148 acres]). The place continued to be inhabited until the late 1st millennium, but at reduced scale and prosperity. Notable features include: the evidence for early settlement in southern Mesopotamia; the extreme wealth of royal and other elite burials, as well as the differences in wealth seen in other graves in the ROYAL CEMETERY; the 3rd millennium religious architecture, principally the ziggurat of NANNA/Sin the moon god; the layout of early Mesopotamian cities and the residential architecture and street plans; and a rich body of texts that range from the early 3rd millennium to the late 1st millennium BC.

Ur III period a period named after the third dynasty of UR according to the SUMERIAN KING LISTS. Ur III denotes the last century of the 3rd millennium during which Ur managed to control much of MESOPOTAMIA and the adjacent Zagros highlands. The dynasty was initiated by Ur-nammu (2112–2095 BC), who extended his power over most of southern Mesopotamia; the empire was largely a creation of his successor SHULGI. The period is marked by close bureaucratic control over many aspects of economic life, reflected in the enormous numbers of economic texts from administrative centres such as DREHEM. The Ur III state collapsed under ELAMITE and AMORITE military pressure, perhaps exacerbated by economic over-intensification and administrative rigidity.

uraeus the coiled serpent shown on the forehead in depictions of Egyptian kings as a symbol of royalty.

uranium series dating a group of ISOTOPIC dating methods based on the decay series of the radioactive uranium isotopes ^{238}U and the far less abundant ^{235}U to the stable isotope of lead. In most cases they are based on measurements of the activity of one of the uranium

isotopes and a relatively short-lived daughter isotope expressed as isotopic ratios. When precipitated as a trace constituent in surface minerals, the uranium begins producing daughter isotopes. Ideally, samples are chosen that chemically have behaved as closed systems, and for which the ratio used to calculate sample age was initially zero.

Dating methods, and respective age ranges, include measurement of $^{230}Th/^{234}U$ (1–350 ka); $^{231}Pa/^{235}U$ (1–300 ka); $^{234}U/^{238}U$ (100–1000 ka); U-trend (10–1000[?] ka); ^{226}Ra (0.5–10 ka); $^{230}Th/^{232}Th$ (5–300 ka); $^{231}Pa/^{230}Th$ (5–300 ka); and $^4He/U$ (20–400[?] ka).

Material datable by uranium series methods includes, in order of reliability, aragonitic coral, SPELEOTHEM, TRAVERTINE, mollusc shells, marl, bone and teeth, caliche and calcretes, organic matter including peat and wood, and detrital sediment. Much of this material has either direct archaeological application, or indirect application through CHRONOMETRIC DATING of archaeological or palaeoenvironmental contexts.

Urartu a kingdom of the 1st millennium BC in the mountains north of ASSYRIA (encompassing northwestern Iran, northeastern Anatolia and Armenia) which represents the last of the important HURRIAN-speaking states of western Asia. Coming into existence probably during the 11th century BC, the Urartu state was a perennial obstacle to Assyrian empire building, especially between 900 and 600 BC; at the same time, Urartian art, especially the iconographic expressions of power, reveals a heavy debt to Assyrian culture. Although the most important centres of the kingdom were around Lake Van (see TOPRAKKALE), other major centres existed elsewhere (especially on the Ararat plain, see KARMIR BLUR). Indeed, the Urartian state seems to have been comparatively decentralized, this being perhaps an adaptation to the nature of its mountainous setting.

Urewe an Early Iron Age pottery style from southwestern Kenya, northwestern Tanzania, Rwanda, eastern Democratic Republic of Congo and southern Uganda, associated with the first iron-making communities in the region. It dates from the last few centuries BC to the first few centuries AD, and gives its name to one of the traditions of the CHIFUMBAZE complex.

Urfirnis the glaze-like paint used on Greek pottery of the middle Neolithic and Early HELLADIC periods. The name comes from the German for primitive glaze.

Urnfield complex a term used to refer to the period between c.1500 and 900 BC in Central Europe, spanning the Late Bronze Age and Early Iron Age, in which the burial rite consisted of cremation burials in urns in large open cemeteries, as at KIETRZ in Poland. The Urnfield complex is generally equated with the HALLSTATT sequence defined by REINECKE, although the pattern of burial spread beyond the core Hallstatt region. Within the Urnfield complex are entities such as the LUSATIAN culture, known also from settlements like BISKUPIN and SENFTENBERG.

Uruk period a period named after the site of WARKA (Uruk) which marks the crystallization of the MESOPOT-AMIAN tradition and the emergence of the Mesopot-amian state societies. Conventionally dated between roughly 3800 and 3100 BC. Calibrated radiocarbon dates suggest that the Uruk period begins in the late 5th millennium BC and ends around 3300 BC. The period is marked by urban development, elaborate religious centres within cities, the development of a writing system and of CYLINDER SEALS and their application to administrative procedures, mass production of pottery and other goods, and sophisticated art. The period is further marked by the appearance of this material culture outside southern Mesopotamia, notably at SUSA, GODIN TEPE and elsewhere to the east and BRAK, HABUBA KABIRA, HACINEBI, SHEIKH HASSAN to the northwest (the 'Uruk expansion'). Occurring prior to the advent of the more literary uses of writing, social and political interpretations of the Uruk period rest largely on archaeological evidence and some backward extrapolation from EARLY DYNASTIC patterns.

Usatovo culture a late regional variant of the ENEO-LITHIC CUCUTENI-TRIPOLYE culture, named after the site of Usatovo, Ukraine, on the northwestern coast of the Black Sea, where there are a settlement, two barrow (or KURGAN) cemeteries and two flat-grave cemeteries. Numerous artifacts point to connections with cultures to the southwest and west, including Central Europe and the Aegean. Usatovo is believed to represent a distinctive local development of social differentiation and long-distance exchange in the period between 3100 and 2600 BC.

usewear analysis or **microwear analysis** the examination of the surface and working edge of an artifact for signs of use, either damage or residue, often by means of a high-powered microscope. The technique is principally used in the study of stone tools, which suffer diagnostic damage or polishing when used to cut, saw or pierce other materials.

ushabti see SHABTI.

Ushki a group of five prehistoric open-air sites in central Kamchatka in Siberia. Cultural layers are buried in sandy loams along the shore of Big Ushki Lake. At Ushki I, four Neolithic levels overlie three levels assigned to the Upper Palaeolithic. The uppermost (5) contains wedge-shaped cores and sidescrapers, and has been dated to the early Holocene (8790 bp). Layer 6 has been dated to 10,760–10,360 bp, and contains a DYUKTAI CULTURE assemblage associated with traces of former dwellings with tunnel entrances. The lowest layer (7) has yielded dates of 14,300–13,600 bp and further evidence of former dwellings; artifacts include stemmed bifacial points and perforated stone ornaments, but microblade technology is lacking. The Ushki sites were discovered and excavated by Dikov in 1961–76.

usnu a platform or small mound found in important INCA sites, on which stood the Inca emperor when holding court. Often the usnu is associated with water channels, and liquid offerings were made there. Astronomical observations may have been made from the usnu in CUZCO.

Ust'-Kan Cave a Middle Palaeolithic site in the Altai region of Siberia. Artifacts and faunal remains are buried in layers of loam and rubble. The most common animals are mountain sheep and hare; the absence of arctic species indicates that the remains date to a relatively mild climatic interval (probably prior to the last GLACIAL). The artifacts include LEVALLOIS cores, sidescrapers and points. Ust'-Kan was discovered and investigated by OK-LADNIKOV in 1954.

Ust'-Kova a prehistoric open-air site on the Angara River in central Siberia. Several cultural layers are contained in deposits of sand and clay on the second terrace. Artifacts of the Iron Age and Bronze Age are buried in the modern soil; beneath the latter lies a sand containing Mesolithic and Neolithic remains. Three Upper Palaeolithic horizons were tentatively identified in the underlying clay. All of the horizons are associated with faunal remains of woolly mammoth, reindeer and other mammals. Artifacts from the lowermost horizon, which yielded radiocarbon dates of 32,865–28,050 bp, include large blades and points. The middle level, dated to 23,920 bp, contains various tool forms, including sidescrapers, endscrapers and bifaces. The upper horizon, dated to 14,220 bp, produced bifaces, burins and other tool types, but not the microblade technology that is so characteristic of the later Upper Palaeolithic in Siberia. Ust'-Kova was discovered in 1937 by OKLADNIKOV, and excavated by Drozdov in 1969–81.

U Thong a large (1,690 by 840 m [1,848 by 919 yds]) late prehistoric/early historic moated settlement in central Thailand located near trade routes to the west. Finds at sites in the old city (Tha Muang) and vicinity include Indian beads similar to those at BAN DON TA PHET (390–360 BC), a Roman coin of Victorinus (3rd century AD), and coins once thought to be from FUNAN, but now dated to the 7th–8th century AD and linked to the MON state of DVARAVATI and contemporaries. The site, which has Buddhist and Hindu remains, and evidence of a bead-producing industry, may have been a palace centre at one time; it was annexed by the state of KAMBUJA early in the 2nd millennium. The name is attached to a style of Buddhist art dating to the 12th-15th centuries.

Utqiagvik an INUIT site, located in Barrow, Alaska, comprising sixty historic and prehistoric house remains. The most significant find at the site was that of the remains of five bodies, trapped in their house by a winter coastal ice-surge. Three of them, belonging to two young girls and an adolescent male, were skeletons only. The other two, however, were the frozen remains of a woman in her twenties and one in her forties. Autopsies revealed that the individuals had been well nourished, although subject to occasional periods of food shortage. They had suffered from excessive consumption of meat and fat and from inhalation of smoke. A radiocarbon date of 440 bp (the same period as the QILAKITSOQ find) was taken from a vertebra of the older woman. Clothing and hunting tools were also well preserved. See also THULE, SKRAELING.

Uttamdi a rockshelter on Kayoya island, northern Moluccas, Indonesia, which yielded red-slipped pottery, stone adzes, shell bracelets and beads dated between 3300 and 2300 BP and which marks the arrival of AUSTRONESIAN-speaking peoples bringing domesticated pigs and dogs, as at BUKIT TENGORAK in Sabah. A later phase of occupation has jar burials with glass beads and iron fragments.

Utu a SUMERIAN god, equivalent to the AKKADIAN god Shamash, an offspring of ENLIL and connected to the sun; the symbol of light, both literally and metaphorically, he was the god of justice, before whom legal contracts had to be sworn and whose name was invoked in the various MESOPOTAMIAN law codes. His symbol, the winged sun disc, became a standard representation of royalty.

Uvarov, Count Aleksei Sergeevich (1828–84) a major figure in the early development of archaeology in pre-revolutionary Russia. Uvarov organized the Imperial Russian Archaeological Society in 1864 and the first archaeological congress in 1869. He also conducted excavations at Chersonese in the 1850s, the Merian graves, and the Upper Palaeolithic site of Karacharovo on the Oka River in 1877.

Uvinza brine springs in western Tanzania, exploited for salt since Early Iron Age times.

Uxmal the largest and best known of the PUUC MAYA sites, occupied during the late CLASSIC. Uxmal enjoyed its heyday in the period AD 800–1000. The site is extremely well planned and an excellent example of the Puuc style of architecture. This style includes large masonry buildings with a veneer of well-cut stone and decoration on the upper portions of the structures. Uxmal is connected by a paved causeway (*sacbe*) to a second Puuc site, KABÁH. Various aspects of Puuc sites suggest that the 'Classic Maya' did not collapse, but rather shifted from south to north during the POSTCLASSIC (or 'Decadent') period.

V

Vădastra culture a middle/late Neolithic culture of southwestern Romania in the late 6th millennium BC, occurring to the north of the VESELINOVO culture of Bulgaria. It was contemporaneous with the early stages (A/B) of the VINČA culture of the western Balkans in its earlier stages, and later part of a complex of late Neolithic groups that include the MARITSA and BOIAN cultures. Cattle phalanges from two Vădastra sites had osteological characteristics that suggested the use of the animals for traction.

Vahangeku'a one of the largest TOHUA in the TAIPIVAL VALLEY, Nuku Hiva, Marquesas, Polynesia. It comprises an artificial terrace, 170 by 25 m (186 by 27 yds), faced by a 3 m (10 ft) wall of basalt blocks. The open area is surrounded by massive PA'EPA'E. Excavations by Robert Suggs in 1957 showed that it was built over several centuries and reached its final form close to European contact.

Vaihingen/Enz see LINEAR POTTERY.

Vailele a series of large earthen mounds built as house platforms on the island of Upolu, Samoa, which date to the most recent aceramic period of Samoan prehistory. Two excavated mounds sealed occupation deposits containing ADZES and plain pottery dating to 300 BC–AD 200.

Vaillant, George Clapp (1901–45) an American archaeologist who worked in the MAYA Lowlands and the BASIN OF MEXICO, and established some of the basic chronologies used in these areas.

Vaisali a city in northern India, the birthplace of Mahavira (the founder of Jainism). Occupation here began around 500 BC (associated with NORTHERN BLACK POLISHED pottery). The oldest known STUPA appears here; initially a pile of clay about 8 m (26 ft) across with projecting square platforms at the cardinal points, it underwent three subsequent enlargements in baked brick during MAURYAN times. Several early Brahminical monuments associated with Vishnu also exist in the city.

Excavation has uncovered post-Mauryan residential sections of the city.

vaisselle blanche pseudo-ceramics produced during the PRE-POTTERY NEOLITHIC (PPNB, c.7600–6000 BC) of Syria, Lebanon and the east bank of the River Jordan (e.g. the sites of ABU HUREYRA, Buqras, Ramad, Labweh, 'AIN GHAZAL). This white ware was made from lime mixed with ashes and built into large vessels in coils; its surface was smoothed, and it was then left to dry rock-hard. These vessels are occasionally decorated with painted bands.

Vaito'otia an early eastern Polynesian (see PACIFIC) site of c.AD 800, on Huahine, Society Islands, with good preservation of organic materials in waterlogged deposits. Structures include wooden storehouses on piles and an enigmatic basalt upright on a coral base. Plant remains found include kava, gourd, coconut and pandanus. Besides fish-hooks and shell artifacts, wood and whalebone hand-clubs similar to MAORI PATU were found.

Valcamonica a glaciated valley in the Alpine foothills of Lombardy, Italy, with a rich collection of prehistoric rock art, conventionally divided into four chronological phases (Neolithic, CHALCOLITHIC, Bronze Age and Iron Age) with subdivisions. Motifs are pecked in the glacially smoothed rock surfaces, and include daggers, chariots, warriors and warfare, sun motifs, ploughing scenes, men and animals, and geometric designs. Some of the daggers resemble those of the Chalcolithic REMEDELLO culture of the Po plain.

Valders Advance the last major GLACIAL advance of the Pleistocene in North America, which lasted until approximately 10,000 BP.

Valdivia an early FORMATIVE period site (c.3200 bc) on the coast of Ecuador, which gives its name to Formative period culture in Ecuador. Early ceramics located at the site by Betty Meggers, Clifford EVANS and Emilio Estrada were, at the time (1960s), the earliest known in the New World (but see PRECERAMIC). Having no known antecedents for this fairly well-made pottery, decorated with a variety of plastic techniques, they suggested that Valdivia ceramics were directly related to the JOMON ceramics of Japan. This idea was never widely accepted, and antecedents to Valdivia ceramics were eventually found.

Vallée des Merveilles see MONT BÉGO.

Valley of Mexico see BASIN OF MEXICO.

Valley of Oaxaca a large plateau lying in the southern part of the Sierra Madres in the state of Oaxaca, Mexico. The valley is a highland area, elevation 1,550 m (5,085 ft) above sea-level.

The valley has a long sequence of occupation, beginning about 5500 BC. Some of the first cities in Mexico emerged in the Valley of Oaxaca. The work of Kent Flannery, especially at SAN JOSÉ MOGOTE and other FORMATIVE sites, has greatly increased our understanding of urban development in MESOAMERICA. The largest centre in the valley was MONTE ALBÁN. The valley was subsequently occupied by the MIXTECS and the ZAPOTECS.

Valley of the Kings part of THEBES (EGYPT)-WEST BANK. With the adjacent West Valley, the Valley of the Kings contained tombs prepared for almost all the known kings of the NEW KINGDOM from TUTHMOSIS I to RAMESSES XI, plus some members of the immediate royal family and high court officials. The best known of the tombs in the Valley of the Kings is that of TUTANKHAMEN.

Vallhagar a Late Iron Age settlement on Gotland, Sweden, consisting of twenty-four foundations with a system of field enclosures which would have corresponded to six to eight farms. The settlement appears to have been occupied during the 4th–6th centuries AD, and most of the buildings were destroyed by fire. Three nearby burial grounds, in which the graves are marked by stone circles and cairns, date to the 2nd and 3rd centuries AD.

Vallonnet a southeastern French Lower Palaeolithic cave-site, discovered in 1958 at Roquebrune-Cap-Martin, Alpes-Maritimes, and excavated by Barral in 1959 and by de Lumley in 1962, which has yielded nine pieces of an unrefined pebble and flake industry and a fauna datable to c.900,000 BP.

vallum **1** a Roman defensive rampart.

2 the flat-bottomed ditch with two parallel banks which ran to the south of HADRIAN'S WALL, in northern Britain. It is thought to have marked the southern boundary of the frontier zone.

Van Heekeren, H. Robert (1902–74) a Dutch archaeologist best known for his work in Indonesia, especially his excavations on Java and Sulawesi, and for his important books *The Stone Age of Indonesia* (1957/1972) and *The Bronze-Iron Age of Indonesia* (1958).

Van Riet Lowe, Clarens 'Peter' (1894–1956) a South African civil engineer and public relations man for archaeology, who discovered many archaeological sites in the course of his work and, with GOODWIN, wrote the 1929 classic *The Stone Age Cultures of South Africa*.

Vapheio the site of a 15th-century BC MYCENAEAN THOLOS tomb in Laconia, Greece, which was excavated by TSOUNTAS. Although plundered, the tomb contained an intact grave-pit in which a rich and no doubt powerful individual had been buried with bronze weapons, fine jewellery and two superb decorated gold cups.

Varna a late ENEOLITHIC cemetery site of the GUMELNIŢA culture (KARANOVO VI) located in eastern Bulgaria, containing some of the richest burials known from the 5th millennium bc. Some 200 graves have been excavated at Varna, a number of which are *cenotaphs* (a mortuary monument to an individual whose remains lie elsewhere). An extraordinary number of gold artifacts were found in the Varna graves, including diadems and earrings, while copper artifacts, pottery and flint tools are common. The differentiation in the richness of grave-goods has led to the interpretation that the Varna cemetery indicates nascent social ranking in southeastern Europe.

varves a SEDIMENTARY structure consisting of rhythmically bedded couplets of LAMINAE or BEDS that demonstrably were deposited in the course of a year. Annually laminated sediments are deposited in freshwater lakes and lakes influenced by proximity to glaciers, and occur as different types, depending on lake chemistry, physical processes and sediment input over the course of the seasons of a year. Varved lake sequences are usually an excellent source of palaeoenvironmental information that can be applied to the interpretation of nearby archaeological sites. In addition to detailed information on seasonal and environmental change, varves provide information on rates of change in vegetation history, the role of fire in forests under natural and management conditions, and the effects of people on erosion and other drainage-basin processes.

Varves can be used in geochronological studies and as a CHRONOMETRIC DATING method because varve couplets are deposited annually. However, unless tied to modern SEDIMENTATION or a known benchmark, varved sequences may be only FLOATING CHRONOLOGIES. Radiocarbon dating of organic constituents can provide a general age estimate for varved sequences. On the other hand, varve sequences can be used to calibrate other dating techniques. The method was developed in 1878 by Baron Gerard de Geer, a Swedish geologist.

vase-support a pottery vessel consisting of a hollow cylindrical (or more rarely cuboid) base supporting a dished upper surface. The outer faces and broad flat rim are often richly decorated with incised triangle, chevron and chequerboard designs. The earlier theory, reflected in the name, that they may have been stands for round-based pots has been superseded by their identification as incense-burners. They are a characteristic feature of the middle Neolithic Chasséen (see CHASSEY) culture.

Vasić, Miloje (1869–1956) a Serbian archaeologist who began the systematic excavation of the TELL site at VINČA in 1908. Vasić recognized the importance of the Vinča site for the establishment of the Neolithic chronology of the western Balkans, but linked it closely with developments in the Aegean area, a theme taken up in the English-language literature by V. G. CHILDE.

Vasiliki the site of a MINOAN settlement on the island of CRETE, excavated by Seager early this century and more recently by Zois, who has demonstrated that the Early Minoan II (c.2900–2300 BC) 'House on the Hill', a multi-storey structure regarded by some as a prototype Minoan palace, is in fact two large houses. The mottled black, red and brown pottery known as Vasiliki ware was abundant in these Early Minoan II levels.

Vatcha a LAPITA site on Île des Pins, New Caledonia, Melanesia. There are two episodes of occupation, the younger of which has a date of 2855 bp.

Vätteryd a large Iron Age cemetery in Scania, southern Sweden, with over 200 monuments, including numerous ship settings and stone circles with cremation burials.

Vedbaek Bøgebakken a Danish Mesolithic cemetery on Zealand which, although there had been at least three previous excavations at Bøgebakken, was discovered only during construction work in 1975 and subsequently excavated by Brinch Petersen. The site, which is dated to c.4800 BC, has yielded seventeen graves with the remains of twenty-two individuals, some accompanied by grave-goods and apparently covered in red ochre. The burials included two young mothers buried with their new-born infants and what appears to be a family group of a father, mother and one-year-old child. The site has been dated to the early ERTEBØLLE phase.

vegetational climax a model which attempts to explain vegetational succession as a series of phases culminating in a terminal phase which exists in a state of dynamic equilibrium with the prevailing environmental conditions. The model has been discounted as an explanation for vegetational community evolution, because it has been demonstrated that they are not predictable systems.

Veii a city in southern ETRURIA situated 18 km (11 miles) to the north of ROME. It seems to have been settled in the VILLANOVAN PERIOD and was destroyed by Rome in 396 BC. The site occupies a large plateau, some 195 ha (482 acres), which in the 5th century BC was enclosed by a wall. A sanctuary has been excavated at Portonaccio.

The ridge of the temple carried large terracotta statues of deities.

Velatice group a regional Late Bronze Age group of the URNFIELD burial tradition in Moravia, dated to the 12th century bc (HALLSTATT A). In addition to burial finds, settlements of the Velatice group are also known, the most important being LOVČIČKY.

Velikent an ENEOLITHIC and Bronze Age settlement along the west side of the Caspian Sea in Dagestan. The Bronze Age settlement belongs to the KURA-ARAXES CULTURE. Houses were built of mud-brick on stone foundations. Eneolithic collective tombs at Velikent contain materials similar to those of the MAIKOP culture of the northern Caucasus.

Vénat a Late Bronze Age metal hoard (c.700 BC) from Charente, France found buried in a large pottery vessel in 1893. The hoard contained 2,720 bronzes including 133 swords, 126 spearheads, 125 socketed axes and 440 bracelets, some with geometric decoration. Among the swords were several of CARP'S TONGUE type, but the hoard as a whole was a mixture of Atlantic and continental bronze-working traditions.

Venedians an ethnonym attached by CLASSICAL authors to the Late Iron Age peoples of the lower Vistula basin in Poland, from the 1st century BC to the 6th century AD, generally corresponding archaeologically to the Oksywie and Przeworsk cultures of this region. Venedian settlements and burials have yielded a rich array of iron and bronze artifacts. Iron working was particularly important at sites in the HOLY CROSS MOUNTAINS such as Słupia Stara. At sites such as Odry in Pomerania, Venedian burials are found beneath tumuli covered with stones. Trade routes brought amber from the Baltic coast to southern Europe, while Venedian mercenaries returning from service in Roman legions brought goods back from Central and western Europe. At Siemiechów in central Poland, a burial dating to the 3rd century AD contained a Roman helmet and weaponry.

Venta Micena see ORCE.

Ventana Cave a stratified site in southwestern Arizona, USA, with occupation levels over 11,000 years old. The lowest level contains stone tools, as well as the bones from numerous extinct Pleistocene animals. The generalized hunting and gathering pattern suggests similarities with the roughly contemporary SAN DIEGUITO COMPLEX of California.

Ventris, Michael (1922–56) a British scholar and architect who, in 1952, deciphered the LINEAR B script as an early form of Greek. This discovery revolutionized our knowledge of the MYCENAEAN civilization.

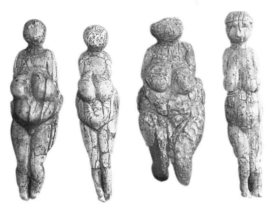

'VENUS' FIGURINES of mammoth ivory, from Avdeevo, Russia.

'Venus' figurines the popular but erroneous name for the small female statuettes of the Upper Palaeolithic. They are found from southwestern France to European Russia, and also in Siberia. Those of western Europe (see BRASSEMPOUY, LESPUGUE, GRIMALDI) are of ivory or stone; very few have any stratigraphic context, but all have been subjectively assigned to the GRAVETTIAN period. In Central Europe (see WILLENDORF, DOLNÍ VĚS-TONICE) they are of stone, baked loess or ivory, while those of the east (see AVDEEVO, GAGARINO, KHO-TYLEVO, KOSTENKI, MAL'TA) are of ivory and span a period from 25,000 to 12,000 BP. Not a homogeneous set of objects, they depict females of a wide variety of ages and physical types. The few with enormous breasts and buttocks are usually seen as emphasizing fertility, but they are not representative of the genre.

Vergina the royal capital of Macedonia in northern Greece. An extensive tumulus cemetery of the Early Iron Age has been explored as well as part of the HELLENISTIC palace. Excavations by Manolis ANDRONIKOS at the so-called Royal Tomb discovered an extremely rich burial which included quantities of ivory and silver items. Inside a gold LARNAX were found the cremated remains of a male. Reconstructions of the skull, and comparisons with royal portraiture, have raised the possibility that this was the burial of Philip II, the father of Alexander the Great.

Vértes, Laszlo (1914–68) a Hungarian archaeologist and Palaeolithic specialist who excavated many of the most important Palaeolithic sites in Hungary, including VÉR-TESSZÖLLÖS, ISTÁLLÓSKÖ, SZELETA CAVE, TATA and JANKOVICH.

Vértesszöllös a Lower Palaeolithic open-air site on the Átalér River, near its confluence with the Danube, in north-central Hungary. Artifacts and faunal remains are buried in loess and spring deposits on the fourth terrace. The fauna (e.g. *Dicerorhinus etruscus*) indicates a Middle Pleistocene age, and the spring deposits yielded URAN-IUM SERIES dates of 350,000–175,000 bp. The artifact assemblages contain pebble chopping tools and un-specialized flake tools, and are included in the BUDA industry. They are associated with human skeletal re-mains considered intermediate between HOMO *erectus* and *H. sapiens*. Vértesszöllös was investigated by VÉRTES in 1963–5.

Verulamium see ST ALBANS.

Veselé an Early Bronze Age fortified site of the MAD'AROVCE culture in southwestern Slovakia, *c.*2000 BC. In the interior of the fortified area were numerous storage pits and houses with beaten earth floors, hearths and burnt wall daub.

Veselinovo culture a middle/late Neolithic culture of southern Bulgaria in the late 5th millennium bc, material of which is found in Layer III at KARANOVO, which is contemporaneous with the early stages (A/B) of the VINČA culture. Veselinovo vessel forms include pear-shaped and cylindrical beakers with flat bases or cylin-drical legs. often with a characteristic curving handle with an upper knob.

Věterov culture an Early Bronze Age culture of Moravia, contemporaneous with the MAD'AROVCE culture of western Slovakia (the two are often considered together). Their material culture contained a mixture of elements from the Hungarian Early Bronze Age and the ÚŇETICE culture of Bohemia.

Victoria West a LEVALLOIS-like technique for preparing cores for the removal of a single flake, often large enough for a handaxe, associated with EARLIER STONE AGE as-semblages from the interior of South Africa.

Vicús a late EARLY HORIZON culture of Piura, on the far north coast of Peru. The modelled and painted ceramics exhibit stylistic similarity to early MOCHE ceramics.

Viet Khe a cemetery of the early DONG SON culture near the Hoa River, Hai Phong Province, northern Vietnam. Five wooden coffins, aligned east-west, contained hun-dreds of bronze weapons, vessels, ladles, ornaments and a small drum. A bronze sword and a ring-handle knife show contacts with late WARRING STATES China. Wood from a coffin indicates a date of between 500 and 300 BC.

Vietnam see ASIA, SOUTHEAST.

vigesimal mathematics a base-20 place-notation system employed in MESOAMERICAN writing systems, primarily that of the MAYA, for counting periods of time. More accurately, it is a *modified* vigesimal system because the 20 x 20 position was calculated as 20 x 18 (known by the Maya as the TUN). Its best-known application was the

LONG COUNT of the Maya calendar: the units were KIN (1 day), UINAL (20 days), tun (360 days), KATUN (7,200 days) and BAKTUN (144,000 days).

Vikings Scandinavians of c.AD 700 to 1100 who were great boat-builders (see CLINKER-BUILT) and navigators. They reached the Mediterranean and the Black Sea, and BYZANTIUM, and also raided the rivers and coasts of western Europe, including LINDISFARNE, the Isle of Man and the Irish coast. In 865 their raids on England led to their conquest of most of the eastern part of the country, with their capital at Jorvik (YORK). In the 10th century they briefly colonized Greenland and portions of the North American coast, but had abandoned these settlements by the mid 15th century because of worldwide climatic deterioration. See also L'ANSE AUX MEADOWS, SCANDINAVIA, SKRAELINGS, THULE, VINLAND.

Vikletice a cemetery of the CORDED WARE culture in Bohemia with 164 graves, 138 of which contained gravegoods. It is difficult to reconcile the existence of such a cemetery with the model of Corded Ware nomadic pastoralism that has often been proposed.

Vila Nova de Foz Côa see CÔA VALLEY.

Vila Nova de São Pedro a CHALCOLITHIC fortress at Santarém, Portugal, consisting of a massive dry-stone rampart with semicircular bastions, on a massive rammed-earth platform surrounded by a rock-cut ditch and traces of concentric outer defensive circuits. Three phases of occupation have been recognized, the first predating the construction of the fortifications. Excavations in the interior have recovered copper axes, chisels and daggers, together with evidence of metal working. Pottery included BEAKER material and local wares, dating to the 3rd millennium BC.

Vilcabamba an INCA site established after the Spanish conquest in the eastern Andes north of CUZCO, Peru. After attempting to defeat the Spanish by means of a siege of Cuzco, the Inca rebels fled north, stopping at various locations, and finally settling at Vilcabamba. Although Hiram Bingham argued that MACHU PICCHU was the location of Vilcabamba, the American explorer Gene Savoy located the actual site in 1964, at a place called Espíritu Pampa.

Vilcas Guamán a large INCA administrative centre near Ayacucho, located along the royal Inca highway north of CUZCO, Peru. It was the symbolic centre of the Inca universe. A large four-stepped USNU of dressed stone was erected at this site.

villa a Roman residence, including palace complexes such as Hadrian's Villa at Tivoli outside Rome, luxurious private dwellings (see OPLONTIS), urban dwellings (see HERCULANEUM, POMPEII), and more humble rural dwellings.

Villanovan period the Early Iron Age phase of the Po Valley, ETRURIA and parts of CAMPANIA in Italy, defined by artifacts from the type-site of Villanova near Bologna (c.900–700 BC). Cremation was often practised and the ashes could be buried in hut-shaped urns (see IMPASTO). Their metalwork, in gold and bronze, often shows affinities with Central Europe as well as with other parts of Italy. The Villanovan culture provided the foundations for the emergence of the Etruscan city-states in the 8th century BC.

Villeneuve-Tolosane a middle Neolithic village covering c.30 ha (74 acres) on a Garonne River terrace in Haute-Garonne, France. Excavations have revealed enclosure ditches, storage pits, a length of palisade trench and over 700 shallow circular and rectangular pits containing cobbles, which probably served as communal hearths. Associated material was of Chasséen (see CHASSEY) type, and radiocarbon dates suggested occupation from c.4250–3600 BC. Thousands of cereal grains were recovered, and one pit contained over 50,000 snailshells.

Vinapu a site with important AHU on EASTER ISLAND. Vinapu II, dating to c.AD 857, has a typically POLYNESIAN facing of rough, vertical slabs, while Vinapu I, of c.AD 1516, has a famous façade of beautifully fitted blocks, often erroneously compared with the CYCLOPEAN blocks of the INCAS at CUZCO. Both ahu carried a series of MOAI.

Vinča a TELL site on the River Danube near Belgrade, Yugoslavia, initially excavated by VASIĆ between 1908 and 1912. The deep (9 m [30 ft]) stratigraphy of the Vinča tell provides a sequence that spans the period between c.6000 and 4500 BC. The lowest levels at Vinča contain STARČEVO material, while the upper levels have yielded habitation levels from all phases of the Vinča culture. V. G. CHILDE attempted to tie the Vinča sequence to the sequence from Troy (HISARLIK) in the Aegean, but the advent of radiocarbon dating showed this correlation to be spurious.

Vinča culture a late Neolithic culture of the western Balkans, centred on the Danube and Morava Valleys in northern-central Yugoslavia, between c.5500 and 4000 BC. The Vinča culture succeeds the STARČEVO culture in this region and is divided into four phases (A–D). Vinča fine pottery is black or dark grey and is decorated by channelling and burnishing. Both extensive open settlements, such as SELEVAC, and compact TELL settlements, such as Vinča itself, are known. Numerous anthropomorphous figurines are found on Vinča sites, suggesting ritual activity. Copper artifacts and evidence for copper mining at sites like RUDNA GLAVA represent some of the earliest metallurgy in prehistoric Europe.

Vindija Cave a Palaeolithic cave-site located near Zagreb in northwestern Croatia. Artifacts and faunal remains are buried in clay, sand and rubble deposits. The lower cultural layers contain tools (primarily scrapers) assigned to the Middle Palaeolithic. The basal layer contains remains of an early rhinoceros (*Dicerorhinus mercki*) and is dated to the last INTERGLACIAL. The uppermost Middle Palaeolithic level, which yielded NEANDERTHAL skeletal fragments, was recently dated by radiocarbon to 28,000 BP, and represents the youngest age for Neanderthal remains from Central Europe (comparable to dates from the late Neanderthal at Zafarraya Cave in Spain). Overlying layers are dated to the middle and late PLENIGLACIAL, containing artifacts assigned to the AURIGNACIAN (lower) and GRAVETTIAN (upper). The latter produced skeletal remains of anatomically modern humans.

Vindolanda a Roman fort and civilian settlement of the late 1st/early 2nd century AD at Chesterholm, northern England, lying just south of HADRIAN'S WALL on the earlier frontier of Stanegate. Excavated by Robin Birley in 1969–89, its main structures include a military bathhouse, an inn, houses and mausolea. A wide range of leather and wooden remains have survived. Among the most important finds are over 1,000 fragments of letters and documents written in ink on thin slivers of wood, which are providing an unparalleled insight into life in a frontier province of the Roman empire.

Vinland the VIKING name for the portion of North America visited by Leif Erikson in the 10th century AD, probably in the vicinity of L'ANSE AUX MEADOWS, although some historians have proposed the coast of Maine as its correct location. See also SKRAELINGS.

Viracochapampa see MARCA HUAMACHUCO.

Viriconium Cornoviorum see WROXETER.

Virú Valley a coastal valley of northern Peru, the site of the pioneering regional survey conducted in 1946 by Gordon R. Willey and a team of archaeologists including BENNETT, STEWARD, STRONG, FORD, Donald Collier and Clifford EVANS. The goals of the project were to describe prehistoric sites with reference to both geographical and chronological position, to outline the development sequence of each site, to reconstruct the cultural institutions reflected in settlement configurations, and to compare the settlement history of Virú with other regions of Peru. The project was one of the first to make extensive use of aerial photography, and intensive pedestrian survey. Such goals and techniques were not only innovative, but they continue to guide settlement research to the present day.

vitrified fort a type of Iron Age HILLFORT with dry-stone timber-laced rampart, found in Scotland, in which the timber-lacing has been fired, probably by accident or hostile action, causing the stone core of the rampart to fuse.

Vix an Iron Age burial mound, 42 m (46 yds) across and 6 m (20 ft) high, at the foot of MONT LASSOIS, Côte-d'Or, France. A sub-rectangular wooden chamber beneath the mound held a rich burial of HALLSTATT D date (late 6th century BC). The body of a woman wearing a solid gold TORC or diadem lay on a dismantled wooden cart. The torc was one of several outstanding imports from the CLASSICAL world, including also ETRUSCAN bronze vessels and an Attic BLACK FIGURE cup. The most notable import, however, was a huge bronze KRATER 1.64 m (5 ft 5 inches) high, decorated around the neck with an embossed frieze of foot soldiers and chariots. The krater, for mixing wine, is of Greek manufacture and is thought to have been made either at SPARTA or at the Greek colony of TARENTUM in southern Italy.

Vladimirovka one of the largest sites of the CUCUTENI-TRIPOLYE culture in Ukraine, with over 200 huts of the PLOSHCHADKI type arranged in five concentric circles.

Vlasac a transitional Mesolithic-Neolithic site located in the gorges of the River Danube known as the Iron Gates in Serbia. The settlement at Vlasac is similar to the one at LEPENSKI VIR, although smaller in size. The large number of human skeletons from the Vlasac cemetery has provided one of the best samples of palaeoanthropological data for this period.

Vogelherd a Palaeolithic cave in Württemberg, southwestern Germany, excavated by G. Riek in 1931, which has yielded MOUSTERIAN layers followed by two important AURIGNACIAN occupation levels: the lower assemblage includes refined retouched blades, burins, endscrapers and many bone points with split bases; the upper assemblage includes a similar stone tool-kit but a different style of bone point with a rounded section. Carved ivory animal figurines, including mammoth, horse and bison, were recovered from both Aurignacian levels. There is MAGDALENIAN occupation above.

Volga-Oka culture a complex of transitional Mesolithic-Neolithic groups of the forest zone of the Central Russian Plain north and east of Moscow. The Volga-Oka culture is related to the 'Forest Neolithic' groups of the Baltic zones, such as the PIT-COMB WARE CULTURE and the NARVA CULTURE, and represents a similar adoption of pottery by local hunter-gatherer populations, but with little evidence of food production. Rather, hunting and fishing appear to have been the central economic activities.

Volgograd see SUKHAYA MECHETKA.

Volgu see LAUREL-LEAF POINT.

Volkov, Fyodor Kondrat'evich (1847–1918) a Ukrainian archaeologist influential in the development of Palaeolithic studies in Russia. A former student of de MORTILLET, Volkov conducted the first excavations at the

Upper Palaeolithic site of MEZIN, and trained the noted Russian Palaeolithic archaeologist EFIMENKO.

Volos the site in Thessaly of ancient Iolkos, in Greek legend the home of Jason, which appears to have been occupied more or less continuously from the Early Bronze Age until the HELLENISTIC period. A large structure, built in the 14th century BC and reconstructed in the 13th century BC, might be a MYCENAEAN palace. An intact THOLOS tomb was discovered at Kapakli, just north of Volos.

Volp Caves a cave system around the Volp River in Ariège (French Pyrenees), comprising three sites. *Enlène*, a MAGDALENIAN occupation site containing numerous hearths, has an area of paving and a wealth of PORTABLE ART including over 1,100 engraved stones. It has produced dates between *c*.12,000 and 11,000 bc. In *Le Tuc d'Audoubert* in 1912 the three Bégouën brothers discovered animal engravings on the walls and, in a chamber at the end of the cave, two clay bison in haut-relief. The Tuc's sparse occupation material has been dated to 12,400 bc; in 1914 the brothers discovered the cave of *Les Trois Frères*, a largely uninhabited extension of Enlène containing hundreds of PARIETAL engravings and some paintings, especially in the profusely engraved 'sanctuary' dominated by a 'sorcerer' figure. Links of style and pigment with Enlène's portable art assign most of the wall art to the 12th millennium bc.

volute a spiral scroll found on CAPITALS of the IONIC ORDER.

vomitorium the access way to the CAVEA of a Roman theatre or AMPHITHEATRE.

Vounous the site of a large Early Cypriot (late 3rd millennium BC) cemetery in northern CYPRUS. The tombs consisted of a roughly oval rock-cut chamber entered through a short DROMOS. The grave-offerings include terracotta models which depict cult scenes.

V-perforation the drilling of two holes into a button at an angle until they converge to form a single v-shape. This technique was used in the BELL BEAKER cultures and the Early Bronze Age of Europe.

Vrysi see AYIOS EPIKTITOS-VRYSI.

Vučedol group a late Neolithic group of the central Balkans, named after the site of Vučedol on the Drava River in northern Croatia and Slovenia. The Vučedol group (or phase) succeeds the BADEN culture and the KOSTOLAC group. Other sites of the Vučedol group are found at LJUBLJANSKO BLAT.

Vulci a city in ETRURIA. Excavations have revealed traces of an Etruscan temple and Roman houses. The exploration of the cemeteries during the 19th century yielded significant quantities of Greek pottery, which were dispersed throughout European collections. It also seems to have been a production centre for bronzes.

Wa the early historic Chinese name for some inhabitants of the Japanese islands in the YAYOI period.

Wace, Alan (1879–1957) a British scholar and archaeologist who was Director of the British School at Athens 1914–23. He undertook excavations in Laconia and in Thessaly and, most extensively, at MYCENAE.

Wadi Kubbaniya an extensive series of Egyptian Late Palaeolithic sites on the west bank of the River Nile south of ASWAN, investigated by F. Wendorf and others since 1978. The sites have yielded rich evidence for early plant domestication, with grinding stones, mortars and pestles and well-preserved carbonized plant remains including wheat and barley, dated by radiocarbon to between 18,250 and 16,960 bp.

Wadi Shatt er-Rigal a dried watercourse in UPPER EGYPT whose valley walls bear over 800 PREDYNASTIC rock engravings and later GRAFFITI, the most important of the latter being of the MIDDLE KINGDOM.

Wadi Sodmein see SODMEIN.

Wairau Bar an Archaic burial ground and MIDDEN site at the mouth of the Wairau River, South Island, NEW ZEALAND. Investigations at this site in the 1940s allowed Roger DUFF to define the so-called 'MOA-hunter period'. Some of the burials have unusually rich grave-goods. The artifacts from Wairau Bar are paralleled in early sites in the Marquesas and Society Islands. Recent new radiocarbon dates have established that Wairau Bar was briefly occupied in the late 13th century AD. These results suggest a late date for the colonization of New Zealand of about 750 years ago.

waisted axe a large stone tool with a flaked cutting edge and a flaked notch on either margin, giving a waist for hafting. Waisted axes have been found in Pleistocene contexts: in New Guinea at KOSIPE, NOMBE and Yuku, and on the HUON PENINSULA. They also occur in Australia, but are undated.

Wajak a now-destroyed site in eastern-central Java, at which two fossilized HOMO *sapiens* crania were found;

associations and dates are lacking, but it is thought that Wajak Man is younger than SOLO MAN, dating from the late part of the Pleistocene or early Holocene.

Wajil a hard-fired, reduced, unglazed earthenware of the Korean PROTO-THREE KINGDOMS period. Compare MUMUN, KIMHAE.

Wakankar Vishnu Sridhar (1919–88) an Indian archaeologist and rock art specialist, best known for his studies and excavations at BHIMBETKA.

Waldalgesheim an Iron Age tumulus in the Moselle Valley of western Germany containing the burial of an elite individual, which has yielded some fine examples of the LA TÈNE style of CELTIC art, datable to the 5th century BC, as well as a bronze SITULA made in northern Italy.

Walker Road an early prehistoric open-air site on the Nenana River in southern-central Alaska, USA. The cultural layer is buried in loess and wind-blown sand deposits overlying an ancient terrace; it has yielded four radiocarbon dates between 11,820 and 11,010 bp. There is evidence of a former dwelling structure with central hearth. The assemblage contains CHINDADN POINTS and endscrapers, and has been assigned to the NENANA COMPLEX. Walker was discovered and initially investigated by Hoffecker in 1980–84; excavations were conducted by Powers in 1985–8.

Wallacea a zone of islands between the Southeast Asian Sunda shelf and the SAHUL SHELF. There has never been a complete land-bridge between the islands, and the resulting water crossings formed a barrier to the spread of animals and humans into Australia and New Guinea. See also WALLACE'S LINE.

Wallace's Line the biogeographical divide between Bali and Lombok, and Borneo and Sulawesi, then running west of the Philippines, marking the eastern boundary of the East Asian faunal zone. The placental mammal fauna progressively diminishes in variety as one moves east into WALLACEA. It also marks the eastern edge of the Sunda shelf, and therefore the edge of the Asian landmass exposed at periods of low sea-level during the Pleistocene. On present evidence, it also seems to mark the limit of the spread of HOMINIDS before the emergence of anatomically modern humans, although recent reports of Early Pleistocene occupation on Flores may dramatically alter this view. The line was modified by Huxley to the west of the Philippines.

Wandersleben see LINEAR POTTERY.

Wandjina figures an Aboriginal term in the Kimberley region of Western Australia for ancestral spirits associated with rain, fertility and increase ceremonies, depicted in large anthropomorphic bichrome or polychrome paintings. The figures have prominent eyes and the head is surrounded by a 'halo', often with radiating lines. Wandjina figures are the most recent art in the area, post-dating BRADSHAW FIGURES, and were repainted periodically.

Wando the site of a late 11th-century AD Koryo shipwreck (see KOREA) off South Cholla Province, Korea. Nine m (30 ft) long and unkeeled, the ship was constructed in traditional Korean fashion with five longitudinal timbers. Cargo consisted of 30,000 CELADON vessels from kilns in Haenam, South Cholla, destined for regional elite use.

Wangman the name of an interloper who seized the Chinese throne, creating the Wangman Interregnum (AD 9–25) in the HAN Dynasty. Coins minted during Wangman's reign are distributed throughout East Asian archaeological sites and provide a diagnostic dating tool.

Wargata Mina or **Judds Cavern** a limestone cave in southwestern TASMANIA, Australia. Hand stencils have been found in this and Ballawinne Cave. The carbonate skin covering the motifs has given a minimum age of 11,000 years, confirming the Pleistocene age of cave occupation in this region.

Wari see HUARI.

Warka or **Uruk** a site near the Euphrates in the southern section of the MESOPOTAMIAN ALLUVIUM, the stratigraphically documented occupation of which begins with the 'UBAID 2 period and continues through PARTHIAN times (early 1st millennium AD). The German work at Warka begun by N. Noldeke in the 1920s provides a fundamental reference for many aspects of southern Mesopotamian archaeology. These investigations have concentrated on two temple precincts, the E-Anna and the Anu ziggurat, with additional investigation of other major architectural units (for example, the early 2nd-millennium palace of Sinkasid, the Karaindash temple of the KASSITE period, the Parthian Gareus). While the size and regional significance of Warka fluctuated through its history, the city was most important during late URUK to EARLY DYNASTIC times, when it grew to cover some 400 ha (990 acres) (by the Early Dynastic I) and formed the regional demographic and probably political centre of gravity. Warka during these periods provides information central to discussion of the origins of the state in southern Mesopotamia (see EANNA SOUNDING).

warranting argument an argument supporting the assumptions about the way the world works. Archaeologists use warranting arguments to support interpretations of empirical observations: e.g. the claim that certain rooms in prehistoric PUEBLOS of the American Southwest were for storage can be supported by analogies concerning room features (size, presence/absence of hearth, number of means of access, location in the site) in more recent local sites. See also ACTUALISTIC STUDY, BRIDGING ARGUMENT.

Warreen a limestone cave in southwestern TASMANIA which is the oldest known site in the region. It was first occupied about 35,000 years ago and was abandoned about 16,000 years ago. The most intense occupation dates to between 24,000 and 22,000 bp. The deposits are extraordinarily rich in cultural material. Almost all the artifacts are made of quartz although DARWIN GLASS appears at about 24,000 bp. Red-necked wallaby dominates the faunal remains. See also KUTIKINA, NUNAMIRA, PARMERPAR MEETHANER, WARGATA MINA.

Warring States see ZHOU.

Wasserburg Buchau see BUCHAU.

Watom Island an island off northeastern New Britain, BISMARCK ARCHIPELAGO, Melanesia, where LAPITA pottery was first reported in 1908. The most recent excavations demonstrate occupation during the middle and late phases of Lapita in the Bismarcks, 2767–1787 bp. Obsidian from both TALASEA and LOU occurs, with Talasea material increasing over time. The largest sample so far of Lapita human skeletal remains comes from the Kainapirina site.

Watsonia a genus of the plant family Iridaceae, with underground storage organs which formed an important part of the diet of Holocene LATER STONE AGE and possibly also earlier Stone Age peoples in the Western and Eastern Cape Provinces of South Africa where FYNBOS vegetation occurs. The corm bases and tunics of *Watsonias* and other seasonally available geophytes are found where conditions have favoured preservation in sites like BOOMPLAAS and MELKHOUTBOOM. *Watsonia* corms look and taste like chestnuts and are best eaten in early summer. The rate of reproduction can be controlled by burning and it has been suggested that fire management was practised by the Stone Age peoples who used these plants.

wattle and daub the construction of walls by plastering mud over a lattice of branches and sticks.

Wayland's Smithy a trapezoidal Neolithic long barrow

of *c.*3500 BC, in Oxfordshire, England, with a flanking kerb and megalithic PASSAGE GRAVE of cruciform plan at its southern end. Excavations beneath the mound revealed an earlier phase consisting of a wooden mortuary house with remains of fourteen individuals, later covered over by an oval chalk mound. This was then in turn buried beneath the central section of the final mound.

Weasel Cave see MYSHTULAGTY LAGAT.

wedge-shaped microcore a small keel- or wedge-shaped core used to produce microblades. It is found in some East European Upper Palaeolithic sites (e.g. AMVROSI-EVKA), but is especially common in Upper Palaeolithic cultures of Siberia and the Far East (Mongolia, northern China and Japan), and also appears in Alaska and other parts of northwestern North America at the close of the Pleistocene.

wedge tomb a type of megalithic tomb common in Ireland, consisting simply of a long narrow chamber of ORTHOSTATs supporting capstones, decreasing in height towards the back and without a separate entrance passage.

Wei see THREE KINGDOMS, CHINESE DYNASTIES.

Weichsel Glaciation the final continental GLACIAL advance, named after the major northern German ice-sheet, and lasting from *c.*115,000 to 10,000 bp. It corresponds broadly to the Alpine WÜRM GLACIATION, the North American WISCONSINAN STAGE and the British Devensian.

Weidenreich, Franz (1873–1948) a German anatomist and palaeoanthropologist, best known for his study of the *Sinanthropus* materials from ZHOUKOUDIAN, China.

Weipa the site, in Cape York Peninsula, Queensland, Australia, of about 500 SHELL MOUNDs, mostly of *Anadara* shell, some of which are up to 9 m (30 ft) high. Excavations by Wright, and later by Bailey, demonstrated that they were human in origin and that they began forming about 1200 bp. The Weipa mounds are among the largest and best-preserved examples of shell middens anywhere in the world. Comparable sites occur in eastern Cape York and in ARNHEM LAND.

Weizhi the *Chronicles of Wei*, compiled between AD 233 and 297 for the Wei Kingdom of China (see THREE KINGDOMS). One section, known as the *Gishi Wajinden* in Japanese, contains references to the Japanese islands, mentioning the country of YAMATAI. The ethnographies reported there can be correlated with YAYOI period Japan as known archaeologically. See also HOUHANSHU.

were-jaguar a creature showing both human and jaguar features. It is an important theme in OLMEC art. Were-jaguar characteristics include an infantile expression combined with fangs, a snarling mouth and other feline

facial features. The were-jaguar has been interpreted as the offspring of a woman and a jaguar, and as a priest or other ritually powerful individual with the ability to transform himself into a jaguar. Scholars suggest that various rain-gods throughout MESOAMERICA derive from it.

Wessex culture an Early Bronze Age culture of central-southern England, essentially an aristocratic burial tradition developed from the earlier BEAKER tradition. It is represented by cemeteries of round barrows covering single graves in Wiltshire and adjacent areas, and is closely related to the Armorican TUMULUS CULTURE (see KERNONEN) with which it shares certain metal types and symbolic equipment. The Wessex I period (*c.*2000–2650 BC), associated with the major rebuilding of STONEHENGE, has richly furnished inhumations containing bronze daggers and axes, beads and buttons of amber and shale, and goldwork as in the famous BUSH BARROW. In the Wessex II period (*c.*1650–1400 BC), cremation replaces inhumation as the dominant rite, segmented FAIENCE beads appear, and goldwork largely disappears from the graves, although the RILLATON CUP is a notable exception.

Western Pluvial Lakes tradition a series of complexes and cultures found throughout western North America, characterized by the exploitation of marshes and lakes in the early part of the POSTGLACIAL period.

Western Pueblo see MOGOLLON.

Western Stream see CHIFUMBAZE.

Western Zhou see ZHOU.

West Kennet a Neolithic long barrow of *c.*3600 BC, in Wiltshire, England, with a megalithic chamber, part of the AVEBURY complex of Neolithic ritual monuments. The mound is 100 m (110 yds) long with a concave megalithic SARSEN façade at the eastern end, blocking an earlier entrance to the passage. This gave access to five burial chambers, arranged one at the end and two either side of a short gallery, and containing remains of at least forty-six disarticulated individuals. The mound was excavated by S. PIGGOTT.

West Point one of the largest and richest SHELL MIDDEN sites in Australia, located in northwestern TASMANIA. Circular depressions on the surface of the midden are probably the remains of huts. The rich bone and shell deposits show that abalone and a range of small animals were eaten, but the main component of the diet was elephant seal, now locally extinct. Fish bones are absent. The site was occupied between 1,800 and 1,200 years ago. See also ROCKY CAPE.

West Slope ware a type of HELLENISTIC pottery, named after the examples found during excavations on the west slope of the Athenian AKROPOLIS. The fabric evolved from the earlier BLACK-GLOSSED pottery produced at ATHENS, although it was enhanced by decoration in added white and yellow as well as occasional incision. It was produced in several centres in the Greek world, such as Athens, CORINTH and CRETE.

Wetherill, Richard (1858–1910) a pioneer archaeologist of the American Southwest who was responsible for locating and excavating some of the most important sites in the area, such as CLIFF PALACE in MESA VERDE and PUEBLO BONITO in CHACO CANYON, and bringing them to the attention of the public and of the profession.

Wharram Percy a deserted medieval village in a valley among the rolling chalklands of the Yorkshire Wolds, England. The village consisted of rows of small rectangular wattle-and-daub houses ranged along the principal streets, with two manor houses of more substantial construction and a 12th-century AD church. Each of the ordinary houses stood within a small yard and was known as a *toft*; at the back of each toft there was an enclosed paddock or *croft*. Beyond tofts and crofts were the large open fields in which the bulk of the community's crops were grown. The village was gradually abandoned during the 14th and 15th centuries, as arable farming gave way in this area to the more profitable but less labour-intensive sheep-rearing.

Wheat, Joe Ben (1916–97) North American archaeologist who made significant contributions to Southwest and Plains archaeology. His excavations at the PALAEO-INDIAN site of OLSEN-CHUBBUCK showed the potential that such sites had for uncovering many facets of human behaviour and ecology.

Wheeler, Sir Robert Eric Mortimer (1890–1976) a British archaeologist whose career started with excavations at COLCHESTER. He later excavated in Wales at the Roman forts of Caernarvon and Brecon as well as the legionary fortress of Caerleon. Later work was conducted at ST ALBANS and the Iron Age HILLFORT of MAIDEN CASTLE. His later British work included the exploration of the Iron Age fortress of STANWICK.

Named Director-General of Archaeology in India (1944–7), Wheeler introduced his scientific and STRATI-GRAPHIC methods of excavation to the subcontinent, where they still serve as a model. He helped train a generation of Indian archaeologists, and undertook excavations at HARAPPA, MOHENJO-DARO and ARIKAMEDU. Later, with colleagues such as Glyn DANIEL, Wheeler also helped popularize archaeology through television programmes.

wheelhouse a stone-built circular house with internal partitions radiating inwards like spokes of a wheel but leaving the central area clear. Wheelhouses are related to BROCHS, are found mainly in the Hebrides and the Shetland Islands of Scotland, and date mostly to the early centuries AD.

White, Leslie Alvin (1900–1975) an American anthropologist who helped to reintroduce evolutionary thinking into American anthropology and archaeology. His views on culture as a system and on the evolutionary development of societies as mechanisms for the capture of greater amounts of energy were important precursors to the development of PROCESSUAL ARCHAEOLOGY. He proposed the term 'culturology' for the study of culture as an independent and discrete entity. See also EVOLUTION.

white-ground a technique used for ATHENIAN POTTERY especially in the 5th century BC. A white SLIP was applied to the surface of the vessel, on to which was painted the decoration in several different colours. The LEKYTHOS is the most common of the shapes to be decorated in this way, and the technique is chiefly linked to funerary vessels. Much of the iconography shows people approaching the tomb, although domestic scenes appear. In the late 5th century the technique was used on monumental funerary lekythoi, which seem to evoke their counterparts in marble. The effect is similar to that found on painted ivory plaques, for example those from Kul Oba in Russia.

White Lady see BRANDBERG.

Wietrzychowice a cluster of Neolithic KUYAVIAN long barrows of the FUNNEL BEAKER culture, located in north-central Poland. Five of the trapezoidal long barrows have been excavated, with the longest (number 3) approximately 115 m (126 yds) in length. The barrows have been reconstructed as an archaeological park.

Wilburton a Late Bronze Age metal hoard from Cambridgeshire, England, which has given its name to the Wilburton bronze industry of southern Britain, c.10th–8th centuries BC. Typical products are bronze leaf-shaped slashing swords, socketed spearheads with a peg for securing to the shaft, horse bits and socketed axes.

Wilgie Mia a red ochre mine in the Weld Range, Western Australia, consisting of a large cavern with caves and galleries branching off it. Ochre from Wilgie Mia was widely traded and it is still a significant site to Aborigines. Excavations by Ian Crawford showed that it has been used for at least 1,000 years.

Willandra Lakes a chain of dry lakes in western New South Wales, Australia, which were filled periodically during the Pleistocene by the Willandra Creek, an ancient distributary channel of the Lachlan River. The lunette dunes provide a record of changing environment over the last 100,000 years. Human activity dates back at least 35,000 years, and the area is rich in archaeological material including hearths, artifact scatters, freshwater SHELL MIDDENS and burials. Extinct species of

MEGAFAUNA also occur. The best-known skeletal remains from the Willandra Lakes are MUNGO 1 and 3 (WLH1, WLH3). These are gracile anatomically modern humans and are crucial to Alan Thorne's theory of a dual origin for Australian Aborigines. At least one robust individual, WLH 50, is also known, although it has not been securely dated. See also COOBOOL CREEK, KEILOR, KOW SWAMP, LAKE MUNGO.

Willendorf II an Upper Palaeolithic open-air site located along the River Danube in northeastern Austria. Artifacts and faunal remains (e.g. reindeer, woolly mammoth) are buried in loess deposits. A small assemblage of uncertain affiliation occurs in the lowest cultural layer. Layers 2–4 contain assemblages (e.g. nosed endscrapers, small retouched blades, bone points) assigned to the AURIGNACIAN; layer 2 recently yielded radiocarbon dates of 41,700–39,500 bp. Layers 5–9 contain assemblages (e.g. small backed blades) assigned to the EASTERN GRAVETTIAN; layer 5 yielded a date of 32,000 bp. Willendorf II provides evidence of early Aurignacian settlement and a classic sequence of industries in Central Europe. Its Gravettian yielded several art objects including a famous obese 'VENUS' FIGURINE in 1908.

Williamsburg see MARTIN'S HUNDRED.

willow-leaf point an elegant and refined long thin SOLUTREAN flake tool. See LAUREL-LEAF POINT.

Wilson, Daniel (1816–92) a Scottish antiquary and author of, among other works, *The Archaeology and Prehistoric Annals of Scotland* (1851), in which the term 'prehistoric' was first used. Wilson was the first to organize the available artifacts of prehistoric Scotland, following the THREE-AGE SYSTEM. He later taught at University College, Toronto, where he wrote *Prehistoric Man: Researches into the Origin of Civilization in the Old and New World* (1862).

Wilson Butte Cave a prehistoric site located in a lava blister on the Snake River Plain of southern-central Idaho, USA. Artifacts and faunal remains (e.g. camel, horse, ground sloth) are buried in deposits of clay, silt and sand. The lowest cultural layer yielded a radiocarbon date of 14,500 bp, and may contain one of the oldest occupations in North America. Stone artifacts are confined to a biface, retouched blade and flake. The five overlying layers contain assemblages dating to the middle–late Holocene.

Wilton a rockshelter in the Eastern Cape Province of South Africa, which has given its name to a microlithic LATER STONE AGE industry of the last 8,000 years, distributed in the Western and Eastern Cape Provinces. Some researchers recognize a widespread Wilton complex distributed in many areas of southern Africa and encompassing Coastal and Interior Wilton industries as well as industries such as the MATOPO/KHAMI/NSWATUGI and ZAMBIAN WILTON. In some areas of southern Africa,

the appearance of pottery some 2,000 years ago is associated with microlithic artifact assemblages labelled 'post-climax Wilton' or 'ceramic Wilton'.

The Wilton industry *sensu stricto* shows changes in the relative percentages and form of certain retouched artifacts over time, especially small convex or 'thumbnail' scrapers, adzes, segments and backed blades. It includes items made from organic materials, many decorative objects and burials, and is also associated with rock painting. Evidence for the wide range of resources exploited includes: plant remains (see MELKHOUTBOOM); faunal remains, especially of small non-gregarious browsing antelope associated with FYNBOS vegetation; and marine and freshwater resources.

Winckelmann, Johann Joachim (1717–68) a German scholar who was appointed Prefect of the Papal Antiquities in 1763. His influential *History of Ancient Art* (1763–4), covering CLASSICAL sculpture as well as the art of Egypt and ETRURIA, provided the basis for stylistic development.

Winde Koroji complex a pastoral tradition in the Inland Niger Delta in West Africa, dated to about 3100–2600 BP.

Windmill Cave, Brixham a cave-site close to KENT'S CAVERN, Devon, England, which was discovered in 1858 and excavated by PENGELLY and a committee of fellow scientists. The site produced stone tools obviously made by humans, associated with the remains of extinct animals, and thus clearly demonstrated the true antiquity of humans in Britain. Thirty-six artifacts were reported as coming from the cave, but these were not fully published and are now mainly lost.

Windmill Hill a Neolithic CAUSEWAYED CAMP of c.3600 BC, in Wiltshire, England, with three widely spaced causewayed ditch circuits, part of the AVEBURY complex of Neolithic ritual monuments. It is the type-site of the Windmill Hill culture, the earliest Neolithic of southwestern England, characterized by plain CARINATED round-based bowls.

Windover a waterlogged site in Florida, USA, where excavations by G. Doran have uncovered America's earliest-known mass burial ground: 168 individuals buried in peat and dating to c.7400 bp. Brain tissue was preserved in ninety-one skeletons, including several complete brains. Studies of their DNA may reveal family relationships and shed light on how and when the New World was colonized. Burials were accompanied by bone, antler and wooden artifacts, and a bottle gourd (*Lagenaria siceraria*). Handwoven fabrics were recovered from many burials. See also REPUBLIC GROVES and LITTLE SALT SPRING.

Winlock, Herbert Eustis (1884–1950) an American Egyptologist, best known for his excavations at DEIR EL-BAHRI and LISHT.

Wisconsinan age a major North American geochrono-logical subdivision of the Pleistocene epoch, ranging from about 75,000 to 10,000 bp. See also WISCONSINAN STAGE.

Wisconsinan stage a major chronostratigraphic subdiv-ision of the Pleistocene series, encompassing deposits of the last GLACIAL episode defined, in the northern American Midwest and adjacent areas of Canada, at the base by the base of material overlying the Sangamon Geosol (see SANGAMONIAN STAGE) and at the summit by the top of non-glacial material overlying the youngest TILL. Remains of early humans and PALAEOINDIANS are contained in deposits belonging to the latest substages. Although the boundaries are recognized to be time-transgressive, they are conceptually placed at about 75,000 and 10,000 bp. The following substages and their general characteristics are recognized:

(a) Altonian substage (c.75,000–25,000 bp) – soil for-mation early followed by loess SEDIMENTATION south and glacial advance and retreat north; cool climate.

(b) Farmdalian substage (c.25,000–22,500 bp) – INTER-STADIAL soil formation; cool climate.

(c) Woodfordian substage (c.22,500–12,500 bp) – major glacial advance and retreat; loess sedimentation and cryogenic processes; cold climate.

(d) Twocreekan substage (c.12,500–11,800 bp) – inter-stadial soil formation; forest beds; cool climate.

(e) Greatlakean substage (c.11,800–7000 or 10,000 bp) – minor glacial readvance; cool climate; replaces Vald-eran substage (see VALDERS ADVANCE, WEICHSEL GLACIATION).

Witów an Upper Palaeolithic open-air site located in Poland. Artifacts are contained in AEOLIAN sand and associated with a buried soil dated to 11,020 bp. Tools include blades with arched backs, burins and endscrapers; remains of four dwelling structures are also present.

Wolstenholme Towne see MARTIN'S HUNDRED.

Wolstonian see SAALIAN.

Wolvercote an ancient river channel exposed in the Wolvercote Brick Pit, Oxford, England, which has yielded a characteristic Lower Palaeolithic pointed biface assem-blage. On typological grounds this assemblage has been linked with late-dating French and German MICOQUIAN industries.

Wonderwerk a huge cave about halfway between the towns of Kuruman and Danielskuil in the Northern Cape Province of South Africa, one of only a few cave-sites with ACHEULIAN stone artifacts, and also containing abun-dant MIDDLE and LATER STONE AGE artifacts and faunal remains. Of particular interest is a small broken slab depicting an unfinished fine line engraving of a mammal, associated with a radiocarbon date of 10,200 bp, the oldest dated rock art in South Africa. Several additional engraved slabs from more recent levels at the site date to between 5180 and 3990 bp. See also MONTAGU CAVE.

Wonoboyo a village near PRAMBANAN, central Java, Indonesia, where finds of gold and silver coins, religious images and utensils, and ornaments were found by vil-lagers in 1990. Later excavations yielded more finds, totalling 35.8 kg (79 lbs) of gold and over 7,000 coins, buried in and around glazed Chinese stoneware jars. The hoard dates to the early 10th century AD, and was prob-ably a royal treasury buried by ash from the nearby volcano of Mount Merapi.

wooden-chamber a form of burial chamber constructed from late Neolithic times onwards in China; it was a log- or board-constructed enclosure into which nested wooden coffins, and grave-goods were packed and sealed from the top. Its use diffused to Korea and Japan in the early centuries AD. See also HEAVENLY HORSE TOMB, XIBEIGANG, MAWANGDUI, SHAFT TOMBS.

Woodhenge a small Neolithic HENGE of c.2500 BC in Wiltshire, England, lying adjacent to the major henge of DURRINGTON WALLS. Discovered by aerial photography in 1925, Woodhenge consists of a series of six concentric rings of POSTHOLES within a circular ditch and bank. The postholes may have held the supports of a roofed timber building, or perhaps an unroofed timber structure with lintels resembling STONEHENGE – hence the name.

Woodland a stage in eastern North America, dated from approximately 1000 BC to AD 800. and characterized by BURIAL MOUNDS, agriculture and pottery. The term should properly be restricted to those cultures in the Eastern Woodlands of North America. The presence of Woodland-derived pottery in other areas has led to some unfortunate terminology, such as the 'Plains Woodland'. See also ADENA, HOPEWELL.

Woodruff Ossuary an ossuary in northwestern Kansas, USA, dating to about AD 600, that belongs to the Keith FOCUS of the WOODLAND stage. It comprises a series of fourteen or more pits, some 2 m (6.5 ft) deep. A large oval pit had then been dug across the tops of the small pits, and in the fill of both the large pit and the small ones were found at least sixty disarticulated human skeletons. Throughout the fill were thousands of beads made from locally available freshwater mussel, both randomly scat-tered and in lines, which suggests that they had once been strung. Other artifacts were relatively scarce.

Woolandale a 13th-century AD Late Iron Age site in central Zimbabwe which has given its name to the second phase of the LEOPARD'S KOPJE complex in that area.

Woolley, Sir Charles Leonard (1880–1960) a British archaeologist most widely known for his work at UR in MESOPOTAMIA between 1922 and 1934, where he re-vealed 5,000 years of history. Woolley presented his Ur excavations in a magnificent ten-volume series, and also in several popular works. Woolley also excavated in Egypt, at CARCHEMISH (with T. E. Lawrence), at Tell AT-CHANA in Syria, and at AL MINA in Turkey.

Wormington, Hannah Marie (1914–94) North American archaeologist. The example she showed, as one of the continent's first female archaeologists, to later generations of women entering the field is perhaps as important as her many significant contributions to North American PALAEOINDIAN studies, her area of specialization.

Worsaae, Jens Jacob Asmussen (1821–86) a Danish pre-historian, Professor of Archaeology at the University of Copenhagen, Inspector-General of Antiquities in Denmark, and successor to C. J. THOMSEN as Director of the National Museum at Copenhagen. Worsaae's major contribution was the application of the THREE-AGE SYSTEM to the understanding of Danish field monuments using excavation, resulting in his influential *Danmarks Oldtid* (1843).

Wrangel Island see MAMMOTH.

Wright, George Ernest (1909–74) an American orientalist, whose best-known excavations are those at SHECHEM and GEZER.

wristguard a long rectangular plaque, usually of stone, with one, two or three small holes at either end for tying to the wrist, as a protection from the recoil of the bowstring. In western Europe, stone wristguards are frequently found together with flint barbed and tanged arrowheads in graves of the BEAKER tradition.

Wroxeter the Roman town of Viriconium Cornoviorum, on the River Severn to the southeast of Shrewsbury, England, was the fourth largest urban centre in Britannia (78 ha [193 acres]), and capital of the Cornovii tribe. It was originally the location for a legionary fortress during the conquest of Wales, but this was moved to the permanent site of Chester on the River Dee. Under the emperor Hadrian, the city constructed a new FORUM, commemorated in an inscription recovered during excavations. A substantial piece of masonry is all that remains of a major bathing-complex.

Unlike most Roman towns in Britain, Wroxeter has survived largely undamaged, with no modern settlement above it, and so has been the subject of extensive excavations, most recently by G. Webster and P. Barker. Aerial survey has also provided much evidence for the layout of the town, while a recent GEOPHYSICAL survey of the whole city has produced an extensive and detailed plan.

Wucheng [Wu-ch'eng] a mid 2nd-millennium BC Bronze Age site in Jiangxi Province, China, distinguished by its stone-mould casting of local styles of bronze weapons and vessels, GEOMETRIC POTTERY including glazed stoneware and incised marks on pottery and stone moulds which are viewed as an indigenous writing system. Contemporaneous with the site of ZHENGZHOU, Wucheng represents a southern bronze civilization comparable with the early SHANG in northern-central China.

Wun Rok Iron Age mounds in southern Sudan dating to the first millennium AD, associated with cattle herding, hunting and fishing. Although iron was present, it seems to have been used mainly for decorative items, and many tools were made from bone. Roulette-decorated pottery is present in contexts dating to the second half of the 1st millennium AD.

Würm Glaciation the final Alpine GLACIAL advance which started c.110,000 years ago and ended with the onset of the POSTGLACIAL Holocene c.10,000 years ago. See also WEICHSEL GLACIATION, WISCONSINAN STAGE.

Wushan hominid site see LONGGUPO.

Wybalenna a settlement established in 1833 on Flinders Island, off TASMANIA, Australia, for the last of the Tasmanian Aborigines rounded up by ROBINSON, who was himself superintendent there in 1835–9. Wybalenna was closed in 1847 and the forty-seven survivors transferred to Oyster Cove. It was the site of one of the first historical excavations in Australia in the early 1970s.

Wylotne a prehistoric rockshelter located on the Sąspówka River, north of Kraków in southern Poland. Artifacts are buried in loess and rubble. The three lowest cultural layers contain Middle Palaeolithic assemblages (e.g. bifaces, scrapers) that probably date to the early GLACIAL and may be assigned to the MICOQUIAN. Upper Palaeolithic and Neolithic remains occur in the upper layers.

Wyrie Swamp a peat deposit in southeastern South Australia, investigated by Roger Luebbers. GAMBIERAN stone artifacts and about twenty-five wooden implements, including BOOMERANGs, barbed and plain spears and digging sticks, were recovered from the 10,000-year-old site. The barbed spears are the oldest known in the world. The site is significant for its extraordinary preservation.

X

X-Group a culture of LOWER NUBIA, dated to *c*.AD 350–600, of uncertain origin but displaying some continuity with the preceding MEROITIC kingdom. The X-Group is chiefly represented archaeologically by cemeteries, especially that of the chiefs of the X-Group at BALLANA AND QUSTUL, but some settlement sites have been explored (e.g. QASR IBRIM).

Xia [Hsia] the first of the CHINESE DYNASTIES of the SANDAI period in China, traditionally dated between 2200 and 1750 BC. Some archaeologists assign early remains of the SHANG culture – such as the ERLITOU site – to the Xia Dynasty; others maintain the Xia Dynasty is a fiction or at least not accessible in the archaeological record without direct corroboration from inscriptional remains.

Xiajiadian [Hsia-chia-tien] a site in Chifeng, Inner Mongolian Autonomous Region of China, giving its name to two quite different cultural entities in the NORTHERN ZONE: an early local Bronze Age culture, the Lower Xiajiadian, contemporaneous with the SHANG in the 2nd millennium BC; and a later Upper Xiajiadian agricultural society with a horse-riding aristocracy (compare XIONGNU) contemporaneous with early ZHOU. Despite the similar names, these two cultures are hypothesized to have different origins.

Xiang Khouang 'Plain of Jars', the upland region east of Luang Prabang in northern Laos, in which a series of late prehistoric burial and ceremonial sites have been found, apparently bordering old trade routes linked to northern Vietnam. These remains, the best known of which lie around the possible early crematorium site of Ban Ang, comprise large stone burial jars (containing locally made iron knives, arrowheads and spearheads, locally cast bronze jewellery, imported beads of glass and carnelian, and cowrie shells), and upright stone slabs or MENHIRS, a type of megalith found more frequently in maritime Southeast Asia. Dates: *c*.300 BC–AD 300.

Xiaotun [Hsiao-t'un] the village in Hebei Province, China, where a palace/temple complex of the late SHANG was discovered near ANYANG City. The complex consists of several building compounds oriented on a longitudinal axis, with watchtowers and altars at the southern end leading into the ancestral worship halls which were backed by residential compounds for the Shang elite. The HANGTU building foundation-platforms incorporated many burials interpreted as human sacrifices, and around the platforms occurred many other burials and some pit-house commoner dwellings.

Xibeigang [Hsi-pei-kang] the village in Hebei Province, China, where the Royal Cemetery of the late SHANG was discovered near ANYANG City. It contains at least seven SHAFT TOMBS with WOODEN-CHAMBER burials and human sacrificial interments, and over 2,000 small pit-graves of further human sacrifices. Most of the shaft tombs have been plundered, but the grave-goods probably included bronze vessels of the Anyang style, jade and carved bone objects.

Xinle [Hsin-lo] a site in Liaoning Province, China, which has given its name to the Neolithic Xinle culture of eastern MANCHURIA, dated to the late 6th millennium

XIANG KHOUANG, Laos: the Plain of Jars.

BC. It is characterized by millet agriculture, coastal SHELL MIDDENS and textured-surface pottery resembling the CHULMUN tradition of the Korean peninsula.

Xiongnu [Hsiung-nu] a nomadic ethnic group occupying the Mongolian region during the HAN Dynasty and later. Constant raids by their predecessors on northern Chinese agricultural populations spurred the construction of the GREAT WALL during the ZHOU period, and the Han initiated the HEQIN system of reverse tribute to pacify them. Compare XIAJIADIAN.

Xochicalco an important late CLASSIC centre in Morelos, Mexico, whose florescence coincided with the decline of TEOTIHUACÁN in the BASIN OF MEXICO. The centre of the site is on an artificially terraced hill. The sculpture and architecture at Xochicalco suggest it was in close contact with the Basin of Mexico, Gulf Coast and MAYA Lowland regions. It is one of the earliest fortified sites in the region.

Xom Trai a cave in Lac Son Province, 150 km (93 miles) southwest of Ha Noi, Vietnam, excavated in the 1980s. The deposits were 5 m (16 ft) deep, very rich in typical HOABINHIAN stone tools, animal bones, freshwater and land molluscs and abundant plant remains. Twenty-two radiocarbon dates place the upper 2.4 m (8 ft) of the deposit in the late Pleistocene between 18,000 and 15,000 BP, and finds of more than thirty grains of carbonized rice, claimed to be domesticated, down to the base of the deposit are difficult to interpret.

x-radiography see RADIOGRAPHY.

x-ray art a style of rock art characteristic of the recent period in northern Australia, especially ARNHEM LAND, in which the skeleton and internal organs of animals and humans are depicted.

x-ray diffraction analysis a physical technique used to identify the mineralogy of crystalline material such as ceramics, stone and weathering products on metals. A small piece of sample is powdered and exposed to a focused beam of monochromatic x-rays which passes over the sample covering a continuous range of incident angles. The spacing between crystal lattice planes in different mineral species and the incident angle of the x-ray beam determines the series of x-ray intensities that are transmitted after passing through the sample to a re-

corder. Diffraction patterns are then compared with reference standards for identification. The sample can initially be mounted on a ceramic or glass slide, in which case the results are recorded on a strip chart with sharp peaks at diagnostic intervals, or it can be mounted in a camera where the diffraction pattern is projected and recorded as series of arcs on photographic film. Mineral identification is based on the spacing between arcs. Relative concentrations of constituents may also be estimated, based on the degree of darkening of the photographically recorded arcs, because the intensity is related to concentration. See also RADIOGRAPHY.

x-ray fluorescence spectrometry a physical technique used to determine the major and TRACE ELEMENTal chemical composition of materials such as ceramics, obsidian and glass which may aid in identifying the material source. A sample is bombarded with x-rays; the wavelengths of the released energy, or fluorescent x-rays, are detected and measured. Constituent elements are identified based on the unique wavelengths of fluorescent x-rays they emit, and concentrations are estimated based on the intensity of the released x-rays. See also RADIOGRAPHY.

x-ray microscopy a physical technique used to identify the composition of crystalline substances by analysing atomic structure. A SCANNING or TRANSMISSION ELECTRON MICROSCOPE is used to render a greatly magnified image of sample atomic structure, based on the differential absorption and emission of x-rays produced by different elements. See also RADIOGRAPHY.

x-ray milliprobe analysis a specialized form of X-RAY FLUORESCENCE SPECTROMETRY using an instrument that directs a highly focused x-ray beam to any desired point on the sample surface. Secondary x-rays emitted from this point are directed to a detector and analysed as in x-ray fluorescence spectrometry. The great advantages of this technique are its flexibility and its ability to analyse microscopic areas.

Xuan La a cemetery of the late DONG SON culture with seven wooden coffins, in Ha Son Binh Province, northern Vietnam, 10 km (6 miles) from CHAU CAN. Two burials contained Chinese coins of WANGMAN (AD 9–25), wooden containers and bowls, bronze weapons and a number of iron spade-ends.

Y

Yabrud see JABRUD.

Yadin, Yigael (1917–84) an Israeli archaeologist and chief of the Israeli Defence Forces, best known for his excavations at HAZOR and MASADA, and for his work on the DEAD SEA SCROLLS.

Yahya, Tepe a 3 ha (7.4 acre) TELL in the Soghun Valley of the Kirman Province of southern Iran, excavated in the 1960s and 1970s by C. C. Lamberg-Karlovsky. It provides a long, if interrupted, cultural sequence of seven periods (Yahya VII–I, with subdivisions) which span the mid 5th millennium BC to early 1st millennium AD. In period IVC (3rd millennium) occurs evidence of PROTO-ELAMITE activities, including texts, seals and sealings, JEMDET NASR painted wares, BEVELLED RIM BOWLS, etc., in a large building; period IVB has evidence for the production of INTERCULTURAL STYLE CARVED CHLORITE vessels, which have an extensive distribution in western Asia.

Yamatai a POLITY in the Japanese islands known from the Chinese chronicles, the WEIZHI and HOUHANSHU. Its location was arguably in northern Kyushu or the KINAI region. The queen of Yamatai is named in the chronicles as Himiko/Pimiko, who interacted with the 3rd-century AD Wei court (see THREE KINGDOMS) through LELANG. This polity has not been documented archaeologically, though the YOSHINOGARI site was contemporaneous. If Yamatai was in Kyushu, then it was a predecessor to the YAMATO state, arising in the Kinai area; if Yamatai was in the Kinai area, then it might have served as an early stage of Yamato state formation.

Yamato the former provincial name of Nara Prefecture, Japan, namesake of the emergent state of the KOFUN period. The Yamato state structure of the 5th century AD was formed through the institutionalization of the BE system for requisitioning goods and services. Yamato kings communicated with the 5th-century CHINESE DYNASTIES and the elite of the KOGURYO, PAEKCHE and SILLA states on the Korean peninsula. With the adoption of the TANG administrative system from China in the late 7th century AD, Yamato was transformed into the RITSURYO state.

Yamazy-Tash see IGNATEVA CAVE.

Yamnaya culture an ENEOLITHIC/Early Bronze Age culture (some refer to it as a 'horizon') of the lower Volga and Don steppes, sometimes also called the Pit-Grave culture. It occupied a vast territory from the Urals to the Dniester River, and in fact was probably not a true culture, but a cultural-historical community with several variants. CHILDE and a number of later prehistorians including GIMBUTAS viewed the Yamnaya as the forebear of the CORDED WARE, SINGLE GRAVE or KURGAN culture, whose dispersal was believed to coincide with the spread of INDO-EUROPEAN languages. This position has been questioned by Renfrew and others.

Yan see ZHOU.

Yangshao the main Neolithic culture of the loess area of northern-central China (c.5000–2700 BC). It is distinguished by millet agriculture, coarse and painted pottery of innumerable regional types, sedentary organization consisting of mother-daughter villages, and kinship groups interpreted to be clans. Some marks on Yangshao pottery are considered to be incipient writing (see WUCHENG, ORACLE BONES). Compare BANPO, HONGSHAN, MACHANG, MIAODIGOU II, DAWENKOU.

Yanik Tepe an 8 ha (20 acre) site northwest of Lake Urmia near Tabriz in northwestern Iran where C. Burney's excavations in the 1960s produced evidence for Neolithic (comparable to the Hajji Firuz phase of the HASANLU sequence, dated to the late 7th/early 6th millennia BC), CHALCOLITHIC (comparable to the Pisdeli phase at Hasanlu, dated to the mid 5th millennium BC), Early Bronze Age, Iron Age (including the initial discovery of the painted 'Triangle ware' of the late Iron Age in the northern Zagros, dated to the second quarter of the 1st millennium BC) occupations. The Early Bronze Age settlement consists of a long sequence of KURA-ARAXES occupations, providing a detailed view of the closely packed circular dwellings equipped with benches and storage bins, the burnished and ornamented pottery, and other materials typical of this culture complex. Burney's exposure also reveals changes through time in the architecture (to rectilinear dwellings) and pottery (a decrease of incised decoration) that may have relevance to the Kura-Araxes culture complex as a whole.

Yaozhou see CELADON.

Yarang a ŚRIVIJAYAN period walled city on the Pattani River, near the east coast of peninsular Thailand. The BUDDHIST brick STUPA-bases were decorated with stucco, and hundreds of inscribed votive tablets were found in excavations. Three main phases of occupation have been identified from the early centuries of the Christian era to an 18th-century fort.

yardang an erosional, streamlined landform created by AEOLIAN abrasion of bedrock residuals. Yardangs are usually associated with desert areas and may have smoothly rounded intervening troughs.

Yarim Tepe six distinct TELLS within the Sinjar region of northern Iraq, where Soviet excavations, begun in 1969 and continued through the 1980s, produced long Neolithic sequences for two of them (Yarim 1 and Yarim 2). Yarim 1 belongs largely to the HASSUNA culture, spanning the 'Archaic' to 'Standard' Hassuna phases (6200–5500 BC), and to the appearance of SAMARRAN elements (late 6th–early 5th millennia BC); HALAF and SASSANIAN burials also occur in eroded surface sediments. The wide architectural exposure and detailed ceramic sequences provide considerable detail of the Hassuna phenomenon. While the Yarim 2 mound begins with traces of 'Archaic' and 'Standard' Hassuna occupation, most of the sequence belongs to the Middle Halaf period; the usual *tholos* architecture, painted pottery, and small finds appear here. 'UBAID deposits cap the sequence.

Yarmoukian a late Neolithic culture (second half of the 6th millennium BC) in the southern Levant. Named after the Yarmuk River in the central Jordan River Valley, it was the first culture to use pottery in the southern Levant, but other aspects of the material culture greatly resembled the preceding ACERAMIC (PPNC) culture. The economic evidence suggests a strong reliance on herding animals for milk and other products (the requirements of milk products may have encouraged use of pottery) in addition to farming. See also 'AIN GHAZAL, SHAAR HA-GOLAN.

Yarmouth see HOLSTEINIAN.

Yarmukian see YARMOUKIAN.

Yarmuth, Tel a 16 ha (40 acre) walled town of the Early Bronze Age II–III (c.3100–2300 BC), located in low hill country 25 km (16 miles) west of Jerusalem, Israel. Starting as a late 4th-millennium village, the settlement expanded rapidly during the first centuries of the 3rd millennium.

French excavations since 1980 have exposed portions of the massive fortifications and town gate, residential and industrial areas, a probable temple, and several palaces. The latest palace, a 85 by 72 m (93 by 79 yd) structure, is the largest known building of this period in the Levant, and clearly reveals a strongly developed social hierarchy. The town was abandoned around 2300 BC as part of a deurbanization process that affected much of the Levant. Thereafter the Yarmuth citadel hosted only intermittent small settlements until Byzantine times.

Yaxchilán a CLASSIC MAYA site on the banks of the Usumacinta River in Chiapas, Mexico. Yaxchilán is best known for its beautiful carved stone STELAS and lintels which document the dynasty of the king Shield Jaguar and his son Bird Jaguar. One famous sequence, from Temple 23, was dedicated to Shield Jaguar's principal wife, Lady Xoc, who is depicted first in a BLOODLETTING ritual passing a thorny cord through her tongue so that it drips onto pieces of paper, and then burning the paper to summon a vision serpent from the smoke.

Yayo a site in northern Chad which has yielded a partial HOMINID cranium of uncertain age and genus. Faunal remains found near by are thought to be some 700,000 years old, but it is not known whether the hominid remains are of a similar age.

Yayoi a PROTOHISTORIC period in Japan (300 BC–AD 300), distinguished by wet-rice agriculture (see ITAZUKE), use of bronze (see DOTAKU) and iron, increasing warfare and social differentiation, and trade interaction with the LELANG COMMANDERY of HAN Dynasty China. Yayoi sites are often moated (see KARAKO, YOSHINOGARI, but compare TORO). Yayoi pottery succeeds JOMON but incorporates manufacturing techniques of MUMUN pottery from the Korean peninsula; it is related to the HAJI pottery of the KOFUN period. The Yayoi peoples are thought to maintain genetic continuity with the Jomon with heavy admixture from the peninsula, especially in western Japan (see DOIGAHAMA, WA). Mound-burials in late Yayoi foreshadow the MOUNDED TOMBS of the Kofun period rulers, in contrast to family burial grounds (see HOKEI SHUKOBO).

Yaz-depe a 16 ha (40 acre) site in the Murghab delta in southeastern Turkmenia excavated by V. M. Masson in the 1950s. It is the type-site for the Iron Age Yaz complex. In its lowest level, Yaz-depe contains a citadel (monumental architecture on a massive platform) surrounded by a residential area; an extensive irrigation system runs near the settlement. Technological and formal changes in the pottery allow definition of three phases (Yaz I–III), which are roughly dated from the mid 2nd to the mid 1st millennium BC. Sites of this and related cultures are distributed between the Kopet Dagh (southeast of the Caspian Sea) and southern Bactria (northwestern Afghanistan), with settlement ranging from farmsteads to small towns (often with citadels) in association with large irrigation works.

Yazılıkaya a HITTITE sanctuary, probably related to the mortuary cult of Tudhaliya IV (1239–1209 BC) about 2 km (1.2 miles) northeast of BOĞAZKÖY, Turkey, and linked to the Hittite capital by a processional way. The sanctuary consists of three monumental structures standing across the entrance to an embayment in a cliff face. The rock face bears portrayals of the Hittite gods carved in relief.

year formula a brief phrase in administrative CUNEIFORM documents of MESOPOTAMIA which often provides a date for a document by describing a significant event (military, cultic, public works, etc.) of a given year in a king's reign. An example of a year formula is 'year when HAMMURABI, by order of ENLIL, destroyed the walls of MARI and Malgi' (the 35th year of Hammurabi's reign). The practice of dating by year formulae, current from AKKADIAN through OLD BABYLONIAN times, provides a basic framework for the political history of southern Mesopotamia, particularly during the period of competing kingdoms in the Old Babylonian period.

Yeavering the 7th-century AD royal seat of ANGLO-SAXON Northumbria, northern England, where excavations by B. Hope-Taylor in the 1950s uncovered a series of great timber halls, and a large semicircular timber grandstand for assemblies.

Yengema a cave in Sierra Leone with both Palaeolithic and Neolithic remains. Crudely flaked picks, hoe-like tools and flake-scrapers present in assemblages dated to around 4500 bp are considered to have been appropriate for a forested environment, while the paucity of microliths in such assemblages has been interpreted to indicate that some form of fallow farming and little hunting took place at that time.

Yiewsley a series of pits in the Yiewsley region of West Middlesex, England, which have yielded large numbers of Lower Palaeolithic artifacts, mainly recovered between 1885 and 1935. The assemblage includes over 2,000 ACHEULIAN bifaces and many LEVALLOIS flakes and cores, and has been dated to c.200–250,000 years ago. The upper layers produced Middle Palaeolithic (MOUSTERIAN) artifacts including BOUT COUPÉ-like bifaces.

Yiftahel an early PRE-POTTERY NEOLITHIC (PPNB, 7th millennium BC) and EARLY BRONZE AGE I (3500–3100 BC) site in northern Israel. The PPNB settlement was a sizeable village, perhaps as much as 4 ha (10 acres) in extent, the large residential units of which often had finely plastered floors. The Early Bronze Age settlement, with its scatter of one-room houses of elliptical shape, provides one of the clearest examples of settlement character in the period just before the rise of town life in the southern Levant.

Yombon a complex of open sites in West New Britain, where Christina Pavlides excavated a sequence in which cultural material alternates with TEPHRA layers from Mount Witori. The area was first occupied about 35,000 bp. This is the oldest evidence in the world of tropical rainforest occupation. Artifacts from Pleistocene layers are made only of local chert and the sequence documents changing patterns of exploitation of this material. Obsidian from TALASEA and MOPIR appears in the mid Holocene.

Yongnam the region of South Korea comprising the southeastern provinces of North and South Kyongsang. The term is widely used in archaeological writings.

York (*Lat.* Eboracum, *Viking* Jorvik) one of the three legionary fortresses in the Roman province of Britain. The thriving civilian settlement was granted the status of colony, perhaps under the emperors Septimius Severus or Caracalla. Remains of the fortress's fortifications were incorporated into the later medieval walls; a particularly fine stretch can be seen adjoining the Multangular Tower. Recent excavations have revealed traces of a large palace-like structure. Development in the city centre has uncovered remains of the VIKING city and these remains have been interpreted in the Jorvik reconstruction.

Yoshinogari a site in Saga Prefecture, Japan, consisting of a double-moated YAYOI period village containing watchtowers, pit-house remains and storage pits, with over 2,000 jar burials in nearby cemeteries. A large oval mound, 30 by 40 m (33 by 44 yds), contained a jar burial with bronze dagger and beads, and is perhaps the earliest mound-burial in Japan, dating to the early 1st century BC. Discovered only in 1986, the site has been inappropriately linked to the country of YAMATAI, known from early Chinese texts; but it belongs to the time period and region of interaction with China, and so is the most important and most well-preserved western Yayoi site in Japan. Compare TORO.

Younger Dryas see DRYAS.

Yuan see CHINESE DYNASTIES.

Yuanmou an Early Palaeolithic site in Yunnan Province, China, at which HOMO *erectus* dental remains were first reported as dated by PALAEOMAGNETISM to 1.7 million years ago. This dating is now under revision to 700,000 bp.

Yubetsu the name of a Late Palaeolithic microlithic technology for working obsidian; also known as the Shirataki technique after the type-site of Shirataki-Hattoridai in Hokkaido, Japan, dated to c.13,000 bp. A bifacial core is prepared, then one lateral edge of the core is removed, producing a triangular cross-sectioned spall; subsequent edge removals produce *ski spalls* of parallel surfaces in order to prepare the striking platform of a now wedge-shaped core when held vertically. This technique was used from Mongolia to Alaska towards the end of the Pleistocene.

Yudinovo two Upper Palaeolithic open-air sites on the Sudost' River (Desna tributary) in European Russia. At each site, the occupation horizon is buried in slope deposits on the first terrace. Yudinovo I has yielded five radiocarbon dates between 15,660 and 12,300 bp. Woolly mammoth remains are abundant at both sites (arctic fox is also common), and three MAMMOTH-BONE HOUSES have been uncovered (one at Yudinovo III). The non-stone artifacts include perforated marine shells from the Black Sea, 680 km (423 miles) to the south.

Yue [Yueh] **1** an ancient ethnic group occupying the southeastern seaboard of mainland China during the HAN Dynasty.

2 a stoneware of southeastern China in the 3rd–6th centuries AD, preceding CELADON and porcelain development. It often has a yellowish-brown feldspathic glaze.

Yurovichi an Upper Palaeolithic site on the Pripyat' River in Belarus. The remains are buried in slope deposits on a low terrace, and appear to be redeposited. A radiocarbon date of 26,470 bp on an associated mammoth tooth indicates that this may be the oldest-known Upper Palaeolithic site of the Dnieper-Desna Basin. Yurovichi was excavated by Polikarpovich in 1929–31, by Bud'ko in 1959–60 and by Ksenzov in 1976.

Z

Zafar the capital city of the Himyar kingdom, located in highland western Yemen near modern Ibb. The Himyarites were the dominant political power of SOUTH ARABIA during the first half of the 1st millennium AD. Zafar has not been the subject of systematic excavation.

Zafarraya see NEANDERTHAL, VINDIJA.

Zakro the site of a MINOAN palace on the island of CRETE, which has been excavated by Platon. Although not as large as the other palaces, Zakro shares the same basic layout of blocks of rooms arranged around a central court. The palace overlooks one of the finest harbours on the east coast of Crete, and was evidently involved in overseas trade. Zakro was destroyed by fire c.1450 BC.

Zambian Wilton a Zambian microlithic LATER STONE AGE industry of the last 6,000 years from sites in the drainage basins of the Kafue and Zambezi Rivers. It is akin to the better-studied WILTON industry of South Africa. See also GWISHO.

Zambujal a CHALCOLITHIC fortress near Lisbon, Portugal, with several walls strengthened by rounded bastions and a wide rock-cut ditch. Successive additions over several centuries of use resulted in walls of stones, in clay mortar, in some places over 10 m (33 ft) thick. The principal bastion on the inner circuit had archery slits in its base overlooking the gateways through the middle wall. Pottery included much BEAKER material along with local wares of c.2700–2200 BC.

Zaminets a settlement of the ENEOLITHIC KRIVODOL group in northwestern Bulgaria, c.4000 BC, located on a promontory with palisade and bank defences. The settlement at Zaminets was rebuilt several times after episodes of destruction by fire.

Zamostje 2 a waterlogged open-air hunter-gatherer site in a peatbog, 110 km (68 miles) northeast of Moscow, Russia, where excavations since 1989 have discovered a continuous stratigraphic sequence from the late Mesolithic (5900 bc) to the end of the middle Neolithic (2700 bc). The excellent conditions of preservation in what was originally a lakeside settlement have yielded thousands of implements and weapons made of organic materials, including bark floats, fish traps, bone hooks and harpoons, and hundreds of varied bone arrow- and spear-heads. There are also flint knives fixed to antler hafts with pine resin and beeswax, and with birch-bark round the handle; and the site has also yielded wooden objects such as paddles, dishes and spoons; an abundance of Neolithic pottery; and numerous art objects of stone or bone, mostly carved elk-heads and ducks. In addition to fish, elk and beaver were the principal prey.

Zapotec an important cultural and linguistic group in Oaxaca, Mexico, from pre-Columbian times to the present day. Zapotec cultural features noted at the time of the Spanish conquest closely resemble aspects of the culture found at MONTE ALBÁN and other sites. It is assumed these sites were built by the Zapotecs. Monte Albán was a Zapotec centre until AD 800. The pre-Columbian Zapotecs worshipped a storm god, Cocijo, who personified the concept of *pii*, signifying the life force. Elite ancestors provided a spiritual conduit between mortals and the supernatural, and ancestral tombs were used as shrines for sequential interment of lineage members as well as consultation with divine ancestors.

Zarzi a cave in southern Kurdistan in western Iraq. GARROD's investigations in 1928 provided the initial definition of the EPIPALAEOLITHIC Zarzian industry, which has since been studied elsewhere in the Zagros (e.g. SHANIDAR, Pa Sangar in KHORRAMABAD). The industry, dating to 10,500–6000 BC, contains high proportions of backed bladelets, a variety of geometric microliths and notched blades.

Zaskal'naya a group of Middle Palaeolithic sites in the Crimea, Ukraine, which consist of former (i.e. collapsed) rockshelters and caves. The most important sites are Zaskal'naya V and VI, which respectively contain seven and six occupation levels buried in layers of loam and rubble. The faunal remains are chiefly of saiga, mammoth and horse. Some of the occupations are associated with a buried soil and appear to date to a mild climatic interval (an INTERSTADIAL preceding the early cold LAST GLA-

CIAL MAXIMUM?). The artifact assemblages are rich in bifacial foliates, as well as sidescrapers, and are assigned to the AK-KAYA CULTURE. Human fossil remains were found at both sites, including a minimum of five individuals ranging from one to fifteen years of age at Zaskal'naya VI, and have been classified as NEANDERTHAL. These sites were discovered and excavated by Kolosov 1969–77.

Závist a HILLFORT of the HALLSTATT D period (c.600 BC) north of Prague in Bohemia. At its centre was an area known as the 'AKROPOLIS', where a large altar was located. Závist was abandoned during LA TÈNE B (c.300 BC) but was reconstructed as an OPPIDUM enclosing 80 ha (198 acres) in the 1st century BC. It was abandoned later in this century with its gate blocked by a clay wall which was destroyed by fire.

Zawi Chemi Shanidar an open-air site near SHANIDAR Cave in the piedmont of northwestern Iraq excavated by Ralph and Ruth Solecki in conjunction with Shanidar. It is a terminal EPIPALAEOLITHIC site (under Iron Age levels) which contains storage pits and a possible circular structure, dating to the 9th millennium BC. Although hunting was the principal source of animal protein during most of the occupation, towards its end sheep become important, and have been suggested to represent 'incipient domestication' of the species. The corresponding levels in Shanidar cave contain some twenty burials that reveal the population's poor state of health.

Zawisza, Count Jan (1820–87) a Polish archaeologist and Palaeolithic specialist who conducted excavations at MAMUTOWA CAVE in 1873–86, bringing to light the first evidence of Upper Palaeolithic industries containing bifacial foliates in this part of Europe.

Zawiyet Umm el-Rakham a site on Egypt's Mediterranean coast, 300 km (186 miles) west of ALEXANDRIA, and probably founded by RAMESSES II as a fortified town, 140 m (153 yds) square, designed to intimidate local Libyan tribes. A range of imported vessels from CRETE, CYPRUS and the Levant suggests that Zawiyet Umm el-Rakham was an important staging point for maritime traders at the same period as the ULU BURUN shipwreck. The site was excavated by HABACHI in the 1950s, with further investigation since 1994 by Liverpool University.

Zazaragi a Palaeolithic site in Miyagi Prefecture, Japan, with tool-yielding strata dated to between 40,000 and 45,000 bp by FISSION TRACK and THERMOLUMINESCENCE.

Zebbug a cemetery of five simple pit graves in Malta, which have given their name to the Zebbug phase of the Maltese pre-temple Neolithic c.4100–3800 BC.

Zeekoei Valley see SEACOW VALLEY.

Zeliezovce style a late regional variant of the LINEAR POTTERY CULTURE, found in Slovakia, Moravia and southern Poland c.4000 bc, with pottery characterized by angular incised lines relieved by lozenge-shaped incisions.

Zemi a principal deity of the ARAWAKAN groups (such as the TAINOS) in northeastern South America and the Caribbean, who took both human and animal form, and was frequently depicted on utensils as well as in places of worship such as caves.

Zenabi Falls a site on the northern Jos Plateau of Nigeria, where river gravels contain undated stone artifacts with MIDDLE STONE AGE and Middle Palaeolithic affinities, made from prepared cores.

Zengövárkony a Neolithic cemetery and settlement of the LENGYEL culture in Hungary. Of the 368 graves, forty-seven had preserved skeletal material. Within these, the grave-goods reflect possible gender differentiation. The faunal remains from the settlement deposits have a high proportion of bones of wild animals.

Zhangguo [Chan-kuo] 'Warring States' in Chinese; see ZHOU.

Zhengzhou [Cheng-chou] a modern city in Henan Province, China, where the remains of an Early SHANG site have been recovered. A walled compound, 1.7 by 1.9 km (1 by 1.2 miles), contains HANGTU foundation platforms of palace buildings; and several workshops of bone, bronze and ceramic crafts are located outside the wall. Zhengzhou is thought to be one of the Shang capitals, and it has been used as the model 'ceremonial centre' by which to understand the beginnings of urbanism. The nearby village of ERLIGANG has given its name to the style of bronze vessels prevalent at Zhengzhou. See also ANYANG, PANLONGCHENG.

Zhenla or **Chenla** the Chinese name for an early, apparently KHMER, state in southeastern Cambodia and southern Vietnam, which Chinese records say conquered FUNAN in the 7th century AD and subsequently broke down to form 'Land Chenla' and 'Water Chenla'. These reports probably conceal considerable fluidity amongst small pre-ANGKOR Khmer states, of which Iśanapura, with its centre at SAMBOR PREI KUK, must have been a dominant example.

Zhizo an Early Iron Age phase in western Zimbabwe and the Limpopo Valley, dating from the 8th–10th centuries AD, and known as the TOUTSWE phase or group in eastern Botswana. See also SCHRODA.

Zhob a valley in northern Baluchistan (Pakistan) where W. Fairservis recorded a regional sequence of CHALCOLITHIC and Bronze Age cultures, based on soundings at Moghul Ghundai and Periano Ghundai. The region gives its name to a style of seated female figurine, commonly identified as a mother-goddess.

ZHOUKOUDIAN, China.

Zhongyuan [Chung-yuan] the Chinese name for the 'Central Plain' of northern China.

Zhou [Chou] the name of a Bronze Age ethnic group which overthrew the SHANG c.1027 BC from QISHAN and established the Zhou Dynasty (see CHINESE DYNASTIES). The Zhou Dynasty is divided into Western or Royal Zhou (1027–771), and historic Eastern Zhou (770–221). It is further divided into the Spring and Autumn (770–476) and Warring States (475–221) periods. The Zhou period is characterized by many small competing states (e.g. Shu, Ba, Yan), organized in feudal subservience to the Royal Zhou during the early period, with hegemonies developing under successively stronger states in the later periods. The Zhou state of QIN eventually conquered its rivals and united the various states in 220 BC. The major advances during the Zhou period were the discovery and development of iron working, construction of the GREAT WALL, coinage and the institution of county-level administration. The earlier Zhou period is considered PROTOHISTORIC from ORACLE BONE and bronze inscriptions.

Zhoukoudian [Chou-k'ou-tien] a Palaeolithic site in Hebei Province, China, discovered by J. C. ANDERSSON in 1921. The first skullcap of HOMO *erectus* – known variously as Peking Man or *Sinanthropus* – was excavated in 1929 by PEI WENZHONG at locality 1. The site has yielded the only large population (fragments of more than forty individuals) of the species worldwide. Most of the actual bones were lost during the Second World War and only the casts have survived; these have been augmented in new excavations through to 1982. Strata at locality 1 range in date from 700,000 to 200,000 bp, and the Upper Cave has been radiocarbon (AMS) dated to between 13,000 and 34,000 bp. The flake tools from locality 1 typify a small-tool tradition in Palaeolithic China (see also JIN-NIUSHAN), in contrast to a heavy-tool tradition manifested at the LANTIAN, KEHE and DINCUN finds. The Upper Cave remains of *H. sapiens sapiens* comprise the first human burials and personal ornamentation known in the East Asian archaeological record.

ziggurat a rectangular stepped temple-tower in MESO-POTAMIA. Though often confused with Egyptian pyramids in the popular imagination, the Mesopotamian ziggurat consists of one or more superimposed brick platforms, on top of which sits the temple of an individual god, with access by a central staircase. These religious structures visually dominated their cities, and form the highest point of many TELLS. Ziggurat architecture is traceable to temples on platforms built during 'UBAID times (second half of the 6th–5th millennia BC) (e.g. at ERIDU), and reached their mature development in the UR III PERIOD (late 3rd millennium BC). Famous examples of ziggurats occur at UR, BABYLON (the 'tower of Babel') and AQAR QUF.

Zillingtal a large AVAR cemetery and settlement about 45 km (28 miles) southeast of Vienna in Austria, dating to the 6th century AD. Nearly 800 graves have been excavated to date. The settlement contains traces of timber houses as well as evidence of iron working.

Zimbabwe (*Dzimbahwe*, pl. *madzimbahwe*) **1** the term used by Shona speakers in Zimbabwe for the court or house of a chief, or *mambo*, which traditionally consisted of a series of stone-walled enclosures built on a hill. More than 150 of these are known, mostly from the central Zimbabwe plateau, the most famous being GREAT ZIMBABWE.

2 The culture or tradition (formerly the Ruins tradition) of which Great Zimbabwe was a capital during the second phase. It is divided into the MAPUNGUBWE (ad 1220–90), Great Zimbabwe (ad 1290–1450) and KHAMI (ad 1450–1820) phases or periods.

Zincirli capital of Sam'al, a Neo-HITTITE state in south-eastern Anatolia during the Early Iron Age, and also important during Hittite (Late Bronze Age) times. Located at the head of the Karasu drainage of the 'Amuq plain, Zincirli possessed a circular wall which enclosed nearly

40 ha (99 acres), and an inner fortified citadel with palaces and other public buildings. A German team working at the end of the 19th century concentrated on public architecture and art; notable finds include reliefs carved on basalt ORTHSTATS and HIEROGLYPHIC inscriptions common to Neo-Hittite capitals.

Zinjanthropus the genus name originally applied by Louis LEAKEY to a 1.8 million-year-old robust australopithecine (see AUSTRALOPITHECUS) found at OLDUVAI GORGE in Tanzania by Mary LEAKEY in 1959. Arguably the most famous hominid fossil from this site, it is also known by the nicknames 'Zinj', 'Nutcracker Man' (for its large molar teeth), as well as Louis Leakey's appellation 'Dear Boy'. It is now known as *Australopithecus* or *Paranthropus boisei*.

Zinken see HAMBURGIAN.

Ziwa a mid 1st-millennium AD Early Iron Age pottery ware of eastern Zimbabwe and Mozambique, closely related to GOKOMERE, with which it is often linked as Gokomere/Ziwa.

Ziwiye or **Ziwiyech** a mounded Iron Age site in Iranian Azerbaijan, near Lake Urmia, and the object of much looting. The 'Ziwiye treasure', one result of looting in 1946, was a hoard of gold, silver and ivory objects contained within a bathtub coffin. The subject of considerable discussion, these items combine stylistic elements of western (ASSYRIAN), northern (URARTIAN) and eastern (SCYTHIAN) inspiration. Some items are similar to the LURISTAN bronzes. The most interesting objects are golden and bronze belts, golden plaques from a sword scabbard, a golden PECTORAL, and other items that can be characterized as signs of power or nobility. They are decorated with images of a very specific eclectic style, mixing features of the Assyrian, Urartian and SCYTHIAN-SIBERIAN ANIMAL STYLE. The Ziwiye treasure is dated to the late 8th–mid 7th centuries BC, and is very important for the study of the ancient art of Iranian tribes – the SCYTHIANS, Medes and PERSIANS. Iranian excavations of the 1990s have recorded a Late Iron Age residence with a pillared hall, but have not yet provided a solid context for the looted artwork.

Złota a late Neolithic cemetery in southeastern Poland on the Vistula River, which gives its name to the Złota culture. Many of the graves at Złota are single inhumations in niches and their grave-goods reflect a mixture of traits from a number of other cultures. The most prominent elements indicate connections to the CORDED WARE and GLOBULAR AMPHORA cultures, while cups with upturned handles are similar to those of the BADEN culture. Copper and amber ornaments are also found.

Zollchow see LINEAR POTTERY.

zong [tsung] a tubular jade artifact of unknown symbolism which appears in the southern Neolithic cultures of China such as LIANGZHU and continues into SHANG and ZHOU times. Its outside profile is square with a circular hollow through the centre. Often it is decorated with the TAOTIE design.

zooarchaeology see ARCHAEOZOOLOGY.

zoomorph 1 an object or picture resembling an animal form.
2 In prehistoric art, a figure providing visual information recognized by contemporary humans as resembling an animal form. See also ANTHROPOMORPH.

zoomorphic *adj.* **1** having or suggesting animal form and appearance.
2 (in prehistoric art) providing visual information recognized by contemporary humans as resembling animal form.
3 attributing the form or nature of an animal to something, especially a deity or superhuman being. See also ANTHROPOMORPHOUS.

Zoser see DJOSER.

Zürich-Utoquai a Neolithic lake-edge settlement, in Zürich, Switzerland, with two layers of occupation separated by an abandonment phase. The lower occupation layer had flat-based 'flower pot' pottery characteristic of the HORGEN culture *c*.3500–2800 BC. Above was a 3rd-millennium BC CORDED WARE occupation with bone and flint tools, cord-decorated BEAKERS, antler sleeves for polished stone axes and wooden bowls and spoons.

Zuttiyeh a very large prehistoric cave in the Wadi Amud north of the Sea of Galilee, Israel, excavated in 1925 by TURVILLE-PETRE, who found the fragmentary GALILEE SKULL (now relatively dated to 300–350,000 BP) at the base of the archaeological sequence, below an industry now recognized as Acheulo-Yabrudian. The skull's morphology is debated but appears to have more early *H. sapiens* characters than NEANDERTHAL.

Zvejnieki a late Mesolithic and Neolithic cemetery located in Latvia. The 304 graves at Zvejnieki, located adjacent to a settlement, have a high degree of organic preservation and have extensive inventories which include perforated elk teeth pendants and bone points. Ochre was used widely. The Zvejnieki cemetery shows similarities to other cemeteries of this period in northern Europe, particularly the one at VEDBAEK.

Zwoleń a Middle Palaeolithic open-air site located on the Zwolenka River (a tributary of the Vistula) in Poland. Artifacts and faunal remains (e.g. woolly mammoth, horse [predominant], reindeer) are buried in loess and stream deposits, dated (THERMOLUMINESCENCE) to 115,000–80,000 bp (i.e. early GLACIAL). The artifacts include bifacial foliates and sidescrapers (?).

Further Reading

General, Method and Theory

Aitken, M. J., 1990. *Science-based Dating in Archaeology.* Longman: London & New York.

Bahn, P. G. (ed.), 1996. *The Cambridge Illustrated History of Archaeology.* Cambridge University Press: Cambridge.

Barker, P., 1993. *Techniques of Archaeological Excavation* (3rd edn). Routledge: London.

Binford, L., 1983. *Working at Archaeology.* Academic Press: Orlando, Florida.

Clark, A., 1996. *Seeing Beneath the Soil: Prospecting Methods in Archaeology.* (2nd edn). Routledge: London.

Hester, T. N. *et al.*, 1997. *Field Methods in Archaeology* (7th edn). Mayfield: Palo Alto, CA.

Hodder, I., 1999. *The Archaeological Process.* Blackwell: Oxford.

Renfrew, C. & Bahn, P., 2000. *Archaeology: Theories, Methods and Practice* (3rd edn). Thames & Hudson: London.

Rosenfeld, A., 1965. *The Inorganic Raw Materials of Archaeology.* Praeger: New York.

Trigger, B., 1989. *A History of Archaeological Thought.* Cambridge University Press: Cambridge.

Willey, G. & Sabloff, J., 1993. *A History of American Archaeology* (3rd edn). Thames & Hudson: London.

Western Europe, Early Periods

Bahn, P. G. & Vertut, J., 1997. *Journey Through the Ice Age.* Weidenfeld & Nicolson: London/University of California Press: Berkeley.

Bhattacharya, D. K., 1977. *Palaeolithic Europe.* Humanities Press: Atlantic Highlands, New Jersey.

Bonsall, C. (ed.), 1989. *The Mesolithic in Europe.* John Donald: Edinburgh.

Bordaz, J., 1970. *Tools of the Old and New Stone Age.* Natural History Press: New York.

Bordes, F., 1961. *Typologie du Paléolithique Ancien et Moyen.* Delmas: Bordeaux.

Campbell, J. B., 1977. *The Upper Palaeolithic of Britain; A study of Man and Nature in the Late Ice Age.* Clarendon Press: Oxford.

Coles, J. M. & Higgs, E. S., 1969. *The Archaeology of Early Man.* Faber and Faber: London.

Collcutt, S. N. (ed.), 1986. *The Palaeolithic of Britain and its Nearest Neighbours: Recent Trends.* Sheffield University: Sheffield.

Cook, J. *et al.*, 1982. 'A review of the chronology of the European Middle Pleistocene hominid record'. *Year Book of Physical Anthropology* 25: 19–65.

Djindjian, F., 1991. *Méthodes pour l'Archéologie.* A. Collin: Paris.

Gamble, C., 1986. *The Palaeolithic Settlement of Europe.* Cambridge University Press: Cambridge.

Gaucher, G., 1990. *Méthodes de recherche en préhistoire.* CNRS: Paris.

Klein, R. G., 1999. *The Human Career: Human Biological and Cultural Origins.* (2nd edn). University of Chicago Press: Chicago.

Lister, A. & Bahn, P., 2000. *Mammoths.* (2nd edn). Marshall Publishing: London.

Oakley, K. P., 1972. *Man the Tool-maker.* British Museum: London.

Otte, M., 1996. *Le Paléolithique Inférieur et Moyen en Europe.* Armand Colin: Paris.

Roe, D. A., 1981. *The Lower and Middle Palaeolithic Periods in Britain.* Routledge & Kegan Paul: London, Boston and Henley.

Trinkaus, E. & Shipman, P., 1992. *The Neanderthals: Changing the Image of Mankind.* Alfred A. Knopf: New York.

Tyldesley, J. A., 1987. *The Bout Coupé Handaxe: a Typological Problem.* British Archaeological Reports British Series 170: Oxford.

Wymer, J., 1985. *Palaeolithic Sites of East Anglia.* Geo Books: Norwich.

Western Europe, Later Periods

Audouze, F. & Büchsenschütz, O., 1992. *Towns, Villages and Countryside of Celtic Europe: From the Beginning of the Second Millennium to the End of the First Century BC.* Batsford: London.

Bradley, R., 1998. *The Significance of Monuments.* Routledge: London.

Burl, A., 1999. *Great Stone Circles*. Yale University Press: New Haven.

Coles, J. M. & Harding, A. F., 1979. *The Bronze Age in Europe*. Methuen: London.

Collis, J., 1984. *The European Iron Age*. Batsford: London.

Cunliffe, B. (ed.), 1994. *The Oxford Illustrated Prehistory of Europe*. Oxford University Press: Oxford.

Darvill, T. C., 1987. *Prehistoric Britain*. Batsford: London.

James, S., 1993. *Exploring the World of the Celts*. Thames & Hudson: London.

Jensen, J., 1982. *The Prehistory of Denmark*. Methuen: London.

Mohen, J.-P., 1989. *The World of Megaliths*. Cassell: London.

Moscati, S. (ed.), 1991. *The Celts*. Thames & Hudson: London.

Renfrew, C., 1987. *Archaeology and Language. The Puzzle of Indo-European Origins*. Cape: London.

Scarre, C. (ed.), 1983. *Ancient France. Neolithic Societies and Their Landscapes*. Edinburgh University Press: Edinburgh.

Scarre, C., 1998. *Exploring Prehistoric Europe*. Oxford University Press: New York.

Waddell, J., 1998. *The Prehistoric Archaeology of Ireland*. Galway University Press: Galway.

Whittle, A., 1996. *Europe in the Neolithic. The Creation of New Worlds*. Cambridge University Press: Cambridge.

Aegean and Cyprus

Barber, R., 1987. *The Cyclades in the Bronze Age*. Duckworth: London.

Cadogan, G., 1976 & 1991. *Palaces of Minoan Crete*. Routledge: London.

Chadwick, J., 1976. *The Mycenaean World*. Cambridge University Press: Cambridge.

Coldstream, J. N., 1977. *Geometric Greece*. Methuen: London.

Dickinson, O. T. P. K., 1977. *The Origins of Mycenaean Civilisation*. Paul Aström Förlag: Gothenburg.

Dickinson, O. T. P. K., 1994. *The Aegean Bronze Age*. Cambridge University Press: Cambridge.

Fitton, J. L., 1995. *The Discovery of the Greek Bronze Age*. British Museum Press: London.

Graham, J. W., 1962 & 1987. *The Palaces of Crete*. Princeton University Press: Princeton.

Hood, M. S. F., 1971. *The Minoans*. Thames & Hudson: London.

Hood, M. S. F., 1978 & 1994. *The Arts in Prehistoric Greece*. Penguin: Harmondsworth.

Hope Simpson, R. & Dickinson, O. T. P. K., 1979. *A Gazetteer of Aegean Civilisation in the Bronze Age 1: The Mainland and the Islands*. Paul Aström Förlag: Gothenburg.

Karageorghis, V., 1982. *Cyprus from the Stone Age to the Romans*. Thames & Hudson: London.

Myers, J. W. *et al.*, 1992. *Aerial Atlas of Ancient Crete*. University of California Press: Berkeley.

Papathanassopoulos, G. A., 1996. *Neolithic Culture in Greece*. Goulandris Foundation: Athens.

Snodgrass, A. M., 1971. *The Dark Age of Greece*. Edinburgh University Press: Edinburgh.

Tatton-Brown, V., 1987 & 1997. *Ancient Cyprus*. British Museum Publications: London.

Taylour, W. D., 1964 & 1983. *The Mycenaeans*. Thames & Hudson: London.

Theocharis, D., 1973. *Neolithic Greece*. National Bank of Greece: Athens.

Thimme, J., 1977. *Art and Culture of the Cyclades*. C. F. Muller: Karlsruhe.

Warren, P. M., 1975 & 1989. *The Aegean Civilisations*. Phaidon: London.

Warren, P. M. & Hankey, V., 1989. *Aegean Bronze Age Chronology*. Bristol Classical Press: Bristol.

Classical World

Biers, W. R., 1996. *The Archaeology of Greece: An Introduction*. (2nd edn). Cornell University Press: Ithaca and London.

Boardman, J. (ed.), 1993. *The Oxford History of Classical Art*. Oxford University Press: Oxford.

Boethius, A., 1978. *Etruscan and Early Roman Architecture*. Penguin: London.

Brendel, O. J., 1978. *Etruscan Art*. Penguin: London.

Elsner, J., 1998. *Imperial Rome and Christian Triumph*. Oxford University Press: Oxford.

Kleiner, D. E. E., 1992. *Roman Sculpture*. Yale University Press: New Haven.

Lawrence, A. W., 1983. *Greek Architecture*. (4th edn). Pelican: London.

Osborne, R. G., 1998. *Archaic and Classical Greek Art*. Oxford University Press: Oxford.

Sear, F., 1982. *Roman Architecture*. Batsford: London.

Snodgrass, A. M., 1987. *An Archaeology of Greece; the present state and future scope of a discipline*. University of California Press: Berkeley.

Spivey, N. & Stoddart, S., 1990. *Etruscan Italy: an Archaeological History*. Batsford: London.

Stewart, A. F., 1990. *Greek Sculpture: an Exploration*. Yale University Press: New Haven and London.

Strong, D. (revised Ling, R.), 1988. *Roman Art*. Penguin: London.

Wycherley, R. E., 1978. *The Stones of Athens*. Princeton University Press: Princeton.

Africa

General

Phillipson, D. W., 1995. *African Archaeology*. (2nd edn). Cambridge University Press: Cambridge.

Robertshaw, P. (ed.), 1990. *A History of African Archaeology*. James Currey: London.

Fossil Hominids

Johanson, D. & Edgar, B., 1996. *From Lucy to Language*. Weidenfeld & Nicolson: London.

Klein, R. G., 2000. 'Archaeology and the Evolution of Human Behavior'. *Evolutionary Anthropology* 9 (1): 17–36.

Tattersall, I., 1995. *The Fossil Trail. How We Know What We Think We Know About Human Evolution*. Oxford University Press: New York and Oxford.

Tobias, P. V., 1991. *Olduvai Gorge. Volume 4*. Cambridge University Press: Cambridge.

Walker, A. & Leakey, R. (eds.), 1993. *The Nariokotome Homo erectus skeleton*. Harvard University Press: Cambridge, Mass.

Wood, B. A., 1991. *Koobi Fora Research Project. Volume 4. Hominid Cranial Remains*. Clarendon Press: Oxford.

Wood, B. & Collard, M., 1999. 'The Human Genus'. *Science* 284: 65–71.

Stone Age

Boonzaier, E., Malherbe, C., Smith, A. & Berens, P., 1996. *The Cape Herders. A History of the Khoikhoi of Southern Africa*. David Philip: Cape Town and Johannesburg.

Close, A. E. (ed.), 1987. *Prehistory of Arid North Africa. Essays in Honor of Fred Wendorf*. Southern Methodist University Press: Dallas.

Deacon, H. J. & Deacon, J., 1999. *Human Beginnings in South Africa. Uncovering the Secrets of the Stone Age*. David Philip: Cape Town and Johannesburg.

Schick, K. D. & Toth, N., 1993. *Making Silent Stones Speak. Human Evolution and the Dawn of Technology*. Weidenfeld & Nicolson: London.

Singer, R. & Wymer, J., 1982. *The Middle Stone Age at Klasies River Mouth in South Africa*. University of Chicago Press: Chicago.

Iron Age and State Formation

Beach, D., 1998. 'Cognitive Archaeology and Imaginary History at Great Zimbabwe'. *Current Anthropology* 39: 47–72.

Chittick, N., 1974. *Kilwa: an Islamic Trading City on the East African Coast*. 2 volumes. British Institute in Eastern Africa: Nairobi.

Connah, G., 1987. *African Civilisations. Precolonial Cities and States in Tropical Africa: an Archaeological Perspective*. Cambridge University Press: Cambridge.

Garlake, P., 1973. *Great Zimbabwe*. Thames & Hudson: London.

Huffman, T. N., 1996. *Snakes and Crocodiles: Power and Symbolism in Ancient Zimbabwe*. Witwatersrand University Press: Johannesburg.

Phillips, T. (ed.), 1995–6. *Africa. The Art of a Continent*. Royal Academy of Arts: London.

Schmidt, P. (ed.), 1996. *The Culture and Technology of African Iron Production*. University of Florida Press: Gainesville.

Shaw, T., 1978. *Nigeria. Its Archaeology and Early History*. Thames & Hudson: London.

Shaw, T., Sinclair, P., Andah, B. & Okpoko, A. (eds.), 1995. *The Archaeology of Africa. Food, Metals and Towns*. Routledge: London & New York.

Egypt

Adams, W. Y., 1977. *Nubia: Corridor to Africa*. Allen Lane: London.

Arnold, D., 1992. *Die Tempel Aegyptens*. Artemis: Zürich.

Baines, J. & Malek, J., 1992. *Atlas of Ancient Egypt*. Facts on File: New York.

Edwards, I. E. S., 1991. *The Pyramids of Egypt*. Penguin: Harmondsworth.

Grimal, N., 1992. *A History of Ancient Egypt*. Blackwell: Oxford.

Helck, W. & Otto, E., 1975–86. *Lexikon der Aegyptologie*. Harrassowitz: Wiesbaden.

Kemp. B. J., 1989. *Ancient Egypt: Anatomy of a Civilisation*. Routledge: London.

Midant-Reynes, B., 1999. *The Prehistory of Egypt*. Blackwell: Oxford.

Porter, B. & Moss, R., 1927–present. *Topographical Bibliography of Ancient Egyptian Hieroglyphic Texts, Reliefs & Paintings*. Oxford University Press: Oxford.

Redford, D., 1992. *Egypt, Canaan and Israel in Ancient Times*. Princeton University Press: Princeton.

Reeves, C. N. & Wilkinson, R. H., 1996. *The Complete Valley of the Kings*. Thames & Hudson: London.

Snape, S. R., 1996. *Egyptian Temples*. Shire: Princes Risborough.

Spencer, A. J., 1982. *Death in Ancient Egypt*. Penguin: London.

Welsby, D., 1996. *The Kingdom of Kush*. British Museum Press: London.

General Near East and Central Asia

Dani, A. H. & Mohen, J.-P. (eds.), 1996. *History of Humanity, Scientific and Cultural Development, Volume II: From the Third Millennium to the Seventh Century BC*. UNESCO and Routledge: Paris and London.

Kuhrt, A., 1995. *The Ancient Near East, c.3000–330 BC*. Routledge: London.

Lloyd, S., 1980. *Foundations in the Dust. The Story of Mesopotamian Exploration*. (Revised edn). Thames & Hudson: London.

Maisels, C. K., 1990. *The Emergence of Civilization: From Hunting and Gathering to Agriculture, Cities, and the State in the Near East*. Routledge: London.

Mellaart, J., 1975. *The Neolithic of the Near East*. Thames & Hudson: London.

Meyers, E. M. (ed.), 1997. *The Oxford Encyclopedia of Archaeology in the Near East* (5 vols.). Oxford University Press: New York.

Nissen, H., 1988. *The Early History of the Ancient Near East 9000–2000 BC*. University of Chicago Press: Chicago.

Redman, C., 1978. *The Rise of Civilization: From Early Farmers to Urban Society in the Ancient Near East*. W. H. Freeman: San Francisco.

Roaf, M., 1990. *Cultural Atlas of Mesopotamia and the Ancient Near East*. Facts on File: New York.

Sasson, J., Barnes, J., Beckman, G. & Rubinson, K. (eds.), 1995. *Civilizations of the Ancient Near East*. Charles Scribner's Sons: New York.

Sherwin-White, S. & Kuhrt, A., 1993. *From Samarkand to Sardis. A New Approach to the Seleucid Empire*. Duckworth: London.

Stein, G. & Rothman, M. (eds.), 1994. *Chiefdoms and Early States in the Near East*. Prehistory Press: Madison, Wisconsin.

Mesopotamia

Adams, R. McC., 1981. *Heartland of Cities: Surveys of Ancient Settlements and Land Use on the Central Flood Plain of the Euphrates*. University of Chicago Press: Chicago.

Crawford, H., 1977. *The Architecture of Iraq in the Third Millennium BC*. Akademisk Forlag: Copenhagen.

Dalley, S., 1984. *Mari and Karana: Two Old Babylonian Cities*. Longman: London.

Lloyd, S., 1984. *Archaeology of Mesopotamia, From the Old Stone Age to the Persian Conquest* (revised edn). Thames & Hudson: New York.

Oates, J., 1986. *Babylon*. Thames & Hudson: London.

Postgate, N., 1992. *Early Mesopotamia. Society and Economy at the Dawn of History*. Routledge: London.

Roux, G., 1993. *Ancient Iraq*. Penguin: London.

Saggs, H., 1990. *The Might that Was Assyria*. Sidgwick & Jackson: London.

van de Mieroop, M., 1997. *The Ancient Mesopotamian City*. Oxford University Press: New York.

Syro-Palestine

Matthiae, P., 1981. *Ebla: An Empire Rediscovered*. Doubleday: Garden City, NY.

Mazar, A., 1992. *Archaeology of the Land of the Bible 10,000–586 B.C.E.* Doubleday: New York.

Stern, E. (ed.), 1993. *The New Encyclopedia of Archaeological Excavations in the Holy Land*. Simon & Schuster: New York.

Weiss, H. (ed.), 1985. *Ebla to Damascus. Art and Archaeology of Ancient Syria*. Smithsonian Institution Traveling Exhibition Service: Washington DC.

Arabia

Daum, W. (ed.), 1988. *Yemen: 3000 Years of Art and Civilisation in Arabia Felix*. Pinguin: Innsbruck.

Doe, B., 1971. *South Arabia*. Thames & Hudson: London.

Doe, B., 1983. *Monuments of South Arabia*. Oleander Press: Cambridge.

Potts, D., 1990. *The Arabian Gulf in Antiquity*. Oxford University Press: Oxford.

Anatolia and Transcaucasia

Burney, C. & Lang, D., 1971. *The Peoples of the Hills. Ancient Ararat and Caucasia*. Weidenfeld & Nicolson: London.

Frankel, D., 1979. *The Ancient Kingdom of Urartu*. British Museum Publications: London.

Joukowsky, M., 1996. *Early Turkey. Anatolian Archaeology from Prehistory through the Lydian Period*. Kendall/Hunt: Dubuque, Iowa.

Kushnareva, K. K., 1997. *The Southern Caucasus in Prehistory*. University of Pennsylvania Museum Press: Philadelphia.

Macqueen, J., 1986. *The Hittites and Their Contemporaries in Asia Minor*. (Revised edn). Thames & Hudson: London.

Mellaart, J., 1978. *The Archaeology of Ancient Turkey*. Rowman & Littlefield: Totowa, New Jersey.

Yakar, J., 1991. *Prehistoric Anatolia: The Neolithic Transformation and the Early Chalcolithic Period*. Institute of Archaeology of Tel Aviv University: Tel Aviv.

Iran and Central Asia

Allchin, B. & Hammond, N. (eds.), 1978. *The Archaeology of Afghanistan from the Earliest Times to the Timurid Dynasty*. Academic Press: London.

Belenitsky, A., 1968. *Archaeologia Mundi: Central Asia*. Nagel Publishers: Geneva.

Carter, E. & Stolper, M., 1984. *Elam. Surveys of Political History and Archaeology*. University of California Press: Berkeley.

Colledge, M., 1977. *Parthian Art*. Cornell University Press: Cornell.

Cook, J., 1983. *The Persian Empire*. Schocken Books: New York.

Frye, R., 1976. *The Heritage of Persia*. (2nd edn). Sphere Books: London.

Frye, R., 1996. *Heritage of Central Asia from Antiquity to the Turkish Expansion*. Markus Weiner Publishers: Princeton.

Ghirshman, R., 1969. *Persia from the Origins to Alexander the Great*. Thames & Hudson: London.

Knobloch, E., 1972. *Beyond the Oxus. Archaeology, Art and Architecture of Central Asia*. Ernest Benn: London.

Kohl, P. (ed.), 1981. *The Bronze Age Civilization of Central Asia: Recent Soviet Discoveries*. Sharpe: New York.

Kohl, P., 1984. *Central Asia, Palaeolithic Beginnings to*

the Iron Age. Éditions Recherche sur les civilisations: Paris.

India

Allchin, R., 1995. *The Archaeology of Early Historic South Asia*. Cambridge University Press: Cambridge.

Allchin, B. & Allchin, R., 1992. *The Rise of Civilization in India and Pakistan*. Cambridge University Press: Cambridge.

Chakrabarti, D. K., 1995. *Archaeology of Ancient Indian Cities*. Oxford University Press: Delhi.

Fairservis, W., 1975. *The Roots of Ancient India. The Archaeology of Early Indian Civilization*. (2nd edn). University of Chicago Press: Chicago.

Ghosh, A. (ed.), 1991. *Encyclopaedia of Indian Archaeology*. E. J. Brill: Leiden.

Kenoyer, J. M., 1998. *Ancient Cities of the Indus Valley Civilization*. Oxford University Press: Karachi.

Possehl, G. (ed.), 1993. *Harappan Civilization*. (2nd edn). Oxford University Press and IBH: Delhi.

Thapar, R., 1966. *A History of India, Vol. 1*. Penguin: Harmondsworth.

Central and Eastern Europe/Asia, Early Periods

Allsworth-Jones, P., 1986. *The Szeletian and the Transition from Middle to Upper Palaeolithic in Central Europe*. Clarendon Press: Oxford.

Boriskowskij, P. I. (ed.), 1984. *Paleolit SSSR*. Nauka: Moscow. (In Russian).

Boriskowskij, P. I. (ed.), 1989. *Paleolit Kavkaza i Severnoi Azii*. Nauka: Leningrad. (In Russian).

Chard, C. S., 1974. *Northeast Asia in Prehistory*. University of Wisconsin Press: Madison.

Derev'anko, A. P., Shimkin, D. B. & Powers, W. R. (eds.), 1998. *The Paleolithic of Siberia: New Discoveries and Interpretations*. Translated by I. P. Laricheva. University of Illinois Press: Urbana.

Gabori, M., 1976. *Les Civilisations du Paléolithique Moyen entre les Alpes et l'Oural*. Akademiai Kiado: Budapest.

Klein, R. G., 1969. *Man and Culture in the Late Pleistocene: A Case Study*. Chandler Publishing Co.: San Francisco.

Klein, R. G., 1973. *Ice-Age Hunters of the Ukraine*. University of Chicago Press: Chicago.

Marks, A. E. & Chabai, V. P. (eds.), 1998. *The Middle Paleolithic of Western Crimea, Vol. 1*. ERAUL 84: Liège.

Roebroeks, W. & van Kolfschoten, T. (eds.), 1995. *The Earliest Occupation of Europe*. University of Leiden: Leiden.

Soffer, O., 1985. *The Upper Paleolithic of the Central Russian Plain*. Academic Press: San Diego.

Soffer, O. & Praslov, N. (eds.), 1993. *From Kostenki to Clovis: Upper Paleolithic – Paleo-Indian Adaptations*. Plenum Press: New York.

Svoboda, J., Lozek, V. & Vlcek, E., 1996. *Hunters between East and West: The Paleolithic of Moravia*. Plenum Press: New York.

West, F. H. (ed.), 1996. *American Beginnings: The Prehistory and Paleoecology of Beringia*. University of Chicago Press: Chicago.

Central and Eastern Europe/Asia, Later Periods

Austin, D. & Alcock, L. (eds.), 1990. *From the Baltic to the Black Sea: Studies in Medieval Archaeology*. Unwin Hyman: London.

Bogucki, P., 1999. *The Origins of Human Society*. Blackwell: Oxford.

Chernykh, E. N., 1992. *Ancient Metallurgy in the USSR*. Cambridge University Press: Cambridge.

Cunliffe, B. (ed.), 1994. *The Oxford Illustrated Prehistory of Europe*. Oxford University Press: Oxford.

Dolukhanov, P., 1996. *The Early Slavs*. Longman: London.

Ehrich, R., 1992. *Chronologies in Old World Archaeology*. (3rd edn). University of Chicago Press: Chicago.

Ellis, L., 1984. *The Cucuteni-Tripolye Culture: a Study in Technology and the Origins of Complex Society*. B.A.R.: Oxford.

Jażdżdewski, K., 1984. *Urgeschichte Mitteleuropas*. Ossolineum: Wroclaw.

Midgley, M. S., 1992. *TRB Culture: the First Farmers of the North European Plain*. Edinburgh University Press: Edinburgh.

O'Shea, J. M., 1996. *Villagers of the Maros. A Portrait of an Early Bronze Age Society*. Plenum Press: New York.

Price, T. D. (ed.), 2000. *Europe's First Farmers*. Cambridge University Press: Cambridge.

Radovanovic, I., 1996. *The Iron Gates Mesolithic*. International Monograph in Prehistory: Ann Arbor.

Rolle, R., 1989. *The World of the Scythians*. Batsford: London.

Rudenko, S. I., 1970. *Frozen Tombs of Siberia. The Pazyryk Burials of Iron Age Horsemen*. University of California Press: Berkeley.

Sherratt, A., 1997. *Economy and Society in Prehistoric Europe. Changing Perspectives*. Princeton University Press: Princeton.

Srejović, D., 1969. *Lepenski Vir*. Thames & Hudson: London.

Tringham, R. E., 1971. *Hunters, Fishers and Farmers of Eastern Europe, 6000–3000 B.C.* Hutchinson: London.

Wells, P. S., 1984. *Farms, Villages, and Cities: Commerce and Urban Origins in Late Prehistoric Europe*. Cornell University Press: Ithaca.

Whittle, A., 1996. *Europe in the Neolithic*. Cambridge University Press: Cambridge.

Zvelebil, M., Dennell, R. & Domanska, L. (eds.), 1998. *Harvesting the Sea, Farming the Forest: the Emergence of Neolithic Societies in the Baltic Region*. Sheffield Academic Press: Sheffield.

Far East

Aikens, C. M. & Higuchi, T., 1982. *Prehistory of Japan*. Academic Press: New York.

Atlas of Primitive Man in China. 1980. Science Press: Beijing.

Barnes, G. L., 1993. *China, Korea and Japan: The Rise of Civilization in East Asia*. Thames & Hudson: London.

Chang, K. C., 1986. *The Archaeology of Ancient China*. (4th edn). Yale University Press: New Haven and London.

Cottrell, A., 1981. *The First Emperor of China*. Macmillan: London.

Debaine-Francfort, C., 1999. *The Search for Ancient China*. Thames & Hudson: London/Abrams: New York.

Imamura, K., 1996. *Prehistoric Japan. New Perspectives on Insular East Asia*. UCL Press: London.

Jia, Lianpo, 1980. *Early Man in China*. Foreign Language Press: Beijing.

Kidder, J. E., 1959. *Japan Before Buddhism*. Thames & Hudson: London.

Kidder, J. E., 1972. *Early Buddhist Japan*. Praeger: New York.

Kim, J.-H., 1978. *The Prehistory of Korea*. University Press of Hawaii: Honolulu.

Nelson, S. M., 1993. *The Archaeology of Korea*. Cambridge University Press: Cambridge.

Nelson, S. M. (ed.), 1995. *The Archaeology of Northeast China, Beyond the Great Wall*. Routledge: London.

Rawson, J., 1980. *Ancient China: Art and Archaeology*. British Museum Press: London.

Rawson, J. (ed.), 1996. *Mysteries of Ancient China. New Discoveries from the Early Dynasties*. British Museum Press: London.

Wu, R. & Olsen, J. W. (eds.), 1985. *Palaeoanthropology and Palaeolithic Archaeology in the People's Republic of China*. Academic Press: Orlando.

Southeast Asia

Allen, J., Golson, J. & Jones, R. (eds.), 1977. *Sunda and Sahul: Prehistoric Studies in South-east Asia, Melanesia and Australia*. Academic Press: London.

Bellwood, P., 1979. *Man's Conquest of the Pacific. The Prehistory of Southeast Asia and Oceania*. Oxford University Press: Auckland.

Bellwood, P., 1985. *Prehistory of the Indo-Malaysian Archipelago*. Academic Press: New York.

Chandler, D., 1983. *A History of Cambodia*. Westview Press: Boulder.

Coèdes, G., 1968. *The Indianized States of Southeast Asia*. East-West Center Press: Honolulu.

Higham, C. F. W., 1989. *The Archaeology of Mainland Southeast Asia*. Cambridge University Press: Cambridge.

Higham, C. F. W., 1996. *The Bronze Age of Southeast Asia*. Cambridge University Press: Cambridge.

Higham, C. & Thosarat, R., 1998. *Prehistoric Thailand, from early Settlement to Sukhothai*. River Books: Bangkok.

Sémah, F. *et al.*, 1990. *They Discovered Java*. Adiwarna: Jakarta.

Smith, R. B. & Watson, W. (eds.), 1979. *Early South East Asia*. Oxford University Press: Oxford.

van de Velde, P. (ed.), 1984. *Prehistoric Indonesia, a Reader*. Foris: Dordrecht.

Australia and the Pacific

Allen, J. & Gosden, C. (eds.), 1991. *Report of the Lapita Homeland Project*. Department of Prehistory, Research School of Pacific Studies, Australian National University: Canberra.

Allen, J. & O'Connell, J. F. (eds.), 1995. 'Transitions'. *Antiquity* 69 (265).

Anderson, A. J., 1989. *Prodigious Birds. Moas and Moa-hunting in Prehistoric New Zealand*. Cambridge University Press: Cambridge.

Bahn, P. & Flenley, J., 1992. *Easter Island, Earth Island*. Thames & Hudson: London and New York.

Bellwood, P., 1978. *Man's Conquest of the Pacific: the Prehistory of Southeast Asia and Oceania*. Collins: Auckland.

Davidson, J., 1984. *The Prehistory of New Zealand*. Longman Paul: Auckland.

Flood, J., 1995. *Archaeology of the Dreamtime*. (Revised edn). Angus & Robertson: Sydney.

Flood, J., 1997. *Rock Art of the Dreamtime*. Angus & Robertson: Sydney.

Frankel, D., 1991. *Remains To Be Seen: Archaeological Insights into Australian Prehistory*. Longman Cheshire: Melbourne.

Goodenough, W. (ed.), 1996. 'Prehistoric Settlement of the Pacific'. *Transactions of the American Philosophical Society* 86 (5).

Irwin, G., 1992. *The Prehistoric Exploration and Colonisation of the Pacific*. Cambridge University Press: Cambridge.

Jennings, J. D. (ed.), 1979. *The Prehistory of Polynesia*. Harvard University Press: Cambridge.

Jones, R. (ed.), 1985. *Archaeological Research in Kakadu National Park*. Australian National Parks and Wildlife Service, Special Publication no. 13.

Kamminga, J., 1982. *Over the Edge. Functional Analysis of Australian Stone Tools*. Occasional Papers in Anthropology 12. Anthropology Museum, University of Queensland: St Lucia.

Kirch, P. V., 1985. *Feathered Gods and Fish-hooks*. University of Hawaii Press: Honolulu.

Lourandos, H., 1997. *Continent of Hunter-gatherers: New Perspectives in Australian Prehistory*. Cambridge University Press: Cambridge.

Morwood, M. J. & Hobbs, D. R. (eds.), 1995. *Quinkan Prehistory: the Archaeology of Aboriginal Art in S.E.*

Cape York Peninsula, Australia. Tempus 3. The Anthropology Museum, University of Queensland: St Lucia.

Mulvaney, D. J. & Kamminga, J., 1999. *Prehistory of Australia.* Allen & Unwin: St Leonards.

Smith, M. A., Spriggs, M. & Fankhauser, B. (eds.), 1993. *Sahul in Review: Pleistocene Archaeology in Australia, New Guinea and Island Melanesia.* Department of Prehistory, Research School of Pacific Studies, Australian National University: Canberra.

Spriggs, M., 1997. *The Island Melanesians.* Blackwell: Oxford.

Spriggs, M., Yen, D. E., Ambrose, W., Jones, R., Thorne, A. & Andrews, A. (eds.), 1993. *A Community of Culture: the People and Prehistory of the Pacific.* Department of Prehistory, Research School of Pacific Studies, Australian National University: Canberra.

Trotter, M. & McCulloch, B., 1989. *Unearthing New Zealand.* Government Printer: Wellington.

North America

Cordell, L. S., 1997. *Archaeology of the Southwest.* Academic Press: San Diego.

Fagan, B. M., 1995. *Ancient North America.* (2nd edn). Thames & Hudson: London.

Frison, G., 1978. *Prehistoric Hunters of the High Plains.* Academic Press: Orlando, Florida.

Jennings, J. (ed.), 1983. *Ancient North Americans.* W. H. Freeman: New York.

Jennings, J. D., 1989. *Prehistory of North America.* (3rd edn). Mayfield Publications: Mayfield, CA.

McGhee, R., 1989. *Ancient Canada.* Canadian Museum of Civilization: Ottawa.

Plog, S., 1997. *Ancient Peoples of the American Southwest.* Thames & Hudson: London.

Silverberg, R., 1986. *The Moundbuilders.* Ohio University Press: Athens, Ohio.

Thomas, D. H., 1999. *Exploring Ancient Native America.* Routledge: London/Prentice-Hall: Paramus, New Jersey.

West, F. H. (ed.), 1996. *American Beginnings: The Prehistory and Paleoecology of Beringia.* University of Chicago Press: Chicago.

Wood, W. R. (ed.), 1998. *Archaeology of the Great Plains.* University Press of Kansas.

Mesoamerica

Adams, R. E. W., 1977. *Prehistoric Mesoamerica.* Little, Brown & Co.: Boston.

Baudez, C. & Picasso, S., 1992. *Lost Cities of the Maya.* Thames & Hudson: London/Abrams: New York.

Fagan, B. M., 1992. *Kingdoms of Gold, Kingdoms of Jade, The Americas before Columbus.* Thames & Hudson: London.

Fash, W. L., 1991. *Scribes, Warriors and Kings. The City of Copán and the Ancient Maya.* Thames & Hudson: London.

Gruzinski, S., 1992. *The Aztecs: Rise and Fall of an Empire.* Thames & Hudson: London/Abrams: New York.

Hammond, N., 1982. *Ancient Maya Civilization.* Cambridge University Press: Cambridge.

Marcus, J. & Flannery, K. V., 1996. *Zapotec Civilization.* Thames & Hudson: London.

Sabloff, J. A., 1989. *The Cities of Ancient Mexico. Reconstructing a Lost World.* Thames & Hudson: London.

Sabloff, J. A., 1990. *The New Archaeology and the Ancient Maya.* Scientific American Library: New York.

Schele, L. & Freidel, D., 1990. *A Forest of Kings. The Untold Story of the Ancient Maya.* William Morrow: New York.

Townsend, R. F., 1992. *The Aztecs.* Thames & Hudson: London.

South America

Bernand, C., 1994. *The Incas. Empire of Blood and Gold.* Thames & Hudson: London/Abrams: New York.

Bruhns, K. O., 1994. *Ancient South America.* Cambridge University Press: Cambridge.

Burger, R. L., 1992. *Chavín and the Origins of Andean Civilization.* Thames & Hudson: London.

Donnan, C. B. (ed.), 1985. *Early Ceremonial Architecture in the Andes.* Dumbarton Oaks Research Library and Collection: Washington DC.

Fagan, B. M., 1992. *Kingdoms of Gold, Kingdoms of Jade, The Americas before Columbus.* Thames & Hudson: London.

Haas, J., Pozorski, S. & Pozorski T. (eds.), 1987. *The Origins and Development of the Andean State.* Cambridge University Press: Cambridge.

Hagen, A. von & Morris, C., 1998. *The Cities of the Ancient Andes.* Thames & Hudson: London.

Keatinge, R. W. (ed.), 1988. *Peruvian Prehistory: an Overview of Pre-Inca and Inca Society.* Cambridge University Press: Cambridge.

Lavallée, D., 2000. *The First South Americans: From Origin to High Culture.* University of Utah Press: Salt Lake City.

Lumbreras, L. G., 1974. *The Peoples and Cultures of Ancient Peru.* Smithsonian Institution Press: Washington DC.

McEwan, C., Borrero, L. A. & Prieto, A. (eds.), 1997. *Patagonia.* Princeton University Press: Princeton.

Moseley, M. E., 1992. *The Incas and Their Ancestors.* Thames & Hudson: London.

Willey, G. R., 1971. *An Introduction to American Archaeology, Volume Two, South America.* Prentice-Hall: Englewood Cliffs, New Jersey.